Spanish-En
English-Sp

D0400663

Medical Dictionary

■ ■ ■

Diccionario Médico

Español-Inglés
Inglés-Español

Spanish-English
English-Spanish
Medical Dictionary

■ ■ ■

Diccionario Médico
Español-Inglés
Inglés-Español

Onyria Herrera McElroy, Ph.D.
Lola L. Grabb, M.A.

Foreword by Vincent A. Fulginiti, M.D.
Dean and Professor of Pediatrics
Tulane University School of Medicine, New Orleans

Introducción por la Dra. Beatriz Varela
Professor of Spanish
University of New Orleans, New Orleans

Little, Brown and Company
Boston / Toronto / London

Library of Congress Cataloging-in-Publication Data
McElroy, Onyria Herrera.
    Spanish-English, English-Spanish medical dictionary = Diccionario médico español-inglés, inglés-español / Onyria Herrera McElroy, Lola L. Grabb.— 1st ed.
        p.   cm.
    ISBN 0-316-55561-4
    1. Medicine—Dictionaries.   2. English language—Dictionaries—Spanish.
    3. Medicine—Dictionaries—Spanish.   4. Spanish language—Dictionaries—English.
    I. Grabb, Lola L.   II. Title.   III. Title: Diccionario médico español-inglés, inglés-español.
    R121.M488   1992
    610'.3—dc20   91-37796
                                                                                                              CIP

Printed in the United States of America

SEM

Contents / Contenido

Foreword

Non-Spanish-speaking physicians are frustrated when attempting to communicate with their Spanish-speaking patients. Not only is there an obvious language barrier, but also the precise definitions of some words that the physician may acquire from dictionaries may not be correct in the medical context. Additionally, patients are uncomfortable with those who do not share their language, and facility with the language may be an incentive to full disclosure. Most of us who are not multilingual pick up phrases and terms that we use loosely in attempting to explore history or reactions to our physical examinations. Now McElroy and Grabb have provided us with a handy reference that will facilitate our ability both to understand our patients and to communicate with them with greater precision and ease.

They have assisted us by providing a well-written, well-structured volume that will provide ready reference to the words, phrases, and constructions that we need. Their use of side by side English-Spanish throughout facilitates ready reference in both directions and can help persons other than the health care worker and the primarily Spanish speaker to move between the two languages. A unique feature is the inclusion of accepted abbreviations, which I have seen in no other text of this type. The abbreviations are placed in context, which makes learning and transition quick and easy. Additionally, the use of conversion tables explains the roots used, the orthographic changes encountered, and the use of prefixes and suffixes.

Finally, the appendixes include a matrix for the physician-patient encounter, with very useful phrases that are commonly employed in gathering historical information and in informing patients of the physician's recommendations and interpretations.

A health care worker armed with this text will find that he or she is more capable of communication than with most other aids to Spanish-English equivalents. I find this a most useful treatment of this important area in medicine for those whose daily professional and personal lives are dependent on accuracy in communication.

Vincent A. Fulginiti, M.D.

Introducción

La importancia del español y del inglés en el mundo de hoy es obvia, no sólo por el número tan considerable de hablantes que posee cada lengua sino también por las contribuciones culturales llevadas a cabo por ambas civilizaciones y con las cuales se ha venido enriqueciendo y beneficiando la humanidad desde hace muchos siglos. La medicina, por ejemplo, se halla entre los campos que cuentan con más adelantos: técnicas nuevas, innovaciones en la cirugía y los tratamientos, conceptos desconocidos que hay que expresar con neologismos y muchas novedades en el diagnóstico y la prevención de enfermedades. Las autoras McElroy y Grabb acertaron, pues, en publicar este diccionario médico-bilingüe en estos momentos tan propicios. Desde luego que la habilidad de escoger el tiempo oportuno no es el único acierto de estas escritoras. Nos encontramos ante un diccionario de calidad, que usa definiciones breves, claras y precisas—en inglés y en español—y que además, en secciones que no he visto en otros diccionarios, estudia las abreviaturas médicas más conocidas, las tablas de conversión con los cambios ortográficos propios de cada lengua y la formación de términos médicos por medio de raíces, prefijos y sufijos. También ofrece orientaciones sencillas para la pronunciación de los sonidos que causan más dificultades al anglo y al hispano respectivamente y una gramática simplificada con las estructuras que contrastan en las dos lenguas. Hay asimismo, tres apéndices en los cuales se traducen pesos y medidas, la temperatura, los números, las tablas de conversión, las frases más comunes que se emplean en el ejercicio de la medicina y los signos y síntomas del paciente. En todas estas divisiones del contenido, las traducciones de cada voz o frase se encuentran una al lado de la otra, de manera que no hay necesidad de acudir a ninguna otra referencia. Cuando se busca una voz en el diccionario, bien sea en español, bien en inglés, aparece en primer lugar el cognado (cuando lo hay) y después la connotación del mismo, expuesta en forma sencilla para que la entienda tanto el científico como el vulgo que nada sabe de estas voces médicas. Se incluye, además, si existe, el vocablo popular de la enfermedad o el tratamiento.

Lo expuesto comprueba que este diccionario médico-bilingüe ha de ser una fuente indispensable no sólo para médicos, trabajadores sociales y enfermeros dedicados a problemas de la salud, sino también para los pacientes y las personas que deseen documentarse sobre distintos aspectos de la medicina contemporánea. Por último, conviene subrayar que la obra ha de beneficiar lo mismo al ciudadano de una nación anglohablante que al de todo país de habla española.

Dra. Beatriz Varela

Preface

The increase of the Hispanic population in the United States has created a real need for communication between Spanish-speaking patients and English-speaking professionals in the various fields of health care. The *Spanish-English English-Spanish Medical Dictionary* provides the vocabulary that will facilitate communication between the patient and the health care provider (doctors, nurses, therapists) in a hospital, a medical office, or a laboratory setting.

The *Spanish-English English-Spanish Medical Dictionary* contains more than twenty thousand entries, which have been selected by consulting other authoritative English and Spanish medical dictionaries, studying current medical publications for new technical words, and consulting with professionals in different fields of specialization.

The definitions have been written in a clear and concise style, and a careful process has been followed to make certain that all the technical words used in each definition are entered in the dictionary. At the same time, the definitions in both languages have been cross referenced, except in areas of idiomatic expressions or terms that have no equivalent in the other language. This feature ensures the bilingual value of this dictionary.

The dictionary also contains a simplified grammar in both languages; conversion tables for translating and interpreting medical terminology; medical abbreviations; a section on topics of communication; and other features to facilitate independent acquisition of English-Spanish communication skills.

The *Spanish-English English-Spanish Medical Dictionary* will be of great use to both English-speaking and Spanish-speaking medical personnel—in the United States and in other countries—who desire to increase their medical vocabulary in English or Spanish. The dictionary will also be an indispensable guide for those who come to the United States from Spanish-speaking countries to further their medical education.

O.H.M.
L.L.G.

Prólogo

El rápido aumento de la población hispana en los Estados Unidos ha creado una verdadera necesidad de comunicación entre pacientes hispano-parlantes y profesionales de habla inglesa que ofrecen servicios en campos relacionados con la medicina. El propósito del *Diccionario Médico Español-Inglés Inglés-Español* es el de proporcionar, además de los términos médicos de mayor uso, los vocablos y expresiones más necesarios para facilitar la comunicación entre paciente y profesional de asistencia médica (médicos, enfermeros, terapeutas) ya sea en un hospital, consultorio o laboratorio.

El *Diccionario Médico Español-Inglés Inglés-Español* incluye más de veinte mil vocablos en ambas lenguas. La selección del vocabulario se ha hecho consultando otros diccionarios médicos autorizados en español e inglés. También se ha hecho un cuidadoso estudio de términos técnicos modernos encontrados en publicaciones profesionales recientes, y se ha consultado a profesionales especialistas en distintas áreas. La selección de las entradas, tanto principales como subalternas, se ha basado en la frecuencia y extensión del uso de las mismas. Términos arcaicos, por regla general, no se han incluído.

Las definiciones se han escrito en un estilo claro y conciso. Cada definición ha sido rigurosamente estudiada teniendo en cuenta el registro de todos los vocablos técnicos componentes de la misma en el diccionario. Al mismo tiempo, se ha seguido la correspondencia en las definiciones de palabras equivalentes en ambos idiomas, con excepción de aquellos casos en los que no existe un término equivalente en el otro idioma, o en expresiones idiomáticas. Esta característica asegura la eficacia de un dicionario bilingüe.

El diccionario contiene una gramática simplificada, abreviaturas médicas, tablas de conversión para la traducción e interpretación de términos médicos, una sección de tópicos de comunicación y otras secciones varias que ayudarán a los lectores a aumentar, con rapidez e independientemente, el vocabulario médico en inglés o en español.

El *Diccionario Médico Español-Inglés Inglés-Español* será de gran utilidad a los profesionales médicos y de asistencia pública que deseen aumentar el conocimiento del idioma inglés o del español en sus propios países. Asimismo, les servirá de guía a aquéllos que viajen a los Estados Unidos a continuar su educación médica o a especializarse.

O.H.M.
L.L.G.

Acknowledgments

The authors would like to express their gratitude to those who by their encouragement, contributions of information, help in the preparation of the manuscript, and editorial assistance have made this dictionary possible.

We give special thanks to the following physicians who answered our questions and guided us to research materials: Gabriel L. Catá, Laurel M. and Steve D. Coleman, Raymundo J. Esquivel (who always responded so enthusiastically to our many inquiries), José J. Fernández, Vincent A. Fulginiti, Harold S. Goldstein, John D. Hamilton, Edward N. Janoff, Horacio Oré-Girón, and Martin S. Stone.

Our gratitude also extends to those who encouraged us in our work, provided information, and assisted in the reading of the manuscript in its early stages: Sylvia T. Alonso, Frances R. Aparicio, Lisa and Kevin Button, Robert C. Coleman, Lauren García, Roseann D. González, Karl C. Gregg, Billie Kozolchyck, Lauren McElroy, Nina Rukas, Matilde A. Sándufer, Allyson Stone, Anita Stone, and María Teresa Velez. To Dana A. Nelson and Beatriz Varela we are particularly grateful for their advice on and help with the grammar section of the dictionary.

We express our thanks to our medical Spanish students throughout the years, whose own experiences and interest in this field increased our awareness of the need for a reference book such as this.

For their professional assistance in carrying out our research, we acknowledge with thanks the staff of the Arizona Health Sciences Center Library at the University of Arizona, especially Bertha Almagro, Hannah Fisher, and Polin Lei; and the staffs of the William D. Perkins Library and the Duke Medical Center Library at Duke University, especially Ginger Matson.

We would like to thank Christopher Davis, our first editor, and Julie E. Hagen and Susan F. Pioli, Production Editor and Executive Editor at Little, Brown and Company, for their support and guidance in the production of the dictionary; and our thanks also to Madela Ezcurra for her copyediting and proofing.

For his enthusiastic encouragement from the very beginning and for his invaluable additional help with the proofing and editing of the text, our heartfelt thanks and appreciation to John Harmon McElroy.

Finally, we express our deepest gratitude to those who collaborated with us most often and who generously and devotedly gave us the benefit of their judgment, experience, and medical knowledge every step of the way. This help from doctors Albert G. Grabb and Samuel J. Grabb sustained our efforts.

How to Use the Dictionary

Main entries

The main entries are printed in **boldface,** in slightly larger type than the rest of the text set flush to the left hand margin. The main entry may consist of:

1. one word **abdomen**
2. words joined by a hyphen **cross-eyed**
3. descriptive phrases **sympathetic nervous system**

The main entries are listed in alphabetical order according to the initial letter of the entry. Two kinds of entries appear: a) strictly medical words and b) common words related to general communication with patients.

When the main entry is a medical term, a simple definition is given with the most important facts pertaining to it. When the main entry has different meanings which are identified as the same part of speech, they are itemized numerically and labeled with an abbreviation if it is needed for clarification (1). When the main entry is a non-medical word or a common term, synonyms are used to define it. If a main entry has more than one meaning, a word or phrase between brackets is given, in italics, in the same language as the entry to clarify its meaning, or in some cases the entry is used in a phrase to clarify its use (2). We have listed new technical words designating programs, products, instruments, or treatments and defined them by following the general rules of language usage.

(1)
> **absorption** *n.* absorción. 1. la acción de un organismo de absorber o pasar líquidos u otras sustancias; 2. *psic.* ensimismación.

(2)
> **fit** *n.* ataque, convulsión; *a.* [*suitable*] adecuado-a; *v.* [*to adjust to shape*] ajustar, encajar.

In some cases, when there is a slight difference in the spelling of words with the same meaning, both spellings are entered together, and the most common one of the two is entered first (3).

(3)
> **exophthalmia, exophthalmus** *n.* exoftalmia, exoftalmus, protrusión anormal del globo del ojo.

Only words that would pertain to communication in a medical situation and to needs related to patients or medical personnel are included in the glossary.

Subentries

Subentries under main entries of medical words are printed in lightface type (4), while subentries under main entries of common words and phrases as well as idiomatic expressions are printed in **boldface type** (5). A slash (/) separates the translation of the subentries from English to Spanish or Spanish to English, while a double space (____) stands for the main entry. Subentries generally are not defined. Their plural forms are indicated by adding **-s** or **-es** after the double space.

(4)
> **dislocation** *n*. luxación, desplazamiento de una articulación; closed
> ____ / ____ cerrada; complicated ____ / ____ complicada; congenital
> ____ / ____ congénita.

(5)
> **around** *prep*. cerca de; en; *adv*. alrededor de, cerca; a la vuelta; más o
> menos; ____ **here** / ____ de aquí; *v*. **to look** ____ / buscar; **to turn**
> ____ / dar la vuelta; voltear; voltearse.

Popular Names

When an entry refers to a sickness which is known by more than one name, only one definition is given. The abbreviation *V*. (See) will guide the reader to the term defined (6).

(6)
> **chickenpox** *n*. varicela. *V*. **varicella.**

Parts of Speech

All main entries, simple or combined, are identified as to part of speech. When the main entry has more than one word, the combined phrase is also identified (7).

(7)
> **robust** *a*.
> **role model** *n*.
> **radioactive iodine excretion test** *n*.

The meanings of a word used as more than one part of speech are indicated in the following order of forms: **noun** *n*.; **adjective** *a*.; **verb** *v*.; **irregular verb** *vi*.; **reflexive verb** *vr*.; **adverb** *adv*. (2).

In the English section of the dictionary, the glossary includes nouns, adjectives, infinitives of verbs, the past participle (classified as an adjective), comparatives and superlatives, prepositions and adverbs. Idiomatic expressions involving the main entry are included following the definitions. Other parts of speech such as pronouns and verb forms can be found in the grammar section of the dictionary.

In the Spanish section nouns and adjectives are identified by their gender *(m., f.)*. In the English section, the translations into Spanish of nouns and adjectives indicate their gender (masculine or feminine) by adding the feminine ending **-a,** accordingly, to nouns and adjectives ending in **-o** that are inflected. In example (8) **rápido-a** means that the masculine is **rápido,** and the feminine is **rápida.** When the adverb is indicated by the ending **-mente,** it means that this ending has to be added to the feminine ending of the adjective, or just added to it if the adjective ends in a consonant.

---

(8)
> **fast** *n.* ayuno; *a.* [*speedy*] rápido-a; ligero-a; color ____ / resistente a un colorante; *v.* [*not to eat anything*] ayunar; to break one's ____/ dejar de ayunar; *adv.* aprisa; rápidamente; **to walk** ____ / andar ____; ____ **sleep** / profundamente dormido-a.

When entries are spelled alike but have a different classification (homographs), the part of speech is indicated by its corresponding abbreviation, definitions follow separated by semicolons without using numerals as is the case when the entry has the same classification regarding part of speech (9).

---

(9)
> **mucoid** *n.* mucoide, glucoprotcína similar a la mucina; *a.* de consistencia mucosa.

Eponyms are entered alphabetically according to last names (10).

---

(10)
> **Babinski's reflex** *n.* reflejo de Babinsky, dorsiflexión del dedo gordo al cstimularse la planta del pie.

Plurals

Irregular plurals in English, and the plurals of Latin and Greek nouns used in medical terminology are indicated in parenthesis after the entry.

---

(11)
> **woman** *n.* (*pl.* **women**) mujer.

---

(12)
> **septum** *L.* (*pl.* **septa**) septum, tabique o membrana que divide dos cavidades o espacios.

Consult the grammar section of the dictionary to find the rules that apply to the formation of plurals in each language.

Capitalization

Most entries in English begin with a lowercase. Capitalization is used in eponyms and trade names of medications; names of plants and animals are capitalized, printed in italics, and given in the singular if referring to the genus, and in the plural if referring to the class, order, family, or phylum (13).

(13) | **Salmonella** *n*. Salmonela, género de bacterias de la familia *Enterobacteriaceae* que causan fiebres entéricas, otras infecciones gastrointestinales y septicemia.

MEDICAL ABBREVIATIONS AND CONVERSION TABLES

To save space and facilitate their use, medical abbreviations and prefixes, suffixes, and roots have been listed in separate sections entitled **Most Common Medical Abbreviations** and **Conversion Tables.**

TOPICS OF COMMUNICATION

This section is intended to satisfy the simplest daily communications that a health professional who speaks either Spanish or English may need to have with a patient who speaks the other language. It is also intended that the use of the dictionary will have the effect of increasing the reader's ability to use the other language in non-clinical contexts as well, such as reading medical literature, attending conferences, and communicating orally and in writing with fellow health professionals in the other language.

APPENDIXES

Numerals, measures, words related to time, words related to signs and symptoms, as well as the idioms and vocabulary for conducting interviews with patients and giving them instructions are found in separate appendices.

WORD TO THE READER

The authors of this dictionary hope that the readers will forward to them via Little, Brown and Company recommendations for improving this dictionary in future editions.

Uso del diccionario

Entradas Principales

Las entradas principales aparecen impresas en letra **negrita** formando el margen izquierdo. La entrada principal puede consistir en:

1. una sola palabra **abdomen**
2. una palabra compuesta **intra-abdominal**
3. una frase descriptiva **cuello uterino**

Las entradas principales siguen un orden alfabético de acuerdo con la primera letra de la palabra. Hay dos tipos de entradas: (a) palabras estrictamente médicas, (b) palabras del lenguaje común necesarias para la comunicación con los pacientes.

Cuando la entrada principal es un vocablo médico, a éste le sigue una definición simple que señala los aspectos más importantes del mismo. Si el vocablo tiene más de una acepción para una misma parte de la oración (sustantivo, adjetivo, etc.), a cada acepción se le atribuye un número y una abreviatura adicional para mayor claridad (1). Cuando la entrada principal es un vocablo común, no médico, se hace uso de sinónimos para traducirla. Si tiene más de un significado, se hace uso de alguna palabra o frase entre corchetes ([]), en *bastardilla* y en el mismo idioma de la entrada, para aclarar su significado, o se emplea la misma entrada en una frase para aclarar su uso (2). En algunos casos incluímos nuevas palabras técnicas que designan programas, productos, instrumentos y tratamientos; estas palabras están definidas de acuerdo con las reglas generales del uso del idioma.

(1)
> **absorción** *f*. absorption, uptake. 1. taking up of fluids and other substances by an organism; 2. *psych.* self-centeredness.

(2)
> **apagar** *v*. [*luces*] to turn off; [*fuego*] to put out.

En algunos casos, cuando hay una pequeña diferencia en la forma escrita de dos palabras con el mismo significado, ambas palabras se presentan en la misma entrada, y se registra primero la palabra de uso más común. (3)

(3)
> **fibrocístico-a, fibroquístico-a** *a*. fibrocystic, cystic and fibrous in nature; enfermedad ___ de la mama / ___ disease of breast.

En el glosario de este diccionario se han incluído solamente términos relacionados con una situación médica, ya sea para la comunicación con los pacientes o para la atención a sus necesidades.

Entradas subalternas

Las entradas subalternas que aparecen bajo las entradas principales aparecen en letra clara si se refieren a terminología médica, mientras que las entradas subalternas referentes a terminología común, así como expresiones idiomáticas, aparecen en letra **negrita**. Una línea inclinada (/) separa la traducción del español al inglés y del inglés al español en las entradas subalternas, y un doble guión (⸺) sustituye la entrada principal; el plural se indica con una **-s** o con **-es** después del doble guión. Las entradas subalternas generalmente no se definen (4).

(4)
> **cuidado** *m.* care, attention; ⸺ intensivo / intensive ⸺; ⸺ post-
> natal / postnatal ⸺; **estar al** ⸺ **de** / to be under the ⸺ of; **tratar**
> **con** ⸺ / to handle with ⸺.
> **febril** *a.* febrile, having a body temperature above normal; convulsions
> ⸺-es / ⸺ convulsions.

Términos populares

Cuando un término médico tiene más de un nombre, solamente se define uno de los términos; la abreviatura *V.* (Véase) en la entrada del otro término guía al lector a la entrada que aparece definida (5).

(5)
> **glucopenia** *f. V.* **hipoglicemia.**

Partes de la oración

Después de cada entrada, consista de una o de más palabras, se indica la parte correspondiente de la oración (6).

(6)
> **emulsión** *f.*
> **enajenamiento mental** *m.*
> **brazalete de identificación** *m.*

Cuando una misma entrada tiene más de una clasificación como parte de la oración, se sigue el siguiente orden: **nombre** *m.,f.*; **adjetivo** *a.*; **verbo** *v.*; **verbo irregular** *vi.*; **verbo refle-xivo** *vr.*; **adverbio** *adv.* Las terminaciones **-a** y **-mente** indican la terminación que se añade a la entrada para formar el adjetivo y el adverbio respectivamente (7).

(7)
> **elástico** *m.* elastic; **-a** *a.* elastic, that can be returned to
> its original shape after being extended or distorted.
> **natural** *a.* natural; **-mente** *adv.* naturally.

En la sección del diccionario en español, el glosario incluye sustantivos, adjetivos, in-finitivos de verbos, el participio pasado (clasificado como adjetivo), preposiciones y adverbios. Las expresiones idiomáticas aparecen como entradas subalternas a continuación de las definiciones. Otras partes de la oración, pronombres y distintas formas de los verbos aparecen en la sección de gramática del diccionario.

En la sección del diccionario en español, los sustantivos y adjetivos se identifican por su género (*m., f.*) En la sección en inglés, la traducción de sustantivos y adjetivos al español indica el género de los mismos (masculino o femenino) mediante el uso de la terminación **-a** añadida a los sustantivos y adjetivos terminados en **o** (8).

(8) | **métrico-a** *a.* metric, rel. to meter or the metric system.

Cuando a una misma entrada se le atribuye más de una clasificación (términos homógrafos) cada parte de la oración se indica con su correspondiente abreviatura, y las definiciones siguen a cada clasificación, separadas por un punto y coma pero sin asignarles números como se hace en los casos en que un mismo término tiene más de una acepción pero mantiene la misma clasificación (véanse ejemplos 1 y 7). Los epónimos están registrados alfabéticamente por apellido (9).

(9) | **Babinski, reflejo de** *m.* Babinski's reflex, dorsiflexion of the big toe on stimulation of the sole of the foot.

Plurales

Los plurales de vocablos incorporados del latín y del griego, así como los plurales irregulares, se indican entre paréntesis a continuación de la entrada (10).

(10) | **septum** *L.* (*pl.* **septa**) septum, partition between two cavities.

En la sección de gramática del diccionario se encuentran las reglas que gobiernan la formación de los plurales en cada idioma.

Letras mayúsculas

La mayoría de las entradas en inglés y en español aparecen en letra minúscula. Las letras mayúsculas se usan en los epónimos y en nombres comerciales de medicinas. Los nombres de plantas y animales se presentan con letra mayúscula, en bastardilla, en singular si se refieren al género y en plural si se refieren a la clase, orden, familia o filo (11).

(11) | **Salmonela** *f.* Salmonella, a gram-negative bacteria of the *Enterobacteriaceae* that causes enteric fever, gastrointestinal infection and septicemia.

ABREVIATURAS MÉDICAS Y TABLAS DE CONVERSIÓN

Para abreviar y facilitar su uso, las abreviaturas médicas y los prefijos, sufijos y raíces aparecen en secciónes aparte tituladas **Abreviaturas médicas mas usuales** y **Tablas de conversión**.

TÓPICOS DE COMUNICACIÓN

Esta sección tiene como propósito facilitar la comunicación entre el profesional médico y el o la paciente cuando el inglés o el español no es el idioma común. Puede, además, servir de ayuda en situaciones no clínicas como en la lectura de literatura médica, durante la asistencia a conferencias o en la comunicación oral con colegas.

APÉNDICES

Los apéndices que se encuentran al final del diccionario comprenden: números, pesos y medidas, palabras relacionadas con el tiempo, síntomas y signos, y una sección de vocabulario y frases, **Tópicos de comunicación.**

PALABRAS A LOS LECTORES

Las autoras de este diccionario agradecen toda sugerencia o comentario que los lectores quieran hacerles llegar a través de Little, Brown and Company con el fin de mejorar ediciones futuras.

Abbreviations / *Abreviaturas*

English		**Spanish**	
a.	adjective	*a.*	adjetivo
abbr.	abbreviation	*abr.*	abreviatura
adv.	adverb	*adv.*	adverbio
approx.	approximate	*aprox.*	aproximadamente
art.	article	*art.*	artículo
aux.	auxiliary	*aux.*	auxiliar
Cast.	Castilian	*Cast.*	castellano
comp.	comparative	*comp.*	comparativo
cond.	conditional	*cond.*	condicional
conj.	conjunction	*conj.*	conjunción
dem.	demonstrative	*dem.*	demostrativo
esp.	especially	*esp.*	especialmente
f.	feminine	*f.*	femenino
		fam.	familiar
Fr.	French	*Fr.*	francés
		form.	formal pronoun
gen.	generally	*gen.*	generalmente
Gr.	Greek	*Gr.*	griego
gr.	grammar	*gr.*	gramática
H.A.	Hispanic America	*H.A.*	Hispanoamérica
imp.	imperative	*imp.*	imperativo
impf.	imperfect	*impf.*	imperfecto
ind.	indicative	*ind.*	indicativo
indef.	indefinite	*indef.*	indefinido
inf.	infinitive	*inf.*	infinitivo
infl.	inflammation	infl.	inflamación
int.	interjection	*int.*	interjección
interr.	interrogative	*interr.*	interrogativo
L.	Latin	*L.*	latín
m.	masculine	*m.*	masculino
Mex.	Mexico	*Mex.*	México
Mex.A.	Mexican-American	*Mex.A.*	Mexicano-americano
n.	noun	*n.*	nombre
neut.	neuter	*neut.*	neutro
obj.	object	*obj.*	objeto
pop.	popular	*pop.*	popular
pp.	past participle	*pp.*	participio de pasado
p.p.	present participle	*p.p.*	participio de presente
pref.	prefix	*pref.*	prefijo
prep.	preposition	*prep.*	preposición

Abbreviations

English		Spanish	
pres.	present	*pres.*	presente
pret.	preterite	*pret.*	pretérito
pron.	pronoun	*pron.*	pronombre
psych.	psychology	*psic.*	psicología
ref.	reflexive	*ref.*	reflexivo
rel.	relative	rel.	relativo
subj.	subjunctive	*subj.*	subjuntivo
sup.	superlative	*sup.*	superlativo
surg.	surgery	*cirg.*	cirugía
U.S.	United States	*E.E.U.U.*	Estados Unidos
usu.	usually	usu.	usualmente
V.	see	*V.*	véase
v.	verb	*v.*	verbo
vi.	irregular verb	*vi.*	verbo irregular
vr.	reflexive verb	*vr.*	verbo reflexivo

Most Common Medical Abbreviations /
Abreviaturas médicas más usuales

Abbreviations in English are commonly used in oral communication as well as in written medical reports. In Spanish, however, they are generally only used in written reports.

Las abreviaturas en inglés se usan comúnmente como medio de expresión oral y escrita. En español, las siglas indicadas sólo se usan generalmente en la forma escrita.

Abbr.	English / Inglés	Abrev.	Spanish / Español
AA	Alcoholics Anonymous	—	Alcohólicos Anónimos (asociación de)
AA	auto accident	—	accidente de automóvil
A&B	apnea and bradycardia	—	apnea y bradicardia
Ab	abortion; antibody	—	aborto; anticuerpo
ABC	artificial beta cells	CBA	células beta artificiales
abd	abdomen	—	abdomen
ABG	arterial blood gases	GSA	gases de sangre arterial
ABMT	autologous bone marrow transplantation	TAMO	transplante autólogo de médula ósea
ac (*ante cibum*)	before meals	—	antes de las comidas
ACBP	aorto-coronary-bypass	DAC	derivación aorto-coronoria
ACG	angiocardiography	—	angiocardiografía
ACTH	adrenocorticotropic hormone	HACT	hormona adrenocorticotrópica
ad (*ad*)	until	—	hasta
AD	right ear	OD	oído derecho
ad effect (*ad effectum*)	until it is effective	—	hasta que produzca efecto
ADH	antidiuretic hormone	HAD	hormona antidiurética
AE	above elbow	EC	por encima del codo
AFB	aorto-femoral bypass	DAF	derivación aorto-femoral
Afeb.	Afebrile	—	afebril
AG	albumin globulin ratio	IAG	índice de albúmina y globulina
agit (*agitatum*)	shake	—	agítese
AHF	antihemophilic Factor VIII	FAH	Factor VIII antihemofílico

Latin expressions (in *italics*), and abbreviations that are the same in both languages appear only on the left.

Las expresiones en latín (en letra *bastardilla*), y las abreviaturas comunes a ambos idiomas aparecen a la izquierda solamente.

Abbr.	English / Inglés	Abrev.	Spanish / Español
AI	aortic insufficiency	IA	insuficiencia aórtica
A.I.D.	artificial insemination by donor	I.A.D	inseminación artificial por donante
AIDS	acquired immunodeficiency syndrome	SIDA	síndrome de inmunodeficiencia adquirida
A.I.H.	artificial insemination by husband	I.A.E.	inseminación artificial por esposo
AK	above knee	ER	por-encima de la rodilla
ALB	albumin	—	albúmina
ALL	acute lymphocytic leukemia	LLA	leucemia linfocítica aguda
am *(ante meridien)*	morning	—	por la mañana
amnio	amniocentesis	—	amniocentesis
AMA	against medical advice	CRM	en contra de la recomendación médica
ANA	antinuclear antibody	—	anticuerpo antinuclear
Anes.	anesthesia	—	anestesia
AO	aorta	—	aorta
AP	anteroposterior	—	anteroposterior
AR	aortic regurgitation	RA	regurgitación aórtica
ARC	AIDS related complex		complejo del SIDA
arf	acute rheumatic fever	fra	fiebre reumática aguda
ARF	acute renal failure	IRA	insuficiencia renal aguda
as	aortic stenosis	EA	estenosis de la aorta
AS	left ear	OI	oído izquierdo
ASAP	as soon as possible	LAP	lo antes posible
ASC	ambulatory surgery center	CCA	centro de cirugía ambulatoria
ASCVD, ASVD	arteriosclerotic vascular disease	ASV	arteriosclerosis vascular
ASD	atrial septal defect	DTA	defecto del tabique auricular
ASHD	arteriosclerotic heart disease	ASC	arteriosclerosis cardíaca
ATB	antibiotic	ATB	antibiótico
ATR	Achilles tendon reflex	RTA	reflejo del tendón de Aquiles
AV	arteriovenous	—	arteriovenoso
AV	atrioventricular	—	auriculoventricular
AVM	arteriovenous malformation	MAV	malformación arteriovenosa
AVR	aortic valve replacement	RVA	reemplazo de la válvula aórtica
AVS	arteriovenous shunt	DAV	derivación arteriovenosa
AZT	Azidothimidine	—	Azidotimidina
BB	blood bank	BS	banco de sangre
BBB	bundle branch block	BR	bloqueo de rama
BE	barium enema	EB	enema de bario
BF	breast feeding	LM	lactancia materna
bid *(bis in die)*	twice a day	—	dos veces al día
BIL	bilateral	—	bilateral
BKA	below knee amputation	ADR	amputación debajo de la rodilla
BM	bowel movement	EF	evacuación, defecación, eliminación fecal

Abbr.	English / Inglés	Abrev.	Spanish / Español
BP	blood pressure	PA	presión arterial
BPH	benign prostatic hyperplasia	HBP	hiperplasia benigna de la próstata
BSO	bilateral salpingo-oophorectomy	SOB	salpingo-ooforectomía bilateral
BUN	blood urea nitrogen	US	urea sanguínea
Bx	biopsy	—	biopsia
c.	with	—	con
CA, Ca	cancer, carcinoma	—	cáncer, carcinoma
CAD	coronary artery disease	—	enfermedad de la arteria coronaria
CATH	catheterize	CAT	cateterizar
CBC	complete blood count	CSC	conteo sanguíneo completo
CC	chief complaint	QP	queja principal
cc	cubic centimeter	—	centímetro cúbico
CCU	coronary care unit	SCC	sala de cuidado coronario
CDC	Centers for Disease Control	CCE	Centros de Control de Enfermedades
CHF	congestive heart failure	ICC	insuficiencia cardíaca congestiva
CHOL	cholesterol	COL	colesterol
cl	clear	—	claro
CMV	cytomegalovirus	—	citomegalovirus
CNS	central nervous system	SNC	sistema nervioso central
CO	cardiac output	GC	gasto cardíaco
COPD	chronic obstructive pulmonary disease	EPCO	enfermedad pulmonar crónica obstructiva
C.P.	chest pain	D.P.	dolor de pecho
CPR	cardiopulmonary resuscitation	RCP	resucitación cardiopulmonar
CRF	chronic renal failure	IRC	insuficiencia renal crónica
C&S	culture and sensitivity	—	cultivo y sensibilidad
CS	cesarean section	OC	operación cesárea
CSF	cerebrospinal fluid	LCR	líquido cefalorraquídeo
CT	computerized tomography	TC	tomografía computada
CV	cardiovascular	—	cardiovascular
CVA	cerebrovascular accident	AP	apoplejía
CVD	cardiovascular disease	ECV	enfermedad cardiovascular
CVI	cerebrovascular insufficiency	ICV	insuficiencia cerebro-vascular
CVP	central venous pressure	PVC	presión venosa central
cysto	cystoscopic examination	cisto	cistoscopía
d.	dose	—	dosis
D	delivery	P	parto
D&C	dilation and curettage	—	dilatación y curetaje
DC	discontinue	SP	suspéndase
DD	differential diagnosis	—	diagnóstico diferencial
ddC 2', 3'	dideoxycytidine	—	dideoxitidina
dE 2'3'	dideoxyinosine	—	dideoxiinosina
DIC	disseminated intravascular coagulopathy	CID	coagulopatía intravascular diseminada

Abbr.	English / Inglés	Abrev.	Spanish / Español
DIFF	differential blood count	CSD	conteo sanguíneo diferenciado
DM	diabetes mellitus	—	diabetes mellitus
DNA	deoxyribonucleic acid	ADN	ácido desoxirribonucleico
DOB	date of birth	FDN	fecha de nacimiento
DOE	dyspnea on exertion	DDE	disnea de esfuerzo
DPT	diphtheria, pertussis, tetanus	—	difteria, pertusis, tétano
DRG	drainage	—	drenaje
DTR	deep tendon reflexes	RTP	reflejos tendinosos profundos
Dx	diagnosis	—	diagnóstico
EBL	estimated blood loss	PES	pérdida estimada de sangre
ECG, EKG	electrocardiogram	ECG	electrocardiograma
EEG	electroencephalogram	—	electroencefalograma
EFW	estimated fetal weight	PEF	peso estimado del feto
ELISA	enzyme-linked immunosorbent assay	—	prueba immuno-sorbente enzimática
EMG	electromyogram	—	electromiograma
ENT	ear, nose, and throat	NGO	nariz, garganta, y oídos
EOM	extraocular muscles	MEO	músculos extraoculares
ER	emergency room	SE	sala de emergencia
ESR	erythrocyte sedimentation rate	IES	índice de eritrosedimentación
EST	electric shock therapy	ECH	electrochoque
ESWL	extracorporeal shock wave lithotripsy	LEOCH	litotripsia extracorpórea con ondas de choque
EXT	extremity	—	extremidad
f	female	SF	sexo femenino
FBS	fasting blood sugar or glucose		glicemia en ayunas
FFP	fresh frozen plasma	PFC	plasma fresco congelado
FHR	fetal heart rate	FCF	frecuencia cardíaca fetal
fl	fluid	—	fluido, líquido
FMH	family medical history	HMF	historia médica de la familia
FSH	follicle stimulating hormone	HFE	hormona folículo estimulante
FTND	full term normal delivery	PAT	parto a término (normal)
FUO	fever of unknown origin	FOD	fiebre de origen desconocido
F / U	follow-up	S / C	seguimiento del caso
Fx	fracture	—	fractura
G	gonorrhea	—	gonorrea
GA	gastric analysis	AG	análisis gástrico
GB	gallbladder	VB	vesícula biliar
GC	gonococcus	—	gonococo
gen	general	—	general
GEN	genetics	—	genética
GH	growth hormone	HC	hormona del crecimiento
GI	gastrointestinal	—	gastrointestinal
GLUC	glucose	—	glucosa

Abbr.	English / Inglés	Abrev.	Spanish / Español
Grx	gravida	—	grávida
GTT	glucose tolerance test	PTG	prueba de tolerancia a la glucosa
Gtt., gtt (*guttatim*)	drops	—	gotas
GU	genitourinary	—	genitourinario
GYN	gynecology	GIN	ginecología
h	hour	—	hora
HCG	human chorionic gonadotropin	GCH	gonadotropina coriónica humana
HCT	hematocrit	—	hematócrito
HCVD	hypertensive cardiovascular disease	ECVH	enfermedad cardiovascular hipertensiva
HD	hemodialysis	—	hemodiálisis
HD	hip disarticulation	DC	desarticulación de la cadera
HGT	height	—	altura
HIV	human immunodeficiency virus	VIH	virus inmuno-deficiente humano
HM	health maintenance	MS	mantenimiento de la salud
H_2O	water	—	agua
HNP	herniated nucleous pulposus	—	hernia del núcleo pulposo
HR	heart rate	IC	índice cardíaco
hs (*hora somni*)	at bed time	—	a la hora de acostarse
hypo	hypodermically		inyectado
Hyst	hysterectomy	Hist	histerectomía
ICF	intracellular fluid	LIC	líquido intracelular
ICH	intracerebral hematoma	HIC	hematoma intracerebral
ICU	intensive care unit	SCI	sala de cuidado intensivo
I&D	incision and drainage	—	incisión y drenaje
ID	identification		identificación
id	infectious disease		enfermedad contagiosa
IgG	immunoglobulin G	—	inmunoglobulina G
IgM	inmunoglobulin M	—	inmunoglobulina M
II	icteric index	—	índice ictérico
IM	intramuscular	—	intramuscular
Imp	impression	—	impresión
INFO	information	—	información
I&O	intake and output	AG	absorción y gasto
IOL	intraocular lens	LIO	lente intraocular
IPD	intermittent peritoneal dialysis	DPI	diálisis peritoneal intermitente
IPPB	intermittent positive pressure breathing	RIPP	respiración intermitente con presión positiva
IQ	intelligence quotient	CI	cociente de inteligencia
IU	international unit	UI	unidad internacional
IUD	intrauterine device	DIU	dispositivo intrauterino
IUM	intrauterine monitoring		monitoreo intrauterino
IUP	intrauterine pregnancy	EIU	embarazo intrauterino
IUT	intrauterine transfusion	TIU	transfusión intrauterina
IV	intravenous	VIV	vía intravenosa

Abbr.	English / Inglés	Abrev.	Spanish / Español
IVC	intravenous cholangiogram	CIV	colangiograma intravenoso
IVP	intravenous pyelogram	PIV	pielograma intravenoso
K	potassium	—	potasio
KCL	potassium chloride	CLP	cloruro de potasio
KD	knee disarticulation	DR	desarticulación de la rodilla
KUB	kidney, ureter, bladder	RUV	riñón, uréter, vejiga, (placa simple de abdomen)
KVO	keep vein open	MVA	mantener la vena abierta
L	left	Iz.	izquierdo-a
LAB	laboratory	—	laboratorio
LAP	laparotomy	—	laparotomía
LBBB	left bundle branch block	BRI	bloqueo de rama izquierda
LDH	lactic dehydrogenase	DHL	dehidrogenasa láctica
LE	lupus erythematosus	—	lupus eritematoso
LE	left eye	OI	ojo izquierdo
LFT	liver function test	PFH	prueba de función hepática
LH	luteinizing hormone	HL	hormona luteinizante
LLE	left lower extremity	EIIz	extremidad inferior izquierda
LLQ	left lower quadrant	CIIz	cuadrante inferior izquierdo
LM	last menstrual period	UPM	último periodo menstrual
LP	lumbar puncture	PL	punción lumbar
LRF	luteinizing releasing factor	FLE	factor luteinizante de descargo
LS	liver scan	EH	escán del hígado
LS	lumbar spine	EL	espina lumbar
LUE	left upper extremity	ESIz	extremidad superior izquierda
LUQ	left upper quadrant	CSIz	cuadrante superior izquierdo
L&W	living and well	V y S	vivo y saludable
MAE	moves all extremities	MTE	mueve todas las extremidades
mc	millicurie	—	milicurie
MCA	middle cerebral artery	ACM	arteria cerebral media
MCH	mean corpuscular hemoglobin	ICH	índice corpuscular de hemoglobina
MCV	mean corpuscular index	IVC	índice de volumen corpuscular
MD	medical doctor	DM	doctor en Medicina
ME	middle ear	OM	oído medio
MED	medicine	—	medicina
MI	myocardial infarction	IC	infarto cardíaco
mi	mitral insuficiency	IM	insuficiencia mitral
min	minute	dim	diminuto-a
MM	mucous membrane	—	membrana mucosa
MR	mitral regurgitation	RM	regurgitación mitral
MS	multiple sclerosis	EM	esclerosis múltiple
MS	mitral stenosis	EM	estenosis mitral
MVI	multivitamins	—	multivitaminas
mx	mixture	—	mezcla

Abbr.	English / Inglés	Abrev.	Spanish / Español
NA	nursing assistant	AE	asistente de enfermería
N / A	not applicable	—	no aplicable
Na	sodium	—	sodio
neurol	neurology	—	neurología
NG	nasogastric	—	nasogástrico
NK	no known allergies	SAC	sin alergia conocida
NPO	nothing by mouth	NPB	nada por la boca
NSR	normal sinus rhythm	RSN	ritmo sinusal normal
NTG	nitroglycerin	—	nitroglicerina
N&V	nausea and vomiting	—	náusea y vómitos
NVD	neck, vein distention	DVY	distensión de las venas yugulares
OB, Obs	obstetrics	—	obstetricia
OC	oral contraceptive	CO	contraceptivo oral
od	once a day	—	una vez al día
omn hor (*omni hora*)	every hour	—	cada hora
on (*omni nocte*)	every night	—	todas las noches
O&P	ova and parasites	P	parásitos
op	operation	—	operación
OR	operating room		sala de operaciones, quirófano
ORTHO	orthopedic	ORTO	ortopédico
OS,RE	right eye	OD	ojo derecho
OS,LE	left eye	OI	ojo izquierdo
OT	occupational therapy	TO	terapia ocupacional
OU	both eyes	—	ambos ojos
P	prognosis	—	prognosis
P	pulse	—	pulso
p (*post*)	after	—	pasado (el tiempo de), después de
P.A.	pernicious anemia	AP	anemia perniciosa
PAC	premature atrial contraction	CAP	contracción atrial prematura
Pap	Papanicolaou	—	Papanicolaou
PAT	paroxysmal atrial tachycardia	TAP	taquicardia auricular paroxística
PATH	pathology	PAT	patología
PA view	posteroanterior view (radiology)	VPA	vista postero-anterior (radiología)
pc (*post cibus*)	after meals	—	después de las comidas
PCO_2	carbon dioxide content of blood	—	contenido de dióxido de carbono en la sangre
PCP	Pneumocystis Carinii pneumonia	—	Pneumocistis Carinii pneumonia
PE	physical examination	EF	examen físico
pe	pulmonary embolism	ep	embolia pulmonar
PERRLA	pupils equal, round, and equally reactive to light and accommodation	PIRRLA	pupilas iguales y redondas de igual reacción a la luz y acomodación

Abbr.	English / Inglés	Abrev.	Spanish / Español
PFC	persistent fetal circulation	CFP	circulación fetal persistente
PGH	pituitary growth hormone	HPC	hormona pituitaria del crecimiento
pH	hydrogen ion concentration (acidity)	—	concentración de iones de hidrógeno (acidez)
PI	present illness	EF	enfermedad actual
PICU	pediatric intensive care unit	SPCI	sala pediátrica de cuidado intensivo
PID	pelvis inflammatory disease	EIP	enfermedad inflamatoria de la pelvis
PLTS	platelets		plaquetas
pm *(post meridien)*	afternoon	—	pasado meridiano
PMH	past medical history	HM	historia médica
PMN	polymorphonuclear	—	polimorfonuclear
PND	paroxysmal nocturnal dyspnea	DPN	disnea paroxística nocturna
PNS	peripheral nervous system	SNP	sistema nervioso periférico
PO *(per os)*	by mouth	—	por vía oral
PO_2	oxygen content of blood	—	contenido de oxígeno en la sangre
POS	positive	—	positivo
Post-OP	after operation	—	post operatorio
PR	per rectum	PVR	por vía rectal
PR	pulse ratio	FP	frecuencia del pulso
Pre-op	before operation	—	anterior a la operación ·
prn *(pro re nata)*	as needed	—	cuando sea necesario
Pro-Time	prothrombin time		tiempo de protrombina
psych	psychiatry	psiq	psiquiatría
P.T.	physical therapy	TF	terapia física
PTA	prior to admission		pre-admisión
PTT	partial thromboplastia time	TPT	tiempo parcial de tromboplastia
PUD	peptic ulcer disease	UP	úlcera péptica
PV	peripheral vision	VP	visión periférica
PVC	premature ventricular contraction	CVP	contracción ventricular prematura
q *(quaque)*	every	—	cada; todo
qd *(quaque die)*	every day	—	diariamente
q.h. *(quaque hora)*	every hour	—	cada hora
qid *(quater in die)*	four times a day	—	cuatro veces al día
qod	every other day	—	días alternos
qns *(quantum non sufficit)*	quantity not sufficient	—	cantidad insuficiente
q.q.h. *(quaque quarta)*	every quarter of an hour	—	cada cuarto de hora

Abbr.	English / Inglés	Abrev.	Spanish / Español
QS *(quantum sufficit)*	enough amount	—	en suficiente cantidad
q 2h	every two hours	—	cada dos horas
R	respiration	—	respiración
rad	radiation absorbed dose	dra	dosis de radiación absorbida
RAM	rapid alternating movements	MAR	movimientos alternos rápidos
RBC	red blood cells	GR	glóbulos rojos (hematíes)
RE	right eye	OD	ojo derecho
RF	renal failure	IR	insuficiencia renal
Rh	blood factor	RH	factor sanguíneo
RHD	rheumatic heart disease	ERC	enfermedad reumática cardíaca
RLE	right lower extremity	EID	extremidad inferior derecha
RLL	right lower lobe	LID	lóbulo inferior derecho
RLQ	right lower quadrant	CID	cuadrante inferior derecho
RNA	ribonucleic acid	ARN	ácido ribonucleico
R / O	rule out		elimínese
ROM	range of motion		alcance en el movimiento
ROS	review of systems		interrogatorio por aparatos
RTA	renal tubular acidosis	ATR	acidosis tubular renal
RU	routine urinalysis	AO	análisis de orina
RUL	right upper lobe	LSD	lóbulo superior derecho
RUP	right upper extremity	ESD	extremidad superior derecha
RV	right ventricle	VD	ventrículo derecho
Rx	prescription	—	receta, prescripción
s *(sine)*	without	—	sin
s. *(signetur)*	label	—	desígnese
S&A	sugar and acetone	A y A	azúcar y acetona
SA	spontaneous abortion	AE	aborto espontáneo
SGOT	serum glutamic oxaloacetic transaminase	TGOS	transaminasa glutámica–oxaloacética del suero
SGPT	serum glutamic pyruvic transaminase	TGPS	transminasa glutámicopirúvica del suero
SH	serum hepatitis	HS	hepatitis sérica
SIADH	syndrome of inappropriate antidiuretic hormone secretion	SSHAI	síndrome de secreción hormonal antidiurética insuficiente
SIDS	sudden infant death syndrome	SMIS	síndrome de muerte infantil súbita
SOB	short of breath	FDR	falta de respiración
sol *(solutio)*	solution	—	solución
sp.gr.	specific gravity	gr.esp.	gravedad específica
ss	half		medio-a
staph	staphylococcus		estafilococo
stat *(statim)*	immediately	—	inmediatamente
strep	streptococcus	estrep	estreptococo

Abbr.	English / Inglés	Abrev.	Spanish / Español
subcu, SC	subcutaneously	—	subcutáneo-a
surg.	surgery, surgical	cirg.	cirugía
Sx	symptoms	—	síntomas
T	temperature	—	temperatura
T&A	tonsillectomy and adenoidectomy	T y A	tonsilectomía y adenoidectomía
TAB	tablet	—	tableta
TB	tuberculosis	TB	tuberculosis
THR	total hip replacement	RTC	reemplazo total de la cadera
TI	tricuspid insufficiency	IT	insuficiencia de la tricúspide
tid (*ter in die*)	three times a day	—	tres veces al día
TPR	temperature, pulse, and respiration	TPR	temperatura, pulso y respiración
TURBT	transurethral resection of bladder tumor	RTUTV	resección transuretral de tumor vesical
TURP	transurethral resection of prostrate	RTUP	resección transuretral de la próstata
TV	tricuspid valve	VT	válvula tricúspide
TWE	tap water enema	E	enema de agua de pila
TX	transplant	trans	transplante
Tx	treatment	—	tratamiento
U	units	—	unidades
UA	urinalysis	—	examen de orina
UC	uterine contractions	CU	contracciones uterinas
UC	ulcerative colitis	—	colitis ulcerativa
UCD	usual childhood diseases	ECI	enfermedades comunes de la infancia
ung	ointment	—	ungüento
ur	urine		orina
URI	upper respiratory infection	ITRS	infección del tracto respiratorio superior
UTI	urinary tract infection	IVU	infección de las vías urinarias
Vag	vaginal	—	vaginal
VD	veneral disease	EV	enfermedad venérea
VHD	ventricular heart disease	EVC	enfermedad ventricular del corazón
VPC	ventricular premature contractions	CVP	contracciones ventriculares prematuras
vs	vital signs	sv	signos vitales
WBC	white blood cells	GB	glóbulos blancos
WC	wheel chair	—	silla de ruedas
WR	Wassermann reaction	RW	reacción de Wassermann
Wt	weight	P	peso
y / o	years old	Ed	edad
Z	zone	—	zona

Conversion Tables

The **Conversion Tables** facilitate vocabulary building in both languages. They also instruct the reader in the recognition of the fundamental orthographic differences between Spanish and English and in the etymological analysis of words.

Consult the **Conversion Tables** when building a vocabulary of medical words or interpreting medical words either in Spanish or in English.

Table 1:   Rules for orthographic changes and differences in spelling between English and Spanish words.

Table 2:   Most commonly used roots.

Table 3:   Most frequently used prefixes.

Table 4:   Most frequently used suffixes in surgical procedures, diagnoses, and symptoms.

The three components listed in Tables 2, 3, and 4, may or may not be together at the same time in a medical term.

Start in Table 1 by learning the orthographic changes and differences in spelling between English and Spanish words. This practice will help you to independently increase your vocabulary in Spanish and English.

When forming or interpreting a medical term it is advisable to find the meaning of the **suffix** first. For example, given the medical term **gastropathy / gastropatía**, the meaning of the suffix (in Table 4) **-pathy / -patía** is **disease / enfermedad;** the root of the term (in Table 2) is **gastr-, stomach / estómago.** The vowel o is added to the root to join another term which begins in a consonant. The interpretation of the medical word results in: **disease of the stomach / enfermedad del estómago.** When interpreting or building a medical term keep in mind that a word root is the main element of the term, often indicating a body part. A medical term may contain more than one root element.

A **prefix** used at the beginning of a medical term either changes its meaning or makes it more specific. In the term **hypodermic,** for example, the three components or elements are present:

prefix	*word root*	*suffix*
hypo	derm	-ic (adjective ending)
(under)	(skin)	(pertaining to)

The meaning of the **word root** becomes more specific after the **prefix,** while the **suffix** indicates, in this case, how the term relates to the root's meaning.

Tablas de conversión

Las **Tablas de conversión** facilitan el aprendizaje continuado del vocabulario en ambos idiomas. Al mismo tiempo, enseñan al lector a reconocer las diferencias ortográficas fundamentales entre el español y el inglés, así como a analizar los vocablos etimológicamente.

Consulte las **Tablas** cuando trate de crear nuevos términos médicos o de interpretar el significado de un término no conocido, ya sea en español o en inglés.

Tabla 1: cambios ortográficos y diferencia en la escritura de palabras entre el inglés y el español.

Tabla 2: raíces más comunes.

Tabla 3: prefijos usados con más frecuencia.

Tabla 4: sufijos usados con más frecuencia en cirugía, síntomas y diagnósticos.

Estos tres últimos elementos (raíces, prefijos y sufijos) pueden o no estar presentes al mismo tiempo en un término médico.

Comience en la Tabla 1 para ver los cambios ortográficos que ocurren entre las palabras inglesas y las españolas. Al componer o interpretar un término médico, es aconsejable encontrar primero el significado del sufijo si se está haciendo su composición o interpretación en inglés. Por ejemplo, dado el término médico **gastropatía / gastropathy**, el significando del sufijo **-patía / -pathy** (V. la Tabla 4) es **enfermedad / disease,** la raíz o radical (V. la Tabla 2) es **gastr-, estómago / stomach.** En este caso, la vocal o se ha añadido a la raíz para unirla a otro vocablo que empieza con una consonante. El significado del término médico es: **enfermedad del estómago / disease of the stomach.** Cuando se crea o interpreta un término médico, se debe tener en cuenta que la raíz es el elemento principal del vocablo y que se refiere generalmente a una parte del cuerpo humano. Un mismo término médico puede tener más de una raíz.

El **prefijo** es un elemento que va delante de la raíz y cuya presencia modifica el significado de la misma o lo hace más específico. Tomemos, por ejemplo, la palabra **hypodermic / hipodérmico**. Si separamos los tres elementos o componentes tendremos:

prefijo	**raíz**	**sufijo**
hipo-	derm-	-ico (terminación adjetiva)
(bajo)	(piel)	(referente a)

El **prefijo** hace más específico el significado de la raíz, mientras que el **sufijo** indica a que se refiere el término o simplemente califica la parte definida por la raíz.

CONVERSION TABLE 1 / TABLA DE CONVERSIÓN 1

Orthographic Changes / Cambios ortográficos

English / Inglés	Spanish / Español	English / Inglés	Spanish / Español
cc	c	accommodate	acomodar
cc[1]	cc before **e** and **i**	accessory	accesorio
		accident	accidente
ch	c	character	carácter
ch before **e** and **i**	qui	chemistry	química
		chiropractor	quiropráctico
comm-	com-	commissure	comisura
im-	in-	immersion	inmersión
qu	cu	quart	cuarto
r[2]	l	paper	papel
s	es[3]	special	especial
		gastrospasm	gastroespasmo
ph	f	phlebitis	flebitis
pn[4]	pn or n	pneumonia	pneumonía, neumonía
ps	ps or s	psychology	psicología, sicología
rh	r	rheumatic	reumático
th	t	therapy	terapia
y[5]	i	typhoid	tifoidea

[1]In Spanish words only two double consonants are used: **cc** and **nn**. The **ll** and the **rr** are considered to be single characters in the Spanish alphabet.
En español sólo hay dos consonantes dobles: **cc** y **nn**. La **ll** y la **rr** se consideran letras separadas en el alfabeto español.
[2]May change to **l** at the end of a word.
Puede cambiar a **l** al final de palabra.
[3]Only before consonants **p** and **t**, including compound words.
Sólo delante de las consonantes **p** y **t** incluso en palabras compuestas.
[4]**pn** and **ps** may drop the initial **p** in Spanish.
En español se puede omitir la **p** inicial en las palabras que comienzan en **pn** o **ps**.
[5]When **y** is not at the end of the word.
Cuando la **y** no es final.

CONVERSION TABLE 2 / TABLA DE CONVERSIÓN 2

A **root** is the main part or element of a term. In medicine, it generally refers to a body part. Compound words (words with more than one root) are common in medical terminology.

La **raíz** o **radical** es el elemento principal de la palabra. En medicina la **raíz** se refiere generalmente a órganos o partes del cuerpo. En la terminología médica abundan palabras compuestas (palabras formadas por más de un elemento o raíz).

Most Commonly Used Roots / Raíces más frecuentes

English / Inglés	Spanish / Español	Meaning / Significado	Example / Ejemplo[1]
acou-	acu-	hearing / sonido	acoustics / acústica
aden-	aden-	gland / glándula	adenoids
aer-	aer-	air / aire	aerogenic / aerogénico

[1]When the words have an identical spelling and meaning in both languages, the Spanish translation is not given.
Cuando las palabras tienen igual significado y se escriben igual en ambos idiomas, la traducción al español se omite.

Conversion Tables

English / Inglés	Spanish / Español	Meaning / Significado	Example / Ejemplo
angi-	angi-	vessel / vaso	angiotitis
ankyl-, anchyl-	anquil-	immobility, stiffness/ inmovilidad, rigidez	anchylosis / anquilosis
arth-	art-	joint / articulación	arthritic / artrítico
brachi-	braqui-	arm / brazo	brachialgia / braquialgia
bronchi-	bronqui-	bronchi / bronquios	bronchopathy/ broncopatía
bucca-	buca-	mouth / boca	buccal / bucal
cardi-	cardi-	heart / corazón	cardiodynia / cardiodinia
carpo-	carpo-	wrist / carpo	carpal
cephal-	cefal-	head / cabeza	cephalitis / cefalitis
cerebr-	cerebr-	brain / cerebro	cerebral
cerv-	cerv-	neck / cerviz, cuello	cervical
cheil-	queil-	lip / labio	cheilectomy/ queilectomía
cost-	cost-	rib / costilla	costal
crani-	crane-	skull / cráneo	cranial / craneal
cysto-	cisto-	bladder / vejiga	cystocele / cistocele
dactyl-	dactil-	finger, toe / dedo	dactylitis / dactilitis
derm-	derm-	dermis / piel	dermatitis
duoden-	duoden-	duodenum / duodeno	duodenohepatic / duodenohepático
encephal-	encefal-	brain / cerebro	encephaloma / encefaloma
enter-	enter-	intestine / intestino	enteritis
fibro-	fibro-	fiber / fibra	fibroma
gastr-	gastr-	stomach / estómago	gastritis
genu-	genu-	knee / rodilla	genuflexion / genuflexión
gloss-	glosa-	tongue / lengua	glossalgia / glosalgia
glyco-	glico-	sugar / glucosa, azúcar	glycogen / glicógeno
hem-, hemo-	hem-, hemo	blood / sangre	hematoxic / hematóxico
hepat-	hepat-	liver / hígado	hepatitis
histo-	histo-	tissue / tejido	histoma
homo-	homo-	same, equal / igual	homologous / homólogo
hydr-	hidro-	water / agua, líquido	hydrocele / hidrocele
hypn-	hipno-	sleep / sueño	hypnosis / hipnosis
hyster-	hister-	uterus / útero	hysterectomy / histerectomía
ili-	ili-	flank / ilíaco	iliocostal
leuk-	leuc-	white corpuscle / leucocito	leukemia / leucemia
lingu-	lingu-	tongue / lengua	lingual
lip-	lip-	fat / grasa	lipoide
lith-	lith-	stone / cálculo	lithotriptor / litotriturador
mening-	mening-	membrane / membrana	meningitis
metr-	metr-	uterus / útero	metrorrhagia / metrorragia
my-.	mi-	muscle / músculo	myocardium / miocardio
myel-	miel-	marrow / médula	myelitis / mielitis
narc-	narc-	sleep / sueño	narcotism / narcotismo
naso-	naso-	nose / nariz	nasopharynx / nasofaringe

English / Inglés	Spanish / Español	Meaning / Significado	Example / Ejemplo
ne-, neo-	neo-	new, recent / nuevo, reciente	neonatal
nephr-	nefr-	kidney / riñón	nephritis / nefritis
neur-	neur-	nerve / nervio	neurotripsy / neurotripsia
noct-	noct-	night / noche	nocturia
nucle-	nucle-, nucleo-	nucleous / núcleo	nucleic / nucleico
oculo-	oculo-	eye / ojo	ocular
oo-	oo-, ovo-	ova, egg / óvulo, huevo	ooplasm / ooplasma
oste-	oste-	bone / hueso	osteosis
oto-	oto-	ear / oído	otodynia / otodinia
ovari-	ovari-	ovary / ovario	ovariectomy / ovariectomía
ox-	ox-	oxygen / oxígeno	oxygenation / oxigenación
path(o)	pato-	disease / enfermedad	pathology / patología
ped-	ped-	child / infante	pediatrics / pediatría
phleb-	fleb-	vein / vena	phlebitis / flebitis
pleur-	pleur-	pleura / pleura	pleuritis
pneum-	pneum-, neum-	air, lung / aire, pulmón	pneumothorax / neumotórax
prostat-	prostat-	prostate / próstata	prostatic / prostático
psych-	psic-, sic-	mind, spirit / mente	psychology / psicología
pupill-	pupil-	pupile / pupila	pupillometer / pupilómetro
pyel-	piel-	renal / renal	pyelitis / pielitis
ren-	ren-	kidney / riñón	renal
retin-	retin-	retina / retina	retinitis
rhin-	rin-	nose / nariz	rhinoclesis / rinoclesis
sarco-	sarco-	flesh / carne	sarcoma
semi-	semi-	half, partial / parcial, medio	semiflexion / semiflexión
sinus-	sinus-	cavity / cavidad	sinusitis
spermat-	espermat-	sperm, semen / esperma, semen	spermatoid / espermatoide
spondylo-	espondilo-	vertebra / vértebra	spondylous / espondiloso
strepto-	estrepto-	twisted / torcido	streptococcal / estreptocócico
techno-	tecno-	skill / técnica	technology / tecnología
teno-	teno-	tendon / tendón	tendonitis
thoraco-	torac-	chest, thorax / pecho, tórax	thoraxic / torácico
thrombo-	trombo-	clot / coágulo	thrombosis / trombosis
toxic-	toxic-	toxic / tóxico	toxicity / toxicidad
ur-, uro-	uro-	urine / orina	urinary / urinario
vas-	vas-	vessel, duct / vaso	vascular
ventro-	ventro-	abdomen, anterior part / abdomen, porción anterior	ventroscopy / ventroscopía
xeno-	xeno-	foreign, strange / extranjero, extraño	xenophtalmia / xenoftalmia

CONVERSION TABLE 3 / TABLA DE CONVERSIÓN 3

Prefixes are placed at the beginning of words; in medical terms the **prefix** is the element which changes the meaning of the term or makes it more specific. Prefixes are generally formed by one or two syllables. Most medical prefixes, roots, and suffixes are derived from Latin and Greek.

Los **prefijos** se colocan al principio de la palabra; en términos médicos el **prefijo** es el elemento que cambia el significado del término y lo hace más específico. Los prefijos tienen generalmente una o dos sílabas. La mayor parte de los prefijos, raíces y sufijos se derivan del latín y del griego.

Most Commonly Used Prefixes / Prefijos de uso más frecuente

English / Inglés	Spanish / Español	Meaning / Significado	Example / Ejemplo[1]
a-, an-	a-	lack of, without / falta de, sin	apathy / apatía
ab-	a-	away from / lejos de, sin	abnormal / anormal
ad-	ad-	toward, near to / hacia, con respecto a	adduction / aducción
ambi-	ambi-	both / ambos	ambidextrous / ambidextro
amphi-	anfi-	on both sides, double / en los dos lados, doble	amphibious / anfibio
ana-	ana-	up, back, again / sobre, otra vez, excesivo	anadipsia
ante-	ante-	before / antes de	antenatal
anti-	anti-	against, reversed / contra, reversión	antibiotic / antibiótico
bi-	bi-	twice, double / dos, doble	bifocal
brady-	bradi-	slow / despacio	bradycardia / bradicardia
circum-	circun-	about, around / alrededor de	circumcision / circuncisión
com-	co-	together, with / junto a, con	commisure / comisura
con-	con-	with, together / junto a, con	congenital / congénito
contra-	contra-	against, opposite / opuesto a, en contra de	contraceptive / contraceptivo
de-	de-, des-	away from, to suppress / separación, suprimir	dehydrated / deshidratado–a
dia-	dia-	through, across / por medio, a través	diaphragm / diafragma
diplo-	diplo-	double / doble	diplocardia
dis-	dis-	away, apart / separado	distention / distensión
dys-	dis-	bad, improper / malo, impropio	dysentery / disentería
e-, ex-	ex-	out, away from / fuera, lejos de	excrete / excretar

[1]When the words have identical spelling and meaning in both languages, the Spanish translation is not given.
Cuando las palabras tienen igual significado y se escriben igual en ambos idiomas, la traducción al español se omite.

Conversion Tables

English / Inglés	Spanish / Español	Meaning / Significado	Example / Ejemplo
ecto-	ecto-	external, outside / afuera, sin	ectoderm / ectodermia
em-	em-	in / adentro de	embolic / embólico
endo-	endo-	inside, within / dentro, entre	endometrium / endometrio
epi-	epi-	upon, on / sobre, encima	epidermia
extra-	extra-	outside / fuera de	extracardial / extracardíaco
hemi-	hemi-	half / medio	hemisphere / hemisferio
hyper-	hiper-	excessive / excesivo	hypertensive / hipertensivo
hypo-	hipo-	under, deficient / falta de, deficiente	hypoglycemia / hipoglicemia
im-, in-	in-	in, into / dentro, junto	infiltration / infiltración
infra-	infra-	below / debajo	infraorbital
intra-	intra-	between / entre	intraglobular
intro-	intro-	into, within / dentro de	introversion / introversión
lingu-	lingu-	tongue / lengua	lingual
mal-	mal-	bad, abnormal / malo, anormal	malocclusion / maloclusión
meso-	meso-	in the middle / en el medio	mesocardia
meta-	meta-	beyond / más allá, extendido	metastasis / metástasis
micro-	micro-	small, minute / pequeño, diminuto	micrococcus / micrococo
neur-	neur-	nerve / nervio	neurosis
para-	para-	beside, near / al lado, cerca	paracardiac / paracardíaco
per-	per-	through, excessive / a través, excesivo	perforation / perforación
peri-	peri-	around / alrededor de	perithelial / peritelial
poly-	poli-	many, several / varios	polyacid / poliácido
post-	post-	after, behind / después, detrás	postfebrile / postfebril
pneum-	neum-	lung / pulmón	pneumonia / neumonía
pre-	pre-	before, in front / antes, en frente	prediastole / prediástole
psych-	psico-	soul, mind / alma, mente	psychotherapy / psicoterapia
pyro-	piro-	heat, fire / calor, fuego	pyrogen / pirógeno
re-	re-	back again / de regreso otra vez	revive / revivir
retro-	retro-	backward; behind / en retroceso, detrás	retrolingual
schizo-	esquizo-	division / división	schizophrenia / esquizofrenia
semi-	semi-	partly, half / medio, parcial	semiflexion / semiflexión
sub-	sub-	under / debajo	subneural
super-	super-	above, upper / encima de, superior	supercentral

English / Inglés	Spanish / Español	Meaning / Significado	Example / Ejemplo
supra-	supra-	above / encima de	supranasal
sym-, syn-	sin-	together, with / junto, con	synovia / sinovia
tachi-	taqui-	accelerated, fast / rápido, acelerado	tachicardia / taquicardia
tetra-	tetra-	four / cuatro	tetralogy / tetralogía
therap-	terap-	treatment / tratamiento	therapeutic / terapéutico
thromb-	tromb-	clot / coágulo	thrombosis / trombosis
trans-	trans-, tras-	across, through / transversal, a través	transuretral
trauma-	trauma-	wound, trauma / herida, trauma	traumatism / traumatismo
tri-	tri-	three / tres	tridimensional
un-	in-, no	against, reversal / contrario, opuesto	unconscious / inconsciente
ultra-	ultra-	beyond, excess / más allá, excesivo	ultrasonic / ultrasónico

CONVERSION TABLE 4 / TABLA DE CONVERSIÓN 4

Suffixes are endings attached to the root or stem of a word to modify its meaning. In medical terminology **suffixes** are added to the root to define terms according to operative, diagnostic, and symptomatic meanings.

Los **sufijos** son terminaciones que al añadirse a la raíz de una palabra modifican el significado de la misma. En la terminología médica los **sufijos** se añaden a la raíz para defininir términos usados en cirugía, diagnosis y síntomas.

Surgical Procedure Suffixes / Sufijos referentes a procedimientos quirúrgicos

English / Inglés	Spanish / Español	Meaning / Significado	Example / Ejemplo
-centesis	-centesis	aspiration, puncture / aspiración, punción	thoracentesis / toracentesis
-ectomy	-ectomía	excision, removal / excisión, extirpación	tonsillectomy / tonsilectomía
-desis	-desis	binding, fixation / ligar, fijar	anthrodesis / antrodesis
-oclasis	-oclasis	to break down / romper, quebrar	osteoclasis
-olysis	-olisis	separate, destroy / separar, destruir	enterolysis / enterolisis
-ostomy	-ostomía	forming an opening / crear un boquete o abertura	colostomy / colostomía
-otomy	-otomía	incision, cut into / incisión, piquete	lithotomy / litotomía
-pexy	-pexia	suspension, fixation/ suspensión, fijación	hysteropexy / histeropexia

English / Inglés	Spanish / Español	Meaning / Significado	Example / Ejemplo
-plasty	-plastia	rebuilding, molding / reformando, moldeando	osteoplasty / osteoplastia
-rraphy	-rrafia	suture, closure / sutura, cierre	perineorraphy / perineorrafia
-stomy	-ostomía	new opening / apertura nueva	enterostomy / enterostomía
-tomy	-tomía	incision, section / incisión, sección	laparectomy / laparectomía
-tripsy	-tripsia	to crush / triturar	lithotripsy / litotripsia

Suffixes Relating to Diagnoses and Symptoms / Sufijos referentes a diagnósticos y síntomas

English / Inglés	Spanish / Español	Meaning / Significado	Example / Ejemplo
-algia	-algia	pain / dolor	cephalalgia / cefalalgia
-cele	-cele	hernia, swelling / hernia, inflamación	metrocele
-dynia	-dinia	pain / dolor	metrodynia / metrodinia
-ectasis	-ectasia	dilation, expansion / dilatación, expansión	bronchiectasis / bronquiectasis
-emia	-emia	blood / sangre	hyperglycemia / hiperglicemia
-iasis	-iasis	condition, presence / condición, presencia	lithiasis / litiasis
-itis	-itis	inflammation / inflamación	dermatitis
-logy	-logía	study of / estudio de	dermatology / dermatología
-malacia	-malacia	softening / reblandecimiento	osteomalacia
-mania	-manía	obsession / obsesión	kleptomania / cleptomanía
-megaly	-megalia	enlargement / engrosamiento	hepatomegaly / hepatomegalia
-oid	-oide	resembling / de tipo similar	lipoide
-oma	-oma	tumorous / tumoroso	nephroma / nefroma
-osis	-osis	abnormal condition / condición anormal	dermatosis
-pathy	-patía	disease / enfermedad	gastropathy / gastropatía
-penia	-penia	decrease, deficiency / disminución, deficiencia	leukopenia / leucopenia
-phagia	-fagia	to eat / comer	dysphagia / disfagia
-phasia	-fasia	speech / habla	aphasia / afasia
-phobia	-fobia	fear / miedo, temor	acrophobia / acrofobia
-plegia	-plejia	paralysis, stroke / parálisis, ataque	hemiplegia / hemiplejía

English / Inglés	Spanish / Español	Meaning / Significado	Example / Ejemplo
-praxia	-praxia	activity, action / actividad, acción	apraxia
-rrhage	-rragia	bursting forth, flooding/ derramamiento	hemorrhage / hemorragia
-rrhea	-rrea	discharge / flujo, descarga	diarrhea / diarrea
-sclerosis	-esclerosis	hardening / endurecimiento	arteriosclerosis
-spasm	-espasmo	contraction / contracción	gastrospasm / gastroespasmo

Notes:
1. When the suffix begins with a vowel, the word root is directly added to the suffix: cephalalgia / cefalalgia.
2. When the suffix begins with a consonant, a connecting vowel is placed between the word root and the suffix (**-o** in the majority of cases): cardiogram / cardiograma.

Notas:
1. Cuando el sufijo comienza con una vocal, la raíz se añade directamente al sufijo: cefalalgia / cephalalgia.
2. Cuando el sufijo comienza en consonante se coloca una vocal, gen. una **-o-**, entre la raíz y el sufijo: cardiograma / cardiogram.

Suffixes that Form a Noun / Sufijos que forman un nombre

English / Inglés	Spanish / Español	Meaning / Significado	Example / Ejemplo
-gram	-grama	record made by an instrument / trazo de un instrumento	cardiogram / cardiograma
-graphy	-grafía	description made by an instrument / descripción hecha por un instrumento	radiography / radiografía
-ia	-a, -ia, -ía	condition or disease/ condición o enfermedad	pneumonia / neumonía
-ician	-ico, -ica	person associated with a given specialty / persona asociada a una especialidad	technician / técnico
-ics	-ia	an art or science / un arte o ciencia	orthopedics / ortopedia
-ine	-ina	substance / sustancia	quinine / quinina
-is, -ismo	-is, -ismo	abnormal condition·/ condición anormal	alcoholism / alcoholismo
-ist	-ista	specialist / especialista	dentist / dentista
-ologist[1]	-ólogo-a	specialist / especialista	cardiologist / cardiólogo

[1]If **-log** precedes **-ist** in English, **-ist** is omitted in Spanish, and the ending **-o** *(m.)* or **-a** *(f.)* is added. Si en una palabra inglesa **-log** precede a **-ist,** esta terminación se omite en español y se añade **-o** *(m.)* o **-a** *(f.)* a **-log.**

English / Inglés	Spanish / Español	Meaning / Significado	Example / Ejemplo
-ology	-ología	study, knowledge / estudio, conocimiento	pathology / patología
-oma	-oma	tumor	adenoma
-osis	-osis	condition, formation / condición formación	tuberculosis
-pathy	-patía	disorder, disease / enfermedad, anomalía	myelopathy / mielopatia
-penia	-penia	deficiency / deficiencia	osteopenia
-philia	-filia	tendency, abnormal liking / tendencia, atracción mórbida	hemophilia / hemofilia
-ty	-dad	condition / condición	senility / senilidad
-y	-ia, -ía	condition or process / condición o proceso	myopathy / miopatía

Suffixes that Form an Adjective / Sufijos que forman un adjetivo

English / Inglés	Spanish / Español	Meaning / Significado	Example / Ejemplo
-iac	-iaco, -iaca	pertaining to, one affected by / en relación con, afectado por	cardiac / cardíaco[1]
-al	-al	related to / que trata de	visual / visual
-ant	-ante	pertaining to, with characteristics / en relación con, con características	abundant / abundante
-ate	-ado, -ada	condition / condición	delicate / delicado
-ic	-ico, -ica	affected by / afectado por	asthmatic / asmático
-ile	-il	state of being / estado	senile / senil

[1]Adjectives ending in **-o** change the **-o** to **-a** to form the feminine.
Los adjetivos que terminan en **-o** cambian la terminación en **-a** para formar el femenino.

Suffixes that Form a Verb / Sufijos que forman un verbo

English / Inglés	Spanish / Español	Example / Ejemplo
-ate	-ar	accommodate / acomodar
-e	-ar	cure / curar
-fy	-ficar	verify / verificar
-ize	-izar	revitalize / revitalizar

SPANISH-ENGLISH
VOCABULARY

VOCABULARIO
ESPAÑOL-INGLÉS

A

a *abr.* **absoluto** / absolute; **acidez** / acidity; **acomodación** / accommodation; **alergia** / allergy; **anterior** / anterior; **aqua** / aqua; **arteria** / artery.

a *prep.* [*hacia*] to, **voy ___ la farmacia** / I am going to the drug-store; [*dirección*] to, **___ la derecha** / to the right, **___ la izquierda** / to the left; [*hora*] at, **voy ___ las tres** / I'm going at three o'clock; [*frecuencia*] a, **tres veces al día** / three times a day.

abajo *adv.* below, down.

abandonar *v.* to abandon, to neglect.

abarcar *vi.* to contain, to include; **___ mucho** / to cover a lot of ground.

abasia *f.* abasia, uncertainty of movement.

abastecer *v.* to supply.

abastecimiento *m.* supply; **artículos para ___** / supplies.

abatido-a *a.* depressed, dejected.

abdomen *m.* abdomen; *pop.* belly; **___ de péndulo** / pendulous **___**; **___ escafoideo** / scaphoid **___**.

abdominal *a.* abdominal, rel. to the abdomen; **cavidad ___** / **___** cavity; **distensión ___** / **___** distention; **respiración ___** / **___** breathing; **retortijón, torsón ___** / **___** cramp; **traumatismos ___-es** / **___** injuries; **vendaje ___** / **___** bandage.

abdominocentesis *f.* abdominocentesis, abdominal puncture.

abdominoplastia *f. surg.* abdominoplasty, plastic surgical repair of the abdominal wall.

abdominovaginal *a.* abdominovaginal, rel. to the abdomen and the vagina.

abduccion *f.* abduction; separation.

abeja *f.* bee.

aberración *f.* aberration. 1. deviation from the norm; **___ cromática** / chromatic **___**;

2. mental disorder; **___ mental** / mental **___**.

aberrante *a.* aberrant, departing from the usual course; wandering.

abertura *f.* opening.

abierto-a *a. pp.* of **abrir,** open.

abiotrofia *f.* abiotrophy, premature loss of vitality.

ablación *f.* ablatio, ablation, detachment, removal; **___ de la placenta** / **___** placentae; **___ de la retina** / **___** retinae.

ablandar *v.* to soften.

abofetear *v.* to slap.

abogado *m.* lawyer, attorney.

aborrecer *vi.* to abhor, to hate.

abortar *v.* to abort, to interrupt the course of a pregnancy or to stop an illness.

abortivo *m.* abortifacient, stimulant to induce abortion.

aborto *m.* abortion; miscarriage; **___ criminal** / criminal **___**; **___ electivo** / elective **___**; **___ espontáneo** / spontaneous **___**; **___ incompleto** / incomplete **___**; **___ inducido** / induced **___**; **___ inevitable** / imminent **___**; **___ por succión** / suction **___**; **___ provocado** / induced **___**; **___ terapéutico** / therapeutic **___**.

abotonar *v.* to button up.

abrasión *f.* abrasion, damage to or wearing away of a surface by injury or friction.

abrasivo-a *a.* abrasive, rel. to or that causes abrasion.

abrazadera *f.* brace.

abrazar *vi.* to embrace.

abrazo *m.* hug, embrace.

abrebocas *m.* gag, jaw-lever, device used to keep the patient's mouth open.

abreviar *v.* to reduce, to shorten; **para ___** / in short.

abreviatura *f.* abbreviation.

abrigarse *vr., vi.* to put on warm clothing; to keep warm.

abrigo *m.* overcoat; cover; **buscar** ___ / to look for shelter.

abrir *v.* to open; ___ **de nuevo** / to reopen.

abrochar *v.* to fasten.

abrumar *v.* to overwhelm; to tax.

abrupción de la placenta *f.* abruptio placentae, premature detachment of the placenta.

abrupto-a *a.* abrupt, brusque.

absceso *m.* abscess, accumulation of pus gen. due to a breakdown of tissue; ___ agudo / acute ___; ___ alveolar / alveolar ___; ___ crónico / chronic ___; ___ de drenaje / drainage ___; ___ enquistado / encysted ___; ___ de las encías / gingival ___; ___ hepático / hepatic ___; ___ mamario / mammary ___; ___ pélvico / pelvic ___; ___ pulmonar / pulmonary ___.

absoluto-a *a.* absolute, unconditional.

absorbente *a.* absorbent.

absorber *v.* to absorb, to take in.

absorción *f.* absorption, uptake. 1. taking up of fluids and other substances by an organism; 2. *psych.* self-centeredness.

abstemio-a *m., f; a.* abstemious.

abstenerse *vr., vi.* to abstain, to refrain; ___ de relaciones sexuales / ___ from sexual intercourse.

abstinencia *f.* abstinence, voluntary restraint.

absurdo-a *a.* absurd.

abuelo-a *m., f.* grandfather; grandmother.

abulia *f.* abulia, loss of will power; ___ cíclica / cyclic ___.

abultado-a *a.* bulky, massive; swollen.

abundancia *f.* abundance.

abundante *a.* abundant, plentiful.

aburrido-a *a.* bored.

aburrirse *vr.* to become bored.

abusado-a *a.* abused; beyond the limits.

abusar *v.* to abuse, to mistreat.

abuso *m.* abuse, overuse; ___ de medicamento / overuse of medication; ___ emocional / emotional ___; ___ físico / physical ___; ___ verbal / verbal ___.

acabar *v.* to finish, to complete; ___ **de llegar** / to have just arrived; ___ **con eso** / to put an end to that; **acabarse** *vr.* to be finished; [*una sustancia*] to run out.

acalasia *f.* achalasia, inability to relax, esp. in reference to the sphincter muscles.

acantoide *a.* acanthoid, thornlike shape.

acantosis *f.* acanthosis, skin condition that is manifested by thick and warty growth.

acapnia *f.* acapnia, state produced by a decrease of carbon dioxide in the blood.

acariasis *f.* acariasis, skin disease caused by acarids.

ácaro *m.* acarid, parasite, mite.

acatarrarse *vr.* to catch a cold.

acceso *m.* 1. access, attack, seizure; ___ de asma / an asthma attack; 2. entrance.

accesorio *m.* accessory.

accidentado-a *m., f.* an injured person.

accidental *a.* accidental, unexpected.

accidente *m.* accident; ___ **automomovilístico** / car ___; ___ **de trabajo** / work related ___; ___ **de tráfico** / traffic ___; **víctima de un** ___ / casualty.

acción *f.* action.

aceite *m.* oil; ___ de hígado de bacalao / cod liver ___; ___ de oliva / olive ___; ___ de ricino / castor ___.

aceituna *f.* olive.

aceleración, aceleramiento *f., m.* acceleration.

acelerador *m.* accelerator, substance or agent acting as an accelerant; **-a** *a.* having the property of accelerating a process.

acelerar *v.* to accelerate, to quicken, to speed up; ___ la cura / to speed the healing process.

acento *m.* accent.

acentuado-a *a.* accented.

acentuar *v.* to accentuate, to emphasize.

aceptable *a.* acceptable.

aceptación *f.* acceptance.

aceptar *v.* to accept.

acera *f.* sidewalk.

acerca (de) *adv.* about, concerning; ___ **de eso** / about that.

acercar *vi.* to bring closer; **acercarse** *vr.* to approach, to get close.

acertado-a *a.* right; un diagnóstico ___ / a correct diagnosis.

acertar *vi.* to be right; to guess.

acetábulo *m.* acetabulum, hip socket.

acético-a *a.* acetic, sour, rel. to vinegar or its acid.

acetona *f.* acetone, fragrant substance used as a solvent and found in excessive amount in diabetic urine.

acetonemia *f.* acetonemia, excess acetone in the blood.

acetonuria *f.* acetonuria, excess acetone in the urine.

acidemia *f.* acidemia, excess acid in the blood.

acidez *f.* acidity, sourness.

ácido *m*. acid; **-a** *a*. bitter; ____ acético / acetic ____ ; ____ ascórbico / ascorbic ____ ; ____ bórico / boric ____ ; ____ butírico / butiric ____ ; ____ clorogénico / chlorogenic ____ ; ____ cólico / cholic ____ ; ____ desoxirribonucleico / deoxyribonucleic ____ ; ____ fólico / folic ____ ; ____ gástrico / gastric ____ ; ____-s grasos / fatty ____-s; ____ láctico / lactic ____ ; ____ nicotínico / nicotinic ____ ; ____ nucleico / nucleic ____ ; ____ resistente / ____ fast; ____ ribonucleico / ribonucleic ____ ; ____ salicílico / salicylic ____ ; ____ sulfónico / sulfonic ____ ; ____ sulfúrico / sulfuric ____ ; a prueba de ____ / ____ proof.

ácido clorhídrico, hidroclórico *m*. hydrochloric acid, a constituent of gastric juice.

ácido gliococólico *m*. glycocholic acid, a compound of glycine and cholic acid.

ácido glucorónico *m*. glucoronic, glycoronic acid, acid that acts as a disinfectant in human metabolism.

ácido hialurónico *m*. hyaluronic acid, acid present in the substance of the connective tissue that acts as a lubricant and connecting agent.

acidosis *f*. acidosis, excessive acidity in the blood and tissues of the body; ____ diabética / diabetic ____ .

ácido úrico *m*. uric acid, a product of protein breakdown present in the blood and excreted in the urine.

acinesia *f*. akinesia, acinesia, partial or total loss of movement.

aclaramiento *m*. clearance, elimination of a given substance from the blood plasma of the kidneys.

aclarar *v*. to clarify, to explain.

aclimatación *f*. acclimatization.

aclimatarse *vr*. to acclimate; to get used to a condition or custom; to adjust.

acloropsia *f*. achloropsia, inability to distinguish the color green.

acné *m*. acne, inflammatory skin condition; ____ rosáceo / ____ , rosacea; ____ vulgar o común / ____ , vulgaris, common acne.

acolia *f*. acholia, absence of bile.

acomodación *f*. accommodation, adjustment.

acomodar *v*. to accommodate, to adjust.

acompañante *m*., *f*. companion.

acompañar *v*. to accompany.

acondicionamiento *m*. conditioning; ____ físico / physical fitness.

acondroplasia *f*. achondroplasia, dwarfism, congenital osseous deformity.

aconsejar *v*. to advise, to recommend; ____ mal / to misguide.

acontecer *v*. to transpire, to occur.

acordar *vi*. to agree; **acordarse** *vr*. to remember, to recall.

acortar *v*. to shorten.

acosamiento *m*. harassment.

acosar *v*. to harass.

acostado-a *a*. reclining; lying down.

acostar *vi*. to lay down, to put to bed; **acostarse** *vr*. to go to bed; to lie down; **hora de** ____ / bed time.

acostumbrado-a *a*. accustomed, used to; no ____ / unaccustomed.

acostumbrarse *vr*. to get used to.

acre *a*. acrid, sour.

acreción *f*. accretion, growth; accumulation.

acreditado-a *a*. accredited, certified; no ____ / unlicensed.

acreditar *v*. to credit, to accredit, to certify.

acrocianosis *f*. acrocyanosis, Raynaud's disease, bluish discoloration and coldness of the extremities due to a circulatory disorder gen. brought about by exposure to cold or by emotional stress.

acrodermatitis *f*. acrodermatitis, infl. of the skin of hands and feet; ____ crónica atrófica / ____ chronica atrophicans.

acrofobia *f*. acrophobia, excessive fear of heights.

acromasia *f*. achromasia, lack or loss of pigmentation in the skin, characteristic of albinos.

acromático-a *a*. achromatic, lacking in color.

acromatopsia *f*. achromatopsia, color blindness.

acromegalia *f*. acromegaly, chronic disease common in middle age, manifested by progressive enlargement of the bones of the extremities and of certain head bones, gen. caused by a malfunction of the pituitary gland.

acromion *m*. acromion, part of the scapular bone of the shoulder.

actina *f*. actin, protein in muscle tissue that together with myosin makes possible muscle contraction.

actitud *f*. attitude, disposition.

activar *v*. to activate.

actividad *f*. activity.

activo-a *a*. active.

acto *m*. act; deed; **en el** ____ / right away.

actual *a.* actual, present, true, real; **-mente** *adv.* actually, presently.

actuar *v.* to act.

acuclillarse *vr.* to squat.

acuerdo *m.* agreement; **estar de** ___ / to be in agreement, to agree.

acumulación *f.* accumulation; pile, heap.

acumular *v.* to accumulate, to pile up, to amass.

acuoso-a *a.* aqueous; humor ___ / ___ humor; intoxicación ___ / water intoxication, condition caused by excessive retention of water in the body.

acupuntura *f.* acupuncture, method of inserting needles into specific points of the body as a means of relieving pain.

acústico-a *a.* acoustic, rel. to sound or hearing.

achacoso-a *a.* sickly, ailing.

achaque *m.* ailment, infirmity.

achicar *vi.* to reduce.

Adán, nuez de *f.* Adam's apple.

adaptabilidad *f.* adaptability; compliance. 1. the ease with which a substance or structure can change its shape, such as the ability of an organ to distend; 2. the degree to which a patient follows a prescribed regimen.

adaptación *f.* adaptation, adjustment.

adaptar *v.* to adapt, to fit, to accommodate; **adaptarse** *vr.* to adapt oneself.

Addison, enfermedad de *f.* Addison's disease, insufficiency or nonfunction of the adrenal glands.

adecuado-a *a.* adequate, suitable.

adelantado-a *a.* advanced, ahead; **por** ___ / in advance.

adelantar *v.* to advance, to move ahead; ___ **la fecha** / to move up the date.

adelante *adv.* forward, ahead; **más** ___ / later on; **de hoy en** ___ / from now on.

adelanto *m.* improvement, progress.

adelgazar *vi.* to lose weight, to get thin.

además *adv.* besides, in addition.

adenectomía *f. surg.* adenectomy, removal of a gland.

adenitis *f.* adenitis, infl. of a gland.

adenoacantoma *m.* adenoacantoma, slow-growing cancer of the uterus.

adenocarcinoma *m.* adenocarcinoma, malignant tumor arising from a gland or organ.

adenocistoma *m.* adenocystoma, benign gland tumor formed by cysts.

adenofibroma *m.* adenofibroma, benign fibrous glandular tumor seen in the breast and uterus.

adenoide *m.* adenoid, gland-like; accumulation of lymphatic tissue located in the throat behind the nose.

adenoidectomía *f. surg.* adenoidectomy, excision of the adenoid.

adenoiditis *f.* adenoiditis, infl. of the adenoid.

adenoma *m.* adenoma, glandular like tumor; ___ **basófilo** / basofil ___; ___ **sebáceo** / sebaceous ___; ___ **tóxico** / toxic ___.

adenomioma *m.* adenomyoma, benign tumor usu. seen in the uterus.

adenopatía *f.* adenopathy, adenopatia, a lymph gland disease.

adenosarcoma *m.* adenosarcoma, malignant tumor.

adenosis *f.* adenosis, enlargement of a gland.

adentro (de) *adv.* inside; inside of.

adherencia *f.* adhesion, attachment.

adherir *vi.* to adhere, to attach.

adhesivo-a *a.* adhesive.

adicción *f.* addiction, dependency, propensity; **dejar la** ___ / *pop.* [*droga*] to kick the habit.

adictivo *m.* addictive, rel. to or causing addiction.

adicto-a *a.* addicted, physically or psychologically dependent on a substance such as alcohol or a narcotic.

adiós *int.* goodbye.

adiposo-a *a.* adipose, fatty; **tejido** ___ / ___ **tissue.**

adjetivo *m.* adjective.

adjuntar *v.* to enclose; to include.

adjutor *m.* adjuvant, helper; substance added to a medication to heighten its action.

administración *f.* administration, management.

administrador-a *m., f.* administrator, manager.

admisión *f.* admission.

admitir *v.* to admit.

adolescencia *f.* adolescence, puberty.

adolescente *m., f.* adolescent.

adolorido-a *a.* sore.

adopción *f.* adoption.

adoptar *v.* to adopt.

adoptivo-a *a.* adoptive.

adormecer *vi.* to put to sleep, [*un nervio*] to deaden; **adormecerse** *vr.* to drowse.

adquirir *vi.* to acquire.

adquisición *f.* acquisition.

adrede *adv.* on purpose.

adrenal *a.* adrenal. V. **suprarrenal.**

adrenalectomía *f. surg.* adrenalectomy, removal of the adrenal gland.

adrenalina *f.* adrenaline, epinephrin, hormone secreted by the adrenal medulla, commonly used as a cardiac stimulant.

adrenalismo *m.* adrenalism, inadequate function of the adrenal glands.

adrenocorticotropina *f.* adrenocorticotropin, hormone secreted by the pituitary gland that has a stimulating effect on the adrenal cortex.

adrenogénico-a *a.* adrenogenous, originating in the adrenal glands.

aductor-a *a.* adductor, a muscle that draws a part towards the median line.

adueñarse *vr.* to take possession.

adulterado-a *a.* adulterated, changed from the original; no ____ / unadulterated.

adulterar *v.* to adulterate, to change the original.

adulterio *m.* adultery.

adulto-a *a.* adult.

adverbio *m. gr.* adverb.

adverso-a *a.* adverse, unfavorable.

advertencia *f.* warning, forewarning; advice.

advertir *vi.* to warn; to advise.

adyacente *a.* adjacent, next to.

aerobio *m.* aerobe, organism that requires oxygen to live.

aeroembolismo *m.* aeroembolism, condition caused by a release of bubbles of nitrogen into the blood gen. due to a sudden change in atmospheric pressure; *pop.* the bends.

aeroenfisema *m.* aeroemphysema, condition caused by a sudden ascent in space without adequate decompression; *pop.* the chokes.

aerofagia *f.* aerophagia, excessive swallowing of air.

aerogénico-a *a.* aerogenic, gas-producing.

afán *m.* eagerness, desire.

afasia *f.* aphasia, inability to coordinate word and thought in speaking.

afebril *a.* afebrile, without fever.

afección *f.* affection, fondness; condition, sickness.

afectado-a *a.* affected.

afectar *v.* to affect; to cause change.

afectivo-a *a.* affective; síntoma ____ / ____ symptom; transtornos ____-s / ____ disorders.

afeitar *v.* to shave; **afeitarse** *vr.* to shave oneself.

afemia *f.* aphemia, loss of speech gen. due to a cerebral hemorrhage, a blood clot or a tumor.

afeminado *a.* effeminate.

aferente *a.* afferent, directing toward the center.

afibrinogenemia *f.* afibrinogenemia, deficiency of fibrinogen in the blood.

afinidad *f.* affinity; similarity.

afirmación *f.* affirmation.

afirmar *v.* to affirm, to make certain.

aflicción *f.* affliction, sorrow, grief, distress; reacción de ____ / grief reaction.

afligido-a *a.* afflicted, distressed, sorrowful, grief-stricken, troubled.

afligir *vi.* to afflict, to cause pain; **afligirse** *vr.* to lament, to be grieved.

aflojar *v.* to loosen, to slacken; **aflojarse** *vr.* to become weak; to lose courage.

afonía *f.* aphonia, loss of voice due to an affection of the larynx.

afónico-a *a.* aphonic, without voice or sound.

afortunado-a *a.* fortunate, lucky.

afrodisíaco *m.* aphrodisiac, any agent that arouses sexual desire.

afrontar *v.* to confront.

afta *f.* aphtha, a small ulcer, sign of fungal infection of the oral mucose.

afuera *adv.* outside.

agacharse *vr.* to bend; to stoop, to squat.

agallas *f. pl.* tonsils; *pop.* tener ____ / to have guts, to be bold.

agalorrea *f.* agalorrhea, cessation or lack of milk in the breasts.

agammaglobulinemia *f.* agammaglobulinemia, deficiency of gamma globulin in the blood.

agarrar *v.* to grab, to grip.

agenesia, agenesis *f.* agenesia, agenesis. 1. congenital failure of an organ to grow or develop; 2. sterility or impotence.

agente *m.* agent, factor.

ágil *a.* agile, nimble; mentally sharp.

agilidad *f.* agility; ____ mental / mental ____ .

agitación *f.* excitement, agitation.

agitar *v.* to stir up, to shake; ____ la botella / to shake the bottle.

aglomeración *f.* agglomeration.

aglutinación *f.* agglutination, the act of binding together.

aglutinante *m.* agglutinant, agent or factor that holds parts together during the healing process.

agobiar *v.* to weigh down; to burden.

agonía *f.* agony, anguish. 1. extreme suffering; 2. state preceding death.

agonizar *vi.* to agonize.

agorafobia *f.* agoraphobia, fear of being alone in a wide open space.

agotado-a *a.* exhausted, tired.

agotador-a *a.* exhausting, tiring.

agotamiento *m.* exhaustion, extreme fatigue; wasting.

agotar *v.* to exhaust; ____ **todos los recursos** / to ____ all means.

agradable *a.* pleasant.

agradecer *vi.* to be grateful, to be thankful.

agradecido-a *a.* grateful, thankful.

agrafia *f.* agraphia, loss of ability to write due to a brain disorder.

agrandamiento *m.* enlargement.

agrandar *v.* to enlargen.

agranulocitosis *f.* agranulocytosis, acute condition caused by the absence of leukocytes in the blood.

agregar *v.* to add.

agresivo-a *a.* aggressive, hostile.

agriarse *vr.* to turn sour.

agrietado-a *a.* chapped; labios ____-s / ____ lips; manos ____-as / ____ hands.

agrio-a *a.* sour.

agua *f.* water; **abastecimiento de** ____ / ____ supply; ____ **alcanforizada** / canphor julep; ____ **corriente o de pila** / tap ____; ____ **de rosa** / rose____; ____ **helada** / ice ____; ____ **oxigenada** / hydrogen peroxide; **bolsa de** ____ / ____ bag; **cama de, colchón de** ____ / ____ bed; **contaminación del** ____ / ____ pollution; **purificación del** ____ / ____ purification; **soluble en** ____ / ____ soluble.

aguado-a *a.* watered down.

aguantar *v.* to hold; to endure.

agudo-a *a.* acute, piercing, sharp.

agüero *m.* omen.

aguja *f.* needle; ____ hipodérmica / hypodermic ____.

agujero *m.* hole.

ahí *adv.* there.

ahijado-a *m., f.* godchild.

ahogamiento *m.* drowning.

ahogar *vi.* to drown; to smother, to extinguish; **ahogarse** *vr.* to drown oneself; to choke.

ahora *adv.* now, presently.

ahorcarse *vr., vi.* to hang oneself.

ahorita *adv.* right away.

ahorrar *v.* to save; to spare; ____ **tiempo** / ____ time.

aire *m.* air, wind; breath; ____ acondicionado / ____ conditioned; ____ contaminado, viciado / contaminated ____, pollution; ____ de ventilación / ventilated ____; ____ respiratorio / tidal ____; bolsa de ____ / ____ pocket; burbujas de ____ / ____ bubbles; cámara de ____ / ____ chamber; conducto de ____ / airway, air passage; enfriado por ____ / ____ cooled; falto de ____ / shortness of breath.

airear *v.* to aerate, to ventilate. 1. to saturate a liquid with air; 2. to change the venous blood into arterial blood in the lungs; 3. to circulate fresh air.

aislado-a *a.* isolated.

aislamiento *m.* isolation; ____ protector / protective ____; sala de ____ / ____ ward.

aislar *v.* to isolate.

ajo *m.* garlic.

ajustado-a *a.* tight-fitting; adjusted.

ajustar *v.* to tighten; to adjust.

ala *m.* wing.

alambre *m.* wire.

alargado-a *a.* elongated, as the digestive tract.

alargar *vi.* to lengthen; to prolong.

alarma *f.* alarm; signal of danger; ____ **de fuego** / fire ____.

alarmante *a.* alarming.

alarmar *v.* to alarm; **alarmarse** *vr.* to become alarmed.

albahaca *f.* sweet basil.

alberca *f.* swimming pool; pond; tank.

albinismo *m.* albinism, lack of pigment in the skin and hair.

albino-a *m., f.* albino, person afflicted with albinism.

albúmina *f.* albumin, protein component.

albuminuria *f.* albuminuria, presence of albumin or globulin in the urine.

alcaloide *m.* alkaloid, one of a group of organic, basic substances found in plants.

alcalosis *f.* alkalosis, physiological disorder in the normal acid-base balance of the body.

alcance *m.* reach; span; **al** ____ **de** / within ____.

alcanfor *m.* camphor, camphor julep.

alcanzar *vi.* to reach; to catch up.

alcohol *m.* alcohol; ____ etílico / ethyl ____.

alcohólico-a *m., f.* an alcoholic; *a.* alcoholic.

alcoholismo *m.* alcoholism, excess intake of alcohol.

aldosterona *f.* aldosterone, hormone produced by the adrenal gland.

aldosteronismo *m.* aldosteronism, anomaly caused by excessive secretion of aldosterone.

alegre *a.* cheerful, joyful, merry.

alelo, alelomorfo *m.* allele, any one of a series of two or more genes situated at the same place in homologous chromosomes, that determine alternative characteristics in inheritance.

alentar *vi.* to encourage, to reassure.

alergia *f.* allergy.

alérgico-a *a.* allergic; reacción ___ / ___ reaction; rinitis ___ / ___ rhinitis.

alerta *a.* alert, vigilant.

aleteo *m.* flutter, cardiac arrhythmia characterized by fast auricular contractions that simulate the flutter of the wings of birds; ___ auricular / ___, atrial, auricular; ___ ventricular / ___, ventricular; ___ y fibrilación / ___ and fibrillation.

aleucemia *f.* aleukemia, absence or deficiency of leukocytes in the blood.

alexia *f.* alexia, inability to understand the written word.

alfiler *m.* pin.

alfombra *f.* rug.

álgido-a *a.* algid, cold.

algodón *m.* cotton.

algor *m.* algor, chill.

algoritmo *m.* algorithm, arithmetical and algebraic method used in the diagnosis and treatment of a disease.

aliento *m.* 1. breath; **sin** ___ / breathless; **mal** ___ / bad ___. 2. encouragement.

aligeramiento *m.* lightening, descent of the uterus into the pelvic cavity in the final stage of pregnancy.

aligerar *v.* to lighten, to ease.

alimentación *f.* feeding, alimentation, nourishment; ___ enteral / enteral ___; ___ forzada / forced ___; ___ intravenosa / intravenous ___; ___ por sonda / tube ___; ___ rectal / rectal ___; requisitos de la ___ / food requirements.

alimentar *v.* to nourish, to feed.

alimento *m.* food, nourishment, nutrient; ___-s enriquecidos / ___ supplements; manipulación de ___-s / ___ handling.

alimenticio-a *a.* alimentary, nourishing; aditivos ___-s / food additives; intoxicación ___ / food poisoning; tracto ___ / ___ tract.

aliviado-a *a.* relieved, alleviated.

aliviar *v.* to relieve, to alleviate; [*un dolor*] to lessen.

alivio *m.* relief; **iqué** ___ / what a relief!

almacenamiento *m.* storage; [*toma*] captura y ___ / uptake and ___.

almanaque *m.* calendar, almanac.

almeja *f.* clam.

almendra *f.* almond.

almidón *m.* starch, main form of storage of carbohydrates.

almohada *f.* pillow.

almohadilla *f.* pad.

almorzar *vi.* to have lunch.

almuerzo *m.* lunch.

alojamiento *m.* lodging.

alojar *v.* to lodge; to accommodate.

alopecia *f.* alopecia, loss of hair.

alquilar *v.* to rent.

alrededor *adv.* around, about.

alteración *f.* alteration, change, modification.

alterar *v.* to alter, to change.

alternar *v.* to alternate.

alternativa *f.* alternative, option.

alto-a *a.* tall.

altura *f.* height.

alucinación, alucinamiento *f., m.* hallucination, subjective feeling not related to a real stimulus; ___ auditiva / auditory ___, imaginary perception of sound; ___ gustativa / gustatory ___, imaginary perception of taste; ___ motor / motor ___, imaginary perception of body movements; ___ olfativa / olfactory ___, imaginary perception of odors; ___ táctil / haptic ___, imaginary perception of pain, temperature or other skin sensations.

alucinar *v.* to hallucinate.

alucinógeno *m.* hallucinogen, drug that produces hallucinations, such as LSD, peyote or mescaline.

alucinosis *f.* hallucinosis, state of persistent hallucinations; ___ alcohólica / alcoholic ___, extreme fear accompanied by auditory hallucinations.

alumbramiento *m.* parturition, the act of giving birth.

alveolar *a.* alveolar, rel. to an alveolus.

alvéolo *m*. alveolus, cavity; ____ pulmonar / air sac.

Alzheimer, enfermedad de *f*. Alzheimer's disease, presenile dementia.

allí *adv*. there.

amable *a*. kind, nice.

amalgamar *v*. to amalgamate, to mix.

amamantar *v*. to nurse, to suckle, to breast-feed.

amar *v*. to love.

amargado-a *m*., *f*. a bitter person; *a*. [*persona*] bitter.

amargar *vi*. to make bitter; **amargarse** *vr*., *vi*. to become bitter.

amargo-a *a*. bitter.

amargura *f*. bitterness.

amarillento-a *a*. yellowish.

amarillo-a *a*. yellow.

amarrar *v*. to tie, to fasten, to secure.

amasadura, amasamiento *f*., *m*. kneading, methodical rubbing and pressing of muscles.

amastia *f*. amastia, absence of breasts.

ambarino-a *a*. amber-colored.

ambición *f*. ambition.

ambicionar *v*. to aspire.

ambidextro *a*. ambidextrous.

ambiente *m*. environment, ambiance, setting.

ambivalencia *f*. ambivalence.

ambliopía *f*. amblyopia, diminished vision.

ambos -as *a*. both.

ambulancia *f*. ambulance.

ambulante, ambulatorio-a *a*. ambulant, ambulatory.

ameba *m*. amoeba, ameba, one-celled organism.

amebiano-a *a*. amebid, rel. to amebae.

amebiasis *f*. amebiasis, infection by amebae.

amenaza *f*. threat; menace.

amenazar *vi*. to threaten.

ameno-a *a*. pleasant, affable.

amenorrea *f*. amenorrhoea, absence of menstrual period.

americano-a *a*. American.

ametropía *f*. ametropia, poor vision due to an anomaly or disturbance in the refractive powers of the eye.

anfetamina *f*. amphetamine, type of drug used as a stimulant of the nervous system.

amígdalas *f*. *pl*. amygdalae, tonsils.

amigdalitis *f*. tonsillitis, infl. of the tonsils.

amigdalotomía *f*. *surg*. tonsillectomy, removal of the tonsils.

amigo-a *m*., *f*. friend.

amiloide *a*. amyloid, starch-like protein.

amiloidosis *m*. amyloidosis, accumulation of amyloid in different tissues of the body.

amina *f*. amine, one of the basic compounds derived from ammonia.

aminoácido *m*. amino acid, an organic metabolic compound that is the end product of protein and necessary for the growth and development of the human body.

amistad *f*. friendship.

amnesia *f*. amnesia, loss of memory.

amniocentesis *m*. amniocentesis, puncture of the uterus to obtain amniotic fluid.

amnios *m*. amnion, membranous sac surrounding the embryo in the womb.

amniótico-a *a*. amniotic, rel. to the amnion; fluido ____ / ____ fluid; saco ____ / ____ sac.

amoldamiento *m*. molding, adjustment of the head of the fetus to the shape and size of the birth canal.

amoníaco *m*. ammonia.

amor *m*. love.

amoratado-a *a*. black and blue.

amorfo-a *a*. amorphous, without shape.

amparar *v*. to protect; to shelter.

ampicilina *f*. ampicillin, semisynthetic penicillin.

ampliación *f*. amplification.

ampliar *v*. to amplify, to magnify, to enlarge.

amplio-a *a*. wide, large, ample.

ampolla *f*. blister, bulla.

ámpula *f*. ampule, vial, small glass container.

amputación *f*. amputation.

amputar *v*. to amputate.

anabólico-a *a*. anabolic, rel. to anabolism; esteroides ____-s / ____ steroids.

anabolismo *m*. anabolism, cellular process by which simple substances are converted into complex compounds; constructive metabolism.

anacidez *f*. anacidity, state of being without acid.

anaeróbico-a *a*. anaerobic, rel. to anaerobes.

anaerobio *m*. anaerobe, germ that multiplies in the absence of air or oxygen.

anafase *f*. anaphase, a stage in cell division.

anafiláctico-a *a*. anaphylactic, rel. to anaphylaxis.

anafilaxis *f.* anaphylaxis, extreme allergic reaction, hypersensitivity.

anal *a.* anal; fístula ____ / ____ fistula.

analfabeto-a *m., f. a.* illiterate.

analgésico *m.* analgesic, pain reliever.

análisis *m.* analysis, test, assay.

analizar *vi.* to analyze, to examine.

analogía *f.* analogy, similarity.

anaplasia *f.* anaplasia, lack or loss of differentiation of cells.

anaplástico-a *a.* anaplastic, rel. to anaplasia.

anaquel *m.* shelf; shelf-like structure.

anaranjado-a *a.* orange.

anasarca *f.* anasarca, generalized edema; dropsy.

anastomosis *f. surg.* anastomosis, creation of a passage or communication between two or more organs; inosculating.

anatomía *f.* anatomy, science that studies the structure of the human body and its organs; ____ macroscópica / gross ____, rel. to structures that can be seen with the naked eye; ____ topográfica / topographic ____, rel. to a specific area of the body.

anatómico-a *a.* anatomic, anatomical, rel. to anatomy.

ancianidad *f.* old age.

anciano-a *m., f.* old man, old woman.

andador *m.* walker, device used to help a person walk.

andar *vi.* to walk, to go, ____ con cuidado / to be careful.

andrógeno *m.* androgen, masculine hormone; *a.* androgenic, rel. to the male sexual characteristics.

androginoide *a.* androgynous, having both male and female characteristics.

androtomía *f.* androtomy, dissection of a cadaver.

anejos, anexos *m. pl.* adnexa, appendages such as found in the uterine tubes.

anemia *f.* anemia, insufficiency of blood cells either in quality, quantity or in hemoglobin content; ____ aplástica / aplastic ____, highly deficient production of blood cells; ____ de glóbulos falciformes / sickle cell ____; ____ hemorrágica o hemolítica / hemorrhagic, hemolitic ____, progressive destruction of red blood cells; ____ hipercrómica / hyperchromic ____, abnormal increase in the hemoglobin content; ____ hipocrómica y microcítica / hipochromic and microcytic ____, small-sized blood cells and insufficient amount of hemo-

globin; ____ macrocítica / macrocytic ____, large-sized blood cells, pernicious anemia; ____ por deficiencia de hierro / iron-deficiency ____.

anestesia *f.* anesthesia; ____ en silla de montar / saddle block ____; ____ epidural / epidural ____ ; ____ general / general ____ ; ____ general intravenosa / general intravenous ____; ____ general por inhalación / general ____ by inhalation; ____ general por intubación / general ____ by intubation; ____ local / local ____ ; ____ raquídea / spinal ____; ____ regional / regional ____.

anestesiar *v.* to anesthetize.

anestésico *m.* anesthetic.

anestesiólogo-a *m., f.* anesthesiologist.

aneurisma *m.* aneurysm, dilation of a portion of the wall of the artery.

aneurismal *a.* aneurysmal, rel. to an aneurysm.

aneurismectomía *f. surg.* aneurysmectomy, excision of an aneurysm.

anexo-a *a.* contiguous, annexive.

angiitis *f.* angiitis, infl. of a blood or lymph vessel.

angina *f.* angina, painful constrictive sensation; ____ intestinal / intestinal ____ , acute abdominal pain caused by insufficient blood supply to the intestines; ____ laríngea / laryngea ____ , infl. of the throat; ____ pectoris / ____ pectoris, chest pain caused by insufficient blood supply to the heart muscle.

angiocardiografía *f.* angiocardiography, X-ray of the heart chambers.

angioedema *f.* angioedema, angioneurotic edema, allergic infl., gen. of the face.

angioespasmo *m.* angiospasm, prolonged contraction of a blood vessel.

angiogénesis *f.* angiogenesis, the development of the vascular system.

angiografía *f.* angiography, X-ray of the blood vessels after injection of a substance to show their outline.

angioma *m.* angioma, benign vascular tumor.

angioplastia *f. surg.* angioplasty, plastic surgery of the blood vessels; ____ coronaria percutánea / percutaneous coronary ____; ____ periférica percutánea / percutaneous peripheral ____.

angioplastia transluminal percutánea *f.* percutaneous transluminal angioplasty, process of dilating an artery or vessel by using a balloon that is inflated by pressure.

angloparlante *m., f.* English speaker.

angosto-a *a.* narrow; tapered.

ángulo *m.* angle.

angustia *f.* anguish, distress.

angustiado-a *a.* distraught, distressed.

anhidrosis *f.* anhidrosis, diminished secretion of sweat.

anillo *m.* ring, margin, verge; ___ anal / anal verge.

animal *m.* animal.

animar *v.* to animate, to cheer up; **animarse** *vr.* to become more lively.

ánimo *m.* spirit; estado de ___ / mood; **no tener** ___ / to be without spirit.

animosidad *f.* animosity, rancor.

aniquilación *f.* annihilation, total destruction.

anisocitosis *f.* anisocytosis, unequal size of red blood cells.

ano *m.* anus.

anoche *adv.* last night.

anodino *m.* anodyne, pain reliever; **-a** *a.* insipid.

anomalía, anormalidad *f.* anomaly, abnormality, irregularity.

anorexia *f.* anorexia, disorder caused by total lack of appetite.

anormal *a.* abnormal, irregular.

anosmia *f.* anosmia, lack of the sense of smell.

anotar *v.* to make or take note.

anovulación *f.* anovulation, cessation of ovulation.

anoxemia *f.* anoxemia, insufficient oxygen in the blood.

anoxia *f.* anoxia, lack of oxygen in body tissues.

anquilosado-a *a.* ankylosed, immobilized.

anquilosis *f.* ankylosis, immobility of an articulation.

ansiedad *f.* anxiety, anguish, state of apprehension or excessive worry; estados de ___ / disorders; neurosis de ___ / ___ neurosis.

ansioso-a *a.* anxious, apprehensive.

anteayer *adv.* the day before yesterday.

antebrazo *f.* forearm.

antecubital *a.* antecubital, preceding the elbow.

anteflexión *f.* anteflexion, bending forward.

antemano *adv.* beforehand.

anteojos *m. pl.* eyeglasses; binoculars. *V.* espejuelos.

antepasados *m. pl.* ancestors.

antepié *m.* ball of the foot.

anterior *a.* preceding, previous.

anteroposterior *a.* anteroposterior, from front to back.

antes *adv.* before, sooner; **lo** ___ **posible** / as soon as possible; ___ **de** / before, prior to; ___ **las comidas** / ___ meals.

anteversión *f.* anteversion, turn towards the front.

antiácido *m.* antacid, acidity neutralizer.

antialérgico *m.* antiallergic, drug used to treat allergies.

antiarrítmico-a *a.* antiarrhythmic, that can prevent or be effective in the treatment of arrhythmia; agentes ___ -s / cardiac depressants.

antiartrítico-a *a.* antiarthritic, rel. to medication used in the treatment of arthritis.

antibiótico *m.* antibiotic, antibacterial drug.

anticarcinógeno *m.* anticarcinogen, drug used in the treatment of cancer.

anticipar *v.* to anticipate.

anticoagulante *m.* anticoagulant, substance used in the prevention of blood clotting.

anticonceptivo *m.* contraceptive; **-a** *a.* that acts as a contraceptive; drogas ___ -s / anovulatory drugs.

anticonvulsante, anticonvulsivo *m.* anticonvulsant, medication used to prevent fits or convulsions.

anticuerpo *m.* antibody, protein substance that is produced by lymph tissue in response to the presence of an antigen; ___ monoclónico / monoclonal ___, derived from hybridoma cells.

antidepresivo *m.* antidepressant, medication or process used in the treatment of depression.

antidiurético *m.* antidiuretic, drug that decreases urine secretion.

antídoto *m.* antidote, substance used to neutralize a poison; ___ universal / universal ___.

antiemético *m.* antiemetic, medication used to treat nausea.

antiespasmódico *m.* antispasmodic, drug used in the treatment of spasms.

antígeno *m.* antigen, toxic substance which stimulates formation of antibodies; ___ carcinoembriogénico / carcinoembryogenic ___.

antihipertensivo *m.* antihypertensive, medication to lower elevated blood pressure.

antihistamínico *m.* antihistamine, medication used in the treatment of some allergies.

antiinflamatorio *m.* anti-inflammatory, agent used to treat inflammations.

antineoplástico *m.* antineoplastic, drug that controls or destroys cancer cells.

antipatía *f.* antipathy, aversion.

antipirético *m.* antipyretic, agent that reduces fever.

antiséptico *m.* antiseptic, agent that destroys bacteria.

antitóxico *m.* antitoxine, neutralizer of the effects of toxines.

antitoxina *f.* antitoxin, antibody that has a neutralizing effect on a given poison introduced in the body by a microorganism.

antracosis *f.* anthracosis, lung condition due to prolonged inhalation of coal dust.

antrectomía *f. surg.* antrectomy, removal of the wall or walls of an antrum.

antro *m.* antrum, cavity.

antropoide *a.* anthropoid, of human resemblance.

anular *v.* to cancel, to make void, to annul.

anuria *f.* anuria, lack of urine production due to kidney malfunction.

año *m.* year.

aorta *f.* aorta, major artery originating from the left ventricle; ____ ascendente / ascending ____; cayado de la ____ / ____ arch; ____ descendente / descending ____.

aórtico-a *a.* aortic, rel. to the aorta.

aortografía *f.* aortography, outline of the aorta on an X-ray.

apagado-a *a.* turned off; dim, unlit.

apagar *vi.* [*luces*] to turn off; [*fuego*] to put out.

aparato digestivo *m.* digestive system.

aparato eléctrico *m.* electrical appliance.

aparente *a.* apparent, manifest, patent, visible.

apariencia *f.* appearance.

apasionado-a *a.* passionate.

apatía *f.* apathy, lack of interest.

apático-a *a.* apathetic, listless, languid.

apelar *v.* to appeal.

apellido *m.* surname, family name.

apenado-a *a.* grieved.

apenas *adv.* barely; no sooner than; as soon as.

apendectomía *f. surg.* appendectomy, removal of the appendix.

apéndice *m.* appendix.

apendicitis *f.* appendicitis, infl. of the appendix.

apendicular *a.* appendicular, rel. to the appendix.

apepsia *f.* apepsia, poor digestion.

aperitivo *m.* aperitive, aperient. 1. mild laxative, physic; 2. aperitif, agent that stimulates the appetite.

apesadumbrado-a *a.* mournful, grieved.

apetito *m.* appetite.

apio *m.* celery.

aplanar *v.* to flatten.

aplasia *f.* aplasia, failure of organ development.

aplazar *vi.* to postpone, to put off.

aplicación *f.* application; ____ de hielo / ice treatment, icing.

aplicador *m.* applicator; ____ de algodón / cotton ____.

aplicar *vi.* to apply.

apnea *f.* apnea, shortness of breath; ____ del sueño / sleep ____, intermittent apnea that occurs during sleep.

apófisis *f.* apophysis, bony outgrowth.

aponeurosis *f.* aponeurosis, connective tissue that attaches the muscles to the bones and to other tissue.

apoplejía *f.* apoplexy, stroke, cerebrovascular accident.

apoyar *v.* to back, to support; **apoyarse** *vr.* to lean on.

apoyo *m.* backing, support.

apraxia *f.* apraxia, lack of muscular coordination and movement.

apreciar *v.* to appreciate, to value; to be grateful.

aprender *v.* to learn.

apretado-a *a.* tight.

apretar *vi.* to tighten, to squeeze, to press down.

aprisa *adv.* fast.

aprobación *f.* approval, consent, acceptance.

aprobar *v.* to approve; to accept.

apropiado-a *a.* appropriate, adequate.

aprovechar *v.* to make use of; to take advantage of.

aproximado-a *a.* approximate; **-mente** *adv.* approximately.

aptitud *f.* aptitude, capacity, ability; prueba de ____ / ____ test.

apto-a *a.* competent, apt.

apurado-a *a.* in a hurry; in difficulty.

apurarse *vr.* to hurry.

apuro *m.* need; hurry; **estar en un** ____ / to be in trouble.

aquí *adv.* here; **por** ____ / this way.

aquietar *v.* to calm down.

Aquiles, tendón de *m.* Achilles tendon, the tendon that originates in the muscles of the calf and attaches to the heel.

aracnoide *m.* arachnoid, weblike membrane that covers the brain and spinal cord.

araña *f.* spider; ____ viuda negra / black widow ____.

arañar *v.* to scratch.

arañazo *m.* scratch.

árbol *m.* 1. anatomical structure resembling a tree; 2. tree.

arcadas *f. pl.* retching, spasmodic abdominal contractions that precede vomiting.

arco *m.* arch.

arder *v.* to have a burning feeling, to itch.

ardor *m.* ardor, burning feeling; ____ en el estómago / heartburn.

arena *f.* sand.

arenilla *f.* minute sand-like particles.

arenoso-a *a.* sandy.

aréola *f.* areola, circular area of a different color around a central point.

Argyll Robertson, pupila de *f.* Argyll Robertson's pupil, a pupil of the eye that accommodates to distance but does not react to the refraction of light.

arma de fuego *m.* firearm.

armazón *f.* frame, supportive structure.

aroma *m.* aroma, pleasant smell.

aromático-a *a.* aromatic, rel. to an aroma.

arquetipo *m.* archetype, original type from which modified versions evolve.

arraigado-a *a.* deep-rooted.

arrancar *vi.* to tear off; to pull out.

arrebato *m.* fit; temporary insanity.

arreglado-a *a.* in order; neat; fixed.

arreglar *v.* to fix, to arrange.

arreglo *m.* settlement, agreement.

arrepentido-a *a.* repentant, regretful.

arrepentirse *vr., vi.* to regret; to repent.

arriba *adv.* above, upstairs; **de** ____ **a abajo** / from top to bottom.

arriesgado-a *a.* risky.

arriesgar *vi.* to risk, to imperil; **arriesgarse** *vr.* to take a risk.

arritmia *f.* arrhythmia, irregular heartbeats.

arrodillarse *vr.* to kneel.

arrojar *v.* to throw up, to vomit.

arroz *m.* rice.

arruga *f.* wrinkle.

arrugado-a *a.* wrinkled.

arrugar *vi.* to wrinkle; **arrugarse** *vr.* to become wrinkled.

arsénico *m.* arsenic; envenenamiento por ____ / ____ poisoning.

arteria *f.* artery; vessel carrying blood from the heart to tissues throughout the body.

arterial *a.* arterial, rel. to the arteries; enfermedades ____-es oclusivas / ____ occlusive diseases; sistema ____ / ____ system.

arterioesclerosis *f.* arteriosclerosis, hardening of the walls of the arteries.

arteriografía *f.* arteriography, X-ray of the arteries.

arteriotomía *f. surg.* arteriotomy, opening of an artery.

arteritis *f.* arteritis, infl. of an artery.

arteriovenoso-a *a.* arteriovenous; rel. to an artery and a vein; anastomosis ____ quirúrgica / ____ shunt, surgical; fístula ____ / ____ fistula; malformaciones ____-s / ____ malformations.

articulación *f.* joint, articulation. 1. joint between two or more bones; ____ de la cadera / hip ____; ____ esferoidea / ball and socket ____; ____ del hombro / shoulder ____; ____ de la rodilla / knee ____; ____ sacroilíaca / sacroiliac ____; 2. articulation, distinctive and clear pronunciation of words in speech.

articular *a.* articular, rel. to the articulations; cápsula ____ / capsular ligament, fibrous structure lined with synovial membrane surrounding the articulations; *v.* to articulate, to pronounce words clearly.

artículo *m.* article.

artificial *a.* artificial.

artrítico-a *a.* arthritic, rel. to or suffering from arthritis.

artritis *f.* arthritis, infl. of an articulation or joint; ____ aguda / acute ____; ____ crónica / chronic ____; ____ degenerativa / degenerative ____; ____ hemofílica / hemophilic ____; ____ reumatoidea / rheumatoid ____; ____ traumática / traumatic ____.

artrodesis *f. surg.* arthrodesis. 1. fusion of the bones of a joint; 2. artificial ankylosis.

artrograma *m.* arthrogram, X-ray of a joint.

artroplastia *f. surg.* arthroplasty, reparation of a joint or building of an artificial one.

artroscopía *f.* arthroscopy, examination of the inside of a joint with an arthroscope.

artroscopio *m.* arthroscope, device used to examine the inside of a joint.

artrotomía *f. surg.* arthrotomy, incision of a joint for therapeutic purposes.

asa *f.* loop.

asado-a *a.* roasted.

asbesto *m.* asbestos.

asbestosis *f.* asbestosis, chronic infection of the lungs caused by asbestos.

ascariasis *f.* ascariasis, intestinal infection caused by a worm of the genus *Ascaris.*

ascárido *m.* ascaris, type of worm commonly found in the intestinal tract.

ascendencia *f.* ancestry, genealogy.

ascendiente *m.* ascendent.

ascitis *f.* ascitis, accumulation of fluid in the abdominal cavity.

asco *m.* nausea; disgust, loathing; **dar ___ /** to produce nausea.

aseado-a *a.* clean, tidy.

asear *v.* to clean; **asearse** *vr.* to clean oneself.

asegurar *v.* to assure; **asegurarse** *vr.* to make sure.

asentaderas *f. pl.* buttocks.

asepsia *f.* asepsia, total absence of germs.

aséptico-a *a.* aseptic, sterile.

asexual *a.* asexual, having no gender; reproducción ___ / ___ reproduction.

asfixia *f.* asphyxia, suffocation; ___ **fetal /** ___ fetalis.

asfixiarse *vr.* to asphyxiate, to suffocate.

así *adv.* like this; ___ **que /** therefore.

asiento *m.* seat, space upon which a structure rests.

asignación *f.* assignment, task, mission.

asignar *v.* to assign.

asilo *m.* nursing home; ___ **para ancianos /** ___ for the aged.

asimilación *f.* assimilation, absorption, and transformation of digested food by the body.

asimilar *v.* to assimilate.

asinergia *f.* asynergia, lack of coordination among normally harmonious organs.

asintomático-a *a.* asymptomatic, without symptoms.

asistencia *f.* 1. assistance, care, help; ___ **social a la infancia /** child welfare; **recibir** ___ / to be on relief; 2. attendance.

asistente *m., f.* attendant, assistant.

asistir *v.* to attend; to help.

asistolia *f.* asystole, asystolia, absence of heart contractions.

asma *m.* asthma, allergic condition that causes bouts of short breath, wheezing, and edema of the mucosa.

asmático-a *a.* asthmatic, rel. to or suffering from asthma.

asociación *f.* association.

asociado-a *m., f.* associate.

asombrar *v.* to amaze; **asombrarse** *vr.* to be amazed.

aspecto *m.* appearance, aspect.

aspereza *f.* roughness, harshness.

aspermia *f.* aspermia, failure to form or emit semen.

áspero-a *a.* rough, harsh; piel ___ / ___ skin.

aspiración *f.* aspiration, inhalation.

aspirar *v.* to breath in, to inhale; ___ por la mucosa nasal / to snort.

aspirina *f.* aspirin, a derivative of salicylic acid.

astigmatismo *m.* astigmatism, defective curvature of the refractive surfaces of the eye.

astilla *f.* splinter.

astrágalo *m.* astragalus, ankle bone.

astringente *m.* astringent, agent that has the power to constrict tissues and mucous membranes.

astrocitoma *f.* astrocytoma, brain tumor.

asunto *m.* subject, matter; business.

asustado-a *a.* frightened, startled.

asustar *v.* to frighten, to scare; **asustarse** *vr.* to become frightened.

ataque *m.* attack, fit, stroke, bout, seizure; ___ **cardíaco /** heart ___.

ataraxia *f.* ataraxia, impassiveness.

atareado-a *a.* busy.

atavismo *m.* atavism, inherited trait from remote ancestors.

ataxia *f.* ataxia, deficiency in muscular coordination; ___ sifilítica / tabes dorsal.

ataúd *m.* coffin, casket.

atelectasia *f.* atelectasis, partial or total collapse of a lung.

atención *f.* attention; care; courtesy; ___ médica / medical care; **falta de** ___ / lack of ___; **prestar** ___ / to pay attention.

atender *v.* to attend, to look after; to pay attention.

atento-a *a.* attentive; polite; **estar** ___ / to be ___ .

atenuación *f.* attenuation, rendering less virulent.

ateo-a *m., f.* atheist.

atérmico-a *a.* athermic, without fever.

ateroma *f.* atheroma, fatty deposits in the intima of an artery.

atetosis *f.* athetosis, infantile spasmodic paraplegia.

atleta *m.* athlete.

atlético-a *a.* athletic.

atmósfera *f.* atmosphere.

atmósferico-a *a.* atmospheric.

atolondrado-a *a.* confused, bewildered.

atolondramiento *m.* confusion, bewilderment.

atomizador *m.* atomizer.

átomo *m.* atom.

atonía *f.* atony, lack of normal tone, esp. in the muscles.

atontado-a *a.* stunned, stupefied.

atorarse *vr.* to gag, to choke.

atormentar *v.* to torment.

atrás *adv.* behind; **ir hacia** ____ / to go backwards.

atrasado-a *a.* backward, late, behind; ____ mental / mentally retarded.

atresia *f.* atresia, congenital absence or closure of a body passage.

atreverse *vr.* to dare, to take a chance.

atravesar *v.* to cross; to go through; ____ **la calle** / to cross the street.

atrevido-a *a.* daring; insolent.

atrial *a.* atrial, rel. to an atrium.

atribuir *vi.* to attribute; to confer.

atrio *m.* atrium. 1. cavity that is connected to another structure; 2. upper chamber of the heart which receives the blood from the veins.

atrioventricular *a.* atrioventricular, rel. to an atrium and a ventricule of the heart.

atrofia *f.* atrophy, deterioration of cells, tissue and organs of the body.

atropellar *v.* to run over, to trample upon.

atropina *f.* atropine sulphate, agent used as a muscle relaxer, esp. applied to the eyes to dilate the pupil and paralyze the ciliary muscle during eye examination.

atún *m.* tuna fish.

aturdido-a *a.* confused, stunned.

aturdimiento *m.* confusion, bewilderment.

aturdir *v.* to stun; to confuse.

audición *f.* audition, sense of hearing; **pérdida de la** ____ / hearing loss.

audífono *m.* hearing aid.

audiograma *m.* audiogram, instrument that records the degree of hearing.

audiovisual *a.* audiovisual, rel. to hearing and vision.

auditivo-a, auditorio-a *a.* auditory, rel. to hearing; conducto ____ / ____ canal; nervio ____ / ____ nerve; tapón ____ / ear plug.

aumentar *v.* to increase, to augment, to magnify; ____ **de peso** / to gain weight.

aumento *m.* increase.

aún *adv.* still, yet; ____ **cuando** / even though.

aunque *conj.* although.

aura *f.* aura, sensation preceding an epileptic attack.

aurícula *f.* auricle. 1. the outer visible part of the ear; 2. either of the two upper chambers of the heart.

auricular *m.* earphone; *a.* 1. rel. to the sense of hearing; 2. rel. to an auricle of the heart.

auscultación *f.* auscultation, the act of listening to sounds arising from organs such as the lungs and the heart for diagnostic purposes.

auscultar *v.* to auscultate, to examine by auscultation.

ausencia *f.* absence.

ausente *a.* absent.

autismo *m.* autism, behavioral disorder manifested by extreme self-centeredness; ____ **infantil** / infantile ____ .

autístico-a *a.* autistic, suffering from or rel. to autism.

autoclave *f.* autoclave, an instrument for sterilizing by steam pressure.

autóctono-a *a.* native, autoctonous, indigenous.

autodigestión *f.* autodigestion, digestion of tissues by their own enzymes and juices.

autógeno-a *a.* autogenous, that is produced within the individual.

autohipnosis *f.* autohypnosis, self-hypnosis.

autoinfección *f.* autoinfection, infection by an agent from the same body.

autoinjerto *m.* autograft, autogenous implant taken from another part of the patient's body.

autoinmunización *f.* autoimmunization, immunity resulting from a substance developed within the affected person's own body.

autoinoculable *a.* autoinoculable, susceptible to a germ from within.

autólogo-a *a.* autologous, derived from the same individual.
automatismo *m.* automatism, behavior not under voluntary control.
automedicación *f.* self-medication.
automóvil *m.* automobile.
autonomía *f.* autonomy.
autónomo-a *a.* autonomic, autonomous, that functions independently; sistema nervioso ___ / ___ nervous system.
autoplastia *f. surg.* autoplasty, implantation of an autograft.
autoplástico-a *a.* autoplastic, rel. to autoplastia.
autopsia *f.* autopsy, postmortem examination of the body.
autorización *f.* authorization.
autorizar *vi.* to authorize.
autosugestión *f.* autosuggestion, self-suggested thought.
auxilio *m.* aid, help; **primeros** ___-s / first ___.
avanzar *vi.* to advance.
avena *f.* oats; **harina de** ___ / oatmeal.
aventado-a *a.* bloated.
aventarse *vr.* to become bloated.
aversión *f.* aversion, dislike.
aviso *m.* notice; **dar** ___ / to notify.
avispa *f.* wasp; **picadura de** ___ / ___ sting.
avispón *m.* hornet.
avitaminosis *f.* avitaminosis, disorder caused by a lack of vitamins.
avivar *v.* to liven up; to strengthen.
avulsión *f. surg.* avulsion, removal or extraction of part of a structure.
axénico-a *a.* axenic, germ free.
axial *a.* axial, rel. to the axis.
axila *f.* axilla, armpit.
axilar *a.* axillary, rel. to the axilla.
axis *m.* axis, imaginary central line passing through the body or through an organ.
ayer *adv.* yesterday.
Ayerza, síndrome de *m.* Ayerza's syndrome, syndrome manifested by multiple symptoms, esp. dyspnea and cyanosis, gen. as a result of pulmonary deficiency.
ayuda *f.* help; **sin** ___ / unassisted.
ayudante *m., f.* helper.
ayudar *v.* to help, to assist.
ayunar *v.* to fast.
ayuno *m.* fast.
azoospermia *f.* azoospermia, lack of spermatozoa in the semen.

azotemia *f.* azotemia, excess urea in the blood.
azúcar *m.* sugar, carbohydrate consisting essentially of sucrose; ___ **de la uva** / grape ___, dextrose.
azufre *m.* sulfur.
azul *a.* blue; mal de ___ / ___ baby.

B

b *abr.* **bacilo** / bacillus; **bucal** / buccal.

baba *f.* spittle.
babear *v.* to slobber.
babero *m.* bib.
Babinski, reflejo de *m.* Babinski's reflex, dorsiflexion of the big toe when the sole of the foot is stimulated.
bacalao *m.* codfish.
bacilar *a.* bacillary, rel. to bacillus.
bacilemia *f.* bacillemia, presence of bacilli in the blood.
bacilo *m.* bacillus (*pl.* bacilli), rod shaped bacteria; ___ **de Calmette-Guérin** / bacille Calmette-Guérin, bacile bilié; ___ **de Koch** / Koch's ___, Mycobacterium tuberculosis; ___ **de la fiebre tifoidea** / typhoid ___, Salmonella typhi; **portador de** ___-s / bacilli carrier.
bacilosis *f.* bacillosis, infection caused by bacilli.
baciluria *f.* bacilluria, presence of bacilli in the urine.
bacín *m.* basin, large bowl; bedpan.
bacitracina *f.* bacitracin, antibiotic effective against some staphylococci.
bacteria *f.* bacterium; germ.
bacteriano-a *a.* bacterial; infecciones ___-s / ___ infections; endocarditis ___ / ___ endocarditis; pruebas de sensibilidad ___ / ___ sensitivity tests.
bacteremia *f.* bacteremia, presence of bacteria in the blood.
bactericida *m.* bactericide, agent that kills bacteria.
bacteriógeno *a.* bacteriogenic. 1. of bacterial origin; 2. that produces bacteria.
bacteriolisina *f.* bacteriolysin, antibody that destroys bacterial cells.
bacteriólisis *f.* bacteriolysis, the destruction of bacteria.
bacteriología *f.* bacteriology, the study of bacteria.

bacteriológico-a *a*. bacteriologic, bacteriological, rel. to bacteria.

bacteriólogo-a *m., f*. bacteriologist, specialist in bacteriology.

bacteriosis *f*. bacteriosis, an infection caused by bacteria.

bacteriostático-a *a*. bacteriostatic, that inhibits the growth or multiplication of bacteria.

bacteriuria *f*. bacteriuria, presence of bacteria in the urine.

baipás *m. surg*. bypass, surgically created alternate channel or route.

bajar *v*. [*escaleras*] to go down; [*movimiento*] to lower; ____ **el brazo** / to lower the arm; ____ **de peso** / to lose weight.

bajo-a *a*. low, short; presión ____ / ____ blood pressure; **bajo** *prep*. under; ____ observación / ____ observation; ____ tratamiento / ____ treatment.

bala *f*. bullet; herida de ____ / ____ wound.

balance *m*. balance, equilibrium; ____ acido-básico / acid-base ____ ; ____ hídrico / fluid ____ .

balanceado-a *a*. balanced; state of equilibrium.

balanitis *f*. balanitis, an infl. of the glans penis, gen. accompanied by infl. of the prepuce.

balanopostitis *f*. balanoposthitis, infl. of the glans penis and prepuce.

balanza *f*. balance, scale.

balbucear *v*. to babble.

baldado-a *a*. maimed, crippled.

balsámico-a *a*. balmy.

bálsamo *m*. balsam, soothing agent.

balón *m*. balloon; ____ insuflable / ____ tamponade.

banana *f*. banana.

banco *m*. bank; bench.

bandeja *f*. tray.

bañar *v*. to bathe; **bañarse** *vr*. to take a bath.

bañadera, bañera *f*. bathtub.

baño *m*. bath; bathroom; ____ antiperético / antipyrectic ____ , to reduce fever; ____ aromático / aromatic ____; ____ con esponja / sponge ____; ____ de agua caliente / hot ____; ____ de agua fría / cold ____; ____ de agua tibia / warm ____; ____ de asiento caliente / Sitz ____, from the waist down; ____ de remolino / whirlpool ____; **cuarto de** ____ / bathroom; **papel de** ____ / toilet tissue.

baragnosis *f*. baragnosis, inability to recognize weight and pressure.

barato-a *a*. inexpensive.

barba *f*. beard.

barbilla *f*. chin, the tip of the chin.

barbituratos *m*. barbiturates, derivatives of barbituric acid.

barbitúrico *m*. barbiturate, hypnotic and sedative agent.

barestesia *f*. baresthesia, the sensation of pressure or weight.

barifonia *f*. baryphonia, thick, heavy voice.

bario *m*. barium.

barorreceptor *m*. baroreceptor, a sensory nerve ending that reacts to changes in pressure.

barrer *v*. to sweep.

barrera *f*. barrier, obstacle.

barriga *f*. belly; **dolor de** ____ / ____ ache.

barrigón-a *a. pop*. pot-bellied.

barrio *m*. neighborhood.

barro *m*. blackhead, pimple; mud.

bartolinitis *f*. bartholinitis, infl. of Bartholin's vulvovaginal gland.

Bartolino, glándula de *f*. Bartholin's vulvovaginal gland.

basal *a*. basal, that which pertains or is close to a base; enfermedad de los ganglios ____-es / ____ ganglia disease; metabolismo ____ / ____ metabolic rate.

basca *f*. nausea. *V*. **arcadas.**

base *f*. base, foundation.

basial, basilar *a*. basal, basilar, rel. to a base.

básico-a *a*. basic.

basofobia *f*. basophobia, fear of walking.

bastante *a*. sufficient, enough.

bastar *v*. to be enough; **bastarse** *vr*. to be self-sufficient.

bastardo-a *m., f*. bastard; *a*. bastard, illegitimate.

bastón *m*. cane.

bastoncillo *m*. rod; ____-s y conos / ____-s and cones, sensitive receptors of the retina.

basura *f*. garbage, trash, refuse; **cesto de** ____ / wastebasket.

bata *f*. gown, housecoat.

batalla *f*. battle, struggle.

batallar *v*. to struggle.

batir *v*. to whip; beat; pound.

bazo *m*. spleen, vascular lymphatic organ situated in the abdominal cavity; ____ accesorio / accessory ____ .

bebé *m*. baby, infant.

beber v. to drink.

bebedero m. drinking fountain.

bebida f. beverage; **dado a la** ____ / that drinks in excess.

beca a. scholarship, grant.

bel m. bel, a unit of sound intensity.

beligerante a. belligerent.

Bell, parálisis de f. Bell's palsy, paralysis of one side of the face caused by an affliction of the facial nerve.

belladona f. belladona, medicinal herb whose leaves and roots contain atropine and related alkaloids.

bello-a a. beautiful.

Bencedrina f. Benzedrine, trade name for amphetamine sulfate.

Benedict, prueba de f. Benedict's test, chemical analysis to determine the presence of sugar in the urine.

benefactor-a m., f. benefactor.

beneficiado-a a. beneficiary.

beneficiar v. to do good; **beneficiarse** vr. to benefit, to profit.

beneficio m. benefit; ____-s de asistencia social / welfare ____-s.

benigno-a a. benign.

benjuí m. benzoin, resin used as an expectorant.

béquico m. cough medicine.

beriberi m. beriberi, endemic neuritis caused by a deficiency of thiamine in the diet.

berrinche m. tantrum, fit of anger.

berro m. watercress.

besar v. to kiss.

beso m. kiss.

bestialidad f. bestiality, sexual relations with an animal.

bezoar m. bezoar, concretion found in the stomach or the intestines constituted by elements such as hair or vegetable fibers.

biaxial a. biaxial, that which has two axes.

biberón m. baby bottle; **suplementación con** ____ / bottle propping.

bibliografía f. bibliography.

biblioteca f. library.

bicarbonato m. bicarbonate, a salt of carbonic acid.

biceps m. biceps muscle.

bicicleta f. bicycle: ____ **estacionaria** / stationary ____.

bicipital a. bicipital. 1. rel. to the biceps muscle; 2. having two heads.

bicóncavo-a a. biconcave, having two concave surfaces as in a lens.

biconvexo-a a. biconvex, with two convex surfaces as in a lens.

bicúspide a. bicuspid, having two points.

bicho m. bug, insect.

bien adv. well; **todo va o está** ____ / all is well.

bienestar m. well-being, welfare, solace.

bienvenida f. welcome.

bienvenido-a a. welcome, pleasant, well received.

bífido-a a. bifid, split in two.

bifocal a. bifocal, having two foci.

bifurcación f. bifurcation, division into two branches or parts.

bigeminia f. bigeminy, two pulse beats occurring in rapid succession.

bigote m. moustache.

bilabial a. bilabial, having two lips.

bilateral a. bilateral, having or rel. to two sides.

bilharziasis f. bilharziasis. V. **esquistosomiasis.**

biliar a. biliary, rel. to the bile, to the bile ducts, or to the gallbladder; **ácidos y sales** ____-es / ____ acids and salts; **conductos** ____-es / bile ducts; **cálculo** ____ / gallstone; **enfermedadades de los conductos** ____ -es / ____ tract diseases; **obstrucción del conducto** ____ / ____ duct obstruction.

bilingüe a. bilingual.

biliosidad f. biliousness, disorder manifested by constipation, headache and indigestion due to excess secretion of bile.

bilioso-a a. bilious, excess bile.

bilirrubina f. bilirubin, a red pigment of the bile.

bilirrubinemia f. bilirubinemia, presence of bilirubin in the blood.

bilirrubinuria f. bilirubinuria, presence of bilirubin in the urine.

bilis f. bile, gall, bitter secretion stored in the gallbladder.

bimanual a. bimanual, performed with both hands.

binario-a a. binary, consisting of two of the same.

bioensayo m. bioassay, sampling the effect of a drug on an animal to determine its potency.

biología f. biology, the study of live organisms; ____ **celular** / cellular ____ ; ____ **molecular** / molecular ____.

biólogo-a m., f. biologist.

biopsia f. biopsy, procedure to remove sample tissue for diagnostic examination; ____ de la mama / ____ of the breast; ____ de la médula ósea / bone marrow ____; ____ del nódulo linfático / ____ of lymph nodes; ____ del cuello uterino / ____ of the cervix; ____ endoscópica / endoscopic ____; ____ por aspiración / needle ____; ____ por excisión / excision ____.

bioquímica *f.* biochemistry, the chemistry of living organisms.

biosíntesis *f.* biosynthesis, formation of chemical substances in the physiological processes of living organisms.

biotipo *m.* biotype, group of individuals with the same genotype.

bípedo *m.* biped, two-legged animal.

birrefringente *a.* birefringent, refracting twice.

bisabuelo-a *m., f.* great-grandfather; great-grandmother.

bisagra *f.* hinge; movimiento de ____ / ____ movement.

bisexual *a.* bisexual. 1. having gonads of both sexes, hermaphrodite; 2. having sexual relations with both sexes.

bisturí *m.* scalpel, surgical knife.

bizco-a *a.* cross-eyed.

biznieto-a *m., f.* great-grandson; great-granddaughter.

bizquera *f.* squint, the condition of being cross-eyed. *V.* **estrabismo.**

blanco *m.* target. 1. an object or area at which something is directed; 2. a cell or organ that is affected by a particular agent such as a drug or a hormone; 3. the color white; **-a** *a.* white.

blancura *f.* whiteness.

blancuzco-a *a.* whitish.

blando-a *a.* soft, bland.

blastema *f.* blastema, primitive mass substance from which cells are formed.

blastomicosis *f.* blastomycosis, infectious fungus disease.

blástula *f.* blastula, an early stage of the embryo.

blefarectomía *f. surg.* blepharectomy, excision of a lesion of the eyelid.

blefaritis *f.* blepharitis, infl. of the eyelid.

blefarocalasis *f.* blepharochalasis, relaxation of the skin of the upper eyelid due to loss of interstitial elasticity.

blefaroplastia *f. surg.* blepharoplasty, plastic surgery of the eyelids.

blefaroplejía *f.* blepharoplegia, paralysis of the eyelid.

blenorragia *f.* blennorrhagia. 1. discharge of mucus; 2. gonorrhea.

bloqueado-a *a.* blocked, obstructed.

bloqueo *m.* block, stoppage, obstruction; ____ atrioventricular / heart ____, atrioventricular, interruption in the A-V node; ____ de rama / heart ____, bundle-branch; ____ interventricular / heart ____, interventricular; ____ sinoatrial / heart ____, sinoatrial.

blusa *f.* blouse.

bobería *f.* foolishness.

bobo-a *m., f.* fool, simpleton; *a.* silly, foolish.

boca *f.* mouth; ____ **abajo** / face down; ____ **arriba** / face up; **por la** ____ / by mouth, orally.

boca de trinchera *f.* trench mouth, infection with ulceration of the mucous membranes of the mouth and the pharynx.

bocado *m.* mouthful, bite.

bocio *m.* goiter, enlargement of the thyroid gland; ____ congénito / congenital ____; ____ exoftálmico / exophthalmic ____; ____ móvil / wandering ____; ____ tóxico / toxic ____.

bochorno *m.* embarrassment.

bofetada *f.* slap.

bofetón *m.* hard blow, forceful slap.

bola *f.* ball; ____ adiposa / fat pad; ____ de pelo / hair ____, a type of bezoar.

bolsa *f.* sac; bag; handbag, pouch, pocket; ____ amniótica (de agua) / amniotic ____ (water bag); ____ **de agua caliente** / hot water bottle; ____ **de hielo** / icepack; ____ **de papel** / paper bag; ____ **eléctrica** / heating pad.

bolsillo *m.* pocket.

bomba *f.* pump.

bombear *v.* to pump; ____ hacia afuera / to ____ out.

bombeo *m.* pumping; ____ del corazón / heart ____; ____ estomacal / stomach ____.

bombero-a *m., f.* fireman, fireperson.

bombilla *f.* light bulb.

bondadoso-a *a.* kind.

boniato *m.* sweet potato.

bonito-a *a.* pretty.

bonito *m.* tuna fish.

boquiabierto-a *a.* open-mouthed.

borato de sodio *m.* borax.

borde *m.* border, edge; ____ bermellón / vermillion ____, the exposed pink margin of a lip.

bordeando *a.* bordering.

borrachera *f.* drunken spree.

borracho-a *a.* drunk.

borradura, borramiento *f., m.* effacement, obliteration of an organ, such as the cervix during labor.

borrar *v.* to erase, scrape; wipe out.

bosquejo *m.* profile.

bostezar *vi.* to yawn.

bostezo *m.* yawn; yawning.

bota *f.* boot; ___ enyesada / short-leg cast.

botar *v.* to throw away; to hurl.

botella *f.* bottle.

botica *f.* drugstore, pharmacy.

boticario-a *m., f.* druggist, pharmacist.

botiquín *m.* medicine cabinet; ___ de primeros auxilios / first aid kit.

botón *m.* button; ___ **para llamar** / push.

botulismo *m.* botulism, food poisoning caused by a toxin that grows in improperly canned or preserved foods.

bóveda *f.* vault, dome-shaped anatomical structure.

bovino *a.* bovine, rel. to cattle.

bracero *m.* farmhand; laborer.

bradicardia *f.* bradycardia, abnormally slow heart beat.

bradipnea *f.* bradypnea, abnormally slow respiration.

braguero *m.* truss, binding device used to keep a reduced hernia in place.

braquiocefálico-a *a.* brachiocephalic, rel. to the arm and the head.

braquidactilia *f.* brachydactyly, abnormally short fingers and toes.

bravo-a *a.* angry; brave.

brazalete de identificación *m.* identification bracelet.

brazo *m. arm.*

brea *f.* tar.

bregma *m.* bregma, the point in the skull at the junction of the sagittal and coronal sutures.

breve *a.* brief; short; **en** ___ / in short, briefly.

Bright, enfermedad de *f.* Bright's disease. *V.* **glomerulonefritis.**

brillante *a.* bright.

brincar *vi.* to hop, to skip.

brindar *v.* to offer.

brisa *f.* breeze.

broma *f.* joke; **en** ___ / jokingly, kidding.

bromidrosis *f.* bromhidrosis, fetid perspiration.

broncodilatador *m.* bronchodilator, agent that dilates the caliber of a bronchus; **-a** *a.* agentes ___-es / ___ agents.

broncoesofagoscopía *f.* bronchoesophagoscopy, examination of the bronchi and esophagus with an instrument.

broncoespasmo *m.* bronchospasm, spasmodic contraction of the bronchi and bronchioles.

broncografía *f.* bronchography, X-ray of the tracheobronchial tree using an opaque medium in the bronchi.

broncolito *m.* broncholith, a bronchial calculus.

bronconeumonía *f.* bronchopneumonia, acute infl. of the bronchi and the alveoli of the lungs.

broncopulmonar *a.* bronchopulmonary, rel. to the bronchi and the lungs.

broncoscopía *f.* bronchoscopy, inspection of the bronchi with a bronchoscope.

broncoscopio *m.* bronchoscope, instrument to examine the interior of the bronchi.

bronquial *a.* bronchial, rel. to the bronchi; árbol ___ / ___ tree; espasmo ___ / ___ spasm; lavado ___ / ___ washing.

bronquiectasia *f.* bronchiectasis, chronic dilation of the bronchi due to an inflammatory disease or obstruction.

bronquio *m.* bronchus, one of the larger tubes through which air enters the lungs.

bronquiocele *m.* bronchiocele, a localized dilation of a bronchus.

bronquiolitis *f.* bronchiolitis, infl. of the bronchioles.

bronquiolo *m.* bronchiole, one of the small branches of the bronquial tree.

bronquitis *f.* bronchitis, infl. of the bronchial tubes.

brotar *v.* to flare up.

brote *m.* flare-up, outburst, outbreak, reddening of the skin due to a lesion, infection or allergic reaction.

brucelosis *f.* brucellosis, Mediterranean fever, undulant fever, disease caused by bacteria obtained through contact with infected animals or their by-products.

brusco-a *a.* abrupt, rude.

brutal *a.* brutal.

bruto-a *a.* stupid; rough.

bubón *m.* bubo, swelling of one or more lymph nodes, esp. in the axilla or groin.

bucal *a*. buccal, rel. to the mouth; **antiséptico** ___ / mouthwash; **higiene** ___ / oral hygiene; **por vía** ___ / by mouth.

buche *m*. mouthful; **un** ___ **de agua** / a ___ of water.

bueno-a *a*. good, kind; **buenos días** / good morning, **buenas tardes** / good afternoon; **buenas noches** / [*saludo*] good evening, [*despedida*] good night; **de buena fé** / in good faith.

bulbo *m*. bulb, circular or oval expansion of a tube or cylinder; ___ **piloso** / hair ___.

bulbouretral *a*. bulbourethral, rel. to the bulb of the urethra and the penis.

bulimia *f*. bulimia, hiperorexia, exaggerated appetite.

bulto *m*. lump; swelling; bundle, package.

bunio *m*. bunion, swelling of the bursa on the first joint of the big toe.

bunionectomía *f*. *surg*. bunionectomy, excision of a bunion.

burbuja *f*. bubble.

burdo-a *a*. coarse; rough.

buril *m*. burr, type of drill used to make openings in bones or teeth.

bursa *L*. bursa, sac-like cavity containing synovial fluid, situated in tissue areas where friction would otherwise occur; ___ del tendón calcáneo / Achille's ___; ___ poplíteal / popliteal ___.

bursitis *f*. bursitis, infl. of a bursa.

buscar *vi*. to look for, to search.

búsqueda *f*. search; persuit.

búster *m*. booster shot, reactivation of an original immunizing agent.

busto *m*. bust.

buzo *m*. diver.

buzón *m*. mailbox.

C

C *abr*. **caloría** / kilocalorie; **centígrado** / centigrade; **carbono** / carbon; **Celsius** / Celsius.

c *abr*. **caloría** / calorie; **cobalto** / cobalt; **cocaína** / cocaine; **contracción** / contraction.

cabalgamiento *m*. [*fracturas*] overriding, the slipping of one part of the bone over the other.

caballero *m*. gentleman.

caballo *m*. horse.

caballo de fuerza *m*. horsepower, a unit of power.

cabecear *v*. to nod; to drop one's head as when snoozing; *pop*. to nod off.

cabecera *f*. head of a bed or table.

cabellera *f*. head of hair.

cabello *m*. hair.

caber *vi*. to fit into something; to have enough room.

cabestrillo *m*. sling, bandage-like support.

cabeza *f*. head; caída de la ___ / ___ drop; traumatismo del cráneo, golpe en la ___ / ___ injury; **apoyo de** ___ / ___ rest; **asentir con la** ___ / to nod one's head.

cabezón-a *a*. big-headed; stubborn.

cabizbajo-a *a*. crestfallen, downcast.

cabra *f*. goat; **leche de** ___ / ___ milk.

caca *f*. excrement, stool of a child.

cacao *m*. cacao. 1. plant from which chocolate is derived; 2. diuretic alkaloid.

cacosmia *f*. cacosmia, perception of imaginary disagreeable odors.

cachetada *f*. slap in the face.

cachete *m*. cheek.

cada *a*. each; ___ **día** / every day; ___ **dos, tres horas** / every two, three, hours; ___ **uno-a** / ___ one; ___ **vez** / ___ time.

cadáver *m*. cadaver, corpse.

cadavérico-a / *a*. cadaverous, rel. to or having the appearance of a cadaver.

cadena *f*. chain; reacción en ___ / ___ reaction; sutura en ___ / ___ suture.

cadera *f*. hip; articulación de la ___ / ___ joint; ___ **de resorte** / ___ snapping; dislocación congénita de la ___ / congenital ___ dislocation; restitución total de la ___ / total ___ replacement.

cadmio *m*. cadmium, a bivalent metal similar to tin.

caducidad *f*. 1. expiration date; 2. old age.

caer *vi*. to fall; **caerse** *vr*. to fall down; ___ **muerto** / to drop dead.

café *m*. coffee.

cafeína *f*. caffeine, alkaloid present chiefly in coffee and tea used as a stimulant and diuretic.

cafetería *f*. cafeteria.

caída *f*. fall.

caído-a *a*. *pp*. of **caer**, fallen.

cajero-a *m*., *f*. cashier.

calabaza *f*. pumpkin, squash.

calambre *m*. cramp, painful contraction of a

muscle; ____ muscular localizado / Charley horse.

calamina *f.* calamine, astringent and antiseptic used for skin disorders.

calavera *f.* skull.

calcáneo *m.* calcaneus, heel bone.

calcáreo-a *a.* calcareous, rel. to lime or calcium.

calcemia *f.* calcemia, presence of calcium in the blood.

calcetines *m.* socks.

cálcico *a.* calcic, rel. to lime.

calciferol *m.* calciferol, derivative of ergosterol, vitamin D^2.

calcificación *f.* calcification, hardening of organic tissue by deposits of calcium salts.

calcificado-a *a.* calcified.

calcinosis *f.* calcinosis, presence of calcium salts in the skin, subcutaneous tissues, or other organs.

calcio *m.* calcium

calcitonina *f.* calcitonin, a hormone secreted by the thyroid gland.

calciuria *f.* calciuria, presence of calcium in the urine.

cálculo *m.* calculus (*pl.* calculi), stone; ____ biliar / biliary ____, gallstone; ____ de cistina / cystine ____; ____ de fibrina / fibrin ____; ____ de oxalato de calcio / calcium oxalate ____; ____ urinario / urinary ____.

caldo *m.* broth, stock; ____ de pollo / chicken ____.

calefacción *f.* heating system; heat.

calendario *m.* calendar.

calentador *m.* heater.

calentar *vi.* to heat; **calentarse** *vr.* to warm oneself up.

calentura *f.* fever, temperature.

calenturiento-a *a.* feverish.

calibrador *m.* calibrator, gauge, measuring device.

calibrar *v.* to calibrate; to gage, to measure the diameter of a canal or tube.

calibre *m.* caliber, the diameter of a tube or canal.

caliceal *a.* caliceal, rel. to the calix.

calicreína *f.* kallicrein, an inactive enzyme present in blood, plasma and urine, that when activated acts as a powerful vasodilator.

calidad *f.* quality, property.

caliente *a.* hot, warm.

calificar *vi.* to qualify; to correct.

caliuresis *f.* kaliuresis, kaluresis, increased urinary excretion of potassium.

cáliz *m.* calyx, a cup-shaped organ, such as the renal calyx.

calma *f.* calm; calmness; **tener** ____ / to be calm.

calmado-a *a.* calm, serene.

calmante *m.* sedative, tranquilizer; *a.* soothing, mitigating.

calmar *v.* to calm down, to soothe; **calmarse** *vr.* to become calm.

calomel *m.* calomel, mercurous chloride used primarily as a local antibacterial element.

calor *m.* heat; warmth; ____ de conducción / ____, conductive; ____ de convención / ____, convective; pérdida de ____ / ____ loss; ____ seco / dry ____; hace ____ / it is hot; **tener** ____ / to be hot.

caloría *f.* calorie, a heat unit, commonly referred to as the energy value of a particular food; gran ____ / large ____ ; ____ pequeña / small ____.

calórico-a *a.* caloric, rel. to the energy value of food; ingestión ____ / ____ intake.

calostro *m.* colostrum, fluid secreted by the mammary glands before the secretion of milk.

calva *f.* bald crown of the head.

calvaria *f.* calvaria, superior portion of the cranium.

calvicie *f.* calvities, baldness.

calvo-a *a.* bald, without hair.

calzoncillos *m. pl.* men's underpants; shorts.

callado-a *a.* quiet, low-key.

callar *v.* to hush, to silence; **callarse** *vr.* to become quiet.

calle *f.* street.

callo, callosidad *m., f.* callus, corn.

calloso-a *a.* callous, rel. to a callus.

cama *f.* bed; orinarse en la ____ / bedwetting; al lado de la ____ / at bedside; **estar en** ____ / to be bedridden; **guardar** ____ / to stay in ____, bedrest; **ocupación de** ____ -s / ____ occupancy; **recluído en** ____ / bed-confined; **ropa de** ____ / bedclothes.

cámara *f.* 1. chamber, cavity; ____ anterior / anterior ____; ____ acuosa / aqueous ____; ____ hiperbárica / hyperbaric ____; ____ -s oculares / ____ -s of the eye; 2. photographic camera.

camarón *m.* shrimp.

cambiar *v.* to change; **cambiarse** *vr.* to change clothes.

cambio *m.* change; [*posición*] shift.
camilla *f.* stretcher.
caminar *v.* to walk; to hike.
caminata *f.* a walk; a hike.
camino *m.* road; course, way.
camión *m.* truck; *Mex.* bus.
camisa *f.* shirt; ___ **de fuerza** / straight-jacket.
camiseta *f.* men's undershirt; T-shirt.
camisón *m.* night gown.
campanilla *f.* uvula, epiglottis.
campo *m.* field. 1. area or open space; 2. specialization.
cana *f.* gray hair.
canal *m.* canal, channel, trough, groove, tubular structure; ___ femoral / femoral ___; ___ del parto / birth ___; ___ inguinal / inguinal ___; ___ radicular / root ___.
canalículo *m.* canaliculus, small channel; ___ biliar / biliary ___, between liver cells; ___ lacrimal, lagrimal / lacrimal ___.
canasta *f.* basket.
cancelación *f.* cancellation.
cancelar *v.* to cancel, to annul.
canceloso-a *a.* cancellous, spongy, resembling a lattice.
cáncer *m.* cancer, tumor; fases o etapas en relación a la extensión del ___ / ___ staging; grado de malignidad del ___ / ___ grading; ___ incipiente / early ___.
cancerofobia *f.* cancerophobia, morbid fear of cancer.
canceroso-a *a.* cancerous, rel. to or afflicted by cancer.
candela *f.* fire; flame.
candente *a.* red hot, burning.
candidiasis *f.* candidiasis, skin infection caused by a yeast-like fungi.
canela *f.* cinnamon.
cangrejo *m.* crab.
canilla *f.* shinbone; tibia.
canino *m.* cuspid tooth; -a *a.* rel. to dogs.
cannabis *L.* cannabis, marihuana, plant whose leaves have a narcotic or hallucinatory effect when smoked.
canoso-a *a.* gray haired.
cansado-a *a.* tired, weary.
cansancio *m.* tiredness, fatigue.
cansar *v.* to tire; **cansarse** *vr.* to get tired.
cantidad *f.* quantity.
canto *m.* canthus. 1. angles at the corner of the eyes formed by the joining of the ex-

ternal and internal eyelids on both sides of the eye; 2. edge, rim.
cánula *f.* cannula, tube through which fluid and gas are put into the body.
canulación *f.* cannulation, the act of introducing a cannula through a vessel or duct; ___ aórtica / aortic ___.
caolín *m.* kaolin, natural hydrated aluminum silicate having absorbing qualities.
caos *m.* chaos.
capa *f.* layer.
capacidad *f.* capacity. 1. ability to contain; ___ vital / vital ___; 2. qualification, competence.
capaz *a.* able, capable.
capilar *m.* capillary, small blood vessel; ___ arterial / arterial ___, tiny channels carrying arterial blood; ___ linfático / lymph ___, minute vessels of the lymphatic system; ___ venoso / venous ___, small channels carrying venous blood; *a.* resembling hair.
capitelum *L.* capitellum. 1. bulb of a hair; 2. part of the humerus.
capítulo *m.* chapter.
caprichoso-a *a.* capricious; stubborn.
cápsula *f.* capsule, membranous enclosure; ___ articular / articular ___, that envolves a synovial joint.
capsulación *f.* capsulation, enclosure in a capsule or sheath.
caquéctico-a *a.* cachectic, rel. to cachexia.
caquexia *f.* cachexia, a grave condition marked by great loss of weight and general weakness.
cara *f.* face; ___ de luna / moon ___, round, puffy face usu. characteristic of someone who has been under steroid treatment for a long period of time; peladura de ___ / ___ peeling; estire de ___ / ___ lift.
caracol *m.* snail.
carácter *m.* character; quality; **tener buen** ___ / to be good-natured; **tener mal** ___ / to be ill-tempered.
característico-a *a.* characteristic.
caramba *int.* good gracious!
caramelo *m.* hard candy.
carbohidrato *m.* carbohydrate, organic substance composed of carbon, hydrogen and oxygen such as starch, sugar and cellulose.
carbólico *a.* carbolic, rel. to phenylic acid.
carbón *m.* coal.
carbonatado-a *a.* carbonated.

carbonización *f.* carbonization.

carbonizado-a *a.* charred.

carbono *m.* carbon; dióxido de ___ / ___ dioxide; monóxido de ___ / ___ monoxide.

carboxihemoglobina *f.* carboxyhemoglobin, a combination of carbon monoxide and hemoglobin that impairs the transportation of oxygen in the blood.

carbunco *m.* carbuncle, large boil of the skin that discharges pus.

cárcel *f.* jail.

carcinogénesis *f.* carcinogenesis, production of cancer.

carcinógeno *m.* carcinogen, cancer producing substance; **-a** *a.* carcinogenic.

carcinoma *m.* carcinoma, cancer derived from living cells of organs; ___ basocelular / basal cell ___ ; ___ broncogénico / ___ of the bronchi; cerebral ___ / ___ del cerebro; ___ cervical / cervical ___ ; ___ de células escamosas epiteliales / squamous cell ___ ; ___ de células transicionales / transitional cell ___ ; ___ de la mama / breast ___ ; ___ endometrial / endometrial ___ ; mucinoso / mucinous ___ ; ___ ovárico / ovarian ___ ; ___ papilar / papillary ___ ; ___ testicular / testicular ___ .

carcinoma in situ *m.* carcinoma in situ, localized tumor cells that have not invaded adjacent structures.

carcinomatosis *f.* carcinomatosis, cancer that has spread throughout the body.

cardíaco-a *a.* cardiac, rel. to the heart; aurícula ___ / heart atrium; ataque ___ / heart attack; cateterización ___ / ___ catheterization; estimulación ___ artificial / ___ pacing, artificial; frecuencia ___ / heart rate; gasto o rendimiento ___ / heart output; insuficiencia o fallo ___ congestivo / heart failure, congestive; insuficiencia ___ , ventricular derecha / heart failure, right sided; insuficiencia ___ , ventricular izquierda / heart failure, left sided; paro ___ / heart arrest, standstill; reanimación ___ / ___ resuscitation; reflejo ___ / heart reflex; taponamiento ___ / ___ tamponade.

cardias *m.* cardia, esophageal orifice of the stomach.

cardioangiograma *m.* cardioangiogram, image by X-rays of the blood vessels and the chambers of the heart taken after injecting a dye.

cardiocentesis, cardiopuntura *f.* cardiocentesis, puncture or incision of a heart chamber.

cardioespasmo *m.* cardiospasm, contraction or spasm of the cardia.

cardiografía *f.* cardiography, recording of the movements of the heart done with the use of a cardiograph.

cardiógrafo *m.* cardiograph, instrument that traces the movements of the heart.

cardiograma *m.* cardiogram, electrical tracing of the impulses of the heart.

cardiología *f.* cardiology, the study of the heart.

cardiólogo-a *m., f.* cardiologist, specialist in cardiology.

cardiomegalia *f.* cardiomegaly, enlarged heart.

cardiomiopatía *f.* cardomyopathy, a disorder of the heart muscle; ___ alcohólica / alcoholic ___ ; ___ congestiva / congestive ___ ; ___ hipertrófica / hypertrophic ___ .

cardiopatía *f.* heart disease; ___ por hipertensión / hypertensive heart disease.

cardioplegia *f.* cardioplegia, heart paralysis.

cardiopulmonar *a.* cardiopulmonary, rel. to the heart and the lungs; máquina ___ / heart-lung machine; puente ___ / ___ bypass; resucitación ___ / ___ resuscitation, reanimación.

cardiotomía *f. surg.* cardiotomy 1. incision in the cardiac end of the stomach; 2. incision of the heart.

cardiotónico-a *a.* cardiotonic, having a tonic or favorable effect on the heart; agente ___ / cardiac stimulant.

cardiovascular *a.* cardiovascular, rel. to the heart and blood vessels.

cardioversión *f.* cardioversion, the act of restoring the heart to a normal synus rhythm by electrical countershock.

carditis *f.* carditis, infl. of the heart.

carecer *vi.* to lack.

carga *f.* load, burden.

cargar *vi.* to load; to carry.

caridad *f.* charity.

caries *f.* caries, dental cavity.

cariñoso-a *a.* affectionate.

cariólisis *f.* karyolysis, breakdown of the nucleus of a cell.

cariolítico-a *a.* karyolytic, rel. to or that produces karyolysis.

carión *m.* karyon, cellular nucleus.

cariotipo *m.* karyotype, chromosome characteristics of an individual species.

caritativo-a *a.* charitable.

carmesí, carmín *m.* carmine.

carne *f.* 1. meat; _____ **asada** / roast beef; _____ **de carnero** / lamb; _____ **de puerco** / pork; _____ **de ternera** / veal; 2. flesh, muscular tissue of the body.

carnívoro-a *a.* carnivorous, that eats meat.

carnosidad *f.* carnosity, fleshy excrescence.

caro-a *a.* expensive, costly.

carótida *f.* carotid, main artery of the neck; arterias _____-s / _____ arteries.

carotina *f.* carotene, yellow-red pigment found in some vegetables that converts into vitamin A in the body.

carpo *m.* carpus, portion of the upper extremity between the hand and the forearm.

carraspera *f.* hoarseness; sore, itchy throat.

carretera *f.* highway.

carro *m.* automobile, car.

carta *f.* letter.

cartera *f.* lady's handbag; wallet.

cartílago *m.* cartilage, elastic semi-hard tissue that covers the bones.

carúncula *f.* caruncle, small irritated piece of flesh; _____ uretral / urethral _____.

casa *f.* house, home; _____ de socorro / first aid station.

casado-a *a.* married.

casarse *vr.* to get married.

cáscara *f.* peel, shell.

cáscara sagrada *f.* cascara sagrada, the bark of *Rhamus Purshiana* shrub, commonly used to treat chronic constipation.

caseína *f.* casein, the main protein found in milk.

caseoso-a *a.* caseous, resembling curd or cheese.

casi *adv.* almost.

caso *m.* case, a specific instant of disease; _____ ambulatorio / ambulatory _____; presentación de un _____ / _____ reporting; **en** _____ **de** / in _____ that; **hacer** _____ / to pay attention; **no viene al** _____ / it is irrelevant.

caspa *f.* dandruff; dander.

castaño-a *a.* brown, chestnut colored.

castigar *vi.* to punish.

castigo *m.* punishment.

castrar *v.* to castrate, to remove the gonads; [*animales hembras*] to spay.

casual *a.* casual, accidental.

casualidad *f.* chance; de _____ / by _____.

catabolismo *m.* catabolism, cellular process

by which complex substances are converted into simpler compounds; destructive metabolism.

catalepsia *f.* catalepsia, a condition characterized by loss of voluntary muscular movement and irresponsiveness to any outside stimuli, gen. associated with psychological disorders.

catálisis *f.* catalysis, alteration of the velocity of a chemical reaction by the presence of a catalyst.

catalítico *m.* catalyst, an agent that stimulates a chemical reaction.

cataplasma *f.* poultice.

cataplexia *f.* cataplexy, sudden loss of muscular tone caused by an exaggerated emotional state.

catarata *f.* cataract, opacity of the lens of the eye; _____ blanda / soft _____; _____ madura / mature _____; _____ senil / senile _____; _____ verde / green _____.

catarral *a.* rel. to catarrh.

catarro *m.* catarrh, cold, sniffle; _____ de pecho, bronquial / chest cold.

catarsis *f.* catharsis, purification. 1. purging the body of chemical or other material; 2. therapeutic liberation of anxiety and tension.

catártico *m.* cathartic, laxative; **-a** *a.* cathartic, rel. to catharsis.

catatonía *f.* catatony, a phase of extreme negativism in schizophrenia in which the patient does not speak, remains in a fixed position, and resists any attempts to activate his or her movement or speech. The same symptoms are present in other mental conditions.

catatónico-a *a.* catatonic, rel. to or affected by catatony.

catecolaminas *f., pl.* catecholamines, amines such as norepinephrine, epinephrine and dopamine, that are produced in the adrenal glands and have a sympathomimetic action.

categoría *f.* category; quality.

catéter *m.* catheter, a rubber or plastic tube used to drain fluid from a body cavity such as urine from the bladder, or to inject fluid, as in cardiac catheterization.

cateterización *f.* catheterization, insertion of a catheter.

cateterizar *vi.* to catheterize, to insert a catheter.

catgut *f.* catgut, type of surgical suture made from the gut of some animals.

cauda *f.* cauda, tail-like structure.

caudal *a.* caudal, rel. to the tail.

causa *f.* cause, reason; **sin** ___ / unreasonable.

causalgia *f.* causalgia, burning pain in the skin.

causar *v.* to cause.

cáustico *m.* caustic, substance used to destroy tissue.

cauterización *f.* cauterization, burning by application of a caustic, heat, or electric current.

cauterizar *vi.* to cauterize, to burn by application of heat or electric current.

cava *f.* cava, hollow organ, cavity. *V.* **vena cava.**

caverna *f.* cavern, cave, pathological cavity or depression.

cavernoso-a *a.* cavernous, having hollow spaces.

cavidad *f.* cavity, hole; ___ abdominal / abdominal ___; ___-es cardíacas: auricular y ventricular / heart chambers; ___-es craneales / cranial cavities; ___ pelviana / pelvic ___; ___ torácica / thoracic ___.

cebada *f.* barley.

cebolla *f.* onion.

cecostomía *f. surg.* cecostomy, surgical opening into the cecum.

cefalea, cefalalgia *f.* cephalea, cephalalgia, headache.

cefálico-a *a.* cephalic, rel. to the head.

cefalorraquídeo-a *a. V.* **cerebroespinal.**

cefalosporina *f.* cephalosporin, wide spectrum antibiotic.

ceguedad, ceguera *f.* blindness; ___ al color / color ___; ___ nocturna / night ___; ___ verde / green ___; ___ roja / red ___.

ceja *f.* eyebrow.

celíaco-a *a.* celiac, rel. to the abdomen.

celiotomía *f. surg.* celiotomy. *V.* **laparotomía.**

celoso-a *a.* jealous.

célula *f.* cell, structural unit of all living organisms; ___ adiposa / adipose ___; ___ anaplástica / anaplastic ___; ___ basal / basal ___; ___ basurera / scavenger ___; ___ caliciforme / goblet ___; ___ columnar / columnar ___; ___ en diana / target ___; ___ ependimaria / ependymal ___; ___ epidérmica / epidermal ___; ___ errante / wandering ___; ___ fagocítica / phagocytic ___; ___ falciforme /

sickle ___; ___ gigante / giant ___; ___ madre / stem ___; ___ piramidal / pyramidal ___.

celular *a.* cellular, rel. to the cell; agua ___ / ___ water; compartimentos ___-es / ___ compartments; crecimiento ___ / ___ growth; tejido ___ / ___ tissue.

celulitis *f.* cellulitis, infl. of connective tissue.

celulosa *a.* cellulose.

cementerio *m.* cemetery.

cemento *m.* cement.

cena *f.* evening meal, supper.

cenar *v.* to have dinner or supper.

cenizas *f. pl.* ashes; ___ radioactivas / fallout.

censo *m.* census.

centeno *m.* rye.

centígrado *a.* centigrade.

central, céntrico-a *a.* central; sistema nervioso ___ / ___ nervous system.

centrífugo-a *a.* centrifugal, going from the center outward.

centrípeto-a *a.* centripetal, going from the outside towards the center.

centro *m.* 1. center: ___ **de servicio de la salud** / community health ___; 2. middle, core.

ceño *m.* brow; **fruncir el** ___ / to frown.

cepa *f.* strain, group of microorganisms within a species or variety characterized by some particular quality.

cepillo *m.* brush; ___ **de dientes** / toothbrush.

cera *f.* wax. 1. beeswax; 2. waxy secretion of the body; ___ depilatoria / depilatory ___.

cerca *f. adv.* near; ___ **de aquí** / close by.

cercanía *f.* vicinity.

cercano-a *a.* close; neighboring, proximate.

cerclaje *m.* cerclage, procedure that consists of encircling a part with a wire loop or catgut, such as in binding together parts of a fractured bone.

cereal *m.* cereal.

cerebelo *m.* cerebellum, posterior brain mass; enfermedades del ___ / cerebellar diseases.

cerebral *a.* cerebral, rel. to the brain; apoplejía ___ / cerebrovascular accident; edema ___ / ___ edema; embolismo y trombosis ___ / ___ embolism and thrombosis; hemorragia o infarto ___ / ___ hemorrhage or infarct; muerte ___ / brain death;

trauma ___ / brain injury; tronco ___ / brain stem; tumor ___ / brain tumor.

cerebro *m*. brain, cerebrum, portion of the central nervous system contained within the cranium that is the chief regulator of body functions; ___ medio / midbrain; escán del ___ (gammagrama) / ___ scan.

cerebroespinal, cefalorraquídeo-a *a*. cerebrospinal, rel. to the brain and the spinal cord.

cerebrovascular *a*. cerebrovascular, rel. to the blood vessels of the brain.

cereza *f*. cherry.

cero *m*. zero.

ceroso-a *a*. waxy.

cerrado-a *a*. closed.

cerradura *f*. lock.

cerrar *vi*. to close; ___ con llave / to lock.

certero-a *a*. accurate.

certeza *f*. certainty; accuracy.

certificado *m*. certificate; ___ de defunción / death ___.

cerumen *m*. cerumen, wax that builds up in the ear.

cerveza *f*. beer.

cervical *a*. cervical. 1. rel. to the cervix; 2. rel. to the area of the neck.

cerviz *f*. nape of the neck.

cesar *v*. to cease, to stop.

cesárea *f*. cesarean section.

cese *m*. stoppage.

cetogénesis *f*. ketogenesis, production of acetone.

cetosa *f*. ketose.

cetosis *f*. ketosis, excessive production of acetone as a result of an incomplete metabolism of fatty acids; acidosis.

cianocobalamina *f*. cyanocobalamin, vitamin B_{12}, complex of cyanide and cobalamin used in the treatment of pernicious anemia.

cianosis *f*. cyanosis, purplish blue discoloration of the skin, often as a result of cardiac, anatomic or functional abnormalities.

cianótico-a *a*. cyanotic, rel. to or afflicted by cyanosis.

cianuro *m*. cyanide.

ciática *f*. sciatica, neuralgia along the course of the sciatic nerve.

cibernética *f*. cybernetics, the study of biological systems such as the brain and the nervous system by electronic means.

cicatriz *f*. scar.

cicatrización *f*. cicatrization.

cicatrizante *m*. cicatrizant, agent that aids the healing process of a wound.

cicatrizar *v*. to scar, the healing process of a wound.

ciclamato *m*. cyclamate, artificial sweetening agent.

ciclectomía *f*. *surg*. cyclectomy, excision of a portion of the ciliary muscle.

ciclitis *f*. cyclitis, infl. of the ciliary body.

ciclo *m*. cycle, recurring period of time; ___ gravídico / pregnancy ___.

cicloforia *f*. cyclophoria, rotation of the eye due to muscle weakness.

ciclofosfamida *f*. cyclophosphamide, antineoplastic drug also used as an immunosuppressive in organ transplants.

ciclofotocoagulación *f*. cyclophotocoagulation, photocoagulation through the pupil with a laser, gen. used in glaucoma.

cicloplejía *f*. cycloplegia, paralysis of the ciliary muscle.

ciclosporina *f*. cyclosporine, immunosuppressive agent used in organ transplant.

ciclotímico-a *m*., *f*. cyclothymic, person afflicted with extreme changes of mood.

ciclotomía *f*. *psych*. cyclothymia, disorder manifested by alternate states of agitation and depression.

ciclotomía *f*. *surg*. cyclotomy, incision through the ciliary body of the eye.

ciclotropía *f*. cyclotropia, deviation of the eye around the anteroposterior axis.

ciego-a *m*., *f*. blind person; *a*. blind.

ciego *m*. cecum. 1. cul-de-sac lying below the terminal ileum forming the first part of the large intestine; 2. any cul-de-sac structure.

cielo *m*. sky.

cien, ciento *a*., *m*. a hundred.

ciencia *f*. science; ___ médica / medical ___; a ___ cierta / for sure.

científico-a *m*., *f*. scientist; *a*. scientific.

cierto-a *a*. certain, true; por ___ / as a matter of fact.

cifosis *f*. kyphosis, exaggerated posterior curvature of the thoracic spine.

cifótico-a *a*. kyphotic, suffering from or rel. to kyphosis.

cigarrillo, cigarro *m*. cigarette.

cigoma, zigoma *m*. zygoma, osseous prominence at the point where the temporal and malar bones join.

cigoto *m*. zygote, the fertilized ovum, cell resulting from the union of two gametes.

ciliar *a.* ciliary, rel. to or resembling the eyelash or eyelid.

cilíndrico-a *a.* cylindrical.

cilindro *m.* cylinder. 1. barrel of a syringe; 2. geometrical form resembling a column.

cilindro granuloso *m.* granular cast, urinary cylinder seen in degenerative or inflammatory nephropathies.

cilindroma *m.* cylindroma, frequently malignant tumor, usu. found in the face or in the orbit of the eye.

cilindruria *f.* cylindruria, presence of cylinders in the urine.

cilio *m.* cilium, eyelid.

cima *f.* summit, top.

Cimetidina *f.* Cimetidine, trade name for an antiacid used in the treatment of gastric and duodenal ulcers.

cimiento *m.* foundation, base.

cinc *m.* zinc.

cinconismo *m.* cinchonism. V. **quinismo.**

cinéreo *m.* cinerea, the gray substance of the nervous system.

cinerradiografía *f.* cineradiography, X-ray of an organ in motion.

cinesis *f.* kinesis, term used to designate physical movements in general, including those that result as a response to a stimulus such as light.

cinestesia *f.* kinesthesia, sensorial experience, sense and perception of a movement.

cinética *f.* kinesics, the study of the body and its static and dynamic positions as a means of communication.

cinético-a *a.* kinetic, rel. to movement or what causes it.

cínico-a *m., f.* cynical person; *a.* cynic.

cinta magnética *f.* audiotape.

cintigrafía *f.* radionucleid imaging, procedure that uses radioisotopes to obtain a two-dimensional image of the distribution of bodily radiation, previously administered as a radiopharmaceutical agent.

cintiescán *m.* scintiscan. V. **gammagrama.**

cinto *m.* belt; waistband.

cintura *f.* waist; waistline.

cinturón *m.* girdle; wide belt.

circinado-a *a.* circinate, ring-shaped.

circuito *m.* circuit.

circulación *f.* circulation; mala ____ / poor ____.

círculo *m.* circle, a round figure or structure.

circuncidar *v.* to circumcise.

circuncisión *f.* *surg.* circumcision, removing part or all of the prepuce.

circundar *v.* to encircle, to surround.

circunferencia *f.* circumference.

circunstancia *f.* circumstance; ____-s atenuantes / mitigating ____-s.

circunvolución *f.* gyrus, elevated portion of the cerebral cortex; ____-es de Broca / ____, Broca's, third, frontal or inferior; ____ frontal, superior / ____, frontal, superior; ____-es occipitales / ____, occipital first, superior.

cirrosis *f.* cirrhosis, progressive disease of the liver characterized by interstitial infl., and associated with failure in the function of hepatocytes and resistance to the flow of blood through the liver; ____ alcohólica / alcoholic ____; ____ biliar / biliary ____.

ciruela *f.* plum; ____ **pasa** / prune.

cirugía *f.* surgery; the branch of medicine that treats diseases, malformations, and injuries and restores or reconstructs body structures through operative procedures; ____ ambulatoria / ambulatory ____; ____ cardiotorácica / cardiotoracic ____; ____ conservadora / conservative ____; ____ cosmética / cosmetic ____; ____ mayor / major ____; ____ menor / minor ____; ____ oral / oral ____; ____ ortopédica / orthopedic ____; ____ plástica / plastic ____; ____ radical / radical ____; ____ torácica / chest

cirujano-a *m., f.* surgeon, specialist in surgery.

cistadenocarcinoma *m.* cystadenocarcinoma, carcinoma and cystadenoma.

cistadenoma *m.* cystadenoma, adenoma that has one or more cysts.

cistectomía *f.* *surg.* cystectomy, total or partial resection of the urinary bladder.

cisteína *f.* cysteine, amino acid derived from cystine and found in most proteins.

cisterna *f.* cistern, a closed space that serves as a reservoir or receptacle.

cístico-a *a.* cystic, rel. to the gallbladder or the bladder.

cistina *f.* cystine, amino acid that is produced by the digestion of proteins, at times found in the urine.

cistinuria *f.* cystinuria, excessive cystine in the urine.

cistitis *f.* cystitis, infl. of the urinary bladder characterized by frequent urination accompanied by pain and burning.

cistocele *m.* cystocele, hernia of the bladder.

cistograma *m.* cystogram, X-ray of the bladder with use of air or a contrasting medium.

cistolitotomía *f. surg.* cystolithotomy, removal of a stone by cutting into the bladder.

cistometría *f.* cystometry, cystometrography, study of the bladder functions through the use of a cystometer.

cistómetro *m.* cystometer, device used to study the pathophysiological functions of the urinary bladder by measuring its capacity and pressure reactions.

cistopexia *f. surg.* cystopexy, fixation of the urinary bladder to the abdominal wall.

cistoscopía *f. surg.* cystoscopy, inspection of the bladder through a cystoscope.

cistoscopio *m.* cystoscope, tube-shaped instrument used to examine the bladder and the urethra.

cistostomía *f. surg.* cystostomy, creation of an opening into the bladder for drainage.

cistotomía *f. surg.* cystotomy, incision in the bladder.

cistouretrografía *f.* cystourethrography, X-ray of the urinary bladder and the urethra.

cistouretroscopio *m.* cystourethroscope, instrument for endoscopic visualization of the bladder and urethra.

cisura *f.* cleft, elongated opening; fissure.

cita *f.* appointment, engagement; **hacer una** ____ / to make an ____; **tener una** ____ / to have an ____.

citocromo *m.* cytochrome, hemochromogen that plays an important part in the oxidation processes.

citolítico-a *a.* cytolytic, having the power to dissolve or destroy a cell.

citología *f.* cytology, the science that deals with the nature of cells.

citómetro *m.* cytometer, a device used for counting and measuring blood cells.

citopenia *f.* cytopenia, deficiency of cellular elements in the blood.

citoplasma *m.* cytoplasm, protoplasm of a cell with exception of the nucleus.

citotoxina *f.* cytotoxin, toxic agent that damages or destroys cells of certain organs.

citrato *m.* citrate, salt of citric acid.

cítrico-a *a.* citric, citrous.

ciudad *f.* city.

ciudadanía *f.* citizenship.

ciudadano-a *m., f.* citizen.

clara *f.* the white of the egg.

claridad *f.* clarity, brightness.

clarificación *f.* clarification.

clarificar *vi.* to clarify.

claro-a *a.* clear.

clase *f.* class, sort, kind.

clasificación *f.* classification.

clasificar *vi.* to classify, to sort out.

claudicación *f.* claudication, limping; ____ intermitente / intermittent ____.

clavícula *f.* clavicle, collarbone.

clavo *m.* nail, slender rod of metal or bone used to fasten together parts of a broken bone; ____ ortopédico / orthopedic pin.

cleidocostal *a.* cleidocostal, rel. to the ribs and the clavicle.

cleptomanía *f. psych.* kleptomania, morbid compulsion to steal.

cleptómano-a *m., f.* kleptomaniac, person afflicted with cleptomania.

clérigo *m.* clergyman.

clima *m.* climate.

climaterio *m.* climacteric, termination of the reproductive period in women.

clímax *m.* climax. 1. crisis in an illness; 2. sexual orgasm.

clínica *f.* clinic, a health-care facility; ____ de consulta externa / outpatient ____.

clínico-a *a.* clinical. 1. rel. to a clinic; 2. rel. to direct observation of patients; cuadro ____ / ____ picture; curso ____ / ____ progress; ensayos ____-s / ____ trials; historia ____, expediente médico / ____ history; procedimiento ____ / ____ procedure.

clitoridectomía *f. surg.* clitoridectomy, excision of the clitoris.

clisis *f.* clysis, the act of supplying fluid to the body by other means than orally.

clítoris *m.* clitoris, small protruding body situated in the most anterior part of the vulva.

cloaca *f.* cloaca. 1. common opening for the intestinal and urinary tracts in the early development of the embryo; 2. sewage.

cloasma *f.* chloasma, skin discoloration seen during pregnancy.

clónico-a *a.* clonic, rel. to clonus.

clono *m.* 1. clonus, a series of rapid and rhythmic contractions of a muscle; 2. clone, an individual derived from a single organism through asexual reproduction.

clonorquiasis *f.* chlonorchiasis, parasitic infection that affects the distal bile ducts.

clorambucil *m.* chlorambucil, a form of nitrogen mustard used to combat some forms of cancer.

cloranfenicol *m.* chloramphenicol, chloromycetin, antibiotic esp. effective in the treatment of typhoid fever.

clorhidria *f.* chlorhydria, excess acidity in the stomach.

cloro *m.* chlorine, gaseous element used as a desinfectant and bleaching agent.

clorofila *f.* chlorophyll, green pigment in plants by which photosynthesis takes place.

cloroformo *m.* chloroform, anesthetic.

cloroma *m.* chloroma, green-colored tumor that can occur in different parts of the body.

clorpromacina *f.* chlorpromazine, tranquilizing and antiemetic agent.

cloroquina *f.* chloroquine, a compound used in the treatment of malaria.

clorosis *f.* chlorosis, type of anemia usu. seen in women and gen. associated with iron deficiency.

clorotetraciclina *f.* chlortetracycline, antibiotic agent.

cloruro *m.* chloride, a compound of chlorine.

coaglutinación *f.* coagglutination, group agglutination.

coaglutinina *f.* coagglutinin, agglutinate that affects two or more organisms.

coagulación *f.* coagulation, clot; ____ diseminada intravascular / disseminated intravascular ____ ; tiempo de ____ / blood ____ time.

coagulante *m.* coagulant, that which causes or precipitates coagulation.

coagular *v.* to coagulate, to clot.

coágulo *m.* coagulation, clot.

coagulopatía *f.* coagulopathy, a disease or condition that affects the coagulation mechanism of the blood.

coalescencia *f.* coalescence, the fusion of parts or elements.

coartación *f.* coarctation, stricture; compression.

cobalto *m.* cobalt.

cobarde *a.* coward.

cobija *f.* cover, blanket.

cobrar *v.* to charge; to collect.

cobre *m.* copper.

coca *f.* coca, bush from whose leaves cocaine is extracted.

cocaína *f.* cocaine, addictive narcotic alkaloid derived from coca leaves.

coccidioidina *f.* coccidioidin, a sterile solution used intracutaneously as a test for coccidioidomycosis.

coccidioidomicosis *f.* coccidioidomycosis,

valley fever, endemic respiratory infection in the Southwest of the United States, Mexico, and parts of South America.

coccigodinia *f.* coccygodynia, pain in the region of the coccyx.

cóccix *m.* coccyx, last bone at the bottom of the vertebral column.

cocer *vi.* to cook; to stew; ____ a fuego lento / to simmer.

cociente *m.* quotient; ____ de inteligencia / intelligence ____ .

cocimiento *m.* concoction made of medicinal herbs.

cocina *f.* kitchen, stove.

cocinado-a *a.* cooked; bien ____ / well done.

cocinar *v.* to cook.

cóclea *f.* cochlea, spiral tube which forms part of the inner ear.

coco *m.* 1. coccus, bacteria; 2. coconut; agua de ____ / ____ milk.

cocoa *f.* cocoa.

coche *m.* automobile.

cochinada *f.* filthy act; dirty trick; filth.

cochino-a *m., f.* pig; *a.* filthy.

codeína *f.* codeine, narcotic analgesic.

codo *m.* elbow; ____ de tenista / tennis ____ ; coyuntura del ____ / ____ joint.

coenzima *f.* coenzyme, a substance that enhances the action of an enzyme.

coerción *f.* duress, coercion; bajo ____ / under ____ .

coger *vi.* to take, to grasp; to get; ____ un resfriado / to catch a cold.

cognado *m.* cognate. 1. that which is of the same nature; 2. *gr.* word that derives from the same root.

cogote *m.* nape, back of neck.

cohabitar *v.* to live together.

coherente *a.* coherent.

cohesión *f.* cohesion, the force that holds molecules together.

cohibido *a.* inhibited; uneasy.

coincidencia *f.* coincidence.

coincidir *v.* to coincide.

coito *m.* coitus, sexual intercourse.

cojear *v.* to limp.

cojera *f.* lameness.

cojinete *m.* cushion.

cojo-a *a.* lame, crippled.

col *f.* cabbage.

cola *f.* 1. glue; inhalar ____ / ____ sniffing; 2. tail.

colaborar *v.* to collaborate.

colador *m.* sieve, strainer.

colágeno *m.* collagen, the main supportive protein of skin, bone, tendon and cartilage.

colangiectasia *f.* cholangiectasis, dilation of the biliary ducts.

colangiografía *f.* cholangiography, X-ray of the biliary ducts.

colangiograma *m.* cholangiogram, X-ray of the biliary ducts with the use of a contrasting medium.

colangitis *f.* cholangitis, infl. of the biliary ducts.

colapso *m.* collapse; ___ nervioso / nervous breakdown.

colar *vi.* to strain; to sift.

colateral *a.* collateral, accessory, or secondary.

colcha *f.* cover, coverlet.

colchón *m.* mattress.

colecistectomía *f. surg.* cholecystectomy, removal of the gallbladder.

colecistitis *f.* cholecystitis, infl. of the gallbladder.

colecistoduodenostomía *f. surg.* cholecystoduodenostomy, anastomosis of the gallbladder and the duodenum.

colecistogastrostomía *f. surg.* cholecystogastrostomy, anastomosis of the gallbladder and the stomach.

colecistografía *f.* cholecystography, X-ray of the gallbladder by administration of a dye, orally or by injection.

colectar, coleccionar *v.* to collect.

colectomía *f. surg.* colectomy, excision of part or all of the colon.

colédoco *m.* choledochus, common bile duct, formed by the union of the hepatic and cystic ducts.

coledocoduodenostomía *f. surg.* choledochoduodenostomy, anastomosis of the choledochus and the duodenum.

coledocolitiasis *f.* choledocholithiasis, presence of calculi in the common bile duct.

coledocoyeyunostomía *f. surg.* choledochojejunostomy, anastomosis of the common bile duct and the jejunum.

colega *m., f.* colleague.

colegio *m.* school.

colelitiasis *f.* cholelithiasis, presence of stones in the gallbladder or in the common bile duct.

colemia *f.* cholemia, presence of bile in the blood.

cólera *f.* cholera. 1. acute infectious disease characterized by severe diarrhea and vomiting; 2. anger, rage.

colestasis *f.* cholestasis, biliary stasis.

colesteatoma *m.* cholesteatoma, a tumor containing cholesterol, found most commonly in the middle ear.

colesterol *m.* cholesterol, component of animal oils, fats and nerve tissue, a precursor of sex hormones and adrenal corticoids; alto nivel de ___ / high ___.

colgajo *m. surg.* flap, detached tissue.

colgar *vi.* to hang.

cólico *m.* colic, acute spasmodic abdominal pain.

coliflor *f.* cauliflower.

colinesterasa *f.* cholinesterase, a family of enzymes.

colirio *m.* colyrium, liquid medicinal preparation for the eye.

colitis *f.* colitis, infl. of the colon; ___ crónica / chronic ___ ; ___ espasmódica / spasmodic ___ ; ___ mucomembranosa / pseudomembranous ___ ; ___ mucosa / mucous ___ ; ___ ulcerativa / ulcerative ___ .

colmena *f.* beehive.

colmillo *m.* canine tooth; tusk, fang.

colocar *vi.* to place, to set; **colocarse** *vr.* to position oneself.

colodión *m.* collodion, liquid substance used to cover or protect skin cuts.

coloide *m.* colloid, gelatin-like substance produced by some forms of tissue decay.

colon *m.* colon, the portion of the intestine extending from the cecum to the rectum; ___ ascendente / ascending ___ ; ___ descendente / descending ___ ; neoplasma del ___ / colonic neoplasma.

colonia *f.* colony, a group of bacteria in a culture, all derived from the same organism.

colónico-a *a.* colonic, rel. to the colon.

colonoscopía *f.* colonoscopy, examination of the inner surface of the colon through a colonoscope.

colonoscopio *m.* colonoscope, instrument used to examine the colon.

color *m.* color.

coloración *f.* coloration, staining.

colorado-a *a.* red; **ponerse** ___ / to blush.

colorante *m.* dye, stain.

colorimétrico-a *a.* rel. to color; guía ___ / color index.

colostomía *f. surg.* colostomy, creation of an artificial anus; bolsa de ____ / ____ bag.

colpitis *f.* colpitis, infl. of the vaginal membrane.

colpocele *m.* colpocele, a hernia into the vagina.

colporrafia *f. surg.* colporrhaphy, suture of the vagina.

colporragia *f.* colporrhagia, vaginal hemorrhage.

colposcopía *f.* colposcopy, examination of the vagina and the cervix through a colposcope.

colposcopio *m.* colposcope, endoscopic instrument that allows direct observation of the vagina and the cervix.

colpotomía *f. surg.* colpotomy, incision in the vagina.

columna *f.* column, pillar-like structure.

columna, espina vertebral *f.* spinal column, osseous structure formed by thirty-three vertebrae that surround and contain the spinal cord.

coluria *f.* choluria, presence of bile in the urine.

colutorio *m.* mouthwash, antiseptic solution for rinsing the mouth.

coma *m.* coma, state of unconsciousness.

comadre *f.* godmother; woman friend.

comadrona *f.* midwife.

comatoso-a *a.* comatose, rel. to or in a state of coma; estado ____ / ____ state.

combatir *v.* to combat, to fight.

combinación *f.* combination.

combinar *v.* to combine.

comedón *m.* blackhead, comedo.

comedor *m.* dining room.

comensal *m.* commensal, host, organism that benefits from living within or on another living organism without either benefiting or harming it.

comentar *v.* to comment.

comentario *m.* commentary, remark.

comenzar *vi.* to commence, to begin.

comer *v.* to eat; dar de ____ / to feed.

comestible *m.* food; *a.* edible.

cometer *v.* to commit.

comezón *f.* itch.

comida *f.* food; meal; hora de ____ / meal time.

comienzo *m.* beginning; start.

comilón-a *a.* big eater.

comisión *f.* commission, assignment.

comisura *f.* commissure, coming together of two parts, such as the labial angles.

comisurotomía *f.* commisurotomy, incision of the fibrous bands of a commisure, such as the labial angles or the commisure of a cardiac valve.

como *adv.* how, as; ____ quiera / as you wish; *conj.* like, as; ____ no / of course; *prep.* about; está ____ a (una milla) / it is about (a mile away); ____ a (las ocho) / about (eight o'clock).

cómodo-a *a.* comfortable.

compacto-a *a.* compact.

compadecer *vi.* to pity; compadecerse *vr.* to feel sorry for; ____ a sí mismo / self-pity.

compadre *m.* godfather; close friend.

compañero *m.* companion, mate.

compañía *f.* company; ____ de seguros / insurance ____.

comparación *f.* comparison.

comparar *v.* to compare.

compartir *v.* to share.

compasión *f.* compassion.

compatible *a.* compatible.

compensación *f.* compensation. 1. that which makes up for a defect or counterbalances some deficiency; 2. defense mechanism; 3. remuneration.

compensar *v.* to compensate.

competente *a.* competent, qualified, able to perform well.

complejo *m. psych.* complex, a series of related mental processes that affect behavior and personality; ____ de castración / castration ____; ____ de culpa / guilt ____; ____ de Edipo / Oedipus ____, morbid love of a son for the mother; ____ de Electra / Electras's ____, morbid love of a daughter for the father; ____ de inferioridad / inferiority ____; -a *a.* complicated; intricate.

complementar *v.* to supplement.

complemento *m.* complement, a serum protein substance that destroys bacteria and other cells with which it comes into contact.

completar *v.* to complete.

completo-a *a.* complete.

complexión *f.* complexion, appearance of the facial skin.

complicación *f.* complication.

complicar *vi.* to complicate; complicarse *vr.*, to become difficult.

componente *m.* component.

componer *vi.* [*una fractura*] to set; to put together; to heal, to restore.

composición *f.* composition.

compostura *f.* composure; serenity.

compota *f.* compote, fruit stew.

comprar *v.* to buy, to purchase.

comprender *v.* to understand.

compresa *f.* compress, pack; ___ fría / cold ___.

compresión *f.* compression, exertion of pressure on a point of the body.

comprimidos *m. pl.* pills.

comprobar *vi.* to prove, to verify.

comprometer *v.* to compromise; **comprometerse** *vr.* to commit oneself.

compromiso *m.* commitment, obligation.

compuesto *m.* compound.

compulsivo-a *a.* compulsive.

computadora *f.* computer.

común *a.* common; **lugar** ___ / ___ place; **nombre** ___ / ___ name; **no** ___ / uncommon; **por lo** ___ / gen.; **sentido** ___ / ___ sense.

comunicación *f.* communication.

comunicar *v.* to communicate, to inform; **comunicarse** *vr.* to communicate with.

comunidad *f.* community.

con *prep.* with, by; ___ **frecuencia** / frequently; ___ **mucho gusto** / gladly; ___ **permiso** / excuse me; ___ **regularidad** / regularly.

cóncavo-a *a.* concave, hollowed.

concebir *vi.* to conceive.

concentración *f.* concentration. 1. increased strength of a fluid by evaporation; 2. the act of concentrating.

concentrado-a *a.* concentrated; ___ **en sí mismo-a** / self-conscious.

concentrar *v.* to concentrate; **concentrarse** *vr.* to concentrate oneself.

concepción *f.* conception.

concepto *m.* concept, idea.

concha *f.* shell; that which resembles a shell.

conciencia *f.* consciousness; conscience, state of awareness.

conciso-a *a.* concise.

concluir *vi.* to conclude; to infer.

conclusión *f.* conclusion.

concreción *f.* concretion, hardening, solidification.

concretio cordis *L.* concretio cordis, partial or complete obliteration of the pericardial cavity due to chronic constrictive periocarditis.

concreto-a *a.* concrete.

concusión *f.* concussion, trauma gen. caused

by a head injury and manifested at times by dizziness and nausea; ___ del cerebro / brain ___; ___ de la médula espinal / spinal ___.

condensar *v.* to condense, to make something more dense.

condición *f.* condition, quality.

condicionar *v.* to condition, to train.

cóndilo *m.* condyle, rounded portion of the bone *usu.* present at the joint.

condiloma *f.* condyloma, warty growth usu. found around the genitalia and the perineum.

condimentado-a *a.* spicy.

condón *m.* condom, contraceptive device.

condral *a.* chondral, of a cartilaginous nature.

condritis *f.* chondritis, infl. of a cartilage.

condrocalcinosis *f.* chondrocalcinosis, condition that resembles gout, characterized by calcification and degenerative alterations in cartilage.

condrocostal *a.* chondrocostal, rel. to the ribs and the costal cartilages.

condromalacia *f.* chondromalacia, abnormal softening of cartilage.

condrosarcoma *m.* chondrosarcoma, malignant tumor of a cartilage.

conducir *vi.* to conduct; to drive.

conducta *f.* conduct, behaviour.

conducto *m.* duct, conduit; ___ biliar / biliary ___; ___ endolinfático / endolymphatic ___; ___ eyaculatorio / ejaculatory ___; ___ hepático / hepatic ___; ___ lacrimal / lacrimal ___; ___ seminal / seminal ___; ___ seminífero / seminiferous tubule.

conectar *v.* to connect; to switch on.

conejillo de Indias *m.* guinea pig.

conejo *m.* rabbit; fiebre de ___ / ___ fever, tularemia; la prueba del ___ / ___ test, pregnancy test.

conexión *f.* connection.

confabulación *f.* confabulation, condition by which the individual fabricates imaginary situations soon to be forgotten.

conferencia *f.* conference, lecture, meeting.

confianza *f.* confidence, trust; ___ en uno, en sí mismo-a / self ___; falta de ___ en sí mismo-a / lack of self-esteem.

confiar *v.* to entrust, to trust.

confidencial *a.* confidential; **comunicación o información** ___ / privileged communication or information.

confinación, confinamiento *f., m.* confinement, restraint.

confirmación *f.* confirmation.

confirmar *v.* to confirm.

conflicto *m.* conflict.

confluencia *f.* confluence, meeting point of several channels.

conformar *v.* to conform, to adapt; **conformarse** *vr.* to resign oneself.

confortar *v.* to comfort.

confrontar *v.* to confront.

confundido-a, confuso-a *a.* confused, at a loss; **estar** ___ / to be at a loss.

confundir *v.* to confuse, to mix up; **confundirse** *vr.* to be or to become confused.

confusión *f.* confusion.

congelación *m.* freezing; corte por ___ / frozen cut; punto de ___ / ___ point; secar por ___ / freeze-drying; sección por ___ / frozen section, thin specimen of tissue that is quickly frozen for the purpose of aiding in the diagnosis of malignancies.

congelado-a *a.* frozen; ___ **al instante** / quick-frozen.

congelar *v.* to freeze; **congelarse** *vr.* to become frozen.

congénito-a *a.* congenital, that which exists from the time of birth; ingrown.

congestión *f.* congestion, excessive accumulation of blood in a given part or organ.

congestionado-a *a.* congested.

conización *f.* conization, removal of a cone shaped tissue such as the mucosa of the cervix.

conjugar *vi. gr.* to conjugate.

conjuntiva *f.* conjunctiva, delicate mucous membrane covering the eyelids and the anterior surface of the eyeball.

conjuntivitis *f.* conjunctivitis, infl. of the conjunctiva; ___ aguda contagiosa / acute contagious ___; ___ alérgica / allergic ___; ___ catarral / catarrhal ___; ___ folicular / follicular ___; ___ vernal / vernal ___.

conjunto *m.* whole, total sum of parts; a set; **en** ___ / as a whole.

conminuto-a *a.* comminuted, broken in many small fragments as in a fracture.

conmoción *f.* commotion.

cono *m.* cone, sensory organ that together with the rods of the retina receives color stimuli.

conocer *vi.* to know; to know about; **conocerse** *vr.* to know each other; to know oneself.

conocimiento *m.* 1. consciousness; **perder el** ___ / to lose ___; 2. knowledge; **no tener** ___ **de** / to be unaware of.

conque *conj.* so, so then.

consanguíneos *m.* blood relatives.

consciencia, conciencia *f.* conscience.

consciente *a.* conscious, aware.

consecuencia *f.* consequence; aftermath; **a** ___ **de** / as a result of.

conseguir *vi.* to obtain, to get.

consejero-a *m., f.* counselor.

consejo *m.* counsel, advice.

consentimiento *m.* consent, permission; ___ autorizado / informed ___.

consentir *vi.* to consent, to permit; to pamper.

conservación *f.* conservation, preservation.

conservar *v.* to keep, to preserve.

consideración *f.* consideration; regard.

considerado-a *a.* considerate.

considerar *v.* to consider.

consistencia *f.* consistency.

consistente *a.* consistent, stable.

consistir *v.* to consist of, to be comprised by.

consolar *v.* to console, to comfort.

consomé *m.* consommé, broth.

constante *a.* constant, invariable.

constitución *f.* constitution, physical make up.

constituir *vi.* to constitute.

constricción *f.* constriction, narrowing, contraction.

consulta *f.* consultation; consulting room; ___ particular / private practice; horas de ___ / office hours.

consultar *v.* to consult, to confer.

consultor-a *m., f.* consultant, person that acts in an advisory capacity.

consultorio *m.* doctor's office; consulting room.

consumación *f.* consummation, completion.

consumir *v.* to consume; **consumirse** *vr.* to waste away.

consunción *f.* consumption, wasting, general emaciation of the body, as seen in patients with tuberculosis.

contacto *m.* contact; ___ inicial / initial ___; **lentes de** ___ / ___ lenses.

contado-a *a.* numbered; scarce; **al** ___ / cash.

contagiar *v.* to transmit, to pass on, to infect.

contagio *m.* contagion, communication of disease.

contagioso-a *a.* contagious, communicable.

contaminación *f.* contamination.

contaminar *v.* to contaminate.

contar *vi.* to count; to tell; ___ **con** / to rely on.

contener *vi.* to contain; **contenerse** *vr.* to restrain oneself, to hold back.

contenido *m.* content.

contento-a *a.* happy, content, pleased.

conteo *m.* count; ___ globular o de células sanguíneas / blood cell ___.

contestación *f.* answer.

contestar *v.* to answer.

contiguo-a *a.* contiguous, adjacent, next to.

continencia *f.* continence, abstinence or moderation.

continuación *f.* continuation.

continuar *v.* to continue.

continuidad *f.* continuity.

contorno *m.* contour, outline.

contra *prep.* against.

contracción *f.* contraction, temporary shortening, as of a muscle fiber; ___ de fondo / deep ___; ___ de hambre / hunger ___; ___ espasmódica / twitching; ___ ulterior / after ___.

contracepción *f.* contraception, birth control.

contraceptivo *m.* contraceptive; **métodos** ___-**s** / methods of contraception.

contráctil *a.* contractile, having the capacity to contract.

contractilidad *f.* contractility, capacity to contract.

contractura *f.* contracture, prolonged or permanent involuntary contraction.

contradecir *vi.* to contradict, to negate.

contradicción *f.* contradiction.

contraer *vi.* to contract, [*una enfermedad*] to catch a sickness; **contraerse** *vr.* to be reduced in size, to shrink up, to crumple up.

contragolpe *m.* countercoup, lesion that occurs as a result of a blow to the opposite point.

contraindicado-a *a.* contraindicated.

contralateral *a.* contralateral, rel. to the opposite side.

contrariado-a *a.* upset.

contrariar *v.* to disappoint, to upset.

contrario-a *a.* contrary; **al** ___ / on the ___; **de lo** ___ / otherwise.

contrarrestar *v.* to counter, to oppose.

contrastar *v.* to contrast.

contraste *m.* contrast; medio de ___ / ___ medium.

contraveneno *m.* counterpoison, antidote.

contribución *f.* contribution.

contribuir *vi.* to contribute.

control *m.* control.

controlar *v.* to control, to regulate; **controlarse** *vr.* to control oneself.

contusión *f.* contusion, bruise.

convalescencia *f.* convalescence, period of time between an illness and the return to health.

convalesciente *a.* convalescent.

convencer *vi.* to convince.

conveniente *a.* convenient, handy.

convergencia *f.* convergence, inclination of two elements toward a common point.

conversación *f.* conversation.

conversión *f.* conversion. 1. change, transformation; 2. *psych.* transformation of an emotion into a physical manifestation.

convertir *vi.* to convert; **convertirse** *vr.* to become.

convexo-a *a.* convex.

convulsión *f.* convulsion, violent involuntary muscular contraction of the muscles; ___ febril / febrile ___; ___ jacksoniana / Jacksonian ___; ___ tónico-clónica / tonic-clonic ___.

convulsivo-a *a.* convulsive, rel. to convulsions.

cooperación *f.* cooperation.

cooperar *v.* to cooperate.

cooperativo-a *a.* cooperative.

coordinación *f.* coordination; falta de ___ / lack of ___.

coordinar *v.* to coordinate.

copa *f.* cup.

copia *f.* copy, imitation.

copiar *v.* to copy; to imitate.

copro-emoliente *m.* stool softener.

coprofagia *f.* *psych.* coprophagy, disorder that drives a person to eat feces.

copulación *f.* copulation, sexual intercourse.

coqueluche *m.* whooping cough.

cor *L.* cor, heart; ___ errante / ___ mobile; ___ juvenil / ___ juvenum; ___ pulmonar / ___ pulmonar / ___ pulmonale.

coracoclavicular *a.* coracoclavicular, rel. to the scapula and the clavicle.

coraje *m.* courage; anger.

corazón *m.* heart; hollow, muscular organ situated in the thorax, the function of which is to maintain the circulation of blood; anormalidades congénitas del ____ / congenital ____ diseases; bloqueo del ____ / ____ block; bulbo del ____ / bulbus cordis; hipertrofia del ____ / ____, hypertrophy; latido del ____ / heartbeat; operación a ____ abierto / open ____ surgery; ruido del ____ / ____ sound; trasplante del ____ / ____ transplant; válvula del ____ / ____ valve.

corazón artificial *m.* artificial heart, instrument or device that pumps blood with the same capacity as a normal heart.

cordal *m.* wisdom tooth.

cordectomía *f. surg.* cordectomy, excision of a vocal chord.

cordel *m.* string, cord.

cordero *m.* lamb; **chuleta de** ____ / ____ chop; **lana de** ____ / ____ 's wool.

cordón *m.* any elongated, rounded structure; cord.

cordón umbilical *m.* umbilical cord, structure that connects the fetus with the placenta during the gestation period.

cordotomía *f. surg.* cordotomy, an operation to cut certain sensory fibers in the spinal cord.

cordura *f.* sanity.

corea *f.* chorea, Huntington's disease, St. Vitus dance, nervous disorder manifested by involuntary rapid and jerky but well coordinated movements of the limbs or facial muscles.

coriocarcinoma *m.* choriocarcinoma, malignant tumor found primarily in the testicle and the uterus.

corion *m.* 1. chorion, one of the two membranes that surround the fetus; 2. corium, dermis or true skin.

coriza *f.* coryza, acute or chronic rhinitis; running nose.

córnea *f.* cornea, transparent membrane on the anterior surface of the eyeball.

córneo-a *a.* corneous, callous.

cornetes nasales *m. pl.* nasal concha.

cornezuelo de centeno *m.* ergot, fungus that in a dry form or as an extract is used as medication to induce uterine contractions or to stop hemorrhaging after delivery.

coroides *f.* choroides, eye membrane that supplies blood to the eye.

coroiditis *f.* choroiditis, infl. of the choroid.

corona *f.* corona, circular-like structure; crown.

coronario-a *a.* coronary, encircling in the manner of a crown; arteria ____ / ____ arte-

ry; trombosis ____ / ____ thrombosis; vasoespasmo ____ / ____ vasospasm.

corporal *a.* corporeal, rel. to the body; líquido ____ / body fluid; peso ____ / body weight; temperatura ____ / body temperature.

corpulento-a *a.* corpulent, stout, robust.

corpus *m.* corpus, the human body.

corpus callosum *L.* corpus callosum, the great commisure of the brain.

corpus luteum *L.* corpus luteum, yellow body, yellow glandular mass in the ovary that is formed by a ruptured follicle and that produces progesterone.

corpúsculo *m.* corpuscle, bud, small mass.

correa *f.* strap, belt.

correctivo-a *m., f.* corrective; antidote.

correcto-a *a.* correct; accurate.

corregir *vi.* to correct, to rectify.

correo *m.* mail.

correr *v.* to run, to jog.

correspondencia *f.* correspondence; reciprocity.

corriente *f.* current, stream, flow of fluid, air, or electricity along a conductor; **al** ____ / current, up to date; *a.* current.

corroído-a *a.* corroded.

corromperse *vr.* to be affected with putrefaction, to taint.

corrosión *f.* corrosion, deterioration by chemical reaction.

corsé *m.* corset, jacket.

cortada, cortadura *f.* cut, slit.

cortado-a *a.* cut, incised.

cortar *v.* to cut, to incise; **cortarse** *vr.* to cut oneself.

corte *m.* cut, slit; ____ transversal / transection.

corteza *f.* cortex, the outer layer of an organ; ____ suprarrenal / adrenal ____; ____ cerebral / cerebral ____.

Corti, órgano de *m.* Corti's organ, the end organ of hearing by which sound is directly perceived.

cortical *a.* cortical, rel. to the cortex.

corticoide, corticosteroide *m.* corticoid, corticosteroid, a steroid produced by the adrenal cortex.

corticotropina *f.* corticotropin, hormonal substance of adrenocorticotropic activity.

cortina *f.* curtain; blinds.

cortisol *m.* cortisol, hormone secreted by the adrenal cortex.

cortisona *f.* cortisone, glycogenic steroid derived from cortisol or produced synthetically.

corto-a *a.* short; ___ **de vista** / nearsighted.

cosa *f.* thing.

coser *v.* to sew.

cosmético *m.* cosmetic; **-a** *a.* cosmetic.

cosquillas *f. pl.* tickle, tickling; **hacer** ___ / to tickle; **tener** ___ / to be ticklish.

cosquilleo *m.* tingling or prickling sensation.

costado *m.* side, flank; **al** ___ / to the ___.

costal *a.* costal, rel. to the ribs.

costalgia *f.* costalgia, neuralgia, pain in the ribs.

costar *vi.* to cost; ___ **trabajo** / to be difficult.

costilla *f.* rib. 1. one of the bones of twelve pairs that form the thoracic cage; 2. chop, a cut of meat.

costo *m.* cost; ___ **de vida** / ___ of living.

costoclavicular *a.* costoclavicular, rel. to the ribs and the clavicle.

costoso-a *a.* costly, expensive.

costovertebral *a.* costovertebral, rel. to the angle of the ribs and the thoracic vertebrae.

costra *f.* crust, scab; ___ **láctea** / cradle cap.

costumbre *f.* custom, habit; **tener la** ___ / to be in the habit of.

costura *f.* seam.

cowperitis *f.* cowperitis, infl. of Cowper's gland.

coyuntura *f.* joint; articulation.

coxa *f.* coxa, hip.

coxalgia *f.* coxalgia, pain in the hip.

coxitis *f.* coxitis, infl. of the hip joint.

craneal *a.* cranial, rel. to the cranium; fractura ___ / skull fracture.

craneales, nervios *m. pl.* cranial nerves, each of the twelve pairs of nerves connected to the brain: I. olfatorio / olfactory; II. óptico / optic; III. motor ocular común / oculomotor; IV. patético / trochlear; V. trigémino / trigeminal; VI. motor ocular externo, abducente / abducens; VII. facial / facial; VIII. auditivo / auditory; IX. glosofaríngeo / glossopharyngeal; X. neumogástrico, vago / vagus; XI. espinal / accessory; XII. hipogloso / hypoglossal.

cráneo *m.* cranium, skull, braincase, the bony structure of the head that covers the brain; base del ___ / base of the ___.

creaneoplastia *f. surg.* craneoplasty, reparation of a cranial bone.

craneotomía *f. surg.* craniotomy, trepanation of the cranium.

cráter *m.* crater, cavity.

creación *f.* creation.

crear *v.* to create.

creatina *f.* creatine, component of muscular tissue very important in the anaerobic phase of muscular contraction.

creatinina *f.* creatinine, substance that is the end product of the metabolism of creatine and is present in urine; depuración de la ___ / ___ clearance, volume of plasma that is clear of creatinine.

crecer *vi.* to grow; ___ **hacia adentro** / to ingrow.

crecido-a *a.* grown; large.

crecimiento *m.* growth, upgrowth.

crecimiento cero de población (CCP) *m.* zero population growth (ZPG), a demographic condition during a certain period of time, in which a population is stable, neither increasing nor diminishing.

crédito *m.* credit.

creer *vi.* to believe; to think.

crema *f.* cream, ointment.

cremastérico *a.* cremasteric, rel. to the cremaster muscle of the scrotal wall.

creosota *f.* creosote, antiseptic oily liquid also used as an expectorant.

crepitación *f.* crepitation, crackling; ___ pleural / pleural ___.

cresta *f.* crest. 1. a bony ridge; 2. the peak of a graph.

cretinismo *m.* cretinism, congenital hypothyroidism due to severe deficiency of the thyroid hormone.

cretino-a *m., f.* cretin, person afflicted with cretinism.

cretinoide *a.* cretinoid, having characteristics similar to cretinism.

cribiforme *a.* cribriform, perforated.

cricoides *a.* cricoid, shaped like a ring.

crimen *m.* crime.

criminal *m.* criminal; felon.

crioanestesia *f.* cryanesthesia. 1. anesthesia applied by means of localized refrigeration; 2. a loss of power to perceive cold.

criocirugía *f.* cryosurgery, destruction of tissue through the application of intense cold.

criógeno *a.* cryogenic, that which produces low temperatures.

crioglobulina *f.* cryoglobulin, a serum globulin that crystallizes spontaneously at low temperatures.

crioterapia *f.* cryotherapy, therapeutic treatment using a cold medium.

cripta *f.* crypt, small tubular recess.

críptico *m.* cryptic, hidden.

criptogénico-a *a.* cryptogenic, of an unknown cause.

criptorquismo *m.* cryptorchism, failure of a testis to descend into the scrotum.

crisis *f.* crisis, turning point in a disease; ___ de identidad / identity ___; ___ nerviosa / nervous breakdown.

crisoterapia *f.* chrysotherapy, treatment with gold salts.

crista *f.* crista, a projecting structure or ridge gen. surmounting a bone.

cristal *m.* crystal.

cristalino *m.* crystalline lense, lense of the eye behind the pupil; **-a** *a.* crystalline, transparent.

cristaloideo-a *a.* crystalloid, resembling crystal.

cromático-a *a.* chromatic, rel. to colors.

cromatina *f.* chromatin, portion of the cell nucleus that stains more readily.

cromocito *m.* chromocyte, a colored or pigmented cell.

cromógeno *m.* chromogen, a substance that produces color.

cromófobo *m.* chromophobe, a cell or tissue that resists stain.

cromosoma *m.* chromosome, part of the nucleus of the cell that contains the genes.

cromosoma X *m.* X-chromosome, differential chromosome that determines the female sex characteristics.

cromosoma Y *m.* Y-chromosome, differential chromosome that determines the male sex characteristics.

cromosómico-a *a.* chromosomic, rel. to the chromosome; aberraciones ___-s / chromosome aberrations.

crónico-a *a.* chronic.

cronológico-a *a.* chronological, rel. to the sequence of time.

cronotropismo *m.* chronotropism, modification of the rate of a regular pace or beat such as the heart beat.

crudo-a *a.* raw; crude; **carne** ___ / ___ meat.

cruel *a.* cruel.

crup *m.* croup, infl. of the larynx in children, usu. accompanied by hoarse coughing, fever, and difficulty in breathing.

crus *L.* crus, leg or a structure resembling one; ___ del cerebro / ___ cereberi; ___ pene / ___ of the penis.

Cruz Roja Internacional *f.* International Red Cross, international organization for medical assistance.

cruzar *vi.* to cross.

cuadra *f.* city block.

cuadrado-a *a.* square.

cuadrángulo *m.* quadrangle.

cuadrante *m.* quadrant, 90°, one-fourth of a circle.

cuadrar *v.* to square; to fit.

cuadriceps *m.* quadriceps, four-headed muscle, extensor of the leg.

cuadriplegia *f.* quadriplegia, paralysis of the four extremities.

cuajado-a *a.* curdled.

cuajar *v.* to curdle; **cuajarse** *vr.* to congeal, to thicken.

cuajo *m.* curd.

cualidad *f.* quality.

cualitativo-a *a.* qualitative, rel. to quality; prueba ___ / ___ test.

cualquier-a *a.* any.

cuando, cuándo *adv.* when, whenever; **de** ___ **en** ___ / from time to time; ___ **usted quiera** / whenever you want; ¿ ___ **empezó?** / ___ did it start?

cuantitativo-a *a.* quantitative, rel. to amount.

cuanto, cúanto-a *a., adv.* how much, how many; ¿___ **tiempo?** / how long?; ___ **antes** / as soon as possible; **en** ___ / as soon as; **en** ___ **a** / in regard to; **unos** ___-s / a few.

cuarentena *f.* quarantine, period of forty days during which a restraint is put upon the activities of persons or animals to prevent the spread of a disease.

cuarto *m.* 1. room; ___ **de baño** / bathroom; ___ **de dormir** / bedroom; ___ **de niños** / nursery room; 2. quart, one-fourth of a whole; **-a** *a.* fourth.

cubeta *f.* basin.

cubierta *f.* covering, sheath, shield.

cubierto-a *a. pp.* of **cubrir,** covered.

cubital *a.* cubital, rel. to the cubital bone or elbow.

cúbito *m.* cubitus, ulna, the inner, long bone of the forearm.

cubrir *v.* to cover, to drape as with a sterilized cloth.

cubreboca *m.* surgical mask.

cucaracha *f.* cockroach.

cuclillas (en) *adv.* in a squatting position.

cuchara *f.* spoon; tablespoon.

cucharada *f.* spoonful; scoop; ___ de postre / cochleare medium; ____ de sopa / cochleare magnum.

cucharita *f.* teaspoon; de café / cochleare parvum.

cuchichear *v.* to whisper.

cuchillita *f.* small knife; razor blade.

cuchillo *m.* knife.

cuello *m.* neck; collar. 1. part that joins the head and the trunk of the body; 2. area between the crown and the root of a tooth.

cuello uterino *m.* uterine neck; cervix uteri; dilatación del ____ / dilation of the cervix.

cuenta *f.* account, bill; **arreglar la** ____ / to settle the ____; ____ **bancaria** / bank ____; **darse** ____ / to realize; **pagar la** ____ / to pay the ____; **tener en** ____ / to take into ____.

cuentacélulas *m.* cell counting device.

cuerda *f.* cord, cordon.

cuerdas vocales *f. pl.* vocal cords, main organ of the voice; ____ superiores o falsas / false ____; ____ inferiores o verdaderas / true ____.

cuerdo-a *a.* sane; wise.

cuerno *m.* horn.

cuero *m.* skin, hide; ____ cabelludo / scalp; **en** ____-s / naked.

cuerpo *m.* body; ____-s extraños / foreign bodies.

cuerpos cetónicos, acetónicos *m. pl.* ketone bodies, known as acetones.

cuerpo amarillo *m.* yellow body. *V.* **corpus luteum.**

cuestión *f.* question; issue, matter.

cuidado *m.* care, attention; ____ intensivo / intensive ____; ____ postnatal / postnatal ____; ____ prenatal / prenatal ____; ____ primario / primary ____; nivel de ____ satisfactorio / reasonable ____; **estar al** ____ **de** / to be under the ____ of; **tratar con** ____ / to handle with care.

cuidadoso-a *a.* careful, mindful.

cuidar *v.* to take care, to look after.

cul-de-sac *Fr.* cul-de-sac. 1. blind pouch, cavity closed on one end; 2. rectouterine pouch.

culdoscopía *f.* culdoscopy, viewing of the pelvic and abdominal cavity with a culdoscope.

culdoscopio *m.* culdoscope, an endoscopic instrument inserted through the vagina to do a visual examination of the pelvis and the abdominal cavity.

culebra *f.* snake.

culebrilla *f.* the shingles, herpes zoster, herpes-like cutaneous disease.

culero *m.* diaper.

culpa *f.* guilt; fault, blame; **tener la** ____ / to be at fault.

culpar *v.* to blame.

cultivar *v.* to cultivate.

cultivo *m.* culture, artificial growth of microorganisms or living tissue cells in the laboratory; ____ de sangre / blood ____; ____ de tejido / tissue ____; medio de ____ / ____ medium.

cuna *f.* crib, cradle, basinet.

cunilinguo-a *a.* cunnilingus, rel. to the practice of oral stimulation or manipulation of the penis or clitoris.

cuña *f.* wedge; bedpan.

cuñado-a *m.*, *f.* brother-in-law; sister-in-law.

cúpula *f.* dome.

cura *f.* 1. cure; 2. *m.* priest.

curable *a.* curable, healable.

curación *f.* cure; healing process.

curanderismo *m.* faith healing.

curandero *m.* faith healer, medicine man, shaman.

curar *v.* to cure, to heal.

curare *m.* curare, venom extracted from various plants used to provide muscle relaxation during anesthesia.

curativo-a *a.* curative, that which has healing properties.

cureta *f.* curette, scoop-like instrument with sharp edges used for curettage.

curetaje *m.* curettage, scraping of a surface or cavity with a sharp-edged instrument; ____ uterino / D&C, dilation and curettage of the uterine cavity.

curioso-a *a.* curious.

curita *f.* bandaid.

curso *m.* course; direction.

curva *f.* curve, bend.

curvatura *f.* curvature, deviation from a straight line.

Cushing, síndrome de *m.* Cushing's syndrome, adrenogenital syndrome manifested by obesity and muscular weakness gen. associated with an excessive production of cortisol.

cuspídeo-a *a.* cuspidal, pointed.

cúspide *f.* cuspid, point.

custodia *f.* custody; bajo ____ del estado / ward of the state.

cutáneo-a *a.* cutaneous, rel. to the skin;

absorción ___ / ___ absorption; glándulas ___-s o sebáceas / ___ glands; manifestaciones ___-s / skin manifestations; pruebas ___-s / skin tests; úlcera ___ / skin ulcer.

cutícula *f.* cuticle, outer layer of the skin.

cutis *m.* cutis, complexion, skin.

CH

ch *f.* fourth letter of the Spanish alphabet.

chalación *f.* chalazion, meibomian cyst, a cyst of the eyelid.

chancro *m.* chancre, the primary lesion of syphilis.

chancroide *m.* chancroid, a nonsyphilitic venereal ulcer.

chaparro-a *a. Mex.* short person.

chaqueta *f.* jacket.

charlatán *m.* charlatan, a quack, someone claiming knowledge and skills he or she does not have.

chasquido *m.* sharp brief sound related to the abrupt opening of the cardiac valve, gen. the mitral valve.

chata *f.* bedpan.

cheque *m.* check.

chequeo *m.* checkup, complete medical examination.

chequear *v.* to check, to verify.

Cheyne-Stokes, respiración de *f.* Cheyne-Stokes respiration, respiration manifested by alternating periods of apnea of increased rapidity and depth, gen. associated with disorders of the neurologic respiration center.

chico-a *m., f.* young boy; young girl; *a.* small.

chicano-a *a. pop.* name given in the U.S.A., to a Mexican-American.

chícharo *n.* green pea.

chichón *m.* bump in the head.

chiflado-a *a. pop.* crazy, nuts.

chile *m.* hot pepper.

chillar *v.* to screech, to scream.

chinche *f.* bedbug.

chiquito-a *a.* small.

chocolate *m.* chocolate.

chochera *f.* senility.

chocho-a *a.* senile.

choque *m.* 1. shock; an abnormal state, gen. following trauma, in which insufficient flow of blood through the body can cause reduced cardiac output, subnormal temperature, descending blood pressure and rapid pulse; ___ alérgico / allergic ___; ___ anafiláctico / anaphylactic ___; ___ eléctrico / electric ___; ___ séptico / septic ___; 2. collision.

chorizo *m.* sausage.

chorrear *v.* to drip; to spout.

chorro *n.* jet, spurt; stream.

chueco-a *a.* crooked, bent.

chupar *v.* to suck; to absorb; **chuparse el dedo** / thumb sucking.

chupete *n.* pacifier.

churre *m.* dirt, grime.

D

d *abr.* **densidad** / density; **difunto** / deceased; **dosis** / dosis.

dacriadenitis *f.* dacryadenitis, infl. of the lacrimal gland.

dacriagogo *m.* dacryagogue, an agent that stimulates tear formation.

dacricistalgia *f.* dacrycystalgia, pain in the lacrimal sac.

dacrioadenectomía *f. surg.* dacryoadenectomy, removal of a lacrimal gland.

dacriocistitis *f.* dacryocystitis, infl. of the lacrimal sac.

dacriocistotomía *f. surg.* dacryocystotomy, incision of the lacrimal sac.

dacriolitiasis *f.* dacryolithiasis, stones in the lacrimal apparatus.

dactilitis *f.* dactylitis, infl. of a finger or toe.

dáctilo *m.* dactyl, finger or toe.

dactilocopista *m., f.* fingerprint expert.

dactilografía *f.* dactylography, study of fingerprints.

dactilograma *f.* dactylogram, fingerprint.

dactilología *f.* dactylology, sign language.

dactilomegalia *f.* dactylomegaly, excessive growth of fingers and toes.

dactiloscopia *f.* dactyloscopy, study of fingerprints for the purpose of identification.

dado-a *a. pp.* of **dar,** given; ___ a / ___ to; ___ que / ___ that.

Dakin, solución de *f.* Dakin's solution, solution used for cleansing wounds.

daltonismo *m.* daltonism, defective perception of the colors red and green.

damiana *f.* damiana, native plant from Mexico the leaves of which are used as a diuretic.

danazol *m.* danazol, Deprancol, Danocrine, synthetic hormone that supresses the action of the anterior pituitary.

dañado-a *a.* hurt; [*comida*] spoiled; tinted.

dañar *v.* to harm; to hurt; to injure.

dañino-a *a.* harmful; noxious.

daño *m.* harm, damage, hurt; *v.* **hacer** ___ / to harm, to hurt.

dapsona *f.* dapsone, sulfone drug used in the treatment of leprosy.

dar *vi.* to give; to minister; ___ a luz / to give birth; ___ **de comer** / to feed; ___ **el pecho** / to breast-feed; ___ de alta / to discharge; ___ **lugar a** / to cause; **darse** *vr.* to give oneself; ___ **por vencido** / to give up; ___ **prisa** / to hurry.

dartos *m.* dartos, a layer of smooth muscle fibers found beneath the skin of the scrotum.

Darvon *m.* Darvon, trade name for dextro propoxyphene hydrochloride, an oral analgesic.

dátil *m.* date.

dato *m.* fact, piece of information.

de *prep.* of, from; [*posesión*], **los rayos-X** ___ **la paciente** / the patient's X rays; [*contenido*] **bicarbonato** ___ **sodio** / sodium bicarbonate; [*procedencia*] **vengo** ___ **la consulta** / I am coming from the doctor's office.

debajo *adv.* underneath; ___ **de** / under; **por** ___ / beneath.

deber *v.* to be obligated; to owe.

débil *a.* debilitated, weak, feeble.

debilidad *f.* debility, weakness.

debilitarse *vr.* to become weak.

decaer *vi.* to weaken; [*en ánimo*] to decline.

decafeinado-a *a.* decaffeinated.

decaído-a *a.* dispirited, dejected.

decaimiento *m.* dejection.

decalcificación *f.* decalcification, loss or reduction of lime salts from bones or teeth.

deceleración *f.* deceleration, diminished velocity, such as of heart frequency.

decidido-a *a.* decided; determined.

decidir *v.* to decide; **decidirse** *vr.* to make up one's mind.

decidua *f.* decidua, mucous membrane of the uterus that develops during pregnancy and is discharged after delivery.

deciduo-a *a.* deciduous, of a temporal nature.

decir *vi.* to say; to tell; **querer** ___ / to mean.

decisión *f.* decision, resolution.

declinación *f.* declination, rotation of the eye.

decorticación *f.* *surg.* decortication, removal of part of the cortical surface of an organ such as the brain.

decrépito-a *a.* decrepit, worn with age.

decúbito *m.* decubitus, lying down position; ___ dorsal / dorsal ___, on the back; ___ lateral / lateral ___, on the side; ___ ventral / ventral ___, on the stomach.

decusación *f.* decussation, crossing of structures in the form of an X; ___ de las pirámides / ___ of pyramids, crossing of nervous fibers from one pyramid to the other in the medulla oblongata; ___ óptica / optic ___, crossing of the fibers of the optic nerves.

dedalera *f.* foxglove, common name for *Digitalis purpurea*.

dedo *m.* finger; toe; caída de los ___-s del pie / toe drop; ___ del pie / toe; ___ en garra, en martillo / hammer, mallet finger or toe; ___ en palillo de tambor / clubbing; ___ gordo / hallux; ___ índice / index ___, forefinger; ___ meñique / little ___; ___ pulgar / thumb; desviación de un ___ / valgus; separación de un ___ / varus.

deducción *f.* deduction, to reason from the general to the particular.

deducir *vi.* to deduce, to infer.

defecación *f.* defecation, bowel movement.

defecar *vi.* to defecate.

defectivo-a *a.* defective.

defecto *m.* defect; blemish; ___ congénito / congenital ___.

defectuoso-a *a.* defective, faulty.

defender *vi.* to defend.

defensa *f.* defense, resistance to a disease; mecanismo de ___ / ___ mechanism; ___ propia / self-___.

deferente *a.* deferent, conveying away from.

defibrilación *f.* defibrilation, the act of changing an irregular heart beat to a normal rhythm.

deficiencia *f.* deficiency; ___ mental / mental ___, enfermedad por ___ / ___ disease.

deficiente *a.* deficient, wanting.

déficit *m.* deficit, deficiency.

definición *f.* definition.

deflexión *f*. deflection, diversion; *psych*. unconscious diversion of ideas.

deformación *f*. deformation, distortion.

deforme *a*. deformed.

deformidad *f*. deformity, irregularity, a congenital or acquired malformation.

defunción *f*. demise, death.

defurfuración *f*. defurfuration, shedding fine bran-like scales from the skin.

degenerado-a *a*. degenerate.

degenerar *v*. to degenerate.

degeneración *f*. degeneration, deterioration.

deglución *f*. deglutition, the act of swallowing.

deglutir *v*. to swallow.

degradación *f*. degradation, reducing a chemical compound to a simpler one.

dehiscencia *f*. dehiscence, splitting open of a wound.

dehidroandrosterona *f*. dehydroandrosterone, previously known as dehydroepiandrosterone, androgenic steroid found in the urine.

dehidrocolesterol *m*. dehydrocholesterol, skin substance that becomes vitamin B complex by the action of sun rays.

dehidrocorticosterona *f*. dehydrocorticosterone, steroid found in the adrenal cortex.

déjà vu *Fr*. déjà vu, an illusory impression of having seen or experienced a new situation before.

dejadez *f*. lassitude, neglect, carelessness.

dejar *v*. to leave; to let, to allow; ____ **dicho** / ____ word; ____ **órdenes** / ____ orders; ____ **de** / to stop from, to quit.

del *gr*. contraction of the *prep*. **de** and the *art*. **el**.

delante *adv*. in front; before.

deletéreo-a *a*. deleterious, harmful, noxious.

delgado-a *a*. thin, slender, slim.

delgaducho-a *a*. thin; delicate.

delicado-a *a*. delicate, tender.

delicioso-a *a*. delicious.

delicuescencia *f*. deliquescence, condition of a substance when it becomes liquified by absorption of water from the air.

deligación *f*. deligation, art of applying ligatures or binders.

delimitación *f*. delimitation, process of marking the limits or circumscribing.

delincuencia *f*. delinquency; ____ **juvenil** / juvenile ____.

delincuente *a*. delinquent.

delirante *a*. delirious, raving.

delirar *v*. to be delirious, to rave.

delirio *m*. delirium, temporary mental disturbance marked by hallucinations and distorted perceptions; ____ **agudo** / acute ____; ____ **crónico** / chronic ____; ____ **de persecución** / persecution complex; ____ **tremens** / ____ tremens, a form of alcoholic psychosis.

deltoideo-a *a*. deltoid. 1. rel. to the deltoid muscle that covers the shoulder; 2. shaped like a triangle.

delusión *f*. delusion, false beliefs.

demacrado-a *a*. gaunt, wasted.

demanda *f*. demand; **alimentación por** ____ / ____ feeding.

demandar *v*. to demand; to sue.

demás *adv*. besides; that which is beyond a certain measure; **lo** ____ / the rest.

demasiado-a *a*. excessive; *adv*. too much.

demencia *f*. dementia, dementia praecox, insanity. *V*. **esquizofrenia**; ____ **alcohólica** / alcoholic ____; ____ **orgánica** / organic ____; ____ **senil** / senile ____.

demente *a*. demented, one suffering from dementia.

Demerol *m*. Demerol, meperdine hydrochloride, trade name for an analgesic drug with properties similar to morphine.

demora *f*. delay.

demorar *v*. to delay; **demorarse** *vr*. to be delayed, to take too long.

demostración *f*. demonstration.

demostrar *vi*. to demonstrate: to prove.

demulcente *m*. demulcent, agent that soothes and softens the skin or mucosa.

dendrita *f*. dendrite, protoplasmic prolongation of the nerve cell that receives the nervous impulses.

dengue *m*. dengue fever, acute febrile and infectious disease caused by a virus and transmitted by the *Aedes* mosquito.

denominación *f*. denomination, name.

densidad *f*. density.

denso-a *a*. dense; thick.

dentado-a *a*. dentiform, toothed. 1. having projections like teeth on the edge; 2. shaped like a tooth.

dentadura *f*. teeth; ____ **postiza** / denture.

dental, dentario-a *a*. dental, rel. to the teeth; **cuidado** ____ / ____ care; **esmalte** ____ / ____ enamel; **hilo** ____ / ____ floss; [*mordisco*] **impresión** ____ / ____ impression; **mecánico** ____ / ____ technician;

placa dentaria / ____ plaque; sarro ____ / ____ tartar; servicios de salud ____ / ____ health services; técnico en profiláctica ____ / ____ hygienist.

dentición f. dentition, time when children's teeth are cut; ____ primaria / primary ____, first teeth; ____ secundaria o dientes permanentes / secondary ____, permanent teeth.

dentilabial a. dentilabial, rel. to the teeth and the lips.

dentina d. dentin, calcified tissue that constitutes the larger portion of the tooth.

dentinogénesis f. dentinogenesis, formation of dentin.

dentinoma m. dentinoma, tumor consisting mainly of dentin.

dentista m., f. dentist; ____ de niños / pedodontist.

dentoide a. dentoid, tooth-shaped.

dentro adv. within; **por** ____ / inside.

denudación f. denudation, deprival of a protecting surface by surgery, trauma or pathologic change.

dependencia f. dependence, subordination.

depender v. to depend; to rely.

depilación f. depilation, removal of hair by the roots.

depilar v. to depilate, to remove hair.

depilatorio m. depilatory, hair remover.

depleción f. depletion.

deporte m. sports; athletics.

deposición f. bowel movement; ____-es blandas o acuosas / loose bowels.

depositar v. to deposit.

depósito m. deposit; precipitate.

depravación f. depravation, perversion.

depravado-a a. depraved, corrupt; perverted.

depresión f. depression. 1. psych. state of sadness and melancholia accompanied by apathy; 2. cavity.

depresor m. depressor. 1. agent used to lower an established level of function or activity of the organism; ____ **de lengua** / tongue ____; 2. tranquilizer; **-a** a. producing or rel. to depression.

deprimente n. depressing.

deprimido-a a. depressed, downcast.

deprimir v. to depress; **deprimirse** vr. to become depressed.

depuración f. depuration, purification.

depurar v. to depurate, to purify.

derecha f. right hand side; **a la** ____ / to the right.

derecho-a a. straight, erect; adv. straight, straight ahead.

derecho m. right; the study of law; los ____-s del paciente / the patient's ____-s; **tener** ____ / to have the right.

derivación f. derivation, bypass; 1. shunt, alternate or lateral course that occurs through anastomosis or through a natural anatomical characteristic; ____ aortocoronaria / aortocoronary bypass; ____ aortoilíaca / aortoiliac ____ bypass; ____ portacava / portacaval shunt; 2. origin or source of a substance.

derivar v. to derive; to infer, to deduce.

dermabrasión f. surg. dermabrasion, procedure to remove acne scars, nevi or fine wrinkles of the skin.

dermal, dermático-a a. dermal, dermatic, rel. to the skin.

dermalgia, dermatalgia f. dermalgia, dermatalgia, pain in the skin.

dermatitis, dermitis f. dermatitis, dermitis, infl. of the skin; ____ actínica / actinic ____, produced by sunlight or ultraviolet light; ____ alérgica / allergic ____; ____ atópica / atopic ____; ____ por contacto / contact ____.

dermatofito m. dermatophyte, fungus that attacks the skin.

dermatofitosis f. dermatophytosis, Athlete's foot, fungal infection of the skin caused by a dermatophyte.

dermatología f. dermatology, the study of skin diseases.

dermatológico-a a. dermatological, rel. to the skin.

dermatólogo m. dermatologist, specialist in dermatology.

dermatomicosis f. dermatomycosis, infl. of the skin by fungi.

dermatomiositis f. dermatomyositis, disease of the connective tissue manifested by edema, dermatitis, and infl. of the muscles.

dermátomo, dermatótomo m. dermatome, dermatotome, instrument used for cutting skin in thin slices.

dermatosífilis f. dermatosyphilis, skin manifestation of syphilis.

dermatosis, dermatopatía f. dermatosis, dermatopathy, general term used for skin disease; ____ eritematosa de los pañales / diaper rash.

dérmico-a *a*. dermic, rel. to the skin.
dermis *f*. dermis, skin.
dermitis *f*. dermitis, infl. of the skin.
dermoflebitis *f*. dermophlebitis, infl. of superficial veins.
dermoideo-a *a*. dermoid, resembling skin; quiste ___ / ___ cyst, congenital, usu. benign.
derramar *v*. to spill.
derrame *m*. spill, overflow, outflow.
derretir *vi*. to melt; **derretirse** *vr*. to become liquified by heat.
desabrido-a *a*. tasteless; insipid.
desabrigado-a *a*. underclothed; too exposed to the elements.
desacostumbrado-a *a*. unaccustomed.
desacuerdo *m*. disagreement.
desadvertidamente *adv*. inadvertently; unintentional.
desafortunado-a *a*. unfortunate, unlucky.
desagradable *a*. disagreeable, unpleasant.
desagradecido-a *a*. ungrateful.
desahogarse *vr., vi*. to release one's grief; *pop*. to let out steam.
desalentar *v. vi*. to discourage; **desalentarse** *vr*. to become discouraged.
desangramiento *m*. excessive bleeding.
desangrarse *vr*. to bleed excessively.
desanimado-a *a*. downhearted, discouraged.
desaparecer *vi*. to disappear.
desaprobar *vi*. to disprove; to refute.
desarrollado-a *a*. developed; no ___ / underdeveloped.
desarrollar *v*. [*síntomas*] to develop; to grow.
desarrollo *m*. development; growth.
desarticulación *f*. disarticulation, separation or amputation of two or more bones from one joint.
desarticulado-a *a*. disarticulated, rel. to a bone that has been separated from its joint.
desaseo *m*. uncleanliness.
desasosiego *m*. uneasiness, unrest.
desastre *m*. disaster.
desatendido-a *a*. unattended.
desatinado-a *a*. lacking good judgement, wild.
desayunar *v*. to have breakfast.
desayuno *m*. breakfast.
desbridamiento *m. surg*. debridgement, removal of foreign bodies or dead or damaged tissue, esp. from a wound.
descalcificación *f*. decalcification, 1. loss of

calcium salts from a bone; 2. removal of calcareous matter.
descalzo-a *a*. barefooted.
descamación *f*. desquamation, the act of shedding scales from the epidermis.
descansado-a *a*. rested, refreshed.
descanso *m*. rest, tranquility.
descarado-a *a*. impudent, shameless.
descarga *f*. discharge, excretion.
descarnado-a *a*. without skin, fleshless; very thin person.
descartar *v*. to reject, to dismiss.
descendente *a*. descending.
descendiente *m*. descendant, offspring.
descentrado-a *a*. decentered, not centered.
descoloración *f*. discoloration.
descolorido-a *a*. discolored, washed out.
descompensación *f*. decompensation, inability of the heart to maintain adequate circulation.
descomponerse *vr., vi*. to decompose.
descomposición *f*. decomposition, decay; índice de ___ / ___ rate.
descompresión *f*. decompression, lack of air or gas pressure such as in deep-sea diving; cámara de ___ / ___ chamber; ___ quirúrgica / surgical ___; enfermedad por ___ / ___ sickness; *pop*. the bends.
desconectar *v*. to disconnect; to switch off.
desconfiar *v*. to distrust; not to have confidence.
descongelación *f*. thawing.
descongelar *v*. to defrost; to thaw.
descongestionante *m*. decongestant.
descongestionar *v*. to decongest.
descontaminación *f*. decontamination, the process of freeing the environment, objects, or persons from contaminated or harmful agents such as radioactive substances.
descontaminar *v*. to decontaminate, to free from contamination.
descontento-a *a*. unhappy.
descontinuado-a *a*. discontinued, suspended.
descontinuar *v*. to discontinue.
descoyuntamiento *m*. luxation, dislocation.
descremar *v*. [*leche*] to skim.
describir *v*. to describe.
descripción *f*. description.
descrito-a *a. pp*. of **describir,** described.
descubierto-a *a. pp*. of **descubrir,** uncovered.
descubrir *vi*. to discover; to uncover.
descuento *m*. discount.
descuidado-a *a*. careless, negligent.

descuido *m.* carelessness.

desde *prep.* since, from; —— **ahora en adelante** / from now on; —— **hace (una semana, un mes)** / it has been (a week, a month); —— **luego** / of course.

desdentado-a *a.* edentulous, toothless.

desdoblamiento *m.* splitting.

desear *v.* to wish, to desire.

desecado-a *a.* desiccated, dried up.

desecante *m.* desiccant, that produces dryness.

desecar *vi.* to desiccate, to dry up.

desechable *a.* disposable.

desechar *v.* to discard, to cast aside.

desempeñar *v.* to perform a given task or role.

desencadenar *v.* to trigger, to initiate a succession of events.

desencajado-a *a.* disengaged; disjointed; gaunt.

desencajar *v.* to disengage.

desenlace *m.* outcome, conclusion.

desensibilizar *v.* to desensitize, to reduce or remove sensitivity, physically or emotionally.

deseo *m.* wish, desire.

deseoso-a *a.* desirous, eager.

desequilibrio *m.* imbalance.

desesperación *f.* desperation, despair, despondency; hopelessness.

desesperado-a *a.* desperate, despaired, despondent.

desesperarse *vr.* to despair, to despond.

desfallecer *vi.* to faint; to become weak.

desfervescencia *f.* defervescence, period of fever decline.

desfibrilación *f.* defibrillation, action of returning an irregular heart beat to its normal rhythm.

desfibrilador *m.* defibrillator, electrical device used to restore the heart to a normal rhythm.

desfiguración, desfiguramiento *f., m.* defacement; disfigurement.

desfigurar *v.* to disfigure, to distort.

desganarse *vr.* to lose appetite.

desgarradura, desgarro *f., m.* tear, laceration.

desgarrar *v.* to tear, to pull apart; to rip.

desgastado-a *a.* worn; eroded; [*persona*] wasted.

desgastar *v.* to erode; **desgastarse** *vr.* to wear down or away.

desgaste *m.* wearing down.

desgracia *f.* adversity, mishap.

desgraciadamente *adv.* unfortunately.

desgrasar *v.* to degrease, to remove the fat.

deshacer *vi.* to undo.

deshecho *m.* waste.

deshidratado-a *a.* dehydrated, free of water.

deshidratar *v.* to dehydrate, eliminate water from a substance.

deshidratarse *vr.* dehydrate, dehidrate, to lose liquid from the body or tissues.

deshumanización *f.* dehumanization, loss of human qualities.

deshumectante *m.* dehumidifier, device to diminish humidity.

desierto *m.* desert.

desigual *a.* uneven; unlike, unequal.

desilusión *f.* disillusion, disenchantment.

desilusionar *v.* to disillusion; **desilusionarse** *vr.* to become disenchanted.

desinfectante *m.* disinfectant, agent that kills bacteria.

desinfectar *v.* to disinfect.

desinflamar *v.* to reduce or remove an inflammation.

desintegración *f.* disintegration; decomposition.

desintoxicar *v.* to detoxicate, to eliminate toxic matter.

deslizarse *vr., vi.* to glide.

deslumbramiento *m.* glare. 1. blurring of the vision with possible permanent damage to the retina; 2. intense light.

desmayarse *vr.* to faint, to pass out; to swoon.

desmayo *m.* fainting.

desmembración, desmembradura *f.* dismemberment.

desmembrar *v.* to dismember, to amputate.

desmielinación, desmielinización *f.* demyelination, demyelinization, loss or destruction of the myelin layer of the nerve.

desmineralización *f.* demineralization, loss of minerals from the body, esp. the bones.

desmoma *f.* desmoma, tumor of the connective tissue.

desmosis *f.* desmosis, disease of the connective tissue.

desnaturalización *f.* denaturation, change of the usual nature of a substance as by adding methanol or acetone to alcohol.

desnervado-a *a.* denervated, deprived of nerve supply.

desnivel *m.* unevenness.

desnudarse *vr.* to undress.

desnudo-a *a.* naked, bare.

desnutrición *f.* malnutrition, undernutrition; ____ proteinocalórica / protein caloric ____.

desnutrido-a *a.* undernourished, malnourished, underfed.

desobedecer *vi.* to disobey.

desobediencia *f.* disobedience.

desobediente *a.* disobedient.

desodorante *m.* deodorant.

desodorizar *vi.* to deodorize, to remove fetid or unpleasant odors.

desorden *m.* disorder, abnormal condition of the body or mind.

desordenado-a *a.* disorderly, unorganized.

desorganización *f.* disorganization.

desorganizado-a *a.* unorganized, not structured.

desorientado-a *a.* disoriented, confused.

desosificación *f.* deossification, loss or removal of minerals from the bones.

desoxicorticosterona *f.* deoxycorticosterone, desoxycorticosterone, steroid hormone produced in the cortex of the adrenal glands that has a marked effect on the metabolism of water and electrolytes.

desoxigenación *f.* deoxidation, process of removing oxygen.

despacio *adv.* slow, slowly.

despejado-a *a.* clear, cloudless; [*persona*] smart, vivacious.

despellejarse *vr.* to peel; to shed skin.

desperdiciar *v.* to waste, to squander.

desperdicio *m.* waste.

despersonalización *f. psych.* depersonalization, loss of identity.

despertarse *vr., vi.* to wake up.

despierto-a *a. pp.* of **despertar,** awake; diligent.

despigmentación *f.* depigmentation, abnormal change in the color of skin and hair.

despiojamiento *m.* delousing, freeing the body from lice.

desplazamiento *m.* 1. displacement; 2. *psych.* transfer of emotion from the original idea or situation to a different one.

desplazar *vi.* to displace.

despliegue *m.* display, exhibition.

desprender *v.* to loosen, to unfasten; **desprenderse** *vr.* to become loose.

desprendimiento *m.* detachment, separation.

despreocupado-a *a.* unconcerned, carefree.

despreocuparse *vr.* to be unconcerned.

desproporción *f.* disproportion.

desproporcionado-a *a.* disproportionate.

después *adv.* after, afterward.

despuntado-a *a.* [*instrumento*] blunt.

destapar *v.* to uncover.

desteñir *vi.* to fade; **desteñirse** *vr.* to become faded.

destetado-a *m., f.* weanling.

destetar *v.* to wean, to adjust an infant to a form of nourishment away from breast or bottle feeding.

destete *m.* delactation, discontinued breast feeding; weaning.

destilado-a *a.* distilled; agua ____ / ____ water.

destilar *v.* to distil, to create vapor by heat.

destino *m.* fate.

destorsión *f.* detorsion, detortion. 1. surgical correction of a testicular or intestinal torsion; 2. correction of the curvature or malformation of a structure.

destoxicación, destoxificación *f.* detoxification, reduction of the toxic quality.

destreza *f.* skill.

destruido-a *a.* destroyed; exhausted, physically or emotionally.

destruir *vi.* to destroy.

destupir *v.* to unclog.

desunión *f.* disengagement. 1. emergence of the fetal head from the vulva; 2. separation.

desvalido-a *a.* destitute, helpless, handicapped.

desvanecerse *vr., vi.* to black out; to swoon.

desvelado-a *a.* unable to sleep, wakeful.

desvelarse *vr.* to stay awake at night.

desvelo *m.* insomnia.

desventaja *f.* disadvantage; diminished capacity.

desvestir *vi.* to strip; **desvestirse** *vr.* to undress.

desviación, desvío *f., m.* deviation, shunt. 1. departure from the established path; 2. *psych.* mental aberration.

desviar *v.* to shunt, to change course; **desviarse** *vr.* to deviate.

detalle *m.* detail.

detectado-a *a.* detected; no ____ / undetected.

detectar *v.* to detect.

detector *m.* detector.

detener *vi.* to detain, to stop.

detergente *m.* detergent, cleaning agent.

deterioración, deterioro *f., m.* deterioration, wear, decay.

deteriorarse *vr.* to deteriorate.

deteriorización *f.* deteriorization. *V.* **deterioración.**

determinación *f.* determination; decision; resolution; _____ propia / self _____.

determinado-a *a.* determined, strong-minded; [*una prueba*] proven.

determinante *m.* determinant, prevailing element; *a.* rel. to a prevailing element or cause.

determinar *v.* to determine.

determinismo *m.* determinism, theory by which all physical or psychic phenomena is predetermined and therefore uninfluenced by the will of the individual.

detestar *v.* to hate, to abhor.

detrás (de) *adv.* behind, in back of.

detrito *m.* detritus, residue of disintegrating matter.

detrusor *m.* detrusor, muscle that expels or projects outward.

deuteranopía *f.* deuteranopia, blindness to the color green.

devitalizar *v.* to devitalize, to debilitate; to deprive from vital force.

devolución *f.* devolution. *V.* **catabolismo.**

devolver *vi.* to return, to give back.

Dexedrina *f.* Dexedrine, amphetamine type drug that stimulates the nervous system.

dextrocardia *f.* dextrocardia, dislocation of the heart to the right.

dextrómano-a *m.* dextromanual, person who gives preference to the use of the right hand.

dextroposición *f.* dextroposition, displacement to the right.

dextrosa *f.* dextrose, form of glucose in the blood popularly called grape sugar.

dextroversión *f.* dextroversion, turn to the right.

deyección *f.* 1. *psych.* dejection, state of depression; 2. the act of defecating.

día *m.* day; **de** _____ / daytime, daylight; **(dos, tres) veces al** _____ / (two, three) times a _____; **todo el** _____ / all day.

diabetes *f.* diabetes, a disease manifested by excessive urination. This term is often used in reference to diabetes mellitus.

diabetes insípida *f.* diabetes insipidus, type of diabetes caused by a deficiency in antidiuretic hormone.

diabetes mellitus *f.* diabetes mellitus, diabetes caused by insufficient production or use of insulin and resulting in hyperglyce-

mia and glycosuria; _____ con dependencia de insulina / insulin dependent _____; _____ sin dependencia de insulina / noninsulin dependent _____.

diabético-a *a.* diabetic, rel. to or suffering from diabetes; angiopatías _____-s / _____ angiopathies; coma _____ / _____ coma; _____ inestable / brittle _____; dieta _____ / _____ diet; neuropatía _____ / _____ neuropathy; retinopatía _____ / _____ retinopathy.

diabetogénico-a *a.* diabetogenic, that produces diabetes.

diabetógrafo *m.* diabetograph, instrument used to determine the proportion of glucose in the urine.

diacetemia *f.* diacetemia, presence of diacetic acid in the blood.

diacetilmorfina *f.* diacetylmorphine, heroin.

diadococinesis *f.* diadochokinesia, ability to make opposing movements in rapid succession.

diáfisis *f.* diaphysis, shaft or middle part of a long, cylindrical bone, such as the humerus.

diaforesis *f.* diaphoresis, profuse perspiration.

diaforético *m.* diaphoretic, agent that stimulates perspiration; **-a** *a.* sweating profusely.

diafragma *m.* diaphragm. 1. muscle that separates the thorax and the abdomen; 2. contraceptive device.

diagnosticar *vi.* to diagnose.

diagnóstico, diagnosis *m., f.* diagnosis, determination of the patient's ailment; _____ computado / computer _____; _____ de imágenes por medios radioactivos / _____ imaging; _____ diferencial / differential _____; _____ equivocado o erróneo / misdiagnosis; _____ físico / physical _____; _____ propio / autodiagnosis; errores de _____ / diagnostic errors.

diagonal *a.* diagonal.

diálisis *f.* dialysis, procedure used to filter and eliminate waste products from the blood of patients with renal insufficiency; aparato de _____ [*riñón artificial*] / _____ machine; _____ peritoneal / peritoneal _____.

dializado *m.* dialysate, the part of the liquid that goes through the dialyzing membrane in dialysis; **-a** *a.* dialyzed. having been separated by dialysis.

dializador *m.* dialyzer, device used in dialysis.

dializar *vi.* to dialyze.

diámetro *m.* diameter.

diapasón *m.* diapason, U-shaped metal device used to determine the degree of deafness.

diapédesis *f.* diapedesis, passage of blood cells, esp. leukocytes, through the intact walls of a capillary vessel.

diaplasis *f.* diaplasis, reduction of a dislocation or fracture.

diapositiva *f.* slide.

diario-a *a.* daily; -mente *adv.* daily.

diarrea *f.* diarrhea; ___ del recién nacido / ___ of the new born; ___ del viajero / traveler's ___; ___ infantil / infant ___; ___ nerviosa / nervous ___; ___ pancreática / pancreatic ___.

diartrosis *f.* diarthrosis, articulation that allows ample movement, such as the hip articulation.

diastasa *f.* diastase, enzyme that acts in the digestion of starches and sugars.

diastasis *f.* diastasis. 1. separation of normally attached bones; 2. the rest period of the cardiac cycle, just before systole.

diástole *f.* diastole, dilation period of the heart during which the cardiac chambers arc filled with blood.

diastólico-a *a.* diastolic, rel. to the diastole; presión ___ / ___ pressure, the lowest pressure point in the cardiovascular system.

diatermia *f.* diathermy, application of heat to body tissues through an electric current.

diátesis *f.* diathesis, organic disposition to contract certain diseases; ___ hemorrágica / hemorrhagic ___; ___ reumática / rheumatic ___.

diatrizoato de meglumina *m.* diatrizoate meglumine, radiopaque substance used to visualize arteries and veins of the heart and the brain as well as the gallbladder, kidneys, and urinary bladder.

diazepam *m.* diazepam, Valium, drug used as a tranquilizer and muscle relaxer.

diccionario *m.* dictionary.

dicigótico-a *a.* dizygotic, rel. to twins derived from two separate fertilized ova.

dicloxacilina *f.* dicloxacillim sodium, semi-synthetic penicillin used against gram-positive organisms.

dicoriónico-a *a.* dichorionic, having two chorions.

dicotomía *f.* dichotomy, dichotomization, process of dividing into two parts.

dicroísmo *m.* dichroism, property of some solutions or crystals to present more than one color in reflected or transmitted light.

dicromatismo *m.* dichromatism, the property of presenting two different colors.

dicrómico-a *a.* dichromic, rel. to two colors.

dicromófilo-a *a.* dichromophil, that can be stainable by both acid and basic dyes.

dicroto-a *a.* dicrotic, having two beats of the pulse for each beat of the heart.

dictioma *m.* dictyoma, diktyoma, tumor of the ciliary epithelium.

Dicumarol *m.* Dicumarol, Dicoumarin, anticoagulant drug used in the treatment of embolism and thrombosis.

dicho *a. pp.* of **decir,** said.

didáctico-a *a.* didactic, rel. to teaching through textbooks and lectures as opposed to a clinical or physical approach.

didelfo-a *a.* didelphic, rel. to a double uterus.

didimitis *f.* V. **orquitis.**

diembrionismo *m.* diembryony, production of two embryos from a single egg.

diencéfalo *m.* diencephalon, part of the brain.

dienestrol *m.* dienestrol, synthetic nonsteroid estrogen.

diente *m.* tooth (*pl.* teeth); ___-s deciduos, de leche / deciduous teeth, baby teeth; ___ desviado / wandering ___; ___ impactado / impacted ___; ___ incisivo / incisor; ___ molar / wall ___; ___ no erupcionado / unerupted ___; ___-s permanentes / permanent teeth; ___-s postizos / denture; ___-s secundarios / second teeth.

diestro-a *a.* dexter, rel. to the right side; right-handed.

dieta *f.* diet; ___ alta en residuos (fibras, celulosas) / high residue ___; ___ balanceada / balanced ___; ___ blanda / bland ___; ___ diabética / diabetic ___; ___ hospitalaria / ward ___; ___ libre de gluten / gluten-free ___; ___ líquida / liquid ___; ___ para bajar de peso / weight reduction ___; ___ rica en calorías / high calorie ___; ___ sin sal / salt-free ___.

dietética *f.* dietetics, the science of regulating diets to preserve or recuperate health.

dietético-a *a.* dietetic, rel. to diets.

dietilamida de acido lisérgico *f.* lisergic acid diethylamide, LSD.

dietilestilbestrol *m*. diethylstilbestrol, synthetic estrogen compound.

dietista *m., f.* dietitian, nutrition specialist.

diezma *f*. decimation, high mortality rate.

difalo *a*. diphallus, partial or complete duplication of the penis.

difásico-a *a*. diphasic, that occurs in two different stages.

difenhidramina *f*. diphenhydramine, Benadryl, antihistamine.

diferencia *f*. difference.

diferenciación *f*. differentiation, distinction of one substance, disease or entity from another.

diferencial *a*. differential, rel. to differentiation.

diferente *a*. different.

diferido-a *a*. deferred, postponed.

diferir *vi,* to disagree.

difícil *a*. difficult.

dificultad *f*. difficulty.

difonía *f*. diphonia, double voice.

difracción *f*. diffraction, the breaking up of a ray of light into its component parts when it passes through a glass or a prism; patrón de _____ / _____ pattern.

difteria *f*. diphtheria, acute infectious and contagious disease caused by the bacillus *Corynebacterium diphtheriae* (Klebs-Loffler bacillus) characterized by the formation of false membranes esp. in the throat; antitoxina contra la _____ / _____ antitoxin.

difterotoxina *f*. diphtherotoxin, toxin derived from cultures of diphtheria bacillus.

difundir *v*. to diffuse.

difunto-a *a*. deceased.

difusión *f*. diffusion. 1. the process of becoming widely spread; 2. dyalisis through a membrane.

digerible, digestible *a*. digestible.

digerido-a *a*. digested; no _____ / undigested.

digerir *vi*. to digest.

digestión *f*. digestion, transformation of liquids and solids into simpler substances that can be absorbed easily by the body; _____ gástrica / gastric _____; _____ intestinal / intestinal _____; _____ pancreática / pancreatic _____.

digestivo *m*. digestant, digestive, an agent that assists in the digestive process.

digitación *f*. digitation, finger-shaped protrusion as in a muscle.

digitalis *f*. digitalis, cardiotonic agent obtained from the dried leaves of *Digitalis purpurea*.

digitalización *f*. digitalization, therapeutic use of digitalis.

digitiforme *a*. finger-shaped.

dígito *m*. digit, finger or toe.

digitoxina *f*. digitoxin, cardiotonic glycoside obtained from *Digitalis purpurea* used in the treatment of congestive heart failure.

digoxina *f*. digoxin, cardiotonic glycoside obtained from *Digitalis purpurea* used in the treatment of cardiac arrhythmia.

dihidroestreptomicina *f*. dihydrostreptomycin, antibiotic derived from and used more commonly than streptomycin as it causes less neurotoxicity.

Dilantina *f*. Dilantin, antispasmodic drug.

dilatación *f*. dilation, stretching; normal or abnormal enlargement of an organ or orifice; _____ de la pupila / _____ of the pupil.

dilatador *m*. dilator, stretcher. 1. muscle that on contraction dilates an organ; 2. device used to enlarge cavities or an opening; _____ de Hegar / Hegar's _____, used to enlarge the cervical canal.

dilatar *v*. to dilate, to expand.

dilaudid *m*. dilaudid, opium derived drug that can produce dependance.

diluente *m*. diluent, agent that has the property of diluting.

diluir *vi*. to dilute; _____ con agua / to water down; sin _____ / undiluted.

dimercaprol *m*. dimercaprol, antidote used in cases of poisoning from heavy metals such as gold and mercury.

dimetilsulfóxido *m*. dimethyl sulfoxide, analgesic and antiinflammatory agent.

dimetría *f*. dimetria, double uterus.

diminuir, disminuir *vi*. to diminish.

diminuto-a *a*. minute, very small.

dimorfismo *m*. dimorphism, occurring in two different forms; _____ sexual, hermafrodismo / sexual _____, hermaphrodism.

dina *f*. dyne, unit of force needed to accelerate one gram of mass one centimeter per second.

dinámica *f*. dynamics, the study of organs or parts of the body in movement.

dinámico-a *a*. dynamic.

dinamómetro *m*. dynamometer. 1. instrument to measure muscular strength; 2. device that determines the magnifying power of a lens.

dinero *m*. money.

dioptómetro *m*. dioptometer, instrument used to measure ocular refraction.

dioptría *f*. diopter, dioptre, unit of the refracting power of a lens.

dióptrica *f*. dioptrics, the science that studies the refraction of light.

dióptrico-a *a*. dioptric, rel. to the refraction of light.

Dios *m*. God.

dióxido de carbono *m*. carbon dioxide.

diplacusia *f*. diplacusis, hearing disorder characterized by the perception of two tones for every sound produced.

diplejía *f*. diplegia, bilateral paralysis; ___ facial / facial ___; ___ espástica / spastic ___.

diplocoria *f*. diplocoria, double pupil.

diploe *m*. diploe, spongy layer that lies between the two flat compact plates of the cranial bones.

diploide *a*. diploid, having two sets of chromosomes.

diplopagos *m*. diplopagus, conjoined twins, each with fairly complete bodies but sharing some organs.

diplopía *f*. diplopia, double vision.

dipsógeno *m*. dipsogen, thirst causing agent.

dipsomanía *f*. dipsomania, recurring uncontrollable urge to drink alcohol.

dipsosis *f*. dipsosis, abnormal thirst.

dirección *f*. direction; address.

directo-a *a*. direct, in a straight line; uninterrupted; **-mente** *adv*. directly.

directrices *f*. guidelines.

dirigir *vi*. to direct; to guide.

disacusia, disacusis *f*. dysacusia, dysacusis, difficulty in hearing.

disafea *f*. dysaphia, impaired sense of touch.

disartria *f*. dysarthria, unclear speech due to an impairment of the tongue or of any other muscle related to speech.

disautonomía *f*. dysautonomy, hereditary disorder of the autonomic nervous system.

disbarismo *m*. dysbarism, condition caused by decompression.

disbasia *f*. dysbasia, difficulty in walking gen. caused by nervous lesions.

disbulia *f*. dysbulia, inability to concentrate.

discalculia *f*. dyscalculia, inability to solve mathematical problems due to brain disease or damage.

discefalia *f*. dyscephalia, malformation of the head and the facial bones.

discinesia, disquinesia *f*. dyscinesia, dys-

kinesia, inability to perform voluntary movements.

disciplina *f*. discipline, strict behavior.

disco *m*. disk; ___ desplazado / slipped ___.

discógeno-a *a*. discogenic, rel. to an intervertebral disk.

discoide *a*. discoid, shaped like a disk.

discordancia *f*. discordance, the absence of a genetic trait in one of a pair of twins.

discoria *f*. dyscoria, abnormal shape of the pupil.

discrasia *f*. dyscrasia, synonym of disease.

discrepancia *f*. discrepancy.

discreto-a *a*. discrete, moderate, subtle; noncontinuous.

discriminación *f*. discrimination, differentiation of race or quality.

discriminar *v*. to discriminate.

discrinismo, disendocrinismo *m*. dyscrinism, abnormal function in the production of secretions, esp. the endocrine glands.

discusión *f*. discussion, argument, debate.

discutir *v*. to discuss; to argue.

disdiadocoquinesia *f*. dysdiadochokinesia, inability to reverse immediately a motor impulse.

disecar *vi. surg.* to dissect, to separate and cut parts and tissues of a body.

disección *f*. dissection, the act of dissecting

diseminación *f*. dissemination, spreading.

diseminado-a *a*. disseminated, spread out over a large area.

disentería *f*. dysentery, painful infl. of the intestines, esp. of the colon, gen. caused by bacteria or parasites and accompanied by diarrhea; ___ amebiana / amebic ___; ___ bacilar / bacillary ___.

disentir *vi*. to disagree, to have an opposite view.

disergia *f*. dysergia, lack of coordination in muscular voluntary movement.

disestesia *f*. dysesthesia, impaired sense of touch.

disfagia *f*. dysphagia, difficulty in swallowing.

disfasia *f*. dysphasia, impairment of the speech caused by a brain lesion.

disfonía *f*. dysphonia, hoarseness.

disforia *f*. dysphoria, severe depression.

disfrutar *v*. to enjoy.

disfunción *f*. dysfunction, malfunction, defective function.

disgenesia *f*. dysgenesis, malformation.

disgerminoma *m*. dysgerminoma, malignant tumor in the ovary.

disgnosia *f*. dysgnosia, impairment of the intellectual function.

dishidrosis *f*. dyshidrosis, anomaly of the sweating function.

dislalia *f*. dyslalia, speech impairment due to functional anomalies of the speech organ.

dislexia *f*. dyslexia, reading disorder, sometimes hereditary or caused by a brain lesion.

dislocación, dislocadura *f*. dislocation, displacement; ____ cerrada / closed ____, simple; ____ complicada / complicated ____; ____ congénita / congenital ____.

dismenorrea, dismenia *f*. dysmenorrhea, painful and difficult menstruation.

dismetría *f*. dysmetria, impaired ability to control range of movement in a coordinated fashion.

dismetropsia *f*. dysmetropsia, disorder that impairs the visual appreciation of size and shape of objects.

disminución *f*. diminution, reducing process.

disminuir *vi*. to diminish, to reduce, to lessen.

dismiotonía *f*. dysmyotonia, abnormal muscular tonicity.

dismnesia *f*. dysmnesia, impaired memory.

dismorfismo *m*. dysmorphism, capacity of a parasite or agent to change its shape.

disnea, dispnea *f*. dispnoea, dyspnea, shortness of breath.

disneico-a *a*. dyspneic, rel. to or suffering from dyspnea.

disoluble *a*. dissoluble.

disolución *f*. dissolution, decomposition; death.

disolvente *m*. dissolvent; *a*. that is capable of being dissolved.

disolver *vi*. to dissolve, to liquify.

disonancia *f*. dissonance, combination of tones that produces an unpleasant sound.

disosmia *f*. dysosmia, impaired smell.

disostosis *f*. dysostosis, abnormal bone growth.

dispareunia *f*. dispareunia, painful coitus.

disparidad *f*. disparity, inequality.

dispensar *v*. to dispense, to distribute.

dispensario *m*. dispensary, a place that provides medical assistance and dispenses medicines and drugs.

dispepsia *f*. dyspepsia, indigestion characterized by irregularities in the digestive process such as eructation, nausea, acidity, flatulence, and loss of appetite.

dispermia *f*. dyspermia, pain on ejaculation.

dispersar *v*. to disperse, to scatter.

dispigmentación *f*. dyspigmentation, abnormal change in the color of the skin and hair.

displasia *f*. dysplasia, abnormal development of the tissues.

disponer *vi*. to arrange, to prepare.

disponible *a*. available.

disposición *f*. disposition, tendency to acquire certain disease.

dispositivo *m*. device, mechanism; ____ intrauterino / intrauterine ____.

dispraxia *f*. dyspraxia, pain or difficulty in performing coordinated movements.

disquiria *f*. dyschiria, inability of a person to distinguish if he or she is being touched on the right or the left side of the body.

disrritmia *f*. dysrhythmia, abnormal rhythm.

distal *a*. distal, farthermost away from the beginning or center of a structure.

distancia *f*. distance.

distasia *f*. dystasia, difficulty in maintaining a standing position.

distensión *f*. distension, distention, dilation; ____ gaseosa / gas ____, resulting from accumulation of gas in the abdominal cavity.

distinguido-a *a*. [*persona o característica*] distinguished.

distinguir *vi*. to distinguish, to differentiate.

distinto-a *a*. different.

distobucal *a*. distobuccal, rel. to the distal and buccal surfaces of a tooth.

distocia *f*. dystocia, difficult labor.

distoclusión *f*. distoclusion, defective closure, irregular bite.

distonía *f*. dystonia, defective tonicity, esp. muscular.

distorsión *f*. distorsion, bending or twisting out ot shape.

distracción *f*. distraction. 1. separation of the surfaces of a joint without dislocation; 2. *psych*. inability to concentrate or fix the mind on a given experience.

distraído-a *a*. absentminded.

distribución *f*. distribution.

distribuir *vi*. to distribute.

distrofia *f*. dystrophy, degenerative disorder caused by defective nutrition or metabolism.

distrofia muscular *f*. muscular dystrophy, slow progressive muscular degeneration.

disturbio *m.* disturbance, confusion.

disuelto-a *a. pp.* of **disolver,** dissolved.

disulfiram *m.* disulfiram, Antabuse, drug used in the treatment of alcoholism.

disuria *f.* dysuria, difficult urination.

disyunción *f.* disjunction, chromosome separation at the anaphase state of cell division.

diuresis *f.* diuresis, increased excretion of urine.

diurético *m.* diuretic, agent that causes increased urination; *pop.* water pill.

divergencia *f.* divergence, spreading apart, separation from a common center.

divergente *a.* divergent, moving in different directions.

diverticulectomía *f. surg.* diverticulectomy, removal of a diverticulum.

diverticulitis *f.* diverticulitis, infl. of a diverticulum.

divertículo *m.* diverticulum (*pl.* diverticula), pouch or sac that originates from a hollow organ or structure.

diverticulosis *f.* diverticulosis, presence of diverticula in the colon.

divertirse *vr., vi.* to have fun.

dividido-a *a.* divided.

dividir *v.* to divide, to disunite; to split.

división *f.* division, separation; split.

divorciado-a *a.* divorced.

divulsión *f.* divulsion, separation or detachment.

doblarse *vr.* to bend; ____ hacia adelante / forward; **hacia atrás** / ____ backward.

doble *m.* double; *a.* double; ____ útero / ____ uterus.

docena *f.* dozen.

doctor-a *m., f.* doctor.

doler *vi.* to be in pain; to ache.

dolicocefálico-a *a.* dolichocephalic, having a narrow, long head.

dolor *m.* pain; ____ errático / wandering ____ ; ____ localizado / localized ____ ; ____ referido / referred ____ , perceived in a different area from where it originates; sin ____ / painless; ____ subjetivo / subjective ____ , of no apparent physical cause.

doloroso-a *a.* painful.

doméstico-a *a.* domestic.

domiciliario-a *a.* domiciliary, taking place in the home.

dominancia *f.* dominance, predominance; ____ cerebral / cerebral ____ ; ____ ocular / ocular ____ .

dominante *a.* dominant, predominant; características ____ -s / ____ characteristics.

donación *f.* donation.

donante *m.* donor; tarjeta de ____ / ____ 's card.

donante universal *m.* universal donor, individual belonging to blood group O or whose blood can be given to persons belonging to any other of the AB blood groups with minimal risk of complication.

donde *adv.* where.

dondequiera *adv.* anywhere; everywhere.

Donovanía granulomatosis *f.* Donovania granulomatosis, Donovan's body, bacterial infection that affects the skin and the mucous membranes of the genitalia and the anal area.

dopamina *f.* dopamine, substance synthesized by the adrenal glands, that increases blood pressure and is gen. used in shock treatment.

dormido-a *a.* asleep; profundamente ____ / sound ____ .

dormir *vi.* to sleep; **dormirse** *vr.* to fall asleep.

dorsal *a.* dorsal, rel. to the back; fisura o corte ____ / ____ slit.

dorsalgia *f.* dorsalgia, backache.

dorsiflexión *f.* dorsiflexion, bending backward.

dorso *m.* dorsum, posterior part, such as the back of the hand or the body.

dorsocefálico-a *a.* dorsocephalic, rel. to the back of the head.

dorsodinia *f.* dorsodynia, pain in the muscles of the upper part of the back.

dorsoespinal *a.* dorsospinal, rel. to the back and the spine.

dorsolateral *a.* dorsolateral, rel. to the back and the side.

dorsolumbar *a.* dorsolumbar, rel. to the lower thoracic and upper lumbar vertebrae area of the back.

dosimetría *f.* dosimetry, precise and systematic determination of doses.

dosímetro *m.* dosimeter, instrument used to detect and measure exposure to radiation; ____ de película / film badge, a badge carrying a film sensitive to X-rays and used to measure the cumulative exposure to the rays.

dosis, dosificación *f.* dose, dosage; ____ de bolo, intravenosa / bolus ____ , intravenous; ____ de refuerzo / booster ____ ; ____ diaria / daily ____ ; ____ dividida / divided

___; ___ individual / unit ___; ___ subletal / sublethal ___, of insufficient amount to cause death; ___ terapéutica / therapeutic ___; ___ umbral / threshold ___, minimal dose needed to produce an effect.

Douglas, placa (saco) de *m.* Douglas, cul de sac, peritoneal pouch between the uterus and the rectum.

Down, síndrome de *m.* Down's syndrome, chromosomal abnormality that causes physical deformity and moderate to severe mental retardation.

dramamina *f.* dramamine, antihistaminic used in the prevention and treatment of motion sickness.

dramatismo *m. psych.* dramatism, pompous behavior and language, gen. seen in mental disorders.

drapetomanía, dromomanía *f.* drapetomania, dromomania, abnormal impulse to wander.

drástico *m.* drastic, strong cathartic; **-a** *a.* extreme, very strong.

drenaje *m.* drainage, outlet; ___ abierto / open ___; ___ postural / postural ___, that allows drainage by gravity; tubo de ___ / ___ tube.

drenar *v.* to drain, to draw off fluid or pus from a cavity or an infected wound.

drepanocito *m.* drepanocyte, sickle cell.

droga *f.* drug; medication; abuso de la ___ / ___ abuse; anomalías causadas por la ___ / ___ anomalies; ___ adictiva / dependence producing ___; ___ neuroléptica / neuroleptic ___, causing symptoms similar to those manifested by nervous diseases; entregarse a la ___ / to become ___ addicted; resistencia microbiana a la ___ / ___ resistance, microbial.

drogadicción *f.* drug addiction.

drogadicto *m.* drug addict.

ductus *m.* ductus, duct.

ducha *f.* douche, jet of water applied to the body for medicinal or cleansing effects; shower; *vr.* **darse una** ___ / to shower.

duda *f.* doubt.

dudar *v.* to doubt, to question.

dudoso-a *a.* doubtful.

duela *f.* fluke, parasitic worm of the *Trematoda* family; ___ hepática / liver ___; ___ intestinal / intestinal ___; ___ pulmonar / lung; ___ sanguínea / blood ___.

dulce *a.* sweet.

dulces *m. pl.* [*glosinas*] sweets.

dulcificante *m.* sweetener.

duodenal *a.* duodenal, rel. to the duodenum.

duodenectomía *f. surg.* duodenectomy, partial or total excision of the duodenum.

duodenitis *f.* duodenitis, infl. of the duodenum.

duodeno *m.* duodenum, essential part of the alimentary tract situated between the pylorus and the jejunum.

duodenoenterostomía *f. surg.* duodenoenterostomy, anastomosis between the duodenum and the small intestine.

duodenoscopía *f.* duodenoscopy, endoscopic examination of the duodenum.

duodenostomía *f. surg.* duodenostomy, opening into the duodenum through the abdominal wall to alleviate stenosis of the pylorus.

duodenotomía *f. surg.* duodenotomy, incision of the duodenum.

duodenoyeyunostomía *f. surg.* duodenojejunostomy, creation of a communication between the duodenum and the jejunum.

duplicar *vi.* to duplicate; to double.

durabilidad *f.* durability; duration.

durable *a.* durable, that lasts.

duración *f.* duration; continuation.

duramadre, duramáter *f.* dura mater, the outer membrane that covers the encephalum and the spinal cord.

durante *adv.* during.

durar *v.* to last; to endure.

durazno *m.* peach.

dureza *f.* hardness.

duro-a *a.* hard, firm.

E

E. *abr.* **emetropía** / emmetropia; **enema** / enema; **enzima** / enzyme.

e *conj.* and.

ebrio-a *a.* drunk.

ebullición *f.* ebullition, boiling; punto de ___ / boiling point.

eclampsia *f.* eclampsia, toxic, convulsive disorder that usu. occurs near the end of pregnancy or right after delivery.

eclámptico-a *a.* eclamptic, rel. to eclampsia.

eco *m.* echo, repercussion of sound.

ecocardiografía *f.* echocardiography, diagnostic procedure that uses sound waves (ultrasound) to visualize the internal structures of the heart.

ecocardiograma *m.* echocardiogram, ultrasonic record obtained by an echocardiography.

ecoencefalografía *f.* echoencephalography, diagnostic procedure that sends sound waves (ultrasound) to the brain structure and records the returning echoes.

ecografía *f.* ecography. *V.* **ultrasonografia.**

ecograma *m.* echogram, graphic representation of an ecography.

ecolalia *f.* echolalia, disorder manifested by involuntary repetition of words spoken by another person.

ecología *f.* ecology, the study of plants and animals and their relationship to the environment.

ecológico-a *a.* ecological; sistema ___ / ___ system.

económico-a *a.* economical, economic.

ecosistema *f.* ecosystem, ecologic microcosm.

ectopia *f.* ectopia, ectopy, displacement of an organ, usu. congenital.

ectópico-a *a.* ectopic, rel. to ectopia.

ectoplasma *m.* ectoplasm, external membrane surrounding the cell cytoplasm.

ectropión *m.* ectropion, eversion of the margin of a body part, such as the eyelid.

ecuador *m.* equator, imaginary line that divides a body in two equal parts.

ecuanimidad *f.* equanimity; steadfastness.

eczema, eccema *m.* eczema, inflammatory noncontagious skin disease.

echar *v.* to throw, to cast; [*líquido*] to pour; ___ **a perder** / to spoil.

Echinococcus *L.* Echinococcus. *V.* **equinococo.**

Echo, virus *m.* echovirus, any of a group of viruses found in the gastrointestinal tract, associated with meningitis and enteritis.

edad *f.* age; ___ **cronológica** / chronological ___; **de** ___ **avanzada** / elderly; **mayor de** ___ / ___ of consent; **menor de** ___ / under ___, a minor.

edema *m.* edema, abnormal amount of fluid in the intercellular tissue; ___ angioneurótico / angioneurotic ___; ___ cardíaco / cardiac ___; ___ cerebral / cerebral ___; ___ dependiente / dependent ___; ___ de fóvea / pitting ___; ___ pulmonar / pulmonary ___.

edematoso-a *a.* edematous, rel. to or affected by edema.

edetate *m.* edetate, calcium disodium, agent used in diagnosing and treating lead poisoning.

edificio *m.* building.

educación *f.* education.

educar *vi.* to educate.

efectivo-a *a.* effective; **en** ___ / cash; **-mente** *adv.* in effect, actually.

efecto *m.* effect, impression; result; ___ secundario / side ___.

efector *m.* effector, nerve ending which produces an efferent action on muscles and glands.

efedrina *f.* ephedrine, adrenalinelike drug used chiefly as a bronchodilator.

eferente *a.* efferent, centrifugal, that pulls away from the center.

efervescente *a.* effervescent, that produces gas bubbles.

eficaz, eficiente *a.* efficacious, efficient.

eficientemente *adv.* efficiently.

efímero-a *a.* ephemeral, of brief duration.

efluente *a.* effluent, flowing out.

efusión *f.* effusion, escape of fluid into a cavity or tissue.

ego *m. psych.* ego, the self, human consciousness.

egocéntrico-a *a.* egocentric, self-centered.

egoísmo *m.* selfishness, self-centeredness.

egoísta *m , f.* selfish person; *a.* selfish.

egomanía *f.* egomania, excessive self-esteem.

egosintónico-a *a. psych.* ego-syntonic, in harmony with the ego.

egreso *m.* output; [*dar de alta*] discharge; sumario de ___ / discharge summary.

eje *m.* axis.

ejemplo *m.* example.

ejercer *vi.* [*una profesión*] to practice; [*autoridad*] to exercise.

ejercicio *m.* exercise; ___ físico / physical ___; ___ para adelgazar / reducing ___.

elación *f.* elation, state of jubilation and exaltation characterized by mental and physical excitement.

elastasa *f.* elastase, enzyme that catalizes the digestion of elastic fibers, esp. of the pancreatic juice.

elasticidad *f.* elasticity, ability to expand easily and resume its normal shape.

elástico *m.* elastic; **-a** *a.* elastic, that can be returned to its original shape after being extended or distorted; tejido ___ / ___ tissue.

elastinasa *f.* elastinase. *V.* **elastasa.**

electivo-a *a.* elective, optional; terapia ___ / ___ therapy; cirugía ___ / ___ surgery.

electricidad *f.* electricity.

eléctrico-a *a.* electric, electrical; corriente ___ / ___ current.

electrocardiógrafo *m.* electrocardiograph, instrument for recording the electrical variations of the heart muscle in action.

electrocardiograma *m.* electrocardiogram, graphic record of the changes in the electric currents produced by the contractions of the heart muscle; ___ de esfuerzo / exercise ___.

electrocauterización *m.* electrocauterization, destruction of tissues by an electric current.

electrocirugía *f.* electrosurgery, use of electric current in surgical procedures.

electrocución *f.* electrocution, termination of life by electric current.

electrochoque *m.* electroshock, electroconvulsive therapy, treatment of some mental disorders by applying an electric current to the brain.

electrodo *m.* electrode, a medium between the electric current and the object to which the current is applied.

electroencefalografía *f.* electroencephalography, registering of the electrical currents produced in the brain.

electroencefalograma *m.* electroencephalogram, graphic record obtained during an electroencephalography.

electrofisiología *f.* electrophysiology, the study of the relationship between physiological processes and electrical phenomena.

electroforesis *f.* electrophoresis, movement of coloidal particles suspended in a medium charged with an electric current that separates them, such as occurs in the separation of proteins in plasma.

electrólisis *f.* electrolysis, destruction or disintegration by means of an electric current.

electrólito *m.* electrolyte, ion that carries an electrical charge.

electromagnético-a *a.* electromagnetic.

electromiografía *f.* electromyography, use of electrical stimulation to record the strength of muscle contraction.

electrónico-a *a.* electronic.

electroquirúrgico-a *a.* electrosurgical; destrucción ___ de lesiones / ___ destruction of lesions.

elefantiasis *f.* elephantiasis, chronic disease produced by obstruction of the lymphatic vessels and hypertrophy of the skin and subcutaneous cellular tissue, that affects most frequently the legs and scrotum.

elegible *a.* eligible, qualified for selection.

elegir *vi.* to elect, to choose.

elemental *a.* elemental; rudimentary.

elemento *m.* element.

elevación *f.* elevation.

elevado-a *a.* elevated, raised.

elevador *m.* elevator. 1. surgical device used for lifting a sunken part or for elevating tissues; 2. elevator.

elevar *v.* to raise, to elevate.

eliminación *f.* elimination, exclusion.

eliminar *v.* to eliminate; to discard waste from the body.

eliptocito *m.* elliptocyte, oval red cell.

elixir *m.* elixir, aromatic and sweet liquor containing an active medicinal ingredient.

emaciación *f.* emaciation, an extreme loss of weight.

embalsamiento *m.* embalming, treatment of a dead body to retard its decay.

embarazada *a.* pregnant.

embarazo *m.* pregnancy; ___ de probeta / test tube ___; ___ ectópico / ectopic ___, extra-uterine; ___ falso / false ___, enlargement of the abdomen simulating pregnancy; ___ intersticial / interstitial ___, that develops in the part of the uterine tube within the wall of the uterus; ___ múltiple / multiple ___, more than one fetus in the uterus at the same time; ___ prolongado / prolonged ___, that goes beyond full term; prueba del ___ / ___ test; ___ subrogado / surrogate ___; ___ tubárico / tubal ___, when the egg develops in the Fallopian tube; ___ tuboabdominal / tuboabdominal ___.

embolia, embolismo *f., m.* embolism, sudden obstruction of a cerebral artery by a loose piece of clot, plaque, fat, or air bubble; ___ cerebral / cerebral ___, stroke; ___ gaseosa / air ___.

émbolo *m.* embolus, clot of blood or other material that when traveling through the bloodstream becomes lodged in a vessel of lesser diameter.

emborrachamiento, embriaguez *m., f.* intoxication, drunkenness.

emborracharse *vr.* to get drunk.

embotamiento *m.* torpor, sluggishness.

embriología *f.* embryology, study of the embryo and its development up to the moment of birth.

embrión *m.* embryo, primitive phase of an organism from the moment of fertilization to about the second month.

embriónico-a *a.* embrional, embryonic, rel. to the embryo.

embudo *m.* funnel.

emergencia *f.* emergency, urgency; línea telefónica de ___ / hotline; servicios de ___ / ___ medicine.

emético *m.* emetic, agent that stimulates vomiting.

emetina *f.* emetine, emetic and antiamebic.

emigración, migración *f.* emigration, escape, such as of leucocytes, through the walls of capillaries and small veins.

eminencia *f.* eminence, prominence or elevation such as on the surface of a bone.

emisión *f.* emission, discharge; ___ seminal nocturna / wet dream, involuntary emission of semen during sleep.

emitir *v.* to emit, to expel; to issue.

emoción *f.* emotion, intense feeling.

emocional, emocionante *a.* emotional, rel. to emotion.

emoliente *a.* emollient, soothing to the skin or mucous membrane.

empachado-a *a.* suffering from indigestion.

empacho *m.* indigestion.

empapar *v.* to soak, to drench; **empaparse** *vr.* to get soaked.

empaste *m.* [*dientes*] filling.

empatía *f.* empathy, understanding and appreciation of the feelings of another person.

empeine *m.* instep, arched medial portion of the foot.

empeorar *v.* to worsen; **empeorarse** *vr.* to get worse.

empezar *vi.* to begin, to start.

empiema *f.* empyema, presence of pus in a cavity, esp. the pleural cavity.

empírico-a *a.* empiric, empirical, based on practical observations.

empleado-a *m., f.* employee.

emplear *v.* to employ, to use.

empleo *m.* employment, job.

emprender *v.* to undertake.

empujar *v.* to push, to press forward.

empuje *m.* impulse; driving force.

empujón *m.* push, shove.

emulsión *f.* emulsion, distribution of a liquid in small globules throughout another liquid.

emulsionar *v.* to emulsify, to convert into an emulsion.

en *prep.* in, on, at; ___ el hospital / in the hospital; ___ la mesa / on the table; ___ casa / at home.

enajenación mental *m.* derangement, mental disorder.

enajenamiento *m.* conversion disorder, the process by which repressed emotions are translated into physical manifestations.

enamorarse *vr.* to fall in love; ___ de / ___ with.

enanismo *m.* dwarfism, impaired growth of the body caused by hereditary or physical deficiencies.

enano-a *m., f.* dwarf, individual who is undersized in relation to the group to which, he or she belongs; ___ acondroplástico-a / achondroplastic ___; ___ asexual / asexual ___; ___ infantil / infantile ___; micromélico-a / micromelic ___.

encadenamiento *m.* linkage.

encadenar *v.* to link; to chain.

encajamiento *m.* engagement. *V.* **aligeramiento.**

encajar *v.* to fit one thing into another; to insert in; to engage; **encajarse** *vr.* to fit in; to become inserted.

encajonamiento *m.* incasement, the act of becoming enclosed in another structure.

encaminar *v.* to put someone or something on the right path.

encapricharse *vr.* to become obstinate or stubborn about something.

encapsulado-a *a.* enclosed in a capsule; walled-off.

encarcelado-a *a.* incarcerated; constricted.

encefalalgia *f.* encephalalgia, intense headache.

encefálico-a *a.* encephalic, rel. to the encephalon.

encefalinas *f.* enkephalins, chemical substances produced in the brain.

encefalitis *f.* encephalitis, infl. of the brain; ___ equina, del este / eastern equine ___; ___ equina, del oeste / western equine ___; ___ infantil / infantile ___.

encéfalo *m.* encephalon, portion of the nervous system contained in the cranium.

encefalocele *m.* encephalocele, protrusion of brain matter through a congenital or traumatic defect in the skull.

encefalografía f. encephalography, X-ray examination of the brain.

encefaloma m. encephaloma, brain tumor.

encefalomalacia f. encephalomalacia, softening of the brain.

encefalomielitis f. encephalomyelitis, infl. of the brain and the spinal cord.

encefalopatía f. encephalopathy, any disease or malfunction of the brain.

encender vi. [una bombilla] to switch on; [un fuego] to kindle.

encerrar vi. to enclose; **encerrarse** vr. to lock oneself up.

encía f. gum.

encigótico-a, enzigótico-a a. enzygotic, rel. to twins developed from the same fertilized ovum.

encima adv. on, upon, on top of.

encinta a. pregnant.

enclenque a. emaciated; feeble.

encondroma f. enchondroma, tumor that develops within a bone.

encogerse vr., vi. to shrink.

enconarse vr. to fester, to become ulcerated.

encontrar vi. to encounter, to find; **encontrarse** vr. to meet with someone; to find.

encopresis f. encopresis, incontinence of feces.

encuesta f. inquest, official investigation.

endarterectomía f. surg. endarterectomy, excision of the thickened inner lining of an artery.

endarteritis f. endarteritis, infl. of the lining of an artery.

endémico-a a. endemic, endemical, rel. to a disease which remains for an indefinite length of time in a given community or region.

endentado-a a. serrated, teeth-like projection.

enderezar vi. to straighten out.

endocardio m. endocardium, the serous inner lining membrane of the heart.

endocarditis f. endocarditis, acute or chronic infl. of the endocardium; ___ aguda bacteriana / ___, acute bacterial; ___ crónica / ___, chronic; ___ no bacteriana / ___, nonbacterial; ___ reumática / ___, rheumatic; ___ subaguda bacteriana / ___, subacute bacterial; ___ valvular / ___, valvular; ___ vegetativa / ___ vegetative.

endocervix m. endocervix, mucous membrane of the cervix.

endocrino-a a. endocrine, rel. to internal secretions and the glands that secrete them; glándulas ___ -s / endocrine glands, glands that secrete hormones directly into the bloodstream.

endocrinología f. endocrinology, the study of the endocrine glands and the hormones secreted by them.

endodermo m. endoderm, the innermost of the three layers of the embryo.

endolinfa f. endolymph, fluid contained in the membranous labyrinth of the ear.

endometrial a. endometrial, rel. to the endometrium; biopsia ___ / ___ biopsy.

endometrio m. endometrium, inner mucous membrane of the uterus.

endometrioma f. endometrioma, mass containing endometrial tissue.

endometriosis f. endometriosis, disorder by which endometrial-like tissue is found in areas outside the uterus.

endometritis f. endometritis, infl. of the mucous membrane.

endomorfo m. endomorph, person whose body is more heavily developed in the torso than in the limbs.

endorfinas f. endorphins, chemical substances produced in the brain which have the property of easing pain.

endoscopía f. endoscopy, examination of a cavity or conduit using an endoscope.

endoscópico-a a. endoscopic, rel. to endoscopy.

endoscopio m. endoscope, instrument used to examine a hollow organ or cavity.

endostio m. endosteum, tissue that covers the medullar cavity of the bone.

endotelial a. endothelial, rel. to the endothelium.

endotelio m. endothelium, thin layer of cells that form the inner lining of the blood vessels, the lymph channels, the heart, and other cavities.

endotérmico-a a. endothermic, that absorbs heat.

endotraqueal a. endotracheal, within or through the trachea; tubo ___ con manguito / ___ tube, cuffed.

endulzar vi. to sweeten.

endurecer vi. to harden; **endurecerse** vr. to become hardened.

endurecimiento m. hardening.

enema f. enema; ___ de bario / barium ___; ___ de contraste doble / double-contrast ___.

energía *f.* energy, vigor.

enérgico-a *a.* energetic, vigorous.

enfadar *v.* to make angry, to upset; **enfadarse** *vr.* to become angry.

énfasis *m.* emphasis; hacer ____ / to emphasize.

enfermar *v.* to cause disease; **enfermarse** *vr.* to become ill, to get sick.

enfermedad *f.* disease, illness, malady; control de ____ -es contagiosas / communicable ____ control; ____ ambulante / walking ____; ____ concomitante / companion ____; ____ de la altura / high altitude sickness, caused by diminished oxygen; ____ de los mineros / coal miner's ____; ____ de red o cadena / heavy chain ____; ____ funcional / functional ____, of unknown origin; ____ renal / renal ____; ____ respiratoria crónica / chronic respiratory ____; ____ venérea / venereal ____; **licencia por** ____ / sick leave.

enfermería *f.* infirmary, a place used for treatment of the sick.

enfermero-a *m., f.* nurse; ____ anestesista / ____ anesthetist; asistente de ____ / orderly; ____ de cirugía / scrub ____ ; ____ de salud pública / community or public health ____; ____ graduado-a / trained ____; ____ práctico-a / practical ____; ____ privado-a / private duty ____; ____ registrado-a / registered ____; jefe-a de ____ -s / chief or head ____.

enfermizo-a *a.* sickly; predisposed to become ill.

enfermo-a *m., f.* sick person; cuidado de ____ -s / nursing.

enfisema *m.* emphysema, chronic lung condition that causes distension of the small air sacs (alveoli) in the lungs and atrophy of the tissue between them, impairing the respiratory process.

enfisematoso-a *a.* emphysematous, affected by emphysema.

enfocar *vi.* to focus.

enfrente *adv.* across from; in front of.

enfriamiento *m.* cold, chill.

enfriar *v.* to cool down.

engañar *v.* to deceive; to fool; **engañarse** *vr.* to deceive oneself.

engordar *v.* to gain weight; to get fat.

engorroso-a *a.* cumbersome, troublesome.

engrama *f.* engram. 1. permanent mark or trace left in the protoplasm by a passing stimulus; 2. *psych.* a latent permanent picture produced by a sensorial experience.

engrasar *v.* to grease; to oil.

engurgitado-a *a.* engorged, distended by excess of liquid.

enjabonar *v.* to soap; **enjabonarse** *vr.* to soap oneself.

enjambrazón *f.* swarming, the act of multiplying or spreading, such as bacteria over a culture.

enjuagar *v.* to rinse; **enjuagarse** *vr.* to rinse oneself out.

enjuague *m.* rinse, mouthwash.

enoftalmia *f.* enophthalmos, receded eyeball.

enojado-a *a.* angry, fretful.

enojar *v.* to anger; **enojarse** *vr.* to get angry.

enorme *a.* enormous, huge.

enquistado-a *a.* encysted, enclosed in a sac or cyst.

enredadera *f.* vine.

enredado-a *a.* tangled; [*situación médica*] complicated.

enredar *v.* to tangle; to make things more difficult; **enredarse** *vr.* to become tangled up or complicated.

enriquecer *vi.* to enrich; **enriquecerse** *vr.* to be enriched; to become rich.

enriquecido-a *a.* enriched; of increased value.

enriquecimiento *m.* enrichment.

enrojecer *vi.* to redden.

enrojecimiento *m.* redness.

ensalada *f.* salad.

ensanchar *v.* to widen.

ensangrentado-a *a.* bloody, stained with blood.

ensartar *v.* to thread.

ensayo *m.* assay.

enseñado-a *a.* taught.

enseñar *v.* to teach; to show; to instruct.

ensimismado-a *a.* absorbed in thought, pensive.

ensordecedor-a *a.* deafening; ruido ____ / ____ noise.

ensuciar *v.* to dirty; to defecate.

entablillar *v.* to splint.

entamebiasis *f.* entamebiasis, infestation by an ameba.

ente *m.* entity, being.

entender *vi.* to understand, to comprehend.

entendido-a *a.* understood; agreed; informed; wise, learned.

enteralgia *f.* enteralgia, neuralgia of the intestine.

entérico-a. enteral *a.* enteral, rel. to the intestine; cubierta ___ / ___ coated.

enteritis *f.* enteritis, infl. of the intestine, esp. the small intestine.

entero-a *a.* whole; undiminished.

enteroclisis *f.* enteroclysis, irrigation of the colon.

enterococo *m.* enterococcus, a streptococcus that inhabits the intestinal tract.

enterocolecistostomía *f. surg.* enterocholecystostomy, opening between the gallbladder and the small intestine.

enterocolitis *f.* enterocolitis, infl. of both the large and small intestine.

enterocutáneo-a *a.* enterocutaneous, that communicates between the intestines and the cutaneous surface.

enteropatía *f.* enteropathy, any anomaly or disease of the intestines.

enterostomía *f. surg.* enterostomy, opening or communication between the intestine and the abdominal wall skin; revisión de una ___ / ___ revision.

enterotoxina *f.* enterotoxin, a toxin produced by or originating in the intestines.

enterovirus *m.* enterovirus, a group of viruses that infect the human gastrointestinal tract, and can cause respiratory diseases and neurological anomalies.

enterrar *vi.* to bury.

entibiar *v.* to make lukewarm.

entidad *f.* entity, that which constitutes the essence of something.

entierro *m.* burial.

entonces *adv.* then, at that time.

entrada *f.* entrance; entry; inlet; access to a cavity.

entrañas *f.* entrails, bowels; insides.

entrar *v.* to go in; to come in.

entre *prep.* between.

entrenamiento *m.* training.

entrenar *v.* to train; **entrenarse** *vr.* to receive training.

entrevista *f.* interview.

entropía *f.* entropy, in thermodinamics, diminished capacity to convert internal energy into work.

entropión *m.* entropion, inversion or turning inward such as that of the eyelid.

entuerto *m.* afterbirth pains.

entumecido-a *a.* numb.

entumecimiento *m.* numbness; torpor.

entusiasmo *m.* enthusiasm.

enucleación *f. surg.* enucleation, removal of a tumor or a structure.

enuclear *v. surg.* to enucleate. 1. to remove a tumor without causing it to rupture; 2. to destroy or take out the nucleus of a cell; 3. to remove the eyeball.

enuresis, enuresia *f.* enuresis, incontinence; bed-wetting; ___ nocturna / nocturnal ___.

envejecer *vi.* to grow old.

envejecido-a *a.* grown old, looking old.

envenenado-a *a.* poisoned.

envenenamiento *m.* poisoning.

envenenar *v.* to poison; **envenenarse** *vr.* to poison oneself.

enviar *v.* to send.

envidia *f.* envy.

enviudar *v.* to become a widow or a widower.

envoltura *f.* pack, cold or hot wrapping.

envolver *vi.* to wrap; to wrap around.

enyesar *v.* to make a cast using plaster of Paris; to plaster.

enzima *f.* enzyme, protein that acts as a catalyst in the vital chemical reactions.

enzimología *f.* enzymology, the study of enzymes.

eosina *f.* eosin, insoluble substance used as a red dye for coloring tissue for microscopic study.

eosinofilia *f.* eosinophilia, presence of a large number of eosinophilic leukocytes in the blood.

eosinófilo-a *a.* eosinophilic, that stains readily with eosin.

ependimario-a *a.* ependymal, rel. to the ependyma; membrana ___ / ___ layer, one of the interior membranes of the neural tube of the embryo.

ependimitis *f.* ependymitis, infl. of the ependyma.

epéndimo *m.* ependyma, membrane that lines the ventricles of the brain and the central canal of the spinal cord.

ependimoma *f.* ependymoma, a tumor of the central nervous system that contains fetal ependymal cells.

epicardio *m.* epicardium, visceral surface of the pericardium.

epicóndilo *m.* epicondyle, a projection or eminence above the condyle of a bone.

epidemia *f.* epidemic, disease that affects a large number of people in a region or community at the same time.

epidémico-a *a.* epidemic; brote ___ / ___ outbreak.

epidemiología *f.* epidemiology, the study of epidemic diseases.

epidérmico-a *a.* epidermal, epidermic, rel. to the epidermis.

epidermis *f.* epidermis, external epithelial covering of the skin.

epidermoide *m.* epidermoid, tumor that contains epidermal cells; *a.* 1. resembling the dermis; 2. rel. to a tumor that has epidermal cells.

epidermólisis *f.* epidermolysis, loosening of the epidermis.

epididimitis *f.* epididymitis, infection and infl. of the epididymis.

epidídimo *m.* epididymis, a tube along the back side of the testes that collects the sperm from the testicle to be transported by the vas deferens to the seminal vesicle.

epidural *a.* epidural, situated above or outside of the dura mater.

epifisario-a *a.* epiphysial, epiphyseal, rel. to the epiphysis.

epífisis *f.* epiphysis, the end of a long bone, usu. wider than the diaphysis.

epifisitis *f.* epiphysitis, infl. of an epiphysis.

epifora *f.* epiphora, watering of the eye.

epigástrico-a *a.* epigastric, rel. to the epigastrium; reflejo ___ / ___ reflex.

epigastrio *m.* epigastrium, upper back portion of the abdomen.

epiglotis *f.* epiglottis, cartilage that covers the entrance to the larynx and prevents food or liquid from entering it during swallowing.

epiglotitis *f.* epiglottitis, infl. of the epiglottis and adjacent tissues.

epilación *f.* epilation, removal of hair by electrolysis.

epilepsia *f.* epilepsy, grand mal, neurological disorder, gen. chronic and in some cases hereditary, manifested by periodic convulsions and sometimes by loss of consciousness.

epilepsia jacksoniana *f.* Jacksonian epilepsy, partial epilepsy without loss of consciousness.

epiléptico-a *m., f.* person affected with epilepsy; *a.* epileptic, rel. to or suffering from epilepsy; ataque o crisis ___ / ___ seizure; ausencia ___ / absentia epileptica, momentary loss of consciousness during an epileptic seizure.

epileptógeno *m.* epileptogenic, epileptogenous, agent that causes epileptic seizures.

epinefrina *f.* epinephrine. *V.* **adrenalina.**

epiploico-a *a.* epiploic, rel. to the epiploon; foramen ___ / ___ foramen, opening that connects the greater and the lesser peritoneal cavities.

epiplón *m.* epiploon, pad of fat that covers the intestines.

episiotomía *f. surg.* episiotomy, incision of the perineum to avoid tearing during parturition.

epispadias *m.* epispadias, abnormal congenital opening of the male urethra on the upper surface of the penis.

epistaxis *f.* epistaxis, nosebleed.

epitálamo *m.* epithalamus, the uppermost portion of the diencephalon.

epitelial *a.* epithelial, rel. to the epithelium.

epitelio *m.* epithelium, the outer layer of mucous membranes; ___ ciliado / ciliated ___, ___ columnar / columnar ___; ___ cuboidal / cuboidal ___; ___ de transición / transitional ___; ___ escamoso / squamous ___; ___ estratificado / stratified ___.

epitelioma *f.* epithelioma, carcinoma consisting mainly of epithelial cells.

epitelización *f.* epithelization, growth of epithelium over an exposed surface, such as a wound.

epitímpano *m.* epitympanum, upper back portion of the eardrum.

epónimo *m.* eponym, a noun that names a medical disorder or device after the name of its discoverer or inventor, such as Down's syndrome.

epoxia *f.* epoxy, compound characterized by its adhesiveness.

Epsom, sales de *f.* Epsom salts, magnesium sulfate used as laxative.

Epstein-Barr, virus de *m.* Epstein-Barr virus, virus thought to be the causative agent of infectious mononucleosis.

equilibrado-a *a.* balanced.

equilibrar *v.* to equilibrate, to balance.

equilibrio *m.* equilibrium, balance.

equimosis *f.* ecchymosis, bruise, gradual blue-black discoloration of the skin due to blood filtering into the cellular subcutaneous tissue.

equinococo *m.* echinococcus, a genus of tape worm.

equinococosis *f.* echinococcosis, infestation by echinococcus; ⸺ hepática / hepatic ⸺; ⸺ pulmonar / pulmonary ⸺.

equinovaro *m.* equinovarus, congenital deformity of the foot.

equitativo-a *a.* equitable.

equivalencia *f.* equivalence.

equivalente *a.* equivalent.

equivocación *f.* mistake, error.

equivocado-a *a.* mistaken, in error.

equivocarse *vr., vi.* to make a mistake; to be in error; to miscalculate.

erección *f.* erection, state of rigidity or hardening of erectile tissue when it is filled with blood, such as the penis.

eréctil *a.* erectile, capable of erection or dilation.

erector *m.* erector, a structure that erects, such as a muscle.

ergonomia *f.* ergonomics, branch of ecology that studies design and operations of machines and the physical environment as related to humans.

ergotamina *f.* ergotamine, alkaloid used chiefly in the treatment of migraine headaches.

ergotismo *m.* ergotism, chronic poisoning due to excessive intake of ergot.

erina *f.* dissecting hook.

erisipela *f.* erysipelas, acute infection of the skin.

eritema *f.* erythema, redness of the skin due to congestion of the capillaries; ⸺ de los pañales / diaper rash; ⸺ solar / sunburn.

eritematoso-a *a.* erythematic, erythematous, rel. to erythema.

eritremia *f.* erythremia, increase of red blood cells due to an excessive production of erythroblasts by the bone marrow.

eritroblasto *m.* erythroblast, primitive red blood cell.

eritroblastosis *f.* erythroblastosis, excessive number of erythroblasts in the blood.

eritrocito *m.* erythrocyte, red blood cell made in the bone marrow that serves to transport oxygen to tissues; índice de sedimentación de ⸺-s / ⸺ sedimentation rate.

eritrocitopenia *f.* erythrocytopenia, deficiency in the number of erythrocytes present in the blood.

eritrocitosis *f.* erythrocytosis, increase in the number of erythrocytes in the blood.

eritroide *a.* erythroid, reddish.

eritroleucemia *f.* erithroleukemia, malignant blood disease caused by abnormal growth of both red and white blood cells.

eritromicina *f.* erithromycin, antibiotic used chiefly in infections caused by grampositive bacteria.

eritrón *m.* erythron, system formed by erythrocytes circulating in the blood and the organ from which they arise.

eritropoyesis *f.* erythropoiesis, red blood cell production.

eritropoyetina *f.* erythropoietin, a non-dialyzable protein that stimulates red blood cell production.

erógeno-a *a.* erogenous, that which produces erotic sensations; zona ⸺ / ⸺ zone.

erosión *f.* erosion, the act of wearing out or away.

erosivo-a *a.* erosive, that causes erosion.

erótico-a *a.* erotic, rel. to eroticism or having the power to arouse sexual impulses.

erotismo *m.* eroticism, erotism, lustful sexual impulses.

erradicar *vi.* to erradicate, to remove, to extirpate.

errante, errático-a *a.* wandering, that deviates from its normal course.

error *m.* error, mistake.

eructación *f.* eructation, belching.

eructar, erutar *v.* to eructate, to belch.

eructo, eruto *m.* eructation, belch.

erupción *f.* eruption, rash, skin outbreak.

escafoide *a.* scaphoid, shaped like a boat, esp. in reference to the bone of the carpus or the tarsus.

escala *f.* scale; ⸺ de diferenciación / range.

escaldadura *f.* scald, skin burn caused by boiling liquid or vapor.

escaldar *v.* to scald; to burn.

escalera *f.* staircase; ladder; ⸺ de escape / fire escape.

escalofrío *m.* chill, a cold shivering sensation.

escalonar *v.* to stagger; to distribute in sequence.

escalpelo, escarpelo *m.* scalpel, surgical blade, dissecting knife.

escama *f.* scale, a thin small lamina shed from the epidermis.

escamoso-a *a.* squamous, scaly.

escán *m.* scan, the process of producing an image of a specific organ or tissue by means of a radioactive substance that is injected as a contrasting element; ___ cardíaco / heart ___; ___ de la tiroides / thyroid ___; ___ de los huesos / bone ___; ___ del cerebro / brain ___; ___ pulmonar / lung ___.

escápula *f.* scapula, shoulder blade.

escara *f.* eschar, dark colored scab or crust that forms in the skin after a burn.

escarificación *f.* scarification, the act of producing a number of small superficial scratches or punctures on the skin.

escarlatina *f.* scarlatina, scarlet fever, an acute contagious disease characterized by fever and a bright red rash on the skin and tongue.

escasez *f.* scarcity, shortage, lack.

escaso-a *a.* scarce, scanty, in short supply.

escatología *f.* scatology; 1. the study of feces; 2. a morbid preoccupation with feces and filth.

escenario *m.* scenario; scene.

escindir *v.* to excise, to cut, to divide.

escirro *m.* scirrhus, hard cancerous tumor.

escirroso-a *a.* scirrhous, hard, rel. to a scirrhus.

escleritis *f.* scleritis, infl. of the sclera.

esclerosis *f.* sclerosis, progressive hardening of organs or tissues; ___ arterial / arterial ___; ___ de Alzheimer / Alzheimer's ___; ___ lateral amiotrófica / amyotrophic lateral ___.

esclerosis múltiple *f.* multiple sclerosis, slow progressive disease of the central nervous system caused by a loss of the protective myelin covering of the nerve fibers of the brain and spinal cord.

esclerosis tuberosa *f.* tuberous sclerosis, familial disease manifested by convulsive seizures, progressive mental deficiency, and multiple tumor formations in the skin and the brain.

escleroterapia *f.* sclerotherapy, the process of injecting chemical solutions to treat varices in order to produce sclerosis.

esclerótica *f.* sclera, sclerotica, the hard, white exterior part of the eye made of fibrous tissue.

esclerótico-a *a.* sclerotic, rel. to or afflicted by sclerosis.

escobillón *m.* swab.

escoger *vi.* to choose, to elect.

escoliosis *f.* scoliosis, pronounced lateral curvature of the spine.

esconder *v.* to hide, to conceal.

escorbuto *m.* scurvy, disease caused by lack of vitamin C and manifested by anemia, bleeding gums and a general state of inanition.

escorpión *m.* scorpion; **picadura de** ___ / ___ sting.

escotoma *m.* scotoma, area of lost or diminished vision within the visual field.

escotopía *f.* scotopia, adjustment to nocturnal vision.

escotópico-a *a.* scotopic, rel. to scotopia; visión ___ / ___ vision.

escribir *v.* to write.

escrito-a *a. pp.* of **escribir**, written.

escrófula *f.* scrofula, tuberculosis of the lymphatic glands.

escrofuloderma *m.* scrofuloderma, a type of scrofula with skin lesions.

escrotal *a.* scrotal, rel. to the scrotum.

escroto *m.* scrotum, the sac surrounding and enclosing the testes.

escrúpulo *m.* scruple.

escrupuloso-a *a.* scrupulous.

escrutinio *m.* scrutiny; screening.

escudo *m.* shield, a protective covering.

escupir *v.* to spit.

esencial *a.* essential, indispensable.

esfacelo *m.* slough, mass of dead tissue that has been shed or fallen off from live tissue.

esfenoidal *a.* sphenoidal, rel. to the sphenoid bone.

esfenoides *m.* sphenoid bone, large bone at the base of the skull.

esfera *f.* sphere. 1. a structure shaped like a globe or ball; 2. sociological environment.

esférico-a *a.* spherical, rel. to a sphere.

esferocito *m.* spherocyte, sphere-shaped erythrocyte.

esferocitosis *f.* spherocytosis, presence of spherocytes in the blood.

esferoide *a.* spheroid, shaped like a sphere.

esférula *f.* spherule, minute sphere.

esfigmomanómetro *m.* sphygmomanometer, instrument for determining blood pressure.

esfínter *m.* sphincter, circular muscle that opens and closes an orifice.

esfinteroplastia *f. surg.* sphincteroplasty, plastic surgery of a sphincter muscle.

esfinterotomía *f. surg.* sphincterotomy, cutting of a sphincter muscle.

esfuerzo *m.* effort; ___ coordinado / teamwork; ___ excesivo / overexertion, strain;

prueba de ____ / stress test; **sin** ____ / effortless.

eslabón *m.* link.

esmalte *m.* enamel, hard substance that covers and protects the dentin of a tooth.

esmegma *m.* smegma, thick cheesy substance secreted by sebaceous glands, esp. seen in the external genitalia.

esofagectomía *f. surg.* esophagectomy, excision of a portion of the esophagus.

esofágico-a *a.* esophageal, rel. to the esophagus; dilatación ____ / ____ dilatation.

esofagitis *f.* esophagitis, infl. of the esophagus.

esófago *m.* esophagus, portion of the alimentary tract between the pharynx and the stomach.

esofagodinia *f.* esophagodynia, pain in the esophagus.

esofagogastritis *f.* esophagogastritis, infl. of the stomach and the esophagus.

esofagogastroduodenoscopía *f.* esophagogastroduodenoscopy, examination of the esophagus, the stomach, and the duodenum by means of an endoscope.

esofagogastroscopía *f.* esophagogastroscopy, endoscopic examination of the esophagus and the stomach.

esoforia *f.* esophoria, crossed eyes, inward deviation of the eyes.

esotropía *f.* esotropia. *V.* **esoforia.**

espacial *a.* spatial, rel. to space.

espacio *m.* space, area.

espalda *f.* back; dolor de ____ / backache.

espanto *m.* fright, excessive fear.

español *m.* [*idioma*] Spanish; [*nativo-a*] Spanish; **-a** *a.* Spanish.

esparadrapo *m.* adhesive tape.

esparcido-a *a.* spread out; scattered.

esparcir *vi.* to scatter, to spread.

espárrago *m.* asparagus.

espasmo *m.* spasm, twitch, involuntary muscular contraction.

espasmódico-a *a.* spasmodic, rel. to spasms.

espasticidad *f.* spasticity, increase in the normal tension of a muscle resulting in stiffness and difficult movement.

espástico-a *a.* spastic. 1. resembling, or of the nature of spasms; 2. that is afflicted with spasms.

espátula *f.* spatula, palette-knife.

especia *f.* spice.

especial *a.* special, especial, unique; **-mente** *adv.* specially.

especialidad *f.* specialty.

especialista *m., f.* specialist.

especialización *f.* specialization.

especializarse *vr., vi.* to specialize.

especie *f.* species, kind, class of organisms belonging to a biological category.

especificar *vi.* to specify.

específico-a *a.* specific; determined; precise; **no** ____ / nonspecific.

espécimen *m.* specimen, sample.

espectro *m.* spectrum. 1. range of activity of an antibiotic against a variety of microorganisms; 2. series of images resulting from the refraction of electromagnetic radiation; 3. series of colors of refracted sunlight that can be seen with the naked eye or with the help of a sensitive instrument.

especular *v.* to speculate.

espéculo *m.* speculum, instrument used for dilating a conduit or cavity.

espejo *m.* mirror.

espejuelos *m. pl.* eyeglasses, spectacles; ____ bifocales / bifocal ____ ; ____ para leer / reading ____ ; ____ trifocales / trifocal ____ .

espera *f.* wait; **salón de** ____ / waiting room.

esperanza *f.* hope; **perder la** ____ / to give up ____ ; **tener** ____ / to have ____ .

esperar *v.* to wait; to hope; to expect.

esperma *f.* sperm. *V.* **semen.**

espermaticida, espermicida *m.* spermaticide, spermicidal, agent that destroys spermatozoa; *a.* spermaticidal, that kills spermatozoa.

espermático-a *a.* spermatic; rel. to sperm or semen.

espermatocele *m.* spermatocele, a cystic tumor of the epididymis containing spermatozoa.

espermatogénesis *f.* spermatogenesis, the process of formation and development of spermatozoa.

espermatoide *a.* spermatoid, resembling spermatozoa.

espermatorrea *f.* spermatorrhea, involuntary loss of semen.

espermatozoide *m.* spermatozoid, spermatozoon, male reproductive cell that fertilizes the ovum.

espermiograma *m.* spermiogram, evaluation of spermatozoa as an aid to determine sterility.

espesar *v.* to thicken; to condense; **espe-**

sarse *vr.* to get thicker; to get condensed.

espeso-a *a.* thick, condensed.

espesor *m.* thickness, consistency.

espica *f.* spica, a type of bandage.

espícula *f.* spicule, a body shaped like a small needle.

espicular *a.* spicular, needle-shaped.

espiga *f.* spike, sharp raise in a curve, such as in the tracing of brain waves.

espina *f.* 1. the spine or vertebral column; 2. spina; thorn; fishbone.

espina bífida *f.* spina bifida, congenital anomaly of the spine with a gap; ___ oculta / ___ occulta, without protrusion, gen. at the lumbar level.

espinaca *f.* spinach.

espinal *a.* spinal, rel. to the spine or the spinal cord; canal ___ / ___ canal; choque ___ / ___ shock; fusión ___ / ___ fusion; médula ___ / ___ cord; nervio accesorio ___ / ___ accesory nerve; nervios ___-es / ___ nerves; punción ___ / ___ puncture.

espinazo *m.* spine, *pop.* backbone.

espinilla *f.* 1. blackhead; 2. shin bone, anterior edge of the tibia.

espinoso-a *a.* spinous, acanthoid, spine-shaped.

espiral *f.* spiral. 1. sphere-like arrangement of cardiac muscular fibers; 2. a type of finger print; *a.* that winds around a center or axis.

espirar *v.* to exhale.

espíritu *m.* spirit. 1. alcoholic solution of a volatile substance; 2. soul; tranquilidad de ___ / peace of mind.

espiritual *a.* spiritual, rel. to the soul; cura ___ / ___ healing.

espirometría *f.* spirometry, the act of measuring the breathing capacity through the use of a spirometer.

espirómetro *m.* spirometer, device used to measure the amount of inhaled and exhaled air.

espiroqueta *f.* spirochete, spiral microorganism that belongs to the order *Spirochaetales* that includes the syphilis causing agent.

espiroquetósico-a *a.* spirochetal, rel. to spirochetes.

esplácnico-a *a.* splanchnic, rel. to or that reaches the viscera; nervios ___-s / ___ nerves.

esplenectomía *f.* *surg.* splenectomy, excision of the spleen.

esplénico-a *a.* splenic, rel. to the spleen.

esplenoportografía *f.* splenoportography, X-ray of the splenic and portal veins following injection of a radiopaque dye into the spleen.

esplenorrenal *a.* splenorenal, rel. to the spleen and the kidneys; derivación ___ / ___ shunt, anastomosis of the splenic veins or artery to the renal vein, esp. used in the treatment of portal hypertension.

espolón *m.* spur, pointed projection, as of a bone; ___ calcáneo / calcaneal ___.

espondilitis *f.* spondylitis, infl. of one or more vertebrae; ___ anquilosante / ankylosing ___, rheumatoid.

espondilólisis *f.* spondylolysis, dissolution or destruction of a vertebra.

espondilolistesis *f.* spondylolisthesis, forward displacement of one vertebra over another, usu. the fourth lumbar over the fifth or the fifth over the sacrum.

espondilopatía *f.* spondylopathy, any disease or disorder of a vertebra.

espondilosis *f.* spondylosis. 1. vertebral ankylosis; 2. any degenerative condition affecting the vertebrae.

esponja *f.* sponge.

esponjar *v.* to sponge, to soak with a sponge.

esponjoso-a *a.* spongy, porous.

espontáneo-a *a.* spontaneous.

espora *f.* spore, unicellular reproductive cell.

esporádico-a *a.* sporadic, occurring irregularly.

esporicida *m.* sporicide, agent that destroys spores.

esposo-a *m., f.* husband; wife.

esprue *m.* sprue, chronic disease that affects the ability to absorb gluten containing foods.

espulgar *vi.* to cleanse of lice or fleas.

espuma *f.* froth, foam; scum.

espurio-a *a.* spurious, false.

esputo *m.* sputum, spittle; ___ sanguinolento / bloody ___.

esquelético-a *a.* skeletal, rel. to the skeleton.

esqueleto *m.* skeleton, the bony structure of the body.

esquema *f.* schema; outline, plan.

esquemático-a *a.* schematic, rel. to a schema.

esquina *f.* corner.

esquirla *f.* bone splinter.

esquistosoma *m.* *Schistosoma,* blood fluke, a trematode larvae which enters the blood through the digestive tract or through the skin by contact with contaminated water.

esquistosomiasis *f.* schistosomiasis, infestation with blood flukes.

esquizofrenia *f.* schizophrenia, a breaking down of the mental functions with different psychotic manifestations such as delusion, withdrawal, and distorted perception of reality.

esquizofrénico-a *a.* *psych.* schizophrenic, rel. to or suffering from schizophrenia.

esquizoide *a.* schizoid, resembling schyzophrenia.

estabilidad *f.* stability, permanence.

estabilización *f.* stabilization, the act of making stable.

estabilizar *vi.* to stabilize, to eliminate fluctuations.

estable *a.* stable, that does not fluctuate.

establecer *vi.* to establish.

estación *f.* station. 1. status of condition; 2. stopping place such as a nurse's station; 3. season of the year.

estacionario-a *a.* stationary, in a fixed position.

estadística *f.* statistics; statistic, figure.

estado *m.* state, condition; ____ crepuscular / twilight ____; ____ de gestación / pregnancy; ____ nutricional / nutritional ____.

estafilococemia *f.* staphylococcemia, presence of staphylococci in the blood.

estafilocócico-a *a.* staphylococcal, staphylococcic, rel. to or caused by staphylococci.

estafilococo *m.* staphylococcus, any pathological micrococci. intoxicación alimentaria por ____-s / staphylococcal food poisoning.

estafilotoxina *f.* staphylotoxin, toxin produced by staphylococci.

estancación, estancamiento *f., m.* stagnation, lack of movement or circulation in fluids.

estándar *a.* standard, normal established way; atención o cuidado ____ / ____ of care; desviación ____ / ____ deviation; error ____ / ____ error; procedimiento ____ / ____ procedure.

estandarización *f.* standardization, uniformity; normalcy.

estanolona *f.* stanolone, anabolic steroid drug.

estapedectomía *f.* *surg.* stapedectomy, excision of the stapes of the ear to improve hearing.

estar *vi.* to be; ____ de guardia / to be on call.

estasis *f.* stasis, stagnation of a body fluid such as blood or urine.

estático-a *a.* static, without movement.

estatura *f.* stature, height.

este *m.* [*punto cardinal*] east; al ____ de / to the ____ of; -a *a.* this; estos-as *pl.* these; éste-a *dem. pron.* this, this one; éstos-as *pl.* these; esto *neut.* this, this one.

estearina *f.* stearine, white crystalline component of fats.

esteatorrea *f.* steatorrhea, excess fat in the stool.

estenia *f.* sthenia, normal strength and vigor.

estenosado-a *a.* stenosed, rel. to stenosis.

estenósico-a *a.* stenotic, produced or characterized by stenosis.

estenosis *f.* stenosis, constriction or abnormal narrowing of a passageway; ____ aórtica / aortic ____; ____ espinal / spinal ____; ____ pilórica / pyloric ____; ____ traqueal / tracheal ____.

éster *m.* ester, compound formed by the combination of an organic acid and alcohol.

estereorradiografía *a.* stereoradiography, a three-dimensional X-ray.

estereotaxia *f.* stereotaxis, technique used in neurological procedures to locate with precision an area in the brain.

estereotipia *f.* stereotype, a type which represents a whole group.

estereotípico-a *a.* stereotypic, rel. to a stereotype.

esterificación *f.* esterification, transformation of an acid into ester.

estéril *a.* sterile. 1. aseptic, free of germs; 2. incapable of producing offspring.

esterilidad *f.* sterility, the condition of being sterile.

esterilización *f.* sterilization. 1. procedure to prevent reproduction; 2. total destruction of microorganisms; ____ por calor / thermosterilization; ____ por gas / gas ____; ____ por vapor / steam ____.

esterilizador *m.* sterilizer.

esterilizar *vi.* to sterilize.

esternal *a.* sternal, rel. to the sternum; punción ____ / ____ puncture.

esternocostal *a.* sternocostal, rel. to the sternum and the ribs.

esternón *m.* sternum, breastbone.

esternotomía *f. surg.* sternotomy, cutting through the sternum.

esteroide *a.* steroid, rel. to steroids.

esteroides *m.* steroids, complex organic compounds that resemble cholesterol and of which many hormones such as estrogen, testosterone, and cortisone are made.

estertor *m.* rale, stertor, an abnormal rattle-like sound heard on auscultation; ____ agónico / death rattle; ____ áspero / coarse ____ ; ____ crepitante / crepitant ____ ; ____ crujiente / crackling ____ ; ____ húmedo / moist ____ ; ____ roncus / rhonchus ____ , rattling in the throat; ____ seco / dry ____ .

estesia *f.* esthesia, perception or sensation, or any anomaly affecting them.

estetoscopio *m.* stethoscope, instrument used for auscultation.

estigma *m.* stigma. 1. a specific sign of a disease; 2. a mark or sign on the body.

estilete *m.* style, stylet, stylus; *surg.* flexible probe.

estiloide *a.* styloid, long and pointed.

estimado *m.* estimate, evaluation.

estimulación *f.* stimulation; motivation.

estimulante *m.* stimulant, agent that incites a reaction; *pop.* upper.

estimular *v.* to stimulate; to motivate, to animate to action.

estímulo *m.* stimulus, agent or factor that produces a reaction; ____ condicionado / conditioned ____ ; ____ subliminal / subliminal ____ .

estíptico *m.* styptic, agent with astringent power.

estirado-a *a.* extended, elongated.

estirar *v.* to stretch, to extend.

estirón *m.* stretch, forceful pull.

estoma *m.* stoma, artificial permanent opening, esp. in the abdominal wall.

estomacal *a.* stomachic, rel. to the stomach.

estómago *m.* stomach, sac-like organ of the alimentary canal; ____ en cascada / cascade ____ ; ____ en bota de vino / leather bottle ____ ; lavado de ____ / ____ pumping.

estomal *a.* stomal, rel. to a stoma.

estomatitis *f.* stomatitis, infl. of the mucosa of the mouth; ____ aftosa / aphthous ____ .

estornudar *v.* to sneeze.

estornudo *m.* sneeze.

estrabismo *m.* strabismus, squint, abnormal alignment of the eyes due to muscular deficiency.

estradiol *m.* estradiol, steroid produced by the ovaries.

estrangulación *f.* strangulation. 1. asphyxia or suffocation gen. caused by obstruction of the air passages; 2. constriction of an organ or structure due to compression.

estrangulado-a *a.* strangulated; constricted.

estrangular *v.* to strangle.

estratificación *f.* stratification; arrangement in layers.

estratificado-a *a.* stratified, arranged in layers; epitelio ____ / ____ epithelium.

estrato *m.* stratum, layer.

estrechamiento *m.* narrowing; tightness.

estrechar *v.* to make narrower.

estrechez, estrechura *f.* stricture, narrowness, closeness.

estrecho-a *a.* narrow.

estrella *f.* star; star-shaped body.

estrellado-a *a.* stellate, shaped like a star.

estremecerse *vr., vi.* to shudder, to tremble.

estreñido-a *a.* constipated; hard bound.

estreñimiento *m.* constipation; infrequent or incomplete bowel movements.

estreptococcemia *f.* streptococcemia, blood infection caused by the presence of streptococci.

estreptocócico-a *a.* streptococcal, rel. to or caused by streptococci; infecciones ____ -s / ____ infections.

estreptococo *m.* streptococcus, organism of the genus *Streptococcus*.

estreptomicina *f.* streptomycin, antibiotic drug used against bacterial infections.

estrés *m.* stress.

estría *f.* stria, streak.

estriado-a *a.* striated, striate, marked by streaks; músculo ____ / ____ muscle.

estribo *m.* stapes, the innermost of the auditory ossicles shaped like a stirrup.

estricnina *f.* strychnine, highly poisonous alkaloid.

estricto-a *a.* strict; exact.

estricturotomía *f. surg.* stricturotomy, the cutting of strictures.

estridor *m.* stridor, whoop, harsh sound during respiration such as following an attack of whooping cough.

estrinización *m.* estrinization, epithelial changes of the vagina due to stimulation by estrogen.

estrogénico-a *a.* estrogenic, rel. to estrogen.

estrógeno *m.* estrogen, female sex hormone produced by the ovaries.

estroma *m.* stroma, the supporting tissue of an organ.

estrona *f.* estrone, oestrone, estrogenic hormone.

estropear *v.* to spoil; to maim; to cripple.

estructura *f.* structure; order.

estudiante *m., f.* student.

estudiar *v.* to study.

estudio *m.* study.

estupidez *f.* stupidity, foolishness.

estúpido-a *a.* stupid, foolish.

estupor *m.* stupor, daze, state of lethargy.

éter *m.* ether, chemical liquid used as a general anesthetic through inhalation of its vapor.

eternal, eterno-a *a.* eternal.

ética *f.* ethics, norms and principles that rule professional conduct.

etileno *m.* ethylene, anesthetic.

etiología *f.* etiology, branch of medicine that studies the cause of diseases.

etiológico-a *a.* ethiologic, rel. to ethiology.

etiqueta *f.* label, tag.

etmoidectomía *f. surg.* ethmoidectomy, removal of ethmoid cells or part of the ethmoid bone.

etmoideo-a *a.* ethmoid, sievelike; seno ___ / ___ sinus, air cavity within the ethmoid bone.

etmoides *m.* ethmoid bone, spongy bone located at the base of the cranium.

eubolismo *m.* eubolism, normal metabolism.

eucalipto *m.* eucalyptus tree.

euforia *f. psych.* euphoria, an abnormal or exaggerated state of well-being.

eugenesia *f.* eugenics, the science that deals with improving and controling procreation to achieve more desirable hereditary characteristics.

eunuco *m.* eunuch, castrated male.

euploidia *f.* euploidy, complete set of chromosomes.

Eustaquio, trompa de *m.* Eustachian tube, part of the auditory conduit.

eutanasia *f.* euthanasia, mercy killing.

eutiroideo-a *a.* euthyroid, rel. to the normal function of the thyroid gland.

evacuación *f.* evacuation. 1. act of emptying or evacuating esp. the bowels; 2. the act of making a vacuum.

evacuante *m.* evacuant, an agent that stimulates bowel movement.

evacuar *v.* to evacuate, to empty; to void.

evaginación *f.* evagination, protrusion of some part or organ from its normal position.

evaluación *f.* evaluation, assessment, rating, score; weighing the physical and mental state and capabilities of an individual; ___ clínica / clinical assessment; ___ del estado de salud / health assessment; ___ del proceso evolutivo / follow-up assessment.

evaluar *v.* to evaluate.

evanescente *a.* evanescent, of brief duration.

evaporación *f.* evaporation, conversion of a liquid or a solid into vapor.

eversión *f.* eversion, outward turning, esp. of the mucosa surrounding a natural orifice.

evidencia *f.* evidence, manifestation; [*legal*] evidence; testimony.

evisceración *f. surg.* evisceration, removal of the viscera or contents of a cavity; disembowelment.

evitar *v.* to avoid.

evocar *vi.* to evoke.

evolución *f.* evolution, gradual change.

evulsión *f.* evulsion, tearing away, pulling out.

exacerbación *f.* exacerbation, increase in the severity of a symptom or disease.

exacto-a *a.* exact; **-mente** *adv.* exactly.

exageración *f.* exaggeration.

exagerar *v.* to exaggerate.

exaltación *f.* exaltation, state of jubilation.

examen *m.* exam, examination; evaluation; investigation; ___ físico completo / complete physical check-up.

examinar *v.* to examine, to view and study the human body to determine a person's state of health; to look into, to investigate.

exsanguinación *f.* exsanguination, severe blood loss.

exsanguinotransfusión *f.* exsanguino-transfusion, exchange transfusion, gradual and simultaneous withdrawal of a recipient's blood with transfusion of a donor's blood.

exantema *f.* exanthem, exanthema, cutaneous eruption.

exasperado-a *a.* exasperated.

exasperar *v.* to exasperate, to aggravate.

exceder *v.* to exceed; to outweigh; to surpass; **excederse** *vr.* to go too far, *pop.* to go overboard.

excéntrico-a *a.* eccentric, odd, different from the norm.

excepción *f.* exception, outside of the rule; **a ___ de** / with the ___ of.

excesivo-a *a.* excessive, too much.

exceso *m.* excess; **en** ___ / excessively.

excisión *f.* excision, removal, ablation.

excitación *f.* excitation, reaction to a stimulus.

excitado-a *a.* excited, worked up.

excitante *m.* stimulant, *pop.* upper; *a.* stimulating, exciting.

excitar *v.* to stimulate; to provoke.

excluir *vi.* to exclude, to leave out.

excoriación *f.* excoriation, abrasion of the skin.

excrecencia *f.* excrescence, tumor protruding from the surface of a part or organ.

excreción *f.* excretion, elimination of waste matter.

excremento *m.* excrement, feces.

excreta *f.* excreta, all waste matter of the body.

excretar *v.* to excrete, to eliminate waste from the body.

excusa *f.* excuse.

excusado *m.* outside toilet; privy.

excusar *v.* to excuse.

exenteración *f. surg.* exenteration. *V.* **evisceración.**

exfoliación *f.* exfoliation, shedding or peeling of tissue.

exhalación *f.* exhalation, the act of breathing out.

exhalar *v.* to exhale.

exhausto-a *a.* exhausted, fatigued.

exhibicionismo *m.* exhibitionism, obsessive drive to expose one's body, esp. the genitals.

exhibicionista *m., f.* exhibitionist, one who practices exhibitionism.

exhumación *f.* exhumation, disinterment.

exigir *vi.* to demand; to require.

existente *a.* existent, on hand.

existir *v.* to exist, to be.

éxito *m.* success; good result.

exocrino-a *a.* exocrine, rel. to the external secretion of a gland.

exoftalmía *f.* exophthalmia, exophthalmos, exophthalmus, abnormal protrusion of the eyeball.

exoftálmico-a *a.* exophthalmic, rel. to or suffering from exophthalmia.

exógeno-a *a.* exogenous, that originates outside the organism.

exostosis *f.* exostosis, cartilaginous osseus hypertrophy that projects outward from a bone, or the root of a tooth.

exótico-a *a.* exotic.

exotoxina *f.* exotoxin, toxic substance secreted by bacteria.

exotropía *f.* exotropia, a type of strabismus, outward turning of the eyes due to muscular imbalance.

expandir *v.* to expand, to dilate; **expandirse** *vr.* to become expanded.

expansión *f.* expansion, extension.

expansivo-a *a.* expansive; [*persona*] outgoing.

expectoración *f.* expectoration, the expulsion of mucus or phlegm from the lungs, trachea or bronchi.

expectorante *m.* expectorant, an agent that stimulates expectoration.

expediente *m.* medical record; file; sumario del ___ / summary of hospital records.

experiencia *f.* experience, knowledge gained by practice.

experimental *a.* experimental, rel. to or known by experiment.

experimentar *v.* to experiment.

experimento *m.* experiment.

experto-a *m., f.* expert.

expiración *f.* expiration, termination; death.

expirar *v.* to expire, to die.

explicación *f.* explanation; interpretation.

exploración *f.* exploration, search, investigation.

exploratorio-a *a.* exploratory, rel. to exploration.

exponer *vi.* to expose.

expresión *f.* expression, facial appearance.

expresividad *f.* expressivity, degree of manifestation of a given hereditary trait in the individual that carries the conditioning gene.

exprimir *v.* to squeeze; to extrude.

expuesto-a *a. pp.* of **exponer,** exposed.

expulsar *v.* to expel, to eject forcefully.

éxtasis *m. psych.* ecstasy, trance accompanied by a pleasurable feeling.

extendedor *m.* stretcher.

extender *vi.* to extend, to stretch out; **extenderse** *vr.* to spread out.

extendido-a *a.* extended; widespread.

extensión *f.* extension, prolongation, straightening of a contracted finger or limb or aligning a dislocated or fractured bone.

extensor-a *a.* extensor, that has the property of extending.

extenuado-a *a.* extenuated, exhausted.

exterior *a.* exterior.

exteriorizar *v. surg.* to exteriorize, to temporarily expose a part or organ.

extinción *f.* extinction, cessation.

extinguir *vi.* to extinguish, to put out.

extirpación *f. surg.* extirpation, removal of a part or organ.

extirpar *v.* to eradicate, to remove.

extracción *f.* extraction, the process of removing, pulling, or drawing out.

extracelular *a.* extracellular, occurring outside a cell.

extracorporal *a.* extracorporeal, occurring outside the body.

extracto *m.* extract, a concentrated product.

extradural *a.* extradural. *V.* **epidural.**

extraer *vi.* to extract, to remove; to dig out.

extrañarse *vr.* to wonder, to question.

extraño-a *a.* extraneous. 1. unrelated to or outside an organism; 2. strange, rare; 3. foreign.

extraocular *a.* extraocular, outside the eye.

extrasístole *f.* extrasystole, arrhythmic beat of the heart, *pop.* skipped beat.

extravasado-a *a.* extravasated, rel. to the escape of fluid from a vessel or organ into the surrounding tissue.

extravascular *a.* extravascular, outside a vessel.

extremidad *f.* extremity; 1. the end portion; 2. a limb of the body; amputación de una ___ / limb amputation; rigidez de una ___ / limb rigidity.

extremo-a *a.* extreme, excessive.

extrínseco-a *a.* extrinsic, that comes from without.

extrofia *f.* extrophy, *V.* **eversión.**

extrovertido-a *a. psych.* extroverted, excessive manifestation and attention outside the self.

extubación *f. surg.* extubation, removal of a tube, such as the laryngeal tube.

exuberante *a.* exuberant, excessive proliferation; overabundant.

exudación *f.* exudation. *V.* **exudado.**

exudado *m.* exudate, inflammatory fluid such as pus or serum.

exudar *v.* to exude, to ooze out gradually through the tissues.

eyaculación *f.* ejaculation, sudden and rapid expulsion, such as the emission of semen.

eyacular *v.* to ejaculate, to expel fluid secretions such as semen.

eyección *f.* ejection, throwing out with force.

F

F *abr.* **Fahrenheit** / Fahrenheit.

f *abr.* **fallo** /failure; **femenino** / feminine; **fórmula** / formula; **función** / function.

fabela *f.* fabella, sesamoid fibrocartilage that can develop in the head of the gastrocnemius muscle.

fabricación *f.* fabrication. *V.* **confabulación.**

faceta *f.* facet, facette *Fr.* small smooth area on the surface of a hard structure such as a bone.

facetectomía *f. surg.* facetectomy, removal of the auricular facet of a vertebra.

facial *a.* facial, rel. to the face; huesos ___-es / ___ bones; nervios ___-es / ___ nerves; parálisis ___ / ___ paralysis; reflejo ___ / ___ reflex; espasmo ___ / ___ spasm.

facies *f.* (*pl.* **facies**) facies, expression or appearance of the face; ___ inexpresiva / masklike ___ ; ___ leontina / ___ leontina.

fácil *a.* easy; **-mente** *adv.* easily.

facilitar *v.* to facilitate, to make easier.

facticio-a *a.* factitious, not natural, artificial.

factor *m.* factor, element that contributes to produce an action; ___ angiogenético tumoral / tumor angiogenetic ___ ; ___ antihemofílico / antihemophilic ___ ; ___ de coagulación de la sangre / clotting ___ ; ___ dominante / dominant ___ ; ___ RH [*erre – ache*] / Rh ___ ; ___ reumatoideo / rheumatoid ___ .

facultad *f.* faculty. 1. capability to perform a normal function; 2. professional staff.

facultativo-a *a.* facultative. 1. not obligatory, voluntary; 2. of a professional nature; asistencia ___ médica / professional medical help; cuidado ___ / professional care.

fagocitario-a, **fagocítico-a** *a.* phagocytic, rel. to phagocytes.

fagocito *m.* phagocyte, cell that ingests and destroys microorganisms or other cells and foreign particles.

fagocitosis *f.* phagocytosis, the process of ingestion and digestion by phagocytes.

Fahrenheit, escala de *f.* Fahrenheit scale, a temperature scale with a freezing point of water at 32° and a normal boiling point at 212°.

faja *f.* girdle; band.

fajero *m.* swaddling band, strip of cloth used to restrain an infant's movements.

falange *f.* phalanx, any of the long bones of the fingers or toes.

falciforme *a.* falciform, shaped like a sickle; ligamento ____ del hígado / ____ ligament of the liver.

fálico-a *a.* phallic, rel. to or resembling the penis.

falda *f.* skirt.

falo *m.* phallus, the penis.

Falopio, trompas de *f.* Fallopian tubes, tubes leading from the uterus to the ovaries.

falsificación *f.* falsification, distortion or alteration of an event or object.

falsificador-a *m., f.* forger.

falsificar *vi.* to forge; to simulate.

falso-a *a.* false, untrue; ____ negativo / ____ negative; ____ positivo / ____ positive.

falta *f.* fault, error; sin ____ / without fail; for sure.

faltar *v.* to be lacking or wanting; to be absent.

falla *f.* defect, deficiency.

fallar *v.* to miss, to fail.

fallecer *vi.* to die.

fallecimiento *m.* death.

fallo *m.* failure; insufficiency; ____ cardíaco / heart ____ ; ____ renal / renal ____ ; ____ respiratorio / respiratory ____ .

Fallot, tetralogía de *f.* tetralogy of Fallot, congenital deformity of the heart involving defects in the great blood vessels and the walls of the heart chambers.

famélico-a *a.* famished.

familia *f.* family.

familiar *m.* family member; *a.* familiar, familial; descendencia ____ / kinship.

fanático-a *m., f.* fanatic; *a.* fanatic, fanatical.

Fanconi, síndrome de *m.* Fanconi's syndrome, congenital hypoplastic anemia.

fantasear *v.* to phantasize, to fancy, to imagine.

fantasía *f.* phantasy, the use of the imagination to transform an unpleasant reality into an imaginary satisfying experience.

fantasma *f.* phantasm, optical illusion, apparition.

fantoma *m.* phantom. 1. mental image; 2. a transparent model of the human body or any of its parts.

farina *f.* farina, corn flour.

faringe *f.* pharynx, part of the alimentary canal extending from the base of the skull to the esophagus.

faríngeo-a *a.* pharyngeal, rel. to the pharynx.

faringitis *f.* pharyngitis, infl. of the pharynx.

farmacéutico-a *m., f.* pharmacist, specialist in pharmacy; *a.* pharmaceutical, rel. to pharmacy.

farmacia *f.* pharmacy. 1. the study of drugs and their preparation and dispensation; 2. drugstore.

farmacocinética *f.* pharmacokinetics, the study *in vivo* of the metabolism and action of drugs.

farmacodependencia *f.* drug dependence.

farmacodinamia *f.* pharmacodynamics, the study of the effects of medication.

farmacogenética *f.* pharmacogenetics, the study of genetic factors as related to drug matabolism.

farmacología *f.* pharmacology, the study of drugs and their effect on living organisms.

farmacólogo-a *m.,f.* pharmacologist, pharmacist, specialist in pharmacology.

farmacopea *f.* pharmacopeia, a publication containing a listing of drugs and formulas as well as information providing standards for their preparation and dispensation.

farmacoterapia *f.* pharmacotherapy, treatment of a disease with the use of medications.

fascia *L.* fascia, fibrous connective tissue that envelops the body beneath the skin and encloses muscles, nerves and blood vessels; ____ aponeurótica / aponeurotic ____ , provides muscle protection; ____ de Buck / Buck's ____ , covers the penis; ____ de Colles / Colle's ____ , inner layer of the perineal fascia; ____ lata / lata ____ , protects the muscles of the thigh; ____ transversalis / transversalis ____ , between the transversalis muscle of the abdomen and the peritoneum.

fasciculación *f.* fasciculation. 1. formation of fascicles; 2. involuntary contraction of muscle fibers.

fascículo *m.* fascicle, fasciculus, a bundle of muscular and nervous fibers.

fasciectomía *f. surg.* fasciectomy, partial or total removal of a fascia.

fascitis *f.* fasciitis, infl. of a fascia.

fasciotomía *f. surg.* fasciotomy, incision or partition of a fascia.

fase *f.* phase, stage.

fásico-a *a.* phasic, rel. to a phase.

fatal *a.* fatal, deadly, mortal.

fatalidad *f.* fatality.

fatiga *f.* fatigue, extreme tiredness.

fatigarse *vr., vi.* to become fatigued, to get tired.

fauces *f.* fauces, the passage from the mouth to the pharynx.

favor *m.* favor, good deed.

favorable *a.* favorable, advantageous.

faz *f.* face.

fe *f.* faith, **de buena** ___ / in good ___.

fealdad *f.* ugliness.

febril *a.* febrile, having a body temperature above normal; convulsiones ___-es / ___ convulsions.

fecal *a.* fecal, containing or rel. to feces.

fecalito *m.* fecalith, intestinal concretion of fecal material.

fecaloma *m.* fecaloma, tumor-like accumulation of feces in the colon or rectum.

fecaluria *f.* fecaluria, presence of fecal material in the urine.

fécula *f.* starch.

feculento-a *a.* starchy; **alimentos** ___-s, almidones / ___ foods.

fecundación *f.* fecundation; fertilization.

fecundidad *f.* fecundity, fertility.

fecundo-a *a.* fruitful; fertile; abundant.

fecha *f.* [*día, mes o año*] date; ___ **de nacimiento** / birth date.

felación *f.* fellatio. *V.* **cunilinguo.**

felino-a *a.* feline, rel. to or resembling a cat.

feliz *a.* happy; felicitous.

femenino-a *a.* feminine.

feminismo *m.* feminism.

feminista *m., f.* feminist, one who fosters feminism.

feminización *f.* feminization, development of feminine characteristics.

femoral *a.* femoral, rel. to the femur; arco ___ profundo / deep ___ arch; arteria ___ / ___ artery; vena ___ / ___ vein.

fémur *m.* femur, the thighbone.

fenestración *f. surg.* fenestration. 1. creation of an opening in the inner ear to restore lost hearing; 2. the act of perforating.

fenestrado-a *a.* fenestrated, having openings.

fénico, fenol *a.* phenic, carbolic.

fenobarbital *m.* phenobarbital, barbiturate used as a hypnotic or sedative.

fenómeno *m.* phenomenon. 1. objective symptom of a disease; 2. event or manifestation; 3. *pop.* freak.

fenotipo *m.* phenotype, characteristics of a species produced by the environment and heredity.

feo-a *a.* ugly.

fermentación *f.* fermentation, splitting a complex compound into simpler ones by the action of enzymes or ferments.

fermentar *v.* to ferment, to produce fermentation.

fermento *m.* ferment, the product of fermentation.

ferritina *f.* ferritin, an iron complex which provides a way to store iron in the body.

ferroproteína *f.* ferroprotein, protein combined with a radical containing iron.

ferruginoso-a *a.* ferruginous, rel. to iron or that contains it.

fértil *a.* fertile, fruitful.

fertilidad *f.* fertility, fruitfulness.

fertilización *f.* fertilization.

fertilizante *m.* fertilizer.

férula *f.* splint, device made of any material such as wood, metal, or plaster, used to immobilize or support a fractured bone or a joint.

fetal *a.* fetal, rel. to the fetus; circulación ___ / ___ circulation; latido del corazón ___ / ___ heart tone; membranas ___-es / ___ membranes; monitorización ___ / ___ monitoring; retardo del crecimiento ___ / ___ growth retardation; viabilidad ___ / ___ viability.

feticidio *m.* feticide, destruction of the fetus in the uterus.

fetiche *m.* fetish.

fétido-a *a.* fetid, having a very bad odor.

feto *m.* fetus, phase of gestation between three months and the moment of birth.

fetoproteína *f.* fetoprotein, an antigen present in the human fetus.

fetor *m.* fetor, stench, offensive odor.

fetoscopio *m.* fetoscope, instrument used to visualize the fetus *in utero* to facilitate prenatal diagnosis.

fiasco *m.* fiasco; gross failure.

fibra *f.* fibre, filament; ___-s ópticas / fiber-optics.

fibrila, fibrilla *f.* fibril, a very small fiber.

fibrilación *f.* fibrillation. 1. involuntary or abnormal muscular contraction; ___ auricular / atrial, auricular ___, irregular movement of the atria; 2. formation of fibrils.

fibrilación-aleteo *f.* flutter-fibrillation, auricular activity that shows signs of flutter and fibrillation.

fibrilar *a.* fibrillar, fibrillary, rel. to a fibril.

fibrina *f.* fibrin, insoluble protein that is essential to the coagulation of blood.

fibrinógeno *m.* fibrinogen, protein present in blood plasma that converts into fibrin during blood clotting.

fibrinogenólisis *f.* fibrinogenolysis, the dissolution of fibrinogen in the circulating blood.

fibrinólisis *f.* fibrinolysis, the dissolution of fibrinogen by the action of enzymes.

fibrinoso-a *a.* fibrous, fibrinous, of the nature of fibers.

fibroadenoma *f.* fibroadenoma, a benign tumor composed of fibrous and glandular tissue.

fibroblasto *m.* fibroblast, a cell from which connective tissue develops.

fibrocartílago *m.* fibrocartilage, a type of cartilage in which the matrix contains a large amount of fibrous tissue.

fibrocístico-a, fibroquístico-a *a.* fibrocystic, cystic and fibrous in nature; enfermedad ___ de la mama / ___ disease of the breast.

fibroide *a.* fibroid, rel. to or of a fibrinous nature.

fibrolipoma *m.* fibrolipoma, tumor that contains fibrous and adipose tissue.

fibroma *m.* fibroma, a benign tumor composed of fibrous tissue.

fibromioma *m.* fibromyoma, tumor that contains muscular and fibrous tissue.

fibromuscular *a.* fibromuscular, of a fibrous and muscular nature.

fibroplasia *f.* fibroplasia, formation of fibrous tissue as seen in the healing of a wound. ___ retrolental / retrolental ___.

fibrosis *f.* fibrosis, abnormal formation of fibrous tissue; ___ cística / cystic ___; ___ intersticial del pulmón / diffuse interstitial pulmonary ___; ___ proliferativa / proliferative ___; ___ pulmonar / pulmonary ___; ___ retroperitoneal / retroperitoneal ___.

fibroso-a, fibrinoso-a *a.* fibrous, fibrinous; 1. rel. to or of the nature of fibrin; 2. threadlike.

fibrótico-a *a.* fibrotic, rel. to fibrosis.

ficticio *a.* fictitious, false.

fidelidad *f.* fidelity; loyalty.

fideo *m.* noodle.

fiebre *f.* fever; ampollas de ___ / ___ blisters; ___ de conejo / rabbit ___, tularemia; ___ de origen desconocido / ___ of unknown origin; ___ del heno / hay ___; ___ entérica / enteric ___, intestinal; ___ familiar del Mediterráneo / familiar Mediterranean ___; ___ intermitente / intermittent ___; ___ ondulante / undulant ___, brucellosis; ___ recurrente / relapsing ___; ___ remitente / remittent ___; ___ reumatoidea / rheumatoid ___; ___ tifoidea / typhoid ___; ___ de trinchera / trench ___; **tener** ___ / to run a temperature.

fiebre amarilla *f.* yellow fever, endemic disease of tropical areas, transmitted by the bite of a female mosquito, *Aedes aegypti,* and manifested by fever, jaundice, and albuminuria.

fiebre del valle *f.* valley fever. *V.* **coccidiomicosis.**

fiebre manchada de las Montañas Rocosas *f.* Rocky Mountain spotted fever, acute febrile disease caused by a germ transmitted by infected ticks.

figura *f.* form, shape; figure.

fijación *f.* fixation. 1. immobilization; 2. the act of focusing the eyes directly upon an object; 3. the act of being strongly attached to a particular person or object; 4. *psych.* interruption of the development of the personality before reaching maturity.

fijador *m.* fixative, a substance that is used to harden and preserve pathological specimens.

fijar *v.* to fix, to affix, [*una fractura*] to set.

filamento *m.* filament, strand, delicate fiber or fine thread.

film *m.* film; thin layer.

filtración *f.* filtration, the act of straining through a filter impeding passage of certain molecules.

filtrar *v.* to strain; **filtrarse** *vr.* to filter through, to filtrate.

filtro *m.* filter, any device used to strain liquids.

fimbria *f.* fimbria. 1. fingerlike structure; 2. appendage of certain bacteria.

fimosis *f.* phimosis, narrowness of the orifice of the prepuce that prevents its being drawn back over the glans penis.

fin *m.* end, conclusion; ¿con qué ___? / for what purpose?; **a** ___ **de** / in order to.

fin de semana *m.* weekend.

final *m.* end; **al** ___ / at the end; *a.* final, conclusive.

financiero-a *a.* financial, monetary; gastos ___ -s / ___ expense.

fingir *vi.* to fake, to malinger.

finito-a *a.* finite, having limits.

fino-a *a.* fine, as opposed to thick or coarse.

firma *f.* signature.

firmar *v.* to sign, to subscribe.

firme *a.* firm, secure.

física *f.* physics, the study of matter and its changes.

físicamente *adv.* physically, referring to the body as opposed to the mind.

físico *m.* 1. physique, appearance, figure; 2. **-a** *m., f.* physicist, specialist in physics; *a.* physical, rel. to the body and its condition; examen ___ / ___ examination; terapia ___ / ___ therapy.

fisicoquímico-a *a.* physicochemical, rel. to physics and to chemistry.

fisiología *f.* physiology, the study of the physical and chemical processes affecting organisms.

fisiológico-a *a.* physiologic, physiological, rel. to physiology; no ___ / unphysiological.

fisiólogo-a *m., f.* physiologist, a specialist in physiology.

fisión *f.* fission, a breaking up into parts; ___ nuclear / nuclear ___.

fisioterapia *f.* physiotherapy, treatment by means of physical manipulation and agents such as heat, light, and water.

fisonomía *f.* physiognomy, facial features.

fístula *f.* fistula, abnormal passage from a hollow organ to the skin or from one organ to another; ___ arteriovenosa / arteriovenous ___; ___ biliar / biliary ___; ___ del ano / anal ___.

fistular, fistuloso-a *a.* fistular, fistulous, rel. to or resembling a fistula.

fistulización *f.* fistulization, pathological or surgical formation of a fistula.

fisura *f.* fissure, cleft, a longitudinal opening.

fitobezoar *m.* phytobezoar, a concretion of undigested vegetable fiber that forms in the stomach or intestine.

fláccido-a, flácido-a *a.* flaccid, limber, lax.

flaco-a *a.* very thin, lanky.

flagelado-a *a.* flagellated, provided with flagella.

flageliforme *a.* flagelliform, shaped like a whip.

flagelo *m.* flagellum, prolongation or tail in the cells of some protozoa or bacteria.

flanco *m.* flank, loin, part of the body situated between the ribs and the upper border of the ilium.

flato *m.* flatus, gas or air in the stomach or intestines.

flatulencia *f.* flatulence, condition marked by distention and abdominal discomfort due to excessive gas in the gastrointestinal tract.

flebitis *f.* phlebitis, infl. of a vein.

flebograma *m.* phlebogram, venogram, a tracing of the venous pulse.

flebolito *m.* phlebolith, phlebolite, a calcareous deposit in a vein.

flebotomía *f. surg.* phlebotomy, venotomy, incision into a vein for the purpose of drawing blood.

flegmasia *f.* phlegmasia, inflammation.

flema *f.* phlegm. 1. thick mucus; 2. one of the four humors of the body.

flemático-a *a.* phlegmatic. 1. that produces phlegm; 2. apathetic.

flemón *m.* phlegmon, an infl. of the cellular tissue.

flexibilidad *f.* flexibility, pliability, the capability to flex.

flexible *a.* flexible, bendable, that can change.

flexión *f.* flexion, flexure, the act of bending.

flexionar *v.* to flex, to bend.

flexor *m.* flexor, a muscle that can flex a joint.

flexura *f.* flexure, fold, curvature, bend; ___ hepática / hepatic ___, right curvature of the colon; ___ esplénica / splenic ___, left curvature of the colon; ___ sigmoidea / sigmoid ___, the curved part of the colon that precedes the rectum.

floculación *f.* flocculation, precipitation and agglomeration of very small invisible particles into large visible flakes.

flogosis *f.* phlogosis. *V.* **flegmasia**.

flojera *f.* weakness.

flojo-a *a.* weak, flaccid; sluggish.

flor *f.* flower.

flora *f.* flora, group of bacteria within a given organ; ___ intestinal / intestinal ___.

florido-a *a.* florid, showing a bright red coloring of the skin.

flotador *m.* floater, macule, specks in the vision.

flotante *a.* floating, free, not adhered.

flotar *v.* to float.

fluctuación, fluctuamiento *f., m.* fluctuation, wavering, wavelike movements produced by vibrations of body fluids on palpation.

fluctuar *v.* to fluctuate, to waver, to go back and forth.

fluidez *f.* fluidity, liquidity.

fluído *m.* fluid, liquid.

fluir *vi.* to flow.

flujo *m.* afflux, flux. 1. large amount of fluid discharge from a cavity or surface of the body; medidor de ____ / flowmeter; 2. the rush of blood or liquid; 3. menstruation.

flúor *m.* fluorine, gaseous chemical element.

fluoresceína *f.* fluorescin, red dye.

fluorescencia *f.* fluorescence, the property of a substance to emit light when exposed to certain types of radiation such as X-rays.

fluorescente *a.* fluorescent, rel. to fluorescence; anticuerpo ____ / ____ antibody; técnica del anticuerpo ____ / ____ treponemal antibody absorption test.

fluoridación *f.* fluoridation, fluoridization, addition of fluorides to water.

fluoroscopía *f.* fluoroscopy, examination of tissues and structures of the body using the fluoroscope.

fluoroscopio *m.* fluoroscope, instrument that makes X-rays visible on a fluorescent screen.

fluorosis *f.* fluorosis, excess fluoride content.

fluoruro *m.* fluoride, combination of fluorine with a metal or a metalloid.

fobia *f.* phobia, abnormal irrational fear.

fóbico-a *a.* phobic, rel. to phobia.

focal *a.* focal, rel. to focus.

foco *m.* focus, the main point or principal spot.

fofo-a *a.* flabby, soft.

fogaje *m.* hot flash.

foliculitis *f.* folliculitis, infl. of a follicle, usu. in reference to a hair follicle.

folículo *m.* follicle, sac or pouchlike secretory depression or cavity; ____ atrésico / atretic ____; ____ de Graaf, ovárico / Graafian, ovaric ____; ____ gástrico / gastric ____; ____ piloso / hair ____; ____ tiroideo / thyroid ____.

folleto *m.* pamphlet.

fomento *m.* hot compress.

fomes *L.* (*pl.* **fomites**) fomes, an element that can absorb and transmit infectious agents.

fondillo *m.* buttocks.

fondo *m.* bottom; ____ del ojo / eyeground.

fonética *f.* phonetics, the study of speech and pronunciation.

fonético-a *a.* phonetic, rel. to the voice and articulated sounds.

fonograma *m.* phonogram, a graphic that indicates the intensity of a sound.

fonoscopio *m.* phonoscope, a device that registers heart sounds.

fontanela *f.* fontanel, fontanelle, soft spot in the skull of a newborn that closes as the cranial bones develop; caída de la ____ / fallen ____.

foramen *m.* foramen, orifice, passage, opening; ____ intervertebral / intervertebral ____; ____ óptico / optic ____; ____ oval / oval ____; ____ sacrociático mayor / sciatic, greater ____; ____ yugular / jugular ____.

fórceps *m.* forceps, a surgical tong-like instrument used to grasp, pull or manipulate tissues or body parts.

forense *a.* forensic, rel. to the courts; laboratorio ____ / ____ laboratory; médico ____ / ____ physician.

forma *f.* form, shape; established manner of doing something; ____ frustrada / forme fruste *Fr.* an aborted or atypical form of a disease.

formación *f.* formation, the manner in which something is arranged.

formaldehido *m.* formaldehyde, antiseptic.

formalina *f.* formalin, formaldehyde compound.

formar *v.* to form, to shape.

formicación *f.* formication, skin sensation comparable to one produced by crawling insects.

fórmula *f.* formula, a prescribed way or model.

formulario *m.* 1. form, [*planilla*] blank; 2. formulary, prescription tablet, a book of formulas.

fórnix *m.* fornix, vault-like structure such as the vagina.

fortalecer *vi.* to fortify, to strengthen.

fortificar *vi.* V. **fortalecer.**

forúnculo *m.* boil.

fosa *f.* fossa, cavity, depression, hole; ____

etmoidal / ethmoid ____; ____ glenoidea / glenoid ____; ____ interpenduncular / interpenduncular ____; ____ mandibular / mandibular ____; ____ nasal / nasal ____; ____ navicular / navicular ____; ____ supraclavicular / supraclavicular ____; ____ yugular / jugular ____.

fósforo *m.* phosphorus.

fotocoagulación *f.* photocoagulation, localized tissue coagulation by an intense controlled ray of light or laser beam, esp. used in surgery of the eye.

fotofobia *f.* photophobia, fear of light.

fotólisis *f.* photolysis, desintegration by rays of light.

fototerapia *f.* phototherapy, light therapy, exposure to sun rays or to an artificial light for therapeutic purposes.

fóvea *f.* fovea, small depression, esp. used in reference to the central fossa of the retina.

fracaso *m.* failure; neurosis del ____ / ____ neurosis.

fracción *f.* fraction, separable part of a unit.

fractura *f.* fracture, breaking or separation of a bone; ____ abierta / open ____; ____ cerrada / closed ____; ____ conminuta / comminuted ____; ____ completa / complete ____; ____ con hundimiento / depressed ____; ____ de línea fina / hairline ____; ____ en caña o tallo verde / greenstick ____; ____ espiral / spiral ____; ____ impactada / impacted ____; ____ con luxación / dislocation ____; ____ patológica / pathologic ____; ____ por avulsión / avulsion ____; ____ por compresión / compression ____; ____ por estallamiento / blow out ____; ____ por herida de bala / gunshot ____; ____ por sobrecarga / stress ____.

fracturar *v.* to fracture, to break a bone.

frágil *a.* fragile, brittle; breakable.

fragilidad *f.* fragility, disposition to tear or break easily.

fragmentación *f.* fragmentation, splitting.

fragmento *m.* fragment, small piece of a whole.

frambesia *f.* frambesia, yaws, pian, infectious tropical disease caused by a spirochete of the genus *Treponema pertenue* and manifested by a primary cutaneous lesion followed by raspberry-like ulcers that spread to different areas of the body.

francés *m.* [*idioma*] French; [*nativo-a*] French; **francés, francesa** *a.* French.

frasco *m.* flask, bottle.

frase *f.* phrase.

frazada *f.* blanket.

frecuencia *f.* frequency; con ____ / frequently.

frecuente *a.* frequent; **-mente** *adv.* frequently.

freír *vi.* to fry.

frémito *m.* fremitus, a vibration that can be detected during auscultation or on palpation, such as the chest vibrations during coughing.

frenectomía *f. surg.* frenectomy, removal of the frenum.

frenesí *m.* frenzy; madness.

frenético-a *a.* phrenetic, frantic, raving, maniacal.

frenillo *m.* frenum of the tongue; con ____ / tongue-tied.

frente *f.* forehead, brow; *prep.* in front; **en** ____ **de** / in ____ of; ____ **a** ____ / face to face; ____ **a** across from.

frenulum *m.* frenulum, frenum, small membranous fold that limits the movement of an organ or part.

fresa *f.* bur, burr. 1. [*dental*] dental drill; 2. strawberry; marca en ____ / strawberry mark.

fresco *m.* refreshing air; hace ____ / it is cool.

freudiano-a *a. psych.* Freudian, rel. to the doctrines of Sigmund Freud, Viennese neurologist, father of psychoanalysis, (1856–1939).

friable *a.* friable, that pulverizes easily.

fricción *f.* friction, rub; ____ de alcohol / alcohol rub.

frigidez *f.* frigidity, coldness, inability to respond to sexual arousement.

frígido-a *a.* frigid, cold.

frijol *m.* bean.

frío-a *a.* cold; [*persona*] without warmth or affection; hace ____ / it is cold.

friolento-a *a.* chilly; too sensitive to cold.

frito-a *a. pp.* of **freír**, fried.

Frohlich, síndrome de *m.* Frohlich's syndrome, adiposogenital dystrophy, manifested by obesity and sexual infantilism.

frontal *a.* frontal, rel. to the forehead; hueso ____ / ____ bone; músculo ____ / ____ muscle; senos ____-es / ____ sinuses.

frotar *v.* to rub; ____ suavemente / to stroke.

frote *m.* rub. 1. friction; massage; 2. sound

heard on auscultation, produced by two dry surfaces rubbing against each other.

frotis *m.* smear, sample of blood or a secretion for the purpose of microscopic study.

fructosa *f.* fructose, sugar of fruits; levulose.

fruta *f.* fruit.

ftiriasis *f.* phthiriasis. V. **pediculosis.**

fuego *m.* fire.

fuente *f.* source, origin; fountain.

fuera *adv.* out, outside; **estar** ___ / to be ___ or away; ___ de sí / beside oneself; **hacia** ___ / outward.

fuerte *a.* strong, vigorous; hard.

fuerza *f.* force, strength; power; ___ catabólica / catabolic ___ ; ___ de gravedad / ___ of gravity; **no tengo** ___ / I feel weak.

fuga *f.* flight; *psych.* ___ de ideas / ___ of ideas, interrupted line of thought and talk.

fulguración *f.* fulguration, use of electric current to destroy or coagulate tissue.

fulminante *a.* fulminant, appearing suddenly and with great intensity, esp. in reference to a disease or pain.

fumador-a *m., f.* person who smokes heavily.

fumante *a.* fuming, that gives forth a visible vapor.

fumar *v.* to smoke.

fumigación *f.* fumigation, extermination or disinfection through the use of vapors.

fumigante *m.* fumigant, agent used in fumigation.

función *f.* function.

funcional *a.* functional, having practical use or value.

funcionamiento *m.* performance; functioning, working.

funcionar *v.* to function, to work.

funda *f.* pillow case; covering.

fundir *v.* to fuse, to liquify with heat.

funeral *m.* funeral.

funeraria *f.* funeral parlor, mortuary; **empresario de** ___ / mortician.

fungemia *f.* fungemia, presence of fungi in the blood.

fungicida *m.* fungicide, agent that destroys fungi.

fungistasis *f.* fungistasis, the action of thwarting the growth of fungi.

fungoso-a *a.* fungous, fungal, rel. to fungi.

furioso-a *a.* furious, frantic.

furor *m.* furor, extreme anger.

furosemida *f.* furosemide, diuretic agent.

fusiforme *a.* fusiform, spindle shaped.

fusión *f.* fusion, the act of melting: ___ nuclear / nuclear ___.

futuro *m.* future; **-a** *a.* future.

G

g *abr.* **género** / gender; **glucosa** / glucosa; **gramo** / gram; **grano** / grain.

gabinete *m.* cabinet.

gafas *f.* spectacles, eyeglasses.

gago-a *m., f.* stutterer.

gaguear *v.* to stutter.

galactagogo, galactógeno *m.* galactagogue, agent that stimulates the flow of milk.

galactasa *f.* galactase, enzyme present in milk.

galactocele *m.* galactocele, breast cyst containing milk.

galactosa *f.* galactose, monosaccharide derived from lactose by the action of an enzyme or mineral acid.

galactosemia *f.* galactosemia, congenital absence of the enzyme necessary to convert galactose to glucose and its derivatives.

galactosuria *f.* galactosuria, milk-like urine due to the presence of galactose.

galactoterapia *f.* galactotherapy. 1. the treatment of breast-fed infants by the administration of medication to the nursing mother; 2. therapeutic use of milk in the diet.

galio *m.* gallium, metallic element.

galvánico-a *a.* galvanic, rel. to galvanism; **batería** ___ / ___ battery; **célula** ___ / ___ cell; **corriente** ___ / ___ current.

galvanismo *m.* galvanism, therapeutic use of a direct electrical current.

galvanocauterización *f.* galvanocautery. V. **electrocauterización.**

galvanómetro *m.* galvanometer, instrument that measures currents by electromagnetic action.

galleta *f.* cracker.

gallina *f.* hen.

gallo *m.* cock, rooster.

gameto *m.* gamete, sexual cell, masculine or feminine.

gametocida *m.* gametocide, agent that kills gametes.

gametocito *m.* gametocyte, a cell that divides to produce gametes, such as the ma larial parasite when taken into the mosquito host.

gametogénesis *f.* gametogenesis, development of gametes.

gamma globulina *f.* gamma globulin, a class of antibodies produced in the lymph tissue or synthetically.

gammagrama *m.* scintiscan, a two dimensional image representation of the interior distribution of a radiopharmaceutical in a previously selected area for diagnostic purposes.

gamopatía *f.* gammopathy, disorder manifested by an excessive amount of immunoglobulins due to an abnormal proliferation of lymphoid cells.

gana *f.* desire, inclination; **tener** ___-s **de** / to desire, to want to; **de buena** ___ / willingly; **de mala** ___ / unwillingly.

ganancia *f.* gain; advantage.

ganar *v.* to win; to earn.

gancho *m.* hook; clasp; -s [*dental*] braces.

gangliectomía, ganglionectomía *f. surg.* gangliectomy, ganglionectomy, excision of a ganglion.

ganglio *m.* ganglion, collection of nerve cells resembling a knot; ___ basal / basal ___; ___ carotídeo / carotid ___; ___ celíaco / celiac ___.

gangliocito *m.* gangliocyte, a ganglion cell.

ganglioctomía *f. surg.* ganglioctomy, excision of a ganglion.

ganglioglioma *m.* ganglioglioma, tumor with a large number of ganglionic cells.

ganglioma *m.* ganglioma, tumor of a ganglion, esp. a lymphatic ganglion.

ganglión *m.* ganglion, a cystic tumor that develops in a tendon or an aponeurosis, often seen in the wrist, the heel or the knee.

ganglionar *a.* ganglionic, rel. to a ganglion; bloqueo ___ / ___ blockade.

gangrena *f.* gangrene, local death, destruction and putrefaction of body tissue due to interrupted blood supply.

Gantrisin *f.* Gantrisin, trade name for sulfisoxazole, an antibacterial agent used in the treatment of urinary infections.

garabato *m.* scribble.

garantía *f.* guarantee, warranty.

garantizar *vi.* to guarantee, to warrant.

garbanzo *m.* chickpea.

garganta *f.* throat, the area of the larynx and the pharynx; anterior part of the neck; dolor de ___ / sore ___.

gárgara, gargarismo *f., m.* gargarism, gargle, gargling, rinsing of the throat and the mouth; **hacer** ___-s / to gargle.

gargolismo *m.* gargoylism, hereditary condition characterized by skeletal abnormalities and sometimes mental retardation.

garra *f.* claw; mano en ___ / ___ hand; pie en ___ / ___ foot.

garrapata *f.* tick, bloodsucking acarid that transmits specific diseases; picadura de ___ / ___ bite.

garrotillo *m.* croup.

gas *m.* gas; ___ lacrimógeno / tear ___; ___ mostaza / mustard ___; ___ neurotóxico / nerve ___; ___-es arteriales / arterial blood ___-es; ___-es en la sangre / blood ___-es.

gasa *f.* gauze; ___ antiséptica / antiseptic ___; compresa de ___ / ___ compress.

gaseoso-a *a.* gaseous, of the nature of gas.

gasolina *f.* gasoline; envenenamiento por ___ / ___ poisoning.

gastado-a *a.* worn out.

gastar *v.* [*dinero*] to spend; **gastarse** *vr.* to wear out.

gasto *m.* [*cardíaco*] output; expenditure.

gastralgia *f.* gastralgia, stomach ache.

gastrectomía *f. surg.* gastrectomy, removal of part or all of the stomach.

gástrico-a *a.* gastric, rel. to the stomach; digestión ___ / ___ digestion; jugo ___ / ___ juice; lavado ___ / ___ lavage; vaciamiento ___ / ___ emptying.

gastrina *f.* gastrin, hormone secreted by the stomach.

gastritis *f.* gastritis, infl. of the stomach; ___ aguda / acute ___; ___ crónica / chronic ___.

gastroanálisis *m.* gastric analysis, analysis of the stomach contents.

gastrocnemio *m.* gastrocnemius, large calf muscle.

gastrocolostomía *f. surg.* gastrocolostomy, anastomosis of the stomach and the colon.

gastroduodenal *a.* gastroduodenal, rel. to the stomach and the duodenum.

gastroduodenoscopía *f.* gastroduodenoscopy, visual examination of the stomach and the duodenum with an endoscope.

gastroenteroanastomosis *f. surg.* gastroenteroanastomosis, anastomosis of the stomach and the small intestine.

gastroenterocolitis *f.* gastroenterocolitis, infl. of the stomach and the small intestine.

gastroenterostomía *f. surg.* gastroenterostomy, anastomosis of the stomach and the small bowel.

gastroepiploico-a *a.* gastroepiploic, rel. to the stomach and the epiplon.

gastroesofagitis *f.* gastroesophagitis. *V.* **esofagogastritis.**

gastrogavage *m.* gastrogavage, artificial feeding into the stomach through a tube.

gastroileostomía *f. surg.* gastroileostomy, anastomosis of the stomach and the ileum.

gastrointestinal *a.* gastrointestinal, rel. to the stomach and the intestine; decompresión ___ / ___ decompression; examen ___ superior / upper ___ examination; sangramiento ___ / ___ bleeding.

gastrorragia *f.* gastrorrhagia, hemorrhaging from the stomach.

gastroscopía *f.* gastroscopy, examination of the stomach and the abdominal cavity with a gastroscope.

gastroscopio *m.* gastroscope, endoscope for visualizing the inside of the stomach.

gastrostomía *f. surg.* gastrostomy, creation of a gastric fistula through the abdominal wall.

gastroyeyunostomía *f. surg.* gastrojejunostomy, anastomosis of the stomach and the jejunum.

gástrula *f.* gastrula, an early stage in embryonic development.

gato-a *m., f.* cat.

gatear *v.* to crawl on all fours, such as babies.

gelatina *f.* gelatin.

gelatinoso-a *a.* gelatinous, having the consistency of or rel. to gelatin.

gemelo-a *m., f.* twin, either of two offspring born of the same pregnancy; ___ dicigótico-a / dizygotic ___; ___ encigótico-a / enzygotic ___; ___ fraternal / fraternal ___; ___ idéntico-a / identical ___; ___ monocigótico-a / monozygotic ___; ___ siamés-a / Siamese ___; ___ verdadero-a / true ___.

gemido *m.* groan, moan.

gemir *vi.* to groan, to moan.

gen, gene *m.* gene, basic unit of hereditary traits; ___ dominante / dominant ___; ___ letal / lethal ___; ___ ligado al sexo / sex-linked ___; ___ recesivo / recessive ___.

generación *f.* generation, procreation. 1. the act of creating a new organism; 2. the whole body of individuals born within a time span of approximately thirty years.

generador *m.* generator.

general *a.* general; estado ___ / ___ condition; tratamiento ___ / ___ treatment; *adv.* -mente generally.

generalización *f.* generalization.

generalizar *v.* to generalize.

genérico-a *a.* generic, rel. to the gender; nombre ___ / ___ name, not protected by a trademark.

género *m.* 1. gender, sex of an individual; 2. genus, a category of biological classification.

generoso-a *a.* generous.

génesis *f.* genesis, origin, beginning; reproduction.

genética *f.* genetics, branch of biology that studies heredity and the laws that govern it; ___ médica / medical ___.

genético-a *a.* genetic, rel. to heredity or genetics; asesoramiento ___ / ___ counseling; ingeniería o construcción ___ / ___ engineering; patrón ___ / ___ code.

genio *m.* genius, extraordinary mental power or faculties.

geniplastia *f. surg.* genyplasty, reconstructive surgery of the jaw.

genital *a.* genital, rel. to the genitals.

genitales *m. pl.* genitals, genitalia, reproductive organs; *pop.* privates; ___ externos / ___ externalia.

genocidio *m.* genocide, systematic extermination of an ethnic or social group of people.

genoma *m.* genome, the complete basic haploid set of chromosomes of an organism.

genotipo *m.* genotype, the basic genetic constitution of an individual.

gentamicina *f.* gentamicin, antibiotic that acts effectively against many gram-negative bacteria.

gente *f.* people, persons in general.

genuflexión *f.* genuflexion, bending of the knee.

genuino-a *a.* genuine, authentic, real.

genu valgum *L.* genu valgum, abnormal inward curvature of the knees that begins at infancy as a result of osseus deficiency, *pop.* knock-knee.

genu varum *L.* genu varum, abnormal outward curvature of the knees, *pop.* bowleg.

geofagia, geofagismo *f., m.* geophagia, geophagism, geophagy, propensity to eat soil or similar substances.

geriatra *m., f.* geriatrician, specialist in geriatrics.

geriatría *f.* geriatrics, a branch of medicine that deals with the problems of aging and the treatment of diseases and ills of old age.

germen *m.* germ. 1. microorganism or bacteria, esp. one that causes diseases; 2. a substance that can develop and form an organism.

germicida *m.* germicide, germicidal, agent that destroys germs.

germinal *a.* germinal, rel. to or of the nature of germs.

germinoma *m.* germinoma, neoplasm of germinal cells in the testis or ovaries.

geromorfismo *m.* geromorphism, premature senility.

gerontología *f.* gerontology. *V.* **geriatría.**

gerundio *m. gr.* gerund, the present participle of the verb.

gestación *f.* gestation, childbearing, pregnancy.

gestacional *a.* rel. to gestation; edad ___ / fetal maturity, chronologic.

Gestalt *m.* Gestalt, *psych,* a school of thought that explains behavior as an integrated response to a situation as a whole.

gesticular *v.* to gesticulate, to communicate or express by means of gestures or signs.

gesto *m.* gesture.

Ghon, foco, lesión, tubérculo de *m.* Ghon's primary lesion, tubercule, first tubercular lesion in children.

giardiasis *f.* giardiasis, common intestinal infection with *Giardia lamblia* that spreads by contaminated food or water or through direct contact.

gibosidad *f.* gibbosity, the condition of having a hump.

giboso-a *a.* gibbous, humpbacked.

Giemsa, coloración de *f.* Giemsa's stain, stain used for blood smears in lab tests.

gigante *m.* giant, unnaturally large; *a.* giant.

gigantismo *m.* gigantism, excessive development of the body or some of its parts; ___ acromegálico / acromegalic ___; ___ eunocoide / eunochoid ___; ___ normal / normal ___.

Gilles de la Tourette, síndrome de *m.* Gilles de la Tourette syndrome, a childhood disease affecting boys more frequently than girls, thought to be of a neurological nature and manifested by muscular anomalies; sometimes accompanied at puberty by involuntary uttering of obscenities and swearing.

Gimbernat, ligamento de *m.* Gimbernat's ligament, membrane attached to the inguinal ligament on one end and the pubis on the other.

gimnasia, gimnástica *f.* gymnastics.

ginandroide *a.* gynandroid, having enough hermaphroditic characteristics to give the appearance of the opposite sex.

ginecología *f.* gynecology, the study of the female reproductive organs.

ginecológico-a *a.* gynecologic, gynecological, rel. to gynecology.

ginecólogo-a *m., f.* gynecologist, specialist in gynecology.

ginecomastia *f.* gynecomastia, excessive development of the mammary glands in the male.

gingiva *L.* gingiva, gum, tissue around the neck of the teeth.

gingivitis *f.* gingivitis, infl. of the gums.

glacial *a.* glacial, resembling or rel. to ice.

glande *m.* glans, gland-like mass located at the distal end of the penis (glans penis), or clitoris (glans clitoridis).

glándula *f.* gland, an organ that secretes or excretes substances that have specific functions or that eliminate products from the organism; ___ inflamada / swollen ___.

glándulas endocrinas *f. pl.* endocrine glands, glands that secrete hormones directly absorbed into the blood or lymph such as the gonads and the pituitary and adrenal glands.

glándulas exocrinas *f. pl.* exocrine glands, glands that discharge their secretion through a duct, such as the mammary and sweat glands.

Glanzmann, trombastenia de *f.* Glanzmann's thrombasthenia, rare congenital disease caused by platelet abnormality.

Glasgow, escala de *f.* Glasgow's scale, instrument used to evaluate the degree of coma.

glaucoma *m.* glaucoma, eye disease caused by intraocular hypertension that results in hardening of the eye, atrophia of the retina, and sometimes blindness; ___ absoluto / absolutum ___, final stage of acute glaucoma; ___ infantil / infantile ___, between birth and three years of age; ____ juvenil / juvenile ____, in older children and young adults without enlargement of the eyeball.

glenohumeral *a.* glenohumeral, rel. to the humerus and the glenoid cavity.

glenoideo-a *a.* glenoid, socket-like cavity; cavidad ____ / ____ cavity; fosa ____ / ____ fossa.

glía *f.* glia. *V.* **neuroglia.**

gliacito *m.* gliacyte, neuroglia cell.

glicemia, glucemia *f.* glycemia, concentration of glucose in the blood.

glicerina, glicerol *f.* glycerine, glycerol, an alcohol found in fats.

glicina *f.* glycine, a nonessential amino acid.

glicógeno, glucógeno *m.* glycogen, polysaccharide usu. stored in the liver that converts into glucose as needed.

glicogenólisis, glucogenólisis *f.* glycogenolysis, the breakdown of glycogen into glucose.

glicólisis *f.* glycolysis, breakdown of sugar into simpler compounds.

glicosuria *f.* glycosuria. *V.* **glucosuria.**

glioblastoma *f.* glioblastoma, a type of brain tumor.

glioma *m.* glioma, malignant brain tumor composed of neuroglia cells.

glioneuroma *f.* glioneuroma, a glioma combined with a neuroma.

globina *f.* globin, protein that is a part of hemoglobin

globo *m.* globe, spherical body.

globular *a.* globular, spherical.

globulina *f.* globulin, one of a class of simple proteins that is insoluble in water but soluble in moderately concentrated salt solutions; ____ antilinfocítica / antilymphocite ____, immunosuppressant; gamma ____ / gamma ____, a family of proteins capable of carrying antibodies.

globulinuria *f.* globulinuria, presence of globulin in the urine.

glóbulo *m.* globule, small spherical mass; ____ blanco / white blood cell, leukocyte; ____ rojo / red blood cell, erythrocyte.

globus *L.* globus, spheric body; ____ histérico / ____ hystericus, sensation of having a lump in the throat.

glomerular *a.* glomerular, rel. or resembling a glomerulus; cluster-like.

glomerulitis *f.* glomerulitis, infl. of the glomeruli, esp. the renal glomeruli.

glomérulo *m.* glomerulus, collection of capillaries in the shape of a tiny ball, present in the kidney.

glomeruloesclerosis *f.* glomerulosclerosis, degenerative process within the renal glomeruli that occurs in renal arteriosclerosis and diabetes.

glomerulonefritis *f.* glomerulonefritis, Bright's disease, infl. of the kidney glomeruli.

glomo *m.* glomus, small mass of arterioles rich in nerve supply and connected directly to veins.

glosa *f.* glossa, tongue.

glosalgia *f.* glossalgia, pain in the tongue.

glosectomía *f. surg.* glossectomy, partial or total excision of the tongue.

glositis *f.* glossitis, infl. of the tongue; ____ aguda / acute ____, associated with stomatitis.

glosodinia *f.* glossodynia. *V.* **glosalgia.**

glosoplejía *f.* glossoplegia, partial or total paralysis of the tongue.

glosotomía *f.* glossotomy, incision in the tongue.

glotis *f.* glottis, opening in the upper part of the larynx between the vocal cords; vocal apparatus of the larynx.

glotitis *f.* glottitis. *V.* **glositis.**

glucagon *m.* glucagón, one of the two hormones produced by the islets of Langerhan that increase the concentration of glucose in the blood and also have an antiinflammatory effect.

glucagonoma *m.* glucagonoma, malignant glucagon secreting tumor.

glucocorticoide *a.* glucocorticoid, adrenal cortical hormones active in protecting against stress and affecting carbohydrate and protein metabolism.

glucofosfato deshidrogenasa *m.* glucose-6-phosphate dehydrogenase, enzyme found in the liver and kidney, important in the conversion of glyceryl to glucosa.

glucogénesis *f.* glucogenesis, formation of glucose from glycogen.

gluconeogénesis *f.* gluconeogenesis, glyconeogenesis, formation of glycogen in the liver from noncarbohydrate sources.

glucopenia *f.* glycopenia. *V.* **hipoglicemia.**

glucopéxico-a *a.* glycopexic, that stores sugar.

glucosa *f.* glucose, dextrose, grape sugar, the main source of energy for living organisms;

nivel de ____ en la sangre / blood level of ____; prueba de tolerancia a la ____ / ____ tolerance test.

glucósido *m.* glucoside, glycoside, natural or synthetic compound that liberates sugar upon hydrolysis.

glucosuria *f.* glucosuria, glycosuria, abnormal amount of sugar in the urine; ____ diabética / diabetic ____; ____ pituitaria / pituitary ____; ____ renal / renal ____.

glutamato *m.* glutamate, salt of glutamic acid.

gluten *m.* gluten, albuminoid vegetable matter.

glúteo-a *a.* gluteal, rel. to the buttocks; pliegue ____ / ____ fold; reflejo ____ / ____ reflex.

gnosia *f.* gnosia, ability to perceive and recognize people and things.

gola *f.* throat; *pop.* gullet.

goloso-a *m.*, *f.* person very fond of sweets and snacks; *a.* fond of snacking; sweet tooth.

golpe *m.* blow; bruise; bang; ____ **en la cabeza** / ____ to the head.

golpear *v.* to beat, to hit.

goma *f.* 1. gumma, syphilitic tumor; 2. gum rubber; [*de borrar*] eraser; glue.

gónada *f.* gonad, a gland that produces sex cells (gametes). In males the gonads are the testes, in females, the ovaries.

gonadal *a.* gonadal, rel. to a gonad gland; disgenesia ____ / ____ dysgenesis, malformation.

gonadotropina *f.* gonadotropin, gonad stimulating hormone; ____ coriónica / chorionic ____, present in the blood and the urine of the female during pregnancy and used in the pregnancy test; ____ hipofisaria / anterior pituitary ____; hormona que estimula la secreción de ____ / ____ releasing hormone.

gonión *m.* gonion, the most inferior, posterior, and lateral point on the external angle of the mandible.

goniopuntura *f. surg.* goniopuncture, puncture of the anterior chamber of the eye as a means to treat glaucoma.

goniotomía *f. surg.* goniotomy, procedure to relieve congenital glaucoma.

gonococo *m.* gonococcus, microorganism of the species *Neisseria gonorrhoeae* that causes gonorrhea.

gonorrea *f.* gonorrhea, highly contagious catarrhal bacterial infection of the genital mucosa, sexually transmitted.

gonorreico-a *a.* gonorrheal, rel. to gonorrhea; artritis ____ / ____ arthritis.

gordiflón-a *m.*, *f.* fat, flabby person.

gordo-a *a.* fat, overweight.

gordura *f.* fatness, corpulence.

gorra *f.* cap, head covering.

gota *f.* gout. 1. a hereditary disease caused by a defect in uric acid metabolism; 2. drop, a very small portion of a liquid.

gotear *v.* to drip; to leak.

goteo *m.* drip, dripping.

gotica *f.* droplet.

gotero *m.* dropper; ____ para los ojos / eye ____.

gozar *vi.* to enjoy, to rejoice.

grabar *v.* to record.

grabadora *f.* tape recorder.

gracias *f. pl.* thanks; **muchas** ____ / thank you very much.

gracilis *m.* gracilis, long internal muscle of the thigh.

grado *m.* [*temperatura*] degree; [*evaluación*] grade.

gradual *a.* gradual; -**mente** *adv.* gradually.

gradiente *a.* gradient, index or curve representing the increase or decrease of a variable.

gráfica, gráfico *f.*, *m.* graph, chart, diagram.

grafología *f.* graphology, the study of handwriting as an indication of an individual's character, also used as an aid in diagnosis.

Gram, método de *m.* Gram's method, a system of coloring bacteria for the purpose of identifying them upon analysis.

gramática *f.* grammar.

gramicidina *f.* gramicidin, antibacterial substance produced by *Bacillis brevis,* active locally against gram-positive bacteria.

gramnegativo *m.* gram-negative, bacteria or tissue that loses coloration when subjected to Gram's method.

gramo *m.* gram, unit of weight in the metrical system.

grampositivo *m.* gram-positive, bacteria or tissue that retains coloration when subjected to Gram's method.

gran, grande *a.* big, large.

grano *m.* grain, granum, a small spherical mass; bead.

granulación *f.* granulation, round, small, fleshy masses that form in a wound.

granular, granuloso-a *a.* granular, made up or marked by grains; cilindro granuloso / _____ cast, urinary cast seen in degenerative and inflammatory nephropathy.

gránulo *m.* granule, small grain or particle; _____ acidófilo / acidophil _____, a stain with acid dyes; _____ basófilo / basophil _____, a stain with basic dyes.

granulocito *m.* granulocyte, leukocyte containing granules.

granulocitopenia *f.* granulocytopenia, deficiency in the number of granulocytes in the blood.

granuloma *m.* granuloma, tumor or neoplasm of granular tissue; _____ de cuerpo extraño / foreign body _____; _____ infeccioso / infectious _____; _____ inguinal / inguinale _____; _____ ulcerativo de los genitales / venereum _____.

granulomatosis *f.* granulomatosis, multiple granuloma.

granulopenia *f.* granulopenia. *V.* **granulocitopenia.**

granulosa *f.* granulosa, ovarian membrane of epithelial cells; tumor de células de la _____ / _____ cell tumor; tumor de la _____ teca / _____ teca cell tumor.

grapar *v.* to staple; surgical procedure.

grasa *f.* fat, adipose tissue.

grasiento-a, grasoso-a *a.* fatty, greasy; degeneración _____ / _____ degeneration.

gratificación *f.* gratification, reward.

gratificar *vi.* to gratify, to reward.

gratis *adv.* gratis, free.

grave *a.* critically ill; of a serious nature.

Grave, enfermedad de *f.* Grave's disease, exophthalmic goiter.

gravedad *f.* gravity. 1. seriousness; estado de _____ / critical condition; 2. force of gravity.

grávida *f.* grávida, pregnant woman.

grieta *f.* crevice, cleft, fissure; _____-s en las manos / chapped hands.

gripe *f.* grippe, flu; _____ asiática / Asiatic flu.

griposis *f.* gryposis, abnormal curvature, esp. as seen in nails.

gris *a.* gray.

gris, materia o sustancia *f.* gray matter, highly vascularized gray tissue of the central nervous system made up primarily of nerve cells and unmyelinated nerve fibers.

griseofulvina *f.* griseofulvin, antibiotic used in fungus skin diseases.

gritar *v.* to scream, to cry out.

grito *m.* scream, cry; **estar en un** _____ / to be in great pain.

grosero-a *a.* gross, coarse.

grosor *m.* thickness; density.

grueso-a *a.* heavy; thick.

grumoso-a *a.* grumose, grumous, lumpy, clotted.

grupo *m.* group, cluster; team, an associated group.

grupo sanguíneo *m.* blood group, the different types of human erythrocytes, genetically determined and differentiated immunologically; _____ RH / Rh _____.

guanetidina *f.* guanethidine, agent used in the treatment of hypertension.

guante *m.* glove; _____-s de goma / rubber _____-s.

guardar *v.* to put away; to keep.

guardería infantil *f.* nursery; children's day care center.

guardián *m.* guardian; custodian.

guayaco *m.* guaiac, substance used in tests as a reagent to detect the presence of blood.

guayacol *m.* guaiacol, antiseptic; expectorant.

gubernaculum *L.* gubernaculum, direction, guidance.

guerra *f.* war.

guía *m., f.* guide, director; _____ **de teléfono** / telephone directory.

guiar *v.* to guide, to direct.

guillotina *f.* guillotine, surgical instrument.

guiñar *v.* to wink.

guisar *v.* to stew.

guisado *m.* stew.

gusano *m.* earthworm, maggot, caterpillar; _____ plano / flatworm, intestinal worm; _____ nematodo que infesta los pulmones / lungworm.

gustar *v.* to like, to enjoy.

gusto *m.* the sense of taste, taste, **buen** _____ / good taste; **mal gusto** / bad taste.

gutapercha *f.* gutta-percha, dried and purified latex of some trees that is used in medical and dental treatments.

gutta *L.* (*pl.* **guttae**) gutta, drop.

gutural *a.* guttural, pronounced in the throat.

H

H *abr.* **heroína** / heroin; **hidrógeno** / hydrogen; **hipermetropía** / hypermetropia; **hipodérmico-a** / hypodermic.

h *abr.* **hora** / hour; **horizontal** / horizontal.

haba *f.* lima bean.

haber *vi. aux.* to have.

habichuela *f.* string bean.

hábil, habilidoso-a *a.* able, skillful.

habilidad *f.* ability, aptitude.

habilitar *v.* to habilitate; to equip.

habitación *f.* room.

hábito *m.* habit.

habitual *a.* habitual, customary; **-mente** *adv.* habitually.

habla *m.* [*locución*] speech; defecto del ___ / ___ defect; patología del ___ / ___ pathology; trastorno del ___ / ___ disorder.

hablar *v.* to speak.

hacer *vi.* to do, to make; ___ **caso** / to mind, to pay attention; ___ **daño** / to harm or hurt; ___ **hincapié** / to emphasize; ___ **lo mejor posible** / to do one's best.

hacia *prep.* towards; ___ **acá** / this way; ___ **allá** / that way; ___ **adelante** / forward; ___ **atrás** / backwards.

hachís *m.* hashish, euphoria producing narcotic extracted from marihuana.

halar *v.* to pull.

hálito *m.* halitus, breath.

halitosis *f.* halitosis, bad breath.

hallar *v.* to find; **hallarse** *vr.* [*en un lugar o condición*] to find oneself.

hallazgos *m. pl.* findings, results of an investigation or inquiry.

hallux valgus *L.* hallux valgus, inward turning of the big toe.

hallux varus *L.* hallux varus, separation of the big toe from the others.

haloide *m.* haloid, salt resulting from the combination of a halogen element and a metal.

halótano *m.* halothane, Fluothane, anesthetic administered by inhalation.

hamartoma *m.* hamartoma, nodule simulating a tumor, usu. benign.

hambre *m.* hunger; **tener** ___ / to be hungry.

hambriento-a *a.* hungry, starved, famished.

Hanot, enfermedad de *f.* Hanot's disease, hypertrophic cirrhosis of the liver accompanied by jaundice; biliary cirrhosis.

Hansen, enfermedad de *f.* Hansen's disease. *V.* **leprosy.**

haploide *a.* haploid, a sex cell that has half the number of chromosomes characteristic of the species.

haptoglobina *f.* haptoglobin, mucoprotein that links itself to the released hemoglobin in the plasma.

haptómetro *m.* haptometer, device used to measure the acuteness of the sense of touch.

haragán-a *m., f.* lazy person; *a.* lazy.

harina *f.* flour, cornmeal.

harmonía, armonía *f.* harmony, congenial communication.

harmonizar, armonizar *v.* to harmonize.

hartarse *vr.* to overeat, to stuff oneself.

hasta *prep.* until; up to; as far as; ___ **ahora** / heretofore, so far; ___ **aquí** / up to this point; ___ **luego** / goodbye, see you later.

haustrum *L.* haustrum, cavity or pouch, esp. in the colon.

Havers, sistema de *m.* Haversian system, concentric formation of small conduits that constitute the base of the compact bone.

hay *v.* there is, there are: ___ **que** / it is necessary; **no** ___ **remedio** / it can't be helped.

haz *m.* bundle; ___ ascendente / ascending tract.

heces *f. pl.* feces.

hecho-a *a. pp.* of **hacer**, done, made; **bien** ___ / well ___ ; **mal** ___ / badly ___ ; **de** ___ / as a matter of fact.

Heimlich, maniobra de *f.* Heimlich's maneuver, technique applied to force the expulsion of a foreign body that is blocking the passage of air from the trachea or pharynx.

helado *m.* ice cream; **-a** *a.* frozen.

helicoideo-a *a.* helical, in the shape of a helix or a spiral.

helicóptero *m.* helicopter.

helio *m.* helium, gaseous inert chemical element mixed with air or oxygen to be used in the treatment of some respiratory disorders.

heliofobia *f.* heliophobia, excessive fear of the sun.

helioterapia *f.* heliotherapy, sun bathing as therapy.

helmintiasis *f.* helminthiasis, intestinal infection with worms.

helminticida *m.* helminthicide, agent that kills parasites; vermicide.

helminto *m.* helminth, worm found in the human intestines.

hemaglutinación, hemoaglutinación *f.* hemagglutination, agglutination of red cells.

hemaglutinina, hemoaglutinina *f.* hemagglutinin, antibody that causes agglutination of red cells.

hemangioma *m.* hemangioma, benign tumor formed by clustered blood vessels that produce a reddish birth mark.

hemangiosarcoma *m.* hemangiosarcoma, malignant tumor of the vascular tissue.

hemartrosis *f.* hemarthrosis, extravasation into a joint cavity.

hematemesis *f.* hematemesis, vomiting of blood.

hematerapia, hemoterapia *f.* hematherapy, hemotherapy, therapeutic use of blood.

hemático *m.* drug used in the treatment of anemia; **-a** *a.* rel. to blood; biometría ____ / complete blood count (CBC).

hematocolpos *m.* hematocolpos, retention of menstrual blood in the vagina due to an imperforated hymen.

hematócrito *m.* hematocrit. 1. centrifuge that is used for separating cells and particles in the blood from the plasma; 2. the volume percentage of erythrocytes in the blood.

hematogénesis *f.* hematogenesis. *V.* **hematopoyesis.**

hematógeno-a *a.* hematogenous. 1. rel. to the production of blood and to its constituents; 2. originating in the blood.

hematología *f.* hematology, the study of the blood and the organs that intervene in its formation.

hematológico-a *a.* hematologic, hematological, rel. to blood; estudios ____-s / ____ studies.

hematólogo-a *m., f.* hematologist, specialist in hematology.

hematoma *m.* hematoma, localized collection of blood that has escaped from a blood vessel into an organ, space, or tissue; ____ pélvico / pelvic ____; ____ subdural / subdural, under the dura mater.

hematomielia *f.* hematomyelia, bleeding into the spinal cord.

hematopoyesis, hemopoyesis *f.* hematopoiesis, hemopoiesis, formation of blood.

hematoquezia *f.* hematochezia, presence of blood in the stool.

hembra *f.* the female of a species.

hemianalgesia *f.* hemianalgesia, insensitivity to pain in one side of the body.

hemianopia, hemanopsia *f.* hemianopia, hemanopsia, loss of vision in one half of the visual field of the left or right eye, or of both.

hemiataxia *f.* hemiataxia, lack of muscular coordination in one side of the body.

hemiatrofia *f.* hemiatrophy, atrophy of half of an organ or half of the body.

hemibalismo *m.* hemiballism, hemiballismus, brain lesion that causes involuntary and rapid movements in half of the body.

hemicolectomía *f. surg.* hemicolectomy, removal of one half of the colon.

hemihipertrofia *f.* hemihypertrophy, hypertrophy of one half of the body.

hemilaminectomía *f. surg.* hemilaminectomy, removal of the vertebral lamina on one side.

hemiparálisis *f.* hemiparalysis, paralysis of one side of the body.

hemiparesia, hemiparesis *f.* hemiparesia, hemiparesis, muscular weakness of one side of the body.

hemiparético-a *a.* hemiparetic, rel. to hemiparesia.

hemiplejía *f.* hemiplegia, paralysis of the side of the body opposite to the affected cerebral hemisphere.

hemipléjico-a *a.* hemiplegic, affected or rel. to hemiplegia.

hemisferio *m.* hemisphere, half of a spherical or spherical-like structure or organ.

hemitórax *m.* hemithorax, each side of the thorax.

hemobilia *f.* hemobilia, bleeding in the bile ducts.

hemoblastosis *f.* hemoblastosis, proliferative disorders of the blood tissues.

hemocitoblasto *m.* hemocytoblast, primordial blood cell from which all others are derived.

hemoconcentración *f.* hemoconcentration, concentration of red blood cells due to a decrease of liquid elements in the blood.

hemoconcentrar *v.* hemoconcentrate, to concentrate red blood cells.

hemocromatosis *f.* hemochromatosis, iron storage disease, bronze diabetes, disorder of iron metabolism due to excess deposition of iron in the tissues accompanied by anomalies such as bronze skin pigmentation, cirrhosis of the liver, diabetes mellitus, and malfunction of the pancreas.

hemocultivo *m.* blood culture.

hemodiálisis *f.* hemodialysis, dialysis process used to eliminate toxic substances from the blood in cases of acute renal disorders.

hemodializador *m.* hemodyalizer, artificial kidney machine used in the dialysis process.

hemodilución *f.* hemodilution, increase in the proportion of plasma to red cells in the blood.

hemofilia *f.* hemophilia, inherited disease characterized by abnormal clotting of the blood and propensity to bleed.

hemofílico-a *m., f.* hemophiliac, person who suffers from hemophilia; *a.* hemophiliac, rel. to or suffering from hemophilia.

hemófilo *m.* hemophilus, haemophilus, one of a group of gram-negative aerobic bacteria.

hemofobia *f.* hemophobia, pathologic fear of blood.

hemoglobina *f.* hemoglobin, important protein element of the blood that gives it its red color and participates in the transportation of oxygen; índice corpuscular de ___ / mean corpuscular ___.

hemoglobinemia *f.* hemoglobinemia, presence of freed hemoglobin in the plasma.

hemoglobinuria *f.* hemoglobinuria, presence of hemoglobin in the urine.

hemograma *m.* hemogram, graphic representation of the differential blood count.

hemólisis *f.* hemolysis, rupture of erythrocytes with release of hemoglobin into the plasma; ___ del recién nacido / hemolitic disease of the new born, gen. caused by incompatibility of the Rh factor.

hemolítico-a *a.* hemolitic, rel. to or that causes hemolysis; anemia ___ / ___ anemia, red cells that rupture easily due to a congenital condition caused by toxic agents.

hemolito *m.* hemolith, concretion in a blood vessel.

hemopneumotórax *m.* hemopneumothorax, accumulation of blood and air in the pleural cavity.

hemoptisis *f.* hemoptysis, bloody expectoration.

hemorragia *f.* hemorrhage, profuse bleeding; ___ cerebral / cerebrovascular accident; ___ intracraneana / intracranial ___; ___ petequial / petechial ___; ___ puerperal / post-partum ___.

hemorrágico-a *a.* hemorrhagic, rel. to hemorrhage.

hemorroide(s) *f.* hemorrhoid, pile, a mass of dilated veins in the inferior anal or rectal wall; ___ de prolapso / prolapsed ___, that protrudes outside the anus; ___ externa / external ___, outside the anal sphincter; ___ interna / internal ___, hidden, proximal to the anorectal line.

hemorroidectomía *f. surg.* hemorrhoidectomy, removal of hemorrhoids.

hemosálpinx *m.* hemosalpinx, accumulation of blood in the fallopian tubes.

hemosiderina *f.* hemosiderin, insoluble iron compound that is stored in the body to be used in the formation of hemoglobin as needed.

hemosiderosis *f.* hemosiderosis, hemosiderin deposit in the liver and the spleen.

hemostasia, hemostasis *f.* hemostasis, cessation of bleeding, natural or otherwise.

hemóstato *m.* hemostat, a surgical clamp or a medication used to suppress bleeding.

hendidura *f.* fissure, crack, cleavage.

heparina *f.* heparin, anticoagulant.

heparinizar *vi.* heparinize, to avoid coagulation by the use of heparin.

hepatectomía *f. surg.* hepatectomy, removal of a part or all of the liver.

hepático-a *a.* hepatic, rel. to the liver; circulación ___ / liver circulation; cirrosis ___ / liver cirrhosis; coma ___ / ___ coma; conducto ___ / ___ duct; fallo ___ / liver failure; lesión ___ / liver damage; lóbulos o subdivisiones ___-s / ___ lobes; manchas ___-s / liver spots; pruebas funcionales ___-s / liver function tests; venas ___-s / ___ veins.

hepatitis *f.* hepatitis, infl. of the liver; ___ tipo A, viral / type A, viral; ___ tipo B, viral / type B ___, viral; ___ no A–no B / non A–non B ___, linked to blood transfusion; ___ amébica / amebic ___; ___ crónica activa / chronic active ___; ___ crónica persistente / chronic persistent ___; ___ fulminante / fulminant ___; ___ sérica / serum ___.

hepatocito *m.* hepatocyte, liver cell.

hepatoentérico-a *a.* hepatoenteric, rel. to the liver and the intestines.

hepatolenticular *a.* hepatolenticular, rel. to the lenticular nucleus of the eye and the liver; degeneración ___ / ___ degeneration.

hepatología *f.* hepatology, the study of the liver.

hepatólogo-a *m., f.* hepatologist, specialist in liver diseases.

hepatomegalia *f.* hepatomegaly, enlargement of the liver.

hepatorrenal *a.* hepatorenal, rel. to the liver and the kidneys.

hepatosplenomegalia *f.* hepatosplenomegaly, enlargement of the liver and the spleen.

hepatotoxina *f.* hepatotoxin, toxin that destroys liver cells.

heredado-a *a.* inherited.

heredar *v.* to inherit.

hereditario-a *a.* hereditary, that is inherited.

herencia *f.* heredity, inheritance, transmission of genetic traits from parents to children; ___ familiar / heredofamilial, rel. to a disease or condition that is inherited.

herida *f.* wound, injury; ___ contusa / contused ___, subcutaneous lesion; ___ de perforación / punctured ___; ___ de bala / gunshot ___; ___ penetrante / penetrating ___.

herido-a *a.* wounded; hurt.

herir *vi.* to injure, to hurt.

hermafrodita *f.* hermaphrodite, an individual that has both ovaric and testicular tissue combined in the same organ or separately.

hermafroditismo *m.* hermaphroditism, condition of being a hermaphrodite.

hermano-a *m., f.* brother; sister.

hermético-a *a.* hermetic, airtight.

hernia *f.* hernia, abnormal protrusion of an organ or viscera through the cavity wall that encloses it; ___ del núcleo pulposo / herniation nucleus pulposus, prolapse or rupture of the intervertebral disk; ___ escrotal / scrotal ___, that descends into the scrotum; ___ estrangulada / strangulated ___, obstructing the intestines; ___ femoral / femoral ___, protruding into the femoral canal; ___ hiatal / hiatus ___, protruding through the esophagic hiatus of the diaphragm; ___ incarcerada / incarcerated ___, frequently caused by adherences; ___ inguinal / inguinal ___, protruding from the viscera into the inguinal canal; ___ lumbar / lumbar ___, in the loin; ___ por deslizamiento / sliding ___, of the colon; ___ reducible / reducible ___, that can be treated by manipulation; saco de la ___ / hernial sac, peritoneal sac into which the hernia descends; ___ umbilical / umbilical ___, occurring at the navel; ___ ventral / ventral ___, protrusion through the abdominal wall.

herniación *f.* herniation, development of a hernia.

herniado-a *a.* herniated, hernial, rel. to or having a hernia.

herniografía *f.* herniography, X-ray of a hernia with the use of a contrasting medium.

herniorrafía *f.* *surg.* herniorrhaphy, reparation or reconstruction of a hernia.

heroico-a *a.* heroic, rel. to very strong medication or extreme medical procedures.

heroína *f.* heroin, diacetylmorphine, addictive narcotic derived from morphine; **adicto-a a la** ___, heroinómano-a / ___ addict.

heroinismo, heroinomanía *m.* heroinism, addiction to heroin.

herpangina *f.* herpangina, infectious disease (epidemic in the summer) that affects the mucous membranes of the throat.

herpes *m.* herpes, inflammatory painful viral disease of the skin that is manifested by the formation of small, cluttered, blisterlike eruptions; ___ genital / ___ genitalis; ___ ocular / ocular ___; ___ simple / ___ simplex, simple vesicles that keep recurring in the same area of the skin; ___ zóster [culebrilla] / ___ zoster, *pop.* shingles, painful eruption along the course of a nerve.

herpético-a *a.* herpetic, rel. to herpes or similar in nature.

hervido-a *a.* boiled.

hervir *vi.* to boil.

heterogéneo-a *a.* heterogeneous, dissimilar, not alike.

heteroinjerto *m.* heterograft, graft that comes from a donor of a different species or type than that of the recipient.

heterólogo-a *a.* heterologous. 1. formed by foreign cell tissue; 2. derived or obtained from a different species.

heteroplasia *f.* heteroplasia, presence of tissue in areas foreign to its normal location.

heteroplastia *f.* *surg.* heteroplasty, transplant of tissue from an individual of a different species.

heteroplástico-a *a.* heteroplastic, rel. to heteroplasia.

heterosexual *a.* heterosexual, that is attracted to the opposite sex.

heterosexualidad *f.* heterosexuality.

heterotaxia *f.* heterotaxis, abnormal or irregular position of some organs or parts of the body.

heterotopia *f.* heterotopia, displacement or deviation of an organ or part of the body from its normal position.

heterotópico-a *a.* heterotopic, rel. to heterotopia.

hético-a *a.* hectic, febrile.

heurístico-a *a.* heuristic, rel. to empirical discoveries or investigations.

hexacloruro de gama-benceno *m.* gama benzene hexachloride, powerful insecticide used in the treatment of scabies.

hialina *f.* hyalin, protein that results from the degeneration of amyloids, colloids and hyaloids.

hialinización *f.* hyalinization, degenerative process by which functioning tissue is replaced by a firm glass-like material.

hialino-a *a.* hyaline, glass-like, or almost transparent; cilindro ___ / ___ cast, found in the urine; enfermedad de la membrana ___ / ___ membrane disease, respiratory disorder of the newborn.

hialoide, hialoideo-a *a.* hyaloid, resembling glass.

hiatus *m.* hiatus, opening, orifice, fissure.

hibernoma *m.* hibernoma, benign tumor localized in the hip or the back.

híbrido-a *a.* hybrid, resulting from the crossing of different species of animals or plants.

hibridoma *m.* hybridoma, hybrid cell capable of producing a continuous supply of antibodies.

hidátide *m.* hydatid, cyst found in tissues, esp. in the liver.

hidatídico-a *a.* hydatid, rel. to a hydatid; enfermedad ___ / ___ disease, echinococcosis; quiste ___ / ___ mole, uterine cyst that produces hemorrhaging.

hidradenitis *f.* hidradenitis, infl. of the sweat glands.

hidramnios *m.* hydramnion, excess of amniotic fluid.

hidratar *v.* to hydrate, to combine a body with water.

hídrico-a *a.* hydric, rel. to water.

hidrocefalia *f.* hydrocephaly, hydrocephalus, abnormal accumulation of cerebrospinal fluid within the ventricles of the brain.

hidrocefálico-a *a.* hydrocephalic, rel. to hydrocephaly.

hidrocortisona *f.* hydrocortisone, corticosteroid hormone produced by the adrenal cortex.

hidroeléctrico-a *a.* hydroelectric, rel. to water and electricity; equilibrio ___ / water-electrolyte balance; desequilibrio ___ / water-electrolyte imbalance.

hidrofílico-a *a.* hydrophilic, having a propensity to attract and retain water.

hidrofobia *f.* hydrophobia. 1. fear of water; 2. rabies, nervous disorder transmitted by an infected animal.

hidrógeno *m.* hydrogen; concentración de ___ / ___ concentration.

hidrólisis *f.* hydrolysis, dissolution of a compound by the action of water.

hidrolizar *vi.* to hydrolyze.

hidromielia *f.* hydromyelia, increase of fluid in the central canal of the spinal cord.

hidronefrosis *f.* hydronephrosis, distension of the renal pelvis and calices due to obstruction.

hidroneumotórax *m.* hydropneumothorax, presence of gas and fluids in the pleural cavity.

hidropesía, hidropsia *f.* hydropsy, dropsy, accumulation of serous fluid in a cavity or cellular tissue.

hidrópico-a *a.* hydropic, rel. to hydropsy.

hidrosálpinx *m.* hydrosalpinx, accumulation of watery fluid in the fallopian tubes.

hidrosis *f.* hidrosis, hydrosis, abnormal sweating.

hidrostático-a *a.* hydrostatic, rel. to the equilibrium of liquids.

hidroterapia *f.* hydrotherapy, therapeutic use of applied external water in the treatment of diseases.

hidrotórax *m.* hydrothorax, collection of fluid in the pleural cavity without inflammation.

hidrouréter *m.* hydroureter, abnormal distension of the ureter due to obstruction.

hidroxiapatita *f.* hydroxyapatite, calcium phosphate, inorganic compound found in teeth and bones.

hiel *f.* bile; gall.

hielo *m.* ice.

hierro *m.* iron.

hifema *f.* hyphema, bleeding in the anterior chamber of the eye.

hígado *m.* liver, largest gland of the body, located in the upper right part of the abdominal cavity. It secretes bile, stabilizes and produces sugar, enzymes, and cholesterol, and eliminates toxins from the body.

higiene *f.* hygiene, the study and practice of

health standards; ___ mental / mental ___; ___ oral / oral ___; ___ pública / public ___.

higiénico-a *a.* hygienic, sanitary; rel. to hygiene; absorbente ___ / sanitary napkin.

higienista *m., f.* hygienist, specialist in hygiene; ___ dental / dental ___, technician in dental profilaxis.

higroma *m.* hygroma, liquid containing sac.

hijo-a *m., f.* son; daughter.

hijastro-a *m., f.* stepson; stepdaughter.

hilio *m.* hilum, hilus, depression or opening in an organ from which blood vessels and nerves enter or leave.

hilo *m.* thread. 1. material used in sutures; 2. filament-like structure.

himen *m.* hymen, membranous fold that covers partially the entrance of the vagina.

himenectomía *f. surg.* hymenectomy, excision of the hymen.

himenotomía *f.* hymenotomy, incision in the hymen.

hinchado-a *a.* swollen, bloated.

hinchar *v.* to swell, to inflate; **hincharse** *vr.* to become swollen or bloated.

hinchazón *f.* swelling.

hioides *m.* hyoid bone, horseshoe-shaped bone situated at the base of the tongue.

hipalgesia, hipalgia *f.* hypalgia, diminished sensitivity to pain.

hiperacidez *f.* hyperacidity, excessive acidity.

hiperactividad *f.* hyperactivity, excessive activity; *psych.*, excessive activity manifested in children and adolescents, usu. accompanied by irritability and inability to concentrate for any length of time.

hiperalbuminosis *f.* hyperalbuminosis, excess albumin in the blood.

hiperalimentación *f.* hyperalimentation, supplemental intravenous feeding; ___ intravenosa / parenteral ___.

hiperbilirrubinemia *f.* hyperbilirubinemia, excessive bilirubin in the blood.

hipercalcemia *f.* hypercalcemia, excessive amount of calcium in the blood.

hipercalemia, hiperpotasemia *f.* hyperkalemia, hyperpotasemia, abnormal elevation of potassium in the blood.

hipercapnia *f.* hypercapnia, excessive amount of carbon dioxide in the blood.

hipercinesia *f.* hyperkinesia, abnormal increase of muscular activity.

hipercloremia *f.* hyperchloremia, excess of chlorides in the blood.

hipercoagulabilidad *f.* hypercoagulability, abnormal increase in the coagulability of the blood.

hipercromático-a *a.* hyperchromatic, having excessive pigmentation.

hiperemesis *f.* hyperemesis, excessive vomiting.

hiperemia *f.* hyperemia, excessive blood in an organ or part.

hiperesplenismo *m.* hypersplenism, exacerbation of spleen function.

hiperestesia *f.* hyperesthesia, abnormal increased sensitivity to sensorial stimuli.

hiperflexión *f.* hyperflexion, exaggerated flexion of a limb, gen. caused by traumatism.

hiperfunción *f.* hyperfunction, excessive function.

hipergammaglobulinemia *f.* hypergammaglobulinemia, excess gamma globulin in the blood.

hiperglucemia *f.* hyperglycemia, excessive amount of sugar in the blood, such as in diabetes.

hiperglucémico-a *a.* hyperglycemic, rel. to. or suffering from hyperglycemia.

hiperglucosuria *f.* hyperglycosuria, excessive amount of sugar in the urine.

hiperhidratación *f.* hyperhydration, abnormal increase of water content in the body.

hiperhidrosis *f.* hyperhidrosis, excessive perspiration.

hiperlipemia *f.* hyperlipemia, excessive amount of fat in the blood.

hipermetropía *f.* hypermetropia, farsightedness, visual defect in which the rays of light come to focus behind the retina making distant objects better seen than closer ones.

hipermovilidad *f.* hypermobility, excessive mobility.

hipernatremia *f.* hypernatremia, excessive amount of sodium in the blood.

hipernefroma *m.* hypernephroma, Grawitz tumor, neoplasm of the renal parenchyma.

hiperopía *f.* hyperopia. V. **hipermetropía.**

hiperópico-a *a.* farsighted.

hiperorexia *f.* hyperorexia, excessive appetite.

hiperosmia *f.* hyperosmia, increased sensitivity of smell.

hiperostosis *f.* hyperostosis, excessive growth of a bony tissue.

hiperpirexia *f.* hyperpyrexia, abnormally high temperature of the body.

hiperpituitarismo *m.* hyperpituitarism, excessive activity of the pituitary gland.

hiperplasia *f.* hyperplasia, excessive proliferation of normal cells of tissues.

hiperpnea *f.* hyperpnea, increase in the depth and rapidity of breathing.

hiperreflexia *f.* hyperreflexia, exaggerated reflexes.

hipersalivación *f.* hypersalivation, excessive secretion of saliva.

hipersecreción *f.* hypersecretion, excessive secretion.

hipersensibilidad *f.* hypersensibility, excessive sensitivity to the effect of a stimulus or antigen.

hipertelorismo *m.* hypertelorism, excessive distance between two parts or organs.

hipertensión *f.* hypertension, high blood pressure; ___ benigna / benign ___; ___ esencial / essential ___; ___ maligna / malignant ___; ___ portal / portal ___; ___ renal / renal ___.

hipertenso-a *a.* hypertensive, rel. to or suffering from hypertension.

hipertermia *f.* hyperthermia. *V.* **hiperpirexia.**

hipertiroidismo *m.* hyperthyroidism, excessive activity of the thyroid gland.

hipertónico-a *a.* hypertonic, rel. to increased tonicity or tension.

hipertrofia *f.* hypertrophy, abnormal growth or development of an organ or structure; ___ cardíaca / cardiac ___, enlarged heart; ___ compensadora / compensatory ___, resulting from a physical defect.

hipertropía *f.* hypertropia, a form of strabismus.

hiperuricemia *f.* hyperuricemia, excessive amount of uric acid in the blood.

hiperventilación *f.* hyperventilation, extremely rapid and deep inspiration and expiration of air.

hiperviscosidad *f.* hyperviscosity, excessive viscosity.

hipnagógico-a *a.* hypnagogic. 1. that induces sleep; estado ___ / ___ state, between wakefulness and sleep; 2. *psych.* rel. to an hallucination or daydream as sleep begins.

hipnosis *f.* hypnosis, an artificially induced passive state during which the subject is responsive to suggestion.

hipnotismo *m.* hypnotism, the practice of hypnosis.

hipnotizar *vi.* to hypnotize, to put a subject under hypnosis.

hipo *m.* hiccups, involuntary contraction of the diaphragm and the glottis.

hipoadrenalismo *m.* hypoadrenalism, condition caused by diminished activity of the adrenal gland.

hipoalbuminemia *f.* hypoalbuminemia, low level of albumin in the blood.

hipocalcemia *f.* hypocalcemia, low amount of calcium in the blood.

hipocalemia, hipopotasemia *f.* hypokalemia, hypopotasemia, deficiency of potassium in the blood.

hipocampo *m.* hippocampus, curved elevation localized in the inferior horn of the lateral ventricle of the brain.

hipocapnia *f.* hypocapnia, deficiency of carbon dioxide in the blood.

hipociclosis *f.* hypocyclosis, deficiency in eye accommodation; ___ ciliar / ciliary ___, weakness of the ciliary muscle; ___ lenticular / lenticular ___, rigidity of the crystalline lens.

hipoclorhidria *f.* hypochlorhydria, deficiency of hydrochloric acid in the stomach, which can be a manifestation of cancer or anemia.

hipocondría *f.* hypochondria, obsessive concern over one's mental and physical health.

hipocondríaco-a *a.* hypochondriac, rel. to or suffering from hypochondria.

hipocondrio *m.* hypochondrium, upper abdominal region on either side of the thorax.

hipocromatismo *m.* hypochromatism, lack of pigmentation, esp. in the cell nucleus.

hipocromía *f.* hypochromia, abnormally pale erythrocytes.

hipocrómico-a *a.* hypochromic, rel. to hypochromia.

hipodérmico-a *a.* hypodermic, beneath the skin.

hipofaringe *f.* hypopharynx, portion of the pharynx situated under the upper edge of the epiglottis.

hipofibrinogenemia *f.* hypofibrinogenemia, low content of fibrinogen in the blood.

hipofisectomía *f. surg.* hypophysectomy, removal of the pituitary gland.

hipófisis *f.* hypophysis, pituitary gland, epithelial body situated at the base of the sella turcica.

hipofunción *f.* hypofunction, deficiency in the function of an organ.

hipogammaglobulinemia *f.* hypogammaglobulinemia, low level of gamma globulin in the blood; ___ adquirida / acquired ___, manifested after infancy.

hipogastrio *m.* hypogastrium, anterior, middle and inferior portion of the abdomen.

hipoglicemia, hipoglucemia *f.* hypoglycemia, abnormally low level of glucose in the blood.

hipoglicémico-a, hipoglucémico-a *a.* hypoglycemic, rel. to or that produces hypoglycemia.

hipoglosal *a.* hypoglossal, rel. to the hyoid bone and the tongue.

hipogloso *m.* hypoglossus, muscle of the tongue that has retractive and lateral action; hypoglossal nerve; **-a** *a.* hypoglossal, beneath the tongue.

hipomanía *f.* hypomania, moderate form of manic-depressive illness.

hiponatremia *f.* hyponatremia, deficiency in the content of sodium in the blood.

hipopituitarismo *m.* hypopituitarism, pathological condition due to diminished secretion of the pituitary gland.

hipoplasia *f.* hypoplasia, defective or incomplete development of an organ or tissue.

hipoplástico-a *a.* hypoplastic, rel. to or suffering from hypoplasia.

hiporreflexia *f.* hyporeflexia, weak reflexes.

hipospadias *m., f.* hypospadias, congenital anomaly by which the wall of the urethra remains open in different degrees in the undersurface of the penis. In the female the urethra opens into the vagina.

hipotálamo *m.* hypothalamus, portion of the diencephalon situated beneath the thalamus at the base of the cerebrum.

hipotensión *f.* hypotension, low blood pressure.

hipotenso-a *a.* hypotensive, rel. to or suffering from low blood pressure.

hipotermia *f.* hypothermia, low body temperature.

hipótesis *f.* hypothesis, a proposition to be proven by experimentation; ___ nula / null ___.

hipotiroideo-a *a.* hypothyroid, rel. to or suffering from hypothyroidism.

hipotiroidismo *m.* hypothyroidism, condition due to a deficiency in the production of thyroxin.

hipotónico-a *a.* hypotonic. 1. rel. to a deficiency in muscular tonicity; 2. having a lower osmotic pressure as compared to another element.

hipotrombinemia *f.* hypothrombinemia, deficiency of thrombin in the blood which can cause a propensity to bleed.

hipoventilación *f.* hypoventilation, reduction of air entering the alveoli.

hipovolemia *f.* hypovolemia, decreased volume of blood in the body.

hipoxemia, hipoxia *f.* hypoxemia, hypoxia, diminished availability of oxygen to the blood.

hirviente *a.* boiling; **agua** ___ / ___ water.

hispano-a *m., f.* Hispanic person; *a.* Hispanic.

hispanoamericano-a *m., f.* Spanish-American person; *a.* Hispanic.

histamina *f.* histamine, substance that acts as a dilator of blood vessels and stimulates gastric secretion.

histerectomía *f. surg.* hysterectomy, partial or total removal of the uterus; ___ abdominal / abdominal ___, through the abdomen; ___ total / total ___, removal of the uterus and the cervix; ___ vaginal / vaginal ___, through the vagina.

histeria *f.* hysteria, extreme neurosis.

histérico-a *a.* hysteric, hysterical, rel. to or suffering from hysteria.

histerismo *m.* hysterics, hysteria.

histerosalpingooforectomía *f. surg.* hysterosalpingoophorectomy, excision of the uterus, ovaries, and oviducts.

histeroscopía *f.* hysteroscopy, endoscopic examination of the uterine cavity.

histeroscopio *m.* hysteroscope, endoscope used in the examination of the uterine cavity.

histerotomía *f.* hysterotomy, incision of the uterus.

histidina *f.* histidin, amino acid essential in the growth and restauration of tissue.

histiocito *m.* histiocyte, large interstitial phagocytic cell of the reticuloendothelial system.

histocompatibilidad *f.* histocompatibility, state in which the tissues of a donor are accepted by the receiver; complejo de ___ mayor / major ___ complex.

histología *f.* histology, study of organic tissues.

histólogo-a *m., f.* histologist, specialist in histology.

histoplasmina *f.* histoplasmin, substance used in the cutaneous test for histoplasmosis.

histoplasmosis *f.* histoplasmosis, respiratory disease caused by the fungus *Histoplasma capsulatum*.

histriónico-a *a.* histrionic, dramatic.

Hodgkin, enfermedad de *f.* Hodgkin's disease, malignant tumors in the lymph nodes and the spleen.

hoja *f.* leaf; [*de papel o metal*] sheet; ___ clínica / medical chart.

hola *int.* hi, hello.

holgazán-a *m., f.* lazy person, loafer; *a.* lazy.

holístico-a *a.* holistic, rel. to a whole or unit.

holocrino-a *a.* holocrine, rel. to the sweat glands.

holodiastólico-a *a.* holodiastolic, rel. to a complete diastole.

holografía *f.* holography, tridimensional representation of a figure by means of a photographic image.

holograma *m.* hologram, production of a holography.

holosistólico-a *a.* holosystolic, rel. to a complete systole.

hombre *m.* man, male.

hombro *m.* shoulder, the union of the clavicle, the scapula, and the humerus.

homeopatía *f.* homeopathy, cure by means of administering medication diluted in minute doses that are capable of producing symptoms of the disease being treated.

homeopático-a *a.* homeopathic, rel. to homeopathy.

homicidio *m.* homicide; ___ sin premeditación / manslaughter.

homocigótico-a *a.* homozygotic, homozygous, rel. to twins that develop from gametes with similar alleles in regard to one or all characters.

homofobia *f.* homophobia, fear of or revulsion regarding homosexuals.

homofóbico-a *a.* that is fearful of or has an aversion to homosexuals.

homogéneo-a *a.* homogeneous, similar in nature.

homoinjerto *m.* homograft, transplant from a subject of the same species or type.

homólogo-a *a.* homologous, similar in structure and origin but not in function.

homosexual *a.* homosexual, sexually attracted to persons of the same sex.

homotónico-a *a.* homotonic, having the same tension.

homotópico-a *a.* homotopic, rel. to or occurring in the same corresponding parts.

homúnculo-a *m., f.* homunculus, dwarf with no deformities and with proportionate parts of the body.

hondo-a *a.* deep.

honesto-a, honrado-a *a.* honest.

hongo *m.* fungus; mushroom; ___ venenoso / toadstool.

honorario *m.* fee, charges; ___-s razonables / reasonable charges.

hora *f.* hour; time; **a cada** ___ / hourly; ___ **de acostarse** / bedtime; **¿qué** ___ **es?** / what time is it?

horario *m.* schedule; timetable.

horizontal *a.* horizontal, parallel to the floor.

hormiga *f.* ant.

hormigueo *m.* tingling sensation.

hormona *f.* hormone, natural chemical substance in the body that produces or stimulates the activity of an organ; ___ del crecimiento / growth ___; ___ estimulante / stimulating ___.

hormona luteinizante *f.* luteinizing hormone produced by the anterior pituitary gland. It stimulates the secretion of sex hormones by the testis (testosterone) and the ovaries (progesterone), and also acts in the formation of sperm and ova.

hormona paratiroidea *f.* parathormona, a hormone that regulates calcium in the body.

hormonal *a.* hormonal, rel. to or acting like a hormone.

hornear *v.* to bake.

Horner, síndrome de *m.* Horner's syndrome, sinking of the eyeball with accompanying eye and facial disorders due to paralysis of the cervical sympathetic nerve.

horno *m.* oven.

horquilla *f.* fourchete, fourchette, posterior junction of the vulva.

horrible *a.* horrible; abominable, hideous.

hospedar *v.* to host; to lodge.

hospicio *m.* hospice, nursing facility.

hospital *m.* hospital.

hospitalizar *vi.* to hospitalize.

hospitalización *f.* hospitalization.

hostil *a.* hostile, unfriendly.

hostilidad *f.* hostility, animosity.

hotel *m.* hotel.

hoy *adv.* today; **de** ___ **en adelante** / from now on; ___ **en día** / nowadays.

hoyo *m.* pit, hole.

hoyuelo *m.* dimple, dimple sign; small hole.

hueco *m.* depression, socket; hole; **-a** *a.* hollow.

huella *f.* impression; print; ___-s dactilares / fingerprints; ___ del pie / footprint.

huérfano-a *m., f.* orphan.

huesecillo *m.* bonelet.

hueso *m.* bone; ___ compacto / hard ___; ___ esponjoso / spongy ___; ___ quebrado / fractured ___.

huésped *m.* [*parásito*] host.

huesudo-a *a.* bony.

huevo *m.* egg, ovum, female sexual cell; **cáscara de** ___ / eggshell; **clara de** ___ / ___ white; ___ **frito** / fried ___; ___ **pasado por agua** / soft boiled ___; **yema de** ___ / ___ yolk.

humanidad *f.* humanity.

humano-a *a.* human; humane; rel. to humanity.

humear *v.* to fume; to emit vapor or gas.

humectante *m.* humidifier, device that controls and maintains humidity in the air within a given area.

humedad *f.* humidity.

humedecer *v.* to moisten, to dampen.

húmedo-a *a.* humid, damp.

húmero *m.* humerus, long bone of the upper arm.

humo *m.* smoke.

humor *m.* humor. 1. any liquid form in the body; ___ acuoso / aqueous ___, clear fluid in the eye chambers; ___ cristalino / crystalline ___, substance that constitutes the lens of the eye; ___ vítreo / vitreous ___, clear, semifluid substance between the lens and the retina; 2. secretion. 3. disposition, mood; **estar de buen** ___ / to be in a good ___; **estar de mal** ___ / to be in a bad mood.

humoral *a.* humoral, rel. to the body fluids.

hundido-a *a.* sunken.

Hunt, neuralgia de *f.* Hunt's neuralgia or syndrome. *V.* **neuralgia.**

Huntington, corea de *f.* Huntington's chorea. *V.* **corea.**

huso *m.* spindle. 1. structure or cell shaped like a round pin with tapered ends; 2. achromatic arrangements of chromosomes in the nuclear cell during mitosis and meiosis.

¡huy! *int.* ouch!

I

I *abr.* **iodo, yodo** / iodine.

iátrico-a *a.* iatric, rel. to medicine, the medical profession or physicians.

iatrogénico-a, iatrógeno-a *a.* iatrogenic. *V.* **yatrógeno.**

Ibuprofén *m.* Ibuprofen, anti-inflammatory, pyrectic, and analgesic agent used in the treatment of rheumatoid arthritis.

ictericia *f.* jaundice, disorder caused by excessive bilirubin in the blood and manifested by a yellow-orange coloring of the skin and other tissues and fluids of the body; ___ del neonato / icterus gravis neonatorum.

ictérico-a *a.* icteric, jaundiced, or rel. to jaundice.

icterogénico-a *a.* icterogenic, agent that causes jaundice.

icterohepatitis *f.* icterohepatitis, hepatitis associated with jaundice.

icterus *L.* icterus. *V.* **ictericia.**

ictiosis *f.* ichthyosis, dry and scaly skin.

ictus *L.* ictus, sudden attack.

idea *f.* idea, concept, thought; ___ fija / fixed ___, idée fixe.

ideación *f.* ideation, process by which ideas are formed.

ideal *a.* ideal.

idem *L.* idem, the same.

idéntico-a *a.* 1. identical, same; 2. rel. to twins that result from the fertilization of only one ovum.

identidad *f.* identity, self recognition.

identificación *f.* *psych.* identification, unconscious process of identifying oneself with another person or group and assuming its characteristics.

identificar *vi.* to identify.

ideocracia *f.* ideocracy, tendency to submit oneself to certain habits and drugs.

ideología *f.* ideology, a set of concepts and ideas.

ideomoción *f.* ideomotion, muscular activity directed by a prevailing idea.

idiograma *f.* idiogram, graphic representation of the chromosomes of a given cell.

idioma *m.* language.
idiopatía *f.* idiopathy, disease or morbid state of unknown origin.
idiopático-a *a.* idiopathic. 1. rel. to idiopathy; 2. of a spontaneous nature.
idiosincracia *f.* idiosyncrasy. 1. set of individual characteristics; 2. an individual's own reaction to a given action, idea, medication, treatment or food.
idiota *m., f.* idiot, fool.
idiotez *f.* idiocy, mental deficiency.
idiotrópico-a *a.* idiotropic. *V.* egocéntrico.
idioventricular *a.* idioventricular, rel. to that which affects ventricles only.
ido-a *a.* absentminded, distracted.
ignorante *a.* ignorant.
ignorar *v.* to ignore.
igual *a.* equal, even, same; **-mente** *adv.* equally.
igualar *v.* to equate.
ileal *a.* ileal, rel. to the ileum.
ilegal *a.* illegal, illicit.
ilegítimo-a *a.* illegitimate.
ileítis *f.* ileitis, infl. of the ileum; ___ regional / regional ___.
ileocecal *a.* ileocecal, rel. to the ileum and the cecum; válvula ___ / ___ valve.
ileocistoplastia *f. surg.* ileocystoplasty, anastomosis of a segment of the ileum to the bladder in order to increase the bladder's capacity.
ileocolitis *f.* ileocolitis, infl. of the mucous membrane of the ileum and the colon.
íleon *m.* ileum, distal portion of the small intestine extending from the jejunum to the cecum; desviación quirúrgica del ___ / ileal bypass.
ileoproctostomía *f. surg.* ileoproctostomy, anastomosis of the ileum and the rectum.
ileosigmoidostomía *f. surg.* ileosigmoidostomy, anastomosis of the ileum and the sigmoid colon.
ileostomía *f. surg.* ileostomy, anastomosis of the ileum and the anterior abdominal wall.
ileotransversostomía *f. surg.* ileotransversostomy, anastomosis of the ileum and the transverse colon.
ilíaco-a *a.* iliac, rel. to the ilium.
ilimitado-a *a.* unlimited, boundless.
iliofemoral *a.* iliofemoral, rel. to the ilium and the femur.
iliohipogástrico-a *a.* iliohypogastric, rel. to the ilium and the hypogastrium.

ilioinguinal *a.* ilioinguinal, rel. to the iliac and inguinal regions.
iliolumbar *a.* iliolumbar, rel. to the iliac and lumbar regions.
ilión *m.* ilium, hip bone.
iluminación *f.* illumination; ___ lateral o indirecta del campo oscuro / lateral or indirect dark field ___.
ilusión *f.* illusion, false interpretation of sensory impressions.
iluso-a *a.* deluded.
ilusorio-a *a.* illusory, illusional or rel. to an illusion.
ilustración *f.* illustration, graph.
imagen *f.* image.
imágenes por resonancia magnética *f. pl.* magnetic resonance imaging, procedure based in the quantitative analysis of the chemical and biological structure of a tissue.
imágenes por ultrasonido *f. pl.* ultrasound imaging, creation of images of organs or tissues through the use of reflex techniques (echogram).
imaginar *v.* to imagine.
imaginario-a *a.* imaginary, illusory; unreal.
imán *m.* magnet, a body that has the property of attracting iron.
imbécil *m., f.* imbecile, stupid person; *a.* imbecilic, stupid.
imbibición *f.* imbibition, absorption of a liquid.
imbricado-a *a.* imbricate, imbricated, in layers.
imitar *v.* to imitate.
imitación *f.* imitation.
impacción *f.* impaction. 1. the condition of being lodged or wedged within a given space; 2. impediment of an organ or part.
impacientarse *vr.* to become impatient.
impaciente *a.* impatient.
impactado-a *a.* impacted; diente ___ / ___ tooth.
impalpable *a.* impalpable, incorporeal, intangible.
impedimento *m.* impediment; handicap; obstacle.
impedir *vi.* to impede, to prevent; to impair.
impenetrable *a.* impenetrable.
imperativo *m. gr.* imperative mood; **-a** *a.* imperative.
imperdible *m.* safety pin.
imperfección *f.* imperfection; defect.
imperfecto-a *m. gr.* past tense; *a.* imperfect; defective.

imperforado-a *a.* imperforate, abnormally closed; himen ___ / ___ hymen.

impermeable *a.* impermeable, not allowing passage, such as fluids; waterproof.

impersonal *a.* impersonal.

impétigo *m.* impetigo, bacterial skin infection marked by vesicles that become pustular and form a yellow crust on rupturing.

ímpetu *m.* impetus, impulse.

impetuoso-a *a.* impetuous, violent.

implacable *a.* implacable, not able to be appeased.

implantación *f.* implantation, insertion and fixation of a part or tissue in an area of the body.

implantar *v.* to implant; to insert.

implante *m.* implant, any material inserted or grafted into the body.

implicación *f.* implication.

implicar *vi.* to imply.

imponer *vi.* to impose; to tax; **imponerse** *vr.* to prevail.

importancia *n.* importance, significance; **sin** ___ / of no significance.

importante *a.* important.

importar *v.* to matter.

imposible *a.* impossible.

impotencia *f.* impotence, inability to have or maintain an erection.

impotente *a.* impotent, rel. to or suffering from impotence.

impráctico-a *a.* impractical.

impregnar *v.* to impregnate; to saturate.

imprescindible *a.* indispensable.

impresión *f.* impression, print; image; ___ **digital** / fingerprint.

impresionante *a.* impressive.

imprevisto-a *a.* unexpected, unforeseen.

improbable *a.* improbable, unlikely.

improvisado-a *a.* improvised.

improvisar *v.* to improvise.

impúbero-a *a.* below the age of puberty.

impuesto *m.* tax; **exempto de** ___ / ___ exempt, free of ___ .

impulsar *v.* to impel; to accelerate.

impulsivo-a *a.* impulsive; driven.

impulso *m.* drive, thrust; sudden pushing force; ___ cardíaco / cardiac ___ ; ___ excitante / excitatory ___; ___ inhibitorio / inhibitory ___; ___ nervioso / nervous ___; ___ vital / élan vital.

impuro-a *a.* impure, contaminated, adulterated.

inaccesible *a.* inaccessible.

inacción *f.* inaction, failure to respond to a stimulus.

inaceptable *a.* unacceptable.

inactivo-a *a.* inactive, passive; in a state of rest.

inactividad *f.* inactivity.

inadaptado-a *a.* maladjusted, unable to adjust to the environment or to endure stress.

inadecuado-a *a.* inadequate.

inanición *f.* inanition, starvation, hunger.

inarticulado-a *a.* inarticulate, 1. unable to articulate words or syllables; 2. disjointed.

in articulo mortis *L.* in articulo mortis, at the moment of death.

incandescente *a.* incandescent, glowing with light.

incansable *a.* tireless, untiring.

incapacitado-a *a.* disabled; unable.

incapaz *a.* incapable, unable.

incendio *m.* fire.

incentivo *m.* incentive.

incertidumbre *f.* uncertainty.

incesante *a.* incessant; continuous.

incesto *m.* incest.

incestuoso-a *a.* incestuous.

incidencia *f.* incidence.

incidental *a.* incidental.

incinerar *v.* to incinerate; to cremate.

incipiente *a.* incipient, just coming into existence.

incisión, incisura *f.* incision; surgical cut; slit; notch.

inclinación *f.* slant, slope, tilt; inclination, predisposition.

inclinado-a *a.* inclined.

incluido *a.* included; enclosed.

incluir *vi.* to include; to embed, to surround a tissue specimen in a firm medium to keep intact in preparation for cutting sections for examination.

inclusión *f.* inclusion, the act of enclosing one thing in another; **cuerpos de** ___ / ___ bodies, present in the cytoplasm of some cells in cases of infection.

incoherencia *f.* incoherence, lack of coordination of ideas.

incoherente *a.* incoherent.

incoloro-a *a.* colorless; achromatic.

incomodar *v.* to disturb, to annoy.

incómodo-a *a.* uncomfortable; annoyed.

incompatible *a.* incompatible.

incompatibilidad *f.* incompatibility.

incompetente *a.* incompetent.

incompleto-a *a.* incomplete, unfinished.

inconsciencia *f.* unconsciousness, impaired consciousness or the loss of it; unawareness.

inconsciente *a.* unconscious. 1. that has lost consciousness; 2. that does not respond to sensorial stimuli.

inconsistencia *f.* inconsistency.

inconsistente *a.* inconsistent.

incontinencia *f.* incontinence, inability to control the emission or expulsion of urine or feces; ___ por rebozamiento / ___, overflow; ___ urinaria de esfuerzo / ___, urinary stress.

incontinente *a.* incontinent, rel. to incontinence.

inconveniencia *f.* inconvenience, hardship.

inconveniente *m.* difficulty, obstacle; *a.* inconvenient.

incorporar *v.* to incorporate, to include.

incorrecto-a *a.* incorrect, inaccurate; **acción** ___ / improper action.

incredulidad *f.* disbelief, skepticism.

incrustación *f.* inlay.

incubación *f.* incubation; 1. latent period of a disease before its manifestation; período de ___ / ___ period; 2. the care of a premature infant in an incubator.

incubadora *f.* incubator, device used to keep optimal conditions of temperature and humidity, esp. in the care of premature infants.

incurable *a.* incurable, not subject to healing.

incus *L.* incus, small bone of the middle ear.

indeciso-a *a.* undecided, undecisive, hesitant.

indefinido-a *a.* indefinite, undefined.

independiente *a.* independent, self-sufficient.

indeseable *a.* undesirable.

indeterminado-a *a.* undetermined; undefined.

indicación *f.* indication; suggestion; hint.

indicado-a *a.* indicated; appropriate.

indicador *m.* marker, indicator.

indicar *vi.* to indicate; to point out.

índice *m.* rate, index; mean; ___ de mortalidad, de mortandad / death ___; ___ de natalidad / birthrate; ___ de natalidad cero / zero population growth.

indiferenciación *f.* undifferentiation. *V.* **anaphasia.**

indiferente *a.* indifferent.

indígena *m., f.* native, aboriginal; *a.* indigenous.

indigestarse *vr.* to suffer from indigestion.

indigestión *f.* indigestion, maldigestion.

indirecto-a *a.* indirect.

indispensable *a.* indispensable, necessary.

indisponer *vi.* to indispose; to make ill.

indispuesto-a *a. pp.* of **indisponer,** indisposed, ill; upset.

individual *a.* individual.

individualidad *f.* individuality.

individuo *m.* individual, person; fellow.

inducido-a *a.* induced.

inducir *vi.* to induce; to force; to provoke.

ineficiente *a.* inefficient, ineffective.

inercia *f.* inertia, stillness; lack of activity.

inerte *a.* inert, rel. to inertia.

inervación *f.* innervation, distribution of nerves or nervous energy in an organ or area.

inervar *v.* to innervate, to stimulate a nerve.

inesperado-a *a.* unexpected, occurring without warning.

inestable *a.* unstable, fluctuating.

inevitable *a.* inevitable, unavoidable.

inexperiencia *f.* inexperience.

infancia *f.* infancy, period of time from birth to one or two years of age; early age.

infantil *a.* infantile. 1. rel. to infancy; 2. childish.

infantilismo *m.* infantilism, infantile characteristics carried into adult life.

infarto *m.* infarct, infarction, necrosis of a tissue area due to a lack of blood supply; ___ blando / bland ___; ___ cardíaco / myocardial ___; ___ cerebral / cerebral ___; ___ hemorrágico / hemorrhagic ___; ___ pulmonar / pulmonary ___.

infección *f.* infection, invasion of the body by pathogenic microorganisms and the reaction of tissue to their presence and effect; ___ aerógena / airborne ___; ___ aguda / acute ___; ___ contagiosa / contagious ___; ___ crónica / chronic ___; ___ de hongos / fungus ___; ___ hídrica / waterborne ___; ___ hospitalaria / cross ___; ___ masiva / massive ___; ___ piógena / pyogenic ___; ___ secundaria / secondary ___; ___ sistémica / systemic ___; ___ subclínica / subclinical ___.

infección oportunista *f.* opportunistic infection, caused by an organism, gen. harmless, that can become pathogenic when resistance to disease is impaired, such as occurs in AIDS.

infeccioso-a *a.* infectious, rel. to an infection; agente ___ / ___ agent; enfermedad ___ / ___ disease.

infectado-a *a.* infected.

infectar *v.* to infect; **infectarse** *vr.* to become infected.

infectivo-a *a.* infectious.

infecundarse *vr.* to become sterile.

infecundidad *f.* infecundity, sterility.

infecundo-a *a.* sterile; barren.

infeliz *a.* unhappy.

inferior *a.* inferior, lower.

inferir *vi.* to infer, to surmise.

infertilidad *f.* infertility, inability to conceive or procreate.

infestación *f.* infestation, invasion of the body by parasites.

infiltración *f.* infiltration, the accumulation of foreign substances in a tissue, organ, or cell.

infiltrar *v.* to infiltrate, to penetrate.

inflación *f.* inflation, distension.

inflamación *f.* inflammation, reaction of a tissue to injury.

inflamarse *vr.* to become inflamed.

inflamatorio-a *a.* inflammatory, rel. to inflammation.

inflexible *a.* inflexible.

inflexión *f.* inflection, inflexion, the act of bending inward.

influencia *f.* influence.

influenza *f.* influenza, acute contagious viral infection of the respiratory tract.

influjo *m.* influx.

información *f.* information.

informar *v.* to inform; **informarse** *vr.* to become informed.

informe *m.* report; account.

infraclavicular *a.* infraclavicular, under the clavicle.

infradiafragmático-a *a.* infradiaphragmatic, under the diaphragm.

infraescapular *a.* infrascapular, situated below the scapula.

infraorbitario *a.* infraorbital, situated under the floor of the orbit.

infrarrojo-a *a.* infrared; rayos ___ -s / ___ rays.

infrecuente *a.* infrequent.

infundíbulo *m.* infundibulum, funnel-like structure.

infusión *f.* infusion. 1. slow gravitational introduction of fluid into a vein; 2. the steeping of an element in water to obtain its soluble active principles.

ingerir *vi.* to ingest, to take in.

ingesta *f.* ingesta, ingestant; oral feeding.

ingestión *f.* ingestion, process of ingesting food or liquids; ___ calórica / caloric ___.

ingle *f.* groin.

inglés *m.* [*idioma*] English; [*nativo*] **inglésa** *m., f.* English; *a.* English.

ingravidez *f.* weightlessness.

ingrávido-a *a.* weightless.

ingrediente *m.* ingredient, component.

ingresar *v.* [*en un hospital*] to be admitted.

ingreso *m.* income; *v.* dar ___ / to admit.

inguinal *a.* inguinal, rel. to the groin; anillo ___ / ___ ring; canal ___ / ___ canal; hernia ___ / ___ hernia; ligamento ___ / ___ ligament.

ingurgitado-a *a.* engorged, distended by excess fluid.

inhábil *a.* unfit.

inhabilidad *f.* inability, incapacity.

inhalación *f.* inhalation, the act of drawing air or other vapor into the lungs.

inhalante *m.* inhalant, medication administered by inhalation.

inhalar *v.* to inhale, to draw in air or vapor.

inherente *a.* inherent, innate, natural to an individual or thing.

inhibición *f.* inhibition, interruption or restriction of a process.

inhibidor *m.* inhibitor, agent that causes inhibition.

inhibir *v.* to inhibit; **inhibirse** *vr.* to restrain from.

inicial *a.* initial.

iniciar *v.* to initiate, to start.

inicio *m.* beginning, start.

injertable *a.* graftable.

injertar *v.* to graft, to implant.

injerto *m.* graft, implant, inlay, any tissue or organ used for transplantation or implantation; ___ alogénico / allogenic ___ , taken from a genetically nonidentical donor: ___ autógeno, autoinjerto / autogenous ___ , taken from the same patient; ___ cutáneo / skin ___ , as in burns; ___ cutáneo de capa gruesa partida / thick-split ___ , thick layer of skin used to cover a bare area; ___ de derivación / bypass ___ ; ___ dermoepidérmico / full thickness ___ , entire layer of the skin without the subcutaneous fat; ___ óseo / bone ___ ; rechazo de ___ / ___ rejection.

inmaduro-a *a.* immature.

inmediato-a *a.* immediate, close; **-mente** *adv.* immediately.

inmersión *f.* immersion, submersion of a body in a liquid.

inmigrante *m., f.* immigrant.

inminente *a.* imminent, about to happen.

inmoderado-a *a.* immoderate, without moderation.

inmoral *a.* immoral, corrupt.

inmóvil *a.* immobile, motionless.

inmovilización *f.* immobilization.

inmovilizar *vi.* to immobilize.

inmundicia *f.* filth, dirt; garbage.

inmune *a.* immune, resistant to contracting a specific disease.

inmunidad *f.* immunity. 1. condition of the organism to resist a particular antigen by activating specific antibodies; 2. resistance to contracting a specific disease; ____ activa / active ____, own production of antibodies; ____ adquirida / acquired ____, such as acquired by vaccination; ____ artificial / artificial ____, such as acquired from vaccination; ____ natural / natural ____, genetic type; ____ pasiva / passive ____, acquired from a donor.

inmunización *f.* immunization, making the organism immune to a given disease.

inmunizar *vi.* to immunize.

inmunocompetencia *f.* immunocompetency, the process of becoming immune following exposure to an antigen.

inmunodeficiencia *f.* immunodeficiency, inadequate cellular immunity reaction that diminishes the ability to respond to antigenic stimuli; enfermedad grave de ____ combinada / severe combined ____ disease.

inmunoelectroforesis *f.* immunoelectrophoresis, the use of electrophoresis as a technique of finding the amount and type of proteins and antibodies in body fluids.

inmunoensayo *m.* immunoassay, the process of identifying a substance by its capacity to act as an antigen and antibody in a tissue; ____ enzimático / enzime ____.

inmunoestimulante *m.* immunostimulant, agent that can stimulate an immune response.

inmunofluorescencia *f.* immunofluorescence, method that uses antibodies labeled with fluorescein to locate antigen in tissues.

inmunoglobulina *f.* immunoglobulin. 1. one of a group of proteins of animal origin that participates in the immune reaction; 2. one of the five types of gamma globulin capable of acting as an antibody.

inmunología *f.* immunology, the study of the body's response to bacteria, virus, or any other foreign invasion, such as transplanted tissue or organ.

inmunológico-a *a.* immunologic, rel. to immunology; respuesta o reacción ____ / immune response.

inmunoproteína *f.* immunoprotein, protein that acts as an antibody.

inmunoquimoterapia *f.* immunochemotherapy, combined process of immunotherapy and chemotherapy used in the treatment of some malignant tumors.

inmunosupresivo *m.* immunosuppressant, agent capable of suppressing an immune response.

inmunoterapia *f.* immunotherapy, prevention or treatment of a disease using passive immunization of agents such as serum or gamma globulin.

innato-a *a.* inborn; congenital; ingrown.

innecesario-a *a.* unnecessary.

inocente *a.* innocent.

inoculación *f.* inoculation, immunization, administration of a serum, vaccine, or some other substance to increase immunization to a given disease.

inocular *v.* to inoculate, to administer an inoculation.

inóculo *m.* inoculum, substance that is inoculated.

inodoro *m.* toilet, commode; **-a** *a.* odorless.

inofensivo-a *a.* harmless.

inoperable *a.* inoperable, lacking potential for surgical treatment.

inoportuno-a *a.* untimely, inopportune.

inorgánico-a *a.* inorganic, that is independent of living organisms.

inotrópico-a *a.* inotropic, that affects the intensity or energy of muscular contractions.

inquieto-a *a.* uneasy, restless, jumpy.

inquietud *f.* unrest, restlessness.

insalubre *a.* insalubrious; unsanitary.

inscribirse *v.* to register.

insecticida *m.* insecticide.

insecto *m.* insect.

inseguridad *f.* insecurity.

inseminación *f.* insemination, fertilization of an ovum.

insensible *a.* insensible, without sensibility.

inseparable *a.* inseparable.
inserción *f.* insertion. 1. the act of inserting; 2. the place where a muscle attaches to the bone.
insertar *v.* to insert.
inservible *a.* useless, unserviceable.
insidioso-a *a.* insidious, rel. to a disease that develops gradually and subtly without warning or early symptoms.
insignificante *a.* insignificant.
insípido-a *a.* insipid, tasteless.
insistir *v.* to insist.
in situ *L.* in situ. 1. in its normal place; 2. that does not extend beyond the place of origin.
insolación *f.* insolation, sunstroke, heat exhaustion, disorder caused by the effect of prolonged exposure to the rays of the sun; ___ con colapso / heat prostration.
insoluble *a.* insoluble, that does not dissolve.
insomne *a.* insomniac, insomnious, rel. to or suffering from insomnia.
insomnio *m.* insomnia, inability to sleep.
insoportable *a.* unbearable.
inspección *f.* inspection.
instalación *f.* installation; facility.
instalar *v.* to install.
instante *m.* instant; **en este** ___ / right now.
instilación *f.* instillation, dripping of a liquid into a cavity or unto a surface.
instintivo-a *a.* instinctive.
instinto *m.* instinct.
institución *f.* institution, establishment.
instrumento *m.* instrument.
insuficiencia *f.* insufficiency, lacking; ___ cardíaca / heart failure; ___ coronaria / coronary ___; ___ hepática / hepatic ___; ___ mitral / mitral ___; ___ pulmonar-valvular / pulmonary valvular ___; ___ renal / renal ___; ___ respiratoria / respiratory ___; ___ suprarrenal / adrenal ___; ___ valvular / valvular ___; ___ venosa / venous ___.
insuficiente *a.* insufficient.
insuflar *v.* to insufflate, to blow into a tube, cavity, or organ of the body.
insufrible *a.* insufferable, unbearable.
ínsula *f.* insula, central lobe of the cerebral hemisphere.
insulina *f.* insulin, hormone secreted by the ·pancreas.
inteligente *a.* intelligent; smart.
intención *f.* intention. 1. goal, purpose; **con**

___ / purposely; 2. natural healing process of a wound.
intensidad *f.* intensity.
intensificar *vi.* to intensify.
intensivo-a *a.* intensive.
intenso-a *a.* intense.
intentar *v.* to attempt, to try.
interacción *f.* interaction; ___ de medicamentos / drug ___.
intercalado-a *a.* intercalated, situated or placed between two parts or elements.
intercostal *a.* intercostal, between two ribs.
intercurrente *a.* intercurrent, that appears during the course of another disease modifying it in some way.
interdigitación *f.* interdigitation, interlocking of parts like the fingers of folded hands.
interés *m.* interest.
interferencia *f.* interference, mutual annulment of, or collision between two parts.
interferir *vi.* to interfere.
interferona *f.* interferon, a natural protein released by cells exposed to viruses that can be used in the treatment of infections and neoplasms.
interfibrilar *a.* interfibrillar, between fibrils.
interín *m.* interim, meantime.
interior *a.* interior.
intermediario-a *a.* intermediary, situated between two bodies.
intermedio-a *a.* intermediate, situated between two extremes.
interminable *a.* endless.
intermitente *a.* intermittent, not continuous; pulso ___ / ___ pulse; ventilación ___ bajo presión positiva / ___ positive-pressure ventilation.
internacional *a.* international; unidad ___ / ___ unit, accepted measured amount of a substance as defined by the international conference of unification of formulae.
internado *m.* internship.
internalización *f. psych.* internalization, unconscious process by which an individual adopts the beliefs, values, and attitudes of another person or of the society in which she or he lives.
internista *m., f.* physician specializing in internal medicine.
interno-a *m., f.* intern; *a.* internal, inside the body; hemorragia ___ / ___ bleeding.
interpretación *f.* interpretation.
interpretar *v.* to interpret.
interrogatorio *m.* questioning.

interrumpir *v.* to interrupt.

intersticial *a.* interstitial, rel. to spaces within an organ, cell, or tissue.

intervalo *m.* interval, period of time.

intervención *f.* surgical intervention, operation.

intervenir *vi.* to intervene; to assist; to supervise.

interventricular *a.* interventricular, between the ventricles; defecto del tabique ___ / ventrical septal defect; tabique ___ del corazón / ___ septum.

intervertebral *a.* intervertebral, between the vertebrae; disco ___ / ___ disk.

intestinal *a.* intestinal, rel. to the intestines; desviación quirúrgica ___ / ___ bypass surgery; flora ___ / ___ flora; obstrucción ___ / ___ obstruction; perforación ___ / ___ perforation.

intestino *m.* intestine, the alimentary canal extending from the pylorus to the anus; ___ delgado / small ___; ___ grueso / large ___; ___ medio del embrión / midgut.

íntima *f.* intima. 1. the innermost of the three layers of a blood vessel; 2. the innermost layer of several organs or parts.

intimal *a.* intimal, *rel.* to the intima.

intolerancia *f.* intolerance, inability to withstand pain or the effects of drugs.

intoxicación *f.* intoxication; poisoning, food poisoning, toxic state produced by the intake of a drug or toxic substance; ___ de pescado / fish poisoning.

intoxicar *vi.* to intoxicate, to poison; **intoxicarse** *vr.* to become intoxicated; to become poisoned.

intra-abdominal *a.* intra-abdominal, within the abdominal cavity.

intra-aórtico-a *a.* intra-aortic, within the aorta.

intra-arterial *a.* intra-arterial, within an artery.

intra-articular *a.* intra-articular, within an articulation or joint.

intracapsular *a.* intracapsular, within a capsule.

intracelular *a.* intracellular, within a cell.

intracraneal *a.* intracranial, within the cranium.

intracutáneo-a *a.* intracutaneous, within the dermis.

intrahepático-a *a.* intrahepatic, within the liver.

intralobular *a.* intralobular, within a lobule.

intraluminal *a.* intraluminal, within the lumen of a tube.

intramuscular *a.* intramuscular, within a muscle.

intranquilidad *f.* restlessness, uneasiness.

intranquilo-a *a.* restless, uneasy.

intraocular *a.* intraocular, within the eye; presión ___ / ___ pressure.

intraoperatorio-a *a.* intraoperative, within the time frame of a surgical procedure.

intraóseo-a *a.* intraosseous, within the bone substance.

intrauterino-a *a.* intrauterine, within the uterus; dispositivo ___ / ___ device, coil.

intravenoso-a *a.* intravenous, within a vein; infusión ___ / ___ infusion; inyección ___ / ___ injection.

intraventricular *a.* intraventricular, within a ventricle.

intrínseco-a *a.* intrinsic, inherent; factor ___ / ___ factor, protein normally present in the gastric juice of humans.

introducir *vi.* to introduce.

introductor, intubador *m.* introducer, intubator, device used to intubate.

introitus *L.* introitus, an entrance or opening to a canal or cavity.

introspección *f.* introspection, self-analysis.

introversión *f. psych.* introversion, the act of turning one's interests inward with diminished interest in the outside world.

introvertido-a *m., f.* introvert; *a.* rel. to introversion.

intubación *f.* intubation, insertion of a tube into a conduit or cavity of the body.

intuición *f.* intuition.

intususcepción *f.* intussusception, invagination of one part of the intestine into the lumen of the adjoining part causing obstruction.

in utero *L.* in utero, within the uterus.

inútil *a.* useless; ineffective.

invadir *v.* to invade, to take over.

invaginación *f.* invagination, process of inclusion of one part into another.

invaginar *v.* invaginate, to introduce one part of a structure into another part of the same structure.

inválido-a *m., f.* invalid; *a.* crippled; void.

invariable *a.* invariable.

invasión *f.* invasion, the act of invading.

invasor-a *a.* invasive, rel. to a germ or substance that invades adjacent tissues; no ___ / noninvasive.

investigación *f.* research; ____ clínica / clinical ____ ; ____ de laboratorio / laboratory ____ .

investigar *vi.* to investigate, to research.

invisible *a.* invisible, that cannot be seen with the naked eye.

in vitro *L.* in vitro, rel. to laboratory tests or biological experimentation occurring outside the living body esp. in a test-tube; fertilización ____ / ____fertilization.

in vivo *L.* in vivo, within the body of living organisms.

involución *f.* involution, a retrogressive change.

involuntario-a *a.* involuntary.

inyección *f.* injection, shot.

inyectar *v.* to inject, to introduce fluid in a tissue, cavity, or blood vessel with an injector.

inyector *m.* injector, device used to inject; syringe.

iodo, yodo *m.* iodine, nonmetallic element used as a germicide and as an aid in the development and function of the thyroid gland.

ión *m.* ion, an atom or group of atoms carrying a charge of electricity.

ionización *f.* ionization, dissociation of compounds into their constituent ions; radiación por ____ / ionizing radiation.

ipeca, jarabe de, *m.* syrup of ipecac, an emetic and expectorant agent.

ipsolateral *a.* ipsolateral, on the same side.

ir *vi.* to go; **irse** *vr.* to go away, to leave.

irascible *a.* irascible, easily angered.

iridectomía *f. surg.* iridectomy, removal of a part of the iris.

iridología *f.* iridology, study of the changes suffered by the iris during the course of an illness.

iris *m.* iris, contractile membrane situated between the lens and the cornea in the aqueous humor of the eye which regulates the entrance of light.

iritis *f.* iritis, infl. of the iris.

irracional *a.* irrational.

irradiación *f.* irradiation, therapeutic use of radiation.

irradiar *v.* to irradiate, to expose to or treat by radiation; to emit rays.

irreducible *a.* irreducible, that cannot be reduced.

irregular *a.* irregular.

irrigación *f.* irrigation, the act of washing out; flushing.

irrigar *vi.* to irrigate, to wash out.

irritabilidad *f.* irritability, property of an organism or tissue to react to its environment.

irritable *a.* irritable, that reacts to a stimulus.

irritación *f.* irritation, intense reaction to a pain or pathological condition.

isla *f.* island, isolated piece of tissue or group of cells.

isométrico-a *a.* isometric, of equal dimensions.

isoniacida *f.* isoniazid, antibacterial medication used in the treatment of tuberculosis.

isotónico-a *a.* isotonic, having equal tension.

isótopo *m.* isotope, one of a group of chemical elements that present almost identical qualities but differ in atomic weight.

isquemia *f.* ischemia, lack of blood supply to a given part of the body.

isquémico-a *a.* ischemic, rel. to or suffering from ischemia; ataque ____ transitorio / transient ____ attack, temporary stoppage of blood supply to the brain.

isquion *m.* ischium, posterior part of the pelvis.

izquierda *f.* left; left hand; **a la** ____ / to the

izquierdo-a *a.* left.

J

jabón *m.* soap.

jadear *v.* to pant.

jadeo *m.* panting, gasping, shortness of breath; wheeze.

jalea *f.* jelly; ____ anticonceptiva /·contraceptive ____ ; ____ vaginal / vaginal ____ .

jamais vu *Fr.* jamais vu, the perception of familiar surroundings as a new experience.

jamás *adv.* never, ever.

jamón *m.* ham.

jaqueca *f.* severe headache.

jarabe *m.* cough syrup; ____ de ipecacuana / ipecac syrup.

jarra *f.* jar, pitcher; ____ **de agua** / a pitcher of water.

jazmín *m.* jasmine; **té de** ____ / ____ tea.

jején *m.* gnat.

jengibre *m.* ginger.

jeringa, jeringuilla *f.* syringe; ____ de aguja

hueca / hollow needle ___ ; ___ con tubo de cristal / glass cylinder ___ ; ___ desechable / disposable ___ ; ___ hipodérmica / hypodermic ___ .

jimaguas *m. pl., Cuba* twins.

joroba *f.* hump.

jorobado-a *a.* hunchbacked; crooked.

joven *a.* young.

jovencito-a *a.* youngster.

juanete *m.* bunion *V.* **hallux valgus.**

jubilado-a *m., f.* retiree; *a.* retired.

juez-a *m., f.* judge.

jugar *vi.* to play.

jugo *m.* juice; ___ gástrico / gastric ___ ; ___ intestinal / intestinal ___ ; ___ pancreático / pancreatic ___ ; ___ **de ciruela** / prune ___ ; ___ **de manzana** / apple ___ ; ___ **de naranja** / orange ___ ; ___ **de piña** / pineapple ___ ; ___ **de tomate** / tomato ___ ; ___ **de toronja** / grapefruit ___ ; ___ **de uva** / grape ___ ; ___ **de zanahoria** / carrot ___ .

jugoso-a *a.* juicy.

juguete *m.* toy.

junta *f.* meeting, gathering.

juntar *v.* to join, to gather together.

junto-a *a.* together.

juntura *f.* joint, juncture.

jurado *m.* jury.

juramento *m.* oath; ___ **hipocrático** / Hippocratic ___ , medical oath.

jurisprudencia médica *f.* medical jurisprudence, the law as applied to the practice of medicine.

justicia *f.* justice.

justificar *vi.* to justify.

justo-a *a.* just, fair; **-mente** *adv.* justly.

juvenil *a.* juvenile; **delincuencia** ___ / ___ delinquency.

juventud *f.* youth.

juzgar *vi.* to judge; **a** ___ **por** / judging by.

K

K *abr.* **potasio** / kalium, potassium.

k *abr.* **kilogramo** / kilogram.

kala-azar *m.* kala-azar, *Hindi* black fever, visceral infestation by a protozoa.

Kaposi, enfermedad de *f.* Kaposi's disease, malignant neoplasm found in the skin of the lower extremities of adult males, very prevalent among individuals suffering from AIDS.

kernicterus *m.* kernicterus, type of jaundice found in the newborn.

kerosén, kerosina *m., f.* kerosene.

kilómetro *m.* kilometer.

Klebsiella *m.* Klebsiella, gram-negative bacilli associated with respiratory and urinary tract infections.

Klebs-Löffler, bacilo de *m.* Klebs-Löffler bacillus, the diphtheria bacillus.

Koch, bacilo de *m.* Koch's bacillus, *Mycobacterium tuberculosis*, the cause of tuberculosis in mammals.

Kussmaul, respiración de *f.* Kussmaul's breathing, deep and gasping respiration seen in cases of diabetic acidosis.

kwashiorkor *m.* kwashiorkor, severe protein deficiency seen in infants after being weaned, esp. in tropical and subtropical areas.

L

l *abr.* **letal** / lethal; **ligero** / light; **litro** / liter.

laberintitis *f.* labyrinthitis. 1. acute or chronic infl. of the labyrinth; 2. internal otitis.

laberinto *m.* labyrinth, maze. 1. communicating channels of the internal ear that function in rel. to hearing and to body balance; 2. channels and cavities that communicate forming a system.

labial *a.* labial, rel. to the lips; **glándulas** ___ **-es** / ___ glands, situated between the labial mucosa and the orbicular muscle of the mouth.

labihendido-a *a.* harelipped.

lábil *a.* labile, unstable, fragile, that changes or is easily altered.

labilidad *f.* lability, condition of being unstable.

labio *m.* lip. 1. fleshy border; 2. lip-like structure.

labio leporino *m.* harelip, cleft lip, congenital anomaly at the level of the upper lip, caused by faulty fusion of the upper jaw and the nasal processes; **cirugía del** ___ / ___ suture.

laboratorio *m.* laboratory.

laboratorista *m., f.* medical laboratory technician.

laborioso-a *a.* labored, laborious; difficult.

laceración *f.* laceration; tear.

lacerar *v.* to lacerate.

lacrimal, lagrimal *a.* lacrimal, lachrymal, rel. to tears or to tear ducts; conducto ____ / ____ duct; hueso ____ / ____ bone; saco ____ / ____ sac.

lacrimógeno-a *a.* lachrymogenous, that produces tears.

lactacidemia *f.* lactacidemia, excessive lactic acid in the blood.

lactancia, lactación *f.* lactation, secretion of milk; ____ materna / breast-feeding.

lactar *v.* to nurse; to suckle.

lactasa *f.* lactase, intestinal enzyme that hydrolizes lactose producing dextrose and galactose.

lácteo-a *a.* lacteal, rel. to milk; **productos** ____ **-s** / dairy products.

lactífero-a *a.* lactiferous, that secretes and conducts milk.

lactocele *m.* lactocele. *V.* **galactocele.**

lacto-ovovegetariano-a *m., f.* lacto-ovovegetarian, person whose diet consists of vegetables, eggs, and dairy products.

lactosa, lactina *f.* lactose, lactine, milk sugar; intolerancia a la ____ / ____ deficiency, characterized by gastrointestinal disorders.

lado *m.* side; **al** ____ / alongside; **al** ____ **de** / next to; **de** ____ / sideways.

lagaña, legaña *f.* lema, gummy secretion of the eye.

lágrima *f.* tear.

lagrimear *v.* to shed tears.

lagrimeo *m.* lacrimation, tearing.

lagrimoso-a *a.* tearful.

laguna *f.* lacuna, small cavity or depression such as those found in the brain.

lalación, lambdacismo *f., m.* lallation. 1. phonetic disorder by which the letter *r* is pronounced as *l;* 2. infantile babbling.

Lamaze, método de *m.* Lamaze technique or method, method of natural childbirth by which the mother is trained in techniques of breathing and relaxation that facilitate the process of delivery.

lamentable *a.* regrettable.

lamentar *v.* to regret; **lamentarse** *vr.* to lament, to complain.

lamento *m.* lament, complaint.

lámina *f.* lamina, thin sheath or layer.

laminado-a *a.* laminated, formed by one or more laminae.

laminectomía *f. surg.* laminectomy, removal of one or more vertebral laminae.

laminilla *f.* lamella. 1. thin layer; 2. disk that is inserted in the eye to apply a medication.

lámpara *f.* lamp; ____ de hendidura / slit ____ ; ____ infrarroja / infrared ____ ; **luz de una** ____ / lamplight.

lana *f.* wool.

lanceta *f.* lancet, lance, surgical instrument.

Landsteiner, clasificación de *f.* Landsteiner's classification, differentiation of blood types: O-A-B-AB.

langosta *f.* lobster.

languidez *f.* languor, languidness, exhaustion, lack of energy.

lánguido-a *a.* languid, weak.

lanolina *f.* lanolin, purified substance obtained from lamb's wool and used in ointments.

lanugo *m.* lanugo, soft fine hair that covers the body of the human fetus.

laparoscopía *f.* laparoscopy, examination of the peritoneal cavity with a laparoscope.

laparoscopio *m.* laparoscope, instrument used to visualize the peritoneal cavity.

laparotomía *f. surg* laparotomy, incision and opening of the abdomen.

lápiz *m.* pencil.

lapso *m.* lapse, span, time interval.

largo-a *a.* long.

laringe *f.* larynx. 1. part of the respiratory tract situated in the upper part of the trachea; 2. voice organ.

laringectomía *f.* surg. laryngectomy, removal of the larynx.

laríngeo-a *a.* laryngeal, rel. to the larynx; reflejo ____ / ____ reflex, cough produced by irritation of the larynx.

laringitis *f.* laryngitis, infl. of the larynx.

laringoespasmo *m.* laryngospasm, spasm of the laryngeal muscles.

laringofaringe *f.* laryngopharynx, inferior portion of the larynx.

laringoplastia *f.* surg. laryngoplasty, plastic reconstruction of the larynx.

laringoscopia *f.* laryngoscopy, examination of the larynx; ____ directa / direct ____ , by means of a laryngoscope; ____ indirecta / indirect ____ , by means of a mirror.

laringoscopio *m.* laryngoscope, instrument used to examine the larynx.

larva *f.* larva, maggot, early stage of some organisms such as insects.

larvado-a *a.* larvate, rel. to an insidious or atypical symptom.

larval *a.* larval, rel. to larvae.

larvicida *m*. larvicide, agent that exterminates larvae.

lasivo-a *a*. lascivious, salacious, lustful.

laser *m*. laser. 1. acronym for Light Amplification by Stimulated Emission of Radiation; 2. microsurgical scalpel used in the cauterization of tumors.

laser, rayos de *m. pl.* laser beams, radiation rays applied for the purpose of destroying tissue or separating parts.

lasitud *f*. lassitude, languor.

lástima *f*. pity, compassion; *v*. **tener** ___ / to feel sorry, to pity; **¡qué** ___**!** / what a ___!

lastimado-a *a*. injured, hurt.

lastimadura *f*. injury, hurt.

lastimar *v*. to hurt, to injure; **lastimarse** *vr*. to get hurt.

lata *f*. [*metal*] tin; [*de alimento*] can.

latencia *f*. latency, the condition of being latent; **período de** ___ / ___ period.

latente *a*. latent, present but not active; with no apparent symptoms or manifestations.

lateral *a*. lateral, rel. to a side.

lateroflexión *f*. lateroflexion, lateral flexion.

latido *m*. beat; throb; ___ **del corazón** / heart ___.

latir *v*. to beat, to throb; to pant.

lavabo *m*. washstand, basin.

lavado *m*. lavage, enema, irrigation of a cavity.

lavado de cerebro *m*. brain washing.

lavadora *f*. washing machine.

lavamanos *m*. washstand, washbowl.

lavaojos *m*. eyecup.

lavar *v*. to wash; **lavarse** *vr*. to wash oneself.

lavativa *f*. enema.

laxante *m*. laxative, mild physic.

laxitud *f*. laxity, relaxation; weakness.

laxo-a *a*. lax, relaxed, loose.

lección *f*. lesson.

lecitina *f*. lecithin, essential substance in the metabolism of fats found in animal tissue, esp. in the nervous tissue.

lectura *f*. reading; **impedimentos de la** ___ / ___ disorders; ___ **labial** / lip ___.

leche *f*. milk; ___ **condensada** / condensed ___; ___ **descremada** / skim ___; ___ **evaporada** / evaporated ___; ___ **materna** / mother's ___.

lechoso-a *a*. milky.

lechuga *f*. lettuce.

leer *vi*. to read.

legal *a*. legal, legitimate, according to the law; **pleito** ___ / law suit.

legaña *f*. lema, gummy secretion of the eye.

legislación médica *f*. medical legislation.

legitimidad *f*. legitimacy.

legítimo-a *a*. legitimate, that goes by the law; authentic.

lego-a *a*. lay, secular.

legumbre *f*. legume, vegetable.

leiomiofibroma *m*. leiomyofibroma, benign tumor of essentially connective fibrous and smooth muscular tissue.

leiomioma *m*. leiomyoma, benign tumor of essentially smooth muscular tissue.

leiomiosarcoma *f*. leiomyosarcoma, combined tumor of leiomyoma and sarcoma.

lejía *f*. lye, bleach; **envenenamiento por** ___ / ___ poisoning.

lejos *adv*. far, afar; **de** ___ / ___ away; **desde** ___ / from afar.

lengua *f*. 1. tongue, lingua; **depresor de** ___ / ___ depressor; 2. language; ___ **materna** / native ___.

lengua geográfica *f*. geographic tongue, tongue characterized by bare patches surrounded by thick epithelium, resembling a geographic map.

lenguaje *m*. language; ___ **hablado** / spoken ___.

lente *m*. lens; ___ **acromático** / achromatic ___; ___ **bicóncavo** / biconcave ___; ___-**s bifocales** / bifocal ___; ___ **de aumento** / magnifying glass; ___-**s de contacto** / contact lens; ___-**s intraoculares** / ___ implantation, intraocular; ___-**s trifocales** / trifocal ___.

lenteja *f*. lentil.

lenticular *a*. lenticular. 1. rel. to a lens; 2. rel. to the lens of the eye.

lento-a *a*. slow; sluggish; inactive; **-mente** *adv*. slowly.

lepra *f*. leprosy, Hansen's disease, infectious disease caused by the *Mycobacterium leprae* and characterized by more or less severe skin lesions.

leproso-a *m., f*. leper, person suffering from leprosy.

leptomeninges *f*. leptomeninges, the thinnest of the cerebral membranes: the pia mater and the arachnoid.

lesbiana *f*. lesbian, homosexual female.

lesbianismo *m*. lesbianism, feminine homosexuality.

lesión *f*. injury, lesion, contusion, wound;

_____ de latigazo / whiplash ____ ; ____ por una explosión próxima / air blast ____ .

letal *a.* lethal, mortal, that causes death; dosis ____ / ____ dose.

letárgico-a *a.* lethargic, lethargical.

letargo *m.* lethargy, torpor.

letra *f.* [*del alfabeto*] letter; [*escritura*] handwriting.

leucaferesis *f.* leukapheresis, separation of leukocytes from a patient's blood and transfusion of the treated blood back into the patient.

leucemia *f.* leukemia, blood cancer.

leucémico-a *a.* leukemic, rel. to or suffering from leukemia.

leucemoide *a.* lcukemoid, with leukemialike signs and symptoms.

leucina *f.* leucine, amino acid that is essential to the growth and metabolism of humans.

leucocito *m.* leukocyte, white blood cell, element of the blood important in the defensive and reparative functions of the body; ____ acidófilo / acidophil ____ , that changes color with acid dye; ____ basófilo / basophil ____ , that changes color with basic dye; ____ eosinofílico / eosinophilic ____ , that stains readily with eosin; ____ linfoide / nongranular lymphoid ____ ; ____ neutrófilo / neutrophil ____ , that has an affinity for neutral stains; ____ polimorfonucleado / polymorphonuclear ____ , having multilobed nuclei.

leucopenia *f.* leukopenia, below normal number of leukocytes in the blood.

leucoplasia *f.* leukoplakia, opalescent, precancerous patches of the mucous membrane of the mouth or tongue.

leucorrea *f.* leukorrhea, whitish vaginal discharge.

levadura *f.* yeast, leaven, minute fungi capable of producing fermentation and used in nutrition as a source of protein and vitamin.

levantar *v.* to raise, to lift, to pull up; **levantarse** *vr.* to get up.

leve *a.* light, slight.

levocardia *f.* levocardia, transposition of the abdominal viscera with normal position of the heart on the left side of the thorax.

levodopa *f.* levodopa, *L.* dopa, chemical substance used in the treatment of Parkinson's disease.

levulosa *f.* levulose. *V.* **fructosa.**

ley *f.* law; ____ del buen Samaritano / good

Samaritan ____ , legal protection to a professional who gives aid in an emergency.

liberación *f.* liberation.

liberado-a *a.* freed.

liberar,*librar *v.* to liberate, to free, to release.

libertad *f.* liberty; *v.* **tener** ____ **para** / to be free to.

libre *a.* free; asociación ____ / ____ association.

librería *f.* bookstore.

libreta *f.* notebook.

libro *m.* book.

licencia *f.* license, permit, licensure, authorization; ____ **para ejercer la medicina** / medical ____ .

licenciado-a *m., f.* attorney, licentiate.

licor *m.* liquor. *V.* **liquor.**

licuar *v.* to liquify, to dissolve.

lidocaína *f.* lidocaine, anesthetic.

Liga de la Leche, La *f.* La Leche League, an organization that promotes breast-feeding.

ligadura *f.* ligature, tie, affixture; linkage.

ligamento *m.* ligament. 1. bands of connective tissue fibers that protect the joints; ____ acromioclavicular / acromioclavicular ____ , extending from the clavicle to the acromion; ____ ancho uterino / broad uterine ____ , peritoneal fold that extends laterally from the uterus to the pelvic wall; 2. protective band of fascia and muscles that connect or support viscerae.

ligar *vi.* to tie, to apply a ligature; ____ las trompas / ____ the tubes.

ligazón *f.* binding, bandage.

ligero-a *a.* light, slight; **-mente** *adv.* lightly, slightly.

lima *f.* [*fruta*] lime; **jugo de** ____ / ____ juice; [*instrumento*] file.

limar *v.* to file; to smooth.

límbico-a *a.* limbic, marginal; sistema ____ / ____ system, group of cerebral structures.

limbo *m.* limbus, the edge or border of a part; ____ de la córnea / ____ cornea.

liminal *a. psych.* liminal, almost imperceptible.

limitación *f.* limitation; restriction.

limitado-a *a.* limited, restricted; **movimiento** ____ / restricted motion.

limitar *v.* to limit, to restrict.

límite *m.* limit; ____ de asimilación / assimilation ____ ; ____ de percepción / ____ of perception; ____ de saturación / saturation ____ .

limón *m.* lemon.

limonada *f.* lemonade.

limpiar *v.* to clean.

limpieza *f.* cleaning; cleanliness.

limpio-a *a.* clean.

linaje *m.* pedigree, ancestral line of descent.

lindo-a *a.* pretty.

línea *f.* line; wrinkle; guide.

linear *a.* lineal, that resembles a line.

linfa *f.* lymph, clear fluid found in lymphatic vessels.

linfadenectomía *f. surg.* lymphadenectomy, removal of lymphatic channels and nodes.

linfadenitis *f.* lymphadenitis, infl. of the lymphatic ganglia.

linfangiectasis *f.* lymphangiectasis, dilation of the lymphatic vessels.

linfangiograma *m.* lymphangiogram, X-ray of the lymph nodes and vessels obtained with the use of a contrasting medium.

linfangitis *f.* lymphangitis, infl. of the lymphatic vessels.

linfático-a *a.* lymphatic, rel. to lymph; ganglios ____-s / lymph nodes; sistema ____ / ____ system.

linfedema *m.* lymphedema, edema caused by blockage of the lymph vessels.

linfoblasto *m.* lymphoblast, early stage of a lymphocyte.

linfocito *m.* lymphocyte, lymphatic cell; ____ B / B cell, important in the production of antibodies.

linfocitopenia, linfopenia *f.* lymphocytopenia, lymphopenia, diminished number of lymphocytes in the blood.

linfocitos T *m. pl.* T cells, lymphocytes differentiated in the thymus that direct the immunological response and alert the B cells to respond to antigens; ____ inductor, (ayudante) / helper ____, enhance production of antibody forming cells from B cells; ____ citotóxico / cytotoxic ____, kill foreign cells (as in rejection of transplanted organs); ____ supresor / suppressor ____, supress production of antibody forming cells from B cells.

linfocitosis *f.* lymphocytosis, excessive number of lymphocytes in the blood.

linfogranuloma venéreo *f.* lymphogranuloma venereum, viral disorder that may lead to elephantiasis of the genitalia and rectal stricture.

linfogranulomatosis *f.* lymphogranulomatosis. *V.* **Hodgkin, enfermedad de.**

linfoide *a.* lymphoid, that resembles the lymphatic tissue.

linfoma *m.* lymphoma, any neoplasm of the lymphatic tissue.

linfomatoide *a.* lymphomatoid, rel. to or resembling a lymphoma.

linfopenia, linfocitopenia *f.* lymphopenia, lymphocytopenia, diminished number of lymphocytes in the blood.

linforeticular *a.* lymphoreticular, rel. to reticuloendothelial cells of the lymph nodes.

linfosarcoma *m.* lymphosarcoma, malignant neoplasm of the lymphoid tissue.

lingual *a.* lingual, rel. to the tongue.

língula *f.* lingula, tongue-like projection or structure.

linimento *m.* liniment, liquid substance for external use.

linitis *f.* linitis. *V.* **gastritis.**

lino *m.* linen.

linterna *f.* flashlight.

lío *m.* mess, confusion.

liodermia *f.* glossy skin, a sign of atrophy or traumatism of the nerves.

liofilización *f.* freeze-drying.

lipectomía *f. surg.* lipectomy, removal of fat tissue; ____ submental / submental ____, under the chin.

lipemia *f.* lipemia, abnormal presence of fat in the blood.

lipidemia *f.* lipidemia, excess lipids in the blood.

lípido *m.* lipid, lipide, organic substance that does not dissolve in water but is soluble in alcohol, ether or chloroform.

lipodistrofia *f.* lipodystrophy, metabolic disorder of fats.

lipoma *m.* lipoma, adipous tissue tumor.

lipomatosis *f.* lipomatosis. 1. condition caused by excessive accumulation of fat in a given area; 2. multiple lipomas.

lipoproteínas *f. pl.* lipoproteins, proteins combined with lipid compounds that contain a high concentration of cholesterol; ____ de densidad baja / low density ____.

liposarcoma *m.* liposarcoma, malignant tumor containing fatty elements.

liposis *f.* liposis, obesity, excessive accumulation of fat in the body.

liposoluble *a.* liposoluble, that dissolves in fatty substances.

liposucción *f.* liposuction, process of extracting fat by high vacuum pressure.

liquen *m.* lichen, noncontagious papular skin lesion; ___ plano / ___ planus.

líquido *m.* fluid, liquid; balance de ___ / ___ balance; ___ amniótico / amniotic ___ ; ___ cefalorraquídeo / cerebrospinal ___ ; ___ extracelular / extracellular ___ ; ___ extravascular / extravascular ___ ; ___ intercelular, intersticial / intercellular, interstitial ___ ; retención de ___ / ___ retention; *v.* **tomar** ___ -s / to take ___ -s; **-a** *a.* liquid.

liquor *L.* liquor. 1. a liquid, esp. an aqueous solution containing a medicinal substance; 2. general term used for certain fluids of the body.

lisiado-a *a.* crippled.

lisina *f.* lysin, antibody that dissolves or destroys cells or bacteria.

lisis *f.* lysis. 1. destruction or dissolution of red cells, bacteria, or any antigen by lysin; 2. gradual cessation of the symptoms of a disease.

lista *f.* list; ___ **de accidentados** / casualty ___ .

listo-a *a.* ready; clever.

litiasis *f.* lithiasis, formation of calculi, esp. in the biliary and urinary tracts.

litio *m.* lithium, metallic element used as a tranquilizer in severe cases of psychosis.

litotomía *f.* *surg.* lithotomy, incision in an organ or conduit to remove stones.

litotripsia *f.* lithotripsy, crushing of calculi present in the kidney, ureter, bladder, or gallbladder.

litotriturador *m.* lithotriptor, machine or device used to crush calculi; ___ extracorporal con ondas de choque / extra corporeal shock wave ___ .

lívido-a *a.* livid, [*una persona*] ash blue.

lobar *a.* lobar, rel. to a lobe; pulmonía ___ / ___ pneumonia.

lobectomía *f.* *surg.* lobectomy, excision of a lobe.

lobotomía *f.* *surg.* lobotomy, incision of a cerebral lobe to correct certain mental disorders; ___ completa / complete ___ ; ___ izquierda anterior / left lower ___ ; ___ parcial / partial ___ .

lobular *a.* lobular, rel. to a lobule.

lobulillo *m.* lobule, small lobe.

lóbulo *m.* lobe, rounded well-defined portion of an organ.

local *a.* local, rel. to an isolated area, such as local anesthesia; aplicación ___ / ___ application; reaparición ___ / ___ recurrence.

localización *f.* localization, location. 1. reference to the point of origin of a sensation; 2. determination of the origin of an infection or lesion.

localizar *vi.* to localize; to locate.

loción *f.* lotion.

loco-a *m., f.* insane person; *a.* mad, insane.

locomoción *f.* locomotion.

locular *a.* locular, loculated, rel. to loculi.

lóculo *m.* loculus, small cavity.

locura *f.* madness, insanity, lunacy.

locus *L.* locus, localization of a gene in a chromosome.

logafasia *f.* logaphasia, motor aphasia gen. caused by a cerebral lesion.

logagrafia *f.* logagraphia, inability to express thoughts in writing.

logamnesia *f.* logamnesia, sensorial aphasia, inability to recognize written or spoken words.

lógico-a *a.* logic, logical; reasonable.

lograr *v.* to achieve; to reach.

lombriz *f.* earthworm; ___ intestinal / pinworm, belly worm; ___ solitaria / tapeworm.

lonche *m.* *H.A.* lunch, midday meal.

longevidad *f.* longevity. 1. long duration of life; 2. life span.

longitudinal *a.* longitudinal, lengthwise.

loquios *m.* lochia, bloody, scrosanguineous discharge from the uterus and the vagina during the first few weeks after delivery.

lordosis *f.* lordosis, abnormally increased curvature of the lumbar spine; saddle back.

lubricación *f.* lubrication.

lubricante *m.* lubricant, oily agent that when applied diminishes friction between two surfaces.

lubricar *vi.* to lubricate, to apply a lubricant to a surface.

lúcido-a *a.* lucid, clear of mind.

lucha *f.* struggle; fight.

luchar *v.* to struggle; to fight.

luego *adv.* in a while; then; *conj.* therefore; **desde** ___ / of course; **hasta** ___ / so long, good-bye.

luético-a *a.* luetic, syphilitic, rel. to or suffering from syphilis.

lugar *m.* place, space; **en** ___ **de** / in ___ of; *v.* **poner en su** ___ / to put in ___ ; **tener** ___ / to take ___ .

lujuria *f.* lust, lewdness, lasciviousness.

lujurioso-a *a.* lustful, lewd, libidinous.
lumbago *m.* lumbago, pain in the lower portion of the back.
lumbar *a.* lumbar, rel. to the part of the back between the thorax and the pelvis; back; punción ___ / ___ puncture; vértebras ___ -es / ___ vertebrae.
lumbricosis *f.* lumbricosis, infestation by earth worms.
lumen *m.* lumen. 1. space in a cavity, conduit, or organ; 2. unit of light.
Luminal *m.* Luminal, trade name for a compound containing phenobarbital and used as a sedative.
luminal *a.* luminal, rel. to light in a conduit or canal.
luminiscencia, luminosidad *f.* luminescense, luminosity, emission of light without production of heat.
luminoso-a *a.* luminous, rel. to luminosity.
luna *f.* moon.
lunar *m.* mole; blemish; *a.* rel. to the moon.
lunático-a *m., f.* lunatic, crazy person.
lupa *f.* magnifying glass.
lupa binocular *f.* loupe, convex magnifying lens used esp. by surgeons and ophthalmologists
lupus *L.* lupus, chronic skin disease of unknown origin that causes degenerative local lesions; ___ eritematoso discoide / ___ erythematosus, discoid, disease that causes irritation of the skin and is characterized by squamous plaques with reddish borders; ___ eritematoso sistémico / ___ erythematosus, systemic, characterized by febrile episodes affecting the viscera and the nervous system.
lúteo-a, luteínico-a *a.* luteal, rel. to the corpus luteum.
luto *m.* mourning; **estar de** ___ / to mourn.
luxación *f.* dislocation, luxation; ___ cerrada / closed ___ ; ___ complicada / complicated ___ ; ___ congénita / congenital ___ .
luz *f.* light; *v.* **dar a** ___ / to give birth.

LL

LL fourteenth letter of the Spanish alphabet.

llaga *f.* sore, ulcer, blain.

llamada *f.* call; ___ **de teléfono** / telephone ___ .
llave *f.* key.
llegada *f.* arrival; coming.
llegar *vi.* to arrive; to reach; to attain; ___ **a ser** / to become; **llegarse** *vr.* to approach.
llenar *v.* to fill; to complete.
lleno-a *a.* full, complete.
llenura *f.* fullness, plenty, abundance; tener ___ / to be very full.
llevar *v.* to carry; to take; to transport; ___ **puesto** / to be wearing; ___ **a cabo** / to carry out; **llevarse** *vr.* to take away; ___ **a cabo** / to take place; ___ **bien** / to get along well; ___ **mal** / not to get along.
llorar *v.* to cry.
lloradera *f.* weeping.
llover *vi.* to rain.
lluvia *f.* rain.
lluvioso-a *a.* rainy.

M

M *abr.* **maduro** / mature; **maligno-a** / malignant; **minuto** / minute; **morfina** / morphin.

macerar *v.* to macerate, to soften by soaking.
macizo-a *a.* compact, solid.
macrocefalia *f.* macrocephalia, abnormally large head.
macrocefálico-a *a.* macrocephalic, having an abnormally large head.
macrocitemia, macrocitosis *f.* macrocythemia, macrocytosis, larger than normal erythrocytes in the blood.
macrocosmo *m.* macrocosm. 1. the universe considered as a whole; 2. the total or entire structure of something.
Macrodantina *f.* Macrodantin, trade name for furantoin, bactericide used in the treatment of urinary infections.
macrófago *m.* macrophage, macrophagus, mononuclear phagocytic cell; migración de ___ -s / ___ migration.
macroglosia *f.* macroglossia, enlargement of the tongue.
macrognatia *f.* macrognathia, enlargement of the jaw.
macromolécula *f.* macromolecule, a large size molecule such as that of a protein.

macroscópico-a *a.* macroscopic, that can be seen with the naked eye.

macrospora *f.* macrospore, large spore.

mácula *f.* macula, macule, speck, small discolored spot in the skin; ___ lútea / ___ lutea, small yellowish area next to the center of the retina.

maculado-a *a.* maculate.

macular *a.* macular, rel. to macules.

maculopapular *a.* maculopapular, rel. to macules and papules.

macho *m.* male; *a.* male; manly.

madera *f.* wood.

madrastra *f.* stepmother.

madre *f.* mother; ___ soltera / unwed ___.

madrugada *f.* daybreak; **de** ___ / at dawn.

madrugar *vi.* to rise early.

madurar *v.* to mature; to ripen.

madurez *f.* maturity; ripeness, stage of full development.

maduro-a *a.* mature, ripened.

magistral *a.* magistral, rel. to medication that is prepared according to the physician's indications.

magma *f.* magma. 1. suspension of particles in a small amount of water; 2. viscous mass composed of organic material.

magnesia *f.* magnesia, magnesium oxide; **leche de** ___ / milk of ___.

magnesio *m.* magnesium; sulfato de ___ / ___ sulfate.

magnético-a *a.* magnetic, magnetical, rel. to or that has the property of a magnet; campo ___ / ___ field.

magnetismo *m.* magnetism, the magnetic property to attract or repeal.

magnetoelectricidad *f.* magnetoelectricity, electricity induced by a magnet.

magnífico-a *a.* superb, wonderful.

magnitud *f.* magnitude.

magulladura *f.* bruise, contusion.

majadero-a *a.* spoiled, cranky.

mal *m.* mal, illness, disease.

mal, malo-a *a.* bad; evil; **mal genio** / ill temper; **mal** *adv.* badly; wrongly; **de** ___ **en peor** / from bad to worse; *v.* **hacer** ___ / to harm, to hurt.

malacia *f.* malacia, softening or loss of consistency of organs or tissues.

malacoplaquia *f.* malacoplakia, formation of soft patches in the mucous membrane of a hollow organ.

malagradecido-a *a.* ungrateful.

malar *a.* malar, rel. to the cheek or the cheek bone.

malaria *f.* malaria. *V.* **paludismo.**

malaricida *a.* malariacidal, that kills the parasites of malaria.

malcriado-a *a.* ill-bred, spoiled.

maleable *a.* malleable.

maléolo *m.* malleolus, hammer-like protuberance, such as the ones on either side of the ankle.

malestar *m.* malaise, discomfort, uneasiness.

maleta *f.* valise, suitcase.

malformación *f.* malformation, anomaly or deformity, esp. congenital.

malfuncionamiento *m.* malfunction, disorder.

malhumor *m.* bad-temper.

malhumorado-a *a.* sullen, bad-tempered.

malignidad *f.* malignancy. 1. quality of being malignant; 2. cancerous tumor.

maligno-a *a.* malignant, virulent, pernicious, with a destructive effect.

malnutrición *f.* malnutrition, deficient nutrition.

maloclusión *f.* malocclusion, defective bite.

malpresentación *f.* malpresentation, abnormal presentation of the fetus at the time of delivery.

malrotación *f.* malrotation, abnormal or defective rotation of an organ or part.

malta *f.* malt.

maltosa *f.* maltose, a type of sugar.

maltratar *v.* to abuse, to mistreat, to manhandle; ___ **de palabra** / verbal abuse.

malunión *f.* malunion, imperfect union of a fracture.

malleus *L.* (*pl.* **mallei**) malleus, one of the three ossicles of the middle ear.

mama *f.* mamma, breast, milk-secreting gland in the female.

mamá *f.* mom, endearing term for mother.

mamalgia *f.* mammalgia, pain in the mamma.

mamaplastia, mamoplastia *f. surg.* mammaplasty, mammoplasty, plastic surgery of the breasts.

mamar *v.* to suckle, to draw milk from the breast; **dar de** ___ / to breast-feed.

mamario-a *a.* mammary, rel. to the mamma; glándulas ___ -s / ___ glands.

mamectomía *f.* mammectomy. *V.* **mastectomía.**

mamífero *m.* mammal.

mamilado-a *a.* mammillated, presenting small protuberances that resemble nipples.

mamilar *a.* mammillary, resembling a nipple.

mamiliplastia *f. surg.* mammilliplasty, plastic surgery of the nipple.

mamilitis *f.* mammillitis, infl. of the nipple.

mamitis, mastitis *f.* mammitis, mastitis, infl. of the mammary gland.

mamograma *m.* mammogram, X-ray of the breast.

manco-a *m., f.* one-handed person.

mancha *f.* spot, blemish, macula, stain.

manchado-a *a.* spotted, soiled.

manchar *v.* to soil, to spot; to stain; **mancharse** *vr.* to become stained or spotted.

mandar *v.* to order, to command; to send.

mandato *m.* order, command.

mandíbula *f.* mandible, mandibula, horseshoe-shaped bone that constitutes the lower jaw; ___ inferior / lower ___ ; ___ superior / upper ___ .

mandibular *a.* mandibular, rel. to the mandible.

manejable *a.* manageable.

manejar *v.* to conduct, to drive.

manera *f.* manner, method, way.

manerismo *m.* mannerism, peculiar manifestation in dress, speech or action.

manga *f.* sleeve.

mango *m.* mango. 1. tropical fruit; 2. handle.

manguito *m.* cuff, handlike structure of skin or subcutaneous tissue encircling a part.

maní *m.* peanut; **mantequilla de** ___ / ___ butter.

manía *f. psych.* mania, emotional disorder characterized by extreme excitement, exalted emotions, rapid succession of ideas and fluctuating moods.

maníaco-a, maniático-a *a.* maniac, maniacal, afflicted by mania; **maníaco-depresivo** / manic-depressive.

manicomio *m.* insane asylum, madhouse.

manifestación *f.* manifestation, revelation.

manifestar *vi.* to manifest, to express; **manifestarse** *vr.* to appear, [*enfermedad*] to reveal itself.

maniobra *f.* maneuver, skillful manual procedure such as executed by the obstetrician in the delivery of a baby.

manipulación *f.* manipulation, professional treatment involving the use of hands.

manipular *v.* to manipulate, to handle.

maniquí *m.* manikin, representative figure of the human body.

mano *f.* hand; deformidades adquiridas de la ___ / acquired ___ deformities; **apoyo de la** ___ / ___ rest; **hecho a** ___ / hand-made.

manómetro *m.* manometer, device used to measure the pressure of liquids or gases.

manteca *f.* lard, animal fat.

mantener *vi.* to sustain, to support; **mantenerse** *vr.* to hold or keep up; to support oneself.

mantenimiento *m.* maintenance, sustenance.

mantequilla *f.* butter.

manto *m.* mantle, covering.

manual *a.* manual.

manubrium *L.* manubrium, handle-shaped structure.

manutención *f.* maintenance, support; child care.

manzana *f.* apple.

manzanilla *f.* camomile, sedative tea used to alleviate gastrointestinal discomfort.

maña *f.* bad habit.

mañana *f.* morning; tomorrow; **por la** ___ / in the morning; **muy de** ___ / very early in the morning.

máquina *f.* machine, apparatus.

mar *m.* sea.

marasmo *m.* marasmus, extreme malnutrition, emaciation, esp. in young children.

maravilloso-a *a.* marvelous, wonderful.

marca *f.* mark, sign; ___ de la viruela / pockmark; ___ de nacimiento / birthmark; ___ en fresa / strawberry ___ ; ___ registrada / trade ___ .

marcador *m.* marker, indicator.

marcapasos *m.* pacemaker, pacer, regulator of cardiac rhythm.

marcar *vi.* to mark; to brand; to point out.

marcha *f.* gait, walk; ___ anserina / waddling ___ , wide spread walk; ___ atáxica / ataxic ___ , staggering; ___ cerebelosa / cerebellar ___ ; ___ espástica / spastic ___ ; ___ hemipléjica / hemiplegic ___ , circular movement of one of the lower extremities.

mareado-a *a.* dizzy, light-headed.

marearse *vr.* to get motion sickness; to become dizzy.

mareo *m.* dizziness; motion sickness; ___ de altura / altitude sickness.

margarina *f.* margarine.

margen *m.* margin, border.

marginación *f.* margination, accumulation and adhesion of leukocytes to the epithelial cells of the blood vessel walls at the beginning of an inflammatory process.

marginal *a.* marginal, rel. to a margin; caso ___ / ___ case.

marido *m.* husband.

mariguana, marijuana *f.* marihuana, marijuana. *V.* **cannabis.**

marisco *m.* shellfish.

marital *a.* marital, rel. to marriage.

marsupialización *f. surg.* marsupialization, conversion of a closed cavity into an open pouch.

martillo *m.* hammer. 1. common name for malleus, small bone of the middle ear; 2. instrument used in physical examination.

más *adv.* more, to a greater degree; **a** ___ **tardar** / at the latest; **por** ___ **que** / however much; ___ **allá** / beyond; ___ **que** / more than; ___ **vale** / better to.

masa *f.* mass, body formed by coherent particles.

masaje *m.* massage, process of manipulation of different parts of the body by rubbing or kneading; ___ cardíaco / cardiac ___ , resuscitation.

masajista *m., f.* masseur, masseuse, person who performs massage.

mascar, masticar *vi.* to chew.

máscara *f.* mask. 1. covering of the face; 2. appearance of the face, esp. as a pathological manifestation.

mascarilla *f.* death mask.

masculinización *f.* masculinization. *V.* **virilización.**

masculino-a *a.* masculine, rel. to the male sex.

masetero *m.* masseter, principal muscle in mastication.

masivo-a *a.* massive.

masoquismo *m. psych.* masochism, abnormal condition by which sexual gratification is obtained from self-inflicted pain or pain inflicted by others.

massa *L.* massa, middle commissure of the brain.

mastadenitis *f.* mastadenitis. *V.* **mamitis.**

mastalgia *f.* mastalgia. *V.* **mamalgia.**

mastectomía *f. surg.* mastectomy, plastic surgery of the breasts.

masticación *f.* mastication, the act of chewing.

mastitis *f.* mastitis. *V.* **mamitis;** ___ cística / cystic ___ , fibrocystic disease of the mamma; ___ por estasis / caked breast.

mastoideo-a *a.* mastoid. 1. rel. to the mastoid process; antro ___ / ___ antrum; células ___ -s / ___ cells, air spaces in the mastoid process; 2. that resembles a breast or nipple.

mastoides *m.* mastoid process, rounded apophysis of the temporal bone.

mastoiditis *f.* mastoiditis, infl. of the air cells of the mastoid process.

mastopatía *f.* mastopathy, any disorder of the mammary glands.

masturbación *f.* masturbation, autostimulation and manipulation of the genitals to achieve sexual pleasure.

matar *v.* to kill.

materia *f.* matter, substance.

material *m.* material; *a.* material.

maternidad *f.* maternity; **hospital de** ___ / ___ hospital.

materno-a *a.* maternal, rel. to the mother; **línea** ___ / matrilineal, tracing descent on the female side.

matidez *f.* dullness, diminished resonance to palpation.

matriz *f.* matrix, basic material; cast.

matutino-a *a.* of the morning, rel. to the early hours of the day; enfermedad ___ del embarazo / morning sickness; rigidez ___ muscular y de las articulaciones / morning stiffness.

maxilar *a.* maxillary, rel. to the maxilla; hueso ___ de la mandíbula / jawbone.

maxilla *L.* maxilla, bone of the upper jaw.

mayonesa *f.* mayonnaise.

mayor *a.* greater, [*edad*] older; **-mente** *adv.* mostly, mainly.

mayoría *f.* majority.

máximo-a *a.* maximum, the most.

meatal *a.* meatal, rel. to a meatus.

meato *m.* meatus, passage or channel in the body.

mecánico-a *m., f.* mechanic; *a.* mechanical.

mecanismo *m.* mechanism. 1. involuntary response to a stimulus; ___ de defensa / defense ___ ; 2. machine-like structure.

meconio *m.* meconium. 1. first feces of the newborn; 2. opium.

media *f.* mean. 1. average; 2. middle coat of a blood vessel or artery.

mediador-a *m., f.* mediator, entity or person that mediates.

medial *a.* medial, rel. to or situated towards the middle.

medianoche *f.* midnight.

mediante *adv.* by means of.

mediar *v.* to mediate.

medias *f. pl.* socks, stockings; ___ elásticas / elastic stockings.

mediastinitis *f.* mediastinitis, infl. of the tissues of the mediastinum.

mediastino *m.* mediastinum. 1. mass of tissues and organs separating the lungs; 2. cavity between two organs.

mediastinoscopía *f.* mediastinoscopy, endoscopic examination of the mediastinum.

medicación, medicamento *f., m.* medication, medicament; medicamento de patente / patent medicine.

Medicaid *m.* Medicaid, U.S. government program to provide health care for the poor.

Medicare *m.* Medicare, U.S. government program that subsidizes health care esp. for the elderly and the disabled.

medicina *f.* 1. medicine, the healing arts; ___ clínica / clinical ___; ___ comunal, al servicio de la comunidad / community ___; ___ deportiva / sport ___; ___ ecológica / environmental ___; ___ del espacio / aerospace ___; ___ familiar / family practice; ___ forense / forensic ___; ___ industrial / industrial ___; ___ interna / internal ___; ___ legal / legal ___; ___ nuclear / nuclear ___; ___ ocupacional / occupational ___; ___ preventiva / preventive ___; ___ socializada / socialized ___; ___ tropical / tropical ___; ___ veterinaria / veterinary ___; 2. medication, medicine, drug; estudiante de ___ / medical student.

medicina holística *f.* holistic medicine, an approach to medicine that considers the human being as an integral functional unit.

medicinal *a.* medicinal, rel. to medicine or with medical properties.

médico-a *m., f.* physician, doctor; cuerpo ___ / medical staff; ___ consultante, asesor / consulting ___; ___ de cabecera o primario / primary ___; ___ de familia / family ___; ___ de guardia / doctor on call; ___ forense / coroner; ___ interno / intern; ___ recomendante / referring ___; ___ residente / resident, physician serving a residency; *a.* medical, medicinal, rel. to medicine or that cures; asistencia

___ / ___ assistance; atención ___ / ___ care.

medicolegal *a.* medicolegal, the practice of medicine as related to law.

medida *f.* measure; measurement; **con** ___ / moderately.

medio *m.* medium; 1. means to attain an effect; 2. substance that transmits impulses; 3. substance used in the culture of bacteria; **en** ___ **de** / in the middle of; **por** ___ **de** / by means of; **-a** *a.* half; in part; **línea** ___ medial line; **punto** ___ / medium.

mediodía *m.* noon.

medir *vi.* to measure; **cinta de** ___ / measuring tape; **taza de** ___ / measuring cup.

médula espinal *f.* spinal cord, a column of nervous tissue that extends from the medulla oblongata to the first or second lumbar vertebrae, and from which arise all the nerves that go to the trunk of the body and to the extremities.

médula oblongata *f.* medulla oblongata, portion of the medulla located at the base of the brain.

médula ósea *f.* bone marrow, sponge-like tissue present in the cavities of bones; punción y aspiración de la ___ / ___ puncture and aspiration; fallo de la ___ / ___ failure; transplante de la ___ / ___ transplant.

medular *a.* medullary, rel. to the medulla.

megacéfalo-a *a.* megacephalic. *V.* **macrocéfalo.**

megacolon *m.* megacolon, abnormally large colon.

megaesófago *m.* megaesophagus, abnormally large dilation of the inferior portion of the esophagus.

megalomanía *f. psych.* megalomania, delusions of grandeur.

megalómano-a *a. psych.* megalomaniac, suffering from megalomania.

megavitamina *f.* megavitamin, a dose of vitamin that exceeds the daily requirement.

meiosis *f.* meiosis, process of cell division that results in the production of gametes.

mejilla *f.* cheek.

mejor *a.* [*comp. of bueno*] better; best; **la** ___ **medicina** / the best medication; *sup.* **es el, la** ___ / it is the best; *adv.* better; *v.* **estar** ___ / to be ___; *vr.* **ponerse** ___ / to get ___; **tanto** ___ / so much the ___.

mejoramiento, mejoría *m., f.* improvement, amelioration.

mejorana *f.* marjoram.

mejorar *v.* to improve; **mejorarse** *vr.* to get better.

mejoría *f.* improvement, amelioration.

melancolía *f.* melancholia, marked depression.

melancólico-a *a.* rel. to or suffering from melancholia.

melanina *f.* melanin, dark pigmentation of the skin, hair and parts of the eye.

melanocito *m.* melanocyte, melanine-producing cell.

melanoma *m.* melanoma, malignant tumor made of melanocytes.

melanosis *f.* melanosis, condition characterized by an unusual deposit of dark pigmentation in various tissues or organs.

melanuria *f.* melanuria, presence of dark pigmentation in the urine.

melena *f.* melena, abnormally dark and pasty stool containing digested blood.

melocotón *m.* peach.

mellizos-as *m., f. pl.* twins. V. **gemelos.**

membrana *f.* membrane, web, thin layer of tissue that covers or protects an organ or structure; ____ -s arteriopulmonares / pulmonary arterial webs; ____ de la placenta / placental ____ ; ____ mucosa / mucous ____ ; ____ nuclear / nuclear ____ ; ____ permeable / permeable ____ ; ____ semipermeable / semipermeable ____ ; ____ sinovial / synovial ____ ; ____ timpánica / tympanic ____ .

membranoso-a *a.* membranous, rel. to or of the nature of a membrane.

memorando *m.* memorandum.

memoria *f.* memory, faculty that allows the registration and recall of experiences; ____ immediata / short term ____ .

memorizar *vi.* to memorize.

menarca *m.* menarche, beginning of menstruation.

mendelismo *m.* Mendelism, set of principles that explains the transmission of certain genetic traits.

menguar *v.* to subside, to diminish.

meníngeo-a *a.* meningeal, rel. to the meninges.

meninges *f.* meninges, three layers of connective tissue that surround the brain and the spinal cord.

meningioma *m.* meningioma, a slow-growing vascular neoplasm arising from the meninges.

meningismo *m.* meningism, meningismus, congestive irritation of the meninges, gen. of a toxic nature, that presents symptoms similar to those of meningitis but without infl., seen esp. in children.

meningitis *f.* (*pl.* **meningitis**) infl. of the meninges.

meningocele *m.* meningocele, protrusion of the meninges through a defect in the skull or the vertebral column.

meningococo *m.* meningococcus, microorganism that causes epidemic cerebral meningitis.

meningoencefalitis *f.* meningoencephalitis, cerebromeningitis, infl. of the encephalum and the meninges.

meningoencefalocele *m.* meningoencephalocele, protrusion of the encephalum and the meninges through a defect in the cranium.

meningomielitis *f.* meningomyelitis, infl. of the spinal cord and the membranes that cover it.

meningomielocele *m.* meningomyelocele, protrusion of the spinal cord and meninges through a defect of the vertebral column.

meniscectomía *f. surg.* meniscectomy, excision of a meniscus.

menisco *m.* meniscus, crescent-shaped, cartilaginous, interarticular structure.

menometrorragia *f.* menometrorrhagia, excessive or irregular menstruation.

menopausia *f.* menopause, cessation of the fertility stage of adult women and decrease in their hormone production.

menor *a.* smaller, less, lesser, [*comp. of pequeño*] younger; smallest, [*sup. of pequeño*] youngest; el hijo ____ / the youngest son.

menorragia *f.* menorrhagia, excessive bleeding in menstruation.

menorralgia *f.* menorrhalgia, painful menstruation.

menorrea *f.* menorrhea, normal menstrual flow without obstruction.

menos *adv.* less; **poco más o** ____ / more or less; **por lo** ____ / at least; **a** ____ **que** / unless.

menospreciar *v.* to underestimate; not to hold in high esteem.

mensaje *m.* message.

menstruación *f.* menstruation, periodic flow of bloody fluid from the uterus; trastornos de la ____ / menstrual disorders.

menstrual *a.* menstrual, rel. to menstruation; ciclo ____ / ____ cycle.

menstruar *v.* to menstruate.

menstruo *m.* menses, menstruation, period.

mensual *a.* monthly; **-mente** *adv.* monthly.

menta *f.* mint.

mental *a.* mental, rel. to the mind; actividad ___ / ___ activity, mentation; edad ___ / ___ age; deficiencia ___ / ___ deficiency; enfermedad ___ / ___ illness; higiene ___ / ___ hygiene; retraso ___ / ___ retardation; trastorno ___ / ___ disorder; **-mente** *adv.* mentally.

mentalidad *f.* mentality, mental capacity.

mente *f.* mind, intellectual power.

mentecato-a *m., f.* numskull.

mentir *vi.* to lie.

mentira *f.* lie, falsehood.

mentol *m.* menthol, an alcohol obtained from peppermint oil and used for its soothing effects.

mentón *m.* mentus, chin.

meñique *m.* small finger.

merbromina *f.* merbromin, odorless red powder, soluble in water, used to kill germs.

mercurial *a.* mercurial, rel. to mercury.

mercurio *m.* mercury, volatile liquid metal.

Mercurocromo *m.* Mercurochrome, trade name for merbromin.

merecer *vi.* to deserve.

mermelada *f.* marmalade.

meridiano *m.* meridian, an imaginary circular line through the poles of a spherical body which connects the opposite ends of its axis.

mes *m.* month.

mesa *f.* table; ___ de operaciones / operating ___ .

mesectodermo *m.* mesectoderm, mass of cells that combine with others to form the meninges.

mesencéfalo *m.* mesencephalon, the midbrain of the embrionary stage.

mesénquima *m.* mesenchyme, embryonic tissue from which the connective tissue and the lymph and blood vessels arise in the adult.

mesentérico-a *a.* mesenteric, rel. to the mesentery.

mesenterio *m.* mesentery, peritoneal folds that fix parts of the intestine to the posterior abdominal wall.

mesial *a.* mesial. V. **medial.**

mesión *f.* mesion, imaginary midlongitudinal plane that divides the body in two symmetrical parts.

mesmerismo *m.* mesmerism, therapy by hypnotism.

mesocardia *f.* mesocardia, displacement of the heart towards the center of the thorax.

mesocolon *m.* mesocolon, mesentery that fixes the colon to the posterior abdominal wall.

mesodermo *m.* mesoderm, middle germ layer of the embryo, between the ectoderm and the endoderm, from which bone, connective tissue, muscle, blood, blood vessels, and lymph tissue, as well as the membranes of the heart and abdomen, arise.

mesotelio *m.* mesothelium, cell layer of the embryonic mesoderm which forms the epithelium covering the serous membranes in the adult.

meta *f.* goal, objective.

metabólico-a *a.* metabolic, rel. to metabolism; índice ___ / ___ rate.

metabolismo *m.* metabolism, physiochemical changes that take place following the digestive process; ___ basal / basal ___ , lowest level of energy waste; ___ de proteína / metabolic protein, digestion of proteins as amino acids.

metabolito *m.* metabolite, substance produced during metabolism or essential to the metabolic process.

metacarpiano-a *a.* metacarpal, rel. to the metacarpus.

metacarpo *m.* metacarpus, the five small metacarpal bones of the hand.

metadona *f.* methadone, highly potent habit-forming synthetic drug with narcotic action weaker than that of morphine.

metafase *f.* metaphase, one of the phases of cell division.

metáfisis *f.* metaphysis, the growing portion of a bone.

metal *m.* metal.

metálico-a *a.* metallic, rel. to or composed of metal.

metamorfosis *f.* metamorphosis; 1. change of form or structure; 2. degenerative process.

metanol *m.* methanol, methyl alcohol, wood alcohol.

metástasis *f.* metastasis, extension of a pathological process from a primary focus to another part of the body through blood or lymph vessels, as occurs in some types of cancer.

metastatizar *vi.* to metastasize, to spread by metastasis.

metatálamo *m.* metathalamus, part of the diencephalon.

metatarsiano-a *a.* metatarsal, rel. to the metatarsus.

metatarso *m.* metatarsus, the five small metatarsal bones located between the tarsus and the toes.

meteorismo *m.* meteorism, bloated abdomen due to gas in the stomach or the intestines.

meter *v.* to put in; to put one thing into another.

meticuloso-a *a.* meticulous, scrupulous.

método *m.* method, procedure, process, treatment.

metópico-a *a.* metopic, frontal, rel. to the forehead.

metria *f.* metria, puerperal infl. of the uterus.

métrico-a *a.* metric, rel. to meter or the metric system; **sistema** ___ / ___ system.

metro *m.* meter.

metritis *f.* metritis, infl. of the walls of the uterus.

metrorragia *f.* metrorrhagia, uterine bleeding other than menstruation.

mezcalina *f.* mescaline, poisonous alkaloid with hallucinatory properties.

mezcla *f.* mixture, compound.

mezclar *v.* to mix, to blend.

mialgia *f.* myalgia, muscle pain.

miastenia *f.* myasthenia, muscle weakness; ___ grave / ___ gravis.

miatonía *f.* myatonia, deficiency or loss of muscle tone.

micetoma *m.* mycetoma, severe infection caused by fungi that affects the skin, the connective tissue, and the bone.

micobacteria *f. V.* **Mycobacterium.**

micología *f.* mycology, the study of fungi and the diseases caused by them.

micoplasmas *m. pl.* mycoplasmas, the smallest free-living organisms some of which produce diseases such as a type of viral pneumonia and pharyngitis.

micosis *f.* mycosis, general term used for any disease caused by fungi.

micótico-a *a.* mycotic, rel. to or affected by mycosis.

micotoxina *f.* mycotoxin, a fungal toxin.

micrencefalia *f.* micrencephaly, abnormal smallness of the encephalon.

microabsceso *m.* microabscess, very small abscess.

microanatomía *f.* microanatomy, histology.

microbacterium *L.* microbacterium, gram-positive bacteria resistant to high temperatures.

microbiano-a *a.* microbian, microbial, rel. to microbes.

microbicida *m.* microbicide, agent that destroys microbes.

microbio *m.* microbe, minute living organism.

microbiología *f.* microbiology, science that studies microorganisms.

microcefalia *f.* microcephalia, microcephaly, congenital abnormally small head.

microcirugía *f.* microsurgery, surgery performed with the aid of special operating microscopes and very small precision instruments.

micrococo *m.* micrococcus, microorganism.

microcolon *m.* microcolon, abnormally small colon.

microcosmo *m.* microcosm, a world in miniature.

microcurie *m.* microcurie, measure of radiation.

microfalo *m.* microfallus, abnormally small penis.

microficha *f.* microfiche, small film capable of storing a large amount of data.

microfilm, microfilme *m.* microfilm, film that contains information reduced to a minimal size.

micrognatia *f.* micrognathia, congenital abnormally small lower jaw.

micrografía *f.* micrography, microscopic study.

microinvasión *f.* microinvasion, invasion of the cellular tissue adjacent to a localized carcinoma that cannot be seen with the naked eye.

micromelia *f.* micromelia, abnormally small limbs.

micromélico-a *a.* micromelic, rel. to micromelia.

microonda *f.* microwave, electromagnetic short wave with a very high frequency.

microorganismo *m.* microorganism, an organism that cannot be seen with the naked eye.

microscopía *f.* microscopy, microscopic examination.

microscópico-a *a.* microscopic, rel. to microscopy.

microscopio *m.* microscope, optical instrument used to amplify objects that cannot be seen with the naked eye; ___ de luz / light ___ ; ___ electrónico / electron ___ .

microsoma *m.* microsome, a fine granular element of the protoplasm.

microsomía *f.* microsomia, condition of having an abnormally small body with otherwise a normal structure.

microtomía *f.* microtomy, cutting thin sections of tissue.

micrótomo *m.* microtome, instrument used to prepare thin sections of tissue for microscopic study.

midriasis *f.* mydriasis, dilation of the pupil of the eye.

midriático *m.* mydriatic, agent that is used to dilate the pupil of the eye; **-a** *a.* that can cause dilation of the pupil of the eye.

miectomía *f. surg.* myectomy, excision of a portion of a muscle.

miedo *m.* fear, apprehension.

miel *f.* honey.

mielina *f.* myelin, the fat-like substance that forms a covering around certain nerve fibers.

mielinación, mielinización *f.* myelination, myelinization, growth of a myelin sheath around a nerve fiber.

mielinolisis *f.* myelinolysis, disease that destroys the myelin cover; ___ aguda / acute ___ .

mielitis *f.* myelitis, infl. of the spinal cord.

mielocele *m.* myelocele, hernia of the spinal cord through a defect in the vertebral column.

mielocítico-a *a.* myelocytic, rel. to myelocytes; leucemia ___ / ___ leukemia.

mielocito *m.* myelocyte, a large granular leukocyte in the bone marrow that is present in the blood in certain diseases.

mielofibrosis *f.* myelofibrosis, fibrosis of the bone marrow.

mielógeno-a *a.* myelogenic, myelogenous, produced in the bone marrow.

mielograma *m.* myelogram, X-ray of the spinal cord with the use of a contrasting medium.

mieloide *a.* myeloid, rel. to or resembling

the spinal cord or the bone marrow; médula ___ / ___ tissue.

mieloma *m.* myeloma, tumor formed by a type of cells usu. found in the bone marrow; ___ múltiple / multiple ___ .

mielomeningocele *m.* myelomeningocele, hernia of the spinal cord and its meninges through a defect in the vertebral canal.

mielopatía *f.* myelopathy, pathological condition of the spinal cord.

mieloproliferativo-a *a.* myeloproliferative, characterized by proliferation of bone marrow inside or outside of the medulla.

mielosupresión *f.* myelosuppression, failure of the bone marrow to produce red blood cells and platelets.

miembro *m.* member. 1. organ or limb of the body; 2. person affiliated with an organization; *vr.* **hacerse** ___ / to become a ___ .

mientras *adv.* meanwhile; ___ **que** / while.

migración *f.* migration, movement of cells from one place to another.

migraña *f.* migraine, severe headache usu. unilateral, accompanied by disturbed vision and in some cases by nausea and vomiting.

migratorio-a *a.* migratory, rel. to migration.

milagro *m.* miracle.

milagroso-a *a.* miraculous.

miliar *a.* miliary, characterized by the presence of small tumors.

miliaria *f.* miliaria, prickly heat, noncontagious cutaneous eruption caused by the obstruction of sweat glands and characterized by small red vesicles and papules accompanied by itching and prickling.

milieu *Fr.* milieu, environment, surroundings.

milla *f.* mile.

mimado-a *a.* pampered.

mimar *v.* to pamper.

mimético-a *a.* mimetic, mimic, that imitates.

minar *v.* to undermine.

mineral *m.* mineral, inorganic element; *a.* rel. to a mineral; **agua** ___ **efervescente** / carbonated ___ water.

mineralización *f.* mineralization, abnormally large deposition of mineral in tissues.

mineralocorticoide *m.* mineralocorticoid, hormone released by the adrenal cortex involved in the regulation of fluids and electrolytes.

minero-a *m., f.* miner.

mínimo-a *a.* minimal, least, smallest; dosis

letal ___ / ___ lethal dose, smallest amount needed to cause death; dosis ___ / ___ dose, smallest amount needed to produce an effect.

ministro-a *m., f.* minister, pastor.

minoría *f.* minority.

minucioso-a *a.* thorough, detailed; examen ___ / ___ exam; **-mente** *adv.* very carefully; thoroughly.

minuto *m.* minute, fraction of time.

miocárdico-a *a.* myocardial, myocardiac, rel. to the myocardium.

miocardio *m.* myocardium, the middle and thickest muscular layer of the heart wall; contracción del ___ / myocardial contraction.

miocardiopatías *f. pl.* myocardial diseases.

miocarditis *f.* myocarditis, infl. of the myocardium.

miocito *m.* myocyte, cell of the muscular tissue.

mioclonus *m.* myoclonus, muscular spasm or contraction as seen in epilepsy.

miodistrofia *f.* myodystrophy, muscular dystrophy.

miofibrilla *f.* myofibril, myofibrilla, minute, slender fiber of the muscle tissue.

miofibroma *m.* myofibroma, tumor containing muscular elements.

miofilamento *m.* myofilament, microscopic element that makes up myofibrils in muscles.

mioglobina *f.* myoglobin, muscle tissue pigment that participates in the transport of oxygen.

miografía *f.* myography, a recording of muscular activity.

miolisis *f.* myolysis, destruction of muscle tissue.

mioma *m.* myoma, benign tumor of muscular tissue.

miomectomía *f. surg.* myomectomy. 1. excision of a portion of a muscle or of muscular tissue; 2. excision of a myoma esp. one localized in the uterus.

miometrio *m.* myometrium, muscle wall of the uterus.

miometritis *f.* myometritis, infl. of the muscular wall of the uterus.

mionecrosis *f.* myonecrosis, necrosis of muscle tissue.

mioneural *a.* myoneural, rel. to muscles and nerves; unión ___ / ___ junction, a nerve ending in a muscle.

miopatía *f.* myopathy, muscle disease.

miope *a.* myopic. 1. nearsighted; 2. rel. to myopia.

miopía *f.* myopia, nearsightedness, a defect in the eyeball that causes parallel rays to be focused in front of the retina.

miosina *f.* myosin, the most abundant protein in muscle tissue.

miosis *f.* miosis, excessive contraction of the pupil.

miositis *f.* myositis, infl. of a muscle or group of muscles.

miotomía *f.* myotomy, dissection of muscles.

miotonía *f.* myotonia, increased rigidity of a muscle following muscle contraction, with diminished power of relaxation.

mirar *v.* to look, to view; ___ **fijamente** / to stare; **mirarse** *vr.* to look at oneself.

miringectomía *f. surg.* myringectomy, myringodectomy, excision of part or all of the tympanic membrane.

miringitis *f.* myringitis, infl. of the ear drum.

miringoplastia *f. surg.* myringoplasty, plastic surgery of the tympanic membrane.

miringotomía *f.* myringotomy, incision of the tympanic membrane.

misantropía *f.* misanthropy, abhorrance of mankind.

miscegenación *f.* miscegenation, sexual relations between individuals of different races.

miscible *a.* miscible, capable of mixing or dissolving.

mismo-a *a.* same; sí ___ / self; dominio de ___ / self-control.

misogamia *f.* misogamy, aversion to marriage.

misoginia *f.* misogyny, hatred of women.

mitad *f.* moiety, half, each of the two halves in which a whole is divided; a la ___ / in half.

mitigado-a *a.* mitigated, diminished, moderated.

mitigar *vi.* to mitigate, to alleviate.

mitocondria *f.* mitochondria, microscopic filaments of the cytoplasm that constitute the main source of energy in cells.

mitogenesia, mitogénesis *f.* mitogenesia, mitogenesis, the cause of cell mitosis.

mitógeno *m.* mitogen, substance that induces cell mitosis.

mitosis *f.* mitosis, cell division process that

results in new cells and replacement of injured tissue.

mitral *a.* mitral, rel. to the mitral valve; estenosis ____ / ____ stenosis, a narrowing of the left atrioventricular orifice; regurgitación ____ / ____ regurgitation, the flow of blood back from the left ventricle into the left atrium due to a lesion of the mitral valve; soplo ____ / ____ murmur.

mittelschmerz *m.* mittelschmerz, lower abdominal pain related to ovulation and occurring midway in the menstrual cycle.

mixedema *m.* myxedema, condition caused by deficient thyroid gland function.

mixoma *m.* myxoma, a tumor of the connective tissue.

mixto-a *a.* mixed.

mixtura *f.* mixture.

mnemónica *f.* mnemonics, recall of memory through free association of ideas and other techniques.

moción *f.* motion, movement.

moco *m.* mucus, viscid matter secreted by the mucous membranes and glands.

modalidad *f.* modality, any form of therapeutic application.

moderación *f.* moderation.

moderado-a *a.* moderate, temperate; **-mente** *adv.* moderately.

modesto-a *a.* modest.

modificación *f.* modification, change.

modificar *vi.* to modify, to change.

modo *m.* mode. 1. manner; way; 2. in a series, the value that is repeated most frequently; **de cualquier** ____ / in any way; anyway; **de ningún** ____ / in no way.

modulación *f.* modulation, the action of adjusting or adapting, such as occurs with the inflection of the voice.

moho *m.* mildew, mold caused by a fungus.

mojar *v.* to wet, to dampen; **mojarse** *vr.* to get wet.

mojado-a *a.* wet.

molar *m.* molar, any of the twelve molar teeth.

molde *m.* 1. cast, hardened bandage made stiff when pouring a hardening material; 2. template, pattern, mold.

moldear *v.* to cast.

molécula *f.* molecule, the smallest unit of a substance above the atomic level.

molécula gramo *m.* gram molecule, weight in grams equal to the molecular weight.

molecular *a.* molecular, rel. to molecules.

moler *vi.* to grind.

molestar *v.* to annoy, to bother.

molestia *f.* discomfort, annoyance.

molesto-a *a.* annoyed, grievous.

momentáneo-a *a.* momentary, of short duration.

momento *m.* moment, fraction of time.

momentum *L.* momentum, impetus, a force of motion.

momificación *f.* mummification, conversion into a state that resembles that of a mummy, as occurs in dry gangrene or in a dead fetus that dries up in the uterus.

mongolismo *m.* mongolism. *V.* **Down, síndrome de.**

mongoloide *a.* mongoloid, rel. to or suffering from mongolism.

moniliasis *f.* moniliasis. *V.* **candidiasis.**

monitor *m.* monitor. 1. electronic device used to monitor a function; 2. person who oversees an activity or function.

monitorear *v.* to monitor, to check systematically with an electronic device an organic function such as the heart beat.

monitoreo, monitorización *m., f.* monitoring; ____ cardíaco / cardiac ____ ; ____ de presión arterial / blood pressure ____ ; ____ fetal / fetal ____ .

monja *f.* nun.

monoarticular *a.* monoarticular, rel. to only one joint.

monocigótico-a *a.* monozygotic, rel. to twins that have identical genetic characteristics.

monocito *m.* monocyte, large granular mononuclear leukocyte.

monoclonal *a.* monoclonal, rel. to a single group of cells; anticuerpos____-es / ____ antibodies.

monocromático-a *a.* monochromatic, having only one color.

monocular *a.* monocular, rel. to only one eye.

monogamia *f.* monogamy, legal marriage to only one person.

mononucleosis *f.* mononucleosis, presence of an abnormally large number of monocytes in the blood; ____ infecciosa / infectious ____ , acute febrile infectious disease.

monosacárido *m.* monosaccharide, simple sugar.

monotonía *f.* monotony; monotone.

monótono-a *a.* monotonous.

monstruo *m.* monster.

montón *m.* heap, pile.

morado *m.* bruise, black and blue spot; the color purple; **-a** *a.* purple.

mórbido-a, morboso-a *a.* morbid, rel. to disease.

morbilidad *f.* morbidity. 1. an illness or disorder; 2. the rate of a disease in a given population or locality.

morbo *m.* illness.

mordedura *f. V.* **mordida.**

morder *vi.* to bite.

mordida *f.* bite; ____ **de perro** / dog bite.

moretón *m.* bruise, black and blue.

morfina *f.* morphine, the main alkaloid of opium, used as a narcotic analgesic.

morfinismo *m.* morphinism, condition caused by addiction to morphin.

morgue *Fr.* morgue, place for temporarily holding dead bodies.

moribundo-a *a.* moribund, dying, on the verge of death.

morir *vi.* to die.

morón, morona *m.,f.* moron, a mentally retarded person with an I.Q. of 50 to 70.

mortal *m.* mortal, a human being; *a.* deadly, mortal; herida ____ / fatal wound; veneno ____ / deadly poison.

mortalidad, mortandad *f.* mortality, death rate; índice de ____ / death rate.

mortífero-a *a.* deadly, that can cause death.

mortinatilidad *f.* natimortality, index of stillbirths.

mortinato-a *m.,f.* stillborn.

morula *f.* morula, solid spheric mass of cells that results from cell division of a fertilized ovum.

mosaico *m.* mosaic, the presence in one individual of different cell populations derived from the same cell as result of mutation.

mosca *f.* fly.

moscardón *m.* gadfly.

mosquito *m.* mosquito.

mostaza *f.* mustard.

mostrar *vi.* to show, to point out.

moteado-a *a.* mottling, mottled, discolored.

motivación *f.* motivation, driving force.

motivar *v.* to motivate, to animate.

motivo *m.* motive, cause, driving force.

motocicleta *f.* motorcycle.

motor *m.* motor, agent that causes or induces movement; **-a** *a.* that causes movement.

mover *vi.* to move, to put in motion; **moverse** *vr.* to move oneself.

movible, móvil *a.* mobile, that can move or be moved.

movilidad *f.* mobility, motility.

movilización *f.* mobilization.

movimiento *m.* movement, move, motion; alcance de ____ / range of motion.

mucina *f.* mucin, glycoprotein that is the chief ingredient of mucus.

mucocele *m.* mucocele, dilation of a cavity due to accumulated mucous secretion.

mucocutáneo-a *a.* mucocutaneous, rel. to the mucous membrane and the skin.

mucoide *m.* mucoid, glycoprotein similar to mucin; *a.* having the consistency of mucus.

mucomembranoso-a *a.* mucomembranous, rel. to the mucous membrane.

mucosa *f.* mucosa, mucous membrane, thin sheets of tissue cells that line openings or canals that communicate to the outside.

mucoso-a *a.* mucous, mucosal, rel. to or of the nature of the mucosa; membrana ____ / ____ membrane, mucosa.

muchacho-a *m.,f.* boy; girl.

mudar *v.* to move; ____ los dientes / to get one's second teeth; ____ la piel / to shed skin.

mudo-a *m.,f.* mute.

mueca *f.* grimace.

muela *f.* molar tooth, grinder; dolor de ____-s / toothache; ____-s del juicio / wisdom teeth.

muerte *f.* death; ____ aparente / apparent ____.

muerto-a *m.,f.* a dead person; *a.* dead.

muestra *f.* sample; tomar ____-s / sampling; tomar ____-s al azar / random sampling.

muestreo *m.* sampling; ____ al azar / random ____.

mugre *f.* grime.

muguet *Fr.* thrush, fungus infection of the oral mucosa, manifested by white patches in the lips, tongue, and the interior surface of the cheek.

mujer *f.* woman.

muletas *f. pl.* crutches.

multicelular *a.* multicellular, that has many cells.

multifactorial *a.* multifactorial, rel. to many factors.

multifocal *a.* multifocal, rel. to many foci.

multilocular *a.* multilocular. *V.* **multicelular.**

multiparidad *f.* multiparity. 1. condition of

having borne more than one living child; 2. multiple birth.

múltiple *a.* multiple, more than one; fallo ___ de órganos / ___ organ failure; personalidad ___ / ___ personality.

mundo *m.* world.

muñeca *f.* 1. wrist; ___ caída / drop ___; V. **carpus**; 2. doll.

muñón *m.* stump of an amputated arm or leg.

mural *a.* mural, rel. to the walls of an organ or part.

muriático-a *a.* muriatic, derived from common salt; ácido ___ / ___ acid.

murino-a *a.* murine, rel. to rodents, esp. mice and rats.

murmullo *m.* murmur, bruit, gen. in reference to an abnormal heart sound.

muscular, musculoso-a *a.* muscular, rel. to the muscles; contracción ___ brusca / jerk; relajador ___ / muscle relaxer.

muscularis *L.* muscularis, muscular layer of an organ or tubule.

musculatura *f.* musculature, the total muscular system.

músculo *m.* muscle, a type of fibrous tissue that has the property to contract allowing movement of the parts and organs of the body; ___ estriado voluntario / striated voluntary ___; ___ flexor / flexor ___; ___ visceral involuntario / visceral involuntary ___.

musculoesquelético-a *a.* musculoskeletal, rel. to the muscles and the skeleton.

musculotendinoso-a *a.* musculotendinous, having both muscle and tendons.

muslo *m.* thigh, the portion of the lower extremity between the hip and the knee.

mutación *f.* mutation, change in genetic structure either spontaneous or induced.

mutágeno *m.* mutagen, substance or agent that causes mutation.

mutante *a.* mutant, rel. to an individual or organism with a genetic structure that has undergone mutation.

mutilación *f.* mutilation, castration.

mutilado-a *a.* mutilated.

mutilar *v.* to mutilate, to maim; to cut in pieces.

mutismo *m.* mutism.

mutuo-a *a.* mutual, reciprocal.

muy *adv.* very.

Mycobacterium *L.* Mycobacterium, grampositive rod-shaped bacteria, including species that cause leprosy and tuberculosis.

N

N *abr.* **nasal** / nasal; **nervio** / nerve; **nitrógeno** / nitrogen; **normal** / normal; **número** / number.

Naboth, quistes de *m.* nabothian cysts, small, usu. benign cysts that form in one of many small mucus-secreting glands of the neck of the uterus due to obstruction.

nacer *vi.* to be born.

nacido-a *a.* born; **recién** ___ / newly ___.

naciente *a.* nascent, incipient. 1. just born; 2. liberated from a chemical compound.

nacimiento *m.* birth; ___ prematuro / premature ___; ___ tardío / post-term ___; **certificado de** ___ / ___ certificate.

nacionalidad *f.* nationality.

nada *f.* nothing, nothingness; *indef. pron.* (after thanks) de ___ / Don't mention it!; not at all; by no means.

nadie *pron.* nobody, no one.

nalgas *f. pl.* buttocks.

nanismo *m.* nanism. *V.* **enanismo**.

naranja *f.* orange.

narcisismo *m.* narcissism. 1. excessive love of self; 2. sexual pleasure derived from contemplation and admiration of one's own body.

narcolepsia *f.* narcolepsy, chronic uncontrollable disposition to sleep.

narcoléptico-a *a.* narcoleptic, rel. to or suffering from narcolepsia.

narcosis *f.* narcosis, unconsciousness caused by a narcotic.

narcótico *m.* narcotic, substance with potent analgesic effects that can become addictive.

narcotismo *m.* narcotism, the stupor-like state caused by narcotics.

naris *L. (pl.* **nares***)* naris, nostril.

nariz *f.* nose; sangramiento por la ___ / nosebleed; *vr.* **sonarse la** ___ / to blow one's nose.

nasal *a.* nasal, rel. to the nose; cavidad ___ / ___ cavity; congestión ___ / ___ congestion; fosa ___ / nostril; goteo ___ / ___ drip; tabique ___ / ___ septum.

nasofaringe *f.* nasopharynx, portion of the pharynx that lies above the soft palate.

nasogástrico-a *a.* nasogastric, rel. to the nose and the stomach; tubo ___ / ___ tube.

nasolabial *a.* nasolabial, rel. to the nose and the lip.

nata *f.* cream.

natal *a.* natal, rel. to birth.

natalidad *f.* natality; control de la ___ / birth control; índice de la ___ / birth rate.

natilla *f.* custard.

natimortalidad *f. V.* **mortinatalidad.**

nativo-a *a.* native. 1. in its natural state; 2. indigenous.

natriurético *m.* natriuretic. *V.* **diurético.**

natural *a.* natural; derechos ___ -es / birth rights; *v.* ser ___ de / to be from; **-mente** *adv.* naturally.

naturaleza *f.* nature.

naturópata *m.* naturopath, practitioner of naturopathy.

naturopatía *f.* naturopathy, therapeutic treatment by natural means.

náusea *f.* nausea, nauseousness; seasickness; *v.* **dar, provocar** ___ / to nauseate; **tener** ___ -s / to be nauseated.

nauseabundo-a *a.* nauseous, that causes nausea.

nauseado-a *a.* nauseated.

nauseoso-a *a.* nauseous, that causes nausea.

navicular *a.* navicular, boat-shaped.

nebulización *f.* nebulization, conversion of liquid into spray or mist.

nebulizador *m.* nebulizer, device used to produce spray or mist from liquid.

nebuloso-a *a.* nebulous.

necesario-a *a.* necessary; **lo** ___ / what is ___ ; *v.* **ser** ___ / to be ___ .

necesidad *f.* necessity, need; *v.* **tener** ___ / to need.

necesitado-a *a.* needy; los ___ -s / the needy.

necesitar *v.* to need.

necrocomio *m.* morgue, place to store dead bodies temporarily.

necrofilia *f.* necrophilia. 1. morbid attraction to corpses; 2. sexual intercourse with a corpse.

necrofobia *f.* necrophobia, morbid fear of death and corpses.

necrógeno-a *a.* necrogenic. 1. rel. to death; 2. formed or composed of dead matter.

necrología *f.* necrology, the study of statistics in mortality.

necropsia, necroscopia *f.* necropsy. *V.* **autopsia.**

necrosar *v.* to necrose, necrotizing, to cause or undergo necrosis.

necrosis *f.* necrosis, death of some or all of the cells in a tissue such as occurs in gangrene.

necrótico-a *a.* necrotic, rel. to necrosis.

nefrectomía *f. surg.* nephrectomy, removal of a kidney.

néfrico-a *a.* nephric, renal.

nefrítico-a *a.* nephritic, rel. to or affected by nephritis.

nefritis *f.* nephritis, infl. of a kidney.

nefrocalcinosis *f.* nephrocalcinosis, renal calcium deposits in the tubules of the kidney that may cause renal insufficiency.

nefroesclerosis *f.* nephrosclerosis, hardening of the arterial system and the interstitial tissue of the kidney.

nefrograma *m.* nephrogram, kidney X-ray.

nefrolitiasis *f.* nephrolithiasis, kidney stones.

nefrolitotomía *f.* nephrolithotomy, incision in the kidney to remove kidney stones.

nefrología *f.* nephrology, the study of the kidney and the diseases affecting it.

nefroma *m.* nephroma, kidney tumor.

nefrona *f.* nephron, the functional and anatomical unit of a kidney.

nefropatía *f.* nephropathy, disease of the kidney.

nefropexia *f. surg.* nephropexy, fixation of a floating kidney.

nefrosis *f.* nephrosis, degenerative renal disorder associated with large amounts of protein in the urine, low levels of albumin in the blood, and marked edema.

nefrostomía *f. surg.* nephrostomy, creation of a fistula in the kidney or renal pelvis.

nefrotomía *f. surg.* nephrotomy, surgical incision into the kidney.

nefrotomografía *f.* nephrotomography, tomography of the kidney.

nefrotóxico-a *a.* nephrotoxic, that destroys kidney cells.

nefrotoxina *f.* nephrotoxin, agent that destroys kidney cells.

negación *f.* negation, denial.

negar *vi.* to deny.

negativismo *m. psych.* negativism, behavior characterized by acting in a manner opposite to the one suggested.

negativo-a *a.* negative; cultivo ___ / ___ culture; **-mente** *adv.* negatively.

negligencia *f.* negligence; ___ **profesional** / malpractice.

negligente *a.* negligent.

negro-a *m., f.* 1. a black person; 2. the color black; *a.* black.

nematelminto *m.* nemathelminth, round-worm, intestinal worm of the phylum *Nemathelminthes.*

nematocida *m.* nematocide, agent that kills nematodes.

Nematoda *Gr.* Nematoda, class of worms of the phylum *Nemathelminthes.*

nemátodo *m.* nematode, worm of the class *Nematoda.*

nematología *f.* nematology, the study of worms of the class *Nematoda.*

nene-a *m., f.* baby.

neoartrosis *f.* nearthrosis, neoarthrosis, false or artificial joint.

neologismo *m.* neologism. 1. *psych.* word or phrase to which a mentally disturbed individual attributes a meaning unrelated to its real meaning; 2. new word or phrase or an old one to which a new meaning has been attributed.

neomicina *f.* neomycin, broad-spectrum antibiotic.

neonatal *a.* neonatal, rel. to the first four to six weeks after birth.

neonato-a *a.* neonate, newborn.

neonatología *f.* neonatology, specialty that studies the care and treatment o˴ newborns.

neonatólogo-a *m., f.* neonathologist, specialist in neonatology.

neoplasia *f.* neoplasia, formation of neoplasms.

neoplasma *m.* neoplasm, abnormal growth of new tissue such as a tumor.

neoplástico-a *a.* neoplastic, rel. to a neoplasm.

nervio *m.* nerve, one or more bundles of fibers that connect the brain and spinal cord with other parts and organs of the body; bloqueo del ___ / ___ block; degeneración del ___ / ___ degeneration; ___ pellizcado / pinched ___ ; terminación del ___ / ___ ending.

nervio ciático *m.* sciatic nerve, nerve that extends from the base of the spine down to the thigh with branches throughout the lower leg and the foot.

nerviosismo *m.* nervousness; *pop.* jitters.

nervioso-a *a.* nervous, rel. to the nerves; crisis ___ / ___ breakdown, collapse; fibra ___ / nerve fiber; impulso ___ / nerve impulse; tejido ___ / nerve tissue.

nestiatría *f.* nestiatria, fasting therapy.

neumático-a *a.* pneumatic, rel. to air or respiration.

neumatización *f.* pneumatization, formation of air cavities in a bone, esp. the temporal bone.

neumatocele *m.* pneumatocele. 1. hernial protuberance of lung tissue; 2. a tumor or sac containing gas.

neumococal, neumocócico-a *a.* pneumococcal, rel. to or caused by pneumococci.

neumococo *m.* pneumococcus, one of a group of gram-positive bacteria that cause acute pneumonia and other infections of the upper respiratory tract.

neumoencefalografía *f.* pneumoencephalography, X-ray of the brain by previous injection of air or gas allowing visualization of the cerebral cortex and ventricles.

neumonía *f.* pneumonia, infectious disease of the upper respiratory tract caused by bacteria or virus that affect the lungs; ___ doble / double ___ ; ___ estafilocócica / staphylococcal ___ ; ___ lobar / lobar ___ .

neumonía neumocística carinii *f.* pneumocystis pneumonia carinii, a type of acute pneumonia caused by the bacillus *Pneumocystis carinii* and one of the opportunistic diseases seen in cases of AIDS.

neumónico-a *a.* pneumonic, rel. to the lungs or to pneumonia.

neumonitis *f.* pneumonitis. *V.* **neumonía.**

neumopatía *f.* lung disease.

neumotórax *m.* pneumothorax, accumulation of gas or air in the pleural cavity that results in the collapse of the affected lung; ___ espontáneo / spontaneous ___ ; ___ por tensión / ___ tension.

neural *a.* neural, rel. to the nervous system.

neuralgia *f.* neuralgia, pain along a nerve.

neurálgico-a *a.* neuralgic, rel. to neuralgia; puntos ___ -s / tender points.

neurapraxia *f.* neurapraxia, temporary paralysis of a nerve without degeneration.

neurastenia *f.* neurasthenia, term usu. associated with increased irritability, tension and anxiety, accompanied by physical exhaustion.

neurasténico-a *a.* neurasthenic, rel. to or afflicted by neurasthenia.

neurilema *f.* neurilemma, thin membranous covering that encloses a nerve fiber.

neurinoma *m.* neurinoma, benign neoplasm of the sheath surrounding a nerve.

neuritis *f.* neuritis, infl. of a nerve.

neuroanatomía *f.* neuroanatomy, the study and practice of the anatomy of the nervous system.

neuroblasto *m.* neuroblast, the immature nerve cell.

neuroblastoma *m.* neuroblastoma, malignant tumor of the nervous system formed mostly of neuroblasts.

neurocirugía *f.* neurosurgery, the study and practice of surgery of the nervous system.

neurocirujano-a *m., f.* neurosurgeon, specialist in neurosurgery.

neurodermatitis *f.* neurodermatitis, chronic skin disease of unknown origin manifested by intense itching in localized areas.

neuroectodermo *m.* neuroectoderm, embrionary tissue from which the nerve tissue derives.

neuroendocrinología *f.* neuroendocrinology, the study of the nervous system as it relates to hormones.

neurofarmacología *f.* neuropharmacology, the study of drugs and medications as they affect the nervous system.

neurofibroma *m.* neurofibroma, tumor of the fibrous tissue of a peripheral nerve.

neurofibromatosis *f.* neurofibromatosis, disease characterized by the presence of multiple neurofibromas along the peripheral nerves.

neurofisiología *f.* neurophysiology, the study of the physiology of the nervous system.

neuroglia *f.* neuroglia, connective supportive cells that constitute the interstitial tissue of the nervous system.

neurohipófisis *f.* neurohypophysis, posterior and nervous portion of the pituitary gland.

neuroléptico *m.* neuroleptic, tranquilizer; -a *a.* anestesia ____ / ____ anesthesia.

neurología *f.* neurology, the study of the nervous system.

neurólogo-a *m., f.* specialist in neurology.

neuroma *f.* neuroma, tumor composed mainly of nerve cells and fibers.

neuromarcapasos *m.* neuropacemaker, instrument used to stimulate electrically the spinal cord.

neuromuscular *a.* neuromuscular, rel. to the nerves and the muscles.

neurona *f.* neuron, nerve cell, the basic functional and structural unit of the nervous system; ____ motor / motor ____ , carries the impulses that initiate muscle contraction.

neuro-oftalmología *f.* neuro-ophthalmology, the study of the relationship between the nervous and visual systems.

neuropatía *f.* neuropathy, a disorder or pathological change in the peripheral nerves.

neurópilo *m.* neuropil, network of nervous fibers (neurites, dentrites, and glia cells) that concentrate in different parts of the nervous system.

neurorradiología *f.* neuroradiology, X-ray study of the nervous system.

neurorregulador *m.* neurotransmitter, a chemical substance that affects the transmission impulses across a synapse between nerves or between a nerve and a muscle.

neurosicofarmacología *f.* neuropsychopharmacology, the study of drugs as they affect the treatment of mental disorders.

neurosífilis *f.* neurosyphilis, syphilis that affects the nervous system.

neurosis *f.* neurosis, condition manifested primarily by anxiety and the use of defense mechanisms.

neurótico-a *a.* neurotic, rel. to or suffering from neurosis.

neurotoxicidad *f.* neurotoxicity, toxic or harmful effect on the nervous system tissue.

neurovascular *a.* neurovascular, rel. to the nervous and vascular systems.

neutral, neutro-a *a.* neutral.

neutralización *f.* neutralization, process that annuls or counteracts the action of an agent.

neutralizar *vi.* to neutralize, to counteract.

neutrofilia *f.* neutrophilia, increase in number of neutrophils in the blood.

neutropenia *f.* neutropenia. V. **agranulocitosis.**

neutrotaxis *f.* neutrotaxis, stimulation of neutrophils by a substance that either attracts or repels them.

nevar *vi.* to snow.

nevo *m.* nevus, mole, birthmark.

nexo *m.* nexus, connection.

ni *conj.* neither, nor; ____ **bueno** ____ **malo** / neither good nor bad; ____ **siquiera** / not even.

niacina *f.* niacin, nicotinic acid.

nicotina *f.* nicotine, toxic alkaloid that is the main ingredient of tobacco.

nictalopía *f.* nictalopia, night blindness.

nicturia, nocturia *f.* nocturia, nycturia, frequent urination during the night.

nicho *m.* niche, small defect or depression esp. in the wall of a hollow organ.

nido *m.* nest, small cellular mass resembling a bird's nest.

niebla *f.* fog.

nieto-a *m., f.* grandson, granddaughter.

nieve *f.* snow; *Mex.* ice cream.

nigua *f.* chigger, chigoe.

ninfa *f.* nympha, inner lip of the vulva.

ninfomanía *f.* nymphomania, excessive sexual desire in the female.

ninfomaníaca *f.* nymphomaniac, rel. to or suffering from nymphomania.

ningún, ninguno-a *a.* not one, not any; **de ___ modo, de ninguna manera** / in no way; *pron.* nobody; none, no one; neither.

niña del ojo *f.* pupil of the eye.

niñez *f.* childhood.

niño-a *m., f.* child; ___ **maltratado-a** / battered ___.

nistagmo *m.* nystagmus, involuntary spasm of the eyeball.

nitrato *m.* nitrate, chemical agent.

nitrógeno *m.* nitrogen.

nitroglicerina *f.* nitroglycerine, a nitrate of glycerin used in medicine as a vasodilator, esp. in angina pectoris.

nivel *m.* level.

no *adv.* no, not; ___ **importa** / it doesn't matter; ___ **obstante** / nevertheless.

nivelación *f.* levelling.

Nocardia *f.* Nocardia, gram-positive microorganism, cause of nocardíasis.

nocardiasis *f.* nocardiasis, infection caused by the species *Nocardia* that gen. affects the lungs but can also expand to other parts of the body.

nocivo-a *a.* noxious, harmful, pernicious.

nocturno-a *a.* nocturnal.

noche *m.* night; **de ___** / at ___; **buenas ___-s** / good evening, good night; **por la ___** / in the evening.

nodal *a.* nodal, rel. to a node.

nodular *a.* nodular, rel. to or resembling a nodule.

nódulo *m.* nodule, small node; ___ **linfático** / lymphatic ___.

nómada *a.* nomadic, free, wandering.

nombre *m.* name; ___ **genérico** / generic ___, common name of a drug or medication which is not registered commercially; ___ **de pila** / given ___.

nomenclatura *f.* nomenclature, terminology.

nonato-a *m., f.* neonate born by Cesarean section.

non compos mentis *L.* non compos mentis, mentally incompetent.

norepinefrina *f.* norepinephrine, vasoconstrictor agent produced in the adrenal gland.

norma *f.* norm, model, standard.

normal *a.* normal.

normalización *f.* normalization, return to a normal state.

normocalcemia *f.* normocalcemia, normal level of calcium in the blood.

normoglicemia *f.* normoglycemia, normal concentration of glucose in the blood.

normopotasemia *f.* normokalemia, normal level of potassium in the blood.

normotenso-a *a.* normotensive, having a normal blood pressure.

normotermia *f.* normothermia, normal temperature.

norte *m.* north; **al ___** / to the ___.

nosocomial *a.* nosocomial, rel. to a hospital or infirmary; **infección ___** / ___ infection, acquired in a hospital.

nostalgia *f.* nostalgia, homesickness.

nota *f.* note; remark.

notable *a.* remarkable.

notar *v.* to note; to become aware of something.

noticias *f. pl.* news.

notificar *vi.* to notify, to make known.

notocordio *m.* notochord, the axial fibrocellular cord in the embryo that is replaced by the vertebral column.

novocaína *f.* novocaine, anesthetic.

núbil *a.* nubile, rel. to female sexual maturity.

nublado-a *a.* bleary; cloudy; **vista ___** / ___ eyed.

nuca *f.* nucha, nape, posterior part of the neck.

nucal *a.* nuchal, rel. to the nape.

nuclear *a.* nuclear. 1. rel. to the nucleus; **envoltura ___** / ___ envelope, the two parallel membranes surrounding the nucleus, as seen under an electron microscope; 2. rel. to atomic power; **desecho ___** / ___ waste.

núcleo *m.* nucleus, the essential part of the cell; ___ **pulposo** / ___ pulpous, central gelatinous mass within an intervertebral disk.

nucléolo *m.* nucleolus, small spherical structure found in the nucleus of cells.

nucleótido *m.* nucleotide, the structural unit of nucleic acid.

nudillo *m.* knuckle.

nudo *m.* node, knotlike mass of tissue; knot.

nudoso-a *a.* nodose, that has nodules or protuberances.

nuevo-a *a.* new.

nuez *f.* walnut; nut.

nuez de Adán *f.* Adam's apple.

nuligrávida *f.* nulligravida, a woman who has never conceived.

nulípara *f.* nullipara, nulliparous, nonparous, a woman who has never borne a living child.

nulo-a *a.* null, void.

número *m.* number; figure.

numeroso-a *a.* numerous.

nunca *adv.* never; at no time; **casi** ___ / hardly ever.

nutrición *f.* nutrition, nourishment.

nutriente *m.* nutrient, nutritious substance; *a.* that nourishes.

nutritivo-a *a.* nutritious, providing nourishment.

Ñ

Ñ seventeenth letter of the Spanish alphabet.

ñame *m.* yam.

ñoñería *f.* childishness; simpleness.

ñoño-a *-a.* child-like; simple-minded.

O

O *abr.* **oral, oralmente** / oral, orally; **ojo** / oculus; **oxígeno** / oxygen.

o *conj.* either, or; ___ **bien** ___ **mal** / one way or another, anyway.

obedecer *vi.* to obey.

obediente *a.* obedient, compliant.

obesidad *f.* obesity, excess fat.

obeso-a *a.* obese, excessively fat.

objetivo *m.* objective, goal; target; **-a** *a.* rel. to the perception of any happening or phenomenon as it is manifested in real life; **-mente** *adv.* objectively.

oblicuo-a *a.* oblique, diagonal; skewed.

obligación *f.* obligation, duty.

obligar *vi.* to obligate, to force.

obliteración *f.* obliteration, destruction, occlusion by degeneration or by surgery.

obliterar *v.* to obliterate, to annul, to destroy.

obrar *v.* to act, to work; *Mex.* to have a bowel movement.

obscuridad, oscuridad *f.* darkness.

obscuro-a, oscuro-a *a.* dark.

observación *f.* observation; remark.

observar *v.* to observe.

obsesión *f.* obsession, abnormal preoccupation with a single idea or emotion; *pop.* hang-up.

obsesivo-compulsivo-a *a. psych.* obsessive-compulsive, rel. to an individual that is driven to repeat actions excessively as a relief of tension and anxiety.

obseso-a *a.* possessed, dominated by an idea or passion.

obsoleto-a *a.* obsolete, outdated; inactive.

obstáculo *m.* obstacle, hurdle.

obstetra *m., f.* obstetrician.

obstetricia *f.* obstetrics, the study of the care of women during pregnancy and delivery.

obstétrico-a *a.* obstetric, rel. to obstetrics.

obstinado-a *a.* obstinate, headstrong, opinionated.

obstipación *f.* obstipation, severe constipation.

obstrucción *f.* obstruction, blockage; ___ crónica del pulmón / obstructive lung disease, chronic condition caused by the physical or functional narrowing of the bronchial tree; ___ en el conducto aéreo superior / upper airway ___.

obstruído-a *a.* obstructed, blocked; no ___ / unobstructed.

obstruir *vi.* to obstruct.

obtener *vi.* to obtain, to attain.

obturación *f.* obturation, occlusion.

obturador-a *a.* obturator, that obstructs an opening.

obtuso-a *a.* obtuse. 1. lacking mental acuity; 2. blunt.

obvio-a *a.* obvious, evident.

ocasión *f.* occasion.

ocasionar *v.* to cause.

occipital *a.* occipital, rel. to the back part of the head; hueso ___ / ___ bone; lóbulo ___ / ___ lobe.

occipitofrontal *a.* occipitofrontal, rel. to the occiput and the forehead.

occipitoparietal *a.* occipitoparietal, rel. to the occipital and parietal bones and lobes.

occipitotemporal *a.* occipitotemporal, rel. to the occipital and temporal bones.

occipucio *m.* occiput, posteroinferior part of the skull.

oclusión *f.* occlusion, obstruction.

octogenario-a *m., f.* octogenarian, individual that is over eighty years old.

ocular *a.* ocular, visual, rel. to the eyes; globo ____ / eyeball; ____ (de un aparato óptico) / eyepiece; órbita ____ / eyesocket; traumatismo ____ / eye injury.

oculista *m., f.* oculist. *V.* **oftalmólogo.**

oculógiro-a *a.* oculogyric, rel. to the rotation of the eyeball.

oculomotor *a.* oculomotor, rel. to the movement of the eyeball.

ocultar *v.* to conceal, to hide.

oculto-a *a.* occult, concealed, not visible.

oculus *L.* oculus, eye.

ocupación *f.* occupation.

ocupacional *a.* occupational, rel. to an occupation.

ocupado-a *a.* busy; occupied.

odiar *v.* to hate.

odinofobia *f. psych.* odynophobia, morbid fear of pain.

odio *m.* hate, hatred.

odontalgia *f.* odontalgia, toothache.

odontectomía *f. surg.* odontectomy, tooth extraction.

odontogénesis *f.* odontogenesis, tooth development.

odontoideo-a *a.* odontoid, dentiform, resembling a tooth.

odontología *f.* odontology, the study of dentistry.

odontólogo-a *m., f.* odontologist, dentist or oral surgeon.

oeste *m.* west; al ____ / to the ____ .

oficial *a.* official, authorized; **no** ____ / unofficial, rel. to medication not listed in the Pharmacopeia or standard formulary.

oficina *f.* office.

oftalmia *f.* ophthalmia. 1. severe conjunctivitis; 2. internal infl. of the eye.

oftálmico-a *a.* ophthalmic, rel. to the eye; nervio ____ / ____ nerve; solución ____ / ____ solution.

oftalmitis *f.* ophthalmitis, infl. of the eye.

oftalmología *f.* ophthalmology, the study of the eye and its disorders.

oftalmólogo-a *m., f.* ophthalmologist, oculist, specialist in eye disorders.

oftalmopatía *f.* ophthalmopathy, eye disorder.

oftalmoplastia *f. surg.* ophthalmoplasty, plastic surgery of the eye.

oftalmoplejía *f.* ophthalmoplegia, paralysis of an eye muscle.

oftalmoscopía *f.* ophthalmoscopy, examination of the eye with an ophthalmoscope.

oftalmoscopio *m.* ophthalmoscope, instrument for viewing the interior of the eye.

oído *m.* ear. 1. hearing organ formed by the inner, middle, and external ear; dolor de ____ / earache; ____ tapado con cerumen / glue ____ ; zumbido en los ____ -s / ringing ____ -s; 2. the sense of hearing.

oir *vi.* to hear.

ojeada *f.* glance; **dar una** ____ / to glance.

ojeras *f. pl.* dark circles under the eyes.

ojeroso-a *a.* haggard, referring to someone with dark circles under their eyes.

ojo *m.* eye; banco de ____ -s / ____ bank; cuenca del ____ / ____ socket; fondo del ____ / eyeground; gotas para los ____ -s / ____ drops; ____ de vidrio / glass ____ ; ____ -s inyectados / blood shot ____ -s; ____ -s llorosos / watery ____ -s; ____ -s saltones / goggle-eyed.

oleada *f.* tide, a space of time; rise and fall.

oleaginoso-a *a.* oleaginous, oily, unctuous.

oleomargarina *f.* oleomargarine.

oler *vi.* to smell, to scent.

olfatear *v.* to sniff.

olfato *m.* 1. the sense of smell; 2. odor.

olfatorio-a *a.* olfactory, rel. to smell.

oligohemia *f.* oligemia, olygohemia. *V.* **hipovolemia.**

oligohidramnios *m.* oligohydramnios, low level of amniotic fluid.

oligomenorrea *f.* oligomenorrhea, deficient or infrequent menstruation.

oligospermia *f.* oligospermia, diminished number of spermatozoa in the semen.

oliguria *f.* oliguria, diminished formation of urine.

oliva *f.* olive. 1. gray body behind the medulla oblongata; 2. green olive color.

olor *m.* odor, smell, scent; ____ penetrante / penetrating smell.

oloroso-a *a.* odorous.

olvidadizo-a *a.* forgetful.

olvidar *v.* to forget.

ombligo *m.* umbilicus, navel, a depression in the center of the abdomen at the point of insertion of the uterine canal at the time of birth; *pop.* belly button.

omento *m.* omentum, a fold of the peritoneum that connects the stomach with some abdominal viscera.

omental *a.* omental, rel. to or formed from omentum.

omentectomía *f. surg.* omentectomy, partial or total removal of the omentum.

omentitis *f.* omentitis, infl. of the omentum.

omisión *f.* omission.

omitir *v.* to omit.

onanismo *m.* onanism, coitus interruptus, interrupted coitus.

oncogénesis *f.* oncogenesis, formation and development of tumors.

oncogénico-a *a.* oncogenic, rel. to oncogenesis.

oncólisis *f.* oncolysis, destruction of tumor cells.

oncología *f.* oncology, the study of tumors.

oncótico-a *a.* oncotic, rel. to or caused by swelling.

onda *f.* wave. 1. ondulant movement or vibration that travels along a fixed direction; 2. ondulant graphic respresentation of an activity, such as seen in an electroencephalogram; guía de ____-s / waveguide; longitud de ____ / wavelength; ____-s cerebrales / brain ____-s; ____-s de excitación / excitation ____-s; ____ sonora / sound ____; ____-s ultrasónicas / ultrasound ____-s.

onda T *f.* T wave, part of the electrocardiogram that represents the repolarization of the ventricles.

onda V *f.* V wave, positive wave that follows the T wave in an electrocardiogram.

ondulado-a *a.* ondulant, having an irregular or wavy border.

onfalectomía *f. surg.* omphalectomy, removal of the umbilicus.

onfálico-a *a.* omphalic, rel. to the umbilicus.

onfalitis *f.* omphalitis, infl. of the umbilicus.

onfalocele *m.* onphalocele, umbilical hernia.

onicosis *f.* onychosis, deformity or sickness of a nail.

oniomanía *f. psych.* oniomania, pathological urge to spend money.

oniquectomía *f. surg.* onychectomy, excision of a nail.

oniquia *f.* onychia, infl. of a nailbed.

onírico-a *a.* oneiric, rel. to dreams.

onirismo *m.* oneirism, dream-like state while awake.

onomatonamía *f. psych.* onomatonamia, obsessive urge to repeat words.

oocito, ovocito *m.* oocyte, female ovum before maturation.

ooforectomía *f. surg.* oophorectomy, partial or total excision of an ovary.

oogénesis, ovogénesis *f.* oogenesis, ovogenesis, formation and development of an ovum.

oospermo *m.* oosperm, a fertilized ovum.

opacidad *f.* opacity, dimness, lack of transparency.

opacificación *f.* opacification, process of rendering something opaque.

opaco-a *a.* opaque, that does not filter light.

operable *a.* operable, that can be treated by surgery.

operación *f.* operation, surgical procedure.

operar *v.* to operate, to intervene surgically.

opérculo *m.* operculum. 1. covering or lid; 2. any of the several parts of the cerebrum covering the insula.

operón *m.* operon, a system of linked genes in which the operator gene regulates the remaining structural genes.

opláceo *m.* opiate, opium-derived drug.

opinar *v.* to express an opinion.

opinión *f.* opinion, judgment.

opio *m.* opium, *Papaver somniferum,* narcotic, analgesic.

opistótonos *m.* opisthotonos, tetanic spasm of the muscles of the back in which the heels and head bend backward and the trunk projects forward.

oponer *vi.* to oppose; **oponerse** *vr.* to be against, to oppose.

oportunidad *f.* opportunity, chance.

oportunista *a.* opportunistic; opportune.

oportuno-a *a.* timely, opportune.

oposición *f.* opposition; objection.

opresión *f.* oppression; heaviness; ____ en el pecho / an ____ in the chest.

opresivo-a *a.* oppressive; overwhelming.

oprimir *v.* to oppress.

opsoclono *m.* opsoclonus, irregular movement of the eyes, esp. seen in some cases of brain lesion.

opsonina *f.* opsonin, antibody that combines with a specific antigen and makes it more susceptible to phagocytes.

óptica *f.* optics, the study of light and its relation to vision; **óptico-a** *a.* optic, optical, rel. to vision; disco ___ / ___ disk, blind spot of the retina; ilusión ___ / ___ illusion; nervio ___ / ___ nerve.

óptimo-a *a.* optimum, the best, the ideal.

optómetra, optometrista *m., f.* optometrist, professional who practices optometry.

optometría *f.* optometry, the practice of examining the eyes for visual acuity and prescribing corrective lenses and other optical aids.

optómetro *m.* optometer, instrument used to measure eye refraction.

opuesto-a *a.* opposite; opposed.

oral *a.* oral, delivered or taken by mouth.

orbicular *a.* orbicular, circular; músculo ___ / ___ muscle, that surrounds a small opening such as the orbicular muscle of the mouth.

órbita *f.* orbit, bony cavity that contains the eyeball and associated structures.

orbital *a.* orbital, rel. to the orbit.

orden *m.* order, arrangement; regulation.

ordenar *v.* to order; to arrange.

ordeño *m.* milking, maneuver to force material out of a tube.

ordinario-a *a.* ordinary, usual, common.

oreja *f.* external ear; lóbulo de la ___ / ear lobe.

orejera *f.* ear protector.

organelo, organito *m.* organelle, minute organ of unicellular organisms.

orgánico-a *a.* organic. 1. rel. to an organ; 2. rel. to organisms of vegetable or animal origin; enfermedad ___ / ___ disease.

organismo *m.* organism, a living being.

organización *f.* organization, association.

organizar *vi.* to organize, to arrange.

órgano *m.* organ, part of the body with a specific function; ___ terminal / end ___; transplante de un ___ / ___ transplant.

organogénesis *f.* organogenesis, growth and development of an organ.

orgasmo *m.* orgasm, sexual climax.

orgulloso-a *a.* proud.

orientación *f.* orientation, direction.

orificio *m.* orifice, aperture, opening.

origen *m.* origin, source, beginning.

original *a.* original.

orín, orina *m., f.* urine, the clear fluid secreted by the kidneys, stored in the urinary bladder, and discharged by the urethra; ___ claro-a / clear ___; especimen de ___ a mitad de chorro / midstream ___ specimen; ___ lechoso-a / milky ___; muestra de ___ / ___ sample; ___ turbio-a / hazy ___.

orinal *m.* urinal, chamber pot, container or receptacle for urine.

orinar *v.* to urinate, to micturate; ardor al ___ / burning on urination; ___ a menudo / frequent urination; ___ con dificultad / difficult urination; ___ con dolor / painful urination; **orinarse** *vr.* to wet oneself; ___ **en la cama** / bed wetting.

orofaringe *m.* oropharynx, central part of the pharynx.

orquidectomía, orquiectomía *f. surg.* orchidectomy, orchiectomy, removal of a testicle.

orquiditis, orquitis *f.* orchiditis, orchitis, infl. of a testicle.

orquidopexia, orquiopexia *f. surg.* orchidopexy, orchiopexy, procedure by which an undescended testicle is lowered into the scrotum and fixed to it.

orquiotomía *f.* orchiotomy, incision in a testicle.

ortocromático-a *a.* orthochromatic, of natural color or that accepts coloration.

ortodoncia *f.* orthodontics, the study of irregularities and corrective procedures of teeth.

ortodoncista *m., f.* orthodontist, specialist in orthodontics.

ortógrado-a *a.* orthograde, that walks in an erect position.

ortopedia *f.* orthopedics, the study of bones, joints, muscles, ligaments, and cartilages and the preventive and corrective procedures that deal with their related disorders.

ortopédico-a, ortopedista *m., f.* orthopedist, specialist in orthopedics; *a.* orthopedic, rel. to orthopedia; calzado ___ / ___ shoes.

ortopnea *f.* orthopnea, difficulty in breathing except when in an upright position.

ortostático-a *a.* orthostatic, rel. to an erect position.

ortotópico-a *a.* orthotopic, in the normal or correct position.

orzuelo *m.* sty, stye, infl. of the sebaceous glands of the eyelid.

os *L.* os, bone.

oscilación *f.* oscillation, a pendulum-like motion.

óseo-a *a.* osseous, rel. to bone; desarrollo ____ / bone development; lesiones ____ -s / bone lesions; placa ____ / bone plate.

osículo *m.* ossicle, small bone.

osificación *f.* ossification. 1. conversion of a substance into bone; 2. bone development.

osificar *vi.* to ossify, to turn into bone.

osífico-a *a.* ossific, rel. to the formation of bone tissue.

osmolar, osmótico-a *a.* osmolar, osmotic, rel. to or of the nature of osmosis.

osmología *f.* osmology, the study of odors.

osmorreceptor *m.* osmoreceptor. 1. a group of cells in the brain that receive olfactory stimuli; 2. a group of cells in the hypothalamus that respond to changes in the osmotic pressure of the blood.

osmosis *f.* osmosis, diffusion of a solvent through a semipermeable membrane separating two solutions of different concentration.

osmótico-a *a.* osmotic, rel. to or of the nature of osmosis.

osteítis, ostitis *f.* osteitis, ostitis, infl. of a bone; ____ fibrosa quistica / ____ fibrosa cystica, with cystic and nodular manifestations.

osteoartritis *f.* osteoarthritis, degenerative hypertrophy of the bones and joints.

osteoartropatía *f.* osteoarthropathy, disease of a joint and a bone, gen. accompanied by pain.

osteoblasto *m.* osteoblast, a cell that forms bone tissue.

osteocarcinoma *m.* osteocarcinoma, bone cancer.

osteocartilaginoso-a *a.* osteocartilaginous, rel. to or formed by bone and cartilage.

osteocito *m.* osteocyte, a mature osteoblast that has become isolated in a lacuna of the bone substance.

osteoclasto *m.* osteoclast, giant multinuclear cell that participates in the formation of bone tissue and replaces cartilage during ossification.

osteocondral *a.* osteochondral, rel. to or made of bone and cartilage.

osteocondritis *f.* osteochondritis, infl. of bone and cartilage.

osteodistrofia *f.* osteodystrophia, osteodystrophy, defective bone formation.

osteófito *m.* osteophyte, bony outgrowth.

osteogénesis *f.* osteogenesis. *V.* **osificación.**

osteoide *a.* osteoid, rel. to or resembling bone.

osteología *f.* osteology, the study of bones.

osteoma *m.* osteoma, a tumor of bone tissue.

osteomalacia *f.* osteomalacia, softening of the bones due to loss of calcium in the bone matrix.

osteomielitis *f.* osteomyelitis, infection of bone and bone marrow.

osteonecrosis *f.* osteonecrosis, destruction and death of bone tissue.

osteópata *m., f.* osteopath, specialist in osteopathy.

osteopatía *f.* osteopathy. 1. an approach to medicine that places emphasis on a favorable environment and on normal structural relationships of the musculoskeletal system, using extensive manipulation as a corrective tool; 2. any sickness of the bones.

osteopenia *f.* osteopenia, diminished calcification of the bones.

osteoporosis *f.* osteoporosis, loss of bone density.

osteotomía *f. surg.* osteotomy, the cutting or sawing of a bone.

ostial *a.* ostial, rel. to an opening or orifice.

ostium *L.* (*pl.* **ostia**) ostium, small opening.

ostomía *f. surg.* ostomy, creation of an artificial opening between the bowel or intestine and the skin, as in ileostomy and colostomy.

ostra *f.* oyster.

otalgia, otodinia *f.* otalgia, otodynia, earache.

otectomía *f. surg.* otectomy, excision of the structural contents of the middle ear.

ótico-a *a.* otic, rel. to the ear.

oticodinia *f.* oticodinia, vertigo caused by an ear disorder.

otitis *f.* otitis, infl. of the external, middle, or inner ear; ____ del nadador / swimmer's ear.

otolaringología *f.* otolaryngology, the study of the ear, nose and throat.

otolaringólogo-a *m., f.* otolaryngologist, specialist in otolaryngology.

otología *f.* otology, the study of the ear and its disorders.

otoneurología *f.* otoneurology, the study of the inner ear as related to the nervous system.

otoplastia *f. surg.* otoplasty, plastic surgery of the ear.

otorragia *f.* otorrhagia, bleeding from the ear.

otorrea *f.* otorrhea, purulent discharge from the ear.

otosclerosis *f.* otosclerosis, progressive deafness due to formation of spongy tissue in the labyrinth of the ear.

otoscopia *f.* otoscopy, examination of the ear with an otoscope.

otoscopio *m.* otoscope, instrument to examine the ear.

ototóxico-a *a.* ototoxic, that has toxic effects on the eighth pair of cranial nerves or on the hearing organs.

otro-a *a.* other; *pron.* another; **el** ___, **la** ___ / the ___ one; **los** ___-s, **las** ___-s / the others.

oval *a.* oval. 1. rel. to an ovum; 2. in the shape of an egg; **ventana** ___ / ___ window, membrane that separates the middle and the inner ear.

ovárico-a *a.* ovarian, rel. to the ovaries.

ovariectomía *f. surg.* ovariectomy. *V.* **ooforectomía.**

ovario *m.* ovary, female reproductive organ that produces the ova.

oviducto *m.* oviduct, uterine conduit.

ovoide *a.* ovoid, egg-shaped.

ovotestis *f.* ovotestis, hermaphroditic gland that contains both ovarian and testicular tissue.

ovulación *f.* ovulation, periodic release of the ovum from the ovary.

óvulo *m.* ovum, egg cell.

oxidación *f.* oxidation, the chemical change resulting from the combination of oxygen with another substance.

oxidado-a *a.* rusty.

oxidante *m.* oxidant, agent that causes oxidation.

oxigenación *f.* oxygenation, saturation with oxygen.

oxigenado-a *a.* oxygenated.

oxigenador *m.* oxygenator, device that oxygenates blood, gen. used during surgery.

oxígeno *m.* oxygen, free element found in the atmosphere as a colorless, tasteless, and odorless gas; **cámara de** ___ / ___ tent; **falta de** ___ / ___ deficiency.

oxímetro *m.* oximeter, instrument used to measure the amount of oxygen in the blood.

oxitocina, ocitocina *f.* oxytocin, pituitary hormone that stimulates uterine contraction.

P

P *abr.* **plasma** / plasma; **positivo-a** / positive; **posterior** / posterior; **presión** / pressure; **psiquiatría** / psychiatry; **pulso** / pulse.

pabulum *L.* pabulum, nutrient.

paciencia *f.* patience; **con** ___ / patiently.

paciente *m., f.* patient; **alta del** ___ / patient's discharge; **cuidado del** ___ / ___'s care; ___ **externo, no hospitalizado** / outpatient; ___ **privado** / private ___; ___ **solvente** / self–paying ___; *a.* patient.

padecer *vi.* to be afflicted by a sickness or injury; ___ **de** / to suffer from.

padecimiento *m.* suffering; affliction.

padrastro *m.* stepfather.

padre *m.* father; **-s** the parents, mother and father.

pagado-a *a.* paid.

pagar *vi.* to pay; ___ **al contado** / ___ in cash.

pago *m.* payment; ___ **compartido** / copayment; ___ **de una vez de la suma total** / lump sum ___.

palabra *f.* word.

paladar *m.* palate, the roof of the mouth; ___ **blando** / soft ___; ___ **duro** / hard ___; ___ **hendido** / cleft ___, congenital fissure; ___ **óseo** / bony ___.

palatino-a *a.* palatine, rel. to the palate.

paliativo-a *a.* palliative, that mitigates.

palidecer *vi.* to become pale.

palidez *f.* pallor.

pálido-a *a.* pallid, pale, sallow.

paliza *f.* beating.

palma *f.* 1. palm, palm of the hand; 2. palm tree; **aceite de** ___ / ___ oil.

palmacristi *f.* castor oil.

palmar *a.* palmar, rel. to the palm of the hand.

palpable *a.* palpable, that can be touched.

palpación *f.* palpation, examination with the hands.

palpar *v.* to palpate, to feel, to touch.

palpitación *f.* palpitation, rapid pulsation or throbbing.

palpitante *a.* throbbing.

palpitar *v.* to palpitate; to pant.

palúdico-a *a.* rel. to or afflicted by malaria.

paludismo *m.* malaria, paludism, highly infectious, febrile, and often chronic disease caused by the bite of an infected mosquito *Anopheles*.

pampiniforme *a.* pampiniform, simulating the structure of a vine.

pan *m.* bread; ____ **y mantequilla** / ____ and butter.

panacea *f.* panacea, a remedy to cure all ills.

panadizo *m.* felon, painful abscess of the distal phalanx of a finger.

panarteritis *f.* panarteritis, infl. of the layers of an artery.

panartritis *f.* panarthritis. 1. infl. of some joints of the body; 2. infl. of all the tissues of a joint.

pancitopenia *f.* pancytopenia, abnormal decrease in the number of blood cells.

páncreas *m.* pancreas, gland of the digestive system that externally secretes the pancreatic juice, and internally secretes insulin and glucagon.

pancreatectomía *f. surg.* pancreatectomy, partial or total removal of the pancreas.

pancreático-a *a.* pancreatic, rel. to the pancreas; conducto ____ / ____ duct; jugo ____ / ____ juice; quiste ____ / ____ cyst.

pancreaticoenterostomía *f. surg.* pancreaticoenterostomy, creation of a passage between the pancreatic duct and the intestines.

pancreatina *f.* pancreatin, digestive enzyme obtained from the pancreas.

pancreatitis *f.* pancreatitis, infl. of the pancreas; ____ aguda / acute ____ ; ____ hemorrágica aguda / acute hemorrhagic ____ .

pandémico-a *a.* pandemic, that occurs over a wide geographical area.

panendoscopio *m.* panendoscope, optical instrument used to examine the urethra and the bladder.

panfleto *m.* pamphlet.

panglosia *f.* panglossia, excessive talking.

panhidrosis *f.* panhidrosis, generalized sweating.

panhipopituitarismo *m.* panhypopituitarism, deficiency of the anterior pituitary gland.

panhisterectomía *f. surg.* panhysterectomy, total excision of the uterus.

pánico *m.* panic, excessive fear; *v.* **tener** ____ / to panic.

paniculitis *f.* paniculitis, infl. of the adipous panniculus.

panículo *m.* panniculus, layer of tissue; ____ adiposo / adipous ____ ; ____ carnoso / carnosus ____ .

pannus *L.* pannus, a membrane of granulation tissue covering a normal surface.

pansinusitis *f.* pansinusitis, infl. of all the paranasal sinuses in one or both sides.

pantalones *m.* pants, slacks.

pantalla *f.* screen.

pantorrilla *f.* calf of the leg.

panza *f.* belly.

panzudo-a *a. pop.* potbellied.

pañal *m.* diaper; ____**-es desechables** / disposable ____ -s.

papa, patata *m.* potato.

papá *m.* dad.

papada *f.* double chin.

Papanicolau, prueba de *f.* Papanicolau's test, Pap smear, sample of mucus from the vagina and the cervix for the purpose of early detection of cancer cells.

papaya *f.* papaya.

papel *m.* paper; ____ **higiénico** / toilet ____ ; role; *v.* **hacer el** ____ **de** / to play the ____ of.

paperas *f.* mumps, acute, febrile, highly contagious disease characterized by swelling of the salivary glands.

papila *f.* papilla, bud, small nipple-like eminence of the skin, esp. seen in the mouth; ____ gustativa / taste bud.

papilar *m.* papillary, rel. to a papilla.

papiledema *m.* papilledema, edema of the optic disk.

papiliforme *a.* papilliform, resembling a papilla.

papilitis *f.* papillitis, infl. of the optic disk.

papiloma *m.* papilloma, benign epithelial tumor.

papilomatosis *f.* papillomatosis, presence of multiple papillomas.

papovavirus *m.* papovavirus, type of virus used in the study of cancer.

pápula *f.* papule, small, hard eminence of the skin.

papular *a.* papular, rel. to papules.

paquete celular *m.* packed cells, red blood cells that have been separated from the plasma.

paquidermia *f.* pachydermia. *V.* **elefantiasis.**

paquigiria *f.* pachygyria, thick convolutions of the cerebral cortex.

par *m.* pair, couple.

para *prep.* to, for; for the purpose of; in order to; ____ **siempre** / forever; ¿ ____ **qué?** / what for?

paracentesis *f.* paracentesis, puncture to obtain or remove fluid from a cavity.

parado-a *a.* in a standing position.

paraesternal *a.* parasternal, adjacent to the sternum.

parafasia *f.* paraphasia, type of aphasia manifested by inability to use words coherently.

parafimosis *f.* paraphimosis. 1. retraction or constriction of the prepuce behind the glans penis; 2. retraction of the eyelid behind the eyeball.

parafina *f.* paraffin.

parainfluenza, virus de *m.* parainfluenza virus, any of several viruses associated with some respiratory infections, esp. in children.

paralaje *m.* parallax, the apparent displacement of an object according to the position of the viewer.

parálisis *f.* palsy, paralysis, partial or total loss of function of a part of the body; ___ cerebral / cerebral ___ , partial paralysis and lack of muscular coordination due to a congenital brain lesion; ___ de los buzos / diver's paralysis, decompression sickness (bends); ___ infantil / infantile paralysis.

paralítico-a *a.* paralytic, invalid, rel. to or suffering from paralysis; íleo ___ / ___ ileus, paralysis of the intestines.

paralizar *vi.* to paralyze.

paramagnético-a *a.* paramagnetic, rel. to substances that are susceptible to magnetism.

paramédico-a *m., f.* paramedic, individual trained and certified to offer emergency medical assistance.

paranasal *a.* paranasal, adjacent to the nasal cavity.

paraneumonía *f.* parapneumonia, illness with clinical characteristics resembling pneumonia.

paranoia *f. psych.* paranoia, mental disorder characterized by delusions of persecution and grandeur.

paranoico-a *a. psych.* paranoid, rel. to or afflicted with paranoia.

parapancreático-a *a.* parapancreatic, adjacent to the pancreas.

paraparesia *f.* paraparesis, partial paralysis esp. of the lower limbs.

paraplejía *f.* paraplegia, paralysis of the legs and the lower half of the body.

parapléjico-a *a.* paraplegic, rel. to or affected with paraplegia.

parapsicología *f.* parapsychology, the study of psychic phenomena such as mental telepathy and extrasensory perception.

parar *v.* to stop, to halt.

pararrectal *a.* pararectal, adjacent to the rectum.

parasimpático-a *a.* parasympathetic, rel. to one of two branches of the autonomic nervous system.

parasístole *f.* parasystole, an irregularity in cardiac rhythm.

parasítico-a *a.* parasitic.

parasitismo *m.* parasitism, infestation with parasites.

parásito *m.* parasite, organism that lives upon another one.

parasitología *f.* parasitology, the study of parasites.

paratífica, fiebre *f.* paratyphoid fever, a fever that simulates typhoid fever.

paratiroidectomía *f. surg.* parathyroidectomy, removal of one or more of the parathyroid glands.

paratiroideo-a *a.* parathyroid, located close to the thyroid gland.

paratiroides *f.* parathyroid, group of small endocrine glands situated behind the thyroid gland.

para-umbilical *a.* parumbilical, close to the navel.

paravertebral *a.* paravertebral, adjacent to the vertebral column.

parcial *a.* partial; **-mente** *adv.* partially.

parco-a *a.* sparing, scanty, moderate.

parche *m.* patch, piece of cloth or adhesive used to protect wounds; prueba del ___ / ___ test, for allergies.

parecer *vi.* to seem, to appear; **parecerse** *vr.* to look alike, to resemble.

parecido-a *a.* resembling.

pared *f.* wall; partition.

paregórico *m.* paregoric, sedative derived from opium.

pareja *f.* pair, couple.

parejo-a *a.* even, equal.

parénquima *m.* parenchyma, the functional elements of an organ.

parenteral *a.* parenteral, that is introduced in the body in a way other than the gastrointestinal route.

parentesco *m.* kindred, family relationship.

paresia *f.* paresis, slight or partial paralysis.

parestesia *f.* paresthesia, sensation of pricking, tingling, or tickling, gen. associated with partial damage to a peripheral nerve.

parético-a *a.* paretic, rel. to or afflicted by paresis.

pariente-a *m., f.* family relative.

parietal *m.* parietal bone; *a.* parietal. 1. rel. to the parietal bone; 2. rel. to the wall of a cavity.

parir *v.* to give birth.

Parkinson, enfermedad de *f.* Parkinson's disease, degenerative process of the brain nerves characterized by tremor, progressive muscular weakness, blurred speech, and shuffling gait.

paro *m.* standstill, arrest.

parodinia *f.* parodynia, difficult or abnormal delivery.

paroniquia *f.* paronychia, infl. of the area adjacent to a fingernail.

parótida *f.* parotid, gland that secretes saliva, situated near the ear.

parotiditis, parotitis *f.* parotiditis, parotitis. V. **paperas.**

paroxismal, paroxístico-a *a.* paroxysmal, rel. to paroxysm.

paroxismo *m.* paroxysm. 1. attack, spasm, or convulsion; 2. recurring intensified symptoms.

parpadear *v.* to blink.

parpadeo *m.* blinking; flicker.

párpado *m.* eyelid; cilium.

parrilla *f.* grill; **a la** ___ / grilled.

pars *L.* part, portion.

parte *f.* part, portion; **por todas** ___-s / everywhere.

partenogénesis *f.* parthenogenesis, unusual reproductive process in which the ovum develops without being fertilized by a spermatozoon; ___ artificial / artificial ___.

partición *f.* partition, sectioning, division.

participar *v.* to participate.

partícula *f.* particle, one of the minute parts that form matter.

particular *a.* particular; **-mente** *adv.* particularly.

particularidad *f.* peculiarity.

partir *v.* to sever, to break; to divide.

parto *m.* labor, delivery, parturition; antes del, después del ___ / before, after ___; canal del ___ / birth canal; dolor de ___ / ___ pains; estar de ___ / to be close to delivery; etapas del ___ / stages of ___; ___ activo / active ___; ___ de un feto sin vida / stillbirth; ___ falso / false ___;

___ inducido / induced ___; ___ laborioso / hard, difficult ___; ___ natural / natural childbirth; ___ normal / normal delivery; ___ prematuro / premature delivery; ___ prolongado, tardío / prolonged ___; ___ seco / dry ___.

parturienta *f.* parturient, a woman in the act of delivering or who has just delivered.

parturifaciente *m.* parturifacient, an agent that induces parturition.

párulis *f.* gumboil, an abscess of the gums.

parvavirus *m.* parvavirus, any of a group of viruses that cause diseases in animals but not in humans.

pasa *f.* raisin.

pasado *m.* the past tense; **-a** *a.* past; ___ **mañana** / the day after tomorrow; **la semana** ___ / last week.

pasaje *m.* passage. 1. conduit or meatus; 2. evacuation of the bowels.

pasar *v.* to pass, to pass by; to happen.

pasear *v.* to go for a stroll or an outing.

paseo *m.* a stroll; an outing.

pasillo *m.* hall, hallway, corridor; coveredway.

pasión *f.* passion, intense emotion.

pasividad *f.* passivity, abnormal dependency on others.

pasivo-a *a.* passive, not spontaneous or active; **ejercicio** ___ / ___ exercise.

paso *m.* step, pace.

pasta *f.* pasta; paste; ___ **de dientes** / toothpaste.

pasteurización *f.* pasteurization, the process of destroying microorganisms by applying regulated heat.

pasteurizar *vi.* to pasteurize, to perform pasteurization.

pastilla *f.* pill, tablet; lozenge; ___ para dormir / sleeping ___; ___ para el dolor / pain ___.

pastoso-a *a.* clammy; doughy.

patada *f.* hard kick.

patear *v.* to kick.

patelectomía *f.* *surg.* patellectomy, excision of the patella.

patelofemoral *a.* patellofemoral, rel. to the patella and the femur.

patella *L.* patella, kneecap.

patente *m.* patent, exclusive right or privilege; medicina de ___ / ___ medicine; *a.* patulous; open, not obstructed; evident.

paternidad *f.* paternity; prueba de ___ / ___ test.

paterno-a *a.* paternal, rel. to the father.

patético-a *a.* pathetic.

patizambo-a *a.* pigeon-toed, feet turned inward.

patofisiología *f.* pathophysiology, the study of the effects of a disease on the physiological processes.

patogénesis *f.* pathogenesis, origin and development of a sickness.

patógeno *m.* pathogen, agent that causes disease; **-a** *a.* pathogenic, that can cause a disease.

patognomónico-a *a.* pathognomonic, rel. to a sign or symptom characteristic of a given disease.

patología *f.* pathology, the study of the origin and nature of disease.

patológico-a *a.* pathologic, pathological, rel. to disease.

patólogo-a *m., f.* pathologist, specialist in pathology.

patrón *m.* pattern, model, type.

pausa *f.* pause, rest; interruption; ___ compensadora / compensatory ___, long interval of the heart, following a heartbeat.

pausado-a *a.* slow, deliberate.

pavo *m.* turkey.

paz *f.* peace; *v.* **dejar en** ___ / to leave alone; **en** ___ / at ___.

peau d'orange *Fr.* peau d'orange, skin condition resembling that of the peel of an orange, an important sign in breast cancer.

peca *f.* freckle, spot, small discoloration of the skin.

pecoso-a *a.* freckled.

pectina *f.* pectin, carbohydrate obtained from the peel of citrus fruits or apples.

pectoral *a.* pectoral, rel. to the chest.

pectus *L.* (*pl.* **pectora**) pectus, breast, chest.

peculiar *a.* peculiar.

pecho *m.* chest; ___ de paloma / pigeon breast; *v.* **dar el** ___ / to breast-feed.

pechuga *a.* breast or white meat of a fowl.

pedal *a.* pedal, rel. to the foot.

pedazo *m.* piece, part of a whole.

pederastia *f.* pederasty, anal intercourse between males, esp. between an adult and a young boy.

pediatra *m., f.* pediatrician, specialist in pediatrics.

pediatría *f.* pediatrics, the study of the care and development of children and the treatment of diseases affecting them.

pediátrico-a *a.* pediatric, rel. to pediatrics.

pedículo *m.* pedicle, narrow stem-like part of a tumor that connects it with its base.

pediculosis *f.* pediculosis, infestation with lice.

pedir *vi.* to ask for something, to request.

pedofilia *f.* pedophilia, morbid sexual attraction to children.

pedunculado-a *a.* pedunculate, pedunculated, rel. to, or having peduncles.

pedúnculo *m.* peduncle, stem-like connection.

pedunculus *L.* pedunculus. *V.* **pedúnculo.**

pegajoso-a *a.* sticky, gummy.

pegar *vi.* to stick together, to glue, to adhere.

peinar *v.* to comb; **peinarse** *vr.* to comb one's hair.

peine *m.* comb.

peladura *f.* peeling, scaling. *V.* **exfoliación;** ___ química / chemical ___.

pelagra *f.* pellagra, illness caused by deficiency of niacin and characterized by dermatitis, gastrointestinal, and mental disorders.

pelar *v.* to peel; to give a haircut; **pelarse** *vr.* to get a haircut.

pelea *f.* fight, quarrel.

pelear *v.* to fight, to quarrel.

película *f.* 1. film, movie; 2. thin layer or membrane.

peligro *m.* danger, risk; hazard; peril; *v.* **estar en** ___ / to be in ___; **poner en** ___ / to endanger, to jeopardize.

peligroso-a *a.* dangerous, risky, hazardous.

pelo *m.* hair; raíz del ___ / ___ root; bola de ___ / ___ ball, type of bezoar; trasplante de ___ / ___ transplant.

pelota *f.* ball.

peloteo *m.* ballottement, maneuver used during examination of the abdomen and pelvis to determine the presence of tumors or enlargement of organs.

peluca *f.* wig.

peludo-a *a.* hairy.

pélvico-a, pelviano-a *a.* pelvic, rel. to the pelvis.

pelvis *f.* pelvis. 1. cavity in the lower end of the trunk formed by the hip bone, the sacrum, and the coccyx; enfermedad inflamatoria de la ___ / inflammatory pelvic disease; 2. basin-shaped cavity.

pelvis menor, verdadera *f.* true pelvis, the inferior and contractile part of the pelvis.

pellejo *m.* peel, hide; *pop.* skin.

pellizcar *vi.* to pinch.

pellizco *m.* pinch.

pena *f.* sorrow, affliction.

penacho *m.* tuft, a small cluster or mass.

pendiente *a.* pending, unfinished.

pendular *a.* pendulous, that oscillates or hangs.

pene *m.* penis, the external part of the male reproductive organ that contains the urethral orifice through which urine and semen pass.

peneal, peneano-a *a.* penile, rel. to the penis.

penetración *f.* penetration. 1. the act of penetrating; 2. the ability of radiation to go through a substance.

penetrante *a.* penetrating; piercing.

penetrar *v.* to penetrate, to go through.

pénfigo *m.* pemphigus, a variety of dermatosis characterized by the presence of blisters that can become infected upon rupturing.

penfigoideo-a *a.* pemphigoid, that is similar to pemphigus but having clinical differences.

penicilina *f.* penicillin, antibiotic derived directly or indirectly from cultures of the fungus *Penicillum.*

pensar *vi.* to think.

peor *a.* *comp.* worse; *sup.* worst; *adv.* worse.

pepino *m.* cucumber.

pepsina *f.* pepsin, the main enzyme of the gastric juice.

péptico-a *a.* peptic, rel. to the action or the digestion of gastric juices.

pequeño-a *a.* small in size.

pera *f.* pear; ___ de goma / bulb syringe.

percepción *f.* perception. 1. the conscious mental recognition of a sensory stimulus; ___ extrasensorial / extrasensory ___; 2. understanding or comprehension of an idea.

percibir *v.* to perceive, to realize.

percusión *f.* percussion, procedure that consists in tapping the surface of the body with the fingers or a small tool, in order to produce sounds or vibrations that indicate the condition of a given part of the body; ___ auscultatoria / auscultatory ___.

percutáneo-a *a.* percutaneous, that is applied through the skin.

percutir *v.* to percuss, to use percussion.

perder *vi.* to lose, to forfeit; ___ sangre / to bleed; ___ la oportunidad / to miss, to

lose an opportunity; ___ tiempo / to waste time; ___ un turno / to miss an appointment.

pérdida *f.* loss; ___ de sangre / ___ of blood; ___ del conocimiento / ___ of conciousness; ___ del contacto con la realidad / ___ of contact with reality; ___ del equilibrio / ___ of balance; ___ del movimiento / ___ of motion; ___ de la audición / of hearing; ___ de la memoria / ___ of memory; ___ de la tonicidad muscular / ___ of muscle tone; ___ de la visión / ___ of vision.

perdido-a *a.* lost.

perfeccionismo *m.* *psych.* perfectionism, excessive drive to attain perfection, regardless of the importance of the task.

perfeccionista *m., f.* perfectionist.

perfecto-a *a.* perfect; -**mente** *adv.* perfectly.

perfil *m.* profile, side view; outline.

perforación *f.* perforation, hole.

perforar *v.* to perforate; to pierce.

perfusión *f.* perfusion, passage of a liquid through a conduit.

periamigdalino-a *a.* peritonsillar, close to the tonsils.

perianal *a.* perianal, located around the anus.

pericárdico-a, pericardial *a.* pericardiac, pericardial, rel. to the pericardium; derrame ___ / ___ effusion.

pericardiectomía *f.* *surg.* pericardiectomy, partial or total excision of the pericardium.

pericardio *m.* pericardium, saclike, double-layered membrane that surrounds the heart and the origins of the large blood vessels.

pericarditis *f.* pericarditis, infl. of the pericardium.

periferia *f.* periphery, part of a body or organ away from the center.

periférico-a *a.* peripheral, rel. to or occurring in the periphery; sistema nervioso ___ / ___ nervous system, the group of nerves situated outside the central nervous system.

perilla *f.* rubber bulb.

perinatal *a.* perinatal, rel. to or occurring before, during, or right after birth.

perineal *a.* perineal, rel. to the perineum.

perinéfrico-a *a.* perinephric, close to the kidney.

perineo *m.* perineum, the pelvic outlet bounded anteriorly by the scrotum in the man and the vulva in the woman, and posteriorly by the anus.

perineural *a.* perineural, around the nerve.

periódico *m.* newspaper; **-a** *a.* periodical; **-mente** *adv.* periodically.

período, periodo *m.* period. 1. interval of time, epoch; _____ de tiempo / time span; 2. menstruation.

periodoncia *f.* periodontics, branch of odontology dealing with areas surrounding the teeth.

periodontal *a.* periodontal, surrounding the tooth.

periostio *m.* periosteum, thick fibrous membrane that covers all the surface of the bone except the articular surface.

peristalsis *f.* peristalsis, wavelike contractions that occur in a tubular structure such as the alimentary canal, by which the contents are forced onward.

peristáltico-a *a.* peristaltic, rel. to peristalsis.

peritoneal *a.* peritoneal, rel. to the peritoneum.

peritoneo *m.* peritoneum, serous membrane that lines the abdominopelvic walls and the viscera.

peritoneoscopía *f.* peritoneoscopy. *V.* **laparoscopía.**

peritonitis *f.* peritonitis, infl. of the peritoneum.

periungual *a.* periungual, around the nail.

periuretral *a.* periurethral, around the urethra.

perjudicial *a.* detrimental, damaging.

perleche *Fr.* perleche, disorder manifested by fissures at the corner of the mouth, seen esp. in children, and gen. as a result of malnutrition.

permanecer *vi.* to remain; to last.

permanente *a.* permanent, lasting; **-mente** *adv.* permanently.

permeabilidad *f.* permeability, patency, the quality of being permeable, not obstructed; _____ capilar / capillary _____ .

permeable *a.* permeable, that allows passage through structures such as a membrane.

permiso *m.* permit; consent.

permitido-a *a.* permissible; permitted.

permitir *v.* to allow, to consent, to agree.

pernicioso-a *a.* pernicious, noxious, harmful.

pero *conj.* but.

peroné *m.* perone, fibula, calf bone, the outer and thinner of the two lower leg bones.

perpendicular *a.* perpendicular.

per rectum *L.* per rectum, by the rectum.

perro *m.* dog.

persecución *f.* persecution.

perseveración *f. psych.* perseveration, mental disorder manifested by the abnormal repetition of an idea or action.

persistir *v.* to persist, to persevere.

persona *f.* person. 1. individual; 2. *psych.* outward personality that conceals the real one.

personal *m.* personnel; _____ médico / medical _____ ; *a.* personal, rel. to a person.

personalidad *f.* personality, traits, characteristics, and individual behavior that distinguishes one person from another; _____ antisocial / antisocial _____ ; _____ compulsiva / compulsive _____ ; _____ esquizoide / schizoid, split _____ ; _____ extrovertida / extroverted _____ ; _____ introvertida / introverted _____ ; _____ neurótica / neurotic _____ ; _____ paranoica / paranoid _____ ; _____ psicopática / psychopathic _____ .

perspectiva *f.* perspective.

perspiración *f.* perspiration, exudation.

persuadir *v.* to persuade.

persuasión *f.* persuasion, therapeutic treatment that tries to deal with the patient through the use of reason.

pertenecer *vi.* to belong.

perteneciente *a.* pertaining or rel. to.

pertinente *a.* pertinent, relevant.

perturbación *f.* perturbation. 1. feeling of uneasiness; 2. abnormal variation from a regular state.

perturbar *v.* to perturb, to disrupt, to disturb.

pertussis *L.* pertussis. *V.* **tos ferina.**

perversión *f.* perversion, deviation from socially accepted behavior; _____ sexual / sexual _____ .

pervertido-a *m., f.* pervert, individual given to sexual perversion.

pervio-a *a.* pervious. *V.* **permeable.**

pes *L.* pes, the foot or a structure resembling it.

pesa *f.* weighing scale.

pesadez *f.* heaviness.

pesadilla *f.* nightmare.

pesado-a *m., f.* a boring person; *a.* heavy; [*conducta*] boring; **sueño** _____ / deep sleep.

pésame *m.* condolences.

pesar *m.* grief, sorrow; *v.* to weigh; **a** ___ **de /** in spite of.

pesario *m.* pessary, uterus-supporting device inserted in the vagina.

pescado *m.* fish.

pescuezo *m.* neck.

pesimismo *m.* pessimism, an inclination to see and judge situations in their most unfavorable light.

pesimista *m., f.* pessimist; *a.* pessimist, rel. to, or that manifests pessimism.

peso *m.* weight; falto de, bajo de ___ / underweight; ___ al nacer / birth ___ .

pestañas *f. pl.* eyelashes.

pestañear *v.* to blink, to wink.

pestañeo *m.* blink; blinking.

peste *f.* 1. bubonic plague, an epidemic infectious disease transmitted by the bite of infected rats or fleas; 2. plague, any epidemic contagious disease with a high rate of mortality; 3. foul smell.

pesticida *m.* pesticide, chemical agent that kills insects and rodents.

petequia *f.* petechiae, minute hemorrhagic spots in the skin and the mucosa that appear in connection with some severe fevers such as typhoid.

petición *f.* petition, request; claim; proceso para revisión de ___ -es / claim review procedure.

petit mal *Fr.* petit mal, benign epileptic attack with loss of consciousness at times, but with no convulsions.

petrificado-a *a.* petrified. 1. made rigid like stone; 2. terrified.

peyote *m.* peyote, plant from which the hallucinatory drug mescaline is obtained.

pezón *m.* nipple; ___ agrietado / cracked ___ ; ___ enlechado / engorged ___ .

piamadre *f.* pia mater, thin vascular membrane, the innermost of the three cerebral meninges.

pica *f.* pica, a craving for inedible substances.

picada, picadura *f.* sting, bite.

picante *a.* piquant, highly seasoned.

picar *vi.* to bite; to pierce, to prick.

picazón *f.* itching.

pie *m.* foot; ___ de atleta / athlete's ___ , dermatofitosis; ___ en extensión / footdrop; ___ plano / flatfoot; planta del ___ / sole; *v.* **estar de** ___ / to be standing; *vr.* **ponerse de** ___ / to stand up; *v.* **ir a** ___ / to go on foot.

pie de trinchera *m.* trench foot, infectious condition of the feet resulting from long exposure to cold.

piedra *f.* stone, calculus.

piel *f.* skin; hide, epidermis; cáncer de la ___ / ___ cancer; injerto de ___ / ___ graft.

pielografía *f.* pyelography. *V.* **pielograma**.

pielograma *m.* pyelogram, X-ray of the renal pelvis and the ureter using a contrasting medium.

pielolitotomía *f. surg.* pyelolithotomy, incision to remove a calculus from the renal pelvis.

pielonefritis *f.* pyelonephritis, infl. of the kidney and the renal pelvis.

pieloplastia *f. surg.* pyeloplasty, plastic surgery of the renal pelvis.

pielostomía *f.* pyelostomy, creation of an opening in the renal pelvis to divert the urine to the exterior.

pielotomía *f. surg.* pyelotomy, incision of the renal pelvis.

pierna *f.* leg, lower extremity that extends from the knee to the ankle; ___ arqueada / bowleg, genu varum; traumatismo de la ___ / ___ injury.

pigmentación *f.* pigmentation.

pigmento *m.* pigment, coloring element.

pijama, piyamas *f.* pajamas.

pila *f.* faucet; battery.

píldora *f.* pill; ___ de control del embarazo / birth control ___ .

piliación *f.* piliation, formation and development of hair.

pilórico-a *a.* pyloric, rel. to the pylorus.

píloro *m.* pylorus, the lower aperture of the stomach that opens into the duodenum.

piloroplastia *f. surg.* pyloroplasty, plastic surgery for reparation of the pylorus.

pilus *L.(pl.* **pili**) pilus, hair.

pimienta *f.* pepper.

pincelación *f.* penciling, pencilling, application of a medical solution to an area of the skin or to a cavity with a medicated pencil, brush, or cotton swab.

pinchar *v.* to prick.

pinchazo *m.* prick, jab; cut.

pinna *L.* pinna, ear lap.

pinocitosis *f.* pinocytosis, absorption of liquids by cells.

pintar *v.* to paint, to apply a medication to the skin.

pinzas *f. pl.* clip, forceps, pincers, tweezers, devices used to assist in the extraction process.

piocito *m.* pyocite, a pus corpuscle.

piógeno-a *a.* pyogenic, that produces pus.

piojo *m.* louse, parasite that is the primary transmitter of some diseases such as typhus.

piorrea *f.* pyorrhea. *V.* **periodontitis.**

pipeta *f.* pipet, pipette, glass tube.

pirámide *f.* pyramid, a cone-shaped structure such as the medulla oblongata.

pirético *m.* pyretic, rel. to fever.

pirexia *f.* pyrexia, high temperature; fever.

pirógeno *m.* pyrogen, agent that elevates a fever.

piromanía *f.* pyromania, obsession with fires.

piscina *f.* swimming pool.

piso *m.* floor; ground.

pistola *f.* pistol, handgun.

pituitaria, glándula *f.* pituitary gland. *V.* **hipófisis.**

piuria *f.* pyuria, presence of pyocites in the urine.

pivote *m.* pivot, part used to support the artificial crown of a tooth.

placa *f.* 1. plate, flat structure such as a thin layer of bone; 2. plate, thin layer of metal used to support a structure; 3. plaque, a patch on the skin or mucous membrane; 4. X-ray.

placebo *m.* placebo, harmless substance of no medical value, gen. used for experimental purposes.

placenta *f.* placenta, vascular organ that develops in the wall of the uterus through which the fetus derives its nourishment; ____ previa / ____ previa, placenta situated before the fetus in relation to the cervical opening causing at times severe hemorrhaging.

placentario-a *a.* placental, rel. to the placenta; insuficiencia ____ / ____ insufficiency.

plaga *f.* plague, epidemic infectious disease.

plan *m.* plan; design.

planeamiento *m.* planning.

planear *v.* to plan.

planificación familiar *f.* planned parenthood; family planning.

planilla *f.* [*formulario*] form.

plano *m.* plane. 1. flat surface; 2. a relatively smooth surface formed by making an imaginary or real cut through a part of the body; ____ axial / axial ____; ____ coronal / coronal ____; ____ frontal / frontal ____; ____ horizontal / horizontal ____; ____ medio / midplane; ____ sagital / sagittal ____.

planta *f.* plant; ____ del pie / sole; ____-s medicinales [*hierbas*] / medicinal ____-s or herbs.

plantar *a.* plantar, rel. to the sole of the foot; reflejo ____ / ____ reflex, Babinski's reflex.

plaqueta *f.* platelet, thrombocyte, an element of the blood in the form of minute disks, essential to coagulation.

plasma *m.* plasma, liquid component of the blood and lymph which is made up of 91 percent of water and 9 percent of a combination of elements such as proteins, salts, nutrients, and vitamins.

plasticidad *f.* plasticity, the capacity to be molded.

plástico *m.* plastic; **-a** *a.* plastic.

plata *f.* silver; nitrato de ____ / ____ nitrate.

plátano *m.* banana.

platicar *vi.* to converse, to talk.

Platelmintos *m. pl.* Platyhelminthes, a phylum of flatworms that includes the *Cestoda* and *Trematoda,* among others.

plegado-a *a.* plicate, folded.

pleomorfismo *m.* pleomorphism, the quality of assuming various forms.

pletismografía *f.* plethysmography, the recording of the changes in size of a part of the body as affected by circulation.

plétora *f.* plethora, an excess of any of the body fluids.

pleura *f.* pleura, doublefold membrane that covers each lung; ____ parietal / parietal ____; ____ visceral / visceral ____.

pleural *a.* pleural, rel. to the pleura; cavidad ____ / ____ cavity, space between the folds of the pleura; derrame ____ / ____ effusion.

pleuresía *f.* pleurisy, infl. of the pleura.

pleurítico-a *a.* pleuritic, rel. to pleurisy.

pleuritis *f. V.* **pleuresía.**

pleuroscopía *f.* pleuroscopy, inspection of the pleural cavity through an incision into the thorax.

plexiforme *a.* plexiform, in the shape of a plexus or net.

plexo *m.* plexus, an interlacing of nerves, blood, or lymphatic vessels.

plica *f.* plica, fold, crease.

pliegue *m.* fold.

plomo *m.* lead; delantal de ____ / ____ apron;

envenenamiento por ___ / ___ poisoning; sonda de ___ / ___ probe.

pluma *f.* pen.

plumbismo *m.* plumbism, chronic lead poisoning.

plural *m.* plural, indicator of the presence of more than one.

pluripotencial *a.* pluripotent, pluripotential, that can take more than one course of action.

población *f.* population.

pobre *a.* poor.

pobreza *f.* poverty.

poción *f.* draft, potion, a single dose of liquid medicine.

poco-a *a.* little, in small quantity; *adv.* little, small; **dentro de** ___ / in a short while; ___ **a** ___ / little by little; **por** ___ / almost.

poder *m.* power, strength; *vi.* to be able to; to have the power to.

podíatra *m.*, *f.* podiatrist, specialist in podiatry.

podiatría *f.* podiatry, the diagnosis and treatment of conditions affecting the feet.

podrido-a *a.* rotten, decomposed.

polar *a.* polar, rel. to a pole.

polaridad *f.* polarity. 1. the quality of having poles; 2. the quality of presenting opposite effects at the two extremities.

polen *m.* pollen.

poli *m.* poly, polymorphonuclear leukocyte.

poliarticular *a.* polyarticular, affecting more than one joint.

poliartritis *f.* polyarthritis, infl. of more than one joint.

policitemia *f.* polycythemia, excess of red blood cells; ___ primaria / primary ___ , vera; ___ rubra / rubra ___ , vera; ___ secundaria / secondary ___ , erythrocythemia; ___ vera / vera ___ , erythremia.

policlínica *f.* polyclinic, a general hospital.

polidactilia *f.* polydactylia, the presence of more than five fingers or toes.

polidipsia *f.* polydipsia, excessive thirst.

poligamia *f.* polygamy, the practive of having more than one spouse at the same time.

polígrafo *m.* polygraph, device that registers simultaneously the arterial and venous pulsations.

polihidramnios *m.* polyhydramnios, an excess of amniotic fluid.

poli – insaturado-a *a.* polyunsaturated, denoting a fatty acid.

poliomiopatía *f.* polymyopathy, any disease that affects several muscles at the same time.

polimorfonucleado-a, polimorfonuclear *a.* polymorphonuclear, having a deeply lobed nucleus; granulocito ___ / ___ granulocyte, having a nucleus with multiple lobes.

polineuropatía *f.* polyneuropathy, any disease that affects several nerves at one time.

polio, poliomielitis *f.* polio, poliomyelitis, contagious disease that attacks the central nervous system and causes paralysis of the muscles, esp. of the legs.

poliovirus *m.* poliovirus, causative agent of poliomyelitis.

polipectomía *f.* *surg.* polypectomy, excision of a polyp.

pólipo *m.* polyp, tag, mass, or growth protruding from a mucous membrane.

poliposis *f.* polyposis, formation of multiple polyps.

poliquístico-a *a.* polycystic, that has many cysts.

polisacárido *m.* polysaccharide, a carbohydrate capable of hydrolysis.

polivalente *a.* polyvalent, that has an effect against more than one agent.

póliza de seguro *f.* insurance policy.

polo *m.* pole, each of the two opposite extremes of a body, organ, or spherical or oval part.

polución *f.* pollution, contamination.

polvo *m.* dust; powder; **en** ___ / powdered.

pollo *m.* chicken.

pomada *f.* ointment, pomade, salve, semisolid medicinal substance for external use; ___ contraceptiva / contraceptive jelly; ___ facial / cold cream; ___ vaginal / vaginal jelly.

pomo *m.* jar; bottle.

pómulo *m.* molar bone, cheekbone.

poner *vi.* to put, to set, to lay down; **ponerse** *vr.* [*vestimenta*] to put on; to become; ___ **viejo** / to grow or become old.

pons *L.* pons, tissue formation that connects two separate parts of an organ.

poplíteo-a *a.* popliteal, rel. to the area behind the knee.

por *prep.* for, by, through, from; ___ **ahora** / for the time being; ___ **atrás** / from or through the back; ___ **delante** / from or through the front; ___ **eso** / because of that; ___ **lo tanto** / therefore.

porcentaje

porcentaje *m.* percentage, percent.
porcino-a *a.* porcine, rel. to swine.
porción *f.* portion.
poro, porus *m.* pore, porus, minute opening of the skin such as the duct of a sweat gland.
poroso-a *a.* porous, permeable.
porque *conj.* because, for the reason that; *interr.* ¿**por qué?** / why?, for what reason?
porta *L.* porta, opening, or entry, esp. one through which blood vessels and nerves penetrate into an organ.
porta, vena *f.* portal vein, short, thick trunk formed by branches of many veins leading from abdominal organs.
portador *m.* carrier, one who or that which carries a disease-causing agent that can be transmitted to other individuals; ___ de bacilos / bacillicarrier.
portal *m.* portal, entryway; *a.* rel. to the portal system.
portal, circulación *f.* portal circulation, flow of blood into the liver by the portal vein and out by the hepatic vein.
portal, hipertensión *f.* portal hypertension, increase in pressure in the portal vein due to an obstruction in blood circulation in the liver.
portaobjeto *m.* slide, specimen holder for microscopic examination.
poseer *vi.* to possess.
poseído-a *a. pp.* of **poseer**, possesed, dominated by an idea or passion.
posesivo *m. gr.* possessive; **-a** *a.* possessive.
posibilidad *f.* possibility.
posible *a.* possible; **-mente** *adv.* possibly.
posición *f.* position; ___ anatómica / anatomic ___; ___ de litotomía / lithotomy ___; ___ distal / distal ___; ___ dorsal recumbente / dorsal recumbent ___; ___ erecta / upright ___; ___ genucubital / genocubital ___, knee-elbow; ___ genupectoral / knee-chest ___; ___ inadecuada / malposition; ___ lateral / lateral ___; ___ prona / prone ___, face down; ___ supina, yacente / supine ___, face up.
positividad *f.* positivity, manifestation of a positive reaction.
positivo-a *a.* positive; certain, without doubt.
posponer *vi.* to postpone, to delay.
posterior *a.* posterior. 1. rel. to the back or the back part of a structure; 2. that follows in sequence.
posthipnótico-a *a.* posthypnotic, following the hypnoptic state.
postictal *a.* postictal, following a seizure or attack.
postmaduro *a.* postmature, rel. to an infant after a prolonged gestation period.
post mortem *L.* post mortem, that occurs after death; autopsy.
postnasal *a.* postnasal, behind the nose.
post partum *L.* post partum, period of time following childbirth; depresión del ___ / ___ depression; psicosis del ___ / ___ psychosis.
postoperatorio-a *a.* postoperative, following surgery; complicación ___ / ___ complication; cuidado ___ / ___ care.
postprandial *a.* postprandial, after a meal.
postración *f.* prostration, exhaustion, extreme fatigue.
postrado-a *a.* prostrate. 1. in prone position; 2. exhausted, debilitated.
postre *m.* dessert.
póstumo-a *a.* posthumous, that occurs after death; examen ___ / post mortem examination.
postura *f.* posture, position of the body.
postural *a.* postural, rel. to position or posture; hipotensión ___ / ___ hypotension, decrease in blood pressure in an erect position.
potable *a.* potable, drinkable, that can be drunk without harm.
potasemia *f.* kaliemia, kalemia, presence of potassium in the blood.
potasio *m.* potassium, mineral which combined with others in the body is essential in the transmission of nerve impulses and in muscular activity.
potencia *f.* potency, strength.
potencial *m.* potential, electric pressure or tension; *a.* having a ready disposition or capacity.
potente *a.* potent, strong.
práctica *f.* practice.
practicar *vi.* to practice.
práctico-a *a.* practical, rel. to meals.
prandial *a.* prandial, rel. to meals.
preagónico-a *a.* preagonal, rel. to a condition preceding death.
preanestésico *m.* preanesthetic, preliminary agent given to ease the administration of general anesthesia.

precanceroso-a *a.* precancerous, that tends to become malignant.

precario-a *a.* precarious, uncertain.

precaución *f.* precaution.

precavido-a *a.* cautious, on guard.

preceder *v.* to precede.

precio *m.* price, cost.

precipitado *m.* precipitate, deposit of solid particles that settles out of a solution; **-a** *a.* that occurs suddenly.

precisión *f.* precision, exactness.

precocidad *f.* precocity, early development of physical or mental adult traits.

precoz *a.* precocious.

precursor *m.* precursor, something that precedes, such as a symptom or sign of a disease; **-a** *a.* introductory, preliminary.

predecir *vi.* to predict.

predisposición *f.* predisposition, propensity to develop a condition or illness caused by environmental, genetic, or psychological factors.

predispuesto-a *a.* predisposed, prone or susceptible to contract a disease.

predominante *a.* predominant.

predominio *m.* predominance.

preeclampsia *f.* preeclampsia, a toxic condition of late pregnancy, manifested by hypertension, albuminuria, and edema.

preferencia *f.* preference.

preferible *a.* preferable.

preferir *vi.* to prefer, to favor one thing, person, or condition over another.

prefijo *m. gr.* prefix.

pregunta *f.* question; *v.* **hacer una** ___ / to ask a ___.

preguntar *v.* to ask, to inquire.

prejuicio *m.* prejudice, bias.

preliminar *a.* preliminary.

premadurez *f.* prematurity, the condition of a viable infant born prior to completion of the thirty-seventh week of gestation.

prematuro-a *m., f.* premature baby; *a.* before term.

premedicación *f.* premedication. *V.* **preanestésico.**

premenstrual *a.* premenstrual; tensión ___ / ___ tension.

premonición *f.* premonition, forewarning.

premonitorio-a *a.* premonitory, advertencia o señal ___ / ___ signal; síntoma ___ / ___ symptom.

premunición *f.* premunition, immunity to a given infection established by the previous presence of the causative agent.

prenatal *a.* prenatal, prior to birth; cuidado ___ / ___ care.

prensil *a.* prehensile, adapted or shaped for grasping or lifting.

preñada *a.* pregnant.

preocupación *f.* preoccupation, concern.

preocupado-a *a.* concerned, worried.

preocuparse *vr.* to worry, to be preoccupied; **no se preocupe, no te preocupes** / don't worry.

preoperativo-a *a.* preoperative; cuidado ___ / ___ care.

preparación *f.* preparation. 1. the act of making something ready; 2. a medication ready for use.

preparar *v.* to prepare, to make ready.

preposición *f. gr.* preposition.

prepubescente *a.* prepubescent, before puberty.

prepucio *m.* prepuce, foreskin, loose fold of skin that covers the glans penis.

prerrenal *a.* prerenal. 1. in front of the kidney; 2. that occurs in the circulatory system before reaching the kidney.

presacro-a *a.* presacral, in front of the sacrum.

presbiopía *f.* presbyopia, farsightedness that occurs with increasing age due to the loss of elasticity of the lens of the eye.

prescribir *vi.* to prescribe.

prescripción *f.* prescription.

prescrito-a *a. pp.* of **prescribir,** prescribed, ordered.

presencia *f.* presence.

presentación *f.* presentation. 1. position of the fetus in the uterus as detected upon examination; 2. position of the fetus in reference to the birth canal at the time of delivery; ___ cefálica / cephalic ___ ; ___ de cara / face ___ ; ___ de nalgas / breech ___ ; ___ transversa / transverse ___ ; 3. oral report.

presente *a.* present, manifest.

preservación *f.* preservation, conservation.

preservar *v.* to preserve.

preservativo *m.* preservative, agent that is added to food or medication to destroy or impede multiplication of bacteria.

presilla *f.* staple.

presión *f.* pressure, stress, strain, tension; ___ alta / high blood ___ ; ___ arterial / blood ___ , pressure of the blood in the arteries; ___ baja / low blood ___ ; ___ central venosa / central venous ___ , blood pressure in the right atrium of the heart; ___ diastólica / diastolic ___ , blood pressure during dilation of the auricles and ventricles; ___ diferencial / wedge ___ ; ___ osmótica / osmotic ___ ; ___ sanguínea / blood ___ ; ___ sistólica / systolic ___ , arterial pressure during contraction of the ventricles; ___ venosa / venous ___ ; *v.* hacer ___ / to exert pressure.

presión del pulso *f.* pulse pressure, the difference between the systolic and diastolic pressures.

presionar *v.* to exert pressure.

presor *a.* pressor, that tends to raise the blood pressure.

pretender *v.* to pretend.

pretérito *m. gr.* preterite.

pretérmino *m.* preterm, what occurs during the period of time prior to the thirty-seventh week in a pregnancy.

prevaleciente *a.* prevailing.

prevalencia *f.* prevalence, the total number of cases of a specific disease present in a given population at a certain time.

prevención *f.* prevention.

prevenir *vi.* to prevent, to forestall.

preventivo-a *a.* preventive; servicios de salud ___ / ___ health services.

prever *vi.* to foresee.

prevertebral *a.* prevertebral, in front of a vertebra.

previo-a *a.* previous, prior.

previsto-a *a. pp.* of **prever,** foreseen.

priapismo *m.* priapism, painful and continued erection of the penis as a result of disease.

primario-a *a.* primary, initial; chief, principal.

primavera *f.* springtime.

primeriza *f.* woman who gives birth to a child for the first time.

primer, primero-a *a.* first, prime.

primeros auxilios *m. pl.* first aid.

primitivo-a *a.* primitive; embryonic.

primo-a *m., f.* cousin.

primogénito-a *a.* first-born.

primordial *a.* primordial, essential.

principal *a.* principal, foremost; -mente *adv.* primarily, mainly.

principiante *m.* beginner, novice.

principio *m.* 1. beginning, start; 2. principle, chief ingredient of a medication or chemical compound; 3. principle, rule.

principio del placer *m. psych.* pleasure principle, behavior directed at obtaining immediate gratification and avoiding pain.

principio de la realidad *m. psych.* reality principle, orientation to reality and self-gratification through awareness of the outside world.

prioridad *f.* priority, precedence.

prisa *f.* haste, rush; a toda ___ / right away; *vr.* darse ___ / to hurry; *v.* tener ___ / to be in a hurry.

privación *f.* privation, hardship; withdrawal.

privado-a *a.* private; cuarto ___ / private room; -mente *adv.* privately.

privilegio *m.* privilege.

probabilidad *f.* probability.

probable *a.* probable; -mente *adv.* probably.

probador *m.* tester.

probar *vi.* [*esfuerzo*] to try; [*gusto*] to taste; [*comprobar*] to prove; to sample.

probeta *f.* pipet, pipette, glass tube.

problema *m.* problem; trouble.

problemático-a *a.* problematic, disputable.

procedente *a.* originating.

proceder *v.* to proceed, to continue.

procedimiento *m.* procedure; ___ clínico / clinical ___ ; ___ quirúrgico / surgical ___ ; ___ terapéutico / therapeutic ___ .

proceso *m.* process, method, system.

procrear *v.* to procreate, to beget.

proctalgia *f.* proctalgia, pain in the rectum and anus.

proctitis *f.* proctitis, infl. of the rectum and anus.

proctología *f.* proctology, the branch of medicine that studies the colon, rectum, and anus, and the treatment of the diseases affecting them.

proctólogo-a *m., f.* proctologist, specialist in proctology.

proctoscopio *m.* proctoscope, endoscope used to examine the rectum.

procurar *v.* to procure; to try.

prodrómico-a *a.* prodromal, rel. to the initial stages of a disease.

pródromo *m.* prodrome, a premonitory symptom.

producción *f.* production, rendering.

producir *vi.* to produce.

productivo-a *a.* productive.

producto *m.* product; result or effect.

profase *f.* prophase, first stage of cell division.

profesión *f.* profession.

profesional *m., f.* professional; *a.* professional.

profiláctico-a *a.* prophylactic. 1. agent or method used to prevent infection; 2. condom.

profilaxis *f.* prophylaxis, preventive treatment.

profunda *L.* profunda, deep, esp. in reference to the location of some arteries.

profundidad *f.* depth.

profundo-a *a.* deep.

profuso-a *a.* profuse, plentiful; **-mente** *adv.* profusely.

progesterona *f.* progesterone, steroid hormone secreted by the ovaries.

prognato-a *a.* prognathous, having a pronounced jaw.

programar *v.* to schedule; to program.

progresar *v.* to advance; to improve; to thrive.

progresivo-a *a.* progressive, advancing.

progreso *m.* progress.

prohibir *v.* to forbid, to prohibit, to ban.

prolapso *m.* prolapse, the falling down or slipping of a body part from its usual position.

proliferación *f.* proliferation, multiplication, esp. of similar cells; ____ excesiva / overgrowth.

prolífico-a *a.* prolific, that multiplies readily.

prólogo *m.* preface.

prolongación *f.* prolongation, extension.

prolongar *vi.* to prolong, to delay.

promedio *m.* average.

promesa *f.* promise.

prometer *v.* to promise, to give one's word.

prominencia *f.* prominence, elevation of a part; projection.

promontorio *m.* promontory, elevation; projection.

pronar *v.* to pronate, to put the body or a body part in a prone position.

prono-a *a.* prone, lying in a face down position.

pronombre *m. gr.* pronoun.

pronosticar *vi.* to prognosticate, to predict.

pronóstico *m.* prognosis, evaluation of the probable course of an illness.

pronto *adv.* soon, fast, quickly; **por lo** ____ / for the time being.

pronunciar *v.* to pronounce, to articulate sounds.

propagación *f.* propagation, reproduction.

propagar *vi.* to propagate.

propenso-a *a.* having a disposition for; ____ a / inclined to.

propio-a *a.* proper, naturally suiting, complying with, relevant to.

propioceptivo-a *a.* proprioceptive, receiving stimulations within the tissues of the body.

propioceptor *m.* proprioceptor, sensory nerve ending that reacts to stimuli and gives information concerning movements and position of the body.

proporción *f.* proportion.

proporcionado-a *a.* proportionate.

próposito *m.* purpose; **a** ____ / on purpose, by the way.

propranolol, clorhidrato de *m.* propranolol hydrochloride, Inderal, blocking agent used in the treatment of high blood pressure and of certain arrhythmias.

proptosis *f.* proptosis, forward displacement of a part, such as the eyeball.

prosencéfalo *m.* prosencephalon, anterior portion of the primary cerebral vesicle from which the diencephalon and the telencephalon develop.

próstata *f.* prostate, male gland that surrounds the bladder and the urethra; hipertrofia de la ____ / prostatic hypertrophy, benign enlargement of the prostate.

prostatectomía *f. surg.* prostatectomy, partial or total excision of the prostate.

prostático-a *a.* prostatic, rel. to the prostate.

prostatismo *m.* prostatism, disorder resulting from obstruction of the bladder neck by an enlarged prostate.

prostatitis *f.* prostatitis, infl. of the prostate.

prostitución *f.* prostitution.

protección *f.* protection.

protector-a *a.* protective.

proteger *vi.* to protect.

proteico-a *a.* protean, that has various forms of manifestation.

proteína *f.* protein, nitrogen compound essential in the development and preservation of body tissues.

proteináceo-a *a.* proteinaceous, of the nature of or resembling protein.

proteinemia *f.* proteinemia, concentration of proteins in the blood.

proteínico-a *a.* proteinic, rel. to protein; balance ____ / protein balance.

proteinosis *f.* proteinosis, excess protein in the tissues.

proteinuria *f.* proteimuria, the presence of protein in the urine.

prótesis *f.* prosthesis, artificial replacement of a missing part of the body such as a limb.

protética *f.* prosthetics, branch of *surg.* concerned with the replacement of parts of the body.

protocolo *m.* protocol. 1. a record taken from notes; 2. a written proposal of a procedure to be performed.

protoplasma *m.* protoplasm, essential part of the cell that includes the cytoplasm and the nucleus.

prototipo *m.* prototype, role, model, example.

protozoario-a *a.* protozoan, rel. to protozoa.

protozoo *m.* protozoan, unicellular organism.

protrombina *f.* prothrombin, one of the four major plasma proteins along with albumin, globulin, and fibrinogen.

protuberancia *f.* protuberance, prominence.

provechoso-a *a.* beneficial.

proveer *vi.* to provide, to administer.

provisional *a.* provisional, temporary.

provisiones *f. pl.* provisions, supplies.

proximal *a.* proximal, closest to the point of reference.

próximo-a *a.* next to, close by.

proyección *f.* projection. 1. protuberance; 2. *psych.* a mechanism by which one's own unacceptable ideas or traits are attributed to others.

prueba *f.* test, proof, trial; indication; ___ cutánea / skin ___ ; ___ de coagulación sanguínea / blood coagulation ___ ; ___ de control sin método / random controlled trial; ___ de la tuberculina / tuberculin ___ ; ___ del esfuerzo / stress ___ ; ___ del rasguño / scratch ___ , allergy ___ ; ___ de tolerancia / tolerance ___ ; ___ eliminatoria / screening ___ ; ___-s sanguíneas cruzadas / crossmatching; ___ serológica / serology ___ ; ___ sin pronóstico o tratamiento cierto / double blind technique; ___ subsecuente, de seguimiento / follow-up ___ ; ___ visual de letras / visual test; **a** ___ **de agua** / water-fast **a** ___ **de fuego** / fireproof; **hay** ___ / there is indication.

prurito *m.* pruritus, severe itching.

pseudoaneurismo *m.* pseudoaneurysm, an aneurysm-like dilation in a vessel.

pseudociesis *f.* pseudocyesis, *V.* **pseudoembarazo.**

pseudoembarazo *m.* pseudopregnancy, false or imaginary pregnancy.

pseudoquiste *m.* pseudocyst, cyst-like formation.

psicoactivo-a *a.* psychoactive, that affects the mind.

psicoanálisis *m.* psychoanalysis, branch of psychiatry founded by Sigmund Freud that endeavors to make the patient conscious of repressed conflicts through techniques such as interpretation of dreams, and free association of ideas.

psicoanalista *m., f.* psychoanalyst, one who practices psychoanalysis.

psicobiología *f.* psychobiology, the study of the mind in relation to biological processes.

psicodélico-a *a.* psychedelic, rel. to a substance that can induce pathological states of altered perception such as hallucinations and delusions.

psicodrama *m.* psychodrama, the psychiatric method of diagnosis and therapy by which the patient acts out conflicting situations of his or her real life.

psicofisiológico-a. *a.* psychophysiologic, rel. to the mind's influence upon bodily processes, as manifested in some disorders or diseases.

psicofisiológicos, desórdenes *m. pl.* psychophysiologic disorders, disorders that result from the relation between psychological and physiological processes.

psicofarmacología *f.* psychopharmacology, the study of the effect of drugs on the mind and behavior.

psicología *f.* psychology, the study of mental processes, esp. as related to the individual's environment.

psicológico-a *a.* psychological, rel. to psychology.

psicólogo-a *m., f.* psychologist, person who practices psychology.

psicomotor-a *a.* psychomotor, rel. to motor actions that result from mental activity.

psicópata *m., f.* psychopath, person suffering from mental illness.

psicopatología *f.* psychopathology, the branch of medicine that deals with the causes and nature of mental illness.

psicosis *f.* psychosis, severe mental disorder of organic or emotional origin in which the patient loses touch with reality and suffers hallucinations and mental aberrations; ___ alcohólica / alcoholic ___ ; ___ depresiva / depressive ___ ; ___ maniacodepresiva / manic-depressive ___ ; ___ orgánica / organic ___ ; ___ por droga / drug related ___ ; ___ senil / senile ___ ; ___ situacional / situational ___ ; ___ tóxica / toxic ___ ; ___ traumática / traumatic ___ .

psicosocial *a.* psychosocial, rel. to both psychological and social factors.

psicosomático-a *a.* psychosomatic, rel. to both mind and body; síntoma ___ / ___ symptom. *V.* **psicofisiológico-a.**

psicoterapia *f.* psychotherapy, the treatment of mental or emotional disorders through psychological means, such as psychoanalysis.

psicótico-a *a.* psychotic, rel. to or suffering from psychosis.

psicotrópicas, drogas *f.* psychotropic drugs, drugs that affect mental stability.

psique *f.* psyche, conscious and unconscious mental life.

psiquiatra *m., f.* psychiatrist, specialist in psychiatry.

psiquiatría *f.* psychiatry, the study of the psyche and its disorders.

psiquiátrico-a *a.* psychiatric, rel. to psychiatry.

psíquico-a *a.* psychic, rel. to the psyche.

psoas *Gr.* psoas, one of the two muscles of the loin.

psoriasis *f.* psoriasis, chronic dermatitis manifested chiefly by red patches covered with white scales.

ptosis *Gr.* ptosis, prolapse of an organ or part, such as the upper eyelid.

púbero-a *a.* pubescent, having reached puberty.

pubertad *f.* puberty, the period of adolescence that marks the development of the secondary sexual characteristics and the beginning of reproductive capacity.

pubescencia *f.* pubescence. 1. beginning of puberty; 2. covering of soft, fine hair, lanugo.

púbico-a *a.* pubic, rel. to the pubis; pelo ___ / ___ hair.

pubis *L.* (*pl.* **pubes**) pubis, osseous structure forming the front of the pelvis.

público-a *a.* public.

pudendum *L.* (*pl.* **pudenda**) pudendum, external sexual organs, esp. the female.

pudrirse *vr.* to rot; to decay.

puente *m.* bridge, [*dental*] pilar de ___ / ___ abutment.

puerco *m.* pig, pork.

pueril *a.* puerile. 1. rel. to a child; 2. childish.

puerperal *a.* puerperal, rel. to the puerperium.

puerperio *m.* puerperium, the period of approximately six weeks following childbirth during which the organs of the mother return to normalcy.

puerta *f.* door.

pues *conj.* therefore; then; so.

puesto-a *a. pp.* of **poner,** placed, put.

pujar *v.* to bear down.

pulga *f.* flea, blood-sucking insect.

pulgada *f.* inch.

pulgar *m.* the thumb.

pulmón *m.* lung, respiratory organ situated inside the pleural cavity of the thorax, connected to the pharynx through the trachea and the larynx; cáncer del ___ / ___ cancer; colapso del ___ / collapse of the ___ .

pulmón de granjero *m.* farmer's lung, hypersensitivity of the pulmonary alveoli caused by exposure to fermented hay.

pulmón de hierro *m.* iron lung, machine used to produce artificial respiration.

pulmonar *a.* pulmonary, pulmonic, rel. to the lungs or to the pulmonary artery; absceso ___ / lung abscess; arteria ___ / ___ artery; elasticidad ___ / lung elasticity; embolismo ___ / ___ embolism; enfisema ___ / ___ emphysema; estenosis ___ / ___ stenosis; hemorragia ___ / ___ hemorrhage; insuficiencia ___ / ___ insufficiency; presión diferencial de la arteria ___ / ___ artery wedge pressure; proteinosis alveolar ___ / ___ alveolar proteinosis; válvula ___ / ___ valve; vena ___ / ___ vein; volumen ___ / lung capacity.

pulmonía *f.* pneumonia. *V.* **neumonía.**

pulpa *f.* pulp. 1. soft part on an organ; 2. chyme; 3. soft inner part of a tooth.

pulsación *f.* pulsation, throbbing, rhythmic beat such as that of the heart.

pulsátil *a.* pulsatile, having a rhythmic pulsation.

pulsímetro *m.* pulsimeter, instrument for measuring the force of the pulse.

pulso *m.* pulse, rhythmic arterial dilation gen. coinciding with the heartbeat; ___

alternante / alternating ___ ; ___ bigeminado / bigeminal ___ ; ___ de la arteria dorsal del pie / dorsalis pedis ___ ; ___ en martillo de agua / water hammer ___ ; ___ femoral / femoral ___ ; ___ filiforme / filiform ___ ; ___ irregular / irregular ___ ; ___ lleno / full ___ ; ___ periférico / peripheral ___ ; ___ radial / radial ___ ; ___ rápido / rapid ___ ; ___ regular / regular ___ ; ___ saltón / bounding ___ .

pulverizar *vi.* to pulverize, to reduce a substance to powder.

punción *f.* puncture, perforation, the act of perforating a tissue with a sharp instrument.

pungente *a.* pungent, sharp.

punta *f.* tip, point, sharp end of an instrument.

punteado *m.* stippling, the condition of being spotted such as seen in red corpuscles.

puntiagudo-a *a.* sharp, pointed.

punto *m.* 1. stitch; 2. point, a position in time and space; *v.* **estar a ___ de** / to be on the verge of; 3. spot; ___ ciego / blind ___ ; 4. *gr.* period.

puntos de presión *m. pl.* pressure points, points in an artery where the pulse can be felt or where pressure can be exerted to control bleeding.

puntual *a.* punctual, prompt, in time.

punzada *f.* twinge; sharp, sudden pain; jab.

punzante *a.* piercing, sharp.

punzar *vi.* to puncture; to tap, to perforate.

puñalada *f.* stab.

puño *m.* fist; cerrar el ___ / to make a fist.

pupila *f.* pupil, contractile opening of the iris of the eye that allows the passage of light; ___ saltona / bounding ___ ; ___ fija / fixed ___ .

pupilar *a.* pupillary, rel. to the pupil.

puré *m.* puree; ___ **de papas** / mashed potatoes.

purgante *m.* purgative, laxative, agent used to cause evacuation of the intestines; ___ de sal / saline cathartic.

purificar *vi.* to purify.

puro-a *a.* pure, uncontaminated.

purpura *L.* purpura, condition characterized by reddish or purple spots that result from escape of blood into tissues.

purulencia *f.* purulence, the condition of being purulent.

purulento-a *a.* purulent, containing pus.

pus *f.* pus, thick yellowish fluid that results from inflammation.

pústula *f.* pustule, sore, small elevation of the skin filled with pus.

putrefacción *f.* putrefaction, the condition of being putrid.

putrefacto-a, pútrido-a *a.* putrid, rotten, foul.

Q

q *abr.* **quaque (cada)** / quaque (every).

quadratus *L.* quadratus. 1. four-sided muscle; 2. four-sided figure.

quantum *L.* quantum, a unit of energy.

quaque *L.* quaque, each; every.

quebradizo-a *a.* brittle, that breaks easily.

quebradura *f.* split; break.

quebrar *vi.* to break, to crack.

quedarse *vr.* to stay, to remain in one place; ___ **atrás** / to lag behind.

queilectomía *f. surg.* cheilectomy, partial excision of the lip.

queilitis *f.* cheilitis, infl. of the lips.

queiloplastia *f. surg.* cheiloplasty, plastic surgery of the lip.

queilosis *f.* cheilosis, disorder caused by a deficiency of vitamin B_2 complex (riboflavin) and marked by fissures at the angles of the lips.

queilosquisis *f.* cheiloschisis. *V.* **labio leporino.**

queirología *f.* cheirology. 1. the study of the hand; 2. sign language.

queja *f.* complaint, grievance; ___ principal / chief ___ .

quejarse *vr.* to complain; to whine.

quejido *m.* groan, moan, whimper, whine.

quelis *m.* kelis, keloid.

queloide *m.* keloid, thick reddish scar formation following a wound or surgical incision.

quemadura *f.* burn; ___ de primer, segundo, tercer grado / first, second, third degree ___ ; ___ por frío / frostbite; ___ por radiación / radiation ___ ; ___ de sol / sunburn; ___ por viento / windburn.

quemar *v.* to burn, to scorch; **quemarse** *vr.* to burn oneself.

quemazón *m.* burning.

queratina *f.* keratin, organic insoluble protein component of nails, skin, and hair.

queratinización *f.* keratinization, process by which cells become horny due to a deposit of keratin.

queratinoso-a *a.* keratinous, rel. to or of the nature of keratin.

queratitis *f.* keratitis, infl. of the cornea; —— micótica / mycotic ——, caused by fungus; —— trófica / trophic ——, caused by the herpes virus.

queratocele *m.* keratocele, hernia of the innermost layer of the cornea.

queratoconjuntivitis *f.* keratoconjunctivitis, simultaneous infl. of the cornea and the conjunctiva.

queratoideo-a *a.* keratose, resembling the cornea.

queratólisis *f.* keratolysis. 1. exfoliation of the skin; 2. congenital anomaly that causes the skin to shed periodically; —— neonatal / —— neonatorum.

queratolítico-a *a.* keratolytic, agent that causes exfoliation of the skin.

queratomalacia *f.* keratomalacia, degeneration of the cornea due to a deficiency of vitamin A.

queratoplastia *f. surg.* keratoplasty, plastic surgery of the cornea.

queratosis *f.* keratosis, horny condition of the skin; —— actínica / actinic ——, precancerous lesion; —— blenorrágica / —— blenorrhagica, manifested by a scaly rash, esp. in the palms of the hands and the soles of the feet.

queratotomía *f. surg.* keratotomy, surgical incision of the cornea.

querer *vi.* to want, to desire; to love.

querido-a *a.* dear, beloved.

querubismo *m.* cherubism, fibro-osseous disease in children that causes an enlargement of the jaw bones.

queso *m.* cheese.

quiasma *m.* chiasm, chiasma, the crossing of two elements or structures; —— óptico / optic ——, the point at which the fibers of the optic nerve cross.

quiescente *a.* quiescent, inactive; latent.

quieto-a *a.* quiet, still; *v.* **estar** —— / to be still.

quijada *f.* jaw, osseous structure of the mouth.

quilemia *f.* chylemia, presence of chyle in the blood.

quilo *m.* chyle, milky fluid which results in the absorption and emulsification of fats in the small intestine.

quilocele *m.* chylocele, presence of chyle within the tunica vaginalis of the testis.

quilomicrón *m.* chylomicron, microscopic particle of fat found in the blood.

quilorrea *f.* chylorrhea, discharge of chyle due to a rupture of the thoracic duct.

quiloso-a *a.* chylous, rel. to or that contains chyle.

quilotórax *m.* chylothorax, accumulation of chyle in the thoracic cavity.

quiluria *f.* chyluria, passage of chyle in the urine.

quimera *f.* chimera, an organism containing cells derived from different zygotes as in the case of twins.

química *f.* chemistry, the science that studies the composition, structure, and properties of matter, and the transformations that they may undergo.

químico-a *m., f.* chemist; *a.* chemical, rel. to chemistry.

quimiocirugía *f. surg.* chemosurgery, removal of diseased tissue through the use of chemicals.

quimiocoagulación *f.* chemocoagulation, coagulation that results from the use of chemicals.

quimionucleólisis *f.* chemonucleolysis, dissolution of the nucleus pulposus of a hernia by injection of a proteolitic enzyme.

quimiorreceptor *m.* chemoreceptor, a cell or a receptor that can be excited by chemical change.

quimiotaxis *m.* chemotaxis, movement by a cell or an organism as a reaction to a chemical stimulus.

quimioterapia *f.* chemotherapy, treatment of a disease by chemical agents.

quimo *m.* chyme, semiliquid substance that results from the gastric digestion of food.

quimografía *f.* kymography, technique or method used to register involuntary movement of an organ or structure, esp. the heart and the diaphragm.

quimotripsina *f.* chymotrypsin, pancreatic enzyme.

quimotripsinógeno *m.* chymotrypsinogen, pancreatic enzyme, precursor of chymotrypsin.

Quincke, edema de *m.* Quincke's edema. *V.* **angioedema.**

quinidina *f.* quinidine, alkaloid derived from the cortex of the cinchona, used in the treatment of cardiac arrhythmia.

quinina *f.* quinine, the most important alkaloid obtained from the cortex of the cinchona, used as an antipyrectic in the treatment of malaria and typhoid fever.

quininismo *m.* quininism, cinchonism, quinine poisoning.

quintana *f.* quintan, fever occurring every fifth day.

quíntuple *m., f.* quintuplet, any of a set of five children born at one birth.

quiropráctica *f.* chiropractic, therapeutic treatment that consists of manipulation and adjustment of body structures, esp. of the spinal column in relation to the nervous system.

quirúrgico-a *a.* surgical, rel. to surgery; colgajo ___ / ___ flap; equipo ___ / ___ equipment; instrumento ___ / ___ instrument; malla ___ / ___ mesh.

quiste *m.* cyst, sac, or pouch containing a fluid or semifluid substance; ___ pilonidal / pilonidal ___, containing hair and gen. occurring in the dermis of the sacroccygeal area; ___ sebáceo / sebaceous ___, gen. localized in the scalp.

quitar *v.* to take away, to remove.

quizás *adv.* perhaps.

R

R *abr.* **radioactivo-a** / radioactive; **resistencia** / resistance; **respiración** / respiration; **respuesta, reacción** / response.

rabadilla *f.* coccyx, the extremity of the backbone.

rábano *m.* raddish.

rabdomioma *m.* rhabdomyoma, benign tumor composed of muscle-striated fiber.

rabdomiosarcoma *m.* rhabdomyosarcoma, malignant tumor of muscle-striated fibers affecting primarily the skeletal muscles.

rabdosarcoma *m.* rhabdosarcoma. *V.* **rabdomiosarcoma.**

rabia *f.* rabies. 1. *V.* **hidrofobia;** 2. rage, anger; *v.* **tener** ___ / to be enraged.

rabieta *f.* tantrum.

rabino *m.* rabbi.

rabioso-a *a.* rabid. 1. rel. to or afflicted by rabies; 2. enraged.

rabo *m.* tail.

racemoso-a, racimoso-a *a.* racemose, that resembles a cluster of grapes.

racial *a.* racial, ethnic, rel. to race; inmunidad ___ / ___ immunity, natural immunity of the members of a race; **prejuicio** ___ / ___ prejudice.

ración *f.* ration, food portion.

racional *a.* rational, reasonable, based on reason.

racionalización *f. psych.* rationalization, defense mechanism by which behavior or actions are justified by explanations that may seem reasonable but are not necessarily based on reality.

racionar *v.* to ration.

rad *L.* rad. 1. unit of absorbed radiation; 2. *abr.* radix, root.

radiación *f.* radiation. 1. emission of particles of radioactive material; 2. propagation of energy; 3. emission of rays from a common center; enfermedad por ___ / ___ sickness, radiation syndrome, illness caused by overexposure to X-rays or radioactive materials; ___ electromagnética / electromagnetic ___; ___ ionizante / ionizing ___; ___ por rayos infrarrojos / infrared ___; ___ por rayos ultravioletas / ultraviolet ___.

radiactividad, radioactividad *f.* radioactiv-*ity, property of some elements to produce radiation.

radiactivo-a *a.* radioactive, rel. to or having radioactivity.

radial *a.* radial. 1. rel. to the radius; 2. that radiates from a center in all directions.

radiante *a.* radiant, that emits rays.

radical *a.* radical. 1. aimed at eradicating the root of a disease or all the diseased tissue; 2. rel. to the root; **-mente** *adv.* radically.

radicular *a.* radicular, rel. to the root or source.

radiculectomía *f. surg.* radiculectomy, excision of the root of a nerve, esp. a spinal nerve.

radiculitis *f.* radiculitis, infl. of a nerve root.

radiculomielopatía *f.* radiculomyelopathy, a disease affecting the spinal cord and the roots of the spinal nerves.

radiculoneuritis *f.* radiculoneuritis, Guillain-Barré syndrome, infl. of the roots of a spinal nerve.

radiculoneuropatía *f.* radiculoneuropathy, disease of the nerves and nerve roots.

radiculopatía *f.* radiculopathy, disease of the roots of the spinal nerves.

radio *m.* 1. radium, metallic radioactive fluorescent element used in the treatment of malignant tumors in some of its variations;

agujas de ____ / ____ needles, needle-shaped radium containing a device used in radiotherapy; 2. radius, the outer bone of the forearm; 3. radio.

radiobiología *f.* radiobiology, the study of the effect of radiation on living tissue.

radiofármaco *m.* radiopharmaceutical, radioactive drug used for diagnosis and treatment of diseases.

radiografía *f.* radiography. *V.* **roentgenograma.**

radioisótopo *m.* radioisotope, radioactive isotope.

radiología *f.* radiology, the study of X-rays and rays emanating from radioactive substances, esp. for medical use.

radiológico-a *a.* radiologic, rel. to radiology.

radiólogo-a *m., f.* radiologist, specialist in radiology.

radiolúcido-a *a.* radiolucent, that allows the passage of most X-rays.

radionecrosis *f.* radionecrosis, disintegration of tissue by radiation.

radiopaco-a *a.* radiopaque, that does not allow the passage of X-rays or any other form of radiation; colorante ____ / ____ dye.

radiorresistente *a.* radioresistant, having the quality of being resistant to the effects of radiation.

radiosensitivo-a *a.* radiosensitive, that is affected by or responds to radiation treatment.

radioterapia *f.* radiotherapy, radiation therapy.

radón *m.* radon, colorless, gaseous radioactive element.

rafe *m.* raphe, joining line of two symmetrical halves of a structure such as the tongue.

raíz *f.* root.

rajadura *f.* crack, slit.

rama *f.* ramus, branch.

ramificación *f.* ramification, separation into branches.

ramificarse *vr., vi.* to ramify.

rancio-a *a.* rancid, stale, having an unpleasant smell, gen. due to decomposition.

ránula *f.* ranula, cystic tumor under the tongue caused by an obstruction of a gland duct.

ranura *f.* groove, slit.

rapidez *f.* speed, velocity.

rápido-a *a.* quick, fast; swift; **-mente** *adv.* quickly.

raptus *L. psych.* raptus, sudden violent attack such as of a maniacal or nervous nature.

raquídeo-a *a.* rachial, rel. to the rachis or the spine.

raquis *m.* rachis, the vertebral column, backbone.

raquítico-a *a.* rachitic. 1. rel. to rachitism; 2. stunted, feeble.

raquitis *f.* rickets. *V.* **raquitismo.**

raquitismo *m.* rachitism, rhachitis, rachitis, a deficiency disease that affects the skeletal growth in the young usu. caused by lack of calcium, phosphorus, and vitamin D; *pop.* rickets.

raro-a *a.* rare, different, unusual; **-mente** *adv.* rarely, seldom.

rascar *vi.* to scratch; **rascarse** *vr.* to scratch oneself.

rasgo *m.* trait, feature, strain; ____ adquirido / acquired ____ ; ____ heredado / inherited ____ .

rasguño, rascuño *m.* scratch.

rash, rasche *Fr.* rash, any eruption of the skin; ____ hemorrágico / hemorrhagic ____ ; ____ medicamentoso / drug ____ .

raspado *m.* curettage, scraping of the interior of a cavity; ____ uterino / D&C, dilation and curettage.

raspador *m.* scraper.

raspadura, rasponazo *f., m.* scrape.

raspante *a.* abrasive.

raspar *v.* to scrape.

rastro *m.* trace. 1. small amount of chemical element; 2. a visible mark.

rastrear *v.* scanning, tracing, and recording with a sensitive detecting device.

rastreo *m.* scan. *V.* **escán.**

rastro *m.* trace. 1. small quantity; 2. a visible sign or mark.

rasura *f.* rasura, scrapings or filings.

rata *f.* rat.

ratio *L.* ratio, quantity of a substance in relation to that of another one.

rato *m.* while, a short space of time.

Rauwolfia serpentina *f. Rauwolfia serpentina*, a plant species that is the source of reserpine, an extract used in the treatment of hypertension and some mental disorders.

raya *f.* streak.

Raynaud, enfermedad de *f.* Raynaud's disease. *V.* **acrocianosis.**

Raynaud, fenómeno de *m.* Raynaud's phenomenon, the symptoms associated with Raynaud's disease.

rayo *m.* ray.

rayos gamma *m. pl.* gamma rays, high energy rays emitted by radioactive substances.

rayos X *m. pl.* 1. X-rays, high energy electromagnetic short waves that are used to penetrate tissues and record densities on film; 2. films obtained through the use of X-rays.

raza *f.* race, a distinctive ethnic group with common inherited characteristics.

razón *f.* the faculty of reason; **a** ___ **de** / at the rate of; *v.* **tener** ___ / to be right.

razonable *a.* reasonable.

razonar *v.* to reason.

reacción *f.* reaction, response; ___ alérgica / allergic ___ ; ___ anafilática / anaphylactic ___ ; ___ de ansiedad / anxiety ___ ; ___ de conversión / conversion ___ ; ___ depresiva psicótica / psychotic depressive ___ ; ___ en cadena / chain ___ ; ___ inmune / immune ___ .

reaccionar *v.* to react, to respond to a stimulus.

reactivar *v.* to reactivate.

reactividad *f.* reactivity, manifestation of a reaction.

reactivo *m.* reagent, agent that stimulates a reaction; **-a** *a.* reactive, that has the property of reacting or causing a reaction.

reagina *f.* reagin, antibody used in the treatment of allergies that causes the production of histamine.

real *a.* real, actual; **-mente** *adv.* really.

realidad *f.* reality.

realimentación, retroalimentación *f.* feedback, regeneration of energy, action of taking the energy or the effects of the process back to its original source.

realzar *vi.* to enhance, to intensify, to increase; to highlight.

reanimar *v.* to reanimate, to bring back to life.

rebelde *a.* rebellious.

reblandecimiento *m.* ripening, softening, dilation, such as of the cervix during childbirth.

reborde *m.* ridge, elongated elevation.

rebote *m.* rebound, a return to a previous condition after the removal of a stimulus; fenómeno de ___ / ___ phenomenon, intensified onward movement of a part when the initial resistance is removed.

rebuscado-a *a.* farfetched.

recado *m.* message.

recaer *vi.* to relapse.

recaída *f.* relapse, setback, the recurrence of a disease after a period of recovery.

recalcificación *f.* recalcification, restoration of calcium compounds to tissues.

recámara *f. Mex.* bedroom.

recapacitar *v.* to reconsider.

receptáculo *m.* receptacle, vessel for liquids.

receptaculum *L.* (*pl.* **receptacula**) receptaculum, container, receptable.

receptivo-a *a.* receptive.

receptor *m.* receptor, a nerve end which receives a nervous stimulus and passes it on to other nerves; ___ auditivo / auditory ___ ; ___ de contacto / contact ___ ; ___ de estiramiento / stretch ___ ; ___ de temperatura / temperature ___ ; ___ gustativo / taste ___ ; ___ propioceptivo / proprioceptive ___ ; ___ sensorial / sensory ___ .

recesión *f.* recession, pathological withdrawal of tissue such as retraction of the gums.

recesivo-a *a.* recessive. 1. tending to withdraw; 2. in genetics, rel. to nondominant genes.

receta *f.* prescription; recipe.

recetar *v.* to medicate, to prescribe medication.

recibir *v.* to receive.

recibo *m.* receipt.

recidiva *f.* recidivation, recidivism, the recurrence of a disease or symptom.

recién *adv.* recently.

recién nacido-a *m., f.* newborn; **sala de** ___ **-s** / nursery.

reciente *a.* recent; **-mente** *adv.* recently.

recipiente *m.* 1. recipient, individual who receives blood, or an implant of tissue or organ from a donor; 2. container.

recipiente universal *m.* universal recipient, person belonging to blood group AB.

reciprocidad *f.* reciprocity.

recíproco-a *a.* reciprocal.

reclamación *f.* claim.

reclinado-a *a.* reclined, reclining, recumbent.

reclinarse *vr.* to recline, to lean back.

recluído-a *a.* confined.

recluir *vi.* to confine.

reclutamiento *m.* recruitment, gradual intensification of a reflex by an unaltered but prolonged stimulus.

recobrar *v.* to regain; ___ **el conocimiento** / ___ consciousness; to retrieve.

recoger *vi.* to gather; to pick up.

recomendable *a.* advisable.
recomendación *f.* recommendation; referral.
recomendar *vi.* to recommend, to advise.
recompresión *f.* recompression, the return to normal environmental pressure.
reconocer *vi.* 1. to examine physically; 2. to recognize; to admit; to acknowledge.
reconocimiento *m.* 1. physical examination; 2. recognition.
reconstitución *f.* reconstitution, restitution of tissue to its initial form.
reconstituir *vi.* to reconstitute; ____ la salud / to build up one's health.
reconstituyente *m.* tonic.
reconstruir *vi.* to reconstruct.
récord *m.* record, chart.
recordar *vi.* to recall; to recollect; to remind; **recordarse** *vr.* to remember.
recostado-a *a.* lying down, recumbent.
recostarse *vr., vi.* to lie down.
recreo *f.* recreation.
recrudescencia *f.* recrudescence, relapse, return of symptoms.
rectal *a.* rectal, rel. to the rectum.
rectificar *vi.* to rectify, to correct.
rectificación *f.* rectification, correction.
recto *m.* rectum, the distal portion of the long intestine that connects the sigmoid and the anus; **-a** *a.* straight.
rectocele *m.* rectocele, herniation of part of the rectum into the vagina.
rectosigmoide *a.* rectosigmoid, rel. to the sigmoid and the rectum.
rectovaginal *a.* rectovaginal, rel. to the rectum and the vagina.
rectovesical *a.* rectovesical, rel. to the rectum and the bladder.
rectus *L.* rectus. 1. straight; 2. rel. to any of a group of straight muscles such as the ones in the eye and the abdominal wall.
recuento sanguíneo completo *m.* complete blood count.
recumbente *a.* recumbent, in a lying down position.
recuperación *f.* recuperation, recovery, restoration to health.
recuperado-a *a. pp.* of **recuperar,** recovered; improved.
recuperar *v.* to recover; ____ **el conocimiento** / to regain consciousness; **recuperarse** *vr.* to get well, *pop.* to pull through, to recoup.
recurrencia *f.* recurrence. 1. the return of symptoms after a period of remission; 2. relapse; repetition.

recurrente *a.* recurrent, intermittent.
recurso *m.* recourse; resource; ____-s económicos / source of income.
rechazar *vi.* to reject, to drive back.
rechazo *m.* rejection. 1. immune reaction of incompatibility to transplanted tissue cells; ____ agudo / acute ____; ____ crónico / chronic ____; 2. denial, refusal.
rechinamiento *m.* [*los dientes*] gnashing.
rechinar *v.* [*los dientes*] to chatter; to squeak.
red *f.* web, network, netlike arrangement of nerve fibers and blood vessels; ____ de membranas arteriopulmonares / pulmonary arterial ____.
redondo-a *a.* round, circular.
reducción *f.* reduction, the act of reducing.
reducible *a.* reducible, that can be reduced.
reducido-a *a.* reduced, diminished.
reducir *vi.* to reduce, to cut down. 1. to restore to its normal position, such as a fragmented or dislocated bone; 2. to weaken the potency of a compound by adding hydrogen or suppressing oxygen; 3. to lose weight.
reductasa *f.* reductase, enzyme that acts as a catalyst in reduction.
reductor *m.* reducer, agent that causes reduction.
reeducación *f.* reeducation, training to regain motor and mental functions.
reemplazar *vi.* to replace, to substitute; to supplant.
reemplazo *m.* replacement, substitution.
reevaluación *f.* reevaluation; reassessment.
referencia *f.* reference; valores de ____ / ____ values.
referir *vi.* to refer; to direct; **referirse** *vr.* to refer to, to cite.
refinar *v.* to refine, to purify.
reflejar *v.* to reflect.
reflejo *m.* reflex, a conscious or unconscious motor response to a stimulus; acto, acción ____ / ____ action; ____ adquirido / behavior ____; arco ____ / ____ arc; ____ condicionado / conditioned ____; ____ de estiramiento / stretch ____; ____ del tendón de Aquiles / Achille's tendon ____; ____ en cadena / chain ____; ____ instintivo / instinctive ____; ____ no condicionado, natural / unconditioned ____; ____ patelar o rotuliano / patellar ____; ____ radial / radial ____; ____ rectal / rectal ____.
reflejo hepatoyugular *a.* hepatojugular reflex, ingurgitation of the jugular veins, pro-

duced by pressure over the liver in cases of right cardiac failure.

reflexión *f.* reflection. 1. the rejection of light or another form of radiant energy from a surface; 2. the turning or bending back, as of the folds of a membrane when it passes over the surface of an organ returning later to the body walls that it lines; 3. introspection.

reflexógeno-a *a.* reflexogenic, that causes a reflex action.

reflujo *m.* reflux, backflow of a fluid substance.

reforzar *vi.* to reinforce, to strengthen.

refracción *f.* refraction, the act of refracting; ___ ocular / ocular ___ .

refractar *v.* to refract. 1. to change the direction from a straight path, such as of a ray of light when it passes from one medium to another one of different density; 2. to detect abnormalities of refraction in the eyes and correct them.

refractario-a *a.* refractory. 1. resistant to treatment; 2. nonresponsive to a stimulus.

refractividad *f.* refractivity, the ability to refract.

refrescante *a.* refreshing, cooling.

refrescar *vi.* to refresh, to revive; **refrescarse** *vr.* to cool off.

refresco *m.* refreshment, soft drink.

refrigeración *f.* refrigeration, reduction of heat by external means.

refrigerante *m.* refrigerant; antipyretic.

refrigerar *v.* to refrigerate.

refringente *a.* refringent, rel. to or that causes refraction.

refugiado-a *m., f.* refugee.

refugiar *v.* to shelter; **refugiarse** *vr.* to seek refuge, to seek shelter.

refugio *m.* shelter, refuge; asylum.

regalo *m.* present, gift.

regazo *m.* lap.

regeneración *f.* regeneration, restoration, renewal; feedback.

regenerar *v.* to regenerate.

régimen *m.* regimen, structured plan, such as a regulated diet.

región *f.* region, a part of the body with more or less definite boundaries.

regional *a.* regional.

registrar *v.* to register, to record.

registro *m.* registry, record; registration.

regla *f.* 1. menstruation; 2. rule; 3. ruler, device for measuring.

reglamento *m.* set of rules, policy.

regresar *v.* to return to a place.

regresión *f.* regression. 1. return to an earlier condition; 2. abatement of the symptoms or process of a disease.

regüeldo *m.* belch.

regulación *f.* regulation.

regular *a.* regular, normal; *v.* to regulate; **-mente** *adv.* regularly.

regurgitación *f.* regurgitation. 1. the act of expelling swallowed food; 2. the backflow of blood through a defective valve of the heart; ___ aórtica / aortic ___ ; ___ mitral / mitral ___ .

regurgitante *a.* regurgitant, rel. to regurgitation.

regurgitar *v.* to regurgitate.

rehabilitación *f.* rehabilitation, the act of rehabilitating.

rehabilitado-a *a.* rehabilitated.

rehabilitar *v.* to rehabilitate, to help regain normal functions through therapy.

rehén *m., f.* hostage.

rehidratación *f.* rehydration, establishment of normal liquid balance in the body.

rehuir *vi.* to evade, to shun.

reimplantación *f.* reimplantation. 1. restoration of a tissue or part; 2. restitution of an ovum into the uterus after having been removed from the body and fertilized *in vitro*.

reinervación *f.* reinnervation, grafting of a nerve to restore the function of a muscle.

reinfección *f.* reinfection, subsequent infestation caused by the same microorganism.

reinfusión *f.* reinfusion, reinjection of blood serum or cerebrospinal fluid.

reinoculación *f.* reinoculation, subsequent inoculation with the same microorganisms.

reírse *vr., vi.* to laugh.

rejuvenecer *vi.* to rejuvenate; **rejuvenecerse** *vr.* to become rejuvenated.

rejuvenecimieno *m.* rejuvenescence.

relación *f.* relation; relationship; ___ armoniosa / rapport.

relacionado-a *a.* rel. to, related.

relacionar *v.* to relate, to establish a relationship; **relacionarse** *vr.* to become acquainted.

relajación *f.* relaxation, act of relaxing or becoming relaxed.

relajado-a *a.* relaxed.

relajante *m.* relaxant, agent that reduces tension.

relajar *v.* to relax, to reduce tension; **relajarse** *vr.* to become less tense, *pop.* to loosen up.

relativo-a *a.* relative; **-mente** *adv.* relatively.

religión *f.* religion.

religioso-a *a.* religious.

reloj *m.* watch; clock.

rellenar *v.* to refill.

relleno *m.* padding; stuffing.

remediador-a *a.* remedial, rel. to remedy.

remediar *v.* to remedy, to help, to alleviate.

remedio *m.* remedy, relief.

remineralización *f.* remineralization, replacement of lost minerals from the body.

remisión *f.* remission. 1. diminution or cessation of the symptoms of a disease; 2. period of time during which the symptoms of a disease diminish.

remitente *a.* remittent, occurring at intervals.

remojar *v.* to soak; to wet again.

remolacha *f.* beet.

remordimiento *m.* remorse.

remoto-a *a.* remote, distant.

removible *a.* removable; that can be removed surgically.

renal *a.* renal, rel. to or resembling the kidney; fallo, insuficiencia ___ / ___ failure, insufficiency; pelvis ___ / ___ pelvis; prueba de aclaramiento o depuración ___ / ___ clearance test.

rendido-a *a.* tired out, exhausted.

rendimiento *m.* output, yield; fallo en el ___ / ___ failure.

renina *f.* renin, an enzyme released by the kidney that is a factor in the regulation of blood pressure.

renograma *m.* renogram, monitoring of the rate at which the kidney eliminates from the blood a radioactive substance previously injected intravenously.

renovar *vi.* to renew, to renovate.

renuente *a.* reluctant.

reñir *vi.* to quarrel, to fight.

reparación *f.* repair, restoration.

reparar *v.* to repair, to restore.

repartir *v.* to distribute, to divide.

repasar *v.* to review, to look over.

repelente *m.* repellent.

repentino-a *a.* sudden; **-mente** *adv.* suddenly.

repetir *vi.* to repeat, to reiterate.

repercusión *f.* repercussion. 1. penetration or spreading of a swelling, tumor, or eruption; 2. ballottement.

repleto-a *a.* replete, full.

repliegue *m.* replication, reproduction, duplication.

reporte *m.* report, account.

reposar *v.* to repose, to rest.

reposo *m.* rest, respose; cura de ___ / ___ cure; **en** ___ / resting.

represión *f.* repression. 1. inhibition of an action; 2. *psych.* exclusion from consciousness of unceptable desires or impulses.

reprimir *v.* to repress, to hold back.

reproducción *f.* reproduction.

reproducir *vi.* to reproduce.

reproductivo-a *a.* reproductive, rel. to reproduction.

reprovisión *f.* feedback. 1. [información] regeneration of information; 2. *V.* **realimentación.**

repugnante *a.* repugnant, disgusting.

repulsión *f.* repulsion, the act of driving back or away; aversion.

repulsivo-a *a.* repulsive, repugnant.

reputación *f.* reputation.

requerido-a *a.* required, mandatory, necessary.

requerimiento *m.* requirement.

requerir *vi.* to require.

requisito *m.* requisite.

resbaladizo-a, resbaloso-a *a.* slippery.

resbalar *v.* to slip; to slide.

rescatar *v.* to rescue, to save.

resecar *v.* to resect. 1. to perform a resection; 2. to cut a portion of tissue or organ; 3. to dry thoroughly.

resección *f.* resection, the act of resecting; ___ en cuña / wedge ___; ___ gástrica / gastric ___; ___ transuretral / transurethral ___.

reseco-a *a.* dried up; parched.

resectoscopía *f.* resectoscopy, resection of the prostate with a resectoscope.

resectoscopio *m.* resectoscope, instrument provided with a cutting electrode used in surgery within cavities, such as the one used for the resection of the prostate through the urethra.

resentimiento *m.* resentment, rancor, hard feelings.

reserpina *f.* reserpine, derivative of *Rauwolfia serpentina* used primarily in the treatment of hypertension and emotional disorders.

reserva *f.* reserve, that which is kept in store for future use.

reservar *v.* to reserve.

resfriado *m.* a cold.

resfriarse *vr.* to catch a cold.

residencia *f.* residency, period of specialized training in a hospital following completion of medical school.

residente *m.* resident, physician completing a residency.

residir *v.* to reside, to live.

residual *a.* residual, remainder; función ___ / ___ function; orina ___ / ___ urine.

residuo *m.* residue; dieta de ___ alto / high ___ diet; dieta de bajo ___ / low ___ diet.

resiliente *a.* resilient, elastic.

resina *f.* resin, resina, organic substance of vegetable origin, insoluble in water, but readily soluble in alcohol and ether that has a variety of uses in medicine and dentistry.

res ipsa loquitor *L.* res ipsa loquitor, evident, that which speaks for itself.

resistencia *f.* resistance, endurance, capacity of an organism to resist harmful effects; ___ adquirida / acquired ___ ; ___ a un colorante / fast resistant; ___ inicial / initial ___ .

resistente *a.* resistant.

resolución *f.* resolution. 1. termination of an inflammatory process; 2. the ability to distinguish fine and subtle details as through a microscope.

resolver *vi.* to resolve. 1. to cause resolution; 2. to become separated into components.

resonancia *f.* resonance, capacity to increase the intensity of a sound; ___ normal / normal ___ ; ___ vesicular / vesicular ___ ; ___ vocal / vocal ___ .

resonante *a.* resonant, ringing, that gives out a vibrant sound on percussion.

resorcinol *m.* resorcinol, agent used in the treatment of acne and other forms of dermatosis.

resorción *f.* resorption, partial or total loss of a process, tissue, or exhudate by biochemical reactions such as lysis and absorption.

respetar *v.* to respect.

respeto *m.* respect.

respiración *f.* breathing, respiration; aguantar o sostener la ___ / to hold one's breath; ___ abdominal / abdominal ___ ; ___ acelerada / accelerated ___ ; ___ aeró-

bica / aerobic ___ ; ___ anaeróbica / anaerobic ___ ; ___ diafragmática / diaphragmatic ___ ; ___ gruesa / coarse ___ ; ___ laboriosa / labored ___ ; ___ profunda / deep ___ .

respirador *m.* respirator, breather, device used to purify the air reaching the lungs or to administer artificial respiration; ___ torácico / chest ___ .

respirar *v.* to breathe; ___ **por la boca** / ___ through the mouth; ___ **por la nariz** / ___ through the nose.

respiratorio-a *a.* respiratory, rel. to respiration; aparato ___ superior / upper ___ tract; cociente ___ / ___ quotient; ejercicios ___ -s / breathing exercises; infección del tracto ___ superior / upper ___ tract infection; infecciones y enfermedades de las vías ___ -s / ___ tract infections and diseases; insuficiencia o fallo ___ / ___ failure, insufficiency; pruebas de función ___ / ___ function tests; unidad de cuidado ___ / ___ care unit.

respiratorio, centro *m.* respiratory center, region in the medulla oblongata that regulates respiratory movements.

responsabilidad *f.* responsibility.

responsable *a.* responsible; **persona** ___ / reliable person.

respuesta *f.* response; answer. 1. reaction of an organ or tissue to a stimulus; 2. reaction of a patient to a treatment; ___ evocada / evoked ___ , sensorial test; ___ no condicionada / unconditioned ___ , nonrestricted reaction.

restablecer *vi.* to restore; **restablecerse** *vr.* to recover.

restablecido-a *a.* [*de una enfermedad*] recovered.

restablecimiento *m.* V. restauración.

restauración *f.* restoration, the act of returning to the original state.

restaurativo-a *a.* restorative, that stimulates restoration.

restitutio ad integrum *L.* restitutio ad integrum, total restitution of health.

resto *m.* rest, remainder.

restricción *f.* restraint, confinement; ___ de movimiento / limitation of motion; ___ en cama / bed confinement.

restringir *vi.* to restrict, to confine.

resucitación *f.* resuscitation. 1. return to life; 2. artificial respiration.

resucitador *m.* resuscitator, an apparatus to provide artificial respiration.

resucitar *v.* to resuscitate, to revive.

resultado *m.* result, outcome.

resumen *m.* resumé; summary.

retardo *m.* V. **retraso.**

rete *L.* (*pl.* **retia**). rete; *V.* **red.**

retención *f.* retention; enema de ____ / ____ enema; ____ urinaria / urinary ____; [dental] *m.* freno de ____ / retainer.

retener *vi.* to retain; to keep.

reticulación *f.* reticulation, reticular formation.

reticular, retiforme *a.* reticular, resembling a network.

retículo *m.* reticulum, a network, esp. of nerve fibers and blood vessels.

retículo endoplásmico *m.* endoplasmic reticulum, a network of canals in the cells in which the functions of anabolism and catabolism take place.

reticulocito *m.* reticulocyte, an immature red blood cell with a network of threads and granules that appears primarily during blood regeneration.

reticulocitopenia *f.* reticulocytopenia, an abnormal decrease in the number of reticulocytes in the blood.

reticulocitosis, reticulosis *f.* reticulocytosis, reticulosis, increase in the number of reticulocytes in the blood.

reticuloendotelial, sistema *m.* reticuloendothelial system, network of phagocytic cells (except circulating leukocytes) throughout the body, involving processes such as blood cell formation, elimination of worn out cells, and immune responses to infection.

reticuloendotelio *m.* reticuloendothelium, tissue of the reticuloendothelial system.

reticuloendotelioma *m.* reticuloendothelioma, tumor of the reticuloendothelial system.

reticulohistiocitoma *m.* reticulohistiocytoma, a large aggregate of granular and giant cells.

reticulopenia *f.* reticulopenia. V. **reticulocitopenia.**

Retin-A *f.* Retin-A, trade name for retinoic acid, esp. used in the treatment of acne.

retina *f.* retina, the innermost layer of the eyeball that receives images and transmits visual impulses to the brain; conmoción de la ____ / commotio retinae, traumatic condition of the retina that produces temporary

blindness; desprendimiento de la ____ / retinal detachment, the retina or part of it becomes separated from the choroid; deterioración de la ____ / retinal degeneration.

retiniano-a *a.* retinal, rel. to the retina; perforación ____ / ____ perforation.

retinitis *f.* retinitis, infl. of the retina.

retinoblastoma *m.* retinoblastoma, gen. inherited malignant tumor of the retina.

retinol *m.* retinol, Vitamin A_1.

retinopatía *f.* retinopathy, any abnormal condition of the retina.

retinoscopía *f.* retinoscopy, determination and evaluation of refractive errors of the eye.

retirado-a *a.* retired; isolated.

retorno *m.* return.

retortijón *m.* brief and acute intestinal cramp.

retracción *f.* retraction, the act of drawing or pulling back; ____ del coágulo / clot ____.

retractable, retráctil *a.* retractile, capable of being retracted.

retractar *v.* to retract, to draw back, to withdraw.

retractor *m.* retractor. 1. instrument for holding back the edges of a wound; 2. retractile muscle.

retraído-a *a.* withdrawn, introverted, that keeps to himself or herself.

retrasado-a, retardado-a *a.* retarded; ____ mental / mentally ____.

retraso *m.* retardation, abnormal slowness of a motor or a mental process.

retroacción *f.* retroaction, retroactive action.

retroactivo-a *a.* retroactive, that acts upon or affects a past event.

retroauricular *a.* retroauricular, rel. to or situated behind the ear or auricle.

retrocecal *a.* retrocecal, rel. to or situated behind the cecum.

retroceso *m.* retrocession, throwback.

retrofaríngeo-a *a.* retropharyngeal, rel. to or situated behind the pharynx.

retroflexión *f.* retroflexion, the flexing back of an organ.

retrógrado-a *a.* retrograde, that moves backward or returns to the past; amnesia ____ / ____ amnesia; aortografía ____ / ____ aortography; pielografía ____ / ____ pyelography.

retrogresión *f.* 1. retrogression, return to a simpler level of development; 2. *psych.*

flashback, retrospection and retroversion of past images.

retrolental *a.* retrolental, rel. to or situated behind the lens of the eye; fibroplasia ___ / ___ fibroplasia.

retroperitoneal *a.* retroperitoneal, rel. to or situated behind the peritoneum.

retroplasia *f.* *V.* **anaplasia.**

retroprovisión *f.* feedback.

retrospectivo-a *a.* retrospective; estudio ___ / ___ study.

retroversión *f.* retroversion, turning backward, such as an organ.

retrovirus *m.* retrovirus, a virus belonging to a group of RNA viruses, some of which are oncogenic.

Retzius, espacio de *m.* Retzius' space, space between the bladder and the pubic bones.

reuma *f.* rheum. 1. aqueous secretion; 2. rheumatism.

reumática, fiebre *f.* rheumatic fever, a fever that gen. follows a streptococcal infection manifested by acute generalized pain of the joints and showing cardiac arrythmia and renal disorders as residual effects.

reumático-a *a.* rheumatic, rel. to or afflicted by rheumatism.

reumátide *f.* rheumatid, any dermatosis associated with rheumatic fever.

reumatismo *m.* rheumatism, painful chronic or acute disease marked by infl. and pain in the joints.

reumatoide *a.* rheumatoid, rel. to or resembling rheumatism; artritis ___ / ___ arthritis.

reunión *f.* 1. reunion; 2. meeting of parts, such as those of a fractured bone or the edges of a wound.

revascularización *f.* revascularization. 1. restoration of blood supply to a part following a lesion or a bypass; 2. bypass.

reventar *vi.* to burst; **reventarse** *vr.* to burst open.

reversión *f.* reversal, restitution to a previously existing condition.

revestimiento *m.* covering; investment.

revisar *v.* to review; to revise.

revisión *f.* revision, review.

revista *f.* magazine.

revivir *v.* to revive, to bring back to life.

revólver *m.* revolver, handgun.

revulsión *f.* revulsion. *V.* **contrairritación.**

revulsivo-a *a.* revulsive, rel. to or causing revulsion.

Reye, síndrome de *m.* Reye's syndrome, acute disease in children and adolescents manifested by severe edema that can affect the brain and other major organs of the body such as the liver.

rezar *vi.* to pray.

riboflavina *f.* riboflavin, component of vitamin B_2 complex, essential to nutrition.

ribonucleasa *f.* ribonuclease, enzyme that catalyzes the hydrolysis of ribonucleic acid.

ribonucleoproteína *f.* ribonucleoprotein, a substance containing both protein and ribonucleic acid.

ricino *m.* castor oil plant; **aceite de** ___ / castor oil.

rickettsia *f.* Rickettsia, any of the gramnegative microorganisms of the group *Rickettsiaceae* that multiply only in host cells of fleas, lice, ticks, and mice, and are transmitted to humans by their bites.

rico-a *a.* rich; affluent; *pop.* very tasty.

riego *m.* flow; ___ sanguíneo / blood ___ .

riesgo *m.* risk; hazard; grupos de alto ___ / high ___ groups; posible ___ / potential ___ ; ___ de contaminación / ___ of contamination; -s / ___ factors.

riesgoso-a *a.* risky.

rifampicina *f.* rifampicin, a semisynthetic antibacterial substance used primarily in the treatment of pulmonary tuberculosis.

rigidez *f.* rigidity, stiffness, inflexibility; ___ cadavérica / cadaveric ___ , rigor mortis.

rígido-a *a.* rigid, stiff.

rigor *m.* rigor. 1. inflexibility of a muscle; 2. chill with high temperature; ___ mortis / ___ mortis.

rinal *a.* rhinal, rel. to the nose.

rinitis *f.* rhinitis, infl. of the nasal mucosa.

rinofaringits *f.* rhinopharyngitis, infl. of the nasopharynx.

rinofima *f.* rhinophyma, severe form of acne rosacea in the area of the nose.

rinolaringitis *f.* rhinolaryngitis, simultaneous infl. of the mucous membrane of the nose and the larynx.

rinoplastia *f.* rhinoplasty, plastic surgery of the nose.

rinorrea *f.* rhinorrhea, liquid mucous discharge from the nose.

rinoscopia *f.* rhinoscopy, examination of the nasal cavities.

riñón *m.* kidney, organ situated in the back of each side of the abdominal cavity; ___

artificial / hemodyalizer; fallo del ___ / ___ failure; necrosis papilar del ___ / renal papillary necrosis; piedras en el ___ / ___ stones; ___ poliquístico /polycystic ___ ; trasplante del ___ / renal transplant.

risa *f.* laugh, laughter; ___ histérica / hysteric ___ ; sardónica / sardonic ___ , contraction of facial muscles that gives the appearance of a smile.

risorio *m.* risorius, muscle inserted at the corners of the mouth.

ristocetina *f.* ristocetin, antibiotic substance used in the treatment of infections by grampositive cocci.

risueño-a *a.* smiling, affable.

Ritalin, clorhidrato de *m.* Ritalin hydrochloride, stimulant and antidepressant.

ritidectomia *f. surg.* rhytidectomy, face lift, removal of wrinkles through plastic surgery.

rítmico-a *a.* rhythmical.

ritmo *m.* rhythm, regularity in the action or function of an organ of the body such as the heart; ___ acoplado / coupled ___ ; ___ atrioventricular / atrioventricular ___ ; ___ de galope / gallop ___ ; ___ ectópico / ectopic ___ ; ___ idioventricular / idioventricular ___ ; ___ nodal / nodal ___ ; ___ sinusal / sinus ___ .

ritual *m.* ritual.

rizotomía *f. surg.* rhizotomy, transection of the root of a nerve.

Robitussin *m.* Robitussin, expectorant.

robustecer *vi.* to strengthen.

robusto-a *a.* robust, stout.

rociar *v.* to spray.

rodar *vi.* to roll; to wheel.

rodeado-a *a.* surrounded.

rodenticida *m.* rodenticide, agent that destroys rodents.

rodilla *f.* knee; dislocación de la ___ / ___ dislocation.

rodillera *f.* knee protector.

rodopsina *f.* rhodopsin, purple-red pigment found in the retinal rods that enhances vision in dim light.

roedor *m.* rodent.

roentgen *m.* roentgen, the international unit of X or gamma radiation; rayos de ___ / ___ rays, X-rays.

roentgenograma *m.* roentgenogram, radiograph, photograph made with X-rays on a fluorescent surface.

rojizo-a *a.* reddish.

rojo-a *a.* red; ___ Congo / Congo ___ ; ___ escarlata / scarlet ___ .

Romberg, signo de *m.* Romberg's sign, swaying of the body when in an erect position with eyes closed and feet close together as a sign of an inability to maintain balance.

romero *m.* rosemary.

romper *v.* to break; **romperse** *vr.* to break into pieces.

roncar *vi.* to snore.

ronco-a *a.* hoarse, with a husky voice.

roncha *f.* blotch; wheal; **-s** hives.

rongeur *Fr.* rongeur, forceps to remove minute bone chips.

ronquera *f.* hoarseness.

ronquido *m.* snore.

ropa *f.* clothing; ___ **de cama** / bed clothes, bed linens; ___ **interior** / underclothing.

Rorschach, prueba de *f.* Rorschach test, psychological test by which personality traits are revealed through the subject's interpretation of a series of ink blots.

rosáceo-a *a.* pinkish, rosy.

rosado-a *a.* pink.

rosario *m.* rosary, structure that resembles a string of beads.

rosbif *m.* roast beef.

roséola *f.* roseola, rose colored skin eruption.

rosette *Fr.* rosette, a rose-shaped cluster of cells.

rostral *a.* rostral, rel. to or resembling a rostrum.

rostro *m.* rostrum. 1. human face; 2. beak or projection.

rotación *f.* rotation.

rotar *v.* to rotate, to turn around.

rotatorio-a *a.* rotatory, that rotates.

roto-a *a. pp.* of **romper,** broken.

rótula *f.* patella, kneecap; ball-and-socket joint.

rotura *f.* breakage; fracture.

rubefaciente *a.* rubefacient, that causes redness of the skin.

rubeola *f.* rubella, German measles, highly contagious benign viral infection manifested by fever, rose-colored eruption, and sore throat. It can have serious effects on the development of the fetus if acquired by the mother during early pregnancy.

rubio-a *a.* fair, blond, of light coloring.

rubor *m.* rubor, redness of the skin; blush.

ruborizado-a *a.* rubescent, that blushes.

ruborizarse *vr., vi.* to blush.

rudimento *m.* rudiment. 1. a partially developed organ; 2. an organ or part with a partial or total loss of function.

ruga *L.* (*pl.* **rugae**) ruga, wrinkle or fold.

ruido *m.* noise; bruit, murmur; ___ sordo / rumble.

ruptura *f.* rupture.

ruta *f.* route, direction.

rutina *f.* routine.

rutinario-a *a.* routine, that is done habitually.

S

S *abr.* **sulfuro** / sulfur.

s *abr.* **sacral** / sacral; **sección** / section; **segundo** / second.

sábana *f.* sheet.

sabañón *m.* chilblain, a hand or foot sore produced by cold.

saber *vi.* to know; **hacer** ___ / to make known; ___ **cómo** / ___ how; ___ **de** / ___ of, about.

Sabin, vacuna de *f.* Sabin vaccine, oral poliomyelitis vaccine.

sabor *m.* taste; flavor, after taste; *v.* **tener** ___ **a, de** / to taste like.

sabroso-a *a.* tasteful, pleasurable to the taste.

sacabocados *m.* punch, surgical instrument used to perforate or cut a resistant tissue.

sacar *vi.* to take out; to draw out.

sacárido *m.* saccharide, chemical compound, one of a series of carbohydrates that includes sugars.

sacarina *f.* saccharin, crystalline substance used as an artificial sweetener; **-o** *a.* saccharine, overly sweet.

sacerdote *m.* priest, clergyman.

saciado-a *a.* satiated.

saciar *v.* to quench; to satiate; ___ **la sed** / ___ the thirst.

saciedad *f.* satiety, the state of being fully satisfied.

saco *m.* sac, pocket, pouchlike structure; jacket.

sacral *a.* sacral, rel. to or near the sacrum; **nervios** ___**-es** / ___ nerves; **plexo** ___ / ___ plexus.

sacralización *f.* sacralization, fusion of the fifth lumbar vertebra and the sacrum.

sacrificar *vi.* to sacrifice.

sacroilitis *f.* sacroilitis, infl. of the sacroiliac joint.

sacro *m.* sacrum, the large triangular bone formed by five fused vertebrae that lies at the base of the spine between the two hip bones.

sacrolumbar *a.* sacrolumbar, rel. to the sacral and the lumbar regions.

sacudida *f.* jerk, jolt.

sacudir *v.* to shake; to jerk.

sáculo *m.* saccule, small sac.

sádico-a *a.* sadistic, rel. to sadism.

sadismo *m.* sadism, perverted sexual pleasure derived from inflicting physical or psychological pain on others.

sadista *m., f.* sadist, person who practices sadism.

sadomasoquismo *m.* sadomasochism, perverted sexual pleasure derived from inflicting pain on oneself or on others.

sadomasoquista *m., f.* person who practices sadomasochism; *a.* sadomasochistic, rel. to the practice of sadomasochism.

safeno-a *a.* saphenous, rel. to or associated with the saphenous veins; **venas** ___**-s** / ___ veins, the veins of the leg.

safismo *m.* sapphism, lesbianism.

sagital *a.* sagittal, resembling an arrow; **plano** ___ / ___ plane, parallel to the long axis of the body.

sal *f.* salt, sodium chloride; ___ **-es aromáticas** / smelling ___**-s**; ___ **corriente** / non-iodized ___; ___ **yodada** / ionized ___; *v.* **echar o poner** ___ / to salt or add salt; **sin** ___ / unsalted.

sala *f.* room; living room; [hospital] ward; ___ **de aislamiento** / isolation ward; ___ **de cuidado cardíaco** / cardiac care unit; ___ **de cuidados intensivos** / intensive care unit; ___ **de emergencia** / emergency ___; ___ **de espera** / waiting ___; ___ **de operaciones** / operating ___; ___ **de parto** / delivery ___; ___ **de recuperación** / recovery ___.

salado-a *a.* salty.

salario *m.* salary, wages.

salcochar, sancochar *v.* to parboil.

salchicha *f.* sausage.

salicilato *m.* salicylate, any salt of salicylic acid.

salicilismo *m.* salicylism, toxic condition produced by excess intake of salicylic acid.

salida *f.* outlet; exit, way out.

saliente *m.* protrusion; *a.* salient, projecting, protruding.

salino-a *a.* saline; solución ____ / ____ solution, distilled water and salt.

salir *vi.* to go out; to leave; to come out.

saliva *f.* saliva, spit, secretion of the salivary glands that moistens and softens foods in the mouth.

salivación *f.* salivation, excessive discharge of saliva.

salival *a.* salivary, rel. to saliva.

Salk, vacuna de *f.* Salk vaccine, poliomyelitis vaccine.

salmón *m.* salmon.

Salmonela *f.* Salmonella, a genus of gramnegative bacteria of the *Enterobacteriaceae* family that causes enteric fever, gastrointestinal disorders, and septicemia.

salmonelosis *f.* salmonellosis, infectious condition caused by ingestion of food contaminated by bacteria of the genus *Salmonella*.

salón *m.* large hall or room.

salpingectomía *f. surg.* salpingectomy, removal of one or both fallopian tubes.

salpingitis *f.* salpingitis, infl. of a fallopian tube.

salpingooforectomía *f. surg.* salpingo-oophorectomy, removal of a fallopian tube and an ovary.

salpingoplastia *f. surg.* salpingoplasty, plastic surgery of the fallopian tubes.

salpinx *Gr.* (*pl.* **salpinges**) salpinx, a tube, such as the fallopian tube.

salpullido, sarpullido *m.* heat rash.

salsa *f.* sauce; gravy.

saltar *v.* to jump; to skip; ____ **un turno** / to skip an appointment or turn.

saltear *v.* to stagger; to alternate.

salto *m.* jump; skip; omission, [*del corazón*] palpitation.

saltón, saltona *a.* jumpy.

salubre *a.* salubrious, healthy.

salubridad *f.* the state of public health.

salud *f.* health; atención a la ____ / ____ care; certificado de ____ / ____ certificate; cuidado de la ____ / ____ care; estado de ____ / ____ status; instituciones de ____ pública / public ____ facilities; servicios de ____ / ____ services; servicios de ____ para los ancianos / ____ services for the aged; ____ pública / public ____ .

saludar *v.* to greet.

saludo *m.* greeting.

salvado *m.* bran, a by-product of the milling of grain.

salvar *v.* to save.

sanar *v.* to cure, to heal.

sanatorio *m.* sanatorium, sanitarium, health establishment for physical and mental rehabilitation.

saneamiento *m.* sanitation.

sangramiento *m.* bleeding; ____ por la nariz / nosebleed.

sangrar *v.* to bleed.

sangre *f.* blood; ____ autóloga / autologous ____ ; coágulo de ____ / ____ clot; conteo de ____ / ____ count; donante de ____ / ____ donor; prueba selecta de ____ / ____ screening; transfusión de ____ / ____ transfusion; ____ vital / lifeblood; **a** ____ **fría** / in cold ____ ; **banco de** ____ / ____ bank.

sangre oculta *f.* occult blood, blood that is present in such a minute amount that it cannot be seen with the naked eye.

sangría *f.* bloodletting.

sangriento-a *a.* bloody.

sanguíneo-a *a.* 1. sanguineous, rel. to blood or that contains it; derivados ____ -s, hemoderivados / blood derivatives; determinación de grupos ____ -s / blood grouping; gases ____ -s / blood gases; plasma ____ / blood plasma; producto ____ / blood product; proteína ____ / blood protein; sustitutos ____ -s / blood substitutes; tipo ____ / blood group; tiempo de coagulación ____ / blood coagulation time; 2. sanguine, of a cheerful nature.

sanguinolento-a *a.* sanguinolent, containing blood; esputo ____ / blood sputum.

sanitario-a *m., f.* sanitarian, person trained in matters of sanitation and public health; *a.* sanitary, hygienic; toalla, servilleta ____ / ____ napkin.

sano-a *a.* healthy; sound; wholesome.

saprófito *m.* saprophyte, vegetable organism that lives on decaying or dead organic matter.

sarampión *m.* measles, highly contagious disease esp. in school age children, caused by the rubeola virus; suero de globulina preventivo al ____ / ____ immune serum globuline administered within five days after exposure to the disease.

sarcoidosis *f.* sarcoidosis. *V.* **Schaumann, enfermedad de.**

sarcoma *m.* sarcoma, malignant neoplasm of the connective tissue.

sardina *f.* sardine.

sarna *f.* scabies, mange, parasitic cutaneous infection that produces itching.

satélite *m.* satellite, a small structure accompanying a larger one.

satisfacer *vi.* to satisfy.

satisfecho-a *a. pp.* of **satisfacer**, satisfied.

saturación *f.* saturation.

saturado-a *a.* saturated, unable to absorb or receive any given substance beyond a given limit; no ____ / unsaturated.

saturar *v.* to saturate.

savia *f.* sap, natural juice.

saya *f.* skirt.

sazonado-a *a.* seasoned.

sazonar *v.* to season.

Schaumann, enfermedad de *f.* Schaumann's disease, chronic disease of unknown cause manifested by the presence of small tubercles, esp. in the lymph nodes, lungs, bones, and skin.

Schilling, prueba de *f.* Schilling test, use of radioactive Vitamin B_{12} for the purpose of diagnosing primary pernicious anemia.

sebáceo-a *a.* sebaceous, rel. to or containing sebum; glándulas ____-s / ____ glands, glands of the skin; quiste ____ / ____ cyst.

sebo *m.* sebum, fatty thick substance secreted by the sebaceous glands.

secar *vi.* to dry; **secarse** *vr.* to dry out.

sección *f.* section, portion, part; ____ media / midsection.

seccionar *v.* to section; to cut.

seco-a *a.* dry.

secreción *f.* secretion. 1. the production of a given substance as a result of glandular activity; 2. substance produced by secretion.

secretagogo *m.* secretagogue, secretogogue, agent that stimulates glandular secretion.

secretar *v.* to secrete.

secretario-a *m., f.* secretary.

secretorio-a *a.* secretory, that has the property of secreting.

secuela *f.* sequela, after effects, condition following or resulting from a disease or treatment.

secuencia *f.* sequence, succession, order.

secuestración *f.* sequestration. 1. the act of isolating; 2. the formation of sequestrum.

secuestrar *v.* to sequester, to isolate.

secuestro *m.* sequestrum, fragment of dead bone that has become separated from adjoining bone.

secundario-a *a.* secondary.

secundinas *f. pl.* afterbirth, placenta and membranes expelled at the time of delivery.

sed *f.* thirst; *v.* **tener** ____ / to be thirsty.

seda *f.* silk.

sedación *f.* sedation, the act and effect of inducing calm through medication.

sedante, sedativo *m.* sedative, agent with a quieting and tranquilizing effect.

sedentario-a *a.* sedentary. 1. having little or no physical activity; 2. rel. to a sitting position.

sediento-a *a.* thirsty.

sedimentación *f.* sedimentation, the process of depositing sediment; índice de ____ / ____ rate.

sedimento *m.* sediment, matter that settles at the bottom of a solution.

segmentación *f.* segmentation, the act of dividing into parts.

segmento *m.* segment, section or part.

seguido-a *a.* continuous, unbroken; following.

seguimiento *m.* follow-up.

seguir *vi.* to follow; to continue.

según *prep.* according to; in accordance with.

segundo *m.* second of time; **-a** *a.* second.

seguridad *f.* safety, security; assurance; **medidas de** ____ / ____ measures.

seguro *m.* insurance; ____ **de vida** / life ____ ; ____ **médico** / health ____ ; ____ **social** / social security; **-a** *a.* safe; certain; **-mente** *adv.* surely.

selección *f.* selection, choice; sampling.

selenio *m.* selenium, a nonmetallic chemical element resembling sulfur, used in electronic devices.

sellar *v.* to seal, to close tightly.

semana *f.* week; **la** ____ **pasada** / last ____ ; **la** ____ **próxima, la** ____ **que viene** / next ____ .

semanal *a.* weekly; **-mente** *adv.* weekly.

semántica *f.* semantics, the study of the meaning of words.

semblante *m.* appearance of the face.

semejante *a.* resembling, similar.

semejar *v.* to resemble.

semen *m.* semen, sperm, thick whitish secretion of the male reproductive organs.

semicoma *m.* semicoma, slight comatose state.

semilla *f.* seed; pit.

seminal *a.* seminal, rel. to or consisting of seed.

seminífero-a *a.* seminiferous, that produces or bears seeds or semen; conductos ___ -s / ___ tubules.

semiótica *f.* semiotics, the branch of medicine concerned with signs and symptoms of diseases.

semiótico-a *a.* semiotic, rel. to the signs and symptoms of a disease.

sencillo-a *a.* simple, plain.

senescencia *f.* senescence, the process of becoming old.

senil *a.* senile, rel. to old age esp. as it affects mental and physical functions.

senilidad *f.* senility, the state of being senile.

seno *m.* breast, bust, bosom; autoexamen de los ___ -s / ___ self-examination.

senos paranasales *m. pl.* paranasal sinuses, any of the air cavities in the adjacent bones of the nasal cavity.

sensación *f.* sensation, feeling, perception through the senses.

sensato-a *a.* sensible, reasonable.

sensibilidad *f.* sensitivity, the condition of being sensitive to touch or palpitation; tenderness; entrenamiento de la ___ / ___ training; ___ profunda / deep ___.

sensibilización *f.* sensitization, the act of making sensible.

sensibilizar *vi.* to sensitize, to make sensitive.

sensible *a.* sensitive, sensible.

sensitivo-a *a.* 1. sensorial, that is perceived through the senses; 2. tender, sensitive to touch or palpation.

sensitivomotor *a.* sensorimotor, rel. to sensory and motor activities of the body.

sensorial, sensorio-a *a.* sensory, rel. to sensation or to the senses; afasia ___ / ___ aphasia; nervio ___ / ___ nerve; privación ___ / ___ deprivation; umbral ___ / ___ threshold.

sensual *a.* sensual, sensuous; carnal.

sentado-a *a.* in a sitting down position.

sentarse *vr., vi.* to sit down.

sentido *m.* sense, a perception or impression received through the senses; ___ de la vista / ___ of sight; ___ del oído / ___ of hearing; ___ del olfato / ___ of smell; ___ del sabor / ___ of taste; ___ del tacto / ___ of touch; ___ **común** / common ___; ___ **del humor** / ___ of humor.

sentimiento *m.* feeling; sentiment.

sentir *vi.* to feel, to perceive through the senses; **sentirse** *vr.* [*estado corporal*] to feel, general state of the body or mind; ___ **bien** / to ___ good; ___ **mal** / to ___ sick.

señal *f.* sign, indication.

señalado-a *a.* conspicuous, pronounced.

señalar *v.* to point out, to indicate; to mark.

señor *m.* mister; *abr.* Mr.

señora *f.* married woman; *abr.* Mrs.

señorita *f.* miss, young lady; *abr.* Miss.

separación *f.* separation; in obstetrics, disengagement.

separado-a *a.* separate; **-mente** *adv.* separately.

separar *v.* to separate, to sever.

sepsis *L.* sepsis, toxic condition caused by bacterial contamination.

septal *a.* septal, rel. to a septum.

septicemia *f.* septicemia, blood poisoning, invasion of the blood by virulent microorganisms.

séptico-a *a.* septic, rel. to sepsis; choque ___ / ___ shock.

septum *L.* (*pl.* **septa**) septum, partition between two cavities.

sequedad *f.* dryness.

sequía *f.* drought.

ser *vi.* to be.

sereno-a *a.* serene, calm; *pop.* cool.

serie *f.* series, a group of specimens or types arranged in sequence; en ___ / serial.

serio-a *a.* serious; [*caso médico*] complicated; en ___ / seriously; **-mente** *adv.* seriously.

seroconversión *f.* seroconversion, development of antibodies as a response to an infection or to the administration of a vaccine.

serología *f.* serology, the science that studies sera.

serológico-a *a.* serologic, serological, rel. to serum.

seroma *m.* seroma, accumulation of blood serum that produces a tumorlike swelling, gen. subcutaneous.

seronegativo-a *a.* seronegative, that presents a negative reaction in serological tests.

seropositivo-a *a.* seropositive, that presents a positive reaction in serological tests.

serosa *f.* serosa, serous membrane.

serosanguíneo-a *a.* serosanguineous, of the nature of serum and blood.

seroso-a *a.* serous. 1. of the nature of serum; 2. producing or containing serum.

serotipo *m.* serotype, type of microorganism determined by the class and combination of antigens present in the cell; determinación del ___ / serotyping.

serpiente *f.* snake, serpent; ___ **de cascabel** / rattlesnake; **mordida de** ___ / ___ bite; ___ **venenosa** / poisonous ___.

serpiginoso-a *a.* serpiginous, that crawls from one place to another.

servible *a.* usable.

servicio *m.* service; ___-s de cuidado exterior / extended care facility; ___-s de emergencia / emergency ___; ___-s de salud preventiva / preventive health ___.

servilleta *f.* napkin.

servir *vi.* to serve; to be of help or service.

sesamoideo-a *a.* sesamoid, rel. to or resembling a small mass in a joint or cartilage.

sésil *a.* sessile, attached by a broad base with no peduncle.

sesión *f.* session.

seso *m.* brain.

severo-a *a.* severe.

sexo *m.* sex; relacionado con el ___ / ___ -linked, transmitted by genes located in the sex chromosome.

sexual *a.* sexual, rel. to sex; características ___-es / ___ characteristics; conducta ___ / ___ behavior; desarrollo ___ / ___ development; educación ___ / ___ education; madurez ___ / ___ maturity; relaciones ___-es / ___ intercourse; trastorno ___ / ___ disorder; vida ___ / ___ life; **-mente** *adv.* sexually; enfermedad ___ transmitida / ___ transmitted disease.

sexualidad *f.* sexuality, collective characteristics of each sex.

shigelosis *f.* shigellosis, bacillary dysentery.

shock *m.* shock, abnormal state generated by insufficient blood circulation that can cause disorders such as low blood pressure, rapid pulse, pallor, abnormally low body temperature, and general weakness; ___ anafiláctico / anaphylactic ___; ___ endotóxico / endotoxic ___; ___ insulínico / insulin ___; ___ séptico / septic ___.

si *conj.* if, in case.

sí *adv.* yes; **diga** ___ **o no, di** ___ **o no** / say ___ or no.

sialadenitis *f.* sialadenitis, sialoadenitis, infl. of a salivary gland.

sialogogo *m.* sialogogue, agent that stimulates secretion of saliva.

sialograma *m.* sialogram, X-ray of the salivary tract.

SIDA *abr.* AIDS, acquired immunodeficiency syndrome, characterized by immunodeficiency, infections (such as pneumonia, tuberculosis, and chronic diarrhea), and tumors esp. lymphoma and Kaposi's sarcoma.

siempre *adv.* always; **para** ___ / forever.

sien *f.* temple, the flattened lateral region on either side of the head.

siesta *f.* nap; break of activities at midday.

sietemesino-a *a.* born after seven months of gestation.

sífilis *f.* syphilis, contagious venereal disease usu. transmitted by direct contact and manifested by structural and cutaneous lesions; ___ terciaria / tertiary ___, the third and most advanced stage of syphilis.

sifilítico-a *m., f.* syphylitic, person infected with syphilis; *a.* rel. to or caused by syphilis.

sifilología *f.* syphilology, branch of medicine that studies the diagnosis and treatment of syphilis.

sifón *m.* syphon.

sigmoide, sigmoideo-a *a.* sigmoid. 1. shaped like the letter *s;* 2. rel. to the sigmoid colon.

sigmoidoscopía *f.* sigmoidoscopy, examination of the sigmoid flexure with a sigmoidoscope.

sigmoidoscopio *m.* sigmoidoscope, long hollow tubular instrument used for the examination of the sigmoid flexure.

significado *m.* meaning, significance.

significar *vi.* to signify, to mean.

significativo-a *a.* significant; meaningful, important.

signo *m.* sign; mark, objective manifestation of a disease; ___-s vitales / vital ___-s.

siguiente *a.* following, next.

sílaba *f. gr.* syllable.

silbar *v.* to whistle.

silbido *m.* whistle.

silencio *m.* silence.

silencioso-a *a.* silent.

silicio *m.* silicon, nonmetallic element found in the soil.

silicón *m.* silicone, organic silicon compound used in lubricants, synthetics and also in plastic surgery and prostheses.

silicosis *f.* silicosis, dust inhalation.

Silvio, acueducto de *m.* aqueduct of Sylvius, narrow channel connecting the third and fourth ventricles of the brain.

silla *f.* chair; ___ **de ruedas** / wheel chair.

silla turca *f.* sella turcica, depression on the superior surface of the sphenoid bone that contains the hypophysis.

sillón *m.* armchair; *Cuba* rocking chair.

simbiosis *f.* symbiosis, close association of two dissimilar organisms.

simbiótico-a *a.* symbiotic, rel. to symbiosis.

simbolismo *m.* symbolism. 1. *psych.* mental abnormality by which the patient conceives occurrences as symbols of his or her own thoughts; 2. in psychoanalysis, symbolic representation of repressed thoughts and emotions.

símbolo *m.* symbol.

simetría *f.* symmetry, perfect correspondence of parts situated on opposite sides of an axis or plane of a body.

simétrico-a *a.* symmetrical.

similar *a.* similar.

simpatectomía *f. surg.* sympathectomy, interruption of the sympathetic nerve pathways.

simpatía *f.* sympathy, relationship, affinity. 1. affinity between mind and body by which one is affected by the other; 2. relationship between two organs by which an anomaly in one affects the other.

simpático-a *a.* sympathetic, rel. to the sympathetic nervous system.

simpatolítico-a *a.* sympatholytic, that offers resistance to the activity produced by the stimulation of the sympathetic nervous system.

simpatomimético-a *a.* sympathomimetic, having the capacity to cause physiological changes similar to those produced by the action of the sympathetic nervous system.

simple *a.* simple; **-mente** *adv.* merely.

simplificar *vi.* to simplify.

simulación *f.* simulation, imitation; feigning an illness or symptom.

simulador-a *m., f.* malingerer, person who deliberately feigns or exaggerates the symptoms of an illness.

sin *prep.* without; ___ **embargo** / nevertheless.

sinapsis *f.* 1. synapse, the point of contact between two neurons, where the impulse traveling through the first neuron originates an impulse in the second one; 2. synapsis, the pairing of homologous chromosomes at the start of meiosis.

sináptico-a *a.* synaptic, rel. to synapse or synapsis.

sinartrosis *f.* synarthrosis, an immovable joint in which the bony elements are fused.

sincitial *a.* syncytial, rel. to or constituting syncytium.

sincitio *m.* syncytium, mass of protoplasm resulting from cell fusion.

sincondrosis *f.* synchondrosis, an immovable joint in which the surfaces are joined by cartilaginous tissue.

sincopal *a.* syncopal, rel. to a syncope.

síncope *m.* syncope, temporary loss of consciousness due to inadequate supply of blood to the brain.

sincrónico-a *a.* synchronous, occurring at the same time.

sindactilia *f.* syndactylism, syndactyly, congenital anomaly consisting in the fusion of two or more fingers or toes.

síndrome *m.* syndrome, the totality of the symptoms and signs of a disease; ___ adiposo / adipose ___; ___ de choque tóxico / toxic shock ___, blood poisoning due to *Staphylococci;* ___ de dificultad respiratoria / respiratory distress ___; ___ de escaldadura / scalded skin ___, burns in the epidermis that gen. do not harm the underlying dermis; ___ de malabsorción / malabsorption ___, gastrointestinal disorder caused by poor absorption of food; ___ de muerte infantil súbita / sudden infant death ___; ___ de niños maltratados / battered children ___; ___ de privación / withdrawal ___, resulting from discontinued use of alcohol or a drug; ___ de transfusión múltiple / transfusion ___, multiple; ___ de vaciamiento gástrico rápido / dumping ___, rapid dumping of the stomach contents into the small intestine; ___ del lóbulo medio del pulmón / middle lobe ___ of the lung; ___ del secuestro subclavicular / subclavian steal ___; ___ nefrótico / nephrotic ___, excessive loss of protein; ___ suprarrenogenital / adrenogenital ___.

síndrome de inmuno-deficiencia adquirida *m.* acquired immunodeficiency syndrome. *V.* **SIDA.**

sinequia *f.* synechia, union or abnormal adherence of tissue or organs, esp. in reference to the iris, the lens, and the cornea.

sinérgico-a *a.* synergistic, synergic, the capacity to act together.

sinergismo *m.* synergism, correlated or harmonious action between two or more structures or drugs.

sínfisis *f.* symphysis, a joint in which adjacent bony surfaces are united by a fibrocartilage.

singular *m. gr.* singular, only one; *a.* singular, not common, unique.

singulto *m.* singultus, hiccup, hiccough.

sinoauricular o sinusal, nódulo *m.* sinoauricular, sinoatrial node located at the meeting point of the vena cava and the right cardiac atrium, point of origin of the impulses that stimulate the heartbeat.

sinograma *m.* sinogram, X-ray of a sinus by means of a contrasting dye.

sinovia *f.* synovia, synovial fluid, transparent and viscid liquid secreted by synovial membranes that lubricates joints and connective tissue.

sinovial *a.* synovial, rel. to or that produces synovia; bursa, saco ____ / ____ bursa; membrana ____ / ____ membrane; quiste ____ / ____ cyst.

sinovitis *f.* synovitis, an infl. of the synovial membrane; ____ purulenta / purulent ____ ; ____ seca / dry ____ ; ____ serosa / serous ____ .

síntesis *f.* synthesis, the composition of a whole by a union of the parts.

sintético-a *a.* synthetic, rel. to or produced by synthesis.

sintetizar *vi.* to synthesize, to produce synthesis.

síntoma *m.* symptom, any manifestation of a disease as perceived by the patient; ____ constitucional / constitutional ____ ; ____ demorado / delayed ____ ; ____ de supresión / withdrawal ____ ; ____ objetivo / objective ____ ; ____ patognomónico / pathognomonic ____ ; ____ presente / presenting ____ ; ____ prodrómico / prodromal ____ ; ____ -s premonitorios / warning ____ -s.

sintomático-a *a.* symptomatic; **-mente** *adv.* symptomatically.

sintomatología *f.* symptomatology, symptoms pertaining to a given condition or case.

sintónico-a *m., f.* syntonic, a type of personality that responds and adjusts normally to his or her environment.

sinuoso-a *a.* sinuous, winding, wavy.

sinus *L.* sinus, cavity or hollow passage.

sinusitis *f.* sinusitis, infl. of a sinus, esp. a paranasal sinus.

sinusoide *m.* sinusoid, a minute passage that carries blood to the tissues of an organ, such as the liver; *a.* resembling a sinus.

siringobulbia *f.* syringobulbia, the presence of abnormal cavities in the medulla oblongata.

siringocele *m.* syringocele. 1. the central canal of the spinal cord; 2. a meningomyelocele containing a cavity in the ectopic spinal cord.

siringomielia *f.* syringomyelia, chronic progressive disease of the spinal cord manifested by formation of liquid filled cavities, gen. in the cervical region and sometimes extending into the medulla oblongata.

sirope *m.* syrup, concentrated solution of sugar.

sistema *m.* system, a group of correlated parts or organs constituting a whole that performs one or more vital functions; ____ cardiovascular / cardiovascular ____ ; ____ digestivo / digestive ____ ; ____ endocrino / endocrine ____ ; ____ genitourinario / genitourinary ____ ; ____ de inmunidad / immune ____ ; hematopoyético / hematopoietic ____ ; ____ linfático / lymphatic ____ ; ____ nervioso / nervous ____ ; ____ óseo / osseous ____ ; ____ portal / portal ____ ; ____ reproductivo / reproductive ____ ; ____ respiratorio / respiratory ____ ; ____ reticuloendotelial / reticuloendothelial ____ ; ____ amortiguador / buffer ____ .

sistemático-a *a.* systematic, that follows a system; **-mente** *adv.* systematically.

sistematización *f.* systematization, the act of following a system.

sistémico-a *a.* systemic, that affects the body as a whole; circulación ____ / ____ circulation.

sístole *f.* systole, the contractive cycle of the heartbeat, esp. of the ventricles; ____ auricular / atrial ____ ; ____ prematura / premature ____ ; ____ ventricular / ventricular ____ .

sistólico-a *a.* systolic, rel. to the systole; murmullo ____ / ____ murmur; presión ____ / ____ pressure.

situación *f.* situation.

situado-a *a.* situated, placed, located.

situs *L.* situs, position or place.

Snellen, prueba de ojo de *f.* Snellen's eye test, a chart of black letters that gradually diminish in size used in testing visual acuity.

sobra *f.* excess, surplus; **hay de** ___ / there is more than enough.

sobrante *m.* surplus, leftover, excess.

sobrar *v.* to be or have in excess.

sobre *prep.* above, over; ___ **todo** / above all.

sobrealimentación *f.* hyperalimentation; ___ intravenosa / parenteral ___.

sobrecierre *m.* overclosure, condition caused when the mandible closes before the upper and lower teeth meet.

sobrecompensación *f.* overcompensation; *psych.* an exaggerated attempt to conceal feelings of guilt or inferiority.

sobrecorrección *f.* overcorrection, use of too powerful a lense to correct an eye defect.

sobredosis *f.* overdose, excessive dose of a drug.

sobreextensión *f.* overextension.

sobrellevar *v.* to endure.

sobremordida *f.* overbite.

sobrenombre *m.* surname, family name.

sobrepeso *m.* overweight.

sobreponerse *vr., vi.* to overcome.

sobreproducción *f.* overreaction.

sobrerrespuesta *f.* overresponse, excessive reaction to a stimulus.

sobresalir *vi.* to protrude; to be conspicuous.

sobresaltado-a *a.* frightened, startled.

sobretodo *m.* coat.

sobrevivir *v.* to survive.

sobrino-a *m., f.* nephew; niece.

sobrio-a *a.* sober.

socavar *v.* to undermine.

sociable *a.* sociable.

social *a.* social; **seguro** ___ / ___ security; asistencia ___ / ___ work; trabajador a ___ / ___ worker.

socialización *f.* socialization, social adaptation.

socializado-a *a.* socialized; medicina ___ / ___ medicine.

sociedad *f.* society; corporation; fellowship.

socio-a *m., f.* member; partner; fellow.

sociobiología *f.* sociobiology, the science that studies genetic factors as determinants of social behavior.

sociología *f.* sociology, the science that studies social relations and phenomena.

sociólogo-a *m., f.* sociologist, specialist in sociology.

sociópata *m., f.* sociopath, an individual that manifests antisocial behavior.

socorrer *v.* to help, to assist, to aid.

soda *f.* soda, sodium carbonate.

sodio *m.* sodium, soft alkaline metallic element found in the fluids of the body; **bicarbonato de** ___ / baking soda; carbonato de ___ / soda.

sodomía *f.* sodomy, term used in reference to sexual relations between males.

sodomita *m., f.* sodomite, one who commits sodomy.

sofisticación *f.* sophistication, the adulteration of a substance.

sofocación *f.* suffocation, asphyxia, shortness of breath.

sofocar *vi.* to suffocate, to smother; to choke.

sofoco *m.* hot flash; suffocation.

soja, soya *f.* soy, soybean.

sol *m.* sun; **bano de** ___ / sunbathing; **mancha del** ___ / sunspot; **quemadura de** ___ / sunburn; **tomar** ___ / to sunbathe.

solar *a.* solar, rel. to the sun; bloqueador ___ / sunscreen.

solaz *m.* solace, comfort, rest from work.

sólido-a *a.* solid; firm; sound.

solo-a *a.* alone, only; **-mente** *adv.* only.

soltar *vi.* to release; to loosen.

soltero-a *a.* single, unmarried.

soluble *a.* soluble.

solución *f.* solution.

solvente *m.* solvent, liquid that dissolves or is capable of producing a solution; thinner; *a.* financially responsible.

sollozar *vi.* to sob; to cry.

somático-a *a.* somatic, rel. to the body.

somatización *f. psych.* somatization; the process of converting mental experiences into bodily manifestations

sombra *f.* shadow; opacity; shade; **a la** ___ / in the shade.

sombrero *m.* hat.

someter *v.* to submit; **someterse** *vr.* to undergo; to submit oneself.

somnífero *m.* sleeping pill.

somnolencia *f.* sleepiness, drowsiness.

sonambulismo *m.* somnambulance, somnabulism, sleep walking.

sonámbulo-a *m., f.* somnambule, person who walks in his or her sleep.

sonar *vi.* to sound, to ring.

sonda *f.* probe, thin, smooth, and flexible instrument used to explore cavities and body passages or to measure the depth and direction of a wound; ____ intestinal / intestinal decompression tube; ____ uretral / urethral catheter.

sonido *m.* sound.

sonografía *f.* sonography. *V.* **ultrasonografía.**

sonograma *m.* sonogram, image obtained by ultrasonography.

sonoluciente *a.* sonolucent, in ultrasonography, having the quality of permitting the passage of ultrasound waves without remitting them back to their source.

sonoro-a *a.* sonorous, resonant, having a radiant sound.

sonreír *vi.* to smile.

sonrisa *f.* smile.

soñar *vi.* to dream; ____ despierto / to daydream.

sopa *f.* soup.

soplar *v.* to blow.

soplo *m.* murmur, bruit, flutter; short, raspy or fluttering sound, esp. an abnormal beat of the heart; ____ aórtico, regurgitante / aortic ____, regurgitant; ____ cardíaco / cardiac ____; ____ continuo / continuous ____; ____ creciente, en crescendo / crescendo ____; ____ diastólico / diastolic ____; ____ en vaivén / to-and-fro ____; ____ funcional / functional ____; ____ mitral /mitral ____; ____ pansistólico / pansystolic ____; ____ presistólico / presystolic ____; ____ sistólico / systolic ____.

sopor *m.* drowsiness, sleepiness.

soporífero, soporífico *m.* soporific, agent that produces sleep.

soportable *a.* bearable, that can be tolerated.

soportar *v.* to endure, to bear, to sustain.

soporte *m.* support.

sorber *v.* to sip; to suck; to absorb.

sorbo *m.* sip.

sordera *f.* deafness.

sordo-a *m., f.* a deaf person; *a.* deaf.

sordomudo-a *m., f.* deaf-mute person.

soso-a *a.* tasteless.

sostén *m.* support, backing; buttress.

sostener *vi.* to sustain; to maintain.

sostenido-a *a.* sustained; maintained.

spina *L.* spina. 1. thornlike projection; 2. the spinal column.

Staphylococcus *Gr.* Staphilococcus, genus of gram-positive bacteria of which several pathogenic species include parasites that are present in the skin and mucous membrane.

status *L.* status, state or condition; ____ asmaticus / ____ asthmaticus, severe asthma condition; ____ epilepticus / ____ epilepticus, series of seizures with loss of consciousness throughout.

Still, enfermedad de *f.* Still's disease, juvenile rheumatoid arthritis.

stratum *L.* (*pl.* **strata**) stratum, layer.

Streptococcus *Gr.* Streptococcus, a genus of gram-positive bacteria of the tribe *Streptocceae* that occur in pairs or chains, many of which are causing agents of serious infection.

stress *m.* stress, physical, chemical, or emotional factor that provokes an immediate or delayed response on the functions of the body or any of its parts.

struma *L.* struma, enlargement of the thyroid gland, goiter.

suave *a.* soft, smooth; **-mente** *adv.* softly.

suavizar *vi.* to soften.

subacromial *a.* subacromial, below the acromion.

subagudo-a *a.* subacute, rel. to a condition that is neither acute nor chronic.

subaracnoideo-a *a.* subarachnoid, situated or occurring below the arachnoid membrane; espacio ____ / ____ space.

subatómico-a *a.* subatomic, smaller than an atom.

subcapsular *a.* subcapsular, located below a capsule.

subclavicular *a.* subclavian, subclavicular, located beneath the clavicle; arteria ____ / ____ artery; vena ____ / ____ vein.

subclínico-a *a.* subclinical, without clinical manifestations.

subconsciencia, subconsciente *f., m. psych.* subconscious. state during which mental processes affecting thought, feeling, and behavior occur without the individual's awareness.

subconsciente *a. psych.* subconscious, partially conscious.

subcostal *a.* subcostal, below the ribs.

subcultivo *m.* subculture, a culture of bacteria derived from another culture.

subcutáneo-a *a.* subcutaneous, under the skin.

subdesarrollado-a *a.* underdeveloped.

subdesarrollo *m.* underdevelopment.

subdural *a.* subdural, under the dura mater; espacio ____ / ____ space.

subependimario-a *a.* subependymal, situated under the ependyma.

subescapular *a.* subscapular, below the scapula.

subesternal *a.* substernal, below the sternum.

subestructura *f.* substructure, supporting structure.

subfrénico-a *a.* subphrenic, situated below the diaphragm; absceso ___ / ___ abscess.

subhepático-a *a.* subhepatic, situated under the liver.

subintimal *a.* subintimal, situated below the intima.

subir *v.* to go up; to lift up; to climb; ___ las escaleras / to climb the stairs.

súbito-a *a.* sudden; muerte ___ / ___ death; -mente *adv.* suddenly.

subjetivo-a *a.* subjective; síntomas ___ -s / ___ symptoms.

sublimación *f.* sublimation. 1. the change from a solid state to vapor; 2. *psych.* a Freudian term indicating a process by which instinctual drives and impulses are modified into socially acceptable behavior.

sublimado *m.* sublimate, substance obtained by sublimation.

sublingual *a.* sublingual, under the tongue; glándula ___ / ___ gland.

subluxación *f.* subluxation, an incomplete dislocation.

submandibular *a.* submandibular, under the mandible.

submental *a.* submental, under the chin.

submucosa *f.* submucosa, layer of cellular tissue situated under a mucous membrane.

subnormal *a.* subnormal, below normal or below average.

subóptimo-a *a.* suboptimal, less than optimum.

subproducto *m.* by-product.

subrogado-a *a.* surrogate, that takes the place of someone or something.

subscripción *f.* subscription, part of the prescription that contains instructions for its preparation.

subsistir *v.* to subsist, to survive.

substantivo, sustantivo *m. gr.* substantive, noun.

subtotal *m.* subtotal.

subungueal *a.* subungual, beneath a nail.

succión *f.* suction.

suceder *v.* to happen.

sucesivo-a *a.* successive, consecutive.

suceso *m.* happening, event.

suciedad *f.* filth.

sucio-a *a.* dirty, filthy.

suco *m.* succus, juice; sap.

sucrosa *f.* sucrose, natural saccharose obtained mostly from sugar cane and sugar beets.

sudado-a *a.* sweaty, moist with perspiration; perspiring.

sudar *v.* to sweat, to perspire.

sudatorio, sudorífico *m.* sudorific, an agent promoting sweat.

sudor *m.* sweat, perspiration, secretion of the sweat glands; ___ -es nocturnos / night ___ -s.

sudoriento-a *a.* sweated, covered with sweat.

sudorífico-a *a.* sudorific, that produces sweat.

sudoroso-a *a.* perspiring, sweaty.

suegro-a *m., f.* father-in-law; mother-in-law.

sueldo *m.* salary, wages.

suelo *m.* ground; floor.

suelto-a *a. pp.* of **soltar,** loose, unattached.

sueño *m.* sleep; dream; ___ crepuscular / twilight ___ ; ___ profundo / deep ___ ; ___ reparador / balmy ___ ; trastornos del ___ / sleeping disorders; *v.* **tener** ___ / to be sleepy.

sueño, enfermedad del *f.* sleeping sickness, endemic acute disease of Africa caused by a protozoon transmitted by the tsetse fly and characterized by a state of lethargy, chills, loss of weight, and general weakness.

suero *m.* serum. 1. clear and watery portion of the plasma that remains fluid after clotting of blood; 2. any serous fluid; 3. immune serum of an animal that is innoculated to produce passive immunization; ___ antitóxico / immune ___ ; ___ de globulina / globulin ___ ; ___ de la verdad / truth ___ .

suerte *f.* luck; *v.* **tener** ___ / to be lucky.

suficiente *a.* sufficient, enough; -mente *adv.* sufficiently.

sufijo *m. gr.* suffix.

sufrible *a.* sufferable, bearable.

sufrimiento *m.* suffering.

sufrir *v.* to suffer; [*herida*] to sustain; [*operación*] to undergo.

sufusión *f.* suffusion, infiltration of a bodily fluid into the surrounding tissues.

sugerencia, sugestión *f.* suggestion, intimation, indication.

sugerir *vi.* to suggest, to indicate, to hint.

sugestivo-a *a.* suggestive, rel. to suggestion or that suggests.

suicida *a.* suicidal, prone to commit suicide.

suicidarse *vr.* to commit suicide.

suicidio *m.* suicide; intento de ___ / attempted ___ .

sujeto *m.* subject. 1. term used in reference to the patient; 2. topic; 3. *gr.* subject of the verb.

sulcus *L.* (*pl.* **sulci**) sulcus, slight depression, fissure.

sulfa, medicamentos de *m. pl.* sulfa drugs, *sulfonamides,* antibacterial drugs of the sulfonamide group.

sulfato *m.* sulfate, a salt of sulfuric acid.

sulfonamidas *f. pl.* sulfonamides, a group of bacteriostatic sulfur organic compounds.

sulfúrico-a *a.* sulfuric, rel. to sulfur.

sulfuro *m.* sulfur.

suma *f.* summation, total amount.

sumamente *adv.* extremely, very.

sumar *v.* to add.

sumario *m.* summary, clinical history of the patient.

sumergir *vi.* to submerge, to immerse.

superar *v.* to overcome.

superfecundación *f.* superfecundation, successive fertilization of two or more ova from the same menstrual cycle in two separate instances of sexual intercourse.

superficial *a.* superficial, rel. to a surface; tensión ___ / surface tension; shallow; **-mente** *adv.* superficially, shallowly.

superficie *f.* surface, outer portion or limit of a structure.

superhembra *f.* superfemale, a female organism that contains more than the normal number of sex-determining chromosomes.

superinfección *f.* superinfection, new infection that occurs while a previous one is still present, gen. caused by a different organism.

superior *a.* superior; upper; higher; greater.

supernumerario-a *a.* supernumerary, that exceeds the normal number.

superolateral *a.* superolateral, situated above and to the side.

supersaturado-a *a.* supersaturated, beyond saturation.

supersaturar *v.* to supersaturate, to add a substance in an amount greater than that which can be dissolved normally by a liquid.

supersensibilidad *f.* supersensitiveness, hypersensibility.

supersónico-a *a.* supersonic, rel. to vibrations of sound space waves above the capacity of human hearing.

superstición *f.* superstition.

supersticioso-a *a.* superstitious.

supervisar *v.* to supervise.

supervisor-a *m., f.* supervisor.

supervivencia *f.* survivorship; annuity.

superyó *m.* superego, in psychoanalysis the part of the psyche concerned with social standards, ethics, and conscience.

supino-a *a.* supine, rel. to the position of lying on the back, face up, with palms of the hands turned upward.

suplemental *a.* supplemental, additional.

suplemento *m.* supplement, supply.

suplicio *m.* torture, punishment, extreme suffering.

suponer *vi.* to suppose, to surmise.

suposición *f.* supposition, guess.

supositorio *m.* suppository, a semisolid, soluble, medicated mass that is introduced in a body passage such as the vagina or the rectum.

supraclavicular *a.* supraclavicular, situated above the clavicle.

suprapúbico-a *a.* suprapubic, above the pubis; catéter ___ / ___ catheter; cistotomía ___ / ___ cystotomy.

suprarrenal *a.* suprarenal, above the kidney; glándula ___ / ___ gland.

suprasillar *a.* suprasellar, above the sella turcica.

supratentorial *a.* supratentorial, above the dura mater.

supresión *f.* suppression; withdrawal; 1. arrest in the production of a secretion, excretion, or any normal discharge; 2. in psychoanalysis, inhibition of an idea or desire.

suprimir *v.* to discontinue, to withdraw.

supuración *f.* suppuration, formation or discharge of pus.

supurar *v.* to suppurate, to fester, to ooze.

supurativo-a *a.* suppurative, rel. to suppuration.

sur *m.* south.

sural *a.* sural, rel. to the calf of the leg.

surco *m.* line, wrinkle; groove, track; ___ bicipital / bicipital ___ ; ___ costal / costal ___ .

suscitar *v.* to rouse, to stir up.

suspender *v.* to suspend, to cancel, to put a halt.

suspensión *f.* suspension. 1. temporary stoppage of a vital process; 2. treatment that consists in immobilizing and suspending a patient in a desired position; 3. the state of a substance when its particles are not dissolved in a fluid or solid; 4. detention, stoppage.

suspenso-a *a.* pending.

suspensorio-a *a.* suspensory, that sustains or provides support; ligamento ___ / ___ ligament.

sustancia *f.* substance, matter; ___ blanca / white matter, neural tissue formed mainly by myelinated fibers that constitutes the conducting portion of the brain and the spinal cord; ___ fundamental / ground ___, gelatinous matter of connective tissue, cartilage, and bone that fills the space between cells and fibers.

sustancioso-a *a.* nutritious.

sustantivo *m. gr.* substantive, noun.

sustentacular *a.* sustentacular, that sustains or supports.

sustentaculum *L.* sustentaculum, support.

sustitución *f.* substitution, the act of replacing one thing for another; terapéutica por ___ / ___ therapy.

sustituir *vi.* to substitute.

sustituto *m.* substitute.

susto *m.* fright, sudden fear.

sustrato *m.* 1. substrate, a substance acted upon by an enzyme; 2. substratum, an underlying foundation.

susurro *m.* whisper, murmur.

sutil *a.* subtile, subtle, fine, delicate; inadvertent.

sutura *f.* suture, line of union; ___ absorbible / absorbable surgical ___; ___ de catgut / catgut ___; ___ compuesta / bolster ___; ___ continua, de peletero / continuous, uninterrupted ___; ___ de colchonero / vertical mattress ___; ___ en bolsa de tabaco / purse-string ___; ___ no absorbible / nonabsorbable ___; ___ de seda / silk ___.

Swan-Ganz, catéter de *m.* Swan-Ganz catheter, soft, flexible catheter with a balloon near the tip used to measure the blood pressure in the pulmonary artery.

T

T *abr.* **temperatura absoluta** / absolute temperature; **T+**, **tensión aumentada** / T+, increased tension; **T−**, **tensión disminuída** / T−, diminished tension.

tabaco *m.* 1. tobacco, the dried and prepared leaves of *Nicotiana tabacum* that contain nicotine; 2. cigar; contaminación por humo de ___ / ___ smoke pollution.

tabaquismo *m.* tabacism, tabacosis, acute or chronic intoxication due to excessive intake of tobacco dust.

tabes *L.* tabes, progressive deterioration of the body or any part of it caused by a chronic illness.

tabético-a *a.* tabetic, rel. to or suffering from tabes.

tabicado-a *a.* septate, that has a dividing wall.

tabique *m.* thin wall; ___ nasal, o de la nariz / nose ridge.

tabla *f.* table. 1. a flat osseous plate or lamina; 2. an arranged collection of many particulars that have a common standard.

tableta *f.* tablet, a solid dosage of medication; ___ de capa entérica / enteric-coated ___.

tabú *m.* taboo, tabu, a forbidden thing or behavior; *a.* forbidden.

tabular *a.* tabular, resembling a table or square; *v.* to tabulate, to make lists or tables.

tacón *m.* heel of a shoe.

táctica *f.* tactic.

táctil *a.* tactile, rel. to touch or to the sense of touch; discriminación ___ / ___ discrimination; sistema ___ / ___ system.

tacto *m.* the sense of touch.

tacha *f.* defect, blemish, imperfection.

taenia *L.* taenia. *V.* **tenia.**

tajada *f.* slice, cut.

tal, tales *a.* such, as, so, so much; ¿qué ___? / how goes it?; ___ cual, ___ como / ___ as; *adv.* thus, in such a way, in such manner.

talámico-a *a.* thalamic, rel. to the thalamus.

tálamo *m.* thalamus, one of the two large oval-shaped masses of gray matter situated at the base of the cerebrum that are the main relay centers of sensory impulses to the cerebral cortex.

talar *a.* talar, rel. to the ankle.

talasemia *f.*, thalassemia, a group of inherited hypochromic anemias caused by genetic factors that produce failure or reduction in the total synthesis of hemoglobin; ____ mayor / major ____ ; ____ menor / minor ____ .

talasoterapia *f.* thalassotherapy, the treatment of disease by sea bathing or by exposure to the sea.

talco *m.* talc, talcum powder.

talidomida *f.* thalidomide, hypnotic sedative known to cause severe malformation in developing fetuses.

talon *m.* talon, posterior part of a molar tooth.

talón *m.* talus, astragalus, heel, ankle bone.

talotibial *a.* talotibial, rel. to the talus and the tibia.

tallo *m.* stalk; stem, an elongated slender structure resembling the stalk or stem of a plant.

tamaño *m.* size.

tambalearse *vr.* to stagger, to waver.

también *adv.* also, as well, too.

tampoco *adv.* neither, not either.

tan *adv.* so, as well, as much.

tanatología *f.* thanatology, branch of medicine that deals with death in all its aspects.

tangible *a.* tangible.

tanto-a *a.* so much, as much, so many, as many; *adv.* so much, as much; ____ mejor / ____ the better; ____ peor / ____ the worse; **estar al** ____ **de** / to be alerted to; **por lo** ____ / therefore.

tapa *f.* cover; lid.

tapado-a *a.* covered; clogged.

tapar *v.* to cover.

tapón *m.* 1. pledget, pack of absorbent material applied to a part of the body or inserted in a cavity to stop hemorrhage or absorb secretions; 2. plug, tampon, buffer.

taponamiento *m.* tamponade, packing. 1. the process of filling a cavity with cotton, gauze or some other material; 2. wrapping.

taponamiento cardíaco *m.* cardiac tamponade, acute compression of the heart due to excess fluid in the pericardium.

taquiarritmia *f.* tachyarrhythmia, arrhythmia combined with a rapid pulse.

taquicardia *f.* tachycardia, acceleration of the heart activity, gen. at a frequency of more than one hundred beats per minute in adults; ____ auricular / atrial ____ ; ____ au-

ricular paroxística / paroxysmal atrial ____ ; ____ ectópica / ectopic ____ ; ____ supraventricular / supraventricular ____ ; ____ ventricular / ventricular ____ .

taquipnea *f.* tachypnea, abnormally rapid respiration.

tarántula *f.* tarantula, large black venomous spider.

tardar *v.* to delay; **a más** ____ / at the latest; **tardarse** *vr.* to be delayed.

tarde *f.* afternoon; *adv.* late; **más** ____ o **más temprano** / sooner or later.

tardío-a *a.* late; delayed.

tardive *Fr.* tardive, late in appearing.

tarea *f.* task.

tarjeta *f.* card; ____ **de crédito** / credit ____ ; ____ **de visita** / calling ____ .

tarsal, tarsiano-a *a.* tarsal, rel. to the connective tissue that supports the eyelid or the tarsus.

tarso *m.* tarsus, posterior part of the foot located between the bones of the lower leg and the metatarsus; huesos del ____ / tarsal bones.

tarsometatarsiano-a *a.* tarsometatarsal, rel. to the tarsus and the metatarsus.

tartamudear *v.* to stammer, to stutter.

tartamudeo, tartamudez *m., f.* stammering, stuttering.

tatuaje *m.* tattooing, the act of puncturing the skin for the purpose of creating designs with permanent colors.

taxis *L.* taxis. 1. manipulation or reduction of a part or an organ to restore it to its normal position; 2. directional reaction of an organism to a stimulus.

taza *f.* cup.

té *m.* tea; ____ de jazmín / jasmine ____ .

tebaína *f.* thebaine, toxic alkaloid obtained from opium.

teca *f.* theca, covering or sheath of an organ.

tecnecio 99m *m.* technetium 99m, a radioisotope that emits gamma rays and that is the most frequently used radioisotope in nuclear medicine.

técnica *f.* technic, technique, method, or procedure.

técnico-a *m., f.* technician, an individual who has the necessary knowledge and skill to carry out specialized procedures and treatments, gen. under the supervision of a health care professional; ____ de rayos-X / X-ray ____ ; ____ dental / dental ____ ; ____ de terapia respiratoria / respiratory therapy ____ .

tecnología *f.* technology, the science of applying technical knowledge for practical purposes.

tecnólogo-a *m., f.* technologist, an expert in technology.

tecoma *m.* thecoma, tumor of an ovary, gen. benign.

tectorium *L.* tectorium, membrane that covers Corti's organ.

tectum *L.* tectum, rooflike structure.

techo *m.* roof; ceiling.

tedioso-a *a.* tedious; tiresome.

tegumento *m.* tegument, the skin.

tejido *m.* tissue, a group of similar cells and their intercellular substance that act together in the performance of a particular function; _____ adiposo / adipose _____ ; _____ cartilaginoso / cartilaginous _____ ; _____ cicatricial / scar _____ ; _____ conectivo / connective _____ ; _____ de granulación / granulation _____ ; _____ elástico / elastic _____ ; _____ endotelial / endothelial _____ ; _____ epitelial / epithelial; _____ eréctil / erectile _____ ; _____ fibroso / fibrous _____ ; _____ glandular / glandular _____ ; _____ linfoide / lymphoid _____ ; _____ mesenquimatoso / mesenchymal _____ ; _____ mucoso / mucous _____ ; _____ muscular / muscular _____ ; _____ nervioso / nerve, nervous _____ ; _____ óseo / bony, bone _____ ; _____ subcutáneo / subcutaneous _____ .

tela *f.* fabric, cloth.

telangiectasia *f.* telangiectasia, telangiectasis, condition caused by an abnormal dilation of the capillary vessels and arterioles that sometimes can produce angioma.

teléfono *m.* telephone; **llamar por** _____ , **telefonear** / to telephone.

telemetría *f.* telemetry, electronically transmitted data.

telencéfalo *m.* telencephalon, anterior portion of the encephalon.

telepatía *f.* telepathy, apparent communication of thought by extrasensory means.

telerradiografía *f.* teleradiography, X-ray taken with the radiation source at a distance of about two meters or more from the subject.

televisión *f.* television.

televisor *m.* television set.

telofase *f.* telophase, last phase of a process.

tembladera *f. pop.* the shakes.

temblar *v.* to quiver, to shiver.

temblor *m.* tremor, an involuntary quivering or trembling; _____ alcohólico / alcoholic _____ ; _____ continuo / continuous _____ ; _____ de aleteo / flapping _____ ; _____ de reposo / rest _____ ; _____ de variaciones rápidas / fine _____ ; _____ esencial / essential _____ ; _____ fisiológico / physiologic _____ ; _____ intencional / intentional _____ ; _____ intermitente / intermittent _____ ; _____ lento y acentuado / coarse _____ ; _____ muscular / muscular _____ .

temblores *m. pl. pop.* the shakes.

temer *v.* to fear, to dread.

temor *m.* fear, dread.

temperamento *m.* temperament, the combined physical, emotional, and mental constitution of an individual that distinguishes him or her from others.

temperatura *f.* temperature. 1. degree of heat or cold as measured on a specific scale; _____ absoluta / absolute _____ ; _____ ambiente / room _____ ; _____ axilar / axillary _____ ; _____ crítica / critical _____ ; _____ del cuerpo / body _____ ; _____ máxima / maximum _____ ; _____ mínima / minimum _____ ; _____ normal / normal _____ ; _____ oral / oral _____ ; _____ rectal / rectal _____ ; _____ subnormal / subnormal _____ ; 2. the natural degree of heat of a living body.

temple *m.* temper; character.

temporal *a.* 1. temporal, rel. to the temple; huesos _____ -es / _____ bones; lóbulo _____ / _____ lobe; músculo _____ / _____ muscle, 2. temporary, limited in time.

temporomandibular *a.* temporomandibular, rel. to or affecting the joint between the temporal bone and the mandible; articulaciones _____ -es / _____ joints.

temprano-a *a.* early.

tenáculo *m.* tenaculum, type of hook used in *surg.* to grasp or hold a part.

tenar *a.* thenar, rel. to the palm of the hand; eminencia _____ / _____ eminence; músculos _____ -es / _____ muscles.

tenaz *a.* tenacious, persistent, determined.

tenaza *f.* clamp, pincers.

tendencia *f.* tendency, propensity; trend.

tendinitis *f.* tendinitis, tendonitis, infl. of a tendon.

tendinoso-a *a.* tendinous, rel. to or resembling a tendon; reflejo _____ / tendon reflex; reflejo _____ profundo / deep tendon reflex; tirón _____ / tendon jerk.

tendón *m.* tendon, sinew, highly resistant fibrous tissue that attaches the muscles to the bones or to other parts; ___ -es de la corva / hamstring; ___ de **Aquiles** / Achilles' ___ .

tenedor *m.* fork.

tener *vi.* to have, to possess; ___ **diez años** / to be ten years old; ___ **dolor** / to be in pain; ___ **ganas de** / to want to; ___ **hambre** / to be hungry; ___ **miedo** / to be afraid; ___ **razón** / to be right; ___ **que** / to have to; ___ **sed** / to be thirsty.

tenesmo *m.* tenesmus, continuously painful, ineffectual, and straining efforts to urinate or defecate.

tenia *f.* flat worm of the class *Cestoda* that in the adult stage lives in the intestines of vertebrates; *pop.* tapeworm.

teniasis *f.* taeniasis, infestation by taenia.

tenosinovitis *f.* tenosynovitis, infl. of a tendon sheath.

tensión *f.* tension, tenseness; 1. the act or effect of stretching or being extended; 2. the degree of stretching; 3. physical, emotional, or mental stress; ___ premenstrual / premenstrual ___ ; ___ superficial / superficial ___ ; 4. the expansive pressure of a gas or vapor.

tenso-a *a.* tense, in a state of tension; rigid, stiff.

tensoactivo *m.* surfactant, an agent that modifies the superficial tension of a liquid.

tensor *a.* tensor, term applied to any muscle that stretches or produces tension.

tentativo-a *a.* tentative, experimental, or subject to change.

tentorial *a.* tentorial, rel. to a tentorium.

tentorium *L.* tentorium, tentlike structure.

tenue *a.* tenuous, slight.

teñir *vi.* to dye; to color.

teoría *f.* theory. 1. an exposition of the principles of any science; 2. hypothesis that lacks scientific proof.

teórico-a *a.* theoretical, rel. to a theory.

terapeuta, terapista *m., f.* therapist, person skilled in giving or applying therapy in a given health field; ___ , patólogo-a del habla y del lenguaje / speech ___ ; ___ físico / physical ___ .

terapéutica *f.* therapeutics, the branch of medicine that deals with treatments and remedies.

terapéutica, terapia *f.* therapy, the treatment of a disease; ___ anticoagulante / anticoagulant ___ ; ___ de conducta / behavioral ___ ; ___ de grupo / group ___ ; ___ del habla y del lenguaje / language / speech ___ ; ___ de oxígeno / oxygen ___ / ___ immunosuspensiva / inmunosupressive ___ ; ___ ocupacional / occupational ___ ; ___ por choque / shock ___ ; ___ por inhalación / inhalation ___ ; ___ por radiación / radiation ___ ; ___ respiratoria / respiratory ___ .

terapéutica por realidad *f.* reality therapy, method by which the patient is confronted with his or her real life situation and helped to accept it as such.

terapéutico-a *a.* therapeutic. 1. rel. to therapy; 2. that has healing properties.

teratogénesis *f.* teratogenesis, the production of gross fetal abnormalities.

teratógeno *m.* teratogen, agent that causes teratogenesis.

teratoide *a.* teratoid, resembling a monster; tumor ___ / ___ tumor.

teratología *f.* teratology, the study of malformations in fetuses.

teratoma *m.* teratoma, neoplasm derived from more than one embryonic layer and therefore constituted by different types of tissues.

terciano-a *a.* tertian, that repeats itself every three days.

terco-a *a.* stubborn, obstinate; *pop.* hardheaded.

teres *L.* teres, term applied to describe some elongated and cylindrical muscles and ligaments.

termal *a.* thermal, thermic, rel. to heat or produced by it.

terminación *f.* ending; [*de un nervio*] twig.

terminal *a.* terminal, final.

terminar *v.* to terminate, to rescind.

término *m.* term. 1. a definite period of time or its completion, such as a pregnancy; 2. word.

terminología *f.* terminology, nomenclature.

termistor *m.* thermistor, a type of thermometer used for measuring minute changes of temperature.

termo *m.* thermos.

termocoagulación *f.* thermocoagulation, coagulation of tissue with high frequency currents.

termodinámica *f.* thermodynamics, the science that studies the relationship between heat and other forms of energy.

termoesterilización *f.* thermosterilization, sterilization by heat.

termografía *f.* thermography, recording obtained by the use of a thermograph.

termógrafo *m.* thermograph, infrared detector that registers variations in temperature by reaction to the blood flow.

termómetro *m.* thermometer; device that measures heat or cold; ____ clínico / clinical ____ ; ____ de Celsius / Celsius ____ , centigrade; ____ de Fahrenheit / Fahrenheit ____ ; ____ de registro automático / self-recording ____ ; ____ rectal / rectal ____ .

termonuclear *a.* thermonuclear.

termorregulación *f.* thermoregulation, regulation by heat and temperature.

termostato *m.* thermostat, instrument used for regulating temperature.

termotaxis *f.* thermotaxis. 1. regulation of the temperature of the body; 2. the reaction of an organism to heat.

termoterapia *f.* thermotherapy, therapeutic use of heat.

ternario-a *a.* ternary, triple, made up of three elements.

ternura *f.* tenderness, sensitivity.

Terramicina *f.* Terramycin, trade name for a tetracycline antibiotic.

terremoto *m.* earthquake.

terrible *a.* terrible.

terror *m.* terror; panic.

tesis *f.* thesis.

testamento *m.* testament, last will.

testarudo-a *a.* hardheaded, stubborn, headstrong.

testicular *a.* testicular, rel. to a testicle; tumores ____ es / tumors.

testículo *m.* testicle, the male gonad, one of the two male reproductive glands that produce spermatozoa and the hormone testosterone; ____ ectópico / ectopic ____ ; ____ no descendido / undescended testis.

testificar *vi.* to testify.

testigo *m., f.* witness.

testis *L.* (*pl.* **testes**) testis, testicle.

testosterona *f.* testosterone, male hormone produced chiefly by the testicle and responsible for the development of male secondary characteristics such as facial hair and a deep voice; implante de ____ / ____ implant.

teta *f.* teat. 1. mammary gland; 2. nipple.

tetania *f.* tetany, a neuromuscular affection

associated with parathyroid deficiencies and diminished mineral balance, esp. calcium, and manifested by intermittent tonic spasms of the voluntary muscles.

tetánico-a *a.* tetanic, rel. to tetanus; antitoxina ____ / tetanus antitoxin; convulsión ____ / ____ convulsion; toxoide ____ / ____ toxoid.

tétano *m.* tetanus, an acute infectious disease caused by the toxin of the tetanus bacillus, gen. introduced in the body through a wound and manifested by muscular spasms and rigidity of the jaw, neck, and abdomen; *pop.* lockjaw; globulina inmune para el ____ / ____ immune globulin.

tetera, teto *f., m.* pacifier; nipple of a nursing bottle.

tetilla *f.* male nipple.

tetraciclina *f.* tetracycline, a type of broadspectrum antibiotic effective against grampositive and gram-negative bacteria, rickettsia, and a variety of viruses.

tétrada *f.* tetrad, a group of four similar elements.

tetralogía *f.* tetralogy, term applied to the combination of four factors or elements.

tetraplejía *f.* tetraplegia, paralysis of the four extremities.

tetraploide *a.* tetraploid, having four sets of chromosomes.

tetravalente *m.* tetravalent, element that has a chemical valence of four.

textura *f.* texture, the composition of a tissue or structure.

tez *f.* complexion.

thrill *m.* thrill, a vibration felt on palpation; ____ aneurismal / aneurysmal ____ ; ____ aórtico / aortic ____ ; ____ arterial / arterial ____ ; ____ diastólico / diastolic ____ .

tibia *f.* tibia, the inner and larger bone of the leg below the knee.

tibial *a.* tibial, rel. to or situated close to the tibia.

tibio-a *a.* tepid, lukewarm.

tic *Fr.* tic, spasmodic, involuntary movement or twitching of a muscle; ____ convulsivo / convulsive ____ ; ____ coordinado / coordinated ____ ; ____ doloroso / douloureux ____ ; ____ facial / facial ____ .

tiempo *m.* 1. time, the duration of an event; ____ de coagulación / coagulation ____ ; ____ de exposición / exposure ____ ; ____ de latencia / ____ lag; ____ de percepción /

perception ___ ; ___ de protrombina / prothrombin ___ ; ___ de sangramiento / bleeding ___ ; a ___ / in time; **a su debido** ___ / in due ___ ; **¿cuánto ___ ?** / how long?; **espacio de** ___ / time frame; **pérdida de** ___ / waste of ___ ; **por algún** ___ / for some ___ ; **regulador de** ___ / timer; ___ **suplementario** / overtime; 2. weather; pronóstico del ___ / weather forecasting; **hace buen** ___ / the ___ is good; **hace mal** ___ / the ___ is bad.

tienda *f.* tent, a cover or shelter made of fabric, gen. used to enclose the patient within a given area; ___ de oxígeno / oxygen ___ .

tierno-a *a.* tender, sensitive.

tierra *f.* soil; earth.

tieso-a *a.* stiff, rigid.

tífico-a *a.* typhoid, rel. to typhus.

tiflitis *f.* typhlitis, infl. of the cecum.

tifoidea, fiebre *f.* typhoid fever, acute intestinal infection caused by a bacterium of the genus *Salmonella,* characterized by fever, prostration, headache, and abdominal pain.

tifus *m.* typhus, acute infectious disease caused by *rickettsia* with manifestations of high fever, delirium, prostration, and severe headache, gen. transmitted by lice, fleas, ticks, and mites.

tijeras *f. pl.* scissors.

tilo *m.* tea made with linden flowers.

timectomía *f. surg.* thymectomy, excision of the thymus.

tímico-a *a.* thymic, rel. to the thymus gland.

tímido-a *a.* timid, bashful, shy

timo *m.* thymus, glandular organ situated in the inferior portion of the neck and the antero-superior portion of the thoracic cavity. It plays an important part in the immunological process of the body.

timocito *m.* thymocyte, a lymphocyte arising in the thymus.

timoma *m.* thymoma, tumor derived from the thymus.

timpanectomía *f. surg.* tympanectomy, excision of the tympanic membrane.

timpánico-a *a.* tympanic, resonant or rel. to the tympanum; membrana ___ / ___ membrane.

timpanismo *m.* tympanites, distension of the abdomen caused by accumulation of gas in the intestine.

timpanítico-a *a.* tympanitic, rel. to or affec-

ted with tympanites; resonancia ___ / ___ resonance.

timpanitis *f.* tympanitis, infl. of the middle ear.

tímpano *m.* tympanum, the eardrum, middle ear.

timpanoplastia *f. surg.* tympanoplasty, reconstruction of the middle ear.

timpanotomía *f. surg.* tympanotomy, incision of the tympanic membrane.

tina *f.* tub.

tinea *L.* tinea, cutaneous fungal infection in the form of a ring; ___ capitis / ___ capitis; ___ corporis / ___ corporis; ___ pedis / ___ pedis, Athlete's foot; ___ versicolor / ___ versicolor.

tinnitus *L.* tinnitus, buzzing or ringling sound in the ears.

tinta *f.* ink.

tinte *m.* dye.

tintura *f.* tincture, an alcoholic extract of animal or vegetable origin.

tiña *f.* tinea, ringworm. *V.* **tinea.**

tío-a *m., f.* uncle; aunt.

típico-a *a.* typical; characteristic.

tipificación *f.* typing, determination by types; ___ de tejido / tissue ___ .

tipo *m.* type; kind, the general character of a given entity.

tira *f.* strap.

tirante *a.* tense, extended; pulling; stretched; [*relación*] strained.

tirar *v.* 1. to throw, to toss; to throw out; 2. to pull, to tug, as in tracheal tugging.

tiritar *v.* to shiver.

tiro *m.* shot from a firearm.

tiroadenitis *f.* thyroadenitis, inf. of the thyroid gland.

tiroglobulina *f.* thyroglobulin. 1. a glycoprotein secreted by the thyroid gland; 2. a substance obtained by the fractioning of the thyroid gland of the hog, used in the treatment of hyperthyroidism.

tirogloso-a *a.* thyroglossal, rel. to the thyroid and the tongue; conducto ___ / ___ duct.

tiroidectomía *f. surg.* thyroidectomy, excision of the thyroid gland.

tiroideo-a *a.* thyroid, rel. to the thyroid gland; cartílago ___ / ___ cartilage; crisis ___ / ___ storm; hormonas ___ -s / ___ hormones.

tiroides, glándula *f.* thyroid gland, one of the endocrine glands situated in the front part of the trachea and made up of two lateral lobules that connect in the middle; prueba del funcionamiento de la ___ / thyroid function test.

tiroiditis *f.* thyroiditis, infl. of the thyroid gland.

tiromegalia *f.* thyromegaly, enlargement of the thyroid gland.

tirón *m.* forceful pull; tugging.

tiroparatiroidectomía *f. surg.* thyroparathyroidectomy, excision of the thyroid and parathyroid glands.

tirotoxicosis *f.* thyrotoxicosis, disorder caused by hyperthyroidism and marked by an enlargement of the thyroid gland, increased metabolic rate, tachycardia, rapid pulse, and hypertension.

tirotropina *f.* thyrotropin, thyroid-stimulating hormone produced in the anterior lobe of the pituitary gland; hormona estimulante de la ___ / ___ releasing hormone.

tiroxina *f.* thyroxine, iodine-containing hormone produced by the thyroid gland, also obtained synthetically for use in the treatment of hypothyroidism.

titulación *f.* titration, determination of volume using standard solutions of known strength.

titular *v.* to titrate, to determine by titration.

título *m.* titer, titre, the required amount of a substance to produce a reaction with a given volume of another substance.

toalla *f.* towel.

tobillera *f.* ankle brace.

tobillo *m.* ankle.

tocar *vi.* to touch, to palpate.

tocino *m.* bacon.

tocógrafo *m.* tocograph, device used to estimate and record the force of uterine contractions.

tocómetro *m.* tocometer. *V.* **tocógrafo.**

todavía *adv.* still, yet.

todo-a *a.* all, entire; **ante** ___ / above all; ___ **el día** / the whole day; ___-**s los días** / every day; ___-**s los meses** / every month.

tofáceo-a *a.* tophaceous, rel. to a tophus or of a gritty nature.

tofo *m.* tophus. 1. deposits of urates in tissues as seen in gout; 2. dental calculus.

toilette *Fr.* toilette, cleansing, as related to a medical procedure.

tolerable *a.* tolerable, bearable.

tolerancia *f.* tolerance, the ability to endure

the use of a medication or a given amount of physical activity without ill effects.

tolerante *a.* tolerant.

tolerar *v.* to tolerate, to endure.

tomar *v.* to take; to eat or drink.

tomate *m.* tomato.

tomografía *f.* tomography, scan, diagnostic technique by which a series of X-ray pictures taken at different depths of an organ are obtained; ___ axial computada / computerized axial ___; ___ computada dinámica auricular / atrial bolus dynamic computerized ___.

tomógrafo *m.* tomograph, X-ray machine used in tomography.

tomograma *m.* tomogram, sectional X-ray of a part of the body.

tonicidad *f.* tonicity, normal quality of tone or tension.

tónico *m.* tonic, medication for restoring tone and vitality; **-a** *a.* 1. that restores the normal tone; 2. characterized by continuous tension.

tono *m.* tone; pitch. 1. the quality of the body with its organs and parts in a normal and balanced state; ___ muscular / muscular ___; 2. a particular quality of sound or voice.

tonoclónico-a *a.* tonoclonic, rel. to muscular spasms that are both tonic and clonic.

tonometría *f.* tonometry, the measurement of tension or pressure.

tonómetro *m.* tonometer, instrument that measures tone, esp. intraocular tension.

tonsila *f.* tonsil. *V.* **amígdala;** ___ cerebelosa / cerebellar ___; ___ faríngea / pharyngeal ___; ___ lingual / lingual ___; ___ palatina / palatine ___.

tonsilar *a.* tonsillar, rel. to a tonsil; cripta ___ o amigdalina / ___ crypt; fosa ___ / ___ fossa.

tonsilectomía *f. surg.* tonsillectomy. *V.* **amigdalotomía.**

tonsilitis *f.* tonsillitis. *V.* **amigdalitis.**

tonsiloadenoidectomía *f. surg.* tonsilloadenoidectomy, excision of the tonsils and adenoids.

tonto-a *a.* foolish, fatuous.

tonus *L.* tonus, tone.

tópico-a *a.* topical, rel. to a specific area.

toracentesis *f.* thoracentesis, surgical puncture and drainage of the thoracic cavity.

torácico-a *a.* thoracic, rel. to the thorax; cavidad ___ / ___ cavity; conducto ___ /

—— duct; pared —— / —— cage, chest wall, osseous structure enclosing the thorax; traumatismos ——-s / —— injuries.

toracicoabdominal *a.* thoracicoabdominal, rel. to the thorax and the abdomen.

Toracina *f.* Thorazine, antiemetic sedative.

toracolumbar *a.* thoracolumbar, rel. to the thoracic and lumbar vertebrae.

toracoplastia *f. surg.* thoracoplasty, plastic *surg.* of the thorax that consists in removing a portion of the ribs to allow the collapse of a diseased lung.

toracostomía *f. surg.* thoracostomy, incision of the chest wall to allow for drainage.

toracotomía *f. surg.* thoracotomy, incision of the thoracic wall.

tórax *m.* thorax, the chest; —— inestable / flail chest, condition of the wall of the thorax caused by multiple fracture of the ribs.

torcedura *f.* strain, sprain, warp, twisting of a joint with distension and laceration of its ligaments, usu. accompanied by pain and swelling.

torcer *vi.* to twist, to strain, to curve, to warp; **torcerse** *vr.* to sprain.

torcido-a *a.* twisted, sprained.

tormenta *f.* storm, abrupt and temporary intensification of the symptoms of a disease.

tormento *m.* torment.

tornillo *m.* screw.

torniquete *m.* tourniquet, tourniquette, device used to apply pressure over an artery to stop the flow of blood.

toronja *f.* grapefruit.

torpe *a.* dull, clumsy, slow.

torpeza *f.* dullness; clumsiness.

tórpido-a *a.* torpid, sluggish, slow.

torpor *m.* sluggishness, cloudiness; —— mental / clouding of consciousness.

torque *m.* torque, a force that produces rotation.

torsión *f.* torsion, twisting or rotating of a part on its long axis; —— ovárica / ovarian ——; —— testicular / testicular ——.

torso *m.* torso, trunk of the body.

tortícolis *f.* torticollis, toniclonic spasm of the muscles of the neck that causes cervical torsion and immobility of the head.

tortuoso-a *a.* tortuous, twisted.

tortura *f.* torture.

torus *L.* (*pl.* **tori**) torus, prominence, swelling.

tos *f.* cough; ataque de —— / coughing spell;

calmante para la —— / —— suppressant; jarabe para la —— / —— syrup; pastillas para la —— / lozenges; —— metálica, bronca / brassy ——; —— seca recurrente / hacking ——.

tos ferina *f.* pertussis, whooping cough, infectious children's disease that gen. begins with a cold followed by a persistent dry cough.

tosecilla *f.* slight cough.

toser *v.* to cough.

tostada *f.* toast.

tostado-a *a.* toasted; **pan** —— / toast.

total *a.* total, whole; **-mente** *adv.* totally.

totipotencia *f.* totipotency, ability of a cell to regenerate or develop into another type of cell.

totipotente *a.* totipotent, that can generate totipotency.

toxemia *f.* toxemia, generalized intoxication due to absorption of toxins formed at a local source of infection.

toxicidad *f.* toxicity, the quality of being poisonous.

tóxico-a *a.* toxic, rel. to a poison or of a poisonous nature.

toxicología *f.* toxicology, the study of poisons and their effects and treatment.

toxicólogo-a *m., f.* toxicologist, a specialist in toxicology.

toxicosis *f.* toxicosis, morbid state caused by a poison.

toxina *f.* toxin, a noxious substance produced by a plant or animal microorganism.

toxina antitoxina *f.* toxin-antitoxin, a nearly neutral mixture of a toxin and its antitoxin used for immunization against the specific disease caused by the toxin.

toxoide *m.* toxoid, a toxin void of toxicity that causes antibody formation and produces immunity to the specific disease caused by the toxin; —— diftérico / diphteria ——; —— tetánico / tetanus ——.

Toxoplasma *m. Toxoplasma,* a genus of parasitic protozoa.

toxoplasmosis *f.* toxoplasmosis, infection with organisms of the genus *Toxoplasma* that can cause minimal symptoms of malaise or swelling of the lymph glands, or serious damage to the central nervous system.

trabajador-a *m., f.* worker; —— social / social ——.

trabajar *v.* to work, to labor.

trabajo *m.* work, job, occupation; ____ de beneficencia social / welfare ____; ____ **de casa** / housework; ____ **excesivo** / overwork.

trabajoso-a *a.* laborious, hard.

trabécula *f.* trabecula, term used to designate a supporting structure of connective tissue that divides or secures an organ.

trabeculado-a *a.* trabeculate, having trabeculae.

tracción *f.* traction. 1. the action of drawing or pulling; 2. a pulling force; ____ cervical / cervical ____; ____ lumbar / lumbar ____.

tracoma *f.* trachoma, a viral contagious disease of the conjunctiva and the cornea, manifested by photophobia, pain, tearing, and, in severe cases, blindness.

tracto *m.* tract, an elongated system of tissue or organs that acts to carry out a common function; ____ alimenticio / alimentary ____; ____ genitourinario / genitourinary; ____ intestinal / intestinal ____.

tractor *m.* tractor, any instrument or machine used to apply traction.

traducción *f.* translation.

traer *vi.* to bring; to fetch.

tragar *vi.* to swallow; ____ **apresuradamente** / to gulp down

trago *m.* tragus, triangular cartilaginous eminence in the outer part of the ear.

traicionero-a *a.* deceitful, treacherous; enfermedad ____ / ____ disease.

trance *m. psych.* trance, hypnotic-like state characterized by detachment from the surroundings and diminished motor activity.

tranquilidad *f.* tranquility, rest; ____ **de espíritu** / peace of mind.

tranquilizante *m.* tranquilizer, sedative.

tranquilizar *vi.* to tranquilize, to calm; **tranquilizarse** *vr.* to quiet down; to ease one's mind.

tranquilo-a *a.* tranquil, calm, restful.

transabdominal *a.* transabdominal, through or across the abdominal wall.

transaminasa glutámica oxalacética *f.* glutamic-oxaloacetic transaminase, enzyme present in several tissues, such as the heart, liver, and brain, that presents a high concentration of serum when there is cardiac or hepatic damage.

transaminasa glutámica pirúvica *f.* glutamic-pyruvic transaminase, enzyme that presents an elevated serum content when

there is an injury or acute damage to liver cells.

transaxial *a.* transaxial, through or across the long axis of a structure.

transcapilar *a.* transcapillary, existing or taking place across the capillary walls.

transcurrir *v.* to elapse; [*tiempo*] to go by.

transcutáneo-a *a.* transcutaneous, through the skin; neuroestimulación eléctrica ____ / ____ electrical nerve stimulation.

transductor *a.* transducer, device that transforms one form of energy to another.

transección *f.* transection, cross section, cutting across the long axis of an organ.

transexual *a.* transexual. 1. individual with a psychological urge to be of the opposite sex; 2. person who has undergone a surgical sex change.

transferencia *f.* transfer, transference. 1. in psychoanalysis, shifting feelings and behavior towards a new object, gen. the psychoanalyst; 2. transmission of symptoms from one part of the body to another.

transferir *vi.* to transfer.

transferrina *f.* transferrin, a type of beta globulin in blood plasma that fixes and transports iron.

transfixión *f. surg.* transfixion, the act of cutting through soft tissues from the inside outwards, such as in amputations and excision of tumors.

transformación *f.* transformation, change of form or appearance.

transformar *v.* to transform, to change the appearance, character, or structure of something or someone.

transfusión *f.* transfusion, the process of transferring fluid into a vein or artery; ____ directa / direct ____; ____ indirecta / indirect ____.

transición *f.* transition.

transicional *a.* transitional, rel. to or subject to change.

transiluminación *f.* transillumination, passage of light through a body part.

transitorio-a *a.* transitory, of a temporal nature.

translocación *f.* translocation, displacement of a chromosome or part of it to another chromosome.

translúcido-a *a.* translucent.

transmigración *f.* transmigration, the passing from one place to another such as of blood cells in diapedesis.

transmisible *a.* transmissible, that can be transmitted.

transmisión *f.* transmission, the act of transmitting, such as an infectious disease or a hereditary condition; ___ placentaria / placental ___; ___ por contacto / ___ by contact; ___ por instilación / droplet ___.

transmural *a.* transmural, that occurs or is administered through a wall.

transmutación *f.* transmutation. 1. transformation, evolutionary change; 2. change of one chemical into another.

transocular *a.* transocular, that occurs or passes through the orbit of the eye.

transonancia *f.* transonance, transmitted resonance.

transorbitorio-a *a.* transorbital, that occurs or passes through the orbit of the eye.

transparencia *f.* transparency; [*diapositiva*] slide.

transparente *a.* transparent, clear.

transplacentario-a *a.* transplacental, that occurs through the placenta.

transpleural *a.* transpleural, that occurs or is administered through the pleura.

transporte *m.* transport, the movement of materials within the body, esp. across the cellular membrane.

transposición *f.* transposition. 1. displacement of an organ to the opposite side; 2. displacement of genetic material from one chromosome to another resulting at times in congenital defects.

transposición de los grandes vasos *f.* transposition of great vessels, congenital defect by which the aorta arises from the right ventricle and the pulmonary artery from the left ventricle.

transuretral *a.* transurethral, that occurs or is administered through the urethra.

transvaginal *a.* transvaginal, that occurs or is done through the vagina.

transversal *a.* transverse, across; plano ___ / ___ plane.

transvestido-a, transvestita *m., f.* transvestite, person who practices transvestism.

transvestismo *m.* transvestism, adoption of modalities of the opposite sex, esp. dress.

trapecio *m.* trapezius, flat triangular muscle essential in the rotation of the scapula.

tráquea *f.* trachea, respiratory conduit between the inferior extremity of the larynx and the beginning of the bronchi; *pop.* windpipe.

traqueal *a.* tracheal, rel. to the trachea.

traqueítis *f.* tracheitis, infl. of the trachea.

traqueoesofágico-a *a.* tracheoesophageal, rel. to the trachea and the esophagus.

traqueomalacia *f.* tracheomalacia, softening of the cartilages of the trachea.

traqueostenosis *f.* tracheostenosis, narrowing of the trachea.

traqueostomía *f. surg.* tracheostomy, incision into the trachea through the neck to allow the passage of air in cases of obstruction.

traqueotomía *f. surg.* tracheotomy, incision into the trachea through the skin and muscles of the neck.

tras *prep.* after, behind.

trasero *m. pop.* buttocks, rear.

trasmitir *v.* to transmit.

trasplantación *f.* transplantation, the act of making a transplant; ___ autoplástica / autoplastic ___; ___ heteroplástica / heteroplastic ___; ___ homotópica / homotopic ___.

trasplantar *v.* to transplant.

trasplante *m.* transplant, the transfer of an organ or tissue from a donor to a recipient, or from one part of the body to another in order to replace a diseased organ or to restitute impaired function.

trastornado-a *a.* deranged, mentally disturbed.

trastorno *m.* disturbance, disorder, derangement; ___ del proceso metabólico / deranged metabollic process; ___ mental / mental disorder.

trasudado *m.* transudate, fluid that has passed through a membrane or that has been forced out from a tissue as a result of infl.

tratado-a *a.* treated; no ___ / untreated.

tratamiento *m.* treatment, method, or procedure used in curing illnesses, lesions, or malformations; método o plan de ___ / ___ plan; ___ de desintoxicación / withdrawal ___; sujeto a ___ / under ___.

tratar *v.* [*a un paciente*] to treat; to try.

trato *m.* care; treatment; **buen** ___ / good ___; **mal** ___ / bad ___.

trauma, traumatismo *m.* trauma. 1. physical injury caused by an external agent; 2. *psych.* severe emotional shock.

traumático-a *a.* traumatic, rel. to, resulting from, or causing trauma.

traumatizar *vi.* to traumatize, to injure.

traumatología *f.* traumatology, the branch

of *surg*. that deals with injuries and wounds and their treatment.

trazador *m*. tracer, a radioisotope that when introduced into the body leaves a trace that can be detected and followed.

trazar *vi*. to trace.

trazo *m*. tracing, the graphic record of movement or change made by an instrument.

trefinación *f*. *surg*. trephination, the act of removing a circular disk of bone, gen. from the skull, or of removing tissue from the cornea or sclera.

Trematoda *Gr*. Trematoda, a class of parasitic worms that includes the flatworms and the flukes, both pathogenic to humans.

tremendo-a *a*. tremendous.

tremor *m*. tremor, trembling.

trémulo-a *a*. tremulous, rel. to or affected by a tremor.

Trendelenburg, posición de *f*. Trendelenburg position, slanted position used in abdominal surgery in which the body and lower extremities are placed higher than the head.

trepanación *f*. *surg*. trepanation, perforation of the skull with a special instrument to relieve increased pressure caused by fracture or accumulation of intracranial blood or pus.

trepanar *v*. to trepan, to perforate with a trepan.

trépano *m*. trepan, bur, burr, type of drill used for trepanation.

Treponema *Gr*. Treponema, microorganisms of the genus *Spirochaetales,* some of which are pathogenic to humans and other animals; ___ pallidum / ___ pallidum, causing agent of syphilis.

treponema *m*. treponema, any organism of the genus *Treponema*.

treponemiasis *f*. treponemiasis, infection with organisms of the genus *Treponema*.

triada *f*. triad, a group of three related elements, objects or symptoms.

triage *Fr*. triage, screening and classification of injured persons during a battle or disaster for the purpose of establishing priority of treatment in order to maximize the number who will survive.

triangular *a*. triangular.

triángulo *m*. triangle.

tribu *f*. tribe.

tríceps *m*. triceps, a three-headed muscle; reflejo del ___ / ___ reflex.

tricobezoar *m*. trichobezoar, concretion or bezoar of hair found in the intestine or stomach.

tricomonas *m*. *V*. **Trichomonas.**

tricomoniasis *f*. trichomoniasis, infestation with *Trichomonas*.

tricromático-a *a*. trichromatic, rel. to or consisting of three colors.

tricúspide *a*. tricuspid. 1. having three points; 2. rel. to the tricuspid valve of the heart; atresia ___ / ___ atresia; soplo ___ / ___ murmur; válvula ___ / ___ valve.

Trichinella *Gr*. Trichinella, a genus of nematode worms parasitic in carnivorous mammals.

Trichomonas *Gr*. **tricomonas** *m*. Trichomonas, a genus of parasitic protozoa that lodge in the alimentary and genitourinary tracts of vertebrates; ___ vaginal / ___ vaginalis.

trifásico-a *a*. triphasic, occurring in three stages, esp. in relation to electric currents.

trifocal *a*. trifocal.

trigémino-a *a*. trigeminal, rel. to the trigeminus nerve; neuralgia ___ / ___ neuralgia.

trigeminus *L*. trigeminus, trigeminus nerve. *V*. **craneales, nervios.**

trigo *m*. wheat; germen de ___ / ___ germ.

trigonitis *f*. trigonitis, infl. of the trigone of the urinary bladder.

trígono *m*. trigone, space or area in a triangular shape.

trigueño-a *a*. dark-complexioned, brunet, brunette.

trimestre *m*. trimester, three-month period.

trinchera *f*. trench, ditch, moat, fiebre de ___ / ___ fever; pie de ___ / ___ foot, infection caused by exposition to severe cold.

tripas *f*. tripe, gut.

Tripanosoma *m*. *V*. **Trypanosoma.**

tripanosomiasis *f*. trypanosomiasis, infection caused by a flagellated organism of the genus *Trypanosoma*.

tripanosómico-a *a*. trypanosomal, caused by or belonging to the genus *Trypanosoma*.

triple *a*. triple, that consists of three components.

triplopia *f*. triplopia, eye disorder by which three images of the same object are seen at one time.

tripsina *f.* trypsin, an enzyme present in the pancreatic juice formed by trypsinogen.

tripsinógeno *m.* trypsinogen, inactive substance released by the pancreas into the duodenum to form trypsin.

triptófano *m.* tryptophan, crystalline amino acid present in proteins essential to animal life.

triquina *f.* trichina, a worm that lives as a parasite in the muscles in the larval stage, and in the intestines when mature.

triquinosis *f.* trichinosis, disease acquired by ingestion of raw or inadequately cooked meat, esp. pork, that contains the larvae of *Trichinella spiralis*.

triquitis *f.* trichitis, infl. of hair bulbs.

trismo *m.* trismus, a spasm of the mastication muscles.

trisomía *f.* trisomy, genetic disorder by which there are three homologous chromosomes per cell instead of the usual two (diploid), causing severe fetal malformation.

triste *a.* sad, sorrowful.

tristeza *f.* sadness; sorrow.

trituración *f.* trituration; pulverization.

triturar *v.* to triturate, to crush, to grind; to shatter in many small fragments.

triunfar *v.* to succeed.

triunfo *m.* success, triumph.

trocánter *m.* trochanter, each of the two outer prominences below the neck of the femur; ____ mayor / major ____ ; ____ menor / lesser ____ .

tróclea *f.* trochlea, structure that functions as a pulley.

trófico-a *a.* trophic, rel. to nutrition.

trombectomía *f. surg.* trombectomy, removal of a thrombus.

trombina *f.* thrombin, an enzyme present in extravasated blood which catalyzes the conversion of fibrinogen to fibrin.

trombinógeno *m.* thrombinogen. *V.* **protrombina.**

trombo *m.* thrombus, a blood clot that causes a total or partial vascular obstruction; ____ blanco / white ____ , pale; ____ estratificado / stratified ____ , layered; ____ mural / mural ____ , attached to the wall of the endocardium; ____ oclusivo / occluding ____ , that closes the vessel completely.

tromboangiítis *f.* thromboangiitis, thrombosis of a blood vessel.

trombocito *m.* thrombocyte, platelet.

trombocitopenia *f.* thrombocytopenia, ab-

normal decrease in the number of blood platelets.

trombocitosis *f.* thrombocytosis, abnormal increase in the number of blood platelets.

tromboembolia *f.* thromboembolism, obstruction of a blood vessel by a blood clot that has broken away from its site of origin.

tromboflebitis *f.* thrombophlebitis, dilation of a vein wall associated with thrombosis.

trombogénesis *f.* thrombogenesis, formation of blood clots.

trombólisis *f.* thrombolysis, dissolution of a thrombus.

trombolítico-a *a.* thrombolytic, rel. to or causing the dissolution of a thrombus.

trombosado-a *a.* thrombosed, rel. to a blood vessel containing a thrombus.

trombosis *f.* thrombosis, formation, development, or presence of a thrombus; ____ biliar / biliary ____ ; ____ cardíaca / cardiac ____ ; ____ coronaria / coronary ____ ; ____ embólica / embolic ____ ; ____ traumática / traumatic ____ ; ____ venosa / venous ____ .

trombótico-a *a.* thrombotic, rel. to or affected by thrombosis.

trompa *f.* tube, conduit; ligadura de las ____ -s / tubal ligation.

troncal *a.* truncal, rel. to the trunk of the body.

tronco *m.* trunk, the human body exclusive of the head and the extremities.

tropezar *vi.* to bump or stumble into something or somebody.

tropical *a.* tropical, rel. to the tropics.

tropismo *m.* tropism, the reaction of a cell or living organism toward or away from the source of an external stimulus.

truncado-a *a.* truncate, having the end squarely cut off; amputated.

truncar *vi.* to truncate, to cut off, to shorten; to amputate.

truncus *L.* truncus, trunk.

Trypanosoma *m. Trypanosoma*, a genus of parasitic protozoa found in the blood of many vertebrates, transmitted to them by insect vectors.

tsetsé *m.* tsetse fly, blood sucking fly of southern Africa that transmits sleeping sickness.

tuba *L.* tuba, tube; ____ acústica / eustachian tube.

tubario-a *a.* tubal, rel. to a tube; embarazo

___ / ___ pregnancy, that occurs in the fallopian tube.

tuber *L*. (*pl*. **tubera**) tuber, enlargement.

tubercular *a*. tubercular, rel. to or marked by tubercles.

tuberculicida *a*. tuberculocidal, that destroys the tubercle bacilli.

tuberculina *f*. tuberculin, compound prepared from the tubercle bacillus and used in the diagnosis of tuberculosis infection; prueba de la ___ / ___ test.

tubérculo *m*. tubercle. 1. small nodule; 2. small knobby prominence of a bone; 3. the characteristic lesion produced by the tuberculosis bacilli.

tuberculosis *f*. tuberculosis, an acute or chronic bacterial infection caused by the germ *Mycobacterium tuberculosis* that gen. affects the lungs, although it can affect other organs as well; ___ espinal / spinal ___ ; ___ infantil / childhood ___ ; ___ meníngea / meningeal ___ ; ___ pulmonar / pulmonary ___ ; ___ urogenital / urogenital ___ .

tuberculosis miliar *f*. miliary tuberculosis, disease that invades the organism through the blood stream and is characterized by the formation of minute tubercles in the different organs affected by it.

tuberculoso-a *a*. tuberculous, rel. to tuberculosis or affected by it.

tuberculum *L*. tuberculum, tubercle.

tuberosidad *f*. tuber, a swelling or enlargement.

tuberoso-a *a*. tuberous, rel. to or resembling a tuber.

tubo *m*. tube, elongated, cylindrical, hollow structure; ___ colector / collecting tubule; ___ contorneado del riñón / convoluted tubule of the kidney; ___ de drenaje / drainage ___ ; ___ de ensayo / test ___ ; ___ de toracostomía / thoracostomy ___ ; ___ de traqueotomía / tracheotomy ___ ; ___ en t / T-___ ; ___ endotraquial / endotracheal ___ ; ___ nasogástrico / nasogastric ___ ; ___ urinífero / uriniferous tubule.

tuboovárico-a *a*. tubo-ovarian, rel. to the fallopian tube and the ovary; absceso ___ / ___ abscess.

tuboplastia *f*. *surg*. tuboplasty, plastic surgery of a tube, esp. the fallopian tube.

túbulo *m*. tubule, a small anatomical tube;

___ colector / collecting ___ ; ___ renal / renal ___ .

tuerto-a *a*. one-eyed or blind in one eye.

tularemia *f*. tularemia, rabbit fever, infection transmitted to humans by the bite of a vector insect or by handling of infected meat.

tumefacción, tumescencia *f*. tumefaction, the process of swelling.

tumor *m*. tumor, swelling, new spontaneous growth of mass or tissue of no physiological use.

tumoral *a*. tumorous, rel. to a tumor.

tumoricida *a*. tumoricidal, that destroys tumorous cells.

tumorigénesis *f*. tumorigenesis, production of tumors.

túnel *m*. tunnel, a bodily channel; ___ del carpo / carpal ___ ; ___ flexor / flexor ___ ; ___ torsal, tarsiano / torsal ___ .

tunica *L*. tunica, tunic, protective membrane; ___ adventicia / ___ adventitia; ___ albugínea / ___ albuginea; ___ dartos / ___ dartos, ___ mucosa / ___ mucosa; ___ muscular / ___ muscularis; ___ serosa / ___ serosa; ___ vaginal / ___ vaginalis.

túnica *f*. tunic, covering, outer layer of an organ or part.

tupido-a *a*. plugged, obstructed; oídos ___ / ___ ears.

turbinado-a *a*. turbinate. 1. rel. to the nasal concha; 2. shaped like a dome.

turbio-a *a*. turbid, cloudy, not transluscent.

túrgido-a *a*. turgid, distended, swollen.

turgor *m*. turgor. 1. swelling, distention; 2. normal cellular tension.

Turner, síndrome de *m*. Turner's syndrome, congenital endocrine abnormality manifested by amenorrhea, failure of sexual maturation, short stature and neck, and the presence of only forty-five chromosomes.

turno *m*. turn; [*cita*] appointment; shift.

tusivo-a *a*. tussive, rel. to cough or caused by it.

tussis *L*. tussis, cough.

tympanum *L*. tympanum, the middle ear. *V*. **tímpano**.

U

U *abr*. **unidad** / unit; **uranio** / uranium; **urología** / urology.

u *conj.* or, used instead of *o* before words beginning with *o* or *ho*.

ubre *f.* udder, mammary gland of female animals, such as cows.

úlcera *f.* ulcer, sore, or lesion of the skin or mucous membrane with gradual desintegration of tissue; ____ duodenal / duodenal ____ ; ____ gástrica / gastric ____ ; ____ perforante / perforating ____ ; ____ por decúbito / decubitus ____ , bedsore; ____ roedora / rodent ____ , that destroys gradually; ____ varicosa crónica de la pierna / chronic varicose leg ____ ; ____ vesical / vesical ____ .

úlcera péptica *f.* peptic ulcer, ulceration of the mucous membranes of the esophagus, stomach, or duodenum caused by excessive acidity of the gastric juice, gen. produced by acute or chronic stress.

ulceración *f.* ulceration, the formation process of an ulcer.

ulcerado-a *a.* ulcerated, rel. to or of the nature of an ulcer.

ulcerar *v.* to ulcerate.

ulcerativo *a.* ulcerative, rel. to an ulcer or that causes it.

ulceroso-a *a.* ulcerous, rel. to an ulcer or affected by one.

uleritema *m.* ulerythema, erimatose dermatitis characterized by formation of scars.

ulnar *a.* ulnar, rel. to the ulna or to the arteries and nerves related to it.

ulocarcinoma *m.* ulocarcinoma, cancer of the gums.

último-a *a.* last, ultimate, final; **-mente** *adv.* lately; **por** ____ / finally.

ultracentrífuga *f.* ultracentrifuge, machine with a centrifugal force capable of separating and sedimenting the molecules of a substance.

ultraestructura *f.* ultrastructure, structure of the smallest elements of a body, visible only through an electron microscope.

ultrafiltración *f.* ultrafiltration, a filtration process that allows the passage of small molecules, holding back larger ones.

ultramicroscopio *m.* ultramicroscope, a microscope that makes visible objects that cannot be seen under a common light microscope.

ultrasónico-a *a.* ultrasonic. *V.* **supersónico.**

ultrasonido *m.* ultrasound, a sound wave with a frequency above the range of human hearing used in ultrasonography for diagnostic and therapeutic purposes; diagnóstico por ____ / ultrasonic diagnosis.

ultrasonografía *f.* ultrasonography, diagnostic technique that uses ultrasound waves to develop the image of a structure or tissue of the body.

ultrasonograma *m.* ultrasonogram, the image produced by ultrasonography.

ultravioleta *a.* ultraviolet, beyond the visible violet end of the spectrum; rayos ____ / ____ rays; terapia de radiación ____ / ____ therapy.

ululación *f.* ululation, the act of screaming hysterically as seen in mental patients.

umbilical *a.* umbilical, rel. to the umbilicus.

umbral *m.* threshold, the minimum degree of stimulus needed to produce an effect or response; ____ absoluto / absolute ____ ; ____ auditivo / auditory ____ ; ____ de la conciencia / ____ of consciousness; ____ renal / renal ____ ; ____ sensorio / sensory ____ .

unánime *a.* unanimous.

unción *f.* unction; ointment.

ungueal *a.* ungual, rel. to the nails.

ungüento *m.* unguent, liniment, salve, medicated preparation for external use.

uniarticular *a.* uniarticular, rel. to a single joint.

unibásico-a *a.* unibasal, rel. to a single base.

unicelular *a.* unicellar, having only one cell.

único-a *a.* only, sole; **-mente** *adv.* only, solely.

unidad *f.* unit. 1. one of a kind; ____ motora / motor ____ , that provides motor activity; 2. standard of measurement; 3. unity.

unidad internacional *f.* international unit, standard measurement of a given substance as adopted by the International Conference for Unification of Formulae.

unido-a *a.* joined; close.

uniforme *m.* uniform; *a.* uniform, even.

unigrávida *f.* unigravida, woman who is pregnant for the first time.

unilateral *a.* unilateral, rel. to one side only.

unión *f.* union. 1. the action or effect of joining two things into one; 2. the growing together of severed parts of a bone or of the lips of a wound.

unípara *f.* uniparous, woman who gives birth to only one child.

unipolar *a.* unipolar, having one pole, such as the nerve cells.

unir *v.* to join; to unite, to merge.

unitario-a *a.* unitary, rel. to a single unit.

universal *a.* universal, general.

universidad *f.* university.

universo *m.* universe.

Unna, bota de pasta de *f.* Unna's paste boot, compression dressing applied to the lower part of the leg in the treatment of varicose ulcers consisting of layers of gauze applied with and covered by Unna's paste.

unsinaria *f.* hookworm, intestinal parasite; enfermedad de la ___ / ___ disease.

untadura *f.* application; ointment.

untar *v.* to oint, to rub, to smear.

untuoso-a *a.* unctuous, greasy, oily.

uña *f.* nail; ___ **del dedo del pie** / toenail; ___ **encarnada** / ingrown ___ ; *vr.* **comerse las** ___ **-s** / to bite one's ___ -s.

uñero *m.* ingrown nail.

uranio *m* uranium, heavy metallic element.

urato *m.* urate, uric acid salt.

urea *f.* urea, crystalline substance found in the blood, lymph, and urine, that is the final product of the metabolism of proteins and is excreted through the urine as nitrogen.

ureico-a *a.* ureal, rel. to urea.

uremia *f.* uremia, toxic condition caused by renal insufficiency that produces retention of nitrogen substances, phosphates, and sulphates in the blood.

urémico-a *a.* uremic, rel. to or affected by uremia.

uréter *m.* ureter, one of the ducts by which urine passes from the kidney to the urinary bladder.

ureteral, uretérico-a *a.* ureteral, rel. to a ureter; obstrucción ___ / ___ obstruction.

ureterectasis *f.* ureterectasis, abnormal dilation of the ureter.

ureterectomía *f.* *surg.* ureterectomy, partial or total excision of the ureter.

ureteritis *f.* ureteritis, infl. of the ureter.

ureterocele *m.* ureterocele, cystic dilation of the distal intravesical portion of the ureter due to stenosis of the ureteral orifice.

ureterocistoneostomía *f.* *surg.* uretercystoneostomy. *V.* **ureteroneocistostomía.**

ureterocistostomía *f.* *surg.* ureterocystostomy. *V.* **ureteroneocistostomía.**

ureterografía *f.* ureterography, X-ray of the ureter with the use of a radiopaque substance.

ureteroheminefrectomía *f.* *surg.* ureteroheminephrectomy, resection of a portion of the kidney and its ureter in cases of duplication of the upper urinary tract.

ureterohidronefrosis *f.* ureterohydronephrosis, distension of the ureter and the kidney due to obstruction.

ureteroileostomía *f.* *surg.* ureteroileostomy, anastomosis of a ureter to an isolated segment of the ileum.

ureterolitiasis *f.* ureterolithiasis, formation of a ureteral calculus.

ureterolitotomía *f.* *surg.* ureterolithotomy, incision into a ureter for removal of a calculus.

ureteronefrectomía *f.* *surg.* ureteronephrectomy, excision of the kidney and its ureter.

ureteroneocistostomía *f.* *surg.* ureteroneocystostomy, reimplantation of the ureter into the bladder.

ureteropieloplastia *f.* *surg.* ureteropyeloplasty, plastic surgery of a ureter and the renal pelvis.

ureteroplastia *f.* *surg.* ureteroplasty, plastic surgery of the ureter.

ureterosigmoidostomía *f.* *surg.* ureterosigmoidostomy, implantation of a ureter in the sigmoid colon.

ureterostomía *f.* *surg.* ureterostomy, formation of a permanent fistula for drainage of a ureter.

ureterotomía *f.* ureterotomy, incision into a ureter.

ureteroureterostomía *f.* *surg.* ureteroureterostomy, anastomosis of two ureters or of extreme parts of the same ureter.

ureterovesical *a.* ureterovesical, rel. to the ureter and the urinary bladder.

uretra *f.* urethra, urinary canal.

uretral *a.* urethral, rel. to the urethra; estrechez ___ / ___ stricture.

uretralgia *f.* urethralgia, pain in the urethra.

uretrectomía *f.* *surg.* urethrectomy, partial or total excision of the urethra.

uretritis *f.* urethritis, chronic or acute infl. of the urethra.

uretrografía *f.* urethrography, X-ray of the urethra after injection of a radiopaque substance.

uretroscopio *m.* urethroscope, instrument for viewing the interior of the urethra.

uretrotomía *f.* *surg.* urethrotomy, incision of the urethra, usu. to alleviate a stricture.

uretrótomo *m.* urethrotome, instrument used in urethrotomy.

urgente *a.* urgent, pressing; **-mente** *adv.* urgently.

uricemia *f.* uricemia, excess uric acid in the blood.

úrico-a *a.* uric, rel. to the urine.

uricosuria *f.* uricosuria, presence of an excessive amount of uric acid in the urine.

urinación *f.* urination, the act of urinating.

urinálisis *m.* urinalysis, analysis of the urine.

urinario-a *a.* urinary, rel. to the urine; infección ___ / ___ infection; órganos ___ -s / ___ organs; sedimento ___ / ___ sediment.

urinario, sistema *m.* urinary system, the group of organs and conduits that participate in the production and excretion of urine.

urinífero-a *a.* uriniferous, that contains or carries urine.

urinogenital, urogenital *a.* urinogenital, urogenital, rel. to the urinary and the genital tracts.

urinoma *m.* urinoma, urine containing cyst or tumor.

urobilinógeno *m.* urobilinogen, pigment derived from the reduction of bilirubin by action of intestinal bacteria.

urocinasa *f.* urokinase, enzyme present in human urine used to dissolve blood clots.

urodinámica *f.* urodynamics, the study of the active process and pathophysyology of urination.

urodinia *f.* urodynia, painful urination.

urogenital *a.* urogenital, rel. to the urinary and the genital tracts; diafragma ___ / ___ diaphragm.

urografía *f.* urography, X-ray of a part of the urinary tract by injection of a radiopaque substance; ___ descendente o excretora / descending or excretory ___ ; ___ retrógrada / retrograde ___ .

urograma *m.* urogram, X-ray record of a urography.

urolitiasis *f.* urolithiasis, formation of urinary calculi and disorders associated with their presence.

urolítico-a *a.* urolithic, rel. to urinary calculi.

urología *f.* urology, the branch of medicine that studies the diagnosis and treatment of diseases of the genitourinary tract in men and the urinary tract in women.

urológico-a *a.* urologic, rel. to urology.

úrologo-a *m., f.* specialist in urology.

uropatía *f.* uropathy, any disease that affects the urinary tract.

urticaria *f.* urticaria, hives, eruptive skin disease characterized by pink patches accompanied by intense itching, gen. allergic in nature, that can be caused by an internal or external agent.

usado-a *a.* used.

usar *v.* to use; [*ropa*] to wear.

uso *m.* use; function; usage.

usual *a.* usual, customary; **-mente** *adv.* usually.

uterino-a *a.* uterine, rel. to the uterus; prolapso ___ / ___ prolapse; ruptura ___ / ___ rupture; sangramiento ___ / ___ bleeding unrelated to menstruation.

útero *m.* uterus, womb, hollow muscular organ of the female reproductive system that contains and nourishes the embryo and fetus during the period of gestation; cáncer del ___ o de la matriz / uterine cancer; ___ didelfo / didelphys ___ , double uterus.

uterosalpingografía *f.* uterosalpingography, X-ray examination of the uterus and the fallopian tubes following injection of a radiopaque substance.

uterovaginal *a.* uterovaginal, rel. to the uterus and the vagina.

uterovesical *a.* uterovesical, rel. to the uterus and the urinary bladder.

útil *a.* useful, practical.

uva *f.* grape.

úvea *f.* uvea, the vascular layer of the eye formed by the iris and the ciliary body together with the choroid coat.

uveítis *f.* uveitis, infl. of the uvea.

úvula *f.* uvula, small, fleshy structure hanging in the middle of the posterior border of the soft palate.

V

V *abr.* **válvula** / valve; **vena** / vein; **visión** / vision; **volumen** / volume.

vaca *f.* cow.

vacaciones *f. pl.* vacations.

vaccinia *L.* vaccinia, cowpox, a virus that causes disease in cattle and that when inoculated in humans gives a degree of immunity against smallpox.

vaciar *v.* to empty; to flush out, to void; **vaciarse** *vr.* to become empty.

vacilante *a.* vacillating, fluctuating; shaky.

vacilar *v.* to vacillate; to fluctuate; to hesitate.

vacío-a *a.* empty; envasado al ___ / vacuum packed.

vacuna *f.* vaccine, a preparation of attenuated or killed microorganisms that when introduced in the body establishes immunity to the specific disease caused by the microorganisms; ___ antipolio oral, trivalente atenuada de Sabin / poliovirus, live oral trivalent ___, Sabin; ___ antirrábica / rabies ___; ___ antisarampión de virus vivo / measles virus ___, live; ___ antisarampión, inactivada / measles virus ___, inactivated; ___ antitífica / typhoid fever ___; ___ antivariólica, antivariolosa / smallpox ___; ___ BCG, contra la tuberculosis / BCG ___ against tuberculosis, ___ contra la influenza / influenza ___; ___ de Salk, contra la poliomielitis / Salk, antipolio; ___ neumocócica polivalente / pneumococcal polyvalent virus ___; ___ de virus vivo contra la rubéola / rubella virus ___, live; ___ triple contra la difteria, el tétano y la tos ferina / DPT ___, against diphteria, pertussis and tetanus.

vacunación *f.* vaccination, inoculation of vaccine.

vacunar *v.* to vaccinate.

vacuola *f.* vacuole, small cavity or space filled with fluid or air in the cellular protoplasm of a cell.

vacuolización *f.* vacuolization, formation of vacuoles.

vacuum *L.* vacuum, emptiness, a space devoid of air or matter.

vagal *a.* vagal, rel. to the pneumogastric or vagus nerve.

vagante *a.* vagrant, that wanders; loose, free.

vagar *vi.* to wander.

vagina *f.* vagina. 1. female canal extending from the uterus to the vulva; 2. structure resembling a sheath.

vaginal *a.* vaginal, rel. to the vagina or to a sheath-like structure.

vaginismus *L.* vaginismus, sudden and painful spasm of the vagina.

vaginitis *f.* vaginitis, infl. of the vagina.

vago-a *a.* vague, indistinct; **-mente** *adv.* vaguely.

vago, nervio *m.* vagus nerve. V. **nervios craneales.**

vagolítico-a *a.* vagolytic, that inhibits the function of the vagus nerve.

vagotomía *f.* *surg.* vagotomy, interruption of the vagus nerve.

vahido *m.* dizziness, fainting spell.

vaina *f.* sheath, a protective covering structure.

vainilla *f.* vanilla.

vaivén *m.* swaying; *pop.* to and fro.

valencia *f.* valence, valency.

valer *vi.* to cost; to be worth; to be valid, good or acceptable; *vr.* **valerse por sí mismo** / to be self-sufficient.

valgus *L.* valgus, bent or twisted outward.

validez *f.* validity.

válido-a *a.* valid, acceptable.

valiente *a.* valiant, brave, courageous.

valioso-a *a.* valuable, of worth.

valor *m.* value, worth.

valorización *f.* valorization, evaluation.

Valsalva, maniobra de *f.* Valsalva's maneuver, procedure to test the patency of the eustachian tubes or to adjust the pressure of the middle ear by forcibly exhaling while holding the nostrils and mouth closed.

válvula *f.* valve, a membranous structure in a canal or orifice that closes temporarily to prevent the backward flow of the contents passing through it; ___ aórtica / aortic ___, between the left ventricle and the aorta; ___ atrioventricular derecha, tricúspide / atrioventricular ___ right, tricuspid; ___ atrioventricular izquierda, bicúspide, mitral / atrioventricular ___ left, bicuspid, mitral; ___ ileocecal / ileocecal ___; ___ pilórica / pyloric ___; ___ pulmonar / pulmonary.

válvula mitral *f.* mitral valve, the left atrioventricular valve of the heart; insuficiencia de la ___ / insufficiency of the ___; prolapso de la ___ / prolapse of the ___.

válvulas conniventes *f. pl.* valvulae conniventes, circular membranous folds found in the small intestine that slow the passage of food along the bowels.

valvuloplastia *f.* *surg.* valvuloplasty, plastic surgery of a heart valve.

valvulótomo *m.* valvulotome, instrument to incise a valve.

vano-a *a.* vain; **en** ___ / in vain, needlessly.

vapor *m.* vapor, gas, fume.

vaporización *f.* vaporization. 1. action and effect of vaporizing; 2. therapeutic use of vapors.

vaporizador *m.* vaporizer, device used to convert a substance into a vapor for therapeutic purposes.

vaporizar *vi.* to vaporize, to change a substance into vapor.

variabilidad *f.* variability.

variable *f.* variable, a changing factor; *a.* that can change.

variación *f.* variation, diversity in the characteristic of related elements.

variado-a *a.* varied.

variante *f.* variant, that which is essentially the same as another but different in form; *a.* different, that changes.

variar *v.* to change, to vary.

várice *f.* varix, an enlarged and tortuous vein, artery or lymphatic vessel.

varicella *L.* varicella, chicken pox, viral contagious disease, gen. manifested during childhood, characterized by an eruption that evolves into small vesicles.

varicocele *m.* varicocele, varicose condition of the veins of the spermatic cord that produces a soft mass in the scrotum.

varicoide *a.* varicoid, that resembles a varix.

varicoso-a *a.* varicose, that resembles or is related to varices; venas ___-s / ___ veins.

varicotomía *f. surg.* varicotomy, excision of a varicose vein.

variedad *f.* variety.

varilla *f.* thin, short rod; wand; ___ de aceite / dipstick.

variola *L.* variola. V. **viruela.**

variólico-a, varioloso-a *a.* variolic, variolous, rel. to smallpox or affected by it.

varioliforme *a.* varioliform, resembling smallpox.

varios-as *a.* several.

varón *m.* male.

varonil *a.* manly.

varus *L.* varus, twisted or turned inward.

vas *L.* (*pl.* **vasa**) vas, vessel; ___ recta / ___ recta; ___ vasorum / ___ vasorum.

vas deferens *L.* vas deferens, the excretory duct of the spermatozoa.

vascular *a.* vascular, rel. to the blood vessels; sistema ___ / ___ system, all the vessels of the body, esp. the blood vessels.

vascularización *f.* vascularization, formation of new blood vessels.

vascularizar *vi.* to vascularize, to develop new blood vessels.

vasculatura *f.* vasculature, arrangement of blood vessels in an organ or part.

vasculitis *f.* vasculitis. V. **angitis.**

vasculopatía *f.* vasculopathy, any disease of a blood vessel.

vasectomía *f. surg.* vasectomy, partial excision and ligation of the vas deferens to prevent the passage of spermatozoa into the semen, usu. done as a means of birth control.

vaselina *f.* vaseline, petroleum jelly.

vasija *f.* receptacle, vessel.

vaso *m.* vessel; conduit. 1. any channel or tube that carries fluid such as blood or lymph; ___ colateral / collateral ___ ; ___ linfático / lymphatic ___ ; grandes ___-s / great ___-s; ___ sanguíneo / blood ___ ; 2. a glass for drinking.

vasoactivo *m.* vasoactive, agent that affects the blood vessels.

vasoconstricción *f.* vasoconstriction, decrease in the caliber of the blood vessels.

vasoconstrictor *m.* vasoconstrictor, that which causes vasoconstriction; **-a** *a.* vasoconstrictive, rel. to constriction of the blood vessels.

vasodilatación *f.* vasodilation, increase in the caliber of the blood vessels.

vasodilatador *m.* vasodilator, that which causes vasodilation; **-a** *a.* that causes vasodilation.

vasomotor *m.* vasomotor, that which regulates the contraction and dilation of blood vessels; **-a** *a.* rel. to dilation or contraction of blood vessels.

vasopresina *f.* vasopressin, hormone secreted by the posterior pituitary gland that increases the reabsorption of water by the kidneys, raising the blood pressure.

vasopresor *m.* vasopressor, that which has a vasoconstrictive effect; **-a** *a.* having a vasoconstrictive effect.

vasospasmo *m.* vasospasm. V. **angioespasmo;** ___ coronario / coronary ___ .

vasotónico-a *a.* vasotonic, rel. to a vessel tone.

vasovagal *a.* vasovagal, rel. to the vessels and the vagus nerve; síncope ___ / ___ syncope, brief fainting spell caused by vascular and vagal disturbances.

vasto-a *a. V.* **vastus.**

vastus *L.* vastus, dilated, large, extensive.

Vater, ámpula de *f.* Vater's ampulla or papilla, the point where the biliar and pancreatic excretory systems enter the duodenum.

vecino-a *m., f.* neighbor.

vector *m.* vector, a carrier that transmits infectious agents.

vegetación *f.* vegetation, a wart-like abnormal growth upon a body part as seen in endocarditis.

vegetal *m.* vegetable; *a.* vegetal, rel. to plants.

vegetarianismo *m.* vegetarianism, the practice of eating only vegetables and fruits. Dairy products may not be excluded.

vegetariano-a *m., f.* individual who eats mainly vegetables; *a.* rel. to vegetables.

vegetativo-a *a.* vegetative. 1. rel. to functions of growth and nutrition; 2. rel. to involuntary or unconscious bodily movements; 3. pertaining to plants.

vehículo *m.* vehicle. 1. agent without therapeutic action that carries the active ingredient of a medication; 2. an agent of transmission.

vejez *f.* old age.

vejiga *f.* bladder; cálculos de la ___ / ___ calculi; irrigación de la ___ / ___ irrigation; ___ llena de aire / air ___ ; ___ neurogénica / neurogenic ___ .

vejiga urinaria *f.* urinary bladder, sac-shaped organ that serves as a receptacle to urine secreted by the kidneys.

vela *f.* candle.

velar *v.* to watch over, to take care of someone.

velo *m.* veil. 1. thin membrane or covering of a body part, 2. a piece of amniotic sac seen sometimes covering the face of a newborn; 3. slight alteration in the voice.

velocidad *f.* speed, velocity.

vello *m.* body hair; ___ púbico / pubic hair.

vellosidad *f.* villus, short, filiform projection from a membranous surface; ___ aracnoidea / arachnoid ___ ; ___ coriónica / chorionic ___ ; ___ -es intestinales (villi intestinales) / intestinal ___ ; ___ -es sinoviales / synovial ___ .

velloso-a, velludo-a *a.* villous, hairy.

vena *f.* vein, fibromuscular vessel that carries blood from the capillaries toward the heart.

vena cava *f.* vena cava, either of two large veins returning deoxygenated blood to the right atrium of the heart; ___ inferior / ___ inferior; ___ superior / ___ superior.

vencimiento *m.* expiration; fecha de ___ / ___ date.

venda *f.* bandage.

vendaje *m.* bandage, dressing, curative protective covering; ___ abdominal / abdominal binder; ___ de yeso / plaster cast; ___ protector / surgical dressing.

vendar *v.* to bandage.

vender *v.* to sell.

veneno *m.* poison, venom, toxic substance; centro de control de ___ -s / ___ control center.

venenoso-a *a.* poisonous, venenous, toxic; hiedra ___ / poison ivy.

venéreo-a *a.* venereal, resulting from or transmitted by sexual intercourse; enfermedad ___ / ___ disease.

venina *f.* venin, venine, toxic substance present in snake venom.

veninantivenina *f.* venin-antivenin, vaccine to counteract the effect of snake poison.

venipuntura *f.* venepuncture, venipuncture, surgical puncture of a vein.

venir *vi.* to come; ___ al caso / to be relevant.

venisección *f.* venisection. *V.* **flebotomía.**

venoclusivo-a *a.* veno-occlusive, rel. to the obstruction of veins.

venografía *f.* venography, recording of a venogram.

venograma *m.* venogram, X-ray of a vein with the use of a contrasting medium.

venoso-a *a.* venous, rel. to the veins; retorno ___ / ___ return; sangre ___ / ___ blood; seno ___ / ___ sinus; trombosis ___ / ___ thrombosis.

venotomía *f. surg.* venotomy. *V.* **flebotomía.**

vent *Fr.* vent, opening.

ventaja *f.* advantage.

ventajoso-a *a.* advantageous.

ventana *f.* window; ___ oval / oval ___ , aperture in the middle ear.

ventilación *f.* ventilation. 1. the act of circulating fresh air in a given area; 2. oxygenation of blood; 3. *psych.*, open discussion and airing of grievances.

ventilador *m.* ventilator, artificial respirator; fan.

ventilar *v.* to ventilate, to air.

ventolera *f.* strong gust of wind.

ventral *a.* ventral, abdominal, rel. to the belly or to the front side of the body; hernia ____ / ____ hernia.

ventricular *a.* ventricular, rel. to a ventricle; defecto del tabique ____ / ____ septal defect.

ventriculitis *f.* ventriculitis, infl. of a ventricle.

ventrículo *m.* ventricle, a small cavity, esp. in reference to such structures as seen in the heart, the brain, or the larynx; cuarto ____ del cerebro / fourth ____ of the brain; tercer ____ del cerebro / third ____ of the brain; ____ de la laringe / ____ of larynx; ____ derecho del corazón / right ____ of heart; ____ izquierdo del corazón / left ____ of heart; ____ lateral del cerebro / lateral ____ of the brain.

ventriculografía *f.* ventriculography. *V.* **neumoencefalografía.**

ventriculotomía *f. surg.* ventriculotomy, incision of a ventricle.

ventrodorsal *a.* ventrodorsal, rel. to the ventral and the dorsal surfaces.

vénula *f.* venule, minute vein that connects the capillaries with larger veins.

ver *vi.* to see; **está por** ____ / it remains to be seen; **tener que** ____ **con** / to have to do with; **verse** *vr.* to see oneself; to see each other.

verano *m.* summer.

verbatim *L.* verbatim, exactly as stated.

verbo *m. gr.* verb.

verdad *f.* truth; **decir la** ____ / to tell the ____ ; **de** ____ / truly, really; **¿no es** ____? / isn't it so?

verdadero-a *a.* true, real; pelvis ____ / ____ pelvis; **-mente** *adv.* truly.

verde *a.* green; not ripe.

verdugón *m.* welt.

verdura *f.* [*vegetales*] greens.

veredicto *m.* verdict.

vergonzoso-a *a.* shameful.

vergüenza *f.* shame; bashfulness; *v.* **tener** ____ / to be ashamed.

verificación *f.* verification, proof.

verificar *vi.* to verify, to prove true.

vermicida, vermífugo *m.* vermicide, agent that destroys worms.

vermiforme *a.* vermiform, worm-like, that resembles a worm; apéndice ____ / ____ appendix.

vermis *L.* vermis. 1. parasitic worm; 2. worm-like structure.

vernix *L.* vernix, varnish; ____ caseosa / ____ caseosa, sebaceous secretion protecting the skin of a fetus.

verruca *L.* (*pl.* **verrucae**) verruca, wart; ____ filiformis / ____ filiformis; ____ plantaris / ____ plantaris; ____ vulgaris / ____ vulgaris.

verruga *f. V.* **verruca.**

verrugoso-a *a.* verrucose, warty, or rel. to warts.

versátil *a.* versatile, that has multiple applications.

versión *f.* version. 1. change of direction of an organ, such as the uterus; 2. change of position of the fetus in utero to facilitate delivery; ____ bimanual / bimanual ____ ; ____ bipolar / bipolar ____ ; ____ cefálica / cephalic ____ ; ____ combinada / combined ____ ; ____ externa / external ____ ; ____ espontánea / spontaneous ____ .

vértebra *f.* vertebra, any of the thirty-three bones of the vertebral column; ____ cervical / cervical ____ ; ____ coccígea / coccygeal ____ ; ____ lumbar / lumbar ____ ; ____ sacra / sacral ____ ; ____ torácica / thoracic ____ .

vertebrado-a *a.* vertebrate, having a vertebral column or resembling one.

vertebral *a.* vertebral, rel. to the vertebrae; arteria ____ / ____ arthery; conducto ____ / ____ canal; costillas ____ -es / ____ ribs.

vertebrobasilar *a.* vertebrobasilar, rel. to the basilar and vertebral arteries.

verter *vi.* to spill; to pour.

vertex *L.* (*pl.* **vertices**) vertex. 1. the highest point of a structure, such as the top of the head; 2. convergence point of the two sides of an angle.

vertical *a.* vertical. 1. upright; 2. rel. to the vertex.

vértice *m. V.* **vertex.**

vertiginoso-a *a.* vertiginous, rel. to vertigo, that is affected by it or that produces it.

vértigo *m.* vertigo, whirling motion of either moving around space (subjective vertigo), or of objects moving around the person (objective vertigo) gen. caused by a disease of the inner ear or by gastric or cardiac disorders.

verumontanitis *f.* verumontanitis, infl. of the verumontanum.

verumontanum *L.* verumontanum, an elevation in the urethra at the point of entry of the seminal ducts.

vesicación *f.* vesication. 1. the formation of blisters; 2. a blister.

vesical *a.* vesical, rel. to or resembling a bladder.

vesicouretral *a.* vesicoureteral, rel. to the urinary bladder and the ureters.

vesicovaginal *a.* vesicovaginal, rel. to the urinary bladder and the vagina.

vesícula *f.* vesicle, vesicula, small sac or elevation of the skin containing serous fluid.

vesícula biliar *f.* gallbladder, pear-shaped receptacle on the lower part of the liver that stores bile.

vesicular *a.* vesicular, rel. to a vesicle.

vesiculoso-a *a.* vesiculate, of the nature of a vesicle.

vestibular *a.* vestibular, rel. to a vestibule; nervio ____ / ____ nerve.

vestíbulo *m.* vestibule. 1. space or cavity that gives access to a duct or canal; 2. lobby, waiting room.

vestigial *a.* vestigial, rudimentary, rel. to a vestige.

vestigio *m.* vestige, remains of a structure that was fully developed in a previous stage of the species or of the individual.

vestimenta *f.* clothing; garment.

vestir *vi.* to dress; **vestirse** *vr.* to dress oneself.

veterano-a *m., f.* veteran.

veterinaria *f.* veterinary, the science that deals with prevention and cure of animal diseases esp. domestic animals.

veterinario-a *m., f.* veterinarian, specialist in veterinary; *a.* rel. to veterinary.

vez *f.* time, occasion; **a la** ____ / at the same ____; **alguna** ____ / sometime; **cada** ____ / each ____; **de una** ____ / all at once; **de** ____ **en cuando** / once in a while; **en** ____ **de** / instead of; **otra** ____ / again; **rara** ____ / rarely; **tal** ____ / perhaps; **una** ____ / once.

vía *f.* tract, via, passage, conduit; ____-s biliares / biliary ____; ____-s digestivas / gastrointestinal ____; ____ olfatoria / olphactory ____; ____ piramidal / pyramidal ____; ____-s respiratorias / respiratory ____; ____-s urinarias / urinary ____.

viabilidad *f.* viability, the quality of being viable.

viable *a.* viable, capable of surviving, gen. in reference to a newborn; no ____ / nonviable.

viajar *v.* to travel.

viaje *m.* trip.

vianda *f.* starchy vegetables such as potatoes.

víbora *f.* viper.

vibración *f.* vibration, oscillation.

vibrante *a.* vibrant.

vibrar *v.* to vibrate.

vibratorio-a *a.* vibratory, vibrative, that vibrates or produces vibration; sentido ____ / ____ sense.

vicario-a *a.* vicarious, that acts or assumes the place of another.

vicio *m.* vice, bad habit.

vicioso-a *a.* given to vice.

víctima *f.* victim; ____ **de accidente** / casualty.

vida *f.* life; vitality; medidas para el sostenimiento de la ____ / ____ saving measures; promedio de duración de ____ / ____ expectancy; que pone la ____ en peligro / ____ threatening; ____ **cotidiana** / daily ____.

vida media *f.* half-life. 1. the time required for half the nuclei of a radioactive substance to disintegrate; 2. the time required for half the amount of a substance taken in by the body to dissolve by natural means.

video *m.* video.

videocinta *f.* videotape.

vidrio *m.* glass; ____ de fibra / fiberglass.

viejo-a *a.* old, aged; stale.

viento *m.* wind; **hace** ____ / it is windy.

vientre *m.* belly; abdomen.

vigente *a.* in force, in effect.

vigilancia *f.* 1. vigilance, state of alertness or responsiveness; 2. surveillance.

vigilar *v.* to watch, to guard; to survey.

vigilia *f.* vigil. 1. the state of being consciously responsive to a stimulus; 2. insomnia.

vigor *m.* vigor, strength; fortitude; stamina.

vigorizar *vi.* to invigorate, to strengthen, to energyze.

vigoroso-a *a.* vigorous, strong; having fortitude; **-mente** *adv.* vigorously.

VIH *m.* HIV, human immuno-deficiency virus-1, a retrovirus considered to be the cause of AIDS that can be transmitted by sexual relations or by blood transfusion from someone who is infected with HIV. The virus can be transmitted to children of mothers with HIV in utero, at birth, or, likely, through breast feeding.

vinagre *m.* vinegar, solution of acetic acid.

vínculo *m*. link.

vino *m*. wine.

violáceo-a *a*. purplish.

violación *f*. rape; violation; ___ estatutaria / statutory ___.

violar *a*. to rape; to harm or injure.

violencia *f*. violence; ___ doméstica / domestic ___.

violento-a *a*. violent.

violeta *a*. [*color*] violet.

viral *a*. viral, rel. to a virus.

virar *a*. to turn; **virarse** *vr*. to turn oneself around.

viremia *f*. viremia, the presence of virus in the blood.

virgen *f*. virgin. 1. uncontaminated, pure; 2. having had no sexual intercourse.

virginal *a*. virginal, pure.

virginidad *f*. virginity.

viril *a*. virile, rel. to the male.

virilidad *f*. virility. 1. sexual potency; 2. the quality of being virile.

virilización *f*. virilization, the process by which secondary male characteristics develop in the female, gen. due to adrenal malfunction or to intake of hormones.

virión *m*. virion, mature viral particle that constitutes the extracellular infectious form of a virus.

virolento-a *a*. 1. rel. to or afflicted with smallpox; 2. pockmarked.

virología *f*. virology, the study of viruses.

virtual *a*. virtual, existing in appearance and effect, but not in reality.

viruela *f*. smallpox, highly contagious viral disease characterized by high temperature and generalized blisters and pustules; ___-s locas / chicken pox.

virulencia *f*. virulence. 1. the power of an organism to produce disease in the host; 2. the quality of being virulent.

virulento-a *a*. virulent, highly poisonous or infectious.

virus *m*. virus, ultramicroscopic microorganisms capable of causing infectious diseases; ___ atenuado / attenuated ___; ___ citomegálico / cytomegalic ___; ___ Coxsackie / Coxsackie ___; ___ de la parainfluenza / parainfluenza ___; ___ ECHO / ECHO ___; ___ entérico / enteric ___; ___ herpético / herpes ___; ___ oncogénico, tumoral / tumor ___; ___ sincitial respiratorio / respiratory syncytial ___; ___ variólico / pox ___.

vísceras *f. pl*. viscera, large internal organs of the body, esp. the abdomen.

visceral *a*. visceral, rel. to viscera.

visceromegalia *f*. visceromegaly, abnormal enlargement of a viscus.

viscosidad *f*. viscosity, the quality of being viscous, esp. the property of fluids to offer resistance due to friction of its molecules.

viscoso-a *a*. viscous, gummy, sticky; slimy.

visibilidad *f*. visibility.

visible *a*. visible; evident; **-mente** *adv*. visibly.

visión *f*. vision, the sense of sight. 1. the ability to see, to perceive things through the action of light on the eyes, and on related centers in the brain; ___ acromática / achromatic ___; ___ binocular / binocular ___; ___ central / central ___; ___ cromática / chromatic ___; ___ diurna / day ___; ___ doble / double ___, diplopia; ___ nocturna / night ___; ___ periférica / peripheral ___; 2. imaginary apparition.

visión en túnel *f*. tunnel vision, eye anomaly manifested by a great reduction in the visual field, as if looking through a tunnel, such as occurs in cases of glaucoma.

visita *f*. visit; call; **horas de** ___ / visiting hours; ___ **médica** / house call.

visitar *v*. to visit.

vista *f*. sight; eyesight; view; **corto de** ___ / nearsighted; ___ cansada / eyestrain; enfermedades de la ___ / eye diseases; ___ nublada / bleary-eyed; *v*. **tener buena** ___ / to have good eyesight; **a primera** ___ / at first ___; **en** ___ **de** / in view of.

visto-a *a. pp*. of **ver,** seen.

vistazo *m*. glance, glimpse; *v*. **dar un** ___ / to take a look.

visual *a*. visual, rel. to vision; campo ___ / ___ field, field of vision; contacto ___ / eye contact; memoria ___ / eye memory.

visualizar *vi*. to visualize. 1. to form a mental image; 2. to make visible, such as through X-rays.

vital *a*. vital, rel. to life or essential to maintaining it; capacidad ___ / ___ capacity; signos ___-es / ___ signs.

vitalicio-a *a*. for life.

vitalidad *f*. vitality. 1. the quality of having life; 2. physical or mental vigor.

vitalizar *vi*. to vitalize, to give life; to reanimate.

vitamina *f*. vitamin, any one of a group of

organic compounds found in small amounts in foods and essential to the growth and development of the body and its functions; pérdida de ___-s / loss of ___-s.

vitáminico-a *a.* vitaminic, rel. to vitamins.

vitíligo *m.* vitiligo, benign skin disease characterized by smooth white spots, gen. in exposed areas.

vítreo-a *a.* vitreous, glassy, hyaline; cámara ___ / ___ chamber; cuerpo ___ / ___ body; humor ___ / ___ humor.

viudo-a *m., f.* widower; widow.

vivificante *a.* vivifying.

vivisección *f.* vivisection, the cutting or operating upon living animals for research purposes.

vivir *v.* to live.

vivo-a *a.* alive; living; *pop.* ingenuous.

vocabulario *m.* vocabulary.

vocación *f.* vocation, profession.

vocal *f. gr.* vowel; *a.* rel. to the voice or produced by it; ligamentos ___-es / ___ ligaments.

vocalización *f.* vocalization.

volar *vi.* to fly; to travel by airplane.

volátil *a.* volatile, that vaporizes readily.

volición *f.* volition, will, the power to determine.

volumen *m.* volume, space occupied by a body or substance; ___ cardíaco / heart ___; ___ de reserva espiratoria o aire de reserva / expiratory air reserve ___; ___ de ventilación pulmonar / tidal ___; ___ residual / residual ___; ___ sanguíneo / blood ___; ___ sistólico / stroke ___.

volumétrico-a *a.* volumetric, rel. to the measurement of volume.

voluntad *f.* will, determination; **fuerza de** ___ / ___ power.

voluntario-a *m., f.* volunteer; *a.* voluntary; músculo ___ / ___ muscle.

voluptuoso-a *a.* voluptuous, sensually provocative.

volver *vi.* to return; to turn; ___ **en sí** / to come to; **volverse** *vr.* to turn over; to return to.

vólvulo *m.* volvulus, intestinal obstruction caused by torsion of the intestines upon its mesentery.

vómer *m.* vomer, the impaired flat bone that forms part of the nasal septum.

vomitar *v.* to vomit.

vomitivo *m.* vomitive, emetic.

vómito *m.* vomit, vomiting.

von Recklinghausen, enfermedad de *f.* von Recklinghausen's disease. *V.* **neurofibromatosis.**

voraz *a.* voracious, having an excessive appetite.

vórtice *m.* vortex, spiral-shaped structure.

voyeur *Fr.* voyeur, one who practices voyeurism.

voyeurismo *m.* voyeurism, sexual perversion by which erotic gratification is derived from observing sexual organs or activity.

voz *f.* voice.

vozarrón *m.* strong, deep voice.

vuelo *m.* flight; trajectory.

vuelta *f.* turning; turn; rotation; **media** ___ / about face; *v.* **dar una** ___ / to take a stroll, ride, or walk; *v.* **estar de** ___ / to be back.

vulnerable *a.* vulnerable, prone to injury or disease.

vulva *f.* vulva, external female organ.

vulvar *a.* vulval, vulvar, rel. to the vulva.

vulvectomía *f. surg.* vulvectomy, excision of the vulva.

vulvitis *f.* vulvitis, infl. of the vulva.

vulvovaginal *a.* vulvovaginal, rel. to the vulva and the vagina.

W

Waldeyer, anillo de *m.* Waldeyer's ring, the ring of lymphatic tissue that consists of the palatine, lingual and pharyngeal tonsils.

Waller, degeneración de *f.* Wallerian degeneration, degeneration of nerve fibers that have been separated from their center of nutrition.

warfarina *f.* warfarin, generic name for Coumadine, anticoagulant used in the prevention of thrombosis and infarcts.

Wasserman, reacción de *f.* Wasserman reaction, serological test for syphilis.

Western Blot *m.* Western Blot, immunoblot, test to confirm HIV infection in patients with evidence of exposure to HIV by a previous enzyme-linked immunosorbent assay (ELISA).

Wharton, conducto de *m.* Wharton's duct, excretory duct of the submandibular gland.

Whipple, enfermedad de *f.* Whipple's disease, rare disease caused by deposit of lipids in the lymphatic and intestinal tissues.

Wilms, tumor de *m.* Wilms tumor, rapidly developing neoplasm of the kidney, seen esp. in children.

Wilson, enfermedad de *f.* Wilson's disease, hereditary disease manifested by severe hepatic and cerebral disorders.

X

xantina *f.* xanthin, one of a group of stimulants of the central nervous system and the heart, such as caffein.

xantoma *m.* xanthoma, condition characterized by the presence of yellowish plaques or nodules in the skin, gen. due to deposit of lipids.

xantocromía *f.* xanthochromia, yellowish decoloration as seen in skin patches or in the cerebrospinal fluid.

xantocrómico-a *a.* xanthochromic, having a yellowish appearance or rel. to xanthochromia.

xantoderma *m.* xanthoderma, yellowish coloration of the skin.

xantosis *f.* xanthosis, yellowing of the skin due to excessive ingestion of foods such as carrots and egg yolks.

xenofobia *f.* xenophobia, morbid fear or aversion to anything foreign.

xenoinjerto *m.* xenograft. *V.* **heteroinjerto.**

xenón *m.* xenon, a dense, colorless element found in small amounts in the atmosphere.

xerodermia *f.* xeroderma, xerosis, excessively dry skin.

xeroftalmía *f.* xerophthalmia, dryness of the conjuctiva due to lack of vitamin A.

xerografía *f.* xerography. *V.* **xerorradiografía.**

xeromamografía *f.* xeromammography, xeroradiography of the breast.

xerorradiografía *f.* xeroradiography, dry process of registering electrostatic images by the use of metal plates covered with a substance such as selenium.

xerosis *f.* xerosis, abnormal dryness as seen in the skin, eyes, and mucous membranes.

xerostomía *f.* xerostomia, abnormal dryness of the mouth due to deficiency of salivary secretion.

xifoide, xifoideo-a *a.* xiphoid, shaped like a sword as the xiphoid process.

xifoides, apéndice *m.* xiphoid process, cartilaginous sword-shaped formation joined to the lowest portion of the sternum.

Y

y *conj.* and.

ya *adv.* already; ____ **que** / as long as.

yarda *f.* yard.

yatrogénico-a, yatrógeno-a *a.* iatrogenic, rel. to the adverse condition of a patient resulting from an erroneous medical treatment or procedure.

yaws *m.* yaws. *V.* **frambesia.**

yema *f.* yolk. 1. the yolk of the egg of a bird; 2. contents of the ovum that supply the embryo.

yerbabuena, hierbabuena *f.* peppermint.

yerno *m.* son-in-law.

yeso *m.* plaster, plaster cast.

yeyunal *a.* jejunal, rel. to the jejunum.

yeyunectomía *f. surg.* jejunectomy, excision of part or all of the jejunum.

yeyuno *m.* jejunum, portion of the small intestine that extends from the duodenum to the ileum.

yeyunostomía *f. surg.* jejunostomy, permanent opening in the jejunum through the abdominal wall.

yo *m.* self, [*el yo*] the ego, Freudian term that refers to the part of the psyche that mediates between the person and reality; *gr. pron.* I.

yodismo *m.* iodism, poisoning by iodine.

yodo *m.* iodine, nonmetallic element used in medications esp. those that stimulate the function and development of the thyroid gland and the prevention of goiter; prueba radiactiva del ____ / radioactive ____ excretion test, used for evaluating the function of the thyroid gland.

yodurar *v.* to iodize, to treat with iodine.

yoga *m.* yoga, Hindu system of beliefs and practices by which the individual tries to reach the union of self with a universal self, through contemplation, meditation, and self control.

yogurt *m.* yogurt, milk that is fermented by the action of *Lactobacillus bulgaricus* and to which nutritious and therapeutic value is attributed.

yugular *a.* jugular, rel. to the throat; venas ____-es / ____ veins, veins that carry blood from the cranium, the face, and the neck to the heart.

yuxtaglomerular *a.* juxtaglomerular, close to a glomerulus; aparato ___ / ___ apparatus; group of cells that participate in the production of renin and in the metabolism of sodium situated around arterioles leading to a glomerulus of the kidney.

yuxtaponer *vi.* to juxtapose, to put next to.

yuxtaposición *f.* juxtaposition, a position that is adjacent or side by side to another.

Z

z *abr.* **zona** / zone.

zambo-a *a.* bandy-legged; bow-legged.

zanahoria *f.* carrot.

zinc, cinc *m.* zinc, crystalline metallic chem-ical element with astringent properties; pomada de ___ / ___ ointment.

Zollinger-Ellison, síndrome de *m.* Zollinger-Ellison syndrome, manifested by gastric hypersecretion and hyperacidity and by peptic ulceration of the stomach and small intestine.

zona *f.* 1. zona, a specific area or layer; 2. zoster; 3. zone, a belt-like anatomical structure.

zona desencadenante *f.* trigger zone, a sensitive area of the body that triggers a reaction in a different part of the body upon stimulation.

zooinjerto *m.* zoograft, graft from an animal.

zoster *f.* zoster, *pop.* shingles *V.* **herpes zoster.**

zumbar *v.* to hum, to buzz, to ring.

zumbido *m.* hum, buzz.

Simplified Spanish Grammar

THE SPANISH ALPHABET / EL ALFABETO ESPAÑOL

Letter / Letra	Name / Nombre	Letter / Letra	Name / Nombre
a	a	n	ene
b	be	ñ	eñe
c	ce	o	o
ch	che o ce hache	p	pe
d	de	q	cu
e	e	r	ere
efe	efe	rr	erre
g	ge	s	ese
h	ache	t	te
i	i	u	u
j	jota	v	ve o uve
k	k	w	doble ve o doble uve
l	ele	x	equis
ll	elle	y	i (i griega)
m	eme	z	zeta

The Spanish alphabet has four more additional characters than the English alphabet: **ch, ll, ñ, rr.** In alphabetizing Spanish words or syllables, those beginning with **ch, ll,** and **ñ** follow words that begin in **c, l, n.** (In Spanish **rr** never begins a word.) The Spanish alphabet like the English alphabet has five vowels: **a, e, i, o, u.** The consonant **y** is pronounced like the vowel **i** at the end of a word. It is also pronounced like **i** when it is used by itself as the word **and.**

Unlike English pronunciation, each vowel in Spanish has, with few exceptions, a single sound.

Vowel	Sound		Example / Meaning
a	ah	as in father	gasa / gauze
e	eh	as in met (without the glide)	leche / milk
i	ee	as in me (without the glide)	mi / my
o	oh	as in spoke	ojo / eye
u	oo	as in food	cura / cure

The Spanish consonants that differ most from English pronunciation are described below. The description of sounds in the Pronunciation Chart are approximations and do not indicate exact equivalence between English and Spanish sounds. The authors of this dictionary believe that a basic understanding of the pronunciation of Spanish and English will better serve the needs of the dictionary users than any attempt to represent the entire phonetic complexities of the two languages. Readers can develop their skills of pronunciation apart from the dictionary by imitating native speakers and using pronunciation tapes available in many libraries.

Consonants That Differ Most from English Pronunciation

Letter	Approx. English Sound	Example / Meaning
c before e, i *(Cast.)*	**th** as in **th**yroid	círculo / circle
c before e, i *(H.A)*	**s** as in **s**eptum	centro (sentro)[1] / center
c before a, o, u	**k** as in **c**ancer	cáncer / cancer
ch	**ch** as in **ch**eck	leche / milk
d between vowel	like **th** in wea**th**er	medio / half
d after n or l	like **d** in **d**art	donde / where
g before e, i	harsher than **h** in **h**emoglobin	germen / germ
gue, gui	hard **g** as in **g**uest	guillotina / guillotine
güe, güi	**gwe**, as in **Gw**en	ungüento / ointment
h	always silent as in **h**our	hora / hour
j	more forcefully than in **h**am	jamón / ham
ll *(Cast.)*	**lli** as in mi**lli**on	millón / million
ll *(H.A)*	**y** as in **y**es	millón (miyón)
ñ	**ny** as in ca**ny**on	muñeca / wrist
p	not aspirated, less explosive than in patient	paciente / patient
q	always pronounced as **k**	queso[2] / cheese
r	if not initial, sound produced by the tip of the tongue against the alveolar ridge	quirúrgico / surgical
r	initial, of multiple trill, roll the r more than in dia**rrh**ea	reuma / rheum
rr	same as initial **r**	diarrea / diarrhea
v as a b bilabial	as in **b**owl	vacuna (bacuna) / vaccine
x	**ks, gs** as in o**x**ygen, e**x**cellent	oxígeno / oxygen excelente / excellent
y	same as **y** in **y**es like **j** in in**j**ection	yeso / plaster inyección / injection
y	by itself or at the end of a word, like **e** in m**e**	y / and soy / I am
z *(Cast.)*	like **th** in **th**umb	zumo / juice
z *(H.A.)*	as **s** in **s**oft	zumbido (sumbido) / buzz

1. Word in parenthesis indicates how it is pronounced in Hispanic America.
2. In the letter combination **qu** the **u** is always silent in Spanish before **e** and **i**.

Linking Words

In Spanish, words are spoken in breath-groups in which two or more words are pronounced as if they were one word. Breath-groups are formed when the ending of one word and the beginning of the following word meet these conditions:

The First Word Ends with:	The Next Word Begins with:
1. a consonant	a vowel
el	estudiante
e-**les**-tu-dian-te	
2. consonant	the letter **h**
el	hospital
e-**lhos**-pi-tal	

3. vowel the same vowel

   enfermera asistente
   en-fer-me-**ra**-sis-ten-te (longer a)

4. strong vowel (a, e, o) weak vowel (i, u)

   persona interesante
   per-so-**nain**-te-re-san-te

5. strong vowel (a, e, o) strong vowel

   la otra
   lao-tra

Comprehensive Example:

> La otra medicina es mejor. / The other medicine is better.
> **lao**-tra (stop) me-di-ci-**naes** (stop) me-jor.

Dividing Words into Syllables

A Spanish word has as many syllables as it has vowels and dipthongs. (A diphthong is the combination of an unstressed **i** or **u** with another vowel **a, e, o**. A diphthong is dissolved, however, if the **i** or the **u** carry a written accent mark.)

How to Separate Syllables

1. An initial vowel in a word is a syllable if it is followed by two consonants the second of which is **l** or **r**.

   aplicar / to apply   a-pli-car

2. The consonants **b, c, f, g, p, t** combine with **l** or **r** to form a syllable with the following vowel. (The letter **d** combines only with **r**.)

   flema / phlegm   fle-ma

3. Any consecutive consonants apart from the combinations described in the preceding rule mark a division between syllables.

   parte / part   par-te
   consult / consultar   con-sul-tar

4. The vowels that make up a diphthong are never separated.

   artery / arteria   ar-te-ria

   Remember, if the vowel (**i** or **u**) has an accent mark, the vowels are divided.

   anatomy / anatomía   a-na-to-mí-a.

5. Two strong vowels form two separate syllables.

   monitoring / monitoreo   mo-ni-to-re-o.

Accentuation

Ending / Terminación	Stress / Sílaba acentuada	Examples / Ejemplos
vowel: a e i o	next to the last syllable	bac-*te*-ria
consonant: n or s	next to the last syllable	*cu*-ran

Ending / Terminación	Stress / Sílaba acentuada	Examples / Ejemplos
consonant other than n or s	on the last syllable	o-fi-*cial*
		a-co-mo-*dar*

All infinitives are stressed in the last syllable. Any words that are exceptions to these two rules carry *a written accent mark* (´) over the stressed vowel:

coffee / ca**fé**   lung / pul**món**   easy / **fá**cil   lamp / **lám**para

A written accent mark is also used to indicate a difference between two words that are written alike but have a different meaning, such as demonstrative adjectives and pronouns—this / **este** paciente (adjective), this one / **éste** (pronoun)—and interrogatives—what / ¿**qué**?, that / **que** (relative pronoun). The same happens with yes / **sí** and if / **si**. All interrogatives require a written accent mark.

Punctuation / Puntuación

(.)	punto	(ü)	diérisis o crema
(;)	punto y coma	(*)	asterisco
(:)	dos puntos	(-)	guión
(¿)	interrogación abierta	(—)	raya
(?)	interrogación cerrada	( )	paréntesis
(¡)	admiración abierta	(" ")	comillas
(!)	admiración cerrada	(. . .)	puntos suspensivos

THE ARTICLE / EL ARTÍCULO

The article (definite or indefinite) precedes the noun. Spanish articles agree with the noun in gender and number.

The Definite Article (the)		
	Feminine (1)	Masculine (2)
Singular	la	el
Plural	las	los

1. the chronic infection / la infección crónica
   the chronic infections / las infecciones crónicas
2. the extreme case / el caso extremo
   the extreme cases / los casos extremos

Note: Singular feminine nouns which begin with stressed **a** or **ha** require the masculine form **el.**

the water / el agua
the speech / el habla

When **de** / of   precedes **el,** they contract to **del;** and when **a** / to   precedes **el,** they contract to **al.**

The Indefinite Article (a, an, some)		
	Feminine (1)	Masculine (2)
Singular	una	un
Plural	unas	unos

1. a complicated situation / una situación complicada
   some complicated situations / unas situaciones complicadas
2. an asthmatic boy / un niño asmático
   some asthmatic boys / unos niños asmáticos

In the first two examples of the definite article, the nouns *infección,* which is feminine, and *caso,* which is masculine, determine the gender and number of the article that precedes them. The descriptive adjectives that follow the nouns have the same gender and number as the noun they modify.The same agreement is demonstrated in the examples for the indefinite article.

Uses of the Definite Article / Usos del artículo definido

1. To refer to parts of the body and articles of clothing.

   Antonia raises her arm. / Antonia levanta el brazo.
   The patient puts on her robe. / La paciente se pone la bata.

2. To refer to days of the week, dates, and seasons.

   Check into the hospital on Thursday. / Ingrese en el hospital el jueves.

3. With nouns of rate, weight, and measure.

   Take half of the pill. / Tome la mitad de la pastilla.

4. With titles when speaking about a person or persons.

   Dr. Ruiz is famous. / El doctor Ruiz es famoso.

5. With cardinal numbers to tell time (feminine forms **la** and **las** only).

   I'll see you at one. / Te veo a la una.
   Come back tomorrow at eleven. / Vuelva mañana a las once.

Uses of the Indefinite Article / Usos del artículo indefinido

1. To indicate some, any, a few, about (meaning approximately).

   The patient is about twenty years old. / El paciente tiene unos veinte años.

2. To stress a person's identity.

   Who is he? He is a famous doctor. / ¿Quién es él? Es un médico famoso.

3. To identify objects or persons after **hay** (there is, there are).

   There is a book, a glass, and some medicines on the table. / Hay un libro, un vaso y unas medicinas en la mesa.

Note: The indefinite article is generally omitted after the verb **ser** with an unmodified noun referring to profession, religion or nationality:

   What is he? He is a doctor. / ¿Qué es él? Es médico.

NOUN / NOMBRES

Gender / Género

In Spanish, nouns are either masculine or feminine. There are no neuter nouns.
Nouns referring to female beings and certain things are classified as feminine; they have the following endings:

Most Common	*Example*	*Exception*
-a	hora / hour	(el) día / day
Others		
-ad	enfermedad / sickness	
-ión	atención / attention	(el) avión / airplane
-is	flebitis / phlebitis	—
-ud	salud / health	—
-umbre	costumbre / custom	—

Nouns referring to masculine beings, days of the week, and names of languages are usually classified as masculine, along with the names of things having the following endings:

ENDINGS OF MASCULINE NOUNS /
TERMINACIONES DE NOMBRES MASCULINOS

Most Common	*Example*	*Exception*
-o	brazo / arm	(la) mano / hand
Others		
-or	doctor	
-ma*	sistema / system	(la) flema / phlegm
-pa*	mapa / map	

*Only nouns ending in **-ma, -pa** of Greek origin are masculine. This rule applies to most scientific names having these endings.

ADJECTIVES / ADJETIVOS

Gender / Género

Adjectives are used in both the masculine and feminine genders. Change the ending **-o** of a masculine adjective to **-a** to form the feminine.

the anemic boy / el niño anémic**o**
the anemic girl / la niña anémic**a**

Add **-a** to an adjective of nationality ending in a consonant to form the feminine. The written accent on the last syllable drops when the feminine ending is added. However, the stress remains on the vowel **e.**

Frenchman / francés   French woman / frances**a**

Adjectives ending in **-e** or a consonant remain unchanged for both the masculine and feminine forms:

intelligent / inteligent**e**   easy / fáci**l**

Adjectives ending in **-án, -ón,** and **-or** (except comparatives), add **-a** to form the feminine. The written accent is omitted when the feminine ending is added.

reductor / reduct**or**, reduct**ora**   lazy / harag**án**, harag**ana**

Note: The adjective may follow or precede the noun; however, nouns and adjectives have the same endings, and are inflected alike.

Number / Número

Nouns and Adjectives / Nombres y adjetivos

Plural Endings

add	-s	if the noun or adjective ends in an unaccented vowel or dipthong, or stressed é:

microbio / microbe	microbios
café / coffee	cafés
amargo / bitter	amargos

add	-es	if the noun or adjective ends in a consonant:

pulmón / lung	pulmones
especial / special	especiales

add	-es	if the noun or adjective ends in z, change z to c before adding -es.

luz / light	luces
feliz / happy	felices

Note: In nouns ending in unstressed -is or -es, the number is indicated by the preceding article; the noun remains unchanged.

la crisis	las crisis
el jueves	los jueves
el análisis	los análisis

Adjectives That Precede the Noun / Adjetivos que preceden al nombre

Demonstratives / Demostrativos

Demonstratives indicate location. A demonstrative adjective indicates persons, animals, or objects in relation to the speaker.

Near the speaker:

	Singular *this*	Plural *these*
Masculine	este	estos
Feminine	esta	estas

this medicine / esta medicina	these medicines / estas medicinas
this doctor / este médico	these doctors / estos médicos

Not far from the person spoken to or the speaker (in time or space):

	Singular *that*	Plural *those*
Masculine	ese	esos
Feminine	esa	esas

that white robe / esa bata blanca	those white robes / esas batas blancas
that week / esa semana	those weeks / esas semanas

Distant from both the speaker and person spoken to:		
	Singular *that*	**Plural** *those*
Masculine	aquel	aquellos
Feminine	aquella	aquellas

that lady (over there) / aquella señora
that case (that was treated) / aquel caso

those ladies (over there) / aquellas señoras
those cases (that were treated) / aquellos casos

Demonstrative Pronouns / Pronombres demostrativos

Demonstrative adjectives and pronouns have the same form. However, the pronouns always carry an accent mark, which distinguishes them from the adjectives: **éste, ése, aquél, ésta, ésa, aquélla; éstos, ésos, aquéllos, éstas, ésas, aquéllas.**

> *a.:* This patient has a fever. / **Este** paciente tiene fiebre.
> *pron.:* That one is anemic. / **Aquél** es anémico.

When referring to a concept, situation, or object whose gender is unknown, the forms **esto, eso,** and **aquello** are used:

> Why do you say that? / ¿Por qué dice **eso?**
> What is this? / ¿Qué es **esto?**
> That was awful! / ¡**Aquello** fue terrible!

Possessive Adjectives / Adjetivos posesivos

Possessive adjectives agree in gender and number with the thing possessed (the noun they modify). The following forms precede the noun.

Singular	Plural	English
mi	mis	my
tu	tus	your (*fam.*)
su	sus	his her
		its, your (*form.*)
nuestro-a	nuestros-as	our
vuestro-a	vuestros-as	your (*fam. Cast.*)
su	sus	their, your

my patient / mi paciente
our evaluation / nuestra evaluación

my patients / mis pacientes
our patients / nuestros pacientes

Note: To clarify **su** (since it can refer to more than one possessor), substitute the preposition **de** and the subject pronoun for **su:**

article + noun + de + pronoun

His temperature is normal. / Su temperatura es normal.
La temperatura **de él** es normal. [*m. sing.*]

Their temperature is normal. / Su temperatura es normal.
La temperatura **de ellas** es normal. [*f. pl.*]

OTHER POSSESSIVE FORMS

There are other possessive forms that are stressed and placed after the noun and are inflected in their endings like adjectives.

Singular	*Plural*	*English*
mío-a	míos-as	my, of mine
tuyo-a	tuyos-as	your (*fam.*), of yours
suyo-a	suyos-as	his, her, your, its, of his, of hers, of yours
nuestro-a	nuestros-as	our, of ours
vuestro-a	vuestros-as	your (*fam.*), of yours
suyo-a	suyos-as	their, your, of theirs, of yours

this patient of mine / este paciente **mío**
that patient of ours / ese paciente **nuestro**

Note: To clarify the meaning of **suyo, suya** (*sing.* or *pl.*) use the corresponding form of the definite article with the preposition **de** and the personal pronoun, as explained in the case of **su** above.

her temperature / la temperatura **suya** / la temperatura **de ella**

The stressed forms of the possessive adjectives can be used as possessive pronouns:

a.:   Your medicine is here / La medicina **suya** está aquí.
pron.:   Yours is here / La **suya** está aquí.
a.:   Our treatment finishes today / El tratamiento **nuestro** termina hoy.
pron.:   Ours finishes today / El **nuestro** termina hoy.

Limiting Adjectives / Adjetivos que limitan al nombre

Numbers and indefinite adjectives which show quantities usually precede the noun.

	Masculine		*Feminine*	
Singular		*Plural*	*Singular*	*Plural*
many, a lot, much / mucho		muchos	mucha	muchas
another / otro		otros	otra	otras
all, every / todo		todos	toda	todas
some, any / algún		algunos	alguna	algunas
(not) any / ningún		(ningunos)	ninguna	(ninguna)
first / primero		primeros	primera	primeras
third / tercero		terceros	tercera	terceras

Note: **Primero** changes to **primer**, and **tercero** to **tercer** when placed in front of a masculine singular noun; **ningunos** and **ningunas** are rarely used.

Go down to the first floor. / Baje al **primer** piso.

Descriptive Adjectives / Adjetivos descriptivos

In Spanish, descriptive adjectives are most frequently placed after the noun, except adjectives denoting quantity, size, or order, which are generally placed before the noun.

You have high blood pressure. / Tiene la presión **alta.**

That sickness has many complications. / Esa enfermedad tiene **muchas** complicaciones.

It is the third time. / Es la **tercera** vez.

Some descriptive adjectives have a different meaning when placed before or after the noun:

bueno-a	un médico bueno / a good doctor (comparing him to others)
	un buen médico (he is definitely good, worth to be recommended)
grande	un hombre grande / a big man (in a physical sense)
	un gran hombre / a great man (in a moral, spiritual, or intellectual sense)
malo-a	una dieta mala / a bad diet (of bad quality)
	una mala dieta / a bad diet (as compared to a good one)

Note: **bueno** and **malo** drop the ending **-o** before a masculine singular noun, **grande** drops the ending **-de** before a singular noun, masculine or feminine.

COMPARISONS THAT ESTABLISH INEQUALITY

> **más** / more + the adjective + **que** / than

John is taller than Joe. / Juan es **más alto que** Pepe.

> **menos** / less + the adjective + **que** / than

Joe is shorter than John. / Pepe es **menos alto que** Juan.

COMPARISONS OF EQUALITY

> **tan** / as + an adjective or adverb + **como** / as

This pill is as effective as that one. / Esta pastilla es **tan eficaz como** ésa.

> **Tanto-a, -os, -as** / as much, as many + noun + **como**

He has as much fever as yesterday. / Tiene **tanta calentura como** ayer.

IRREGULAR COMPARATIVES

Adjectives	Comparative	Superlative
low / bajo	lower / inferior	(the) lowest / ínfimo
good / bueno	better / mejor	(the) best / (el) (la) mejor
bad / malo	worse / peor	(the) worst / (el) (la) mejor
big / grande	greater / major	(the) greatest / (el) (la) mayor
small / pequeño	smaller / menor	(the) smallest / (el) (la) menor
young / joven	younger / menor	(the) youngest / (el) (la) menor
much / mucho	more / más	(the) most / (el) (la) más
little / poco	less / menos	(the) least / (el) (la) menos

Article and adjective agree with the noun in gender and number.

This is the best treatment. / Este es **el mejor** tratamiento.
These are the best pills. / Estas son **las mejores** pastillas.

Note: In Spanish the preposition **de** is generally used after the superlative; before numerals, **de** is the translation of the English *than*.

The sickest of all. / El **más** enfermo **de** todos.
There are more than ten cases. / Hay **más de** diez casos.

The absolute superlative refers only to a quality possessed by a person or object in a high degree, without comparison to others. To form the absolute superlative, the ending **-ísimo -a** is added to the radical of the adjective:

mucho → muchísimo   rápido → rapidísimo
excelente → excelentísimo   inteligente → inteligentísimo

Note: Adjectives ending in **-co** and **-go** change the **c** to **qu** and the **g** to **gu** before adding **ísimo**:

poco → po**qu**ísimo   largo → lar**gu**ísimo

Adverbs	*Superlatives*
well / bien	better, best / mejor
bad, badly / mal	worse, worst / peor
much / mucho	more, most / más
little / poco	less, least / menos

Do you feel well today? / ¿Se siente **bien** hoy?
I feel better. / Me siento **mejor.**
I feel worse today. / Me siento **peor** hoy.

PRONOUNS / PRONOMBRES

A pronoun is a word that takes the place of a noun. There are different types of pronouns, according to the use of the noun that the pronoun replaces.

Subject Pronouns / Pronombres personales

Subject pronouns tell who is performing the action of the verb. They are not used as commonly as subject pronouns in English, since the form of the verb in Spanish indicates person and number without reliance on the form of the subject pronoun. Subject pronouns are used in Spanish for clarification and emphasis. The familiar **tú** is used when speaking to a friend, a relative, or a child. **Vosotros-as** is rarely used in Hispanic America, where **ustedes** is used for the plural of **tú.** There is no translation in Spanish for the English subject pronoun *it.*

It is a complicated case. / Es un caso complicado.
It is I. / Soy yo.

Direct Object Pronouns / Pronombres de objeto directo

A direct object pronoun is used instead of a noun object of the verb:

Did you bring the sample? / ¿Trajo la muestra?
Yes, I brought it. / Sí, la traje.

Indirect Object Pronouns / Pronombres de objeto indirecto

An indirect object pronoun is used instead of a noun indirect object of the verb.

Did you give María (to her) the prescription? Yes, I gave it to her. /
¿Le dio la receta a María? Sí, se la di.

Note: When two object pronouns are used together, the indirect object pronoun generally precedes the direct. **Se** replaces **le, les** when preceding **lo, la, los, las.**

Subject Pronouns	Direct Object Pronouns	Indirect Object Pronouns
I / yo	me / me	to me, for me / me
you / tú	you / te	to you, for you / te
we / nosotros-as	us / nos	to us, for us / nos
you / vosotros-as	you / os	to you, for you / os

Note: **Me, te, nos** and **os,** can be used as direct and indirect object pronouns, or as reflexive pronouns.

THIRD AND SECOND PERSON (FORMAL)

Subject Pronouns	Direct Object Pronouns	Indirect Object Pronouns
you / usted	you / lo, la	to you, for you / le
he / él	him / lo	to him, for him / le
She / ella	her / la	to her, for her / le
	it / lo, la	to it, for it / le
you / ustedes	them / los, las	to you, for you / les
they / ellos	them / los	to them, for them / les
they / ellas	them / las	to them, for them / les

Note: The subject pronoun is used with the preposition **a** either for emphasis or clarification (although redundant), in addition to the indirect object pronoun.

The doctor examined him many times. / El médico **lo** examinó **a él** varias veces.

Note: **Le, les** are also used as direct object pronouns for the second person: **usted, ustedes,** and for the third person masculine. In Hispanic America they are less frequently used as such than in Spain.

Reflexive pronouns / Pronombres reflexivos

A reflexive pronoun is used when the subject acts upon itself. The forms **me, te, nos, os,** are also used in the reflexive, meaning myself, yourself, ourselves, yourselves. For the other persons **se** is used meaning yourself (for *usted*), herself, and himself for the singular forms; yourselves (for *ustedes*), and themselves for the plural forms.

Subject Pronouns	Reflexive Pronouns
I / yo	myself / me
you / tú	yourself / te
you / usted	yourself / se
he / él	himself / se
she / ella	herself / se
we / nosotros-as	ourselves / nos
you / vosotros-as	yourselves / os
you / ustedes	yourselves / se
they / ellos-as	themselves / se

She washed her hands. / Ella **se** lavó las manos.
They get up early. / Ellos **se** levantan temprano.

Relative Pronouns / Pronombres relativos

A relative pronoun (**que; el, la cual; quien** / that; which; who) introduces an adjective clause that refers back to an antecedent noun; it can be the subject or direct object of the clause's verb, or the object of a preposition.

I know a nurse who can assist you. / Conozco a una enfermera **que** puede asistirlo.
The medicine (that) you took. / La medicina **que** usted tomó.
The case which we are talking about . . . / El caso **del cual** estamos hablando . . .

Possessive pronouns and **demonstrative pronouns** have already been explained under Adjectives.

VERBS / VERBOS

In Spanish as in English, the mood of a verb states

1. a fact:

INDICATIVE

> The doctor is in his office. /
> El doctor está en su consulta.

2. a condition expressed by the speaker involving some doubt, wish, hope, or possibility:

SUBJUNCTIVE

> I hope you feel better tomorrow. /
> Espero que se sienta mejor mañana.

Expressions of willing that are generally followed by the infinitive in English are followed by the subjunctive in the dependent clause in Spanish:

I want you to come next week. / Quiero que **venga** la semana próxima.

The subjunctive is generally used when the subject of the dependent clause is not the subject of the main clause. The subjunctive is more frequently used in Spanish than it is in English. It appears in the main clause to express a formal command, after certain adverbs implying uncertainty (**tal vez, quizás**), or after interjections which introduce non-factual statements.

Perhaps he can leave tomorrow. / Quizás él **pueda** salir mañana.

3. what might happen, without establishing when it would or could happen:

CONDITIONAL

> I would call the doctor. / Yo llamaría al médico.

4. a command or a request:

IMPERATIVE

> Take the medication now. / Tome la medicina ahora.

Verb Tenses / Tiempos del verbo

Tense means the time when the action takes place: present, past, or future. See how the verb changes in the following examples using a regular verb in the indicative.

Present The doctor speaks to the pacient now. /
La doctora **habla** con el paciente ahora.
Past The doctor spoke to the patient. /
La doctora **habló** con el paciente.
Future The doctor will speak to the patient. /
La doctora **hablará** con el paciente.

To indicate the tense of the verb in Spanish add to the stem of the verb, or to its infinitive in the case of the future and conditional, the ending that belongs to the appropriate tense, person and number:

Present habl + a (third person singular) → habla
Past habl + ó (third person singular) → habló
Future hablar (infinitive) + á (third person singular) → hablará
Conditional hablar (infinitive) + ía (third person singular) → hablaría

The Spanish tenses are divided into simple and compound tenses. The compound tenses of the indicative and subjunctive are formed with the auxiliary verb **haber** (used in the simple tenses) and the past participle of the conjugated verb. In the indicative and the conditional, they are generally translated as follows:

SIMPLE TENSES

To examine / **examinar** has the following forms in the third person singular:

Present examina he, she examines; he, she is examining; he, she does examine
Imperfect examinaba he, she examined; he, she was examining; he, she did examine
Preterit examinó he, she examined; he, she did examine
Future examinará he, she will examine
Conditional examinaría he, she would (could) examine

COMPOUND TENSES

Perfect ha examinado he, she has examined
Pluperfect había examinado he, she had examined
Future perfect habrá examinado he, she will have examined
Conditional perfect habría examinado he, she would (could) have examined

Note: See Verb Charts at the end of this section for complete conjugation of compound tenses of the indicative, subjunctive, and conditional.

Conjugation of Verbs / Conjugación del verbo

The infinitive of verbs in Spanish end in: **-ar** as in **curar** / to cure, **-er** as in **comer** / to eat, and **-ir** as in **admitir** / to admit. The letters preceding the infinitive ending are the root or stem of a Spanish verb. The tenses of regular verbs are formed by adding endings to the root, except for the future and the conditional tenses, which use the whole infinitive as a root. Only most common verbs and irregularities are shown here.

Regular Verbs	*Root*	*Infinitive ending*
to cure, to heal / curar	cur-	-ar
to eat / comer	com-	-er
to admit / admitir	admit-	-ir

Moods / Modos del verbo

INDICATIVE / INDICATIVO:
PRESENT / PRESENTE

cur- + Endings

curar:	Singular Endings			Plural Endings
I / yo	curo		we / nosotros	curamos
you / tú *(fam.)*	curas		you / vosotros	curáis
you / usted	cura		you / ustedes	curan
he / él	cura		they / ellos	curan
she / ella	cura		they / ellos	curan

com- + Endings

comer:	Singular Endings			Plural Endings
I / yo	como		we / nosotros-as	comemos
you / tú *(fam.)*	comes		you / vosotros-as	coméis
you / usted	come		you / ustedes	comen
he / él	come		they / ellos	comen
she / ella	come		they / ellas	comen

admit- + Endings

admitir:	Singular Endings			Plural Endings
I / yo	admito		we / nosotros-as	admitimos
you / tú *(fam.)*	admites		you / vosotros-as	admitís
you / used	admite		you / ustedes	admiten
he / él	admite		they / ellos	admiten
she / ella	admite		they / ellas	admiten

Note: Except for the forms of the plural, **nosotros** and **vosotros**, the forms of the -er and -ir verbs are the same (-**er**: -emos, éis; -**ir**: -imos, -ís). The **vosotros** form is seldom used in Hispanic America.

IMPERFECT AND PRETERIT / IMPERFECTO Y PRETÉRITO

There are two tenses of the indicative that refer to the past. The imperfect is one of them, frequently called the past descriptive because it describes actions and conditions which took place in a continuous or customary way.

> I used to work from 8 A.M. until 3 P.M. / Yo **trabajaba** desde las ocho de la mañana hasta las tres de la tarde.

The preterit refers in a narrative way to an action in the past which ended at a definite time. Historical facts are generally narrated in the preterit.

> Yesterday I worked from 2 P.M. until 10 P.M. / Ayer **trabajé** desde las dos de la tarde hasta las diez de la noche.

IMPERFECT / IMPERFECTO

curar / to cure, to heal

cur- + Endings

curar:	Singular Endings			Plural Endings
I / yo	curaba		we / nosotros-as	curábamos
you / tú *(fam.)*	curabas		you / vosotros-as	curábais
you / usted	curaba		you / ustedes	curaban
he / él	curaba		they / ellos	curaban
she / ella	curaba		they / ellas	curaban

Verbs ending in **-er** and **-ir** have the same endings in the imperfect.

comer / to eat   admitir / to admit

com- + *Endings*

comer:	*Singular Endings*			*Plural Endings*
I / yo	comía	we / nosotros-as		comíamos
you / tú *(fam.)*	comías	you / vosotros-as		comíais
you / usted	comía	you / ustedes		comían
he / él	comía	they / ellos		comían
she / ella	comía	they / ellos		comían

admit- + *Endings*

admitir:	*Singular Endings*			*Plural Endings*
I / yo	admitía	we / nosotros-as		admitíamos
you / tú *(fam.)*	admitías	you / vosotros-as		admitíais
you / usted	admitía	you / ustedes		admitían
he / él	admitía	they / ellos		admitían
she / ella	admitía	they / ellas		admitían

Note: The only irregular verbs in the imperfect indicative are: **ser, ver,** and **ir:** yo era, yo iba, yo veía. See verb charts at the end of this section for complete conjugation.

PRETERIT / PRETÉRITO

curar / to cure, to heal

cur- + *Endings*

curar:	*Singular Endings*			*Plural Endings*
I / yo	curé	we / nosotros-as		curamos
you / tú *(fam.)*	curaste	you / vosotros-as		curasteis
you / usted	curó	you / ustedes		curaron
he / él	curó	they / ellos		curaron
she / ella	curó	they / ellos		curaron

com- + *Endings*

comer:	*Singular Endings*			*Plural Endings*
I / yo	comí	we / nosotros-as		comimos
you / tú *(fam.)*	comiste	you / vosotros-as		comisteis
you / usted	comió	you / ustedes		comieron
he / él	comió	they / ellos		comieron
she / ella	comió	they / ellas		comieron

admit- + *Endings*

admitir:	*Singular Endings*			*Plural Endings*
I / yo	admití	we / nosotros-as		admitimos
you / tú *(fam.)*	admitiste	you / vosotros-as		admitisteis
you / usted	admitió	you / ustedes		admitieron
he / él	admitió	they / ellos		admitieron
she / ella	admitió	they / ellas		admitieron

Note: Regular verbs ending in **-er** and **-ir** have the same endings in the preterit.

FUTURE / FUTURO

The Spanish future expresses not only actions that will take place in the future, but often also probability or speculation.

She will be here at 9 A.M. / **Estará** aquí a las nueve de la mañana.
I wonder what time it is? / ¿Qué hora **será?**
It is probably one o'clock. / **Será** la una.
I wonder if the surgery will take a long time. / ¿**Durará** mucho la operación?

The present tense is also used to express the immediate future.

He will arrive at 10 A.M. / **Llega** a las diez de la mañaua.

Note: When translating English expressions in which *will* refers to willingness of someone to do something, use the verb **querer** and not the future tense; Will you please bring me some water? / ¿**Quieres** traerme agua, por favor?

All verbs use the same endings to form the future tense. **Comer** and **admitir** take the same endings as **curar,** shown here.

Infinitive + Endings	*Singular*	*Endings*	
curar +	I / yo	-é	curar**é**
comer +	you / tú *(fam.)*	-ás	curar**ás**
admitir +	you / usted	-á	curar**á**
	he, she / él, ella	-á	curar**á**

	Plural	*Endings*	
	we / nosotros-as	-emos	curar**emos**
	you / vosotros-as	-éis	curar**éis**
	you / ustedes	-án	curar**án**
	they / ellos-as	-án	curar**án**

CONDITIONAL

All verbs use the same endings to form the conditional. The conditional is formed by adding to the infinitive the same endings used to form the imperfect indicative of **-er** and **-ir** verbs.

The conditional often refers to probability in the past:

Joey felt bad last night. Could it be something he ate? /
Pepito se sintió mal anoche. ¿**Sería** algo que comió?

Infinitive + Endings	*Singular*	*Endings*	
curar +	yo	-ía	curar**ía**
comer +	tú (fam.)	-ías	curar**ías**
admitir +	usted	-ía	curar**ía**
	él	-ía	curar**ía**
	ella	-ía	curar**ía**

	Plural	*Endings*	
	nosotros-as	-íamos	curar**íamos**
	vosotros-as	-íais	curar**íais**
	ustedes	-ían	curar**ían**
	ellos-as	-ían	curar**ían**

Note: Use the infinitive to form the future and the conditional. Only twelve verbs have irregularities in their radical in the future and the conditional: **caber** / cabr-; **haber** / habr-; **saber** / sabr-; **poder** / podr-; **poner** / pondr-; **salir** / saldr-; **tener** / tendr-; **valer** / valdr-; **venir** / vendr-; **hacer** / har-; **decir** / dir- **querer** / querr-. See verb charts at the end of this section for complete conjugation.

PRESENT SUBJUNCTIVE

All persons of the present subjunctive have the same root as the first person singular of the present indicative except for the verbs: **dar, ser, estar, haber, ir, saber.** To form the present subjunctive, drop the **-o** of the first person singular of the present indicative before adding the endings of the subjunctive.

For verbs ending in **-ar,** start with the first person of the present indicative: **curo.** Drop the **-o,** and add the endings of the present subjunctive.

curar:	*Singular*	*Endings*	
cur- +	I / yo	-e	cure
	you / tú *(fam.)*	-es	cures
	you / usted	-e	cure
	he / él	-e	cure
	she / ella	-e	cure

	Plural	*Endings*	
	we / nosotros-as	-emos	cur**emos**
	you / vosotros-as	-éis	cur**éis**
	you / ustedes	-en	cur**en**
	they / ellos ellas	-en	cur**en**

Verbs ending in **-er** and **-ir** have the same endings in the present subjunctive.

com- + *Endings*

comer:	*Singular Endings*	*Plural Endings*	
I / yo	coma	we / nosotros	com**amos**
you / tú	com**as**	you / vosotros	com**áis**
you / usted	coma	you / ustedes	com**an**
he / él	coma	they / ellos	com**an**
she / ella	coma	they / ellas	com**an**

admit- + *Endings*

admitir:	*Singular Endings*	*Plural Endings*	
I / yo	admita	we / nosotros-as	admit**amos**
you / tú *(fam.)*	admit**as**	you / vosotros-as	admit**áis**
you / usted	admita	you / ustedes	admit**an**
he / él	admita	they / ellos	admit**an**
she / ella	admita	they / ellas	admit**an**

Note: Observe that the subjunctive endings are the reverse of the indicative endings, except for the first person singular.

IMPERFECT SUBJUNCTIVE / IMPERFECTO DE SUBJUNTIVO

The subjunctive has only one simple past tense, el imperfecto de subjuntivo. The endings are identical for all the verbs with infinitives ending in **-ar, -er,** or **-ir.** However, the endings are not added to the root of the verb, but to the third person plural of the preterit indicative, after dropping the ending **-on.**

curar, comer, admitir

Singular	*Endings*	*Plural*	*Endings*
I / yo	**-a**	we / nosotros-as	**-amos**
you / tú (fam.)	**-as**	you / vosotros-as	**-ais**
you / usted	**-a**	you / ustedes	**-an**
he / él	**-a**	they / ellos	**-an**
she / ella	**-a**	they / ellas	**-an**

I was hoping that he would eat more. / Esperaba que él comiera más.

Drop the ending **-on** of the third person plural of the preterit in: cur**aron,** com**ieron,** admit**ieron;** add the endings: **-a, -as, -a, -amos, -ais, -an:**

curara	curáramos	comiera	comiéramos	admitiera	admitiéramos
curaras	curarais	comieras	comierais	admitieras	admitierais
curara	curaran	comiera	comieran	admitiera	admitieran

How to give an order or make a request

IMPERATIVE / EL IMPERATIVO

A command is given generally to a second person, the person spoken to. There are two forms of addressing a second person in Spanish: a familiar way, **tú**, and a formal way, **usted.** A physician or health care person addresses his or her patients in a formal way unless the patient is a child or an old friend. After a command is given, the polite form **por favor** (please) may be used.

COMMAND FORMS FOR USTED AND USTEDES
WITH REGULAR VERBS

If the infinitive ending is **-ar**, add **-e** to form the command of **usted,** and **-en** to form the command of **ustedes.** If the infinitive ending is either **-er** or **-ir**, add **-a** to form the command of **usted,** and **-an** to form the command of **ustedes.**

Infinitive	Drop ending	Add	usted	ustedes (+n)
curar / to cure	-ar	-e	cure	curen
comer / to eat	-er	-a	coma	coman
admitir / to admit	-ir	-a	admita	admitan

COMMAND FORMS OF IRREGULAR VERBS

To form the command of **usted** of irregular verbs, use the first person singular of the present indicative and drop the **-o** ending. Add **-e** to **-ar** verbs and **-a** to **-er** and **-ir** verbs. To form the command of **ustedes,** add **-n** to the command form of **usted.**

Infinitive	*1st p. sing.*	*usted*	*Command Forms* *ustedes (+n)*
to say, tell / decir	digo	diga	digan
to do, make / hacer	hago	haga	hagan
to put / poner	pongo	ponga	pongan
to leave / salir	salgo	salga	salgan
to have / tener	tengo	tenga	tengan
to bring / traer	traigo	traiga	traigan
to come / venir	vengo	venga	vengan
to think / pensar	pienso	piense	piensen
to move / mover	muevo	mueva	muevan
to sleep / dormir	duermo	duerma	duerman

Exceptions: Special Forms of Commands

Infinitive	*usted*	*ustedes*
to give / dar	dé	den
to be / estar	esté	estén
to have / haber	haya	hayan
to go / ir	vaya	vayan
to know / saber	sepa	sepan
to be / ser	sea	sean
to see / ver	vea	vean

Formal commands with root-vowel changing verbs (**e-ie, o-ue, e-i**) have the same form as with the first person singular of the present indicative.

to sleep / dormir   **duerma** Ud.   to think / pensar   **piense** Ud.

Verbs ending in **-car, -gar,** and **-zar** require spelling changes to keep the same sounds of the **c, g,** and **z** of the infinitive.

c → qu
to look for / buscar   Look for the prescription. / **Busque** la receta.

g → gu
to pay / pagar   Pay the bill / **Pague** la cuenta.

z → c
to begin / empezar   Begin now. / **Empiece** ahora.

NEGATIVE FORMAL COMMANDS

Negative formal commands are formed by placing **no** before the command.

   Take the medicine. / **Tome** la medicina.   Don't take the medicine. / **No tome** la medicina.

NEGATIVE TÚ COMMANDS

   No + command of **usted** + **s**
   No + tome   + **s** → **No tomes** (tú).

AFFIRMATIVE TÚ COMMANDS

Use an informal command with persons whom you address by their first name, using the same form as the third person singular of the present indicative.

   tomar   Take the medicine. / **Toma** (tú) la medicina.
   comer   Eat less. / **Come** (tú) menos.
   dormir Sleep more. / **Duerme** (tú) más.

SPECIAL FORMS OF COMMANDS OF TÚ IN THE AFFIRMATIVE

   to say / decir   Tell me. / **Dime.**
   to do, to make / hacer Do it. / **Hazlo.**
   to go / ir   Go home. / **Ve** a la casa.
   to put / poner   Put your hand here. / **Pon** la mano aquí.
   to leave / salir   Leave now. / **Sal** ahora.
   to be / ser   Be attentive. / **Sé** atento.

PLURAL OF TÚ COMMANDS

Affirmative commands for **vosotros** are formed by substituting **-d** for the final **-r** of the infinitive. In Hispanic America, the plural form of the formal command is used for the plural of **tú** commands.

NOSOTROS COMMANDS

Translate *let us* in either of two ways:

1. **Vamos** a + infinitivo:
   Let's examine her. / **Vamos a** examinarla.
2. Using the present subjunctive of the first person plural:
   Let's study the case. / **Estudiemos** el caso.

Root-Vowel Changing Verbs and Spelling Change Verbs /
Verbos de cambio vocálico y ortográfico

1. **Root-Vowel Changing Verbs** are classified according to the pattern of changes in the root vowel.
   a. **First class:** Verbs with infinitive ending **-ar** and **-er.** When the root is stressed, root vowel **e** changes to **ie,** and **o** to **ue,** in all the forms of the present indicative, and subjunctive,

except the first and second person plural. **Apretar, entender, mostrar, volver,** and others belong to this class. See chart for conjugation of these verbs after spelling change verbs.

b. **Second class:** Verbs with infinitive ending in **-ir.** When the root is stressed the changes occur in the same tenses as verbs in the first class: **e** changes to **ie, o** to **ue,** in the singular and the third person plural of the present indicative. The changes in the subjunctive are the same except in the first and second person plural (the changes take place while they do not in the indicative). The **e** changes to **i,** and the **o** to **u,** in the third person singular and plural of the preterit and in the present participle (gerund). Examples of the second class are **sentir (ie)** and **dormir (ue).**

c. **Third class:** Verbs ending in **-er** and **-ir.** When the root is stressed, the change is **e** to **i,** in the same forms in which changes take place in the second class. See conjugation of **repetir** as a model verb for this class.

2. **Spelling Change Verbs:** Changes in spelling occur in Spanish in certain verbs to keep the sound of the final consonant of the root:

Verbs with Infinitive Ending in -ar

Ending	Change	When	Tenses
car	c-qu	followed by **e**	1st. person pret., and
gar	g-gu	followed by **e**	all persons pres. subj.
guar	gu-gü	followed by **e**	for all these endings
zar	z-c	followed by **e**	

Examples:

Verb	Preterit	Pres. Subj.
buscar / to look for	bus**qué**	bus**que**
		bus**ques**
		bus**que**
pagar / to pay	pa**gué**	pa**gue**
		pa**gues**
		pa**gue**
averiguar / to find out	averi**güé**	averi**güe**
		averi**gües**
		averi**güe**
abrazar / to embrace, to hug	abra**cé**	abra**ce**
		abra**ces**
		abra**ce**

Verbs with Infinitive Ending in -er and -ir

Ending	Change	When	Tenses
cer	c-z	preceded by	1st. person sing.
cir	c-z	consonant and	pres. indic.,
ger	g-j	followed by **a**	all persons
gir	g-j	or **o, i** is be-	pres. subj.,
guir	gu-g	tween vowels	3rd person sing. and plural
eer	i-y		preterit,
ocer	+**z** before **c**		all persons
ucir			imperf. subj.,
			1st person pres. ind.,
			all persons pres. subj.

Examples:

Verb	Pres. Ind.	Pres. Subj.
conocer / to know, to be acquainted with	conozco	conozca
		conozcas
		conozca
reducir / to reduce	reduzco	reduzca
		reduzcas
		reduzca
proteger / to protect	protejo	proteja
		protejas
		proteja

Verb	Preterit	Imp. Subj.
creer / to believe	creyó	creyera
	creyeron	creyeras
		creyera
	Gerund	
	creyendo	

All tenses not given are regular. Only the first three persons singular of tenses will be given; once the root change is made, regular endings are added.

Root-Vowel Changing Verbs

	apretar / *to squeeze*	*mostrar /* *to show*	*entender/* *to understand*
Gerund	apretando	mostrando	entendiendo
Past Participle	apretado	mostrado	entendido
Pres. Indic.	aprieto	muestro	entiendo
	aprietas	muestras	entiendes
	aprieta	muestra	entiende
	apretamos	mostramos	entendemos
	apretáis	mostráis	entendéis
	aprietan	muestran	entienden
Pres. Subj.	apriete	muestre	entienda
	aprietes	muestres	entiendas
	apriete	muestre	entienda
	apretemos	mostremos	entendamos
	apretéis	mostréis	entendáis
	aprieten	muestren	entiendan

Note: Use **apretar** as a model to conjugate: **cerrar** / to close; **comenzar** / to begin; **despertar** / to wake up; **empezar** / to begin; **pensar** / to think; **sentar** / to settle, to fit; **sentarse** / to sit down.

Other verbs like **mostrar: acordar** / to agree; **acordarse** / to remember; **acostarse** / to lie down; **apostar** / to bet; **encontrar** / to find; **encontrarse** / to run across, to meet; **probar** / to test; to taste; **recordar** / to remember; **rogar** / to beg; **volar** / to fly.

Other verbs like **entender: atender** / to attend; **defender** / to defend; **encender** / to light, to set fire to; **perder** / to lose.

	volver/ *to return*	*sentir/* *to feel*	*dormir/* *to sleep*	*repetir/* *to repeat*
Gerund	volviendo	sintiendo	durmiendo	repitiendo
Past Participle	vuelto	sentido	dormido	repetido
Pres. Indic.	vuelvo	siento	duermo	repito
	vuelves	sientes	duermes	repites
	vuelve	siente	duerme	repite
	volvemos	sentimos	dormimos	repetimos
	volvéis	sentís	dormís	repetís
	vuelven	sienten	duermen	repiten
Pres. Subj.	vuelva	sienta	duerma	repita
	vuelvas	sientas	duermas	repitas
	vuelva	sienta	duerma	repita
	volvamos	sintamos	durmamos	repitamos
	volváis	sintáis	durmáis	repitáis
	vuelvan	sientan	duerman	repitan
Pret.	volví	sentí	dormí	repetí
	volviste	sentiste	dormiste	repetiste
	volvió	sintió	durmió	repitió
	volvimos	sentimos	dormimos	repetimos
	volvisteis	sentisteis	dormisteis	repetisteis
	volvieron	sintieron	durmieron	repitieron

Note: Other verbs that follow the same changes: **mover** / to move; **disolver** / to disolve; **doler** / to hurt; **moler** / to grind; **morder** / to bite; **promover** / to promote; and other verbs formed by adding a prefix to **volver**. Volver and its derivatives have an irregular past participle as well as **disolver** (disuelto).

Verbs conjugated like **sentir: advertir** / to advice, to take notice; **consentir** / to consent; **convertir** / to convert; **digerir** / to digest; **divertirse** / to have a good time; **herir** / to wound, hurt, stab; **hervir** / to boil; **mentir** / to lie; **preferir** / to prefer; **referir** / to refer.

Like **dormir** are **dormirse** / to fall sleep, and **morir** / to die.

Use **repetir** as a model verb for: **competir** / to compete; **concebir** / to conceive; **derretir** / to melt; **conseguir** / to obtain; **medir** / to measure; **pedir** / to ask, to request; **reír** / to laugh.

LIST OF USEFUL VERBS / LISTA DE VERBOS ÚTILES

English	*Spanish*	*English*	*Spanish*
to abstain, to refrain	abstenerse de	to admit	admitir
		to advise	aconsejar
to accelerate, to speed up	acelerar	to age	envejecer
		to affect	afectar
to accept	aceptar	to aggravate	empeorar, agravar
to accompany, to go with	acompañar	to aid	ayudar
		to alleviate	aliviar
to accumulate, to gather	acumular	to amputate	amputar
		to anesthetize	anestesiar
to ache, to hurt	doler *(ue)*	to announce	anunciar; informar; *(to warn)*[2] avisar
to acquire	adquirir *(ie)*[1]		
to add	añadir, agregar	to annoy	molestar

[1] Vowels between parentheses indicate root-changing verbs.
[2] Brackets clarify the meaning of the verb. Parentheses indicate a synonym.

English	Spanish	English	Spanish
to appear	aparecer	to bleed	sangrar
to apply for	solicitar	to blink	parpadear
to approach, to draw near	acercarse	to bother, to annoy	molestar
to approve	aprobar	to break	romper; quebrar
to arouse	excitar	to breathe	respirar
to arrange	arreglar	to bring	traer
to arrest	arrestar; (*to stop*) parar	to buy	comprar
to arrive	llegar; [*on time*] llegar a tiempo	to bruise	magullarse; amoratarse
to ask for, to request	pedir	to brush	cepillar
		to burn	quemar; quemarse
to ask (*to question*)	preguntar	to burp	eructar; repetir
to aspirate	aspirar	to call	llamar
to aspire to	aspirar a	to carry, to wear	llevar
to assimilate	asimilar	to cause	causar
to assume	asumir	to change [*one's clothes*]	cambiarse (de ropa)
to assure	asegurar		
to astonish	asombrar	to chat	charlar
to attack	atacar	to check [*to examine*]	examinar, revisar
to attend	asistir		
to attract	atraer	to choke	atragantarse; ahogar; sofocar
to bathe	bañarse		
to be	estar; ser	to choose	escoger, elegir (*i*)
to be able, can	poder	to clean	limpiar
to be absent	estar ausente	to climb up	subirse
to be afraid	tener miedo	to close	cerrar (*ie*)
to be at fault, to blame	tener la culpa, culpar	to come	venir
		to complain [*of, about*]	quejarse (*de*)
to be born	nacer		
to be hungry	tener hambre	to complete	completar
to be in a hurry	tener prisa	to conceive	concebir
to be long [*time*]	tardar	to consider	considerar
to be lucky	tener suerte	to contain	contener
to be quiet	callarse; (*to calm*) calmarse	to continue	continuar, seguir (*i*)
		to convalesce	convalecer; recuperarse
to be silent	callarse		
to be right	tener razón	to cost	costar (*ue*)
to be sick	estar enfermo-a	to count	contar (*ue*)
to be sleepy	tener sueño	to cough	toser
to be [*weather*]	hacer (frío, calor)	to create	crear
to be . . .years old	tener . . .años	to cry	llorar
to become [*something*]	hacerse; ponerse (+ *adj.*)	to cut	cortar
		to deliver [*to give birth*]	dar a luz; estar de parto; *pop.* aliviarse
to begin	empezar (*ie*), comenzar (*ie*)		
		to deny	negar (*ie*)
to behave	portarse	to depend on	depender de
to belch	eructar	to develop	desarrollar; [*a photo*] revelar
to believe	creer		
to bend, to flex	doblar; doblarse	to die	morir (*ue, u*)
to bite	morder (*ue*)	to diet	estar a dieta; hacer una dieta
		to discharge [*secretion*]	tener secreciones

English	Spanish	English	Spanish
to discharge [*a patient*]	dar de alta	to hide	esconder; esconderse
to disinfect	desinfectar	to hope	esperar
to do, to make	hacer	to hurry	apurarse, darse prisa
to doubt	dudar	to hurt	doler (*ue*); lastimar
to dream	soñar (*ue*)	to immobilize	inmobilizar
to dress [*with clothes*]	vestir; vestirse (*i*)	to improve	mejorar
to dress [*a wound*]	vendar	to increase	aumentar
to drink	beber; tomar	to inform	informar
to earn	ganar	to inject	inyectar
to eat	comer	to insert	insertar, introducir, meter
to eat breakfast	desayunar	to itch	picar
to eat dinner	cenar	to kill	matar
to eat lunch	almorzar (*ue*)	to know	saber; [*to be acquainted with*] conocer
to ejaculate	eyacular		
to enter	entrar	to lack	faltar
to examine	examinar	to leak	gotear
to exercise	hacer ejercicio	to lean to	apoyarse en
to exist	existir	to learn	aprender
to expect	esperar	to leave	salir
to explain	explicar	to let	dejar, permitir
to fail	dejar de	to lie	mentir (*ie, i*)
to fall asleep	dormirse (*ue, u*)	to lie down	acostarse (*ue*)
to fall down	caerse	to lift	levantar, alzar
to fear	temer; tener miedo	to like	gustar
to feel	sentir (*ie, i*)	to listen	escuchar, atender (*ie*)
to follow	seguir (*i*)		
to forget	olvidar	to live	vivir
to form	formar	to look at	mirar
to fracture	fracturar; quebrar; romper	to look for	buscar
		to lose	perder (*ie*)
to function	funcionar	to love	amar; querer
to gargle	hacer gárgaras	to lower [*arm, leg*]	bajar
to get	obtener, conseguir (*i*)	to marry	casarse
		to masturbate	masturbarse
to get angry	enfadarse, enojarse	to menstruate	menstruar
to get better	mejorarse	to miscarry	abortar
to get up	levantarse	to move	mover (*ue*)
to get well	curarse, sanarse, ponerse bien	to need	necesitar
		to nurse [*a baby*]	amamantar
to give	dar	to nurse [*the sick*]	cuidar
to go	ir; salir	to nurture	nutrir
to go away	irse	to obtain	conseguir (*i*), obtener
to go to bed	acostarse (*ue*)		
to grow	crecer	to obstruct	obstruir
to happen, to turn out	suceder	to open	abrir
		to oppose	oponerse
to hand over	entregar	to order	ordenar, mandar
to have	tener; [*aux.*] haber	to owe	deber
to hear	oír	to palpate	palpar
to heat	calentar	to pant	jadear
to help	ayudar		

217

English	Spanish	English	Spanish
to paralyse	paralizar	to shower	ducharse
to participate	participar	to sit down	sentarse (*ie*)
to pay	pagar	to smoke	fumar
to penetrate	penetrar	to sneeze	estornudar
to permit	permitir, dejar	to solve	resolver (*ue*)
to plan	planear	to speak	hablar
to practice	practicar	to spend	gastar; [*time*] pasar
to prefer	preferir (*ie*)	to spit	escupir
to prescribe	recetar, prescribir	to sprain	torcer (*ue*)
to promise	prometer	to spray	rociar
to push [*down-*	pujar	to stand up	levantarse
wards]		to stimulate	estimular
to put	poner	to study	estudiar
to put in	poner; meter	to suck	chupar, absorber
to put on [*clothing*]	ponerse	to suffer	sufrir
to put to bed	acostar (*ue*)	to suppose	suponer
to qualify	capacitar	to surprise	sorprender
to question	preguntar	to swallow	tragar
to raise	levantar	to sweat	sudar
to react	reaccionar	to sweeten	endulzar
to read	leer	to swell	hinchar
to receive	recibir	to take	tomar
to recover	recobrar	to take off	quitar, quitarse
to recuperate	recuperar, recobrar	to talk	hablar
to relax	relajar, aflojar	to teach	enseñar
to remain	quedar	to tell	decir
to remember	recordar (*ue*)	to think	pensar (*ie*)
to remove, take off	quitar; quitarse	to throw [*into*]	echar
to repeat	repetir (*i*)	to try	tratar de; probar
to reply	contestar, respon-		(*ue*)
	der	to turn	virar; virarse
to respond	responder	to turn around	dar vuelta; vol-
to rest	descansar		tearse
to restore	restaurar, reparar	to turn down	rechazar
to return	volver (*ue*)	to urinate	orinar
to run	correr	to use	usar, emplear
to say	decir	to visit	visitar
to scratch	arañar	to vomit	vomitar
to see	ver	to wait	esperar
to seem	parecer	to wake up	despertarse (*ie*)
to send	mandar	to want	querer (*ie*), desear
to serve	servir (*i*)	to wear	llevar
to shake	agitar	to wheeze	resollar (*ue*)
to shout	gritar	to wish	querer (*ie*), desear
to show	mostrar (*ue*), seña-	to work	trabajar
	lar, enseñar	to write	escribir

VERB CHARTS / CUADROS DE VERBOS

Regular Verbs

SIMPLE TENSES

The gerund is formed by adding **-ando** to the stem of the infinitive of verbs ending in **-ar,** and adding **-iendo** to the stem of the infinitive of verbs ending in **-er** and **-ir.**

The past participle of regular verbs is formed by adding **-ado** to the stem of the infinitive of verbs ending in **-ar,** and adding **-ido** to the stem of verbs ending in **-er** and **-ir.**

Infinitive	**tomar**	**comer**	**admitir**
	(to take, to drink)	*(to eat)*	*(to admit)*
Gerund	tomando	comiendo	admitiendo
Past participle	tomado	comido	admitido

Indicative

Present

tomo	como	admito
tomas	comes	admites
toma	come	admite
tomamos	comemos	admitimos
tomáis	coméis	admitís
toman	comen	admiten

Preterit

tomé	comí	admití
tomaste	comiste	admitiste
tomó	comió	admitió
tomamos	comimos	admitimos
tomasteis	comisteis	admitisteis
tomaron	comieron	admitieron

Imperfect

tomaba	comía	admitía
tomabas	comías	admitías
tomaba	comía	admitía
tomábamos	comíamos	admitíamos
tomabais	comíais	admitíais
tomaban	comían	admitían

Future

tomaré	comeré	admitiré
tomarás	comerás	admitirás
tomará	comerá	admitirá
tomaremos	comeremos	admitiremos
tomaréis	comeréis	admitiréis
tomarán	comerán	admitirán

Conditional

tomaría	comería	admitiría
tomarías	comerías	admitirías
tomaría	comería	admitiría
tomaríamos	comeríamos	admitiríamos
tomaríais	comeríais	admitiríais
tomarían	comerían	admitirían

PERFECT FORMS

Indicative

Present Perfect
he
has
ha
hemos   tomado   comido   admitido
habéis
han

Past Perfect
había
habías
había
habíamos   tomado   comido   admitido
habíais
habían

Future Perfect
habré
habrás
habrá
habremos   tomado   comido   admitido
habréis
habrán

Conditional Perfect
habría
habrías
habría
habríamos   tomado   comido   admitido
habríais
habrían

Subjunctive

Present

tome	coma	admita
tomes	comas	admitas
tome	coma	admita
tomemos	comamos	admitamos
toméis	comáis	admitáis
tomen	coman	admitan

Imperfect (-ra)

tomara	comiera	admitiera
tomaras	comieras	admitieras
tomara	comiera	admitiera
tomáramos	comiéramos	admitiéramos
tomarais	comierais	admitierais
tomaran	comieran	admitieran

Note: The form ending in **-ra** is the most commonly used.

Imperfect (-se)

tomase	comiese	admitiese
tomases	comieses	admitieses

220

tomase	comiese	admitiese
tomásemos	comiésemos	admitiésemos
tomaseis	comieseis	admitieseis
tomasen	comiesen	admitiesen

PERFECT FORMS

Present Perfect
haya
hayas
haya   tomado   comido   admitido
hayamos
hayáis
hayan

Past Perfect (-ra)
hubiera
hubieras
hubiera
hubiéramos   tomado   comido   admitido
hubierais
hubieran

Past Perfect (-se)
hubiese
hubieses
hubiese
hubiésemos   tomado   comido   admitido
hubieseis
hubiesen

Irregular Verbs / Verbos irregulares

The following verbs and their compounds have other irregularities that do not allow their inclusion in any of the classifications given before. For this particular kind of verb, twenty in our list, only the tenses with irregular forms will be given. Apply the rule of regular verbs to tenses not given here. Only the singular forms will be given when the ordinary rules of those tenses are followed in their formation. The auxiliary verb **haber** belongs to this group.

1. **andar** / to walk

Pret. Ind.	Imp. Subj.
anduve	anduviera
anduviste	anduvieras
anduvo	anduviera
anduvimos	anduviéramos
anduvisteis	anduviérais
anduvieron	anduvieran

2. **caber** / to fit, to be contained in

Pres. Ind.	Pres. Subj.	Fut.
quepo	quepa	cabré
	quepas	cabrás
	quepa	cabrá

Pret. Ind.	Imp. Subj.	Cond.
cupe	cupiera	cabría
cupiste	cupieras	cabrías
cupo	cupiera	cabría
cupimos		
cupisteis		
cupieron		

3. **caer** / to fall

		Pres. Ind.	**Pres. Subj.**
Gerund	cayendo	caigo	caiga
Past Participle	caído		caigas
			caigas
			caigamos
			caigáis
			caigan

Pret. Ind.	**Imp. Subj.**
cayó	cayera
cayeron	cayeras
	cayera

4. **dar** / to give

Pres. Ind.	**Pres. Subj.**	**Pret. Ind.**	**Imp. Subj.**
doy	dé	di	diera
	des	diste	dieras
	dé	dio	diera
	demos	dimos	
	deis	disteis	
	den	dieron	

5. **decir** / to say, to tell

		Pres. Ind.	**Pret. Ind.**
Gerund	diciendo	digo	dije
Past Participle	dicho	dices	dijiste
		dice	dijo
		decimos	dijimos
		decís	dijisteis
		dicen	dijeron

Fut.	**Cond.**
diré	diría
dirás	dirías
dirá	diría

6. **estar** / to be

Pres. Ind.	**Pres. Subj.**
estoy	esté
estás	estés
está	esté
estamos	estemos
estáis	estéis
están	estén

Pret. Ind.	**Imp. Subj.**
estuve	estuviera
estuviste	estuvieras
estuvo	estuviera
estuvimos	
estuvisteis	
estuvieron	

7. **hacer** / to do, to make

		Pres. Ind.	**Pret. Ind.**	**Imp. Subj.**
Past Participle	hecho	hago	hice	hiciera
			hiciste	hicieras
			hizo	hiciera
			hicimos	
			hicisteis	
			hicieron	

		Fut.	*Cond.*	
		haré	haría	
		harás	harías	
		hará	haría	

8. **ir** / to go

		Pres. Ind.	*Pres. Subj.*	*Pret. Ind.*
Gerund	yendo	voy	vaya	fui
		vas	vayas	fuiste
		va	vaya	fue
		vamos	vayamos	fuimos
		vais	vayáis	fuisteis
		van	vayan	fueron

	Imp. Ind.	*Imp. Subj.*
	iba	fuera
	ibas	fueras
	iba	fuera
	íbamos	fuéramos
	ibais	fuerais
	iban	fueran

9. **oír** / to hear

		Pres. Ind.	*Pres. Subj.*
Gerund	oyendo	oigo	oiga
Past Participle	oído	oyes	oigas
		oye	oiga
		oímos	oigamos
		oís	oigáis
		oyen	oigan

	Pret. Ind.	*Imp. Subj.*
	oyó	oyera
	oyeron	oyeras
		oyera

10. **poder** / to be able

		Pres. Ind.	*Pres. Subj.*	*Pret. Ind.*
		puedo	pueda	pude
Gerund	pudiendo	puedes	puedas	pudiste
		puede	pueda	pudo
		podemos	podamos	pudimos
		podéis	podáis	pudisteis
		pueden	puedan	pudieron

	Imp. Subj.	*Fut.*	*Cond.*
	pudiera	podré	podría
	pudieras	podrás	podrías
	pudiera	podrá	podría

11. **poner** / to put, to place

		Pres. Ind.	*Pres. Subj.*	*Pret. Ind.*
Past Participle	puesto	pongo	ponga	puse
			pongas	pusiste
			ponga	puso
			pongamos	pusimos
			pongáis	pusisteis
			pongan	pusieron

	Imp. Subj.	*Fut.*	*Cond*
	pusiera	pondré	pondría
	pusieras	pondrás	pondrías
	pusiera	pondrá	pondría

12. **querer** / to wish,
to want

Pres. Ind.	Pres. Subj.	Pret. Ind.
quiero	quiera	quise
quieres	quieras	quisiste
quiere	quiera	quiso
queremos	queramos	quisimos
queréis	queráis	quisisteis
quieren	quieran	quisieron

Imp. Subj.	Fut.	Cond
quisiera	querré	querría
quisieras	querrás	querrías
quisiera	querrá	querría

13. **saber** / to know

Pres. Ind.	Pres. Subj.	Fut.
sé	sepa	sabré
	sepas	sabrás
	sepa	sabrá
	sepamos	
	sepáis	
	sepan	

Pret. Ind.	Imp. Subj.	Cond.
supe	supiera	sabría
supiste	supieras	sabrías
supo	supiera	sabría
supimos	supiéramos	
supisteis	supierais	
supieron	supieran	

14. **salir** / to go out,
to leave

Pres. Ind.	Pres. Subj.
salgo	salga
	salgas
	salga
	salgamos
	salgáis
	salgan

Fut.	Cond.
saldré	saldría
saldrás	saldrías
saldrá	saldría

15. **ser** / to be

Pres. Ind.	Imp. Ind.	Pret. Ind.
soy	era	fui
eres	eras	fuiste
es	era	fue
somos	éramos	fuimos
sois	érais	fuisteis
son	eran	fueron

Pres. Subj.	Imp. Subj.
sea	fuera
seas	fueras
sea	fuera
seamos	fuéramos
seais	fuerais
sean	fueran

16. **tener** / to have

Pres. Ind.	Pres. Subj.	Pret.
tengo	tenga	tuve
tienes	tengas	tuviste
tiene	tenga	tuvo
tenemos	tengamos	tuvimos
tenéis	tengáis	tuvisteis
tienen	tengan	tuvieron

Imp. Subj.	Fut.	Cond.
tuviera	tendré	tendría
tuvieras	tendrás	tendrías
tuviera	tendrá	tendría

17. **traer** / to bring

		Pres. Ind.	Pres. Subj.
Gerund	trayendo	traigo	traiga
Past Participle	traído		traigas
			traiga
			traigamos
			traigáis
			traigan

Pret. Ind.	Imp. Subj.
traje	trajera
trajiste	trajeras
trajo	trajera
trajimos	
trajisteis	
trajeron	

18. **valer** / to be worth

Pres. Ind.	Pres. Subj.
valgo	valga
	valgas
	valga
	valgamos
	valgáis
	valgan

Fut.	Cond.
valdré	valdría
valdrás	valdrías
valdrá	valdría

19. **venir** / to come

Pres. Ind.	Pres. Subj.	Pret.
vengo	venga	vine
vienes	vengas	viniste
viene	vanga	vino
	vengamos	vinimos
	vengáis	vinisteis
vienen	vengan	vinieron

Imp. Subj.	Fut.	Cond.
viniera	vendré	vendría
vinieras	vendrás	vendrías
viniera	vendrá	vendría

225

20. **ver** / to see	Pres. Ind.	Pres. Subj.	Imp. Ind.
Past Participle visto	veo	vea	veía
		veas	veías
		vea	veía
		veamos	veíamos
		veáis	veíais
		vean	veían

Spanish verbs with irregular past participles

Infinitivo / Infinitive	*Past Participle*
abrir / to open	abierto
bendecir / to bless	bendito
cubrir / to cover	cubierto
descubrir / to discover	descubierto
encubrir / to hide, to cover up	encubierto
decir / to say	dicho
predecir / to predict	predicho
despertar / to awake	despierto, despertado
dividir / to divide	dividido, diviso
escribir / to write	escrito
inscribir / to inscribe	inscrito
prescribir / to prescribe	prescrito
subscribir / to subscribe	subscrito
expresar / to express	expresado, expreso
freir / to fry	frito
sofreir / to refry	sofrito
hacer / to do, to make	hecho
deshacer / to undo	deshecho
rehacer / to redo	rehecho
satisfacer / to satisfy	satisfecho
imprimir / to print	impreso
juntar / to join	junto, juntado
oprimir / to oppress	oprimido, opreso
poner / to put	puesto
componer / to fix	compuesto
disponer / to dispose	dispuesto
exponer / to expose	expuesto
imponer / to impose	impuesto
oponer / to oppose	opuesto
reponer / to improve	repuesto
suponer / to suppose	supuesto
prender / to apprehend	preso, prendido
proveer / to provide	proveído, provisto
pudrir / to rot	podrido
absolver / to absolve	absuelto
disolver / to dissolve	disuelto
resolver / to resolve	resuelto
romper / to break	roto
soltar / to release	suelto
torcer / to twist	torcido, tuerto

Infinitivo / Infinitive	*Past Participle*
ver / to see	visto
prever / to foresee	previsto
volver / to return	vuelto
devolver / to give back	devuelto
envolver / to wrap around	envuelto
revolver / to stir, to agitate	revuelto

Note: Verbs in **boldface** serve as models to the derivate compound forms not appearing on this list. / Los verbos en **negrita** sirven de modelo para los derivados que no aparecen en esta lista.

ENGLISH-SPANISH VOCABULARY

VOCABULARIO

INGLÉS-ESPAÑOL

A

a *abbr.* **absolute** / absoluto; **acidity** / acidez; **accommodation** / acomodación; **allergy** / alergia; **anterior** / anterior; **aqua** / agua; **artery** / arteria.

a *art.indef.* un, una; **a contagious disease** / una enfermedad contagiosa; **a good doctor** / un médico bueno; (antes de vocal o *h* muda) **an; an abdominal pain** / un dolor abdominal; *a.* algún, alguna; **Is there a doctor on duty?** / ¿Hay algún médico de guardia?; *prep.* a; **three times a day** / tres veces al (a + el) día.

abandon *v.* abandonar, dejar; desamparar.

abandoned *a.* abandonado-a; irresponsable.

abasia *n.* abasia, movimiento incierto.

abbreviate *v.* abreviar, acortar, reducir, resumir.

abbreviation *n.* abreviación, abreviatura.

abdomen *n.* abdomen, vientre. *pop.* barriga, panza; **pendulous** ___ / ___ colgante, pendular; **scaphoid** ___ / ___ escafoideo.

abdominal *a.* abdominal, rel. al abdomen; ___ **bandage** / vendaje ___ ; ___ **breathing** / respiración ___ ; ___ **cavity** / cavidad ___ ; ___ **cramps** / retortijón, torzón; ___ **distention** / distención ___ ; ___ **injuries** / traumatismos ___ -es.

abdominocentesis *n.* abdominocentesis, punción abdominal.

abdominohysterectomy *n.* *cirg.* abdominohisterectomía, excisión del útero por medio de una incisión abdominal.

abdominoplasty *n.* *cirg.* abdominoplastia, operación de reparación de la pared abdominal.

abdominovaginal *a.* abdominovaginal, rel. al abdomen y la vagina.

abduce *v.* abducir, desviar, separar.

abducent *a.* abducente; abductor.

abduction *n.* abducción, separación.

aberrant *a.* aberrante, desviado del curso normal; anómalo.

aberration *n.* aberración. 1. visión defectuosa o imperfecta; **chromatic** ___ / ___ cromática; 2. desviación de lo normal; 3. trastorno mental; **mental** ___ / ___ mental.

abhor *v.* aborrecer; tener aversión a algo o a alguien.

ability *n.* habilidad, aptitud; talento, capacidad.

abiotrophy *n.* abiotrofia, pérdida prematura de la vitalidad.

ablatio *n.* ablación, separación, desprendimiento; ___ **placentae** / desprendimiento de la placenta; ___ **retinae** / desprendimiento de la retina.

ablation *n.* ablación.

able *a.* hábil, capaz, apto-a; *v.* **to be** ___ / [*to be or do something*] ser capaz de; poder.

abnormal *a.* anormal, disforme, irregular, anómalo-a.

abnormality *n.* anormalidad, anomalía; irregularidad; deformidad.

abort *v.* abortar; hacer abortar, interrumpir el curso de una gestación o de una enfermedad antes del término natural.

abortifacient *n.* abortivo, estimulante para inducir un aborto.

abortion *n.* aborto, expulsión prematura; **caused** ___ / ___ provocado; **criminal** ___ / ___ criminal; **elective** ___ / ___ electivo, por elección; **imminent** ___ / ___ inevitable; **induced** ___ / ___ inducido; **incomplete** ___ / ___ incompleto; **spontaneous** ___ / ___ espontáneo; **suction** ___ / ___ por succión; **therapeutic** ___ / ___ terapéutico.

about *prep.* cerca de; junto a; alrededor de; a eso de, sobre; **it is** ___ **a block from here** / está cerca de una cuadra de aquí; *adv.* [*time*] **it is** ___ **one thirty** / es alrededor de la una y media; *v.* **to speak** ___ / hablar de.

above *n.* antecedente, precedente; *a.* antedicho-a, anterior; *prep.* sobre, por encima de; ____ the heart / encima del corazón; *adv.* arriba; la parte alta; más de o más que; ____ **all** / sobre todo; **from** ____ / desde lo alto, desde arriba.

abrasion *n.* abrasión, excoriación, irritación o raspadura de las mucosas o de una superficie a causa de una fricción o de un trauma.

abrasive *a.* abrasivo-a, irritante, raspante, rel. a una abrasión o que la causa.

abreast *adv.* de frente; en frente.

abrupt *a.* abrupto-a, precipitado-a, repentino-a.

abruptio *L.* abruptio, abrupción, acción violenta de separación, desprendimiento; ____ placentae, placental abruption / desprendimiento prematuro de la placenta.

abruption *n.* abrupción.

abscess *n.* absceso, acumulación de pus gen. debido a una desintegración del tejido; acute ____ / ____ agudo; alveolar ____ / ____ alveolar; chronic ____ / ____ crónico; drainage ____ / ____ de drenaje; encysted ____ / ____ enquistado; gingival ____ / ____ de las encías; hepatic ____ / ____ hepático; mammary ____ / ____ mamario; pelvic ____ / ____ de la pelvis; pulmonary ____ / ____ pulmonar o en un pulmón.

absence *n.* ausencia, falta; pérdida momentánea del conocimiento.

absent *a.* ausente; distraído-a, absorto-a; ____ **minded** / distraído-a; absorto-a.

absentia epileptica *n.* absencia epiléptica, (epilepsia menor) pérdida momentánea del conocimiento en ciertos casos de ataques epilépticos.

absolute *a.* absoluto-a, incondicional; ____ alcohol (ethyl) / alcohol ____ (alcohol etílico).

absorb *v.* absorber, sorber, chupar.

absorbency *n.* absorbencia.

absorbent *a.* absorbente; que puede absorber.

absorption *n.* absorción. 1. acto de ingerir o introducir líquidos u otras sustancias en el organismo; 2. *psic.* ensimismación.

abstain *v.* abstenerse, privarse de; ____ from sexual intercourse / ____ de relaciones sexuales; *Mex.* cuidarse.

abstainer, abstemious *a.* abstemio-a; persona sobria.

abstention *n.* abstinencia, abstención, privación.

abstinence *n.* abstinencia, privación voluntaria, templanza, moderación.

abstract *n.* extracto, cantidad pequeña; resumen; *a.* abstracto-a; *v.* separar, alejar; extractar; resumir.

abstracted *a.* pensativo-a, abstraído-a; puro-a, sin mezcla alguna.

absurd *a.* absurdo-a, ridículo-a.

abulia *n.* abulia, pérdida de la voluntad; cyclic ____ / ____ cíclica.

abundance *n.* abundancia.

abundant *a.* abundante, copioso-a.

abuse *n.* abuso, uso exagerado; maltrato; ____ of medication / uso exagerado de medicamentos o drogas; **verbal** ____ / maltrato de palabra, insulto; *v.* [*to take advantage of*] abusar de; maltratar; seducir.

abutment *n.* refuerzo, remate; [*dentistry*] soporte.

acanthoid *n.* acantoide, espinoso-a, en forma de espina.

acanthosis *n.* acantosis, enfermedad que causa una condición áspera y verrugosa en la piel.

acapnia *n.* acapnia, estado producido por una disminución de ácido carbónico en la sangre.

acariasis *n.* acariasis, infección causada por ácaros; comezón, sarna.

acarid *n.* ácaro, parásito; *a.* acárido-a.

accelerate *v.* acelerar, apresurar, aumentar la velocidad; to ____ the healing process / ____ la cura.

acceleration *n.* aceleración, aceleramiento.

accelerator *n.* acelerador, sustancia o agente que tiene la propiedad de acelerar un proceso.

accent *n.* acento, énfasis, intensificación; *v.* acentuar, hacer énfasis; recalcar.

accented *a.* acentuado-a.

accept *v.* aceptar, admitir, acoger, aprobar.

acceptable *a.* aceptable, permitido-a; admitido-a.

access *n.* 1. ataque, acceso; paroxismo; 2. [*entrance*] entrada.

accessible *a.* accesivo-a, acequible, accesible.

accessory *a.* accesorio-a, adicional, adjunto-a.

accident *n.* accidente; **by** ____ / por casualidad, sin querer; **car** ____ / ____ automovilístico; **occupational** ____ / ____ del trabajo, ocupacional; **traffic** ____ / ____ de tráfico.

accidental *a.* accidental, inesperado-a, casual.

acclimate *v.* aclimatar.

acclimatization *n.* aclimatación.

accommodate *v.* acomodar, ajustar, cuadrar; [*to lodge*] alojar, hospedar.

accommodation *n.* acomodación, ajustamiento; [*lodging*] alojamiento.

accompany *v.* acompañar.

accomplish *v.* acabar, realizar, lograr, cumplir, finalizar.

accomplishment *n.* realización, éxito, logro.

accord *n.* acuerdo, convenio, arreglo, transacción; *v.* acordar, poner de acuerdo; **of one's own** ____ / espontáneamente, voluntariamente; **of mutual** ____ / dc acuerdo mutuo.

accordingly *adv.* de acuerdo con, por consiguiente; conformemente, en conformidad.

account *n.* cuenta, cálculo; nota, relación; **bank** ____ / ____ bancaria; **current** ____ / ____ corriente; **on** ____ **of** / por motivo de; *v.* **to pay the** ____ / pagar la ____ ; **to settle the** ____ / arreglar la ____ ; **to take into** ____ / tener en ____ , tener en consideración.

accountable *a.* responsable, contable.

accredit *v.* dar crédito, acreditar; certificar; dar credenciales.

accreditation *n.* crédito; credencial.

accredited *a.* acreditado-a.

accretion *n.* aumento, acrecentamiento; acumulación.

accumulate *v.* acumular, añadir, aumentar.

accumulation *n.* acumulación, amontonamiento; hacinamiento.

accuracy *n.* exactitud, precisión, cuidado.

accurate *a.* exacto-a, preciso-a, correcto-a.

accurateness *n.* precisión, exactitud, esmero.

accusation *n.* acusación, imputación.

accuse *v.* acusar, denunciar, culpar.

accustom *v.* acostumbrar, hacer algo de costumbre.

accustomed *a.* acostumbrado-a; *v.* **to be** ____ **to** / estar acostumbrado-a a.

acentric *a.* acéntrico, fuera del centro.

acerbic *a.* agrio-a, ácido-a, áspero-a.

acetabulum *n.* acetábulo, hueso cóncavo de la cadera.

acetic *a.* acético, agrio, relacionado con el vinagre; ____ **acid** / ácido ____ .

acetone *n.* acetona, sustancia fragante que se usa como solvente y se observa en cantidad excesiva en casos de diabetes.

acetonemia *n.* acetonemia, exceso de acetona en la sangre.

acetonuria *n.* acetonuria, exceso de acetona en la orina, característico de la diabetes.

acetylsalicylic acid *n.* ácido acetilsalicílico, aspirina.

achalasia *n.* acalasia, falta de capacidad de relajación esp. de una abertura o esfínter.

ache *n.* dolor constante, padecimiento, *pop.* achaque.

achieve *v.* llevar a cabo, realizar, lograr un éxito.

achievement quotient (A.Q.) *n.* cociente de inteligencia.

Achilles' tendon *n.* tendón de Aquiles, tendón mayor que se une a los músculos posteriores de la pierna y se inserta en el talón del pie.

achillobursitis *n.* aquilobursitis, infl. de la bursa situada en la parte anterior del tendón de Aquiles.

achillodynia *n.* aquilodinia, dolor en la región del tendón de Aquiles.

aching *a.* doloroso-a, doliente; mortificante.

achlorhydria *n.* aclorhidria, ausencia de ácido hipoclorhídrico en las secreciones estomacales.

achloropsia *n.* acloropsia, inhabilidad de distinguir el color verde.

acholia *n.* acolia, ausencia de bilis.

achondroplasia *n.* acondroplasia, deformidad ósea de nacimiento; enanismo.

achromasia *n.* acromasia, falta o pérdida de la pigmentación de la piel, característica de los albinos.

achromatic *a.* acromático-a, sin color.

achromatopsia *n.* acromatopsia, ceguera cromática.

achylia *n.* aquilia, deficiencia de jugos estomacales.

acid *n.* ácido; ____ **fast** / ____ resistente; ____ **proof** / a prueba de ____ ; **acetic** ____ / ____ acético; **aminoacetic** ____ / ____ aminoacético (suplemento dietético); **ascorbic** ____ / ____ ascórbico; **boric** ____ / ____ bórico; **butyric** ____ / ____ butírico; **chlorogenic** ____ / ____ clorogénico; **cholic** ____ / ____ cólico o coleico; **citric** ____ / ____ cítrico; **deoxyribonucleic** ____ / ____ desoxirribonucleico; **fatty** ____ / ____ graso; **folic** ____ / ____ fólico; **gastric** ____ / ____ gástrico; **glucuramic** ____ / ____ glucurámico;

glutamic ___ / ___glutámico; lactic ___ / ___ láctico; nicotinic ___ / ___ nicotínico; nitric ___ / ___ nítrico; nucleic ___ / ___ nucleico; phenilic ___ / ___ fenílico; ribonucleic ___ / ___ ribonucleico; salicylic ___ / ___ salicílico; sulfoni̧c ___ / ___ sulfónico; sulfuric ___ / ___ sulfúrico; uric ___ / ___ úrico.

acidemia *n.* acidemia, exceso de ácido en la sangre.

acidify *v.* acedar, agriar, acidular.

acidity *n.* acidez, exceso de ácido, acedia, agrura.

acidosis *n.* acidosis, exceso de acidez en la sangre y tejidos del cuerpo; diabetic ___ / ___ diabética.

acknowledge *v.* reconocer, agradecer; [*correspondence*] acusar recibo.

acne *n.* acné, condición inflamatoria de la piel; ___ rosacea / ___ rosácea; ___ vulgaris / ___ vulgar o común.

acoustic *a.* acústico-a, rel. al sonido o la audición.

acquaint *v.* dar a conocer, enterar, informar.

acquaintance *n.* conocimiento; trato; [*person*] un conocido, una conocida.

acquainted *a.* conocido-a, informado-a; to be ___ with a case / tener conocimiento del caso.

acquire *v.* adquirir, obtener, conseguir.

acquired *a.* adquirido-a; contraído-a.

acquired immuno-deficiency syndrome (AIDS) *n.* síndrome de inmuno deficiencia adquirida (SIDA), colapso del sistema inmune del organismo que lo incapacita a responder a la invasión de infecciones.

acquisition *n.* adquisición.

acrid *a.* amargo-a, agrio-a, acre, irritante.

acridity *n.* acritud, amargura.

acroarthritis *n.* acroartritis, infl. de las articulaciones de las extremidades.

acrocyanosis, Raynaud's disease *n.* acrocianosis, Raynaud, enfermedad de, cianosis y frialdad en las extremidades a causa de un trastorno circulatorio asociado con una tensión emocional o por exposición al frío.

acrodermatitis *n.* acrodermatitis, infl. de la piel de las manos y los pies; chronic ___ / ___ crónica atrófica.

acromegaly *n.* acromegalia, enfermedad crónica de la edad madura manifestada por un agrandamiento progresivo de las extremidades óseas y los huesos de la cabeza debido a un malfuncionamiento de la pituitaria.

acromion *n.* acromión, parte del hueso escapular del hombro.

acrophobia *n.* acrofobia, temor excesivo a la altitud.

across *adv.* a través, de una parte a otra, al otro lado de; *prep.* a través de, por, sobre, contra; *v.* to come ___ / encontrarse con.

act *n.* acto; ___ of God / fuerza mayor; *v.* actuar, obrar, ejecutar, hacer algo; portarse; do not ___ like that / no se porte así, no te portes así.

actine *n.* actina, proteína del tejido muscular que unida a la miosina hace posible la contracción muscular.

action *n.* acción, actuación.

activate *v.* activar.

active *a.* activo-a; diligente, hábil, enérgico-a.

activity *n.* actividad, ejercicio, ocupación.

actual *a.* actual, real, verdadero-a; **-ly** *adv.* en realidad, actualmente; the ___ symptom / el síntoma verdadero.

acuity *n.* agudeza; precisión; visual ___ / ___ visual.

acupuncture *n.* acupuntura, método de cura por inserción de agujas en áreas determinadas del cuerpo con el propósito de reducir o suprimir un dolor.

acute *a.* agudo-a, punzante; an ___ pain / un dolor ___ ; ___ care facility / centro de cuidado crítico; ___ care center / centro de emergencia.

Adam's apple *n.* nuez de Adán.

adapt *v.* adaptar; *vr.* adaptarse, ajustarse.

adaptation *n.* adaptación, ajuste.

add *v.* añadir, sumar, agregar.

addict *n.* adicto-a; vicioso-a; *a.* adicto-a, entregado-a, dependiente física o psicológicamente de una sustancia, esp. referente a una persona alcohólica o narcómana.

addicted *a.* enviciado-a; entregado-a, habituado-a a una sustancia. esp. alcohol o narcóticos; *v.* to become ___ / enviciarse, entregarse a una droga.

addiction *n.* adicción, propensión, dependencia.

Addison's disease *n.* enfermedad de Addison, hipofunción de las glándulas suprarrenales.

additive *n.* aditivo, sustancia que se agrega.

address *n.* dirección, señas; *v.* [*to speak or write to*] dirigirse a; hablar con; [*to write*] escribir a; [*to speak to an audience*] hablar en público.

adductor *n.* músculo aductor, músculo que tira hacia una línea media o centro.

adenectomy *n. cirg.* adenectomía, extirpación de una glándula.

adenitis *n.* adenitis, infl. de una glándula.

adenoacanthoma *n.* adenoacantoma, cáncer en el útero que crece lentamente.

adenocarcinoma *n.* adenocarcinoma, cáncer maligno que se origina en una glándula.

adenocystoma *n.* adenocistoma, tumor benigno de una glándula formado por quistes.

adenofibroma *n.* adenofibroma, tumor benigno formado por tejido fibroso y glandular, visto en el útero y en los pechos.

adenoid *a.* adenoideo, semejante a una glándula.

adenoidectomy *n. cirg.* adenoidectomía, extirpación de la adenoide.

adenoids *n. pl.* acumulación de tejido linfático localizado en la nasofaringe en la niñez.

adenoiditis *n.* adenoiditis, infl. de la adenoide.

adenoma *n.* adenoma, tumor de una consistencia parecida a la del tejido glandular; basofil ___ / ___ basófilo; sebaceous ___ / ___ sebáceo; toxic ___ / ___ tóxico.

adenomyoma *n.* adenomioma, tumor benigno visto con frecuencia en el útero.

adenopathy, adenopalia *n.* adenopatía, adenopalia, enfermedad de una glándula linfática.

adenosarcoma *n.* adenosarcoma, tumor maligno.

adenosis *n.* adenosis, engrosamiento de una glándula.

adequate *a.* adecuado-a, proporcionado-a.

adherent lens *n.* lente de contacto.

adhesion *n.* adhesión, adherencia.

adhesive *n.* adhesivo, tela adhesiva; ___ strips / esparadrapo.

adipose tissue *n.* tejido adiposo, grasa.

adiposogenital *a.* adiposogenital. *V.* **syndrome.**

adjacent *a.* adyacente, contiguo, al lado de.

adjective *n. gr.* adjetivo.

adjoin *v.* juntar, asociar, unir.

adjunct *a.* adjunto-a, unido-a, asociado-a, arrimado-a.

adjust *v.* ajustar, arreglar, acomodar.

adjuvant *n.* adjutor, agente o sustancia que acentúa la potencia de un medicamento.

administer *v.* administrar, proveer, dar algo necesario.

administration *n.* administración.

admirable *a.* admirable, digno-a.

admission *n.* admisión, internación, ingreso.

admit *v.* admitir, dar entrada o ingreso a una institución.

admittance *n.* entrada, admisión.

admix *v.* mezclar, juntar.

admonish *v.* advertir, amonestar.

admonition *n.* advertencia, admonición, consejo.

adnexa *n. pl.* anejos, anexos, apéndices tales como los tubos uterinos.

adolescence *n.* adolescencia, pubertad.

adolescent *n.* adolescente; pubescente.

adopt *v.* adoptar, prohijar.

adoption *n.* adopción.

adoptive *a.* adoptivo-a.

adrenal *a.* suprarrenal, adrenal; ___ cortex hormones / corticosteroides; ___ gland diseases / enfermedades de la glándula ___ ; ___ glands / glándulas ___ -es; ___ glands neoplasms / neoplasmas de las glándulas ___ -es.

adrenalectomy *n.* adrenalectomía, *cirg.* extirpación de las glándulas suprarrenales.

adrenaline *n.* adrenalina, marca registrada de la epinefrina, hormona usada como vasoconstrictor secretada por la médula suprarrenal.

adrenalism *n.* adrenalismo, disfunción de la glándula suprarrenal que ocasiona síntomas de debilidad y decaimiento.

adrenocorticotropin (ACTH) *n.* adrenocorticotropina, hormona secretada por la pituitaria, estimulante de la corteza suprarrenal.

adrenogenic *a.* adrenogénico, que proviene de las glándulas suprarrenales.

adsorbent *a.* adsorbente.

adult *n., a.* adulto-a.

adulterate *v.* adulterar, cambiar el original, viciar; falsificar.

adultery *n.* adulterio.

advance *v.* avanzar, adelantar, pasar adelante; **in** ___ / por adelantado.

advancement *n.* [*improvement*] mejora, mejoría, progreso; promoción, ascenso.

advantage *n.* ventaja, ganancia, beneficio; *v.* **to take** ___ / aprovecharse, valerse de.

adverb *n. gr.* adverbio.

adverbial *a.* adverbial.

adverse *a.* desfavorable, adverso-a, contrario-a, opuesto-a.

advisable *a.* recomendable, conveniente.

advise *n.* advertencia, consejo; opinión, parecer; *v.* advertir; aconsejar, recomendar.

aerate *v.* airear, ventilar. 1. saturar un líquido de aire; 2. cambiar la sangre venosa en sangre arterial en los pulmones.

aerobe *n.* aerobio, organismo que requiere oxígeno para vivir.

aerocele *n.* aerocele, hernia de la tráquea.

aeroembolism *n.* aeroembolismo, "enfermedad de los buzos", condición causada por burbujas de nitrógeno liberadas en la sangre debido a un cambio brusco de presión atmosférica; *pop.* the bends.

aeroemphysema *n.* aeroenfisema, "enfermedad de los aviadores", condición causada por un ascenso súbito en el espacio sin decompresión adecuada; *pop.* the chokes.

aerogenic *a.* aerógeno-a, que produce gas.

aerophagia *n.* aerofagia, tragar aire en exceso.

afebril *a.* afebril, sin fiebre, sin calentura.

affair *n.* asunto, cuestión.

affect *v.* afectar, causar un cambio en la salud; conmover, excitar.

affectation *n.* artificio, afectación.

affected *a.* afectado-a, que padece de una enfermedad física o de un sufrimiento emocional; _____ **by** / _____ por.

affection *n.* [*sickness*] afección, dolencia, enfermedad; [*feeling*] expresión de cariño, afecto o afección.

affectionate *a.* afectuoso,-a, cariñoso-a.

affective *a.* afectivo-a; _____ disorders / trastornos _____-s; _____ symtoms / síntomas _____-s.

afferent *a.* aferente, que se dirije hacia el centro, hacia adentro.

affinity *n.* afinidad, conformidad; conexión.

affirm *v.* afirmar, asegurar.

affirmation *n.* afirmación, confirmación, ratificación de una medida.

affirmed *a.* afirmado-a, confirmado-a, ratificado-a.

affix *v.* aplicar, colocar, adaptar; ligar, unir.

affixture *n.* ligadura, adición.

afflict *v.* afligir, causar dolor o sufrimiento; [*lament*] afligirse, inquietarse.

afflicted *a.* afligido-a, sufrido-a.

affliction *n.* aflicción, padecimiento, sufrimiento.

afflux *n.* flujo.

afford *v.* poder costear, tener solvencia; soportar.

affront *v.* hacer frente, confrontar; encararse.

afibrinogenemia *n.* afribrinogenemia, deficiencia de fibrinógeno en la sangre.

afire *a.* encendido-a; *adv.* en llamas.

afraid *a.* temeroso-a, miedoso-a, intimidado-a, *v.* **to be** _____ / tener miedo.

after *prep.* después; *adv.* después, más tarde; _____ care / convalescencia, restablecimiento; *cirg.* _____ care / *surg.* tratamiento post-operatorio; _____ effects / consecuencias, secuelas; acción retardada de una droga; _____ image / impresión mantenida por la retina; [*birth*] _____ pains / entuertos, dolores de parto; _____ sleep / sueño secundario; _____ sound / impresión auditiva que persiste después de cesar el estímulo; _____ taste / permanencia de la sensación del gusto; _____ treatment / tratamiento de recuperación.

afterbirth *n.* secundinas, placenta y membranas que se expelen en el parto.

aftermath *n.* secuela, consecuencias de una enfermedad.

afterwards *adv.* después, luego, más tarde.

again *adv.* otra vez; _____ **and** _____ / una y otra vez, muchas veces; **do it** _____ / hágalo, hazlo _____ .

against *prep.* contra, enfrente; *v.* **to be** _____ / oponerse; enfrentarse a, con.

agalorrhea *n.* agalorrea, cesación o falta de leche en los pechos.

agamic *a.* agámico-a, rel. a la reproducción sin unión sexual.

agammaglobulinemia *n.* agammaglobulinemia, deficiencia de gamma globulina en la sangre.

age *n.* edad; generación; **full** _____ / mayor de edad; **tender** _____ / infancia, primera edad; **under** _____ / menor de _____, minoría de _____; _____ **of consent** / mayor de _____, mayoría de _____; **legal** _____ / _____ legal.

agenesis, agenesia *n.* agénesis, agenesia. 1. defecto congénito en el desarrollo de un órgano o parte del cuerpo; 2. esterilidad; impotencia.

agent *n.* agente, factor.

agglomeration *n.* aglomeración, acumulación.

agglutinants *n. pl.* aglutinantes, agentes o

factores que unen partes separadas en un proceso de curación.

agglutinate *v.* aglutinar; causar unión.

agglutination *n.* aglutinación, acción, de aglutinar o causar unión.

aggravate *v.* agravar, empeorar, irritar.

aggression *n.* agresión, actitud y acción hostil.

aggressive *a.* agresivo-a, hostil.

agile *a.* ágil, ligero-a, expedito-a.

aging *n.* envejecimiento.

agitate *v.* [*to shake*] agitar, sacudir; [*to upset*] inquietar, perturbar.

agitation *n.* agitación, perturbación; alboroto.

agony *n.* agonía. 1. sufrimiento extremo; 2. estado que precede a la muerte.

ago *adv.* atrás; [*with time*] hace, **ten years** ___ / [*hace + length of time*] hace diez años.

agonize *v.* agonizar, estar en agonía; sufrir en extremo.

agoraphobia *n.* agorafobia, temor excesivo a los espacios abiertos.

agranulocytosis *n.* agranulocitosis, condición aguda causada por la disminución excesiva de leucocitos en la sangre.

agraphia *n.* agrafia, pérdida de la habilidad de escribir causada por un trastorno cerebral.

agree *v.* acordar; estar de acuerdo; sentar bien, caer bien; **we** ___ / estamos de acuerdo; **coffee does not** ___ **with me** / el café no me sienta bien; el café no me cae bien.

agreeable *a.* agradable, ameno-a, placentero-a, grato-a.

agreement *n.* acuerdo, pacto, consolidación, ajustamiento; **to come to an** ___ / llegar a un acuerdo; acordar.

ahead *adv.* adelante, enfrente, hacia adelante; *v.* **look** ___ / mire, mira ___ .

aid *n.* ayuda, asistencia; **government** ___ / subsidio del gobierno; **nurse** ___ / enfermero, enfermera asistente.

AIDS *abbr.* **acquired immunodeficiency syndrome** *n.* SIDA *abr.* síndrome de inmunodeficiencia adquirida, estado avanzado de infección por el virus VIH, caracterizado por inmuno deficiencia, infecciones (tales como neumonía, tuberculosis y diarrea crónica), y tumores (esp. linfoma y sarcoma de Kaposi).

ailing *a.* achacoso-a, enfermizo-a.

ailment *n.* dolencia, achaque, indisposición.

air *n.* aire; ___ **bladder** / vejiga llena de ___ ; ___ **blast injury** / lesión por una explosión; ___ **bubbles** / burbujas de ___ ; ___ **chamber** / cámara de ___ ; ___ **conditioned** / acondicionado; ___ **contamination** / contaminado; contaminación del aire, polución; **cool** ___ / ___ **fresco**; ___ **dressing** / vendaje; ___ **embolism** / embolia gaseosa; ___ **hole** / respiradero; ___ **mail** / correo aéreo; ___ **matress** / colchón neumático; ___ **passages** / conductos de ___ ; ___ **pocket** / bolsa de ___ ; ___ **pollution** / polución atmosférica; ___ **sickness** / mareo de altura; ___ **sac** [*lung*] / alvéolo pulmonar; **tidal** ___ / ___ **respiratorio**; ___ **tight** / hermético-a; **ventilated** ___ / ___ **de ventilación**; *v.* [*to ventilate*] airear, ventilar.

airborne *a.* en vuelo; [*transported*] llevado-a por el aire.

airing *n.* aireo, ventilación, oreo.

airless *a.* falto de respiración, sin aire.

airplane *n.* avión, aeroplano.

airway *n.* conducto de aire.

akin *a.* consanguíneo, de cualidades uniformes.

akinesthesia *n.* aquinestesia, falta del sentido de movimiento.

alalia *n.* pérdida del habla.

alarm *n.* alarma, peligro; **fire** ___ / ___ de fuego.

alarm *v.* alarmar, inquietar, impacientar; turbar.

alarming *a.* alarmante, inquietante, desesperante; sorprendente.

albinism *n.* albinismo, falta de pigmentación en la piel, el cabello y los ojos.

albino *n.* albino-a, persona afectada por albinismo.

albumin *n.* albúmina, componente proteínico.

albuminuria *n.* albuminuria, presencia de proteína en la orina, esp. albúmina o globulina.

alcohol *n.* alcohol.

alcoholic *n.*, *a.* alcohólico-a.

alcoholism *n.* alcoholismo, uso excesivo de bebidas alcohólicas.

aldosterone *n.* aldosterona, hormona producida por la corteza suprarrenal.

aldosteronism *n.* aldosteronismo, trastorno

causado por una secreción excesiva de aldosterona.

alert *a.* alerta, dispuesto-a.

aleukemia *n.* aleucemia, falta o deficiencia de leucocitos en la sangre.

alexia *n.* alexia, inhabilidad de comprender la palabra escrita.

algesia *n.* algesia, hipertesia.

algid *a.* álgido-a, frío-a.

algor *n.* escalofrío, algor.

algorithm *n.* algoritmo, método aritmético y algebraico que se usa en el diagnóstico y tratamento de una enfermedad.

alien *a.* incompatible; extranjero-a, forastero-a.

alienation *n.* separación; *psic.* ofuscación.

alimentary *a.* alimenticio-a, rel. a los alimentos; ___ tract / tubo digestivo, tracto ___.

alimentation *n.* alimentación, nutrición; forced ___ / ___ forzada; rectal ___ / ___ por el recto.

alimony *n.* manutención, pensión alimenticia, apoyo monetario.

alive *a.* vivo-a, con vida; *v.* to be ___ / estar ___.

alkaloid *n.* alcaloide, grupo de sustancias orgánicas básicas de origen vegetal.

alkalosis *n.* alcalosis, trastorno patológico en el balance acidobásico del organismo.

all *n.* el todo, compuesto de partes iguales; *a.* todo-a, todos-as; [*everyone*] todo el mundo; **before** ___ / ante todo; ___ **day** / todo el día; ___ **night** / toda la noche; **at** ___ **risks** / a todo riesgo; *adv.* todo, del todo, completamente; enteramente; ___ **along** / todo el tiempo; ___ **the better** / tanto mejor; **by** ___ **means** / sin duda, por supuesto; ___ **right** / está bien; ___ **of a sudden** / de pronto, de golpe, de repente; ___ **the worse** / tanto peor.

allele *n.* alelo, alelomorfo, uno de dos o más genes de una serie que ocupan la misma posición en cromosomas homólogos y que determinan características alternantes en los descendientes.

allergic *a.* alérgico-a; ___ reaction / reacción alérgica; ___ rhinitis / rinitis ___.

allergy *n.* alergia.

alleviate *v.* aliviar, calmar, mejorar, atenuar.

alliance *n.* alianza, unión; acuerdo.

allow *v.* admitir, aceptar, consentir.

allowance *n.* asignación, regalía, dieta alimenticia.

almanac *n.* almanaque, calendario.

Almighty *n.* Dios; Almighty *a.* todopoderoso-a, omnipotente.

almond *n.* almendra.

almost *adv.* casi, cerca de, alrededor de.

alone *a.* solo-a, solitario-a.

along *adv.* a lo largo de, próximo a, junto a; *v.* to get ___ / llevarse bien; come ___ / venga; ven.

alongside *adv.* al costado de, junto a.

aloof *a.* apartado-a, aislado-a, lejos de todo o de todos.

alopecia *n.* alopecia, caída del cabello.

aloud *adv.* en voz alta; to speak ___ / hablar recio.

already *adv.* ya.

also *adv.* del mismo modo, también.

alter *v.* cambiar, variar; reformar.

alteration *n.* alteración, modificación, reforma, cambio.

alternate *v.* alternar, turnar.

alternative *n.* alternativa, opción.

although *conj.* aunque, si bien, bien que.

altitude *n.* altitud, altura, elevación.

alveolar *a.* alveolar, rel. a un alvéolo.

alveolus *n.* alvéolo, cavidad.

always *adv.* siempre, para siempre.

Alzheimer's disease *n.* enfermedad de Alzheimer, deteriorización cerebral progresiva con características de demencia senil.

am *v.* soy, estoy, *primera persona pres. ind.* *v.* to be / ser; estar.

amalgamate *v.* amalgamar, mezclar, juntar.

amastia *n.* amastia, ausencia de los pechos.

amateur *a.* aficionado-a; principiante.

amaze *v.* asombrar, maravillar, pasmar.

amazement *n.* asombro, pasmo, admiración.

amber *n.* ámbar; *a.* ambarino-a.

ambiance *n.* ambiente.

ambidextrous *a.* ambidextro-a.

ambisexual *a.* ambisexual, bisexual.

ambition *n.* ambición, aspiración; *v.* ambicionar, aspirar.

ambivalence *n.* ambivalencia.

amblyopia *n.* ambliopía, visión reducida.

ambulance *n.* ambulancia.

ambulant *a.* ambulante.

ambulatory *a.* ambulatorio-a; ambulante.

amebiasis *n.* amebiasis, amibiasis, estado infeccioso causado por amebas.

amebic *a.* amebiano-a, rel. a la ameba o causado por ésta.

ameliorate *v.* mejorar; adelantar; mejorarse.

amend *v.* enmendar, corregir.

amenorrhea *n.* amenorrea, ausencia del período menstrual.

American *n., a.* americano-a.

ametropia *n.* ametropía, falta de visión causada por una anomalía de los poderes refractores del ojo.

amine *n.* amina, uno de los compuestos básicos derivados del amoníaco.

amino acid *n.* aminoácido, compuesto orgánico metabólico necesario en el desarrollo y crecimiento humano esencial en la digestión e hidrólisis de proteínas.

ammonia *n.* amoníaco, gas alcalino que se forma por la descomposición de sustancias nitrogenadas y por aminoácidos.

amnesia *n.* amnesia, pérdida de la memoria.

amniocentesis *n.* amniocentesis, punción del útero para obtener líquido amniótico.

amnion *n.* amnios, saco membranoso que envuelve al embrión.

amniotic *n.* amniótico, en relación con el amnios; ___ sac / saco ___ ; ___ fluid / fluído ___ .

amoeba, ameba *n.* ameba, organismo de una sola célula.

amorphous *a.* amorfo-a, sin forma.

amphetamine *n.* anfetamina, tipo de droga usada como estimulante del sistema nervioso.

ampicillin *n.* ampicilina, penicilina semisintética.

ample *a.* amplio-a, ancho-a; abundante, copioso-a.

amplification *n.* amplificación, ampliación, extensión.

amplify *v.* ampliar, extender, dilatar.

ampoule, ampule *n.* ámpula, ampolla, tubo de jeringuilla.

amputate *v.* amputar, desmembrar.

amputation *n.* amputación, desmembración.

amygdala *n.* amígdala. *V.* **tonsil.**

amyloid *n.* amiloide, proteína que se asemeja a los almidones.

amyloidosis *n.* amiloidosis, acumulación de amiloide en los tejidos.

anabolic *a.* anabólico-a, rel. al anabolismo; ___ steroid / esteroide ___ .

anabolism *n.* anabolismo, proceso celular por el cual sustancias simples se convierten en complejas, fase constructiva del metabolismo.

anacidity *n.* anacidez, sin ácido.

anaerobe *n.* anaerobio, microorganismo que se multiplica en ausencia de aire u oxígeno.

anaerobic *a.* anaeróbico, rel. a los anaerobios o de la naturaleza de éstos.

anal *a.* anal, rel. al ano; ___ fistula / fístula ___ .

analgesic *n.* analgésico, calmante.

analogy *n.* analogía, semejanza.

analphabet *n.* analfabeto-a.

analysis *n.* análisis, prueba.

analyze *v.* analizar, hacer análisis.

anaphase *n.* anafase, etapa de la división celular.

anaphylactic *a.* anafiláctico-a, rel. a la anafilaxis.

anaphylaxis *n.* anafilaxis, hipersensibilidad, reacción alérgica extrema.

anaplasia *n.* anaplasia, falta de diferenciación en las células.

anaplastic *a.* anaplástico-a, rcl. a la anaplasia.

anasarca *n.* anasarca, edema generalizado, hidropesía.

anastomosis *n. cirg.* anastomosis, pasaje o comunicación entre dos o más órganos.

anatomic, anatomical *a.* anatómico-a, rel. a la anatomía.

anatomy *n.* anatomía, ciencia que estudia la estructura del cuerpo humano y de sus órganos; macroscopic ___ / ___ macroscópica, estudio de estructuras que se distinguen a simple vista; topographic ___ / ___ topográfica, estudio de estructuras y partes de las mismas en las distintas regiones del cuerpo.

ancestors *n. pl.* antepasados, padres o abuelos, *pop.* los mayores.

ancestry *n.* ascendencia; extracción étnica, raza; alcurnia.

anconal *a.* anconal, referente al codo.

and *conj.* y; e (*gr. used instead of y before words beginning with i or hi*); **two thirty /** las dos **y** media; **father and son /** padre **e** hijo.

androgen *n.* andrógeno, hormona masculina.

androgenic *a.* androgénico-a, rel. a las características sexuales masculinas.

androgynous *a.* androginoide, que tiene las características de ambos sexos.

androtomy *n.* androtomía, disección de un cadáver.

anemia *n.* anemia, insuficiencia hemática o de glóbulos rojos en calidad, cantidad o en hemoglobina; aplastic ____ / ____ aplástica, falta anormal de producción de glóbulos rojos; hemorrhagic, hemolytic ____ / ____ hemorrágica, hemolítica, destrucción progresiva de glóbulos rojos; hyperchromic ____ / ____ hipercrómica, aumento anormal en la hemoglobina; hypochromic microcytic ____ / ____ hipocrómica microcítica, [*células pequeñas*], deficiencia de glóbulos rojos en menor cantidad que de hemoglobina; macrocytic ____ / ____ macrocítica, glóbulos rojos de un tamaño exagerado [*anemia perniciosa*]; sickle cell ____ / ____ de glóbulos falciformes; iron deficiency ____ / ____ por deficiencia de hierro.

anesthesia *n.* anestesia; epidural ____ / ____ epidural; general ____ / ____ general; general ____ by inhalation / ____ general por inhalación; general ____ by intubación / ____ general por intubación; intravenous general ____ / ____ general intravenosa; local ____ / ____ local; regional ____ / ____ regional; saddle block ____ / ____ en silla de montar; spinal ____ / ____ raquídea.

anesthesiologist *n.* anestesista, anestesiólogo-a.

anesthesiology *n.* anestesiología.

anesthetic *n.* anestésico.

anesthetize *v.* anestesiar.

aneurysm *n.* aneurisma, dilatación de una porción de la pared de una arteria.

aneurysmal *a.* aneurismal, rel. a un aneurisma.

aneurysmectomy *n. cirg.* aneurismectomía, extirpación de un aneurisma.

anger *n.* ira, cólera.

angina *n.* angina, sensación de dolor constrictivo o ahogo; intestinal ____ / ____ intestinal, dolor abdominal agudo debido a insuficiencia de flujo sanguíneo a los intestinos; laryngea ____ / ____ laríngea, infl. de la garganta; ____ pectoris, angor pectoris / angina de pecho, dolor en el pecho causado por insuficiencia de flujo sanguíneo al músculo cardíaco.

angiitis *n.* angiitis, infl. de un vaso linfático o de un vaso sanguíneo.

angiocardiography *n.* angiocardiografía, visión rayos-X de las aurículas y ventrículos del corazón.

angioedema *n.* edema angioneurótico, infl. alérgica localizada gen. en la cara.

angiogenesis *n.* angiogénesis, desarrollo del sistema vascular.

angiography *n.* angiografía, radiografía de los vasos sanguíneos haciendo resaltar su contorno.

angioma *n.* angioma, tumor vascular benigno.

angioplasty *n. cirg.* angioplastia, intervención quirúrgica para reconstrucción de vasos sanguíneos enfermos o traumatizados; percutaneous coronary ____ / ____ coronaria percutánea; peripheral percutaneous ____ / ____ periférica percutánea.

angiospasm *n.* angioespasmo, contracción prolongada y fuerte de un vaso sanguíneo.

angiotensin *n.* angiotensina, agente presor en los trastornos hipotensivos, estimulante de la aldosterona.

angle *n.* ángulo, abertura formada por dos líneas que salen separadamente de un mismo punto.

anguish *n.* agonía, angustia.

anhidrosis *n.* anhidrosis, deficiencia o falta de secreción sudoral.

animal *n.* animal.

animate *v.* animar, dar vida.

animosity *n.* animosidad, rencor, aversión, mala voluntad; *v.* to have ____ / tener ____ .

ankle *n.* tobillo; ____ bone / hueso del ____ .

ankylosis *n.* anquilosis, inflexibilidad o falta de movimiento de una articulación.

ankylous *a.* anquiloso-a, anquilosado-a.

annexive *a.* anexo, contiguo.

annihilation *n.* aniquilación, destrucción total.

annotate *v.* anotar, hacer un comentario.

annotation *n.* anotación, nota.

announce *v.* anunciar, publicar.

announcement *n.* anuncio, aviso, declaración pública.

annoy *v.* importunar, fastidiar, molestar.

annual *a.* anual; **-ly** *adv.* anualmente, cada año.

annul *v.* anular, cancelar, revocar.

anodyne *n.* anodino, agente mitigador del dolor; *a.* insípido-a.

anoint *v.* untar, administrar la extremaunción.

anomalous *a.* anómalo-a, irregular, disforme.

anomaly *n.* trastorno, anomalía, irregularidad contraída o congénita.

anorexia *n.* anorexia, trastorno causado por falta de apetito; ____ nervosa / ____ nerviosa, aversión histérica a la comida.

anosmia *n.* anosmia, falta de olfato.

another *a.* otro-a, otros-as; *pron.* el otro, la otra.

anovulation *n.* anovulación, cese de ovulación.

anovulatory drugs *n. pl.* drogas anticonceptivas, drogas para evitar la ovulación.

anoxemia *n.* anoxemia, insuficiencia de oxígeno en la sangre.

anoxia *n.* anoxia, ausencia de oxígeno en los tejidos.

answer *n.* contestación, respuesta.

ant *n.* hormiga.

antacid *n.* antiácido, neutralizador de acidez.

antagonist *a.* antagonista, droga que neutraliza los efectos de otra.

antecubital *a.* antecubital, en posición anterior al codo.

anteflexion *n.* anteflexión, acto de doblarse hacia adelante.

antemetic *n.* antiemético, medicamento para controlar las naúseas.

anterior *a.* anterior, precedente, previo-a.

anteversion *n.* anteversión, vuelta hacia el frente.

anthracosis *n.* antracosis, condición pulmonar causada por la inhalación prolongada de polvo de carbón.

anthropomorphic *a.* antropomórfico-a, de forma humana.

antiallergic *a.* antialérgico-a, rel. a los medicamentos que se usan para combatir alergias.

antiarrythmic *a.* antiarrítmico-a, que previene la arritmia cardíaca o es efectivo en tratamientos contra ésta; ____ agents / agentes ____-s.

antiarthritics *n. pl.* antiartríticos, medicamentos para combatir la artritis o aliviarla.

antibiotic drugs *n. pl.* antibióticos, drogas antibacterianas.

antibody *n.* anticuerpo, sustancia de proteína que actúa como respuesta a la presencia de antígenos; ____ formation / formación de ____-s; monoclonal ____ / ____ monoclónico, derivado de células de hibridoma.

anticancer drug, anticarcinogen *n.* anticarcinógeno, droga usada en el tratamiento del cáncer.

anticipate *v.* anticipar, prevenir.

anticoagulant *n.* anticoagulante, medicamento usado para evitar coágulos.

anticonvulsant *n.* anticonvulsivo, medicamento usado en la prevención de convulsiones o ataques.

antidepressant *n.* antidepresivo, medicamento o proceso curativo usado para evitar estados de depresión.

antidiabetic *n.* antidiabético, medicamento usado en el tratamiento de la diabetes.

antidiuretic *n.* antidiurético, sustancia que evita la emisión excesiva de orina.

antidote *n.* antídoto, contraveneno.

antiemetic *n.* antiemético, medicamento usado en el tratamiento de la naúsea.

antigen *n.* antígeno, sustancia tóxica que estimula la formación de anticuerpos; carcinoembriogenic ____ (CEA) / ____ carcinoembriogénico.

antiglobulin test *n.* prueba de la antiglobulina.

antihistamine *n.* antihistamina, medicamento usado en el tratamiento de reacciones alérgicas.

antihypertensive *n.* antihipertensivo, medicamento para bajar la presión arterial.

anti-inflammatory agents *n. pl.* agentes antiinflamatorios.

antineoplastic *a.* antineoplástico, droga que controla o mata células cancerosas.

antioncotic *n.* antioncótico, agente reductor de la tumefacción.

antipathy *n.* antipatía, aversión.

antipyretic *n.* antipirético-a, agente reductor de la fiebre.

antiseptic *n.* antiséptico, agente desinfectante que destruye bacterias.

antispasmodic *n.* antiespasmódico, medicamento usado para aliviar o prevenir espasmos.

antitoxic *n.* antitóxico, neutralizador de los efectos de las toxinas.

antitoxin *n.* antitoxina, anticuerpo que actúa como neutralizante de la sustancia tóxica introducida por un microorganismo.

antrectomy *n. cirg.* antrectomía, excisión de la pared de un antro.

antrum *n.* antro, cavidad o cámara casi cerrada; mastoid ____ / ____ mastoideo.

anuria *n.* anuria, escasez o ausencia de orina.

anus *n.* ano, orificio del recto.

anxiety *n.* ansiedad, angustia; estado de preocupación excesiva; aprehensión, abatimiento de ánimo, desasosiego; ___ disorders / estados de ___ ; ___ neurosis / neurosis de ___ .

anxious *a.* ansioso-a, anheloso-a, abatido-a, perturbado-a.

any *a.* algún, alguna, cualquier, cualquiera; are you taking **any** medicine? / ¿toma, tomas **alguna** medicina?; ¿toma, tomas **algún** medicamento?; ___ **further** / más lejos; don't go ___ **further** / no vaya, no vayas más lejos; ___ **more** / más; you don't need ___ **more** pills / no necesita, no necesitas **más** pastillas; [*after negation*] ningún, ninguno-a; **don't take** ___ of **those pills** / no tome, no tomes ninguna de esas pastillas.

anybody *pron.* alguien, alguno-a; cualquiera; **did** ___ **call?** / ¿llamó alguien?; [*negative*] nada, nadie, ninguno-a; **no one called** / no llamó nadie.

anysocytosis *n.* anisocitosis, tamaño desigual de los glóbulos rojos.

anything *pron.* algo, alguna cosa, cualquier cosa; [*negative*] nada; **do you feel** ___? / ¿siente, sientes algo?; **don't you feel** ___? / ¿no siente, sientes nada?

anyway *adv.* de todas maneras, de cualquier modo, sea lo que fuera.

anywhere *adv.* dondequiera, en cualquier parte.

aorta *n.* aorta, arteria mayor que se origina en el ventrículo izquierdo del corazón; ascending ___ / ___ ascendiente; arch of the ___ / cayado de la ___ ; descending ___ / ___ descendiente, descendente.

aortic *a.* aórtico-a, rel. a la aorta; ___ murmur / soplo, ruido ___ ; ___ stenosis / estenosis o estrechamiento ___ .

aortogram *n.* aortograma, rayos-X de la aorta.

aortography *n.* aortografía, técnica empleada con rayos-X para ver el contorno de la aorta.

apart *adv.* aparte, separadamente; hacia un lado.

apathetic *a.* apático-a, indolente, insensible.

apathy *n.* apatía, insensibilidad.

apepsia *n.* apepsia, mala digestión.

aperitive *n.* aperitivo. 1. purgante suave; 2. estimulante del apetito.

aperture *n.* apertura, abertura, paso, boquete.

apex *n.* apex, extremidad puntiaguda de una estructura.

aphasia *n.* afasia, incapacidad de coordinar el pensamiento y la palabra.

aphemia *n.* afemia, pérdida del habla, gen. debido a una hemorragia cerebral, coágulo o tumor.

aphonia *n.* afonía, pérdida de la voz debido a una afección localizada en la laringe.

aphonic *a.* afónico-a, sin sonido, sin voz.

aphrodisiac *a.* afrodisíaco-a, que estimula deseos sexuales.

aphtha *n.* afta, úlcera pequeña que aparece como señal de infección en la mucosa oral.

aphthous stomatitis *n.* estomatitis aftosa, dolor de garganta acompañado de pequeñas aftas en la boca.

aplasia *n.* aplasia, falta de desarrollo normal en un órgano.

apnea *n.* apnea, falta de respiración.

aponeurosis *n.* aponeurosis, membrana que cubre los músculos.

apophysis *n.* apófisis, parte saliente de un hueso.

apoplexy *n.* apoplejía, hemorragia cerebral.

appalling *a.* espantoso-a, aterrador-a, atemorizante.

apparent *a.* aparente, evidente, preciso-a; claro-a; patente.; **-ly** *adv.* aparentemente, evidentemente, precisamente.

appeal *n.* apelación, recurso, súplica; *v.* apelar, recurrir, suplicar.

appear *v.* aparecer, parecer, responder; manifestarse.

appearance *n.* apariencia, aspecto.

appendage *n.* apéndice; dependencia; accesorio.

appendectomy *n. cirg.* apendectomía, extirpación del apéndice.

appendicitis *n.* apendicitis, infl. del apéndice.

appendicular *a.* apendicular, rel. al apéndice.

appendix *n.* apéndice.

appetite *n.* apetito, deseos de, ganas de comer; **altered** ___ / ___ alterado; **excessive** ___ / ___ excesivo; **poor** ___ , **loss of** ___ / falta de ___ , pérdida del ___ .

appetizing *a.* grato-a, gustoso-a.

apple *n.* manzana.

appliance *n.* aplicación; accesorio, instrumento, aparato eléctico.

application *n.* aplicación, solicitud; ___ blank / formulario; [*ointment*] untadura.

applicator *n.* aplicador; cotton ___ / ___ de algodón.

applicable *a.* aplicable, adecuado-a, apropiado-a para utilizarse.

apply *v.* aplicar, solicitar, requerir.

appointment *n.* cita, consulta, turno; [*job related*] nombramiento, cargo.

appraise *v.* apreciar, estimar, evaluar, ponderar.

appreciate *v.* apreciar, agradecer, reconocer.

approach *n.* [*avenue*] acceso, entrada; [*words*] las palabras acertadas; método; [*decision*] las medidas necesarias; *v.* abordar; *vr.* acercarse, aproximarse.

appropriate *a.* apropiado-a, adecuado-a, apto-a.

approval *n.* aprobación, aceptación, consentimiento, admisión.

approve *v.* aprobar, aceptar, dar estimación.

approximate *a.* aproximado-a.

apraxia *n.* apraxia, falta de coordinación muscular en los movimientos causada por una afección cerebral.

apricot *n.* albaricoque; *Mex.* chabacano.

apron *n.* delantal.

aptitude *n.* aptitud, capacidad, destreza para hacer algo; ___ test / prueba de ___.

aqua *n. L.* agua; aq. *abbr.* / aq. *abr.;* aq. bull, aqua bulliens / ___ hirviendo; aq. dest., ___ destillata / ___ destilada; aq. pur., ___ pura / ___ pura; aq. tep., ___ tepid / ___ tépida, tibia. *V.* **water.**

aqueous *a.* acuoso-a, aguado-a; ___ humor / humor ___.

aquiline *a.* aquilino-a; ___ nose / nariz aguileña.

arachnoid *n.* aracnoides, membrana media cerebral que cubre el cerebro y la médula espinal.

arch *n.* arco, estructura de forma circular o en curva.

archetype *n.* arquetipo, tipo original ideal del que se derivan versiones modificadas.

ardor *n.* ardor, sensación quemante.

areola *n.* aréola, areola, área circular alrededor de un centro.

argue *v.* razonar, discutir, sostener.

Argyll-Robertson, symptom *n.* signo de Argyll-Robertson, condición de la pupila de acomodarse a una distancia pero no a refracciones de la luz.

arise *vi.* subir, levantarse, surgir.

arm *n.* brazo, una de las extremidades superiores; ___ less / sin ___-s; ___ pit / axila, *pop.* sobaco; ___ sling / cabestrillo; ___ span / de mano a mano, distancia de la mano derecha a la izquierda con los ___-s extendidos; **open arms** / ___-s abiertos.

aroma *n.* aroma, olor agradable.

aromatic *a.* aromático-a, rel. al aroma.

around *prep.* en, cerca de; *adv.* alrededor, cerca, a la vuelta; más o menos; ___ **here** / por aquí, en los alrededores; *v.* **to look** ___ / buscar; *v.* **to turn** ___ / voltear, dar la vuelta; virarse.

arrange *v.* arreglar, colocar, poner en su sitio.

arrest *n.* paro, arresto; detención; cardiac ___ / ___ del corazón, ___ cardíaco.

arrhythmia *n.* arritmia, falta de ritmo, esp. latidos irregulares del corazón.

arrival *n.* arribo, llegada; **dead on** ___ / paciente que llega sin vida, que llega muerto-a; [*new born*] new ___ / neonato-a, recién nacido-a.

arsenic *n.* arsénico; ___ poisoning / envenenamiento por arsénico.

arterial *a.* arterial, referente a las arterias; ___ blood gases / gases ___ ; ___ occlusive diseases / enfermedades oclusivas ___-es; ___ system / sistema ___ .

arteriography *n.* arteriografía, radiografía de las arterias.

arteriosclerosis *n.* arterioesclerosis, endurecimiento de las paredes de las arterias.

arteriotomy *n.* arteriotomía, *cirg.* apertura de una arteria.

arteriovenous *a.* arteriovenoso-a, relacionado con una arteria y una vena; ___ fistula / fístula ___ ; ___ malformations / malformaciones ___-s; ___ shunt, surgical / anastomosis ___ quirúrgica.

arteritis *n.* arteritis, infl. de una arteria. ___

artery *n.* arteria, uno de los vasos mayores que llevan la sangre del corazón a otras partes del cuerpo.

arthritic *a.* artrítico-a, que padece artritis.

arthritis *n.* artritis, infl. de una articulación o coyuntura; acute ___ / ___ aguda; chronic ___ / ___ crónica; degenerative ___ / ___ degenerativa; hemophilic ___ / ___ hemofílica; rheumatoid ___ / ___ reumatoidea; juvenile rheumatoid ___ / ___ reumatoidea juvenil; traumatic ___ / ___ traumática.

arthrodesis *n.* artrodesis. 1. *cirg.* fusión de

los huesos que hacen una articulación; 2. anquilosis artificial.

arthrogram *n.* artrograma, radiografía de una articulación por medio de un tinte opaco.

arthroplasty *n.* artroplastia, *cirg.* reparación de una articulación o construcción de una coyuntura artificial.

arthroscope *n.* artroscopio, instrumento para examinar el interior de una articulación.

arthroscopy *n.* artroscopia, examen del interior de una articulación.

arthrotomy *n.* artrotomía, *cirg.* incisión en una articulación con fines terapéuticos.

articular *a.* articular, rel. a las articulaciones.

articulate *a.* articulado-a, que se pronuncia con precisión; ___ person / persona que tiene facilidad de palabra, que puede expresarse bien; *v.* articular, pronunciar palabras claramente.

articulation *n.* articulación. 1. unión de dos o más huesos; 2. pronunciación clara y distinta de los sonidos de las palabras; ___ disorders / trastornos de la ___.

artificial *a.* artificial, artificioso-a; ___ limb / extremidad o parte ___.

artificial heart *n.* corazón artificial, aparato que bombea la sangre con la capacidad funcional de un corazón normal.

as *conj.* como, del mismo modo; ___ a child / de niño; *comp.* ___ much / tanto; ___ much ___ possible / lo más posible; ___you please / como Ud. quiera, tú quieras; ___ soon ___ you can / tan pronto como pueda, puedas; ___ usual / como de costumbre; not ___ yet / todavía no.

asbestos *n.* asbesto, amianto.

asbestosis *n.* asbestosis, infección crónica de los pulmones causada por el polvo del asbesto.

ascariasis *n.* ascariasis, infección causada por parásitos del género *Ascaris*.

ascaris *n. Ascaris,* género de parásitos que se aloja en el intestino de animales vertebrados.

ascend *v.* ascender, subir, escalar.

ascendent *a.* ascendiente, ascendente.

ascitis *n.* ascitis, acumulación de líquido en la cavidad abdominal.

ascorbic acid *n.* ácido ascórbico, vitamina C.

asepsia `*n.* asepsia, ausencia total de gérmenes.

aseptic *a.* aséptico-a, estéril.

asexual *a.* asexual, sin género; ___ reproduction / reproducción sin unión sexual.

ash *n.* ceniza; ___ colored / ceniciento-a.

ashamed *a.* avergonzado-a, apenado-a; *v.* to be ___ / tener vergüenza, tener pena.

Asiatic flu *n.* gripe asiática.

aside *adv.* aparte, a un lado; *v.* to lay ___ / dejar de lado.

ask *v.* preguntar, interrogar, hacer preguntas; [*about someone*] preguntar por; to ___ for; [*to request*] pedir.

asking *n.* súplica, petición, demanda.

asleep *a.* dormido-a; *v.* to fall ___ / dormirse, quedarse ___.

aspect *n.* aspecto, apariencia.

aspermia *n.* aspermia, fallo en la emisión de semen.

asphyxia *n.* asfixia, sofocación, falta de respiración; ___ fetalis / ___ del feto.

asphyxiate *v.* asfixiarse.

aspirate *v.* aspirar.

aspiration *n.* aspiración, inhalación, succión, extracción de un líquido sin dejar entrar el aire; ___ biopsy / biopsia con aguja.

aspirin *n.* aspirina, ácido acetilsalicílico.

assay *n.* ensayo; análisis.

assert *v.* afirmar, sostener.

assessment *n.* evaluación; clinical ___ / ___ clínica; health ___ / ___ del estado de salud.

assets *n.* capital existente, fondos.

assign *v.* asignar, indicar, señalar.

assignment *n.* asignación, tarea, misión.

assimilate *v.* asimilar, convertir los alimentos en sustancias.

assimilation *n.* asimilación, transformación y absorción por el organismo de los alimentos digeridos.

assist *v.* ayudar, asistir, socorrer.

assistance *n.* asistencia, ayuda.

assistant *n., a.* asistente, ayudante.

associate *a.* asociado-a, socio-a.

association *n.* asociación, sociedad, unión.

assurance *n.* seguridad, confianza, certeza.

assure *v.* asegurar, dar confianza.

astasia *n.* astasia, condición histérica.

asthenia *n.* astenia, pérdida de vigor.

asthma *n.* asma, condición alérgica con ataques de coriza, y falta de la respiración a causa de la infl. de las membranas mucosas.

asthmatic *a.* asmático-a, rel. al asma.

astigmatism *n.* astigmatismo, defecto de la

visión a causa de una irregularidad en la curvatura del ojo.

astragalus *n.* astrágalo, calus, hueso del tobillo.

astringent *a.* astringente, agente con poder de constricción de los tejidos y las membranas mucosas.

astrocytoma *n.* astrocitoma, tumor cerebral.

asylum *n.* asilo.

asymmetry *n.* asimetría, falta de simetría.

asymptomatic *a.* asintomático-a, sin síntoma alguno.

asynergy *n.* asinergia, falta de coordinación entre órganos gen. armónicos.

asystole, asystolia *n.* asístole, asistolia, paro del corazón, ausencia de contracciones cardíacas.

ataraxia *n.* ataraxia; *psic.* impasividad.

atavism *n.* atavismo, reproducción de rasgos y características ancestrales.

ataxia *n.* ataxia, deficiencia de coordinación muscular.

atelectasis *n.* atelectasis, colapso parcial o total de un pulmón.

athermic *a.* atérmico-a, sin fiebre.

atheroma *n.* ateroma, depósito graso o lípido en la capa íntima de una arteria que causa endurecimiento de la misma.

atherosclerosis *n.* aterosclerosis, condición causada por la deposición de grasa en las capas interiores de las arterias y fibrosis de las mismas.

athetosis *n.* atetosis, condición con síntomas de contracciones involuntarias en las manos y los dedos y movimientos sin coordinación de las extremidades, esp. los brazos.

athlete's foot *n.* pie de atleta. V. **dermatophytosis.**

atmosphere *n.* atmósfera.

atmospheric *a.* atmosférico-a.

atom *n.* átomo.

atomic *a.* atómico-a.

atomizer *n.* atomizador.

atonia, atony *n.* atonía, falta de tono, esp. en los músculos.

atresia *n.* atresia, cierre congénito anormal de una abertura o conducto del cuerpo.

atrial *a.* auricular, atrial, rel. al atrio o la aurícula.

atrioventricular *a.* atrioventricular, rel. a la aurícula y ventrículo del corazón; ____ node / nudo aurículoventricular.

atrium *n.* (*pl.* **atria**) atrio. 1. cavidad que

tiene comunicación con otra estructura; 2. cavidad superior del corazón.

atrophy *n.* atrofia, deteriorización de las células, tejidos y órganos del cuerpo.

atropine sulfate *n.* atropina, agente usado como relajador muscular, esp. aplicado para dilatar la pupila y paralizar el músculo ciliar durante un examen de la vista.

attach *v.* añadir, juntar, pegar, unir.

attached *a.* añadido-a, pegado-a, unido-a.

attack *n.* ataque, acceso; heart ____ / ataque al corazón; *v.* atacar, combatir.

attempt *v.* intentar, tratar de obtener algo; hacer un esfuerzo; esforzarse, arriesgarse.

attend *v.* atender, asistir, cuidar, tener cuidado; **to** ____ **the sick** / asistir, cuidar a los enfermos.

attendant *n.* auxiliar, asistente.

attending physician *n.* médico-a de cabecera.

attention *n.* atención, cuidado; **lack of** ____ / falta de ____ ; *v.* **to pay** ____ / atender, prestar atención.

attentive *a.* atento-a.

attentively *adv.* atentamente, con cuidado.

attenuation *n.* atenuación, acto de disminución, esp. de una virulencia.

attitude *n.* actitud; ____ of health personnel / ____ del personal de salud; ____ **toward death** / ____ frente a la muerte.

attorney *n.* abogado-a, agente legal.

attract *v.* atraer.

attraction *n.* atracción.

attribute *n.* atributo, característica.

atypical *a.* atípico-a, que no es común; *adv.* fuera de lo corriente.

audiogram *n.* audiograma, instrumento para anotar la agudeza de la audición.

audiovisual *a.* audiovisual, rel. a la vista y a la audición.

auditory *a.* auditivo-a, rel. a la audición; ____ canal / conducto ____ ; ____ nerve / nervio ____ .

augment *n.* aumento, crecimiento; *v.* aumentar, crecer; agrandarse.

aunt *n.* tía.

aura *n.* aura, síntoma premonitorio de un ataque epiléptico.

aural, auricular *a.* aural, auricular. 1. rel. al sentido del oído; 2. rel. a una aurícula del corazón.

auricle, auricula *n.* aurícula. 1. oreja, la

parte externa del oído. 2. cavidad superior del corazón: aurícula derecha e izquierda.

auscultate *v.* auscultar, examinar, detectar sonidos de órganos tales como el corazón y los pulmones con el propósito de hacer un diagnóstico.

auscultation *n.* auscultación, acto de auscultar, detección de sonidos en un examen directo o por medio del estetoscopio.

authority *n.* autoridad, facultad.

authorization *n.* autorización.

authorize *v.* autorizar, permitir.

autism *n.* autismo, trastorno de la conducta que se manifiesta en un egocentrismo extremo; infantile ___ / ___ infantil.

autistic *a.* autístico-a, rel. al autismo o que padece de éste.

autoclave *n.* autoclave, aparato de esterilización al vapor.

autodiagnosis *n.* autodiagnosis, diagnóstico propio, de sí mismo-a.

autodigestion *n.* autodigestión, digestión de tejidos por las mismas sustancias que los producen.

autogenous *n.* autógeno-a, que se produce en el mismo organismo.

autogenous vaccine *n.* vacuna autógena, inoculación que proviene del cultivo de bacterias del mismo paciente y se hace para crear anticuerpos.

autograft *n.* autoinjerto, injerto que se transfiere de una parte a otra del cuerpo del mismo paciente.

autohypnosis *n.* autohipnosis, hipnotismo propio, de sí mismo-a.

autoimmunization *n.* autoinmunización, inmunidad producida por una sustancia desarrollada dentro del organismo de la persona afectada.

autoinfection *n.* autoinfección, infección causada por un agente del propio organismo.

autoinoculable *a.* autoinoculable, suceptible a organismos que provienen del propio cuerpo.

autologous *a.* autólogo-a, que indica algo que proviene del propio individuo.

automatic *a.* automático, de movimiento propio.

automatism *n.* automatismo, conducta que no está bajo control voluntario.

automobile *n.* automóvil, carro, *Cuba* máquina, *Spain* coche.

autonomic, autonomous *a.* autonómico-a, autónomo-a, que funciona independientemente; ___ nervous system / sistema nervioso ___.

autonomy *n.* autonomía, de funcionamiento propio.

autoplastic *a.* autoplástico-a, rel. a la autoplastia.

autoplasty *n.* autoplastia, *cirg.* cirugía plástica con el uso de un injerto que se obtiene de la misma persona que lo recibe.

autopsy *n.* autopsia, examen de un cadáver.

autosuggestion *n.* autosugestión, acto de sugestionarse.

auxiliary *a.* auxiliar; ayudante.

available *a.* disponible, servicial; a la mano.

avaricious *a.* avaricioso-a, ruin, miserable.

average *n.* promedio, término medio; de mediana proporción.

aversion *n.* aversión, aborrecimiento, odio.

avitaminosis *n.* avitaminosis, trastorno o enfermedad causada por una deficiencia vitamínica.

avoid *v.* evitar.

avulsion *n. cirg.* avulsión, extracción, o remoción de una estructura o parte de ésta.

awake *a.* despierto-a.

aware *a.* enterado-a; conocedor-a; *v.* to be ___ / estar al tanto.

away *adv.* lejos; *a.* distante, ausente; *v.* to go ___ / irse, ausentarse; *interj.* get ___! / quítese, quítate; váyase, vete.

awful *a.* terrible, desagradable; tremendo-a.

awhile *adv.* por un rato, por algún tiempo.

awkward *a.* [*movement*] torpe; desmañado-a; [*appearance*] extraño-a; ___ feeling / sentimiento extraño.

axial *a.* axil, axial, rel. al axis o a un eje.

axilla *n.* (*pl.* **axillae**) axila, *pop.* sobaco.

axillary *a.* axilar, rel. a la axila.

axis *n.* axis, eje, línea central imaginaria que pasa através del cuerpo o de un órgano.

ay, aye *adv.* sí, claro, desde luego, seguramente.

Ayerza's syndrome *n.* síndrome de Ayerza, síndrome caracterizado por multiples síntomas esp. dispnea y cianosis, gen. como resultado de insuficiencia pulmonar.

azoospermia *n.* azoospermia, falta de espermatozoos en el esperma.

azotemia *n.* azotemia, exceso de urea en la sangre.

azure *n.* azul celeste.

B

b *abbr.* **bacillus** / bacilo; **behavior** / conducta; **buccal** / bucal

babble *n.* balbuceo; *v.* balbucear.

Babinski sign *n.* reflejo de Babinski, dorsiflexión del dedo gordo al estimularse la planta del pie.

baby, babe *n.* bebé, *dim.* bebito-a; nene-a.

bachelor *n.* soltero-a, célibe; [*degree*] bachiller.

bacillar, bacillary *a.* bacilar, rel. a un bacilo.

bacillemia *n.* bacilemia, presencia de bacilos en la sangre.

bacillicarrier *n.* portador de bacilos.

bacillosis *n.* bacilosis, infección provocada por bacilos.

bacilluria *n.* baciluria, presencia de bacilos en la orina.

bacillus *n.* (*pl.* **bacilli**) bacilo, microbio, bacteria en forma de bastoncillo; Calmette-Guérin, bacile bilié (BCG) ___ / ___ de Calmette Guérin, bacile bilié; Koch's ___ , Mycobacterium tuberculosis / ___ de Koch, micobacteria de la tuberculosis; typhoid ___ , Salmonella typhi / ___ de la fiebre tifoidea, Salmonela tifoidea.

bacitracin *n.* bacitracin, antibiótico efectivo en contra de ciertos estafilococos.

back *n.* espalda; ___ ache / dolor de ___ ; *adv.* atrás, detrás.

backboard *n.* respaldar.

backbone *n.* columna vertebral, espina dorsal.

background *n.* fondo; [*knowledge*] preparación, experiencia.

backing *n.* apoyo, sostén.

backlash *n.* contragolpe.

backside *n.* nalgas, *pop.* sentaderas, posaderas, trasero.

backslide *v.* resbalar o caer hacia atrás.

backtooth *n.* muela.

backward *a.* atrasado-a, tardío-a, lento-a, retraído-a; *adv.* atrás, hacia atrás, al revés; [*direction*] en sentido contrario.

backwardness *n.* atraso, retraso, ignorancia, torpeza.

bacon *n.* tocino.

bacteremia *n.* bacteremia, presencia de bacterias en la sangre.

bacteria *n. pl.* bacterias, gérmenes.

bacterial *a.* bacteriano-a; ___ infections / infecciones ___ -s; ___ endocarditis / endocarditis ___ ; ___ sensitivity tests / pruebas de sensibilidad ___ .

bactericidal *n.* bactericida, exterminador de bacterias.

bacteriogenic *a.* bacteriogénico-a. 1. de origen bacteriano; 2. que produce bacterias.

bacteriological *a.* bacteriológico-a, rel. a las bacterias.

bacteriologist *n.* bacteriólogo-a, especialista en bacteriología.

bacteriology *n.* bacteriología, ciencia que estudia las bacterias.

bacteriolysin *n.* bacteriolisina, anticuerpo antibacteriano que destruye bacterias.

bacteriolysis *n.* bacteriolisis, destrucción de bacterias.

bacteriosis *n.* bacteriosis, toda infección causada por gérmenes o bacterias.

bacteriostatic *a.* bacteriostático-a, que detiene el desarrollo o multiplicación de bacterias.

bacterium *n.* (*pl.* **bacteria**) bacteria, germen.

bacteriuria *n.* bacteriuria, presencia de bacterias en la orina.

bad *a.* malo-a, nocivo-a, [*harmful*] dañino-a; **it is** ___ **for your health** / dañino a la salud; **from** ___ **to worse** / de mal en peor; *v.* **to look** ___ / tener mal aspecto, tener mala cara; ___ **breath** / mal aliento; ___ **looking** / mal parecido; ___ **mood** / de mal humor; ___ **taste in the mouth** / mal sabor en la boca; *slang* ___ **trip** / mala experiencia con una droga; *adv.* mal; *v.* **to feel** ___ / sentirse mal; **-ly** *adv.* mal, malamente; *v.* **to need** ___ / necesitar con urgencia.

bag *n.* bolsa, bolso; saco; colostomy ___ / bolso de colostomía; ___ of waters / saco amniótico, *pop.* ___ de aguas; ice ___ / ___ de hielo.

baked *a.* asado-a, guisado-a al horno, horneado-a.

balance *n.* balance. 1. estado de equilibrio; acid base ___ / ___ acidobásico; fluid ___ / ___ hídrico; 2. balanza, pesa.

balanced *a.* balanceado-a; en control; ___ diet / dieta ___ .

balanitis *n.* balanitis, infl. del glande gen. acompañada de infl. del prepucio.

balanoposthitis *n.* balanopostitis, infl. del glande y del prepucio.

baldhead *a.* calvo-a, sin pelo.

baldness *n.* calvicie.

ball *n.* bola; asiento del pie; ____ forceps / pinzas sacabalas; ____ of the foot / antepié; ____ and socket joint / articulación esférica.

ballistocardiogram *n.* balistocardiograma, registro fotográfico del volumen sistólico para calcular el volumen minuto.

balloon *n.* balón; *slang* [*heroin*] globo.

ballottement *Fr.* peloteo, movimiento manual de rebote por palpación usado en el examen de abdomen y pelvis para determinar la presencia de un tumor o el agrandamiento de un órgano.

balm *n.* bálsamo, ungüento, calmante de uso externo.

balmy *a.* balsámico; suave, reparador; ____ sleep / sueño reparador.

balsam *n.* bálsamo, agente suavizante.

ban *v.* prohibir, suspender, suprimir.

banana *n.* banana, plátano.

bandage *n.* venda, vendaje, faja; *v.* vendar, ligar, atar.

bandaid *n.* curita, parche.

bandyleg *n.* zambo-a, patizambo-a.

bane *n.* veneno; ruina.

baneful *a.* venenoso-a, dañino-a, destructivo-a.

bang *n.* golpe; detonación.

bank *n.* banco.

baragnosis *n.* baragnosis, pérdida de la capacidad de reconocer pesos y presiones.

barbiturate *n.* barbitúrico, hipnótico, sedante.

bare *a.* desnudo-a, descubierto-a; ____ **foot** / descalzo-a, sin zapatos; ____ **legged** / sin medias; **-ly** *adv.* apenas.

baresthesia *n.* barestesia, sensación de presión o peso.

barium *n.* bario; ____ enema / enema de ____.

barley *n.* cebada.

barometer *n.* barómetro, instrumento para medir la presión atmosférica.

baroreceptor *n.* barorreceptor, terminación nerviosa sensorial que reacciona a los cambios de presión.

barrel *n.* [*part of a syringe*] cilindro; barril.

barren *a.* estéril, infecundo-a.

barrier *n.* obstrucción, barrera.

bartholinitis *n.* bartolinitis, infl. de la glándula de Bartolino o glándula vulvo vaginal.

baryphonia *n.* barifonía, tipo de voz gruesa.

basal, basilar *a.* basal, basilar, rel. a una

base; ____ ganglia diseases / enfermedades de los ganglios ____ -es; ____ metabolic rate / índice del metabolismo ____.

base, basis *n.* base.

bashful *a.* tímido-a, *pop.* corto-a.

basic *a.* básico-a, fundamental.

basil *n.* albahaca.

basilar *a.* basilar, rel. a la base o parte basal.

basin *n.* 1. vasija redonda tal como una palangana; 2. cavidad de la pelvis.

basophobia *n.* *psic.* basofobia, temor excesivo de caminar.

bassinet *n.* bacinete, cuna.

bastard *n.* bastardo-a; hijo o hija ilegítimo-a.

bath *n.* baño; aromatic ____ / ____ aromático; alcohol ____ / fricción de alcohol; antipyretic ____ / ____ antipirético, para reducir la fiebre; cold ____ / ____ de agua fría; Sitz ____ / ____ de asiento caliente; sponge ____ / ____ con esponja; warm ____ / ____ tibio.

bathe *v.* bañar, lavar; bañarse, lavarse.

bathrobe *n.* bata de baño.

bathroom *n.* baño, cuarto de baño.

bathtub *n.* tina, bañadera.

battered *a.* abatido-a, maltratado-a.

battle *n.* batalla, lucha; *v.* batallar, combatir, luchar.

bay leaves *n. pl.* hojas de laurel.

bay-salt *n.* sal marina.

be *vi.* ser, estar; **there is, there are** / hay; **there was** / hubo, había; **there will be** / será, estará; habrá; *pp.* **been** / sido, estado; *p.p.* **being** / siendo, estando; **to ____ afraid** / tener miedo; **to ____ calm** / calmarse; **to ____ careful** / tener cuidado; **to ____ cold** / tener frío; **to ____ hot** / tener calor; **to ____ hungry** / tener hambre; **to be at a loss** / estar confundido-a; **to ____ quiet** / callarse; estar tranquilo-a; **to ____ right** / tener razón; **to ____ all right** / estar bien; **to ____ years old** / tener años; **to ____ sick** / estar enfermo-a; **to ____ sleepy** / tener sueño; **to ____ successful** / tener éxito; **to ____ thirsty** / tener sed; **to ____ warm** [*with a temperature*] / tener fiebre, tener calentura; tener calor; **to want to ____** / querer ser; **to want to ____** [*somewhere*] / querer estar.

bean *n.* frijol.

bear *vi.* soportar; aguantar; ____ **down** pujar, empujar hacia afuera con fuerza.

bearable *a.* soportable, tolerable.

beard *n.* barba.

bearded *a.* barbudo.

bearer *n.* soporte, apoyo.

bearing *n.* gestación; conexión; [*in obstetrics*] ____ down / pujo, expulsión hacia afuera, (segunda etapa del parto).

beat *n.* [*heart*] latido, pulsación; heart ____ / ____ del corazón; *vi.* pulsar; [*heart*] palpitar; pegar, golpear.

beaten *a. pp.* de **to beat,** maltratado-a; golpeado-a; vencido-a, derrotado-a.

beating *n.* pulsación, latido; paliza, zurra.

beautiful *a.* hermoso-a, bello-a.

beauty *n.* belleza, hermosura, beldad.

become *vi.* hacerse, convertirse; ____ a doctor / hacerse médico-a; [*conversion*] ____ a / convertirse; ____ **accustomed** / acostumbrarse; ____ **crazy** / volverse loco-a; ____ **frightened** / asustarse; ____ **ill** / ponerse enfermo-a; enfermarse; ____ **inflamed** / inflamarse; ____ **swollen** / hincharse.

becoming *a.* apropiado-a, conveniente, que sienta o cae bien.

bed *n.* cama; lecho; ____ **bug** / chinche; ____ **clothes** / ropa de cama; ____ **fast** / recluído-a en ____ ; ____ **pan** / bacín, chata, cuña; ____ **ridden** / postrado-a en ____ ; ____ **side** / al lado de la ____ ; ____ **sore** / úlcera por decúbito; ____ **spread** / colcha, sobrecama, cubrecama; ____ **occupancy** / ocupación de ____ -s; ____ **rest** / guardar ____ ; ____ **time** / hora de acostarse; ____ **wetting** / enuresis, orinarse en la ____ ; mo jar la ____ .

bedding *n.* ropa de cama; colchón y almohada.

bedroom *n.* cuarto de dormir, alcoba, dormitorio; *Mex.* recámara.

bee *n.* abeja; ____ **venoms** / venenos de ____ .

beef *n.* carne de res, carne de vaca; ____ **broth** / caldo de carne; **roast** ____ / carne asada, rosbif; ____ **steak** / biftec.

beer *n.* cerveza.

beet *n.* remolacha.

before *adv.* delante; enfrente de; antes de; anterior a; *conj.* antes que; antes de que.

beforehand *adv.* con anterioridad, con anticipación; de antemano.

beg *v.* pedir, rogar, mendigar.

begin *vi.* comenzar, empezar, principiar.

beginner *n.* principiante, novicio-a; autor-a, iniciador-a.

beginning *n.* principio, origen, génesis.

behalf *n.* en beneficio, a favor; **on your** ____ / a su favor, por usted.

behavior *n.* conducta, comportamiento; ____ reflex / reflejo adquirido; ____ therapy / terapia de la ____ ; high risk ____ / comportamiento arriesgado.

behind *adv., prep.,* detras, trás, atrás, hacia atrás.

bel, belio *n.* bel, unidad que expresa la intensidad relativa de un sonido.

belch *n.* eructo, regüeldo; *v.* eructar.

belief *n.* creencia, opinión.

belittle *n.* dar poca importancia, humillar.

belladonna *n.* belladona, yerba medicinal cuyas hojas y raíces contienen atropina y alcaloides.

bellied *a.* panzudo-a, barrigón-a, con barriga.

belligerent *a.* beligerante.

Bell's palsy *n.* parálisis de Bell, parálisis de un lado de la cara causada por una afección del nervio facial.

belly *n.* abdomen, barriga, vientre, *pop.* panza; ____ ache / dolor de estómago, de barriga; ____ button / ombligo; ____ worm / lombriz intestinal.

below *prep.* después de, debajo de; *adv.* abajo, bajo, debajo; **down** ____ / en la parte baja; más abajo.

bend *vi.* doblarse, inclinarse; ____ back / ____ hacia atrás; ____ forward / ____ hacia adelante.

beneath *prep., adv.* abajo, debajo, bajo.

Benedict test *n.* prueba de Benedict, análisis químico para encontrar la presencia de azúcar en la orina.

beneficial *a.* beneficioso-a, favorable, provechoso-a.

beneficiary *n., a.* beneficiado-a, favorecido-a.

benefit *n.* beneficio, favor; servicio, provecho.

benign *a.* benigno-a, que no es de naturaleza maligna.

bent *n.* inclinación, curvatura; *a.* encorvado-a; inclinado-a.

Benzedrine *n.* Bencedrina, nombre comercial del sulfato de anfetamina.

benzoin *n.* benjuí, recina usada como expectorante.

beri-beri *n.* beriberi, tipo de neuritis múltiple causada por deficiencia de vitamina B_1 (tiamina).

beside *adv.* además, *prep.* al lado de, cerca

de, junto a; ____ **oneself** / fuera de sí, estar loco-a.

best *a. sup.* mejor, superior, óptimo; *v.* **to do one's** ____ / hacer lo ____ posible.

bestial *a.* bestial, irracional, brutal.

bestiality *n.* bestialidad, relaciones sexuales con animales.

better *a. comp.* mejor, superior; [*better than*] mejor que; *v.* **to be** ____ / estar mejor, ponerse mejor; **to make** ____ / mejorar, aliviar; **so much the** ____ / tanto mejor; *v.* **to change for the** ____ / recuperarse, restablecerse; **to be** ____ **than** / ser mejor que; **to be** ____ **than before** / estar, ser mejor que antes; **to like** ____ / preferir.

between *adv.* en medio; *prep.* entre, en medio de.

beverage *n.* bebida; **alcoholic** ____-**s** / bebidas alcoholicas; **non-alcoholic** ____ / refresco, soda.

beware of *vi.* cuidarse de.

bewilder *v.* confundir, perturbar, turbar.

bewildered *a.* perplejo-a, confundido-a; atolondrado-a.

beyond *adv.* más allá, más lejos.

bezoar *n.* bezoar, concreción formada de distintas materias como fibras vegetales y pelo, presente en el estómago y en el intestino humano y el de los animales.

bias *n.* parcialidad, prejuicio, tendencia.

biaxial *a.* biaxil, que tiene dos ejes.

bib *n.* babero; pechera.

bibliography *n.* bibliografía.

bicarbonate *n.* bicarbonato, sal de ácido carbónico.

biceps *n.* músculo bíceps.

bicipital *a.* bicipital. 1. rel. al músculo bíceps; 2. bicípite, que tiene dos cabezas.

biconcave *a.* bicóncavo-a, de dos superficies cóncavas.

biconvex *a.* biconvexo-a, de dos caras convexas, tal como los lentes para la presbicia.

bicuspid *a.* bicúspide, que presenta dos puntas.

bicycle *n.* bicicleta; stationary ____ / ____ estacionaria.

bifid *a.* bífido-a, partido en dos.

bifocal *a.* bifocal, referente a dos focos o enfoques.

bifurcation *n.* bifurcación, división en dos ramas o bifurcaciones.

big *a.* grande, enorme; mayor; ____ **bellied** / barrigón-a, panzudo-a; ____ **head** / cabezón-a; ____ **sister, brother** / hermana

mayor, hermano mayor; ____ **toe** / dedo gordo; ____ **with child** / encinta, en estado.

bigeminy *n.* bigeminia, pulsación duplicada en sucesión rápida.

bigger *a. comp.* mayor, más grande.

bilabial *a.* bilabial.

bilateral *a.* bilateral, de dos lados.

bile *n.* bilis, hiel, producto de la secreción del hígado; ____ **acids and salts** / ácidos y sales biliares; ____ **ducts** / conductos biliares.

bilharziasis *n.* bilharziasis. *V.* **schitosomiasis.**

biliary *a.* biliar, rel. a la bilis, los conductos biliares o la vesícula ____; ____ **duct obstruction** / obstrucción del conducto ____; ____ **stasis** / colestasis; ____ **tract diseases** / enfermedades de las vías ____-es; ____ **tract hemorrhage** / hemobilia.

bilingual *a.* bilingüe.

bilious *a.* bilioso-a, con exceso de bilis.

biliousness *n.* biliosidad, trastorno con síntomas de estreñimiento, dolor de cabeza e indigestión atribuidos a un exceso de secreción biliar.

bilirubin *n.* bilirrubina, pigmento rojo de la bilis.

bilirubinemia *n.* bilirrubinemia, presencia de bilirrubina en la sangre.

bilirubinuria *n.* bilirrubinuria, presencia de bilirrubina en la orina.

bill *n.* [*statement*] cuenta; [*currency*] billete.

bimanual *a.* bimanual, rel. a las dos manos.

binary *a.* binario, doble.

bind *vi.* unir, ligar, vendar.

binding *n.* enlace; ligazón; venda.

binocular *n.* binocular, lentes, gemelos.

bioassay *n.* bioensayo, prueba de determinación de la potencia de una droga en animales.

biochemistry *n.* bioquímica, ciencia que estudia los organismos vivos.

biologist *n.* biólogo-a.

biology *n.* biología, ciencia que estudia los organismos vivos; cellular ____ / ____ celular; molecular ____ / ____ molecular.

biopsy *n.* biopsia, proceso para obtener un espécimen de tejido con fines de diagnóstico; ____ **of the bone marrow** / ____ de la médula ósea; ____ **of the breast** / ____ de la mama, del seno; ____ **of the cervix** / ____ del cuello uterino; ____ **of the lymph**

nodes / ____ de los ganglios linfáticos; needle ____ / ____ por aspiración; endoscopic ____ / ____ endoscópica; excision ____ / ____ por excisión.

biosynthesis *n.* biosíntesis, formación de sustancias químicas en los procesos fisiológicos de los organismos.

biotype *n.* biotipo, grupo de individuos con igual genotipo.

biped *n.* bípedo, animal de dos pies.

birefringent *a.* birrefringente, de refracción doble.

birth *n.* nacimiento, parto, alumbramiento; ____ canal / canal del parto; ____ certificate / certificado de ____ ; ____ control / control de la natalidad, planeamiento familiar; ____ death ratio / índice de mortalidad; post-term ____ / ____ tardío; premature ____ / ____ prematuro; ____ rate / natalidad; ____ right / derechos naturales; ____ weight / peso al nacer; *v.* **to give** ____ / dar a luz, estar de parto.

birth date *n.* fecha de nacimiento.

birthday *n.* cumpleaños, natalicio.

birthplace *n.* lugar de nacimiento.

bisect *v.* bisecar, dividir en dos partes.

bisexual *a.* bisexual, con gónadas de los dos sexos.

bite *n.* mordida, picadura; [*snake*] mordida de serpiente; [*insect*] picadura; ____ block / bloque de ____ ; ____ rim / reborde de la ____ ; *vi.* morder, picar.

biting *a.* penetrante, picante.

bitter *a.* agrio-a, amargo-a; [*person*] amargado-a.

black *a.* negro-a; ____ **and blue** / amoratado; ____ **eye** / ojo amoratado; ____ death / peste bubónica; ____ urine / melanuria.

blackhead *n.* barro, espinilla, comedón.

blackout *n.* desmayo, vértigo, condición caracterizada por la falta de visión y pérdida momentánea del conocimiento; desmayarse.

bladder *n.* vejiga; saco músculo-membranoso situado en la cavidad pélvica; ____ calculi / cálculos, piedras de la ____ ; ____ infection / infección de la ____ ; ____ irrigation / irrigación de la ____ ; ____ , neurogenic / ____ neurogénica.

blain *n.* llaga, ampolla, pústula.

bland *a.* blando-a, suave; ____ diet / dieta ____ .

blanket *n.* manta, frazada, cobija.

blastema *n.* blastema, sustancia primaria de la que se originan las células.

blastomycosis *n.* blastomicosis, infección causada por hongos que se inicia gen. en los pulmones.

blastula *n.* blástula, etapa primitiva del óvulo.

bleach *n.* lejía.

bleariness *n.* lagaña, secreción pegajosa del ojo; vista nublada.

bleary-eyed *a.* [*eye*] legañoso; [*sight*] vista nublada; vista cansada.

bleed *vi.* sangrar, derramar, perder sangre; [*profusely*] desangrarse.

bleeding *n.* sangramiento.

blemish *n.* mancha, imperfección, defecto.

blend *n.* mezcla; *v.* mezclar, combinar.

blennorrhagia *n.* blenorragia, flujo de mucus.

blepharectomy *n.* blefarectomía, *cirg.* excisión de una parte o de todo el párpado.

blepharitis *n.* blefaritis, infl. de los párpados.

blepharochalasis *n.* blefarocalasis, relajación o caída del párpado superior por pérdida de elasticidad del tejido intersticial.

blepharoplasty *n. cirg.* blefaroplastia, operación plástica de los párpados.

blepharoplegia *n.* blefaroplejía, parálisis del párpado.

blind *a.* ciego-a, sin vista, ofuscado-a; *v.* cegar, deslumbrar; ____ in one eye / tuerto-a; ____ spot / punto ____ .

blindness *n.* ceguera; color ____ / acromatopsia, ____ al color; night ____ / nictalopía, ____ nocturna; red ____ / ____ roja; total ____ / pérdida completa de la visión.

blinds *n. pl.* cortinas.

blink *v.* parpadear.

blinking *n.* parpadeo.

blister *n.* ampolla, vesícula, flictena.

bloat *n.* aventación. V. **tympanites;** *v.* entumecerse, hincharse.

bloated *a.* aventado-a, abotagado-a.

block *n.* bloqueo, obstrucción; *v.* obstruir, bloquear.

blocked *a.* bloqueado-a, obstruído-a; ____ bowel / obstrucción intestinal; ____ ureter / obstrucción ureteral.

blond *a.* rubio-a, *Mex.* güero-a.

blood *n.* sangre; autologous ____ / ____ autóloga; ____ bank / banco de ____ ; ____ cell count / conteo globular, conteo de células sanguíneas; ____ count / conteo sanguíneo; ____ culture / hemocultivo; ____ clot / coágulo de ____ ; ____ coagulation time / tiempo de coagulación sanguínea; ____ derivatives / derivados sanguíneos, hemoderivados; ____ donor / donante de ____ ; ____ gases / gases sanguíneos; ____ groups / grupos sanguíneos; ____ grouping / determinación de grupos sanguíneos; ____ oxygen analysis / análisis del oxígeno contenido en la ____ ; ____ packed cells / células paquete, células compactadas sanguíneas; ____ plasma / plasma sanguíneo; ____ pressure / presión arterial; ____ products / productos sanguíneos; ____ proteins / proteínas sanguíneas; ____ relation / consanguíneo-a; ____ screening / prueba selecta de ____ ; ____ sputum / esputo sanguinolento; ____ substitutes / substitutos sanguíneos; ____ sugar / glucemia; ____ transfusion / transfusión sanguínea; ____ type / grupo sanguíneo; ____ typing / determinación del grupo sanguíneo; ____ vessel / vaso sanguíneo.

bloodless *a.* exangüe, debilitado-a.

bloodletting *n. pop.* sangría.

bloodshot *a.* [*eye*] inyectado de sangre.

bloody *a.* ensangrentado-a, con sangre, sanguinolento-a.

blotch *n.* marca, roncha.

blouse *n.* blusa, corpiño.

blow *n.* golpe; *vi.* soplar, **to give a** ____ / golpear. **to** ____ **one's nose** / soplarse, sonarse la nariz.

blown *a., pp.* de **to blow,** soplado-a; ____ **up** / hinchado-a.

blue *n.* color azul; triste, melancólico-a; ____ **baby syndrome** / cianosis congénita, *pop.* mal azul.

blunder *n.* disparate, desatino.

blunt *a.* despuntado-a; embotado-a; ____ injuries / heridas contusas.

blur *v.* empañar, nublar los ojos.

blurred *a., pp.* de **to blur,** borroso-a, nublado-a, empañado-a.

blush *vr.* sonrojarse, ruborizarse.

blushing *n.* rubor.

board *n.* tabla.

body *n.* cuerpo; [*dead*] cadáver; tronco; materia, sustancia; ____ fluid / líquido corporal; ____ height / estatura; ____ temperature / temperatura corporal; ____ weight / peso corporal; ____ wall / tronco.

bogus *a.* falso-a; podrido-a.

boil *n.* forúnculo, *Cuba* nacido; *Mex.* elacote; *v.* hervir, cocer.

boiled *a.* hervido-a; ____ water / agua ____ .

boiling point *n.* punto de ebullición.

bolster *n.* cabezal; sostén, refuerzo; ____ suture / sutura compuesta.

bond *n.* vínculo, unión.

bone *n.* hueso; ____ cell / osteoblasto; ____ development / desarrollo óseo; ____ fracture / fractura, ____ quebrado; ____ fragility / fragilidad ósea; ____ graft / injerto óseo; ____ hook / gancho óseo; ____ lesions / lesiones en los ____ -s; ____ marrow / médula ósea, *pop.* tuétano; ____ marrow failure / fallo de la médula ósea; ____ plate / placa ósea; ____ splinter / esquirla, astilla ósea; hard ____ / ____ compacto; spongy ____ / ____ esponjoso; *v.* **to make no** ____ **-s about it** / hablar sin rodeos; **skin and** ____ **-s** / piel y ____ -s, muy delgado *pop.* estar en el hueso; *v.* deshuesar; sacar los ____ -s.

bonelet *n. dim.* huesecillo.

bonesetter *n.* componedor de huesos; curandero-a.

book *n.* libro.

booster shot *n.* búster, inyección de refuerzo; dosis suplementaria; reactivación de una vacuna o agente inmunizador.

boot *n.* bota.

booze *n.* bebida alcohólica.

borax *n.* bórax, borato de sodio.

border *n.* borde, margen; frontera; ____ line case / caso incierto.

bordering *a.* cercano-a, fronterizo-a, adyacente.

bored *a.* aburrido-a.

boredom *n.* fastidio, aburrimiento.

boric acid *n.* ácido bórico.

born *a.* nacido-a; **new** ____ / recién nacido-a; *v.* **to be** ____ / nacer.

borne *a.* acarreado-a, transmitido-a; llevado-a.

bosom *n.* seno, pecho.

both *a., pron.* ambos, los dos.

bothersome *a.* incómodo-a, molesto-a.

bottle *n.* botella, frasco, [*infant*] biberón, mamadera; *Mex. A.* pote, tele; ____ feeding / lactancia; ____ propping / suplementación con biberón.

bottom *n.* fondo, parte inferior; asiento; *pop.* posaderas, asentaderas; *Cuba* fondillo.

botulin *n.* botulina, toxina causante del botulismo.

botulism *n.* botulismo, intoxicación ocasionada por la ingestión de alimentos contaminados por *Clostridium botulinum* que se desarrolla en alimentos que no han sido propiamente conservados.

bougie *n.* bujía; candelilla, instrumento usado en la dilatación de la uretra.

bouillon *n.* caldo, líquido alimenticio.

boulimia *n.* bulimia, apetito insaciable.

bounding pulse *n.* pulso saltón.

bounding pupil *n.* pupila saltona.

bout *n.* acceso, ataque, episodio.

bovine *n.* bovino, referente al ganado.

bowel *n.* intestino. ___ movement / evacuación, deposición; ___ obstruction / obstrucción intestinal.

bowels *n. pl.* intestinos.

bowl *n.* bacín, taza.

bowleg *n. V.* **genu-varum.**

box *n.* caja, estuche.

boy *n.* niño, muchacho.

boyfriend *n.* amigo, novio.

brace *n.* braguero, corsé, vendaje; abrazadera; ankle ___ / tobillera; **braces** *n. pl.* [*dentistry*] ganchos; aros.

brachiocephalic *a.* braquiocefálico, rel. a la cabeza y al brazo.

brachydactyly *n.* braquidactilia, condición de manos y pies anormalmente pequeños.

bracing *n.* aplicación de una abrazadera.

bradycardia *n.* bradicardia, espanocardia, lentitud anormal en los latidos del corazón.

bradypnea *n.* bradipnea, movimientos respiratorios lentos.

brain *n.* cerebro, parte del sistema nervioso central que se localiza en el cráneo y actúa como regulador principal de las funciones del cuerpo; ___ death / muerte cerebral; ___ edema / edema cerebral; ___ injuries / traumatismo cerebral; ___ scan / escán del ___ ; ___ stem / tronco cerebral; ___ tumor / tumor cerebral.

braincase *n.* cráneo, parte que encierra el cerebro.

brainless *a.* tonto-a, insensato-a.

brainwashing *n.* lavado de cerebro.

brainy *a.* inteligente, listo-a, talentoso-a.

braise *v.* asar al fuego; a la brasa.

bran *n.* salvado, producto procesado del trigo.

branch *n.* rama, bifurcación; sección, dependencia.

brassiere *n.* sostén, ajustador, corpiño.

brassy cough *n.* tos metálica, tos bronca.

bread *n.* pan; ___ **and butter** / pan y mantequilla.

break *n.* fractura, rotura; quebradura; *vi.* romper, quebrar, fracturar; *v.* fracturarse, romperse, quebrarse; **to** ___ **down** / [*health*] perder la salud; **to** ___ **in** / forzar, abrir; **to** ___ **loose** / separarse, desprenderse; **to** ___ **through** / avanzar; **to** ___ **up** / fraccionar; nervous ___ down / crisis nerviosa.

breakable *a.* frágil, quebradizo.

breakage *n.* rotura, quebradura.

breakfast *n.* desayuno.

breakout *n.* erupción.

breast *n.* pecho, seno, busto, *slang* teta; caked ___ / mastitis por estasis; *v.* to ___ feed / dar el pecho, dar de mamar, dar la teta, *Mex. A.* criar con pecho; ___ pump / sacaleche, mamadera; ___ self examination / autoexamen de los senos.

breastbone *n.* esternón.

breastfeeding *n.* lactancia materna.

breath *n.* respiración, aliento, soplo *pop.* resuello, coarse ___ / ___ gruesa; short of ___ / corto de resuello, falto de aliento; out of ___ / falto de ___ , sin aliento; *v.* to be out of ___ / faltar la ___ , estar sofocado-a; to gasp for ___ / jadear, resollar; to take a deep ___ / respirar profundamente; to hold one's ___ / sostener, aguantar la ___ .

breathe *v.* respirar; [*to exhale*] exhalar; [*to inhale*] aspirar; *pop.* resollar; **to** ___ **through the mouth** / ___ por la boca; **to** ___ **through the nose** / ___ por la nariz.

breather *n.* respirador; tregua, reposo.

breathing *n.* respiración, aliento, respiro; *pop.* resuello; inhalación, aspiración; ___ exercises / ejercicios respiratorios; ___ **space,** ___ **time** / descanso, parada, reposo.

breathless *a.* sofocado-a, sin aliento; falto de respiración.

breathlessness *n.* sofocación.

breech *n.* trasero, posaderas, nalgas; [*in obstetrics*] ___ birth / presentación de nalgas, presentación trasera.

breed *vi.* criar, producir, engendrar.

breeding *n.* cria, crianza.

breeze *n.* brisa, aire suave.

bregma *Gr.* bregma, intersección de las suturas coronal y sagital del cráneo.

bridge *n.* puente; ___ abutment / pilar de ___ , anclaje.

brief *n.* sumario, resumen; *a.* breve, corto-a, conciso-a.

briefly *adv.* brevemente, concisamente; en pocas palabras.

bright *a.* brillante, lustroso-a, luminoso-a.

Bright's disease *n.* enfermedad de Bright. *V.* **glomerulonephritis.**

brim *n.* borde.

bring *vi.* traer; inducir; **to ____ down** / bajar; **to ____ down the fever** / bajar la fiebre; [*raise children*] **to ____ up** / educar, criar.

bromhidrosis *n.* bromhidrosis, perspiración fétida; sudor fétido.

bronchial *a.* bronquial, rel. a los bronquios. ____ **spasm** / espasmo ____ ; ____ **tree** / árbol ____ ; ____ **washing** / lavado ____ .

bronchiectasia *n.* bronquiectasia, dilatación crónica de los bronquios debida a una obstrucción o a una condición inflamatoria.

bronchiocele *n.* bronquiocele, dilatación localizada de un bronquiolo.

bronchiole *n.* bronquiolo, una de las ramas menores del árbol bronquial.

bronchiolitis *n.* bronquiolitis, infl. de los bronquiolos.

bronchitis *n.* bronquitis, infl. de los tubos bronquiales.

bronchodilator *n.* broncodilatador, medicamento que dilata el calibre de un bronquio; ____ **agents** / agentes ____ -es.

bronchography *n.* broncografía, radiografía del árbol bronquial usando un medio de contraste.

broncholith *n.* broncolito, cálculo bronquial.

bronchopneumonia *n.* bronconeumonía, infl. aguda de los bronquiolos y de los lóbulos pulmonares que afecta gen. ambos pulmones.

bronchopulmonary *a.* broncopulmonar, rel. a los bronquios y los pulmones.

bronchoscopy *n.* broncoscopía, examen del árbol bronquial por medio del broncoscopio.

bronchospasm *n.* broncoespasmo, contracción espasmódica de los bronquios y los bronquiolos.

bronchus *n.* (*pl.* **bronchia**) bronquio, uno de los tubos por los cuales el aire pasa a los pulmones.

brother *n.* hermano; ____ -in-law / cuñado; half ____ / medio ____ .

brow *n.* ceño; frente.

brown *n.* castaño, café, carmelita; [*skin*] moreno-a.

Brown Sequard syndrome *n.* síndrome de Brown Sequard, hemisección de la médula espinal que causa hiperestesia en el lado lesionado y pérdida de la sensibilidad en el lado opuesto.

brucellosis *n.* brucelosis, fiebre ondulante o fiebre mediterránea, condición infecciosa bacteriana que se contrae por contacto con ganado vacuno o sus productos.

bruise *n.* magulladura, morado.

brunet, brunette *a.* trigueño-a, de piel oscura.

brush *n.* cepillo; *v.* cepillar; cepillarse.

brutal *a.* brutal, bruto-a.

bubble *n.* burbuja, ampolla; **to ____ over with joy** / rebozar de gozo.

bubo *n.* bubón, infl. linfática de la ingle.

bubonic plague *n.* peste bubónica.

bucca *n.* boca.

buccal *a.* bucal.

bucket *n.* cubeta, cubo, balde.

buckle *n.* hebilla; *v.* **to ____ together** / unir, atar, juntar

bud *n.* brote, retoño.

budget *n.* presupuesto.

buffer *n.* tampón, tope; *v.* neutralizar, tamponar; ____ **system** / sistema amortiguador.

build *vi.* construir; **to ____ up one's health** / reconstituir la salud; ____ **up phase** / fase de ascenso.

bulb *n.* bulbo, pera; bombillo; 1. [*syringe*] pera de goma; 2. expansión oval o circular de un conducto o cilindro.

bulbourethral *a.* bulbouretral, uretrobulbar, rel. al bulbo del pene y la uretra.

bulbus cordis *n. L.* bulbo del corazón.

bulge *n.* hinchazón, protuberancia.

bulging *n.* protuberancia; ____ **abdomen** / abdomen prominente, vientre abombado; ____ **eyes** / ojos saltones.

bulimia *n.* bulimia, apetito exagerado.

bulla *n.* ampolla.

bullet *n.* bala; ____ **wound** / balazo, herida de ____ .

bump *n.* golpe, [*on the head*] chichón; *v.* tropezar; golpearse, darse un golpe.

bundle *n.* manojo, haz; bulto; ____ **branch block** / bloque de rama.

bunion *n.* bunio, juanete, infl. de la bursa en la primera coyuntura del dedo pulgar del pie. *V.* **Hallux valgus.**

bunionectomy *n. cirg.* extirpación de un juanete.

burden *v.* agobiar.

burn *n.* quemadura; ____ -s, chemical / ____ -s por sustancias químicas; ____, dry heat / ____ por calor seco; sun ____ / insolación, eritema solar; first, second and third degree ____ -s / ____ -s de primer, segundo y tercer grado; *vi.* arder, quemar, incendiar.

burning *n.* ardor, quemadura; irritación; a ____ feeling / sensación de ____, quemazón; ____ on urination / ____ al orinar.

burp *n.* eructo, eructación; *v.* eructar, sacar el aire.

burr *n.* taladro; [*dentistry*] fresa.

bursa *L.* bursa, bolsa o saco en forma de cavidad que contiene líquido sinovial en áreas de los tejidos donde puede ocurrir una fricción.

bursitis *n.* bursitis, infl. de una bursa.

burst *v.* reventar, reventarse, abrirse; to ____ out / brotar, reventar; to ____ open / abrirse, reventarse; to ____ into tears / deshacerse en lágrimas.

butter *n.* mantequilla.

buttocks *n. pl.* nalgas, *pop. Mex.* asentaderas, *Cuba* fondillo.

button *n.* botón.

buttress *n.* contrafuerte, resfuerzo, sostén.

buy *vi.* comprar.

buzz *n.* murmullo, zumbido.

by *prep.* por, cerca de, al lado de, según; ____ day / de día, por el día; ____ night / de noche, por la noche.

bypass *n.* 1. baipás, derivación, puente externo; 2. creación de una nueva vía o derivación; ____ graft / injerto de derivación; aortocoronary ____ / derivación aortocoronaria; *v.* desviar; esquivar.

by-product *n.* subproducto.

C

C *abbr.* Kilo**calorie** / kilocaloría; **carbon** / carbono; **centigrade** / centígrado; **Celsius** / Celsius

c *abbr.* **cobalt** / cobalto; **cocaine** / cocaína; **contraction** / contracción; **calorie** / caloría

cabbage *n.* col, repollo.

cacao *n.* cacao, planta de la cual se deriva el chocolate, alcaloide diurético.

cachexia *n.* caquexia, condición grave que se caracteriza por pérdida excesiva de peso y debilidad general progresiva.

cacosmia *n.* cacosmia, percepción de olores imaginarios, esp. olores fétidos.

cadaver *n.* cadáver.

cadaverous *a.* cadavérico-a.

cafeteria *n.* cafetería.

caffeine *n.* cafeína, alcaloide presente esp. en café y té, estimulante y diurético.

calamine *n.* calamina, antiséptico astringente secante que se usa en afecciones de la piel.

calcaneus *n.* calcáneo, hueso del talón; *pop.* calcañal, calcañar.

calcareous *n.* calcáreo, que contiene calcio o lima.

calcemia *n.* calcemia, presencia de calcio en la sangre.

calcic *a.* cálcico, rel. a la lima.

calciferol *n.* calciferol, producto derivado de ergosterol, vitamina D_2.

calcification *n.* calcificación, endurecimiento de tejidos orgánicos por depósitos de sales de calcio.

calcified *a.* calcificado-a.

calcinosis *n.* calcinosis, presencia de sales cálcicas en la piel, los tejidos subcutáneos y los órganos.

calcitonin *n.* calcitonina, hormona segregada por la glándula tiroides que estimula el transporte del calcio de la sangre a los huesos.

calcium *n.* calcio, sustancia mineral necesaria en el desarrollo de los huesos y tejidos.

calciuria *n.* calciuria, presencia de calcio en la orina.

calculate *v.* calcular.

calculation *n.* calculación.

calculus *n.* (*pl.* **calculi**) cálculo, concreción o pequeña piedra que puede formarse en las secreciones y fluídos del organismo; biliary ____ / ____ biliar; calcium oxalate ____ / ____ de oxalato de calcio; cystine ____ / ____ de cistina; fibrin ____ / ____ de fibrina; urinary ____ / ____ urinario.

calendar *n.* calendario, almanaque.

calf *n.* pantorrilla; [*animal*] ternero-a.

caliber *n.* calibre, diámetro de un conducto o canal.

calibrator *n.* calibrador, instrumento para medir el diámetro de un conducto o canal.

caliceal *n.* caliceal, rel. a un cáliz.

call *n.* llamada; *v.* llamar; to ____ for / pedir; to be on ____ / estar de guardia.

callous *a.* calloso-a.

callosity *n.* callosidad.

callus *n.* callo, callosidad.

calm *n.* calma, serenidad; *v.* calmar, tranquilizar; calmarse, serenarse, tranquilizarse.

calmative *a.* calmante, sedante.

calomel *n.* calomel, cloruro mercurioso, usado como agente local antibacteriano.

caloric *n.* calórico-a, rel. al calor o las calorías; ⸺ intake / ingestión ⸺.

calorie *n.* caloría, unidad de calor a la que se refiere al evaluar la energía alimenticia; kilocalorie, large ⸺ / gran ⸺; small ⸺ / pequeña ⸺.

calorific *n.* calorífico.

calvaria, skull cap *n.* calvaria, bóveda craneal.

calvities *n.* calvicie, pérdida del pelo en la corona o parte superior de la cabeza.

calyx *n.* cáliz, colector en forma de copa.

camera *n.* cámara. 1. espacio abierto o ventrículo; 2. cámara fotográfica.

camphor *n.* alcanfor; ⸺ julep / agua alcanforada.

can *n.* lata, bote, envase; *vi.* poder.

canal *n.* canal, pasaje, estructura tubular; birth ⸺ / ⸺ del parto; femoral ⸺ / ⸺ femoral; inguinalis ⸺ / ⸺ inguinal; root ⸺ / ⸺ radicular.

canaliculus *n.* canalículo, canal o pasaje diminuto; biliary ⸺ / ⸺ biliar, entre las células del hígado; lacrimal ⸺ / ⸺ lacrimal, lagrimal.

cancel *v.* cancelar, suprimir.

cancellation *n.* cancelación.

cancellous *a.* canceloso-a, esponjoso-a, reticulado-a; ⸺ bone / hueso ⸺ .

cancer *n.* cáncer, tumor maligno; early ⸺ / ⸺ incipiente; grading / evaluación en relación con el grado maligno de las células cancerosas; ⸺ staging / evaluación en cuanto a la extensión de un cáncer.

cancerous *a.* canceroso-a.

cancerphobia *n.* cancerofobia, fobia a contraer cáncer.

candid *a.* cándido-a; sincero-a.

candidiasis *n.* candidiasis, infección de la piel producida por un hongo semejante a la levadura.

candy *n.* dulce, confite, caramelo.

cane *n.* bastón; caña; ⸺ sugar / azúcar de caña, sucrosa, sacarosa.

canine *n.* canino; cúspide; diente; *a.* rel. a los perros.

canker *n.* ulceración de la boca o los labios; ⸺ sore / afta, llaga ulcerosa.

cannabis, marijuana *n.* canabis, marijuana, mariguana, marihuana, planta de hojas que producen un efecto narcótico y halucinógeno al fumarse; *slang* **grass; bomber** / marijuana cigarrete; *v. slang* **to blast, to blow weed** / fumar marijuana.

cannula *n.* (*pl.* **cannulae**) cánula, sonda, tubo que insertado en el cuerpo conduce o saca líquidos.

cannulation *n.* canulación, acto de introducir una cánula a través de un vaso o conducto; aortic ⸺ / ⸺ aórtica.

canthus *n.* 1. canto, borde; 2. ángulo formado por el párpado externo y el interno al unirse en ambas partes del ojo.

cap *n.* gorra; tapa.

capable *a.* capaz.

capacity *n.* capacidad; vital ⸺ / ⸺ vital.

capillary *n.* capilar; vaso capilar; *a.* semejante a un cabello; arterial ⸺ / ⸺ arterial; lymph ⸺ / ⸺ linfático; venous ⸺ / ⸺ venoso.

capitellum *n.* capitelum. 1. bulbo de un pelo. 2. parte del húmero.

capsula, capsule *n.* cápsula. 1. envoltura membranosa. 2. pastilla; articular ⸺ / ⸺ articular, que envuelve una articulación sinovial; enclosed in a ⸺ / encapsulado.

capsulation *n.* encapsulación, acto de envolver en una cápsula o envoltura.

car *n.* automóvil, carro; *Spain* coche; ⸺ accident / accidente automovilístico.

carbohydrase *n.* carbohidrasa.

carbohydrate *n.* carbohidrato, grupo de compuestos de carbono, hidrógeno y oxígeno entre los que se encuentran los almidones, azúcares y celulosas.

carbolic *a.* carbólico-a, rel. al fenol o ácido fenílico.

carbon *n.* carbono; ⸺ dioxide / dióxido de ⸺ ; ⸺ monoxide / monóxido de ⸺ .

carbonated *a.* carbonatado-a.

carbonic *a.* carbónico-a.

carbonization *n.* carbonización.

carboxyhemoglobin *n.* carboxihemoglobina, combinación de monóxido de carbono y hemoglobina que desplaza el oxígeno e interrumpe la función oxidante de la sangre.

carbuncle n carbunco, furúnculo, inflamación con pus, *pop.* avispero.

carcinogen n. carcinógeno, cualquier sustancia que puede producir cáncer.

carcinogenesis n. carcinogénesis, origen del cáncer.

carcinogenic n. carcinógeno-a, de origen canceroso.

carcinoma n. carcinoma, tumor canceroso; basal cell ___ / ___ basocelular; breast ___ / ___ de la mama; bronchial ___ / ___ broncogénico; cervical ___ / ___ cervical; endometrial ___ / ___ endometrial; mucinous ___ / ___ mucinoso; ovarian ___ / ___ ovárico; papillary ___ / ___ papilar; squamous cell ___ / ___ de células escamosas epiteliales; testicular ___ / ___ testicular; transitional cell ___ / ___ de células transicionales.

carcinoma in situ L. carcinoma in situ, células tumorales localizadas en estado de desarrollo que no han invadido aún estructuras adyacentes.

carcinomatosis n. carcinomatosis, invasión de cáncer diseminado en varias partes del cuerpo.

cardiac a. cardíaco-a, referente al corazón; ___ arrest, stand still / paro ___ ; ___ catherization / caterización ___ ; ___ depressants / agentes antiarrítmicos; ___ chambers / cavidades ___ -s; ___ failure / insuficiencia ___ ; ___ output / gasto, rendimiento ___ ; ___ pacing, artificial / estimulación ___ artificial; ___ stimulants / agentes cardiotónicos; ___ tamponade / taponamiento ___ .

cardias n. cardias, desembocadura del esófago en el estómago.

cardiataxia n. cardiataxia, falta de coordinación de los movimientos cardíacos.

cardiectomy n. *cirg.* cardiectomía, extirpación de la región superior extrema del estómago.

cardioangiogram n. cardioangiograma, imagen por rayos-X de los vasos sanguíneos y las cámaras del corazón usando un medio de contraste.

cardiocentesis n. *cirg.* cardiocentesis, cardiopuntura, punción de una cavidad del corazón.

cardiogram n. cardiograma, trazado que representa los impulsos del corazón.

cardiograph n. cardiógrafo, instrumento que traza gráficamente los movimientos del corazón.

cardiography n. cardiografía, uso del cardiógrafo para registrar los movimientos del corazón.

cardiologist n. cardiólogo-a, especialista del corazón.

cardiology n. cardiología, ciencia que estudia el corazón, sus funciones y enfermedades.

cardiomegaly n. cardiomegalia, hipertrofia cardíaca.

cardiomyopathy n. cardiomiopatía, alteración del músculo del corazón; alcoholic ___ / ___ alcohólica; congestive ___ / ___ congestiva; hypertrophic ___ / ___ hipertrófica.

cardioplegia n. cardioplegia, paro cardíaco o traumatismo.

cardiopulmonary a. cardiopulmonar, rel. al corazón y los pulmones; ___ bypass / puente cardiopulmonar; ___ resuscitation / resucitación ___ ; ___ resuscitator / resucitador, reanimador ___ .

cardiospasm n. cardiospasmo, espasmo o contracción del cardias.

cardiotomy n. *cirg.* cardiotomía, incisión en el corazón.

cardiotonic a. cardiotónico-a, de efecto tónico o favorable al corazón.

cardiovascular a. cardiovascular, rel. al corazón y los vasos sanguíneos.

cardioversion n. cardioversión, restauración del ritmo sinusal normal del corazón por medio de una corriente directa.

carditis n. carditis, infl. del pericardio, miocardio y endocardio; rheumatic ___ / ___ reumática.

care n. cuidado, asistencia, atención; cardiac ___ unit (CCU) / sala de ___ cardíaco; free of ___ / libre de ___ ; intensive ___ unit (ICU) / sala de ___ intensivo; prenatal ___ / ___ y atención prenatal; postnatal ___ / ___ después del parto; proper ___ / ___ apropiado; *v.* **to be under the** ___ **of** / estar bajo el ___ de.

career n. profesión.

careful a. cuidadoso-a; esmerado-a; atento-a.

careless a. descuidado-a; desatento-a.

carelessness n. descuido; negligencia.

caries n. *pl.* caries. 1. destrucción progresiva de tejido óseo. 2. caries dentales, *pop.* dientes picados.

carmine *n.* carmín, carmesí.

carnivorous *a.* carnívoro-a.

carnosity *n.* carnosidad, excrecencia carnosa.

carotene *n.* caroteno, pigmento amarillo rojizo presente en vegetales que se convierte en vitamina A en el cuerpo.

carotid *n.* carótida, arteria principal del cuello; ___ arteries / arterias ___ -s.

carpal *a.* carpal, rel. al carpo.

carpus *n.* (*pl.* **carpi**) carpo, muñeca de la mano, porción de la extremidad superior stiuada entre el antebrazo y la mano.

carrier *n.* portador, agente transmisor; ___ state / estado portador.

carrot *n.* zanahoria.

carry *v.* llevar; cargar; **to** ___ **out** / llevar a cabo.

cartilage *n.* cartílago, tejido semiduro que cubre los huesos.

caruncle *n.* carúncula, pequeña irritación de la piel; urethral ___ / ___ uretral.

cascara sagrada *n.* cáscara sagrada, corteza de la planta *Rhamnus purshiana,* comúnmente usada como medicamento en casos de estreñimiento crónico.

case *n.* caso; ___ fatality rate / índice de mortalidad por ___ ; ___ history / historia clínica; ___ reporting / presentación del ___ ; ___ control study / estudio comparativo de ___ -s; **in** ___ **of** / en ___ de; **just in** ___ / por si ___ .

casein *n.* caseína, proteína principal de la leche.

caseous *a.* caseoso, de queso o parecido al queso.

cash *n.* dinero al contado; ___ **payment** / ___ , pago al contado; *v.* **to pay** ___ / pagar al contado.

casket *n.* ataúd, caja.

cast *n.* molde; yeso; cilindro; *v.* to put in a ___ / enyesar, moldear; **to** ___ **aside** / desechar.

castor oil *n.* aceite de ricino, palmacristi.

castrate *v.* castrar.

casual *a.* casual, accidental.

casualty *n.* víctima; accidentado-a; [*wounded*] herido-a; ___ list / lista de accidentados.

cat *n.* gato-a.

catabolism *n.* catabolismo, proceso por el cual sustancias complejas se reducen a compuestos más simples.

catalepsy *n.* catalepsia, condición caracterizada por la pérdida de la capacidad de movimiento muscular voluntario y disminución acentuada de la habilidad de reaccionar a estímulos, gen. asociada con transtornos psicológicos.

catalysis *n.* catálisis, alteración de la velocidad de una reacción química por la presencia de un catalítico.

catalyst, catalitic *a.* catalítico-a, agente estimulante de una reacción química sin afectarla.

cataplexy *n.* cataplejía, pérdida repentina del tono muscular causada por un estado emocional intenso.

cataract *n.* catarata, opacidad del cristalino; green ___ / ___ verde; mature ___ / ___ madura; senile ___ / ___ senil; soft ___ / ___ blanda.

catarrh *n.* catarro, resfriado, constipado.

catarrhal *a.* catarral, referente a un catarro.

catatonia *n.* catatonía, esquizofrenia caracterizada por mutismo, postura rígida y resistencia a cooperar para activar los movimientos o el habla. Los mismos síntomas se asocian con otras enferinedades mentales.

catch *vi.,* contraer; agarrar; coger; ___ una enfermedad.

catecholamines *n. pl.* catecolaminas, aminas de acción simpatomimética producidas en las glándulas suprarrenales, (incluyen la dopamina, la epinefrina y la norepinefrina).

category *n.* categoría, clase.

catgut *n.* catgut, tipo de ligadura que se hace con la tripa del intestino de algunos animales.

catharsis *n.* catarsis. 1. acción purgativa; 2. *psic.* análisis con el fin terapéutico de liberar al paciente de un estado de ansiedad.

cathartic *n.* catártico, medicamento con efectos laxativos o purgativos; *a.* catártico-a, rel. a la catarsis.

catheter *n.* catéter, sonda, tubo usado para drenar o introducir líquidos.

catheterization *n.* cateterización, inserción de un catéter.

catheterize *v.* cateterizar, insertar un catéter.

cauda *n.* cauda, apéndice similar a una cola.

caudal *a.* caudal, rel. a la cola.

cauliflower *n.* coliflor.

causal *a.* causal.

causalgia *n.* causalgia, dolor con ardor en la piel.

cause *n.* causa, principio. origen; **without** ___ / sin ___.

cause *v.* causar, ocasionar.

caustic *a.* caústico-a.

cauterization *n.* cauterización, quemadura producida por medio de un agente cauterizante tal como el calor, la corriente eléctrica, o un caústico.

cauterize *v.* cauterizar, quemar por medio de un agente cauterizante.

caution *n.* advertencia, precaución.

cautious *a.* precavido-a, cuidadoso-a.

cava *n. pl.* de **cavum**, cavidad, hueco. *V.* **vein, cava.**

cave *n.* depresión.

cavern *n.* caverna, cavidad patológica.

cavernous *a.* cavernoso-a, que contiene espacios huecos.

cavity *n.* cavidad, lugar hueco; abdominal ___ / ___ abdominal; cranial ___ / ___ craneal; pelvic ___ / ___ pelviana; thoracic ___ / ___ torácica.

cease *v.* cesar, parar, detener.

cecostomy *n. cirg.* cecostomía, creación de una apertura artificial en el ciego.

cecum *n.* ciego, bolsa que forma la primera parte del intestino grueso.

celery *n.* apio.

celiac *a.* celíaco, abdominal, rel. al abdomen.

celiotomy *n. cirg.* celiotomía. *V.* **laparotomía.**

cell *n.* célula, unidad estructural de todo organismo viviente; adipose ___ / ___ adiposa; anaplastic ___ / ___ anaplástica; B ___ / linfocito B, tipo de linfocito importante en la producción de anticuerpos; basal ___ / ___ basal; columnar ___ / ___ columnar; giant ___ / ___ gigante; goblet ___ / ___ calciforme; ependymal ___ / ___ ependimaria; epidermal ___ / ___ epidérmica; interstitial ___ / ___ intersticial; phagocyte ___ / ___ fagocitaria; pyramidal ___ / ___ piramidal; red blood ___ -s / ___ -s sanguíneas (eritrocitos y leucocitos); reproductive ___ / ___ reproductiva; scavenger ___ / ___ basurera; sickle ___ / ___ falciforme.

cellular *a.* celular, de naturaleza semejante o referente a la célula; ___ compartmentation / compartimentos ___ -es; ___ counting device / cuenta células; ___ growth / crecimiento ___ ; ___ like / en forma ___ ; ___ tissue / tejido ___ ; ___ water / agua ___ .

cellulitis *n.* celulitis, infl. del tejido conectivo celular.

cellulose *n.* celulosa.

cement *n.* cemento.

cemetery *n.* cementerio, camposanto.

census *n.* censo.

center *n.* centro.

Center for Disease Control *n.* Centro para Control de Enfermedades.

centigrade *n.* centígrado.

centimeter *n.* centímetro.

central *a.* central; céntrico-a; ___ nervous system / sistema nervioso ___ .

centrifugal *a.* centrífugo-a, rel. al movimiento de repulsión, del centro hacia afuera.

centripetal *a.* centrípeto-a, con movimiento de atracción hacia el centro.

cephalalgia, cephalea *n.* cefalalgia, dolor de cabeza, *pop.* jaqueca.

cephalic *a.* cefálico-a, rel. a la cabeza.

cephalosporin *n.* cefalosporina, antibiótico de espectro amplio.

cerclage *n.* cerclaje, en ortopedia procedimiento usado en ciertas fracturas por el cual se unen partes rodeándolas con un hilo metálico o con catgut.

cereal *n.* cereal.

cerebellum *n.* cerebelo, parte posterior del cerebro, centro de coordinación de los movimientos musculares voluntarios.

cerebral *a.* cerebral, rel. al cerebro; ___ edema / edema ___ ; ___ embolism and thrombosis / embolia y trombosis ___ ; ___ hemorrhage / hemorragia ___ ; ___ palsy / parálisis ___ ; ___ tumor / tumor ___ .

cerebrospinal *a.* cefalorraquídeo, cerebroespinal; ___ fluid / líquido ___ .

cerebrovascular *a.* cerebrovascular; ___ accident (CVA) / apoplegía, hemorragia cerebral.

cerebrum *n.* cerebro, encéfalo, centro de coordinación de actividades sensoriales e intelectuales.

certain *a.* cierto-a; seguro-a; *v.* **to be** ___ / estar seguro-a; **-ly** *adv.* ciertamente, seguramente.

certainty *n.* certeza.

certificate *n.* certificado; **death** ___ / ___ de defunción.

cerumen *n.* cerumen, segregación cerosa que lubrica y protege el oído.

cervical *a.* cervical. 1. referente al área del cuello; 2. rel. al cuello uterino.

cervicovesical *a.* cervicovesical, rel. al cuello uterino y a la vejiga.

cervix *n.* cuello uterino, parte baja del útero en forma de cuello; dilation of the ____ / dilatación del ____.

cesarean *n.* cesárea; ____ section / cirugía de parto.

chain *n.* cadena; ____ reaction / reacción en ____; ____ suture / sutura en ____.

chair *n.* silla.

chalazion *n.* chalazión, quiste del párpado, quiste meiboniano.

chalk *n.* yeso.

chamber *n.* cámara, cavidad; anterior ____ / ____ anterior, situada entre la córnea y el iris; aqueous ____ / ____ acuosa; ____-s of the eye / ____-s oculares; hyperbaric ____ / ____ hiperbárica; ____-s of the heart / cavidades del corazón: aurículas y ventrículos del corazón.

chamomile *n.* manzanilla, té sedante gastrointestinal.

chancre *n.* chancro; lesión primaria de la sífilis.

chancroid *n.* chancroide, úlcera venérea no sifilítica.

change *n.* cambio, alteración; ____ of life / menopausia; *v.* cambiar, mudar.

changeless *a.* invariable, inmutable.

channel *n.* canal; estructura tubular; birth ____ / ____ del parto.

chaos *n.* caos, desorden.

chaotic *n.* caótico-a, desordenado-a.

chap *n.* hendidura, raja, grieta.

chapel *n.* capilla.

chapped *a.* agrietado-a, cuarteado-a; rajado-a; ____ hands / manos ____-s; ____ lips / labios ____-s.

chapter *n.* capítulo.

character *n.* carácter; personalidad; personaje.

characteristic *n.* característica, peculiaridad; *a.* característico-a; peculiar.

charcoal *n.* carbón vegetal.

charge *n.* costo; *v.* cobrar.

charitable *a.* caritativo-a.

charity *n.* caridad; beneficiencia.

charlatan *n.* charlatán-a; dícese de una persona que pretende tener cualidades o conocimientos para curar enfermedades.

charley horse *n.* dolor y sensibilidad en un músculo; *pop.* calambre.

charred *a.* carbonizado-a.

chart *n.* plano, gráfico; medical ____ / hoja clínica.

chat *n.* charla, plática; *v.* charlar, platicar.

chatter *v.* [*teeth*] rechinar los dientes.

cheap *a.* barato-a.

check *n.* control; acción o efecto de regular; [*bank*] cheque; ____ book / chequera; ____ up / *Am.* chequeo, examen físico completo; *v.* controlar; chequear, verificar.

cheek *n.* mejilla.

cheekbone *n.* carrillo, pómulo, hueso malar.

cheer up *v.* animarse, alegrarse.

cheese *n.* queso.

cheilectomy *n.* *cirg.* queilectomía, excisión parcial del labio.

cheilitis, chelitis *n.* queilitis, infl. de los labios.

cheiloplasty *n.* *cirg.* queiloplastia, operación de reparación del labio.

cheiloschisis *n.* queilosquisis. V. **harelip.**

cheilosis *n.* queilosis, manifestación con marcas y fisuras en la comisura de los labios debido a deficiencia de vitamina B_2 (riboflavina).

cheirology *n.* quirología. 1. estudio de la mano; 2. uso del lenguaje por señas como medio de comunicación con los sordomudos.

chemical *a.* químico-a; ____ peel / peladura ____.

chemist *n.* químico-a; farmacéutico-a, boticario-a.

chemistry *n.* química, ciencia que estudia los elementos, estructura y propiedades de las sustancias y las transformaciones que éstas sufren.

chemocoagulation *n.* quimiocoagulación, coagulación por medio de agentes químicos.

chemonucleolysis *n.* quimionucleólisis, disolución por inyección de una enzima proteolítica del núcleo pulposo de una hernia.

chemoreceptive *n.* quimiorreceptor-a, célula susceptible a cambios químicos o que puede ser afectada por éstos.

chemosurgery *n.* quimiocirugía, extirpación o remoción de tejidos por medio de sustancias químicas.

chemotaxis *n.* quimiotaxis, movimiento de un organismo o célula como reacción a un estímulo químico.

chemotherapy *n.* quimioterapia, tratamiento

de una enfermedad por medio de agentes químicos.

cherubism *n.* querubismo, condición fibró-ósea infantil que causa agrandamiento de los huesos de la mandíbula.

chest *n.* tórax, pecho; ____ cold / catarro bronquial, *pop.* catarro al pecho; ____ respirator / respirador torácico; ____ surgery / cirugía torácica; ____ wall / pared torácica.

chew *v.* masticar, mascar.

Cheyne-Stokes respiration syndrome *n.* síndrome de respiración Cheyne-Stokes, respiración cíclica con períodos de apnea y aumento rápido y profundo de la respiración gen. asociada con trastornos del centro neurológico respiratorio.

chiasm, chiasma *n.* quiasma. 1. cruzamiento de dos vías o conductos; 2. punto de cruzamiento de las fibras de los nervios ópticos.

chiasma opticum *n.* quiasma óptico.

chicken *n.* pollo; ____ **breast** / pechuga.

chickenpox, varicella *n.* varicela, enfermedad viral contagiosa que se manifiesta gen. en la infancia, y se caracteriza por una erupción que se convierte en pequeñas vesículas; *pop.* viruelas locas.

chief *n.* jefe-a; ____ **complaint** / queja principal.

chilblain *n.* sabañón, eritema debido a frío intenso que gen. se manifiesta en las manos y los pies.

child *n.* niño-a; ____ bearing / gestación, embarazo; ____ nurse / niñera; ____ nursery / guardería infantil, jardín de la infancia; ____ support / manutención, pensión alimenticia; ____ welfare / asistencia social a la infancia.

childbirth *n.* parto, nacimiento, alumbramiento.

childhood *n.* infancia, niñez.

chill *n.* enfriamiento, escalofrío.

chin *n.* barba, mentón, barbilla.

chiropodist *n.* quiropodista. *V.* **podiatrist.**

chiropractic *n.* quiropráctica, sistema terapéutico que recurre a la manipulación y ajustamiento de las estructuras del cuerpo esp. la columna vertebral en relación con el sistema nervioso.

chloasma *n.* cloasma, hiperpigmentación facial que puede ocurrir en algunas mujeres durante el embarazo.

chlorambucil *n.* clorambucil, forma de mos-

taza nitrogenada usada para combatir algunas formas de cáncer.

chloramphenicol, chloromycetin *n.* cloranfenicol, cloromicetina, antibiótico esp. efectivo en el tratamiento de la fiebre tifoidea.

chlorhydria *n.* clorhidria, exceso de ácido clorhídrico en el estómago.

chloride *n.* cloruro.

chlorine *n.* cloro, agente desinfectante y blanqueador.

chloroform *n.* cloroformo, anestésico.

chloroma *n.* cloroma, tumor de color verde que puede manifestarse en distintas partes del cuerpo.

chlorophyll *n.* clorofila, pigmento verde de las plantas esencial en la producción de carbohidratos por fotosíntesis.

chloroquine *n.* cloroquina, compuesto usado en el tratamiento de la malaria.

chlorosis *n.* clorosis, tipo de anemia vista esp. en la mujer y usu. relacionada con deficiencia de hierro.

chlorpromazine *n.* cloropromacina, antiemético y tranquilizante.

chlortetracycline *n.* clorotetraciclina, antibiótico antimicrobiano de espectro amplio.

chocolate *n.* chocolate.

choice *n.* opción, alternative; elección.

choke *v.* ahogar, sofocar, estrangular; [*choke on something*] atragantarse.

cholangiectasis *n.* colangiectasis, dilatación de los conductos biliares.

cholangiogram *n.* colangiograma, radiografía de las vías biliares usando un medio de contraste.

cholangiography *n.* colangiografía, rayos-X de las vías biliares.

cholangitis *n.* colangitis, infl. de los conductos biliares.

cholecystectomy *n. cirg.* colecistectomía, extirpación de la vesícula biliar.

cholecystitis *n.* colecistitis, infl. de la vesícula biliar.

cholecystoduodenostomy *n. cirg.* colecistoduodenostomía, anastomosis de la vesícula y el duodeno.

cholecystogastrostomy *n. cirg.* colecistogastrostomía, anastomosis de la vesícula y el estómago.

cholecystogram *n.* colecistograma, radiografía de la vesícula biliar.

choledochojejunostomy *n. cirg.* coledocoyeyunostomía, anastomosis del colédoco y el yeyuno.

choledocholithiasis *n.* coledocolitiasis, cálculos en el colédoco.

choledochus *n.* colédoco, conducto biliar formado por la unión de los conductos hepático y cístico.

cholelithiasis *n.* colelitiasis, litiasis biliar, presencia de cálculos en la vesícula biliar o en un conducto biliar.

cholemia *n.* colemia, presencia de bilis en la sangre.

cholera *n.* cólera, enfermedad infecciosa grave caracterizada por diarrea severa y vómitos; ____ fulminans / ____ fulminante.

choleric *a.* colérico-a.

cholestasis *n.* colestasis, estasis biliar.

cholesteatoma *n.* colesteatoma, tumor que contiene colesterol, situado comúnmente en el oído medio.

cholesterol *n.* colesterol, lípido precursor de las hormonas sexuales y corticoides adrenales, componente de las grasas y aceites animales, del tejido nervioso y de la sangre.

cholic acid *n.* ácido cólico, uno de los ácidos no conjugados de la bilis.

cholinesterase *n.* colinesterasa, familia de enzimas.

choluria *n.* coluria, presencia de bilis en la orina.

chondritis *n.* condritis, infl. de un cartílago.

chondrocalcinosis *n.* condrocalcinosis, condición semejante a la gota, con manifestaciones de cicatrización por calcificación y deteriorización o alteraciones degenerativas de los cartílagos.

chondrocostal *a.* condrocostal, rel. a los cartílagos costales y las costillas.

chondrodynia *n.* condrodinia, dolor en un cartílago.

chondromalacia *n.* condromalacia, reblandecimiento anormal de los cartílagos.

choose *vi.* escoger, elegir.

chord *n.* cuerda; vocal ____ / ____ vocal.

chorea, Huntington's disease *n.* corea; enfermedad de Huntington, padecimiento nervioso que se manifiesta en movimientos abruptos coordinados aunque involuntarios de las extremidades y los músculos faciales; *pop.* baile de San Vito.

choriocarcinoma *n.* coriocarcinoma, tumor maligno visto gen. en el útero y en los testículos.

chorion *n.* corión, una de las dos membranas que rodean al feto.

choroid *n.* coroides, membrana situada en el ojo al que nutre con la sangre.

choroiditis *n.* coroiditis, infl. de la coroides.

chromatic *a.* cromático-a, rel. al color.

chromatin *n.* cromatina, parte del núcleo de la célula más propensa a absorber color.

chromocyte *n.* cromocito, célula pigmentada.

chromogen *n.* cromógeno, sustancia que produce color.

chromophobe *n.* cromófobo, tipo de célula que ofrece resistencia al color.

chromophobia *n.* cromofobia, aversión anormal a ciertos colores.

chromosome *n.* cromosoma, la parte dentro del núcleo de la célula que contiene los genes.

chromosomic *a.* cromosómico-a, rel. al cromosoma; ____ aberrations / aberraciones ____ -s.

chronic *a.* crónico-a, de larga duración.

chronological *a.* cronológico-a, rel. a la secuencia del tiempo.

chronotropism *n.* cronotropismo, modificación de funciones regulares tal como los latidos del corazón.

chubby *a.* regordete-a, macizo-a.

chyle *n.* quilo, sustancia lechosa que resulta de la absorción y emulsión de las grasas, presente en el intestino delgado.

chylemia *n.* quilemia, presencia de quilo en la sangre.

chylomicron *n.* quilomicrón, pequeña partícula de lípido vista en la sangre después de la ingestión de grasas.

chylorrhea *n.* quilorrea, derrame de quilo debido a una ruptura del conducto torácico.

chylous *a.* quiloso-a, que contiene quilo o de la naturaleza de éste.

chyluria *n.* quiluria. V. galacturia.

chyme *n.* quimo, sustancia o materia semilíquida que proviene de la digestión gástrica.

chymotrypsin *n.* quimotripsina, tripsina, enzima de la secreción pancreática.

chymotrypsinogen *n.* quimotripsinógeno, enzima pancreática precursor de la quimotripsina.

cicatrix *L.* (*pl.* **cicatrices**) cicatriz.

cicatrizant *n.* cicatrizante, agente que contribuye a la cicatrización.

cicatrization *n.* cicatrización.

cigar *n.* tabaco.

cigarette *n.* cigarro, cigarrillo.

ciliary *n.* ciliar, rel. a las pestañas o al párpado.

cilium *L.* (*pl.* **cilia**) párpado.

Cimetidine *n.* Cimetidina, nombre comercial de un antiácido usado en el tratamiento de úlceras gástricas y duodenales.

cineradiography *n.* cinerradiografía, película radiográfica de un órgano en movimiento.

cinerea *n.* cinérea, la sustancia gris del sistema nervioso.

cinnamon *n.* canela.

circinate *a.* circinado-a, semejante a un anillo o círculo.

circle *n.* círculo, circunferencia.

circuit *n.* circuito, vuelta, rotación.

circulation *n.* circulación; poor ___ / mala ___ ; ___ rate / volumen circulatorio por minuto.

circulatory *a.* circulatorio-a; circular.

circumcise *v.* circuncidar.

circumcision *n.* circuncisión, excisión del prepucio.

circumference *n.* circunferencia; círculo.

cirrhosis *n.* cirrosis, enfermedad asociada con infl. intersticial, fallo en la función de hepatocitos y trastornos en la circulación de la sangre en el hígado; alcoholic ___ / ___ alcohólica; biliary ___ / ___ biliar.

cistern *n.* cisterna, receptáculo de agua, aljibe.

cite *v.* citar, referirse a.

citizen *n.* ciudadano-a.

citizenship *n.* ciudadanía.

citric, citrous *a.* cítrico-a; ___ acid / ácido ___ .

city *n.* ciudad.

claim *n.* reclamación; petición; ___ review procedure / proceso para revisión de peticiones (reclamaciones); *v.* reclamar, demandar.

clam *n.* almeja.

clamp *n.* pinza; presilla.

clamping *n.* pinzado.

clap *n. pop.* gonorrea, blenorragia; [*hand*] palmada.

clarification *n.* aclaración, clarificación.

clarify *v.* aclarar, clarificar.

clarity *n.* claridad.

clasp *n.* gancho.

class *n.* clase; tipo.

classification *n.* clasificación; distribución.

classify *v.* clasificar, distribuir.

claudication *n.* claudicación; intermittent ___ / ___ intermitente.

claustrophobia *n.* claustrofobia, miedo o fobia a espacios cerrados.

clavicle *n.* clavícula, hueso de la faja pectoral que conecta al esternón con la escápula.

clavicular *a.* clavicular, rel. a las clavículas.

claw *n.* garra; ___ foot / pie en ___ ; ___ hand / mano en ___ .

clean *a.* limpio-a, aseado-a; *v.* limpiar, asear.

clear *a.* claro-a.

clearance *n.* aclaramiento, eliminación renal de una sustancia en el plasma sanguíneo.

cleft *n.* fisura, abertura alargada.

cleft lip *n.* labio leporino. *V.* **harelip.**

cleft palate *n.* paladar hendido, defecto congénito del velo del paladar por falta de fusión en la línea media.

cleidocostal *a.* cleidocostal, rel. a la clavícula y las costillas.

cleptomania, kleptomania *n.* cleptomanía, impulso mórbido al robo.

cleptomaniac *n.* cleptómano-a, persona que padece de cleptomanía.

clergyman *n.* clérigo.

climacteric *a.* climatérico-a.

climacterium *L.* climaterio, menopausia, cese de actividad reproductiva.

climate *n.* clima.

climax *L.* climax. 1. crisis de una enfermedad; 2. orgasmo sexual.

climb *v.* subir; trepar; subirse, treparse.

clinic *n.* clínica, small ___ / dispensario.

clinical *a.* clínico-a. 1. rel. a una clínica; 2. rel. a la observación directa de pacientes; ___ history / historia ___ , expediente; ___ picture / cuadro ___ ; ___ procedure / procedimiento ___ ; ___ trials / ensayos ___ -s.

clip *n.* pinza; *v.* sujetar con pinzas.

clitoridectomy *n. cirg.* clitoridectomía, excisión del clítoris.

clitoris *n.* clítoris, pequeña protuberancia situada en la parte anterior de la vulva.

cloaca *n.* cloaca, abertura común del intestino y de las vías urinarias en la fase de desarrollo primario del embrión.

clock *n.* reloj.

clone *n.* clono, derivación de un organismo simple por reproducción asexual.

clonic *a.* clónico-a, rel. a un clono.

clonorchiasis *n.* clonorquiasis, infección parasitaria que afecta los conductos biliares distales.

clonus *Gr.* clono, serie de contracciones rápidas y rítmicas de un músculo.

close *v.* cerrar.

closed *a.* cerrado-a; ___ ecological system / sistema ecológico ___ ; ___ circuit television / televisión en circuito ___ .

closure *n.* acto de cerrar o sellar; encierro.

clot *n.* coágulo, cuajo, grumo, *pop.* cuajarón.

clothes, clothing *n.* ropa.

clotting *n.* coagulación; ___ time / tiempo de ___ ; ___ factor / factor de ___ .

cloudiness *n.* nebulosidad, enturbamiento.

cloudy *a.* turbio-a, nebuloso-a, oscuro-a.

clove *n.* clavo de especia.

club feet *n.* pie torcido, *pop.* patizambo, *slang* chueco.

club hand *n.* mano zamba, *pop.* mano de gancho.

clubbing *n.* dedo en palillo de tambor.

cluster *n.* racimo, grupo.

cluster headache, Horton's syndrome *n.* cefalalgia de Horton, dolor de cabeza producido por histaminas.

clysis *n.* clisis, administración de líquidos por cualquier vía excepto la oral.

coagglutination *n.* coaglutinación, aglutinación de grupos.

coagglutinine *n.* coaglutinina, aglutinante que afecta a dos o más organismos.

coagulant *a.* coagulante, que produce coagulación.

coagulate *v.* coagular, coagularse.

coagulation *n.* coagulación, coágulo; disseminated intravascular ___ (DIC) / ___ intravascular diseminada.

coagulopathy *n.* coagulopatía, enfermedad o condición que afecta el mecanismo de la coagulación de la sangre.

coalescense *n.* coalescencia, fusión de dos o más partes.

coal miners' disease *n.* enfermedad de los mineros. *V.* **anthracosis.**

coarctation *n.* contracción, estrechez.

coarse *a.* grueso-a; rudo-a, tosco-a, burdo-a, ordinario-a.

coat *n.* membrana, cubierta; [*clothing*] abrigo.

cobalt *n.* cobalto.

coca *n.* coca, planta de cuyas hojas se extrae la cocaína.

cocaine *n.* cocaína, narcótico alcaloide adictivo complejo obtenido de las hojas de coca; *slang* nieve.

coccidioidin *n.* coccidioidina, solución estéril suministrada por medio intercutáneo en la prueba de la coccidioidomicosis (fiebre del valle).

coccidioidomycosis, valley fever *n.* coccidioidomicosis, fiebre del valle, infección respiratoria endémica en el suroeste de los Estados Unidos, México y algunas partes de América del Sur.

coccus *L.* (*pl.* **cocci**) coco, bacteria de forma esférica.

coccygeal *a.* coccígeo, rel. al cóccix.

coccygodynia *n.* coccigodinia, dolor en la región coccígea.

coccyx *Gr.* cóccix; último hueso de la columna vertebral; *pop.* rabadilla.

cochlea *n.* coclea, parte del oído interior en forma de caracol.

cochleare *L.* cucharada; ___ magnum / ___ de sopa; ___ medium / ___ de postre; ___ parvum / cucharita de café.

cockroach *n.* cucaracha.

cod *n.* bacalao; ___ liver oil / aceite de hígado de ___ .

codeine *n.* codeína, narcótico analgésico.

coefficient *n.* coeficiente, indicación de cambios físicos o químicos producidos por variantes de ciertos factores.

coenzyme *n.* coenzima, sustancia que activa la acción de una enzima.

coffee *n.* café.

coffin *n.* ataúd, caja.

cognac *n.* cognac, aguardiente.

cognate *n.* cognado, palabra que proviene del mismo tronco o raíz; *a.* cognado-a, de la misma naturaleza o calidad.

cohabit *v.* cohabitar, vivir en unión sin matrimonio legal.

coherence *n.* coherencia, cohesión.

coherent *a.* coherente.

cohesion *n.* cohesión, unión, fuerza que une a las moléculas.

coil *n.* espiral, serpentina, dispositivo intrauterino.

coincide *v.* coincidir.

coincidence *n.* coincidencia; **by** ___ / por casualidad.

coitus *L.* coito, acto sexual.

cold *n.* catarro; resfriado; [*weather*] frío; *a.* [*temperature*] frío-a; ___ blooded / de sangre fría o de temperatura muy baja; ___ sore / úlcera de herpes simple; ___ sweat /

sudor frío; ___ **cream** / crema, pomada facial; ___ **pack** / compresa fría; *v.* **to be** ___ / tener frío; **it is** ___ / hace frío.

coldness *n.* frialdad.

colectomy *n. cirg.* colectomía, extirpación de una parte o de todo el colon.

colic *n.* cólico, dolor espasmódico abdominal agudo.

colicky *a.* rel. al cólico.

colitis *n.* colitis, infl. del colon; chronic ___ / ___ crónica; spasmodic ___ / ___ espasmódica; pseudomembranous ___ / ___ mucomembranosa; ulcerative ___ / ___ ulcerativa.

collaborate *v.* colaborar, cooperar.

collagen *n.* colágeno, principal proteína de sostén del tejido conectivo de la piel, huesos, tendones y cartílagos.

collapse *n.* colapso; postración; desplome; ___ therapy / terapia de ___; *v.* sufrir un ___.

collapsed *a.* desplomado-a; derrumbado-a; estado de vacuidad.

collar *n.* cuello.

collarbone *n.* clavícula.

collateral *a.* colateral, al lado; accesorio-a.

colleague *n.* colega; compañero-a.

collect *v.* coleccionar, recoger, juntar; acumular.

colloid *n.* coloide, sustancia gelatinosa producida por ciertas formas de degeneración de los tejidos.

collodion *n.* colodión, sustancia usada para proteger heridas en la piel.

collyrium *n.* colirio, medicamento aplicado a los ojos.

colon *n.* colon, porción del intestino grueso entre el ciego y el recto, ascending ___ / ___ ascendente; descending ___ / ___ descendente.

colonic *a.* colónico, referente al colon; ___ neoplasms / neoplasmas del colon.

colonoscopy *n.* colonoscopía, examen de la superficie interna del colon a través del colonoscopio.

colony *n.* colonia, cultivo de bacterias derivadas del mismo organismo.

color *n.* color; ___ index / guía colorimétrica; *v.* colorar; teñir o dar color.

coloration *n.* coloración.

colostomy *n. cirg.* colostomía, creación de un ano artificial.

colostrum *n.* colostro, secreción de la glándula mamaria anterior a la leche.

colpitis *n.* colpitis, vaginitis, infl. de la vagina.

colpocele *n.* colpocele, hernia vaginal.

colporrhagia *n.* colporragia, hemorragia vaginal.

colporrhaphy *n. cirg.* colporrafia, sutura de la vagina.

colposcope *n.* colposcopio, instrumento que se usa para examinar visualmente la vagina y el cuello uterino.

colposcopy *n.* colposcopía, examen de la vagina y el cuello uterino a través de un coldoscopio.

colpotomy *n. cirg.* colpotomía, incisión de la vagina.

column *n.* columna.

coma *n.* coma, en estado de coma; sueño profundo o estado inconsciente.

comatose *a.* comatoso-a; in a ___ state / en estado de coma.

comb *n.* peine; *v.* peinar; peinarse.

combat *v.* combatir; *n.* combate, lucha.

combating *p. p.* de **to combat,** combatiendo.

combine *v.* combinar, unir.

come *vi.* venir; **to** ___ **to terms** / ponerse de acuerdo; ___ **in!** / pase, pasa; entre, entra.

comfort *n.* comodidad, alivio, bienestar; *v.* confortar, alentar.

comfortable *a.* cómodo-a; a gusto.

comfortless *a.* incómodo-a.

command *n.* orden; *gr.* mandato.

commensal *n.* comensal, organismo que vive a expensas de otro sin beneficiarlo ni perjudicarlo.

comment *n.* comentario; *v.* comentar; hacer un comentario.

comminute *v.* pulverizar, triturar.

comminuted *a.* conminuto-a, roto-a en fragmentos tal como en una fractura.

commiserate *v.* tener compasión, tener lástima; apiadarse, compadecerse; tenerse lástima.

commission *n.* comisión, encargo.

commissure *n.* comisura, punto de unión de estructuras tal como la unión de los labios.

commisurotomy *n. cirg.* comisurotomía, incisión de las bandas fibrosas de una comisura tal como la de los labios o la de los bordes de válvulas cardíacas.

commit *v.* cometer; [*intern*] internar, encerrar.

commitment *n.* obligación, compromiso.

commode *n.* inodoro, servicio.

common *a.* común, corriente; ____ name / nombre ____ ; ____ place / lugar ____ ; ____ sense / sentido ____ .

commotion *n.* conmoción; agitación.

commotio retinae *n. L.* conmoción retinal, condición traumática que produce ceguera momentánea.

communicable *a.* contagioso-a; comunicable; ____ disease control / control de enfermedades ____ .

communicate *v.* comunicar; *vr.* comunicarse con.

communication *n.* comunicación; acceso; entrada.

community *n.* comunidad, sociedad, barrio; ____ health center / centro de servicio de la salud; ____ medicine / medicina comunitaria.

companion *n.* compañero-a; acompañante; ____ disease / enfermedad concomitante.

company *n.* compañía, establecimiento.

comparative *a.* comparativo-a.

compare *v.* comparar.

compassion *n.* compasión, lástima.

compatible *a.* compatible.

compensate *v.* compensar, recompensar.

compensation *n.* compensación. 1. cualidad de compensar o equilibrar un defecto; 2. mecanismo de defensa; 3. remuneración.

competent *a.* competente, capaz.

complain *v.* quejarse, lamentarse.

complainer *a.* quejoso-a.

complaint *n.* queja, síntoma; trastorno, molestia.

complement *n.* complemento, sustancia proteínica presente en el plasma que destruye las bacterias y las células con que se pone en contacto.

complex *n.* complejo, serie de procesos mentales interrelacionados que afectan la conducta y la personalidad; castration ____ / ____ de castración; guilt ____ / ____ de culpa; inferiority ____ / ____ de inferioridad; Electra's ____ / ____ de Electra; Oedipus ____ / ____ de Edipo; *a.* complejo-a; complicado-a.

complexion *n.* cutis, complexión, tez.

compliance *n.* adaptabilidad, conformidad, grado de elasticidad de un órgano para distenderse o de una estructura para perder la forma; ____ with standards / ____ con las normas.

complicate *v.* complicar.

complication *n.* complicación.

component *n.* componente.

composition *n.* composición, mezcla, compuesto.

composure *n.* compostura, serenidad.

compote *n.* compota.

compound *n.* compuesto.

comprehension *n.* comprensión.

compress *n.* compresa, apósito; cold ____ / ____ fría; hot ____ / fomento; *v.* comprimir, apretar.

compromise *v.* comprometerse, obligarse.

compulsion *n.* compulsión.

compulsive *a.* compulsorio-a, compulsivo-a; obsesivo-a.

computer diagnosis *n.* diagnóstico computado.

concave *a.* cóncavo-a.

conceive *v.* concebir.

concentrate *v.* concentrar.

concentration *n.* concentración.

concept *n.* concepto, opinión, noción, idea.

conception *n.* concepción, acto de concebir.

concern *n.* preocupación, cuidado.

concise *a.* conciso-a; definido-a.

conclusion *n.* conclusión.

concoction *n.* cocimiento, mezcla, concocción.

concrete *a.* concreto-a; definido-a.

concretio cordis *L.* concretio cordis, obliteración parcial o total de la cavidad del pericardio debido a una pericarditis constrictiva.

concretion *n.* concreción, bezoar o masa inorgánica que se acumula en partes del cuerpo.

concubitus *L.* concúbito.

concussion *n.* concusión, conmoción, traumatismo esp. del cerebro causado por una lesión en la cabeza que puede presentar síntomas de naúsea y mareos; ____ of the brain / ____ cerebral.

condemn *v.* condenar.

condense *v.* condensar, hacer más denso o compacto.

condition *n.* condición, cualidad; guarded ____ / en estado de gravedad.

conditioning *n.* acondicionamiento, condicionamiento.

condole *v.* condolerse; dar el pésame.

condolence *n.* condolencia, pésame.

condom *n.* condón, contraceptivo masculino.

conduct *v.* dirigir, conducir.

conduit *n.* conducto; airway ____ / ____ para aire; tear ____ / ____ lagrimal.

condyle *n.* cóndilo, porción redondeada de un hueso, usu. en la articulación.

condyloma *n.* condiloma, tipo de verruga vista alrededor de los genitales y el perineo.

cone *n.* cono, uno de los órganos sensoriales que junto a los bastoncillos de la retina facilitan la visión del color; ____ cells / ____ -s de la retina.

confabulation *n. psic.* confabulación, condición en la que el individuo imagina situaciones que olvida fácilmente.

confer *v.* consultar; conferenciar.

confess *v.* admitir, reconocer; confesar.

confidential *a.* confidencial; en secreto.

confine *v.* recluir, internar, confinar; **to** ____ **in bed** / ____ en la cama.

confined *a.* recluído-a, confinado-a.

confinement *n.* confinación, reclusión, internación.

confirm *v.* confirmar.

conflict *n.* conflicto, problema.

confluence *n.* confluencia, punto de reunión de varios canales.

confront *v.* confrontar.

confuse *v.* confundir, trastornar, aturdir.

confused *a.* confuso-a, confundido-a, distraído-a; *v.* **to be** ____ / estar ____, confundirse.

confusion *n.* confusión; atolondramiento; aturdimiento.

congenital *a.* congénito-a; engendrado-a, rel. a una característica que se hereda y existe desde el nacimiento.

congested *a.* congestionado-a; en estado de congestión.

congestion *n.* congestión, aglomeración; acumulación excesiva de sangre en un órgano.

congestive *a.* congestivo-a, rel. a la congestión; ____ heart failure / insuficiencia cardíaca ____ .

conical, conic *a.* cónico-a, semejante a un cono.

conization *n.* conización, extirpación de tejido que tiene forma cónica, semejante al de la mucosa del cuello uterino.

conjunctiva *n.* conjuntiva, membrana mucosa protectora del ojo.

conjunctival *a.* conjuntivo-a, rel. a la conjuntiva; ____ diseases / enfermedades de la conjuntiva.

conjunctivitis *n.* conjuntivitis, infl. de la conjuntiva; ____ acute, contagious / ____ aguda contagiosa; allergic ____ / ____ alérgica; catarrhal ____ / ____ catarral; follicular ____ / ____ folicular; vernal ____ / ____ vernal.

consanguineous *a.* consanguíneo-a, de la misma sangre u origen.

conscious *a.* consciente, en posesión de las facultades mentales.

consciousness *n.* consciencia, conocimiento, sentido; estado consciente; *v.* **to lose** ____ / perder el conocimiento; perder el sentido; **clouding of** ____ / torpor, confusión, entorpecimiento mental.

consent *n.* consentimiento, autorización; *v.* permitir, consentir; informed ____ / ____ autorizado.

consequences *n. pl.* consecuencias, secuelas.

conservation *n.* conservación, preservación.

conservative *a.* conservador-a; preservativo-a.

conserve *v.* conservar, mantener.

consider *v.* considerar, ponderar.

considerate *a.* considerado-a; moderado-a.

consideration *n.* consideración.

consist *v.* consistir; estar formado de; componerse.

consistency *n.* consistencia; solidez.

consistent *a.* consistente, firme, estable.

console *v.* consolar, confortar; dar aliento.

consomme *n.* consomé, caldo.

conspicuous *a.* sobresaliente, señalado-a, conspicuo-a.

constant *a.* constante, persistente.

constipate *v.* estreñir, constipar.

constipated *a.* estreñido-a; constipado-a; *v.* to be ____ / estar ____ .

constipation *n.* estreñimiento, trastorno intestinal caracterizado por la imposibilidad de evacuar con facilidad.

constitute *v.* constituir, componer, formar.

constitution *n.* constitución, fortaleza.

constrain *v.* restringir; impedir.

constrict *v.* apretar, estrangular.

constriction *n.* constricción.

consult *v.* consultar.

consultant *n.* consultor-a, consejero-a.

consultation *n.* consulta.

consulting room *n.* consultorio médico.

consume *v.* consumir.

consummation *n.* consumación.

consumption *n.* consunción; desgaste progresivo; tisis, tuberculosis.

contact *n.* contacto; close ___ / ___ íntimo; ___ lenses / lentes de ___; initial ___ / ___ inicial.

contagion *n.* contagio, transmisión de una enfermedad por contacto.

contagious *a.* contagioso-a; infeccioso-a; que se comunica por contagio.

contain *v.* contener; reprimir.

container *n.* recipiente, envase.

contaminate *v.* contaminar, infectar.

contamination *n.* contaminación; infección.

content *n.* contenido.

contented *a.* satisfecho-a.

contiguous *a.* contiguo-a, adyacente.

continence *n.* continencia, control o automoderación en relación con actividades sexuales o físicas.

continuation *n.* continuación.

continue *v.* continuar.

continuity *n.* continuidad.

continuous *a.* continuo-a, seguido-a.

contour *n.* contorno.

contraception *n.* contracepción, anticoncepción.

contraceptive *n.* contraceptivo, anticonceptivo, agente o método para impedir la concepción; ___ agents / agentes anticonceptivos; ___ methods / métodos ___-s, métodos anticonceptivos.

contract *v.* [*a disease*] contraer.

contracted *n.* contraído-a; retenido-a.

contractile *a.* contráctil, que tiene la capacidad de contraerse.

contractility *n.* contractilidad, capacidad de contraerse.

contraction *n.* contracción; after ___ / ___ ulterior; deep ___ / ___ de fondo; hunger ___ / ___ de hambre; muscular ___ / ___ muscular; spasmodic ___ / ___ espasmódica.

contracture *n.* contractura, contracción prolongada involuntaria.

contradict *v.* contradecir, negar.

contradiction *n.* contradicción, oposición.

contraindicated *a.* contraindicado-a.

contralateral *a.* contralateral, rel. al lado opuesto.

contrary *a.* contrario-a, adverso-a, opuesto-a.

contrast *n.* contraste; ___ medium / medio de ___; *v.* contrastar, resaltar.

contribute *v.* contribuir.

control *n.* control, regulación; *v.* controlar,

regular, dominar; to ___ oneself / controlarse, dominarse.

contuse *v.* magullar.

contusion *n.* contusión, magulladura.

convalesce *v.* convalecer, reponerse.

convalescence *n.* convalescencia, proceso de restablecimiento, estado de recuperación.

convalescent *a.* convalesciente.

convergence *n.* convergencia, inclinación de dos o más elementos hacia un punto común.

conversion *n.* conversión. 1. cambio, transformación; 2. *psic.* transformación de una emoción en una manifestación física; ___ disorder / enajenamiento.

convex *a.* convexo-a.

convict *n.* preso-a, detenido-a, presidiario-a.

convulsant *a.* convulsivo-a, rel. a la convulsión.

convulsion *n.* convulsión, contracción involuntaria de un músculo; febril ___ / ___ febril; Jacksonian ___ / ___ Jacksoniana; tonic-clonic ___ / ___ tónico-clónica.

cook *n.* cocinero-a; *v.* cocinar.

cooked *a.* cocinado-a; guisado-a; **well** ___ / bien ___.

cool *a.* fresco-a; refrescado-a; [*weather*] it is ___ / hace fresco; [*body temperature*] he, she, it is ___ / está fresco-a; ___ **headed** / sereno-a, calmado-a.

cooler *n.* refrigerante, refresco.

coolness *n.* frialdad; serenidad.

cooperate *v.* cooperar, ayudar.

coordinate *v.* coordinar.

coordination *n.* coordinación; lack of ___ / falta de ___.

co-payment *n.* pago compartido.

copious *a.* abundante, copioso-a.

coprophagy *n.* coprofagia, trastorno mental manifestado en la ingestión de heces fecales.

copulation *n.* copulación, relaciones sexuales.

copy *n.* copia; imitación; *v.* copiar; imitar.

cor *L.* cor, corazón.

coracoclavicular *a.* coracoclavicular, referente a la escápula y la clavícula.

coracoid *n.* coracoides, apófisis del omóplato.

Coramine *n.* Coramina, nombre comercial de la niquetamida.

cord *n.* cordón, cuerda, cordel; umbilical ___ / ___ umbilical.

cordectomy *n.* *cirg.* cordectomía, excisión de una cuerda vocal o parte de ésta.

core *n.* centro, corazón, núcleo.

corium *L.* corion, dermis o piel.

corn *n.* callo, callosidad; [*grain*] maíz.

cornea *n.* córnea, parte anterior transparente del globo del ojo.

corneous *a.* córneo, rel. a la córnea; calloso-a.

coronary *a.* coronario-a, que circunda tal como una corona; ___ artery / arteria ___; ___ care unit / unidad de cuidado ___; ___ thrombosis / trombosis ___; ___ vasospasm / vasoespasmo ___.

coroner *n.* médico-a forense.

corporeal *a.* corporal, físico-a, rel. al cuerpo.

corpse *n.* cadáver, muerto-a.

corpus *L.* (*pl.* **corpora**) corpus, el cuerpo humano.

corpus callosum *L.* corpus callosum, comisura mayor del cerebro.

corpuscle *n.* corpúsculo, cuerpo diminuto.

corpuscular *a.* corpuscular, diminuto-a.

corpus luteum *L.* corpus luteum, cuerpo lúteo, cuerpo amarillo, masa glandular amarillenta que se forma en el ovario por la ruptura de un folículo y produce progesterona.

correct *a.* correcto-a, exacto-a.

correction *n.* corrección.

corrective *a.* correctivo-a.

correspondence *n.* correspondencia; reciprocidad.

corroded *a.* corroído-a, desgastado-a.

corrosion *n.* corrosión, desgaste.

corset *n.* corsé.

cortex *n.* corteza, córtex, la capa más exterior de un órgano; adrenal ___ / ___ suprarrenal; cerebral ___ / ___ cerebral.

cortical *a.* cortical, rel. a la corteza.

corticoid, corticosteroid *n.* corticoide, corticoesteroide, esteroide producido por la corteza suprarrenal.

corticotropin *n.* corticotropina, sustancia hormonal de actividad adrenocorticotrópica.

cortisol *n.* cortisol, hormona secretada por la corteza suprarrenal.

cortisone *n.* cortisona, esteroide glucogénico derivado del cortisol, también se obtiene sintéticamente.

Corti's organ *n.* órgano de Corti, órgano terminal de la audición a través del cual se perciben directamente los sonidos.

cosmetic *n.* cosmético; *a.* cósmetico-a.

cosmetic surgery *n.* cirugía plástica con fines estéticos.

cost *n.* coste, costo, precio; *v.* costar.

costal *a.* costal, rel. a las costillas.

costalgia *n.* costalgia, neuralgia, dolor en las costillas.

costly *a.* costoso-a, caro-a; *adv.* costosamente.

costoclavicular *a.* costoclavicular, rel. a las costillas y la clavícula.

costovertebral *a.* costovertebral, rel. a las costillas y vértebras toráxicas.

cotton *n.* algodón.

cough *n.* tos; ___ drops / gotas para la ___; hacking ___ / ___ seca recurrente; ___ lozenges / pastillas para la ___; ___ suppressant / calmante para la ___; ___ syrup / jarabe para la ___, *v.* toser; to ___ up phlegm / expectorar la flema; coughing spell / ataque de ___.

count *v.* contar.

counter *n.* contador; *v.* **to** ___ **attack** / luchar en contra de; oponerse.

counteract *n.* contraataque; *v.* oponerse a; contraatacar.

countercoup *n.* contragolpe.

counterpoison *n.* antídoto, contraveneno.

counterreaction *n.* reacción opuesta; reacción en contra de.

countershock *n.* contrachoque, corriente eléctrica aplicada al corazón para normalizar el ritmo cardíaco.

courage *n.* coraje, valor, firmeza.

courageous *a.* valiente, valeroso-a.

course *n.* curso, dirección.

cousin *n.* primo-a.

cover *n.* cobertor, manta, cobija; *v.* cubrir, proteger; tapar; abrigar.

covered *a.* cubierto-a; protegido-a.

cow *n.* vaca.

coward *a.* cobarde.

cowperitis *n.* cowperitis, infl. de las glándulas de Cowper (bulbouretrales).

Cowper's glands *n.* glándulas de Cowper, (bulbouretrales) pequeñas glándulas adyacentes al bulbo de la uretra masculina en la que vacían una secreción mucosa.

cowpox *n.* vacuna, cowpox.

coxa *n.* *L.* (*pl.* **coxae**) coxa, cadera.

coxalgia *n.* coxalgia, dolor en la cadera.

coxitis *n.* coxitis, infl. de la articulación coxofemoral, (articulación de la cadera).

crab *n.* cangrejo, cámbaro.

crack *n.* rajadura, quebradura; *v.* rajar, quebrar.

cracker *n.* galleta.

cradle *n.* cuna; ____ cap / costra láctea.

cramp *n.* calambre, entumecimiento; contracción dolorosa de un músculo.

cranial *a.* craneal, craneano-a, del cráneo o rel. al mismo.

cranial nerves *n.* nervios craneales, cada uno de los doce pares de nervios que salen de la región inferior del cerebro; I. olfactory / olfatorio; II. optic / óptico; III. oculomotor / motor ocular común; IV. trochlear / patético; V. trigeminal / trigémino; VI. abducens / motor ocular externo abducente; VII. facial / facial; VIII. auditory / auditivo; IX. glossopharyngeal / glosofaríngeo; X. vagus / neumogástrico; XI. spinal accessory / espinal; XII. hypoglossal / hipoglosal.

cranioplasty *n. cirg.* craneoplastia, reparación de defectos en los huesos del cráneo.

craniotomy *n. cirg.* craneotomía. trepanación del cráneo.

cranium *n.* cráneo, parte ósea de la cabeza que cubre el cerebro.

cranky *a.* majadero-a; inquieto-a.

crash *n.* choque violento; accidente de tráfico.

crater *n.* cráter. *V.* **niche.**

crave *v.* apetecer; ansiar; desear algo excesivamente.

craving *n.* deseo exagerado.

crawl *v.* arrastrarse; andar a gatas, gatear.

craze *n.* manía, locura.

crazy *a.* loco-a, demente.

cream *n.* crema, nata.

create *v.* crear.

creatine *n.* creatina, componente del tejido muscular, esencial en la fase anaeróbica de la contracción muscular.

creatinine *n.* creatinina, sustancia presente en la orina que representa el producto final del metabolismo de la creatina; ____ clearance / depuración de ____, volumen de plasma libre de ____.

creation *n.* creación, obra; universo.

credit *n.* crédito; *v.* acreditar, dar crédito.

cremasteric *a.* cremastérico, referente al músculo cremastérico del escroto.

cremate *v.* incinerar.

cremation *n.* incineración.

creosote *n.* creosota, líquido aceitoso gen.

usado como desinfectante y como expectorante catarral.

crepitation *n.* crepitación, chasquido, crujido; pleural ____ / ____ pleural.

crest *n.* cresta, prominencia; copete. 1. reborde o prominencia de un hueso; 2. la elevación máxima de una línea en un gráfico.

crestfallen *a.* decaído-a, alicaido-a; acobardado-a.

cretin *n.* cretino-a, persona con manifestaciones de cretinismo.

cretinism *n.* cretinismo, hipotiroidismo congénito debido a una deficiencia acentuada de la hormona tiroidea.

cretinoid *a.* cretinoide, con características similares a un cretino.

crib *n.* cuna, camita.

cribriform *a.* cribriforme, perforado-a.

cricoid *a.* cricoide, de forma anular.

crime *n.* crimen, delito.

criminal *n.* criminal.

cripple *a.* lisiado-a, paralítico-a, inválido-a, tullido-a; *v.* lisiar, baldar, paralizar; tullir.

crisis *n.* crisis; identity ____ / ____ de identidad.

crisscross *a.* cruzado-a, entrelazado-a; *adv.* en cruz.

crista *n.* cresta, proyección.

critical *a.* crítico-a; ____ condition / estado ____, gravedad extrema.

cross-eye, strabismus *n.* estrabismo, *pop.* bizquera, debilidad de los músculos que controlan la posición del ojo impidiendo la coordinación visual.

cross-eyed *a.* bizco-a.

cross-legged *a.* patizambo-a; cruzado-a de piernas.

cross matching *n.* pruebas sanguíneas cruzadas que comprueban la compatibilidad de la sangre antes de una transfusión.

crotch *n.* bifurcación, horquilla.

croup *n.* crup, pop. garrotillo, síndrome respiratorio visto en los niños, causado gen. por una infección o una reacción alérgica.

crown *n.* corona.

crucial *a.* crucial, definitivo-a.

crude *a.* rudo-a, crudo-a.

cruel *a.* cruel, inhumano-a.

crus *L.* crus, 1. pierna o parte semejante a una pierna; 2. parte de la pierna entre la rodilla y el tobillo.

crush *v.* triturar, moler, aplastar.

crust *n.* costra.

crutches *n. pl.* muletas.

cry *v.* llorar; lamentarse.

cryoanesthesia *n.* crioanestesia, 1. anestesia producida por aplicación de frío localizado; 2. pérdida de la sensibilidad al frío.

cryogenic *n.* criogénico, que produce temperaturas bajas.

cryoglobulin *n.* crioglobulina, globulina que se precipita del suero por acción del frío.

cryoprecipitate *n.* crioprecipitado, precipitado producido por enfriamiento.

cryosurgery *n.* criocirugía, destrucción de tejidos por aplicación de temperatura fría local o general.

cryotherapy *n.* crioterapia, tratamiento terapéutico por aplicación de frío local o general.

crypt *n.* cripta, pequeño receso tubular.

cryptic *a* críptico-a, escondido-a.

cryptogenic *a.* criptogénico, de causa desconocida.

cryptorchism *n.* criptorquismo, falta de descenso testicular al escroto.

crystal *n.* cristal, vidrio.

crystalline *a.* cristalino-a, transparente.

crystalline lens *n.* cristalino, lente del ojo.

cubiform *a.* cúbico-a, rel. a la forma cúbica.

cubital *a.* cubital, codal.

cubitus, ulna *L.* cubitus, cúbito, hueso interno del antebrazo.

cucumber *n.* pepino, pepinillo.

cul-de-sac *Fr.* 1. cul-de-sac, fondo de saco, bolsa sin boquete de salida; 2. saco rectouterino.

culdoscope *n.* culdoscopio, instrumento endoscópico que se inserta en la vagina para examinar visualmente la pelvis y la cavidad abdominal.

culdoscopy *n.* culdoscopía, examen de la pelvis y la cavidad abdominal por medio del culdoscopio.

cultivate *v.* cultivar; estudiar.

culture *n.* cultivo, crecimiento artificial de microorganismos o células de tejido vivo en el laboratorio; blood ___ / ___ de sangre; ___ medium / medio de ___ ; ___ tissue / ___ de tejido.

cunnilingus *a.* cunilinguo-a, rel. a la práctica de estimulación oral del pene o el clítoris.

cup *n.* copa; ventosa; **optic** ___ / ___ de ojo, ___ ocular; **measuring** ___ / taza de medir.

cupful *n.* una taza llena.

curable *a.* curable, sanable.

curare *n.* curare, veneno extraído de varios tipos de plantas y usado como relajante muscular y anestésico.

curative *n.* curativo, remedio, agente que tiene propiedades curativas.

curd *n.* cuajo, cuajarón, coágulo sanguíneo grande; [*milk*] leche cuajada.

curdle *v.* cuajarse, coagularse, engrumecerse.

cure *n.* curación, remedio; *v.* curar, sanar, remediar.

cureless *a.* incurable.

curettage *n. cirg.* curetaje, raspado de una superficie o cavidad con uso de la cureta.

curette *n.* cureta, instrumento quirúrgico en forma de cuchara o pala usado para raspar los tejidos de una superficie o cavidad.

curious *a.* curioso-a, extraño-a.

current *n.* corriente, trasmisión de fluído o electricidad que pasa por un conductor; *a.* corriente, actual; **-ly** *adv.* actualmente.

curvature *n.* curvatura.

curve *n.* curva; *v.* torcer, encorvar.

Cushing's syndrome *n.* síndrome de Cushing, síndrome adrenogenital asociado con una producción excesiva de cortisol, caracterizado por obesidad y debilitamiento muscular.

cushion *n.* cojinete, cojín.

cusp *n.* cúspide, punta.

cuspid *n.* [*tooth*] colmillo.

cuspidal *a.* cuspídeo, puntiagudo.

custard *n.* flan, natilla.

custom *n.* costumbre, hábito.

cut *n.* cortada, cortadura; *vi.* cortar; **to ___ down** / rebajar, reducir; **to ___ off** / extirpar, amputar; [*oneself*] cortarse.

cutaneous *a.* cutáneo-a; ___ absorption / absorción ___ ; ___ glands / glándulas ___ -s o sebáceas.

cuticle *n.* cutícula, capa exterior de la piel.

cutis *n.* cutis; piel de la cara.

cyanide *n.* cianuro, compuesto extremadamente venenoso.

cyanocobalamin *n.* cianocobalamina, vitamina B_{12} usada en el tratamiento de la anemia perniciosa.

cyanosis *n.* cianosis, condición azulada o amoratada de la piel y las mucosas a causa de anomalías cardíacas o funcionales.

cyanotic *a.* cianótico-a, rel. a la cianosis o causado por ésta.

cybernetics *n.* cibernética, estudio del uso de medios electrónicos y mecanismos de comunicación aplicados a sistemas biológicos tales como los sistemas nervioso y cerebral.

cyclamate *n.* ciclamato, agente artificial dulcificante.

cycle *n.* ciclo, período; pregnancy ____ / ____ gravídico.

cyclectomy *n. cirg.* cicletomía, excisión de una parte del músculo ciliar.

cyclic *a.* cíclico-a, que ocurre en períodos o ciclos.

cyclitis *n.* ciclitis, infl. del músculo ciliar.

cyclophoria *n.* cicloforia, rotación del globo ocular debido a debilidad muscular.

cyclophosphamide *n.* ciclofosfamida, droga antineoplástica usada también como inmunosupresor en trasplantes.

cyclophotocoagulation *n.* ciclofotocoagulación, fotocoagulación a través de la pupila con un laser, procedimiento usado en el tratamiento de glaucoma.

cycloplegia *n.* cicloplejía, parálisis del músculo ciliar.

cyclosporin *n.* ciclosporina, agente inmuno supresivo usado en trasplantes de órganos.

cyclothymia *n. psic.* ciclotimia, personalidad cíclica con trastornos de agitación y depresión.

cyclotomy *n. cirg.* ciclotomía, incisión a través del músculo ciliar.

cyclotropia *n.* ciclotropia, desviación del ojo alrededor del eje anteroposterior.

cylinder *n.* cilindro. 1. émbolo de una jeringa; 2. forma geométrica semejante a una columna.

cylindrical *a.* cilíndrico-a.

cylindroma *n.* cilindroma, tumor generalmente maligno visto en la cara o en la órbita del ojo.

cylindruria *n.* cilindruria, presencia de cilindros en la orina.

cynic *a.* cínico-a.

cyst *n.* quiste, saco o bolsa que contiene líquido o materia semilíquida; pilonidal ____ / ____ pilonidal, que contiene pelo, gen. localizado en el área sacrococcígea; sebaceous ____ / ____ sebáceo, gen. localizado en el cuero cabelludo.

cystadenocarcinoma *n.* cistadenocarcinoma, carcinoma y cistadenoma combinados.

cystadenoma *n.* cistadenoma, adenoma que contiene uno o varios quistes.

cystectomy *n. cirg.* cistectomía, extirpación o resección de la vejiga.

cysteine *n.* cisteína, aminoácido derivado de la cistina, presente en la mayor parte de las proteínas.

cystic *a.* cístico-a, rel. a la vesícula biliar o la vejiga urinaria; ____ duct / conducto ____.

cystic fibrosis *n.* fibrosis cística del páncreas, fibroquiste.

cystine *n.* cistina, aminoácido producido durante la digestión de las proteínas, presente a veces en la orina.

cystinuria *n.* cistinuria, exceso de cistina en la orina.

cystitis *n.* cistitis, infl. de la vejiga urinaria caracterizada por ardor, dolor y micción frecuente.

cystocele *n.* cistocele, hernia de la vejiga.

cystogram *n.* cistograma, rayos X de la vejiga.

cystolithotomy *n.* cistolitotomía, extracción de una piedra o cálculo por medio de una incisión en la vejiga.

cystometer *n.* cistómetro, instrumento usado para estudiar la patofisiología de la vejiga que mide la capacidad y las reacciones de ésta a presiones aplicadas.

cystometry *n.* cistometría, estudio de las funciones de la vejiga con uso del cistómetro.

cystopexy *n. cirg.* cistopexia, fijación de la vejiga urinaria a la pared abdominal.

cystoscope *n.* cistoscopio, instrumento en forma de tubo usado para examinar y tratar trastornos de la vejiga, los uréteres y los riñones.

cystoscopy *n.* cistoscopía, examen por medio del cistoscopio.

cystostomy *n. cirg.* cistostomía, creación de un boquete o fístula en la vejiga para permitir el drenaje urinario.

cystotomy *n. cirg.* cistotomía, incisión en la vejiga.

cystourethrography *n.* cistouretrografía, radiografía de la vejiga y la uretra.

cystourethroscope *n.* cistouretroscopio, instrumento usado en la exploración de la vejiga y la uretra.

cytochrome *n.* citocromo, hemocromógeno importante en el proceso de oxidación.

cytology *n.* citología, ciencia que estudia la estructura, forma y función de las células.

cytolytic *a.* citolítico-a, que tiene la cualidad de disolver o destruir células.

cytomegalic *a.* citomegálico-a, caracterizado-a por células agrandadas.

cytometer *n.* citómetro, dispositivo usado en el conteo y medida de los hematíes.

cytopenia *n.* citopenia, deficiencia de elementos celulares en la sangre.

cytoplasm *n.* citoplasma, protoplasma de una célula con exclusión del núcleo.

cytotoxin *n.* citotoxina, agente tóxico que afecta las células de ciertos órganos.

D

d *abbr.* **death** / muerte; **deceased** / difunto-a; **degree** / grado; **density** / densidad; **dose** / dosis.

dacryadenitis *n.* dacriadenitis, infl. de una glándula lagrimal

dacryagogue *n.* dacriagogue, agente estimulante de las glándulas lagrimales.

dacrycystalgia *n.* dacricistalgia, dolor en el saco lagrimal.

dacryoadenectomy *n.* *cirg.* dacrioadenectomía, extirpación de una glándula lagrimal.

dacryocystitis *n.* dacriocistitis, infl. del saco lagrimal.

dacryocystotomy *n.* *cirg.* dacriocistotomía, incisión del saco lagrimal.

dacryolithiasis *n.* dacriolitiasis, formación de cálculos lacrimales.

dactyl *n.* dáctilo, dedo de la mano o del pie.

dactylogram *n.* dactilograma, proceso de determinación de las huellas digitales.

dactylography *n.* dactilografía, estudio de las huellas digitales.

dactylology *n.* dactilología, lenguaje mímico o por señas.

dactilomegaly *n.* dactilomegalia, dedos de los pies o las manos de tamaño anormalmente grande.

dad *n.* papá; **daddy** / *H.A.* papi, papacito, tata.

daily *a.* diario-a, cotidiano-a; ___ **life** / vida cotidiana; *adv.* diariamente, todos los días, cada día, cotidianamente.

dairy products *n. pl.* productos lácteos.

daltonism *n.* daltonismo, dificultad para percibir colores.

dam *v.* acción de detener, estancar, tapar.

damage *n.* daño, deterioro, lesión; *v.* dañar, perjudicar; dañarse, perjudicarse.

damaging *a.* perjudicial.

damiana *n.* damiana, planta originaria de *Mex.* cuyas hojas tienen acción diurética.

damp *a.* húmedo-a.

dampen *v.* humedecer, mojar.

danazol *n.* danazol, nombre comercial Danocrina, hormona sintética que suprime la acción de la pituitaria anterior.

dance *v.* bailar, danzar; St. Vitus' ___ *n.* baile de San Vito. V. **chorea.**

dandruff *n.* caspa.

danger *n.* peligro, riesgo; *v.* **to be in** ___ / correr ___ .

dangerous *a.* peligroso-a, arriesgado-a.

dapsone *n.* dapsona, sulfonildianilina, droga usada en el tratamiento de la lepra.

dare *v.* atreverse, arriesgarse.

dark *a.* obscuro-a; ___ **adaptation** / adaptación a la obscuridad; ___ **field illumination** / iluminación del campo ___ , iluminación lateral u oblicua.

darken *v.* obscurecer.

darkness *n.* obscuridad.

Darvon *n.* Darvón, Deprancol, nombre comercial de dextro propoxifeno hidroclórido, analgésico oral.

data *n. pl.* datos.

date *n.* fecha; **up to** ___ / hasta la fecha; [*current*] al corriente.

daughter *n.* hija; ___ **in-law** / nuera.

dawn *n.* amanecer.

day *n.* día, **all** ___ / todo ___ ; **by** ___ / por el ___ , de ___ ; ___ **after tomorrow** / pasado mañana; ___ **before yesterday** / anteayer; ___ **in** ___ **out** / ___ tras ___ ; **each** ___ / cada ___ ; **every** ___ / todos los ___ -s; **every other** ___ / un ___ sí y un ___ no; ___ **time** / de ___ ; **three times a** ___ / tres veces al ___ ; **twice a** ___ / dos veces al ___ .

daybreak *n.* amanecer, alba.

daydream *n.* ilusión, ensueño; *v.* **to** ___ / soñar despierto-a.

daylight *n.* luz del día.

daze *n.* ofuscación, deslumbramiento.

deacidify *v.* neutralizar un ácido.

deactivation *n.* desactivación, proceso de transformar lo activo en inactivo.

dead *a.* difunto-a; muerto-a.

deaden *v.* [*sound*] amortiguar; [*nerve*] adormecer; anestesiar.

deadly *a.* mortífero-a; mortal, que puede causar la muerte; ___ **poison** / veneno ___ ; ___ **wound** / herida ___ .

deaf *n., a.* sordo-a.

deafen *v.* ensordecer.

deaf-mute *n.* sordomudo-a.

deaf-muteness, deaf-mutism *n.* sordomudez.

deafness *n.* sordera.

deal *n.* cantidad, porción; **a good** ___ / bastante; **a great** ___ **of time** / mucho tiempo; *v.* repartir, distribuir; **to** ___ **with** / tratar con.

deambulatory *a.* ambulatorio-a; móvil.

dear *a.* querido-a; estimado-a.

death *n.* muerte, fallecimiento; apparent ___ / ___ aparente; ___ certificate / certificado de defunción; fetal ___ / ___ del feto; ___ instinct / instinto mortal; ___ rate / mortalidad; ___ rattle / estertor agónico.

debilitate *v.* debilitar; debilitarse.

debilitated *a.* debilitado-a.

debility *n.* debilidad; atonía.

debridement *n.* desbridamiento, proceso quirúrgico de limpieza de una herida o quemadura para prevenir una infección.

debt *n.* deuda.

decalcification *n.* descalcificación, pérdida o disminución de sales de calcio en los huesos o dientes.

decay *n.* deteriorización, deterioro, descomposición gradual; [*teeth*] caries; dental ___ / carie dental, *pop.* dientes picados; ___ rate / índice de descomposición gradual; *v.* deteriorar, descomponer, decaer, declinar; deteriorarse, descomponerse, [*teeth*] cariarse; [*wood*] carcomerse; [*matter*] podrirse, pudrirse.

decayed *a.* deteriorado-a, decaído-a; empeorado-a; cariado-a; carcomido-a; podrido-a; putrefacto-a.

deceased *n.* difunto-a, persona muerta.

deceit *n.* engaño, fraude.

deceitful *a.* traicionero-a, engañador-a; ___ sickness / enfermedad ___ .

deceive *v.* engañar, defraudar, embaucar.

deceleration *n.* desaceleración, disminución de la velocidad tal como en la frecuencia cardíaca.

decency *n.* decencia.

decent *a.* decente.

decentered *a.* descentrado-a, fuera del centro.

decide *v.* decidir, determinar.

decided *a.* decidido-a.

decidua *n.* decidua, tejido membranoso formado por la mucosa uterina durante la gestación que es expulsado después del parto.

deciduous *a.* deciduo-a, de permanencia temporal; ___ dentition / primera dentición; ___ teeth / dientes ___ -s, dientes de leche.

decimate *v.* diezmar.

decimation *n.* gran mortalidad, diezma.

decipher *v.* descifrar, resolver un problema.

decision *n.* decisión, resolución.

decisive *a.* decisivo-a, terminante.

declination *n.* declinación. 1. rotación del ojo; 2. declive, descenso.

decline *n.* declinación; decadencia, decaimiento; [*invitation*] excusa; *v.* declinar, decaer; [*invitation, offer*] declinar, rehusar, rechazar; [*health*] desmejorarse.

decoction *n.* cocimiento, té de yerbas medicinales.

decompensation *n.* descompensación, inhabilidad del corazón para mantener una circulación adecuada.

decompose *v.* descomponerse, corromperse; [*food*] podrirse, pudrirse.

decomposed *a.* descompuesto-a; [*food*] podrido-a, putrefacto-a.

decompression *n.* descompresión, reducción de presión; ___ chamber / cámara de ___ ; surgical ___ / ___ quirúrgica; ___ sickness / condición por ___ , *pop.* the bends.

decongest *v.* descongestionar.

decongestant *n.* descongestionador, descongestionante.

decontaminate *v.* descontaminar, librar de contaminación.

decontamination *n.* descontaminación, proceso de librar el ambiente, objetos o personas de sustancias o agentes contaminados o nocivos tales como sustancias radioactivas.

decrepit *a.* decrépito-a, senil.

decrepitude *n.* decrepitud.

decubitus *n.* decúbito, posición acostada; ___ dorsal / dorsal, de espalda o boca arriba; ___ lateral / lateral, ___ de lado; ___ ventral / ___ de vientre o boca abajo; ___ ulcer / úlcera o escara por ___ .

decussation *n.* decusación, cruzamiento de estructuras en forma de X; ___ of pyramids / ___ de las pirámides, cruzamiento de fibras nerviosas de una pirámide a otra en la médula oblongata; optic ___ / ___

óptica, cruzamiento de las fibras del nervio óptico.

dedicate *v.* dedicar.

deduce *v.* deducir, inferir.

deduct *v.* descontar; rebajar.

deep *a.* profundo-a, hondo-a; ____ breathing / respiración ____ ; ____ contractions / contracciones ____ -s, de fondo; ____ chested / ancho-a de pecho; ____ dredging / dragado; ____ rooted / arraigado-a; ____ sensibility / sensibilidad ____ ; ____ sleep / sueño ____ , sopor; ____ X-ray therapy / terapia ____ ; ____ tendon reflex / reflejos tendónicos ____ -s.

deface *v.* mutilar, deformar, desfigurar.

defacement *n.* deformación; deterioro; mutilación.

defecate *v.* defecar, evacuar *Mex.* obrar.

defecation *n.* defecación, evacuación intestinal

defect *n.* defecto; insuficiencia; fallo.

defective *a.* defectuoso-a; incompleto-a.

defense *n.* defensa; protección; resistencia; ____ mechanism / mecanismo de ____ ; [*organic*] antitoxina; *psic.* autoprotección.

defenseless *a.* indefenso-a, inerme.

defend *v.* defender.

defer *v.* diferir, aplazar.

deferent *a.* deferente, hacia afuera.

deferred *a.* aplazado-a, diferido-a.

defibrillation *n.* desfibrilación, acción de cambiar latidos irregulares del corazón a su ritmo normal.

deficiency *n.* deficiencia, falta de algún elemento esencial al organismo; ____ disease / enfermedad por deficiencia; mental ____ / ____ mental; oxygen ____ / falta de oxígeno.

deficient *a.* deficiente, careciente.

deficit *n.* déficit, deuda; falta; deficiencia.

definition *n.* definición.

deflate *v.* desinflar, deshinchar.

deflect *v.* desviar, apartar.

deflection, deflexion *n.* desviación, desvío; *psic.* diversión inconsciente de ideas.

deform *v.* deformar.

deformed *a.* deformado-a, irregular.

deformity *n.* deformidad, irregularidad, defecto congénito o adquirido.

defurfuration *n.* defurfuración, acto de soltar escamas de la piel semejantes a hojuelas.

degenerate *a.* degenerado-a; anómalo-a.

degeneration *n.* degeneración, deteriorización.

deglutition *n.* deglución, acto de ingerir.

degree *n.* grado. 1. unidad de medida de una temperatura; 2. intensidad.

dehiscence *n.* dehiscencia, abertura espontánea de una herida.

dehumidifier *n.* deshumectante, aparato para disminuir la humedad.

dehydrate, dihydrate *v.* deshidratar, eliminar el agua de una sustancia; deshidratarse, perder líquido del cuerpo o de los tejidos.

dehydrated *a.* deshidratado-a.

dehydrocholesterol *n.* dehidrocolesterol, esterol presente en la piel que se convierte en vitamina D por la acción de rayos solares.

déjà vu *Fr.* déjà vu, impresión ilusoria de haber experimentado antes una situación que es totalmente nueva.

dejection *n.* deyección. 1. estado de abatimiento, depresión; 2. expulsión de excremento.

delay *n.* demora; *v.* demorar, atrasar; postergar.

delayed *a.* tardío-a, demorado-a; ____ delivery / parto ____ .

deleterious *a.* deletéreo-a, nocivo-a, dañino-a.

delicate *a.* delicado-a.

delicious *a.* delicioso-a; exquisito-a.

delight *n.* deleite; delicia; *v.* agradar, deleitar.

delighted *a.* encantado-a; *v.* **to be** ____ / tener mucho gusto.

delinquency *n.* delincuencia; juvenile ____ / ____ juvenil.

delirious *a.* delirante, en estado de delirio.

delirium *n.* delirium, estado de confusión mental acompañado gen. de alucinaciones y sensaciones distorsionadas; ____ tremens / ____ tremens, tipo de psicosis alcohólica.

deliver *v.* extraer; partear; [*in childbirth*] to be delivered / dar a luz, estar de parto, *Mex.A.* aliviarse.

delivery *n.* parto, alumbramiento; after ____ / después del ____ ; before ____ / antes del ____ ; false ____ / ____ falso; hard ____ / ____ laborioso; induction of ____ / ____ inducido; normal ____ / ____ normal; ____ of the placenta / expulsión de la placenta; premature ____ / ____ prematuro; prolonged ____ / ____ prolongado; ____ room / sala de ____ -s; stages of ____ / etapas del ____ .

deltoid *a.* deltoideo-a. 1. en forma de delta; 2. rel. al músculo deltoides.

delusion *n.* decepción, engaño; creencias falsas; ____ of persecution / delirio de persecución.

demand *n.* petición, demanda; ____ feeding / alimentación por demanda.

demented *a.* demente, enajenado-a; que sufre de demencia.

dementia *n.* demencia, locura; declinación de las funciones mentales; organic ____ / ____ orgánica; ____ paralytica / ____ paralítica; ____ praecox / ____ precoz, esquizofrenia; senil ____ / ____ senil.

Demerol *n.* Demerol, hidrocloruro de meperidina, nombre comercial de un analgésico con efecto similar al de la morfina.

demineralization *n.* desmineralización, pérdida de sales minerales del organismo.

demulcent *n.* emoliente, demulcente, aceite u otro agente que suaviza y alivia molestias de la piel.

demyelination *n.* desmielinización, pérdida de la capa de mielina de un nervio.

dendrite *n.* dendrita, prolongación protoplasmática de la célula de un nervio que recibe los impulsos nerviosos.

dengue fever *n.* dengue, fiebre endémica producida por un virus, transmitida por el mosquito *Aedes*.

denomination *n.* denominación, nombre.

dense *a.* denso-a, espeso-a.

density *n.* densidad.

dental *a.* dental, dentario-a rel. a los dientes; ____ care / cuidado ____; ____ caries / caries ____ -es; ____ drill / taladro, torno; ____ enamel / esmalte dentario; ____ floss / hilo ____, hilo de seda encerada; ____ health services / servicios de salud ____; ____ hygienist / técnico-a en profiláctica ____; ____ impression / impresión, mordisco; ____ plaque / placa dentaria; ____ surgeon / odontólogo; ____ tartar / sarro ____; ____ technician / mecánico ____.

dentiform *a.* odontoide, dentado-a, de proyección similar a un diente.

dentifrice *n.* dentífrico, pasta dental.

dentilabial *a.* dentilabial, rel. a los dientes y los labios.

dentin *n.* dentina, marfil dentario, tejido calcificado de un diente.

dentinogenesis *n.* dentinogénesis, formación de la dentina.

dentinoma *n.* dentinoma, tumor benigno que consiste mayormente de dentina.

dentist *n.* dentista.

dentistry *n.* arte o profesión de un dentista.

dentition *n.* dentición, brote de los dientes; ____, primary / ____ primaria [*first teeth*] o dientes de leche; ____, secondary / ____ secundaria o dientes permanentes.

denture *n.* dentadura, prótesis; [*artificial*] dentadura postiza; ____ plates / ____ parcial, *pop.* plancha dental.

denudation *n.* denudación, privación de la cubierta de una superficie de una manera traumática sea por cirugía, trauma, o por un cambio patológico.

denutrition *n.* desnutrición, malnutrición, deficiencia alimenticia; protein calorie ____ / ____ proteino-calórica.

deny *v.* negar, rehusar.

deodorant *n.* desodorante.

deodorize *v.* desodorizar, destruir olores fétidos o desagradables.

deoxycorticosterone *n.* desoxicorticosterona, hormona producida en la corteza de las glándulas suprarrenales de efecto marcado en el metabolismo del agua y los electrolitos.

depart *v.* partir, salir.

departed *a.* difunto-a; ausente.

depend *v.* depender.

dependence, dependency *n.* dependencia, subordinación; ____ producing drugs / drogas adictivas, de dependencia.

dependent *a.* dependiente.

depersonalization *n.* despersonalización, pérdida de la personalidad.

depilate *v.* depilar, acción de quitar o extirpar pelo.

depilation *n.* depilación, procedimiento de extirpación del pelo y la raíz.

depilatory *n.* depilatorio.

deplete *v.* agotar, vaciar; depauperarse.

depleted *a.* agotado-a, vaciado-a, depauperado-a.

depletion *n.* depleción. 1. acción de vaciar; 2. pérdida o remoción de los líquidos del cuerpo.

deposit *n.* depósito; *v.* depositar.

depravation *n.* depravación.

depress *v.* deprimir; desalentar, desanimar.

depressant *n.* depresor; tranquilizante; ____ drug / medicamento tranquilizante.

depressed *a.* deprimido-a, abatido-a; *v.* **to become** ____ / deprimirse.

depression *n.* depresión. 1. *psic.* sensación de tristeza o melancolía acompañada de apatía y estados de abatimiento; 2. cavidad.

depressive *a.* depresivo-a, deprimente; ___ disorder / trastorno ___ .

depressor *n.* depresor. 1. agente usado para reducir un nivel establecido de una función o actividad del organismo; 2. tranquilizante que produce depresión.

depurate *v.* depurar.

depurated *a.* depurado-a.

depuration *n.* depuración, purificación.

derange *v.* perturbar, desordenar, causar trastorno.

deranged *a.* perturbado-a; trastornado-a; ___ metabolic process / trastorno del proceso metabólico.

derangement *Fr.* trastorno, desequilibrio, irregularidad de una función del cuerpo.

derivation *n.* derivación. 1. desviación, curso alterado o lateral que tiene lugar por anastomosis o por una característica anatómica natural; 2. descendencia.

derive *v.* derivar, inferir, deducir; descender, proceder.

dermabrasion *n.* dermabrasión, abrasión cutánea, proceso empleado para eliminar los nevos y cicatrices de la acné.

dermatitis *n.* dermatitis, dermitis, cualquier infl. de la piel.

dermatological *a.* dermatológico-a, rel. a la dermis.

dermatologist *n.* dermatólogo-a, especialista en dermatología.

dermatology *n.* dermatología, parte de la medicina que estudia la piel, su estructura, sus funciones y el tratamiento de la misma.

dermatoma *n.* dermatoma, neoplasma de la piel.

dermatome *n.* dermátomo, instrumento quirúrgico empleado para cortar capas o tejidos finos de la piel.

dermatomere *n.* dermatomera, segmento del tegumento embrionario.

dermatomycosis *n.* dermatomicosis, infl. de la piel producida por hongos.

dermatomyositis *n.* dermatomiositis, enfermedad del tejido conectivo con manifestaciones de dermatitis, edema e infl. de los músculos.

dermatopathy, dermatosis *n.* dermatopatía, dermatosis, cualquier enfermedad de la piel.

dermatophiliasis *n.* dermatofiliasis, infección de la piel producida por pulgas o niguas.

dermatophyte *n.* dermatófito, hongo parásito que ataca la piel.

dermatophytosis *n.* dermatofitosis, pie de atleta, infección fungosa producida por dermatófilos.

dermatosyphilis *n.* dermatosífilis, manifestación sifilítica en la piel.

dermic *a.* dermal, dermático-a, cutáneo-a.

dermis, derma *n.* dermis, piel.

dermoid *a.* dermoideo-a, semejante o rel. a la piel; ___ cyst / quiste ___ , de origen congénito, gen. benigno.

descend *v.* descender, bajar; derivarse.

descendant *n., a.* descendiente.

descending *a.* descendente, descendiente; ___ aorta / aorta ___ , parte mayor de la aorta; ___ colon / colon ___ .

descent *n.* descenso, bajada; descendencia, sucesión.

describe *v.* describir.

described *a.* descrito-a, narrado-a.

desensitize *v.* desensibilizar, reducir o eliminar una sensibilidad de origen físico o emocional.

desert *n.* desierto, yermo, páramo.

deserve *v.* merecer.

desexualizing *n.* desexualización, 1. eliminación de un impulso sexual; 2. castración.

desiccant *a.* desecante, que tiene la propiedad de secar.

desiccate *v.* desecar, secar, quitar la humedad.

desiccated *a. pp.* de **to desiccate**, desecado-a.

desirable *a.* deseado-a; conveniente.

desire *n.* deseo, ansia; *v.* desear, ansiar.

desk *n.* escritorio; **front** ___ / mesa de admisión.

desmoid *a.* desmoide, en forma de ligamento.

desmoma *n.* desmoma, tumor del tejido conjuntivo.

despair *n.* desesperación; *v.* [*to lose hope*] perder la esperanza; desesperarse.

despondency *n.* desaliento; desesperación.

despondent *a.* desesperado-a, desalentado-a; *v.* **to be** ___ / estar ___ .

desquamation *n.* descamación, exfoliación, desprendimiento de la piel en forma de escamas.

destroy *v.* destruir, aniquilar; arruinar.

detach *v.* separar, desprender, despegar; desprenderse; soltarse.

detachment *n.* desprendimiento, separación; ___ of the retina / ___ de la retina.

detail *n.* detalle; **in** ___ / con detalle, detalladamente; *v.* detallar, destacar; **to go into** ___ / explicar todo detalladamente.

detain *v.* detener, parar.

detect *v.* detectar, descubrir.

detector *n.* detector, revelador, descubridor.

detergent *n.* detergente, agente limpiador, *a.* detergente, limpiador-a.

deteriorate *v.* deteriorar, desmejorar; deteriorarse; desmejorarse.

deteriorization *n.* deteriorización, deterioro, desmejoramiento.

determinant *n.* determinante, elemento que predomina o causa una determinación.

determination *n.* determinación, decisión, resolución.

determine *v.* determinar, decidir; resolver; concluir.

determined *a.* decidido-a; [*in tests*] comprobado-a.

determinism *n.* determinismo, teoría que establece que todo fenómeno físico o psíquico está predeterminado y no es influído por la voluntad individual.

detorsion *n.* destorsión, 1. corrección de la curvatura o malformación de una estructura; 2. corrección quirúrgica de la torsión de un testículo o del intestino.

detoxicate *v.* desintoxicar.

detoxification *n.* destoxificación, reducción de las propiedades tóxicas de una sustancia.

detoxify *v.* destoxificar, desentoxicar, extraer sustancias tóxicas.

detrimental *a.* perjudicial, nocivo-a.

detritus *n. pl.* desechos.

detrusor *n.* detrusor, músculo que expulsa o echa hacia afuera.

deuteranopia *n.* deuteranopía, ceguera al color verde.

develop *v.* [*to expand, to grow*] desarrollar, crecer, progresar; evolucionar; avanzar, progresar; [*film*] revelar; [*symptom*] surgir; manifestarse.

developed *a.* desarrollado-a; revelado-a, manifestado-a.

development *n.* desarrollo; adelanto; progreso, crecimiento; [*germs*] proliferación.

deviation *n.* desviación, desvío. 1. alejamiento de una pauta establecida; 2. *psic.* aberración mental; mala conducta, mal comportamiento.

device *n.* dispositivo; mecanismo.

devious *a.* desviado-a; descaminado-a; extraviado-a.

devise *v.* idear, inventar, considerar.

devitalize *v.* devitalizar, debilitar, privar de la fuerza vital.

devolution *n.* devolución. *V.* **catabolism.**

Dexedrine *n.* Dexedrina, tipo de anfetamina, estimulante del sistema nervioso.

dexter *a.* diestro-a; a la derecha.

dextrocardia *n.* dextrocardia, dislocación del corazón hacia la derecha.

dextromanual *a.* dextromanual, preferencia por el uso de la mano derecha.

dextroposition *n.* dextroposición, desplazamiento hacia la derecha.

dextrose *n.* dextrosa, glucosa, forma de azúcar simple, *pop.* azúcar de uva.

diabetes *n.* diabetes, enfermedad que se manifiesta por excesiva emisión de orina.

diabetes insipidus *n.* diabetes insípida nefrógena, causada por una deficiencia en el gasto de hormona antidiurética.

diabetes mellitus *n.* diabetes mellitus, diabetes causada por una deficiencia en la producciòn de insulina que resulta en hiperglucemia y glucosuria; ___ non insulin dependant / ___ sin dependencia de insulina.

diabetic *a.* diabético-a; rel. a la diabetes o que padece de ella; ___ angiopathies / angiopatías ___ -s; brittle ___ / ___ inestable; ___ coma / coma ___ , por falta de insulina; ___ diet / dieta ___ ; ___ neuropathy / neuropatía ___ ; ___ retinopathy / retinopatía ___ .

diabetogenic *a.* diabetogénico-a, que produce diabetes.

diabetograph *n.* diabetógrafo, aparato para medir la proporción de glucosa en la orina.

diacetemia *n.* diacetemia, presencia de ácido diacético en la sangre.

diacetic acid *n.* ácido diacético.

diacetylmorphine *n.* diacetilmorfina, heroína.

diagnose *v.* diagnosticar, dar un diagnóstico, hacer un diagnóstico o diagnosis.

diagnosis *n.* diagnóstico, diagnosis, determinación de la enfermedad del paciente; computer ___ / ___ por computadora; differential ___ / ___ diferencial, por comparación; ___ error / errores de ___ ; physical ___ / ___ físico, por medio de un examen físico completo.

diagnostic *n.* diagnóstico; ___ chart / ficha de ___ ; ___ imaging / ___ de imágenes por medios radioactivos.

diagonal *a.* diagonal, sección transversal.

diagram *n.* diagrama.

dialysated *a.* dializado-a, que ha sido separado por diálisis.

dialysis *n.* diálisis, procedimiento para filtrar y eliminar toxinas presentes en la sangre de pacientes con insuficiencia renal; ___ machine / aparato de ___ (riñon artificial); peritoneal ___ / ___ peritoneal; renal ___ / ___ renal.

dialyzated *a.* dializado-a, en diálisis rel. al líquido que pasa por la membrana separadora o dializadora.

dialyze *v.* dializar, hacer una diálisis.

dialyzer *n.* dializador, instrumento usado en el proceso de diálisis.

diameter *n.* diámetro.

diapedesis *n.* diapédesis, paso de células sanguíneas, esp. leucocitos a través de la pared intacta de un vaso capilar.

diaper *n.* pañal; culero; *Mex. A.* pavico; *Mex.* zapeta; ___ rash / eritema de los pañales, erupción.

diaphoretic *n.* diaforético, agente que estimula la transpiración.

diaphragm *n.* diafragma. 1. músculo que separa el tórax del abdomen; 2. anticonceptivo uterino.

diaphragmatic *a.* diafragmático-a, rel. al diafragma.

diaphysis *n.* diáfisis, porción media de un hueso largo tal como se presenta en el húmero.

diaplasis *n.* diaplasis, reducción de una luxación o fractura.

diarrhea *n.* diarrea; acute ___ / ___ severa; dysenteric ___ / ___ disentérica; ___ of the new born / ___ epidémica del recién nacido; ___ infantile / ___ infantil; ner vous ___ / ___ nerviosa; pancreatic ___ / ___ pancreática; travelers' ___ / ___ del viajero.

diarrheal *a.* diarreico-a rel. a la diarrea.

diarthrosis *n.* diartrosis, tipo de articulación que permite movimiento amplio, tal como la de la cadera.

diastase *n.* diastasa, enzima que actúa en la digestión de almidones y azúcares.

diastasis *n.* diastasis. 1. separación anormal de partes unidas esp. huesos; 2. tiempo de descanso del ciclo cardíaco inmediatamente anterior a la sístole.

diastole *n.* diástole, fase de dilatación del corazón durante la cual se llenan de sangre las cavidades cardíacas.

diastolic *a.* diastólico-a, rel. a la diástole del corazón; ___ pressure / presión ___ .

diathermy *n.* diatermia, aplicación de calor a los tejidos del cuerpo por medio de una corriente eléctrica.

diathesis *n.* diátesis, propensión constitucional u orgánica a contraer ciertas enfermedades; hemorrhagic ___ / ___ hemorrágica; rheumatic ___ / ___ reumática.

diatrizoate meglumine *n.* diatrizoate de meglumina, sustancia radiopaca que se usa para hacer visibles las arterias y venas del corazón y del cerebro así como la vesícula, los riñones y la vejiga.

diazepam *n.* diazepam, nombre comercial Valium, sedante y relajador muscular.

dichorionic *n.* dicoriónico, que tiene dos coriones.

dichotomy, dichotomization *n.* dicotomía, dicotomización, división en dos partes; bifurcación.

dichroism *n.* dicroísmo, propiedad de algunas soluciones o cristales de diferenciar colores a través de la luz reflejada o transmitida.

dichromic *a.* dicrómico-a, rel. a dos colores.

dichromophil *a.* dicromófilo-a, que permite la coloración básica y ácida.

dictate *v.* dictar, ordenar.

Dicumarol *n.* Dicumarol, Dicoumarin, anticoagulante usado en el tratamiento de embolismo y trombosis.

didactic *a.* didáctico-a, instructivo-a, que se enseña por medio de libros de texto y conferencias a diferencia de un planteamiento clínico.

didelphic *a.* didélfico-a, rel. a un útero doble.

didymitis *n.* didimitis. *V.* **orchitis.**

die *n.* molde, troquel; *v.* morir, fallecer, dejar de existir; morirse.

diembryony *n.* diembrionismo, producción de dos embriones de un solo óvulo.

diencephalon *n.* diencéfalo, parte del cerebro.

dienestrol *n.* dienestrol, estrógeno sintético.

diet *n.* dieta, régimen; balanced ___ / ___ balanceada, equilibrada; bland ___ / ___ blanda; diabetic ___ / ___ diabética; gluten-free ___ / ___ libre de gluten; low

salt ____ / ____ baja de sal; liquid ____ /
____ líquida; salt free ____ / ____ sin sal;
weight reduction ____ / ____ para bajar de
peso.

dietary *a.* dietético-a; alimenticio-a; ____
vitamins / vitaminas ____ -s.

dietetic *a.* dietético-a, rel. a la dieta o aplicado a ésta.

dietetics *n.* dietética, ciencia que regula el régimen alimenticio para preservar o recuperar la salud.

dietitian *n.* dietista, especialista en nutrición.

different *a.* diferente, distinto-a.

differential *a.* diferencial, rel. a la diferenciación; ____ diagnosis / diagnóstico ____.

differentiate *v.* diferenciar.

differentiation *n.* diferenciación, comparación y distinción de una sustancia, enfermedad o entidad con otra o de otra.

difficult *a.* difícil.

difficulty *n.* dificultad; penalidad; obstáculo.

diffraction *n.* difracción. 1. desviación de dirección; 2. la descomposición de un rayo de luz y sus componentes al atravesar un cristal o prisma; ____ pattern / patrón de ____.

diffusion *n.* difusión. 1. proceso de difundir; 2. diálisis a través de una membrana.

dig *vi.* excavar, extraer.

digest *v.* digerir.

digestant *n.* digestivo, agente que facilita la digestión.

digestion *n.* digestión, transformación de líquidos y sólidos en sustancias más simples para ser asimiladas por el organismo; gastric ____ / ____ gástrica; intestinal ____ / ____ intestinal, del intestino; pancreatic ____ / ____ pancreática.

digestive *a.* digestivo-a; rel. a la digestión; ____ system / sistema ____.

digit *n.* dedo.

digital *a.* digital, rel. a los dedos.

digitalis *n.* digitalis, agente cardiotónico que se obtiene de las hojas secas de la *Digitalis purpurea*.

digitalization *n.* digitalización, uso terapeútico de digitalis.

digitation *n.* digitación, proceso en forma de dedos.

digitoxin *n.* digitoxina, glucósido cardiotónico obtenido de digitalis y usado en el tratamiento de la congestión pasiva del corazón.

digitus *n.* dígito, dedo; ____ malleus, mallet

finger / dedo en martillo; ____ valgus, varus / desviación de un dedo.

Digoxin *n.* Digoxina, nombre comercial de un derivado de digitalis que se emplea en el tratamiento de arritmias cardíacas.

dihydrostreptomycin *n.* dihidroestreptomicina, antibiótico derivado de la estreptomicina más usado que ésta por causar menos neurotoxicidad.

Dilantin *n.* Dilantin, droga antiespasmódica.

dilatation, dilation *n.* dilatación, aumento o expansión anormal de un órgano u orificio.

dilate *v.* dilatar, expandir.

dilation and curettage (D&C) *n.* dilatación y curetaje, *pop.* raspado.

dilator *n.* dilatador. 1. músculo que dilata un órgano al contraerse. 2. instrumento quirúrgico para expandir o dilatar un orificio o paredes; Hegar's ____ / ____ de Hegar, instrumento usado para dilatar el canal uterino.

diluent *a.* diluente, diluyente, agente o medicamento que tiene la propiedad de diluir.

dim *a.* débil, mortecino-a; confuso-a; opaco-a.

dimension *n.* dimensión, medida de un cuerpo.

Dimercaprol *n.* Dimercaprol, antídoto usado en el envenenamiento producido por metales tales como oro y mercurio.

dimethyl sulfoxide *n.* dimetilsulfóxido, medicamento antiinflamatorio y analgésico.

dimetria *n.* dimetría, útero o matriz doble.

diminish *v.* disminuir, reducir; amortiguar.

diminution *n.* disminución, proceso de disminuir o reducir.

diminutive *n. gr.* diminutivo; *a.* diminuto-a, pequeño-a.

dimness *n.* opacidad; obscurecimiento de la vista.

dimorphism *n.* dimorfismo, caracterización de dos formas diferentes; sexual ____ / ____ sexual, hermafrodismo.

dimple *n.* hoyuelo o hendidura en la piel, esp. en la mejilla o la barbilla.

dinner *n.* cena.

diopter, dioptre *n.* dioptría, unidad de medida de refracción en un lente.

dioptometer *n.* dioptómetro, instrumento usado para medir la refracción ocular.

dioptric *a.* dióptrico, referente a la refracción de la luz.

dioptrics *n.* dióptrica, ciencia que trata de la formación de imágenes y lentes.

diphallus *n.* difalo, duplicación parcial o completa del pene.

diphasic *a.* difásico-a, que tiene lugar en dos etapas diferentes.

diphenhydramine *n.* difenhidramina, nombre comercial Benadryl, antihistamínico.

diphonia *n.* difonía, producción de dos tonos diferentes.

diphtheria *n.* difteria, enfermedad contagiosa e infecciosa aguda, causada por el bacilo *Corynebacterium diphtheriae* (Klebs-Löffler), caracterizada por la formación de membranas falsas esp. en la garganta; ____ antitoxin / antitoxina contra la ____.

diphtherotoxin *n.* difterotoxina, toxina derivada del cultivo de bacilos de la difteria.

diplacusis *n.* diplacusia, desorden auditivo caracterizado por la percepción de dos tonos por cada sonido producido.

diplegia *n.* diplejía, parálisis bilateral; facial ____ / ____ facial, parálisis de ambos lados de la cara; spastic ____ / ____ espástica.

diplocoria *n.* diplocoria, pupila doble.

diploc *n.* diploc, tejido esponjoso localizado entre las dos capas compactas de los huesos craneales.

diploid *a.* diploide, que posee dos combinaciones de cromosomas.

diplopagus *n.* diplópagos, mellizos unidos, cada uno de cuerpo casi completo, pero que comparten algunos órganos.

diplopia *n.* diplopía, visión doble.

dipsesis, dipsosis *n.* dipsesis, dipsosis, sed insaciable.

dipsomania *n.* dipsomanía, tipo de alcoholismo en el cual el paciente sufre una urgencia incontrolable por consumir sustancias alcohólicas.

direct *a.* directo-a; *v.* dirigir, ordenar; instruir.

direction *n.* dirección; instrucción.

directory *n.* directorio; junta; telephone ____ / guía telefónica.

dirty *a.* sucio-a, mugriento-a; *pop.* cochino-a.

disability *n.* incapacidad, inhabilidad; invalidez, impedimento; disminución de una capacidad física o mental.

disabled *a.* inválido-a; impedido-a; incapacitado-a.

disadvantage *n.* desventaja; alguna capacidad disminuída.

disagree *v.* no estar de acuerdo; disentir; altercar, argumentar.

disagreeable *a.* desagradable; ofensivo-a.

disappoint *v.* contrariar, desengañar.

disappointment *n.* contrariedad; desengaño, desilusión.

disarticulated *a.* desarticulado-a, dislocado-a, rel. a un hueso separado de la articulación.

disarticulation *n.* desarticulación, separación o amputación de dos o más huesos articulados entre sí.

disaster *n.* desastre; desdicha, infortunio.

disbelief *n.* incredulidad, escepticismo.

disbelieve *v.* desconfiar, dudar.

discard *n.* desecho, descarte; *v.* descartar, desechar.

discharge *n.* flujo; supuración; excreción; descarga; derrame; ____ summary / sumario o nota de egreso; *v.* [*fluid, pus*] secretar, supurar; [*from the hospital*] dar de alta; librar; soltar; [*electricity*] descargar.

discipline *n.* disciplina, comportamiento estricto.

discitis *n.* discitis, infl. de un disco.

disclose *v.* revelar, descubrir; destapar, abrir.

discogenic *a.* discogénico, rel. a un disco intervertebral.

discolor *v.* cambiar de color, quitar el color.

discolored *a.* descolorido-a, [*skin*] ensombrecido-a, sin color, empañado-a.

discomfort *n.* incomodidad, malestar, aflicción.

discomposed *a.* descompuesto-a; desordenado-a.

disconnect *v.* desconectar, desunir, quitar la conexión; separar.

disconnected *a.* desconectado-a, separado-a, sin conexión, desunido-a.

discontented *a.* descontento-a; insatisfecho-a; disgustado-a.

discontinue *v.* suspender, interrumpir, descontinuar; to ____ the medication / ____ la medicina.

discontinued *a.* suspendido-a, interrumpido-a, descontinuado-a.

discourage *v.* desanimar, desalentar; to ____ from / disuadir.

discouraged *a.* desanimado-a, desalentado-a.

discredit *v.* desacreditar.

discreet *a.* discreto-a, prudente.

discrepancy *n.* desacuerdo, discrepancia, diferencia.

discretion *n.* discreción, prudencia; acuerdo.

discriminate *v.* discriminar; mostrar prejuicio; hacer notar diferencias.

discrimination *n.* discriminación; diferenciación de raza o cualidad.

discuss *v.* discutir, argumentar.

discussion *n.* discusión, debate, argumento.

disease *n.* enfermedad, dolencia, anomalía; indisposición; a crippling ___ / ___ que causa invalidez; *v.* causar una enfermedad, contagiar, enfermar, dañar, hacer daño.

disengage *v.* librar, separar, desplazar.

disengagement *n.* desencajamiento, separación, desunión; [*in obstetrics*] desplazamiento de la cabeza del feto de la vulva.

disfiguration *n.* desfiguración, desfiguramiento.

disfigure *v.* desfigurar, afear.

disillusion *n.* desencanto, desilusión; *v.* perder la ilusión; desilusionarse.

disinfect *v.* desinfectar, esterilizar.

disinfectant *n.* desinfectante, antiséptico, esterilizante.

disintegrate *v.* desintegrar, reducir a fragmentos o partículas; desintegrarse; separarse.

disintegration *n.* desintegración, descomposición, separación.

disjoint *v.* desunir, separar, desarticular.

disjointed *a.* desarticulado-a, descoyuntado-a, dislocado-a.

disjunction *n.* disyunción, desunión, separación de cromosomas en la anafase de la división celular.

disk, disc *n.* disco; herniated ___ / desplazamiento del ___ intervertebral.

dislike *n.* aversión, antipatía; *v.* aborrecer, desagradar, repugnar; I ___ this medicine / no me gusta, me desagrada, me repugna esta medicina.

dislocate *v.* dislocar, descoyuntar, desencajar.

dislocation *n.* luxación, desviación, desplazamiento de una articulación; closed ___ / ___ cerrada; complicated ___ / ___ complicada; congenital ___ / ___ congénita.

dismember *v.* desmembrar, amputar; [*to break apart*] despedazar.

dismemberment *n.* desmembración, amputación.

dismiss *v.* rechazar; descartar; [*an employee*] despedir.

disobedience *n.* desobediencia.

disobedient *a.* desobediente.

disorder *n.* desorden, desarreglo, trastorno; mental ___ / desarreglo emocional, trastorno mental.

disorganized *a.* desorganizado-a.

disorient *v.* desorientar.

disorientation *n.* desorientación, incapacidad de encontrar una dirección o local, de reconocer a otras personas, y de establecer una relación temporal lógica.

disoriented *a.* desorientado-a; confundido-a, confuso-a.

dispensary *n.* dispensario, clínica, establecimiento que proporciona asistencia médica y dispensa medicamentos.

dispense *v.* dispensar; distribuir.

disperse *v.* dispersar, disipar.

dispirited *a.* descorazonado-a, desalentado-a.

displace *v.* desplazar; poner fuera de lugar.

displaced *a.* desplazado-a; dislocado-a; *v.* to be ___ / estar fuera de lugar, estar ___; [*bone, joint*] estar dislocado-a.

displacement *n.* desplazamiento; dislocación; *psic.* transferencia de una emoción a otra distinta de la inicial.

display *n.* muestra, exhibición; *v.* mostrar, exhibir, extender.

displease *v.* desagradar; incomodar.

displeased *a.* descontento-a; insatisfecho-a.

disposable *a.* desechable; disponible.

dispose *v.* disponer; desechar; to ___ of / deshacerse de.

disposition *n.* disposición; tendencia.

disproportion *n.* desproporción; desproporcionamiento.

disproportionate *a.* desproporcionado-a, desigual, sin simetria.

disprove *v.* refutar, desaprobar.

disregard *v.* ignorar; no prestar atención, descuidar.

disrespect *n.* falta de respeto, irreverencia; *v.* desatender; dejar de respetar, faltar el respeto.

dissect *v. cirg.* disecar, acto de dividir y cortar; hacer una disección.

dissecting hook *n.* erina.

dissecting knife *n.* escalpelo, bisturí.

dissection *n.* disección.

disseminated *a.* diseminado-a, difundido-a; ___ intravascular coagulation / coagulación intravascular ___.

dissemination *n.* diseminación, esparción.

dissipation *n.* disipación, vida disipada; dispersión.

dissociation *n.* disociación, separación.

dissolution *n.* disolución; descomposición; muerte.

dissolve *v.* disolver, diluir, deshacer; destruir.

dissolved *a. pp.* de **to dissolve,** disuelto-a, diluido-a.

dissolvent *a.* disolvente, capaz de disolver.

distal *a.* distal, distante, rel. a la parte más lejana; ____ end / extremo ____.

distance *n.* distancia, lejanía; **at a** ____ / a lo lejos; *v.* **to keep a** ____ / mantener a ____.

distaste *n.* aversión, disgusto.

distend *v.* distender, dilatar; distenderse, dilatarse.

distension, distention *n.* distensión, condición de dilatación o expansión.

distill *v.* destilar, crear vapor por medio de calor.

distillation *n.* destilación.

distinct *a.* diferente; definido-a; **-ly** *adv.* definidamente; con diferencia, con precisión.

distinguish *v.* distinguir; diferenciar, clasificar.

distinguished *a.* [*person*] distinguido-a; [*characteristics*] señalado-a, marcado-a.

distobuccal *a.* distobucal, rel. a la superficie distal y bucal de un diente.

distoclusion *n.* distoclusión, mordida irregular.

distort *v.* torcer, deformar, desfigurar.

distorted *a.* torcido-a; deformado-a; desfigurado-a.

distortion *n.* distorsión, deformación, desfiguración.

distract *v.* distraer, interrumpir.

distracted *a.* distraído-a, [*madness*] trastornado-a.

distraction *n.* distracción. 1. *psic.* inhabilidad para concentrarse en una experiencia determinada; 2. separación de articulaciones sin dislocación.

distraught *a.* atolondrado-a, confundido-a, desconcertado-a; [*irrational*] demente.

distress *n.* angustia, apuro, preocupación, aflicción; *v.* **to be in** ____ / estar angustiado-a, estar afligido-a.

distressed *a.* adolorido-a, angustiado-a, afligido-a.

distribute *v.* distribuir, dispensar, repartir.

distrust *n.* desconfianza, falta de confianza; *v.* desconfiar.

disturb *v.* perturbar, incomodar, molestar, inquietar.

disturbance *n.* confusión; disturbio.

diuresis *n.* diuresis, aumento en la secreción de orina.

diuretic *a.* diurético, rel. a agentes que provocan aumento en la secreción de orina.

diuria *n.* diuria, frecuencia de excreción de orina durante el día.

diver *n.* buzo-a; ____ 's paralysis / parálisis de los ____ -s.

divergence *n.* divergencia, separación de un centro común.

divergent *a.* divergente, movimiento en sentido opuesto; ____ reactor / reactor de potencia ____.

diverticulitis *n.* diverticulosis, diverticulitis, infl. de un divertículo, esp. de pequeños sacos que se forman en el colon.

diverticulum *n.* (*pl.* **diverticula**) divertículo, saco o bolsa que se origina en la cavidad de un órgano o estructura.

divide *v.* dividir, repartir.

divided *a.* dividido-a, separado-a.

division *n.* división, desunión; separación.

divorce *n.* divorcio, disolución.

divulsion *n.* divulsión, separación o desprendimiento.

dizygotic twins *n. pl.* gemelos dicigóticos, mellizos de embriones producidos por dos óvulos.

dizziness *n.* mareo, sensación de desvanecimiento, vahído.

dizzy *a.* mareado-a.

do *vi. aux.* hacer; **How do you** ____? / ¿cómo está usted?, ¿cómo estás tú? [*introduction*] mucho gusto; **What do you** ____? / ¿Qué hace usted?, ¿ qué haces tú?; **whatever you** ____ / cualquier cosa que haga; hagas; ____ **it!** / ¡hágalo!,¡hazlo!; ____ **not** ____ **it!** / ¡No lo haga!,¡ no lo hagas!, **to** ____ **one's best** / hacer lo mejor posible; **to** ____ **harm** / hacer daño; **to** ____ **without** / pasar sin, prescindir de; **that will** ____ / eso es suficiente; ____ **you cough a lot?** / ¿Tose mucho?, ¿toses mucho?; **he, she does** / él, ella hace. (**Do** is not translated in Spanish when used as an auxiliary verb.)

doctor *n.* doctor-a, médico-a; ____ 's discretion / al criterio del ____; según opinión facultativa.

document *n.* documento

documentation *n.* documentación.

doer *n.* hacedor-a, agente, ejecutor-a.

dog *n.* perro-a; ___ **bite** / mordida de ___.

dolichocephalic *a.* dolicocefálico-a, de cráneo alargado y estrecho.

domestic *a.* doméstico-a.

domiciliary *a.* domiciliario-a, rel. a lo que se trata en el domicilio.

dominance *n.* dominancia, predominio.

dominant *a.* dominante, característica primordial; ___ **characteristics** / características ___ -s, con tendencia a heredarse; ___ **factor** / factor ___.

donate *v.* donar, regalar.

donative *n.* donativo, donación.

donor *n.* donante, donador; persona contribuyente; ___ **card** / tarjeta de ___.

Donovania granulomatosis, Donovan's body *n.* Donovania granulomatosis, cuerpos de Donovan, infección bacteriana que afecta la piel y las membranas mucosas de los genitales y el ano.

door *n.* puerta; [*entrance*] ___ de entrada; back ___ / ___ de atrás.

dopamine *n.* dopamina, neurotransmisor, sustancia sintetizada por la glándula suprarrenal que aumenta la presión arterial; gen. usada en el tratamiento de choque.

dope *n.* narcótico; ___ **fiend** / narcómano-a; ___ **addict** / drogadicto-a.

dormancy *n.* sueño pesado, estupor, letargo.

dorsal *a.* dorsal, situado-a en la parte posterior del cuerpo o rel. a ésta; ___ **recumbent position** / posición recumbente; ___ **slit** / fisura o corte ___.

dorsalgia *n.* dorsalgia, dolor de espalda.

dorsiflexion *n.* dorsiflexión, movimiento de doblar o de doblarse hacia atrás.

dorsocephalad *a.* dorsocefálico-a, situado-a en la parte posterior de la cabeza.

dorsodynia *n.* dorsodinia, dolor en los músculos de la parte superior de la espalda.

dorsolateral *a.* dorsolateral, rel. a la espalda y un costado.

dorsolumbar *a.* dorsolumbar, lumbodorsal, rel. a la espalda y la región lumbar de la columna.

dorsospinal *a.* dorsoespinal, rel. a la espalda y la espina dorsal.

dorsum *n.* (*pl.* **dorsa**) dorso. 1. porción posterior, tal como el dorso de la mano o el pie; 2. espalda.

dose, dosage *n.* dosis, dosificación; average ___ / ___ promedio, media; booster ___ / ___ de refuerzo; daily ___ / ___ diaria; divided ___ / ___ dividida; lethal ___ /

___ letal; radiation ___ / ___ de radiación; therapeutic ___ / ___ terapéutica; unit ___ / ___ individual; volume ___ / ___ volumen.

dosimeter *n.* dosímetro, instrumento usado para detectar y medir la exposición a radiaciones.

dosimetry *n.* dosimetría, determinación precisa y sistemática de las dosis de radiación.

dossier *n.* expediente.

dot *n.* cúmulo, mancha.

dotage *n.* senilidad, chochera, chochez.

double *a.* doble; ___ **edged** / con dos bordes; ___ **personality** / desdoblamiento de la personalidad; ___ **uterus** / útero didelfo, útero o matriz doble; *v.* duplicar.

doubt *n.* duda, incertidumbre.

douche *n.* 1. ducha, regadera; 2. lavado vaginal; irrigación; *v.* tomar una ducha; ducharse.

Douglas cul-de-sac *n.* saco de Douglas, pliegue del peritoneo que se introduce entre el recto y el útero.

down *adv.* abajo, hacia abajo; ___ **below** / más abajo; *v.* **to cut** ___ / recortar; reducir; **to lie** ___ / acostarse, recostarse.

downcast *a.* deprimido-a, alicaído-a, abatido-a.

Down's syndrome *n.* síndrome de Down, anormalidad citogenética del cromosoma 21 caracterizada por retraso mental y facciones mongoloides.

downstairs *adv.* abajo; *v.* **to go** ___ / bajar las escaleras.

downtown *n.* centro (de la ciudad).

doze *v.* dormitar, quedarse medio dormido.

dozen *n.* docena.

draft *n.* 1. líquido prescripto para ser tomado en una sola dosis; 2. [*air*] corriente de aire; 3. [*art design*] diseño, bosquejo.

drain *n.* desagüe, escurridor; *v.* drenar, desaguar, eliminar una secreción o pus de una parte infectada.

drainage *n.* drenaje; open ___ / ___ abierto; continuous ___ / ___ continuo; postural ___ / ___ postural, por gravedad; ___ **tube** / tubo de ___; tidal ___ / ___ periódico.

Dramamine, dimenhydrinate *n.* Dramamina, dimenhidrinato, anthistamínico usado en el tratamiento de naúsea.

dramatism *n. psic.* dramatismo, conducta espectacular y lenguaje dramatizado manifestados en ciertos trastornos mentales.

drape *v. cirg.* cubrir el campo operatorio con paños esterilizados.

drastic *a.* drástico-a; ____ therapy / tratamiento ____.

draw *vi.* extraer, sacar; [*air*] aspirar; [*art*] dibujar, trazar; **to** ____ **back** / retroceder; **to** ____ **in** / atraer; incitar; **to** ____ **near** / acercarse, arrimarse.

drawer *n.* gaveta, cajón.

dream *n.* sueño, ilusión; *v.* soñar, imaginar, hacerse ilusiones.

dreary *a.* monótono-a, escabroso-a, pesado-a.

drenched *a.* empapado-a, mojado-a.

drepanocyte *n.* drepanocito, glóbulo rojo de células falciformes.

dress *n.* vestido; *v.* [*a wound*] vendar, curar; [*a corpse*] amortajar; [*put on clothes*] vestirse.

dressing *n.* venda de gasa u otro material para cubrir una herida.

dribble *n.* goteo.

drill *n.* taladro; [*dentistry*] fresa.

drink *n.* bebida, trago; *v.* beber, tomar.

drinker *a.* bebedor, tomador.

drip *n.* gota, goteo; gotera; *v.* gotear.

drive *n.* paseo, vuelta; *v.* **to go for a** ____ / dar un paseo; *psic.* impulso; [*haste*] exigencia; [*energy*] energía, vigor; *vi.* [*vehicles*] conducir, manejar, guiar; **to** ____ **someone crazy** / enloquecer, volver loco-a.

drivel *n.* baba o saliva que sale por los extremos de la boca.

drop *n.* gota; caída; ____ **by** ____ / gota a gota; *v.* dejar caer; [*from school*] dejar la escuela; caerse.

droplet *n.* partícula, gotica; ____ infection / infección trasmitida por goticas o partículas.

dropper *n.* gotero.

dropsy *n.* hidropesía, acumulación excesiva de fluído seroso en una cavidad o tejido celular.

drought *n.* sequía.

drown *v.* ahogar; anegar; sumergir; sofocar; ahogarse.

drowning *n.* ahogamiento, acción de ahogar o ahogarse.

drowse *v.* adormecerse, adormitarse.

drowsiness *n.* sopor, somnolencia, abotagamiento, pesadez.

drug *n.* droga, medicamento, narcótico, barbitúrico; ____ abuse / uso excesivo de una ____ por adicción; ____ addict / narcóma-

no-a, drogadicto-a; ____ induced abnormality / anomalía causada por el uso de ____ -s; ____ interactions / interacciones de medicamentos; ____ resistance, microbial / resistencia microbiana a las ____.

drugged *a.* endrogado-a, drogado-a.

drunk *n.* borracho-a, ebrio-a.

drunkenness *n.* borrachera, embriaguez.

drunkometer *n.* instrumento que analiza el aliento de una persona para indicar el grado de consunción de alcohol.

dry *a.* seco-a; árido-a; *v.* secar; **to** ____ **out** / secarse.

dryness *n.* sequedad; aridez.

duct *n.* conducto, canal.

ductal *a.* rel. a un conducto o canal.

dues *n. pl.* deuda; obligación.

dull *a.* aburrido-a; [*pain*] dolor sordo; [*blade*] mellado-a.

dullness *n.* 1. matidez, resonancia disminuida en la palpación; 2. estado de aburrimiento, torpeza, estupidez; 3. [*instrument's edge*] melladura.

dumb *a.* mudo-a; torpe, estúpido-a.

dumping syndrome *n.* síndrome de vaciamiento gástrico demasiado rápido del contenido estomacal en el intestino delgado.

duodenal *a.* duodenal, rel. al duodeno.

duodenal ulcer *n.* úlcera duodenal.

duodenectomy *n. cirg.* duodenectomía, excisión del duodeno o una parte de éste.

duodenitis *n.* duodenitis, infl. del duodeno.

duodenoenterostomy *n. cirg.* duodenoenterostomía, anastomosis entre el duodeno y el intestino delgado.

duodenography *n.* duodenografía, radiografía del duodeno.

duodenojejunostomy *n. cirg.* duodenoyeyunostomía, operación para construir un pasaje artificial entre el yeyuno y el duodeno.

duodenoplasty *n. cirg.* duodenoplastia, operación para reparar el duodeno.

duodenostomy *n. cirg.* duodenostomía, creación de una salida en el duodeno, para aliviar la estenosis del píloro.

duodenum *n.* duodeno, parte esencial del canal alimenticio y del intestino delgado situado entre el píloro y el yeyuno.

duplication *n.* doblez, pliegue; duplicación.

durability *n.* durabilidad, duración.

durable *a.* durable, duradero-a; estable.

dura mater *n.* duramadre, membrana externa que cubre el encéfalo y la médula espinal.

duration *n.* duración, continuación.

duress *n.* coerción; coacción, **under** ___ / bajo ___.

during *prep.* durante; mientras, entre tanto.

dust *n.* polvo [*mortal remains*] cenizas, restos mortales; ___ count / conteo de partículas de ___ en el aire.

duty *n.* deber, obligación; [*tax*] impuesto; on ___ / de guardia.

dwarf *n.* enano-a, persona de estatura inferior a la normal; achondroplastic ___ / ___ acondroplástico-a; asexual ___ / ___ asexual; infantile ___ / ___ infantil; micrometic ___ / ___ micromético-a.

dwarfism *n.* enanismo, insuficiencia del desarrollo en el crecimiento de una persona.

dye *n.* tinte, color saturado; colorante.

dying *a.* moribundo-a, agonizante, mortal.

dynamics *n.* dinámica, estudio de órganos o partes del cuerpo en movimiento.

dyne *n.* unidad de fuerza necessria para acelerar un gramo de masa un centímetro por segundo.

dysacousis, dysacousia *n.* disacusis, disacusia, trastorno o dificultad para oír.

dysaphia *n.* disafia, entorpecimiento del sentido del tacto.

dysarthria *n.* disartria, dificultad del habla a causa de una afección de la lengua u otro músculo esencial al lenguaje.

dysautonomia *n.* disautonomía, trastorno del sistema nervioso autónomo.

dysbarism *n.* disbarismo, condición causada por decompresión.

dyscalcúlia *n.* discalculia, incapacidad de resolver problemas matemáticos debido a una anomalía cerebral.

dyscephalia *n.* discefalia, malformación de la cabeza y los huesos de la cara.

dyschiria *n.* disquiria, incapacidad de percibir sensaciones táctiles en ciertas áreas.

dyscinesia, dyskinesia *n.* discinesia, disquinesia, inhabilidad de realizar movimientos voluntarios tal como sucede en la enfermedad de Parkinson.

dyscoria *n.* discoria, pupila deformada.

dyscrasia *n.* discrasia, sinónimo de enfermedad.

dyscrinism *n.* discrinismo, funcionamiento anormal en la producción de secreciones esp. de las glándulas endocrinas.

dysdiadochokinesia *n.* disdiadocoquinesia, alteración de la función de detener un im-

pulso motor y substituirlo por otro diametralmente opuesto.

dysentery *n.* disentería, condición inflamatoria del intestino grueso causada por bacilos o parásitos con síntomas de diarrea y dolor abdominal; amebic ___ / ___ amebiana; bacilar ___ / ___ bacilar.

dysergia *n.* disergia, falta de coordinación en los movimientos musculares voluntarios.

dysesthesia *n.* disestesia, reacción excesiva de molestia a algunas sensaciones que por lo común no producen dolor.

dysfunction *n.* desorden, trastorno, malfuncionamiento de un órgano o parte.

dysgenesis *n.* disgénesis, defecto, malformación hereditaria.

dysgerminoma *n.* disgerminoma, tumor maligno del ovario.

dysgnosia *n.* disgnosia, cualquier impedimento relacionado con el intelecto.

dyshidrosis *n.* dishidrosis. 1. trastorno transpiratorio; 2. erupción recurrente de vesículas y picazón tal como en el pie de atleta.

dyslalia *n.* dislalia, impedimento en el habla debido a trastornos vocálicos funcionales.

dyslexia *n.* dislexia, impedimento en la lectura, dificultad que puede ser una condición hereditaria o causada por una lesión cerebral.

dysmenorrhea, dysmenorrhoea *n.* dismenorrea, menstruación difícil, acompañada de dolor y trastornos.

dysmetria *n.* dismetría, afección del cerebelo que incapacita el control de la distancia en movimientos musculares.

dysmetropsia *n.* dismetropsia, defecto en la apreciación visual del tamaño y forma de objetos.

dysmnesia *n.* dismnesia, trastorno de la memoria.

dysmorphism *n.* dismorfismo, malformación anatómica.

dysmyotomia *n.* dismiotonía, distonía muscular con tonicidad muscular anormal.

dysosmia *n.* disosmia, malfuncionamiento de la función olfatoria.

dysostosis *n.* disostosis, desarrollo deficiente de los huesos y dientes.

dyspareunia *n.* dispareunia, relaciones sexuales dolorosas.

dyspepsia *n.* dispepsia, indigestión caracterizada por irregularidades digestivas tales como eructos, náuseas, acidez, flatulencia y pérdida del apetito.

dyspermia *n.* dispermia, dolor durante la eyaculación.

dysphagia *n.* disfagia, dificultad al tragar a causa de una obstrucción.

dysphasia *n.* disfasia, defecto del habla causado por una lesión cerebral.

dysphonia *n.* disfonía, ronquera.

dysphoria *n.* disforia, excesiva depresión o angustia.

dyspigmentation *n.* despigmentación, decoloración anormal de la piel y el pelo.

dysplasia *n.* displasia, cambio o desarrollo anormal de los tejidos.

dyspnea, dyspnoea *n.* disnea, dificultad en la respiración.

dyspneic *a.* disneico-a, rel. a o que padece de disnea.

dyspraxia *n.* dispraxia, impedimento o dolor al realizar cualquier movimiento coordinado.

dysrhythmia *n.* disritmia, sin coordinación o ritmo.

dysstasia *n.* distasia, dificultad de mantenerse en pie.

dyssynergia *n.* disinergia. *V.* **ataxia.**

dystocia *n.* distocia, parto difícil, laborioso.

dystonia *n.* distonía, tonicidad alterada, esp. muscular.

dystrophy *n.* distrofia. 1. anomalía causada por malnutrición; 2. desarrollo defectuoso o de malformación.

dysuria *n.* disuria, dificultad o dolor al orinar.

E

E *abbr.* **emmetropia** / emetropía; **enema** / enema; **enzyme** / enzima; **eye** / ojo.

each *a.* cada; todo; cualquier-a; *pron.* cada uno, cada una; cada cual.

eager *a.* ansioso-a, deseoso-a; impaciente.

ear *n.* oreja; oído, órgano de la audición formado por el oído interior, el medio, y el externo; ____ cup / audífono; ____ lap / pabellón de la oreja; ____ lobe / lóbulo de la oreja; ____ plug / tapón auditivo; ____ protector / orejera; *a.* ____ deafening / ensordecedor-a.

earache *n.* dolor de oído.

eardrum *n.* tímpano del oído.

early *adv.* temprano, pronto; **at the earliest** / lo más ____ ; **as** ____ **as possible** / lo más ____ posible; ____ **age** / infancia; ____ can-

cer / cáncer incipiente; ____ **death** / muerte prematura; ____ **stage of** / la primera fase de, al principio de.

earn *v.* ganar, merecer.

earphone *n.* auricular, audífono.

earthquake *n.* terremoto, temblor de tierra, sismo.

earthworn *n.* lombriz de tierra; gusano.

ease *n.* alivio; descanso; facilidad; *v.* aliviar, facilitar; **to** ____ **one's mind** / tranquilizarse.

easily *adv.* fácilmente, sin dificultad.

east *n.* este, oriente; **to the** ____ / al ____ .

easy *a.* fácil; **within** ____ **reach** / al alcance de la mano.

easygoing *a.* sereno-a, tranquilo-a, de buena disposición.

eat *vi.* comer, sustentarse, ingerir alimentos; **to** ____ **breakfast** / desayunarse, tomar el desayuno; **to** ____ **lunch** / almorzar; tomar el almuerzo; **to** ____ **supper** / cenar.

eating *n.* acto de comer; *a.* rel. a comer o para comer.

ebullient *a.* hirviente; ____ **water** / agua ____ .

ebullition *n.* ebullición, acto de hervir.

eccentric *a.* excéntrico-a; extravagante.

ecchymosis *n.* equimosis, *pop.* morado, moratón. 1. cambio de color de la piel de azulado a verde debido a extravasación de sangre en el tejido subcutáneo celular; 2. contusión.

eccrine sweat glands *n.* glándulas sudoríparas ecrinas, secretoras de la transpiración.

echinococcosis *n.* equinococosis, infestación de equinococos; hepatic ____ / ____ hepática.

Echinococcus *n.* Equinococo, especie de tenia o trematodo.

echo *n.* eco, repercusión del sonido; *v.* **to make an** ____ / hacer eco.

echocardiogram *n.* ecocardiograma, gráfico producido por una ecocardiografía.

echocardiography *n.* ecocardiografía, método de diagnóstico por sonido ultrasónico para hacer visuales estructuras internas del corazón.

echoencephalography *n.* ecoencefalografía, técnica de diagnóstico por medio de ultrasonido para examinar estructuras intracraneales.

echogram *n.* ecograma, registro de una ecografía.

echography *n.* ecografía. V. **ultrasonography.**

echolalia *n.* ecolalia, trastorno de repetición involuntaria de sonidos y palabras después de oirlas.

Echo virus *n.* Echo virus, virus presente en el tracto gastrointestinal asociado con la meningitis, enteritis e infecciones respiratorias agudas.

eclampsia *n.* eclampsia, desorden convulsivo tóxico que se presenta gen. al final del embarazo o pocos días después del parto.

eclamptic *a.* eclámptico-a, rel. a la eclampsia.

ecology *n.* ecología, estudio de plantas y animales en relación con el ambiente.

economic *a.* económico-a; módico-a, moderado-a.

ecosystem *n.* ecosistema, microcosmo ecológico.

ecstasy *n. psic.* éxtasis, trance acompañado de un sentimiento de placer.

ectopic pregnancy *n.* embarazo ectópico, gestación fuera del útero.

ectoplasm *n.* ectoplasma, capa externa del citoplasma en una célula viva.

ectopy *n.* ectopia, desplazamiento de un órgano, condición gen. congénita.

ectropion *n.* ectropión, anomalía de eversión congénita o adquirida, gen. vista en la comisura del párpado.

eczema, eccema *n.* eczema, infección cutánea inflamatoria no contagiosa.

edema *n.* edema, acumulación anormal de líquido en los tejidos intracelulares; angioneurotic ____ / ____ angioneurótico; brain ____ / ____ cerebral; cardiac ____ / ____ cardíaco; dependent ____ / ____ dependiente; pitting ____ / ____ de fóvea; pulmonary ____ / ____ pulmonar.

edematous *a.* edematoso-a, rel. a un edema o afectado por éste.

edentulous *n.* desdentado, sin dientes.

edetate, calcium disodium *n.* disodio de calcio, agente usado en el tratamiento de envenenamiento por plomo.

edge *n.* borde, orilla, canto; [*of cutting instruments*] filo; **on** ____ / irritable, impaciente, nervioso-a.

edible *a.* comestible; edible.

educate *v.* educar, enseñar, instruir.

education *n.* educación, enseñanza; medical ____ / ____ médica.

effacement *n.* borradura, deformación de las características de un órgano tal como la del cuello uterino durante el parto.

effect *n.* efecto, impresión, resultado; *v.* **to carry into** ____ / llevar a cabo; **to this** ____ / en este sentido; **in** ____ / en ____ , en realidad; **no** ____ / sin ____ .

effective *a.* efectivo-a.

effector *n.* efector, terminación nerviosa que produce un efecto eferente en una glándula de secreción o en una célula muscular.

effeminate *a.* afeminado, *pop.* invertido-a.

efferent *a.* eferente, de fuerza centrífuga.

effervescence *n.* efervescencia, producción de burbujas.

effervescent *a.* efervescente, que produce efervescencia.

efficacious, efficient *a.* eficaz, eficiente, competente.

efficiency *n.* eficiencia, competencia; **-ly** *adv.* eficientemente.

effluent *a.* efluente, que tiene salida de dentro hacia afuera.

effort *n.* esfuerzo, empeño; *v.* **to make every** ____ **to** / hacer todo lo posible por.

effortless *a.* fácil, sin esfuerzo.

effusion *n.* efusión, derrame, escape de líquido a una cavidad o tejido.

egg *n.* huevo; *Mex.* blanquillos; ____ **cell** / óvulo; **fried** ____ / huevo frito; **hardboiled** ____ / huevo duro; ____ **shaped** / ovoide; **soft-boiled** ____ / ____ pasado por agua; ____ **white** / clara de ____ ; ____ **yolk** / yema de ____ .

eggplant *n.* berenjena.

eggshell *n.* cáscara de huevo.

ego *n. psic.* ego, el yo; la conciencia humana; término freudiano que se refiere a la parte de la psique mediadora entre la persona y la realidad.

egocentric *a.* egocéntrico-a, concentrado-a en sí mismo-a.

egoism *n.* egoísmo.

egomania *n.* egomanía, concentración excesiva en sí mismo-a.

ego-syntonic *a. psic.* egosintónico-a, en armonía o correspondencia con el ego.

either *a., pron.* uno-a u otro-a; *conj.* o; *adv.* también; [*after negation*] tampoco.

ejaculate *v.* eyacular, expeler.

ejaculation *n.* eyaculación, expulsión rápida y súbita tal como la emisión del semen.

ejaculatory duct *n.* conducto eyaculatorio.

ejection *n.* eyección, acto de expulsar con fuerza.

elaborate *v.* elaborar, tratar o explicar con detalle.

elastase *n.* elastasa, enzima que cataliza la digestión de las fibras elásticas, esp. del jugo pancreático.

elastic *n.* elástico, cinta de goma; *a.* elástico-a, capaz de extenderse y de volver luego a la forma inicial; ___ tissue / tejido elástico.

elasticity *n.* elasticidad, habilidad de expandirse.

elastinase *n.* elastinasa; *V.* **elastase.**

elation *n.* estado de exaltación o euforia, caracterizado por excitación física y mental.

elbow *n.* codo; ___ joint / coyuntura del ___ ; ___ room / espacio suficiente; **tennis** ___ / ___ de tenista.

elder *a.* mayor, de más edad; anciano-a; **elders** *pl.* antepasados, los mayores.

elderly *adv.* de avanzada edad.

eldest *a. sup.* el mayor, la mayor.

elect *v.* elegir, escoger.

elective *a.* electivo-a, elegido-a; ___ surgery / cirugía ___ , planeada; ___ therapy / terapia ___ .

electric *a.* eléctrico-a; ___ current / corriente ___ ; ___ eye / ojo mágico, ojo ___ .

electrical *a.* eléctrico-a.

electricity *n.* electricidad.

electrocardiogram (ECG) *n.* electrocardiograma, gráfico de cambios eléctricos que se producen durante las contracciones del músculo cardíaco.

electrocardiograph *n.* electrocardiógrafo, instrumento para registrar las variaciones eléctricas del músculo cardíaco en acción.

electrocauterization *n.* electrocauterización, destrucción de tejidos por medio de una corriente eléctrica.

electroconvulsive therapy *n.* terapéutica de choque, electrochoque, tratamiento de ciertos desórdenes mentales con aplicación de corriente eléctrica al cerebro.

electroencephalogram *n.* electroencefalograma, registro obtenido de una encefalografía.

electroencephalography *n.* electroencefalografía, gráfico descriptivo de la actividad eléctrica desarrollada en el cerebro.

electrolysis *n.* electrólisis, descomposición de una sustancia por medio de una corriente eléctrica.

electrolyte *n.* electrolito, ión que conduce una carga eléctrica.

electrolyzation *n.* electrolización, descomposición por electricidad.

electromagnetic *a.* electromagnético-a.

electromyography *n.* electromiografía, uso de estimulación eléctrica para registrar la fuerza de contracción muscular.

electronic *a.* electrónico-a.

electrophoresis *n.* electroforesis, movimiento de partículas coloidales en un medio que al someterse a una corriente eléctrica las separa, tal como ocurre con la separación de proteínas en el plasma.

electrophysiology *n.* electrofisiología, estudio de la relación entre procesos fisiológicos afectados por fenómenos eléctricos.

electrosurgery *n.* electrocirugía, uso de electricidad en procesos quirúrgicos.

electrosurgical *a.* electroquirúrgico-a; ___ destruction of lesions / destrucción ___ de lesiones.

element *n.* elemento, componente.

elementary *a.* elemental; rudimentario-a.

elephantiasis *n.* elefantiasis, enfermedad crónica caracterizada por obstrucción de los vasos linfáticos e hipertrofia de la piel y tejido celular subcutáneo que afecta gen. las extremidades inferiores y los órganos genitales externos.

elevate *v.* elevar, levantar, alzar.

elevation *n.* elevación; altura.

elevator *n.* elevador. 1. instrumento quirúrgico que se usa para levantar partes hendidas o para extirpar tejido óseo; 2. ascensor.

eligible *a.* elegible, electivo-a.

eliminate *v.* eliminar, expeler del organismo; suprimir.

elimination *n.* eliminación; exclusión.

elixir *n.* elixir, licor dulce y aromático que contiene un ingrediente medicinal activo.

elliptocyte *n.* eliptocito, eritrocito, célula roja ovalada.

elongated *a.* alargado-a, estirado-a, como el sistema de las vías digestivas.

else *a.* otro-a; más; **Who** ___ **needs help?** / ¿Quién más necesita ayuda?; **anyone** ___ / alguien más; **anything** ___ / algo más; **nothing** ___ / nada más.

elsewhere *adv.* en otra parte, a otra parte.

emaciated *a.* enflaquecido-a; excesivamente delgado-a.

emasculation *n.* emasculación; castración; mutilación.

embalm *v.* embalsamar.

embalming *n.* embalsamiento, preservación del cuerpo después de la muerte por medio de sustancias químicas.

embarrass *v.* avergonzar, trastornar, turbar, interferir, desconcertar.

embolism, embolia *n.* embolismo, embolia, oclusión súbita de un vaso por un coágulo, placa o aire; cerebral ____ / ____ cerebral.

embolus *n.* émbolo, coágulo u otro tipo de materia que al circular a través de la corriente sanguínea se aloja en un vaso de menor diámetro.

embrace *n.* abrazo; *v.* abrazar; [*each other*] abrazarse.

embryo *n.* embrión; 1. fase primitiva de desarrollo del ser humano desde la concepción hasta la séptima semana; 2. organismo en la fase primitiva de desarrollo.

embryology *n.* embriología, estudio del embrión y su desarrollo hasta el momento del nacimiento.

embryonic *a.* embriónico-a, embrional.

emerge *v.* brotar, emerger, surgir.

emergency *n.* emergencia, urgencia; ____ room / sala de ____; ____ care / servicio de ____.

emetic *a.* emético-a, que estimula el vómito.

emetine *n.* emetina, droga emética y antiamébica.

emigration *n.* emigración o migración, escape tal como el de leucocitos a través de las paredes de los capilares y las venas.

eminence *n.* eminencia o prominencia, forma de elevación semejante a la de la superficie de un hueso.

emission *n.* emisión, salida de líquido; derrame; nocturnal ____ / ____ nocturna, escape involuntario de semen durante el sueño.

emit *v.* emitir, descargar; manifestar una opinión.

emollient *a.* emoliente, que suaviza la piel o mucosas interiores.

emotion *n.* emoción, sentimiento intenso.

emotional *a.* emocional, rel. a las emociones; ____ disturbances / síntomas afectivos; ____ life / vida afectiva.

emotive *a.* emotivo-a.

empathy *n.* empatía, compresión y apreciación de los sentimientos de otra persona.

emphasis *n.* énfasis; acentuación.

emphatic *a.* enfático-a, acentuado-a, marcado-a.

emphysema *n.* enfisema, enfermedad crónica pulmonar en la cual los alvéolos pulmonares se distienden y los tejidos localizados entre los mismos se atrofian y dificultan el proceso respiratorio.

emphysematous *a.* enfisematoso-a, rel. al enfisema.

empiric *a.* empírico-a, que se basa en observaciones prácticas.

emplacement *n.* colocación, ubicación.

employ *v.* emplear, ocupar.

employee *n.* empleado-a.

employment *n.* empleo, ocupación.

empty *a.* vacío-a, desocupado-a.

empty *v.* vaciar, desocupar; to ____ itself / vaciarse, desocuparse.

empyema *n.* (*pl.* **empyemata**) empiema, acumulación de pus en una cavidad, esp. la cavidad torácica.

emulsify *v.* emulsionar, convertir en emulsión.

emulsion *n.* emulsión, mezcla de dos líquidos, uno de los cuales permanece suspendido.

enamel *n.* esmalte, sustancia dura que protege la dentina del diente.

encephalalgia *n.* encefalalgia, dolor de cabeza intenso.

encephalic *a.* encefálico-a, rel. al encéfalo o cerebro.

encephalitis *n.* encefalitis, infl. del encéfalo; ____ equine, eastern / ____ equina, del este, viral aguda; ____ equine, western / ____ equina, del oeste, viral benigna.

encephalocele *n.* encefalocele, hernia del encéfalo, protrusión del encéfalo a través de una abertura congénita o traumática en el cráneo.

encephalography *n.* encefalografía, examen radiográfico del cerebro.

encephaloma *n.* encefaloma, tumor del encéfalo.

encephalomalacia *n.* encefalomalacia, reblandecimiento del encéfalo.

encephalomyelitis *n.* encefalomielitis, infl. del encéfalo y la médula espinal.

encephalon *n.* encéfalo, porción del sistema nervioso contenido en el cráneo.

encephalopatia *n.* encefalopatía, cualquier enfermedad cerebral.

enchondroma *n.* encondroma, tumor que se desarrolla en un hueso.

encircle *v.* rodear, circundar.

enclose *v.* encerrar, cercar; [*in a letter*] incluir, adjuntar.

enclosed *a. pp.* de **to enclose,** [*in a letter*] incluído-a, adjunto-a.

encopresis *n.* encopresis, incontinencia de heces fecales.

encounter *n.* encuentro; *v.* encontrar, salir al encuentro.

encourage *v.* alentar, animar.

encouragement *n.* aliento, incentivo.

encysted *a.* enquistado-a, que se encuentra envuelto en un saco o quiste.

end *n.* fin, término, extremidad; extremo; **at the** ___ **of** / al extremo de; [*date*] a fines de; **To what** ___? / ¿Con qué ___?; *a.* terminal, final; ___ artery / arteria ___; ___ organ / órgano ___.

endanger *v.* poner en peligro; arriesgarse.

endarterectomy *n. cirg.* endarterectomía, extirpación de la túnica interna (intima) engrosada de una arteria.

endarteritis *n.* endarteritis, infl. de la túnica (intima) de una arteria.

endeavor *n.* empeño, esfuerzo.

endemic, endemical *a.* endémico-a, rel. a una enfermedad que permanece por un tiempo indefinido en una comunidad o región.

ending *n.* final; terminación, conclusión.

endless *a.* interminable, inacabable, sin fin.

endocarditis *n.* endocarditis, inflamación aguda o crónica del endocardio; acute bacterial ___ / ___ aguda bacteriana; chronic ___ / ___ crónica; rheumatic ___ / ___ reumática; subacute bacterial ___ / ___ subaguda bacteriana; valvular ___ / ___ valvular; vegetative ___ / ___ vegetativa.

endocardium (*pl.* **endocardia**) *n.* endocardio, membrana serosa interior del corazón.

endocervix *n.* endocérvix, mucosa glandular del cuello uterino.

endocrine *a.* endocrino-a, rel. a secreciones internas y a las glándulas que las producen.

endocrine glands *n.* glándulas endocrinas, glándulas que segregan hormonas directamente en la corriente sanguínea (gónadas, pituitaria y suprarrenales).

endocrinology *n.* endocrinología, estudio de las glándulas endocrinas y las hormonas segregadas por éstas.

endoderm *n.* endodermo, la más interna de las tres membranas del embrión.

endolymph *n.* endolinfa, fluído contenido en el laberinto membranoso del oído.

endolymphatic duct *n.* conducto endolinfático localizado en el oído.

endometrial *a.* endometrial, rel. al endometrio; ___ biopsy / biopsia ___.

endometrioma *n.* endometrioma, tumor constituído por tejido endometrial.

endometriosis *n.* endometriosis, trastorno por el cual tejido similar al del endometrio se manifiesta en otras partes fuera del útero.

endometritis *n.* endometritis, infl. de la mucosa uterina.

endometrium *n.* endometrio, membrana mucosa interior del útero.

endomorph *a.* endomorfo-a, de torso más pronunciado que las extremidades.

endoplasmic reticulum *n.* retículo endoplásmico, sistema de canales en los cuales se llevan a cabo las funciones de anabolismo y catabolismo de la célula.

endorphins *n. pl.* endorfinas, sustancias químicas naturales del cerebro a las que se le atribuye la propiedad de aliviar el dolor.

endoscope *n.* endoscopio, instrumento usado para examinar un órgano o una cavidad interior hueca.

endoscopic *a.* endoscópico-a, rel. a la endoscopía.

endoscopy *n.* endoscopía. examen interior hecho con el endoscopio.

endosteum *n.* (*pl.* **endostea**) endostio, capa de tejido conectivo que protege la cavidad medular de un hueso.

endothelial *a.* endotelial, rel. al endotelio.

endothelium *n.* (*pl.* **endothelia**) endotelio, capa celular interna que reviste los vasos sanguíneos, los canales linfáticos, el corazón y otras cavidades.

endothermic *a.* endotérmico-a, rel. a la absorción de calor.

endotracheal *a.* endotraqueal, dentro de la tráquea; ___ tube, cuffed / tubo ___ con manguito.

endurable *a.* soportable, aguantable, tolerable.

endurance *n.* resistencia; tolerancia; **beyond** ___ / más allá de lo que puede soportarse, intolerable.

endure *v.* soportar, sobrellevar, resistir, aguantar.

enema *n.* enema, lavado, lavativa; ayuda; barium ___ / ___ de bario; cleansing ___ / lavativa, lavado; double contrast ___ / ___ de contraste doble; retention ___ / ___ de retención.

energetic *a.* enérgico-a, vigoroso-a, lleno-a de energía.

energize *v.* desplegar energía; vigorizar.

energy *n.* energía, vigor.

engage *v.* encajar, ajustar, conectar; [*in a relationship*] comprometerse.

engaged *a.* encajado-a, ajustado-a, conectado-a; [*undertaken*] comprometido-a.

engender *v.* engendrar, procrear.

English *n.* [*language*] inglés; [*native*] *a.* inglés, inglesa.

engorged *a.* ingurgitado-a. 1. distendido por exceso de líquidos; 2. congestionado de sangre.

engram *n.* engrama. 1. marca permanente hecha en el protoplasma por un estímulo pasajero; 2. vestigio o visión imborrable producida por una experiencia sensorial.

enhance *v.* aumentar el valor, intensificar; [*beautify*] realzar.

enhancement *n.* aumento de un efecto tal como el de radiaciones por oxígeno u otro elemento químico.

enjoy *v.* disfrutar, gozar de.

enkephalins *n. pl.* encefalinas, sustancias químicas (polipéptidos) producidas en el cerebro.

enlarge *v.* ampliar, expandir, agrandar; ensanchar.

enlargement *n.* agrandamiento; ampliación, expansión, ensanchamiento.

enophthalmos *n.* enoftalmia, hundimiento del globo ocular.

enormous *a.* enorme, muy grande.

enough *a., adv.* bastante, suficiente; *int.* ¡basta!; ¡no más!

enrich *v.* enriquecer.

enriched *a.* [*added qualities*] enriquecido-a, de valor aumentado.

enrichment *n.* enriquecimento.

enter *v.* entrar, introducir, penetrar.

enteral, enteric *a.* entérico-a, rel. al intestino.

enteric coated *n.* cubierta entérica, revestimiento de ciertas tabletas y cápsulas para evitar que se disuelvan antes de llegar al intestino.

enteritis *n.* enteritis, infl. del intestino delgado.

enterocholecystostomy *n. cirg.* enterocolecistotomía, abertura entre la vesícula biliar y el intestino delgado.

enteroclysis *n.* enteroclisis. 1. irrigación del colon; 2. enema intenso.

enterococcus *n.* (*pl.* **enterococci**) enterococo, clase de estreptococo que se aloja en el intestino humano.

enterocolitis *n.* enterocolitis, infl. del intestino grueso y delgado.

enterocutaneous *a.* enterocutáneo-a, que comunica la piel y el intestino.

enteropathy *n.* enteropatía, cualquier anomalía o enfermedad del intestino.

enterostomy *n. cirg.* enterostomía, apertura o comunicación entre el intestino y la piel de la pared abdominal.

enterotoxin *n.* enterotoxina, toxina producida en el intestino.

enterovirus *n.* enterovirus, grupo de virus que infecta el tubo digestivo y que puede ocasionar enfermedades respiratorias y trastornos neurológicos.

enthusiasm *n.* entusiasmo.

entire *a.* entero-a, completo-a, íntegro-a; **-ly** *adv.* completamente, del todo, totalmente.

entity *n.* entidad, integridad, esencia o cualidad de algo.

entrance *n.* [*local*] entrada; [*acceptance*] ingreso; acceso a una cavidad.

entropion *n.* entropión, inversión del párpado.

entropy *n.* entropía, disminución de la capacidad de convertir la energía en trabajo.

entry *n.* entrada, acceso.

enucleate *v. cirg.* enuclear. 1. extirpar un tumor sin causar ruptura; 2. destruir o separar el núcleo de una célula; 3. extirpar el globo ocular.

enucleation *n.* enucleación, extirpación de un tumor o estructura.

enumerate *v.* enumerar, contar.

enuresis *n.* enuresis, incontinencia de orina; nocturnal ___ / ___ nocturna.

environment *n.* ambiente.

envy *n.* envidia.

enzygotic *a.* encigótico-a, que se deriva del mismo óvulo fecundado.

enzyme *n.* enzima, proteína que actúa como catalítico en reacciones químicas vitales.

enzymology *n.* enzimología, estudio de las enzimas.

eosin *n.* eosina, sustancia insoluble usada como colorante rojo en algunos tejidos que se estudian bajo el microscopio.

eosinophil *n.* eosinófilo, célula granulocítica que acepta fácilmente la acción colorante de la eosina.

eosinophilia *n.* eosinofilia, aumento en exceso de eosinófilos en la sangre por unidad de volumen.

eosinophilic leukocytes *n.* leucocitos eosinofílicos, leucocitos con abundante granulación ácida que con los colorantes básicos se tiñen de color violeta.

ependyma *n.* epéndimo, membrana que cubre los ventrículos del cerebro y el canal central de la médula espinal.

ependymal *a.* ependimario-a, rel. al epéndimo: _____ cells / células _____ -s; _____ layer / membrana _____.

ependymitis *n.* ependimitis, infl. del epéndimo.

ependynoma *n.* ependinoma, tumor del sistema nervioso central que se origina de inclusiones fetales ependimarias.

ephedrine *n.* efedrina, alcaloide, tipo de adrenalina de efecto broncodilatador.

ephemeral *a.* efímero-a, pasajero-a.

epicardium *n.* (*pl.* **epicardia**) epicardio, cara visceral del pericardio.

epicondyle *n.* epicóndilo, eminencia sobre el cóndilo de un hueso.

epidemic *n.* epidemia, enfermedad que se manifiesta con alta frecuencia y que afecta a un número considerable de personas en una región o comunidad; *a.* epidémico-a; _____ outbreak / brote _____.

epidemiologist *n.* epidemiólogo-a, especialista en el estudio de enfermedades epidémicas.

epidemiology *n.* epidemiología, estudio de las enfermedades epidémicas.

epidermic *a.* epidérmico-a, rel. a la epidermis.

epidermis *n.* epidermis, cubierta externa epitelial de la piel.

epidermoid *a.* epidermoide. 1. semejante a la piel; 2. rel. a un tumor que contiene células epidérmicas.

epidermolysis *n.* epidermólisis, descamación de la piel.

epididymis *n.* epidídimo, conducto situado en la parte posterior del testículo que recoge el esperma que es transportado por el conducto deferente a la vesícula seminal.

epididymitis *n.* epididimitis, infección e infl. del epidídimo.

epidural *a.* epidural, situado-a sobre o fuera de la duramadre.

epigastric *a.* epigástrico-a, rel. al epigastrio; _____ reflex / reflejo _____.

epigastrium *n.* (*pl.* **epigastria**) epigastrio, región superior media del abdomen.

epiglottis *n.* epiglotis, cartílago que cubre la laringe e impide la entrada de alimentos en la misma durante la deglución.

epiglottitis *n.* epiglotitis, infl. de la epiglotis.

epilation *n.* epilación, depilación por medio de electrolisis.

epilepsy, Grand Mal *n.* epilepsia, desorden neurológico gen. crónico y con frecuencia hereditario que se manifiesta con ataques o convulsiones y a veces con pérdida del conocimiento.

epileptic *n.* epiléptico-a, persona que padece de epilepsia; *a.* epiléptico-a, rel. a la epilepsia o que sufre de ella; _____ seizure / ataque _____, crisis _____.

epileptogenic, epileptogenous *a.* epileptógeno-a, causante de crisis epilépticas.

epinephrine *n.* epinefrina. *V.* **adrenaline.**

epiphora *n.* epifora, lagrimeo.

epiphysial *a.* epifisiario-a, rel. a la epífisis.

epiphysis *n.* epífisis, extremo de un hueso largo, gen. parte más ancha que la diáfisis.

epiphysitis *n.* epifisitis, infl. de una epífisis.

epiploic *a.* epiploico-a, rel. al epiplón.

epiploic foramen *n.* foramen epiploico, abertura que comunica la cavidad mayor peritoneal con la menor.

epiploon *n.* epiplón, repliegue de grasa que cubre el intestino.

episiotomy *n.* *cirg.* episiotomía, incisión del perineo durante el parto para evitar desgarros.

epispadias *n.* epispadias, abertura congénita anormal de la uretra en la parte superior del pene.

epistaxis *n.* epistaxis, sangramiento por la nariz.

epithalamus *n.* epitálamo, porción extrema superior del diencéfalo.

epithelial *a.* epitelial, rel. al epitelio.

epithelial casts *n.* cilindro epitelial, cilindro urinario constituído por células epiteliales renales y células redondas.

epithelialization *n.* epitelialización, epitelización, crecimiento de epitelio sobre una superficie expuesta tal como en la cicatrización de una herida.

epithelioma *n.* epitelioma, carcinoma compuesto mayormente de células epiteliales.

epithelium *L.* (*pl.* **epithelia**) epitelio, tejido que cubre las superficies expuestas e interiores del cuerpo; ciliated ___ / ___ ciliado; columnar ___ / ___ columnar; cuboidal ___ / ___ cuboidal; squamous ___ / ___ escamoso; stratified ___ / ___ estratificado; transitional ___ / ___ de transición, transicional.

epitympanum *n.* epitímpano, porción superior del tímpano.

eponym *n.* epónimo, uso del nombre propio de una persona para nombrar instrumentos médicos, anomalías o síndromes tal como el síndrome de Down.

epoxy *n.* epoxia, adhesivo.

epsilon-amino caproic acid *n.* ácido epsilón-amino caproico; ácido sulfúrico.

Epsom salt *n.* sal de Epsom; sal de higuera; sulfato de magnesio; medicamento usado como catártico.

Epstein-Barr virus *n.* virus de Epstein-Barr, posible causante de la mononucleosis.

equal *n.* igualdad, uniformidad; *a.* igual; parejo-a; uniforme; ___ rights / ___ de derechos; **-ly** *adv.* igualmente.

equalize *v.* igualar, emparejar, uniformar.

equanimity *n.* ecuanimidad; entereza.

equator *n.* ecuador, línea imaginaria que divide un cuerpo en dos partes iguales.

equilibrate *v.* equilibrar, balancear.

equilibration *n.* equilibración, mantenimiento del equilibrio.

equilibrium *n.* equilibrio, balance.

equinovarus *n.* equinovarus, deformidad congénita del pie.

equipment *n.* equipo, provisión; accesorios.

equitable *a.* equitativo-a; justo-a.

equivalence *n.* equivalencia.

equivalent *a.* equivalente, del mismo valor.

eradicate *v.* erradicar, extirpar; desarraigar.

erase *v.* borrar; raspar.

erectile *a.* eréctil, capaz de ponerse en erección o de dilatarse; ___ tissue / tejido ___.

erection *n.* erección, estado de rigidez, endurecimiento o dilatación de un tejido eréctil cuando se llena de sangre, tal como el pene.

erector *n.* erector, con propiedad de erección.

ergonomics *n.* ergonomía, rama de la ecología que estudia la creación y diseño de maquinarias en su ambiente físico y la relación de las mismas con el bienestar humano.

ergot *n.* cornezuelo de centeno, hongo que en forma seca o en extracto se usa como medicamento para detener hemorragias o para inducir contracciones uterinas.

ergotamine *n.* ergotamina, alcaloide usado en el tratamiento de migraña.

ergotism *n.* ergotismo, intoxicación crónica producida por el uso excesivo de alcaloides del cornezuelo de centeno.

erode *v.* desgastar.

erogenous *a.* erógeno-a, que produce sensaciones eróticas; ___ zone / zona erótica.

erosion *n.* erosión, desgaste

erosive *a.* erosivo-a, que causa erosión.

erotic *a.* erótico-a, rel. al erotismo o capaz de despertar impulsos sexuales.

eroticism, erotism *n.* erotismo, gozo de un deseo sexual.

erratic *a.* errático-a, que no sigue un curso o ritmo estable.

error *n.* error, falta, equivocación.

eructation *n.* eructación, eructo.

erupt *v.* brotar salir con fuerza, hacer erupción.

eruption *n.* erupción, brote; salpullido.

erysipelas *n.* erisipela, enfermedad infecciosa de la piel.

erythema *n.* eritema, enrojecimiento de la piel debido a una congestión de los capilares.

erythematic, erythematous *a.* eritematoso-a, rel. al eritema.

erythremia *n.* eritremia. V. **polycythemia**.

erythroblast *n.* eritroblasto, hematíe, globulo rojo primitivo.

erythroblastosis *n.* eritroblastosis, número excesivo de eritoblastos en la sangre.

erythrocyte *n.* eritrocito, célula roja producida en la médula ósea que actúa como transportadora de oxígeno a los tejidos; ___ sedimentation rate / índice de sedimentación de ___ -s.

erythrocytopenia *n.* eritrocitopenia, deficiencia en la cantidad de glóbulos rojos circulantes.

erythrocytosis *n.* eritrocitosis, aumento de eritrocitos en la sangre.

erythroid *n.* eritroide, de color semejante al rojo.

erythroleukemia *n.* eritroleucemia, enfermedad sanguínea maligna caracterizada por el crecimiento anormal de glóbulos rojos y blancos.

erythromycin *n.* eritromicina, antibiótico usado en el tratamiento de bacterias grampositivas.

erythron *n.* eritrón, concepto de la sangre como un sistema compuesto por los eritrocitos y sus precursores, así como también los órganos de los que provienen.

erythropoiesis *n.* eritropoyesis, producción de eritrocitos.

erythropoietin *n.* eritropoyetina, proteína no dializable que estimula la producción de eritrocitos

eschar *n.* escara, costra de color oscuro que se forma en la piel después de una quemadura.

esophageal *a.* esofágico-a, rel. al esófago: —— dilatation / dilatación ——.

esophagectomy *n. cirg.* esofagectomía, excisión de una porción del esófago.

esophagitis *n.* esofagitis, infl. del esófago.

esophagodynia *n.* esofagodinia, dolor en el esófago.

esophagogastritis *n.* esofagogastritis, infl. del estómago y el esófago.

esophagogastroduodenoscopy *n.* esofagogastroduodenoscopía, examen del estómago, esófago y duodeno por medio de un endoscopio.

esophagogastroscopy *n.* esofagogastroscopía, examen del esófago y del estómago por medio de un endoscopio.

esophagus *n.* esófago, porción del tubo digestivo situado entre la faringe y el estómago.

esophoria *n.* esoforia, movimiento del ojo hacia adentro; *pop.* bizquera.

esotropia *n.* esotropia. V. **esophoria.**

essence *n.* esencia, cualidad indispensable.

essential *a.* esencial, indispensable.

establish *v.* establecer, determinar.

estate *n.* estado, condición de una persona, animal o cosa.

ester *n.* éster, compuesto formado por la combinación de un ácido orgánico con alcohol.

esterification *n.* esterificación, transformación de un ácido en un éster.

esthesia *n.* estesia. 1. percepción, sensación; 2. cualquier anomalía que afecte las sensaciones.

esthetics *n.* estética, rama de la filosofía que se refiere a la belleza y el arte.

estradiol *n.* estradiol, esteroide producido por los ovarios.

estrinization *n.* estrinización, cambios epiteliales de la vagina producidos por estimulación de estrógeno.

estrogen *n.* estrógeno, hormona sexual femenina producida por los ovarios.

estrogenic *a.* estrogénico-a, rel. al estrógeno.

estrone *n.* estrona, hormona estrogénica.

eternal *a.* eterno-a.

ethanol *n.* alcohol etílico.

ether *n.* éter, fluído químico cuyo vapor es usado en anestesia general.

ethics *n.* ética, normas y principios que gobiernan la conducta profesional.

ethmoid *n.* etmoides, hueso esponjoso situado en la base del cráneo.

ethmoidectomy *n. cirg.* etmoidectomía, extirpación de las células etmoideas o de parte del hueso etmoide.

ethmoid sinus *n.* seno etmoideo, cavidad aérea situada dentro del etmoide.

ethylene *n.* etileno, anestésico.

etiologic *a.* etiológico-a, rel. a la etiología.

etiology *n.* etiología, rama de la medicina que estudia la causa de las enfermedades.

eubolism *n.* eubolismo, metabolismo normal.

eucalyptus *n.* eucalipto.

eugenics *n.* eugenesia, ciencia que estudia el mejoramiento de la especie humana de acuerdo con las leyes biológicas de la herencia.

eunuch *n.* eunuco, hombre castrado.

euphoria *n. psic.* estado exagerado de sensación de bienestar.

euploidy *n.* euploidia, grupos completos de cromosomas.

Eustachian tube *n.* trompa de Eustaquio, parte del conducto auditivo.

euthanasia *n.* eutanasia, muerte infringida sin sufrimiento en casos de una enfermedad incurable.

euthyroid *a.* eutiroideo-a, rel. a la función normal de la glándula tiroides.

evacuant *a.* evacuante, catártico, estimulante de la evacuación.

evacuate *v.* evacuar, eliminar; defecar; vaciar, *Mex.* obrar.

evacuation *n.* evacuación. 1. acción de vaciar esp. los intestinos; 2. acción de hacer un vacío.

evagination *n.* evaginación, salida o protuberancia de un órgano o parte de éste de la localización propia.

evaluate *v.* evaluar, estimar.

evaluation *n.* evaluación, consideración del

estado de salud mental y físico de una persona enferma o sana.

evanescent *a.* evanescente, que se desvanece, efímero-a.

evaporation *n.* evaporación, conversión de un estado líquido a vapor.

even *a.* igual, uniforme; [*same*] mismo-a, parejo-a; *adv.* ___ **so** / aun cuando; ___ **though** / aun cuando.

evening *n.* tardecita, anochecer, por la noche; **last** ___ / ayer por la noche; **this** ___ / esta noche.

ever *adv.* siempre; **for** ___ / para ___; **for** ___ **and** ___ / por ___ jamás; **hardly** ___ / casi nunca; ___ **since** / desde entonces.

eversion *n.* eversión, versión hacia afuera, esp. la de una mucosa que rodea un orificio natural.

every *a.* todo; cada; ___ **day** / ___ -s los días; ___ **once in a while** / a veces, de vez en cuando; ___ **other day** / día por medio, cada dos días, un día sí y otro no.

everybody *pron.* todos, todo el mundo.

everything *pron.* todo.

evidence *n.* evidencia, manifestación; [*legal*] evidencia, testimonio.

evil *n.* mal; *a.* malo-a, maligno-a; **-ness** *n.* maldad.

evisceration *n. cirg.* evisceración, extirpación del contenido de una víscera o de una cavidad.

evoke *v.* evocar.

evoked response *n.* respuesta evocada.

evolution *n.* evolución, cambio gradual.

evultion *n.* evulsión, acción de sacar hacia afuera, arranque.

exacerbation *n.* exacerbación, agravamiento de un síntoma o enfermedad.

exact *a.* exacto-a; **-ly** *adv.* exactamente.

exaggerate *v.* exagerar.

exaggeration *n.* exageración, alarde.

exam *n.* examen, evaluación, investigación.

examine *v.* examinar, evaluar, investigar, indagar.

examination *n.* examen; medical ___ / médico, examen físico completo, reconocimiento o inspección del cuerpo para establecer el estado de salud de una persona.

example *n.* ejemplo, muestra.

exanthem, exanthema *Gr.* exantema, erupción cutánea, salpullido.

exasperate *v.* exasperar, agravar.

exasperated *a.* exasperado-a.

excellent *a.* excelente, óptimo-a.

except *prep.* excepto, menos.

exception *n.* excepción; **with the** ___ **of** / a ___ de.

excess *n.* exceso, sobrante.

excessive *a.* excesivo-a.

exchange *v.* cambiar, trocar.

exchange transfusion *n.* ex-sanguinotransfusión, transfusión gradual y simultánea de sangre que se hace al recipiente mientras se saca la sangre del donante.

excise *v.* extirpar, cortar, dividir.

excision *n.* excisión, extirpación, ablación.

excitation *n.* excitación, reacción a un estímulo.

excite *v.* excitar, estimular; provocar.

excited *a.* excitado-a; acalorado-a.

exclude *v.* excluir, suprimir.

exclusive *a.* exclusivo-a.

excoriation *n.* excoriación, abrasión de la epidermis.

excrement *n.* excremento, heces fecales, *pop.* [*infant's*] caca.

excrescence *n.* excrecencia, tumor saliente en la superficie de un órgano o parte.

excreta *n.* excreta, todo lo excretado por el cuerpo.

excrete *v.* excretar, eliminar desechos del cuerpo.

excretion *n.* excreción, expulsión de lo secretado.

excretory *a.* excretorio-a, rel. a la excreción.

excuse *v.* excusar, perdonar, dispensar; ___ **me** / con permiso.

exenteration *n. cirg.* exenteración. V. **evisceration.**

exercise *n.* ejercicio; ___ electrocardiogram, stress test / prueba de esfuerzo máximo; physical ___ / ___ físico; ___ tolerance test / prueba física de ___ tolerado.

exfoliation *n.* exfoliación, descamación del tejido.

exhalation *n.* exhalación, proceso de salida del aire hacia afuera.

exhale *v.* espirar, exhalar.

exhaust *v.* agotar; extraer; vaciar; **to** ___ **all means** / agotar todos los recursos.

exhausted *a.* agotado-a, exhausto-a, extenuado-a.

exhaustion *n.* agotamiento, postración, fatiga extrema.

exhibition *n.* exhibición, exposición.

exhibitionism *n.* exhibicionismo, deseo obsesivo de exhibir partes del cuerpo esp. los genitales.

exhibitionist *n.* exhibicionista, persona que practica el exhibicionismo.

exhumation *n.* exhumación, desenterramiento.

exist *v.* existir, ser, vivir.

existent *a.* existente.

exit *n.* salida.

exocrine *a.* exocrino-a, rel. a la secreción externa de una glándula.

exocrine glands *n.* glándulas exocrinas, glándulas que secretan hormonas a través de un conducto o tubo tal como las mamarias y las sudoríparas.

exogenous *a.* exógeno-a, externo-a, que se origina fuera del organismo.

exomphalos *n.* exónfalo. *V.* **omphalocele.**

exophthalmia, exophthalmos *n.* exoftalmia, protrusión anormal del globo del ojo.

exophthalmic *a.* exoftálmico-a, rel. a la exoftalmia.

exophthalmic goiter *n.* bocio exoftálmico.

exostosis *n.* exóstosis, hipertrofia ósea cartilaginosa que sobresale hacia afuera de un hueso o de la raíz de un diente.

exotic *a.* exótico-a, raro-a, extraño-a.

exotoxin *n.* exotoxina, toxina secretada por bacterias.

exotropia *n.* exotropía, tipo de estrabismo divergente, rotación anormal de un ojo o de ambos hacia afuera por falta de balance muscular.

expand *v.* ensanchar, expandir, dilatar; expandirse.

expansion *n.* expansión, extensión.

expect *v.* esperar; suponer.

expectorant *n.* expectorante, agente que estimula la expectoración.

expectoration *n.* expectoración, esputo, expulsión de mucosidades o flema de los pulmones, tráquea y bronquios.

expel *v.* expulsar.

experience *n.* experiencia, práctica.

experiment *n.* experimento; *v.* experimentar.

expert *a.* experto-a, perito-a.

expiration *n.* expiración, terminación; espiración. 1. acto de dar salida al aire aspirado por los pulmones; 2. acto de fallecer o morir.

expire *v.* 1. espirar, expeler el aire aspirado; 2. expirar, morir, dejar de existir.

explain *v.* explicar, aclarar.

explanation *n.* explicación; interpretación.

exploration *n.* exploración, investigación, búsqueda.

exploratory *a.* exploratorio-a, rel. a una exploración.

expose *v.* exponer, mostrar; expulsar bajo presión.

expression *n.* expresión, aspecto o apariencia que se registra en la cara; medio de expresar algo.

expressivity *n.* expresividad, apreciación de un rasgo heredado según se manifiesta en el descendiente portador del gene.

extended care facility *n.* centro de atención médica externa.

extension *n.* 1. prolongación, extensión; 2. acto de enderezar un dedo o alinear un miembro o hueso dislocado.

extensor *a.* extensor-a, que tiene la propiedad de extender.

exterior *a.* exterior, externo-a; visible.

exteriorize *v. cirg.* exteriorizar, exponer un órgano o una parte temporalmente.

externalia *n. pl.* genitales externos.

externalize *v.* externalizar, *V.* **exteriorize.**

extinction *n.* extinción; supresión; cesación.

extinguish *v.* extinguir, apagar.

extirpation *n.* extirpación, ablación de una parte u órgano.

extra *a.* extraordinario-a; adicional.

extracellular *a.* extracelular, fuera de la célula.

extracorporeal *a.* extracorporal, fuera del cuerpo.

extract *n.* extracto, producto concentrado.

extraction *n. cirg.* extracción, proceso de extraer, separar o sacar afuera.

extradural *a.* extradural, *V.* **epidural.**

extraneous *a.* extraño-a, sin relación con un organismo o fuera del mismo.

extraocular *a.* extraocular, fuera del ojo.

extrasensory perception (ESP) *n.* percepción extrasensorial, percepción o conocimiento de las acciones o pensamientos de otras personas adquirido sin participación sensorial.

extrasystole *n.* extrasístole, latido arrítmico del corazón.

extravasated *a.* extravasado-a, rel. al escape de fluído de un vaso a tejidos circundantes.

extravascular *a.* extravascular, que ocurre fuera de un vaso o vasos.

extreme *a.* extremo-a, excesivo-a; último-a; **-ly** *adv.* extremadamente, excesivamente; sumamente.

extremity *n.* extremidad, la parte terminal de algo.

extrinsic *a.* extrínseco-a, que proviene de afuera.

extrophy *n.* extrofia. *V.* **eversion.**

extrovert *a.* extrovertido-a, tipo de personalidad que dirige la atención a sucesos u objetos fuera de sí mismo-a.

extrude *v.* exprimir, forzar hacia afuera.

extrusion *n.* extrusión, expulsión.

extubation *n.* *cirg.* extubación, extracción de un tubo.

exuberant *a.* exuberante, de proliferación excesiva.

exudate *n.* exudado, fluído inflamatorio tal como el de secreciones y supuraciones.

exudation *n.* exudación.

exude *v.* exudar, sudar, supurar a través de los tejidos.

eye *n.* ojo; ____ bank / banco de ojos; blood shot ____ / ____ inyectado; ____ contact / contacto visual; ____ diseases / enfermedades de los ojos, enfermedades de la vista; ____ **drops** / gotas para los ojos; **glass** ____ / ____ de vidrio; ____ injuries / traumatismos oculares; ____ sight / vista; ____ socket / cuenca del ____; ____ water / colirio; *v.* **to keep an ____ on** / cuidar, vigilar.

eyeball *n.* globo del ojo, globo ocular.

eyeband *n.* venda para los ojos.

eyebrow *n.* ceja.

eyecup *n.* copita para los ojos.

eyeglasses *n. pl.* espejuelos, gafas, lentes, anteojos; bifocal ____ / ____ bifocales; trifocal ____ / ____ trifocales.

eyeground *n.* fondo del ojo.

eyelash *n.* pestaña.

eyelid *n.* párpado.

eye memory *n.* memoria visual.

eyepiece *n.* ocular.

eyesight *n.* vista; *v.* **to have good ____** / tener buena ____.

eyesocket *n.* órbita ocular.

eyestrain *n.* vista cansada.

eyewash *n.* solución ocular, colirio, solución para los ojos.

eyewitness *n.* testigo ocular o visual.

F

F *abbr.* **Fahrenheit** / Fahrenheit.

f *abbr.* **failure** / fallo; **feminine** / femenino; **formula** / fórmula; **function** / función.

fabella *n.* fabela, fibrocartílago sesamoideo que puede desarrollarse en la cabeza del músculo gastronecmio.

face *n.* cara, ˏrostro, faz; ____ down / boca abajo; ____ lifting / estire de la cara, *cirg.* ritidectomía; ____ **peeling** / peladura de la ____; ____ to face / frente a frente; ____ up / boca arriba.

facet, facette *n.* faceta, pequeña parte lisa en la superficie de una estructura dura semejante a la de los huesos.

facetectomy *n.* *cirg.* extirpación de la faceta auricular.

facial *a.* facial, rel. a la cara; ____ bones / huesos de la cara, huesos ____ -es; ____ injuries / traumatismos ____ -es; ____ nerves / nervios ____ -es; ____ paralysis / parálisis ____.

facies *n.* (*pl.* **facies**) facies, expresión o apariencia de la cara; leontina ____ / ____ leontina; masklike ____ / ____ inexpresiva.

facilitate *v.* facilitar; proporcionar.

facility *n.* facilidad; instalación; [*conveniences*] *pl.* comodidades; servicios en general.

fact *n.* hecho, realidad; **in ____** / en efecto, en realidad.

factitious *a.* facticio-a, artificial, no natural.

factor *n.* factor, elemento que contribuye a producir una acción; antihemophilic ____ / ____ antihemofílico; clotting, coagulation ____ / ____ de coagulación; rheumatoid ____ / ____ reumatoideo; Rh ____ / ____ Rh [*erre ache*]; tumor angiogenesis ____ / ____ angiogenético tumoral.

factual *a.* objetivo-a, real.

facultative *a.* facultativo. 1. voluntario, que no es obligatorio; 2. de naturaleza profesional.

faculty *n.* facultad. 1. cuerpo facultativo; 2. aptitud o habilidad para llevar a cabo funciones normales.

fade *v.* descolorar; perder el color, atenuar la imagen o el color, desteñirse.

Fahrenheit scale *n.* escala de Fahrenheit, escala de temperatura que usa el punto de congelación a 32° y el de ebullición a 212°.

fail *v.* [*to be deficient*] fallar, faltar; dejar de; **without ____** / sin falta.

failing *n.* debilidad; deterioro; flaqueza; falla, falta.

failure *n.* insuficiencia, fallo; omisión; fracaso; heart ____ / ____ cardíaca, fallo cardíaco; ____ neurosis / neurosis de fracaso;

renal ___ / ___ renal; respiratory ___ / ___ respiratoria; **gross** ___ / fiasco.

faint *n*. desmayo, desvanecimiento, vahído; *v*. dar un vahído; desmayarse, desvanecerse.

fainting *n*. desmayo; desfallecimiento; ___ spell / desmayo.

faintly *adv*. débilmente, lánguidamente; escasamente.

faintness *n*. desaliento, [*weakness*] debilidad.

fair *a*. [*blonde*] rubio-a; [*light skin*] de tez blanca; [*average*] regular; ___ complexion / rubio-a, de tez clara; [*weather*] claro, despejado, favorable; [*decision*] favorable, razonable, justa.

faith *n*. fe; **in good** ___ / de buena ___.

faithful *a*. exacto-a, veraz; **-ly** *adv*. fielmente, exactamente.

faith healer *n*. curandero-a.

faith healing *n*. curanderismo.

fake *v*. fingir; falsificar, simular.

falciform *a*. falciforme, en forma de hoz; ___ ligament of liver / ligamento ___ del hígado.

fall *n*. caída; [*season*] otoño; ___ out / cenizas radioactivas; *vi*. caer; caerse; **to** ___ **asleep** / quedarse dormido-a; **to** ___ **back** / echarse atrás; **to** ___ **behind** / atrasarse, quedarse atrás; **to** ___ **short** / faltar, ser deficiente.

fallen *a. pp*. de **to fall**, caído-a.

falling *n*. caída; [*temperature*] descenso.

Fallopian tubes *n*. trompas de Falopio, conductos que se extienden del útero a los ovarios.

Fallot, tetralogy of *n*. tetralogía de Fallot, deformación cardíaca congénita que comprende cuatro defectos en los grandes vasos sanguíneos y de las paredes de las aurículas y ventrículos.

false *a*. falso-a, incorrecto-a. no real; ___ negative / ___ negativo; ___ positive / ___ positivo.

falsification *n*. falsificación, distorsión o alteración de un suceso u objeto.

fame *n*. fama, nombre.

familial, familiar *a*. familiar, rel. a la familia; frecuente; ___ Mediterranean fever / fiebre ___ del Mediterráneo; ___ periodic paralysis / parálisis periódica ___ .

family *n*. familia; ___ **man** / padre de familia; ___ **name** / apellido.

family planning *n*. planificación familiar, planeamiento de la concepción de los hijos gen. con el uso de métodos contraceptivos.

family practice *n*. medicina familiar, atención médica especial de la familia como unidad.

famine *n*. hambre, carestía.

famished *a*. famélico-a, hambriento-a.

fanatic, fanatical *a*. fanático-a.

Fanconi's syndrome *n*. síndrome de Fanconi, anemia hipoplástica congénita.

fancy *v*. imaginar, fantasear.

fantasy, phantasy *n*. fantasía, uso de la imaginación para transformar una realidad desagradable en una experiencia satisfactoria.

far *adv*. lejos; distante; ___ **apart** / infrecuente; **from** ___ **away** / de lejos, a lo lejos; ___ **better** / mucho mejor; ___ **cry** / gran diferencia; ___ **off** / a lo lejos, distante; **so** ___ / hasta ahora, hasta aquí.

farfetched *a*. rebuscado-a; inconcebible.

farina *n*. farina, harina, combinación de harina de trigo con otro cereal.

farmer *n*. campesino-a, granjero-a.

farmer's lung *n*. pulmón de granjero, hipersensibilidad de los alvéolos pulmonares causada por exposición a heno fermentado.

farsighted *a*. hiperópico-a, que sufre de hipermetropía.

farsightedness *n*. presbiopía, hiperopía, hipermetropía, defecto visual en el cual los rayos de luz hacen foco detrás de la retina y objetos lejanos se ven mejor que los que están a corta distancia.

fascia *n*. fascia, tejido fibroso conectivo que envuelve el cuerpo bajo la piel y protege los músculos, los nervios y los vasos sanguíneos; ___ , aponeurotic / ___ aponeurótica, tejido fibroso que sirve de soporte a los músculos; ___ , Buck's / ___ de Buck, tejido fibroso que cubre el pene; ___ , Colles' / ___ de Colles, cubierta interna de la fascia perineal; ___ , lata / ___ lata, protectora de los músculos del muslo; ___ , tranversalis / ___ tranversal, localizada entre el peritoneo y el músculo transverso del abdomen.

fascicle, fasciculum *n*. (*pl*. **fascicula**) fascículo, haz de fibras musculares y nerviosas.

fasciculation *n*. fasciculación. 1. formación de fascículos; 2. contracción involuntaria breve de fibras musculares.

fascietomy n. cirg. fascietomía, excisión parcial o total de una fascia.

fasciitis n. fascitis, infl. de una fascia.

fasciotomy n. cirg. fasciotomía, incisión de una fascia.

fast n. ayuno; a. [speed] rápido-a, ligero-a; [of a color] que tiene resistencia a un colorante: ____ **asleep** / profundamente dormido-a; ____ **day** / día de ayuno; v. ayunar, estar en ayunas.

fasten v. sujetar; amarrar; abrochar; abotonar.

fasting n. ayuno.

fastness n. resistencia.

fat n. [grease] grasa; a. gordo-a, grueso-a, obeso-a; [greasy] grasoso-a; v. **to get** ____ / engordar.

fatal a. fatal

fatality n. fatalidad, desgracia; muerte.

fate n. destino.

father n. padre; papá; tata.

father-in-law n. suegro.

fatherless n. huérfano-a de padre.

fatigability n. fatigabilidad, predisposición a la fatiga.

fatigue n. fatiga; cansancio; v. fatigarse, cansarse.

fatness n. gordura.

fatty a. adiposo-a, grasoso-a; ____ acids / ácidos grasos; ____ degeneration / degeneración ____ ; ____ tumor / lipoma; ____ tissue / tejido ____ .

fauces L. fauces, región intermedia entre la boca y la faringe.

faucet n. pila, llave de agua.

fault n. falta, defecto, culpa; v. **to be at** ____ / ser culpable.

faultless a. perfecto-a; intachable.

faulty a. defectuoso-a, imperfecto-a.

favor n. favor.

favorable a. favorable; propicio-a.

fear n. temor, miedo, aprehensión.

fearful a. temeroso-a, miedoso-a.

fearless a. sin temor, intrépido-a.

feasible a. posible, factible.

feast n. banquete.

feather n. pluma.

feature n. rasgo, característica.

febrile a. febril, calenturiento-a; ____ convulsion / convulsión ____ .

fecal a. fecal, que contiene heces fecales.

fecalith n. fecalito, concreción intestinal formada alrededor de materia fecal.

fecaloma n. fecaloma, acumulación de heces fecales en el recto con apariencia de tumor abdominal.

fecaluria n. presencia de materia fecal en la orina.

feces n. pl. heces, excremento.

fecund a. fecundo-a; fértil.

fecundity n. fecundidad, fertilidad.

fed a. pp. de to feed; to be ____ up / estar harto-a, pop. estar hasta la coronilla.

fee n. honorario, cuota.

feeble a. débil, endeble.

feed vi. alimentar, dar de comer; proveer materiales o asistencia.

feedback n. 1. [information] reprovisión de material informativo distribuído; 2. retroalimentación, retorno parcial del rendimiento o efectos de un proceso a su fuente de origen o a una fase anterior; v. proveer de nuevo material informativo; regenerar la energía.

feeding n. alimentación; breast ____ / lactancia materna; enteral ____ / ____ enteral; forced ____ / ____ forzada; intravenous ____ / ____ intravenosa; rectal ____ / por el recto; tube ____ / ____ por sonda.

feel vi. sentir, percibir; **to** ____ **hungry** / tener hambre; **to** ____ **the effects of** / sentir los efectos de; **Do you** ____ **the effects of the medication?** / ¿Siente, sientes los efectos de la medicina?; **to** ____ **like** / tener ganas de; **to** ____ **sleepy** / tener sueño; **to** ____ **sorry for** / compadecerse de; tener lástima de; **to** ____ **the pulse** / tomar el pulso; **to** ____ **thirsty** / tener sed; sentirse; **to** ____ **bad** / sentirse mal; **to** ____ **better** / ____ mejor; **to** ____ **good, fine** / ____ bien; **to** ____ **uncomfortable** / ____ incómodo-a.

feeling n. sensación; [emotion] sentimiento, emoción, sensibilidad.

feet n. pl. de foot pies.

feline a. felino-a, rel. a la familia de los gatos o con características semejantes a éstos.

fellatio n. felación. V. **cunnilingus**.

felon n. 1. panadizo, absceso doloroso de la falange distal de un dedo; 2. felón, criminal.

female n. hembra; a. femenino-a, rel. a la mujer.

feminine a. femenino-a; afeminado.

feminist a. feminista.

feminization n. feminización, desarrollo de características femeninas.

femoral *a.* femoral, rel. al fémur; _____ artery / arteria _____; deep _____ arch / arco _____ profundo; _____ vein / vena _____.

femur *n.* fémur, hueso del muslo.

fenestrated *a.* fenestrado-a; que tiene orificios o aperturas.

fenestration *n. cirg.* fenestración. 1. creación de una abertura en el laberinto del oído para restaurar la audición; 2. acto de perforar.

ferment *n.* fermento. 1. sustancia o agente que activa la fermentación; 2. producto de fermentación; *v.* fermentar, hacer fermentar.

fermentation *n.* fermentación, descomposición de sustancias complejas por la acción de enzimas o fermentos.

ferritin *n.* ferritina, una de las formas en que el hierro se almacena en el organismo.

ferroprotein *n.* ferroproteína, proteína compuesta de un radical ferruginoso.

ferruginous *a.* ferruginoso-a, rel. al hierro o que lo contiene.

fertile *a.* fértil, fecundo-a, productivo-a.

fertility *n.* fertilidad.

fertilization *n.* fertilización, fecundación.

fertilize *v.* fecundar, hacer fértil.

fertilizer *n.* fertilizante.

fester *v.* enconarse, supurar superficialmente.

fetal *a.* fetal, rel. al feto; _____ alcohol syndrome / síndrome alcohólico _____; _____ circulation / circulación _____; _____ drug syndrome / síndrome _____ del abuso de droga; _____ heart tone / latido del corazón _____; _____ growth retardation / retardo del crecimiento _____; _____ maturity, chronologic / edad gestacional; _____ monitoring / monitorización _____; _____ transfusion / transfusión de sangre *in utero*; _____ viability / viabilidad _____.

feticide *n.* feticidio, destrucción del feto en el útero.

fetid *a.* fétido-a, hediondo-a, de mal olor.

fetish *n.* fetiche.

fetoprotein *n.* fetoproteína, antígeno presente en el feto humano.

fetor *n.* fetor, mal olor, hedor.

fetoscope *n.* fetoscopio, instrumento usado para visualizar al feto y facilitar diagnosis prenatales.

fetus *n.* feto, embrión en desarrollo, fase de la gestación desde los tres meses hasta el parto.

fever *n.* fiebre, calentura; _____ blister / herpes febril; enteric _____ / _____ entérica, intestinal; _____ of unknown origin (FUO) / _____ de origen desconocido; intermittent _____ / _____ intermitente; rabbit _____ / _____ de conejo, tularemia; rheumatoid _____ / _____ reumatoidea; remittent _____ / _____ remitente; Rocky Mountain _____ / _____ manchada de las Montañas Rocosas; scarlet _____ / escarlatina; yellow _____ / _____ amarilla, paludismo, malaria; typhoid _____ / _____ tifoidea; undulant _____ / brucelosis.

fiber *n.* fibra, filamento en forma de hilo.

fiberoptic *a.* fibróptico, rel. a las fibras ópticas.

fiberoptics *n. pl.* fibras ópticas, filamentos flexibles de cristal o plástico que conducen una imagen transmitida.

fibril *n.* filamento, fibrilla, fibra pequeña.

fibrillar, fibrillary *a.* fibrilar, rel. a una fibra.

fibrillation *n.* fibrilación. 1. contracción muscular involuntaria que afecta fibras musculares individuales; 2. formación de fibrillas; atrial _____ / _____ auricular; flutter _____ / _____ de aleteo; ventricular _____ / _____ ventricular.

fibrin *n.* fibrina, proteína insoluble indispensable en la coagulación de la sangre.

fibrinogen *n.* fibrinógeno. 1. proteína presente en el plasma sanguíneo que se convierte en fibrina en el proceso de coagulación; 2. el Factor I.

fibrinogenolysis *n.* fibrinogenólisis, disolución o inactivación del fibrinógeno en la corriente sanguínea.

fibrinolysis *n.* fibrinólisis, disolución de fibrina por la acción de enzimas.

fibrinous, fibrous *a.* fibrinoso-a, fibroso-a. 1. rel. a la naturaleza de una fibra; 2. semejante a un hilo.

fibroadenoma *n.* fibroadenoma, tumor benigno formado por tejido fibroso y glandular.

fibroblast *n.* fibroblasto, células de soporte de las que proviene el tejido conectivo.

fibrocartilage *n.* fibrocartílago, tipo de cartílago en el que la matriz contiene abundante tejido fibroso.

fibrocyst *n.* fibroquiste. 1. fibroma formado por quistes; 2. neoplasma de degeneración cística.

fibrocystic *a.* fibrocístico-a, fibroquístico-a, de naturaleza fibrosa con degeneración cística; —— disease of the breast / enfermedad —— de la mama.

fibrocystoma *n.* fibrocistoma, tumor benigno con elementos císticos.

fibroid *a.* fibroide, de naturaleza fibrosa.

fibrolipoma *n.* fibrolipoma, tumor que contiene tejido fibroso y adiposo en exceso.

fibroma *n.* fibroma, tumor benigno compuesto de tejido fibroso.

fibromuscular *a.* fibromuscular, de naturaleza muscular y fibrosa; —— dysplasia / displasia ——.

fibromyoma *n.* fibromioma, tumor benigno formado por tejido muscular y fibroso.

fibroplasia *n.* fibroplasia, producción de tejido fibroso tal como en la cicatrización de una herida.

fibrosis *n.* fibrosis, formación anormal de tejido fibroso; diffuse interstitial pulmonary —— / —— intersticial del pulmón; proliferative —— / —— proliferativa; retroperineal —— / —— retroperineal.

fibrositis *n.* fibrositis, infl. de tejido blanco conjuntivo esp. en el área de las articulaciones.

fibrotic *a.* fibrótico-a, rel. a la fibrosis.

fibula *a.* peroné, el hueso más externo y más delgado de la pierna.

fictitious *a.* ficticio-a, falso-a.

fidelity *n.* fidelidad, lealtad; precisión.

field *n.* campo. 1. área o espacio abierto; —— of vision / —— visual; 2. área de especialización.

fight *n.* pelea, lucha; *vi.* pelear, combatir, luchar con.

figure *n.* figura; cifra, número.

filament *n.* filamento, fibra o hilo fino.

file *n.* [*instrument*] lima; [*record*] expediente, ficha; *v.* limar, suavizar; clasificar.

fill *v.* llenar; rellenar; llenarse.

filling *n.* [*dental*] empaste; obturación; restauración.

film *n.* 1. película; 2. telilla, membrana o capa fina.

filter *n.* filtro; *v.* filtrar; to —— through / filtrarse.

filth *n.* suciedad, inmundicias, mugre; *H.A.* cochinada.

filthy *a.* sucio-a, mugriento-a, mugroso-a.

filtration *n.* filtración, colación, acción de pasar a través de un filtro.

fimbria *n.* (*pl.* **fimbriae**) fimbria, borde o canto; apéndice de ciertas bacterias.

final *a.* final, último-a; conclusivo-a; definitivo-a.

financial *a.* financiero-a, monetario-a; —— expenses / gastos ——-s; —— income / ingresos, honorarios; —— responsibility / solvencia, capacidad ——; **-ly** adv. financieramente; —— responsible / solvente, persona responsable de los gastos.

find *vi.* hallar, encontrar, descubrir.

findings *n. pl.* hallazgos, resultados de una investigación o indagación.

fine *a.* fino-a, delicado-a; *v.* to feel —— / sentirse bien.

finger *n.* dedo de la mano; **first** —— / dedo índice; **little** —— / dedo meñique; **mallet** —— / dedo en martillo; —— **-shaped** / digitiforme.

fingernail *n.* uña.

fingerprint *n.* impresión, huella digital; *v.* tomar las impresiones digitales; —— expert / dactiloscopista.

finish *n.* final, terminación; *v.* acabar, terminar.

finished *a.* acabado-a, terminado-a.

finite *a.* finito-a, que tiene límites.

fire *n.* fuego; [*conflagration*] incendio; —— **alarm** / alarma de ——; —— **department** / cuerpo de bomberos; —— **escape** / escalera de ——-s; *v.* **to catch** —— / encenderse, prenderse; **to set** —— **to** / encender, quemar.

firearm *n.* arma de fuego.

firm *a.* firme, fijo-a, consistente.

first *n.* primero-a; *a.* primero-a, primer *(before a m. singular n.)* —— **degree** / de primer grado; —— **name** / nombre de pila.

first aid *n.* primeros auxilios; —— **kit** / botiquín de ——.

first born *n.* primogénito-a.

fish *n.* (*pl.* **fish**) pez; [*fish caught*] pescado.

fish poisoning *n.* intoxicación de pescado.

fission *n.* fisión. 1. división en partes. 2. división de un átomo para ser descompuesto y desplazar energía y neutrones.

fissura, fissure *n.* fisura. *V.* **cleft.**

fist *n.* puño; *v.* **to make a** —— / cerrar el ——.

fistula *n.* fístula, canal o pasaje anormal que permite el paso de secreciones de una cavidad a otra o a la superficie exterior; anal —— / —— anal; arteriovenous —— / —— arteriovenosa; biliary —— / —— biliar.

fistulization *n.* fistulización, formación de

una fístula por un medio quirúrgico o patológico.

fistulous *a.* fistuloso-a, rel. a una fístula.

fit *n.* ataque súbito; convulsión; *a.* [*suitable*] adecuado-a: *vi.* [*to adjust to shape*] ajustar, encajar.

fitness *n.* aptitud, vigor físico; physical ___ / ___ física.

fix *v.* [*fasten*] fijar, asegurar; **to fix up** / arreglar; convenir.

fixation *n.* fijación. 1. inmovilización de una parte; 2. acción de fijar la vista en un objeto; 3. *psic.* interrupción del desarrollo de la personalidad antes de alcanzar la madurez.

fixative *n.* fijador, sustancia usada para endurecer muestras de exámenes patológicos.

fixed *a.* fijo-a; decidido-a [*resolved*] resuelto; arreglado-a, determinado-a; compuesto-a; ___ **fee** / honorario ___ o definido; ___ **term** / plazo ___ .

flabby *a.* blando-a, flojo-a; *pop.* fofo-a.

flaccid *a.* flácido-a; débil, flojo-a; ___ paralysis / parálisis ___ .

flagellated *a.* flagelado-a, provisto de flagelo o flagelos.

flagelliform *n.* flageliforme, en forma de látigo.

flagellum *n.* (*pl.* **flagella**) flagelo, prolongación o cola en la célula de algunos protozoos.

flail chest *n.* tórax inestable, condición de la pared del tórax causada por la fractura múltiple de costillas.

flake *n.* escama; copo; **snow**___ **-s** / copos de nieve.

flaky *a.* escamoso-a.

flank *n.* flanco, parte del cuerpo entre las costillas y el borde superior del íleo.

flap *n.* [*sound of wings*] aleteo; sonido de alas; cubierta; colgajo.

flare *n.* brote, irritación rosácea o área difundida; destello, fulgor; ___-up / ___ con irritación; *v.* brotar, irritar.

flash *n.* fulguración, destello; hot ___ / fogaje, rubor.

flashback *n.* retrogresión; retroversión; *psic.* retrospección y actualización de imágenes pasadas.

flashlight *n.* linterna eléctrica.

flask *n.* frasco, pomo.

flat *a.* plano-a, llano-a; extendido-a; ___ **foot** / pie ___ .

flatulence *n.* flatulencia, distensión y moles

tias abdominales por exceso de gas en el tracto gastrointestinal.

flatus *n.* flato, *pop.* aventación, gas o aire en los intestinos.

flatworm *n.* gusano plano que se aloja en los intestinos.

flavor *n.* sabor, gusto.

flaw *n.* falta, defecto, falla.

flea *n.* pulga, insecto chupador de sangre; ___ **bite** / picadura de ___ .

flesh *n.* carne, tejido muscular suave del cuerpo; ___ wound / herida superficial.

fleshless *a.* descarnado-a.

flex *v.* flexionar, doblar.

flexibility *n.* flexibilidad, propiedad de flexionar.

flexion *n.* flexión, acto de flexionar o de ser flexionado.

flexor *n.* flexor, músculo que hace flexionar una articulación.

flexure *n.* flexura, pliegue o doblez de una estructura u órgano; hepatic ___ / ___ hepática, ángulo derecho del colon; sigmoid ___ / sigmoidea, curvatura del colon que antecede al recto; splenic ___ / ___ esplénica, ángulo izquierdo del colon.

flicker *v.* fluctuar, vacilar; [*to quiver*] oscilar; causar una sensación visual de contraste con interrupción de la luz.

flight *n.* escape, fuga; vuelo; trayectoria; viaje aéreo.

flight of ideas *n. psic.* fuga de ideas, interrupciones en el pensamiento y la expresión de palabras.

float *n.* flotador; *v.* flotar.

floaters *n. pl.* flotadores, manchas visuales, máculas.

floating *a.* flotante, libre, sin adhesión; ___ ribs / costillas ___-s.

flocculation *n.* floculación, precipitación o aglomeración en forma de copos de partículas usu. invisibles.

floor *n.* piso, suelo.

flora *n.* flora, grupo de bacterias que se alojan en un órgano; intestinal ___ / ___ intestinal.

florid *a.* florido-a; encarnado-a; de color rojo vivo.

floss *n.* seda floja; **dental** ___ / hilo dental.

flour *n.* harina.

flow *n.* flujo, salida; riego; [*menstrual*] *pop.* pérdida; *v.* fluir; correr; derramar; blood ___ / riego sanguíneo.

flower *n.* flor, órgano reproductor de la planta.

flowmeter *n.* medidor de flujo.

fluctuate *v.* fluctuar, cambiar.

fluctuation *n.* fluctuación. 1. acto de fluctuar, variación de un curso a otro; 2. sensación de movimiento ondulante producido por líquidos en el cuerpo que se percibe en un examen de palpación.

fluid *n.* líquido, fluído; secreción; amniotic ___ / ___ amniótico; cerebrospinal ___ / ___ cerebroespinal; extracellular ___ / ___ extracelular; extravascular ___ / ___ extravascular; interstitial ___ / ___ intersticial; intracellular ___ / ___ intracelular; seminal ___ / ___ seminal; serous ___ / ___ seroso; synovial ___ / ___ sinovial.

fluid balance *n.* balance hídrico.

fluid retention *n.* retención de líquido.

fluke *n.* duela, gusano de la orden *Trematoda;* blood ___ / ___ sanguínea; intestinal ___ / ___ intestinal; liver ___ / ___ hepática; lung ___ / ___ pulmonar.

fluorescence *n.* fluorescencia, propiedad de emisión de luminosidad de ciertas sustancias cuando son expuestas a cierto tipo de radiación, tal como los rayos X.

fluorescent *a.* fluorescente, rel. a la fluorescencia; ___ antibody / anticuerpo ___; ___ troponemal antibody absorption test / técnica del anticuerpo ___.

fluoridation *n.* fluoridización, adición de fluoruro al agua.

fluoride *n.* fluoruro, combinación de flúor con un metal o metaloide.

fluorine *n.* flúor, elemento químico gaseoso.

fluoroscope *n.* fluoroscopio, instrumento que hace visibles los rayos X en una pantalla fluorescente.

fluoroscopy *n.* fluoroscopía, uso del fluoroscopio para examinar los tejidos y otras estructuras internas del cuerpo.

fluorosis *n.* fluorosis, exceso de absorción de flúor.

flush *n.* rubor; [*cleansing*] irrigación; [*to empty out*] vaciar; irrigar; ruborizarse, sonrojarse.

flutter *n.* aleteo, acción similar al movimiento de las alas de los pájaros; atrial ___ / ___ auricular; ventricular ___ / ___ ventricular; ___ and fibrillation / fibrilación y ___; *v.* aletear, sacudir; agitarse.

flux *n.* flujo excesivo proveniente de una cavidad u órgano del cuerpo.

fly *n.* mosca; *vi.* volar.

foam *n.* espuma.

focal *a.* focal, rel. a un foco.

focus *n.* (*pl.* **foci**) foco; *v.* enfocar.

fold *n.* pliegue de un margen; aryepiglottic ___ / ___ ariepiglótico; gastric ___ / ___ gástrico; gluteal ___ / ___ glúteo.

folic acid *n.* ácido fólico, miembro del complejo de vitaminas B.

follicle *n.* folículo, saco, bolsa, depresión o cavidad excretora; atretic ___ / ___ atrésico; gastric ___ / ___ gástrico; hair ___ / ___ piloso; ovarian ___ / ___ ovárico; thyroid ___ / ___ tiroideo.

follicular *a.* folicular, rel. a un folículo.

folliculitis *n.* foliculitis, infl. de un folículo, gen. un folículo piloso.

follow *v.* seguir, continuar; ___-up / acción continuada, seguimiento, (estudio, procedimiento del caso); ___-up evaluation / evaluación del proceso evolutivo; **to ___ through** / continuar el procedimiento; llevar hasta el final; continuar la observación de un caso.

fomes L. (*pl.* **fomites**) fomes, cualquier sustancia que puede absorber y luego transmitir agentes infecciosos.

fontanel, fontanella *n.* fontanel, fontanela, *pop.* mollera, parte suave en el cráneo del recién nacido que normalmente se cierra al desarrollarse los huesos craneales.

food *n.* alimento; comida; ___ additives / aditivos alimenticios; ___ contamination / contaminación de ___-s; ___ handling / manipulación de ___-s; ___ poisoning / intoxicación alimenticia; ___ requirements / requisitos alimenticios; ___ supplements / alimentos enriquecidos.

foolishness *n.* tontería, bobería.

foot *n.* (*pl.* **feet**) pie; athlete's ___ / ___ de atleta; flat ___ / ___ plano.

footdrop *n.* pie caído.

footprint *n.* impresión o huella del pie, pisada.

footsore *a.* que presenta molestia o dolor en el pie.

footstep *n.* paso, pisada; [*print*] huella del pie.

for *prep.* [*intended for or for the use of*] para, **the medicine is ___ the patient** / la medicina es ___ el paciente; [*for the purpose of*] para; **a thermometer for taking the temperature** / un termómetro ___ tomar la temperatura; [*for the benefit of*] para; **an**

antibiotic ____ the infection / un antibiótico ____ la infección; [*in exchange for*] por; **you pay a dollar** ____ **each pill** / paga un dólar ____ pastilla; [*for the sake of*] por; **do it** ____ **her** / hágalo, házlo ____ ella; ____ **the time being** / por ahora, por el momento.

foramen *n.* foramen, orificio, pasaje, abertura; intervertebral ____ / ____ intervertebral; jugular ____ / ____ yugular; optic ____ / ____ óptico; ovale ____ / ____ oval; sciatic, greater ____ / ____ sacrociático mayor; sciatic, lesser ____ / ____ sacrociático menor.

forbid *vi.* prohibir, impedir; **God** ____! / ¡no lo permita Dios!

force *n.* fuerza, vigor, energía; *v.* forzar violentar, obligar; *v.* **to** ____ **out** / echar a la fuerza; **to** ____ **through** / hacer penetrar a la fuerza.

forceps *n. pl.* fórceps, pinza en forma de tenaza que se emplea para sujetar y manipular tejidos o partes del cuerpo.

forearm *n.* antebrazo.

forebrain *n.* prosencéfalo, porción anterior de la vesícula primaria cerebral de donde se desarrollan el diencéfalo y el telencéfalo.

forecast *n.* pronóstico, predicción; *v.* predecir, pronosticar.

forefinger *n.* dedo índice.

forefoot *n.* antepié, parte anterior del pie.

foregut *n.* intestino anterior, porción cefálica del tubo digestivo primitivo en el embrión.

forehead *n.* frente.

foreign *a.* extranjero-a; extraño-a.

foreign bodies *n. pl.* cuerpos extraños, máculas, materia o pequeños objetos ajenos al lugar en que se alojan.

forensic *a.* forense, rel. a asuntos legales; ____ laboratory / laboratorio ____ ; ____ medicine / medicina legal; ____ physician / médico ____ .

foreplay *n.* estímulo erótico que precede al acto sexual.

foresee *vi.* prever; prevenir

foreseen *a. pp.* de **to foresee**, previsto-a.

foresight *n.* precaución, previsión.

foreskin *n.* prepucio. *V.* **prepuce.**

forever *adv.* siempre, para siempre, por siempre.

forge *v.* falsificar, falsear

forger *n.* falsificador, -a, falsario-a.

forget *vi.* olvidar; olvidarse de; ____ **it** / olvídese, olvídate de eso; no se preocupe, no te preocupes.

forgetful *a.* olvidadizo-a; negligente.

forgive *vi.* perdonar.

fork *n.* tenedor; bifurcación.

forked *a.* bifurcado-a.

form *n.* forma; [*document*] formulario; *v.* formar, dar forma; establecer.

formaldehyde *n.* formaldehído, antiséptico.

formalin *n.* formalina, solución compuesta de formaldehído.

formation *n.* formación; composición; conjunto.

forme fruste *Fr.* forma frustrada, enfermedad abortada o manifestada de manera atípica.

formication *n.* formicación, sensación de hormigueo en la piel.

formula *n.* fórmula, forma prescrita o modelo a seguir.

fornix *L.* (*pl.* **fornices**) fornix. 1. estructura en forma de arco; 2. concavidad en forma de bóveda semejante a la vagina.

forth *adv.* [*forward*] hacia adelante: [*out, away*] afuera, hacia afuera.

forthcoming *a.* venidero-a; disponible.

fortify *v.* fortalecer, fortificar.

fossa *n.* (*pl.* **fossae**) fosa, cavidad, hueco, depresión; ____ , glenoid / ____ glenoidea; ____ , interpeduncular / ____ interpeduncular; ____ , jugular / ____ yugular; ____ , mandibular / ____ mandibular; ____ , nasal / ____ nasal; ____ , navicular / ____ navicular.

fourchete, fourchette *Fr.* horquilla, comisura posterior de la vulva.

fovea *n.* fóvea, fosa o depresión pequeña, esp. en referencia a la fosa central de la retina.

foxglove *n.* dedalera, nombre común de *Digitalis purpurea.*

fraction *n.* fracción, parte separable de una unidad.

fracture *n.* fractura, rotura; *pop.* quebradura; avulsion ____ / ____ por avulsión; blow-out ____ / ____ por estallamiento; closed ____ / ____ cerrada; comminuted ____ / ____ conminuta; complete ____ / ____ completa; compression ____ / ____ por compresión; depressed ____ / ____ con hundimiento; dislocation ____ / ____ por luxación; greenstick ____ / ____ en tallo verde o ____ de caña; hair line ____ / ____ de raya fina; impacted ____ / ____ impactada; open ____ / ____ expuesta; pathologic ____ / ____ pato-

fracture — fumes

lógica; spiral ___ / ___ en espiral; stress ___ / ___ por sobrecarga.

fracture *v.* fracturar, quebrar.

fragility *n.* fragilidad, con disposición a romperse o quebrarse con facilidad.

fragment *n.* fragmento, parte; *v.* fragmentar, romper, dividir en pedazos.

frambesia, yaws *n.* frambesia, enfermedad cutánea tropical infecciosa que se manifiesta con lesiones aframbuesadas ulcerosas.

frame *n.* armazón. estructura de soporte.

frank *a.* obvio-a, rel. a una condición física presente.

frantic *a.* frenético-a.

fraternal twins *n. pl.* mellizos fraternales, desarrollados de dos óvulos fecundados separadamente.

freckle *n.* peca, mácula pigmentada que se manifiesta en el exterior de la piel esp. en la cara.

freckled *a.* pecoso-a.

free *a.* libre, suelto-a; [*of charge*] gratis; ___ association / ___ asociación; **-ly** *adv.* libremente.

freedom *n.* libertad, independencia; *v.* **to have** ___ **to** / tener ___ para.

freeze *n.* helada; congelación; ___ drying / secar por congelación; *vi.* congelar, helar; congelarse, helarse; **to** ___ **to death** / morirse de frio.

freezing *n.* congelación; ___ point / punto de congelación.

fremitus *n.* fremitus, frémito, vibración detectable por palpación o auscultación tal como las vibraciones del pecho al toser.

French *n.* [*language*] francés; [*native*] francés, francesa; *a.* francés, francesa.

frenectomy *n. cirg.* frenectomía, excisión de un frenillo.

frenulum, frenum *L.* (*pl.* **frenulla**) frenulum, pliegue membranoso que impide los movimientos de un órgano o parte; ___ of the tongue / frenillo de la lengua.

frenzy *n.* locura, frenesí, extravío, arrebato.

frequency *n.* frecuencia.

frequent *a.* frecuente, habitual, regular; **-ly** *adv.* frecuentemente, con frecuencia.

fresh *a.* fresco-a, reciente.

freshen *v.* refrescar; renovar; refrescarse; renovarse.

Freudian *a.* freudiano, *psic.* rel. a las doctrinas de Sigmund Freud, neurólogo vienés (1856–1939).

friable *a.* friable, que se pulveriza o rompe fácilmente.

friction *n.* fricción, rozamiento.

fried *a. pp.* de **to fry**, frito-a.

fright *n.* espanto, temor excesivo.

frighten *a.* asustado-a, atemorizado-a.

frigid *a.* frígido-a.

frigidity *n.* frigidez, frialdad, esp. de la mujer incapaz de responder a estímulos sexuales.

frivolous *a.* frívolo-a; tonto-a; vano-a.

Frohlich's syndrome *n.* síndrome de Frolich, distrofia adipogenital manifestada en infantilismo sexual con cambios en las características sexuales secundarias.

front *n.* frente; **in** ___ **of** / en ___ de, delante de.

frontal *a.* frontal, rel. a la frente; ___ bone / hueso ___; ___ muscle / músculo ___; ___ sinuses / senos ___ -es.

frost *n.* escarcha, helada.

frostbite *n.* quemadura por frío.

froth *n.* espuma; *v.* echar espuma, espumar; **to** ___ **at the mouth** / echar ___ por la boca.

frozen *a. pp.* de **to freeze,** congelado-a; *v.* **to become** ___ / congelarse, helarse.

frozen section *n. cirg.* corte por congelación, espécimen de tejido fino que se toma y congela inmediatamente para ser usado en el diagnóstico de tumores.

fructose *n.* fructosa, azúcar de frutas; lebulosa.

fruit *n.* fruta; *v.* **to eat** ___ **-s** / comer ___ -s.

fruitful *a.* productivo-a; provechoso-a.

fry *v.* freir.

fulfill *v.* cumplir; llevar a cabo; realizar.

fulguration *n.* fulguración, uso de corriente eléctrica para destruir tejido vivo.

full *a.* completo-a; lleno-a, pleno-a; **in full** / completamente, por completo; ___ **answer** / respuesta ___; ___ **payment** / pago total.

full-grown *a.* completamente desarrollado-a; crecido-a.

full term *n.* a término, [*in obstetrics*] embarazo a término, de 38 a 41 semanas de duración incluyendo el nacimiento.

fulminant *a.* fulminante, que aparece súbitamente con extrema intensidad tal como un dolor o enfermedad.

fume *v.* humear, emitir vapores o gases.

fumes *n. pl.* vapores.

306

fumigant *n.* fumigante, agente usado en la fumigación.

fumigation *n.* fumigación, exterminación por medio de vapores.

fuming *a.* fumante, que desprende vapores visibles.

fun *n.* diversión, entretenimiento; *v.* **to have** ___ / divertirse, entretenerse.

function *n.* función; facultad; *v.* funcionar, desempeñar un trabajo.

functional *a.* funcional, de utilidad o valor práctico.

functional disease *n.* enfermedad funcional, desorden o trastorno que no tiene una causa orgánica conocida.

functioning *n.* funcionamiento.

funeral *n.* funeral, entierro; ___ **parlor** / funeraria.

fungal, fungous *a.* fungoso-a, rel. a hongos o causado por éstos.

fungate *v.* reproducirse rápidamente como los hongos.

fungemia *n.* fungemia, presencia de hongos en la sangre.

fungicide *n.* fungicida, exterminador de hongos.

fungistasis *n.* fungistasis, acto de impedir o arrestar el desarrollo de hongos.

fungus *n.* (*pl.* **fungi**) hongo.

funnel *n.* embudo

furious *a.* furioso-a; enfurecido-a.

furor *n.* furor, ira extrema.

furosemide *n.* furoscmida, diurético.

furuncle *n.* furúnculo; *pop.* grano enterrado.

furunculous *a.* foruncular, rel. a un forúnculo.

fuse *v.* fundir, fusionar, derretir un metal por medio de calor.

fusiform *a.* fusiforme, en forma de huso.

fusion *n.* fusión. 1. reacción termonuclear en la cual núcleos atómicos de luz se unen para formar átomos más potentes; 2. acto de fusionar o fundir; nuclear ___ / ___ nuclear.

future *n.* futuro, porvenir.

fuzzy *a.* 1. nublado-a, que no es claramente visible. 2. velloso-a; cubierto de pelusa.

G

G *abbr.* **constant of gravitation** / constante de gravitación.

g *abbr.* **gender** / género; **glucose** / glucosa; **grain** / grano.

gadfly *n.* tábano, moscardón; moscón.

gag *n.* abrebocas, instrumento para mantener la boca abierta durante ciertas intervenciones quirúrgicas; ___ **reflex** / reflejo de ___ .

gage *v.* medir, calibrar.

gain *n.* ganancia, ventaja; provecho; *v.* ganar; **to** ___ **weight** / aumentar de peso.

gainful *a.* ventajoso-a, provechoso-a.

gait *n.* marcha, andar; abnormal ___ / porte, paso irregular; ___ , ataxic / ___ atáxica, tambaleante; ___ , cerebellar / ___ cerebelosa, andar tambaleante, relacionado con trastornos cerebrales; ___ , hemiplegic / ___ hemiplégica, movimiento semicircular de una de las extremidades inferiores al andar; ___ , spastic / ___ espasmódica, andar rígido; ___ , waddling / ___ anserina, de pies excesivamente separados al andar, *pop.* andar de pato.

galactagogue *n.* galactagogo, galactógeno, agente que promueve la secreción de leche.

galactase *n.* galactasa, enzima presente en la leche.

galactocele *n.* galactocele, quiste de la mama que contiene leche.

galactose *n.* galactosa, monosacárido derivado de la lactosa por acción de una enzima o un ácido mineral.

galactosemia *n.* galactosemia, ausencia congénita de la enzima necesaria en la conversión de galactosa a glucosa o sus derivados.

galactosuria *n.* galactosuria, orina con apariencia lechosa.

galactotherapy *n.* galactoterapia. 1. tratamiento dirigido a un lactante mediante administración de medicamentos a la madre; 2. uso terapéutico de la leche en una dieta especial.

gall *n.* bilis, hiel; ___ **ducts** / conductos biliares.

gallbladder *n.* vesícula biliar; ___ **attack** / ataque de la vesícula.

gallium *n.* galio, metal.

gallop rhythm *n.* ritmo de galope, sonido anormal del corazón percibido en casos de taquicardia.

gallstone *n.* cálculo biliar.

galvanic *a.* galvánico-a, rel. al galvanismo; ___ **battery** / batería; ___ **cell** / célula ___ ; ___ **current** / corriente___ .

galvanism *n.* galvanismo, uso terapéutico de corriente eléctrica directa.

galvanocautery *n.* galvanocauterización. *V.* **electrocautery.**

galvanometer *n.* galvanómetro, instrumento que mide la corriente por acción electromagnética.

gamete *n.* gameto, célula sexual masculina o femenina.

gametocide *n.* gametocida, agente que destruye gametos.

gametocyte *n.* gametocito, célula que al dividirse produce gametos tal como el parásito de la malaria cuando se divide y pasa al mosquito portador.

gametogenesis *n.* gametogenesis, desarrollo de gametos.

gamma benzene hexachloride *n.* hexacloruro de gamma-benceno, insecticida poderoso utilizado contra la sarna.

gamma globulin *n.* gamma globulina, tipo de anticuerpo producido en el tejido linfático o sintéticamente.

gamma rays *n. pl.* rayos gamma. rayos emitidos por sustancias radioactivas.

gammopathy *n.* gammopatía, trastorno manifestado por un exceso de inmunoglobulinas como resultado de una proliferación anormal de células linfoides.

gangliectomy *n. cirg.* gangliectomía, ganglionectomía, excisión de un ganglio.

gangliocyte *n.* gangliocito, célula ganglionar.

ganglioglioma *n.* ganglioglioma, ganglioneuroma, tumor caracterizado por un gran número de células ganglionares.

ganglioma *n.* ganglioma, tumor de un ganglio, esp. linfático.

ganglion *n.* (*pl.* **ganglia**) ganglio. 1. masa de tejido nervioso en forma de nudo; 2. quiste en un tendón o en una aponeurosis, que se observa a veces en la muñeca, en el talón o en la rodilla; ____, celiac / ____ celíaco; ____-a, basal / ____-s basales; ____, carotid / ____ carotídeo.

ganglionic blockade *n.* bloqueo ganglionar.

gangrene *n.* gangrena, destrucción de un tejido debido a riego sanguíneo interrumpido gen. por infección bacteriana y putrefacción.

Gantrisin *n.* Gantricin, nombre comercial de sulfisoxazol, agente antibacteriano usado en el tratamiento de infecciones urinarias.

gap *n.* laguna, vacío; intervalo, abertura.

gargarism *n.* gargarismo, gárgara, gargarización con enjuague de la boca y la garganta.

gargle *n.* gargarización; *v.* hacer gárgaras.

gargolysm *n.* gargolismo, condición hereditaria caracterizada por anormalidades físicas, en algunos casos con retraso mental.

garlic *n.* ajo.

gas *n.* gas, sustancia con propiedades de expansión indefinida; **mustard** ____ / ____ de mostaza; **nerve** ____ / ____ neurotóxico; **tear** ____ / ____ lacrimógeno.

gaseous *a.* gaseoso-a, rel. a o de la naturaleza del gas.

gasoline *n.* gasolina; ____ poisoning / envenenamiento por ____.

gastralgia *n.* gastralgia, dolor de estómago.

gastrectomy *n. cirg.* gastrectomía, extirpación de una parte o de todo el estómago.

gastric *a.* gástrico-a, rel. o concerniente al estómago; ____ acid / ácido ____; ____ analysis / gastroanálisis; ____ digestion / digestión ____; ____ emptying / vaciamiento ____; ____ juice / jugo ____; ____ lavage / lavado ____; ____ ulcer / úlcera ____.

gastrin *n.* gastrina, hormona segregada por el estómago.

gastritis *n.* gastritis, infl. del estómago; **acute** ____ / ____ aguda; **chronic** ____ / ____ crónica.

gastrocolostomy *n. cirg.* gastrocolostomía, anastomosis del estómago y el colon.

gastroduodenal *a.* gastroduodenal, rel. al estómago y el duodeno.

gastroduodenoscopy *n.* gastroduodenoscopía, uso del endoscopio para examinar visualmente el estómago y el duodeno.

gastroenteroanastomosis *n. cirg.* gastroenteroanastomosis, unión quirúrgica del estómago al intestino delgado.

gastroenterocolitis *n.* gastroenterocolitis, infl. del estómago y el intestino delgado.

gastroepiploic *a.* gastroepiploico-a, rel. al estómago y el epiplón.

gastroesophagitis *n.* gastroesofagitis. *V.* **esophagogastritis.**

gastrogavage *n.* gastrogavaje, alimentación artificial al estómago por tubo o a través de una abertura.

gastroileostomy *n. cirg.* gastroileostomía, anastomosis entre el estómago y el íleo.

gastrointestinal *a.* gastrointestinal, rel. al estómago y el intestino; ____ barrier / barrera ____; ____ bleeding / sangramiento

———; ——— decompression / descompresión
———.

gastrojejunostomy *n. cirg.* gastroyeyunostomía, anastomosis del estómago y el yeyuno.

gastrorrhagia *n.* gastrorragia, hemorragia estomacal.

gastrostomy *n. cirg.* gastrostomía, creación de una fístula gástrica.

gastrula *n.* gástrula, etapa primitiva del desarrollo embriónico.

gauze *n.* gasa: absorbable ——— / ——— absorbible; absorbent ——— / ——— absorbente; antiseptic ——— / ——— antiséptica; ——— compress / compresa de ———.

gel *n.* jalea.

gelatin *n.* gelatina.

gelatinous *a.* gelatinoso-a, de consistencia semejante a la gelatina o que la contiene.

gender *n.* género, denominación del sexo masculino o femenino.

gene *n.* gen, gene, unidad básica de rasgos hereditarios; dominant ——— / ——— dominante; ——— frequency / frecuencia del ———; lethal ——— / ——— letal; recessive ——— / ——— recesivo; sex linked ——— / ——— ligado al sexo.

general *a.* general; ——— appearance / aspecto ———; ——— condition / estado ———; ——— treatment / tratamiento ———; ——— practitioners / médicos de familia.

generalize *v.* generalizar.

generalization *n.* generalización.

generation *n.* generación. 1. acción de crear un nuevo organismo; 2. producción por proceso natural o artificial; 3. conjunto de personas nacidas dentro de un período de unos treinta años aproximadamente.

generator *n.* generador, máquina que convierte energía mecánica en eléctrica.

generic *n.* nombre común de un producto o medicamento no patentado; *a.* genérico-a, rel. al género; ——— name / nombre genérico.

genesis *n.* génesis, acto de creación, reproducción y desarrollo.

genetic *a.* genético-a, rel. a la génesis y a la genética; ——— code / patrón ———; ——— counseling / asesoramiento ———; ——— engineering / construcción ———.

genetics *n.* genética, rama de la biología que estudia la herencia y las leyes que la gobiernan; medical ——— / ——— médica.

genital *a.* genital, rel. a los genitales; ——— herpes / herpes ———.

genitals, genitalia *n. pl.* genitales, órganos de la reproducción.

genocide *n.* genocidio, exterminación sistemática de un grupo étnico.

genom, genome *n.* genoma, el conjunto básico completo de cromosomas haploides en un organismo.

genotype *n.* genotipo, constitución genética de un organismo.

gentamicin *n.* gentamicina, antibiótico efectivo en varios tipos de bacterias gramnegativas.

gentle *a.* suave, sutil, tierno-a; moderado-a; **-ly** *adv.* suavemente, sutilmente, tiernamente; moderadamente.

genucubital *a.* genucubital, rel. a los codos, las rodillas y su posición; ——— position / posición ———.

genuine *a.* auténtico-a, genuino-a; legítimo-a.

genupectoral *a.* genupectoral, rel. a las rodillas y el tórax y su posición; ——— position / posición ———.

genu valgum, knock knee *n.* genu valgum, curvatura anormal hacia adentro de las rodillas y separación de los tobillos al caminar que comienza en la infancia a causa de una deficiencia ósea.

genu varum, bow-leg *n.* piernas arqueadas, *pop.* zambo-a, curvatura anormal de las rodillas hacia afuera.

genus *n.* (*pl.* **genera**) género, categoría perteneciente a una clasificación biológica.

genyplasty *n. cirg.* geniplastia, reconstrucción plástica de la mandíbula.

geographic tongue *n.* lengua geográfica, lengua caracterizada por áreas desnudas rodeadas de epitelio grueso que simulan áreas terrestres.

geophagia, geophagism, geophagy *n.* geofagia, geofagismo, propensión a comer sustancias terrosas tales como tierra o barro.

geriatrics *n.* geriatría, rama de la medicina que trata de las enfermedades que se manifiestan en la vejez y de los problemas que la afectan.

germ *n.* germen, microorganismo o bacteria esp. causante de enfermedades.

German measles *n.* rubela, rubéola, *pop.* sarampión de tres días, infección viral benigna muy contagiosa en los niños de 3 a 10 años. Puede causar trastornos serios en el desarrollo del feto al contraerla la madre; ____ vaccination / vacunación antirubeólica.

germ free *n.* axénico.

germinal *a.* germinal, rel. a o de la naturaleza de un germen o gérmenes; ____ vesicle / vesícula o núcleo ____.

germination *n.* germinación, brote de una planta o desarrollo de una persona o animal.

germinoma *n.* germinoma, neoplasma de tejido o células germinales usu. localizado en los testículos u ovarios

geromorphism *n.* geromorfismo, senilidad prematura.

gerontology *n.* gerontología. *V.* **geriatrics.**

gestalt *n.* gestalt, *psic.* teoría que mantiene que la conducta responde a la percepción íntegra de una situación y no es posible analizarla atendiendo sólo a las partes componentes de la misma.

gestation *n.* embarazo, gestación, estado de gravidez. *V.* **pregnancy.**

gesticulate *v.* gesticular, expresar por medio de gestos o señas.

gesticulation *n.* gesticulación, seña, gesto, ademán.

gesture *n.* gesto, ademán.

get *vi.* obtener, adquirir, conseguir; [*communication*] **to** ____ **across** / lograr comunicarse, hacer comprender; **to** ____ **ahead** / prosperar; **to** ____ **back something** / recobrar; [*to return*] **to** ____ **back** / volver: [*to swallow*] **to** ____ **down** / tragar; [*steps*] **to** ____ **down** / bajar; **to** ____ **into** / meterse; **to** ____ **it over** / acabar de una vez; **to** ____ [*someone, something*] **out of the way** / sacar de, quitar de, apartar de; **to** ____ **sick** / enfermarse; **to** ____ **underway** / empezar, comenzar; **to** ____ **up** / levantarse; **to** ____ **well** / curarse, sanarse.

giant *a.* gigante, de un tamaño grande anormal; ____ **cell** / célula ____ ; ____ **cell tumor** / tumor de células ____ -s.

giardiasis *n.* giardasis, infección intestinal común causada por la *Giardia lamblia* que se trasmite por contaminación de alimentos, de agua o por contacto directo.

gibbosity *n.* gibosidad, corcova, condición de joroba.

Giemsa's stain *n.* coloración de Giemsa, usada en frotis de sangre en análisis microscópicos.

gigantism *n.* gigantismo, desarrollo en ex-

ceso del cuerpo o de una parte de éste; ____ , acromegalic / ____ acromegálico; ____ , eunochoid / ____ eunocoide, gigantismo acompañado de características e insuficiencia sexual propias del eunuco; ____ , normal / ____ normal, desarrollo normal de los órganos sexuales y proporción normal de los órganos y partes del cuerpo, gen. causado por secreción excesiva de la glándula pituitaria.

Gimbernat's ligament *n.* ligamento de Gimbernat, membrana que se adhiere por un extremo al ligamento inguinal y por otro al pubis.

ginger *n.* jengibre.

gingiva *n.* (*pl.* **gingivae**) gingiva, encía, porción de tejido que rodea el cuello de los dientes.

gingivitis *n.* gingivitis, infl. de las encías.

girdle *n.* faja, cinturón; **pelvic** ____ / cinturón pélvico; **shoulder** ____ / cinturón toráxico.

Gitaligin *n.* Gitalina, glucósido extraído de la digitalis.

give *vi.* dar; ____ **birth** / dar a luz, estar de parto; **to** ____ **and take** / hacer concesiones mutuas; **to** ____ **out** / repartir; **to** ____ **up** / renunciar a, perder la esperanza; darse por vencido.

given *a., pp.* de **to give**, dado-a; ____ **name** / nombre de pila.

glacial *a.* glacial, rel. al hielo o semejante al mismo.

glad *a.* alegre, contento-a; *v.* **to be** ____ **of** / alegrarse de; **to be** ____ **to** / tener mucho gusto en; **-ly** *adv.* con mucho gusto; con satisfacción; alegremente.

glance *n.* mirada, ojeada, vistazo; *v.* dar un vistazo, dar una ojeada; **at first** ____ / a primera vista.

gland *n.* glándula, órgano que segrega o secreta sustancias que realizan funciones fisiológicas específicas o que eliminan productos del organismo; **eccrine** ____ / ____ ecrina; **endocrine** ____ / ____ endocrina; **swollen** ____ / ____ inflamada.

glans *n.* glande, masa redonda de estructura similar a una glándula situada en la extremidad del pene (glans penis) y del clítoris (glans clitorides).

glare *n.* resplandor, deslumbramiento, relumbrón; resol, excesiva exposición a un objeto luminoso que puede resultar en daño permanente a la retina.

glaring *a.* deslumbrante, intenso-a; brillante.

Glasgow coma scale *n.* escala de coma de Glasgow, método para evaluar el grado de un estado de coma.

glass *n.* vidrio, cristal; **magnifying** ___ / lente de aumento.

glasses *n. pl.* lentes, espejuelos, gafas; bifocal ___ / ___ bifocales; trifocal ___ / ___ trifocales.

glaucoma *n.* glaucoma, enfermedad de los ojos producida por hipertensión del globo ocular, atrofia de la retina y ceguera; absolutum ___ / ___ absoluto, etapa final del glaucoma agudo que resulta en ceguera; chronic ___ / ___ crónico; congenital ___ / ___ congénito; juvenil ___ / ___ juvenil, se manifiesta en niños mayores y jóvenes sin agrandamiento del globo ocular; infantil ___ / ___ infantil, se manifiesta a partir del nacimiento o desde los tres años.

glenohumeral *a.* glenohumeral, rel. al húmero y la cavidad glenoide.

glenoid *a.* glenoideo-a, con apariencia de fosa o cuenca; ___ cavity / cavidad ___; ___ fossa / fosa ___.

glia *n.* glia. V. **neuroglia.**

gliacyte *n.* gliacito, célula de una neuroglia.

glide *v.* resbalar; deslizarse.

glimpse *n.* mirada fugaz.

glioblastoma *n.* glioblastoma, tipo de tumor cerebral.

gliocytoma *n.* gliocitoma, tumor de células de neuroglia.

glioma *n.* glioma, neoplasma del cerebro compuesto de células de neuroglia.

gliomyoma *n.* gliomioma, combinación de glioma y mioma.

glioneuroma *n.* glioneuroma, glioma combinado con neuroma.

globin *n.* globina, proteína que constituye la hemoglobina.

globule *n.* glóbulo, pequeña masa esférica.

globulin *n.* globulina, una de las cuatro proteínas más importantes que componen el plasma; antilymphocyte ___ / ___ antilinfocítica; gamma ___ / gamma ___.

globulinuria *n.* globulinuria, presencia de globulina en la orina.

globus *n.* globo, esfera; ___ hystericus / ___ histérico, sensación subjetiva de tener una bola en la garganta.

glomerular *a.* glomerular. rel. a un glomérulo; en forma de racimo

glomerulonephritis *n.* glomerulonefritis, enfermedad de Bright, infl. del glomérulo renal.

glomerulosclerosis *n.* glomeruloesclerosis, proceso degenerativo del glomérulo renal que se asocia con arterioesclerosis y diabetes.

glomerulus *n.* (*pl.* **glomeruli**) glomérulo, colección de capilares en forma de bola pequeña localizados en el riñón.

glomus *n.* (*pl.* **glomera**) glomo, bola, grupo de arteriolas conectadas directamente a las venas, ricas en inervación.

gloom *n.* tristeza, desaliento.

gloomy *a.* triste, abatido-a.

glossa *n.* glosa, lengua.

glossalgia *n.* glosalgia, dolor en la lengua.

glossectomy *n. cirg.* glosectomía, excisión parcial o completa de la lengua.

glossitis *n.* glositis, infl. de la lengua; acute ___ / ___ aguda, asociada con estomatitis.

glossodynia *n.* glosodinia, V. **glosalgia.**

glossopathy *n.* glosopatía, enfermedad de la lengua.

glossoplegia *n.* glosoplejía, parálisis total o parcial de la lengua.

glossorrhaphy *n. cirg.* glosorrafía, sutura de la lengua.

glossotomy *n.* glosotomía, *cirg.* incisión de la lengua.

glossy skin *n.* liodermia, apariencia brillante de la piel. síntoma de atrofia o traumatismo de los nervios.

glottal *a.* glótico-a; ___ stop / oclusión ___ .

glottis *n.* glotis, hendidura en la parte superior de la laringe entre las cuerdas vocales verdaderas; aparato vocal de la laringe.

glottitis *n.* glotitis. V. **glossitis.**

glove *n.* guante; *v.* **to handle with kid** ___ -s / tratar con mucho cuidado, tratar delicadamente; *v.* **to fit like a** ___ / ajustar.

glucagon *n.* glucagón, una de dos hormonas producida por los islotes de Langerhans cuya función consiste en aumentar la concentración de glucosa en la sangre y que tiene un efecto antiinflamatorio.

glucagonoma *n.* glucagonoma, tumor que secreta glucagón.

glucocorticoid *n.* glucocorticoide, grupo de hormonas segregadas por la corteza suprarrenal que intervienen en el proceso metabólico del organismo y tienen un efecto antiinflamatorio.

glucogenesis *n.* glucogénesis, proceso de desdoblamiento del glucógeno.

gluconeogenesis *n.* gluconeogénesis. 1. formación hepática de glucógeno a partir de fuentes distintas de los carbohidratos; 2. formación de azúcar por desdoblamiento de glucógeno.

glucoronic acid, glycoronic acid *n.* ácido glucorónico, ácido de efecto desintoxicante en el metabolismo humano.

glucose *n.* glucosa, dextrosa, azúcar de fruta, fuente principal de energía en organismos vivos; ____, blood level of / nivel de ____ en la sangre; ____, tolerance test / prueba de tolerancia a la ____.

glucose-6-phosphate dehydrogenase *n.* glucofosfato de deshidrogenasa, enzima presente en el hígado y los riñones necesaria en la conversión de glicerol a glucosa.

glucoside, glycoside *n.* glucósido, compuesto natural o sintético que al hidrolizarse libera azúcar.

glucosuria, glycosuria *n.* glucosuria, presencia excesiva de glucosa en la orina; ____ diabetic / ____ diabética; ____ pituitary / ____ pituitaria; ____ renal / ____ renal.

glue *n.* cola, goma de pegar; ____ ear / oído tupido o tapado con cerumen: ____ sniffing / adicción a inhalar ____.

gluey *a.* gomoso-a, viscoso-a, glutinoso-a.

glutamate *n.* glutamato, sal de ácido glutámico.

glutamic-oxaloacetic transaminase *n.* transaminasa glutámica oxalacética (GOT o SGOT), enzima presente en varios tejidos y líquidos del organismo cuya concentración elevada en el suero indica daño cardíaco o hepático.

glutamic-pyruvic transaminase *n.* transaminasa glutámica pirúvica (GPT o SGPT), enzima cuyo aumento en la sangre es indicio de daño cardíaco o hepático.

gluteal *a.* glúteo-a, rel. a las nalgas; ____ fold / pliegue ____; ____ reflex / reflejo ____.

gluten *n.* gluten, materia vegetal albuminoidea; ____ free diet / dieta libre de ____.

glycemia *n.* glicemia, glucemia, concentración de glucosa en la sangre.

glycerin *n.* glicerina, glicerol, alcohol que se encuentra en las grasas.

glycine *n.* glicina, ácido aminoacético, aminoácido no esencial.

glycocholic acid *n.* ácido glicocólico, combinación de glicina y ácido cólico.

glycogen *n.* glucógeno, polisacárido usu. almacenado en el hígado que se convierte en glucosa según lo necesite el organismo; ____ storage disease / hepatina, almacenamiento de glucógeno en el hígado.

glycolysis *n.* glicólisis, subdivisión de azúcar en compuestos más simples.

glycopenia *n.* glucopenia. *V.* **hypoglicemia.**

glycopexic *n.* glucopéxico, que fija o acumula azúcar.

gnashing *n.* rechinamiento de los dientes.

gnat *n.* [*insect*] jején.

gnosia *n.* gnosia, facultad de reconocer y distinguir objetos y personas.

go *vi.* ir; irse; **to ____ after** / seguir; **to ____ about** / andar, caminar; [*to accompany*] **to ____ along with** / acompañar; **to ____ against** / ir en contra de; **to ____ ahead** / adelantar; emprender; **to ____ along with a decision** / aceptar, aprobar una decisión; **to ____ bad** / echarse a perder; **to ____ back** / volver, retroceder; **to ____ crazy** / enloquecer; **to ____ in** or **into** / entrar; **to ____ deep into** / ahondar; **to ____ down with** / enfermarse, caer enfermo-a; [*distance*] **to ____ far** / ir lejos; [*to succeed*] tener éxito, progresar; **to ____ on** / continuar; **to let ____** / soltar, dejar; **to ____ over** / examinar, estudiar; **to ____ through** / examinar o estudiar con cuidado; **to let oneself ____** / soltarse; dejarse; relajarse.

goat *n.* cabra; ____ milk / leche de____.

goblet cell *n.* célula caliciforme secretora que se localiza en el epitelio del tubo digestivo y del tubo respiratorio.

godchild *n.* ahijado-a.

godfather *n.* padrino.

godless *a.* ateo-a; incrédulo-a.

godmother *n.* madrina.

goggle-eyed *a.* de ojos saltones.

goiter *n.* bocio, engrosamiento de la glándula tiroides; congenital ____ / ____ congénito; exophtalmic ____ / ____ exoftálmico; toxic ____ / ____ tóxico (de síntomas similares a la tirotoxicosis); wandering ____ / ____ móvil.

gold *n.* oro.

gonad *n.* gónada, glándula productora de gametos: los ovarios en la mujer y los testículos en el hombre.

gonadal *a.* gonadal, rel. a una glándula

gónada; ___ dysgenesis / distenesia, malformación ___.

gonadotropin *n.* gonadotropina, hormona estimulante de las gónadas; ___ of the anterior pituitary / ___ hipofisaria; chorionic ___ / ___ coriónica, presente en la sangre y orina de la mujer durante el embarazo, base de la prueba del embarazo.

gonadotropin-releasing hormone *n.* hormona que estimula la secreción de gonadotropina.

gonion *n.* gonión, punto extremo inferior, posterior y lateral del ángulo de la mandíbula.

goniopuncture *n. cirg.* goniopuntura, tratamiento de glaucoma por punción en la cámara anterior del ojo.

goniotomy *n. cirg.* goniotomía, procedimiento para tratar el glaucoma congénito.

gonococcus *n.* (*pl.* **gonococci**) gonococo, microorganismo de la especie *Neisseria gonorrhoeae*, causante de la gonorrea.

gonorrhea *n.* gonorrea, enfermedad infecciosa catarral contagiosa de la mucosa genital.

gonorrheal *a.* gonorreico-a, rel. a la gonorrea; ___ arthritis / artritis ___.

good *a.* bueno-a; **all in** ___ **time** / todo a su debido tiempo; **in** ___ **time** / a buen tiempo, puntual; *v.* **to be** ___ **at** / tener talento para; **to put in a** ___ **word** / recomendar; **to do someone** ___ / hacer bien a alguien; **good!** / ¡muy bien! ___ **afternoon** / buenas tardes; ___ **behavior** / ___ conducta, buen comportamiento; ___ **cause** / causa justificada; **in** ___ **faith** / de ___ fe; ___ **luck** / buena suerte; ___ **morning** / buenos días, buen día; ___ **night** / buenas noches; ___ **-by** / adiós.

Good Samaritan Law *n.* Ley del buen samaritano, protección legal al facultativo o a otras personas que prestan ayuda médica en casos de emergencia.

gooseflesh *n. pop.* carne de gallina.

gout *n.* gota, enfermedad hereditaria causada por defecto del metabolismo de ácido úrico.

gracilis *n.* gracilis, músculo largo interno del muslo.

gradient *a.* gradiente, línea que indica aumento o disminución en una variable.

graft *n.* injerto, tejido u órgano usado en un trasplante o implante; ___, allograft, allogenic / ___ alogénico, de un donante genéticamente desigual al paciente; ___,

autogenous / ___ autógeno, injerto que se toma del propio paciente; bone ___ / ___ óseo; bypass ___ / ___ de derivación; ___, full thickness / ___ de capa gruesa completa, dermoepidérmico; ___, skin / ___ cutáneo, esp. en quemaduras; ___, thick-split / ___ de capa gruesa partida, que se injerta en un área descarnada; *v.* injertar.

graftable *a.* injertable.

graftage *n.* práctica de hacer injertos.

grain *n.* grano. cereal.

gram *n.* gramo, unidad de medida métrica.

gramicidin *n.* gramicidina, antibiótico producido por *Bacillus brevis,* localmente activo contra bacterias gram-positivas.

grammar *n. gr.* gramática.

gram-molecule *n.* molécula gramo, el peso en gramos de una sustancia igual a su peso molecular.

gram-negative *n.* gram-negativo, resultado de la aplicación del método de Gram de decoloración de una bacteria o tejido por medio de alcohol.

gram-positive *n.* gram-positivo, retención del color o resistencia a la decoloración en la aplicación del método de Gram.

Gram's method *n.* método de Gram, proceso de coloración de bacterias para identificarlas en un análisis.

granular *a.* granuloso-a, granulado-a, hecho o formado de gránulos.

granular cast *n.* cilindro granuloso, cilindro urinario visto en nefropatías degenerativas o de tipo inflamatorio.

granulation *n.* granulación, masa redonda y carnosa que se forma en la superficie de un tejido, membrana u órgano; ___ tissue / tejido de ___.

granule *n.* gránulo, partícula pequeña formada de gránulos; ___, acidophil / ___ acidófilo, que acepta colorantes ácidos; ___, basophil / ___ basófilo, que acepta colorantes básicos.

granulocyte *n.* granulocito, leucocito que contiene gránulos.

granulocytopenia *n.* granulocitopenia, deficiencia de granulocitos en la sangre.

granuloma *n.* granuloma, tumor o neoplasma de tejido granular; foreign body ___ / ___ de cuerpo extraño; infectious ___ / ___ infeccioso; inguinale ___ / ___ inguinal; venereum ___ / ___ ulcerativo de los genitales.

granulomatosis *n.* granulomatosis, granuloma múltiple.

granulopenia *n.* granulopenia. *V.* **granulocytopenia.**

granulosa *n.* granulosa, membrana ovárica de células epiteliales que rodea el folículo ovárico.

granulosa cell tumor *n.* tumor de la granulosa.

granulosa-teca cell tumor *n.* tumor de células de la granulosa-teca, tumor ovárico de células que provienen del folículo de Graaf.

grape *n.* uva.

grape sugar *n.* dextrosa, azúcar de uva y de otras frutas.

graphology *n.* grafología, estudio de la escritura como indicación de la personalidad del paciente y como ayuda en el diagnóstico de enfermedades nerviosas.

grass *n.* hierba, yerba.

grateful *a.* agradecido-a.

gratefulness *n.* gratitud.

gravamen *n.* agravio, motivo de queja.

grave *a.* severo-a, serio-a, peligroso-a.

Grave's disease *n.* enfermedad de Grave, hipertiroidismo. *V.* **exophthalmic goiter.**

graveyard *n.* cementerio, camposanto.

gravida *n.* mujer embarazada, preñada, encinta, en estado.

gravidity *n.* gravidez, embarazo.

gravity *n.* fuerza de gravedad.

gravy *n.* salsa, jugo de carne.

gray *n.* color gris; *a.* gris.

gray matter *n.* materia o sustancia gris, tejido nervioso muy vascularizado de color gris pardo compuesto de células nerviosas y fibras nerviosas amielínicas.

great *a.* grande, grandioso-a; **in ___ detail** / muy minucioso; **it is going ___** / todo va muy bien.

green *n.* verde.

green blindness *n.* ceguera al color verde.

green pepper *n.* pimiento verde.

greet *v.* saludar; recibir.

greeting *n.* saludo.

grid *n.* rejilla.

grief *n.* pesar, aflicción.

grief reaction *n.* reacción de aflicción.

grief stricken *a.* desconsolado-a; afligido-a; acongojado-a; lleno-a de pesar.

grieve *v.* afligirse, apenarse.

grievous *a.* penoso-a, doloroso-a.

grilled *a.* asado-a a la parrilla.

grime *n.* mugre, tizne.

grind *vi.* moler; triturar; picar.

grinder *n.* [*dental*] molar, *pop.* muela; pulverizador.

grinder's disease *n.* enfermedad de los pulmones producida por inhalación de polvo.

grip *n.* apretón de la mano; *v.* agarrar, apretar.

grip, grippe *n.* gripe, *Mex. A.* gripa; influenza.

griseofulvin *n.* griseofulvina, antibiótico usado en el tratamiento de algunas enfermedades de la piel.

gristle *n.* cartílago.

groan *v.* gemir; quejarse.

groggy *a.* atontado-a, vacilante, tambaleante.

groin *n.* ingle.

groove *n.* surco, ranura; **bicipital ___** / ___ bicipital; **costal ___** / ___ costal.

gross *a.* grave; grueso-a, denso-a; grotesco-a; **___ negligence** / imprudencia o negligencia ___.

gross anatomy *n.* anatomía macroscópica, estudio de los órganos y partes del cuerpo que se ven a simple vista.

ground *n.* base; suelo; terreno; *a. pp.* de **to grind,** molido-a.

ground substance *n.* sustancia fundamental que llena los espacios intercelulares de los huesos, cartílagos y tejido fibroso.

group *n.* grupo, conglomerado.

group therapy *n. psic.* terapia de grupo.

grow *vi.* crecer, desarrollar; **to ___ old** / envejecer.

growth *n.* desarrollo, crecimiento.

growth hormone *n.* hormona del crecimiento, secreción de la glándula pituitaria que estimula el crecimiento.

grumose, grumous *a.* grumoso-a, coagulado-a.

gryposis *n.* griposis, curvatura anormal esp. rel. a una uña.

guaiacol *n.* guayacol, antiséptico y anestésico.

guanethidine *n.* guanetidina, agente usado en el tratamiento de la hipertensión.

guarantee *n.* garantía; *v.* garantizar; acreditar.

guard *v.* [*protect*] guardar, proteger, cuidar; guardarse, cuidarse; **to ___ against** / tomar precauciones, cuidarse de, guardarse de.

guarded *a.* de cuidado; guardado-a; vigilado-a; protegido-a; in ____ condition / en estado de cuidado; en estado grave.

guardian *n.* guardián-a, custodio-a; tutor-a.

gubernaculum *n.* gubernaculum, dirección o guía.

guess *n.* suposición. *v.* adivinar, suponer; acertar.

guest *n.* invitado-a, huésped, comensal; parásito.

guidance *n.* guía, consejo, dirección.

guide *n.* guía; *v.* guiar, dirigir.

guideline *n.* pauta, guía, directriz.

guillotine *n.* guillotina, instrumento quirúrgico.

guinea pig *n.* conejillo de Indias.

gullet *n.* esófago; *pop.* garguero, gaznate.

gulp down *v.* engullir, tragar apresuradamente.

gum *n.* encía. *V.* **gingiva;** goma; **chewing** ____ / goma de mascar, *pop.* chicle.

gumboil *n.* absceso en la encía, flemón.

gumma *n.* (*pl.* **gummata**) goma, tumor sifilítico.

gummy *a.* pegajoso-a, gomoso-a, viscoso-a.

gun *n.* escopeta; revólver; pistola.

gunshot wound *n.* herida de bala.

gush *v.* salir a borbotones, derramar, verter.

gustation *n.* gustación, sentido del gusto.

gut *n.* intestino, *pop.* tripas.

gutta *n.* (*pl.* **guttae**) gutta, gota.

gutta-percha *n.* gutapercha, látex vegetal seco y purificado, que se usa en tratamientos dentales y médicos.

guttural *a.* gutural.

gymnastics *n.* gimnasia, calistenia.

gynandroid *n.* ginandroide, persona de características hermafroditas que muestra la apariencia del sexo opuesto.

gynecologic, gynecological *a.* ginecológico-a, rel. al estudio de enfermedades del tracto reproductivo femenino.

gynecologic operative procedures *n.* procedimientos quirúrgicos ginecológicos.

gynecologist *n.* ginecólogo-a, especialista en ginecología.

gynecology *n.* ginecología, estudio de los trastornos que afectan los órganos reproductivos femeninos.

gynecomastia *n.* ginecomastia, desarrollo excesivo de las glándulas mamarias en el hombre.

gyrus *n.* circunvolución, porción, elevada de la corteza cerebral; Broca's ____ / ____ de

Broca, tercera, frontal inferior; frontal, superior ____ / ____ frontal superior; inferior, lateral occipital ____ / ____ occipital inferior lateral; superior occipital ____ / ____ occipital superior.

H

H *abbr.* **hydrogen** / hidrógeno; **heroin** / heroína; **hypermetropia** / hipermetropía; **hypodermic** / hipodérmico.

h *abbr.* **height** / altura; **hour** / hora; **horizontal** / horizontal.

habilitate *v.* habilitar, equipar.

habit *n.* hábito, uso, costumbre; adicción al uso de una droga o bebida; *v.* **to be in the** ____ **of** / tener la costumbre de; acostumbrarse a; habituarse; [*drugs*] *pop.* **to kick the** ____ / dejar la adicción; curarse.

habit forming *a.* adictivo-a, rel. a una sustancia que envicia, que crea una adicción.

habit training *n.* entrenamiento de hábitos, enseñanza impartida a los niños para realizar actividades básicas tales como comer, dormir, vestirse, asearse y usar el servicio sanitario.

habitual *a.* habitual, usual, acostumbrado-a; **-ly** *adv.* habitualmente.

hacking cough *n.* tos seca recurrente.

had *pret., pp.* de **to have.**

haggard *a.* ojeroso-a; desfigurado-a; desaliñado-a.

hair *n.* pelo, cabello, vello; **curly** ____ / ____ rizado; **gray** ____ / cana; **pubic** ____ / vello púbico; **straight** ____ / ____ lacio, liso; **wavy** ____ / ____ ondeado.

hair ball *n.* bola de pelo, tipo de bezoar.

hairbrush *n.* cepillo para el cabello.

hair bulb *n.* bulbo piloso.

hair follicle *n.* folículo piloso.

hairless *a.* pelón -ona, pelado-a, calvo-a.

hairline *n.* raya del pelo; línea fina; trazo fino; ____ fracture / fractura de línea fina.

hair remover *n.* depilatorio.

hair root *n.* raíz del pelo.

hair transplantation *n. cirg.* trasplante de pelo, trasplante de epidermis que contiene folículos pilosos de una parte del cuerpo a otra.

hairy *a.* peludo-a, velludo-a; ____ tongue / lengua velluda, lengua infectada de hongos parásitos.

half *n.* mitad, medio; **in** ___ / en dos mitades; ___ **as much** / la mitad; ___ **and** ___ / a mitades, en igual proporción; ___ **brother** / medio hermano; ___ **sister** / media hermana; ___ **hour** / media hora; ___ **starved** / medio muerto de hambre.

half-life *n.* 1. vida media, tiempo requerido para que la mitad de una sustancia ingerida o inyectada en el organismo se elimine por medios naturales; 2. semidesintegración, tiempo requerido por una sustancia radioactiva para perder la mitad de su radioactividad por desintegración.

halide *n.* haloide, sales producidas por la combinación de un elemento halógeno y un metal.

halitosis *n.* halitosis, mal aliento.

halitus *n.* hálito, aire aspirado.

hall *n.* vestíbulo; recepción; pasillo.

hallucinate *v.* alucinar, desvariar.

hallucination *n.* alucinación, alucinamiento, sensación subjetiva que no tiene precedencia o estímulo real; auditory ___ , imaginary perception of sounds / ___ auditiva, percepción imaginaria de sonidos; gustatory ___ , imaginary sensation of taste / ___ gustativa, sensación imaginaria del gusto; haptic ___ , imaginary perception of pain, temperature or skin sensations / ___ táctil, percepción imaginaria de dolor, de temperatura o de sensaciones en la piel; motor ___ , imaginary movement of the body / ___ de movimiento, percepción imaginaria de movimiento del cuerpo; olfactory ___ , imaginary smells / ___ olfativa, de olores imaginarios.

hallucinatory *a.* alucinante, alucinador-a.

hallucinogen *n.* alucinógeno, droga que produce alucinaciones o desvaríos tal como LSD, peyote, mescalina y otras.

hallucinosis *n.* alucinosis, delirio alucinatorio crónico; acute alcoholic ___ / ___ alcohólica, manifestación de temor patológico acompañada de alucinaciones auditivas.

hallux *n.* (*pl.* **halluces**) dedo gordo del pie; ___ **valgus** / ___ valgus, desviación del dedo gordo hacia los otros dedos; ___ **varus** / varus, separación del dedo gordo de los demás dedos.

halo *n.* aréola. 1. área del seno de tono más oscuro que rodea el pezón; 2. círculo de luz.

halothane *n.* halótano, anestésico administrado por inhalación, nombre comercial Fluotane.

ham *n.* 1. corva de la pierna, región poplítea detrás de la rodilla; 2. jamón.

hamartoma *n.* hamartoma, nódulo de tejido superfluo semejante a un tumor usualmente benigno.

hamate bone *n.* hueso medio del carpo de la muñeca.

hammer *n.* martillo. 1. huesecillo del oído medio; 2. instrumento empleado en exámenes físicos; ___ **finger** or **toe** / dedo en garra; **percussion** ___ / ___ de percusión; **reflex** ___ / ___ de reflejo; ___ **toe** / dedo en martillo.

hamstring *n.* 1. tendones de la corva; 2. músculos flexores y aductores de la parte posterior del muslo.

hand *n.* mano; **give me a** ___ / ayúdeme, ayúdame; **at close** ___ / muy de cerca; **in good** ___-**s** / en buenas manos; *v.* **to have a free** ___ / tener libertad para, tener carta blanca; **to have one's** ___-**s tied** / tener atadas las manos, sin poder hacer nada; **to keep one's** ___-**s off** / no meterse; **to shake** ___-**s** / dar la ___ ; **on the other** ___ / por otra parte; ___ **deformities, acquired** / deformidades adquiridas de la ___ ; ___ **made** / hecho a mano; ___ **rest** / apoyo de la ___ ; *v.* **to** ___ **in a report** / presentar un informe; **to** ___ **news** / facilitar noticias; **to** ___ **out information** / facilitar información.

handful *n.* puñado, manojo.

handicap *n.* impedimento; obstáculo, desventaja; **handicapped person** / persona desvalida, inválida, baldada, impedida.

handle *n.* asa, mango; *v.* tratar, manejar, manipular; ___ **with care** / trátese con cuidado.

handling *n.* manejo, manipulación.

handmade *a.* hecho a mano.

handpiece *n.* [*dental*] pieza de mano.

handsome *a.* guapo, hermoso, distinguido.

handwriting *n.* escritura a mano.

handy *a.* a la mano; conveniente; cercano-a.

hang *vi.* colgar, suspender; ahorcar; ahorcarse.

hanging *n.* suspensión, colgajo; ejecución en la horca.

hangnail *n.* uñero, uña encarnada.

hangover *n.* malestar después de una borrachera.

hang-up *n.* obsesión o problema que irrita.

Hanot's disease *n.* enfermedad de Hanot,

cirrosis biliar, cirrosis hipertrófica del hígado acompañada de ictericia.

Hansen's disease *n.* enfermedad de Hansen. *V.* **leprosy.**

haploid *n.* haploide, célula sexual que contiene en el cromosoma la mitad de las características somáticas de la especie.

happen *v.* suceder, acontecer, ocurrir.

happening *n.* suceso, hecho, acontecimiento; **What is** ___? / ¿Qué sucede?, ¿qué pasa?

happiness *n.* alegría, felicidad.

happy *a.* contento-a, alegre, feliz.

haptoglobin *n.* haptoglobina, mucoproteína que se une a la hemoglobina libre en el plasma.

haptometer *n.* haptómetro, instrumento para medir la agudeza del sentido del tacto.

harass *v.* acosar, perturbar, hostigar, hostilizar.

harassment *n.* acosamiento, perturbación, vejamen.

hard *a.* duro-a, endurecido-a, sólido; trabajoso-a, difícil; [*bone*] osificado; ___ **of hearing** / medio sordo; *v.* **to grow** ___ / endurecerse; [*parturition*] ___ **labor** / parto laborioso; **-ly** *adv.* a duras penas, difícilmente, escasamente.

hard bone *n.* hueso compacto.

hardbound *a.* estreñido-a.

hard contact lens (HCL) *n.* lentes duros de contacto.

harden *v.* endurecer, solidificar.

hardening *n.* endurecimiento, solidez.

hard feelings *n. pl.* resentimiento.

hardheaded *a.* obstinado-a, terco-a, testarudo-a.

hard palate *n.* paladar óseo.

hard pressed *a.* acosado-a, apremiado-a.

hardship *n.* sufrimiento, privación, penalidad.

harelip *n.* labio leporino, deformidad congénita a nivel del labio superior causada por falta de fusión del proceso nasal interno y el lateral maxilar; ___ **suture** / sutura del ___.

harelipped *a*: labihendido-a, que tiene labio leporino.

harm *n.* daño, mal, perjuicio; *v.* dañar, perjudicar.

harmful *a.* perjudicial, dañino-a.

harmless *a.* inofensivo-a, inocuo-a.

harmonize *v.* armonizar; [*relations*] llevarse bien.

harmony *n.* armonía, reunión o comunicación agradable.

harness *n.* cinturón corrector.

harvest *n.* recolección, obtención o separación de bacterias u otros microorganismos de un cultivo; cosecha.

hashish *n.* hachís, *pop.* yerba, narcótico de efecto eufórico extraído de la marihuana.

hate, hatred *n.* odio, aversión; *v.* odiar, repudiar.

haustrum *L.* haustrum, cavidad o saco, esp. en el colon.

have *vi. aux.* haber; tener; **to** ___ **to** / tener que.

haversian system *n.* sistema de Havers, serie de canículos o pequeños conductos y láminas en formación concéntrica que forman la base estructural del hueso compacto.

hay fever *n.* fiebre del heno, asma del heno, catarro del heno, catarro primaveral, alergia causada por un agente irritante externo, gen. polen.

hazard *n.* riesgo, peligro; a ___ **to your** health / un ___ para su salud.

hazardous *a.* arriesgado-a, peligroso-a.

head *n.* 1. cabeza; 2. parte principal de una estructura; ___ **birth** / presentación cefálica; ___ **drop** / caída de la ___; **from** ___ **to toe** / de la ___ a los pies; ___ **injury** / traumatismo del cráneo, golpe en la ___; ___ **of the family** / ___ de familia; rest / apoyo para la ___; *v.* **to nod one's** ___ / asentir con la ___.

headache *n.* cefalalgia, dolor de cabeza, jaqueca.

head-shrinker *n.* psiquiatra.

headstrong *a.* voluntarioso-a, testarudo-a.

heal *v.* curar, sanar, recobrar la salud; [*a wound*] cicatrizar; curarse, sanarse; recobrarse.

healer *n.* curador-a; curandero-a.

healing *n.* 1. curación, recuperación de la salud; ___ **process** / proceso de ___; 2. curanderismo.

health *n.* salud; [*government*] ___ authorities / autoridades de Sanidad; Department of ___ / Ministerio de Salud o Salubridad; ___ assessment / evaluación del estado de salud; ___ care / atención o cuidado de la ___; ___ certificate / certificado de ___; ___ education / educación de la ___; ___ facilities / instituciones de ___; ___ laws / estatutos sanitarios; ___ personnel / profesionales médicos y de asistencia pública; ___ planning / planeamiento de métodos de ____ ; ____ services / servicios o atención de la ____ ; ____ services for the aged / servicios de salud a los ancianos; ____ status / estado de ____ .

healthy *a.* sano-a, saludable, fornido-a.

hear *vi.* oír, escuchar.

hearing *n.* audición, oído; ____ aid / audífono, dispositivo para aumentar la audición; ____ loss / pérdida de la audición.

heart *n.* corazón, órgano muscular cóncavo cuya función es mantener la circulación de la sangre; ____ atrium / aurícula cardíaca; ____ block / bloqueo del ____ ; ____ block, atrioventricular / bloqueo atrioventricular, interrupción en el nódulo A-V; ____ block, bundle-branch / bloqueo de rama; ____ block, interventricular / bloqueo interventricular; ____ block, partial / bloqueo parcial; ____ block, sinoatrial / bloqueo sinoatrial, interferencia completa o parcial del paso de impulsos del nódulo sinoatrial; ____ catherization / caterización o cateterismo cardíaco; congenital ____ disease / anomalías congénitas del ____ ; ____ disease / cardiopatías; ____ failure, congestive / insuficiencia cardíaca congestiva, colapso o fallo cardíaco; ____ failure, low output / deficiencia en mantener un flujo sanguíneo adecuado; ____ failure, left / insuficiencia ventricular izquierda, deficiencia en mantener un gasto normal del ventrículo izquierdo; ____ failure, right sided / insuficiencia del ventrículo derecho; hypertensive ____ disease / cardiopatía por hipertensión; ____ , hypertrophy / hipertrofia del ____ ; ____ , low output / gasto bajo; ____ murmur / soplo cardíaco; ____ output / gasto cardíaco; ____ pacemaker / estimulador cardíaco, marcapasos; ____ palpitation / palpitación cardíaca; ____ pump, nuclear powered / bomba del ____ de fuerza nuclear; ____ rate / frecuencia cardíaca; ____ reflex / reflejo cardíaco; ____ scan / escán cardíaco; ____ sound / ruido del ____ ; ____ transplant / trasplante del ____ ; ____ valve / válvula del ____ .

heartbeat *n.* latido del corazón, [*rapid*] palpitación.

heartburn *n.* acedía, acidez, *pop.* ardor en el estómago; agruras.

heart-lung machine *n.* máquina corazón-pulmón, máquina cardio-pulmonar que se usa para mantener artificialmente las funciones del corazón y los pulmones.

heat *n.* calor; ____ , conductive / ____ de conducción; ____ cramps / espasmo muscular (debido a trabajos realizados en altas temperaturas); dry ____ / ____ seco; ____ exhaustion / colapso por calor; ____ loss / pérdida de ____ ; ____ prostration / insolación con colapso; ____ stroke / insolación; ____ unit / caloría; ____ therapy / termoterapia; *v.* calentar; dar calor.

heater *n.* calentador; aparato de calefacción.

heating pad, electric *n.* almohadilla eléctrica.

heavier *a.* muy pesado; *comp.* más pesado que.

heaviness *n.* pesadez, pesantez, peso; [*sleep*] sueño pesado, modorra; [*feelings*] abatimiento, decaimiento.

heavy *a.* pesado-a, grueso-a, fornido-a; ____ chain disease / enfermedad de red o cadena.

hectic *a.* hético-a, febril; agitado-a; consumido-a, tísico-a.

heel *n.* talón, calcañal, parte posterior redondeada del pie.

hefty *a.* fuerte, macizo-a.

height *n.* altura, alto; estatura.

Heimlich maneuver *n.* maniobra de Heimlich, técnica que se usa para sacar o forzar la expulsión de un cuerpo extraño que impide el paso del aire de la tráquea o la faringe.

helical *a.* helicoideo-a, en forma de hélice o espiral.

heliophobia *n.* heliofobia, temor exagerado al sol de personas que han sufrido de insolación.

heliotherapy *n.* helioterapia, exposición o baños de sol con propósito terapéutico

helium *n.* helio, elemento gaseoso inerte empleado en tratamientos respiratorios y en cámaras de descompresión para facilitar el aumento o disminución de la presión del aire.

helminth *n.* helminto, gusano que se localiza en el intestino humano.

helminthiasis *n.* helmintiasis, condición parasítica intestinal.

helminthicide *n.* helminticida, vermicida, medicamento que extermina parásitos.

help *n.* ayuda, asistencia, socorro, auxilio; *v.* ayudar, asistir, auxiliar; remediar.

helpful *a.* útil, provechoso-a.

helpless *a.* desamparado-a, indefenso-a; desvalido-a, abandonado-a.

hemacytometer *n.* hemacitómetro, instrumento contador de las células sanguíneas.

hemagglutination *n.* hemoaglutinación, aglutinación de células rojas sanguíneas.

hemagglutinin *n.* hemoaglutinina, anticuerpo de células rojas o hematíes que causa aglutinación.

hemangioblastoma *n.* hemangioblastoma, hemangioma localizado generalmente en el cerebelo.

hemangioma *n.* hemangioma, tumor benigno formado por vasos capilares en racimo que producen una marca de nacimiento de color rojo púrpura en la piel.

hemangiosarcoma *n.* hemangiosarcoma, tumor maligno del tejido vascular.

hemarthrosis *n.* hemartrosis, derrame de sangre en la cavidad de una articulación.

hematemesis *n.* hematemesis, vómito de sangre.

hematherapy, homotherapy *n.* hematerapia, hemoterapia, uso terapéutico de la sangre.

hemathochezia *n.* hematoquezia, presencia de sangre en el excremento.

hematic *n.* hemático, droga usada en el tratamiento de anemia; *a.* hemático-a, relacionado con la sangre.

hematocolpos *n.* hematocolpos, retención del flujo menstrual en la vagina debido a imperforación del himen.

hematocrit *n.* hematócrito, 1. aparato centrifugador que se usa en la separación de células y partículas del plasma; 2. promedio de eritrocitos en la sangre.

hematocyst *n.* hematoquiste. 1. quiste sanguinolento; 2. hemorragia dentro de un quiste.

hematogenesis *n.* hematogénesis. *V.* **hematopoiesis.**

hematologic, hematological *a.* hematológico-a, rel. a la sangre.

hematologist *n.* hematólogo-a, especialista en hematología.

hematology *n.* hematología, ciencia que estudia la sangre y los órganos que intervienen en la formación de ésta.

hematoma *n.* hematoma, hinchazón por sangre coleccionada fuera de un vaso; *pop.* chichón; pelvic ___ / ___ pélvico; subdural ___ / derrame subdural.

hematomyelia *n.* hematomielia, derrame de sangre dentro de la médula espinal.

hematopoiesis, hemopoiesis *n.* hematopoyesis, hemopoyesis, formación de sangre.

hemianalgesia *n.* hemianalgesia, insensibilidad al dolor en un lado del cuerpo.

hemianopia, hemianopsia *n.* hemianopia, hemianopsia, pérdida de la visión en la mitad del campo visual de uno o ambos ojos.

hemiataxia *n.* hemiataxia, falta de coordinación muscular que afecta un lado del cuerpo.

hemiatrophy *n.* hemiatrofia, atrofia de la mitad de un órgano o de la mitad del cuerpo.

hemiballism *n.* hemibalismo, lesión en el cerebro que afecta la mitad del cuerpo con movimientos involuntarios rápidos sin coordinación, esp. en las extremidades superiores.

hemicolectomy *n. cirg.* hemicolectomía, extirpación de una mitad del colon.

hemihypertrophy *n.* hemihipertrofia unilateral con desarrollo excesivo de una mitad del cuerpo.

hemilaminectomy *n. cirg.* hemilaminectomía, extirpación de un lado de la lámina vertebral.

hemiparalysis *n.* hemiparálisis, parálisis de un lado del cuerpo.

hemiparesis *n.* hemiparesis, debilidad muscular que afecta un lado del cuerpo.

hemiparetic *a.* hemiparético-a, rel. a la hemiparesis o de la naturaleza de la misma.

hemiplegia *n.* hemiplejía, parálisis gen. ocasionada por una lesión cerebral que afecta la parte del cuerpo opuesta al hemisferio cerebral afectado.

hemiplegic *a.* hemipléjico-a, que sufre de hemiplejía.

hemisphere *n.* hemisferio, mitad de una estructura u órgano de forma estérica.

hemithorax *n.* hemitórax, cada mitad del tórax.

hemobilia *n.* hemobilia, sangramiento en los conductos biliares.

hemoblastosis *n.* hemoblastosis, desórdenes proliferativos de los tejidos que forman la sangre.

hemochromatosis, iron storage disease *n.* hemocromatosis, trastorno del metabolismo férrico acompañado por exceso de depósitos de hierro en los tejidos que causa anomalías de pigmentación de la piel, cirrosis hepática y diabetes.

hemoconcentrate *v.* hemoconcentrar, concentrar hematíes.

hemoconcentration *n.* hemoconcentración, concentración de hematíes a causa de una disminución en los elementos líquidos sanguíneos.

hemocytoblast *n.* hemocitoblasto, célula sanguínea primitiva de la cual se derivan las demás.

hemodialysis *n.* hemodiálisis, proceso de diálisis usado para eliminar sustancias tóxicas de la sangre.

hemodialyzer *n.* hemodializador, riñón artificial, aparato que se usa en el proceso de diálisis.

hemodilution *n.* hemodilución, aumento del plasma sanguíneo en relación al de los glóbulos rojos.

hemoglobin *n.* hemoglobina, la proteína de mayor importancia en la sangre a la que da color y por la que transporta el oxígeno.

hemoglobinemia *n.* hemoglobinemia, presencia de hemoglobina libre en el plasma sanguíneo.

hemoglobinuria *n.* hemoglobinuria, presencia de hemoglobina en la orina.

hemogram *n.* hemograma, representación gráfica de un conteo sanguíneo diferencial.

hemolith *n.* hemolito, concreción en un vaso sanguíneo.

hemolysis *n.* hemólisis, ruptura de eritrocitos con liberación de hemoglobina en el plasma.

hemolytic *a.* hemolítico-a, rel. a hemólisis o que la produce.

hemolytic anemia *n.* anemia hemolítica, anemia congénita causada por agentes tóxicos de eritrocitos frágiles de forma esferoidal.

hemolytic disease of the newborn *n.* hemólisis en el recién nacido, trastorno gen. causado por la incompatibilidad del factor Rh. *V.* **RH factor.**

hemophilia *n.* hemofilia, condición hereditaria caracterizada por deficiencia de coagulación y tendencia a sangrar.

hemophiliac *a.* hemofílico-a, persona afectada por hemofilia.

hemophilus, haemophilus *n.* hemófilo, bacteria anaeróbica gram-negativa del género *Haemophilus.*

hemophobia *n.* hemofobia, temor patológico a la sangre.

hemopneumothorax *n.* hemoneumotórax, acumulación de sangre y de aire en la cavidad pleural.

hemoptysis *n.* hemoptisis, expectoración sanguinolenta de color rojo vivo.

hemorrhage *n.* hemorragia, derrame profuso de sangre; internal ___ / ___ interna; cerebral ___ / ___ cerebral, accidente cerebrovascular; intracranial ___ / ___ intracraneana; petechial ___ / ___ petequial; post-partum ___ / ___ puerperal.

hemorrhagic *a.* hemorrágico-a.

hemorrhoid *n.* hemorroide, *pop.* almorrana, masa de venas dilatadas en la pared rectal; external ___ / ___-s externas, fuera del esfínter anal; internal ___ / ___ interna; prolapsed ___ / ___ de prolapso, protusión de almorranas internas por el ano.

hemorrhoidectomy *n. cirg.* hemorroidectomía, extirpación de hemorroides.

hemosalpinx *n.* hemosálpinx, acumulación de sangre en las trompas de Falopio.

hemosiderin *n.* hemosiderina, compuesto insoluble de hierro derivado de la hemoglobina que se almacena para ser usado en la formación de hemoglobina en el momento necesario.

hemosiderosis *n.* hemosiderosis, depósitos de hemosiderina en el hígado y el vaso.

hemostasis, hemostasia *n.* hemostasis, hemostasia, detención o contención (artificial o natural) de sangramiento.

hemostat *n.* hemóstato, instrumento o medicamento que se emplea para contener un sangramiento.

hen *n.* gallina; [*broth*] caldo de ___.

heparin *n.* heparina, sustancia que actúa como anticoagulante.

heparinize *n.* heparinizar, evitar la coagulación por medio del uso de heparina.

hepatectomy *n. cirg.* hepatectomía, extirpación de una parte o de todo el hígado.

hepatic *a.* hepático-a, rel. al hígado; ___ coma / coma ___; ___ duct / conducto ___; ___ lobes / lóbulos o subdivisiones ___-s; ___ veins / venas ___-as.

hepatitis *n.* hepatitis, infl. del hígado; fulminant ___ / ___ aguda fulminante; infectous ___ / ___ infecciosa o viral; non A-non B ___ / ___ no A-no B, asociada con transfusiones de sangre; ___ A(HAV) / ___ A, viral, afecta primordialmente a los niños; ___ B(HBV) / ___ B, causada por un virus y trasmitida en líquidos del organismo; saliva, lágrimas, semen; serum ___ / ___ sérica.

hepatocholangiogastrostomy *n. cirg.* hepatocolangiogastrostomía, establecimiento de drenaje de las vías biliares hacia el estómago.

hepatocyte *n.* hepatocito, célula del hígado.

hepatojugular reflex *n.* reflejo hepatoyugular, ingurgitación de las venas yugulares producida por el hígado en casos de insuficiencia cardíaca derecha.

hepatolenticular degeneration *n.* degeneración hepatolenticular.

hepatologist *n.* hepatólogo-a, especialista en trastornos hepáticos.

hepatology *n.* hepatología, estudio del hígado.

hepatomegaly *n.* hepatomegalia, agrandamiento del hígado.

hepatorenal *a.* hepatorrenal, rel. a los riñones y el hígado.

hepatosplcnomegaly *n.* hepatosplenomegalia, agrandamiento del hígado y el bazo.

hepatotoxin *n.* hepatotoxina, toxina destructora de células hepáticas.

herb *n.* yerba, hierba, planta clasificada como medicinal o usada como condimento; _____ tea / infusión.

here *adv.* aquí; _____ **and now** / ahora mismo; _____ **and there** / aquí y allá.

hereditary *a.* hereditario-a; que se trasmite por herencia.

heredity *n.* herencia, trasmisión de características o rasgos genéticos de padres a hijos.

heredofamilial *a.* herencia familiar, rel. a cualquier enfermedad o condición cuya manifestación indica un proceso heredado.

hermaphrodite *n.* hermafrodita, persona cuyo cuerpo presenta los tejidos ovárico y testicular combinados en un mismo órgano o separadamente.

hermaphroditism *n.* hermafroditismo, condición de hermafrodita.

hermetic *a.* hermético-a, que no deja pasar el aire.

hernia *n.* hernia, protrusión anormal de un órgano o víscera a través de la cavidad que la contiene; cystic _____ / _____ cística; hiatus _____ / _____ hiatal, a través del hiato esofágico del diafragma; incarcerated _____ / _____ incarcerada, gen. causada por adherencias; inguinal _____ / _____ inguinal, de una víscera con protrusión en la ingle o el escroto; lumbar _____ / _____ lumbar, protrusión en la región lumbar; reducible _____ / _____ reducible, que puede tratarse por mani-

pulación; scrotal _____ / _____ escrotal; sliding _____ / _____ por deslizamiento, de una víscera intestinal; strangulated _____ / _____ estrangulada, que obstruye los intestinos; umbilical _____ / _____ umbilical; ventral _____ / _____ ventral, protrusión a través de la pared abdominal.

hernial, herniated *a.* herniado-a, rel. a una hernia o que padece de ella; _____ sac / saco de la hernia, bolsa peritoneal en la cual desciende la hernia.

herniation *n.* herniación, desarrollo de una hernia; _____ of nucleus pulposus / _____ del núcleo pulposo, prolapso o ruptura del disco intervertebral.

herniography *n.* herniografía, radiografía de una hernia usando un medio de contraste.

herniorrhaphy *n. cirg.* herniorrafía, reconstrucción o reparación quirúrgica de una hernia.

heroic *a.* heroico-a, rel. a medicamentos de acción muy intensa.

heroin, dyacetylomorphine *n.* heroína, diacetilomorfina, narcótico adictivo derivado de la morfina; _____ addict / heroinómano-a.

heroinism *n.* heroinismo, heroinomanía, adicción a la heroína.

herpangina *n.* herpangina, enfermedad infecciosa, epidémica en el verano, que afecta las membranas mucosas de la garganta.

herpes *n.* herpes, enfermedad inflamatoria viral dolorosa dc la piel que se manifiesta con erupción y ampollas; _____ genitales / _____ de los genitales; _____ ocular / _____ ocular; _____ simplex / _____ simple, de simples vesículas que recurren una y otra vez en la misma área de la piel; _____ zoster, *pop.* shingles / _____ zóster, erupción dolorosa a lo largo de un nervio, *pop.* culebrilla.

herpetic *a.* herpético-a, rcl. al herpes o de naturaleza similar; _____ gingivostomatitis / gingivostomatitis _____, infl. de la boca y las encías causada por herpes simple.

hesitant *a.* indeciso-a, vacilante.

hesitate *v.* vacilar, mostrarse indeciso-a; **Don't** _____ **to call us** / No deje, no dejes de llamarnos; no vacile, no vaciles en llamarnos.

heterogeneous *a.* heterogéneo-a, de naturaleza diferente.

heterograft *n.* heteroinjerto, injerto de un donante de especie o tipo diferente al del receptor.

heterologous *a.* heterólogo-a; derivado de un organismo o especie diferente.

heteroplasia *n.* heteroplasia, presencia anormal de tejido en un área diferente a la que le corresponde según su origen.

heteroplastia *n.* heteroplastia, trasplante de tejido obtenido de un donante que pertenece a una especie diferente.

heterosexual *n.* heterosexual, inclinación sexual hacia el sexo opuesto.

heterosexuality *n.* heterosexualidad.

heterotaxis *n.* heterotaxia, posición anormal o irregular de vísceras o partes del cuerpo.

heterotopia *n.* heterotopia, desplazamiento de un órgano o parte de la posición normal.

heterotopic *a.* heterotópico-a, rel. a la heterotopía.

heuristic *a.* heurístico-a, que descubre una investigación o la estimula.

hiatus *n.* hiatus, abertura, orificio, fisura.

hibernoma *n.* hibernoma, tumor benigno localizado en la cadera o en la espalda.

hiccough, hiccups *n.* hipo, contracción involuntaria del diafragma y la glotis.

hidden *a. pp.* de **to hide,** oculto-a, escondido-a, latente.

hide *vi.* esconder; ocultar; esconderse.

hideous *a.* horrible; abominable.

hidradenitis *n.* hidradenitis, infl. de las glándulas sudoríparas.

hidrosis, hydrosis *n.* hidrosis, sudor excesivo.

high *a.* alto-a, elevado-a; ___ blood pressure / presión alta; ___ calorie diet / dieta rica en calorías; ___ color / de color subido; ___ cholesterol / nivel de colesterol; ___ risk / peligro o riesgo; ___ risk behavior / conducta o actividades de ___ riesgo; ___ residue diet / dieta ___ en residuos (fibras, celulosas); ___ nuclear waste / desechos nucleares de alta radiactividad; **-ly** *adv.* altamente, sumamente, excesivamente.

high altitude sickness *n.* enfermedad de la altura, trastorno por altura excesiva manifestado en dificultades respiratorias por imposibilidad de adaptarse a la disminución de la presión del oxígeno.

high risk groups *n. pl.* pacientes o personas con alto riesgo de contraer VIH: personas de actividades sexuales múltiples sin adecuada protección; drogadictos que intercambian agujas y jeringuillas; feto *in utero* o infante lactante de madre drogadicta o infectada por el virus.

highlight *v.* destacar, realzar, subrayar.

hike *n.* caminata; *v.* **to go on a** ___ / ir a caminar, ir andando.

hilum, hilus *n.* (*pl.* **hila**) hilio, depresión o apertura en un órgano que sirve de entrada o salida a nervios, vasos y conductos.

hindwater *n.* aguas posteriores, líquido amniótico.

hinge *n.* bisagra; ___ joint / coyuntura; ___ movement / movimiento de bisagra; ___ position / posición de gozne.

hint *n.* insinuación; indicación.

hip *n.* cadera, región lateral de la pelvis; ___ dislocation / dislocación de la ___ ; ___ dislocation, congential / dislocación congénita de la ___ ; ___ joint / articulación de la ___ ; snapping ___ / ___ de resorte; total ___ replacement / restitución total de la ___ .

hippocampus *n.* (*pl.* **hippocampi**) hipocampo, circunvolución de materia gris que forma la mayor parte de la corteza cerebral olfatoria.

hippocratic facies *n.* facies hipocrática, máscara facial que precede a la muerte.

hippocratic oath *n.* juramento hipocrático, juramento ético de la medicina.

hirsute *a.* hirsuto-a, peludo-a.

hirsutism *n.* hirsutismo, desarrollo excesivo del pelo en áreas no comunes, esp. en la mujer.

histamine *n.* histamina, sustancia que produce efecto dilatador en los vasos capilares y estimula la secreción gástrica.

histidine *n.* histidina, aminoácido esencial en el crecimiento y en la restauración de los tejidos.

histocompatibility *n.* histocompatibilidad, estado en el cual los tejidos de un donante son aceptados por el receptor; major ___ complex (MHC) / complejo de ___ mayor.

histologist *n.* histólogo-a, especialista en histología.

histology *n.* histología, estudio de los tejidos orgánicos.

histoplasmin *n.* histoplasmina, sustancia que se usa en la prueba cutánea de histoplasmosis.

histoplasmosis *n.* histoplasmosis, enfermedad de las vías respiratorias causada por el hongo *histoplasma capsulatum.*

histrionic *a.* histriónico-a, dramático-a.

HIV *n. abbr.* human immunodeficiency virus / VIH *abr.* virus de inmunodeficiencia humano, retrovirus del SIDA. Se transmite a través de relaciones sexuales o por intercambio de agujas y jeringuillas con una persona infectada. Puede transmitirse también a través de transfusiones de sangre obtenida de donantes infectados. El virus puede ser transmitido igualmente al feto *in utero,* durante el parto o en la lactancia a través de la leche materna de una madre afectada.

hives *n. pl.* ronchas, erupción alérgica.

hoarse *a.* ronco-a; áspero-a.

hoarseness *n.* ronquera, manifestación en la voz de una afección de la laringe.

Hodgkin's disease *n.* enfermedad de Hodgkin, presencia de tumores malignos en los nódulos linfáticos y el bazo.

hold *vi.* aguantar, sujetar; detener, mantener; sostener; contener; **to get ___ of** / agarrar; **to ___ off** / mantener a distancia; **to ___ an interview** / tener una entrevista; **to ___ responsible** / hacer responsable.

hole *n.* hueco, agujero.

holistic *a.* holístico-a, rel. a un todo o unidad.

holistic medicine *n.* medicina holística, sistema médico que considera al ser humano integrado como una unidad funcional.

hollow *a.* hueco-a, cóncavo-a.

holocrine *a.* holocrino-a, rel. a las glándulas secretorias.

holodiastolic *a.* holodiastólico-a, rel. a una diástole completa.

hologram *n.* holograma, producción de una holografía.

holography *n.* holografía, figura tridimensional de un objeto por medio de una imagen fotográfica.

holosystolic *a.* holosistólico-a, rel. a una sístole completa.

homeopathy *n.* homeopatía, curación por medio de medicamentos diluídos en cantidades ínfimas que producen efectos semejantes a los síntomas producidos por la enfermedad.

homeopatic *a.* homeopático-a, rel. a la homeopatía.

homogeneous *a.* homogéneo-a, semejante, de la misma naturaleza.

homograft *n.* homoinjerto, transplante tomado de la misma especie o tipo.

homologous *a.* homólogo-a, similar en estructura y origen pero no en funcionamiento.

homophobia *n.* homofobia, temor o repulsión a los homosexuales.

homophobic *a.* homofóbico-a, que tiene repulsión o temor a homosexuales.

homosexual *n.* homosexual, invertido-a, atracción sexual por las personas del mismo sexo.

homotonic *a.* homotónico-a, de la misma tensión.

homotopic *a.* homotópico-a, que ocurre en o corresponde al mismo lugar o parte.

homozygote *n.* homocigoto-a, que presenta aleles idénticos en una característica o en varias.

homozygous *a.* homocigótico-a, rel. a un homocigoto.

homunculus *n.* homúnculo-a, enano-a sin deformidades y proporcionado-a en todas las partes del cuerpo.

honest *a.* honesto-a, honrado-a.

honey *n.* miel de abeja.

hook *n.* gancho.

hookworm *n.* uncinaria, lombriz de gancho, nemátodo del intestino; **___ disease** / enfermedad de la ___ .

hope *n.* esperanza; *v.* esperar, tener esperanzas.

hopelessness *n.* estado de desesperanza; desesperación.

hordeolum *n.* hordeolo, orzuelo. V. **sty.**

horizontal *n., a.* horizontal; **___ position** / posición acostada.

hormonal *a.* hormonal, rel. a una hormona o que actúa como tal.

hormone *n.* hormona, sustancia química natural del cuerpo que produce o estimula la actividad de un órgano; **growth ___** / ___ del crecimiento.

hornet *n.* avispa, avispón.

hospice *n.* hospicio.

hospital *n.* hospital.

hospitalization *n.* hospitalización.

hospitalize *v.* hospitalizar, ingresar en un hospital; dar ingreso en un hospital.

host *n.* [*parasite*] huésped.

hostage *n.* rehén.

hostile *a.* hostil; enemigo-a.

hostility *n.* hostilidad, agravio, animosidad.

hot *a.* caliente, de temperatura alta; contaminado-a por material radioactivo; **___ flashes** / fogaje, sofoco; rubores, bochorno.

hot line *n.* línea telefónica de emergencia.

hour *n.* hora; **by the ___** / por hora; **-ly** *adv.* a cada hora.

house *n.* casa, vivienda, domicilio; ____ call / visita médica.

household *n.* familia.

housewife *n.* ama de casa, madre de familia.

housework *n.* tareas domésticas, trabajo de la casa.

how *adv.* cómo, cuánto; ____ **are you?** / ¿Cómo está?, ¿cómo estás?; ____ **many?** / ¿Cuántos-as?; ____ **late?** / ¿Hasta qué hora?; ____ **often?** / ¿Cuántas veces?, ¿Con qué frecuencia?

however *adv.* sin embargo, no obstante.

huge *a.* inmenso-a; enorme.

hum *n.* susurro; tarareo; zumbido; *v.* [*music*] tararear; zumbar; murmurar, susurrar.

human *a.* humano-a, rel. a la humanidad.

human immunodeficiency virus, HIV *n.* virus de immunodeficiencia humana, VIH, retrovirus del SIDA. *V.* **HIV.**

humanity *n.* humanidad.

humeral *a.* humeral, rel. al húmero.

humerus *n.* (*pl.* **humeri**) húmero, hueso largo del brazo.

humid *a.* húmedo-a, que contiene humedad.

humidifier *n.* humectante, humedecedor, aparato que controla y mantiene la humedad en el aire de una habitación.

humidity *n.* humedad.

humor *n.* humor. 1. cualquier forma líquida en el cuerpo; aqueous ____ / ____ acuoso, líquido claro en las cámaras del ojo; crystalline ____ / ____ cristalino, sustancia que forma el cristalino; vitreus ____ / ____ vítreo, sustancia transparente semilíquida localizada entre el cristalino y la retina; 2. secreción; 3. disposición de carácter; *v.* **to be in good** ____ / estar de buen ____; **to be in bad** ____ / estar de mal ____.

humoral *a.* humoral, rel. a los fluidos del cuerpo.

hump *n.* joroba, corcova, jiba.

hunchback *n.* corcova, joroba, deformación con curvatura de la espina dorsal.

hunger *n.* hambre.

hungry *a.* hambriento-a; **to be** ____ / tener hambre; **to go** ____ / pasar hambre.

Huntington's chorea *n.* corea de Huntington, *V.* **chorea.**

Hunt's neuralgia, syndrome *n.* neuralgia de Hunt. *V.* **neuralgia.**

hurdle *n.* obstáculo.

hurry *n.* prisa, apuro; **Are you in a** ____**?** / ¿Tiene prisa?, ¿tienes prisa?; *v.* apresurar; **to** ____ **him, her in** / traerlo, traerla inmediatamente.

hurt *vi.* lastimar, herir, hacer daño, dañar.

husband *n.* esposo, marido.

hyalin *n.* hialina, sustancia proteínica producto de la degeneración de amiloides, coloides y hialoides.

hyaline *a.* hialino-a, vítreo-a o casi transparente; ____ cast / cilindro ____, que se observa en la orina; ____ membrane disease / enfermedad de la membrana hialina, trastorno respiratorio que se manifiesta en recién nacidos.

hyalinization *n.* hialinización, conversión a una sustancia semejante al vidrio.

hyalinosis *n.* hialinosis, degeneración hialina.

hyalitis *n.* hialitis, infl. del humor vítreo.

hyaloid *a.* hialoide, hialoideo-a, semejante al vidrio.

hyaluronic acid *n.* ácido hialunórico, presente en la sustancia del tejido conjuntivo, actúa como lubricante y agente conector.

hybrid *a.* híbrido-a, rel. al producto de un cruzamiento de diferentes especies en animales y plantas.

hybridization *n.* hibridación, cruzamiento de especies.

hybridoma *n.* hibridoma, célula somática híbrida capaz de producir anticuerpos.

hydatid *n.* hidátide, quiste que se manifiesta en los tejidos esp. en el hígado; *a.* hidatídico, rel. a un tumor enquistado; ____ disease / equinococcosis; ____ mole / quiste ____ en el útero que produce hemorragia.

hydramnion *n.* hidramnios, exceso de líquido amniótico.

hydrate *v.* hidratar, combinar un cuerpo con el agua.

hydrocephalus *Gr.* hidrocéfalo, acumulación de líquido cefalorraquídeo en los ventrículos del cerebro.

hydrochloric acid *n.* ácido clorhídrico o hidroclórico, constituyente del jugo gástrico.

hydrocortisone *n.* hidrocortisona, hormona corticosteroide producida por la corteza suprarrenal.

hydroelectric *a.* hidroelétrico-a, rel. a la electricidad y el agua.

hydrogen *n.* hidrógeno; ____ concentration / concentración de ____.

hydrogen peroxide *n.* peróxido de hidrógeno, agua oxigenada, limpiador y desinfectante.

hydrolysis *n.* hidrólisis, disolución química de un compuesto por acción del agua.

hydrolyze *v.* hidrolizar.

hydromyelia *n.* hidromielia, aumento de líquido cefalorraquídeo en el canal central de la médula espinal.

hydronephrosis *n.* hidronefrosis, distensión en la pelvis renal y cálices a causa de una obstrucción.

hydrophilic *a.* hidrofílico-a, que tiene tendencia a retener agua.

hydrophobia *n.* hidrofobia, 1. temor excesivo al agua; 2. *pop.* rabia.

hydropic *a.* hidrópico-a, rel. a la hidropesia.

hydropneumothorax *n.* hidroneumotórax, acumulación de líquido y de gas en la cavidad pleural.

hydrops, hydropsy *n.* hidropesía, hidropsia o edema.

hydrosalpinx *n.* hidrosálpinx, acumulación de fluído seroso en la trompa de Falopio.

hydrosis *n.* hidrosis, secreción y excreción del sudor.

hydrostatic *a.* hidrostático-a, rel. al equilibrio de líquidos, o a la presión ejercida por un líquido estacionario.

hydrotherapy *n.* hidroterapia, uso terapéutico del agua con aplicaciones externas en el tratamiento de enfermedades.

hydrothorax *n.* hidrotórax, colección de fluído en la cavidad pleural sin producir inflamación.

hydroureter *n.* hidrouréter, distensión por obstrucción del uréter.

hydroxyapatite *n.* hidroxiapatita, forma de fosfato de calcio, compuesto inorgánico presente en los dientes y los huesos.

hygiene *n.* higiene, estudio de la salud y la conservación de un cuerpo sano; mental ___ / ___ mental; oral ___ / ___ oral; public ___ / ___ pública.

hygienic *a.* higiénico-a, sanitario-a, rel. a la higiene.

hygienist *n.* higienista, especialista en higiene; dental ___ / ___ dental, técnico en profiláctica-dental.

hygroma *n.* hidroma, saco o bursa que contiene líquido.

hymen *n.* himen, repliegue membranoso que cubre parcialmente la entrada de la vagina.

hymenectomy *n. cirg.* himenectomía, excisión del himen.

hymenotomía *n. cirg.* himenotomía, incisión del himen.

hyoglossal *a.* hioglosal, rel. al hioides y la lengua.

hyoglossus *n.* hiogloso, músculo de la lengua de acción retractora y lateral.

hyoid *a.* hioideo-a, rel. al hueso hioides.

hyoid bone *n.* hioides, hueso en forma de herradura situado en la base de la lengua.

hypalgia, hypalgesia *n.* hipalgia, hipalgesia, disminución en la sensibilidad del dolor.

hyperacidity *n.* hiperacidez, acidez excesiva.

hyperactive *a.* hiperactivo-a, excesivamente activo-a.

hyperactivity *n.* actividad excesiva; *psic.* desorden caracterizado por actividad excesiva que se manifiesta en niños y adolescentes acompañado de irritabilidad e incapacidad de mantener la atención.

hyperacuity *n.* desarrollo anormal de uno de los sentidos esp. la vista o el olfato.

hyperacute *a.* sobreagudo-a, extremadamente agudo-a.

hyperalbuminosis *n.* hiperalbuminosis, exceso de albúmina en la sangre.

hyperalimentation *n.* hiperalimentación, sobrealimentación por vía intravenosa.

hyperbilirubinemia *n.* hiperbilirrubinemia, exceso de bilirrubina en la sangre.

hypercalcemia *n.* hipercalcemia, cantidad excesiva de calcio en la sangre.

hypercapnia *n.* hipercapnia, cantidad excesiva de dióxido de carbono en la sangre.

hyperchloremia *n.* hipercloremia, exceso de cloruros en la sangre.

hyperchromatic *a.* hipercromático-a, con exceso de colorante o pigmentación.

hypercoagulability *n.* hipercoagulabilidad, aumento anormal de la coagulabilidad.

hyperemesis *n.* hiperemesis, vómitos excesivos.

hyperemia *n.* hiperemia, exceso de sangre en un órgano o parte.

hyperesthesia *n.* hiperestesia, aumento exagerado de la sensibilidad sensorial.

hyperflexion *n.* hiperflexión, flexión excesiva de una articulación, gen. causada por un traumatismo.

hyperfunction *n.* hiperfunción, funcionamiento excesivo.

hypergammaglobulinemia *n.* hipergammaglobulinemia, exceso de gamma globulina en la sangre.

hyperglycemia *n.* hiperglucemia, aumento excesivo de azúcar en la sangre.

hyperglycemic *a.* hiperglucémico-a, que sufre de hiperglucemia, o rel. a la misma.

hyperglycosuria *n.* hiperglcosuria, exceso de azúcar en la orina.

hyperhidrosis *n.* hiperhidrosis, sudor excesivo.

hyperhydration *n.* hiperhidración, aumento excesivo del contenido de agua en el cuerpo.

hyperkalemia *n.* hipercalemia, hiperpotasemia, aumento excesivo de potasio en la sangre.

hyperkinesia *n.* hipercinesia, aumento en exceso de actividad muscular.

hyperlipemia *n.* hiperlipemia, cantidad excesiva de grasa en la sangre.

hypermobility *n.* hipermobilidad, movilidad excesiva.

hypernatremia *n.* hipernatremia, cantidad excesiva de sodio en la sangre.

hypernephroma *n.* hipernefroma, tumor de Grawitz, neoplasma del parénquima renal.

hyperopia *n.* hiperopia, hipermetropía, *V.* **nearsightedness.**

hyperorexia *n.* hiperorexia, apetito excesivo.

hyperosmia *n.* hiperosmia, sensibilidad olfativa exagerada.

hyperostosis *n.* hiperostosis, desarrollo excesivo del tejido óseo.

hyperpituitarism *n.* hiperpituitarismo, actividad excesiva de la glándula pituitaria.

hyperplasia *n.* hiperplasia, proliferación excesiva de células normales en un tejido.

hyperpnea *n.* hiperpnea, aumento de la respiración en rapidez y profundidad.

hyperpyrexia *n.* hiperpirexia, temperatura del cuerpo excesivamente alta.

hyperreflexia *n.* hiperreflexia, reflejos exagerados.

hypersalivation *n.* hipersalivación, excesiva secreción de las glándulas salivales.

hypersecretion *n.* hipersecreción, secreción excesiva.

hypersensibility *n.* hipersensibilidad, sensibilidad excesiva al efecto de un antígeno o a un estímulo.

hypersensitive *a.* hipersensible, hiperestésico-a.

hypersplenism *n.* hiperesplenismo, funcionamiento exagerado del bazo.

hypertelorism *n.* hipertelorismo, distancia exagerada en la localización de dos órganos o partes.

hypertension *n.* hipertensión, presión arterial alta; benign ___ / ___ benigna; essential ___ / ___ esencial; malignant ___ / ___ maligna; portal ___ / ___ portal; primary ___ / ___ primaria; renal ___ / ___ renal.

hypertensive *a.* hipertenso-a. 1. que causa elevación en la presión; 2. rel. a la hipertensión o que padece de ella.

hyperthermia *n.* hipertermia. *V.* **hyperpiresia.**

hyperthyroidism *n.* hipertiroidismo, actividad excesiva de la glándula tiroides.

hypertonic *a.* hipertónico-a, rel. a o caracterizado por aumento de tonicidad o tensión.

hypertrophy *n.* hipertrofia, desarrollo excesivo o agrandamiento anormal de un órgano o parte; cardiac ___ / ___ cardíaca, corazón agrandado; compensatory ___ / ___ compensatoria, como resultado de un defecto físico.

hypertropia *n.* hipertropia, tipo de estrabismo.

hyperuricemia *n.* hiperuricemia, exceso de ácido úrico en la sangre.

hyperventilation *n.* hiperventilación, respiración excesivamente rápida y profunda con expiración del aire igualmente rápida.

hyperviscosity *n.* hiperviscosidad, viscosidad excesiva.

hyphema *n.* hifema. 1. ojo inyectado; 2. sangramiento en la cámara anterior del ojo.

hypnagogic *a.* hipnagógico-a. 1. adormecedor-a, que induce el sueño; 2. *psic.* que experimenta alucinaciones o sueños antes de perder el conocimiento o de pasar a un sueño profundo.

hypnosis *n.* hipnosis, estado sugestivo durante el cual la persona sometida responde a mandatos siempre que éstos no contradigan convicciones arraigadas.

hypnotherapy *n.* hipnoterapia, tratamiento terapéutico con práctica de hipnosis.

hypnotism *n.* hipnotismo, práctica de la hipnosis.

hypnotize *v.* hipnotizar, producir hipnosis.

hypoadrenalism *n.* hipoadrenalismo, desorden causado por deficiencia de la glándula suprarrenal.

hypoalbuminemia *n.* hipoalbuminemia, deficiencia de albúmina en la sangre.

hypocalcemia *n.* hipocalcemia, calcio en la sangre anormalmente bajo.

hypocapnia *n.* hipocapnia, disminución del dióxido de carbono en la sangre.

hypochlorhydria *n.* hipocloridria, deficiencia en la secreción de ácido clorídrico en el estómago, condición que puede indicar una fase primaria de cáncer.

hypochondria *n.* hipocondría, excesiva preocupación por la salud propia, con síntomas imaginarios de enfermedades.

hypochondriac *n. a.* hipocondríaco-a, hipocóndrico-a, que cree haber contraído alguna enfermedad cuando goza de salud y se preocupa por ello.

hypochondrium *n.* hipocondrio, parte del abdomen a cada lado del epigastrio.

hypochromatism *n.* hipocromatismo, falta o disminución de color o pigmentación, esp. en el núcleo de la célula.

hypochromia *n.* hipocromía, deficiencia de hemoglobina en la sangre.

hypochromic *a.* hipocrómico-a rel. a la hipocromía.

hypocyclosis *n.* hipociclosis, deficiencia en la acomodación visual; lenticular ___ / ___ por deficiencia muscular o rigidez del cristalino.

hypodermic *a.* hipodérmico-a, que se aplica por debajo de la piel.

hypofibrinogenemia *n.* hipofibrinogenemia, contenido bajo de fibrinógeno en la sangre.

hypofunction *n.* hipofunción, deficiencia en el funcionamiento de un órgano.

hypogammaglobulinemia *n.* hipogammaglobulinemia, nivel anormalmente bajo de gamma globulina en la sangre; acquired ___ / ___ adquirida, que se manifiesta después de la infancia.

hypogastrium *n.* hipogastrio, área inferior media y anterior del abdomen.

hypoglossal *a.* hipoglosal, rel. a una posición debajo de la lengua.

hypoglossal nerve *n.* nervio hipogloso.

hypoglycemia *n.* hipoglicemia, hipoglucemia, disminución anormal del contenido de glucosa en la sangre.

hypoglycemic *a.* hipoglicémico-a, hipoglucémico-a, que produce o tiene relación con la hipoglicemia; ___ agents / agentes ___ -s; ___ shock / choque ___ .

hypokalemia *n.* hipocalemia, deficiencia en el contenido de potasio en la sangre.

hypomania *n.* hipomanía, manía moderada.

hyponatremia *n.* hiponatremia, deficiencia en el contenido de sodio en la sangre.

hypopharynx *n.* hipofaringe, parte de la faringe situada bajo el borde superior de la epiglotis.

hypophysectomy *n. cirg.* hipofisectomía, extirpación de la glándula pituitaria.

hypophysis *n.* hipófisis, glándula pituitaria, cuerpo epitelial localizado en la base de la silla turca.

hypopituitarism *n.* hipopituitarismo, condición patológica debida a disminución de la secreción de la glándula pituitaria.

hypoplasia *n.* hipoplasia, desarrollo incompleto de un órgano o parte.

hypoplastic *a.* hipoplástico-a, rel. a la hipoplasia.

hypoprothombinemia *n.* hipoprotombinemia, deficiencia en la cantidad de protombina en la sangre.

hyporeflexia *n.* hiporreflexia, reflejos débiles.

hypospadias *n.* hipospadias, anomalía congénita de la uretra masculina que consiste en el cierre incompleto de la cara ventral de la uretra en distintos grados de longitud. (En la mujer la uretra tiene salida a la vagina.)

hypotelorism *n.* hipotelorismo, disminución anormal de la distancia entre dos órganos o partes.

hypotension *n.* hipotension, presión arterial baja.

hypotensive *a.* hipotenso-a, rel. a la presión baja o que sufre de ella.

hypothalamus *n.* hipotálamo, parte del diencéfalo.

hypothermia *n.* hipotermia, temperatura baja.

hypothesis *n.* (*pl.* **hypotheses**) hipótesis, suposición asumida en el desarrollo de una teoría.

hypothrombinemia *n.* hipotrombinemia, deficiencia de trombina en la sangre que causa una tendencia a sangrar.

hypothyroid *a.* hipotiroideo-a, rel. al hipotiroidismo.

hypothyroidism *n.* hipotiroidismo, deficiencia en el funcionamiento de la glándula tiroides.

hypotonic *a.* hipotónico-a. 1. rel. a la deficiencia en tonicidad muscular; 2. de presión osmótica más baja en comparación con otros elementos.

hypoventilation *n.* hipoventilación, reducción en la entrada de aire a los pulmones.

hypovolemia *n.* hipovolemia, disminución del volumen de la sangre en el organismo.

hypoxemia *n.* hipoxemia, insuficiencia de oxígeno en la sangre.

hysterectomy *n. cirg.* histerectomía, extirpación del útero; abdominal ___ / ___ abdominal, a través del abdomen; total ___ / ___ total, del útero y del cuello uterino; vaginal ___ / ___ vaginal, a través de la vagina.

hysteria *n.* histeria, neurosis extrema.

hysteric, hysterical *a.* histérico-a, rel. a la histeria o que padece de ella; ___ laughter / risa ___ ; *v.* to get ___ / ponerse ___ ; **-ly** *adv.* histéricamente.

hysterics *n.* histerismo, histeria.

hysteroid *n.* histeroide, semejante a la histeria.

hysteromania *n.* histeromanía, ninfomanía.

hysterosalpingo-oophorectomy *n. cirg.* histerosalpingo-ooforectomía, excisión del útero, tubos uterinos y ovarios.

hysteroscopy *n.* histeroscopía, examen endoscópico de la cavidad uterina.

hysterotomy *n. cirg.* histerotomía, incisión del útero.

I

I *abbr.* símbolo químico del iodo.

i *abbr.* **iatric** / iátrico; **immune** / inmune; **implant** / implante; **impotence** / impotencia; **incomplete** / incompleto

I *pron.* yo, primera persona del singular.

iatric *a.* iátrico-a, rel a la medicina, a la profesión médica, o a los que la ejercen.

iatrogenic *a.* yatrógeno-a, iatrogénico-a, rel. a un trastorno o lesión producido por tratamiento o instrucción errónea del facultativo.

ibuprofen *n.* ibuprofén, agente antiinflamatorio, antipirético y analgésico usado en el tratamiento de artritis reumatoidea.

ice *n.* hielo; ___ **cap**, ___ **bag** / bolsa de ___ ; ___ **cream** / helado; ___ **water** / agua helada, agua con hielo; ___ **treatment** / aplicación de hielo; **My hands are like ___** . / Tengo las manos heladas.

ichthyosis *n.* ictiosis, dermatosis congénita caracterizada por sequedad y peladura escamosa esp. de las extremidades.

icing *n.* aplicación de hielo.

icteric *a.* ictérico-a, rel. a la ictericia.

icterogenic *a.* icterogénico-a, causante de ictericia.

icterohepatitis *n.* icterohepatitis, hepatitis asociada con ictericia.

icterus *n.* icterus; ___, gravis neonatorum / ictericia del neonato. *V.* **jaundice.**

ictus *n.* ictus, ataque súbito.

idea *n.* idea, concepto; fixed ___ / ___ fija.

ideal *n., a.* ideal; perfecto-a.

ideation *n.* ideación, proceso de formación de ideas.

idée fixe *Fr.* idea fija.

identical *a.* idéntico-a, igual, mismo-a.

identical twins *n. pl.* gemelos idénticos formados por la fertilización de un solo óvulo.

identification *n.* identificación; *psic.* proceso en el cual una persona adopta inconscientemente características semejantes a otra persona o grupo; ___ papers / documento oficial de identidad.

identify *v.* identificar; reconocer.

identity *n.* identidad, reconocimiento propio; ___ crisis / crisis de ___ .

ideology *n.* ideología, formación de conceptos e ideas.

ideomotion *n.* ideomoción, actividad muscular dirigida por una idea predominante.

idiocracy *n.* idiocracia, tendencia a someterse a ciertos hábitos o drogas.

idiocy *n.* idiotez, deficiencia mental.

idiogram *n.* idiograma, gráfico representativo de los cromosomas de una célula en particular.

idiopathic *a.* idiopático-a. 1. rel. a la idiopatía; 2. que tiene origen espontáneo propio.

idiopathy *n.* idiopatía, enfermedad espontánea o de origen desconocido.

idiosyncrasy *n.* idiosincrasia. 1. características individuales; 2. reacción peculiar de cada persona a una acción, idea, medicamento, tratamiento o alimento.

idiot *a.* idiota, imbécil.

idiotropic *a.* idiotrópico-a. *V.* **egocentric.**

idioventricular *a.* idioventricular, rel. a los ventrículos o que afecta exclusivamente a éstos.

ignorance *n.* ignorancia.

ignorant *a.* ignorante.

ignore *v.* desatender, ignorar, desconocer, no hacer caso.

ileal *a.* ileal, rel. al íleon.

ileal bypass *n.* desviación quirúrgica del íleon.

ileitis *n.* ileitis, infl. del íleon; regional ___ / ___ regional.

ileocecal *a.* ileocecal, rel. al íleon y al ciego; ___ valve / válvula ___.

ileocolitis *n.* ileocolitis, infl. de la mucosa del íleon y el colon.

ileocystoplasty *n. cirg.* ileocistoplastia, sutura de un segmento del íleon a la vejiga para aumentar la capacidad de ésta.

ileoproctostomy *n. cirg.* ileoproctostomía, anastomosis entre el íleon y el recto.

ileosigmoidostomy *n.* ileosigmoidostomía, anastomosis del íleon al colon sigmoide.

ileostomy *n. cirg.* ileostomía, anastomosis del íleon y la pared abdominal anterior.

ileotransversostomy *n. cirg.* ileotransversostomía, anastomosis del íleon y el colon transverso.

ileum *n.* (*pl.* **ílea**) íleon, porción distal del intestino delgado que se extiende desde el yeyuno al ciego.

iliac *a.* ilíaco-a, rel. al ilión.

iliofemoral *a.* iliofemoral, rel. al ilión y el fémur.

iliohypogastric *a.* iliohipogástrico, rel. al ilión y el hipogastrio.

ilioinguinal *n.* ilioinguinal, rel. a las regiones inguinal e ilíaca.

iliolumbar *a.* iliolumbar, rel. a las regiones ilíaca y lumbar.

ilium *n.* (*pl.* **ilia**) ilión, porción del iliaco.

ill *a.* enfermo-a, insano-a; *v.* **to be** ___ / estar enfermo-a; **to become** ___ / enfermarse; **to feel** ___ / sentirse indispuesto-a; sentirse mal.

ill-advised *a.* mal aconsejado; mal informado-a; desacertado; imprudente.

ill-behaved *a.* de mala conducta.

illegal *a.* ilegal.

illegible *a.* ilegible.

illegitimate *a.* ilegítimo-a.

ill health *n.* mala salud; *v.* **to be in** ___ / no estar bien de salud.

illicit *a.* ilícito, ilegal.

illiterate *a.* analfabeto-a.

ill-mannered *a.* descortés.

illness *n.* enfermedad, dolencia.

ill-tempered *a.* de mal carácter, de mal genio.

illumination *n.* iluminación; dark field ___ / iluminación lateral u oblicua del campo oscuro.

illusion *n.* ilusión, interpretación imaginaria de impresiones sensoriales.

illusory *a.* ilusorio-a, rel. a la ilusión.

illustration *n.* ilustración, gráfico.

image *n.* imagen, figura; representación.

imaginary *a.* imaginario-a, ilusorio-a.

imagination *n.* imaginación.

imbalance *n.* desequilibrio.

imbecile *a.* imbécil.

imbed *v.* V. **embed.**

imbibition *n.* imbibición, absorción de un líquido.

imbricated *a.* imbricado-a, en forma de capas.

imitable *a.* imitable.

imitate *v.* imitar, copiar.

imitation *n.* imitación, copia.

immature *a.* inmaturo-a, inmaduro-a; prematuro-a; sin madurez.

immediate *a.* inmediato-a, cercano-a.

immediately *adv.* inmediatamente, en seguida.

immerse *v.* sumergir, hundir.

immersion *n.* inmersión, sumersión de un cuerpo o materia en un líquido.

immigrant *n.* inmigrante.

imminent *a.* inminente; irremediable.

immoblle *a.* inmóvil, estable, fijo-a; que no se puede mover.

immobility *n.* inmovilidad, sin movimiento.

immobilization *n.* inmovilización.

immobilize *v.* inmovilizar.

immoderate *a.* inmoderado-a, sin moderación.

immoral *a.* inmoral, corrompido-a, vicioso-a.

immorality *n.* inmoralidad.

immortal *a.* inmortal, imperecedero-a.

immune *a.* inmune. resistente a contraer una enfermedad; ___ response / respuesta ___; ___ reaction / reacción ___.

immunity *n.* inmunidad. 1. condición del organismo de resistir a un determinado antígeno por activación de anticuerpos específicos; 2. resistencia creada por el organismo en contra de una enfermedad específica; active ___ / ___ activa, producción propia de anticuerpos; acquired ___ / ___ adquirida, presencia de anticuerpos y reactivación de células que forman anticuerpos; natural ___ / ___ natural, de tipo genético; passive ___ / ___ pasiva, adquirida de un donante; artificial ___ /

artificial, tal como la inmunidad adquirida en una vacunación.

immunization *n.* inmunización, proceso para activar la producción de inmunidad en el organismo en contra de una determinada enfermedad.

immunize *v.* inmunizar, hacer inmune.

immunoassay *n.* inmunoensayo, proceso para determinar la capacidad de una sustancia para actuar como antígeno y anticuerpo en un tejido; enzime ___ / ___ enzimático.

immunochemotherapy *n.* inmunoquimoterapia, proceso combinado de inmunoterapia y quimoterapia aplicado en el tratamiento de ciertos tumores malignos.

immunocompetency *n.* inmunocompetencia, proceso de alcanzar inmunidad después de la exposición a un antígeno.

immunodeficiency *n.* inmunodeficiencia, reacción inmune celular inadecuada que limita la habilidad de responder a estímulos antigénicos; severe combined ___ disease / enfermedad grave de ___ combinada.

immunoelectrophoresis *n.* inmunoelectroforesis, uso de electroforesis como técnica para investigar el número y tipo de proteínas y anticuerpos presentes en los líquidos del organismo.

immunofluorescence *n.* inmunofluorescencia, método que usa anticuerpos marcados con fluorescina para localizar antígenos en los tejidos.

immunoglobuline *n.* inmunoglobulina. 1. proteína de origen animal que pertenece al grupo sistema de respuesta inmune; 2. uno de los cinco tipos de gamma globulina capaz de actuar como anticuerpo.

immunologic *a.* inmunológico-a, rel. a la inmunología.

immunology *n.* inmunología, rama de la medicina que estudia las reacciones del cuerpo a cualquier invasión extraña, tal como la de bacterias, virus o trasplantes.

immunoprotein *n.* inmunoproteína, proteína que actúa como anticuerpo.

immunostimulant *n.* inmunoestimulante, agente capaz de inducir o estimular una respuesta inmune.

immunosuppressant *n.* inmunosupresivo, agente capaz de suprimir una respuesta inmune.

immunotherapy *n.* inmunoterapia, inmunización pasiva del paciente por medio de

anticuerpos preformados (suero o gamma globulina).

impact *n.* colisión, impacto; efecto; golpe; *v.* impactar, fijar rellenar, asegurar; incrustar.

impacted tooth *n.* diente impactado.

impaction *n.* impacción. 1. condición de estar alojado o metido con firmeza en un espacio limitado; 2. impedimento de un órgano o parte.

impair *v.* dañar; debilitar, desmejorar.

impaired *a.* impedido-a, baldado-a; desmejorado-a, debilitado-a.

impalpable *n.* impalpable.

impartial *a.* imparcial.

impatient *a.* impaciente; *v.* **to get, to become** ___ / impacientarse, perder la paciencia.

impede *v.* impedir, obstruir.

impediment *n.* impedimento, obstáculo, obstrucción.

impenetrable *a.* impenetrable, que no puede ser penetrado.

imperative *n. gr.* imperativo; *a.* imperativo-a; requerido-a.

imperfect *n. gr.* tiempo imperfecto; *a.* imperfecto-a; defectuoso-a.

imperfection *n.* imperfección, deformidad, defecto.

imperforate *a.* imperforado-a; ___ hymen / himen ___.

imperil *v.* poner en peligro, arriesgar, hacer daño.

impermeable *a.* impermeable, impenetrable, que no deja pasar líquidos.

impersonal *a.* impersonal.

impetigo *n.* impétigo, infección bacteriana de la piel que se caracteriza por pústulas dolorosas de tamaño diferente que al desecarse forman costras amarillentas.

impetuous *a.* impetuoso-a.

implant *n.* implante, cualquier material insertado o injertado en el cuerpo; *v.* implantar, injertar, insertar.

implantation *n.* implantación, inserción o fijación de una parte o tejido en un área del cuerpo.

implanted *a. pp.* de **to implant,** implantado-a.

implication *n.* implicación.

imply *v.* implicar, insinuar.

importance *n.* importancia.

important *a.* importante.

impose *v.* imponer.

impossible *a.* imposible.
impotence *n.* impotencia, incapacidad de tener o mantener una erección.
impotent *a.* impotente.
impractical *a.* poco práctico-a.
impregnate *n.* impregnar; saturar.
impression *n.* impresión; imagen.
impressive *a.* impresionante.
improbable *a.* improbable.
improper action *n.* acción incorrecta.
improve *v.* mejorar; adelantar; mejorarse, recuperarse; restablecerse.
improved *a. pp.* de **to improve,** mejorado-a, recuperado-a.
improvement *n.* mejoría, restablecimiento, recuperación.
improvise *v.* improvisar.
improvised *a.* improvisado-a.
impulse *n.* impulso; fuerza súbita impulsiva; cardiac ____ / ____ cardíaco; excitatory ____ / ____ excitante; inhibitory ____ / ____ inhibitorio; nervous ____ / ____ nervioso; *v.* **to act on** ____ / dejarse llevar por un ____.
impulsive *a.* impulsivo-a; irreflexivo-a.
impure *a.* impuro-a; contaminado-a, adulterado-a.
in *prep.* [*inside of*] dentro de; [*in time*] con; [*in the night, day, etc.*] durante, por; [*in place*] en; *adv.* dentro; adentro; ____ **the meantime** / mientras tanto; ____ **the care of** / al cuidado de.
inability *n.* inhabilidad, incapacidad.
inaccurate *a.* inexacto-a, incorrecto-a.
inaction *n.* inacción, fallo en responder a un estímulo.
inactive *a.* inactivo-a, pasivo-a.
inadequate *a.* inadecuado-a, impropio-a.
inanition *n.* inanición; debilidad; malnutrición.
inarticulate *a.* desarticulado-a, incapaz de articular palabras o sílabas.
in articulo mortis *L.* in articulo mortis, a la hora de la muerte, al instante de morir.
inborn *a.* innato-a, cualidad adquirida desde el nacimiento.
incandescent *a.* incandescente, con brillo de luz.
incapable *a.* incapaz.
incapacitate *v.* incapacitar, imposibilitar, inhabilitar.
incapacitated *a.* incapacitado-a.
incarcerated *a.* constricto-a; encarcelado-a; limitado-a.
incase *v.* encajar, encajonar.

incasement *n.* encajonamiento, encerramiento.
incentive *n.* incentivo, estímulo; incitante, estimulante.
incessant *a.* incesante, constante.
incest *n.* incesto.
incestuous *a.* incestuoso-a.
inch *n.* pulgada.
incidence *n.* incidencia; frecuencia.
incidental *a.* incidental, casual.
incinerate *v.* incinerar.
incipient *a.* incipiente, principiante, que comienza a existir.
incise *v.* cortar, hacer un corte.
incised *a.* cortado-a, inciso-a.
incision *n.* incisión, corte, cortadura.
incisor *n.* diente incisivo.
incisura *n. L.* incisura, corte, raja.
inclination *n.* inclinación.
inclusion *n.* inclusión, acto de contener una cosa dentro de otra; ____ bodies / cuerpos de inclusión, presentes en el citoplasma de ciertas células en casos de infección.
incoherence *n.* incoherencia, falta de coordinación de las ideas.
incoherent *a.* incoherente, que no coordina las ideas.
income *n.* ingreso, entrada; ____ **tax** / impuestos.
incompatibility *n.* incompatibilidad.
incompatible *a.* incompatible.
incompetent *a.* incompetente, incapacitado-a.
incomplete *a.* incompleto-a.
inconsiderate *a.* desconsiderado-a.
inconsistency *n.* inconsistencia.
inconsistent *a.* inconsistente.
incontinence *n.* incontinencia, emisión involuntaria, inhabilidad de controlar la orina o las heces fecales; ____ , overflow / ____ por rebosamiento; ____ , urinary stress / ____ urinaria de esfuerzo.
incontinent *a.* incontinente, rel. a la incontinencia.
inconvenience *n.* inconveniencia.
inconvenient *a.* inconveniente.
incoordinate *a.* incoordinado, sin coordinación.
incoordination *n.* falta de coordinación.
incorporate *v.* incorporar, añadir.
incorrect *a.* incorrecto-a.
increase *v.* aumentar, agrandar.
incubation *n.* incubación. 1. período de latencia de una enfermedad antes de mani-

festarse; 2. mantenimiento de un ambiente especial ajustado a las necesidades de recién nacidos, esp. prematuros; ____ period / período de ____ .

incubator *n.* incubadora, receptáculo usado para asegurar las condiciones óptimas en el cuidado de prematuros.

incurable *a.* incurable, que no tiene cura.

incus *L.* incus, huesecillo del oído medio.

indecision *n.* indecisión; irresolución.

indecisive *a.* indeciso-a; irresoluto-a.

indefinite *a.* indefinido-a; indeterminado-a.

indemnity *n.* indemnización, resarcimiento; ____ benefits / beneficios de ____ ; ____ insurance / seguro de ____ .

independent *a.* independiente.

indeterminate *a.* indeterminado-a, desconocido-a.

index *n.* índice; sumario.

indicate *v.* indicar, señalar.

indicated *a.* indicado-a; apropiado-a.

indication *n.* indicación; señal.

indicator *n.* indicador, señalador.

indifferent *a.* indiferente.

indigenous *a.* autóctono-a, indígena.

indigestion *n.* indigestión.

indirect *a.* indirecto-a.

indispensable *a.* indispensable, necesario-a.

indispose *v.* indisponer, enfermar.

indisposed *a.* maldispuesto-a; indispuesto-a; to become ____ / enfermarse.

indisposition *n.* indisposición, desorden o enfermedad pasajera.

indissoluble *a.* indisoluble.

individual *n.* individuo; *a.* individual.

individuality *n.* individualidad.

indivisible *a.* indivisible.

indolent *a.* indolente, perezoso-a; inactivo-a, lento-a en desarrollarse, tal como sucede en ciertas úlceras.

induce *v.* inducir, provocar, suscitar, ocasionar.

induced *a. pp.* de **to induce,** inducido-a, provocado-a.

induction *a.* inducción, acción o efecto de inducir.

ineffective *a.* inefectivo-a; inútil.

inefficient *a.* deficiente; ineficaz.

inert *a.* inerte, rel. a la inercia.

inertia *n.* inercia, falta de actividad.

inexperience *n.* inexperiencia, sin experiencia.

infancy. *n.* infancia, menor edad, primera

edad, período desde el nacimiento hasta los primeros dos años.

infant *n.* infante, lactante.

infanticide *n.* infanticidio.

infantile *a.* infantil, pueril; ____ paralysis / parálisis ____ .

infantilism *n.* infantilismo, manifestación de características infantiles en la edad adulta.

infarct, infarction *n.* infarto, necrosis de un área de tejido por falta de irrigación sanguínea (isquemia); ____ , bland / ____ blando; ____ , cardiac / ____ cardíaco; ____ , cerebral / ____ cerebral; ____ , hemorrhagic / ____ hemorrágico; ____ , myocardial / ____ cardíaco; ____ , pulmonary / ____ pulmonar.

infect *v.* infectar; infectarse.

infected *a.* infectado-a.

infection *n.* infección, invasión del cuerpo por microorganismos patógenos y la reacción y efecto que provocan en los tejidos; acute ____ / ____ aguda; airborne ____ / ____ aerógena; chronic ____ / ____ crónica; contagious ____ / ____ contagiosa; cross ____ / ____ hospitalaria; fungus ____ / ____ de hongos parásitos; massive ____ / ____ masiva; opportunistic ____ / enfermedad oportunista infecciosa; pyogenic ____ / ____ piogénica; secondary ____ / ____ secundaria; subclinical ____ / ____ subclínica; systemic ____ / ____ sistémica; water-borne ____ / ____ hídrica.

infectious *a.* infeccioso-a, rel. a una infección; ____ agent / agente ____ ; ____ disease / enfermedad ____ .

infecundity *n.* infecundidad, esterilidad.

infer *v.* inferir, deducir.

inferior *a.* inferior.

inferiority complex *n.* complejo de inferioridad.

infertility *n.* infertilidad, inhabilidad de concebir o procrear.

infestation *n.* infestación, invasión del organismo por parásitos.

infiltrate *v.* infiltrar, penetrar.

infiltration *n.* infiltración, acumulación de sustancias extrañas en un tejido o célula.

infirmary *n.* enfermería, establecimiento de salud, local donde se atiende a personas enfermas o lesionadas.

inflame *v.* inflamar; inflamarse.

inflammation *n.* inflamación, reacción de un tejido lesionado.

inflammatory *a.* inflamatorio-a, rel. a la inflamación.

inflation *n.* inflación, distensión.

inflection *n.* inflexión, torcimiento.

inflict *v.* infligir, causar sufrimiento.

inflow *n.* flujo, afluencia, entrada.

influenza *n.* influenza, infección viral aguda del tracto respiratorio.

inform *v.* informar, comunicar, avisar.

information *n.* información; informe.

infraclavicular *a.* infraclavicular, localizado debajo de la clavícula.

infraction *n.* infracción, fractura ósea incompleta sin desplazamiento.

infradiaphragmatic *a.* infradiafragmático-a, localizado debajo del diafragma.

infraorbital *a.* infraorbital, infraorbitario-a, localizado debajo de la órbita.

infrared rays *n. pl.* rayos infrarrojos.

infrascapular *n.* infraescapular, localizado debajo de la escápula.

infrequent *a.* infrecuente, raro-a.

infundibulum *n.* (*pl.* **infundibula**) infundíbulo, estructura en forma de embudo.

infusion *n.* infusión; 1. introducción lenta, por gravedad, de líquidos en una vena; 2. sumersión de un elemento en agua para obtener los principios activos solubles.

ingest *v.* ingerir.

ingestant, ingesta *n* alimentación oral.

ingestion *n.* ingestión, proceso de ingerir alimentos.

ingredient *n.* ingrediente, componente.

ingrowing *a.* rel. a una parte que crece hacia adentro y no hacia afuera, en forma opuesta a lo normal.

ingrown nail *n.* uñero; uña encarnada, uña enterrada.

inguinal *a.* inguinal, rel. a la ingle; ____ canal / conducto, canal ____ ; ____ hernia / hernia ____ ; ____ ligament / ligamento ____ ; ____ ring / anillo ____ .

inhalant *n.* inhalante, medicamento administrado por inhalación.

inhalation *n.* inhalación, aspiración de aire o vapor a los pulmones.

inhale *v.* inhalar, aspirar.

inherent *a.* inherente, rel. a una cualidad natural o innata.

inherit *v.* heredar.

inheritance *n.* herencia. *V.* **heredity.**

inherited *a.* heredado-a, rel. a la herencia.

inhibit *v.* inhibir; inhibirse, cohibirse.

inhibition *n.* inhibición, interrupción o restricción de una acción o hábito.

inhibitor *n.* inhibidor, agente que causa una inhibición.

initial *a.* inicial, primero-a.

initiate *v.* iniciar, comenzar, empezar.

inject *v.* inyectar, acto de introducir líquidos en un tejido, vaso, o cavidad por medio de un inyector.

injection *n.* inyección, acción de inyectar una droga o líquido en el cuerpo.

injector *n.* inyector, jeringa, dispositivo que se usa para inyectar.

injure *v.* dañar; lastimar, herir.

injured *a. pp.* de **to injure,** lastimado-a, dañado-a; herido-a.

injury *n.* lesión, lastimadura; herida.

ink *n.* tinta.

inlaid *a.* incrustado-a; embutido-a.

inlet *n.* entrada, acceso.

innate *a.* innato-a, inherente.

inner *a.* interior.

innervate *v.* inervar, estimular un área o parte con energía nerviosa.

innervation *n.* inervación. 1. acto de inervar; 2. distribución de nervios o de energía nerviosa en un órgano o área.

innocent *a.* inocente.

inoculate *v.* inocular, inmunizar, vacunar.

inoculation *n.* inoculación, vacunación, inmunización, acción de administrar sueros, vacunas u otras sustancias para producir o incrementar inmunidad a una enfermedad determinada.

inoculum *n.* (*pl.* **inocula**) ínoculo, la sustancia introducida por inoculación.

inoperable *a.* inoperable, que no puede tratarse quirúrgicamente.

inorganic *a.* inorgánico-a; que no pertenece a organismos vivos.

inosculating *n.* comunicación directa, anastomosis.

inotropic *a.* inotrópico-a, que afecta la intensidad o energía de las contracciones musculares.

inquest *n.* encuesta, investigación oficial.

insalubrious *a.* insalubre; antihigiénico-a.

insane *a.* loco-a, demente.

insanitary *a.* antihigiénico-a.

insanity *n.* locura, demencia.

insatiable *a.* insaciable, insatisfecho-a.

insect *n.* insecto.

insecticide *n.* insecticida.

insecurity *n.* inseguridad.

insemination *n.* inseminación, fertilización de un óvulo.

insensible *n.* insensible, que carece de sensibilidad.

inseparable *a.* inseparable.

insertion *n.* inserción; 1. acto de insertar; 2. punto de unión de un músculo y un hueso.

inside *prep.* por dentro, hacia adentro; adentro.

insider *n.* persona bien informada.

insidious *a.* insidioso-a, rel. a una enfermedad que se desarrolla gradualmente sin producir síntomas obvios.

insight *n.* conocimiento; penetración; v. to get an ___ into / formarse una idea de; hacer un estudio detenido.

insignificant *a.* insignificante, sin importancia.

insipid *a.* insípido-a, sin sabor; *pop.* soso-a.

insist *v.* insistir; to ___ on / ___ en; to ___ that / ___ en que.

in situ *L.* in situ. 1. en el lugar normal; 2. que no se extiende más allá del sitio en que se origina.

insolation *n.* insolación. *V.* **sunstroke.**

insoluble *a.* insoluble, que no se disuelve.

insomnia *n.* insomnio, desvelo.

inspection *n.* inspección.

install *v.* instalar, colocar.

installation *n.* instalación; montaje.

instant *n.* instante; *a.* instantáneo-a, inmediato-a; urgente.

instep *n.* empeine, parte anterior del pie.

instillation *n.* instilación, goteo de un líquido en una cavidad o superficie.

instinct *n.* instinto.

instinctive *a.* instintivo-a.

institution *n.* institución; fundación; establecimiento; [*mental*] asilo, manicomio; [*home of the aged*] asilo de ancianos.

instruct *v.* instruir, enseñar, dar instrucciones.

instrument *n.* instrumento.

insufficiency *n.* insuficiencia, falta de; adrenal ___ / ___ suprarrenal; cardiac ___ / ___ cardíaca; coronary ___ / ___ coronaria; hepatic ___ / ___ hepática; mitral ___ / ___ mitral; pulmonary valvular ___ / ___ pulmonar-valvular; renal ___ / ___ renal; respiratory ___ / ___ respiratoria; valvular ___ / ___ valvular; venous ___ / ___ venosa.

insufficient *a.* insuficiente.

insufflate *v.* insuflar, soplar hacia el interior de una cavidad, parte u órgano.

insula *n.* ínsula, lóbulo central del hemisferio cerebral.

insulin *n.* insulina. hormona secretada en el páncreas.

insurance *n.* seguro; compañía de seguros; *Mex.* aseguranza; life ___ / ___ de vida; medical ___ / ___ médico; ___ policy / póliza de ___.

insure *v.* asegurar; asegurarse.

intelligence *n.* inteligencia.

intelligent *a.* inteligente, listo-a.

intense *a.* intenso-a.

intensify *v.* intensificar.

intensity *n.* intensidad.

intensive *a.* intensivo-a.

intention *n.* intención. 1. meta o propósito; 2. proceso natural en la curación de heridas.

intentional *a.* intencional, a propósito.

interaction *n.* interacción; drug ___ / ___ de medicamentos.

intercalated *a.* intercalado-a, colocado-a entre dos partes o elementos.

intercostal *a.* intercostal, entre dos costillas.

intercourse *n.* [*sexual*] coito, relaciones sexuales; intercambio, comunicación.

intercurrent *a.* intercurrente, que aparece en el curso de una enfermedad y que la modifica.

interdigitation *n.* interdigitación, entrecruzamiento de partes esp. los dedos.

interest *n.* interés; *v.* to take an ___ in / interesarse por.

interfere *v.* interferir.

interference *n.* interferencia, anulación o colisión entre dos partes.

interferon *n.* interferón, proteína natural liberada por células expuestas a la acción de virus usada en el tratamiento de infecciones y neoplasmas.

interfibrillar *a.* interfibrilar, localizado entre fibrillas.

interim *L.* interim, entretanto.

interior *a.* interior.

intermediary *a.* intermediario-a, situado entre dos cuerpos.

intermediate *a.* intermedio-a, situado entre dos extremos; después del principio y antes del final.

intermittent *a.* intermitente, que no es continuo; ___ positive-pressure breathing / ventilación ___ bajo presión positiva; ___ pulse / pulso ___.

intern *n.* interno-a; médico-a interno-a.

internal *a*. interno-a, dentro del cuerpo; ____ bleeding / hemorragia ____.

internalization *n*. *psic*. internalización, proceso inconsciente por el cual una persona adapta las creencias y valores de otra persona o de la sociedad en que vive.

International Red Cross *n*. Cruz Roja Internacional, organización mundial de asistencia médica.

international unit (I.U) *n*. unidad internacional, medida de una sustancia definida aceptada por la Conferencia Internacional de Unificación de Fórmulas (C.I.U.F.)

interpret *v*. interpretar, traducir oralmente.

interpretation *n*. interpretación.

interpreter *n*. intérprete.

interruption *n*. interrupción.

interstices *n*. *pl*. intersticios, intervalos o pequeños espacios.

interstitial *a*. intersticial, rel. a los espacios dentro de un tejido, órgano o célula.

interval *n*. intervalo; espacio; período de tiempo.

intervene *v*. intervenir; asistir; supervisar.

interventricular *a*. interventricular, localizado entre los ventrículos; ____ optum / tabique ____ del corazón.

intervertebral disk *n*. disco intervertebral.

interview *n*. entrevista.

intestinal *a*. intestinal, rel. a los intestinos; ____ bypass surgery / desviación quirúrgica ____ ; ____ flora / flora ____ ; ____ juice / jugo ____ ; ____ obstruction / obstrucción ____ ; ____ perforation / perforación ____ .

intestine *n*. intestino, tubo digestivo que se extiende del píloro al ano; large ____ / ____ grueso; small ____ / ____ delgado.

intima *L*. (*pl*. **intimae**) íntima, la membrana o túnica más interna de las capas de un órgano tal como en un vaso capilar.

intimal *a*. íntimal, rel. a la íntima.

intolerance *n*. intolerancia, incapacidad de soportar dolor o los efectos de una droga.

intoxicate *v*. intoxicar.

intoxication *n*. intoxicación, envenenamiento o estado tóxico producido por una droga o sustancia tóxica.

intra-abdominal *a*. intrabdominal, localizado dentro del abdomen.

intra-aortic *a*. intraórtico-a, rel. a o situado dentro de la aorta.

intra-arterial *a*. intra arterial, dentro de una arteria.

intra-articular *a*. intra articular, dentro de una articulación.

intracapsular *a*. intracapsular, dentro de una cápsula.

intracellular *a*. intracelular, dentro de una célula o células.

intracranial *a*. intracraneal, dentro del cráneo.

intrahepatic *a*. intrahepático-a, dentro del hígado.

intralobular *a*. intralobular, dentro de un lóbulo.

intraluminal *a*. intraluminal. 1. dentro de la luz o estructura lumínica; 2. semejante al lumen de un vaso arterial o venoso.

intramuscular *a*. intramuscular, dentro del músculo.

intraocular *a*. intraocular, dentro del ojo; ____ pressure / presión ____ .

intraoperative *a*. intraoperatorio-a, que tiene lugar durante un proceso quirúrgico.

intraosseous *a*. intraóseo-a, dentro de la sustancia ósea.

intrauterine *a*. intrauterino-a, dentro del útero; ____ device (IUD) / dispositivo ____ .

intravenous *a*. intravenoso-a, dentro de una vena; ____ infusion / infusión ____ ; ____ injection / inyección ____ .

intraventricular *a*. intraventricular, dentro de un ventrículo.

intrinsic *a*. intrínseco-a, esencial, exclusivo-a. *V*. **inherent**.

intrinsic factor *n*. factor intrínseco, proteína normalmente presente en el jugo gástrico humano.

introducer *n*. intubador, divisa utilizada para intubar.

introitus *L*. introito, abertura o entrada a un canal o cavidad.

introspection *n*. introspección, análisis propio o de sí mismo-a.

introversion *psic*. inversion, introversión, acto de concentración de una persona en sí misma, con disminución del interés por el mundo externo.

intubation *n*. intubación, inserción de un tubo en un conducto o cavidad del cuerpo.

intussusception *n*. intususcepción, invaginación tal como la de una porción del intestino que causa una obstrucción intestinal.

in utero *L*. in utero, dentro del útero.

invade *v*. invadir, penetrar; atacar.

invaginate *v*. invaginar, replegar una porción de una estructura en otra parte de la misma.

invagination *n.* invaginación, proceso de inclusión de una parte dentro de otra.

invalid *a.* inválido-a; debilitado-a; incapacitado-a.

invariable *a.* invariable, que no cambia.

invasive *a.* invasor-a, germen o sustancia que invade tejidos adyacentes.

invasion *n.* invasión, acto de invadir.

inversion *n.* inversión, proceso de volverse hacia adentro.

invert *v.* invertir.

investigation *n.* investigación, indagación.

investment *n.* revestimiento, cubierta.

invisible *a.* invisible, que no puede verse a simple vista.

in vitro *L.* in vitro, dentro de una vasija de vidrio, término aplicado a pruebas de laboratorio.

in vivo *L.* in vivo, en el cuerpo vivo.

involuntary *a.* involuntario-a.

involution *n.* involución, cambio retrógrado.

involutional melancholia *n. psic.* melancolía involucional, trastorno emocional depresivo que se observa en mujeres de 40 a 55 años y en hombres de 50 a 65 años.

iodine *n.* iodo, yodo. 1. elemento no metálico que pertenece al grupo halógeno usado como componente en medicamentos para contribuir al desarrollo y funcionamiento de la tiroides; 2. tintura de yodo usada como germicida y desinfectante.

iodism *n.* yodismo, envenenamiento por yodo.

iodize *v.* yodurar, tratar con yodo.

ion *n.* ion, átomo o grupo de átomos provistos de carga eléctrica.

ionization *n.* ionización, disociación de compuestos en los iones que los componen.

ionizing radiation *n.* radiación por ionización.

ipecac, syrup of *n.* jarabe de ipecacuana, emético y expectorante.

ipsilateral *a.* ipsilateral, ipsolateral, que afecta el mismo lado del cuerpo.

irascible *a.* irascible, que se irrita fácilmente.

iridectomy *n. cirg.* iridectomía, extirpación de una parte del iris.

iridology *n.* iridología, estudio del iris y de los cambios que éste sufre en el curso de una enfermedad.

iris *n.* iris, membrana contráctil del humor acuoso del ojo situada entre el cristalino y la córnea, que regula la entrada de la luz.

iritis *n.* iritis, infl. del iris.

iron *n.* hierro; *v.* **to have an** ___ **constitution** / tener una constitución de hierro.

iron-deficiency anemia *n.* anemia por deficiencia de hierro.

iron lung *n.* pulmón de hierro, máquina que se usa para producir respiración artificial.

irradiate *v.* irradiar; exponer a o tratar por uso de radiación.

irradiation *n.* irradiación, uso terapéutico de radiaciones.

irrational *n.* irracional.

irreducible *a.* irreducible, que no puede reducirse.

irregular *a.* irregular.

irrelevant *a.* ajeno-a, no pertinente, que no tiene relación con lo que se discute; que no viene al caso.

irrigate *v.* irrigar, lavar con un chorro de agua.

irrigation *n.* irrigación, acto o proceso de irrigar.

irritability *n.* irritabilidad, propiedad de un organismo o tejido de reaccionar al ambiente.

irritable *n.* irritable, que reacciona a un estímulo.

irritate *v.* irritar.

irritation *n.* irritación, reacción extrema a un dolor o a una condición patológica.

ischemia *n.* isquemia, insuficiencia de riego sanguíneo a un tejido o parte.

ischium *n.* (*pl.* **ischia**) isquion, parte posterior de la pelvis.

island *n.* isla, nombre dado a un grupo celular o a un tejido aislado.

Islets of Langerhans *n. V.* **Langerhans, islets of.**

isolate *v.* aislar, separar.

isolated *a.* aislado-a, separado-a.

isolation *n.* aislamiento, proceso de aislar o separar; ___ **ward** / sala de ___ .

isometric *a.* isométrico-a, de dimensiones iguales.

isoniazid *n.* isoniazida, medicamento antibacteriano usado en el tratamiento de tuberculosis.

isotonic *a.* isotónico-a, que tiene la misma tensión que otra dada; ___ **exercise** / ejercicio ___ .

isotope *n.* isótopo, elemento químico que pertenece a un grupo de elementos que presentan propiedades casi idénticas pero que difiere de éstos en el peso atómico.

issue *n.* emisión; cuestión; ___ of blood / pérdida de sangre; **to avoid the** ___ / esquivar la cuestión; *v.* brotar, fluir; emitir.

issued *a.* expedido-a, emitido-a.

issuing *n.* salida.

it *pron. neut.* (*pl.* **they**); **the best of** ___ / lo mejor; **the worst of** ___ / lo peor; **it's,** *abr.* de **it is** / eso es; es.

itch *n.* picazón.

itching *n.* sensación de picazón.

itself *pron. m.* (él) mismo, sí mismo; *f.* (ella) misma; sí misma.

ivy *n.* hiedra.

J

j *abbr.* **joint** / articulación.

jab *n.* pinchazo, punzada; golpe corto; *v.* pinchar; dar golpes cortos.

jacket *n.* forro; corsé, soporte del tronco y la espina dorsal usado para corregir deformidades.

Jacksonian epilepsy *n.* epilepsia jacksoniana, epilepsia parcial sin pérdida del conocimiento.

jam *n.* conserva, compota; *v.* **to be in a** ___ / estar en apuros.

jamais vu *Fr.* jamais vu, nunca visto, percepción de una experiencia familiar o conocida como si fuera una experiencia nueva.

jar *n.* jarro, frasco, pomo, recipiente de cristal.

jargon *n.* jerigonza; parafasia. *V.* **paraphasia.**

jasmine *n.* jazmín; ___ **tea** / té de ___.

jaundice *n.* ictericia, derrame biliar por exceso de bilirrubina en la sangre que causa pigmentación amarillo-anaranjada de la piel y otros tejidos y fluidos del cuerpo; obstructive ___ / ___ obstructiva, obstrucción de la bilis. *V.* **icterus.**

jaundiced *a.* ictérico-a, rel. a la ictericia o que padece de ella.

jaw *n.* mandíbula, quijada, maxilar inferior.

jawbone *n.* hueso maxilar de la mandíbula.

jaw-lever *n.* abrebocas. *V.* **gag.**

jealous *a.* celoso-a.

jealousy *n.* celos.

jejunal *a.* yeyunal, rel. al yeyuno.

jejunectomy *n. cirg.* yeyunectomía, excisión de todo el yeyuno o parte del mismo.

jejunostomy *n.* yeyunostomía, creación de

una abertura permanente en el yeyuno a través de la pared abdominal.

jejunum *n.* yeyuno, porción del intestino delgado que se extiende del duodeno al íleon.

jelly *n.* jalea, sustancia gelatinosa; contraceptive ___ / ___ anticonceptiva; petroleum ___ / vaselina.

jerk *n.* sacudida, reflejo súbito, contracción muscular brusca; *a.* [*slang*] tonto-a, imbécil; *v.* sacudir, tirar de, mover bruscamente.

jest *n.* broma, chiste; *v.* bromear.

jet *n.* chorro; avión de propulsión.

jet lag *n.* estado de cansancio que sufren los viajeros aéreos después de jornadas largas a través de diferentes zonas de tiempo.

jitters *n.* [*slang*] nerviosidad.

job *n.* trabajo, empleo; [*task*] tarea.

jog *v.* correr acompasadamente como medio de ejercicio.

jogger *n.* corredor-a.

jogging *n.* acción de correr como medio de ejercicio.

join *v.* unir, juntar; [*as a member*] hacerse miembro, hacerse socio-a; [*meet*] encontrarse.

joint *n.* articulación, coyuntura, punto de unión entre dos huesos; arthrodial ___ / artrodia, que permite un movimiento de deslizamiento; ball-and-socket ___ / ___ esferoidea, que permite movimientos en varias direcciones; hip ___ / ___ de la cadera; knee ___ / ___ de la rodilla; sacroiliac ___ / ___ sacroilíaca; shoulder ___ / ___ del hombro.

joint capsule *n.* cápsula articular, cubierta en forma de bolsa que envuelve una articulación.

joint mice *n.* partículas sueltas de cartílago o hueso que se alojan generalmente en algunas articulaciones.

jolly *a.* alegre, jovial.

jolt *n.* sacudida, tirón.

journal *n.* diario.

jovial *n.* jovial, alegre.

jowl *n.* cachete, carrillo.

joy *n.* alegría.

judge *n.* juez, magistrado-a; *v.* juzgar, hacer juicio.

judgment, judgement *n.* juicio; decisión, opinión.

jug *n.* jarro

jugular *a.* yugular, rel. a las venas yugulares.

jugular veins *n.* venas yugulares, venas que llevan la sangre de la cabeza y del cuello al corazón.

juice *n.* jugo, zumo, líquido extraído o segregado; **apple** ___ / ___ de manzana; **carrot** ___ / ___ de zanahoria; **grape** ___ / ___ de uva; **grapefruit** ___ / ___ de toronja; **pineapple** ___ / ___ de piña; **plum** ___ / ___ de ciruela; gastric ___ / ___ gástrico; intestinal ___ / ___ intestinal; pancreatic ___ / ___ pancreático.

juiciness *n.* jugosidad.

juicy *a.* jugoso-a.

jump *n.* salto, brinco; *v.* saltar, brincar.

jumpy *a.* inquieto-a, intranquilo-a.

junction *n.* unión, entronque, punto de contacto de dos partes.

junctura *n.* juntura; coyuntura.

junkie *a.* *slang,* [*rel. to drug addiction*], vicioso-a, narcómano-a, *Mex.* tecato-a.

jurisprudence, medical *n.* Jurisprudencia Médica, ciencia del Derecho Judicial que se aplica a la medicina.

just *a.* justo-a; preciso-a, exacto-a; **-ly** *adv.* justamente.

justice *n.* justicia.

justify *v.* justificar.

juvenile *a.* juvenil, joven; ___ delincuency / delincuencia ___.

juvenile rheumatoid arthritis *n.* artritis reumatoidea juvenil; V. **rheumatoid arthritis.**

juxtaglomerular *a.* yuxtaglomerular, junto a un glomérulo.

juxtaglomerular apparatus *n.* aparato yuxtaglomerular, grupo de células localizadas alrededor de arteriolas aferentes del riñón, que intervienen en la producción de renina y en el metabolismo del sodio.

juxtaglomerular cells *n.* células yuxtaglomerulares, localizadas cerca de o junto a glomérulos del riñón.

juxtaposition *n.* yuxtaposición, aposición; posición adyacente.

K

K *abbr.* **kalium** / potasio.
k *abbr.* **kilogram** / kilogramo.

kala-azar *n.* kala-azar, infestación visceral por un protozoo.

kalemia *n.* potasemia, presencia de potasio en la sangre.

kaliuresis *n.* caliuresis, aumento en la excreción de potasio en la orina.

kallikrein *n.* calicreína, enzima potente de acción vasodilatadora.

kaolin *n.* caolín, silicato de aluminio hidratado, agente de cualidades absorbentes de uso interno y externo.

Kaposi's disease *n.* enfermedad de Kaposi, neoplasma maligno localizado en las extremidades inferiores de hombres adultos que se desarrolla rápidamente en casos de SIDA.

karyolitic *a.* cariolítico-a, rel. a cariolisis o que la causa.

karyolysis *n.* cariolisis, disolución del núcleo de una célula.

karyon *n.* carión, núcleo celular.

karyotype *n.* cariotipo, cromosoma característico de un individuo o de una especie.

keep *vi.* [*a record*] mantener; [*guard*] guardar; **to** ___ **down** / limitar; **to** ___ **from** / abstenerse de, guardarse de, evitar; **to** ___ **off** /alejarse, apartarse; **to** ___ **on** / continuar; **to** ___ **quiet** / estarse quieto-a, quedarse callado-a; **to** ___ **up** / mantener.

keeping *n.* cuidado, custodia.

keloid *n.* queloide, cicatriz de tejido grueso rojizo que se forma en la piel después de una incisión quirúrgica o de una herida.

keloidosis *n.* queloidosis, formación de queloides.

kelp *n.* cenizas de un tipo de alga marina rica en yodo.

keratectomy *n.* *cirg.* queratectomía, incisión de una parte de la córnea.

keratin *n.* queratina, proteína orgánica insoluble que es un elemento componente de las uñas, la piel y el cabello.

keratinization *n.* queratinización, proceso por el cual las células se vuelven callosas por depósitos de queratina.

keratinous *a.* queratinoso-a, rel. a o de la naturaleza de la queratina.

keratitis *n.* queratitis, infl. de la córnea; mycotic ___ / ___ micótica, queratomicosis, infección fungal de la córnea; trophic ___ / ___ trófica, causada por el virus del herpes.

keratocele *n.* queratocele, hernia de la membrana anterior de la córnea.

keratohemia *n.* queratohemia, presencia de sangre en la córnea.

keratolitic *n.* queratolítico, agente que provoca exfoliación.

keratolysis *n.* queratolisis. 1. exfoliación de la epidermis; 2. anomalía congénita por la cual se muda la piel periódicamente; ___ neonatorum / ___ neonatal.

keratoma *n.* queratoma, callosidad, tumor córneo.

keratomalacia *n.* queratomalacia, degeneración de la córnea causada por deficiencia de vitamina A.

keratoplasty *n. cirg.* queratoplastia, cirugía plástica de la córnea.

keratoscope *n.* queratoscopio, instrumento para examinar la córnea.

keratoses *n.* queratoses, enfermedad no contagiosa de la piel con escamación y posible inflamación.

keratosis *n.* queratosis, condición callosa de la piel tal como callos y verrugas; actinic ___ / ___ actínica, lesión solar precancerosa; blenorrhagic ___ / ___ blenorrágica, manifestada en la palma de las manos y los pies con erupción escamosa.

keratotomy *n. cirg.* queratotomía, incisión a través de la córnea.

keratous *a.* queratoso-a, semejante a la córnea.

kernicterus *n.* kernícterus, forma de ictericia del recién nacido.

ketogenesis *n.* cetogenesis, producción de acetona.

ketone bodies *n.* cuerpos cetónicos o acetónicos, comúnmente llamados acetonas, productos desintegrados de las grasas en el catabolismo celular.

ketosis *n.* cetosis, producción excesiva de cuerpos acetónicos como resultado del metabolismo incompleto de ácidos lípidos; acidosis.

key *n.* llave; [*clue, reference*] clave.

kick *n.* patada, puntapié; *v.* patear, dar puntapiés; [*addiction*] to ___ the habit / [*to abstain or stay away*] dejar la droga.

kid *n.* [*child*] niño, niña, chiquillo, chiquilla.

kidney *n.* riñón, órgano par situado a cada lado de la región lumbar y que sirve de filtro al organismo; artificial ___ / ___ artificial; polycystic ___ / ___ poliquístico; ___ stones / piedras o cálculos renales; ___ failure / fallo renal; ___ stone / cálculo renal, *pop.* piedras en los riñones.

kill *v.* matar; [*germs*] exterminar; **to ___ time** / pasar el tiempo.

kilo *n.* kilogramo, kilo.

kilometer *n.* kilómetro.

kind *n.* clase, tipo; *a.* bondadoso-a; *v.* **to be so ___ as to** / tener la bondad de; **-ly** *adv.* bondadosamente.

kindness *n.* bondad.

kindred *n.* parentesco.

kinesiology *n.* cinesiología, estudio de los músculos y los movimientos musculares.

kinesthesia *n.* cinestesia, experiencia sensorial, sentido y percepción de un movimiento.

kinetic *n.* cinético-a, rel. al movimiento.

kingdom *n.* reino, categoría en la clasificación de animales, plantas y minerales.

kinship *n.* [*family relationship*] parentesco.

kit *n.* equipo.

kitchen *n.* cocina.

klebsiella *n.* klebsiela, bacilo gram-negativo asociado con infecciones respiratorias y del tracto urinario.

Klebs-Löffler bacillus *n.* bacilo de Klebs-Löffler, bacilo de la difteria.

kleptomania *n. psic.* cleptomanía, deseo incontrolable de robar.

kleptomaniac *n., a,* cleptómano-a, persona afectada por cleptomanía; rel. a la cleptomanía.

knead *v.* amasar, sobar.

kneading *n.* amasijo, proceso de masaje y frotación.

knee *n.* rodilla, articulación del fémur, la tibia y la patela; ___ dislocation / dislocación de la ___; ___ protector / rodillera.

kneecap *n.* rótula.

knee jerk *n.* reflejo de la rodilla que se produce con el toque de un martillo de goma en el ligamento de la patela.

knife *n.* cuchillo.

knob *n.* protuberancia, bulto.

knock-knee *n.* V. **genus valgum.**

knot *n.* nudo; surgical ___ / ___ quirúrgico.

know *vi.* saber, [*to be acquainted*] conocer; **to ___ how to** / saber + *inf.*; **to ___ of** / tener noticias de, estar enterado-a de.

knowledge *n.* conocimiento; **to the best of my ___** / a mi entender, por lo que sé; *v.* **to have ___ of** / saber.

knuckle *n.* nudillo.

Koch's bacillus *n.* bacilo de Koch, *Mycobacterium tuberculosis,* causa de la tuberculosis en los mamíferos.

kolpitis *n.* colpitis, infl. de la mucosa vaginal.

Kussmaul breathing *n.* respiración Kussmaul, respiración jadeante y profunda vista en casos de acidosis diabética.

kwashiorkor *n.* Kwashiorkor, deficiencia proteínica o malnutrición durante la infancia que se manifiesta después del destete esp. en áreas tropicales y subtropicales.

kyphosis, hunchback *n.* cifosis, exageración en la curvatura posterior de la espina dorsal que da lugar a una corcova.

kyphotic *a.* cifótico-a; *pop.* corcovado-a, que sufre de una corcova.

L

l *abbr.* **left** / izquierdo-a; **lethal** / letal; **light** / ligero-a; **liter** / litro; **lower** / más bajo.

label *n.* etiqueta; *v.* poner etiqueta.
labial *a.* labial, rel. a los labios.
labial glands *n.* glándulas labiales, situadas entre la mucosa labial y el músculo orbicular de la boca.
labile *a.* lábil, inestable, frágil, que cambia o se altera fácilmente.
lability *n.* labilidad, condición de inestabilidad.
labium *n.* (*pl.* **labia**) labio; 1. borde carnoso; 2. estructura semejante a un labio.
labor *n.* parto; active ___ / ___ activo; induction of ___ / ___ inducido; after ___ / después del ___; before ___ / antes del ___; complicated ___ / ___ complicado; contractions during ___ / contracciones durante el ___; dry ___ / ___ seco; during ___ / durante el ___; hard ___ / ___ laborioso; painless ___ / ___ sin dolor; ___ pains / dolores de ___; ___ room / sala de ___; stages of ___ / etapas del ___; *v.* estar de parto; *V.* **childbirth.**
laboratory *n.* laboratorio; ___ technician / técnico de ___; ___ findings / resultados del análisis.
labored *a.* laborioso-a, trabajoso-a; ___ breathing / respiración jadeante.
laborious *a.* laborioso-a, trabajoso-a.
labyrinth *n.* laberinto. 1. red de conductos del oído interno cuya función relaciona la audición con el equilibrio del cuerpo; 2. conductos y cavidades que forman un sistema comunicándose entre sí.

labyrinthitis *n.* laberintitis. 1. infl. aguda o crónica del laberinto; 2. otitis interna.
lacerate *v.* lacerar, desgarrar.
laceration *n.* laceración, desgarro.
lachrymogenous *a.* lacrimógeno-a, que produce lágrimas.
lachrymose *a.* lacrimoso-a, lagrimoso-a.
lack *n.* falta, carencia; necesidad; ___ of medication / falta de o carencia de medicina; *v.* carecer de; faltar; **they** ___ **everything** / carecen de todo.
lacrimal *a.* lagrimal, rel. a las lágrimas y a los órganos y partes relacionados con éstas; ___ bone / hueso ___; ___ duct / conducto ___; ___ gland / glándula ___; ___ sac / saco ___.
lacrimation *n.* lagrimeo, producción de lágrimas.
lactacidemia *n.* lactacidemia, exceso acumulado de ácido láctico en la sangre.
lactase *n.* lactasa, enzima intestinal que hidroliza la lactosa y produce dextrosa y galactosa.
lactation *n.* lactancia, crianza, secreción de leche.
lactial *a.* lácteo-a, rel. a la leche.
lactic acid *n.* ácido láctico.
lactiferous *a.* lactífero-a, que segrega y conduce leche.
lactocele *n.* lactocele. *V.* **galactocele.**
lacto-ovovegetarian *a.* lacto-ovovegetariano-a; que sigue una dieta de vegetales, huevos y productos lácteos.
lactose, lactine *n.* lactosa, lactina, azúcar de leche; ___ deficiency / intolerancia a la ___.
lacuna *L.* (*pl.* **lacunes**) lacuna, laguna, depresión pequeña tales como las cavidades del cerebro.
lady *n.* dama, señora.
lag *n.* atraso, retraso; [*slow growth*] latencia; ___ time / período de latencia.
laid up *a.* inactivo-a; *pop.* en cama; enfermo-a.
laity *n.* [*non-professional*] lego.
La Leche League *n.* La Liga de la Leche, organización que promueve la lactancia materna.
lallation, lambdacism *n.* lalación, lambdacismo. 1. defecto y cambio fonético de la *l* por la *r*; 2. balbuceo, tartamudeo infantil.
Lamaze technique, Lamaze method *n.* método de Lamaze, procedimiento de parto natural con adiestramiento de la madre en

técnicas respiratorias que facilitan el proceso del parto.

lamb *n*. cordero-a, oveja, borrego-a.

lamb chop *n*. chuleta de cordero.

lamb's wool *n*. lana de cordero.

lame *a*. cojo-a, lisiado-a; *v*. **to go** ___ / cojear, andar cojeando.

lamella *n*. laminilla. 1. capa fina; 2. disco que se inserta en el ojo para aplicar un medicamento.

lament *n*. lamento, queja; lamentarse, quejarse.

lamina *n*. (*pl*. **laminae**) lámina, placa o capa fina.

laminated *a*. laminado-a, que está formado por una o varias láminas.

laminectomy *n*. *cirg*. laminectomía, extirpación de una o varias láminas vertebrales.

lamp *n*. lámpara; **lamplight** / luz de una ___; **infrared** ___ / ___ infrarroja; **slit** ___ / ___ de hendidura; **sun** ___ / ___ solar.

lancet, lance *n*. lanceta, instrumento quirúrgico; *v*. abrir con una lanceta.

Landztainer's classification *n*. clasificación de Landztainer, diferenciación de grupos sanguíneos: O-A-B-AB.

language *n*. lenguaje.

languid *a*. lánguido-a, débil, flojo-a; decaído-a.

languidness *n*. languidez, decaimiento.

lanolin *n*. lanolina, sustancia purificada que se obtiene de la lana de la oveja y se usa en pomadas.

lantern *n*. linterna, farol.

lanugo *n*. lanugo, vellosidad, pelusilla suave que cubre el cuerpo del feto.

lap *n*. regazo, falda; [*sitting*] sentado-a en las piernas de; **mother's** ___ / el ___, la ___ de la madre.

laparoscope *n*. laparoscopio, instrumento usado para visualizar la cavidad peritoneal.

laparoscopy *n*. laparoscopía, examen de la cavidad peritoneal por medio de un laparoscopio.

laparotomy *n*. *cirg*. laparotomía, incisión y abertura del abdomen.

lapse *n*. [*time*] lapso, intervalo de tiempo.

lard *n*. manteca, grasa de origen animal.

large *a*. grande, grueso-a, abultado-a; ___ intestine / intestino grueso.

larger, largest *comp*., *sup*., de **large** más grande; mayor; **the tumor is** ___ **now** / el tumor está más grande ahora.

larva *L*. (*pl*. **larvae**) larva, primera fase o forma de ciertos organismos tal como los insectos.

larval *a*. larval, larvado-a, rel. a una larva.

larvate *a*. larvado-a, rel. a un síntoma atípico o insidioso.

larvicide *n*. larvicida, agente que destruye las larvas, esp. las de los insectos.

laryngeal *a*. laríngeo-a; ___ reflex / reflejo ___, tos producida por irritación de la laringe.

laryngectomy *n*. *cirg*. laringectomía, extirpación de la laringe.

laryngitis *n*. laringitis; 1. infl. de la laringe; 2. afonía, ronquera.

laryngopharynx *n*. laringofaringe, porción inferior de la faringe.

laryngoplasty *n*. *cirg*. laringoplastia, reconstrucción plástica de la laringe.

laryngoscope *n*. laringoscopio, instrumento usado para examinar la laringe.

laryngoscopy *n*. laringoscopía, examen de la laringe; direct ___ / ___ directa, por medio de un laringoscopio; indirect ___ / ___ indirecta, por medio de un espejo.

laryngospasm *n*. laringoespasmo, espasmo de los músculos de la laringe.

laryngotomy *n*. *cirg*. laringotomía, incisión de la laringe.

larynx *n*. laringe. 1. parte del tracto respiratorio situada en la parte superior de la tráquea; 2. órgano de la voz.

laser *n*. laser. 1. sigla del inglés "Light Amplification by Stimulated Emission of Radiation" (amplificación de la luz por estimulación de emisión de radiación); 2. bisturí microquirúrgico usado en la cauterización de tumores.

laser beams *n*. *pl*. rayos de laser, rayos de luz por efecto radioactivo de calor intenso que se usan para destruir tejidos o separar partes.

lassitude *n*. lasitud, languidez, agotamiento.

last *a*. último-a; final, pasado-a; **the** ___ **treatment** / el ___ tratamiento; **the** ___ **word** / la ___ palabra; ___ **night** / anoche.

late *a*. tardío-a, último-a; *adv*. tarde; *v*. **to be** ___ / atrasarse, retrasarse; **-ly** *adv*. últimamente, hace poco.

latency *n*. latencia, acto de permanecer latente; ___ period / período de ___ .

latent *a*. latente, presente pero no activo-a; sin síntomas aparentes; sin manifestación.

later *a., comp.* de **late**; *adv.* más tarde, luego, después.

lateral *a.* lateral, rel. a un lado o costado.

lateroflexion *n.* lateroflexión, flexión lateral o de inclinación hacia un costado.

latest *a., sup.* de **late**, último; **at the** ___ / a más tardar; **the** ___ **drug in the market** / el medicamento más reciente en el mercado.

lather *n.* jabonadura, espuma de jabón.

latter *pron.* éste, ésta; el la más reciente, el más moderno, la más moderna.

laugh *n.* risa; *v.* reír; **to** ___ **at** / reírse de, mofarse.

laughter *n.* risa, carcajada.

lavage *n.* lavado, irrigación de una cavidad.

lavatory *n.* [*basin*] lavatorio, lavabo, lavamanos; [*restroom*] inodoro, servicio, baño, excusado.

law *n.* ley, regla, norma.

lawsuit *n.* pleito legal, litigio.

lawyer *n.* abogado-a, *Mex.* licenciado-a.

lax *a.* laxo-a, suelto-a, relajado-a.

laxative *n.* laxante, laxativo, purgante suave.

laxity *n.* laxitud, aflojamiento, flojedad; relajación.

lay *vi.* poner, colocar; **to** ___ **aside** / desechar; apartar; **to** ___ **off** / suspender despedir.

layer *n.* capa, estrato.

laying *n.* colocación, acto de colocar.

laziness *n.* pereza, holgazanería, haraganería.

lazy *a.* perezoso-a, flojo-a, holgazán, holgazana, haragán, haragana.

lazy eye *n.* ambliopía, falta de coordinación en la percepción de la profundidad visual.

lead *n.* 1. plomo; ___ **apron** / delantal de ___, usado como protección a radiaciones; ___ **poisoning** / envenenamiento por ___; 2. conductor, guía que se usa en una electrocardiografía; *vi.* conducir, llevar de la mano, guiar.

leading *a.* principal, primero-a, más importante.

leaf *n.* hoja.

leak *n.* [*of gas*] escape; [*water*] gotera, filtración; salirse, derramarse, escaparse.

lean *a.* [*meat*] magro-a, sin grasa; [*without flesh*] enjuto, flaco-a; seco-a; *v.* [*aptitude*] **to** ___ **toward** / tener propensión o disposición hacia algo o hacia alguien;

[*on against*] apoyarse, recostarse, arrimarse a; [*over*] inclinarse.

learn *vi.* aprender; [*to have knowledge of*] saber; [*to learn about something new*] tener noticias de, enterarse de.

learning *n.* aprendizaje; ___ disability / impedimento en el ___.

leather *n.* cuero, piel curtida.

leave *n.* [*of absence*] licencia, permiso de ausencia del trabajo; *vi.* [*to go away from*] salir; [*to give up*] dejar, renunciar; descontinuar, abandonar; **to** ___ **alone** / dejar en paz; **to** ___ **behind** / dejar atrás; **Nothing was left behind** / No se dejó nada; **to** ___ **off** / dejar.

lecithin *n.* lecitina, elemento esencial en el metabolismo de las grasas presente en los tejidos de los animales, esp. el tejido nervioso.

lecture *n.* conferencia, disertación.

ledge *n.* borde.

leech *n.* sanguijuela, gusano anélido acuático chupador de sangre; artificial ___ / ventosa.

left *a.* izquierdo-a; **to the** ___ / a la izquierda; ___ **hand** / mano izquierda; ___ **side** / lado ___.

left-handed *a.* zurdo-a.

leg *n.* pierna, extremidad inferior que se extiende de la rodilla al tobillo; ___ **injuries** / traumatismos de la ___; *v.* **to pull one's** ___ / tomar el pelo; **to get back on one's** ___**-s** / levantarse; ponerse bien; recobrar la salud.

legal *a.* legal, legítimo-a, de acuerdo con la ley; ___ **medicine**, forensic medicine / medicina ___; ___ **suit** / litigio, demanda, pleito.

legislation, medical *n.* legislación médica.

legitimacy *n.* legitimidad.

legitimate *a.* legítimo-a, auténtico-a.

legume *n.* legumbre.

leiomyofibroma *n.* leiomiofibroma, tumor benigno compuesto de tejido conectivo fibroso y muscular liso.

leiomyoma *n.* leiomioma, tumor benigno compuesto esencialmente de tejido muscular liso.

leiomyosarcoma *n.* leiomiosarcoma, tumor formado por leiomioma y sarcoma.

leisure *n.* holganza, ociosidad; **at** ___ / a conveniencia, cómodamente; *a.* ___ **hours** / tiempo libre, horas desocupadas.

lema *n.* legaña, lagaña, secreción de los ojos.

lemon *n.* [*fruit*] limón; [*tree*] limonero.

lemonade *n.* limonada.

lend *vi.* prestar; **to** ___ **a hand** / prestar ayuda, ayudar, dar ayuda.

length *n.* longitud, largo; extensión, distancia; ___ **of time** / período de tiempo; ___ **of stay** [*in a hospital*] / tiempo de internamiento.

lengthen *v.* alargar, extender, dilatar, prolongar.

lengthy *a.* largo-a; prolongado-a.

lenient *a.* indulgente, lenitivo-a; consentidor-a.

lens *n.* 1. lente; achromatic ___ / ___ acromático; adherent ___ / ___ adherido; biconcave ___ / ___ bicóncavo; biconvex ___ / ___ biconvexo; bifocal ___ / ___ bifocal; contact ___ / ___ de contacto, lentillas; dislocation of ___ / dislocación del ___; ___ implantation, intraocular / ___ -s intraoculares; trifocal ___ / ___ -s trifocales; 2. cristalino, lente transparente del ojo.

lent *a. pp.* de **to lend,** prestado-a.

lenticula *n.* lente pequeño.

lenticular *a.* lenticular, rel. a un lente.

lentil *n.* lenteja.

leper *a.* leproso-a, lazarino-a; que sufre de lepra.

leprosy *n.* lepra, enfermedad infecciosa conocida también como enfermedad de Hansen causada por el bacilo *Mycobaterium leprae* caracterizada por lesiones cutáneas de pústulas y escamas.

leptomeninges *n.* leptomeninges, las membranas más finas del cerebro: la piamadre y la aracnoide.

leptomeningitis *n.* leptomeningitis, infl. de las leptomeninges.

lesbian *n.* lesbiana, mujer homosexual.

lesbianism *n.* lesbianismo, homosexualidad femenina.

lesion *n.* lesión, herida, contusión.

less *a. comp.* menos, menor; **more or** ___ / más o menos; ___ **complicated** / ___ complicado; ___ **difficult** / ___ difícil; ___ **and** ___ / cada vez menos; *adv.* menos, en grado menor; *sufijo* menos, sin.

lessen *v.* aliviar, aminorar, disminuir, acortar; **a pill to** ___ **the pain** / una pastilla para ___ el dolor.

lesser *a. comp.* de **less,** menor; más pequeño.

lesson *n.* lección, enseñanza, instrucción.

let *vi.* permitir, dejar, conceder; **to** ___ **down** / dejar bajar; dejar caer; desilusionar, abandonar; **let us +** inf. / vamos a + *inf.*; **to** ___ **be** / dejar tranquilo-a; **to** ___ **blood** / hacer sangrar; **to** ___ **go** / soltar; **to** ___ **in** / dejar entrar, admitir; **to** ___ **out** / dejar salir; ___ **us go** / vámonos.

lethal *a.* letal, mortal; ___ **dose** (LD) / dosis ___.

lethargic, lethargical *a.* letárgico-a, aletargado-a.

lethargy *n.* letargo, estupor.

letter *n.* letra; carta; ___ **opener** / abrecartas.

lettuce *n.* lechuga.

leucine *n.* leucina, aminoácido esencial en el crecimiento y metabolismo.

leukapheresis *n.* leucaferesis, separación de leucocitos de la sangre de un paciente con subsecuente retransfusión al mismo paciente.

leukemia *n.* leucemia, cáncer de la sangre.

leukemic *a.* leucémico-a, rel. a la leucemia o que padece de ella.

leukemoid *n.* leucemoide, semejante a la leucemia.

leukocyte *n.* leucocito, glóbulo blanco, célula importante en la defensa y reparación del organismo; acidophil ___ / ___ acidófilo, que cambia de color con ácidos colorantes; basophil ___ / ___ basófilo, que cambia de color con colorantes básicos; lymphoid ___ / ___ linfoide, sin gránulos; neutrophil ___ / ___ neutrófilo, de afinidad con colorantes neutros; polymorphonuclear ___ / ___ polimorfonucleado, con núcleos de más de un lóbulo.

leukopenia *n.* leucopenia, número anormalmente bajo de glóbulos blancos.

leukoplakia *n.* leucoplasia, áreas de color opaco en la membrana mucosa de la lengua gen. de carácter precanceroso.

leukorrhea *n.* leucorrea, flujo vaginal blancuzco.

levator *n.* elevador, músculo que eleva o levanta una parte.

level *n.* nivel, plano; *v.* nivelar, ajustar; ___ **of health** / estado de salud.

leveling *n.* nivelación.

levocardia *n.* levocardia, transposición de

las vísceras abdominales y conservación de la posición normal del corazón en el lado izquierdo del tórax.

levodopa *n.* levodopa, sustancia química usada en el tratamiento de la enfermedad de Parkinson.

levulose *n.* levulosa. *V.* **fructose.**

lewd *a.* lujurioso-a, deshonesto-a, libidinoso-a, obsceno-a.

lewdness *n.* lujuria, impudicia, sensualidad, lascivia.

liability *n.* riesgo, responsabilidad de pago.

liable *a.* responsable, sujeto-a a cargos.

liar *n., a.* embustero-a, mentiroso-a.

liberation *n.* liberación.

liberty *n.* libertad; **at** ___ **to** / tener libertad para.

librarian *n.* bibliotecario-a.

library *n.* biblioteca.

lice *n. pl.* piojos.

license, licence *n.* licencia, permiso; medical ___ / ___ para ejercer la medicina.

licensure *n.* autorización, permiso legal para ejercer la medicina o ejecutar actos sólo permitidos a médicos o personal médico.

lichen *n.* liquen, lesiones o erupciones de la piel no contagiosas de forma papular; ___ planus / ___ plano.

licit *a.* lícito-a, permitido-a.

lick *v.* lamer; golpear, *pop.* dar una tunda.

lid *n.* 1. párpado del ojo; 2. tapa, tapadera.

lidocaine *n.* lidocaína, anestésico.

lie *n.* mentira, embuste; ___ detector / polígrafo, detector de ___-s; *v.* mentir; *v.* tenderse; **to** ___ **down** / echarse, acostarse, descansar.

life *n.* vida, modo de vivir, existencia; ___ expectancy / expectativa de ___; promedio de ___; ___ insurance / seguro de ___; ___ preservers, ___ support devices / aparatos para prolongar la ___; ___ saving measure / medida para prolongar o salvar la ___; ___ span / longevidad; ___ threatening / que puede causar la muerte.

life insurance *n.* seguro, póliza de seguro;- *Mex. A.* aseguranza.

lifeless *a.* muerto-a, sin vida.

lifetime *n.* toda la vida, curso de la vida; *a.* vitalicio-a.

lift *v.* levantar, alzar, elevar; ___ **your hand** / levante, levanta la mano; **to give one a** ___ / ayudar, animar, alentar.

lifting *n.* acto de levantar, levantamiento.

ligament *n.* ligamento. 1. banda de fibras de

tejido conjuntivo que protege las articulaciones y evita que sufran torceduras o luxaciones; 2. banda protectora de fascias y músculos que conectan o sostienen vísceras.

ligate *v.* ligar, aplicar una ligadura.

ligature, ligation *n.* ligadura; acción o proceso de ligar.

light *n.* luz; lumbre; ___ absorption / absorción de la ___; ___ adaptation / adaptación de la ___; ___ perception / percepción de la ___; ___ reflex / reflejo de la ___; ___ therapy / fototerapia; *a.* ligero-a, liviano-a claro-a, pálido-a; ___ **in the head** / [*dizzy*] mareado-a; **-ly** *adv.* ligeramente, levemente.

lighten *v.* iluminar, prender la luz; [*color*] aclarar.

lightening *n.* [*childbirth*] aligeramiento, descenso del útero en la cavidad pélvica, gen. en la etapa final del embarazo.

lighter *a. comp.* más ligero-a, más claro-a, más pálido-a.

likable *a.* agradable, amable, simpático-a.

like *a.* parecido-a, igual, semejante; **to look** ___ / parecerse a; [*to look alike*] **The boy looks** ___ **the father** / El niño se parece al padre; *v.* **to** ___ **someone, something** / gustar, agradar; **I** ___ **this medicine** / Me gusta esta medicina; *adv.* como, como si, del mismo modo.

lima beans *n. pl.* habas de lima.

limb *n.* 1. extremidad, miembro del cuerpo; 2. porción terminal o distal de una estructura; ___ amputation / amputación de una ___; ___ rigidity / rigidez de la ___ o del miembro.

limber *a.* flojo-a, flexible.

limbic *a.* marginal.

limbic system *n.* sistema límbico, grupo de estructuras cerebrales.

limbus *n.* limbo, filo o borde de una parte; ___ corneae / ___ de la córnea.

lime *n.* lima. 1. ___ **juice** / jugo, zumo de ___; 2. cal, óxido de calcio.

liminal *a.* liminal, casi imperceptible.

limit *n.* límite, frontera; ___, assimilation / ___ de asimilación; ___, saturation / ___ de saturación; ___ of perception / umbral perceptivo.

limitation *n.* limitación, restricción; ___ of motion / ___ de movimiento.

limited *a.* limitado-a, restricto-a; ___ activity / actividad ____; ____ autopsy / autopsia parcial.

limp *n.* cojera, flojera; *v.* cojear, renquear, renguear.

linden tea *n.* té de flores de tilo.

line *n.* línea; rasgo; arruga; límite o guía.

linear *a.* lineal, semejante a una línea.

linen *n.* lienzo, lino; **bed** ____ / ropa de cama.

linger *v.* [*to suffer*] consumirse, padecer lentamente; [*to delay*] demorarse.

lingering *v.* prolongación, tardanza, morosidad; *a.* prolongado-a, retardado-a, moroso-a.

lingua *n.* (pl. **linguae**) lengua o estructura semejante a la lengua.

lingual *a.* lingual, rel. a la lengua.

lingula *n.* língula, proyección o estructura en forma de lengüeta.

liniment *n.* linimento, untura de uso externo.

lining *n.* túnica, capa, forro, cubierta, revestimiento.

linitis *n.* linitis, *V.* **gastritis.**

link *n.* eslabón, vínculo.

linkage *n.* vínculo, unión, asociación de genes.

lint *n.* 1. fibra de algodón; 2. partículas desprendidas de la ropa.

lip *n.* labio, parte externa de la boca.

lipectomy *n. cirg.* lipectomía, excisión de tejido graso; submental ____ / ____ submental, del cuello.

lipemia *n.* lipemia, presencia anormal de grasa en la sangre.

lipid, lipide *n.* lípido, sustancia orgánica que no se disuelve en el agua pero que es soluble en alcohol, éter o cloroformo.

lipodystrophy *n.* lipodistrofia, trastorno del metabolismo de las grasas.

lipoid *n.* lipoide, sustancia que se asemeja a la grasa.

lipoma *n.* lipoma, tumor de tejido adiposo.

lipomatosis *n.* lipomatosis. 1. condición causada por depósito excesivo de grasa; 2. lipomas múltiples.

lipomatous *a.* lipomatoso-a, obeso-a.

lipoproteins *n. pl.* lipoproteínas, proteínas combinadas con compuestos lípidos que contienen una concentración alta de colesterol.

liposarcoma *n.* liposarcoma, tumor maligno que contiene elementos grasos.

liposis *n.* obesidad, acumulación excesiva de grasa en el cuerpo.

liposoluble *a.* liposoluble, que se disuelve en sustancias grasas.

liposuction *n.* liposucción, proceso de extraer grasa por medio de alta presión al vacío.

lip reading *n.* lectura labial, interpretación del movimiento de los labios.

liquefy *v.* licuar, disolver; descoagular.

liquid *n.* líquido, fluido; ____ balance / balance de ____; ____ retention / retención de ____.

liquor *n.* 1. licor, líquido acuoso que contiene sustancias medicinales; 2. término general aplicado a algunos líquidos del cuerpo.

lisping *n.* ceceo, sustitución de sonidos debido a un defecto en la articulación de las palabras, tal como el sonido de la *z* por la *c*, o el sonido de la *c* por la *s*.

list *n.* lista; casualty ____ / lista de accidentados.

listen *v.* escuchar, atender, prestar atención.

listless *a.* apático-a, lánguido-a, sin ánimo; indiferente.

liter *n.* litro.

lithiasis *n.* litiasis, formación de cálculos, esp. biliares o del tracto urinario.

lithium *n.* litio, elemento metálico usado como tranquilizante para tratar casos severos de psicosis.

lithotomy *n. cirg.* litotomía, incisión en un órgano o conducto para extraer cálculos.

lithotripsy *n.* litotripsia, trituración de cálculos en el riñón, el uréter, la vejiga y la vesícula biliar.

lithotriptor *n.* litotriturador, aparato o mecanismo para triturar cálculos; extracorporal shock wave ____ / ____ extracorporal con ondas de choque.

litter *n.* [*stretcher*] camilla; *v.* tirar basura.

little *a.* [*size*] pequeño-a; [*quantity*] poco, muy poco, un poquito; ____ by ____ / poco a poco.

live *v.* vivir, existir; ____ birth / nacimiento con vida.

livelihood *n.* vida; existencia; subsistencia.

lively *a.* vivo-a; vivaracho-a, animado-a.

liver *n.* hígado, glándula mayor del cuerpo que segrega bilis y sirve de estabilizador y productor de azúcar, enzimas, proteínas y colesterol además de eliminar las sustancias tóxicas del organismo; ____ circulation / circulación hepática; ____ cirrhosis / cirrosis hepática; ____ damage / lesión hepática;

enlarged ___ / ___ agrandado; ___ failure / insuficiencia hepática; ___ function tests / pruebas funcionales hepáticas; ___, infantile biliary cirrhosis / cirrosis biliar infantil; ___ spots / manchas hepáticas.

livid *a.* lívido-a; *pop.* amoratado-a.

living *n.* vida; con vida; modo de vivir; **cost of** ___ / costo de ___ ; ___ **expenses** / gastos de mantenimiento; ___ **under stress** / ___ agitada, ___ con estrés.

living will *n.* testamento hecho por una persona en completo estado de salud en el que dispone que en caso de peligro de muerte no se use ningún medio artificial para prolongarle la vida.

load *n.* carga, peso; ___ **dose** / dosis de ___ ; *v.* cargar, recargar.

loading *n.* carga por administración de una sustancia en una prueba metabólica; ___ **test** / prueba de carga.

loan *n.* préstamo; *v.* prestar.

lobar *a.* lobar, lobular, rel. a un lóbulo; ___ **pneumonia** / pulmonía ___.

lobby *n.* salón de entrada, sala de espera, vestíbulo.

lobe *n.* lóbulo, porción redondeada de un órgano; **middle** ___ **syndrome** / síndrome del lóbulo medio del pulmón.

lobectomy *n. cirg.* lobectomía, excisión de un lóbulo; **complete** ___ / ___ completa; **left lower** ___ / ___ izquienda anterior; **partial;** ___ / ___ parcial.

lobotomy *n. cirg.* lobotomía, incisión de un lóbulo cerebral con el fin de aliviar ciertos trastornos mentales.

lobster *n.* langosta.

lobular *a.* lobular, rel. a un lóbulo.

lobule *n.* lobulillo, lóbulo pequeño.

local *a.* local, rel. a una parte aislada; ___ **anethesia** / anestesia ___ ; ___ **application** / aplicación ___ ; ___ **recurrence** / reaparición ___ .

localization *n.* localización. 1. rel. al punto de origen de una sensación; 2. determinación de la procedencia de una infección o lesión.

localize, locate *v.* localizar.

lochia *n.* loquios, flujo serosanguíneo del útero en las primeras semanas después del parto.

lock *n.* cerradura; *v.* cerrar, trancar; encerrar, cerrar con llave; encerrarse, trancarse; cerrarse.

lockjaw *n.* tétano; pasmo; *V.* **tetanus.**

locomotion *n.* locomoción.

loculated, locular *a.* locular, rel. a un lóculo.

loculus *n. (pl.* **loculi**) lóculo, cavidad pequeña.

locus *n.* 1. lugar, sitio; 2. localización de un gene en el cromosoma.

logagraphia *n.* logagrafía, incapacidad de reconocer palabras escritas o habladas.

logamnesia *n.* logamnesia, afasia sensorial.

logaphasia *n.* logafasia, afasia motora, gen. causada por una lesión cerebral.

logic *a.* lógico-a, acertado-a.

logical *a.* lógico-a, preciso-a, exacto-a.

loin *n.* flanco, ijar, ijada, parte inferior de la espalda y de los costados entre las costillas y la pelvis.

long *a.* largo-a, extenso-a, prolongado-a; ___ **ago** / hace tiempo; **How** ___ **ago?** / ¿Cuánto tiempo hace?; ___ **after** / mucho después; ___ **standing** / de larga duración; **not** ___ **before** / poco tiempo antes; ___ **distance** / larga distancia.

longevity *n.* longevidad, ancianidad, duración larga de la vida.

longing *n.* deseo, anhelo, ansia.

longitudinal *a.* longitudinal, a lo largo del eje del cuerpo.

longus *a.* largo-a, extenso-a.

look *n. [appearance]* aspecto, apariencia, cara; mirada, ojeada. *v.* mirar; revisar; **to** ___ **for** / buscar; **to take a** ___ **at** / mirar, echar una mirada; **to** ___ **bad** / tener mal aspecto; **to** ___ **through** / examinar con cuidado.

loop *n.* asa; estructura en forma de lazo semejante a la curvatura de una cuerda.

loose *a.* suelto-a, desatado-a, libre; ___ **bowels** / deposiciones blandas o aguadas; *v.* desatar, desprender, aflojar.

lordosis *n.* lordosis, aumento exagerado hacia adelante de la concavidad de la columna lumbar.

lose *vi.* perder.

loss *n.* pérdida; ___ **of balance** / ___ del equilibrio; ___ **of blood** / ___ de sangre; ___ **of consciousness** / ___ del conocimiento; ___ **of contact with reality** / ___ del contacto con la realidad; ___ **of grip** / ___ de la retención; ___ **of hearing** / ___ de la audición; ___ **of memory** / ___ de la memoria; ___ **of motion** / ___ del movimiento; ___ **of muscle tone** / ___ de la tonicidad muscular; ___ of vision / ___ de la visión; **at a** ___ / confundido-a.

lost *a. pp.* de **to lose**, perdido-a, desorientado-a, extraviado-a.

lotion *n.* loción, ablución.

loud *a.* ruidoso-a, escandaloso-a.

loupe *n.* lupa binocular, lente convexa de aumento usada esp. por cirujanos y oculistas.

louse *n.* (*pl.* **lice**) piojo, insecto parásito que se aloja en el pelo, trasmisor de enfermedades infecciosas tales como la fiebre tifoidea.

love *n.* amor, cariño, afecto; *v.* amar, querer; **to fall in** ___ / enamorarse; **to fall in** ___ **with** / enamorarse de.

low *a.* bajo-a; [*in spirits*] abatido-a; ___ **opinion** / mala opinión.

lower *a., comp.* de **low**, inferior; bajo-a; *v.* bajar, poner más bajo; [*in quantity, price*] reducir, disminuir; **to** ___ **the arm** / ___ el brazo.

loyal *a.* leal, fiel, constante.

lozenge *n.* pastilla que se disuelve en la boca.

lubricant *n.* lubricante, agente oleaginoso que al lubricar disminuye la fricción entre dos superficies.

lubricate *v.* lubricar, untar, saturar una superficie con un líquido, especialmente aceite.

lubrication *n.* lubrificación, lubricación.

lucid *a.* lúcido-a, claro-a, inteligible; cuerdo-a.

lucidity *n.* claridad, esp. mental.

lucidness *n.* lucidez, claridad mental.

luck *n.* suerte, dicha; casualidad; **good** ___ / buena ___ ; **out of** ___ / de mala suerte; **worse** ___ / la peor ___ .

lucky *a.* afortunado-a, dichoso-a; *v.* **to be** ___ / tener suerte.

lues *n.* lues, sífilis.

luetic *a.* luético-a, sifilítico-a, rel. a o que padece de sífilis.

lukewarm *a.* tibio-a, templado-a; [*feelings*] indiferente.

lumbago *n.* lumbago, dolor en la parte inferior de la espalda.

lumbar *a.* lumbar, región de la espalda entre el tórax y la pelvis; ___ **puncture** / punción ___ ; ___ **vertebrae** / vértebras ___ -es.

lumbriscosis *n.* lumbricosis, infestación por lombrices.

lumen *n.* lumen. 1. unidad de flujo luminoso; 2. espacio en una cavidad, canal, conducto u órgano.

Luminal *n.* Luminal, patente comercial de un compuesto de fenobarbital usado como sedativo.

luminal *a.* luminal, rel. a la luz de un conducto.

luminescence *n.* luminosidad, emisión de luz sin producción de calor.

luminous *a.* luminoso-a, rel. a la luminosidad.

lump *n.* bulto, protuberancia, chichón; [*in the throat*] nudo en la garganta; [*of sugar*] terrón de azúcar.

lumpectomy *n. cirg.* extirpación de un tumor gen. de la mama.

lunacy *n.* locura, demencia.

lunar *a.* lunar, rel. a la luna.

lunatic *a.* lunático-a, demente, loco-a.

lunch *n.* almuerzo, comida del mediodía.

lung *n.* pulmón, órgano par de la respiración contenido dentro de la cavidad pleural del tórax que se conecta con la faringe a través de la tráquea y la laringe; ___ **abscess** / absceso pulmonar; **air containing** ___ / ___ **aireado**; ___ **cancer** / cáncer del ___ ; ___ **capacities** / volumen pulmonar; ___ **collapse** / colapso del ___ ; ___ **diseases** / neumopatías; ___ **elasticity** / elasticidad pulmonar; ___ **hemorrhage** / hemorragia pulmonar.

lungworm *n.* gusano nematodo que infesta los pulmones.

lupus *n.* lupus, enfermedad crónica de la piel de origen desconocido que causa lesiones degenerativas locales.

lupus erythematosus, discoid *n.* lupus eritematoso discoide, condición caracterizada por placas escamosas de bordes enrojecidos que causa irritación de la piel.

lupus erythematosus, systemic *n.* lupus eritematoso sistémico, condición caracterizada por episodios febriles que afecta las vísceras y el sistema nervioso.

lust *n.* lujuria, codicia, deseo incontenible.

luteal *a.* lúteo-a, rel. al cuerpo lúteo.

luteinizing hormone *n.* hormona luteinizante producida por la pituitaria anterior que estimula la secreción de hormonas sexuales por los testículos (testosterona) y el ovario (progesterona) e interviene en la formación de esperma y óvulos.

luxation *n.* luxación, dislocación.

lye *n.* lejía; ___ **poisoning** / envenenamiento por ___ .

lying *a.* acostado-a; recostado-a; extendido-a.

lymph *n.* linfa, líquido claro que se encuentra en los vasos linfáticos; ⸺ nodes / ganglios linfáticos.

lymphadenectomy *n. cirg.* linfadenectomía, extirpación de vasos linfáticos y ganglios.

lymphadenitis *n.* linfadenitis, infl. de los ganglios linfáticos.

lymphangiectasis *n.* linfangiectasis, dilatación de los vasos linfáticos.

lymphangiogram *n.* linfangiograma, representación filmada de ganglios y vasos linfáticos usando un medio de contraste inyectado.

lymphangitis *n.* linfangitis, infl. de vasos linfáticos.

lymphatic *a.* linfático-a, rel. a la linfa; ⸺ spaces / espacios ⸺ -s; ⸺ system / sistema ⸺.

lymphedema *n.* linfedema, edema causado por una obstrucción en los vasos linfáticos.

lymphoblast *n.* linfoblasto, forma primitiva del linfocito.

lymphocyte *n.* linfocito, célula linfática; ⸺ B cell / ⸺ B, importante en la producción de anticuerpos.

lymphocyte T *n.* linfocitos de células T, linfocitos diferenciados en el timo que dirigen la respuesta inmunológica y alertan a las células B a responder a los antígenos; ⸺ T helper / ayudante de ⸺, inductores, aumentan la producción de anticuerpos de las células B; cytotoxic ⸺ / ⸺ citotóxicos, ayudan a exterminar células extrañas tal como en el rechazo de órganos transplantados; supressor ⸺ / represores de ⸺, detienen la producción de anticuerpos de las células B.

lymphocytosis *n.* linfocitosis, cantidad excesiva de linfocitos en la sangre periférica.

lymphogranulomatosis, Hodgkin's disease *n.* linfogranulomatosis, enfermedad de Hodgkin, granuloma infeccioso del sistema linfático.

lymphogranuloma venereum *n.* linfogranuloma venéreo, enfermedad viral trasmitida sexualmente que puede producir elefantiasis de los genitales y estrechez rectal.

lymphoid *a.* linfoide, que se asemeja al tejido linfático.

lymphoma *n.* linfoma, neoplasma del tejido linfático.

lymphomatoid *n.* linfomatoide, rel. a un linfoma o semejante a éste.

lymphopenia, lymphocytopenia *n.* linfope-

nia, linfocitopenia, disminución en el número de linfocitos en la sangre.

lymphoreticular *a.* linforeticular, rel. a células reticuloendoteliales de los nódulos linfáticos.

lymphosarcoma *n.* linfosarcoma, neoplasma maligno del tejido linfoide.

lysergic acid, diethylamide (LSD) *n.* dietilamida del acido lisérgico.

lysin *n.* lisina, anticuerpo que disuelve o destruye células y bacterias.

lysis *n.* lisis. 1. proceso de destrucción o disolución de glóbulos rojos, bacterias o cualquier antígeno por medio de lisina; 2. desaparición gradual de los síntomas de una enfermedad.

M

m *abbr.* **male** / hombre; **malignant** / maligno; **married** / casado-a; **mature** / maduro; **melts at** / se derrite a; **minute** / minuto **molecular weight** / peso molecular; **morphine** / morfina.

macerate *v.* macerar; suavizar una materia por medio de inmersión en un líquido.

machine *n.* aparato, máquina.

macrocephalia *n.* macrocefalia, cabeza anormalmente grande.

macrocephalic *a.* macrocefálico-a, megalocefálico-a, de cabeza anormalmente grande.

macrocosm *n.* macrocosmo. 1. el universo como representación del ser humano; 2. el universo considerado como un todo.

macrocythemia *n.* macrocitemia, macrositosis, glóbulos rojos anormalmente grandes.

Macrodantin *n.* Macrodantina, nombre comercial Furantoína, bactericida usado en el tratamiento de infecciones urinarias.

macroglossia *n.* macroglosia, agrandamiento excesivo de la lengua.

macrognathia *n.* macrognatia, mandíbula demasiado grande.

macromolecule *n.* macromolécula, molécula de tamaño grande tal como la de una proteína.

macrophage, macrophagus *n.* macrófago, célula mononuclear fagocítica; ⸺ migration / migración de ⸺ -s.

macroscopic *a.* macroscópico-a, que se ve a simple vista, antónimo de microscópico.

macrospore *n.* macroespora, espora grande.

macula, macule *n.* mácula, pequeña mancha descolorida de la piel.

macula lutea, yellow spot *n.* mácula lútea, pequeña zona amarillenta situada en el centro de la retina.

macular *a.* macular, rel. a una mácula.

maculopapular *a.* maculopapular, rel. a máculas y pápulas.

mad *a.* [*insane*] loco-a, demente, perturbado-a; [*moody*] enojado-a, furioso-a; *v.* **to become** _____ / enloquecer; enloquecerse, enfurecerse; volverse loco-a; enojarse.

made *v., pret., pp.* de **to make**, hecho-a, producido-a.

madhouse *n.* manicomio, asilo de locos.

maggot *n.* larva de un insecto.

magistral *a.* magistral, rel. a medicamentos que se preparan de acuerdo a indicaciones médicas.

magma *n.* magma. 1. suspensión de partículas en una cantidad pequeña de agua; 2. sustancia viscosa compuesta de material orgánico.

magnesia *n.* magnesia, óxido de magnesio; **milk of** _____ / leche de _____ .

magnesium *n.* magnesio; _____ sulfate / sulfato de _____ .

magnet *n.* imán.

magnetic, magnetical *a.* magnético-a; _____ field / campo _____ .

magnetic resonance imaging *n.* imágenes por resonancia magnética, procedimiento por imágenes basado en el análisis cualitativo de la estructura química y biológica de un tejido.

magnetism *n.* magnetismo, propiedad de atracción y repulsión magnéticas.

magnetize *v.* magnetizar, imantar.

magnetoelectricity *n.* magnetoelectricidad, electricidad inducida por medios magnéticos.

magnification *n.* magnificación, ampliación de un objeto.

magnifier *n.* amplificador; vidrio de aumento.

magnify *v.* amplificar, agrandar, ampliar, aumentar.

magnifying glass *n.* lente de aumento; lupa.

magnitude *n.* magnitud.

mail *n.* correo, correspondencia; *v.* **to** _____ **a letter** / echar una carta al _____ .

maim *v.* mutilar; estropear; lisiar.

main *a.* principal; esencial; **-ly** *adv.* principalmente, esencialmente.

maintenance *n.* mantenimiento; [*feeding*] alimentación; sostén, apoyo; [*of a building*] conservación, mantenimiento.

make *vi.* hacer; [*money*] ganar; **to** _____ **mistakes** / hacer errores; equivocarse; [*earn*] **How much do you** _____ **?** / ¿Cuánto gana usted?, ¿cuánto ganas tú?; **to** _____ **believe** / fingir; **to** _____ **fun of** / burlarse de; **to** _____ **known** / declarar; **to** _____ **no difference** / no tener importancia; **to** _____ **a prescription** / llenar, preparar una receta; **to** _____ **sense** / tener sentido; **to** _____ **sure** / asegurarse; **to** _____ **up** [*time*] / recobrar el tiempo perdido; **to** _____ **up one's mind** / decidirse.

mal *n.* enfermedad, trastorno, desorden.

malabsorption syndrome *n.* síndrome de malabsorción, condición gastrointestinal con trastornos múltiples causada por absorción inadecuada de alimentos.

malacia *n.* malacia, reblandecimiento o pérdida de consistencia en órganos o tejidos.

malacoplakia *n.* malcoplaquia, formación de áreas blandas en la membrana mucosa de un órgano hueco.

maladjusted *a.* inadaptado-a, incapaz de adaptarse al medio social y de soportar tensiones.

malady *n.* enfermedad, trastorno, desorden.

malaise *n.* malestar, indisposición, molestia.

malar *a.* malar, rel. a la mejilla o a los pómulos.

malar bone *n.* pómulo, hueso en ambos lados de la cara.

malaria *n.* malaria, infección febril aguda a veces crónica causada por protozoos del género *Plasmodium* y trasmitida por el mosquito *Anófeles*.

malariacidal *a.* malaricida, que destruye parásitos de malaria.

malassimilation *n.* malasimilación, asimilación deficiente.

maldigestion *n.* indigestión.

male *n.* varón; hombre; macho; _____ nurse / enfermero.

malformation *n.* deformación, anomalía o enfermedad esp. congénita.

malfunction *n.* disfunción, funcionamiento defectuoso; *v.* funcionar mal.

malice *n.* malicia, malos deseos.

malicious *a.* malicioso-a.

malignancy *n.* 1. cualidad de malignidad; 2. tumor canceroso.

malignant *a.* maligno-a, pernicioso-a, de efecto destructivo.

malinger *v.* fingirse enfermo-a; fingir una enfermedad.

malingerer *n.* simulador-a, persona que finge o exagera los síntomas de una enfermedad.

malleable *a.* maleable.

malleolus *n.* (*pl.* **malleoli**) maléolo, protuberancia en forma de martillo tal como la que se ve a ambos lados de los tobillos.

mallet finger *n.* dedo en martillo; **mallet toe** / dedo del pie en martillo.

malleus *n.* (*pl.* **mallei**) malleus, uno de los huesecillos del oído medio.

malnourished *a.* desnutrido-a, malnutrido-a.

malnutrition *n.* malnutrición; mala alimentación; deficiencia nutricional.

malocclusion *n.* maloclusión, mordida defectuosa.

malposition *n.* posición inadecuada.

malpractice *n.* negligencia profesional.

malpresentation *n.* presentación anormal del feto durante el parto.

malrotation *n.* malrotación, rotación anormal o defectuosa de un órgano o parte.

malt *n.* malta; **malted milk** / leche malteada.

maltose *n.* maltosa, tipo de azúcar.

malunion *n.* malunión, fijación imperfecta de una fractura.

mamma *n.* mama, glándulas secretoras de leche en la mujer localizadas en la parte anterior del tórax.

mammal *n.* animal manífero.

mammalgia *n.* mamalgia, dolor en la mama.

mammaplasty, mammoplasty *n. cirg.* mamaplastia, cirugía plástica de los senos.

mammary *a.* mamario-a, rel. a los pechos o senos. ____ glands / glándulas ____-s.

mammectomy, mastectomy *n. cirg.* mamectomía, mastectomía, excisión de la mama o de una porción de la glándula mamaria.

mammillary *a.* mamilar, que se asemeja a un pezón.

mammillated *a.* mamilado-a, que presenta protuberancias similares a un pezón.

mammilliplasty *n. cirg.* mamiliplastia, operación plástica del pezón.

mammillitis *n.* mamilitis, infl. del pezón.

mammitis, mastitis *n.* mastitis, infl. de la mama.

mammogram *n.* mamograma, rayos X de la mama.

mammography *n.* mamografía, rayos X de la glándula mamaria.

mammoplasty *n. cirg.* mamoplastia, operación plástica de la mama.

man *n.* (*pl.* **men**) hombre.

manageable *a.* manejable; dócil.

manager *n.* administrador-a, gerente-a.

mandatory *a.* necesario-a, requerido-a.

mandible *n.* mandíbula, hueso de la quijada en forma de herradura.

mandibular *a.* mandibular, rel. a la mandíbula.

maneuver *n.* maniobra, movimiento preciso hecho con la mano.

mange *n.* sarna, roña.

mangy *a.* sarnoso-a, roñoso-a.

manhandle *v.* maltratar.

manhood *n.* virilidad; edad viril.

mania *n.* manía, trastorno emocional caracterizado por excitación excesiva, ansiedad y altas y bajas de espíritu.

maniac *a.* maníaco-a, persona afectada de manía.

manic-depressive psychosis *n.* psicosis maníaco-depresiva cíclica, condición caracterizada por estados de depresión y manía.

manifest *v.* manifestar; expresar; revelar; manifestarse, revelarse.

manifestation *n.* manifestación; revelación.

manikin *n.* maniquí, figura representativa del cuerpo humano.

manipulate *v.* manipular, manejar.

manipulation *n.* manipulación, tratamiento por medio del uso diestro de las manos.

manliness *n.* masculinidad, virilidad.

manly *a.* varonil.

manner *n.* manera, modo; hábito, costumbre; [*behavior*] **bad** ____-s / malos modales.

mannerism *n.* manerismo, expresión peculiar en la manera de hablar, de vestir o de actuar.

manometer *n.* manómetro, instrumento para medir la presión de líquidos o gases.

manslaughter *n.* homicidio sin premeditación.

mantle *n.* manto, capa.

manual *a.* manual, manuable.

manubrium *n.* (*pl.* **manubria**) manubrium, estructura en forma de mano.

many *a.*, *pron.* muchos-as; tantos, tantas; **a great** ___ / muchos, muchas; **as** ___ **as** / tantos-as como, igual número de.

marasmus *n.* marasmo, emaciación debida a malnutrición, esp. en la infancia.

march *n.* marcha,   progreso; *v.* marchar, poner en marcha.

margarine *n.* margarina.

margin *n.* margen, borde.

marginal *a.* marginal; **a** ___ **case** / un caso ___.

margination *n.* marginación, acumulación y adherencia de leucocitos a las paredes de los vasos capilares en un proceso inflamatorio.

marijuana, marihuana *n.* mariguana. *V.* **Cannabis sativa.**

marital *a.* matrimonial, marital; ___ relations / relaciones ___ -es.

marjoram *n.* mejorana.

mark *n.* marca, seña, señal, signo; *v.* marcar; señalar.

marker *n.* marcador, indicador.

marmalade *n.* mermelada, conserva de frutas.

marriage *n.* matrimonio; [*ceremony*] boda, casamiento.

married *a.* casado-a; ___ **couple** / matrimonio; ___ **life** / vida conyugal, vida matrimonial.

marrow *n.* médula, tejido esponjoso que ocupa las cavidades medulares de los huesos; *pop.* tuétano; ___ aspiration / aspiración de la ___; ___ puncture / punción de la ___ ósea; ___ transplant / transplante de la ___.

marsupialization *n. cirg.* marsupialización, conversión de una cavidad cerrada en una forma de bolsa abierta.

masculation *n.* masculación, desarrollo de características masculinas.

masculine *a.* masculino-a, viril.

masculinization *n.* masculinización. *V.* **virilización.**

mash *v.* mezclar ingredientes; amasar; **mashed** *a.*, *pp.* de **to mash**, [*vegetables*] ___ potatoes / puré de patatas.

mask *n.* máscara. 1. cubierta de la cara; 2. aspecto de la cara, esp. como manifestación patológica; death ___ / mascarilla; pregnancy ___ / manchas de la cara durante el embarazo; surgical ___ / cubreboca.

masked *a.* enmascarado-a; oculto-a.

masochism *n.* masoquismo, condición anor-

mal de placer sexual por abuso infligido a otros o a sí mismo-a.

mass *n.* masa, cuerpo formado de partículas coherentes.

massage *n.* masaje, proceso de manipulación del cuerpo por medio de fricciones; cardiac ___ / ___ cardíaco de resuscitación; *v.* dar masaje, sobar.

masseter *n.* músculo masetero, músculo principal de la masticación.

masseur, masseuse *Fr.* masajista, persona que da masajes.

massive *a.* maciso-a, abultado-a.

mastadenitis *n.* mastadenitis, infl. de una glándula mamaria. V. **mastitis.**

mastadenoma *n.* mastadenoma, tumor de la mama, tumor del seno.

mastalgia *n.* mastalgia, V. **mammalgia.**

mastectomy *n. cirg.* mastectomía. V. **mammectomy.**

masticate *v.* masticar, mascar.

mastication, chewing *n.* masticación.

masticatory *a.* masticatorio-a, rel. a la masticación.

mastitis, cystic *n.* mastitis cística, enfermedad fibroquística de la mama.

mastoid *n.* mastoides, apófisis del hueso temporal; *a.* 1. mastoideo-a, rel. a la mastoides o que ocurre en la región del proceso mastoideo; 2. semejante a una mama.

mastoid antrum *n.* antro mastoideo, cavidad que sirve de comunicación entre el hueso temporal, el oído medio y las células mastoideas.

mastoid cells *n. pl.* células mastoideas, bolsas de aire en la prominencia mastoidea del hueso temporal.

mastoiditis *n.* mastoiditis, infl. de las células mastoideas.

mastopathy *n.* mastopatía, afección de las glándulas mamarias.

masturbate *v.* masturbarse.

masturbation *n.* masturbación, autoestimulación y manipulación de los genitales para obtener placer sexual.

match *n.* semejante; [*by pairs*] pareja; [*game*] juego, partido; copia; *v.* igualar, asemejar, [*colors*] armonizar, hacer juego.

matching *n. a.* semejante, igual; ___ pair / compañero-a, pareja.

material *n.* materia; asunto; *a.* material; esencial.

maternal *a.* maternal, materno-a, rel. a la madre; ___ fetal exchange / intercambio materno-fetal; ⎯ welfare / bienestar materno.

maternity *n.* maternidad; ⎯ hospital / hospital de ⎯.

mating *n.* emparejamiento de sexos opuestos esp. para la reproducción.

matricide *n.* matricidio.

matrilineal *a.* de línea materna, descendiente de la madre.

matrix *n.* matriz; molde.

matter *n.* materia, sustancia; asunto; **gray** ⎯ / ⎯ gris; **as a** ⎯ **of fact** / en realidad; **What is the** ⎯? / ¿Qué pasa?, ¿qué ocurre?; **Let's take care of this** ⎯ / Vamos a hacernos cargo de este asunto.

mattress *n.* colchón.

maturate *v.* madurar; sazonar; supurar.

mature *a.* maduro-a; [*fruit*] sazonado-a.

maturity *n.* madurez; etapa de desarrollo completo.

maxilla *n.* maxila, hueso del maxilar superior.

maximum *a. sup.* máximo.

may *v. aux.* poder, [*possibility*] it ⎯ be / puede ser; [*permission*] ⎯ I see you? / ¿Puedo verlo-a?, ¿puedo verte?; ⎯ I come in? / ¿Puedo entrar?.

maybe *adv.* quizás, tal vez.

maze *n.* laberinto.

me *pron.* me, mí; **The doctor is going to see** ⎯ / El doctor me va a ver; **The medicine is for** ⎯ / La medicina es para mí; **Come with** ⎯ / Venga, ven conmigo.

meager *a.* escaso-a, insuficiente, pobre.

meal *n.* comida; **at** ⎯ **time** / a la hora de la ⎯.

mean *n.* media, índice, término medio; ⎯ corpuscular hemoglobin / índice corpuscular de hemoglobina; *a.* malo-a, desconsiderado-a, de mal humor.

meaning *n.* significado.

measles *n.* sarampión; *pop. Mex.* tapetillo de los niños, enfermedad sumamente contagiosa esp. en niños de edad escolar causada por el virus de la rubéola.

measles immune serum globulin *n.* suero de globulina preventivo contra el sarampión, se inyecta en uno de los cinco días siguientes a la exposición al contagio.

measles virus vaccine, live *n.* vacuna antisarampión de virus vivo, de uso en la inmunización contra el sarampión.

measure *n.* medida, dimensión, capacidad de algo; *v.* medir.

meat *n.* carne; **roast** ⎯ / ⎯ asada.

meatal *a.* meatal, concerniente al meato.

meatus *n.* meato, pasaje, abertura, apertura.

mechanic *n.* mecánico-a.

mechanical *a.* mecánico-a.

mechanism *n.* mecanismo. 1. respuesta involuntaria a un estímulo; defense ⎯ / ⎯ de defensa; 2. estructura semejante a una máquina.

meconium *n.* meconio. 1. primera fecalización del recién nacido; 2. opio.

medial *a.* medial, localizado-a hacia la línea media.

median *n.* mediana, intermedio; ⎯ plane / plano medio.

mediastinal *a.* mediastínico-a, rel. al mediastino.

mediastinitis *n.* mediastinitis, infl. del tejido del mediastino.

mediastinoscopy *n.* mediastinoscopía, examen del mediastino por medio de un endoscopio.

mediastinum *n.* mediastino. 1. cavidad entre dos órganos; 2. masa de tejidos y órganos que separa los pulmones.

mediate *v.* mediar, interceder.

mediator *a.* mediador-a; intercesor-a.

medic *n.* técnico-a entrenado para dar primeros auxilios.

Medicaid *n.* Asistencia Médica, programa del gobierno de los Estados Unidos que provee asistencia médica a los pobres.

medical *a.* médico-a; medicinal, curativo-a; ⎯ assistance / asistencia ⎯; ⎯ examiner / médico forense; ⎯ history / hoja clínica; ⎯ records / registros ⎯-s; [*patient's record*] expediente del paciente; ⎯ staff / cuerpo médico; ⎯ student / estudiante de medicina.

Medicare *n.* Programa de asistencia médica del gobierno de los Estados Unidos a personas desde los 65 años de edad o a adultos incapacitados para trabajar.

medicate *v.* recetar, medicinar.

medication *n.* medicina, medicamento; *pop.* remedio.

medicinal *a.* medicinal, rel. a la medicina, o con propiedades curativas.

medicine *n.* medicina. 1. ciencia que se dedica al mantenimiento de la salud por medio de tratamienos de curación y prevención de enfermedades; aerospace ⎯ / ⎯ del espacio; clinical ⎯ / ⎯ clínica; community ⎯ / ⎯ comunal, al servicio de la comunidad; environmental ___ / ___ ecológica; forensic ___ / ___ forense; legal ___ / ___ legal; nuclear ___ / ___ nuclear; preventive ___ / ___ preventiva; socialized ___ / ___ socializada; sports ___ / ___ deportiva; tropical ___ / ___ tropical; veterinary ___ / ___ veterinaria; 2. una droga o medicamento; ___ chest / botiquín.

medicine man *n.* curandero; **medicine woman** / curandera.

medicolegal *a.* médico-legal, rel. a la medicina en relación con las leyes.

mediolateral *a.* mediolateral, rel. a la parte media y a un lado del cuerpo.

medium *n.* (*pl.* **media**) medio. 1. intermediario-a, elemento mediante el cual se obtiene un resultado; 2. sustancia que transmite impulsos; 3. sustancia que se usa en un cultivo de bacterias.

medulla *n.* médula, *pop.* tuétano, parte interna o central de un órgano; ___ ossium, bone marrow / ___ ósea; ___ oblongata / ___ oblongata, bulbo raquídeo, porción de la médula localizada en la base del cráneo.

medullar, medullary *a.* medular, rel. a la médula.

meet *n.* reunión; concurso; *vi.* encontrar; reunirse con; **I am glad to** ___ **you** / Mucho gusto en conocerlo-a.

meeting *n.* reunión, junta; conferencia.

megabladder, megalocystis *n.* megalocisto, vejiga distendida.

megacephalic *a.* megacefálico-a. *V.* **macrocephalus.**

megacolon *n.* megacolon, colon anormalmente agrandado.

megaesophagus *n.* megaesófago, dilatación anormal de la parte inferior del esófago.

megalomania *n.* megalomanía, delirio de grandeza.

megavitamin *n.* megavitamina, dosis de vitamina en exceso de la cantidad normal requerida diariamente.

meibomian cyst *n.* quiste meiboniano, quiste del párpado.

meiosis *n.* meiosis, proceso de subdivisión celular que resulta en la formación de gametos.

melancholia *n. psic.* melancolía, depresión acentuada.

melancholic *a.* melancólico-a, rel. a la melancolía.

melanin *n.* melanina, pigmento oscuro de la piel, el pelo y partes del ojo.

melanocyte *n.* melanocito, célula que produce melanina.

melanoma *n.* melanoma, tumor maligno compuesto de melanocitos.

melanosis *a.* melanosis, condición que se caracteriza por la pigmentación oscura presente en varios tejidos y órganos.

melanuria *n.* melanuria, presencia de pigmentación oscura en la orina.

melena *n.* melena, masa de heces fecales negruscas y pastosas que contiene sangre digerida.

mellow *a.* dulce, suave, tierno-a.

melon *n.* melón.

melt *v.* derretir, disolver.

member *n.* miembro. 1. órgano o parte del cuerpo; 2. socio-a de una organización.

membrane *n.* membrana, capa fina que sirve de cubierta o protección a una cavidad, estructura u órgano; elastic ___ / ___ elástica; mucous ___ / ___ mucosa; nuclear ___ / ___ nuclear; permeable ___ / ___ permeable; placental ___ / ___ de la placenta; semipermeable ___ / ___ semipermeable; sinovial ___ / ___ sinovial; tympanic ___ / ___ timpánica.

membranous *a.* membranoso-a, rel. a una membrana o de la naturaleza de ésta.

memorandum *n.* memorando, nota.

memorial *n.* memoria, recuerdo.

memorize *v.* memorizar, aprender de memoria.

memory *n.* memoria, retentiva, facultad de la mente para registrar y recordar experiencias; **good** ___ / buena ___ ; **bad** ___ / mala ___ ; **short-term** ___ / ___ inmediata; *v.* **to lose the** ___ / perder la ___ ; **to have memories from** / tener recuerdos de; **Do you have a good** ___ ? / ¿Tiene, tienes buena ___ ?

men *pl.* de **man**, hombres.

menace *n.* amenaza; *v.* amenazar, atemorizar.

menarche *n.* menarca, inicio de la menstruación.

mend *v.* reparar, componer, mejorar.

mendable *a.* reparable, componible.

Mendelism *n.* mendelismo, principios que explican la trasmisión genética de ciertos rasgos.

meningeal *a.* meníngeo-a, rel. a las meninges.

meninges *n. pl.* meninges, las tres capas de tejido conjuntivo que rodean al cerebro y la médula espinal.

meningioma *n.* meningioma, neoplasma vascular gen. benigno de desarrollo lento que se origina en las meninges.

meningism *n.* meningismo, irritación congestiva de las meninges gen. de naturaleza tóxica con síntomas similares a los de la meningitis pero sin inflamación.

meningismus *L.* meningismus. *V.* **meningism.**

meningitic *a.* meningítico-a, rel. a las meninges.

meningitis *n.* meningitis, infl. de las meninges cerebrales o espinales.

meningocele *n.* meningocele, protrusión de las meninges a través del cráneo o de la espina dorsal.

meningococcus *n.* meningococo, uno de los microorganismos causantes de la meningitis cerebral epidémica.

meningoencephalitis *n.* meningoencefalitis, cerebromeningitis, infl. del encéfalo y las meninges.

meningoencephalocele *n.* meningoencefalocele, protrusión del encéfalo y meninges a través de un defecto en el cráneo.

meningomyelitis *n.* meningomielitis, infl. de la médula espinal y las membranas que la cubren.

meningomyelocele *n.* meningomielocele, protrusión de la médula espinal y las meninges a través de un defecto en la columna vertebral.

meniscectomy *n. cirg.* meniscectomía, extirpación de un menisco.

meniscus *n.* (*pl.* **menisci**) menisco, estructura cartilaginosa de forma lunar.

menometrorrhagia *n.* menometrorragia, menstruación irregular o excesiva.

menopause *n.* menopausia, cambio de vida en la mujer adulta, terminación de la etapa de reproducción y disminución de la producción hormonal

menorrhagia *n.* menorragia, períodos o reglas muy abundantes.

menorrhalgia *n.* menorralgia, menstruación dolorosa.

menorrhea *n.* menorrea, flujo menstrual normal

menses *n.* menses, menstruo, menstruación, período, regla.

menstrual *a.* menstrual, rel. a la menstrua-ción; ____ cycle / ciclo ____; ____ disorder / trastorno ____.

menstruate *v.* menstruar.

menstruation *n.* menstruación, flujo sanguíneo periódico de la mujer.

mental *a.* mental, rel. a la mente; ____ age / edad ____; ____ disorder / trastorno ____; ____ deficiency / retraso ____; ____ health / salud ____; ____ hygiene / higiene ____; ____ illness / enfermedad ____; ____ retardation / retraso ____; ____ test / examen de capacidad ____.

mentality *n.* mentalidad, capacidad mental.

mentation *n.* actividad mental.

menthol *n.* mentol, sustancia que se obtiene del alcanfor de menta y que tiene efecto sedativo.

mentum *n.* mentón, barbilla, prominencia de la barba.

merbromin *n.* merbromina, polvo rojo inodoro, soluble en agua, usado como germicida.

merciful *a.* misericordioso-a, compasivo-a.

merciless *a.* inhumano-a, despiadado-a.

mercurial *a.* mercurial, perteneciente o rel. al mercurio.

mercurochrome *n.* mercurocromo, nombre registrado de la merbromina.

mercury *n.* mercurio, metal líquido volátil; ____ poisoning / envenenamiento por ____.

mercy *n.* misericordia, compasión; ____ killing / eutanasia.

merge *v.* unir, unificar.

meridian *n.* meridiano, línea imaginaria que conecta los extremos opuestos del axis en la superficie de un cuerpo esférico.

mescaline *n.* mescalina, alcaloide alucinogénico, *pop.* peyote.

mesectoderm *n.* mesectodermo, masa de células que componen las meninges.

mesencephalon *n.* mesencéfalo, el cerebro medio en la etapa embrionaria.

mesenchyme *n.* mesénquima, red de células embrionarias que forman el tejido conjuntivo y los vasos sanguíneos y linfáticos en el adulto.

mesenteric *a.* mesentérico-a, concerniente al mesenterio.

mesentery *n.* mesenterio, repliegue del peritoneo que fija el intestino a la pared abdominal posterior.

mesial *a.* mesial *V.* **medial.**

mesion *n.* mesión, plano imaginario medio

que divide el cuerpo en dos partes simétricas.

mesmerism *n.* mesmerismo, uso del hipnotismo como método terapéutico.

mesocardia *n.* mesocardia, desplazamiento anormal del corazón hacia el centro del tórax.

mesocolon *n.* mesocolon, mesenterio que fija el colon a la pared abdominal posterior.

mesoderm *n.* mesodermo, capa media germinativa del embrión situada entre el ectodermo y endodermo de la cual provienen el tejido óseo, el muscular, los vasos sanguíneos y linfáticos, y las membranas del corazón y abdomen.

mesothelium *n.* mesotelio, capa celular del mesodermo embrionario que forma el epitelio que cubre las membranas serosas en el adulto.

mess *n.* lío, confusión; *v.* **to make a** ___ / hacer un ___ ; desordenar, revolver, ensuciar.

message *n.* mensaje, recado.

messy *a.* revuelto-a, desordenado-a, sucio-a.

metabolic *a.* metabólico-a, rel. al metabolismo; ___ rate / índice ___ .

metabolism *n.* metabolismo, suma de los cambios físicoquímicos que tienen efecto a continuación del proceso digestivo; ___ basal / ___ basal, el nivel más bajo del gasto de energía; constructive ___ / anabolismo, asimilación; destructive ___ / ___ destructivo, catabolismo; protein ___ / ___ de proteínas, digestión de proteínas y conversión de éstas en aminoácidos.

metabolite *n.* metabolito, sustancia producida durante el proceso metabólico.

metacarpal *a.* metacarpiano-a, rel. al metacarpio.

metacarpus *n.* metacarpo, la parte formada por los cinco huesecillos metacarpianos de la mano.

metal *n.* metal; ___ fume fever / fiebre por aspiración de vapores metálicos.

metallic *a.* metálico-a, rel. a un metal o de la naturaleza de éste.

metamorphosis *n.* metamorfosis. 1. cambio de forma o estructura; 2. cambio degenerativo patológico.

metaphase *n.* metafase, una de las etapas de la división celular.

metaphysis *n.* metáfisis, zona de crecimiento del hueso.

metastasis *n.* metástasis, extensión de un proceso patológico de un foco primario a otra parte del cuerpo a través de los vasos sanguíneos o linfáticos como se observa en algunos tipos de cáncer.

metastasize *v.* metastatizar, esparcirse por metástasis.

metatarsial *a.* metatarsiano-a, rel. al metatarso.

metatarsus *n.* metatarso, la parte formada por los cinco huesecillos del pie situados entre el tarso y los dedos.

meteorism *n.* meteorismo, abdomen distendido causado por acumulación de gas en el estómago o los intestinos.

methadone *n.* metadona, droga sintética potente de acción narcótica menos intensa que la morfina.

methanol, wood alcohol *n.* metanol, alcohol de madera.

method *n.* método, procedimiento; proceso; tratamiento.

meticulous *a.* meticuloso-a.

metopic *a.* metópico-a, frontal, rel. a la frente.

metria *n.* metria, infl. del útero durante el puerperio.

metric *a.* métrico-a; ___ system / sistema ___ .

metritis *n.* metritis, infl. de la pared uterina.

metroflebitis *n.* metroflebitis, infl. de las venas uterinas.

micrencephaly *n.* micrencefalia, cerebro anormalmente pequeño.

microabscess *n.* microabsceso, absceso diminuto.

microanatomy *n.* microanatomía, histología.

microbe *n.* microbio, microoganismo, organismo diminuto.

microbial, microbian *a.* microbiano-a, rel. a los microbios.

microbiology *n.* microbiología, ciencia que estudia los microorganismos.

microbizide *n.* microbicida, agente exterminador de microbios.

microcephaly *n.* microcefalia, cabeza anormalmente pequeña de origen congénito.

micrococcus *n.* micrococo, microorganismo.

microcolon *n.* microcolon, colon anormalmente pequeño.

microcosmus *n.* microcosmo. 1. universo en miniatura; 2. cualquier entidad o estructura considerada en sí misma un pequeño universo.

microcurie *n.* microcurie, medida de radiación.

microfiche *n.* microficha, ficha en la que se acumulan datos para ser vistos bajo un lente amplificador.

microfilm *n.* microfilm, microfilme, película que contiene información reducida a un tamaño mínimo.

micrognathia *n.* micrognatia, mandíbula inferior anormalmente pequeña.

micrography *n.* micrografía, estudio microscópico.

microinvasion *n.* microinvasión, invasión de tejido celular adyacente a un carcinoma localizado que no puede verse a simple vista.

micromelia *n.* micromelia, extremidades normalmente pequeñas.

micromelic *a.* micromélico-a, rel. a la micromelia.

micrometer *n.* micrómetro, instrumento para medir distancias cortas.

microorganism *n.* microorganismo, organismo que no puede verse a simple vista.

microphallus *n.* microfalo, pene anormalmente pequeño.

microscope *n.* microscopio, instrumento óptico con lentes que amplifican objetos que no pueden verse a simple vista; electron ___ / ___ electrónico; light ___ / ___ con luz o lumínico.

microscopic *a.* microscópico-a, rel. al microscopio.

microscopy *n.* microscopía, examen que se realiza con un microscopio.

microsome *n.* microsoma, elemento fino granular del protoplasma.

microsomia *n.* microsomía, cuerpo anormalmente pequeño de proporciones normales.

microsurgery *n.* microcirugía, operación efectuada con el uso de microscopios quirúgicos e instrumentos minúsculos de precisión.

microtome *n.* micrótomo, instrumento de precisión que se usa en la preparación de secciones finas de tejido para ser examinadas bajo el microscopio.

microtomy *n.* microtomía, corte de secciones finas de tejido.

microwave *n.* microonda, onda corta electromagnética de frecuencia muy alta.

micturate *v.* orinar.

middle *n.* medio, centro; **in the** ___ **of** / en el ___ de.

middle age *n.* mediana edad, madurez.

middle ear *n.* oído medio, parte del oído situada más allá del tímpano.

middle finger *n.* el dedo cordial.

middle lobe syndrome *n.* síndrome del lóbulo medio del pulmón.

midget *n.* enano-a.

midgut *n.* intestino medio del embrión.

midline *n.* línea media del cuerpo.

midnight *n.* medianoche.

midplane *n.* plano medio.

midriff *n.* diafragma.

midsection *n.* sección media.

midstream specimen *n.* especimen de orina que se toma después de comenzar la emisión y poco antes de terminarse.

midwife *n.* comadrona, partera.

midyear *n.* mediados de año.

migraine *n.* migraña, jaqueca, ataques severos de dolor de cabeza que gen. se manifiestan en un solo lado acompañados de visión alterada y en algunos casos de naúseas y vómitos.

migration *n.* migración, se dice de las células al moverse de un lugar a otro.

mild *a.* [*pain*] leve, tolerable; moderado-a, indulgente.

mildew *n.* moho, añublo.

miliary *a.* miliar, caracterizado-a por pequeños tumores o nódulos.

miliary tuberculosis *n.* tuberculosis miliar, enfermedad que invade el organismo a través de la sangre y se caracteriza por la formación de tubérculos diminutos en los órganos afectados.

milieu *n.* medio ambiente.

milk *n.* leche; **boiled** ___ / ___ hervida; **condensed** ___ / ___ condensada; **evaporated** ___ / ___ evaporada; ___ **of magnesia** / ___ de magnesia; **skim** ___ / ___ desnatada; **sterilized** ___ / ___ esterilizada; **mother's** ___ / leche materna.

milking *n.* ordeño, maniobra para forzar sustancias fuera de un tubo.

milky *a.* lechoso-a, lácteo-a.

mimetic, mimic *a.* mimético-a, que imita.

mind *n.* mente, entendimiento; *v.* atender, tener en cuenta; **to bear in** ___ / tener presente; **to be out of one's** ___ / volverse loco-a; **to make up one's** ___ / decidirse; **to speak one's** ___ / dar una opinión; dar su parecer.

miner *n.* minero.

mineral *n.* mineral, elemento inorgánico; *a.* mineral; ___ **water** (carbonated) / agua ___ efervescente.

mineralization *n.* mineralización, depósitos de minerales en los tejidos.

mineralocorticoid *n.* mineralocorticoide, tipo de hormona liberada por la glándula suprarrenal que participa en la regulación del volumen de la sangre.

minimal *a. comp.* mínimo-a, más pequeño-a.

minimal dose *n.* dosis mínima, la menor dosis necesaria para producir un efecto determinado.

minimal lethal dose *n.* dosis letal mínima, la menor dosis de una sustancia que puede ocasionar la muerte.

minimize *v.* aliviar, atenuar, mitigar; reducir al mínimo; **This pill is to** ___ **the pain** / Esta pastilla es para ___ el dolor.

minister *n.* ministro; pastor.

minor *n.* [*in age*] menor de edad; *a.* [*smaller, youngest*] menor, más pequeño; **a** ___ **problem** / un problema sin importancia; ___ **surgery** / cirugía menor.

minority *n.* minoría, minoridad.

mint *n.* [*herb*] menta.

minute *n.* [*time*] minuto, momento; *a.* menudo-a, mínimo-a, diminuto-a.

miosis *n.* miosis, contracción excesiva de la pupila.

miracle *n.* milagro, prodigio.

miraculous *a.* milagroso-a, prodigioso-a.

mirror *n.* espejo.

misadventure *n.* infortunio, desgracia; accidente.

misanthropia *n.* misantropía, aversión a la humanidad.

misbehave *v.* portarse mal, conducirse mal.

misbehaved *a.* mal criado-a, majadero-a; mal educado-a.

misbehavior *n.* mala conducta, mal comportamiento.

miscalculate *v.* hacer un error o falta; equivocarse.

miscalculation *n.* error, falta, equivocación.

miscarriage *n.* aborto, malparto, expulsión del feto por vía natural.

miscegenation *n.* miscegenatión, relaciones sexuales entre personas de razas diferentes.

miscible *a.* capaz de mezclarse o disolverse.

misdiagnosis *n.* diagnóstico equivocado o erróneo.

misery *n.* sufrimiento, pena; desesperación; miseria.

misfit *a.* mal adaptado-a.

misguide *v.* dirigir mal, aconsejar mal.

misguided *a.* mal aconsejado-a, mal dirigido-a.

misinform *v.* dar una información errónea.

misinformed *a.* mal informado-a.

misjudge *v.* juzgar mal, tener una opinión errónea.

misogamy *n.* misogamia, aversión al matrimonio.

misogyny *n.* misoginia, aversión a las mujeres.

misplace *v.* extraviar, poner algo fuera de lugar.

miss *n.* señorita, jovencita; *v.* [*to fail, to overlook*] perder; **to** ___ **an appointment** / perder el turno; [*sentiment*] echar de menos; **to** ___ **one's family** / echar de menos a la familia; [*to skip*] **to** ___ **a period** / faltar la regla, faltar el periodo.

misshape *v.* deformar, desfigurar.

misshaped, misshapen *a.* deforme, desfigurado-a.

missing *a.* desaparecido-a; extraviado-a.

mission *n.* misión; destino.

mistake *n.* error, equivocación, desacierto, falta; *vi.* equivocar entender mal, confundir; equivocarse, confundirse.

mistaken *a. pp.* de **to mistake,** equivocado-a, desacertado-a, incorrecto-a.

mister *n.* señor.

mistimed *a.* inoportuno, fuera de tiempo.

mistranslation *n.* traducción incorrecta.

mistrustful *a.* desconfiado-a, receloso-a.

misunderstand *vi.* no comprender, entender mal

mitigate *v.* mitigar, aliviar, calmar.

mitigated *a.* mitigado-a, aliviado-a, calmado-a; disminuído-a.

mitochondria *n.* mitocondria, filamentos microscópicos del citoplasma que constituyen la fuente principal de energía de la célula.

mitogen *n.* mitógeno, sustancia que induce mitosis celular.

mitogenesis, mitogenia *n.* mitogénesis, causa de la mitosis celular.

mitosis *n.* mitosis, división celular que da lugar a nuevas células y reemplaza tejidos lesionados.

mitral *a.* mitral, rel. a la válvula mitral o bicúspide; ___ **disease** / enfermedad de la válvula ___ del corazón; ___ **murmur** /

soplo; ⸻ orifice / orificio ⸻; ⸻
valve insuficiency / insuficiencia de la válvula ⸻; ⸻ valve prolapse (MVP) /
prolapso de la válvula ⸻, cierre defectuoso de la válvula ⸻.

mitral regurgitation *n.* regurgitación mitral,
flujo sanguíneo retrógrado del ventrículo izquierdo a la aurícula izquierda causado por
lesión de la válvula mitral.

mitral stenosis *n.* estenosis mitral, estrechez
del orificio izquierdo aurículo-ventricular.

mitral valve *n.* válvula mitral, válvula aurículo-ventricular izquierda del corazón.

mittelschmerz *n.* dolor en el vientre relacionado con la ovulación que ocurre gen.
a mitad del ciclo menstrual.

mix *v.* mezclar, juntar, asociar.

mixed *a.* mezclado-a, asociado-a.

mixture *n.* mezcla, mixtura; poción.

mnemonics *n.* mnemónica, adiestramiento de
la memoria por medio de asociación de
ideas y otros recursos.

moan *n.* quejido, gemido, queja, lamento;
v. quejarse, lamentarse.

mobility *n.* movilidad.

mobilization *n.* movilización.

mobilize *v.* movilizar; movilizarse, moverse.

modality *n.* modalidad, cualquier método de
aplicación terapéutica.

mode *n.* 1. moda, manera. valor repetido con
mayor frecuencia en una serie; 2. modo.

model *n.* modelo, patrón, molde.

moderated *a.* moderado-a, mesurado-a;
[*price*] módico, [*weather*] templado; ⸻
temperature / temperatura ⸻.

moderation *n.* moderación, sobriedad.

modern *a.* moderno-a, reciente.

modest *a.* modesto-a, recatado-a.

modification *n.* modificación, cambio.

modify *v.* modificar, cambiar.

modulation *n.* modulación, acto de ajustar o
adaptar tal como ocurre en la inflexión de la
voz.

moiety *n.* mitad, una de las porciones de un
todo.

molar *n.* diente molar, muela.

mold *n.* moho, cualquier moho.

molding *n.* amoldamiento de la cabeza del
feto para adaptarla a la forma y tamaño del
canal del parto.

mole *n.* mancha, lunar.

molecular *a.* molecular, rel. a una molécula;
⸻ **biology** / biología ⸻.

molecule *n.* molécula, unidad mínima de una
sustancia.

molest *v.* dañar físicamente, vejar; humillar;
asaltar.

mollusc, mollusk *n.* (*pl.* **mollusca.**) molusco.

moment *n.* momento, instante.

momentary *a.* momentáneo-a.

momentum *L.* momentum; ímpetu; fuerza
de movimiento.

monarticular *a.* monarticular, que concierne
o afecta a una sola articulación.

money *n.* dinero; moneda; divisas.

mongolism *n.* mongolismo. *V.* **Down's
syndrome.**

mongoloid *a.* mongoloide, rel. a mongolismo o que sufre del mismo.

moniliasis *n.* moniliasis. *V.* **candidiasis.**

monitor *n.* monitor. 1. instrumento electrónico usado para monitorear una función; 2.
persona que supervisa una función o actividad; *v.* monitorear, chequear sistemáticamente con un instrumento electrónico una
función orgánica, tal como los latidos del
corazón.

monitoring *n.* monitoreo, acción de monitorear; blood pressure ⸻ / ⸻ de la presión arterial; cardiac ⸻ / ⸻ cardíaco;
fetal ⸻ / ⸻ del corazón fetal.

monochromatic *a.* monocromático-a, de un
solo color.

monoclonal *a.* monoclonal, rel. a un solo
grupo de células; ⸻ antibodies / anticuerpos ⸻ -es.

monocular *a.* monocular, rel. a un solo ojo.

monocyte *n.* monocito, glóbulo blanco mononuclear granuloso.

monogamy *n.* monogamia, unión matrimonial legal con una sola persona.

mononucleosis *n.* mononucleosis, presencia
de un número anormalmente elevado de
leucocitos mononucleares en la sangre; infectious ⸻ / ⸻ infecciosa, infección
viral aguda.

monosaccharide *n.* monosucárido, azúcar
simple.

monotone *n.* monotonía.

monotonous *a.* monótono-a.

monozygotic twins *n. pl.* gemelos monoci-
góticos con características genéticas idénticas.

monster *n.* monstruo.

month *n.* mes.

monthly *a.* mensual; *adv.* mensualmente.

mood *n.* estado de ánimo, disposición, humor; *v.* **to be in the** ___ / tener deseos de; *gr.* modo.

moody *a.* triste, deprimido-a; irritable, de mal humor.

moon *n.* luna; **moonlight** / luz de la luna.

moonface *n.* cara de luna, cara llena redonda característica de pacientes sometidos a un tratamiento prolongado de un esteroide.

moonlighter *n.* persona que tiene más de un empleo.

moral *a.* moral, honesto-a, honrado-a.

morality *n.* ética, rectitud, moral.

morbid *a.* mórbido, insano-a, morboso-a, rel. a una enfermedad.

morbidity *n.* morbidez, morbosidad, enfermedad.

mordacious *a.* mordaz, satírico-a.

more *a.* más; *adv.* más; **more and more** / cada vez ___ ; **once** ___ / una vez ___ ; [*before numeral*] ___ **than a hundred** / ___ de cien; [*before a verb*] ___ **than** / más de lo que; ___ **than he needs** / más de lo que necesita.

moreover *adv.* además, además de eso; también.

morgue *Fr.* morgue, necrocomio, depósito temporal de cadáveres.

moribund *a.* moribundo-a, cercano-a a la muerte, agonizante.

morning *n.* mañana, madrugada; **Good** ___ / buenos días, buen día; **early in the** ___ / muy de ___ ; **in the** ___ / por la ___ , en la ___ ; ___ **stiffness** / rigidez matutina muscular y de las articulaciones; **tomorrow** ___ / ___ por la ___ .

morning sickness *n.* trastorno matutino de náuseas y vómitos que sufren algunas mujeres en la primera etapa del embarazo.

moron *n.* morón-a, persona con retraso mental de un cociente intelectual de 50 a 70.

morphine *n.* morfina, alcaloide que se obtiene del opio y se usa como analgésico y sedativo.

morphinism *n.* morfinismo, condición morbosa ocasionada por la adicción a la morfina.

mortal *a.* mortal, mortífero-a, fatal, letal.

mortality *n.* mortalidad, mortandad. 1. estado de ser mortal; 2. índice de mortalidad.

mortify *v.* mortificar; mortificarse, sentirse mortificado-a.

mortuary *n.* mortuorio, funeraria.

morula *n.* mórula, masa esférica y sólida de células que resulta de la división celular del óvulo fecundado.

mosaic *n.* mosaico, la presencia en una persona de distintos tejidos adyacentes derivados de la misma célula como resultado de mutaciones.

mosquito *n.* mosquito.

most *a. sup.* de **more**, el, la más; lo más; el, la mayor; el mayor número de, la mayor parte de; *adv.* más, muy, a lo sumo; **-ly** sumamente, principalmente.

mother *n.* madre, mamá; **mother-in-law** / suegra.

motherhood *n.* maternidad.

motility *n.* movilidad.

motion *n.* movimiento; [*sign*] seña, indicación; moción; ___ **sickness** / mareo.

motionless *a.* sin movimiento, inmóvil.

motivate *v.* motivar, animar.

motivation *n.* motivación, estimulación externa.

motive *n.* motivo; ánimo, fuerza mayor.

motor *n.* motor, agente que produce o induce movimiento; *a.* motor-a, que causa movimiento.

motor neuron *n.* neurona motora, células nerviosas que conducen impulsos que inician las contracciones musculares.

mottling *a.* moteado-a, descolorido-a.

mountain *n.* montaña.

mourn *v.* estar de duelo; guardar luto.

mouse *n.* (*pl.* **mice**) ratón, [*small*] ratoncito.

moustache *n.* bigote.

mouth *n.* boca. 1. cavidad bucal; 2. abertura de cualquier cavidad; **by** ___ / por vía bucal; **Open your** ___ / Abra, abre la boca.

mouthwash *n.* antiséptico bucal; enjuague.

move *n.* movimiento; paso; *v.* mover; mudar; **to** ___ **about, to** ___ **around** / caminar, andar, ir; **to** ___ **away** / irse, trasladarse, mudarse; **to** ___ **down** / bajar; ___ **your hand** / Mueva, mueve la mano; ___ **your fingers** / Mueva, mueve los dedos.

movement *n.* movimiento, moción, acción, maniobra; [*of the intestines*] evacuación, defecación.

much *a.* mucho-a; abundante; *adv.* excesivamente, demasiado, en gran cantidad; **as** ___ **as** / tanto como; **How** ___ / ¿Cuánto? **not as** ___ **as before** / no tanto como antes; **too** ___ / en exceso, excesivamente; **How** ___ **does it hurt?** / ¿Cuánto le duele?

mucin *n.* mucina, glucoproteína, ingrediente esencial del mucus.

mucocele *n.* mucocele, dilatación de una cavidad ósea debida a una acumulación de secreción mucosa.

mucocutaneous *a.* mucocutáneo-a, rel. a la membrana mucosa y la piel.

mucoid *n.* mucoide, glucoproteína similar a la mucina; *a.* de consistencia mucosa.

mucomembranous *a.* mucomembranoso-a, rel. a la membrana mucosa.

mucosa *n.* mucosa, membrana mucosa. *V.* **mucous membrane.**

mucosal *a.* mucosal, rel. a cualquier membrana mucosa.

mucosity *n.* mucosidad.

mucous *n.* mucoso-a, flemoso-a; ___ colitis / colitis ___.

mucous membrane *n.* membrana mucosa, láminas finas de tejido celular que cubren aberturas o canales que comunican con el exterior.

mucus *n.* moco, mucosidad, sustancia viscosa segregada por las membranas y glándulas mucosas.

multicellular *a.* multicelular, que consiste de muchas células.

multifactorial *a.* multifactorial, rel. a varios factores.

multifocal *a.* multifocal, rel. a más de un foco.

multilocular *a.* multilocular, *V.* **multicellular.**

multiparity *n.* multiparidad. 1. condición de una mujer que ha tenido más de un parto logrado; 2. parto múltiple.

multiple *a.* múltiple, más de uno; ___ organ failure / fallo ___ de órganos; ___ personality / personalidad ___.

multiple sclerosis *n.* esclerosis múltiple, enfermedad progresiva lenta del sistema nervioso central causada por pérdida de la capa de mielina que cubre las fibras nerviosas del cerebro y la médula espinal.

mummification *n.* momificación, conversión a un estado similar al de una momia tal como en la gangrena seca o en el estado de un feto que muere y permanece en la matriz.

mumps *n.* paperas, parotiditis, enfermedad febril aguda de alta contagiosidad que se caracteriza por la infl. de las glándulas parótidas y otras glándulas salivales.

mural *a.* mural, rel. a las paredes de un órgano o parte.

muriatic *n.* muriático, derivado de sal común; ácido muriático.

murmur *n.* soplo, ruido; sonido breve raspante, esp. un sonido anormal del corazón; aortic ___, regurgitant / ___ aórtico, regurgitante; cardiac ___ / ___ cardíaco; continuous ___ / ___ creciente, in crescendo; diastolic ___ / ___ diastólico; functional ___ / ___ funcional; mitral ___ / ___ mitral; pansystolic ___ / ___ pansístolico; presystolic ___ / ___ presístolico; systolic ___ / ___ sistólico.

muscle *n.* músculo, tipo de tejido fibroso capaz de contraerse y que permite el movimiento de las partes y órganos del cuerpo; cardiac ___ / ___ cardíaco; flexor ___ / ___ flexor; involuntary, visceral ___ / ___ involuntario, visceral; striated, voluntary ___ / ___ estriado, voluntario; relaxants / relajadores musculares, medicamentos para aliviar espasmos musculares.

muscular *a.* muscular, musculoso-a, rel. al músculo; ___ contractions / contracciones ___-es; ___ dystrophy / distrofia ___.

muscularis *n.* muscularis, capa muscular de un órgano.

musculature *n.* musculatura; aparato muscular del cuerpo.

musculoskeletal *a.* musculoesquelético-a, rel. a los músculos y el esqueleto.

musculotendinous *a.* musculotendinoso-a, que está formado por músculo y tendón.

mushroom *n.* hongo, seta, champiñón; ___ poisoning / envenenamiento por ___-s.

mussel *n.* almeja.

must *v. aux.* deber, ser necesario, tener que; **You must take the medication** / Usted debe, tú debes tomar la medicina.

mustard *n.* mostaza.

mutagen *n.* mutágeno, sustancia o agente que causa mutación.

mutant *a.* mutánte, rel. a un organismo que ha pasado por mutaciones.

mutation *n.* mutación, alteración, cambios espontáneos o inducidos en la estructura genética.

mute *n.* mudo-a.

mutilate *v.* mutilar, cortar, cercenar.

mutilation *n.* mutilación.

mutism *n.* mutismo, mudez.

mutter *v.* murmurar, musitar; decir entre dientes; *pop.* cuchichear.

my *a.* mi, mis; mío-a, míos-as.

myalgia *n.* mialgia, dolor muscular.

myasthenia *n.* miastenia, debilidad muscular; ____ gravis / ____ grave.

myatonia *n.* miatonía, deficiencia o pérdida del tono muscular.

mycetoma *n.* micetoma, infección causada por hongos parásitos que afectan la piel, el tejido conjuntivo y los huesos.

mycobacterium *L. Mycobacterium,* especie de bacterias gram-positivas en forma de bastoncillo que incluyen las causantes de lepra y tuberculosis.

mycology *n.* micología, estudio de hongos y de las enfermedades que ellos producen.

mycoplasmas *n. pl.* micoplasmas, la más diminuta forma de organismos vivos libres a la cual pertenecen los virus que causan enfermedades como la pulmonía y la faringitis.

mycosis *n.* micosis, cualquier enfermedad causada por hongos.

mycotic *a.* micótico-a, rel. a la micosis.

mycotoxins *n. pl.* micotoxinas, toxinas producidas por hongos parásitos.

mydriasis *n.* midriasis, dilatación prolongada de la pupila del ojo.

mydriatic *a.* midriático-a, que causa dilatación de la pupila del ojo.

myectomy *n. cirg.* miectomía, extirpación de una porción de un músculo.

myelin *n.* mielina, sustancia de tipo grasoso que cubre fibras nerviosas.

myelination, mielinization *n.* mielinización, crecimiento de mielina alrededor de una fibra nerviosa.

myelinolysis *n.* mielinolisis, enfermedad que destruye la mielina alrededor de ciertas fibras nerviosas; acute ____ / ____ aguda; ____ transverse / ____ transversa.

myelitis *n.* mielitis, infl. de la espina dorsal.

myelocele *n.* mielocele, hernia de la médula espinal a través de la columna vertebral.

myelocyte *n.* mielocito, leucocito granular de la médula ósea presente en la sangre en ciertas enfermedades.

myelocytic *a.* mielocítico-a, rel. a mielocitos; ____ leukemia / leucemia ____ .

myelofibrosis *n.* mielofibrosis, fibrosis de la médula ósea.

myelogenic, myelogenous *a.* mielógeno-a, que se produce en la médula.

myelogram *n.* mielograma, radiografía de la médula usando un medio de contraste.

myeloid *n.* mieloide; *a.* rel. a la médula espinal o similar a la médula espinal o a la médula ósea; ____ tissue / médula roja.

myeloma *n.* mieloma. 1. cualquier tumor de la médula espinal u ósea; 2. tumor formado por el tipo de células que se encuentran en la médula ósea; multiple ____ / ____ múltiple.

myelomeningocele *n.* mielomeningocele, hernia de la médula espinal y de las meninges con protrusión a través de un defecto en el canal vertebral.

myelopathy *n.* mielopatía, cualquier condición patológica de la médula espinal o de la médula ósea.

myeloproliferative *a.* mieloproliferativo-a, que se caracteriza por una proliferación de la médula ósea dentro o fuera de la médula.

myelosuppression *n.* mielosupresión, inhabilidad de la médula ósea de producir glóbulos rojos y plaquetas.

myocardial, myocardiac *a.* miocárdico-a, rel. al miocardio; ____ contraction / contracción del miocardio; ____ diseases / miocardiopatías.

myocardial infarction *n.* infarto cardíaco, necrosis de células del músculo cardíaco debido a un bloqueo del abastecimiento de sangre que lo irriga, condición usu. conocida como "ataque al corazón."

myocarditis *n.* miocarditis, infl. del miocardio.

myocardium *n.* miocardio, capa media de la pared cardíaca.

myoclonus *n.* mioclonus, contracción o espasmo muscular tal como se manifiesta en la epilepsia.

myocyte *n.* miocito, célula del tejido muscular.

myodystrophy *n.* miodistrofia, distrofia muscular.

myofibril *n.* miofibrilla, fibrilla diminuta delgada del tejido muscular.

myofibroma *n.* miofibroma, tumor compuesto de elementos musculares.

myofilament *n.* miofilamento, filamentos microscópicos que constituyen las fibrillas musculares.

myoglobin *n.* mioglobina, pigmento del tejido muscular que participa en la distribución de oxígeno.

myography *n.* miografía, gráfico que registra la actividad muscular.

myolysis *n.* miolisis, destrucción de tejido muscular.

myoma *n.* mioma, tumor benigno compuesto de tejido muscular.

myomectomy *n. cirg.* miomectomía. 1. excisión de una porción de un músculo o de tejido muscular; 2. extirpación de un tumor miomatoso localizado gen. en el útero.

myometrium *n.* miometrio, pared muscular del útero.

myonecrosis *n.* mionecrosis, necrosis del tejido muscular.

myoneural *a.* mioneural, rel. a una terminación nerviosa en un músculo; ___ junction / unión ___ .

myopathy *n.* miopatía, cualquier enfermedad muscular.

myope *n.* miope, persona que tiene miopía.

myopia *n.* miopía, defecto del globo ocular por el cual los rayos de luz hacen foco enfrente de la retina lo que causa dificultad para ver objetos a distancia.

myopic *a.* miope. 1. que padece de miopía; 2. rel. a la miopía.

myosin *n.* miosina, la proteína más abundante del tejido muscular.

myositis *n.* miositis, infl. de uno o de más músculos.

myotomy *n. cirg.* miotomía, sección o disección de un músculo.

myotonia *n.* miotonía, condición muscular con aumento en rigidez y contractibilidad muscular y disminución de relajamiento.

myringectomy, myringodectomy *n.* miringectomía, extirpación de la membrana timpánica o de una parte de ésta.

myringitis *n.* miringitis, infl. del tímpano.

myringoplasty *n. cirg.* miringoplastia, cirugía plástica de la membrana del tímpano.

myxedema *n.* mixedema, condición causada por deficiencia funcional de la glándula tiroides.

myxoma *n.* mixoma, tumor compuesto de tejido conjuntivo.

N

N *abbr.* **nasal** / nasal; **nerve** / nervio; **nitrogen** / nitrógeno; **normal** / normal; **number** / número.

Nabothian cysts *n. pl.* quistes de Naboth, quistes pequeños gen. benignos formados por obstrucción de las glándulas secretoras de mucus del cuello uterino.

nail *n.* 1. uña de los dedos del pie o de la mano; ___ **scratch** / arañazo; ___ **biting** / comerse las uñas; **ingrown** ___ / uñero, ___ encarnada; 2. clavo. V. **pin.**

nailbed *n.* matriz de la uña, porción de epidermis que cubre la uña.

naive *a.* ingenuo-a; cándido-a; inocente.

naked *a.* desnudo-a, descubierto-a; *pop.* en cuero, en pelota; **with the** ___ **eye** / a simple vista; *v.* **to strip** ___ / desnudarse.

name *n.* nombre; [*first name and surname*] nombre completo, nombre y apellido; **What is your** ___? / ¿Cómo se llama usted?, ¿cómo te llamas tú?, ¿cuál es su, tu nombre?

nanism *n.* nanismo. V. **dwarfism.**

nap *n.* siesta; *v.* **to take a** ___ / echar una ___ , dormir una ___ .

nape *n.* nuca, cerviz, parte posterior del cuello; *pop.* pescuezo, cogote.

napkin *n.* servilleta.

narcissism *n.* narcisismo. 1. amor excesivo a sí mismo; 2. placer sexual derivado de la contemplación del propio cuerpo.

narcolepsy *n.* narcolepsia, padecimiento crónico de accesos de sueño.

narcoleptic *a.* narcoléptico-a, rel. a la narcolepsia o que padece de ella.

narcosis *n.* narcosis, estado inconsciente causado por un narcótico o droga.

narcotic *a.* narcótico-a, estupefaciente de efecto analgésico que puede producir adicción.

naris *n.* (*pl.* **nares**) naris, orificios o ventanas de la nariz.

narrow *a.* angosto-a, estrecho-a.

nasal *a.* nasal, rel. a la nariz; ___ **cavity** / cavidad ___ ; ___ **congestion** / congestión ___ ; ___ **drip** / goteo ___ , *pop.* moquera.

nascent *a.* 1. naciente, incipiente; 2. liberado de un compuesto químico.

nasogastric *a.* nasogástrico-a, rel. a la nariz y el estómago; ___ **tube** / tubo ___ .

nasolabial *a.* nasolabial, rel. a la nariz y el labio.

nasopharynx *n.* nasofaringe, parte de la faringe localizada sobre el velo del paladar.

nasty *a.* agresivo-a, de mal carácter; ___ illness / enfermedad grave, seria; ____ weather / mal tiempo.

natal *a.* natal, rel. a la natalidad.

natality *a.* natalidad, índice de nacimientos en una comunidad.

natimortality *n.* mortinatalidad, porcentaje de nacimientos no viables o no logrados.

nationality *n.* nacionalidad.

native *a.* nativo-a, natural de, [*indigenous*] indígena, autóctono-a; ____ **born** / nacido-a en; oriundo-a de; ____ **tongue** / lengua materna.

nativity *n.* natividad, nacimiento.

natriuretic *n.* natriurético-a. *V.* **diuretic.**

natural *a.* natural; sencillo-a; ____ **childbirth** / parto ____ ; **-ly** *adv.* naturalmente.

nature *n.* naturaleza.

naturopath *n.* naturópata, persona que practica la naturopatía.

naturopathy *n.* naturopatía, tratamiento terapéutico por medio de recursos naturales.

naughtiness *n.* malacrianza, travesura, majadería.

naughty *a.* travieso-a, majadero-a.

nausea *n.* naúsea, asco, ganas de vomitar.

nauseate *v.* dar o causar naúseas, dar asco; **to be nauseated** / tener naúseas.

nauseating *a.* nauseabundo-a.

nauseous *a.* nauseoso a. 1. propenso a tener naúseas; 2. que produce naúsea o asco.

navel *n.* ombligo.

navicular *a.* navicular, en forma de nave.

near *a.* cercano-a, próximo-a, a corta distancia; **a** ____ **relative** / un pariente ____ ; [*almost*] casi; *prep.* cerca de, junto a; [*at hand*] a la mano; [*toward*] ____ **the right** / hacia la derecha, cerca de la derecha; **-ly** *adv.* casi, por poco; **He, she** ____ **died** / por poco se muere.

nearsighted *a.* miope, corto-a de vista.

nearsightedness *n.* miopía. *V.* **myopia.**

neat *a.* pulcro-a, cuidadoso-a, aseado-a; [*very pleasing*] bueno-a.

nebulization *n.* nebulización, atomización, conversión de un líquido a una nube de vapor.

nebulizer *n.* nebulizador, atomizador de líquido.

nebulous *a.* nebuloso-a.

necessary *n.* necesidad; *a.* necesario-a, indispensable; **It is** ____ / Es necesario; **what is** ____ / lo necesario; **whatever is** ____ / lo que sea necesario.

necessity *n.* necesidad.

neck *n.* cuello, pescuezo. 1. parte del cuerpo que une la cabeza al tronco; 2. región de un diente entre la corona y la raíz.

necklace *n.* collar, gargantilla.

neck of uterus *n.* cuello uterino.

necrogenic *a.* necrógeno-a / rel. a la muerte; 2. que se forma o compone de materia muerta.

necrology *n.* necrología, estudio de estadísticas referentes a la mortalidad.

necrophilia *n.* necrofilia. 1. atracción mórbida por los cadáveres; 2. relación sexual con un cadáver.

necrophobia *n.* necrofobia, temor anormal a la muerte y a los cadáveres.

necropsy *n.* necropsia, *V.* **autopsia.**

necrose *v.* necrosar, causar o experimentar necrosis.

necrosis *n.* necrosis, muerte parcial o total de las células que forman un tejido tal como ocurre en la gangrena.

necrotic *a.* necrótico-a, rel. a la necrosis o a un tejido afectado por ésta.

necrotize *v.* necrosar, causar la muerte, producir necrosis.

need *n.* necesidad; **a person in** ____ / un-a necesitado-a; *v.* necesitar.

needle *n.* aguja; **hypodermic** ____ / ____ hipodérmica.

needless *a.* inútil, innecesario.

needy *a.* necesitado-a; pobre; *n. pl.* **the** ____ / los ____ **-s.**

negation *n.* negación.

negative *a.* negativo-a; ____ **culture** / cultivo ____ ; **-ly** *adv.* negativamente.

negativism *n. psic.* negativismo, conducta caraterizada por una actuación opuesta a la sugerida.

neglect *n.* negligencia, descuido, desamparo.

neglectful *a.* negligente, descuidado-a.

negligence *n.* negligencia, descuido.

negligent *a.* negligente, descuidado-a.

neighbor *n.* vecino-a.

nemathelminth *n.* nematelminto, gusano intestinal de forma redondeada que pertenece al orden de los *Nemathelmintes.*

nematocide *n.* nematocida, agente que destruye nematodos.

Nematoda *n. Nematoda,* clase de gusanos del orden de los *Nemathelmintes.*

nematode *n.* nematodo, gusano de la clase *Nematoda.*

nematology *n.* nematología, estudio de los gusanos de la clase *Nematoda*.

neoarthrosis, nearthrosis *n.* neoartrosis, neartrosis, articulación artificial o falsa.

neologism *n.* neologismo. 1. *psic.* vocablos a los cuales el paciente mental atribuye nuevos significados no relacionados con el verdadero; 2. vocablo al cual se le atribuye un giro nuevo.

neomycin *n.* neomicina, antibiótico de espectro amplio.

neonatal *a.* neonatal, rel. a las primeras seis semanas después del nacimiento.

neonate *n.* neonato-a, recién nacido-a, de seis semanas o menos de nacido-a.

neonatologist *n.* neonatólogo-a, especialista en neonatología.

neonatology *n.* neonatología, estudio y cuidado de los recién nacidos.

neoplasia *n.* neoplasia, formación de neoplasmas.

neoplasm *n.* neoplasma, crecimiento anormal de tejido nuevo tal como un tumor.

neoplastic *a.* neoplástico-a, rel. a un neoplasma.

nephew *n.* sobrino.

nephralgia *n.* nefralgia, dolor en el riñón.

nephrectomy *n. cirg.* nefrectomía, extirpación de un riñón.

nephric *a.* néfrico-a, renal.

nephritic *n.* nefrítico-a, rel. a la nefritis o afectado por ella.

nephritis *n.* nefritis, infl. del riñón.

nephrocalcinosis *n.* nefrocalcinosis, depósitos de calcio en los túbulos renales que pueden causar insuficiencia renal.

nephrogram *n.* nefrograma, radiografía del riñón.

nephrolithiasis *n.* nefrolitiasis, presencia de cálculos renales.

nephrolithotomy *n. cirg.* nefrolitotomía, incisión en el riñón para extraer cálculos renales.

nephrology *n.* nefrología, estudio del riñón y de las enfermedades que lo afectan.

nephroma *n.* nefroma, tumor del riñón.

nephron *n.* nefrona, unidad funcional y anatómica del riñón.

nephropathy *n.* nefropatía, cualquier enfermedad del riñón.

nephropexy *n. cirg.* nefropexia, fijación de un riñón flotante.

nephrosclerosis *n.* nefroesclerosis, endurecimiento del sistema arterial y tejido intersticial del riñón.

nephrosis *n.* nefrosis, afección renal degenerativa asociada con gran cantidad de proteína en la orina, niveles bajos de albúmina en la sangre y edema pronunciado.

nephrostomy *n. cirg.* nefrostomía, formación de una fístula en el riñón o en la pelvis renal.

nephrotic syndrome *n.* síndrome nefrótico, afección del riñón caracterizada por un exceso de pérdida de proteína.

nephrotomography *n.* nefrotomografía, tomografía del riñón.

nephrotomy *n. cirg.* nefrotomía, incisión en el riñón.

nephrotoxic *a.* nefrotóxico, que destruye células renales.

nephrotoxin *n.* nefrotoxina, toxina que destruye células renales.

nerve *n.* nervio, cada una de las fibras libres o fibras en haz que conectan al cerebro y la médula espinal con otras partes y órganos del cuerpo; ____ block / bloqueo del ____ ; ____ cells / neuronas; ____ degeneration / degeneración nerviosa; ____ ending / terminación ____ ; ____ fiber / fibra nerviosa; pinched ____ / ____ pellizcado; ____ tissue / tejido nervioso.

nervous *a.* nervioso-a, ansioso-a, excitable; ____ breakdown / colapso ____ , crisis ____ ; ____ debility / fatiga ____ ; ____ disorder / trastorno ____ ; ____ impulse / impulso ____ ; ____ system / sistema ____ .

nervousness *n.* nerviosismo, nerviosidad.

nest *n.* nido de células, masa de células en forma de nido de pájaro.

nestiatria *n.* nestiatría, terapia con ayuno.

network *n.* red, encadenación; arreglo de fibras en forma de malla.

neural *a.* neural, rel. al sistema nervioso.

neuralgia *n.* neuralgia, dolor intenso a lo largo de un nervio.

neuralgic *a.* neurálgico-a, rel. a la neuralgia.

neurapraxia *n.* neurapraxia, parálisis temporal de un nervio sin causar degeneración.

neurasthenia *n.* neurastenia, término asociado con un estado general de irritabilidad y agotamiento nervioso.

neurasthenic *a.* neurasténico-a, rel. a o con síntomas de neurastenia.

neurilemma *n.* neurilema, membrana fina que cubre una fibra nerviosa.

neurinoma *n.* neurinoma, neoplasma benigno de las capas que rodean un nervio.

neuritis *n.* neuritis, infl. de un nervio.

neuroanatomy *n.* neuroanatomía, estudio anatómico del sistema nervioso.

neuroblast *n.* neuroblasto, célula nerviosa primitiva.

neuroblastoma *n.* neuroblastoma, tumor maligno del sistema nervioso formado en gran parte por neuroblastos.

neurodermatosis *n.* neurodermatosis, erupción crónica cutánea de origen desconocido que se caracteriza por una picazón intensa en áreas localizadas.

neuroectoderm *n.* neuroectodermo, tejido embrionario del cual se deriva el tejido nervioso.

neuroendocrinology *n.* neuroendocrinología, estudio del sistema nervioso y su relación con las hormonas.

neurofibroma *n.* neurofibroma, tumor del tejido fibroso que cubre un nervio periférico.

neurofibromatosis *n.* neurofibromatosis, condición que se caracteriza por la manifestación de múltiples neurofibromas a lo largo de los nervios periféricos.

neuroglia *n.* neuroglia, células que sirven de sostén y constituyen el tejido intersticial del sistema nervioso.

neurohypophysis *n.* neurohipófisis, porción nerviosa posterior de la glándula pituitaria.

neuroleptic *n.* neuroléptico-a, agente tranquilizante; ____ anesthesia / anestesia con el uso de un ____ .

neurologist *n.* neurólogo-a, especialista del sistema nervioso.

neurology *n.* neurología, rama de la medicina que estudia el sistema nervioso.

neuroma *n.* neuroma, tumor constituído principalmente por fibras y células nerviosas.

neuromuscular *a.* neuromuscular, rel. a nervios y músculos.

neuron *n.* neurona, célula que constituye la unidad básica funcional del sistema nervioso.

neuro-ophthalmology *n.* neurooftalmología, rama de la oftalmología que se especializa en la parte del sistema nervioso relacionada con la visión.

neuropacemaker *n.* neuromarcapasos, instrumento para estimular eléctricamente la médula espinal.

neuropathology *n.* neuropatología, ciencia que estudia las enfermedades nerviosas.

neuropathy *n.* neuropatía, trastorno o cambio patológico en los nervios periféricos.

neuropharmacology *n.* neurofarmacología, estudio farmacológico del efecto de drogas en el sistema nervioso.

neuro-physiology *n.* neurofisiología, fisiología del sistema nervioso.

neuropil *n.* neurópilo, red de fibras nerviosas (dendritas y neuritas) y de las células de la glia interrumpidas por sinapses en partes del tejido nervioso.

neuropsychopharmacology *n.* neurosicofarmacología, estudio de medicamentos y del efecto que causan en el tratamiento de trastornos mentales.

neuroradiology *n.* neurorradiología, radiología del sistema nervioso.

neurosis *n.* neurosis, condición que se manifiesta principalmente por ansiedad y por el uso de mecanismos de defensa.

neurosurgeon *n.* neurocirujano-a, especialista en neurocirugía.

neurosurgery *n.* neurocirugía, *cirg.* del sistema nervioso.

neurosyphilis *n.* neurosífilis, sífilis que afecta el sistema nervioso central.

neurotic *a.* neurótico-a, que sufre de neurosis.

neurotoxicity *n.* neurotoxicidad, acción tóxica destructiva del sistema nervioso.

neurotransmitter *n.* neurorregulador, sustancia química que modifica la transmisión de impulsos a través de una sinapsis entre nervios o entre un nervio y un músculo.

neurovascular *a.* neurovascular, rel. a los sistemas nervioso y vascular.

neutral *a.* neutral.

neutralization *n.* neutralización, proceso de anular o contrarrestar la acción de un agente.

neutralize *v.* neutralizar; contrarrestar.

neutropenia *n.* neutropenia. *V.* **agrunolocitosis.**

neutrophil *n.* neutrófilo, leucocito-fagocito que se tiñe con colorantes neutrales.

neutrophilia *n.* neutrofilia, aumento de neutrófilos en la sangre.

neutrotaxis *n.* neutrotaxis, estimulación de neutrófilos con una sustancia que los atrae o repele.

never *adv.* nunca, jamás; ____ **fear** / pierda cuidado; ____ **mind** / no importa.

nevertheless *adv.* sin embargo, no obstante.

nevus *n.* (*pl.* **nevi**) nevo, lunar, marca de nacimiento.

new *a.* nuevo-a; **What is new?** / ¿Qué hay de ____?

newborn *n.* recién nacido-a; neonato-a.

news *n. pl.* noticias; **bad** ____ / malas ____; **good** ____ / buenas ____; *v.* **to break the** ____ / dar la noticia.

newspaper *n.* diario, periódico.

next *a.* próximo-a, siguiente; **Who is** ____? / ¿Quién es el, la ____? ____ **door** / al lado; **The table is** ____ **to the bed** / La mesa está al lado de la cama; ____ **of kin** / el pariente más cercano; ____ **to nothing** / casi nada.

nexus *n.* (*pl.* **nexus**) nexo, conexión, unión.

niacin *n.* ácido nicotínico.

nice *a.* delicado-a, fino-a, bueno-a; **-ly.** *adv.* finamente, delicadamente; **nicely done** / bien hecho.

niche *n.* nicho, depresión o defecto pequeño esp. en la pared de un órgano hueco.

nicotine *n.* nicotina, alcaloide tóxico, ingrediente principal del tabaco.

niece *n.* sobrina.

night *n.* noche; **by** ____ / de noche, por la noche; ____ **fall** / atardecer, anochecer; **Good** ____ / Buenas noches; **last** ____ / anoche; ____ **before last** / anteanoche.

nightgown *n.* bata de dormir, camisa de dormir.

nightmare *n.* pesadilla.

night watch *n.* guardia nocturna.

nipple *n.* pezón; [*of male*] tetilla; [*nursing bottle*] mamadera, tetera; **cracked** ____ / ____ agrietado; **engorged** ____ / ____ enlechado.

nitric acid *n.* ácido nítrico.

nitrogen *n.* nitrógeno.

nitroglycerine *n.* nitroglicerina, nitrato de glicerina usado como vasodilatador esp. en la angina de pecho.

no *adv.* no, de ningún modo, de ninguna manera; **no good** / no vale; ____ **one** / nadie; **Say yes or** ____ / Diga, di que sí o que no.

Nocardia *n.* Nocardia, microorganismo grampositivo que causa nocardiosis.

nocardiosis *n.* nocardiosis, infección generalmente pulmonar causada por Nocardia que puede expandirse a varias partes del cuerpo.

nocturia, nycturia *n.* nocturia, nicturia, frecuencia aumentada de emisión de orina esp. durante la noche.

nocturnal *a.* nocturno-a, nocturnal, de noche; ____ **emission**, emiction / micciones nocturnas, orinarse en la cama; emisión ____ involuntaria de semen.

nod *v.* inclinar la cabeza; aprobar.

node *n.* nudo, nódulo, ganglio; lymphatic ____ / ____ linfático.

nodose *a.* nudoso-a, formado por nódulos o protuberancias.

nodular *a.* nodular, semejante a un nudo.

nodule *n.* nódulo o nudo pequeño.

noise *n.* ruido; *v.* **to make** ____ / hacer ____.

noiseless *a.* callado-a, tranquilo-a.

noisy *a.* ruidoso-a, turbulento-a, bullicioso-a.

nomadic *a.* nómada, errante.

nomenclature *n.* nomenclatura, terminología.

non compos mentis *L.* non compos mentis, mentalmente incompetente.

none *pron.* nadie, ninguno-a.

noninvasive *a.* no invasor, que no se propaga o invade.

nonparous *a.* nulípara. *V.* **nulliparous.**

nonsense *n.* tontería, bobería, disparate.

nonspecific *a.* sin especificación.

nonviable *n.* que no puede sobrevivir.

noodle *n.* fideo, tallarín; pasta.

noon *n.* mediodía.

norm *n.* norma, regla.

normal *a.* normal, natural, regular.

normalization *n.* normalización, regreso al estado normal.

normocalcemia *n.* normocalcemia, nivel normal de calcio en la sangre.

normoglycemia *n.* normoglucemia, concentración normal de azúcar en la sangre.

normokalemia *n.* normopotasemia, nivel normal de potasio en la sangre.

normotensive *a.* normotenso-a, de presión arterial normal.

normothermia *n.* normotermia, temperatura normal.

normotonic *a.* normotónico-a, de tono muscular normal.

nose *n.* nariz; **bridge of the** ____ / tabique nasal, puente de la nariz; **running** ____ / nariz destilante; coriza.

nosebleed *n.* sangramiento por la mariz.

nosocomial *a.* nosocomial, rel. a un hospital o clínica; ____ **infection** / infección ____, enfermedad adquirida en un hospital.

nostalgia *n.* nostalgia, tristeza, añoranza.

nostril *n.* naris, fosa nasal, ventana de la nariz.

not *adv.* no, de ningún modo; **Why not?** / ¿Por qué no?; ___ **at all** / de ninguna manera.

notch *n.* incisión, incisura, ranura.

note *n.* nota, apunte, aviso; progress ___ -s / informe del progreso clínico; *v.* notar, apreciar; **to take** ___ **of** / tomar ___ de, darse cuenta de, observar.

nothing *n.* nada, niguna cosa; *adv.* en nada, de ningún modo, de ninguna manera.

notice *n.* aviso, informe, nota; observación; *v.* notar, hacer caso, observar.

noticeable *a.* notorio-a, que se distingue.

notification *n.* notificación, aviso, información.

notify *v.* avisar, informar, notificar; ___ **your doctor at once** / Avise a su médico en seguida.

notion *n.* noción, concepto, opinión.

notochord *n.* notocordio, sostén fibrocelular del embrión que se convierte más tarde en la columna vertebral.

noun *n.* nombre, sustantivo.

nourish *v.* alimentar, nutrir, sustentar.

nourishable *a.* nutritivo-a, alimenticio-a.

nourishing *a.* alimenticio-a, nutritivo-a.

nourishment *n.* alimento, nutrición, sustento.

novice *a.* principiante, novicio-a.

novocaine *n.* novocaína, anestésico.

now *adv.* ahora, ahorita, en este momento, actualmente; **from** ___ **on** / de ___ en adelante; **just** ___ / ___ mismo, hace un momento; ___ **and then** / de vez en cuando; ___ **then** / ahora bien.

nowadays *adv.* hoy en día, al presente.

noway *adv.* de ningún modo, de ninguna manera.

nowhere *adv.* en ninguna parte; ___ **else** / en ninguna otra parte.

nubile *a.* núbil. rel. a la madurez sexual femenina.

nucha *n.* nuca, parte posterior del cuello.

nuclear *a.* nuclear. 1, rel. al núcleo de la célula; 2. rel. a la fuerza atómica.

nuclear envelope *n.* envoltura nuclear, forma que toman las dos membranas nucleares que envuelven al núcleo de la célula al examinarse bajo el microscopio electrónico.

nucleated *a.* nucleado-a, que posee un núcleo.

nucleic acid *n.* ácido nucleico.

nucleolus *n.* nucléolo, pequeña estructura esférica en el núcleo celular.

nucleotide *n.* nucleótido, unidad estructural de ácido nucleico.

nucleus *n.* (*pl.* **nuclei, nucleuses**) núcleo, parte esencial de una célula; ___ **pulpous** / ___ **pulposo**, masa gelatinosa contenida dentro de un disco intervertebral.

nude *a.* desnudo-a, *pop,* en cuero, en cuero vivo.

nudity *n.* desnudez.

nuisance *n.* molestia, incomodidad, estorbo; **What a** ___ **!** / ¡Qué lata!

null *a.* nulo-a, sin valor, inútil; ___ **hypothesis** / hipótesis ___.

nulligravida *n.* nuligrávida, mujer que nunca ha concebido.

nulliparous *n.* nulípara, mujer que nunca ha dado a luz un feto con vida.

numb *a.* [*extremity*] entumecido-a, adormecido-a; aturdido-a; **My fingers are** ___ / mis dedos están ___ -s; **I feel** ___ / Me siento entumecido-a; me siento aturdido-a.

number *n.* número, cifra.

numbness *n.* [*in a part*] entumecimiento, adormecimiento; [*confusion*] aturdimiento, entorpecimiento.

numerous *a.* numeroso-a.

numskull *a.* mentecato-a, tonto-a.

nun *n.* monja, hermana religiosa.

nurse *n.* enfermero-a; ___ **aid** / asistente de ___; ___ **anesthetist** / ___ anesesista; **chief** ___, **head** ___ / jefe-a de ___ -s; **community health** ___ / ___ de salud pública; ___ **practitioner** / practicante de ___; *v.* [*care*] cuidar a una persona enferma; [*breast feeding*] amamantar, dar el pecho, dar de mamar.

nursery *n.* guardería; [*in a hospital*] sala de niños recién nacidos.

nursing *n.* 1. cuidado de los enfermos; 2. lactancia.

nut *n.* [*fruit*] nuez; [*mad*] loco-a, maniático-a; [*screw*] tuerca.

nutrient *n.* alimento, nutriente, sustancia nutritiva.

nutriment *n.* nutrimento, alimento, sustancia nutritiva.

nutrition *n.* nutrición, mantenimiento, alimentación.

nutritious *a.* nutritivo-a, alimenticio-a, que proporciona nutrición.

nutritive *a.* nutritivo-a, sustancioso-a, alimenticio-a.

nutty *a.* abundante en nueces, con sabor a nueces; *pop.* [*crazy*] loco-a, chiflado-a.

nympha *n.* ninfa, labio interior de la vulva.

nymphomania *n. psic.* ninfomanía, fuego uterino, deseo sexual mórbido en la mujer.

nymphomaniac *a.* ninfómana, mujer afectada por ninfomanía.

nystagmus *n.* nistagmo, espasmo involuntario del globo ocular.

O

O *abbr.* oculus / ojo; **oral** / oral; **orally** / oralmente, por la boca; **oxygen** / oxígeno.

oath *n.* juramento, promesa; Hippocratic ___ / ___ hipocrático; **under** ___ / bajo ___; *v.* **to take an** ___ / jurar, prestar ___.

oatmeal *n.* harina de avena.

obedience *n.* obediencia.

obedient *a.* obediente.

obese *a.* obeso-a, excesivamente grueso-a.

obesity *n.* obesidad, grasa excesiva en el cuerpo.

obey *v.* obedecer; **You must** ___ / usted debe ___, tú debes ___.

obfuscation *n.* ofuscación, confusión mental.

object *n.* objeto, cosa; *v.* objetar, oponerse, tener inconveniente.

objective *n.* objetivo, propósito; *a.* objetivo-a, rel. a la percepción de fenómenos y sucesos tal como se manifiestan en la vida real; ___ sign / señal ___; ___ symptoms / síntomas. ___ -s, **-ly** *adv.* objetivamente.

obligate *v.* obligar, exigir.

obligation *n.* obligación, deber, compromiso.

obligatory *a.* obligatorio-a.

oblique *a.* oblicuo-a, diagonal.

obliterate *v.* obliterar, anular, destruir.

obliteration *n.* obliteración, destrucción; oclusión por degeneración o por cirugía.

obscure *a.* oscuro-a; oculto-a, escondido-a.

observation *n.* observación, examen, estudio.

observe *v.* observar, estudiar, examinar.

obsession *n.* obsesión, preocupación excesiva con una idea o emoción fija.

obsessional *a.* obsesivo-a, rel. a una obsesión o causante de ésta.

obsessive-compulsive *n.* estado neurótico obsesivo-compulsivo con repetición morbosa de acciones como desahogo de tensiones y ansiedades.

obsolete *a.* obsoleto-a, anticuado-a, en desuso, inactivo-a.

obstacle *n.* obstáculo, *pop.* traba.

obstetric *a.* obstétrico-a, rel. a la obstetricia.

obstetrician *n.* obstetra, partero-a, tocólogo-a, especialista en obstetricia.

obstetrics *n.* obstetricia, rama de la medicina que se refiere al cuidado de la mujer durante el embarazo y el parto.

obstinate *a.* obstinado-a, *pop.* cabeza dura, cabeciduro-a.

obstipation *n.* obstipación, estreñimiento rebelde.

obstruct *v.* obstruir, impedir.

obstructed *a.* obstruído-a, tupido-a.

obstruction *n.* obstrucción, bloqueo, obstáculo, impedimento; intestinal ___ / ___ intestinal.

obstructive lung disease, chronic *n.* obstrucción crónica del pulmón que impide la entrada libre del aire a causa de un estrechamiento físico o funcional del árbol bronquial.

obtain *v.* obtener, adquirir, conseguir.

obturation *n.* obturación, obstrucción o bloqueo de un pasaje.

obturator *a.* obturador-a, bloqueador-a, que obstruye una abertura.

obtuse *a.* obtuso-a. 1. que le falta agudeza mental; 2. romo-a, mellado-a.

obvious *a.* obvio-a, evidente.

occasion *n.* ocasión, circunstancia, casualidad; *v.* causar, ocasionar.

occasional *a.* infrecuente, casual, accidental; **-ly** *adv.* a veces; de vez en cuando, ocasionalmente.

occipital *a.* occipital, rel. a la parte posterior de la cabeza; ___ bone / hueso ___; ___ condyle / cóndilo ___; ___ lobe / lóbulo ___.

occipitofrontal *a.* occipitofrontal. rel. al occipucio y la frente.

occipitoparietal *a.* occipitoparietal, rel. a los huesos y lóbulos occipital y parietal.

occipitotemporal *a.* occipitotemporal, rel. a los huesos occipital y temporal.

occiput *n.* occipucio, porción postero-inferior del cráneo.

occlusion *n.* oclusión, cierre, obstrucción.

occult *a.* oculto-a, desconocido-a; escondido-a.

occult blood *n.* sangre oculta, presencia de sangre en cantidad tan ínfima que no puede verse a simple vista.

occupation *n.* ocupación, trabajo, profesión, oficio; ____ neurosis / neurosis del trabajo, de la profesión.

occupational *a.* ocupacional, rel. a una ocupación; ____ therapist / terapeuta ____ ; ____ therapy / terapia ____ .

occupy *v.* ocupar, llenar.

occurrence *n.* ocurrencia, suceso, acontecimiento; of frequent ____ / que sucede con frecuencia.

octogenarian *n.* octogenario-a, persona de ochenta años de edad o más; *a.* octogenario-a.

ocular *a.* ocular, visual, rel. a los ojos o a la vista.

oculist *n.* oculista. *V.* **ofthalmologist.**

oculogyric *a.* oculógiro-a, rel. a la rotación del globo ocular.

oculomotor *a.* oculomotor, rel. al movimiento del globo ocular.

oculus *L.* oculus, ojo, órgano de la visión.

odd *a.* extraño-a, irregular, raro-a, inexacto-a; **an** ____ **case** / un caso ____ ; ____ **or even** / nones o pares; **thirty** ____ **pills** / treinta píldoras más o menos, treinta y tantas píldoras; **at** ____ **times** / en momentos imprevistos, a horas inprevistas.

odontalgia *n.* odontalgia, dolor de dientes; dolor de muelas.

odontectomy *n. cirg.* odontectomía, extracción de una pieza dental.

odontogenesis *n.* odontogénesis, proceso de desarrollo dentario.

odontoid *a.* odontoideo-a, semejante a un diente.

odontologist *n.* odontólogo-a, dentista o cirujano-a dental.

odontology *n.* odontología, estudio de los dientes y del tratamiento de las enfermedades dentales.

odor *n.* olor.

odorless *a.* sin olor, inodoro-a.

odorous *a.* oloroso-a, fragante.

odynophobia *n. psic.* odinofobia, temor excesivo al dolor.

Oedipus complex *n.* complejo de Edipo, amor intenso del hijo a la madre acompañado de celos y antipatía al padre.

of *prep.* de; [*possession*] ____ **the** / del, de la; [*telling time*] menos; **Call at a quarter** ____ **six** / Llame, llama a las seis menos cuarto.

off *adv.* fuera de aquí, lejos; ____ **and on** / a veces, a intervalos; ____ **the record** / confidencial; *v.* [*work*] **to be** ____ ausente, [*without work*] sin trabajo; **The operation is** ____ / Se ha suspendido la operación; **to put** ____ / aplazar, posponer, diferir; **to turn** ____ / cerrar, apagar; *int.* ¡fuera!, ¡salga!, ¡sal!

offence, offense *n.* ofensa, agravio, afrenta.

offend *v.* ofender, insultar, agraviar.

offensive *a.* ofensivo-a.

offer *n.* oferta, ofrecimiento.

office *n.* oficina; **doctor's** ____ / consulta, consultorio. [*business*] ____ **hours** / horas de ____ ; horas de consulta.

official *a.* oficial, autorizado-a.

offspring *n.* descendencia, sucesión, hijos.

often *adv.* con frecuencia, frecuentemente, a menudo; **How** ____ ? / ¿Cuántas veces?; **as** ____ **as needed** / tantas veces como sea necesario; **not** ____ / pocas veces; **too** ____ / demasiado, demasiadas veces.

oil *n.* aceite; **castor** ____ / ____ de ricino; **cod liver** ____ / ____ de hígado de bacalao; **mineral** ____ / ____ mineral; **olive** ____ / ____ de oliva; **salad** ____ / ____ para ensalada; *v.* aceitar, lubricar, engrasar, untar con aceite.

oily *a.* grasoso-a, grasiento-a, oleaginoso-a, lubricante.

ointment *n.* ungüento, pomada, unto, untura; medicamento oleaginoso semisólido de uso externo.

old *a.* viejo-a, anciano-a; antiguo-a; **an** ____ **man** / un anciano, un hombre ____ ; **an** ____ **method** / un método antiguo; **How** ____ **are you?** / ¿Cuántos años tiene, tienes?; **I am fifty years** ____ / Tengo cincuenta años; ____ **wives' tale** / cuento de ____ .

oleaginous *a.* oleaginoso-a, aceitoso-a, derivado del aceite o rel. al mismo.

oleomargarine *n.* oleomargarina, margarina.

olfactory *a.* olfatorio-a, rel. al sentido del olfato.

oligohemia, oligemia *n.* oligohemia. *V.* **hypovolemia.**

oligohydramnios *n.* oligohidramnios, bajo nivel de líquido amniótico al término de la gestación.

oligomenorrhea *n.* oligomenorrea, deficiencia en la menstruación.

oligospermia *n.* oligospermia, disminución del número de espermatozoos en el semen.

oliguria *n.* oliguria, disminución en la formación de orina.

olive *n.* oliva. 1. materia gris localizada detrás de la médula oblongata; 2. color aceitunado, verde oliva; 3. árbol del olivo; 4. aceituna.

omen *n.* agüero.

omental *a.* omental, rel. a un omento o formado por él.

omentectomy *n. cirg.* omentectomía, extirpación total o parcial de un omento.

omentitis *n.* omentitis, infl. del omento.

omentum *n.* omento, repliegue del peritoneo que conecta el estómago con ciertas vísceras abdominales.

ominous *a.* ominoso-a, nefasto-a.

omission *n.* omisión; exclusión.

omit *v.* omitir, suprimir, excluir.

omnivorous *a.* omnívoro-a, que come alimentos de origen vegetal y animal.

omphalectomy *n. cirg.* onfalectomía, extirpación del ombligo.

omphalic *n.* onfálico-a, rel. al ombligo.

omphalitis *n.* onfalitis, infl. del ombligo.

omphalocele *n.* onfalocele, hernia congénita del ombligo.

on *prep.* sobre, encima, en, hacia; [*before inf.*] después de; al; ____ **an average** / por término medio; ____ **the contrary** / al contrario; ____ **the left foot** / en el pie izquierdo; ____ **the right eye** / en el ojo derecho; ____ **the table** / sobre la mesa, encima de la mesa; *adv.* ____ **account of** / a causa de; ____ **all sides** / por todos lados; *v.* **to be** ____ **call** / estar de guardia; **caught** ____ / atrapado-a en; ____ **condition that you come back** / con tal de que vuelva; **later** ____ / más tarde; **off and** ____ / a intervalos, de vez en cuando; ____ **and** ____ / contínuamente, sin cesar, sin parar; ____ **purpose** / a propósito; [*function*] funcionando; **The machine is on** / El aparato está funcionando; *a.* [*clothing*] puesto-a; **She has the robe on** / Ella tiene la bata ____ ; [*after a verb*] **Go** ____ ! / ¡Siga, sigue!; ¡Continúe, continúa!

onanism *n.* onanismo, coito interrumpido.

once *n.* una vez; *adv.* **all at** ____ / al mismo tiempo, de pronto; **at** ____ / en seguida,

ahora mismo; ____ **in a while** / algunas veces, de vez en cuando.

oncogenesis *n.* oncogénesis, formación y desarrollo de un tumor.

oncogenic *a.* oncogénico-a, rel. a la oncogénesis.

oncology *n.* oncología, rama de la medicina que estudia los neoplasmas.

oncolysis *n.* oncólisis, destrucción de las células de un tumor.

oncotic *a.* oncótico-a, rel. a una tumefacción o la causa de ésta.

oncotomy *n. cirg.* oncotomía, incisión en un tumor, absceso o quiste.

one *n.* [*number*] uno; *a.* un, uno-a, solo, único-a; **just** ____ / solamente uno; **only** ____ **form** / una sola forma; **from** ____ **day to another** / de un día a otro; **He is** ____ **good patient** / Él es un buen paciente; *pron.* **the only** ____ / el único, la única; **the** ____ **I have** / el que tengo; **this** ____ / éste; ____ **and all** / todos; ____ **of them** / ____ de ellos.

one-eyed *n.* tuerto-a.

oneiric *a.* onírico-a, rel. a los sueños.

oneirism *n.* onirismo, estado de ensoñación; soñar despierto.

onerous *a.* oneroso-a, gravoso-a.

oniomania *n. psic.* oniomanía, psicosis de urgencia de gastar dinero.

onion *n.* cebolla.

onlay *n.* injerto, esp. en la reparación de defectos óseos.

only *a.* único-a, solo-a; *adv.* sólo, solamente.

onomatomania *n. psic.* onomatomanía, repetición obsesiva de palabras.

onychectomy *n. cirg.* oniquectomía, extirpación de una uña.

onychia *n.* oniquia, infl. de la matriz de una uña.

onychosis *n.* onicosis, enfermedad o deformidad de las uñas.

oocyte *n.* oocito, ovocito, el óvulo antes de la madurez.

oogenesis *n.* oogénesis, formación y desarrollo del óvulo.

oophorectomy *n. cirg.* ooforectomía, excisión parcial o total de un ovario.

oosperm *n.* oospermo, óvulo fecundado.

ooze *v.* exudar, supurar.

oozing *n.* exudado; supuración.

opacification *n.* opacificación proceso de opacar.

opacity *n.* opacidad, falta de transparencia.

opaque *a.* opaco-a, sin brillo, que no deja pasar la luz.

open *a.* abierto-a, descubierto-a, destapado-a, libre de paso; ___ heart surgery / operación a corazón ___ ; *v.* abrir, descubrir, destapar, abrir paso; cortar, rajar.

opening *n.* abertura, orificio de entrada o salida.

open reduction *n.* reducción abierta, [*in fractures*] técnica de reducir fracturas con exposición de la dislocación o del hueso.

operable *a.* operable, que puede tratarse con cirugía.

operate *v.* operar, intervenir, proceder.

operating room *n.* sala de operaciones, quirófano.

operation *n.* operación, intervención quirúrgica, procedimiento quirúrgico.

operculum *n.* opérculo. 1. cubierta o tapadera; 2. una de las partes del cerebro que cubre la ínsula.

operon *n.* operon, sistema de genes combinados en el cual el gene operador regula los demás genes estructurales.

ophthalmia *n.* oftalmia. 1. conjuntivitis severa; 2. infl. interna del ojo.

ophthalmic *a.* oftálmico-a, visual, rel. al ojo; ___ nerve / nervio ___ ; ___ solutions / soluciones ___ -s.

ophthalmitis *n.* oftalmitis, condición inflamatoria del ojo.

ophthalmologist *n.* oftalmólogo-a, médico oculista especializado en trastornos y enfermedades de la vista.

ophthalmology *n.* oftalmología, rama de la medicina que trata del estudio del ojo y trastornos de la vista.

ophthalmoneuritis *n.* oftalmoneuritis, infl. del nervio óptico.

ophthalmopathy *n.* oftalmopatía, enfermedad de los ojos.

ophthalmoplastia *n.* oftalmoplastia, cirugía plástica del ojo.

ophthalmoplegia *n.* oftalmoplegia, parálisis de un músculo ocular.

ophthalmoscope *n.* oftalmoscopio, instrumento usado para visualizar el interior del ojo.

ophthalmoscopy *n.* oftalmoscopía, examen del ojo con un oftalmoscopio.

opiate *n.* opiáceo, opiato, cualquier droga

derivada del opio; ___ abstinence syndrome / síndrome provocado por la abstinencia de opio o sus derivados.

opinion *n.* opinión, juicio, parecer; *v.* to have an ___ / opinar, hacer juicio, dar el parecer; to be of the same ___ / estar de acuerdo, acordar.

opinionated *a.* obstinado-a, inflexible.

opioids *n. pl.* drogas que no son derivadas del opio pero pueden producir efectos similares a éste.

opisthotonos *n.* opistótonos, espasmo tetánico de los músculos de la espalda por el cual los talones se viran hacia atrás y el tronco se proyecta hacia adelante.

opium *n.* opio, *Papaver somniferum,* narcótico, analgésico, estimulante venenoso y alucinógeno cuya adicción produce deteriorización física y mental; *slang* goma.

opiumism, opiomania *n.* opiomanía. 1. adicción al uso de opio o sus derivados; 2. condición física deteriorada por el uso de opio.

opponent *n.* oponente, antagonista, contrario-a; *a.* opuesto-a, contrario-a.

opportune *a.* oportuno-a, conveniente.

opportunist *n.* oportunista.

opportunistic *a.* oportunista.

opportunistic infectious disease *n.* enfermedad oportunista infecciosa, infección parasítica oportunista producida por un microorganismo gen. no dañino que no causa una enfermedad severa o prolongada pero se convierte en patógeno cuando la inmunidad del organismo ha sido ya quebrantada.

opportunity *n.* oportunidad, ocasión.

oppose *v.* oponer, resistir; oponerse, resistirse.

opposite *a.* opuesto-a, adverso-a, contrario-a.

opposition *n.* oposición, objeción.

oppress *v.* oprimir, afligir, agobiar; apretar.

oppression *n.* opresión, pesadez; an ___ in the chest / una ___ , una sofocación en el pecho.

oppressive *a.* opresivo-a, sofocante, molesto-a, gravoso-a.

opsoclonus *n.* opsoclono, movimiento irregular del ojo, esp. relacionado con algunos casos de trastorno cerebral.

opsonin *n.* opsonina, anticuerpo que al combinarse con un antígeno hace que éste sea más suceptible a los fagocitos.

optic, optical *a.* óptico-a, rel. a la visión;

_____ disk / disco _____, punto ciego de la retina; _____ illusion / ilusión _____; _____ nerve / nervio _____.

optics *n.* óptica, ciencia que estudia la luz y la relación de ésta con la visión.

optimist *a.* optimista.

optimum *a.* óptimo-a, el mejor, la mejor; _____ temperature / temperatura _____.

option *n.* opción, alternativa.

optometer *n.* optómetro, instrumento usado para medir el poder de refracción del ojo.

optometrist *n.* optometrista, optómetra, profesional que practica optometría.

optometry *n.* optometría, práctica de examinar los ojos para determinar la agudeza visual y para la prescripción de lentes correctivos y otros auxilios visuales.

or *conj.* o, u (used instead of *o* before words beginning in *o* or *ho*).

oral *a.* oral, bucal, rel. a la boca; verbal, hablado; _____ contraceptive / píldora contraceptiva; _____ diagnosis / diagnóstico bucal; _____ hygiene / higiene bucal.

orange *n.* naranja; _____ **grove** / naranjal; **orangeade** / naranjada.

orbicular *a.* orbicular, circular; _____ muscle / músculo _____, rodea una pequeña abertura tal como la de la boca.

orbit *n.* órbita, cavidad ósea de la cara que contiene los ojos.

orbital *a.* orbital. rel. a la órbita; _____ fractures / fracturas _____ -es.

orchidectomy *n. cirg.* orquidectomía, orquectomía, extirpación de un testículo.

orchiditis, orchitis *n.* orquiditis, orquitis, infl. de los testículos.

orchidopexy, orchiopexy *n. cirg.* orquidopexia, orquipexia, procedimiento por el cual se baja y se fija al escroto un testículo que no ha descendido.

orchiotomy *n.* orquiotomía, incisión en un testículo.

order *n.* orden, reglamento, disposición; **in** _____ **that** / para que, a fin de que; **in** _____ **to** / para; *v.* ordenar, disponer, mandar; [*arrange*] arreglar; **to be in good** _____ / estar en buen estado; **to get out of** _____ / descomponerse.

orderly *n.* asistente de enfermero-a.

ordinary *a.* ordinario-a, corriente, común.

organ *n.* órgano, parte del cuerpo que realiza una función específica; end _____ / _____ terminal; _____ transplant / transplante de un _____.

organelle *n.* organelo, organito, órgano diminuto de los organismos unicelulares.

organic *a.* orgánico-a. 1. rel. a un órgano u órganos; 2. rel. a organismos de origen vegetal o animal; _____ disease / enfermedad _____.

organism *n.* organismo, ser vivo.

organization *n.* organización; asociación.

organize *v.* organizar, disponer, arreglar.

organogenesis *n.* organogénesis, desarrollo y crecimiento de un órgano.

orgasm *n.* orgasmo, clímax sexual.

orient *n.* oriente, este.

oriental *a.* oriental.

orientation *n.* orientación, dirección.

orifice *n.* orificio, salida, boquete, abertura.

origin *n.* origen, principio.

original *n.* original, prototipo; *a.* original; primitivo-a.

originality *n.* originalidad

originate *v.* originar, engendrar; provenir de.

originator *n.* originador, productor.

oropharynx *n.* orofaringe, parte central de la faringe.

orphan *n.* huérfano-a.

orphanage *n.* orfanato, hospicio, asilo de huérfanos.

orthochromatic *a.* ortocromático-a, de color normal o que acepta coloración sin dificultad.

orthodontia *n.* ortodoncia, rama de la odontología que trata las irregularidades dentales por medio de procedimientos correctivos.

orthopedia, orthopedics *n.* ortopedia, rama de la medicina que trata de la prevención y corrección de trastornos en los huesos, articulaciones, músculos, ligamentos y cartílagos.

orthopedic *a.* ortopédico-a, rel. a la ortopedia; _____ **shoes** / calzado _____; _____ surgery / cirugía _____.

orthopedist *n.* ortopédico-a, ortopedista, especialista en ortopedia.

orthopnea *n.* ortópnea, dificultad para respirar excepto en posición erecta.

orthoscopic *a.* ortoscópico, rel. a los instrumentos que se usan para corregir distorsiones ópticas.

orthosis *n.* ortosis, corrección de una deformidad o impedimento.

orthotopic *a.* ortotópico-a, que ocurre en una posición normal o correcta.

os *L.* (*pl.* **ossa**) os, hueso.

oscillate *v.* oscilar; fluctuar.

oscillation *n.* oscilación, movimiento de vaivén, tal como el de un péndulo.

osmolar *a.* osmolar, de naturaleza o propiedad osmótica.

osmology *n.* osmología, estudio de los olores.

osmoreceptor *n.* osmorreceptor. 1. grupo de células cerebrales que reciben estímulos olfatorios; 2 grupo de células en el hipotálamo que responden a cambios en la presión osmótica de la sangre.

osmosis *n.* osmosis, difusión de un solvente a través de una membrana semipermeable interpuesta entre soluciones de concentración diferente.

osmotic *a.* osmótico-a, rel. a la osmosis.

osseous *a.* óseo-a, rel. a los huesos; ___ tissue / tejido ___.

ossicle *n.* huesillo, osículo.

ossific *a.* osífico-a, rel. a la formación del tejido óseo.

ossification *n.* osificación, proceso de desarrollo óseo.

ossification, ostosis *n.* osificación. 1. conversión de una sustancia en hueso; 2. desarrollo del hueso.

ossify *v.* osificar, transformarse en hueso.

osteal *a.* óseo-a, rel. a los huesos.

osteitis *n.* osteítis, ostitis, infl. de un hueso; ___ fibrosa cystica / ___ fibrosa cística, con degeneración fibrosa y manifestación de quistes y nódulos en el hueso.

ostensive *a.* ostensivo-a, evidente, aparente.

osteoarthritis *n.* osteoartritis, hipertrofia degenerativa del hueso y de las articulaciones esp. en la vejez.

osteoarthropathy *n.* osteoartropatía, enfermedad gen. dolorosa que afecta las articulaciones y los huesos.

osteoblast *n.* osteoblasto, célula desarrollada aisladamente en una lacuna de la sustancia ósea.

osteocarcinoma *n.* osteocarcinoma, cáncer del hueso.

osteocartillaginous *a.* osteocartilaginoso-a, rel. a la formación de huesos y cartílagos.

osteochondral *n.* osteocondral, rel. a o compuesto de hueso y cartílago.

osteochondritis *n.* osteocondritis, infl. del hueso y el cartílago.

osteoclast *n.* osteoclasto, célula gigante multinucleada que participa en la formación de tejido óseo y reemplaza al cartílago durante la osificación.

osteocyte *n.* osteocito, célula ósea desarrollada.

osteodystrophy *n.* osteodistrofia, hipertrofia múltiple degenerativa con formación defectiva del hueso.

osteogenesis *n.* osteogénesis. *V.* **ossification.**

osteoid *a.* osteoide, rel. o semejante a un hueso.

osteology *n.* osteología, rama de la medicina que estudia la estructura y funcionamiento de los huesos.

osteoma *n.* osteoma, tumor formado de tejido óseo.

osteomalacia *n.* osteomalacia, reblandecimiento de los huesos debido a la pérdida de calcio en la matriz del hueso.

osteomyelitis *n.* osteomielitis, infección del hueso y de la médula ósea.

osteonecrosis *n.* osteonecrosis, destrucción y muerte del tejido óseo.

osteopath *n.* osteópata, especialista en osteopatía.

osteopathy *n.* osteopatía. 1. sistema terapéutico médico con énfasis en la relación entre los órganos y el sistema muscular esquelético que hace uso de la manipulación como medio de corrección; 2. cualquier enfermedad de los huesos.

osteopenia *n.* osteopenia, disminución de la calcificación ósea.

osteophyte *n.* osteófito, prominencia ósea.

osteoporosis *n.* osteoporosis. pérdida en la densidad del hueso.

osteotomy *n.* *cirg.* osteotomía, cortar o serruchar un hueso.

ostial *a.* ostial, rel. o concerniente a un orificio o abertura.

ostium *L.* (*pl.* **ostia**) ostium, pequeña abertura.

ostomy *n.* *cirg.* ostomía, creación de una abertura entre un órgano y la piel como medio de salida exterior, tal como se efectúa en colostomías e ileostomías.

otalgia, otodynia, otoneuralgia *n.* otalgia, otodinia, otoneuralgia, dolor de oídos.

otectomy *n.* *cirg.* otectomía, extirpación del contenido estructural del oído medio.

other *a.* otro-a, diferente, nuevo-a; **every** ___ **day** / un día sí y otro no; *pron.* **the** ___ **one** / el otro, la otra; **the** ___ **ones** / los otros, las otras.

otherwise *adv.* de otra manera, de otro modo, por otra parte.

otic *a.* ótico-a, rel. al oído.

oticodinia *n.* oticodinia, vértigo causado por una enfermedad del oído.

otitis *n.* otitis, infl. del oído externo, medio o interno.

otolaryngologist *n.* otolaringólogo-a, especialista en otolaringología.

otolaryngology *n.* otolaringología, estudio de la garganta nariz y oídos.

otologist *n.* otólogo-a, especialista en enfermedades del oído.

otology *n.* otología, rama de la medicina que estudia el oído, su función y las enfermedades que lo afectan.

otoneurology *n.* otoneurología, estudio del oído interno en su relación con el sistema nervioso.

otoplasty *n.* otoplastia, cirugía plástica del oído.

otorrhagia *n.* otorragia, sangramiento por el oído.

otosclerosis *n.* otosclerosis, sordera progresiva debida a la formación de tejido esponjoso en el laberinto del oído.

otoscope *n.* otoscopio, instrumento para examinar el oído.

otoscopy *n.* otoscopia, uso del otoscopio en un examen del óido.

ototomy *n. cir.* ototomía, incisión en el oído.

ototoxic *a.* ototóxico-a, que tiene efecto tóxico en el octavo par craneal o en los órganos de la audición.

ouch *int.* ¡ay!

ought *v.* deber, deber de + *inf.*; ser necesario, tener la obligación de + *inf.*

ounce *n.* onza.

oust *v.* expulsar, sacar, echar fuera.

out *adv.* afuera, fuera, [*light, appliance*] apagado-a; [*unconscious*] inconsciente, sin conocimiento; ____ of / de; **three** ____ of **ten cases** / tres de diez casos; ____ of **work** / sin trabajo, sin empleo, desempleado-a; *v.* **to be** ____ / estar ausente; **to go** ____ / salir; **Get** ____! / ¡Salga!, ¡sal!

outbreak *n.* [*of an epidemic*] brote epidémico; erupción.

outbreathe *v.* dejar sin aliento; *pop.* dejar sin resuello.

outburst *n.* erupción; estallido; arranque; manifestación abrupta, brote.

outcome *n.* resultado, consecuencia; [*good*] éxito.

outdated *a.* anticuado-a.

outdo *vi.* superar, exceder.

outdoors *a.* al aire libre; externo-a; *adv.* afuera de la casa.

outer *a.* externo-a; exterior.

outfit *n.* traje, equipo, habilitación.

outflow *n.* derrame, salida, flujo.

outgoing *n.* salida, ida, partida; *a.* saliente, cesante; expansivo-a.

outgrow *vi.* sobrepasar, crecer más.

outgrowth *n.* excrecencia, bulto.

outlet *n.* orificio de salida; [*electric*] tomacorriente.

outlive *v.* sobrevivir, vivir más que; durar más.

outlook *n.* punto de vista, expectativa, opinión.

outnumber *v.* exceder en número.

outpass *v.* pasar más allá de; avanzar.

outpatient *n.* paciente externo, paciente de consulta externa, paciente no hospitalizado.

outpour *n.* derramamiento, chorro; *v.* chorrear, derramar, verter.

output *n.* rendimiénto; ____ failure / fallo en el ____ .

outrageous *a.* [*shocking*] atroz; increíble.

outright *a.* sincero-a, franco-a, cabal; *adv.* francamente, sinceramente.

outroot *v.* sacar de raíz, desarraigar, extirpar.

outside *n.* exterior, apariencia; *prep.* fuera de, más allá de.

outspoken *a.* franco-a, que habla sin rodeos.

outstretch *v.* extender, alargar, expandir.

outweigh *v.* pesar más que; exceder.

oval *a.* oval; rel. al óvulo.

oval window *n.* ventana oval; abertura del oído medio.

ovarian *a.* ovárico-a, rel. a los ovarios.

ovariectomy *n. cirg.* ovariectomía. V. **oophorectomy**.

ovary *n.* ovario, órgano reproductor femenino que produce el óvulo.

over *a.* acabado-a, terminado-a; *prep.* sobre, encima, por; a través de; *adv.* por encima, de un lado a otro; al otro lado; al revés; ____ **again** / otra vez; ____ **and** ____ **again** / muchas veces; *v.* [*years*] **to be** ____ / tener más de; **It is** ____ / ya se pasó, ya se acabó; **Turn** ____ / Vuélvase, vuélvete.

overact *v.* exagerar demasiado.

overanxious *a.* demasiado inquieto-a, excitado-a, muy ansioso-a.

overbearing *a.* insoportable.

overbite *n.* sobremordida.

overboil *v.* hervir demasiado, hervir más de lo necesario.

overburden *v.* agobiar, sobrecargar.

overcareful *a.* demasiado cuidadoso-a, *pop.* puntilloso-a.

overcharge *n.* precio excesivo, recargo de precio; *v.* sobrecargar, cobrar demasiado.

overclosure *n.* sobrecierre, cierre de la mandíbula antes de que los dientes superiores e inferiores se junten.

overcoat *n.* abrigo, sobretodo.

overcome *vi.* vencer, rendir; sobreponerse; **You must ____ this** / Debe sobreponerse, debes sobreponerte a esto; **You must ____ this sickness** / Debe, debes ____ a esta enfermedad.

overcompensation *n.* sobrecompensación, *psic.* intento exagerado de ocultar sentimientos de inferioridad o de culpa.

overcorrection *n.* sobrecorrección, acción de corregir en exceso un defecto visual por medio de lentes.

overdose *n.* dosis excesiva; dosis tóxica; sobredosis.

overdue *a.* retrasado-a, tardío-a.

overeat *vi.* comer con exceso; hartarse.

overexposure *n.* superexposición; exposición excesiva.

overextension *n.* sobreextensión.

overfeed *vi.* sobre alimentar, alimentar en exceso.

overflow *n.* rebosamiento; derramamiento; *pop.* desparramo.

overgrown *a.* demasiado crecido-a, muy grande o agrandado-a.

overgrowth *n.* proliferación excesiva.

overhear *vi.* oír por casualidad; alcanzar a oír.

overjoyed *a.* rebosante de alegría.

overnight *n.* velada, la noche completa; *adv.* durante la noche; la noche pasada.

overpowering *a.* abrumador-a; irresistible.

overproduction *n.* superproducción.

overreact *v.* reaccionar en exceso.

overresponse *n.* sobrerespuesta, reacción excesiva a un estímulo.

oversight *n.* descuido, equivocación, inadvertencia.

overtime *n.* tiempo suplementario; horas extras de trabajo.

overweigh *v.* pesar más que; sobrecargar.

overweight *n.* peso excesivo, sobrepeso.

overwhelm *v.* abrumar; colmar.

overwork *n.* trabajo excesivo, trabajo en exceso.

ovicular, ovoid *a.* ovicular, en forma de huevo.

oviduct *n.* oviducto, conducto uterino; trompas de Falopio.

ovotestis *n.* ovotestis, glándula hermafrodita que contiene tejido ovárico y testicular.

ovulation *n.* ovulación, liberación periódica del óvulo o gamete por el ovario.

ovulatory *a.* ovulatorio-a, rel. al proceso de ovulación.

ovum *n.* (*pl.* **ova**) óvulo, gamete fecundado.

oxalic acid *n.* ácido oxálico.

oxidant *a.* oxidante, que causa oxidación o rel. a ésta.

oxidation *n.* oxidación, combinación de una sustancia con oxígeno.

oxidize *v.* oxidar, combinar con oxígeno.

oximeter *n.* oxímetro, instrumento para medir la cantidad de oxígeno en la sangre.

oxygen *n.* oxígeno, elemento o gas incoloro e inodoro no metálico que circula libremente en la atmósfera; ____ deficiency / falta de ____ .

oxygenator *n.* oxigenador, instrumento para oxigenar la sangre gen. usado durante cirugía.

oxygen tent *n.* cámara de oxígeno, tienda de oxígeno.

oxygen therapy *n.* terapia de oxígeno.

oxytocin, ocitocina *n.* oxitocina, ocitocina, hormona pituitaria que estimula las contracciones del útero.

oyster *n.* ostra, ostión.

P

P *abbr.* **part** / parte; **phosphorous** / fósforo; **plasma** / plasma; **population** / población; **positive** / positivo; **posterior** / posterior; **postpartum** / postpartum; **pressure** / presión; **psychiatry** / psiquiatría; **pulse** / pulso

pabulum *L.* pabulum, alimento o sustancia alimenticia.

pace *n.* marcha, paso, el andar; *v.* andar, marchar.

pacemaker, pacer *n.* marcapasos, estabilizador del ritmo cardíaco.

pachyderma *n.* paquidermia. *V.* **elephantiasis.**

pachygyria *n.* paquigiria, circunvoluciones gruesas en la corteza cerebral.

pacifier *n.* chupete, tetera, teto.

pacify *v.* apaciguar, tranquilizar.

pack *n.* envoltura. 1. cubierta fría o caliente en la cual se envuelve el cuerpo; 2. compresa; *v.* [*to wrap*] envolver.

packing *n.* tapón, taponamiento. 1. acto de llenar una cavidad con gasa o algodón; 2. envoltura.

pad *n.* cojín, almohadilla; *v.* [*to fill*] rellenar.

padding *n.* relleno.

pain *n.* [*ache*] dolor; [*suffering*] sufrimiento, pena; burning ___ / ___ quemante, con ardor; [*colicky*] cólico; constant ___ / ___ constante, que no se quita; dull ___ / ___ sordo; gnawing ___ / punzada; localized ___ / ___ localizado; mild ___ / ___ leve, dolorcito; pressure-like ___ / ___ opresivo; radicular ___ / radicular; referred ___ / ___ referido, que se percibe en un lugar distinto al que se origina; sharp ___ / ___ agudo; severe ___ / ___ fuerte, severo; subjective ___ / ___ subjetivo, sin causa física aparente; a ___ that comes and goes / un ___ que viene y se va; a ___ that irradiates / un ___ que se corre; a ___ like a knife / ___ como un cuchillo, lancinante; **Where do you have the ___?** / ¿Dónde tiene, tienes el ___?; *v.* **to be in ___** / tener dolor; [*to suffer*] sufrir, apenar, afligir; estar apenado-a; estar afligido-a. *V.* **Appendix B.**

painful *a.* doloroso-a, penoso-a, aflictivo-a.

pain killer *n.* calmante, sedante, remedio, pastilla para el dolor.

painless *a.* sin dolor; [*easy*] fácil.

paint *n.* pincelación, aplicación a la piel de una solución medicinal; *v.* pintar, aplicar una solución.

pair *n.* par, pareja.

pajamas *n. pl.* piyamas, pijamas.

palatable *a.* sabroso-a, apetitoso-a; gustoso-a.

palate *n.* paladar; velo del paladar; *pop.* cielo de la boca; bony ___ / ___ óseo; hard ___ / ___ duro; soft ___ / ___ blando.

palatine *a.* palatino, rel. al paladar.

pale *a.* pálido-a, descolorido-a.

paleface *n.* rostro pálido, carapálida.

palindromic *a.* palindrómico-a, recurrente.

palliative *a.* paliativo-a, lenitivo-a, que alivia.

pallid *a.* pálido-a, descolorido-a.

pallor *n.* palidez.

palm *n.* palma, parte inferior de la mano; ___ oil / aceite de ___.

palmar *a.* palmar, rel. a la palma de la mano.

palpable *a.* palpable.

palpate *v.* palpar, acto de palpación.

palpation *n.* palpación, acto de tocar y examinar con las manos un área del cuerpo.

palpitate *v.* palpitar, latir.

palpitation *n.* palpitación, latido; pulsación; aleteo rápido.

palsy *n.* perlesía, parálisis, pérdida temporal o permanente de la sensación, de la función o control de movimiento de una parte del cuerpo; cerebral ___ / ___ cerebral, parálisis parcial y falta de coordinación muscular debida a una lesión cerebral congénita.

paludism *n.* paludismo, enfermedad infecciosa febril gen. crónica, transmitida por la picadura de un mosquito Anófeles infectado por un protozooario *Plasmodium.*

pamper *v.* mimar; malcriar.

pampered *a. pp.* de **to pamper**, mimado-a, consentido-a.

pamphlet *n.* folleto.

pampiniform *a.* pampiniforme, semejante a la estructura de un zarcillo de la vid.

panacea *n.* panacea, remedio para todas las enfermedades.

panarteritis *n.* panarteritis, infl. de las capas de una arteria.

panarthritis *n.* panartritis. 1. infl. de varias articulaciones del cuerpo; 2. infl. de los tejidos de una articulación.

pancreas *n.* páncreas, glándula del sistema digestivo que secreta externamente el jugo pancreático e interiormente la insulina y el glucagón.

pancreatalgia *n.* pancreatalgia, dolor en el páncreas.

pancreatectomy *n. cirg.* pancreatectomía, excisión parcial o total del páncreas.

pancreatic *a.* pancreático-a, rel. al páncreas; ___ cyst / quiste ___; ___ duct / conducto ___; ___ juice / jugo ___; ___ neoplasms / neoplasmas ___-s.

pancreaticoenterostomy *n. cirg.* pancreaticoenterostomía, anastomosis entre el conducto pancreático y el intestino.-

pancreatin *n.* pancreatina, enzima digestiva del páncreas.

pancreatitis *n.* pancreatitis, infl. del páncreas; acute ___ / ___ aguda; hemorrhagic, acute ___ / ___ hemorrágica aguda.

pancytopenia *n.* pancitopenia, disminución anormal del número de células sanguíneas.

pandemic *a.* pandémico-a, de contagiosidad epidémica en un área geográfica extensa.

panendoscope *n.* panendoscopio, instrumento óptico usado para examinar la vejiga.

pang *n.* dolor agudo penetrante.

panglossia *n.* panglosia, verborrea.

panhidrosis *n.* panhidrosis, transpiración generalizada.

panhypopituitarism *n.* panhipopituitarismo, deficiencia de la pituitaria anterior.

panhysterectomy *n. cirg.* panhisterectomía, excisión total del útero.

panic *n.* pánico, temor excesivo; *v.* tener un miedo excesivo; sobrecogerse de pánico.

panicked *a. pp.* de **to panic**, sobrecogido a de pánico; *pop.* muerto-a de miedo.

panniculitis *n.* paniculitis, infl. del panículo grasoso.

panniculus *n.* panículo, capa de tejido adiposo; ___ adiposus / ___ adiposo; ___ carnosus / ___ carnoso.

pannus *L.* pannus, paño, membrana de tejido granulado que cubre una superficie normal.

pansinusitis *n.* pansinusitis, infl. de los senos paranasales de un lado o de ambos.

pant *v.* jadear, resollar.

panting *n.* jadeo, respiración rápida.

pants *n. pl.* pantalones, calzones.

Papanicolaou test, Pap smear *n.* prueba de Papanicolaou, (frotis, unto) recolección de mucosa de la vagina y el cuello uterino para detectar un cáncer incipiente.

papaya *n.* papaya, *Cuba* frutabomba.

paper *n.* papel; **toilet** ___ / ___ higiénico.

papilla *n.* (*pl.* **papillae**) papila, protuberancia esp. en la lengua.

papillary *a.* papilar, rel. a una papila.

papilledema *n.* papiledema, edema del disco óptico.

papilliforme *a.* papiliforme, similar a una papila.

papillitis *n.* papilitis, infl. del disco óptico.

papilloma *n.* papiloma, tumor epitelial benigno.

papillomatosis *n.* papilomatosis, presencia de múltiples papilomas.

papovavirus *n.* papovavirus, miembro de un grupo de virus de gran importancia en el estudio del cáncer.

papular *a.* papular, rel. a una pápula.

papule *n.* pápula, protuberancia en la piel compuesta de materia sólida.

paracentesis *n.* paracéntesis, punción para obtener o eliminar líquido de una cavidad.

paraffin *n.* parafina.

parainfluenza viruses *n. pl.* virus de parainfluenza, virus asociados con infecciones respiratorias, esp. en los niños.

parallax *n.* paralaje, posición de desplazamiento aparente de un objeto de acuerdo con la posición del observador.

paralysis *n.* parálisis, pérdida parcial o total de movimiento o de función de una parte del cuerpo.

paralytic *a.* paralítico-a, inválido-a; impedido-a, rel. a o que sufre de parálisis; ___ ileus / parálisis del intestino.

paralyze *v.* paralizar, inmovilizar.

paralyzer *a.* paralizador, que causa parálisis.

paramagnetic *a.* paramagnético-a, rel. a una sustancia suceptible al magnetismo.

paramedic *n.* paramédico-a, profesional con entrenamiento para ofrecer asistencia médica esp. de emergencia.

paranasal *a.* paranasal, adyacente a la cavidad nasal.

paranasal sinuses *n. pl.* senos paranasales, cualquiera de las cavidades aéreas en los huesos adyacentes a la cavidad nasal.

paranoia *n. psic.* paranoia, trastorno mental caracterizado por delirio de persecución o de grandeza.

paranoid *a.* paranoico-a, persona afectada por paranoia.

parapancreatic *a.* parapancreático-a, adyacente al páncreas.

paraparesis *n.* paraparesis, parálisis parcial esp. de las extremidades inferiores.

paraphasia *n.* parafasia, tipo de afasia que se caracteriza por el uso incoherente de palabras.

paraphimosis *n.* parafimosis. 1. constricción del prepucio detrás del glande del pene; 2. retracción del párpado por detrás del globo ocular.

paraplegia *n.* paraplejía, parálisis de la parte inferior del tronco y las piernas.

paraplegic *a.* parapléjico-a, rel. a, o afectado por paraplejía.

parapsychology *n.* parapsicología, estudio de fenómenos psíquicos tales como la telepatía y la percepción extrasensorial.

pararectal *a.* pararrectal, adyacente al recto.

parasite *n.* parásito, organismo que vive a expensas de otro.

parasitic *a.* parasítico-a, parasitario-a.

parasitism *n.* parasitismo, infección de parásitos.

parasitology *n.* parasitología, estudio de los parásitos.

parasternal *a.* parasterno-a, adyacente al esternón.

parasympathetic *a.* parasimpático, rel. a una de las dos ramas del sistema nervioso autónomo; ___ nervous system / sistema nervioso autónomo.

parasympatholytic *a.* parasimpatolítico, que destruye o bloquea las fibras nerviosas del sistema nervioso parasimpático.

parasystole *n.* parasístole, irregularidad en el ritmo cardíaco.

parathormone *n.* hormona paratiroidea, hormona reguladora del calcio.

parathyroid *n.* paratiroides, grupo de glándulas endocrinas pequeñas situadas junto a la tiroides; *a.* paratiroideo-a, localizado-a cerca de la tiroides; ___ hormone / hormona ___, reguladora de calcio.

parathyroidectomy *n. cirg.* paratiroidectomía, extirpación de una o más de las glándulas paratiroideas.

paratyphoid *n.* paratífica, fiebre similar a la tifoidea.

paravertebral *a.* paravertebral, situado-a al lado de la columna vertebral.

parched *a.* reseco-a.

paregoric *n.* paregórico, narcótico, calmante derivado del opio.

parenchyma *n.* parénquima, partes funcionales de un órgano.

parent *n.* padre o madre; *pl.* ___-s / padres.

parenteral *a.* parenteral, rel. a la introducción de medicamentos o sustancias en el organismo por otra vía que no sea la del canal alimenticio; ___ hyperalimentation / sobrealimentación intravenosa.

parenthood *n.* paternidad o maternidad.

paresis *n.* paresia, parálisis parcial o leve.

paresthesia *n.* parestesia, sensación de hormigueo o de calambre que se asocia a una lesión de un nervio periférico.

paretic *a.* parético-a, rel. o afectado por paresis.

parietal *a.* parietal, rel. al hueso parietal; rel. a la pared de una cavidad.

parietal bone *n.* hueso parietal, uno de los dos huesos situados en la parte superior y lateral del cráneo.

Parkinson's disease *n.* enfermedad de Parkinson, atrofia o degeneración de los nervios cerebrales que se manifiesta con temblores, debilidad muscular progresiva, cambios en el habla, la manera de andar y la postura.

parodynia *n.* parodinia, parto difícil.

paronychia *n.* paroniquia, infl. del área adyacente a la uña.

parotid *n.* parótida, glándula secretora de saliva localizada cerca del oído.

parotiditis *n.* parotiditis, parotitis. *V.* **mumps.**

paroxysm *n.* paroxismo, ataque. 1. espasmo o convulsión; 2. síntomas que se repiten y se intensifican.

pars *L.* pars, parte, porción.

parsley *n.* perejil.

part *n.* parte, porción; [*component of an instrument*] pieza; **-ly** *adv.* parcialmente, en parte.

parthenogenesis *n.* partenogénesis, reproducción en la cual el óvulo se desarrolla sin ser fecundado por un espermatozoo; artificial ___ / ___ artificial.

partial *a.* parcial; **-ly** *adv.* parcialmente.

participate *v.* participar, tomar parte.

particle *n.* partícula, porción ínfima de una materia.

particular *a.* particular; **-ly** *adv.* particularmente.

parturient *a.* parturienta, mujer que acaba de dar a luz o está en el acto de dar a luz.

parturifacient *n.* parturifaciente, droga que induce el parto.

parturition *n.* parto, alumbramiento.

parumbilical *a.* paraumbilical, adyacente al ombligo.

parvovirus *n.* parvovirus, grupo de virus patógenos que originan enfermedades en animales aunque no en personas.

pass *v.* pasar, aprobar; **to** ___ **away** / morir, fallecer; **to** ___ **on** / contagiar, pegar; **to** ___ **out** / desmayarse; **to** ___ **over** / pasar por, atravesar.

passage *n.* pasaje. 1. conducto o meato; 2. evacuación del intestino.

passion *n.* pasión, emoción intensa.

passionate *a.* apasionado-a.

passive *a.* pasivo-a; sumiso-a; inactivo-a, que no es espontáneo o activo; ____ exercise / ejercicio ____ .

passivity *n.* pasividad, estado anormal de dependencia de otros.

past *n.* pasado; *a.* pasado-a.

pasta *n.* pasta, preparación de sustancias medicinales gen. para aplicación a la epidermis.

pasteurization *n.* pasteurización, proceso de destrucción de microorganismos nocivos por medio de la aplicación de calor regulado.

patch *n.* placa, mancha. 1. pequeña porción de tejido que se caracteriza por pigmentación diferente a la del área que lo rodea; 2. parche, adhesivo aplicado para proteger heridas; ____ test / prueba alérgica.

patella *L.* patella, rótula.

patellectomy *n.* patelectomía, excisión de la patella.

patellofemoral *a.* patelofemoral, rel. a la rótula y el fémur.

patency *n.* permeabilidad. *V:* **permeability.**

patent *n.* patente, producto de marca autorizada o derecho exclusivo; ____ medicine / medicina de ____ , ____ médico; *a.* patente; accesible; abierto-a.

paternal *a.* paterno, rel. al padre.

paternity *n.* paternidad.

paternity test *n.* prueba de la paternidad, comparación del tipo sanguíneo de un niño o niña con el de un hombre para comprobar si éste puede ser el padre.

path *n.* vía, curso.

pathetic *a.* patético-a.

pathogen *n.* patógeno, agente capaz de producir una enfermedad.

pathogenesis *n.* patogénesis, origen y desarrollo de una enfermedad.

pathogenic *a.* patógeno-a, que causa una enfermedad.

pathognomonic *a.* patognomónico-a, rel. a un signo o síntoma característico de una enfermedad.

pathologic, pathological *a.* patológico-a, rel. a o producido por enfermedades.

pathology *n.* patología, ciencia que estudia la naturaleza y causa de las enfermedades.

pathophysiology *n.* patofisiología, estudio de los efectos de una enfermedad en los procesos fisiológicos.

pathway *n.* curso, comunicación; senda.

patience *n.* paciencia.

patient *n.* paciente, enfermo-a, ____ 's care / cuidado del ____ ; ____ discharge / alta, egreso del ____ ; private ____ / ____ privado-a; self-paying ____ / ____ solvente; **-ly** *adv.* con paciencia, pacientemente.

patrilineal *a.* de descendencia paterna; rel. a rasgos heredados del padre.

patronize *v.* tratar con condescendencia.

pattern *n.* patrón, modelo, tipo.

patulous *a.* abierto-a, distendido-a.

pause *n.* pausa, interrupción; paro; compensatory ____ / ____ compensatoria; *v.* **to give** ____ / dar que pensar.

pay *vi.* pagar; **to** ____ **attention** / prestar atención; **to** ____ **in cash** / ____ al contado.

payment *n.* pago.

pea *n.* chícharo, guisante.

peace *n.* paz; ____ **of mind** / tranquilidad de espíritu; *v.* **to be at** ____ / estar en paz, tranquilizarse; **to keep, to hold one's** ____ / quedarse tranquilo-a.

peaceful *a.* pacífico-a; tranquilo-a, calmado-a.

peach *n.* melocotón, *H.A.* durazno.

peak *n.* [*sickness*] crisis, [*diagram*] cresta; cima, punta.

peanut *n.* maní, *Mex.* cacahuete; ____ **butter** / mantequilla de ____ .

pear *n.* pera.

peau d'orange *Fr.* piel de naranja, condición cutánea que asemeja la cáscara de naranja y que es señal importante en el cáncer de la mama.

pectin *n.* pectina, carbohidrato que se obtiene de la cáscara de frutas cítricas y de manzana.

pectoral *a.* pectoral, rel. al pecho.

pectus *L.* pecho, tórax.

peculiar *a.* peculiar.

pedal *a.* pedal; rel. al pie.

pederasty *n.* pederastia, relación homosexual anal esp. entre un hombre adulto y un muchacho.

pediatric *a.* pediátrico-a, rel. a la pediatría.

pediatrician *n.* pediatra, médico-a especialista en enfermedades de la infancia.

pediatrics *n.* pediatría, rama de la medicina relacionada con el cuidado y desarrollo de los niños y el tratamiento de las enfermedades que los afectan.

pedicle *n.* pedículo, porción estrecha que conecta un tumor o colgajo con su base.

pediculosis *n.* pediculosis, infestación de piojos.

pedodontist *n.* dentista infantil.

pedophilia *n. psic.* pedofilia, atracción mórbida sexual de un adulto hacia los niños.

peduncle *n.* pedúnculo, conexión en forma de tallo.

pedunculated *a.* pediculado-a, pedunculado-a, rel. a o provisto de pedúnculo.

pedunculus *L.* pedúnculo.

peel *n.* [*fruits*] cáscara, hollejo, corteza; *v.* pelar; [*to shed skin*] despellejarse, pelarse.

peeling *n.* peladura; chemical ___ / ___ química. V. **exfoliation.**

pellagra *n.* pelagra, enfermedad causada por deficiencia de niacina y caracterizada por dermatitis, trastornos gastrointestinales y finalmente mentales.

pelvic *a.* pélvico-a, pelviano-a, rel. a la pelvis.

pelvic inflammatory disease *n.* enfermedad inflamatoria de la pelvis.

pelvis *n.* pelvis. 1. cavidad en la parte inferior del tórax formada por los huesos de la cadera, el sacro y el cóccix; 2. cavidad en forma de vasija o copa.

pemphigoid *a.* penfigoideo, semejante al pénfigo con diferencias clínicas.

pemphigus *L.* pénfigo, término usado para definir una variedad de dermatosis, cuya característica común consiste en la manifestación de ampollas que se infectan y revientan.

pendent, pending *a.* [*hanging*] pendiente, colgante, suspenso-a, dependiente; [*waiting*] pendiente.

pendulous *a.* pendular, que oscila o cuelga.

peneal, penial *a.* peneano-a, rel. al pene.

penetrate *v.* penetrar, pasar, atravesar.

penetrating *a.* [*as a pain*] penetrante, agudo-a.

penetration *n.* penetración. 1. acción de penetrar; 2. paso de radiación a través de una sustancia.

penicillin *n.* penicilina, antibiótico que se obtiene directa o indirectamente de un grupo de cultivos del hongo de la especie *Penicillium.*

penile *a.* V. **peneal.**

penis *n.* pene, parte exterior del aparato re-

productor masculino que contiene la uretra a través de la cual pasan el semen y la orina.

people *n.* [*of a nation*] pueblo; [*population*] población, personas, habitantes; gente.

pepper *n.* [*spice*] pimienta; pimiento.

peppermint *n.* hierbabuena, yerbabuena.

pepsin *n.* pepsina, enzima principal del jugo gástrico.

peptic *a.* péptico-a, rel. a la acción o a la digestión de los jugos gástricos.

peptic ulcer *n.* úlcera péptica, ulceración de las membranas mucosas del esófago, estómago o duodeno causada por acidez excesiva en el jugo gástrico y producida por tensión aguda o crónica; ___ perforation / perforación de la ___.

per *prep.* por; ___ rectum / ___ el recto, ___ vía rectal.

perceive *v.* darse cuenta de, percibir, advertir.

percentage *n.* porcentaje, tanto por ciento.

perception *n.* percepción, acción de reconocer conscientemente un estímulo sensorial; extrasensory ___ (ESP) / ___ extrasensorial.

perceptivity *n.* perceptibilidad, capacidad de percibir.

perceptual *a.* perceptivo-a, que recibe o transmite sensaciones.

percuss *v.* percutir, producir una percusión.

percussion *n.* percusión, procedimiento de palpación de toque firme en la superficie del cuerpo para producir sensaciones vibratorias que indiquen el estado de una parte interior determinada; auscultatory ___ / ___ auscultatoria.

percutaneous *a.* percutáneo-a, aplicado-a a través de la piel.

percutaneous transluminal angioplasty *n.* angioplastia transluminal percutánea, proceso de dilatación de una arteria por medio de un balón inflado a presión.

perfect *a.* perfecto-a, completo-a, acabado-a; **-ly** *adv.* perfectamente, completamente.

perfectionism *n. psic.* perfeccionismo, tendencia al fervor exagerado en la ejecución de actividades sin distinción de importancia entre las mismas.

perfectionist *a.* perfeccionista.

perforate *v.* perforar, abrir un agujero.

perforation *n.* perforación, agujero.

perform *v.* llevar a cabo, realizar, hacer; **to ___ an operation** / operar, intervenir quirúrgicamente.

perfusion *n.* perfusión, pasaje de un líquido o sustancia a través de un conducto.

perianal *a.* perianal, situado alrededor del ano.

pericardial, pericardiac *a.* pericárdico-a, pericardial, rel. al pericardio; _____ effusion / derrame _____.

pericardiectomy *n. cirg.* pericardiectomía, excisión parcial o total del pericardio.

pericarditis *n.* pericarditis, infl. del pericardio.

pericardium *n.* pericardio, membrana delicada de capa doble en forma de saco que envuelve el corazón y el inicio de los grandes vasos.

peril *n.* peligro, riesgo.

perimetrium *n.* perimetrio, membrana exterior del útero.

perinatal *n.* perinatal, rel. a o que ocurre antes, durante o inmediatamente después del nacimiento.

perineal *a.* perineal, rel. al perineo.

perinephric *a.* perinefrítico-a, rel. a o cercano al riñón.

perineum *n.* perineo, suelo pelviano delimitado anteriormente por la raíz del escroto en el hombre y la vulva en la mujer y posteriormente por el ano.

period *n.* período. 1. intervalo de tiempo; época; incubation _____ / _____ de incubación; latency _____ / _____ de latencia; 2. período, menstruación, menses, regla; 3. *gr.* punto.

periodic *a.* periódico-a.

periodical *n.* publicación, periódico.

periodontal *a.* periodontal, localizado alrededor de un diente.

periodontics *n.* periodoncia, rama de la odontología que estudia las enfermedades que atacan las áreas que envuelven los dientes.

periosteum *n.* periosteo, membrana fibrosa gruesa que cubre la superficie de los huesos excepto la superficie articular.

peripheral *a.* periférico-a, rel. a la periferia.

peripheral nervous system *n.* sistema nervioso periférico, nervios situados fuera del sistema nervioso central.

periphery *n.* periferia, parte de un cuerpo fuera del centro.

perishable *a.* perecedero-a, de fácil descomposición debido al contenido orgánico.

peristalsis *n.* peristalsis, contracciones ondulantes de estructuras tubulares tal como el canal alimenticio, cuyo movimiento fuerza el contenido almacenado hacia afuera en dirección descendiente.

peristaltic *a.* peristáltico-a, rel. a la peristalsis.

peritoneal *a.* peritoneal, rel. al peritoneo _____ cavity / cavidad _____.

peritoneoscopy *n.* peritoneoscopía. *V.* **laparoscopy.**

peritoneum *n.* peritoneo, membrana que cubre la pared abdominal y las vísceras.

peritonitis *n.* peritonitis, infl. del peritoneo.

peritonsillar *a.* periamigdalino-a, que rodea o está cerca de una amígdala.

periungual *a.* periungueal, localizado cerca de una uña.

periurethral *a.* periuretral, alrededor de la uretra.

perlèche *Fr.* perlèche, *pop.* boquera, infección en la comisura de los labios y manifestaciones de inflamación y fisuras, gen. causada por malnutrición.

permanent *a.* permanente; **-ly** *adv.* permanentemente.

permeability *n.* permeabilidad, cualidad de ser permeable; capillary _____ / _____ capilar.

permeable *a.* permeable, que permite el paso de sustancias a través de una membrana u otras estructuras.

permissible *a.* permisible; permitido-a.

permit *n.* permiso, consentimiento; *v.* permitir, autorizar.

pernicious *a.* pernicioso-a, nocivo-a, destructivo-a.

peroxide, hydrogen *n.* peróxido de hidrógeno, agua oxigenada.

perpendicular *a.* perpendicular.

per rectum *L.* per rectum, por el recto, por vía rectal.

persecution *n.* persecución, acosamiento.

perseveration *n. psic.* perseveración, tipo de trastorno mental que se manifiesta con repetición anormal de palabras y acciones.

persist *v.* persistir, perseverar, insistir.

persistence *n.* persistencia, insistencia, constancia.

person *n.* persona.

persona *n. psic.* persona, personalidad adoptada que encubre la verdadera.

personal *a.* personal, privado-a.

personality *n.* personalidad, rasgos, características y conducta individual que distinguen a una persona de otras; antisocial _____ / _____ antisocial; compulsive _____ /

____ compulsiva; extroverted ____ / ____ extrovertida; introverted ____ / ____ introvertida; neurotic ____ / ____ neurótica; paranoid ____ / ____ paranoica; psychopathic ____ / ____ psicopática; split ____ / ____ desdoblada; schizoid ____ / ____ esquizoide.

personnel *n.* personal; medical ____ / equipo médico, cuerpo facultativo.

perspective *n.* perspectiva.

perspiration *n.* sudor, transpiración.

perspire *v.* sudar, transpirar.

persuade *v.* persuadir.

persuasion *n.* persuasión, técnica terapéutica que consiste en un acercamiento racional al paciente para orientarle en sus actuaciones.

pertaining *a.* perteneciente; referente a.

pertubation *n.* pertubación, acto de insuflar oviductos para hacerlos permeables.

perturbation *n.* perturbación. 1. sentimiento de inquietud; 2. variación anormal de un estado regular a otro.

pertussis, whooping cough *n.* pertusis, tos ferina, enfermedad infantil infecciosa que se inicia con un estado catarral seguido de una tos seca persistente.

perversion *n.* perversión, desviación depravada, gen. de índole sexual.

pervert *n.* pervertido-a, persona que manifiesta alguna forma de perversión.

pervious *a.* pervio-a. *V.* **permeable.**

pes *L.* (*pl.* **pedes**) pes, pie o estructura similar a éste.

pessary *n.* pesario, instrumento que se introduce en la vagina para sostener el útero o como contraceptivo.

pessimism *n.* pesimismo, propensión a juzgar situaciones negativamente.

pessimist *n.* pesimista, persona que muestra pesimismo.

pessimistic *a.* pesimista.

pest *n.* 1. insectos nocivos; 2. peste. *V.* **plague.**

pesticide *n.* pesticida, exterminador de insectos y roedores.

pet *n.* 1. animal doméstico favorito; 2. niño-a mimado-a.

petechia *n.* (*pl.* **petechiae**) petequia, mancha hemorrágica pequeña que se manifiesta en la piel y las mucosas en casos de estado febril esp. en la tifoidea.

petit mal *Fr.* petit mal, ataque epiléptico benigno con pérdida del conocimiento pero sin convulsiones.

petrified *a.* petrificado-a, convertido-a en piedra.

peyote *n.* peyote, planta de la que se extrae la mescalina, droga alucinatoria.

phage *n.* bacteriófago. *V.* **bacteriophage.**

phagocyte *n.* fagocito, célula que ingiere y destruye otras células, sustancias y partículas extrañas.

phagocytic *a.* fagocítico-a, fagocitario-a, rel. a fagocitos.

phagocytosis *n.* fagocitosis, proceso de ingestión y digestión realizado por fagocitos.

phalanx *n.* (*pl.* **phalanxes, phalanges**) falange, uno de los huesos largos de los dedos de los pies o las manos.

phallic *a.* fálico, rel. al pene.

phantasm *n.* fantasma, ilusión óptica, aparición.

phantom *n.* fantasma, fantoma. 1. imagen mental; 2. patrón transparente del cuerpo y sus partes.

pharmaceutical *a.* farmacéutico-a, rel. a la farmacia.

pharmaceutics *n.* 1. farmacia; 2. preparaciones farmacéuticas.

pharmacist *n.* farmacéutico-a, boticario-a.

pharmacokinetics *n.* farmacocinética, estudio *in vivo* del metabolismo y acción de las drogas.

pharmacology *n.* farmacología, estudio de drogas, medicamentos, su naturaleza, origen, efectos y usos.

pharmacopeia *n.* farmacopea, compendio de drogas, agentes químicos y medicamentos regidos por una autoridad oficial que sirve de estándar en la preparación y dispensación de productos farmacéuticos.

pharmacy *n.* farmacia, botica.

pharyngitis *n.* faringitis, infl. de la faringe.

pharynx *n.* faringe, pasaje del aire de las fosas nasales a la laringe y de la boca al esófago en el tracto alimenticio.

phase *n.* fase, estado de desarrollo, estado transitorio.

phasic *a.* fásico-a, rel. a una fase.

phenobarbital *n.* fenobarbital, hipnótico, sedante, nombre comercial Luminal.

phenomenon *n.* (*pl.* **phenomena**) fenómeno. 1. evento o manifestación de cualquier índole; 2. síntoma objetivo de una enfermedad.

phenotype *n.* fenotipo, características visibles de un organismo como resultado de interacción entre el ambiente y los factores hereditarios.

phimosis *n.* fimosis, estrechamiento del orificio del prepucio que impide que éste pueda extenderse hacia atrás sobre el glande.

phlebitis *n.* flebitis, infl. de una vena, trastorno común esp. en las extremidades.

phlebogram *n.* flebograma, trazado del pulso venoso.

phlebolith *n.* flebolito, depósito calcáreo en una vena.

phlebotomy *n. cirg.* flebotomía, venotomía, incisión en una vena para sacar sangre.

phlegm *n.* flema. 1. mucus; 2. uno de los cuatro humores del cuerpo.

phlegmon *n.* flemón, infl. del tejido celular.

phobia *n.* fobia, temor exagerado e irracional.

phobic *a.* fóbico-a, rel. a la fobia.

phone *n.* teléfono; ___ **call** / llamada telefónica.

phonetic *a.* fonético-a, rel. a la voz y a los sonidos articulados.

phonetics *n.* fonética, ciencia que estudia la articulación de los sonidos y su pronunciación.

phonocardiogram *n.* fonocardiograma, representación gráfica que describe los sonidos del corazón.

phonogram *n.* fonograma, representación gráfica de la intensidad de un sonido.

phonoscope *n.* fonoscopio, instrumento para registrar los sonidos del corazón.

phosphate *n.* fosfato, sal del ácido fosfórico.

phosphorus *n.* fósforo, elemento no metálico que se encuentra en alcaloides.

photocoagulation *n.* fotocoagulación, proceso usado en cirugía óptica por el cual un rayo intenso de luz controlada (laser) produce una coagulación localizada.

photophobia *n.* fotofobia, intolerancia a la luz.

phototherapy *n.* fototerapia, exposición a los rayos del sol o a una luz artificial con propósito terapéutico.

phrase *n. gr.* frase.

phrenetic *a.* frenético-a, maníaco-a.

phthiriasis *n.* ftiriasis. V. **pediculosis.**

phylaxis *n.* filaxis, autodefensa del organismo.

physic *n.* medicamento, esp. un catártico o purgante.

physical *a.* físico-a, rel. al cuerpo y su condición; ___ examination / examen ___ ; ___ fitness / acondicionamiento ___ ; ___ therapist / terapeuta ___ ; ___ therapy / terapia ___.

physician *n.* médico-a; attending ___ / ___ de cabecera; consulting ___ / ___ consultante, consultor; family ___ / ___ de familia; ___ on call / ___ de guardia; referring ___ / ___ recomendante.

physiognomy *n.* fisionomía, semblante, rasgos faciales.

physiologist *n.* fisiólogo-a, especialista en fisiología.

physiology *n.* fisiología, ciencia que estudia las funciones de los organismos vivos y los procesos químicos o físicos que los caracterizan.

physiotherapy *n.* fisioterapia, tratamiento por medio de agentes físicos como agua, calor o luz.

physique *n.* físico, presencia, figura.

phytobezoar *n.* fitobezoar, concreción formada por fibra vegetal que se deposita en el estómago o el intestino y se digiere.

pia mater *L.* piamáter, piamadre, membrana vascular fina, la más interna de las meninges.

pian *n.* V. **frambesia.**

pica *n.* pica, deseo insaciable de ingerir sustancias que no son comestibles.

pick *n.* [*axe*] pico; [*choice*] selección; *v.* seleccionar, escoger; **to** ___ **out** / sacar, entresacar; **to** ___ **up** / recoger; captar.

picture *n.* fotografía; lámina; retrato.

piece *n.* pedazo, parte.

pierce *v.* agujerear, perforar.

piercing *a.* penetrante, agudo-a.

pigeon-toed *a.* patizambo-a.

pigment *n.* pigmento, colorante.

pigmentation *n.* pigmentación, coloración.

piles *n. pl.* almorranas, hemorroides.

piliation *n.* piliación, formación y desarrollo de pelo.

pill *n.* pastilla, píldora; birth control ___ / la píldora, píldora de control del embarazo; sleeping ___ / sedativo, ___ para dormir; pain ___ / calmante, sedativo, ___ para el dolor.

pillar *n.* columna, pilar.

pillow *n.* almohada; [*inflatable*] almohadilla, cojín.

pilus *L.* (*pl.* **pili**). pilus, pelo.

pimple *n.* barrillo, [*blackhead*] espinilla, grano de la cara.

pin *n.* clavo ortopédico, pieza de metal o hueso que se usa para unir partes de un hueso fracturado.

pinch *n.* pellizco; *v.* pellizcar; comprimir, apretar.

pinched nerve *n.* nervio pellizcado.

pineal *a.* pineal, en forma de piña o cono.

pineal gland *n.* glándula o cuerpo pineal.

pink *a.* rosado-a, sonrosado-a.

pinkeye *n.* conjuntivitis catarral, oftalmia purulenta.

pinna *L.* pinna, pabellón de la oreja.

pipet, pipette *n.* pipeta, probeta, tubo de ensayo.

pit *n.* hueco, hoyo; [*seed*] semilla de frutas.

pitch *n.* tono, diapasón, cualidad de un sonido de acuerdo con la frecuencia de las ondas que lo producen.

pith *n.* médula, parte principal.

pitiful *a.* lastimoso-a, pobre.

pituitary gland *n.* glándula pituitaria. *V.* **hypophysis.**

pity *n.* lástima, compasión; **What a __!** / ¡Qué __!

pivot *n.* pivote, eje, parte que sostiene la corona de un diente.

place *n.* lugar, sitio; **in __ of** / en __ de; *v.* colocar; **to put in __** / colocar en su __.

placebo *n.* placebo, sustancia anodina sin valor medicinal gen. usada en experimentos por comparación.

placenta *n.* placenta, órgano vascular que se desarrolla en la pared del útero a través del cual el feto se nutre de la madre por medio del cordón umbilical; early, previa __ / __ previa, anterior al feto en relación con la apertura externa del cuello uterino lo que puede causar una hemorragia grave.

placental *a.* placentario-a, de la placenta, rel. a la placenta; __ insufficiency / insuficiencia __.

plague *n.* peste. 1. peste bubónica, infección epidémica transmitida por la picadura de pulgas de ratas; 2. enfermedad epidémica que causa alta mortalidad.

plain *a.* común, ordinario-a.

plan *n.* plan, planificación; intento; *v.* planear.

plane *n.* plano. 1. superficie lisa y plana; 2. superficie relativamente lisa formada por un corte imaginario o un corte real a través de una parte del cuerpo; axial __ / __ axial;

coronal __ / __ coronal, frontal; sagittal __ / __ sagital.

planned parenthood *n.* planificación familiar.

planning *n.* planeamiento, planificación; organización; family __ / __ familiar.

plant *n.* planta; medicinal __ / __ , yerba medicinal.

plantar *a.* plantar, rel. a la planta del pie; __ reflex / reflejo plantar. *V.* **Babinski's sign.**

plaque, placque *n.* placa; plaqueta. 1. cualquier superficie de la piel o membrana mucosa; 2. plaqueta sanguínea.

plasma *n.* plasma, componente líquido de la sangre y linfa que se compone en su mayor parte (91%) de agua; __ proteins / proteínas sanguíneas.

plaster *n.* yeso, emplaste, molde; __ cast / vendaje enyesado, tablilla de __.

plastic *n.* plástico; *a.* plástico-a.

plasticity *n.* plasticidad, capacidad para moldearse.

plastic surgery *n.* cirugía plástica, proceso quirúrgico para reparar o reconstruir estructuras del cuerpo.

plate *n.* placa. 1. estructura lisa tal como una lámina ósea; 2. pieza de metal que se usa como soporte de una estructura.

platelet *n.* plaqueta, elemento celular esencial en la coagulación de la sangre.

platinum *n.* platino.

Platyhelminthes *n.* Platelmintos, *phylum* de gusanos planos que incluye las clases *Cestoda* y *Trematoda.*

play *v.* jugar; [*an instrument*] tocar.

play therapy *n. psic.* terapia infantil aplicada en un ambiente de juguetes y juegos infantiles por medio de los cuales se estimula a los niños a revelar conflictos interiores.

please *int.* por favor; **Come in, __!** / ¡Entre, entra por favor!; *v.* gustar, agradar, satisfacer; tener placer, tener gusto en.

pleasing *a.* agradable, placentero-a, gustoso-a.

pleasure principle *n. psic.* principio del placer, conducta dirigida a satisfacer deseos propios y a evadir el dolor.

pledget *n.* tapón de algodón absorbente o de gasa.

pleomorphism *n.* pleomorfismo, cualidad de asumir o tener formas diferentes.

plethora *n.* plétora, exceso de cualquiera de los líquidos del organismo.

plethysmography *n.* pletismografía, registro de las variaciones de volumen que ocurren en una parte u órgano en relación con la cantidad de sangre que pasa sobre los mismos.

pleura *n.* pleura, membrana doble que cubre los pulmones y la cavidad torácica; parietal ___ / ___ parietal; visceral ___ / ___ visceral.

pleural *a.* pleural, rel. a la pleura; ___ cavity / cavidad ___; ___ effusion / derrame ___.

pleuralgia *n.* pleuralgia, dolor en la pleura o en un costado.

pleurisy *n.* pleuresía, infl. de la pleura.

pleuritic *a.* pleurítico-a, rel. a o de la naturaleza de la pleuresía.

pleuritis *n.* plcuritis. *V.* **pleurisy.**

pleuroscopy *n.* pleuroscopía, examen de la cavidad pleural a través de una incisión en el tórax.

plexiform *a.* plexiforme, en forma de plexo o red.

plexus *n.* plexo, red de nervios o de vasos sanguíneos o linfáticos.

pliability *n.* flexibilidad; docilidad.

plica *n.* (*pl.* **plicae**) plica, doblez o pliegue.

plicate *v.* doblar, plegar.

plug *n.* tapón.

plumbism *n.* plumbismo, envenenamiento crónico con plomo.

plural *gr.* plural, más de uno en número.

pluripotent, pluripotential *a.* pluripotencial, que puede tomar más de un curso de acción.

pneumatic *a.* neumático-a, rel. al aire o a la respiración.

pneumatization *n.* neumatización, formación de cavidades llenas de aire en un hueso esp. en el hueso temporal.

pneumatocele *n.* neumatocele. 1. hernia de tejido pulmonar; 2. saco o tumor que contiene gas.

pneumococcal *a.* neumocócico-a, rel. a la neumonía o que la causa.

pneumococcus *n.* (*pl.* **pneumococci**) neumococo, microorganismo o tipo de bacteria gram-positiva que causa neumonía aguda y otras infecciones del tracto respiratorio superior.

pneumocystis carinii pneumonia *n.* neumonía neumocística carinii, tipo de pulmonía aguda intersticial causada por el bacilo *Pneumocysti- carinii*, considerada una de las infecciones oportunistas comunes del SIDA.

pneumoencephalograpy *n.* neumoencefalografía, rayos X del cerebro por medio de aire o gas inyectado para permitir distinguir visualmente la corteza y ventrículos cerebrales.

pneumomediastinum *L.* neumomediastinum, presencia de gas o de aire en los tejidos del mediastino.

pneumonia *n.* pulmonía, neumonía, enfermedad infecciosa causada por bacterias o virus presentes en el tracto respiratorio superior; doble ___ / ___ doble; ___, lobar / ___ lobar; ___, staphylococcal / ___ estafilocócica.

pneumonic *a.* neumónico-a, rel. a los pulmones o a la pneumonía.

pneumonitis *n.* neumonitis *V.* **pneumonia.**

pneumothorax *n.* neumotórax, acumulación de aire o gas cn la cavidad pleural que resulta en colapso del pulmón afectado; ___ spontaneous / ___ espontáneo; ___ tension / ___ por tensión.

pocket *n.* saco, bolsa; [*clothing*] bolsillo.

pockmark *n.* marca, señal o cicatriz. 1. marca de una pústula; 2. señal que deja la viruela.

podiatrist *n.* podíatra, especialista cn podiatría.

podiatry *n.* podiatría, diagnóstico y tratamiento de afecciones de los pies.

point *n.* punto, punta.

poison *n.* veneno; [*insect, reptile bite*] ponzoña; substancia tóxica; ___ ivy / hiedra venenosa.

poisoning *n.* envenenamiento.

poisonous *a.* venenoso-a; tóxico-a.

polar *a.* polar, rel. a un polo.

polarity *n.* polaridad. 1. cualidad de poseer polos; 2. presentación de efectos opuestos en dos extremos o polos.

polarization *n.* polarización.

pole *n.* polo. 1. cada uno de los extremos opuestos de un cuerpo u órgano o de una parte esférica u oval.

policy *n.* póliza; reglamento; insurance ___ / ___ de seguros.

polio, poliomyelitis *n.* polio, poliomielitis, parálisis infantil, enfermedad contagiosa que ataca el sistema nervioso central y causa parálisis en los músculos esp. de las piernas.

poliovirus *n.* poliovirus, agente causante de la poliomielitis.

polite *a.* cortés.

pollen *n.* polen.

pollute *v.* contaminar, corromper.

pollution *n.* polución, contaminación; **air** ___ / ___ del aire; **water** ___ / ___ del agua.

poly *n.* poli, leucocito polimorfonuclear.

polyarthritis *n.* poliartritis, infl. de varias articulaciones.

polyarticular *a.* poliarticular, que afecta varias articulaciones.

polyclinic *n.* policlínica, hospital general.

polycystic *a.* poliquístico-a que está formado-a por varios quistes.

polycythemia *n.* policitemia, aumento excesivo de glóbulos rojos; primary ___ / ___ primaria; ___ rubra / ___ vera secundaria; ___ vera. *V.* **erythrocythosis.**

polydactyly *n.* polidactilia, condición anormal de poseer más de cinco dedos en la mano o el pie.

polydipsia *n.* polidipsia, sed insaciable.

polygamy *n.* poligamia, práctica de poseer más de un cónyuge a la vez.

polygraph *n.* polígrafo, instrumento para obtener diversas pulsaciones arteriales y venosas simultáneamente.

polyhydramnios *n.* polihidramnios, exceso de líquido amniótico.

polymorphonuclear *a.* polimorfonucleado-a, que tiene un núcleo lobular complejo.

polymorphonuclear leukocyte *n.* leucocito polimorfonucleado, granulocito con núcleo de lóbulos múltiples.

polymyopathy *n.* polimiopatía, cualquier enfermedad que afecta varios músculos simultáneamente.

polyneuropathy *n.* polineuropatía, enfermedad que afecta varios nervios a la vez.

polyp *n.* pólipo, cualquier protuberancia o bulto que se desarrolla de una membrana mucosa.

polypectomy *n.* *cirg.* polipectomía, excisión de un pólipo.

polyposis *n.* poliposis, formación numerosa de pólipos.

polysaccharide *n.* polisacárido, carbohidrato que puede disolverse en agua.

polyunsaturated *a.* poli -no saturado, que denota un ácido graso.

polyvalent *a.* polivalente, que tiene efecto en contra de más de un agente.

pomade *n.* pomada, sustancia medicinal semisólida para uso externo.

pons *L.* pons, formación de tejido que sirve de puente entre dos partes.

poor *a.* pobre, necesitado-a; deficiente; **in** ___ **condition** / en mala condición, en mal estado.

popliteal *a.* poplíteo-a, área posterior de la rodilla.

popper *n.* *pop.* nombre atribuído a algunas drogas adictivas.

population *n.* población, habitantes de un área.

porcine *a.* porcino-a, rel. al cerdo.

pore, porus *n.* poro, abertura diminuta tal como la de una glándula sudorípara.

pork *n.* cerdo, puerco; ___ **chop** / chuleta o costilla de cerdo.

porosis *n.* porosis, formación de una cavidad.

porous *a.* poroso-a, permeable.

porta *L.* porta, entrada, esp. la parte de un órgano por donde penetran vasos sanguíneos y nervios.

portal *a.* portal, rel. al sistema portal.

portal circulation *n.* circulación portal, curso por el cual la sangre entra al hígado por la vena porta y sale por la vena hepática.

portal hypertension *n.* hipertensión portal, aumento de la presión en la vena porta debido a una obstrucción.

portal vein *n.* vena porta, vena formada por varias ramas de venas que provienen de órganos abdominales.

portion *v.* porción.

position *n.* posición. 1. actitud o postura del cuerpo; anatomic ___ / ___ anatómica; central ___ / ___ central; decubitus ___ / decúbito; deep ___ / ___ dentro de, profundamente; distal ___ / ___ distal; genupectoral ___ / ___ genupectoral; inferior ___ / ___ inferior; lateral ___ / ___ lateral, de un lado; lithotomy's ___ / ___ de litotomía; lying down ___ / ___ yacente, acostada; medial ___ / ___ media; posterior ___ / ___ posterior, detrás de; prone ___ / ___ prona, boca abajo; superficial ___ / ___ superficial; superior ___ / ___ superior, encima de; supine ___ / ___ supina, boca arriba; upright ___ / ___ erecta; 2. posición y presentación del feto. *V.* **presentation.**

positive *a.* positivo-a, afirmativo-a.

positivity *n.* positividad, manifestación de una reacción positiva.

possess *v.* poseer, tener.

possessed *a.* poseído-a, dominado-a por una idea o pasión.

possession *n.* posesión.

possessive *n.* *gr.* adjetivo o pronombre posesivo; *a.* posesivo-a.

posterior *a.* posterior. 1. rel. a la parte dorsal o trasera de una estructura; 2. que continúa.

posthypnotic *a.* posthipnótico-a, que sigue al estado hipnótico.

posthumous *a.* póstumo, que ocurre después de la muerte.

post ictal *a.* post ictal, después de un ataque.

post mature *a.* postmaduro-a, rel. a un recién nacido después de un embarazo prolongado.

postmortem *L.* post mortem, después de la muerte; autopsia.

postnasal *a.* postnasal, detrás de la nariz.

postoperative *a.* postoperatorio-a, que ocurre después de la operación; ____ care / cuidado ____ ; ____ complication / complicación ____ .

postpartum *L.* postpartum, después del parto; ____ blues / estado de depresión que sigue al parto.

postpartum period, puerperium *n.* puerperio, período de aproximadamente seis semanas después del parto durante el cual los órganos de la madre vuelven a su estado normal.

postpartum psychosis *n.* psicosis del postpartum.

postpone *v.* posponer, demorar, aplazar.

postprandial *a.* postprandial, después de una comida.

postural *a.* postural, rel. a la postura del cuerpo; ____ hypotension / hipotensión ____ , descenso de la presión arterial en posición erecta.

posture *n.* postura, posición del cuerpo.

potable *a.* potable, salubre, que puede beberse.

potassium *n.* potasio, mineral que se encuentra en el cuerpo combinado con otros, esencial en la conducción de impulsos nerviosos y actividad muscular.

potato *n.* patata, *H.A.* papa.

potbelly *n.* panza, barriga.

potency *n.* fuerza, potencia.

potent *a.* potente, fuerte; eficaz.

potential *a.* potencial, que existe en forma de cierta capacidad o disposición.

potion *n.* poción, dosis de líquido medicinal.

pouch *n.* bolsa, saco, cavidad.

poultice *n.* cataplasma, emplasto.

pound *n.* libra, medida de peso; *v.* machacar, golpear.

pour *v.* verter, vaciar, derramar.

poverty *n.* pobreza, carencia.

powder *n.* polvo; **powdered** *a.* en polvo.

power *n.* poder, fuerza.

pox *n.* enfermedad eruptiva de la piel caracterizada por manifestación de vesículas que se convierten en pústulas.

practical *a.* práctico-a.

practice *n.* práctica; costumbre; private ____ / ____ privada; *v.* practicar.

prandial *a.* prandial, rel. a las comidas.

preagonal *a.* preagónico-a; moribundo-a, al borde de la muerte.

preanesthetic *n.* preanestésico, agente preliminar que se administra con anticipación a la anestesia general.

precancerous *a.* precanceroso-a, susceptible a o que puede convertirse en un cáncer.

precarious *a.* precario-a.

precaution *n.* precaución.

precede *v.* preceder, anteceder.

precipitate *n.* precipitado, depósito de partes sólidas que se asientan en una solución; *a.* precipitado-a, que sucede con rapidez.

precise *a.* preciso-a, correcto-a.

precision *n.* precisión, exactitud.

precocious *a.* precoz, de un desarrollo más avanzado que el normal para la edad; ____ child / niño-a ____ .

precocity *n.* precocidad, desarrollo de rasgos físicos o facultades mentales más avanzados que lo normal en comparación con la edad cronólogica.

precursor *n.* precursor-a, predecesor-a, manifestación tal como la aparición de un síntoma o señal antes de desarrollarse una enfermedad; *a.* precursor-a, predecesor-a; preliminar.

predict *v.* predecir.

predispose *v.* predisponer.

predisposed *a.* predispuesto-a, que tiene susceptibilidad o tendencia a contraer una enfermedad.

predisposition *n.* predisposición, inclinación a desarrollar una condición o enfermedad debido a factores genéticos, ambientales o psicológicos.

predominant *a.* predominante.

preeclampsia *n.* preeclampsia, condición tóxica que se ve en la última etapa del embarazo y que se manifiesta con hipertensión, albuminuria y edema.

prefer *v.* preferir, seleccionar.

preferable *a.* preferible, favorito-a.

preference *n.* preferencia.

prefix *n. gr.* prefijo.

pregnancy *n.* embarazo, gravidez, estado de gestación; ectopic ___ / ___ ectópico; extrauterine ___ / ___ extrauterino; incomplete ___ / ___ incompleto; interstitial ___ / ___ intersticial; false ___ / ___ falso; multiple ___ / ___ múltiple; prolonged ___ / ___ prolongado; surrogate ___ / ___ subrogado; tubal ___ / ___ tubárico.

pregnant *a.* embarazada, encinta, en estado de gestación; grávida.

prehensile *a.* prensil, adaptado para agarrar o asir.

prejudice *n.* prejuicio.

preliminary *a.* preliminar.

premature *a.* [*newborn*] prematuro-a, nacido antes de llegar a término.

prematurity *n.* prematurez, condición del feto antes de alcanzar el término de treinta y siete semanas de la gestación.

premedication *n.* premedicación. *V.* preanesthetic.

premenstrual *n.* premenstrual, antes de la menstruación; ___ tension / tensión ___.

premonition *n.* premonición, presentimiento.

premunition *n.* premunición, inmunidad a una infección específica debida a la presencia previa del agente que la causa en el organismo.

prenatal *a.* prenatal, anterior al nacimiento. ___ care / cuidado ___.

preoccupation *n.* preocupación.

preoccupied *a.* preocupado-a.

preoccupy *v.* preocupar; preocuparse.

preoperative care *n.* cuidado preoperatorio, cuidado preliminar a la operación.

prep *abbr.* término que se usa esp. para referirse a todo lo relacionado con el proceso preoperatorio.

preparation *n.* preparación. 1. acción de preparar algo; 2. un medicamento que se prepara para ser administrado.

prepare *v.* preparar.

prepared childbirth *n.* parto natural. *V.* natural childbirth.

preposition *n. gr.* preposición.

prepubescent *a.* prepubescente, anterior a la pubertad.

prepuce *n.* prepucio, pliegue de piel sobre el glande del pene.

prerenal *a.* prerrenal. 1. situado frente al riñón; 2. que tiene lugar en la circulación antes de llegar al riñón.

presacral *a.* presacro, frente al sacro.

presbiopia *n.* presbiopía, presbicia, condición de la visión que ocurre en la vejez a causa de una deficiencia en la elasticidad del cristalino.

prescribe *v.* prescribir, recetar.

prescribed *a. pp.* de **to prescribe**, prescrito-a, ordenado-a.

prescription *n.* receta; ___ tablet / formulario.

presence *n.* [*looks*] presencia, aspecto; [*attendance*] asistencia.

present *n. gr.* tiempo presente; at ___ / hoy, actualmente, por ahora; [*gift*] regalo, obsequio; *v.* to be ___ / asistir, concurrir; -ly *adv.* ahora, actualmente.

presentation *n.* presentación. 1. reporte oral; 2. posición del feto en el útero según se detecta en un examen, o posición de salida en relación con el canal del parto en el momento del nacimiento; breech ___ / ___ de nalgas; brow ___ / ___ de cejas o frente; cephalic ___ / ___ de cabeza; face ___ / ___ de cara; footling ___ / ___ de pies; shoulder ___ / ___ de hombro; transverse ___ / ___ transversa.

preservation *n.* preservación, conservación.

preservative *n.* preservativo, conservador. 1. agente que se añade a un alimento o medicamento para impedir el desarrollo de bacterias; 2. profiláctico.

preserve *v.* preservar, conservar.

press *v.* hacer presión, comprimir, oprimir.

pressor *a.* presor, que tiende a aumentar la presión sanguínea.

pressure *n.* presión, tensión, compresión; arterial ___ / ___ arterial, presión o tensión de la sangre en las arterias; blood ___ / ___ sanguínea, tensión de la sangre sobre las paredes de los vasos capilares; central venous ___ / ___ venosa central, presión de la sangre en la aurícula derecha del corazón; diastolic ___ / ___ diastólica, presión arterial durante la dilatación de las aurículas y ventrículos; intrathoracic ___ / ___ intratorácica; osmotic ___ / ___ osmótica; pulse ___ / ___ de pulso; systolic ___ / ___ sistólica, presión arterial durante la contracción de los ventrículos; venous ___ / ___ venosa, presión de la sangre en las venas; ___ wedge / ___ diferencial; *v.* hacer presión, presionar.

pressure point *n.* punto de presión, área donde puede sentirse el pulso o hacer presión para contener un sangramiento.

pressure sore *n.* úlcera decúbito.

pretend *v.* pretender, fingir, aparentar.

preterit *gr.* préterito, tiempo pasado.

preterm *n.* pretérmino, lo que concierne a sucesos anteriores a completar el término de treinta y siete semanas en un embarazo.

prevalence *n.* prevalencia, número de casos en una población afectados por la misma enfermedad en un tiempo determinado.

prevent *v.* prevenir, precaver, evitar.

preventive *a.* preventivo-a; ___ health services / servicios de salud ___.

prevertebral *a.* prevertebral, situado enfrente de una vertebra.

previous *a.* previo-a, anterior.

priapism *n.* priapismo, erección prolongada y dolorosa del pene a consecuencia de una enfermedad.

price *n.* precio, valor, costo.

prick *n.* pinchazo; punzada; picadura, aguijón; *v.* picar, punzar, aguijonear, pinchar.

prickly heat *n.* salpullido, sarpullido.

priest *n.* sacerdote, padre, cura.

primarily *adv.* primeramente; principalmente, primordialmente.

primary *a.* inicial, primario-a, rel. al contacto o atención de un caso en su principio; ___ physician / médico de cabecera, facultativo que atiende al paciente inicialmente, esp. un pediatra o médico de la familia.

primary care *n.* atención inicial del paciente.

prime *a.* primero-a, principal; *v.* **to be in one's** ___ / estar en la flor de la vida.

primitive *a.* primitivo-a; embriónico-a.

primordial *a.* primordial, esencial.

principal *a.* principal, más importante.

principle *n.* principio. 1. ingrediente esencial de un compuesto químico; 2. regla; orden.

print *n.* impresión, marca.

prior *n.* antecesor, predecesor; *a.* previo-a; ___ **to** / anterior a, antes de.

priority *n.* prioridad, preferencia, precedencia.

prism *n.* prisma.

privacy *n.* vida privada; aislamiento.

private *a.* privado-a, particular, exclusivo-a; ___ **hospital** / clínica; ___ **practice** / consulta particular; ___ **room** / cuarto ___; **-ly** *adv.* privadamente.

privation *n.* privación, necesidad.

privilege *n.* privilegio; derecho.

privileged *a.* confidencial, privilegiado-a; reservado-a; ___ **information** / información ___ o reservada.

probability *n.* probabilidad.

probable *a.* probable, casi posible; **-ly** *adv.* probablemente.

probe *n.* sonda, instrumento flexible que se usa para explorar cavidades o conductos y para medir la penetración de una herida.

problem *n.* problema; cuestión; trastorno.

problematic *a.* problemático-a; dificultoso-a.

procedure *n.* procedimiento; **clinical** ___ / ___ clínico; **surgical** ___ / ___ quirúrgico; **therapeutic** ___ / ___ terapeútico.

proceed *v.* proceder, continuar, seguir adelante, avanzar.

process *n.* proceso, método, sistema.

procreate *v.* engendrar, procrear, reproducir.

procreation *n.* procreación, reproducción.

proctalgia *n.* proctalgia, dolor en el recto y el ano.

proctitis *n.* proctitis, infl. de la mucosa del recto y el ano.

proctologist *n.* proctólogo-a; especialista en proctología.

proctology *n.* proctología, estudio del colon, recto y ano, de las enfermedades que los afectan y su tratamiento.

proctoscope *n.* proctoscopio, tipo de endoscopio usado para examinar el recto.

procure *v.* procurar, tratar de obtener.

prodromal *a.* prodrómico-a, rel. a la fase inicial de una enfermedad.

prodrome *n.* pródromo, señal o síntoma preliminar.

produce *n.* producto, esp. vegetales, frutas y legumbres; producción; *v.* producir, crear; causar.

product *n.* producto; resultado, efecto.

production *n.* producción, rendimiento.

productive *a.* productivo-a, fecundo-a.

profession *n.* profesión, carrera, oficio.

professional *n.* profesional, facultivo-a; *a.* profesional, facultativo-a; ____ care / cuidado ____ ; ____ help / asistencia médica, asistencia ____ .

profile *n.* perfil, bosquejo, esbozo.

profit *n.* beneficio, ganancia; ventaja.

profunda *L.* (*pl.* **profunda**) muy interior, en referencia esp. a algunas arterias.

profundus *L.* profundo, interior.

profuse *a.* profuso-a; abundante; **-ly** *adv.* profusamente; abundantemente.

progeny *n.* descendencia, prole.

progesterone *n.* progesterona, hormona esteroide segregada por los ovarios.

prognathous *a.* prognato-a, que tiene la mandíbula prominente.

prognose *v.* pronosticar o predecir el desarrollo de una enfermedad.

prognosis *n.* pronóstico, evaluación del curso probable de una enfermedad.

prognosticate *v.* pronosticar.

progress *n.* progreso; *v.* **to make** ____ / progresar, mejorar.

progressive *a.* progresivo-a, que avanza.

projection *n.* proyección. 1. protuberancia; 2. *psic.* mecanismo por el cual el (la) paciente atribuye inconscientemente a otras personas u objetos las cualidades y sentimientos propios que rechaza.

prolapse *n.* prolapso, caída de un órgano o parte.

proliferation *n.* proliferación, multiplicación en número por reproducción esp. de células similares.

proliferous, prolific *a.* prolífero-a, que se reproduce fácilmente.

prolong *v.* prolongar, extender; retardar.

prolongation *n.* prolongación, extensión.

prominence *n.* prominencia, proyección; *pop.* bulto.

promise *n.* promesa; *v.* prometer, dar la palabra.

promontory *n.* promontorio, elevación.

prompt *a.* puntual, a tiempo.

pronate *v.* pronar, poner el cuerpo o parte del mismo en posición prona.

prone *a.* acostado-a, postrado-a. 1. en posición acostada boca abajo; 2. con la mano virada, apoyada en el dorso; 3. propenso, susceptible a contraer una enfermedad.

pronoun *n.* *gr.* pronombre.

pronounce *v.* pronunciar, articular sonidos de letras.

pronunciation *n.* pronunciación.

proof *n.* prueba, comprobación; *v.* probar, demostrar.

propagate *v.* propagar, diseminar.

propagation *n.* propagación, reproducción.

proper *a.* propio-a, particular, apropiado-a.

prophase *n.* profase, primera fase en la mitosis celular.

prophylactic *n.* profiláctico. 1. agente o método para evitar infecciones; 2. contraceptivo.

prophylaxis *n.* profilaxis, medidas para prevenir enfermedades o su propagación.

proportion *n.* proporción, tamaño determinado, medida.

proprietary medicine *n.* medicamento de patente.

proprioceptive *a.* propioceptivo-a, que recibe estímulos.

proprioceptor *n.* propioceptor, terminación nerviosa receptora que responde a estímulos y trasmite información de los movimientos y posiciones del cuerpo.

proptosis *n.* proptosis, desplazamiento de un órgano hacia adelante tal como el globo ocular.

proscribe *v.* prohibir, cancelar.

prosencephalon *n.* prosencéfalo, porción anterior de la vesícula cerebral de la que se desarrollan el diencéfalo y el telencéfalo.

prostate *n.* próstata, glándula masculina que rodea el cuello de la vejiga y la uretra.

prostatectomy *n.* *cirg.* prostatectomía, excisión parcial o total de la próstata.

prostatic *a.* prostático-a, rel. a la próstata; ____ hypertrophy / hipertrofia ____ , agrandamiento benigno de la próstata debido a la vejez.

prostatism *n.* prostatismo, trastorno debido a una obstrucción del cuello de la vejiga por agrandamiento de la próstata.

prostatitis *n.* prostatitis, infl. de la próstata.

prosthesis *n.* prótesis, reemplazo de una parte del cuerpo con un sustituto artificial.

prosthetics *n.* protética, rama de la cirugía que se dedica al reemplazo de partes del cuerpo.

prostitution *n.* prostitución.

prostrate *a.* postrado-a. 1. en posición prona o supina; 2. débil, abatido-a; *v.* postrar; abatir; postrarse; abatirse; debilitarse.

prostration *n.* postración, debilidad, abatimiento.

protean *n.* proteico, que se manifiesta en distintas formas.

protect *v.* proteger, cuidar.

protection *n.* protección, cuidado.

protective *a.* protector-a.

protective isolation *n.* aislamiento protector, estado que se recomienda en casos de pacientes de baja resistencia o inmunidad.

protein *n.* proteína, complejo compuesto nitrogenado esencial en el desarrollo y preservación de los tejidos del cuerpo; ___ balance / balance de las ___-s.

proteinaceous *a.* proteináceo-a, de la naturaleza o semejante a una proteína.

proteinemia *n.* proteinemia, proteínas en la sangre.

proteinosis *n.* proteinosis, acumulación en exceso de proteínas en los tejidos.

proteinuria *n.* proteinuria, presencia de proteínas en la orina.

prothrombin *n.* protrombina, una de las cuatro proteínas principales del plasma junto a la albúmina, globulina y fibrinógeno.

protocol *n.* protocolo, notas oficiales de un procedimiento.

protoplasm *n.* protoplasma, parte esencial de la célula que incluye el citoplasma y el núcleo.

prototype *n.* prototipo, modelo, ejemplo.

protozoon *n.* (*pl.* **protozoa.**) protozoo, organismo unicelular.

protrude *v.* sobresalir; salirse de su lugar.

protruding *a.* saliente.

protuberance *n.* protuberancia, prominencia.

proud *a.* orgulloso-a, arrogante.

prove *v.* demostrar, comprobar, probar.

provide *v.* proveer, dar, abastecer.

providence *n.* providencia.

provision *n.* provisión, abastecimiento.

provisional *a.* provisional, interino; **-ly** *adv.* provisionalmente, por lo pronto.

proximal *a.* próximo-a, cerca del punto de referencia.

prune *n.* ciruela pasa.

pruritus *n.* prurito, comezón, picazón.

pseudoaneurysm *n.* pseudoaneurisma, condición semejante a la dilatación de un aneurisma.

pseudocyesis *n.* pseudociesis. *V.* **pseudopregnancy.**

pseudocyst *n.* pseudo quiste, formación semejante a la de un quiste.

pseudopregnancy *n.* embarazo falso o imaginario.

psoriasis *n.* psoriasis, dermatitis crónica que se manifiesta con manchas rojas cubiertas de escamas blancas.

psyche *n.* psique, mente, proceso mental consciente o inconsciente.

psychedelic *a.* psicodélico-a, rel. a substancias o drogas que pueden inducir alteraciones perceptuales tales como alucinaciones y delirios.

psychiatric *a.* psiquiátrico-a, siquiátrico-a.

psychiatrist *n.* psiquiatra, siquiatra, especialista en psiquiatría.

psychiatry *n.* psiquiatría, rama de la medicina que estudia los trastornos mentales.

psychic *a.* psíquico-a, rel. a la mente o psique.

psychoactive *a.* psicoactivo-a, que afecta la condición mental.

psychoanalysis *n.* psicoanálisis, método de análisis psicológico creado por Sigmund Freud que se vale de la interpretación de los sueños y de la libre asociación de ideas para hacer al paciente consciente de conflictos reprimidos y tratar de ajustar su conducta emocional.

psychoanalyst *n.* psicoanalista, analista.

psychoanalyze *v.* psicoanalizar, sicoanalizar.

psychobiology *n.* psicobiología, estudio de la psique en relación a otros procesos biológicos.

psychodrama *n.* psicodrama, método de terapia psíquica en el cual se dramatizan situaciones conflictivas de la vida del paciente con la participación de éste.

psychological *a.* psicológico-a, rel. a la psicología.

psychologist *n.* psicólogo-a, profesional que practica la psicología.

psychology *n.* psicología, sicología, ciencia que estudia los procesos mentales y la conducta de un individuo.

psychomotor *a.* psicomotor-a, rel. a acciones motoras como resultado de actividades mentales.

psychopath *n.* psicópata, persona que padece de trastornos mentales.

psychopathology *n.* psicopatología, rama de la medicina que trata de las causas y naturaleza de las enfermedades mentales.

psychopharmacology *n.* psicofarmacología, estudio del efecto de drogas y medicamentos en la mente y la conducta.

psychophysiological *a.* psicofisiológico-a, rel. a la influencia mental sobre procesos físicos tal como se manifiesta en algunos desórdenes y enfermedades.

psychosis *n.* psicosis, trastorno mental severo de origen orgánico o emocional en el cual el paciente pierde contacto con la realidad y sufre de alucinaciones o aberraciones mentales; alcoholic ____ / ____ alcohólica; depressive ____ / ____ depresiva; drug ____ / ____ por drogas; manic-depressive ____ / ____ maníacodepresiva; organic ____ / ____ orgánica; senile ____ / ____ senil; situational ____ / ____ situacional; toxic ____ / ____ tóxica; traumatic ____ / ____ traumática.

psychosocial *a.* psicosocial, rel. a factores psicológicos y sociales.

psychosomatic *a.* psicosomático-a, rel. al cuerpo y a la mente; ____ symptom / síntoma ____. *V.* **psychophysiological.**

psychotherapy *n.* psicoterapia, tratamiento de trastornos mentales o emocionales por medios psicológicos tales como el psicoanálisis.

psychotic *a.* psicótico-a, rel. a o que sufre de una psicosis.

psychotropic drugs *n.* drogas psicotrópicas, compuestos químicos que afectan la estabilidad mental.

ptosis *Gr.* ptosis, prolapso de un órgano o parte, esp. visto en el párpado superior.

puberty *n.* pubertad, adolescencia, desarrollo de las características sexuales secundarias y comienzo de la capacidad reproductiva.

pubescense *n.* pubescencia, pubertad. 1. principio de la pubertad; 2. vellosidad, lanugo.

pubic *a.* púbico-a, rel. al pubis; ____ hair / pelo ____.

pubis *n.* (*pl.* **pubes**) pubis, región púbica, estructura ósea frontal de la pelvis.

public *a.* público-a.

public health *n.* salubridad pública, rama de la medicina que se dedica a la atención social, física y mental de los miembros de una comunidad.

pudendum *L.* (*pl.* **pudenda**) pudendum, órganos genitales externos, esp. los femeninos.

puerile *a.* pueril, infantil.

puerperal *a.* puerperal, concerniente al puerperio.

puerperium *n.* puerperio. *V.* **post partum.**

pull *n.* tirón; *v.* tirar, halar, arrancar, sacar; to ____ in / tirar hacia adentro; to ____ oneself together / calmarse; to ____ through [*as in a sickness*] / recuperarse; to ____ up one's knees / levantar las rodillas.

pulmonary, pulmonic *a.* pulmonar, pulmónico-a, rel. al pulmón o a la arteria pulmonar; ____ alveolar proteinosis / proteinosis alveolar ____; ____ artery wedge pressure / presión diferencial de la arteria ____; ____ edema / edema ____; ____ embolism / embolia ____; ____ emphysema; enfisema ____; ____ insufficiency / insuficiencia ____; ____ stenosis / estenosis ____; ____ valve / válvula ____; ____ vein / vena ____.

pulp *n.* pulpa. 1. parte blanda de un órgano; 2. quimo; 3. pulpa dental, parte central blanda de un diente.

pulsatile *a.* pulsátil, de pulsación rítmica.

pulsation *n.* pulsación, latido rítmico tal como el del corazón.

pulse *n.* pulso, dilatación arterial rítmica que gen. coincide con los latidos cardíacos; alternating ____ / ____ alternante; bigeminal ____ / ____ bigeminado; dorsalis pedis ____ / ____ de la arteria dorsal del pie; femoral ____ / ____ femoral; filiform ____ / ____ filiforme; full ____ / ____ lleno; peripheral ____ / ____ periférico; radial ____ / ____ radial; regular ____ / ____ regular; ____ pressure / presión del pulso, diferencia entre la presión sistólica y la diastólica.

pulverize *v.* pulverizar, reducir a polvo, hacer polvo.

pump *n.* bomba; *v.* bombear; to ____ out / ____ hacia afuera, sacar por bomba.

pumping *n.* bombeo; heart ____ / ____ del corazón; stomach ____ / ____ estomacal.

punch *n.* sacabocados, instrumento quirúrgico que se usa para perforar o cortar un disco o un segmento de tejido.

punctuate *n.* puntuar, acto de perforar un tejido con un instrumento afilado.

puncture *n.* punción, perforación; *v.* punzar, pinchar; agujerear.

punctured wound *n.* herida por perforación con un instrumento afilado.

pungent *a.* pungente, acre; penetrante.

pupil *n.* pupila, abertura contráctil del iris que da entrada a la luz.

pupillary *a.* pupilar, rel. a la pupila.

pure *a.* puro-a, sin contaminación.

purgative *n.* purgante, catártico que causa evacuación.

purge *n.* purga, medicamento o catártico; *v.* purgar, forzar la evacuación de los intestinos por medio de un purgante.

purification *n.* purificación, destilación.

purify *v.* purificar, destilar.

purple *n.* color púrpura; morado.

purpose *n.* propósito, intención.

purposeful *a.* intencional, con intención; determinado-a.

purpura *n.* púrpura, condición caracterizada por manchas rojizas o de color púrpura en la piel, debida al escape de sangre a los tejidos.

purulence *n.* purulencia, pus.

purulent *a.* purulento, que está supurando.

pus *n.* pus, excreción, fluido amarillento espeso que se forma por supuración.

push *n.* empujón; pujo; ___ **button** / botón de llamada; *v.* [*as to bear down*] pujar.

pustule *n.* pústula, costra, elevación pequeña de la piel que contiene pus; *pop.* postilla.

put *vi.* poner; **to** ___ **in** / poner dentro de, echar en, meter; **to** ___ **off** / aplazar, cancelar; **to** ___ **on** [clothes] / ponerse la ropa, vestirse; **to** ___ **out** [*light, fire*] / apagar; **to** ___ **together** / unir, juntar; **to** ___ **up with** / aguantar, soportar, tolerar.

putrefaction *n.* putrefacción, condición de ser pútrido-a, corrompido-a.

putrid *a.* pútrido-a, corrompido-a.

pyelogram *n.* pielograma, radiografía de la pelvis renal y uréter usando un medio de contraste.

pyelolithotomy *n.* *cirg.* pielolitotomía, incisión para extraer un cálculo de la pelvis renal.

pyelonephritis *n.* pielonefritis, infl. del riñón y la pelvis renal.

pyeloplastia *n.* *cirg.* pieloplastia, operación de reparación plástica de la pelvis renal.

pyelostomy *n.* *cirg.* pielostomía, formación o establecimiento de una abertura en la pelvis renal para desviar la orina hacia el exterior.

pyelotomy *n.* *cirg.* pielotomía, incisión de la pelvis renal.

pyloric *a.* pilórico, rel. al píloro.

pyloroplasty *n.* *cirg.* piloroplastia, reparación del píloro.

pylorus *n.* píloro, abertura u orificio circular entre el estómago y el duodeno.

pyocyte *n.* piocito, corpúsculo de pus.

pyoderma *n.* pioderma, cualquier enfermedad de la piel que presenta supuración.

pyogenic *a.* piógeno-a, purulento-a.

pyorrhea *n.* piorrea, periodontitis.

pyramid *n.* pirámide, estructura semejante a un cono, tal como la médula oblongata.

pyrectic, pyretic *a.* pirético-a, rel. a la fiebre.

pyretolysis *n.* piretolisis. 1. reducción de fiebre; 2. proceso de curación que se acelera con la fiebre.

pyrexia *n.* pirexia, condición febril.

pyrogen *n.* pirógeno, sustancia que produce fiebre.

pyromania *n.* piromanía, obsesión con el fuego.

pyuria *n.* piuria, presencia de piocitos en la orina.

Q

q *abbr.* **quantity** / cantidad; **quaque** / cada.

quack *n.* charlatán, persona que pretende tener cualidades o conocimientos para curar enfermedades.

quackery *n.* curanderismo, charlatanería.

quadrangle *n.* cuadrángulo, figura geométrica formada por cuatro ángulos.

quadrant *n.* cuadrante, cuarta parte de un círculo.

quadratus *L.* quadratus. 1. músculo de cuatro lados; 2. figura de cuatro lados.

quadriceps *n.* cuadríceps, músculo de cuatro cabezas, extensor de la pierna.

quadriplegia *n.* cuadriplegia, parálisis de las cuatro extremidades.

quadruplet *a.* cuádruple, cada uno de los cuatro hijos nacidos en un parto múltiple.

quake *n.* [*earthquake*] temblor de tierra, terremoto; *v.* temblar; sacudirse.

qualification *n.* calificación; [*competence*] capacidad.

qualified *a.* competente, capaz.

qualify *v.* calificar; capacitar.

qualitative *a.* cualitativo-a, rel. a cualidad o clase.

qualitative test *n.* prueba cualitativa.

quality *n.* cualidad, propiedad.

quantitative test *n.* prueba cuantitativa.

quantity *n.* cantidad.

quantum *L.* quantum, unidad de energía.

quarantine *n.* cuarentena, período de cuarenta días durante los cuales se restringen las actividades de personas o animales para prevenir la propagación de una enfermedad contagiosa.

quarrel *n.* pelea, riña, disputa, querella; *v.* reñir, disputar, pelear.

quartan *a.* cuartana, que recurre cada cuatro días tal como la fiebre palúdica.

quarter *n.* cuarto, cuarta parte de un todo.

quash *v.* suprimir, sofocar.

quaver *n.* vibración, temblor; *v.* vibrar, temblar.

queasy *a.* nauseabundo-a; _____ stomach / tener naúseas, asco.

queer *a.* raro-a, excéntrico-a; *slang* homosexual, invertido, maricón.

queilotomy *n.* queilotomía. *V.* **cheilotomy.**

quench *v.* extinguir, apagar; [*thirst*] saciar.

query *n.* pregunta; duda.

quest *n.* indagación, búsqueda, pesquisa.

question *n.* pregunta; cuestión, problema; *v.* interrogar, preguntar.

quick *a.* rápido-a, ligero-a, [*alert*] listo-a; _____-frozen / congelado-a al instante; **-ly** *adv.* pronto, rápidamente, al instante.

quicken *v.* acelerar; animar, avivar, estimular.

quickening *n.* 1. animación; 2. percepción por la madre del primer movimiento del feto en el útero.

quiescent *a.* quiescente, en estado de reposo; inactivo-a.

quiet *a.* quieto-a, sosegado-a, tranquilo-a; *v.* calmar, tranquilizar.

quinidine *n.* quinidina, alcaloide derivado de una *Cinchona* que se usa en irregularidades cardíacas.

quinine *n.* quinina, alcaloide que se obtiene de la corteza de una *Cinchona* usado como antiséptico y antipirético esp. en el tratamiento de paludismo, tifoidea y malaria.

quininism *n.* quininismo, chinchonismo, intoxicación de sales de quinina.

quintan *n.* quintana, fiebre recurrente cada cinco días.

quintuplet *a.* quíntuple, cada uno de los cinco hijos nacidos en un parto múltiple.

quit *v.* desistir, dejar, parar.

quota *n.* cuota.

quotient *n.* cuociente, cociente, cifra que resulta de una división; achievement _____ / _____ de realización; blood _____ / _____ san-

guíneo; growth _____ / _____ de crecimiento; intelligence _____ / _____ de inteligencia.

R

R *abbr.* **radioactive** / radioactivo; **resistance** / resistencia; **respiration** / respiración; **response** / respuesta, reacción;

rabbi *n.* rabí, rabino.

rabbit *n.* conejo-a; _____ test / prueba del embarazo.

rabbit fever *n.* fiebre de conejo. *V.* **tularemia.**

rabid *a.* rabioso-a, rel. a la rabia o afectado por ella.

rabies *n.* rabia. *V.* **hydrophobia.**

race *n.* raza, grupo étnico diferenciado por características comunes heredadas.

racemose *a.* racemoso-a, racimoso-a, similar a un racimo de uvas.

rachicentesis *n.* raquicentesis, punción lumbar.

rachiotomy *n.* *cirg.* raquiotomía. *V.* **laminectomy.**

rachis *n.* raquis, la columna vertebral.

rachitic *a.* raquítico-a. rel. al raquitismo; débil, endeble.

rachitism, rhachitis, rachitis *n.* raquitismo, enfermedad por deficiencia que afecta el desarrollo óseo en los adolescentes, causada por falta de calcio, fósforo y vitamina D.

racial *a.* racial, étnico-a, de la raza; _____ **prejudice** / prejuicio _____; _____ **immunity** / inmunidad _____, tipo de inmunidad natural de los miembros de una raza.

rad *n.* rad. 1. dosis de radiación absorbida; 2. rad. *abbr.* de radix, raíz.

radial *a.* radial. 1. rel. al hueso del radio; 2. que se expande en todas direcciones a partir de un centro.

radiant *a.* radiante, que emite rayos.

radiate *v.* irradiar, expandirse.

radiation *n.* radiación. 1. emisión de materiales o partículas radioactivas; 2. propagación de energía; 3. emisión de rayos desde un centro común; _____ dosage / dosis de _____; _____ hazards / riesgos y peligros causados por una _____; _____ therapy / radioterapia; electromagnetic _____ / _____ electromagnética; infrared _____ / _____ por rayos infrarrojos; ionizing ___ / ___ ionizante; ultraviolet ___ / ___ de rayos ultravioleta.

radiation sickness *n.* enfermedad por radiación causada por exposición a rayos X o materiales radioactivos.

radical *n. gr.* raiz de una palabra; *a.* radical, dirigido a erradicar la raíz de una enfermedad o de todo tejido enfermo; ___ treatment / tratamiento ___.

radicle *n.* radícula, estructura semejante a una raíz.

radicular *a.* radical, rel. a la raíz u origen.

radiculectomy *n. cirg.* radiculectomía, excisión de la raíz de un nervio, esp. de la raíz de un nervio espinal.

radiculitis *n.* radiculitis, infl. de la raíz de un nervio.

radiculomyelopathy *n.* radiculomielopatía, enfermedad que afecta la médula espinal y la raíz de los nervios espinales.

radiculoneuritis, Guillain-Barré syndrome *n.* radiculoneuritis, síndrome de Guillain-Barré, infl. de raíces de nervios espinales.

radiculoneuropathy *n.* radiculoneuropatía, condición patológica de los nervios y sus raíces.

radiculopathy *n.* radiculopatía, cualquier enfermedad de las raíces de los nervios espinales.

radioactive *a.* radiactivo-a, rel. a la radiactividad o que la posee.

radioactive iodine excretion test. *n.* prueba radiactiva del yodo, evaluación de la función de la tiroides por medio del uso de yodo radiactivo.

radioactivity *n.* radiactividad, propiedad de ciertos elementos de producir radiaciones.

radiobiology *n.* radiobiología, estudio del efecto de la radiactividad en tejidos vivos.

radiocarbon *n.* carbono radiactivo.

radiodermatitis *n.* radiodermatitis, dermatitis causada por la exposición a radiaciones.

radioelement *n.* radioelemento, cualquier elemento que tiene propiedades radiactivas.

radiography *n.* radiografía, uso de rayos X para producir imágenes en placas o en una pantalla fluorescente.

radioimmunity *n.* radioinmunidad, disminución de la sensibilidad a las radiaciones.

radioimmunoassay *n.* radioinmunoensayo.

radioisotope *n.* radioisótopo, isótopo radioactivo.

radiologic *a.* radiológico-a, rel. a la radiología.

radiologist *n.* radiólogo-a, especialista en radiología.

radiology *n.* radiología, ciencia que trata de los rayos X o rayos que provienen de sustancias radiactivas, esp. para uso médico.

radiolucent *a.* radiolúcido-a, que permite el paso de la mayor parte de rayos X.

radionecrosis *n.* radionecrosis, desintegración de tejidos por radiación.

radionuclide imaging *n. V.* **scintigraphy.**

radiopaque *a.* radiopaco-a, que no deja pasar rayos X u otra forma de radiación; ___ dye / colorante ___.

radiopharmaceutical agents *n.* radiofármacos, drogas radiactivas usadas en el tratamiento y diagnóstico de enfermedades.

radioreceptor *n.* radiorreceptor, receptor que recibe energía radiante como la de los rayos X, de la luz o del calor.

radioresistance *n.* radiorresistencia, resistencia a los efectos de una radiación.

radioresistant *a.* radiorresistente, que tiene la propiedad de resistir efectos radiactivos.

radioscopy *n.* radioscopía. *V.* **fluoroscopy.**

radiosensitive *a.* radiosentitivo-a, que es afectado por o que responde a un tratamiento de radiación.

radiotherapy *n.* radioterapia, tratamiento de una enfermedad por medio de rayos X o por otras sustancias radiactivas.

radish *n.* rábano.

radium *L.* radium, radio, elemento metálico radiactivo y fluorescente usado en algunas de sus variaciones en el tratamiento de tumores malignos; ___ needle / aguja de radio, divisa en forma de aguja que contiene radio usada en radioterapia.

radium therapy *n.* radioterapia, terapia con el uso de radio.

radius *n.* radio. 1. hueso largo del antebrazo; 2. línea recta que une el centro y cualquier punto de la circunferencia.

radon *n.* radón, elemento radiactivo gaseoso.

rage *n.* rabia, ira, cólera.

rain *n.* lluvia; *v.* llover.

raise *v.* levantar; [*increase*] aumentar, subir.

raisin *n.* pasa, uva seca.

rale *n.* estertor, sonido anormal originado en el pulmón que se percibe durante la auscultación; coarse ___ / ___ áspero; rackling ___ / ___ crujiente; crepitant ___ /

___ crepitante; dry ___ / ___ seco; moist ___ / ___ húmedo.

ramification *n.* ramificación, distribución en ramas.

ramify *v.* ramificar; ramificarse.

ramus *n.* (*pl.* **rami**) rama, bifurcación, división.

rancid *a.* rancio, de olor desagradable; que denota descomposición.

rancor *n.* rencor, resentimiento.

random control test *n.* prueba de control sin método.

range *n.* escala de diferenciación; ___ of motion / alcance de movimiento.

ranine *n.* ranino-a, rel. a la ránula o parte inferior de la lengua.

ranula *n.* ránula, quiste situado debajo de la lengua causado por la obstrucción de un canal glandular.

rape *n.* violación; *v.* violar, abusar sexualmente.

raphe *n.* rafe, línea de unión de dos mitades simétricas de una estructura tal como la lengua.

rapid *a.* rápido-a, veloz.

rapidity *n.* rapidez, velocidad.

rapport *n.* relación armoniosa.

raptus *L.* raptus, arrebato, ataque súbito violento.

rare *a.* raro-a; único-a; **-ly** *adv.* raramente, casi nunca.

rash, rasche *Fr. n.* rasche, erupción; diaper ___ / eritema de los pañales; heat ___ / salpullido; hemorrhagic ___ / ___ hemorrágica.

raspberry *n.* frambuesa; ___ **mark** / marca de nacimiento de color rosado.

rasura *n.* rasura, raspadura, limadura.

rat *n.* rata.

rate *n.* índice, proporción; tasa; birth ___ / ___ de natalidad; death ___ / ___ de mortalidad; **at any** ___ / de todos modos; no obstante; **at the** ___ **of** / a razón de; *v.* estimar, evaluar, tasar.

rather *adv.* algo, un tanto; bastante; más bien.

ratify *v.* ratificar, confirmar.

rating *n.* evaluación; clasificación, determinación.

ratio *L.* (*pl.* **ratios.**) ratio, expresión de la cantidad de una sustancia en relación con otra.

ration *n.* ración, porción alimenticia.

rational *a.* racional, cuerdo-a, basado-a en la razón.

rationalization *n. psic.* racionalización, mecanismo de defensa por el cual se justifica la conducta o actividades propias con explicaciones que aunque razonables no se ajustan a la realidad.

rattle snake *n.* serpiente de cascabel; ___ **poison** / veneno de la ___.

Rauwolfia serpentina *n. Rauwolfia serpentina,* planta tropical de la cual se obtiene la reserpina, extracto que se usa en el tratamiento de hipertensión y en algunos casos de trastornos mentales.

rave *v.* delirar, hablar irracionalmente.

raw *a.* crudo-a; [*skin*] en carne viva; [*fruit*] sin madurar; [*material*] materia prima.

ray *n.* rayo.

Raynaud's disease *n.* síndrome de Raynaud. *V.* **acrocyanosis.**

Raynaud's phenomenon *n.* fenómeno de Raynaud, síntomas asociados con el síndrome de Raynaud.

razor *n.* navaja, cuchilla.

reach *n.* alcance; **within** ___ / al ___ de; *v.* alcanzar, obtener.

react *v.* reaccionar, responder a un estímulo.

reaction *n.* reacción, respuesta; allergic ___ / ___ alérgica; anaphylactic ___ / ___ anafiláctica; anxiety ___ / ___ de ansiedad; chain ___ / ___ en cadena; conversion ___ / ___ de conversión; immune ___ / ___ inmune; runaway ___ / ___ de escape.

reactivate *v.* reactivar, volver a activar.

reactive *a.* reactivo-a, que tiene la propiedad de reaccionar o de causar una reacción.

reactive depression *n. psic.* reacción depresiva psicótica a consecuencia de una experiencia traumática.

reactivity *n.* reactividad, manifestación de una reacción.

read *vi.* leer; ___ **the letters** / Lea, lee las letras.

reader *n.* lector, lectora.

reading *n.* lectura; ___ **glasses** / anteojos, espejuelos. gafas para leer; ___ **disorders** / transtornos o impedimentos en la ___.

ready *a.* listo-a, preparado-a; *v.* **to get** ___ / prepararse; arreglarse.

reaffirm *v.* reafirmar, asegurar.

reagent *n.* reactivo, agente que produce una reacción.

reagin *n.* reagina, anticuerpo usado en el tra-

tamiento de alergias que estimula la producción de histamina.

real *a.* real, verdadero-a, cierto-a; **-ly** *adv.*
realmente, verdaderamente, ciertamente.

realistic *a.* verdadero-a, realista.

reality *n.* realidad.

reality principle *n.* principio de realidad,
método de orientación del paciente hacia el
mundo externo para provocar el reconocimiento de objetos y actividades olvidados,
esp. dirigido a personas severamente deso-
rientadas.

reality therapy *n.* terapéutica por realidad,
método por el que se enfrenta al paciente
con la realidad ayudándolo a aceptarla.

realize *v.* realizar; llevar a cabo; darse cuenta
de.

reanimate *v.* reanimar, revivir.

rear *a.* posterior, trasero-a.

reason *n.* razón; justificación; *v.* razonar;
justificar.

reasonable *a.* razonable; justificado-a; sensato-a; _____ care / cuidado justificado; _____
charge / honorarios _____ -s; _____ cost /
costo _____ .

reassessment *n.* estimado; reevaluación; _____
of the case / reevaluación del caso.

reassure *v.* asegurar, alentar, reestablecer la
confianza.

reawaken *v.* volver a despertar.

rebel *n.* rebelde.

rebellion *n.* rebelión.

rebound *n.* rebote, regreso a una condición
previa después que el estímulo inicial se
suprime; *v.* rebotar, repercutir.

rebound phenomenon *n.* fenómeno de rebote, movimiento intensificado de una parte
hacia adelante cuando se elimina la fuerza
inicial contra la cual ésta hacía resistencia.

recalcification *n.* recalcificación, restauración de compuestos de calcio en los tejidos.

recall *v.* recordar; reclamar; hacer volver;
acordarse de.

receipt *n.* recibo, carta de pago.

receive *v.* recibir, admitir; acoger; aceptar.

recent *a.* reciente; moderno; nuevo-a; **-ly**
adv. recientemente, hace poco tiempo.

receptaculum *L.* (*pl.* **receptacula**) receptaculum. receptáculo, recipiente.

receptionist *n.* recepcionista.

receptive *a.* receptivo-a, acogedor-a.

receptor *n.* receptor, terminación nerviosa
que recibe un estímulo y lo transmite a otros

nervios; auditory _____ / _____ auditivo; contact _____ / _____ de contacto; proprioceptive
_____ / _____ propioceptivo; sensory _____ /
_____ sensorial; taste _____ / _____ gustativo;
temperature _____ / _____ de temperatura.

recess *n.* suspensión; cavidad, espacio vacío.

recession *n.* receso, retroceso patológico de
tejidos tal como la retracción de la encía.

recessive *a.* recesivo-a. 1. que tiende a retraerse; 2. en genética, rel. al gene que
permanece latente.

recidivation *n.* recidiva, tendencia a recaer
en una condición, enfermedad o síntoma
previos.

recipe *n.* receta, prescripción.

recipient *n.* 1. receptor; vasija; recipiente; 2.
persona que recibe una transfusión, un implante de tejido o un órgano de un donante.

reciprocal *a.* recíproco-a, mutuo-a.

reciprocity *n.* reciprocidad.

reckless *a.* descuidado-a, imprudente.

recklessness *n.* descuido; indiferencia; imprudencia; temeridad.

reclaim *v.* reclamar.

reclamation *n.* reclamación.

recline *n.* reclinación; *v.* reclinar, inclinar;
recostarse.

reclining *a.* recostado-a, inclinado-a.

recognition *n.* reconocimiento, estado de ser
reconocido.

recognize *v.* reconocer; admitir.

recollection *n.* recuerdo, memoria.

recombination *n.* recombinación.

recommend *v.* recomendar; aconsejar.

recommendation *n.* recomendación.

recompense *n.* recompensa, compensación,
reparación.

recompression *n.* recompresión, vuelta a la
presión ambiental normal.

reconcile *v.* reconciliar; reconciliarse; resignarse, conformarse

reconciliation *n.* reconciliación, conformidad.

reconsider *v.* recapacitar; volver a considerar.

reconstitution *n.* reconstitución, restitución
de un tejido a la forma inicial.

reconstruct *v.* reconstruir, reparar, restablecer.

reconstruction *n.* reconstrucción.

record *n.* [*trace of an instrument*] registro;
[*medical history*] historia clínica, expediente; informe; anotación; evidencia;
v. registrar, inscribir; [*on tape*] grabar; **to**

go on ____ / expresar públicamente; **off the** ____ / confidencialmente.

recorder *n.* anotador-a; archivero-a; registrador-a; tape ____ / grabador-a.

recoup *v.* recuperar; recobrar; recuperarse, recobrarse; restablecerse.

recourse *n.* recurso, auxilio.

recover *v.* recobrar, recuperar, restablecer; restablecerse, recobrarse, reponerse.

recovery *n.* recuperación, restablecimiento, recobro, mejoría; **past** ____ / sin remedio, sin cura; ____ **room** / sala de ____.

recreation *n.* recreo, pasatiempo, entretenimiento.

recrudescence *n.* recrudescencia, relapso, reaparición de síntomas.

rectal *a.* rectal, del recto, rel. al recto.

rectification *n.* rectificación, corrección; enmienda.

rectify *v.* rectificar, corregir, enmendar.

rectocele *n.* rectocelo, hernia del recto con protrusión en la vagina.

rectosigmoid *a.* rectosigmoide, rel. al sigmoide y al recto.

rectovaginal *a.* rectovaginal, rel. a la vagina y el recto.

rectovesical *a.* rectovesical, rel. al recto y la vejiga.

rectum *n.* recto, la porción distal del intestino grueso que se extiende de la flexura sigmoidea al ano.

rectus *L.* (*pl.* **recti**) músculo recto; ____ muscles / músculos ____-s; grupo de músculos rectos tales como los situados alrededor del ojo y en la pared abdominal.

recumbent *a.* yacente, acostado-a, recostado-a, reclinado-a, recumbente; ____ position / posición ____.

recuperate *v.* recuperar, recobrar las fuerzas; recuperarse, reponerse.

recuperation *n.* recuperación, restablecimiento.

recur *v.* repetir, volver a ocurrir; recaer, repetirse.

recurrence *n.* recurrencia. 1. reaparición de síntomas después de una remisión; 2. relapso, recaída.

recurrent *a.* recurrente, repetido-a.

red *n.* [*color*] rojo; ____ **cell** / glóbulo rojo, hematíe, eritrocito; Congo ____ / ____ Congo; scarlet ____ / ____ escarlata.

redden *v.* enrojecer, dar color rojo.

reddish *a.* rojizo-a, enrojecido-a.

red-eyed *a.* de ojos enrojecidos; con los ojos inyectados.

red faced *a.* ruborizado-a, con la cara encendida.

redhead *a.* pelirrojo-a.

red-hot *a.* muy caliente, candente.

redness *n.* enrojecimiento.

redress *v.* volver a vendar; poner un nuevo vendaje; remediar.

reduce *v.* reducir, rebajar; disminuir. 1. restaurar a la situación normal, tal como un hueso fracturado o dislocado; 2. disminuir la potencia al dar hidrógeno o quitarle oxígeno a un compuesto; 3. bajar de peso.

reducible *a.* reducible, susceptible a la reducción.

reducing exercises *n. pl.* ejercicios para adelgazar, ejercicios para bajar de peso.

reductase *n.* reductasa, enzima que actúa como catalítico en el proceso de reducción.

reduction *n.* reducción, disminución, acción de reducir.

reductor *n.* reductor, agente que causa reducción en otras sustancias.

reeducation *n.* reeducación, enseñanza con entrenamiento para recobrar funciones motoras o mentales.

refer *v.* referir, atribuir, asignar, referirse a.

reference *n.* referencia; ____ values / valores de ____.

referral *n.* recomendación; remisión; ____ and consultation / ____ y consulta.

refill *n.* repuesto; repetición; relleno; repetición de una receta; *v.* reponer; repetir; rellenar.

refine *v.* refinar, purificar.

reflect *v.* reflejar; **to** ____ **upon** / reflexionar.

reflection *n.* reflexión. 1. acomodamiento o vuelta hacia atrás tal como una membrana que después de llegar a la superficie de un órgano se repliega sobre sí misma; 2. rechazo de la luz u otra forma de energía radiante de una superficie; 3. introspección.

reflex *n.* reflejo, respuesta motora involuntaria a un estímulo; Achilles tendon ____ / ____ del tendón de Aquiles; ____ action / acto, acción ____; ____ arch / arco ____; behavior ____ / ____ adquirido; chain ____ / ____ en cadena; conditioned ____ / ____ condicionado; instinctive ____ / ____ instintivo; patelar ____ / ____ patelar o rotuliano; radial ____ / ____ radial; rectal ____ /

_____ rectal; stretch _____ / _____ de estiramiento; unconditioned _____ / _____ no condicionado.

reflexogenic _n._ reflexógeno, agente que causa un reflejo.

reflux _n._ reflujo, flujo retrógrado.

reform _n._ reforma, cambio; _v._ reformar, cambiar; reformarse.

refract _v._ refractar, desviar. 1. cambiar una dirección tal como la de un rayo de luz al pasar de un medio a otro de diferente densidad; 2. rectificar anormalidades de refracción en el ojo y corregirlas.

refraction _n._ refracción, acto de refractar; ocular _____ / _____ ocular.

refractivity _n._ refractividad, habilidad de refractar.

refractory _a._ refractario-a. 1. resistente a un tratamiento; 2. que no responde a un estímulo.

refresh _v._ refrescar; renovar, revivir; refrescarse; renovarse.

refreshing _a._ refrescante.

refreshment _n._ refresco; refrigerio.

refrigerant _a._ refrigerante; antipirético-a.

refrigerate _v._ refrigerar, mantener en el frío.

refrigeration _n._ refrigeración, reducción del calor a una temperatura fría por medios externos.

refringent _a._ refringente, rel. a la refracción o que la causa.

refuge _n._ refugio; asilo; _v._ **to take** _____ / refugiarse.

refugee _n._ refugiado-a.

refuse _n._ desecho, basura; desperdicios.

regain _v._ recuperar, recobrar; **to** _____ **consciousness** / recobrar el conocimiento.

regard _n._ respeto, consideración; **in** _____ **to** / respecto a; **regards** / recuerdos.

regarding _prep._ respecto a.

regenerate _v._ regenerar.

regeneration _n._ regeneración, restauración, renovación.

regime _n._ régimen, regla, plan, esp. en referencia a una dieta o ejercicio físico.

region _n._ región, parte del cuerpo más o menos delimitada.

regional _a._ regional; _____ **medical programs** / programas médicos _____ -es.

registration _n._ registro, inscripción; [_courses_] matrícula.

regression _n._ regresión, retrogresión. 1. vuelta a una condición anterior; 2. apaci-

guamiento de síntomas o de un proceso patológico.

regret _n._ sentimiento de pesar; remordimiento; _v._ sentir, lamentar deplorar; **I** _____ **to tell you** / Siento decirle, decirte.

regrettable _a._ lamentable; infortunado-a.

regular _a._ regular, común; **-ly** _adv._ regularmente, con regularidad.

regularity _n._ regularidad, normalidad.

regulate _v._ regular, ordenar.

regulation _n._ regulación, norma o regla.

regulator _n._ regulador-a.

regurgitant _a._ regurgitante, rel. a la regurgitación.

regurgitate _v._ regurgitar.

regurgitation _n._ regurgitación. 1. acto de devolver o expulsar la comida de la boca; 2. flujo retrógrado de la sangre a través de una válvula defectuosa del corazón; aortic _____ / _____ aórtica; mitral _____ / _____ mitral.

rehabilitate _v._ rehabilitar, ayudar a recobrar funciones normales por medio de métodos terapéuticos.

rehabilitation _n._ rehabilitación, acto de rehabilitar.

rehabilitee _n._, _a._ rehabilitado-a.

rehydration _n._ rehidratación, restablecimiento del balance hídrico del cuerpo.

reimplantation _n._ reimplantación. 1. restauración de un tejido o parte; 2. restitución de un óvulo al útero después de extraerlo y fecundarlo _in vitro._

reinfection _n._ reinfección, infección subsecuente por el mismo microorganismo.

reinforce _v._ reforzar; enforzar.

reinfusion _n._ reinfusión, reinyección de suero sanguíneo o líquido cefalorraquídeo.

reinnervation _n._ reinervación, injerto de un nervio para restaurar la función de un músculo.

reinnoculation _n._ reinoculación, inoculación subsecuente con el mismo microorganismo.

reject _n._ rechazar, rehusar.

rejection _n._ rechazo, reacción inmunológica de incompatibilidad a células de tejidos transplantados; acute _____ / _____ agudo; chronic _____ / _____ crónico.

rejuvenate _v._ rejuvenecer; rejuvenecerse.

rejuvenescense _n._ rejuvenecimiento.

relapse _n._ relapso, recaída, volver a sufrir una enfermedad o los síntomas de ésta después de cierta mejoría.

relapsing fever _n._ fiebre recurrente.

relate v. relacionar; establecer una relación; relacionarse.

related a. relacionado-a; emparentado-a.

relation n. relación; comparación.

relationship n. relación, parentesco, lazo familiar.

relative n. pariente, familiar; a. relativo-a; gr. pronombre relativo.

relax v. relajar el cuerpo, reducir tensión; relajarse.

relaxant n. relajante, tranquilizante; droga que reduce la tensión.

relaxation n. relajación, acto de relajar o de relajarse; reposo, descanso.

relaxed a. relajado-a.

release n. información; liberación; v. soltar, librar, desprender; [*to inform*] informar, dar a conocer.

releasing hormone n. hormona estimulante.

reliable a. [*person*] formal, responsable; seguro-a.

relief n. alivio, mejoría; ayuda, auxilio; **What a ___! / ¡Ay, qué ___!;** v. **to be on ___ /** recibir asistencia social.

relieve v. [*pain*] aliviar, mejorar.

religion n. religión.

religious a. religioso-a.

reluctant a. renuente; resistente; contrario-a.

rely v. depender, contar con, confiar en.

remain v. permanecer; **to ___ in bed /** guardar cama.

remainder n. resto, residuo.

remains n. pl. restos, despojos.

remarkable a. extraordinario-a, notable.

remedial a. remediador-a, reparador-a, curativo-a.

remedy n. remedio, cura, medicamento; v. remediar, curar.

remember v. recordar, acordarse; **___ correctly! / ¡Acuérdese, acuérdate bien!; Don't you ___? / ¿No se acuerda?, ¿no te acuerdas?**

remineralization n. remineralización, reemplazo de minerales perdidos en el cuerpo.

reminisce v. recordar; divagar.

remission n. remisión. 1. disminución o cesación de los síntomas de una enfermedad; 2. período de tiempo durante el cual los síntomas de una enfermedad disminuyen.

remittent a. remitente, que se repite a intervalos.

remorse n. remordimiento.

remote a. remoto-a, distante.

removal n. extirpación, remoción.

remove v. sacar; quitar, extraer; extirpar.

renal a. renal, rel. a o semejante al riñón; **___ clearance test /** prueba de aclaramiento o depuración **___; ___ failure, acute /** insuficiencia **___** aguda; **___** insufficiency / insuficiencia **___; ___** papillary necrosis / necrosis papilar **___; ___** pelvis / pelvis **___; ___** transplantation / transplante **___.**

renew v. renovar.

renin n. renina, enzima segregada por el riñón que interviene en la regulación de la presión arterial.

renogram n. renograma, proceso de monitoreo del índice de eliminación sanguínea a través del riñón usando una sustancia radiactiva inyectada previamente.

renovate v. reformar, innovar.

reopen v. volver a abrir, abrir de nuevo.

repair n. reparación, restauración; v. reparar, restaurar.

repeat v. repetir, reiterar.

repellent a. repelente.

repercussion n. repercusión. 1. penetración o dispersión de una inflamación, tumor o erupción; 2. peloteo.

replace v. reemplazar, reponer, substituir.

replacement n. reemplazo, substitución, repuesto; v. reemplazar, substituir, reponer.

replete a. repleto-a, lleno-a en exceso.

replication n. reproducción, duplicación.

reply n. contestación, respuesta; v. contestar, responder.

repolarization n. repolarización, restablecimiento de la polarización de una célula, o de una fibra nerviosa o muscular después de su depolarización.

report n. informe, reporte; v. informar, reportar.

reprehensible a. reprobable, censurable.

repress v. reprimir.

repression n. represión. 1. inhibición de una acción; 2. *psic.* mecanismo de defensa por el que se eliminan del campo de la conciencia deseos e impulsos en conflicto.

reproduce v. reproducir; reproducirse.

reproducer n. reproductor.

reproduction n. reproducción; sexual **___ / ___** sexual.

reproductive a. reproductivo-a, rel. a la reproducción.

repudiate v. repudiar, repeler.

repugnant a. repugnante, repulsivo-a.

repulsion *n.* repulsión, aversión, repugnancia.

repulsive *a.* repulsivo-a, chocante.

reputation *n.* reputación, fama, nombre.

reputed *a.* reputado-a, distinguido-a, de buena fama.

request *n.* petición, encargo; solicitud; *v.* pedir, hacer una petición, [*of supplies*] encargar.

require *v.* requerir, solicitar.

required *a.* requerido-a, necesario-a; mandatorio-a.

requirement *n.* requerimiento.

requisite *n.* requisito.

rescind *v.* rescindir, anular; terminar.

rescue *v.* salvar, rescatar, librar.

research *n.* investigación, indagación, pesquisa; *v.* investigar, indagar, hacer in vestigaciones.

resect *n.* resecar. 1. cortar una porción de un órgano o tejido; 2. hacer una resección.

resection *n.* resección, acto de resecar; gastric ___ / ___ gástrica; transurethral ___ / ___ transuretral; wedge ___ / ___ en cuña.

resectoscope *n.* resectoscopio, instrumento quirúrgico provisto de un electrodo cortante como el que se usa para la resección de la próstata a través de la uretra.

resectoscopy *n.* resectoscopía, resección de la próstata con un resectoscopio.

resemblance *n.* semejanza, parecido.

resemble *v.* tener semejanza; parecerse a.

resentment *n.* resentimiento, rencor.

reserpine *n.* reserpina, derivado de la *Rauwolfia serpentina* que se usa principalmente en el tratamiento de la hipertensión y de desórdenes emocionales.

reservation *n.* reservación, reserva.

reserve *n.* reserva, sustancia, objeto o idea que se guarda para uso futuro; *v.* reservar; conservar, guardar.

reserved *a.* reservado- a, [*personality*] reservado-a, callado-a.

reside *v.* residir, vivir.

residency *n.* residencia, período de entrenamiento médico especializado que se hace gen. en un hospital.

resident *n.* médico-a residente, que cursa una residencia.

residual *a.* residual, restante, remanente; ___ function / función ___ ; ___ urine / orina ___ .

residue *n.* residuo; ___ diet, high / dieta de

___ alto; ___ diet, low / dieta de ___ bajo.

resign *v.* renunciar, resignar, desistir; resignarse.

resilience *n.* elasticidad. *V.* **elasticity.**

resilient *a.* elástico-a.

resin *n.* resina, sustancia vegetal insoluble en el agua aunque soluble en alcohol y éter que tiene una variedad de usos medicinales y dentales.

res ipsa loquitur *L.* res ipsa loquitor, evidente, que habla por sí mismo.

resist *v.* resistir; rechazar.

resistance *n.* resistencia, oposición; capacidad de un organismo para resistir efectos dañinos; initial ___ / ___ inicial; acquired ___ / ___ adquirida; *v.* **to offer** ___ / oponerse; hacer resistencia.

resistant *a.* resistente; fast ___ / resistencia a un colorante.

resolute *a.* resuelto-a, determinado-a.

resolution *n.* resolución. 1. terminación de un proceso inflamatorio; 2. habilidad de distinguir detalles pequeños y sutiles tal como se hace a través de un microscopio; 3. descomposición sin supuración.

resolve *v.* resolver. 1. encontrar una solución; 2. descomponer, analizar, separar en componentes.

resonance *n.* resonancia, capacidad de aumentar la intensidad de un sonido; normal ___ / ___ normal; vesicular ___ / ___ vesicular; vocal ___ / ___ vocal.

resonant *a.* resonante, que da un sonido vibrante a la percusión.

resorcinol *n.* resorcinol, agente usado en el tratamiento de acné y otras dermatosis.

resorption *n.* resorción, pérdida total o parcial de un proceso, tejido o exudado por resultado de reacciones bioquímicas tales como lisis y absorción.

resort *n.* recurso; **health** ___ / lugar de recuperación física; **the last** ___ / el último ___ ; *v.* acudir, pedir ayuda, recurrir.

resource *n.* recurso, medio.

respect *n.* respeto, consideración; *v.* respetar, considerar.

respectable *a.* respetable, acreditado-a.

respiration *n.* respiración, proceso respiratorio; abdominal ___ / ___ abdominal; aerobic ___ / ___ aeróbica; accelerated ___ / ___ acelerada; anaerobic ___ / ___ anaeróbica; diaphragmatic ___ / ___ diafragmática; air hunger, gasping ___ / ___ jadeante; labored ___ / ___ laboriosa.

respirator *n.* respirador, aparato para purificar el aire que se inhala o para producir respiración artificial; chest___ / ___ torácico.

respiratory *a.* respiratorio-a, rel. a la respiración; ___ care unit / unidad de cuidado ___ ; ___ quotient / cociente ___ ; ___ distress syndrome / síndrome de dificultad ___ ; ___ failure, acute / insuficiencia ___ aguda; ___ failure, chronic / insuficiencia ___ crónica; ___ function tests / pruebas de función ___ ; ___ system / sistema ___ ; ___ tract infections and diseases / infecciones y enfermedades de las vías ___ -s.

respiratory center *n.* centro respiratorio, área en la médula oblongata que regula los movimientos respiratorios.

response *n.* respuesta. 1. reacción o cambio de un órgano o parte a un estímulo; immune ___ / ___ inmune; 2. reacción de un paciente a un tratamiento.

responsibility *n.* responsabilidad.

responsible *a.* responsable.

rest *n.* descanso, reposo; residuo, resto; ___ cure / cura de reposo; *v.* descansar, reposar.

restful *a.* tranquilo-a, quieto-a.

resting *a.* inactivo-a, en reposo, en estado de descanso.

restitutio ad integrum *L.* restitutio ad integrum, recuperación total de la salud.

restoration *n.* restauración, restitución, restablecimiento, acción de restituir algo a su estado original.

restorative *n.* restaurativo, agente que estimula la restauración.

restore *v.* restituir, restablecer.

restraint *n.* restricción; confinamiento; ___ in bed / ___ en cama; mechanical ___ / ___ mecánica; medicinal ___ / ___ con uso de medicamentos.

restrict *v.* restringir, confinar.

restricted *a.* limitado-a, confinado; ___ area / área ___ .

result *n.* resultado, conclusión.

resuscitate *v.* resucitar; reanimar.

resuscitation *n.* resucitación. 1. devolver la vida; reanimar el corazón; 2. respiración artificial.

resuscitator *n.* resucitador, aparato automático de asistencia respiratoria.

retain *v.* retener, guardar; quedarse con.

retainer *n.* [*dentistry*] aro, freno de retención.

retardate *a.* retardado-a, retrasado-a, atrasado-a.

retardation *n.* retraso, atraso, retardo anormal de una función motora o mental. *V.* **mental retardation.**

retch *n.* arcada, basca, contracciones abdominales espasmódicas que preceden al vómito.

rete *L.* (*pl.* **retia**) rete. *V.* **network.**

retention *n.* retención, conservación; ___ enema / enema de ___ ; urinary ___ / ___ urinaria.

reticular *a.* reticular, retiforme, en forma de red.

reticulation *n.* reticulación, disposición reticular.

reticulocyte *n.* reticulocito, célula roja inmadura, eritrocito en red o gránulos que aparece durante la regeneración de la sangre.

reticulocytopenia, reticulosis *n.* reticulocitopenia, reticulosis, disminución anormal del número de reticulocitos en la sangre.

reticulocytosis *n.* reticulocitosis, aumento en el número de reticulocitos.

reticuloendothelial system *n.* sistema reticuloendotelial, red de células fagocíticas (excepto leucocitos circulantes) esparcidas por todo el cuerpo que intervienen en procesos tales como la formación de células sanguíneas, destrucción de grasas, eliminación de células gastadas y restauración de tejidos que son participantes esenciales en el proceso inmunológico del organismo.

reticuloendothelioma *n.* reticuloendotelioma, tumor del sistema reticuloendotelial.

reticuloendothelium *n.* reticuloendotelio, tejido del sistema reticuloendotelial.

reticulohistiocytoma *n.* reticulohistiocitoma, agregación de células granulares y gigantes.

reticulopenia *n.* reticulopenia. *V.* **reticulocytopenia.**

reticulum *n.* retículo. 1. red de nervios y vasos sanguíneos; 2. tejido reticular.

Retin-A *n.* Retin-A, nombre comercial del ácido retinoico, medicamento usado en el tratamiento de acné.

retina *n.* retina, la capa más interna del ojo que recibe imágenes y transmite impulsos visuales al cerebro; detachment of the ___ / desprendimiento de la ___ .

retinal *a.* de la retina, retiniano-a; rel. a la retina; ____ degeneration / deterioramiento ____ ; ____ perforation / perforación ____ .

retinitis *n.* retinitis, infl. de la retina.

retinoblastoma *n.* retinoblastoma, tumor maligno de la retina gen. hereditario.

retinol *n.* retinol, vitamina A₁.

retinopathy *n.* retinopatía, cualquier condición anormal de la retina.

retinoscopy *n.* retinoscopía, determinación y evaluación de errores visuales de refracción.

retinosis *n.* retinosis, proceso degenerativo de la retina.

retire *v.* retirar; [*from work*] retirarse, jubilarse; [*to bed*] irse a acostar.

retired *a. pp.* de **to retire**, retirado-a; [*from work*] retirado-a, jubilado-a; [*withdrawn*] reservado-a; retirado-a; [*secluded*] alejado-a, apartado-a.

retiree *n.* jubilado-a; retirado-a.

retract *v.* retraer, retractar; retraerse, volverse hacia atrás.

retractile *a.* retráctil, retractable.

retraction *n.* retracción, encogimiento, contracción; acto de echarse hacia atrás; clot ____ / ____ del coágulo; uterine ____ / ____ uterina.

retractor *n.* retractor. 1. instrumento para separar los bordes de una herida; 2. tipo de músculo que retrae una parte u órgano.

retrieval *n.* recuperación de algo.

retroaction *n.* retroacción, acción retroactiva.

retroactive *a.* retroactivo-a, de acción retroactiva.

retroauricular *a.* retroauricular, rel. a o situado detrás de la oreja o aurícula.

retrocecal *a.* retrocecal, rel. a o situado detrás del ciego.

retrocession *n.* retroceso.

retroflexion *n.* retroflexión, flexión de un órgano hacia atrás.

retrograde *a.* retrógrado-a, que se mueve hacia atrás o retorna al pasado; ____ amnesia / amnesia ____ ; ____ aortography / aortografía ____ ; ____ pyelography / pielografía ____ .

retrogression *n.* retrogresión, regreso a un estado más primitivo de desarrollo.

retrolental *a.* retrolental, situado detrás del cristalino; ____ fibroplasia / fibroplasia ____ .

retroperitoneal *a.* retroperitoneano-a, rel. a o situado detrás del perineo.

retroplasia *n.* retroplasia. *V.* **anaplasia.**

retrospective *a.* retrospectivo-a; ____ study / estudio ____ .

retroversion *n.* retroversión, vuelta hacia atrás; ____ of uterus / desplazamiento del útero hacia atrás.

retrovirus *n.* retrovirus, virus que pertenece al grupo ácido ARN, algunos de los cuales son oncogénicos.

retry *v.* ensayar de nuevo.

return *n.* regreso, retorno; *v.* regresar.

Retzius, space of *n.* espacio de Retzius, área entre la vejiga y los huesos del pubis.

reunion *n.* reunión, unión de partes o tejidos esp. en un hueso fracturado o partes de una herida al cicatrizar.

revascularization *n.* revascularización, proceso de restauración de la sangre a una parte del cuerpo después de una lesión o una derivación quirúrgica.

reversal *n.* reversión, restitución a un estado anterior.

review *n.* revisión, análisis, repaso; [*literary*] reseña; *v.* repasar, volver a ver.

revise *v.* revisar, repasar, mirar con detenimiento.

revision *n.* revisión.

revitalize *n.* revitalizar, vivificar, volver a dar fuerzas.

revive *v.* revivir.

revulsion *n.* revulsión.

revulsive *a.* revulsivo-a, rel. a la revulsión o que la causa.

Reye's syndrome *n.* síndrome de Reye, enfermedad aguda que se manifiesta en niños y adolescentes con edema agudo en órganos importantes esp. en el cerebro y el hígado.

rhabdomyosarcoma *n.* rabdomiosarcoma, tumor maligno de fibras musculares estriadas que afecta gen. los músculos esqueléticos.

rhachitis *n.* raquitismo. *V.* **rickets.**

RH blood group *n.* grupo sanguíneo Rh. *V.* **blood group.**

rheum, rheuma *n.* 1. reuma, secreción catarral o acuosa por la nariz; 2. reumatismo.

rheumatic *a.* reumático-a, rel. a o afectado por reumatismo.

rheumatic fever *n.* fiebre reumática, fiebre o condición acompañada de dolores en las articulaciones que puede dejar como secuela trastornos cardíacos y renales.

rheumatism *n.* reumatismo, enfermedad aguda crónica caracterizada por infl. y dolor en las articulaciones.

rheumatoid *a.* reumatoide, de naturaleza semejante al reumatismo.

RH genes *n. pl.* genes Rh, determinantes de los distintos tipos sanguíneos Rh.

rhinal *a.* rinal, rel. a la nariz.

rhinitis *n.* rinitis, infl. de la mucosa nasal.

rhinolaryngitis *n.* rinolaringitis, infl. simultánea de las mucosas nasales y laríngeas.

rhinopharyngitis *n.* rinofaringitis, infl. de la nasofaringe.

rhinophyma *n.* rinofima, acné rosácea aguda en el área de la naris.

rhinoplasty *n. cirg.* rinoplastia, cirugía plástica de la nariz.

rhinorrhea *n.* rinorrea, secreción mucosolíquida por la nariz.

rhinoscopy *n.* rinoscopía, examen de los pasajes nasales a través de la nasofaringe o de los orificios nasales.

rhizotomy *n. cirg.* rizotomía, división o transección de la raíz de un nervio.

rhodopsin *n.* rodopsina, pigmento de color rojo púrpura que se encuentra en los bastoncillos de la retina y que facilita la visión en luz tenue.

rhythm *n.* ritmo, regularidad en la acción o función de un órgano u órganos del cuerpo tal como el corazón.

rhythmical *a.* rítmico-a.

rhytidectomy *n.* ritidectomía, estiramiento de la piel de la cara por medio de cirugía plástica.

rib *n.* costilla, uno de los huesos de una serie de doce pares que forman la pared torácica.

riboflavin *n.* riboflabina, vitamina B_2, componente del complejo vitamínico B esencial en la nutrición.

ribonucleoprotein *n.* ribonucleoproteína, sustancia que contiene proteína y ácido ribonucleico.

rich *a.* [*wealth*] rico-a, opulento-a; [*food*] muy sazonado-a, muy condimentado-a.

rickets *n.* raquitismo. *V.* **rachitism.**

rickettsia *n.* ricketsia, rickettsia, uno de los organismos gram-negativos que se reproducen solamente en células huéspedes de pulgas, piojos, garrapatas y ratones, y se transmiten a humanos a través de las mordidas de éstos.

ridge *n.* borde, reborde, elevación prolongada.

rifampicin *n.* rifampicina, sustancia semisintética, antibacteriana que se usa en el tratamiento de la tuberculosis pulmonar.

right *n.* justicia; derecho; *a.* derecho-a, rel. a la parte derecha del cuerpo; recto-a, correcto-a; ___-**handed** / diestro-a, que usa con preferencia la mano derecha; **on the** ___ **side** / al costado o lado derecho; [*health*] sano-a; *v.* **to be in one's** ___ **mind** / estar en su juicio, estar cuerdo-a; **the** ___ **medication** / la medicina necesaria; **the** ___ **treatment** / el tratamiento adecuado; [*in a problem*] **taking the** ___ **direction** / la solución indicada; **Everything is all** ___ / Todo está bien; ___ **or wrong** / con o sin razón; *adv.* bien, correctamente; mismo; **It is going all** ___ / Todo sigue bien; ___ **here** / aquí mismo.

rights of the patient *n. pl.* derechos del paciente.

rigid *a.* rígido-a, tieso, inmóvil.

rigidity *n.* rigidez, tesura, inmovilidad, inflexibilidad; **cadaveric** ___ / ___ cadavérica, rigor mortis.

rigor *n.* rigor. 1. escalofrío repentino con fiebre alta; 2. tesura, inflexibilidad muscular.

ring *n.* anillo, círculo; *vi.* sonar; zumbar.

ringing *a.* resonante, retumbante; ___ **ears** / tintineo, zumbido, ruido en los oídos.

ringworm *n.* tiña.

rip *v.* rasgar, desgarrar.

ripe *a.* [*fruit*] maduro-a; [*boil, cataract*] madurado-a.

ripen *v.* madurar; madurarse.

ripening *n.* reblandecimiento, dilatación tal como la del cuello uterino durante el parto.

ripping *n.* laceración, rasgadura; descosedura.

rise *n.* ascensión, subida, salida, crecimiento; *vi.* ascender, subir; [*from bed*] levantarse o salir de la cama; **to** ___ **to one's feet** / ponerse de pie.

risk *n.* riesgo, peligro; ___ **of contamination** / riesgo o peligro de contaminación; ___ **factors** / factores de ___; **high** ___ **groups** / grupos de alto ___; **potential** ___ / ___ posible. *v.* poner en peligro; arriesgarse.

risky *a.* arriesgado-a, peligroso-a.

risorious *n.* risorio, músculo que se inserta en la comisura de la boca.

ristocetin *n.* ristocetina, antibiótico que se

usa en el tratamiento de infecciones producidas por un estreptococo gram-positivo.

Ritalin hydrochloride *n.* clorhidrato de Ritalin, estimulante y antidepresivo benigno.

ritual *n.* ritual, rito.

rivalry *n.* rivalidad; competencia.

roach *n.* cucaracha.

road *n.* camino, carretera; curso.

roast *a.* asado-a ____ **meat** / carne ____; *v.* asar, hornear.

robe *n.* [*dressing gown*] bata.

robust *a.* robusto-a, vigoroso-a.

rod *n.* bastoncillo; varilla.

rodent *n.* roedor; *a.* roedor-a; ____ ulcer / úlcera roedora, que destruye poco a poco.

rodenticide *n.* rodenticida, agente que destruye roedores.

roentgenography *n.* radiografía.

role *n.* [*theatre*] papel; *v.* **to play the** ____ **of** / hacer el ____ de.

role model *n.* prototipo, modelo.

roll *n.* panecillo; *v.* rodar.

Romberg's sign *n.* signo de Romberg, oscilación del cuerpo que indica inhabilidad de mantener el equilibrio en posición erecta, con los pies juntos y los ojos cerrados.

rongeur *Fr.* rongeur, fórceps o pinzas para extraer astillas de hueso y tejidos endurecidos.

room *n.* cuarto, sala; **bath** ____ / ____ de baño; **delivery** ____ / sala de partos; **operating** ____ / sala de operaciones, quirófano; **the patient's** ____ / ____ del paciente; **recovery** ____ / sala de recuperación; ____ **temperature** / temperatura ambiente; **waiting** ____ / sala de espera.

root *n.* raíz; radical.

Rorschach test *n.* prueba de Rorschach, prueba psicológica por la cual se revelan rasgos de la personalidad a través de la interpretación de una serie de borrones de tinta.

rosary *n.* rosario, estructura que se asemeja a cuentas enlazadas.

rosemary *n.* romero.

roseola *n.* roséola, condición de la piel caracterizada por manchas rosáceas de varios tamaños.

rosette *F.* rosette, células en formación semejante a una rosa.

rose water *n.* agua de rosa.

rostral *a.* rostral, rel. o semejante a un rostro.

rostrum *L.* rostro. 1. cara; 2. pico, proyección.

rosy *a.* rosado-a, de color de rosa

rot *v.* podrirse, pudrirse, echarse a perder.

rotary *a.* rotatorio-a; giratorio-a.

rotate *v.* rotar, girar, voltear.

rotation *n.* rotación; fetal ____ / ____ de la cabeza del feto.

rotten *a.* podrido-a, putrefacto-a, corrompido-a; [*tooth*] cariado-a.

rough *a.* [*surface, skin*] áspero-a, escabroso-a; [*character*] rudo-a. grosero-a; *v.* **to have a** ____ **time** / pasarla mal.

round *a.* redondo-a, circular; ____ **shouldered** / cargado de espaldas; **all year** ____ / todo el año.

route *n.* ruta.

routine *n.* rutina, hábito, costumbre; *a.* rutinario-a.

rub *n.* 1. fricción, frote, frotación, masaje; 2. sonido producido por el roce de dos superficies secas que se detecta en auscultación; *v.* frotar, hacer penetrar un unguento o pomada en la piel; friccionar; **to** ____ **off** / limpiar frotando; borrar; **to** ____ **down** / dar un masaje.

rubber *n.* goma; ____ **bulb** / perilla de ____; ____ **gloves** / guantes de ____.

rubbing *n.* masaje.

rubbing alcohol *n.* alcohol para fricciones.

rubefacient *n.* enrojecedor, agente que enrojece la piel.

rubella *n.* rubéola, sarampión alemán; *pop. Mex.* pelusa, enfermedad infecciosa viral que se manifiesta con dolor de garganta, fiebre y una erupción rosácea y que puede ocasionar serios trastornos fetales si la madre la contrae durante los primeros tres meses del embarazo.

rubella virus vaccine, live *n.* vacuna de virus vivo contra la rubéola.

rubescent *a.* ruborizado-a, que se enrojece.

rubor *n.* rubor, enrojecimiento de la piel.

rudiment *n.* rudimento. 1. órgano parcialmente desarrollado; 2. órgano o parte que ha perdido total o parcialmente su función anterior.

ruga *n.* L. (*pl.* **rugae**) arruga, pliegue.

rugose *a.* arrugado-a, lleno-a de arrugas.

rugosity *n.* rugosidad, arruga.

rule *n.* régimen, regla, precepto; **rules and regulations** / según el reglamento; **as a** ____ / por lo general; *v.* gobernar, administrar; **to** ____ **out** / prohibir, desechar; **to**

be ruled by one's emotions / dejarse llevar por las emociones.

rumble *n.* ruido sordo; estruendo.

run *n.* carrera; *vi.* correr, hacer correr; to ___ a fever / tener calentura.

rupture *n.* [*hernia*] ruptura; [*bone*] rotura, fractura; [*boil*] reventazón; *v.* reventar, romper, fracturar; abrirse, reventarse, romperse, fracturarse.

rush *n.* precipitación, agolpamiento, torrente; oleada; **with a** ___ / de golpe, de repente; *v.* darse prisa; **to** ___ **in** / entrar de golpe, entrar con precipitación.

rusty *a.* oxidado-a.

rye *n.* centeno.

S

S *abbr.* **sacral** / sacral; **second** / segundo; **section** / sección; **singular** / singular; **stimulus** / estímulo; **subject** / sujeto; **sulphur** / sulfuro, azufre

Sabin vaccine *n.* vacuna de Sabin, vacuna oral contra la poliomielitis.

sac *n.* saco, bolsa; estructura u órgano en forma de saco o bolsa.

saccades *n.* sacades. *V.* **nystagmus.**

saccharide *n.* sacárido, compuesto químico que pertenece a una serie de carbohidratos que incluye los azúcares.

saccharine *n.* sacarina, sustancia sumamente dulce, agente dulcificante artificial, *a.* sacarino-a, azucarado-a.

saccule *n.* sáculo, saco o bolsa pequeña.

sacral *a.* sacral, rel. al sacro o situado cerca de éste; ___ nerves / nervios ___ -es; plexus ___ / plexo ___.

sacralization *n.* sacralización, fusión de la quinta vértebra lumbar con el sacro.

sacrifice *n.* sacrificio; *v.* sacrificar.

sacroilitis *n.* sacroilitis, infl. de la articulación sacroilíaca.

sacrolumbar *a.* sacrolumbar, rel. a las regiones sacra y lumbar.

sacrum *n.* sacro, hueso triangular formado por cinco vértebras fusionadas en la base de la espina dorsal y entre los dos huesos de la cadera.

sad *a.* triste, desconsolado-a.

saddle back *n.* espalda caída. *V.* **lordosis.**

sadism *n.* sadismo, perversión por la cual se obtiene placer sexual inflingiendo dolor físico o psicológico a otros.

sadist *n.* sadista, persona que practica sadismo.

sadistic *a.* sádico-a, rel. al sadismo.

sadness *n.* tristeza, melancolía.

sadomasochism *n.* sadomasoquismo, derivación de placer sexual inflingiendo dolor físico a sí mismo o a otros.

sadomasochist *n.* sadomasoquista, persona que practica sadomasoquismo.

safe *a.* seguro-a, sin peligro; sin riesgo; **-ly** *adv.* seguramente.

safety *n.* seguridad, protección; ___ **pin** / imperdible.

sag *v.* perder elasticidad, perder la forma; combarse; pandearse; [*to weaken*] debilitarse.

sage *n.* salvia.

sagittal *a.* sagital, semejante a una saeta; ___ **plane** / plano ___ paralelo al eje longitudinal del cuerpo.

said *a. pp.* de **to say,** dicho; dicho-a, citado-a, antes mencionado.

salacious *a.* lascivo-a, libidinoso-a.

salad *n.* ensalada.

salary *n.* sueldo, salario.

salicylate *n.* salicilato, cualquier sal de ácido salicílico; ___ **poisoning** / envenenamiento por aspirina.

salicylic acid *n.* ácido salicílico, ácido cristalino blanco derivado del fenol.

salicylism *n.* salicilismo, condición tóxica causada por ingestión excesiva de ácido salicílico.

salient *a.* saliente, pronunciado-a.

saline *a.* salino-a; ___ **solution** / solución ___; agua destilada con sal; ___ **cathartic** / purgante ___.

saliva *n.* saliva, secreción de las glándulas salivales que envuelve y humedece el bolo alimenticio en la boca y facilita la deglución.

salivant *a.* salivoso-a, rel. a la saliva.

salivary glands *n. pl.* glándulas salivales o salivares.

salivation *n.* salivación. 1. acto de secreción de saliva; 2. secreción excesiva de saliva.

Salk vaccine *n.* vacuna de Salk, vacuna contra la poliomielitis.

sallow *a.* pálido-a, lívido-a.

salmon *n.* salmón.

salmonella *n.* Salmonela, género de bacterias gram-negativas de la familia *Enterobac-*

teriaceae que causan fiebres entéricas, otras infecciones gastrointestinales y septicemia.

salmonellosis *n.* salmonelosis, infección causada por ingestión de comida contaminada por bacterias del género Salmonela.

salpingectomy *n. cirg.* salpingectomía, extirpación de una o de ambas trompas de Falopio.

salpingitis *n.* salpingitis, infl. de las trompas de Falopio.

salpingo-oophorectomy *n. cirg.* salpingo-ooforectomía, extirpación de un ovario y un tubo uterino.

salpingoplasty *n. cirg.* reparación plástica de las trompas de Falopio.

salpinx *Gr.* (*pl.* **salpinges**) trompa, estructura similar a la trompa de Eustaquio o a la trompa dc Falopio.

salt *n.* sal, cloruro de sodio; iodized ___ / ___ yodada; noniodized ___ / ___ corriente; **smelling** ___-s / ___-es aromáticas; ___ **shaker** / salero; ___ free diet / dieta libre de ___ o sin ___; low ___ diet / dieta hiposódica; *v.* salar, echar sal; [*to season with*] condimentar con sal, sazonar.

salty *a.* salado-a, salobre, salino-a.

salubrious *a.* salubre, saludable.

salutary *a.* saludable.

salve *n.* ungüento, pomada.

same *a.* mismo-a, idéntico-a, igual.

sample *n.* espécimen, muestra; *v.* probar; sacar o tomar una muestra.

sampling *n.* muestreo; hacer muestras; selección partitiva; random ___ / ___ al azar.

sanatorium *n.* sanatorio, institución de rehabilitación física o mental.

sanction *n.* sanción, pena.

sand *n.* arena.

sandy *a.* arenoso-a.

sane *a.* sano-a; [*mentally*] cuerdo-a.

sanguine *a.* sanguíneo-a. 1. rel. a la sangre; 2. de complexión rosácea, con disposición alegre.

sanguineous *a.* sanguíneo-a, rel. a la sangre o de abundante sangre.

sanguinolent *a.* sanguinolento-a, que contiene sangre.

sanitarian *n.* sanitario-a, persona entrenada en problemas de salubridad.

sanitarium *n.* sanatorio, institución de salud de rehabilitación física o mental.

sanitary *a.* higiénico-a; ___ napkin / servilleta ___ absorbente, toalla ___.

sanitation *n.* saneamiento, sanidad.

sanity *n.* cordura, sensatez, bienestar mental.

sap *n.* savia, jugo natural de algunas plantas.

saphenous *a.* safeno-a, rel. a las venas safenas.

saphenous veins *n. pl.* venas safenas, dos venas superficiales de la pierna.

sapphism *n.* safismo, lesbianismo.

saprophyte *n.* saprófito, organismo vegetal que vive en materia orgánica pútrida.

sarcoidosis *n.* sarcoidosis. *V.* **Schaumann's disease.**

sarcoma *n.* sarcoma, neoplasma maligno formado por tejido conectivo.

sardonic laugh *n.* risa sardónica, contracción espasmódica de los músculos risorios en forma dc una sonrisa.

sat *a., pp.* de **to sit,** sentado-a.

satellite *n.* satélite, estructura asociada con otra o situada cerca de ella.

satiate *v.* saciar.

satiated *a.* saciado-a.

satiety *n.* saciedad, hartura, hartazgo.

satisfactory *a.* satisfactorio-a.

satisfied *a.* satisfecho-a, contento-a.

satisfy *v.* satisfacer.

saturate *v.* saturar; empapar.

saturated *a.* saturado-a, empapado-a, incapaz de absorber o recibir una sustancia más allá de un límite; ___ solution / solución ___.

saturation *n.* saturación, acto de saturar; ___ index / índice dc ___; ___ time / tiempo de ___.

sauce *n.* salsa; [*dressing*] aderezo.

sausage *n.* salchicha; chorizo.

save *v.* salvar, [*energy, money*] ahorrar; [*time*] aprovechar el tiempo.

say *vi.* decir; **You don't say!** / ¡No me diga!, ¡no me digas!.

scab *n.* costra, escara.

scabies *n.* sarna, infección cutánea parasitaria muy contagiosa que causa picazón.

scald *n.* escaldadura, quemadura de la piel causada por vapor o por un líquido caliente; *v.* lavar en agua hirviendo, quemar con un líquido caliente.

scale *n.* 1. escala, balanza; 2. escama, costra, lámina que se desprende de la piel seca.

scaling *n.* peladura.

scalp *n.* cuero cabelludo; ___ dermatoses / dermatosis del ___ .

scalpel *n.* escalpelo; bisturí, instrumento quirúrgico.

scaly *a.* escamoso-a.

scan, scintiscan *n.* escán; rastreo, proceso que reproduce la imagen de un tejido u órgano específico usando un detector de la sustancia radiactiva tecnecio 99 m. inyectada como medio de contraste; bone ___ / ___ de los huesos; brain ___ / ___ del cerebro; heart ___ / ___ cardíaco; lung ___ / ___ pulmonar; thyroid ___ / ___ de la tiroide.

scanning *n.* escanografía, escrutinio y registro por medio de un instrumento de detección de la emisión de ondas radiactivas de una sustancia específica que ha sido inyectada y que se concentra en partes o tejidos en observación.

scant *a.* escaso-a, parco-a, insuficiente.

scanty *a.* escaso-a, limitado-a, no abundante.

scaphoid *a.* escafoide, en forma de bote esp. en referencia al hueso del carpo y al del tarso.

scapula *n.* escápula, hueso del hombro.

scar *n.* cicatriz, marca en la piel; *v.* cicatrizar.

scare *v.* asustar, atemorizar.

scarification *n.* escarificación, acto de hacer punturas o raspaduras en la piel.

scarlet fever, scarlatina *n.* escarlatina, enfermedad contagiosa aguda caracterizada por fiebre y erupción con enrojecimiento de la piel y la lengua.

scatology *n.* escatología. 1. estudio de las heces fecales; 2. obsesión con el excremento y las inmundicias.

scatter *v.* esparcir, diseminar; dispersar, desparramar.

scattered *a.* esparcido-a, diseminado-a; desparramado-a, regado-a; derramado-a.

scene *n.* escena, escenario.

scent *n.* olor; aroma, perfume.

Schaumann's disease *n.* enfermedad de Schaumann, enfermedad crónica manifestada con pequeños tubérculos esp. en los pulmones, los nódulos linfáticos, los huesos y la piel.

schedule *n.* horario; *v.* hacer un horario; programar.

schema *n.* esquema, plan, planeamiento.

schematic *a.* esquemático-a, rel. a un esquema.

Schilling test *n.* prueba de Schilling; uso de vitamina B_{12} radiactiva en el diagnóstico de anemia perniciosa primaria.

schirrhus *n.* escirro, tumor canceroso duro.

schistosoma *n. Schistosoma,* esquistosoma, duela, especie de trematodo cuyas larvas entran en la sangre del huésped por contacto con agua contaminada a través del tubo digestivo o la piel.

schistosomiasis *n.* esquistosomiasis, infestación producida por la duela.

schizoid *a.* esquizoide, semejante a la esquizofrenia.

schizophrenia *n. psic.* esquizofrenia, desintegración mental que transforma la personalidad con varias manifestaciones psicóticas tales como alucinaciones, retraimiento y distorsión de la realidad.

schizophrenic *a.* esquizofrénico-a, rel. a la esquizofrenia o que padece de ella.

sciatica *n.* ciática, neuralgia que se irradia a lo largo del nervio ciático.

sciatic nerve *n.* nervio ciático, nervio que se extiende desde la base de la columna vertebral a lo largo del muslo y se ramifica en la pierna y el pie.

scintigraphy *n.* cintigrafía, técnica de diagnóstico que emplea radioisótopos para obtener una imagen bidimensional de la distribución de un radiofármaco en un área designada del cuerpo.

scintiscan *n.* cintiescán, gammagrama, registro de la imagen bidimensional de la distribución interior de un radiofármaco en un área seleccionada previamente para fines de diagnóstico.

scissors *n. pl.* tijeras.

sclera, sclerotica *n.* esclerótica, parte blanca del ojo compuesta de tejido fibroso.

scleritis *n.* escleritis, infl. de la esclerótica.

sclerosing solutions *n. pl.* soluciones esclerosantes.

sclerosis *n.* esclerosis, endurecimiento progresivo de los tejidos y órganos; Alzheimer's ___ / ___ de Alzheimer; amyotrophic lateral ___ / ___ lateral amiotrófica; arterial ___ / ___ arterial; multiple ___ / ___ múltiple.

sclerotherapy *n.* escleroterapia, tratamiento con una solución química que se inyecta en las várices para producir esclerosis.

sclerotic *a.* esclerótico-a, rel. a la esclerosis o afectado por ella.

scoliosis *n.* escoliosis, desviación lateral pronunciada de la columna vertebral.

scoop *n.* paletada, cucharada.

scorch *v.* chamuscar, quemar, abrasar.

score *n.* valoración, evaluación; *v.* llevar la cuenta; [*in a game*] anotar.

scorpion *n.* escorpión, alacrán; ___ sting / picadura de ___.

scotoma *n.* (*pl.* **scotomata**) escotoma, área del campo visual en la cual existe pérdida parcial o total de la visión.

scotopia *n.* escotopia, visión nocturna, adaptación visual a la oscuridad.

scotopic *a.* escotopico-a, rel. a la escotopia; ___ vision / visión ___.

scrape *n.* raspadura, rasponazo, raspado; *v.* raspar, rasguñar.

scraper *n.* descarnador, raspador.

scratch *n.* rasguño, arañazo; *v.* raspar, rascar, rascarse; ___ test / prueba del rasguño, gen. para uso en pruebas alérgicas.

scream *n.* grito, chillido; *v.* gritar, chillar.

screech *v.* chillar.

screen *n.* pantalla; *v.* examinar sistemáticamente un grupo de casos; escrutar.

screening *n.* escrutinio, averiguación, selección; multiphasic ___ / ___ múltiple; prescriptive ___ / ___ prescrito.

screw *n.* tornillo, rosca.

scribble *n.* garabato.

scrofula *n.* escrófula, tuberculosis de la glándula linfática.

scrofuloderma *n.* escrofuloderma, *pop.* lamparón, tipo de escrófula cutánea.

scrotal *a.* escrotal, rel. al escroto.

scrotum *n.* escroto, saco o bolsa que envuelve o contiene los testículos.

scrub *v.* limpiar, fregar, restregar; ___ nurse / enfermera de cirugía.

scrubbing *n.* limpieza rigurosa de las manos y brazos antes de la cirugiqa.

scruple *n.* escrúpulo.

scrupulous *a.* escrupuloso-a.

scrupulousness *n.* escrupulosidad.

scum *n.* espuma; escoria.

scurvy *n.* escorbuto, enfermedad causada por deficiencia de vitamina C que se manifiesta con anemia, encías sangrantes y un estado general de laxitud.

seal *n.* sello; *v.* cerrar herméticamente.

seam *n.* costura, línea de costura.

search *n.* búsqueda, investigación; registro; *v.* buscar, registrar; investigar.

seasickness *n.* mareo; mareo por movimiento.

season *n.* estación; temporada; *v.* [*cooking*] sazonar.

seasoned *a.* sazonado-a; ___ foods / alimentos ___ -s.

seat *n.* asiento; localidad.

sebaceous *a.* sebáceo-a, seboso-a, rel. al sebo o de la naturaleza de éste; ___ cyst / quiste ___; ___ gland / glándula ___.

seborrhea *n.* seborrea, secreción excesiva de las glándulas sebáceas.

sebum *n.* sebo, secreción espesa que segregan las glándulas sebáceas.

second *n.* segundo; *a.* segundo-a.

secondary *a.* secundario-a.

secretagogue, secretogogue *n.* secretogogo, agente que estimula la secreción glandular.

secrete *v.* secretar, segregar.

secretion *n.* secreción. 1. producción de un tejido o sustancia como resultado de una actividad glandular; 2. sustancia producida por secreción.

secretory *a.* secretorio-a, que tiene la propiedad de secretar.

section *n.* sección, porción, parte; *v.* cortar; seccionar.

sectioning *n.* partición, división, corte.

secure *a.* seguro-a; *v.* asegurar.

security *n.* seguridad; ___ measures / medidas de ___.

sedation *n.* sedación, acción o efecto de calmar o sedar; *v.* to put under ___ / dar un sedante, calmante o soporífero.

sedative *n.* calmante, sedante, agente con efectos tranquilizantes.

sedentary *a.* sedentario-a. 1. de poca actividad física; 2. rel. a la posición sentada.

sediment *n.* sedimento, materia que se deposita en el fondo de un líquido.

sedimentation *n.* sedimentación, acción o proceso de depositar sedimentos; ___ rate / índice de ___.

see *vi.* ver; **to** ___ **to it** / atender, ver que, hacer que; **I see!** / ¡Ya veo!; Let's ___ / Vamos a ver.

seed *n.* semilla, simiente.

seeing *n.* vista, visión.

seen *a., pp.* de **to see**, visto-a.

segment *n.* segmento, porción, sección.

segmentation *n.* segmentación, acto de dividir en partes.

seizure *n.* ataque repentino, acceso.

seldom *adv.* rara vez, con rareza, raramente.

select *v.* seleccionar, escoger.

selection *n.* selección, elección.

self *n.* el yo; *pron.* uno-a mismo-a; *a.* sí mismo-a; mismo-a; propio-a; ____ assurance / confianza en ____; ____ centered / egoísta, egocéntrico-a; ____ conscious / concentrado-a en ____, cohibido-a; ____ contained / autónomo; [*personality*] reservado-a; ____ contamination / autocontaminación; ____ control / dominio de ____; ____ defense / defensa propia; ____ delusion, deception / engaño a ____; ____ denial / abnegación; ____ determination / autodeterminación; ____ distrust / falta de confianza en ____; ____ esteem / reconocimiento de valores propios; ____ identity / conciencia de la identidad del yo; ____ induced / auto-inducido-a; ____ medication / auto-medicación; ____ pity / compasión por ____; *v.* to be ____ sufficient / valerse por ____.

selfish *a.* egoísta.

sella turcica *n.* silla turca, depresión en la superficie superior del esfenoide que contiene la hipófisis.

semantics *n.* semántica, estudio del significado de las palabras.

semen *n.* semen, esperma, secreción espesa blanca segregada por los órganos reproductivos masculinos.

semester *n.* semestre.

semi-coma *n.* semicoma, estado comatoso leve.

semidesintegration *n.* semidesintegración, tiempo requerido por una sustancia radiactiva para perder la mitad de la radioactividad por desintegración.

seminal *a.* seminal, rel. a una semilla o que consiste de una semilla.

seminiferous *a.* seminífero-a, que produce semen.

semiotic *n.* semiótico-a, rel. a los síntomas o señales de una enfermedad.

semiotics *n.* semiótica, rama de la medicina que trata de las señales y síntomas de una enfermedad.

send *vi.* enviar, mandar.

senescence *n.* senescencia, senectud, proceso de envejecimiento.

senile *a.* senil, rel. a la vejez esp. en lo que afecta a las funciones mentales y físicas.

senility *n.* senilidad, cualidad de ser senil.

senior citizen *n.* persona mayor; jubilado-a.

sensation *n.* sensación, percepción de una estimulación por un órgano sensorial.

sense *n.* sentido, facultad de percibir por medio de los órganos sensoriales; ____ of hearing / ____ del oído; ____ of smell / ____ del olfato; ____ of sight / ____ de la vista; ____ of taste / ____ del gusto; ____ of touch / ____ del tacto; **common** ____ / ____ común; ____ **of humor** / ____ del humor; *v.* sentir.

sensibility *n.* sensibilidad, capacidad de recibir sensaciones.

sensitive *a.* sensitivo-a, sensible.

sensitivity training *n.* entrenamiento de la sensibilidad o capacidad sensorial.

sensitization *n.* sensibilización, acto de hacer sensible o sensorial.

sensorial *a.* sensorial, sensitivo-a; que se percibe por los sentidos.

sensorimotor *a.* sensitivomotor, rel. a las actividades motoras y sensitivas del cuerpo.

sensory *a.* sensorial, sensorio-a, rel. a las sensaciones o los sentidos; ____ aphasia / afasia ____.

sensory threshold *n.* umbral sensorial.

sensual *a.* sensual, carnal.

sensuous *a.* sensual.

sentiment *n.* sentimiento.

separate *v.* separar, dividir.

separation *n.* separación, división; selección.

sepsis *L.* sepsis, condición tóxica producida por una contaminación bacteriana.

septal *a.* septal, rel. a un septum.

septate *a.* septado-a, rel. a una estructura dividida por un septum.

septic *n.* séptico-a, rel. a la sepsis; ____ shock / choque ____.

septicemia, blood poisoning *n.* septicemia, envenenamiento de la sangre, invasión de la sangre por microorganismos virulentos.

septum *L.* (*pl.* **septa**) septum, tabique o membrana que divide dos cavidades o espacios; ventricular ____ / ____ ventricular.

sequela *n.* (*pl.* **sequelae**) secuela, condición que resulta de una enfermedad, lesión o tratamiento.

sequence *n.* secuencia, sucesión.

sequester *v.* secuestrar, aislar.

sequestration *n.* secuestro, aislamiento. 1. acto de aislar; 2. formación de un sequestrum.

sequestrum *n.* sequestrum, secuestro, fragmento de un hueso necrosado que se separa de un hueso sano adyacente.

serene *a.* sereno-a, tranquilo-a.

serial *a.* en serie.

series *n. pl.* series, grupo de espécimenes en una secuencia.

serious *a.* serio-a; complicado-a; **-ly** *adv.* seriamente.

seroconversion *n.* seroconversión, desarrollo de anticuerpos como respuesta a una infección o a la administración de una vacuna.

serologic, serological *a.* serológico-a, rel. a un suero; ___ test / prueba ___.

serology *n.* serología, ciencia que estudia las propiedades de los sueros.

seroma *n.* seroma, acumulación gen. subcutánea de suero sanguíneo que produce una hinchazón que se asemeja a un tumor.

seronegative *a.* seronegativo-a, que presenta una reacción negativa en pruebas serológicas.

seropositive *a.* seropositivo-a, que presenta una reacción positiva a pruebas serológicas.

seropositivity *n.* seropositividad, resultado positivo en un examen serológico.

serosa *n.* membrana serosa.

serosanguineous *a.* serosanguíneo-a, de naturaleza serosa y sanguínea.

serotype *n.* serotipo, tipo de microorganismo que se determina por las clases y combinaciones de antígenos presentes en la célula.

serotyping *n.* determinación del serotipo.

serous *a.* seroso-a, que produce o contiene suero.

serpiginous *n.* serpiginoso-a, sinuoso-a, de movimiento semejante a una serpiente.

serrated *a.* serrado-a, endentado-a, con proyección similar a los dientes de un serrucho.

serum *n.* suero, líquido seroso. 1. elemento del plasma que permanece líquido y claro después de la coagulación; 2. cualquier líquido seroso; 3. suero inmune de animales o personas que se inocula para producir inmunizaciones pasivas o temporales.

sesamoid *a.* sesamoideo, semejante a una pequeña masa o semilla incrustada en una articulación o cartílago.

sessile *a.* sésil, insertado o fijo en una base ancha que carece de pedúnculo.

session *n.* sesión.

set *n.* conjunto, equipo; grupo; instrumentos y accesorios; [*surgical*] instrumental quirúr-

gico; **a** ___ **back** / una recaída; un retraso, una contrariedad; **it is all** ___ / todo está arreglado; *vi.* poner, colocar; [*a broken bone*] encasar, fijar, ajustar; ___ a fracture / componer una fractura.

setting *n.* [*environment*] ambiente; montaje.

settle *v.* asentar, fijar; asegurar.

settlement *n.* [*account*] arreglo, ajuste.

sever *v.* cortar, romper; separar.

several *a.* varios-as, muchos-as, algunos-as.

severe *a.* grave, severo-a.

severe combined immunodeficiency disease *n.* enfermedad grave de inmuno deficiencia combinada, una de las enfermedades genéticas raras que se caracteriza por el desarrollo defectivo de las células que generan anticuerpos.

sew *vi.* coser.

sewage *n.* aguas de alcantarilla, cloacas.

sewing *n.* costura, puntada.

sex *n.* sexo; ___ determination / determinación del ___; ___ disorders / trastornos o anomalías sexuales; ___ distribution / distribución según el ___.

sex-linked *a.* 1. relacionado con el sexo; 2. que se refiere a cromosomas sexuales o es transmitido por ellos.

sexual *a.* sexual, rel. al sexo; ___ behavior / conducta ___; ___ characteristics / características ___-es; ___ development / desarrollo ___; ___ intercourse / relaciones ___-es, coito; ___ life / vida ___; ___ maturity / madurez ___; **-ly** *adv.* sexualmente; ___ transmitted disease / enfermedad transmitida ___.

sexuality *n.* sexualidad, características de cada sexo.

shadow *n.* sombra; opacidad.

shaft *n.* caña. V. **diaphysis.**

shake *vi.* agitar; [*hands*] dar la mano; [*from cold*] temblar, tiritar de frío; ___ well before using / agítese bien antes de usarse.

shaken *a.* sacudido-a; afectado-a; debilitado-a.

shakes *n. pl.* temblores, *pop.* tembladera; escalofríos; fiebre intermitente.

shaky *a.* vacilante, temeroso-a; [*untrustful*] que no merece confianza.

shall *v. aux.* deber.

shaman *n.* curandero.

shamanism *n.* curanderismo.

shame *n.* vergüenza; **What a** ___! / ¡Qué pena!, ¡Qué lástima!; *v.* avergonzar.

shameful *a.* vergonzoso-a, penoso-a.

shank *n.* canilla de la pierna.

shape *n.* forma, aspecto; condición [*health*] **in bad** ___ / enfermo-a; destruido-a; **out of** ___ / deformado-a, imperfecto; [*physically*] desajuste físico; *v.* formar, moldear.

sharp *a.* [*pain*] agudo-a; [*instrument*] afilado-a.

shave *v.* afeitar; afeitarse.

shears *n. pl.* tijeras.

sheath *n.* cubierta, capa o membrana protectora.

shed *vi.* [*blood, tears*] derramar; [*light*] dar, esparcir; difundir; [*skin, hair*] mudar; pelar; soltar; descamar.

shedding *n.* [*hair*] exfoliación; [*skin*] peladura.

sheep *n.* oveja, carnero.

sheet *n.* lámina, hoja de metal.

shelf *n.* anaquel, estructura en forma horizontal alargada.

shell *n.* cáscara; concha marina.

shellfish *n.* molusco.

shield *n.* escudo, cubierta.

shift *n.* cambio de posición, desviación; [*work period*] turno; *v.* cambiar, desviar.

shigellosis *n.* shigelosis, disenteria bacilar.

shinbone *n.* espinilla, borde anterior de la tibia.

shingles *n.* culebrilla, herpes zóster, erupción inflamatoria de la piel con vesículas o ampollas gen. localizadas en el tronco.

shirt *n.* camisa; **under** ___ / camiseta.

shiver *n.* estremecimiento, escalofrío, temblor; *v.* tener escalofríos; tiritar de frío; estremecerse.

shock, choc *Fr. n.* shock, choque, estado anormal generado por una insuficiencia circulatoria sanguínea que puede causar descenso en la presión arterial, pulso rápido, palidez, temperatura anormalmente baja y debilidad; anaphylactic ___ / ___ anafiláctico; endotoxic ___ / ___ endotóxico; septic ___ / ___ séptico; ___ therapy, electric / terapia electroconvulsiva.

shoe *n.* zapato, calzado; orthopedic ___ -s / calzado ortopédico.

short *a.* corto-a; [*time*] breve; [*height*] bajo-a; **in a** ___ **time** / en breve, dentro de poco; **in** ___ **notice** / en corto plazo; ___ **of breath** / falto-a de respiración; sin resuello.

shortage *n.* carencia, falta, déficit.

shorten *v.* acortar.

shortsightedness, nearsightness *n. V.* **myopia.**

shot *n.* tiro, disparo, [*wound*] balazo; [*injection*] inyección.

should *v. aux., cond., pret.* de **shall,** deber.

shoulder *n.* hombro, unión de la clavícula, la escápula y el húmero.

shout *n.* grito, alarido: *v.* gritar.

show *vi.* mostrar, enseñar, manifestar; revelar.

shower *n.* ducha; *v.* darse una ducha.

shrimp *n.* camarón.

shrink *n. pop.* psiquiátra o alienista, psicólogo; *vi.* encoger; encogerse.

shudder *v.* estremecerse.

shunt *n.* desviación, derivación; *v.* desviar, derivar.

shut *vi.* cerrar.

shy *a.* tímido-a, temeroso-a; cauteloso-a.

sialadenitis, sialoadenitis *n.* sialodenitis, infl. de una glándula salival.

sialogogue *n.* sialogogo, agente que estimula la secreción salival.

sialogram *n.* sialograma, rayos X del conducto de la glándula salival.

sick *n., a.* enfermo-a; ___ **leave** / licencia por enfermedad.

sickly *a.* enfermizo-a, achacoso-a, endeble.

sickness *n.* enfermedad, dolencia, mal.

side *n.* lado, costado; **by the** ___ **of** / al ___ de; **right** ___ / ___ derecho; **left** ___ / ___ izquierdo; ___ **effect** / efecto secundario, reacción gen. adversa a un medicamento, tratamiento o droga.

sideways *a.* al lado de; de lado.

sieve *n.* colador; *v.* colar, pasar por un tamiz.

sight *n.* vista; **at first** ___ / a primera ___ .

sigmoid *a.* sigmoide, sigmoideo. 1. que tiene forma de *s;* 2. rel. al colon sigmoide.

sigmoidoscope *n.* sigmoidoscopio, instrumento tubular largo que se usa para examinar la flexura sigmoide.

sigmoidoscopy *n.* sigmoidoscopía, uso de un sigmoidoscopio para examinar la flexura sigmoide.

sign *n.* señal., signo, indicación, manifestación objetiva de una enfermedad; vital ___ -s / signos vitales.

signature *n.* 1. firma; 2. parte de una receta médica que contiene las instrucciones.

significance *a.* significado; **of no** ___ / sin importancia.

significant *a.* importante, significativo-a.

signify *v.* significar.

sign language *n.* lenguaje mímico por señales. *V.* **dactilology.**

silence *n.* silencio.

silent *a.* silencioso-a.

silicon *n.* silicio, elemento no metálico encontrado en la tierra.

silicone *n.* silicón, silicona, compuesto orgánico que se usa en lubricantes, productos sintéticos, cirugía plástica y en prótesis.

silicosis *n.* silicosis, inhalación de partículas de polvo.

silk *n.* seda.

silly *a.* tonto-a.

silver *n.* plata; ____ nitrate / nitrato de ____.

similar *a.* similar, scmejante, parecido-a.

simmer *v.* cocer a fuego lento.

simple *a.* simple, sencillo-a; **simply** *adv.* simplemente, meramente.

simplify *v.* simplificar.

simulate *v.* fingir, simular, pretender.

simulation *n.* simulación, fingir un síntoma o enfermedad.

since *adv.* desde; ____ **then; ever** ____ / ____ entonces; ____ **when?** / ¿ ____ cuándo?

sinew *n. V.* **tendon.**

single *a.* sencillo-a, simple, solo-a; [*unmarried*] soltero-a.

singular *a.* singular, único.

singultus *n. L.* hipo.

sinoatrial *a.* sinoatrial, rel. a la región del seno auricular.

sinoatrial, sinoauricular node *n.* nódulo sinusal o senoauricular, localizado en la unión de la vena cava y la aurícula derecha y que se considera el punto de origen de los impulsos que estimulan los latidos del corazón.

sinogram *n.* sinograma, radiografía de un seno paranasal usando un medio de contraste.

sintomatology *n.* sintomatología, conjunto de síntomas que se refieren a una enfermedad o a un caso determinado.

sinuous *a.* sinuoso-a, ondulado-a.

sinus *L.* sinus, seno, cavidad de abertura estrecha; ____ rhythm / ritmo sinusal.

sinusal *a.* sinusal, rel. a un sinus.

sinusitis *n.* sinusitis, infl. de la mucosa de un seno o cavidad, esp. los senos paranasales.

sinusoid *n.* sinusoide, conducto diminuto que lleva sangre a los tejidos de un órgano; *a.* rel. a un sinus.

sip *n.* sorbo, trago; *v.* sorber.

siphon *n.* sifón.

sister *n.* hermana; ____ **-in-law** / cuñada.

sit *vi.* sentar, asentar; **to** ____ **down** / sentarse.

situated *a.* situado-a, localizado-a.

situation *n.* situación, localización.

situs *L.* situs, posición, sitio.

size *n.* tamaño; [*garments*] talla.

skeletal *a.* esquelético-a.

skeleton *n.* esqueleto, armazón ósea del cuerpo.

skew *n.* movimiento oblicuo-a, movimiento sesgado-a, de lado.

skill *n.* destreza, habilidad.

skin *n.* piel, epidermis, cutis; *pop.* pellejo; ____ cancer / cáncer de la ____ ; ____ diseases / enfermedades de la ____ , dermatosis; ____ graft / injerto de la ____ ; ____ rash / erupción cutánea, urticaria; ____ tests / pruebas cutáncas; ____ ulcer / úlcera cutánea.

skinny *a.* flaco-a, delgado-a, descarnado-a.

skip *v.* omitir, pasar por alto; [*jump*] saltar.

skirt *n.* falda.

skull *n.* cráneo; calavera, estructura ósea de la cabeza; ____ fractures / fracturas del ____ ; base of the ____ / base del ____ .

slant *n.* inclinación, plano inclinado; *v.* inclinar; [*words*] distorsionar; inclinarse.

slanted *a.* oblicuo-a, inclinado-a; sesgado-a.

slap *n.* bofetada, manotazo; *v.* pcgar, dar una bofetada, dar un manotazo.

sleep *n.* sueño; ____ apnea / apnea intermitente que ocurre durante el sueño; balmy ____ / ____ reparador; ____ disorders / trastornos del ____ ; ____ stages / fases del ____ ; twilight ____ / ____ crepuscular; *vi.* dormir; dormirse; **to** ____ **soundly** / ____ profundamente.

sleepiness *n.* somnolencia, adormecimiento.

sleeping pill *n.* soporífero, somnífero, pastilla para dormir.

sleeping sickness *n.* enfermedad del sueño, dolencia aguda endémica de África que se manifiesta con fiebre, letargo, escalofríos, pérdida de peso y debilidad general, causada por un protozoo transmitido por la picadura de la mosca tsetse.

sleep walking *n.* sonambulismo.

sleeve *n.* manga; **Put up your** ____ / Súbase, súbete la manga.

slender *a.* esbelto-a; delgado-a.

slice *n.* pedazo, tajada, rebanada.

slide *n.* diapositiva, laminilla; [*specimen holder*] portaobjeto.

slight *a.* ligero-a, leve; ____ fever / fiebrecita, fiebre ____.

slim *a.* delgado-a; esbelto-a; insuficiente; **a** ____ **chance** / poco probable.

slimy *a.* viscoso-a; enlodado-a.

sling *n.* cabestrillo, soporte de vendaje.

slippery *a.* resbaladizo-a, resbaloso-a.

slit *n.* incisión, rajadura; *v.* **to make a** ____ / hacer una incisión, hacer una hendidura; rajar, cortar en tiras.

slope *n.* inclinación; declive; *v.* estar inclinado-a; estar en declive.

slough *n.* esfacelo, masa de tejido muerto que se ha desprendido de un tejido vivo.

slow *a.* lento-a, pausado-a, despacioso-a; [*clock*] atrasado, retrasado; *v.* **to** ____ **down** / ir más despacio; tener más calma; **-ly** *adv.* lentamente, pausadamente, más despacio.

sluggish *a.* flojo-a, inactivo-a, de movimiento lento.

small *a.* pequeño-a; **smaller** *comp.* / más pequeño; **smallest** *sup.* / el menor, el más pequeño.

smallpox *n.* viruela, enfermedad infecciosa viral que se manifiesta con un cuadro febril agudo y erupción de ampollas y pústulas diseminadas por todo el cuerpo.

smart *a.* inteligente, listo-a.

smear *n.* frotis, unto; *v.* untar, embarrar.

smegma *n.* esmegma, secreción producida por las glándulas sebáceas vista esp. en los órganos genitales exteriores.

smell *n.* 1. olor, aroma; penetrating ____ / ____ penetrante; 2. sentido del olfato; *v.* oler, percibir un olor.

smile *n.* sonrisa; *v.* sonreír.

smiling *a.* risueño-a.

smog *n.* mezcla de niebla y humo.

smoke *n.* humo; ____ **screen** / cortina de ____ ; *v.* fumar; **Do not** ____ **here** / No fume, no fumes aquí.

smooth *a.* liso-a; [*cutis*] suave, terso-a, delicado-a.

snake *n.* serpiente, culebra; ____ **bite** / mordedura de ____ ; ____ **venom** / ponzoña de ____ ; **poisonous** ____ / ____ venenosa.

snap *n.* chasquido, ruido cardíaco relacionado con la apertura de una válvula del corazón, gen. la válvula mitral.

sneeze *n.* estornudo; *v.* estornudar.

sniff *v.* olfatear, oler; absorber por la nariz; resoplar.

sniffle *n.* catarro nasal; *v.* sorber repetidàmente por la nariz.

snooze *v.* adormecerse.

snore *n.* ronquido; *v.* roncar.

snort *v.* aspirar a través de la mucosa nasal.

snow *n.* nieve; *v.* nevar.

snuff *v.* inhalar; resoplar hacia adentro; **to** ____ **up** / tomar por la nariz.

so *adv.* así, de este modo, de esta manera; ____ **that** / de manera que; **not** ____ **much** / no tanto; **it is not** ____ / no es ____ ; **so-so** / más o menos, regular.

soak *v.* remojar, empapar; **to** ____ **in, to** ____ **up** / absorber, chupar.

soap *n.* jabón; *v.* enjabonar; **to** ____ **oneself** / enjabonarse.

sob *n.* sollozo; *v.* sollozar.

sober *a.* sobrio-a, serio: *v.* **to get** ____ / dejar de beber, dejar de tomar bebidas alcohólicas.

sociable *a.* sociable, amigable.

social *a.* social, sociable; ____ **behavior** / conducta o comportamiento ____ ; ____ **security** / seguro ____ ; ____ **work** / asistencia ____ ; ____ **worker** / trabajador-a ____ .

socialization *n.* socialización, adaptación social.

socialized *a.* socializado-a; ____ **medicine** / medicina ____ .

society *n.* sociedad; organización social.

sociobiology *n.* sociobiología, ciencia que estudia los factores genéticos como determinantes de la conducta.

sociologist *n.* sociólogo-a, especialista en sociología.

sociology *n.* sociología, ciencia que trata de las relaciones sociales y de los fenómenos de tipo social.

sociopath *n.* sociópata, persona caracterizada por una conducta antisocial.

sock *n.* media, calcetín.

socket *n.* hueco, [*of a bone*] fosa; [*electric*] enchufe.

soda *n.* soda, carbonato de sodio; **baking** ____ / bicarbonato de sodio.

sodium *n.* sodio, elemento metálico alcalino que se encuentra en los líquidos del cuerpo.

sodomite *n.* sodomita, persona que comete sodomía

sodomy *n.* sodomía. término que denota relación sexual entre hombres; bestialidad o felación.

soft *a.* blando-a, suave, delicado-a; [*metals*] flexible, maleable; ____ **diet** / dieta ____ ;

_____ **drinks** / refrescos, bebidas no alcohólicas; **-ly** _adv._ suavemente, blandamente.

soften _v._ ablandar, suavizar.

softening _n._ reblandecimiento, ablandamiento; suavidad.

soggy _a._ saturado-a, empapado-a.

soil _n._ tierra, terreno; [_dirt_] suciedad.

solace _n._ consuelo; solaz; esparcimiento; _v._ consolar; alegrar.

solar _a._ solar, rel. al sol.

sole _n._ suela, planta del pie.

solid _a._ sólido-a, macizo-a; [_person_] serio-a, formal.

soluble _a._ soluble.

solution _n._ solución.

solvent _n._ solvente, líquido que disuelve o es capaz de producir una solución.

somatic _a._ somático-a, rel. al cuerpo.

somatization _n._ somatización, _psic._ proceso de conversión de experiencias mentales en manifestaciones corporales.

some _a._ alguno-a; algún, algo de, un poco de; unos, unos cuantos, unas, unas cuantas, algunos-as.

somebody _n._ alguien; _____ **else** / otro, otra.

somehow _adv._ de algún modo, de alguna manera.

something _n._ alguna cosa, algo; _____ **else** / otra cosa.

somnambulance, somnambulism _n._ somnambulismo.

somnambule _n._ sonámbulo-a, persona que anda mientras está dormida.

somniferous _n._ soporífero.

somnolence _n._ somnolencia.

son _n._ hijo; _____-**in-law** / yerno; **sonny** / hijito.

sonogram _n._ sonograma, registro de una imagen producida por ultrasonido.

sonography _n._ sonografía. _V._ **ultrasonography**.

sonolucent _a._ sonoluciente, [_ultrasonography_] que puede dar paso a las ondas sonoras sin reflejarlas de nuevo en la fuente de origen.

sonorous _a._ sonoro-a, resonante, con un sonido vibrante.

soon _adv._ pronto, dentro de poco, en poco tiempo.

soothe _v._ calmar, aliviar, mitigar; suavizar.

sophistication _n._ sofisticación, adulteración de una sustancia.

soporific _n._ soporífico, agente que produce el sueño.

sore _a._ [_feeling_] adolorido-a, doloroso-a, con dolor; _____ eyes / malestar en los ojos, ojos adoloridos; _____ throat / dolor de garganta; _____ all over / malestar general, dolor en todo el cuerpo; _____ wound / llaga, úlcera, herida; _v._ to be sore / estar adolorido-a.

sorrow _n._ pena, aflicción, pesar, dolor.

sorrowful _a._ apenado-a, afligido-a, apesadumbrado-a, adolorido-a.

sorry _a._ apesadumbrado-a; arrepentido-a; **I am** _____ / Lo siento; _v._ **to be** _____ / arrepentirse de; **to be** _____ **for** (someone) / tener lástima de (alguien).

sort _n._ clase. especie, género; **all** _____-**s of** / una variedad de; **out of** _____-**s** / malhumorado-a, indispuesto-a; _v._ separar, clasificar, distribuir.

soul _n._ alma, espíritu.

sound _n._ sonido, ruido; ruido de soplo percibido por auscultación; _v._ sonar.

soup _n._ sopa.

sour _a._ agrio-a, ácido, avinagrado-a.

source _n._ origen; foco; fuente.

sourness _n._ acedía, agrura, acidez.

south _n._ sur.

soy _n._ soja, soya.

space _n._ área, espacio, segmento, lugar.

spacial _a._ espacial, rel. al espacio.

span _n._ lapso, instante, momento; tiempo limitado; intervalo; distancia.

Spanish _n._ [_language_] español; / [_native_] español-a; _a._ español-a; **Spanish-American** / hispanoamericano-a.

spasm _n._ espasmo, convulsión, contracción muscular involuntaria.

spasmodic _a._ espasmódico-a.

spastic _a._ espástico-a, convulsivo-a, espasmódico-a; 1. de naturaleza espasmódica; _____ colon / colon espasmódico o espástico; 2. que sufre espasmos.

spasticity _n._ espasticidad, aumento en la tensión normal de un músculo que causa movimientos rígidos y dificultosos.

spatula _n._ espátula.

speak _vi._ hablar; _____ **slowly** / Hable, habla más despacio; _____ **louder** / Hable, habla más alto.

special _a._ especial, único-a; extraordinario-a; **-ly** _adv._ especialmente.

specialist _n._ especialista.

specialize _v._ especializarse.

specialty _n._ especialidad.

species _n._ (_pl._ **species**) especie, clasificación

de organismos vivos pertenecientes a una categoría biológica.

specific *a.* específico-a; determinado-a; preciso-a.

specify *v.* especificar.

specimen *n.* espécimen, muestra.

speck *n.* mácula, mancha.

spectacles *n. pl.* lentes, espejuelos, gafas.

spectrum *n.* (*pl.* **spectra**) espectro. 1. amplitud en la actividad de un antibiótico contra variedades de microorganismos; 2. serie de imágenes que resultan de la refracción de radiación electromagnética; 3. banda matizada de rayos solares discernibles a simple vista o con un instrumento sensitivo.

speculate *v.* argumentar, especular.

speculum *n.* espéculo, instrumento para dilatar un conducto o cavidad.

speech *n.* habla, lenguaje; ___ defect / defecto del ___ ; ___ disorder / trastorno del ___ ; ___ therapy / terapéutica del ___ .

spell *n.* ataque súbito; *v.* **to have a** ___ / tener un ataque o acceso de; deletrear; **to** ___ **a word** / deletrear una palabra.

spend *vi.* [*money*] gastar, [*energy*] gastar, consumir; [*time*] pasar.

sperm *n.* esperma, semen; ___ count / espermiograma V. **semen.**

spermatic *a.* espermático, rel. al esperma.

spermaticidal, spermaticide *n.* espermaticida, que destruye o causa la muerte de espermatozoos.

spermatocele *n.* espermatocele, quiste del epidídimo que contiene espermatozoos.

spermatogenesis *n.* espermatogénesis, proceso de formación y desarrollo de espermatozoos.

spermatoid *a.* espermatoide, con apariencia de semen.

spermatorrhea *n.* espermatorrea, pérdida involuntaria de esperma.

spermatozoid, spermatozoon *n.* (*pl.* **spermatozoa**) espermatozoo, célula sexual masculina que fertiliza el óvulo.

spermicidal *n.* espermicida V. **spermaticidal.**

spermiogram *n.* espermiograma, evaluación de los espermatozoides en el proceso de determinación de la esterilidad.

sphenoid *n.* esfenoide, hueso situado en la base del cráneo.

sphere *n.* esfera. 1. estructura en forma de globo; 2. ambiente sociológico.

spherical *a.* esférico-a, rel. a una esfera.

spherocyte *n.* esferocito, eritrocito de forma esférica.

spherocytosis *n.* esferocitosis, presencia de esferocitos en la sangre.

spheroid *n.* esferoide, de forma esférica.

spherule *n.* esfera diminuta.

sphincter *n.* esfínter, músculo circular que abre y cierra un orificio.

sphincteroplasty *n. cirg.* esfinteroplastia, operación plástica de un esfínter.

sphincterotomy *n. cirg.* esfinterotomía, corte de un esfínter.

sphygmomanometer *n.* esfigmomanómetro, instrumento para determinar la presión arterial.

spica *n.* espica, tipo de vendaje.

spice *n.* especia, condimento.

spicular *a.* espicular, en forma de aguja.

spicule *n.* espícula, cuerpo en forma de aguja.

spider *n.* araña; **black** ___ / araña negra.

spike *n.* espiga; [*in a graphic*] cresta o elevación brusca.

spill *n.* derrame; *v.* derramar, verter.

spina *n.* spina, espina. 1. protuberancia en forma de espina; 2. la espina o columna vertebral.

spina bifida *n.* espina bífida, malformación congénita en el cierre de un conducto de la estructura ósea de la espina vertebral, con o sin protrusión de las meninges medulares, gen. a nivel lumbar; occult ___ / ___ oculta, sin protrusión.

spinach *n.* espinaca.

spinal *a.* espinal, raquídeo-a, rel. a la médula espinal o a la espina o columna vertebral; ___ anesthesia / anestesia raquídea; ___ canal / canal raquídeo; ___ cord / médula ___ ; ___ fluid / líquido cefalorraquídeo; ___ fusion / fusión ___ ; ___ puncture / punción ___ ; ___ shock / choque ___ ; ___ stenosis / estenosis ___ .

spinal column *n.* columna o espina vertebral, estructura ósea formada por treinta y tres vértebras que rodean y contienen la médula espinal.

spinal cord *n.* médula espinal, columna de tejido nervioso que se extiende desde el bulbo raquídeo hasta la segunda vértebra lumbar y de la cual parten todos los nervios que van al tronco y a las extremidades; ___ compression / compresión de la ___ .

spindle *n.* huso. 1. estructura o célula en forma de rodillo; 2. forma que toman los cromosomas durante la mitosis y la meiosis.

spine *n.* columna o espina vertebral; *pop.* espinazo.

spine-shaped *a.* espinoso-a, acantosa-a

spinous *a.* espinoso-a, en forma de espina.

spiral *a.* espiral, que se envuelve alrededor de un centro o axis.

spirit *n.* 1. espíritu, alma; 2. solución alcohólica de una sustancia volátil.

spiritual healing *n.* cura mental, cura espiritual.

spirochetal *a.* espiroquetósico-a, rel. a espiroquetas.

spirochete *n.* espiroqueta, microorganismo espiral de la especie *Spirochaetales* que incluye el microorganismo causante de la sífilis.

spirometer *n.* espirómetro, instrumento que se usa para medir la cantidad de aire que se inhala y la que se expele del pulmón.

spirometry *n.* espirometría, medida de la capacidad respiratoria tomada por medio de un espirómetro.

spit *n.* saliva, escupo; *vi.* escupir, expectorar.

spittle *n.* saliva; expectoración; salivazo, escupitazo.

splanchnic *a.* esplácnico-a, rel. a las vísceras o que llega a éstas; _____ nerves / nervios _____ -s.

spleen *n.* bazo, órgano vascular linfático, situado en la cavidad abdominal; accesory _____ / _____ accesorio.

splenectomy *n. cirg.* esplenectomía, excisión del bazo.

splenic *a.* esplénico-a, rel. al bazo.

splenoportography *n.* esplenoportografía, radiografía de las venas esplénica y cava usando un medio de contraste radiopaco inyectado en el bazo.

splenorenal *a.* esplenorrenal, rel. al bazo y al riñón.

splenorenal shunt *n.* derivación esplenorrenal, anastomosis de la vena o arteria esplénica a la vena renal esp. en el tratamiento de la hipertensión portal.

splint *n.* férula, tablilla, soporte de madera, metal, plástico, vidrio de fibra o yeso usado para dar apoyo, inmovilizar un hueso fracturado o proteger una parte del cuerpo.

splinter *n.* espina; esquirla; astilla.

split *n.* división, desunión; abertura; *v.* dividir, desunir, separar; dividirse, separarse.

splitting *n.* fragmentación; desdoblamiento.

spoil *v.* echar a perder.

spoken *v. pp.* de to speak, hablado.

spoken language *n.* lenguaje hablado.

spondylitis *n.* espondilitis, infl. de una o más vértebras; _____ ankylosing / _____ anquilosante, reumatoide.

spondylolisthesis *n.* espondilolistesis, desplazamiento anterior de una vértebra sobre otra, gen. la cuarta lumbar sobre la quinta o ésta sobre el sacro.

spondylolysis *n.* espondilólisis, disolución o destrucción de una vértebra.

spondylopathy *n.* espondilopatía, cualquier enfermedad que afecta las vértebras.

spondylosis *n.* espondilosis. 1. anquilosis vertebral; 2. toda lesión degenerativa de la columna vertebral.

sponge *n.* esponja; *v.* esponjar, remojar con una esponja.

spongy *a.* esponjoso-a; poroso-a.

spontaneous *a.* espontáneo-a.

spoon *n.* cuchara; _____ full / cucharada.

sporadic *a.* esporádico-a, infrecuente.

spore *n.* espora, célula reproductiva unicelular.

sporicide *n.* esporicida, agente que destruye esporas.

sport *n.* 1. mutación; 2. deporte; _____ medicine / medicina del deporte.

spot *n.* mancha, marca, pápula; blind _____ / punto ciego; liver _____ / _____ hepática; *v.* [*stain*] manchar; [*notice*] notar.

spotting *n.* manchas de flujo vaginal sanguinolento.

sprain *n.* torcedura, torción de una articulación con distensión y laceración parcial de los ligamentos; *v.* torcer; torcerse; **to** _____ **one's ankle** / _____ el tobillo.

spray *n.* atomizador de líquido para rociar; *v.* rociar con un líquido.

spread *n.* extensión, diseminación, esparcimiento; *a.* extendido-a, esparcido-a; diseminado-a; *vi.* diseminar; esparcir, extender; diseminarse, esparcirse, extenderse.

sprue *n.* esprue, enfermedad digestiva crónica caracterizada por la inhabilidad de absorber alimentos que contienen gluten.

spur *n.* espolón, protuberancia esp. de un hueso; calcaneal _____ / _____ calcáneo.

spurious *a.* espurio-a, falso-a.

sputum *n.* esputo, flema; bloody ___ / ___ sanguinolento.

squamous *a.* escamoso-a; ___ cell / célula ___.

square *n.* cuadrado; *a.* cuadrado-a; correcto-a, justo, -a.

squash *n.* calabaza; *v.* aplastar; estrujar.

squat *v.* agacharse; sentarse en cuclillas; acuclillarse.

squeak *n.* chirrido; *v.* chirriar, rechinar.

squeal *n.* chillido, alarido; *v.* chillar.

squeeze *v.* apretar, comprimir: [*cloth, fruit*] exprimir.

squint *n.* estrabismo; acción de encoger los ojos como protección contra una luz intensa o para tratar de ver mejor. *V.* **strabismus**.

stab *n.* puñalada; *v.* apuñalar, acuchillar.

stability *n.* estabilidad, permanencia, seguridad.

stabilization *n.* estabilización, acto de hacer algo estable.

stabilize *v.* estabilizar, evitar cambios o fluctuaciones.

stabilizer *n.* estabilizador, agente que estabiliza.

stable *a.* estable, que no fluctúa.

staff *n.* personal de una institución.

stage *n.* [*sickness*] fase; **in a recuperating** ___ / en una ___ de recuperación.

stagger *v.* escalonar, saltear, distribuir con una secuencia; vacilar; tambalear; tambalearse.

stagnation *n.* estancación, estancamiento, falta de circulación en los líquidos.

stain *n.* 1. colorante, tinte; 2. mancha, mácula.

staining *n.* coloración, tintura.

stalk *n.* tallo, estructura alargada que se asemeja al tallo de una planta.

stammer *n.* tartamudeo, balbuceo; *v.* tartamudear, balbucear.

stand *n.* sitio, puesto, situación; *vi.* ponerse o estar de pie; sostenerse; **to ___ back /** retroceder; **to ___ still /** no moverse, estarse quieto-a.

standalone *n.* estandona, droga esteroide anabólica.

standard *n.* estándar, norma, criterio, pauta a seguir; lo normal, lo usual o común; ___ of care / atención o cuidado ___; ___ deviation / desviación ___; ___ error / error ___; ___ procedure / procedimiento ___, procedimiento usual establecido.

standardization *n.* estandarización, uniformidad; normalización.

standing *n.* [*position*] de pie; [*pending*] vigente; ___ orders / órdenes o reglamento vigente.

standstill *n.* paro, cese de actividad.

stapedectomy *n.* *cirg.* excisión del estribo para mejorar la audición.

stapes *n.* estribo, el más interno de los huesecillos del oido.

staphylococcal *a.* estafilocócico-a, rel. a o causado por estafilococos; ___ food poisoning / intoxicación alimenticia por ___ -s.

staphylococcemia *n.* estafilococemia, presencia de estafilococos en la sangre.

Staphylococcus *Gr.* estafilococo. 1. especie de bacteria gram-positiva que puede causar diferentes clases de infecciones, incluye parásitos que se alojan en la piel y las mucosas; 2. término aplicado a cualquier micrococo patológico.

staphylotoxin *n.* estafilotoxina, toxina producida por estafilococos.

staple *n.* presilla, grapa; *v.* presillar, engrapar.

star *n.* estrella.

starch *n.* almidón, fécula, elemento principal de los carbohidratos.

starchy *a.* feculento-a; almidonado-a; ___ foods / alimentos ___ -s, almidones que contienen carbohidratos.

stare *n.* mirada fija; *v.* mirar fijamente.

start *n.* comienzo principio, inicio; *v.* empezar, comenzar, iniciar; hacer andar o funcionar un aparato; [*motor*] arrancar, poner en marcha.

starvation *n.* malnutrición, inanición, hambre, privación de alimentos.

starve *v.* pasar hambre, privar de alimentos.

stasis *n.* estasis, estancamiento de la circulación de un líquido tal como la sangre y la orina en una parte del cuerpo.

state *n.* estado, condición; nutritional ___ / ___ nutricional.

station *n.* estación; **nursing ___** / puesto de enfermeras.

stationery *a.* estacionario-a, estacionado-a, que permanece en una posición fija.

statistics *n.* estadística.

stature *n.* estatura, altura.

status *L.* status, estado o condición; ___ asthmaticus / ___ asmaticus, condición de un ataque de asma agudo; ___ epilepticus /

_____ epilepticus, serie de ataques sucesivos con pérdida del conocimiento.

stay _v._ permanecer; quedarse; **to** _____ **awake** / desvelarse; **to** _____ **in bed** / _____ en cama, guardar cama.

steam _n._ vapor.

stearine _n._ estearina, componente blanco y cristalino de las grasas.

steatorrhea _n._ esteatorrea, exceso de grasa en las heces fecales.

stellate _a._ estrellado-a, semejante a una estrella.

stem _n._ tallo, pedúnculo, estructura semejante al tallo de una planta; **brain** _____ / _____ encefálico; _____ **cell** / célula madre.

stenosed _a._ estenosado-a, rel. a una estenosis.

stenosis _n._ estenosis, estrechamiento o contracción anormal de un pasaje; **aortic** _____ / _____ aórtica; **piloric** _____ / _____ pilórica.

stenotic _a._ estenósico-a, producido por o caracterizado por estenosis.

step _n._ paso; [_stairs_] escalón, peldaño; _____ **by** _____ / paso a paso; _v._ **to** _____ **down** / bajar; reducir: **to** _____ **in** / entrar; intervenir; **to** _____ **up** / subir; apurar, acelerar.

stereoradiography _n._ estereorradiografía, radiografía tridimensional.

stereotaxis _n._ esterotaxia, técnica de localización de áreas cerebrales usada en procedimientos neurológicos.

stereotype _n._ estereotipo; cliché.

sterile _a._ estéril. 1. que no es fértil; 2. aséptico-a, que no contiene ni produce microorganismos.

sterility _n._ esterilidad, incapacidad de concebir o procrear.

sterilization _n._ esterilización. 1. procedimiento que impide la reproducción; 2. destrucción completa de microorganismos; **dry heat** _____ / _____ por calor seco; **vapor** _____ / _____ por vapor; **gas** _____ / _____ por gas.

sterilize _v._ esterilizar.

sternal _a._ esternal, rel. al esternón; _____ **puncture** / punción _____ .

sternocostal _a._ esternocostal, rel. al esternón y las costillas.

steroid _n._ esteroide, compuesto orgánico complejo del cual se derivan varias hormonas como el estrógeno, la testosterona, y la cortisona.

stertor _n._ estertor. V. **rale.**

stethoscope _n._ estetoscopio, instrumento médico usado en la auscultación.

stew _n._ guisado, cocido; _v._ guisar, cocer.

sticky _a._ pegajoso-a.

stiff _a._ tieso-a, rígido-a; _____ **neck** / cuello _____ .

stigma _n._ estigma, huella. 1. señal específica de una enfermedad; 2. marca o señal en el cuerpo.

still _a._ inmóvil, quieto-a, tranquilo-a.

stillbirth _n._ nacimiento sin vida.

stillborn _a._ mortinato-a, muerto-a al nacer.

Still's disease _n._ enfermedad de Still, artritis reumatoidea juvenil.

stimulant _n._ estimulante, agente que produce una reacción.

stimulate _v._ estimular; motivar; excitar.

stimulation _a._ estimulación; motivación.

stimulus _n._ (_pl._ **stimuli**) estímulo, cualquier agente o factor que produce una reacción; **conditioned** _____ / _____ condicionado; **subliminal** _____ / _____ sublimado.

sting _n._ picadura; **bee** _____ / picadura de abeja; **wasp** _____ / _____ de avispa.

stink _n._ olor desagradable, mal olor.

stippling _n._ punteado, condición de apariencia con manchas.

stipulate _v._ negociar, estipular.

stir _n._ movimiento; excitación; _v._ revolver, agitar.

stirrup bone _n._ estribo. V. **stapes.**

stitch _n._ punto de sutura; _v._ dar puntos.

stock _n._ caldo.

stocking _n._ medias; **elastic** _____ / calceta, media elástica.

stocky _a._ robusto-a.

stoma _n._ estoma, abertura hecha por cirugía, esp. en la pared del abdomen.

stomach _n._ estómago, órgano en forma de saco que forma parte del tubo digestivo; _____ **ulcer** / úlcera gástrica; _____ **ache** / dolor de _____ ; **on an empty** _____ / en ayunas; _____ **pump** / bomba estomacal; _____ **pumping** / lavado de _____ ; _v._ **pop.** soportar, tolerar.

stomachal _a._ estomacal, rel. al estómago; _____ **tonic** / tónico _____ .

stomal _n._ estomal, rel. a un estoma.

stomatitis _n._ estomatitis, infl. de la mucosa de la boca; **aphthous** _____ / _____ aftosa.

stone _n._ piedra, cálculo.

stool _n._ heces fecales, excremento; _____ **softener** / copro-emoliente.

stop _n._ parada, alto, interrupción; _v._ dete-

ner, parar, interrumpir; **to make a** ___ /
hacer alto, hacer una parada; detenerse, pa-
rarse.

stoppage *n*. bloqueo; obstrucción; taponamiento.

storm *n*. tormenta; intensificación repentina
de síntomas de una enfermedad.

strabismus *n*. estrabismo, alineamiento a-
normal de los ojos debido a una deficiencia
muscular; *pop*. bizquera.

straight *a*. derecho-a, recto-a; estirado-a,
erguido-a.

straightjacket *n*. camisa de fuerza.

strain *n*. esfuerzo, torcedura, *V*. **sprain;**
[*inherited trait*] rasgo, cepa; *v*. forzar; **to**
___ **the eyes** / forzar la vista; **to** ___ **a**
muscle / torcer un músculo; [*filter*] colar,
pasar; esforzarse demasiado.

strainer *n*. colador, coladera.

strand *n*. filamento, hilo; fibra delicada.

strange *a*. extraño-a, raro-a; extranjero-a; no
relacionado-a con un organismo o situado-a
fuera del mismo.

strangle *v*. estrangular.

strangulated *n*. estrangulado-a; constreñi-
do-a; ___ hernia / hernia ___.

strangulation *n*. estrangulación. 1. asfixia o
sofocación gen. causada por obstrucción de
las vías aéreas; 2. constricción de un órgano
o estructura debido a compresión.

strap *n*. faja, banda, correa, tira; *v*. poner
una faja; amarrar, atar.

stratification *n*. estratificación, formación
en capas.

stratified *a*. estratificado-a, colocado-a en
capas; ___ epithelium / epitelio ___.

stratum *n*. estrato; capa.

strawberry *n*. fresa; ___ mark / marca en
forma de ___.

stream *n*. chorro, flujo, corriente.

strength *n*. fuerza, vigor, resistencia.

strep throat *n*. infección y dolor de garganta
causados por un estreptococo.

streptococcal *a*. estreptocócico-a, rel. a estreptococos. ___ infections / infecciones
___-s.

streptococcemia *n*. estreptococemia, infección de la sangre debida a la presencia de
estreptococos.

streptococcus *n*. estreptococo, género de microorganismo de la tribu *Streptococceae,*
bacterias gram-positivas que se agrupan en
pares o cadenas, y que causan enfermedades serias.

streptomycin *n*. estreptomicina, antibiótico
que se usa contra infecciones bacterianas.

stress *n*. estrés, tensión emocional, compulsión. 1. factor químico. físico o emocional
que provoca un cambio como respuesta inmediata o demorada en las funciones del
cuerpo o en sus partes; ___ test / prueba de
esfuerzo; 2. *gr*. énfasis, acento tónico.

stretch *n*. tirón, estirón, esfuerzo; *v*. extender, alargar, estirar; **to** ___ **forth, to** ___
out / estirarse, extenderse, alargarse; ___
receptor / receptor de estiramiento.

stretcher *n*. camilla, andas; dilatador, extendedor.

stretching *n*. dilatación, extendimiento.

stria *n*. lista, fibra.

striated *a*. estriado-a, enlistado-a; ___ muscle / músculo ___.

stricken *a*. afectado-a súbitamente; afligido-
a.

strict *a*. estricto-a; exacto-a.

stricture *n*. estrechez, estrechamiento, constricción.

stridor *L*. stridor, estridor, ruido sordo respiratorio.

strike *n*. golpe, ataque repentino: *vi*. golpear, atacar súbitamente.

string *n*. cuerda, cordel.

string bean *n*. habichuela verde.

stroke *n*. 1. embolia cerebral, apoplejía; ataque súbito; 2. choque golpe.

stroking *n*. acto de frotar suavemente.

stroma *n*. estroma, armazón de tejido que
sirve de soporte a un órgano.

strong *a*. fuerte, fornido-a, robusto-a; ___
minded / determinado-a, decidido-a

structural *a*. estructural, rel. a la estructura
de un órgano.

structure *n*. estructura; orden.

struggle *n*. lucha, esfuerzo; *v*. luchar, esforzarse.

struma *L*. struma, engrosamiento de la tiroides; *pop*. bocio.

strychnine *n*. estricnina, alcaloide cristalino
muy venenoso.

stubborn *a*. obstinado-a, testarudo-a, caprichoso-a; *v*. **to become** ___ / obstinarse,
encapricharse.

student *n*. estudiante; medical ___ / ___ de
medicina.

study *n*. estudio; *v*. estudiar.

stuff *n*. material, elemento; *v*. embutir, llenar, empaquetar; **to** ___ **oneself** / hartarse.

stump *n.* muñón, parte que queda de una extremidad amputada.

stun *v.* aturdir, pasmar.

stupid *n.* estúpido-a, imbécil.

stupidity *n.* estupidez.

stupor *n.* estupor, letargo.

sturdy *a.* fuerte, vigoroso-a.

stutter *v.* tartamudear.

stuttering *n.* tartamudeo.

sty *n.* orzuelo, condición inflamatoria de las glandulas sebáceas del párpado.

styloid *a.* estiloide, de forma larga y puntiaguda.

subacromial *a.* subacromial, rel. al acromión o localizado debajo de éste.

subacute *a.* subagudo-a, rel. a una condición que no es ni aguda ni crónica.

subarachnoid *a.* subaracnoideo-a, que ocurre debajo de la membrana aracnoidea o de posición inferior a ésta; ____ hemorrhage / hemorragia ____; ____ space / espacio ____.

subatomic *a.* subatómico-a, menor que un átomo.

subcapsular *n.* subcapsular, situado debajo de una cápsula.

subclavian, subclavicular *a.* subclavicular, localizado debajo de la clavícula; ____ steal syndrome / síndrome del secuestro ____; ____ artery / arteria ____; ____ vein / vena ____.

subclinical *a.* subclínico-a, sin manifestación clínica.

subconscious *n. psic.* subconsciente, subconsciencia, donde se lleva a cabo la elaboración de procesos mentales que afectan la conducta y que no son reconocidos en un nivel consciente; *a.* subconsciente, parcialmente consciente.

subcostal *a.* subcostal, debajo de las costillas.

subculture *n.* subcultivo, cultivo de bacterias que se deriva de otro.

subcutaneous *a.* subcutáneo-a, debajo de la piel.

subdivide *v.* subdividir.

subdue *a.* sumiso-a, dominado-a, subyugado-a; *v.* dominar, subyugar.

subdural *a.* subdural, situado debajo de la dura madre; ____ hematoma / hematoma ____; ____ space / espacio ____.

subependymal *a.* subependimario-a, situado debajo del epéndimo.

subhepatic *a.* subhepático-a, situado debajo del hígado.

subject *n.* sujeto. 1. término usado en referencia al paciente; 2. tópico; 3. *gr.* sujeto del verbo.

subjective *a.* subjetivo-a; ____ symptoms / síntomas ____-s.

sublethal dose *a.* dosis subletal, cantidad insuficiente de una sustancia para causar la muerte.

sublimate *n.* sublimado, sustancia adquirida por sublimación; *v.* sublimar, depurar.

sublimation *n.* sublimación. 1. cambio de un estado sólido a vapor; 2. *psic.* término freudiano que se refiere al proceso de transferir un impulso o deseo instintivo a una conducta aceptada socialmente.

sublingual *a.* sublingual, situado-a debajo de la lengua; ____ gland / glándula ____.

subluxation *a.* subluxación, dislocación incompleta.

submandibular *a.* submandibular, debajo de la mandíbula.

submental *a.* submental, debajo del mentón.

submerge *v.* sumergir, colocar debajo de un líquido.

submission *n.* sumisión, sometimiento.

submit *v.* someter; someterse.

submucosa *n.* submucosa, capa de tejido celular situado debajo de una mucosa.

subnormal *a.* subnormal, menos que el promedio normal.

subphrenic *a.* subfrénico-a, situado-a debajo del diafragma; ____ abscess / absceso ____.

subscapular *a.* subescapular, debajo de la escápula.

subscription *n.* subscripción, parte de la receta médica que da instrucciones para la preparación de un medicamento.

subside *v.* menguar, apaciguar, bajar, cesar.

subsist *v.* subsistir, sobrevivir.

substance *n.* sustancia, líquido; droga; ____ abuse / abuso de drogas; ____ dependence / dependencia de drogas; ____ withdrawal syndrome / síndrome de abstinencia de drogas; ground ____ / ____ fundamental.

substantive *n. gr.* substantivo, sustantivo, nombre.

substernal *a.* subesternal, debajo del esternón.

substitute *n.* sustituto-a; reemplazo; *v.* sustituir, reemplazar.

substitution *n.* substitución; ____ therapy / terapia por ____.

substratum *n.* sustrato, fundación, base en la que vive un organismo.

substructure *n.* subestructura, soporte o material que sirve de base.

subtile, subtle *a.* sutil, delicado-a; inadvertido-a, desapercibido-a.

subungual *a.* subungual, debajo de una uña.

succeed *v.* tener éxito, salir bien; lograr.

success *n.* éxito, acierto, triunfo.

successful *a.* afortunado-a, de excelente resultado.

successive *a.* sucesivo-a, consecutivo-a.

succus *L.* succus, jugo.

such *a.* tal, semejante; **in** ___ **manner** / en ___ forma.

suck *v.* chupar, [*mother's milk*] mamar; **to** ___ **out** / chupar sacando; vaciar, extraer.

sucrose *n.* sucrosa, sacarosa que se obtiene de la caña de azúcar o la remolacha.

suction *n.* succión, aspiración.

sudden *a.* súbito-a, imprevisto-a, repentino-a; ___ **death** / muerte ___.

sudor *n.* sudor, secreción de las glándulas sudoríparas.

sudorific *a.* sudorífico-a, que promueve el sudor.

sudoriparous *a.* sudoríparo-a, que secreta sudor; ___ **gland** / glándula ___.

sue *v.* demandar, poner pleito.

suffer *v.* sufrir, padecer; **to** ___ **from** / padecer de.

suffering *n* sufrimiento, padecimiento.

sufficient *a.* suficiente; **-ly** *adv.* suficientemente.

suffix *n. gr.* sufijo.

suffocate *v.* sofocar, asfixiar; faltar la respiración.

suffocation *n.* asfixia, paro de la respiración.

suffusion *n.* sufusión, infiltración de un líquido del cuerpo en los tejidos circundantes.

sugar *n.* azúcar, carbohidrato que consiste esencialmente de sucrosa; **beet** ___ , **cane** ___ / sucrosa; **fruit** ___ / fructosa; **grape** ___ / glucosa; **milk** ___ / lactosa.

suggest *v.* sugerir, indicar, aconsejar.

suggestion *n.* sugerencia, consejo, indicación; sugestión.

suggestive *a.* sugestivo-a, rel. a la sugestión o que sugiere.

suicidal *a.* suicida, rel. al suicidio o con tendencia al mismo.

suicide *n.* suicidio; suicidarse; **attempted** ___ / tentativa o intento de ___.

sulcus *L.* (*pl.* **sulci**) sulcus, depresión leve, sisura.

sulfacetamide *n.* sulfacetamida, sulfonamida antibacteriana.

sulfa drugs *n.* sulfa, medicamentos del grupo sulfonamida, antibacterianos.

sulfate *n.* sulfato, sal de ácido sulfúrico.

sulfonamides *n. pl.* sulfonamidas, grupo de compuestos orgánicos sulfuro-bacteriostáticos.

sulfur *n.* azufre, sulfuro.

sulfuric *a.* sulfúrico-a, rel. al sulfuro.

sullen *a.* malhumorado-a; resentido-a.

summary *n.* sumario, historia clínica del paciente; ___ **of hospital records** / sumario del expediente.

summation *n.* suma total, acción o efecto acumulativo.

sun *n.* sol; ___ **bathing** / baño de ___ ; ___ **burn** / quemadura de ___ , eritema solar; ___ **burnt** / quemado-a, tostado-a por el sol; *v.* **to** ___ **bathe** / tomar el ___ .

sunscreen *n.* bloqueador solar.

sunspot *n.* mancha de sol.

sunstroke *n.* insolación.

superb *a.* magnífico-a, superior.

super ego *L.* el yo, término freudiano que se refiere a la parte de la psique que concierne a los valores sociales, morales y éticos.

superfecundation *n.* superfecundación, fertilización sucesiva de dos óvulos que pertenecen al mismo ciclo menstrual en dos actos sexuales distintos.

superfemale *n.* superhembra, organismo femenino que tiene más del número necesario de cromosomas que determinan el sexo.

superficial *a.* superficial, rel. a la superficie; **-ly** *adv.* superficialmente.

superinfection *n.* superinfección, infección subsecuente producida gen. por un microorganismo diferente que ocurre durante el curso de una infección presente.

superior *n.* superior, más alto; [*position*] hacia arriba; al exterior.

superiority complex *n.* complejo de superioridad.

supernatural *a.* sobrenatural.

supernumerary *a.* supernumerario-a, en número mayor que el normal.

superolateral *a.* superolateral, en posición superior y lateral.

supersaturate *v.* supersaturar, saturar excesivamente, añadir una sustancia en una cantidad mayor de la que puede ser disuelta normalmente por un líquido.

supersaturated *a.* supersaturado-a.

supersensitiveness *n.* supersensibilidad, hipersensibilidad.

supersonic *a.* supersónico-a, ultrasónico, rel. a ondas de frecuencia demasiado alta para ser captadas por el oído humano.

superstition *n.* superstición.

superstitious *a.* supersticioso-a.

supervise *v.* supervisar, dirigir.

supervisor *n.* supervisor-a, jefe-a.

supine *a.* supino-a, de posición acostada de espalda, boca arriba y con la palma de la mano hacia arriba.

supper *n.* cena, la comida.

supplant *v.* reemplazar, substituir.

supplement *n.* suplemento; *v.* complementar.

supplemental *a.* suplemental, adicional.

supply *n.* abastecimiento; **supplies** / artículos de ____ , provisiones; *v.* proveer, surtir, abastecer.

support *n.* soporte, sostén.

suppose *v.* suponer.

suppository *n.* supositorio, medicamento semisólido que se inserta en una cavidad natural del cuerpo (vagina, recto).

suppression *n.* supresión. 1. fallo súbito del cuerpo en la producción de una excreción o secreción normal; 2. en psicoanálisis, la inhibición de una idea o deseo.

suppurate *v.* supurar, excretar.

suppuration *n.* supuración, formación o salida de pus.

suppurative *a.* supurativo-a, rel. a la supuración.

supraclavicular *a.* supraclavicular, situado-a encima de la clavícula.

suprapubic *a.* suprapúbico-a, localizado-a encima del pubis; ____ catheter / cáteter ____ ; ____ cystostomy / cistostomía ____ .

supratentorial *a.* supratentorial, que ocurre encima del tentorio.

sural *a.* sural, rel. a la pantorrilla.

sure *a.* seguro-a, decidido-a; positivo-a.

surface *n.* superficie. porción o límite exterior de una estructura; ____ tension / tensión superficial.

surfactant *n.* agente tensoactivo que modifica la tensión superficial de un líquido.

surgeon *n.* cirujano-a.

surgery *n.* cirugía. rama de la medicina que

comprende procesos operatorios de reparación, diagnosis de enfermedades y corrección de estructuras del cuerpo; ambulatory ____ / ____ ambulatoria; chest ____ / ____ cardiotoráxica; conservative ____ / ____ conservadora; major ____ / ____ mayor; minor ____ / ____ menor; orthopedic ____ / ____ ortopédica; oral ____ / ____ oral; plastic ____ / ____ plástica; radical ____ / ____ radical.

surgical *a.* quirúrgico-a; ____ dressing / vendaje ____ ; protector; ____ equipment / equipo ____ ; ____ flaps / colgajos ____ -s ; ____ incision / incisión ____ ; ____ instruments / instrumentos ____ -s; ____ mesh / malla ____ ; ____ resident / residente de cirugía.

surname *n.* apellido, nombre de familia.

surpass *v.* sobrepasar, exceder.

surplus *n., a.* sobrante, excedente.

surprise *n.* sorpresa.

surrogate *a.* subrogado-a, que sustituye algo o a alguien; *v.* subrogar, sustituir.

surveillance *n.* vigilancia.

survey *n.* encuesta; cuestionario.

survival *n.* supervivencia.

survive *v.* sobrevivir.

survivor *n.* sobreviviente.

survivorship *n.* supervivencia; anualidad, renta o pensión anual.

suspect *a.* sospechoso-a.

suspend *v.* suspender, cancelar.

suspicion *n.* sospecha.

sustain *v.* sostener, mantener; [*a wound*] sufrir una herida.

sustained *a.* sostenido-a; ininterrumpido-a; sufrido-a.

suture *n.* sutura; puntada; línea de unión; absorbable surgical ____ / ____ absorbible quirúrgica; bolster ____ / ____ compuesta; catgut ____ / ____ de catgut; purse-string ____ / ____ en bolsa de tabaco; uninterrupted continuous ____ / ____ continua, de peletero; vertical mattress ____ / ____ de colchonero.

swab *n.* escobillón; *v.* limpiar, fregar.

swaddling band *n.* fajero.

swallow *n.* trago; deglusión; *v.* tragar, deglutir.

swallowing *n.* deglución.

Swan-Ganz catheter *n.* cáteter de Swan-Ganz, sonda flexible que contiene un balón cerca de la punta y que se emplea para medir la presión sanguínea en la arteria pulmonar.

swaying *n*. vaivén, movimiento acompasado.

sweat *n*. sudor, secreción de las glándulas sudoríparas; night ___ -s / ___ -es nocturnos; *v*. sudar; hacer sudar.

sweated *a*. *pp*. de **to sweat**, sudoriento-a; sudoroso-a.

sweat glands *n*. *pl*. glándulas sudoríparas.

sweating *n*. sudor, perspiración, transpiración.

sweaty *a*. sudado-a, sudoroso-a.

sweep *vi*. barrer; recoger; limpiar.

sweet *a*. dulce, azucarado-a; [*tempered*] dulce, agradable, gentil.

sweet basil *n*. albahaca.

sweetener *n*. dulcificante.

sweeten *v*. endulzar, azucarar.

sweets *n*. *pl*. golosinas, dulces.

swell *vi*. hinchar, abultar, entumecer, agrandar; hincharse, entumecerse, agrandarse.

swelling *n*. hinchazón; tumefacción; *pop*. bulto, chichón.

swift *a*. ligero-a; fácil, sin complicación; **a** ___ **operation** / una operación fácil, sin complicaciones.

swim *vi*. nadar.

swimmer *n*. nadador-a; ___ 's ear / otitis del ___ .

switch *n*. [*instrumento*] cambio; conector eléctrico; *v*. cambiar; **to** ___ **on** / conectar; **to** ___ **off** / desconectar; cambiar.

swollen *a*. *pp*. de **to swell**, hinchado-a.

swoon *n*. desmayo, síncope; *v*. desfallecer; desmayarse, desvanecerse.

syllable *n*. *gr*. sílaba.

Sylvian aqueduct *n*. acueducto de Silvius, conducto estrecho que conecta los ventrículos cerebrales tercero y cuarto.

symbiosis *n*. simbiosis, unión estrecha de dos organismos que pertenecen a especies diferentes.

symbiotic *a*. simbiótico-a, rel. a la simbiosis.

symbol *n*. símbolo, representación o señal que sustituye o representa en la práctica otra cosa o idea.

symbolism *n*. simbolismo. 1. uso de símbolos en la práctica para dar una representación a las cosas; 2. *psic*. anormalidad mental por la cual el paciente

percibe todos los sucesos y cosas como símbolos de sus propios pensamientos.

symmetrical *a*. simétrico-a.

symmetry *n*. simetría, correspondencia perfecta entre partes de un cuerpo colocadas en posición opuesta a un centro o axis.

sympathectomy *n*. *cirg*. simpatectomía, extirpación de una porción del simpático.

sympathetic *a*. simpático-a, rel. al sistema nervioso simpático.

sympathetic nervous system *n*. sistema nervioso simpático, abastecedor de los músculos involuntarios, formado por nervios motores y sensoriales.

sympatholytic *a*. simpatolítico-a, que ofrece resistencia a la actividad producida por la estimulación del sistema nervioso simpático.

sympathomimetic *a*. simpatomimético-a, que puede causar cambios fisiológicos similares a los causados por el sistema nervioso simpático.

sympathy *n*. simpatía, asociación, relación. 1. afinidad; 2. relación entre dos órganos afines por la cual una anomalía en uno afecta al otro; 3. afinidad entre la mente y el cuerpo que causa que se afecten entre sí.

symphysis *n*. sínfisis, articulación en la cual las superficies óseas adyacentes se unen por un fibrocartílago; pubic ___ / ___ púbica.

symptom *n*. síntoma, manifestación o indicio de una enfermedad según se percibe por el paciente; constitutional ___ / ___ constitucional; delayed ___ / ___ demorado; objective ___ / ___ objetivo; pathognomic ___ / ___ patognómico; presenting ___ / ___ presente; prodormal ___ / ___ prodrómico; withdrawal ___ / ___ de supresión.

symptomatic *a*. sintomático-a, de la naturaleza de un síntoma o rel. a éste.

symptom complex *n*. complejo de síntomas o síntomas concurrentes que se manifiestan al mismo tiempo y que caracterizan una enfermedad.

synapse *n*. sinapsis, punto de contacto entre dos neuronas donde el impulso que pasa por la primera neurona origina un impulso en la segunda.

synapsis *n*. sinapsis, aparejamiento de cromosomas homólogos al comienzo de la meiosis.

synaptic *a*. sináptico-a, rel. a la sinapsis.

synarthrosis *n*. sinartrosis, articulación inmóvil en la cual los elementos óseos están fusionados.

synchondrosis *n.* sincondrosis, articulación inmóvil de superficies unidas por tejido cartilaginoso.

syncopal *a.* sincopal, rel. a un síncope.

syncope *n.* síncope, desmayo o pérdida temporal del conocimiento.

syncytial *a.* sincitial, rel. a un sincitio o que lo constituye.

syncytium *n.* sincitio, masa protoplasmática nucleada que resulta de la fusión celular.

syndactylism *n.* sindactilia, anomalía congénita que consiste en la fusión de dos o más dedos de la mano o los pies.

syndrome *n.* síndrome, síntomas y señales que caracterizan una enfermedad; acquired immune deficiency ___ (AIDS) / ___ de inmuno deficiencia adquirida (SIDA); adipous ___ / ___ adiposo; adrenogenital ___ / ___ suprarrenogenital; battered children ___ / ___ de niños maltratados; dumping ___ / ___ de vaciamiento gástrico rápido; hepatorenal ___ / ___ hepatorrenal; malabsorption ___ / ___ de malabsorción gastrointestinal; middle lobe ___ / ___ del lóbulo medio del pulmón; nephrotic ___ / ___ nefrótico; respiratory stress ___ / ___ de dificultad respiratoria; scalded skin ___ / ___ de escaldadura, quemadura de la epidermis; sick sinus ___ / ___ del seno carotídeo; subclavian steal ___ / ___ del secuestro subclavicular; sudden death ___ / ___ de muerte súbita; transfusion ___ , multiple / ___ de transfusión múltiple; toxic shock ___ / ___ de choque tóxico, envenenamiento de la sangre causado por estafilococos; withdrawal ___ / ___ de privación.

synechia *n.* sinequia, unión o adherencia anormal de tejidos u órganos esp. referente al iris, al cristalino y a la córnea.

synergic *n.* sinérgico-a, que posee la propiedad de actuar en cooperación.

synergism *n.* sinergismo, correlación o unión armoniosa entre dos o más estructuras o sustancias.

synovia *n.* sinovia, líquido que lubrica las articulaciones y tendones.

synovial *a.* sinovial, rel. a la membrana sinovial; ___ bursa / bursa ___ ; ___ cyst / quiste ___ .

synovial fluid *n.* líquido sinovial, líquido viscoso transparente.

synovitis *n.* sinovitis, infl. de la membrana sinovial; dry ___ / ___ seca; purulent ___ / ___ purulenta; serous ___ / ___ serosa.

synovium *n.* membrana sinovial.

synthesis *n.* síntesis, composición de un todo por la unión de las partes.

synthesize *v.* sintetizar, producir síntesis.

synthetic *a.* sintético-a, rel. a una síntesis o producido por ésta.

syntonic *a.* sintónico-a, rel. a un tipo de personalidad estable que se adapta normalmente al ambiente.

syphilis *n.* sífilis, enfermedad venérea contagiosa que se manifiesta en lesiones cutáneas, usu. transmitida por contacto directo.

syphilitic *n.* *a.* sifilítico-a, rel. a la sífilis o causado por ella.

syphilology *n.* sifilología, rama de la medicina que se dedica al tratamiento y diagnosis de la sífilis.

syphiloma *n.* tumor sifilítico.

syringe *n.* jeringa, jeringuilla; disposable ___ / ___ desechable; glass cylinder ___ / ___ con tubo de cristal; hypodermic ___ / ___ hipodérmica.

syringobulbia *n.* siringobulbia, presencia de cavidades en la médula oblongata.

syringocele *n.* siringocele. 1. conducto central de la médula espinal; 2. meningomielocele que contiene una cavidad en la médula espinal ectópica.

syringomyelia *n.* siringomielia, enfermedad crónica progresiva de la columna vertebral caracterizada por cavidades llenas de líquido en la región cervical y que a veces se extiende a la médula oblongata.

syrinx *Gr.* (*pl.* **syringes**) syrinx. 1. fístula; 2. tubo o conducto.

syrup *n.* jarabe, almíbar.

system *n.* sistema, grupo de partes u órganos combinados que constituyen un conjunto que desempeña una o más funciones vitales en el organismo; cardiovascular ___ / ___ cardiovascular; digestive ___ / ___ digestivo; endocrine ___ / ___ endocrino; genitourinary ___ / ___ genitourinario; hematopoietic ___ / ___ hematopoyético; immune ___ / ___ de inmunidad; limphatic ___ / ___ linfático; nervous ___ / ___ nervioso; osseous ___ / ___ óseo; portal

___ / ___ portal; respiratory ___ / ___ respiratorio; reticuloendothelial ___ / ___ reticuloendotelial.

systematic *a.* sistemático-a, que se ajusta a un régimen o sistema.

systematization *n.* sistematización, acción de seguir un sistema.

systematize *n.* sistematizar, hacer una síntesis.

systemic *a.* sistémico-a; que afecta el cuerpo en general; ___ circulation / circulación ___.

systole *n.* sístole, contracción del corazón esp. de los ventrículos; atrial ___ / ___ auricular; premature ___ / ___ prematura; ventricular ___ / ___ ventricular.

systolic *a.* sistólico-a, rel. a la sístole; ___ murmur / murmullo ___; ___ pressure / presión ___.

T

T *abbr.* **absolute temperature** / temperatura absoluta; **T+, increased tension** / tensión aumentada; **T–, diminished tension** / tensión disminuída.

tabacism *n.* tabaquismo, intoxicación aguda o crónica causada por una excesiva inhalación de polvo de tabaco.

tabes *n.* tabes, deterioro progresivo del organismo o de una parte del mismo debido a una enfermedad crónica.

tabetic *a.* tabético-a, rel. a tabes o que padece de éste.

table *n.* tabla. 1. capa o lámina ósea; 2. mesa; operating ___ / ___ de operaciones; 3. tabla, colección de datos o de referencia con una variante determinada.

tablespoon *n.* cuchara; ___ ful *n.* cucharada; *V.* **Appendix A.**

tablet *n.* tableta, comprimido, dosis en un compuesto sólido; enteric coated ___ / ___ de capa entérica.

taboo, tabu *n.* tabú, prohibición; *a.* prohibido-a.

tabular *a.* tabular, dispuesto en forma de tabla o cuadro.

tabulate *v.* tabular, hacer tablas o listas.

tache *n.* tacha, mancha, peca; imperfección.

tachyarrythmia *n.* taquiarritmia, forma de arritmia acompañada de pulso rápido.

tachycardia *n.* taquicardia, aceleración de la

actividad cardíaca, gen. a una frecuencia de más de 100 por minuto en una persona adulta; atrial ___ / ___ auricular; ectopic ___ / ___ ectópica; paroxismal atrial ___ / ___ auricular paroxística; sinusal ___ / ___ sinusal; supraventricular ___ / ___ supraventricular; ventricular ___ / ___ ventricular.

tachypnea *n.* taquipnea, respiración anormalmente acelerada.

tact *n.* tacto; diplomacia, discreción.

tactful *a.* discreto-a.

tactic *n.* táctica.

tactil, tactile *a.* táctil, palpable; rel. al sentido del tacto; ___ discrimination / discriminación ___; ___ system / sistema ___.

tactless *a.* indiscreto-a.

taenia, tenia *n.* tenia, parásito de la clase *Cestoda* que en la etapa adulta vive en el intestino de los vertebrados.

tag *n.* [*label*] etiqueta.

tail *n.* [*appendage*] cola, rabo.

taint *n.* [*stain*] mancha, mácula; *v.* manchar, podrirse o causar putrefacción; corromperse.

take *vi.* [*to get*] tomar; [*to seize*] coger, agarrar; [*to carry something, to take someone*] llevar; [*to remove*] quitar; **to** ___ **notes** / anotar; **to** ___ **a trip** / viajar; **to** ___ **a walk** / dar un paseo; **to be taken ill** / enfermarse.

talar *a.* talar, rel. al tobillo.

talc *n.* talco.

talcum *n.* polvo.

tale *n.* [*story*] cuento; [*gossip*] *pop.* chisme.

talent *n.* talento, habilidad.

talk *n.* charla, plática; *v.* charlar, hablar, platicar.

tall *a.* alto-a; elevado-a.

talon *n.* talón, parte posterior de un diente molar.

talotibial *a.* talotibial, rel. al talón y la tibia.

talus *n.* (*pl.* **tali**) talón, astrágalo, tobillo.

tambour *n.* tambor. 1. tímpano del oído medio; 2. instrumento de precisión que se usa para registrar y transmitir movimientos ligeros tales como las contracciones peristálticas.

tampon *n.* tapón, gasa o algodón prensado que se aplica o inserta en la vagina u otra cavidad para absorber secreciones.

tamponade *Fr.* taponamiento, aplicación de tapones a una herida o cavidad para detener una hemorragia o absorber secreciones; balloon ___ / ___ por balón insuflable; cardiac ____ / ____ cardíaco, compresión aguda del corazón causada por un exceso de sangre acumulada en el pericardio.

tangible *a*. tangible.

tangle *n*. enredo, confusión; *v*. enredarse; confundirse.

tangled *a*. enredado-a; confundido-a.

tangy *a*. [*smell*] fuerte, penetrante.

tantrum *n*. rabieta; *pop*. berrinche, pataleta.

tap *v*. tocar ligeramente; punzar, perforar, hacer una punción; ____ **water** / agua corriente.

tape *n*. [*audiotape*] cinta magnética; [*adhesive*] esparadrapo; ____ **recorder** / grabadora.

tapeworm *n*. tenia, solitaria. *V*. **taenia**.

tarantula *n*. tarántula, araña negra venenosa.

tardive *Fr*. tardío, retardado-a, que tarda en aparecer.

target *n*. 1. [*area*] blanco; 2. objetivo de una investigación; 3. célula "en diana" u órgano afectado por un agente definido (droga u hormona).

tarsal *a*. tarsal, tarsiano-a. 1. rel. al tarso; 2. rel. al tejido conectivo que soporta el párpado del ojo.

tarsal bones *n. pl*. huesos del tarso.

tarsometatarsal *a*. tarsometatarsiano-a, rel. al tarso y al metatarso.

tarsus *n*. tarso, parte posterior del pie situada entre los huesos de la pierna y los huesos metatarsianos.

tart *a*. agrio-a, ácido-a.

task *n*. tarea, labor, trabajo.

taste *n*. gusto; ____ **buds** / papilas gustativas; **in good** ____ / de buen ____ ; *v*. probar, saborear.

tasteful *a*. gustoso-a, sabroso-a.

tasteless *a*. insípido-a, sin sabor.

tasty *a*. gustoso-a, apetitoso-a, sabroso-a.

tattooing *n*. tatuaje, diseño con colorantes permanentes en la epidermis.

taught *pret., pp*. de **to teach**, enseñado.

tax *n*. impuesto, contribución; **tax-exempt** *a*. exento de impuesto; *v*. imponer; cargar, abrumar.

taxis *L*. taxis. 1. manipulación o reducción de una parte u órgano para llevarlo a la posición normal; 2. reflejo direccional del movimiento de un organismo en respuesta a un estímulo.

T cells *n. pl*. linfocitos T, linfocitos diferenciados en el timo que dirigen la respuesta inmunológica y que asisten a los linfocitos B a responder a antígenos; helper ____ / ____ inductores, ayudantes, estimulan la producción de anticuerpos formados por células que se derivan del linfocito B; cytotoxic ____ / ____ citotóxicos, destruyen células extrañas al cuerpo (como en el caso de órganos transplantados); suppressor ____ / ____ supresores, detienen la producción de anticuerpos formados por células que se derivan del linfocito B.

tea *n*. té.

teach *vi*. enseñar.

team *n*. equipo; grupo asociado; *v*. **to** ____ **up** / asociarse en cooperación.

teamwork *n*. esfuerzo coordinado; trabajo en coordinación.

tear *n*. lágrima; desgarramiento, desgarro; ____ **gas** / gas lacrimógeno; *vi*. rasgar, desgarrar, romper; **to** ____ **off** / arrancar; **to shed** ____ **-s** / lagrimear.

tear duct *n*. conducto lacrimal.

tearful *a*. lagrimoso-a.

tearing *n*. lagrimeo.

tease *v*. rasgar, separar un tejido o espécimen con agujas para examinarlo bajo el microscopio.

teaspoon *n*. cucharita; ____ **ful** / cucharadita.

teat *n*. tetilla. 1. glándulas mamarias; 2. pezón.

technetium 99 m *n*. tecnecio 99 m., radioisótopo que emite rayos gamma, de uso frecuente en medicina nuclear.

technician *n*. técnico-a, persona entrenada en la administración de tratamientos o pruebas de laboratorio y que gen. actúa bajo la supervisión de un facultativo; dental ____ / ____ dental; electrocardiographic ____ / ____ electrocardiógrafo-a; emergency medical ____ / ____ de emergencia; medical laboratory ____ / laboratorista; radiologic ____ / ____ radiólogo-a; respiratory therapy ____ / ____ de terapia respiratoria.

technique *n*. técnica, método o procedimiento.

technologist *n*. techólogo-a, persona experta en tecnología.

technology *n*. tecnología, ciencia que trata de la aplicación de procedimientos técnicos.

tectorium _L._ tectorium, membrana que cubre el órgano de Corti.

tectum _L._ tectum, estructura en forma de techo.

tedious _a._ tedioso-a, aburrido-a, engorroso-a.

teenage _n._ adolescencia.

teenager _n._ jovencito-a de trece a diecinueve años de edad.

teeth _n. pl._ dientes; deciduous ___ / ___ de leche o primera dentición; permanent ___ / ___ permanentes; secondary ___ / ___ secundarios; wisdom ___ / ___ cordales, _pop._ muelas del juicio.

teething _n._ dentición.

tegument _n._ tegumento, la piel.

telangiectasia _n._ telangiectasia, telangiectasis, condición causada por dilatación de los vasos capilares y arteriolas que puede formar un angioma.

telemetry _n._ telemetría, información transmitida electrónicamente a distancia.

telencephalon _n._ telencéfalo, porción anterior del encéfalo.

telepathy _n._ telepatía, comunicación aparente de pensamientos de una persona a otra por medios extrasensoriales.

telephone _n._ teléfono; ___ **call** / llamada telefónica; _v._ telefonear, llamar por teléfono.

teleradiography _n._ telerradiografía, rayos X tomados a dos o más metros de distancia del objetivo para disminuir distorsiones.

television _n._ televisión; ___ **set** / televisor.

tell _vi._ decir; relatar, contar.

telophase _n._ telofase, fase final de un proceso.

temper _n._ carácter, disposición; temple, humor; genio; _v._ **to have bad** ___ / tener mal ___ ; **to have good** ___ / tener buen ___ .

temperament _n._ temperamento, combinación de la constitución física, mental y emocional de una persona que la distingue entre otras.

temperate _a._ moderado-a; sobrio-a, abstemio-a.

temperature _n._ temperatura. 1. grado de calor o frío según se mide en una escala específica; 2. calor natural de un cuerpo vivo; 3. fiebre o calentura; absolute ___ / ___ absoluta; ambient ___ / ___ ambiental; axillary ___ / ___ axilar; body ___ / ___ del cuerpo; critical ___ / ___

crítica; maximum ___ / ___ máxima; minimum ___ / ___ mínima; normal ___ / ___ normal; oral ___ / ___ oral; rectal ___ / ___ rectal; subnormal ___ / ___ subnormal.

tempest _n._ tempestad, tormenta.

template _n._ patrón, molde; _a._ templado-a.

temple _n._ sien, superficie lisa a cada lado de la parte lateral de la cabeza.

temporal _a._ temporal. 1. rel. a la sien; ___ bone / hueso ___ ; ___ lobe / lóbulo ___ ; 2. rel. al tiempo.

temporary _a._ temporal; pasajero-a; [_transition period_] interino-a; transitorio-a.

temporomandibular joint _n._ articulación temporomaxilar, rel. a la articulación entre la mandíbula y el hueso temporal.

tempting _a._ tentador-a; atractivo-a.

tenacious _a._ tenaz, persistente; determinado-a.

tend _v._ cuidar, atender; vigilar.

tendency _n._ tendencia.

tender _a._ sensitivo-a al tacto o la palpación; ___ points / puntos neurálgicos; [_soft_] blando-a, tierno-a.

tenderness _n._ blandura; delicadeza. 1. sensibilidad, condición sensible al tacto o palpación; 2. ternura.

tendinitis, tendonitis _n._ tendinitis, tendonitis, infl. de un tendón.

tendinous _a._ tendinoso-a, rel. a o semejante a un tendón.

tendon _n._ tendón, tejido fibroso que sirve de unión a los músculos y los huesos y a otras partes; deep ___ reflexes / reflejos profundos de los ___ -es; ___ jerk / tirón tendinoso; ___ reflex / reflejo tendinoso.

tenesmus _n._ tenesmo, condición dolorosa e ineficaz al orinar o defecar.

tennis elbow _n._ codo de tenista.

tenosynovitis _n._ tenosinovitis, infl. de la vaina que cubre un tendón.

tense _a._ tenso-a, rígido-a, tirante, en estado de tensión.

tenseness _n._ tensión.

tension _n._ tensión. 1. acto o efecto de estirarse o ser extendido; 2. grado de estiramiento; 3. sobreesfuerzo mental, emocional o físico; premenstrual ___ / ___ premenstrual; 4. expansión de un gas o vapor; surface ___ / ___ superficial.

tension headache _n._ dolor de cabeza causado por una tensión nerviosa mental.

tensor *n.* tensor, músculo que estira o hace tensión.

tent *n.* tienda, cámara esp. para cubrir un espacio en el cual se incluye al paciente; oxygen ___ / ___ o cámara de oxígeno.

tentaculum *n.* tentáculo, tipo de gancho quirúrgico para sujetar o prensar una parte.

tentative *a.* tentativo-a, experimental, sujeto-a a cambios.

tentorial *a.* tentorial, rel. a un tentorium.

tentorium *L.* tentorium, estructura que se asemeja a una tienda.

tenuous *a.* tenue, delicado-a.

tepid *a.* tibio-a.

teratogen *n.* teratógeno, agente que causa teratogénesis.

teratogenesis *a.* teratogénesis, producción de anomalías severas en el feto.

teratoid *a.* teratoide. 1. semejante a un monstruo; 2. que proviene de un embrión malformado; ___ tumor / tumor ___.

teratology *n.* teratología, estudio de malformaciones en el feto.

teratoma *n.* teratoma, neoplasma que deriva de más de una capa embrionaria y por lo tanto se compone de tejidos de distintas clases.

teres *L.* teres, término empleado para describir ciertos tipos de músculos o ligamentos alargados y cilíndricos.

term *n.* término. 1. período de tiempo de duración efectiva o limitada tal como en el embarazo; 2. vocablo.

terminal *a.* terminal, final.

terminal illness *n.* enfermedad maligna que causa la muerte.

terminate *v.* terminar, acabar.

termination *n.* terminación.

terminology *n.* terminología, nomenclatura.

ternary *a.* ternario-a, que se compone de tres elementos.

Terramycin *n.* Terramicina, nombre comercial de un antibiótico derivado de la tetraciclina.

terrible *a.* terrible.

terror *a.* terror, pánico.

tertian *a.* terciano-a, que se repite cada tercer día; ___ fever / fiebre ___.

tertiary syphillis *n.* sífilis terciaria, el estado más avanzado de la sífilis.

test *n.* prueba; examen; análisis; double blind ___ / ___ de pronóstico incierto; endurance ___ / ___ de resistencia; follow up ___ / ___ subsecuente; glucose tolerance ___ / ___ de tolerancia a la glucosa; pregnancy ___ / ___ del embarazo; random ___ / ___ de control sin método; skin ___ / ___ cutánea; scratch ___ / ___ de rasguño, ___ de alergia; screening ___ / ___ eliminatoria; stress ___ / ___ de esfuerzo; ___ tube / tubo de ensayo; ___ type / ___ de tipo, prueba visual de letras; visual ___ / ___ visual.

testament *n.* testamento.

tester *n.* probador, ensayador.

testicle *n.* testículo, una de las dos glándulas reproductivas masculinas que produce espermatozoos y la hormona testosterona; ectopic ___ / ___ ectópico; undescended ___ / ___ no descendido.

testicular *a.* testicular, rel. al testículo; ___ tumors / tumores ___-es.

testify *v.* declarar, testificar.

testis *L.* (*pl.* **testes**) testis, testículo.

testosterone *n.* testosterona, hormona producida en el testis estimulante del desarrollo de algunas características masculinas secundarias tales como el vello facial y la voz grave; ___ implant / implante de ___.

test-tube baby *n.* fertilización *in vitro*, embarazo en probeta o que resulta de un óvulo fecundado fuera de la madre en el laboratorio, y reimplantado en el útero.

tetanic *a.* tetánico-a, rel. al tétano; ___ antitoxin / antitoxina ___; ___ convulsion / convulsión ___ toxoid / toxoide ___.

tetanus, lockjaw *n.* tétano, enfermedad infecciosa aguda causada por el bacilo del tétano gen. introducido a través de una lesión y que se manifiesta con espasmos musculares y rigidez gradual de la mandíbula, el cuello y el abdomen.

tetanus immune globulin *n.* globulina inmune contra el tétano.

tetany *n.* tetania, afección neuromuscular que se manifiesta con espasmos intermitentes de los músculos voluntarios asociada con deficiencia paratiroidea y disminución del balance de calcio.

tetracycline *n.* tetraciclina, antibiótico de espectro amplio usado para combatir microorganismos gram-positivos y gram-negativos, ricketsia y cierta variedad de virus.

tetrad *n.* tétrada, grupo de cuatro elementos similares.

tetralogy *n.* tetralogía, término aplicado a

una combinación de cuatro factores o elementos.

tetraplegia *n*. tetraplejía, parálisis de las cuatro extremidades.

tetraploid *n*. tetraploide, que posee cuatro grupos de cromosomas.

tetravalent *n*. tetravalente, que posee una valencia química igual a cuatro.

texture *n*. textura, composición de la estructura de un tejido.

thalamic *a*. talámico-a, rel. al tálamo.

thalamus *n*. tálamo, una de las dos estructuras formadas por masas de materia gris que se encuentran en la base del cerebro y que constituyen el centro principal por donde los impulsos sensoriales pasan a la corteza cerebral.

thalassemia *n*. talasemia, grupos de anemias hipocrómicas causadas por factores genéticos que producen reducción o fallo en la síntesis total de hemoglobina; major ___ / ___ mayor; minor ___ / ___ menor.

thalassotherapy *n*. talasoterapia, tratamiento de una enfermeded por medio de baños de mar o exposición al aire marino.

thalidomide *n*. talidomida, sedativo e hipnótico, causante probado de malformaciones en niños de madres que tomaron la droga durante el embarazo.

than *conj*. que; *comp*. que. *V.* grammar section.

thanatology *n*. tanatología, rama de la medicina que trata de la muerte en todos sus aspectos.

thank *v*. dar gracias; agradecer.

thankful *a*. agradecido-a.

thanks *n*. *pl*. gracias; agradecimiento, gratitud.

thaw *n*. deshielo, descongelación; *v*. descongelar, deshelar, derretir.

theca *n*. teca, envoltura o capa que actúa esp. como protectora de un órgano.

thecoma *n*. tecoma, tumor ovárico gen. benigno.

thenar *a*. tenar, rel. a la palma de la mano; ___ eminence / eminencia ___ ; ___ muscles / músculos ___ -es.

theoretical *a*. teórico-a, rel. a una teoría.

theory *n*. teoría. 1. conocimientos relacionados con un tema sin verificación práctica de los mismos; 2. especulación u opinión que no ha sido probada científicamente.

therapeutic *a*. terapéutico-a. 1. que tiene

propiedades curativas; 2. rel. a la terapéutica.

therapeutics *n*. terapéutica, rama de la medicina que estudia tratamientos y curaciones.

therapist *n*. terapeuta, persona experta en una o más áreas de aplicación de tratamientos en el campo de la salud; physical ___ / ___ físico; speech ___ / ___ del lenguaje.

therapy *n*. terapia, terapéutica, tratamiento de una enfermedad; anticoagulant ___ / ___ anticoagulante; behavior ___ / ___ de conducta; electric convulsive ___ (E.C.T.) / electrochoque; X-ray ___ / radioterapia; group ___ / ___ de grupo; inhalation ___ / ___ por inhalación; occupational ___ / ___ ocupacional; physical ___ / fisioterapia; shock ___ / ___ por choque.

thermal, thermic *a*. termal, térmico-a, rel. al calor o producido por éste.

thermistor *n*. termistor, tipo de termómetro para medir cambios mínimos en la temperatura.

thermocoagulation *n*. termocoagulación, coagulación de tejidos por medio de corrientes de alta frecuencia.

thermodynamics *n*. termodinámica, ciencia que trata de la relación entre el calor y otras formas de energía.

thermograph *n*. termógrafo, detector infrarrojo que registra variaciones de la temperatura corporal según reacciona a los cambios de la circulación sanguínea.

thermography *n*. termografía, registro obtenido con un termógrafo.

thermometer *n*. termómetro, instrumento usado para medir el grado de calor o frío; Celsius ___ / ___ de Celsius o centígrado; clinical ___ / ___ clínico; Fahrenheit ___ / ___ de Fahrenheit; rectal ___ / ___ rectal; self-recording ___ / ___ de registro automático.

thermonuclear *a*. termonuclear, rel. a reacciones termonucleares.

thermoregulation *n*. termorregulación, regulación del calor o de la temperatura; termotaxis.

thermos *n*. termo.

thermostat *n*. termostato, instrumento regulador de temperaturas.

thermosterilization *n*. termoesterilización, esterilización por medio del calor.

thermotaxis *n*. termotaxis. 1. mantenimiento de la temperatura del cuerpo; 2. reacción de un organismo al estímulo del calor.

thermotherapy *n*. termoterapia, uso terapéutico del calor.

thesis *n*. (*pl*. **theses**) tesis; postulado.

thick *a*. grueso-a; macizo-a; [*liquid*] espeso-a.

thicken *v*. engrosar, espesar; condensar.

thickness *n*. espesor, densidad; consistencia.

thigh *n*. muslo, porción de la extremidad inferior entre la cadera y la rodilla; ___ bone / fémur.

thin *a*. delgado-a, flaco-a; [*liquid*] aguado-a, aclarado-a; [*light*] ligero-a.

thing *n*. cosa, objeto.

think *vi*. pensar; [*believe*] creer; **to ___ it over** / pensarlo bien; **to ___ nothing of** / tener en poco; **to ___ through** / considerar; **to ___ well of** / tener buena opinión de.

thinner *n*. solvente, diluyente.

third degree burn *n*. quemadura de tercer grado.

thirst *n*. sed.

thirsty *a*. sediento-a; *v*. **to be ___** / tener sed.

thoracentesis *n*. toracéntesis, punción y drenaje quirúrgicos de la cavidad torácica.

thoracic *a*. torácico-a, rel. al tórax; ___ **cage** / caja o pared ___; ___ **cavity** / cavidad ___; ___ **duct** / conducto ___; ___ **injuries** / traumatismos ___-s; ___ **neoplasms** / neoplasmas ___-s.

thoracicoabdominal *a*. toracicoabdominal, rel. al tórax y el abdomen.

thoracolumbar *a*. toracolumbar, rel. a las vértebras torácicas y lumbares.

thoracoplasty *n*. *cirg*. toracoplastia, cirugía plástica del tórax por medio de excisión de costillas para provocar la caída de un pulmón afectado.

thoracostomy *n*. *cirg*. toracostomía, incisión en la pared del tórax usando la abertura como drenaje.

thoracotomy *n*. *cirg*. toracotomía, incisión de la pared torácica.

thorax *n*. tórax, el pecho.

Thorazine *n*. Torazina, sedativo y antiemético.

thorough *a*. completo-a, minucioso-a, acabado-a; **-ly** *adv*. completamente, minuciosamente, a fondo.

thought *n*. pensamiento, concepto, idea; *a.*, *pp.* de. **to think**, pensado.

thoughtful *n*. atento, solícito-a, esmerado-a.

thread *n*. hilo; fibra, filamento; línea fina. 1. material de sutura; 2. cualquier filamento fino semejante a un hilo; *v*. enhebrar, ensartar; ___ **-like** / hiliforme, fibroso-a, filamentoso-a.

threat *n*. amenaza.

threaten *v*. amenazar.

threshold *n*. umbral. 1. grado mínimo necesario de un estímulo para producir un efecto; 2. dosis mínima que puede producir un efecto; absolute ___ / ___ absoluto; auditory ___ / ___ auditivo; ___ of consciousness / ___ de la consciencia; ___ dose / dosis mínima; renal ___ / ___ renal; sensory ___ / ___ sensorio.

thrill *n*. "thrill", estremecimiento, vibración o ruido especial que se siente por palpación; aneurysmal ___ / ___ aneurismal; aortic ___ / ___ aórtico; arterial ___ / ___ arterial; diastolic ___ / ___ diastólico; presystolic ___ / ___ presistólico; systolic ___ / ___ sistólico; *v*. emocionar, excitar; *v*. emocionarse, excitarse.

thrive *v*. prosperar, progresar.

throat *n*. garganta, área que incluye la faringe y la laringe.

throat culture *n*. muestra de cultivo del mucus extraído de la garganta y detección en el laboratorio de la presencia o no de agentes infecciosos en el mismo.

throb *n*. latido, pulsación, palpitación; *v*. latir, palpitar, pulsar.

throbbing *a*. palpitante.

thrombectomy *n*. *cirg*. trombectomía, extracción de un trombo.

thrombin *n*. trombina, enzima presente en la sangre extravasada que cataliza en la conversión de fibrinógeno en fibrina.

thrombnogen *n*. trombinogeno. *V*. **prothrombin.**

thromboangiitis *n*. tromboangiitis, infl. de un vaso sanguíneo con trombosis; trombosis de un vaso sanguíneo.

thrombocyte *n*. trombocito, plaqueta.

thrombocytopenia *n*. trombocitopenia, disminución anormal del número de las plaquetas sanguíneas.

thrombocytosis *n*. trombocitosis, aumento excesivo de plaquetas en la sangre.

thromboembolism *n*. tromboembolia, obstrucción de un vaso sanguíneo por un coágulo desprendido del lugar de origen.

thrombogenesis *n*. trombogénesis, formación de coágulos o trombos.

thrombolysis *n.* trombólisis, lisis o disolución de un coágulo.

thrombolytic *a.* trombolítico-a, rel. a un trombo o que causa la disolución de éste.

thrombophlebitis *n.* tromboflebitis, dilatación de la pared de una vena asociada con trombosis.

thrombosed *a.* trombosado, rel. a un vaso sanguíneo que contiene un trombo.

thrombosis *n.* trombosis, formación, desarrollo y presencia de un trombo; biliary ___ / ___ biliar; cardiac ___ / ___ cardíaca; coronary ___ / ___ coronaria; embolic ___ / ___ embólica; traumatic ___ / ___ traumática; venous ___ / ___ venosa.

thrombotic *a.* trombótico-a, rel. a la trombosis o que padece de ella.

thrombus *n.* (*pl.* **thrombi**) trombo, coágulo que causa una obstrucción vascular parcial o total.

throw *vi.* tirar; arrojar.

thrush *n.* muguet, afta, infección fungosa de la mucosa oral que se manifiesta con placas blancas en la cavidad bucal y la garganta.

thumb *n.* dedo pulgar; ___ sucking / chuparse el dedo gordo.

thumbnail *n.* uña del pulgar.

thymectomy *n. cirg.* timectomía, extirpación del timo.

thymic *a.* tímico-a, rel. al timo.

thymocyte *n.* timocito, linfocito que se origina en el timo.

thymoma *n.* timoma, tumor que se origina en el timo.

thymus *n.* timo, glándula situada en la parte inferior del cuello y anterosuperior de la cavidad torácica que desempeña un papel de importancia en la función inmunológica.

thyroglobulin *n.* tiroglobulina. 1. iodina que contiene glicoproteína secretada por la tiroides; 2. sustancia que se obtiene de tiroides porcinas y se administra como suplemento en el tratamiento de hipertiroidismo.

thyroglossal *a.* tirogloso-a, rel. a la tiroides y la lengua.

thyroid *n.* glándula tiroides, una de las glándulas endocrinas situadas delante de la tráquea y constituída por dos lóbulos laterales conectados en el centro; ___ function tests / pruebas del funcionamiento de la ___ ; *a.* tiroideo-a, rel. a la tiroides; ___

cartilage / cartílago ___ ; ___ hormones / hormonas ___-as; ___ storm / tormenta ___ , crisis ___ .

thyroidectomy *n. cirg.* tiroidectomía, extirpación de la tiroides.

thyroidism *n.* tiroidismo, condición por exceso de secreción tiroidea.

thyroiditis *n.* tiroiditis, infl. de la tiroides.

thyroid-stimulating hormone *n.* hormona estimulante de la secreción tiroidea. *V.* **thyrotropin.**

thyromegaly *n.* tiromegalia, agrandamiento de la tiroides.

thyroparathyroidectomy *n. cirg.* tiroparatiroidectomía, excisión de la tiroides y la paratiroides.

thyrotoxicosis *n.* tirotoxicosis, trastorno causado por hipertiroidismo que se manifiesta con agrandamiento de la tiroides, aumento en el metabolismo, taquicardia, pulso rápido e hipertensión.

thyrotropin *n.* tirotropina, hormona estimulante de la tiroides secretada por el lóbulo anterior de la pituitaria; ___ releasing hormone / hormona estimulante de ___ .

thyroxine *n.* tiroxina, hormona producida por la tiroides que contiene iodo, se obtiene sintéticamente de la tiroides de animales y se usa en el tratamiento de hipotiroidismo.

tibia *n.* tibia, hueso triangular anterior de la pierna situado debajo de la rodilla.

tibial *a.* tibial, rel. a la tibia o localizado cerca de ella.

tic *Fr.* tic, espasmo súbito o involuntario de un músculo que ocurre esp. en la cara; convulsive ___ / ___ convulsivo; coordinated ___ / ___ coordinado; douloureux ___ / ___ doloroso; facial ___ / ___ facial.

tick *n.* garrapata, acárido chupador de sangre transmisor de enfermedades; ___ bite / picadura de ___ .

tickle *n.* cosquilleo; *v.* hacer cosquillas, cosquillear; sentir un cosquilleo.

tickling *n.* cosquilla.

tidiness *n.* aseo, pulcritud; limpieza.

tidy *a.* aseado-a, pulcro-a; limpio-a.

tie *n.* ligadura, lazo; conexión *v.* amarrar, atar, enlazar; **to be tied up** / estar muy ocupado-a.

tight *a.* [*fitted*] apretado-a, ajustado-a; [*airtight*] hermético-a; tirante; **a ___ situation** / una situación grave; ___ **squeeze** /

pop. aprieto; *v.* **to hold on** ___ / agarrarse bien.

tighten *v.* apretar, ajustar.

time *n.* tiempo, medida de duración; bleeding ___ / ___ de sangramiento; coagulation ___ / ___ de coagulación; ___ exposure / ___ de exposición; ___ frame / espacio de ___ ; ___ lag / ___ de latencia; perception ___ / ___ de percepción; prothrombin ___ / ___ de protrombina; **at** ___ **-s** / a veces; **at the same** ___ / a la vez; **behind** ___ / atrasado-a; **for some** ___ / por algún ___ ; **for the** ___ **being** / por el momento, por ahora; **from** ___ **to** ___ / de vez en cuando; **in due** ___ / a su debido ___ ; **on** ___ / a tiempo; **What** ___ **is it?** / ¿Qué hora es?; **At what** ___ **?** / ¿A qué hora?

timely *a.* oportuno-a.

timer *n.* regulador de tiempo, minutero.

timid *a.* tímido-a.

tincture *n.* tintura, extracto de origen animal o vegetal que contiene alcohol.

tinea *L.* tinea, tiña, infección cutánea fungosa; ___ capital / ___ capitis; ___ pedis / ___ pedis, *pop.* pie de atleta; ___ versicolor / ___ versicolor.

tingle *n.* hormigueo, comezón, sensación de picazón.

tinnitus *n.* zumbido, chasquido, sonido que se siente en el oído.

tint *n.* tinte, colorante; *v.* teñir, colorar, dar color.

tiny *a.* diminuto-a.

tip *n.* punta, extremo; [*light touch*] toque ligero.

tired *a.* cansado-a, fatigado-a.

tiredness *n.* cansancio, fatiga.

tireless *a.* incansable, infatigable.

tiresome *a.* pesado-a, tedioso-a.

tiring *a.* agotador-a, que cansa o fatiga.

tissue *n.* tejido, grupo de células similares de función determinada unidas por una sustancia intercelular que actúan conjuntamente; adipous ___ / ___ adiposo; bone ___ , bony ___ / ___ óseo; carthilaginous ___ / ___ cartilaginoso; connective ___ / ___ conectivo; epithelial ___ / ___ epitelial; endothelial ___ / ___ endotelial; erectile ___ / ___ eréctil; fibrous ___ / ___ fibroso; glandular ___ / ___ glandular; granulation ___ / ___ de granulación; lymphoid ___ / ___ linfoide; mesenchymal ___ / ___ mesenquimatoso;

muscular ___ / ___ muscular; nervous ___ , nerve ___ / ___ nervioso; scar ___ / ___ cicatrizante; subcutaneous ___ / ___ subcutáneo.

tissue typing *n.* tipificación, clasificación por tipo; tipificación de tejido.

titer, titre *n.* título, la cantidad de una sustancia que se requiere para producir una reacción con un volumen determinado de otra sustancia.

titrate *v.* titular, determinar por titración.

titration *n.* titulación, determinación de volumen usando soluciones estandarizadas de valor conocido.

toad stool *n.* seta venenosa; hongo venenoso.

toast *n.* tostada.

tobacco *n.* tabaco, planta americana de la *Nicotiana tabacum* cuyas hojas preparadas contienen nicotina, sustancia tóxica perjudicial a la salud; ___ smoke pollution / contaminación por humo de tabaco; ___ use disorder / trastorno por uso de ___ .

tocograph *n.* tocógrafo, instrumento para estimar la fuerza de las contracciones uterinas.

tocometer *n.* tocómetro. *V.* **tocograph.**

today *adv.* hoy.

toddler *n.* niño-a que comienza a caminar.

toe *n.* dedo del pie.

toe drop *n.* caída de los dedos del pie.

toe nail *n.* uña de un dedo del pie.

toilet *n.* 1. servicio, inodoro; 2. limpieza relacionada con un procedimiento médico o quirúrgico; ___ **paper** / papel higiénico.

toilet training *n.* entrenamiento de los niños para controlar el acto de orinar y el de defecar.

tolerable *a.* tolerable.

tolerance *n.* tolerancia, capacidad de soportar una sustancia o un ejercicio físico sin sufrir efectos dañinos, tal como el uso de una droga o actividad física prolongada.

tolerant *a.* tolerante.

tolerate *v.* tolerar.

tomato *n.* tomate; ___ **soup** / sopa de ___ .

tomogram *n.* tomograma, radiografía seccionada de una parte del cuerpo.

tomograph *n.* tomógrafo, máquina radiográfica que se usa para hacer una tomografía.

tomography *n.* tomografía, técnica de diagnóstico por la cual se hacen radiografías de un órgano por secciones del mismo a profundidades distintas; computerized axial

· ___ (CAT) / ___ axial computarizada (TAC).

tomorrow *adv*. mañana; **day after** ___ / pasado ___.

tone *n*. tono. 1. grado normal de vigor y tensión en el funcionamiento de los órganos y músculos de un cuerpo sano; muscular ___ / ___ muscular; 2. cualidad definida de un sonido o voz.

tongue *n*. lengua; ___ **depressor** / depresor de ___; dry ___ / ___ seca; geographic ___ / ___ geográfica; black hairy ___ / ___ negra velluda; lengua infectada de hongos parásitos; red ___ / ___ roja o enrojecida; sticky ___ / ___ pegajosa.

tonic *n*. tónico, reconstituyente que restaura la vitalidad del organismo; *a*. tónico-a. 1. que restaura el tono normal; 2. caracterizado-a por una tensión continua.

tonicity *a*. tonicidad, cualidad normal de tono o tensión.

tonight *adv*. esta noche.

tonoclonic *a*. tonoclónico-a, rel. a espasmos musculares que son tónicos y clónicos.

tonometer *n*. tonómetro, instrumento usado para medir la tensión o presión esp. intraocular.

tonometry *n*. tonometría, medida de la presión o tensión.

tonsil *n*. amígdala, tonsila; cerebelar ___ / ___ cerebelosa; lingual ___ / ___ lingual; palatine ___ / ___ palatina; pharyngeal ___ / ___ faríngea.

tonsillar *a*. tonsilar, rel. a una tonsila; ___ crypt / cripta ___ o amigdalina; ___ fossa / fosa amigdalina.

tonsillectomy *n. cirg*. amigdalectomía, extirpación de las amígdalas.

tonsillitis *n*. amigdalitis, infl. de las amígdalas.

tonsilloadenoidectomy *n. cirg*. tonsiloadenoidectomía, extirpación de las adenoides y las amígdalas.

tonus *L*. tonus. *V*. **tone**.

too *adv*. además; también; asimismo.

tooth *n*. (*pl*. **teeth**) diente; impacted ___ / ___ impactado; ___ unerupted / ___ no erupcionado.

toothache *n*. dolor de muelas.

toothbrush *n*. cepillo de dientes.

toothpaste *n*. pasta de dientes, dentífrico.

tophaceous *a*. tofacio, rel. a un tofo o de naturaleza arenosa.

tophus *n*. tofo. 1. depósito de sal de ácido úrico en los tejidos, gen. visto en casos de gota; 2. cálculo dental.

topical *a*. tópico-a, rel. a un área localizada.

topographic anatomy *n*. anatomía topográfica.

torment *n*. tormento; *v*. atormentar.

torpid *a*. tórpido-a, torpe en los movimientos.

torpor *n*. embotamiento; estancamiento, inactividad física.

torque *Fr*. torque, fuerza rotatoria.

torsion *n*. torsión, rotación de una parte sobre su propio eje longitudinal; ovarian ___ / ___ ovárica; testicular ___ / ___ testicular.

torso *n*. torso, el tronco humano.

torticollis *n*. torticolis, espasmo tonicoclónico de los múculos del cuello que causa torsión cervical e inmovilidad de la cabeza.

tortuous *a*. tortuoso-a; torcido-a; sinuoso-a.

torture *n*. tortura, gran sufrimiento; castigo.

torus *L*. (*pl*. **tori**) torus, eminencia, protuberancia, abultamiento.

total *a*. total; completo-a; *v*. sumar, añadir.

totipotency *n*. totipotencia, habilidad de una célula de regenerarse o desarrollarse en otro tipo de célula.

totipotent *a*. totipotente, que puede generar totipotencia.

touch *n*. 1. sentido del tacto, percepción a través de la piel o de las membranas mucosas; 2. [*act of touching*] toque; *v*. tocar, palpar.

tourniquet *n*. torniquete, dispositivo usado para aplicar presión sobre una arteria y contener la salida de la sangre.

towel *n*. toalla.

toxemia *n*. toxemia, condición tóxica provocada por la absorción de toxinas que provienen de un foco infeccioso.

toxic *a*. tóxico-a, venenoso-a, rel. a un veneno o de naturaleza venenosa.

toxicity *n*. toxicidad, cualidad de ser venenoso.

toxicologist *n*. toxicólogo-a, especialista en toxicología.

toxicology *n*. toxicología, estudio de los venenos o sustancias tóxicas, los efectos que causan en el organismo, y su tratamiento.

toxicosis *n*. toxicosis, estado morboso debido a un veneno.

toxin *n.* toxina, veneno, sustancia nociva de origen animal o vegetal.

toxin-antitoxin *n.* toxina antitoxina, mezcla casi neutra de toxina diftérica y antitoxina que se usa en inmunizaciones contra la difteria.

toxoid *n.* toxoide, toxina desprovista de toxicidad que al introducirse en el organismo causa la formación de anticuerpos; *a.* toxoide, de naturaleza tóxica o venenosa; diphtheria ____ / ____ diftérico; tetanus ____ / ____ tetánico.

toxoplasma *n. Toxoplasma,* género de parásito protozoario.

toxoplasmosis *n.* toxoplasmosis, infección causada por un microorganismo de la familia *Toxoplasma* que invade los tejidos, con síntomas leves de malestar o posible infl. de las glándulas linfáticas y que puede ocasionar daños a la vista y al sistema nervioso central.

toy *n.* juguete.

trace *n.* rastro, vestigio. 1. cantidad diminuta de un elemento químico; 2. marca visible; *v.* trazar; rastrear, investigar.

tracer *n.* trazador, radioisótopo que al introducirse en el cuerpo crea un rastro que puede detectarse.

trachea *n.* tráquea, conducto respiratorio entre la parte extrema inferior de la laringe y el comienzo de los bronquios.

tracheal *a.* traqueal, rel. a la tráquea; ____ stenosis / estenosis ____ .

tracheitis *n.* traqueitis, infl. de la tráquea.

tracheoesophageal *a.* traqueoesofágico-a, rel. a la tráquea y al esófago.

tracheomalasia *n.* traqueomalasia, reblandecimiento de los cartílagos traqueales.

tracheostenosis *n.* traqueostenosis, estrechez de la tráquea.

tracheostomy *n. cirg.* traqueostomía, incisión en la tráquea para permitir el paso de aire en caso de obstrucción.

tracheotomy *n. cirg.* traqueotomía, incisión en la tráquea a través de la piel y los músculos del cuello.

trachoma *n.* tracoma, infección viral contagiosa de la conjuntiva y la córnea que se manifiesta con fotofobia, dolor, lagrimeo y, en casos severos, ceguera total.

tracing *n.* trazo, gráfica descriptiva que hace un instrumento al registrar un movimiento.

tract *n.* tracto, tubo, vía, vías, sistema alargado compuesto de tejidos y órganos que

actúan coordinadamente para desempeñar una función; alimentary ____ / ____ alimenticio; ascending ____ / ____ ascendiente; biliary ____ / ____ biliar; digestive ____ / ____ digestivo; genitourinary ____ / ____ genitourinario; olfactory ____ / vía olfatoria; pyramidal ____ / ____ piramidal; respiratory ____ / ____ o vía respiratoria.

traction *n.* tracción. 1. acto de tirar o halar; 2. fuerza que tira con tensión; cervical ____ / ____ cervical; lumbar ____ / ____ lumbar.

tractor *n.* tractor, instrumento o máquina usada para aplicar tracción.

trademark *n.* marca registrada.

tragus *n.* (*pl.* **tragi**) trago, protuberancia triangular en la parte externa del oido.

train *v.* entrenar; entrenarse.

trained nurse *n.* enfermero-a graduado-a.

training *n.* entrenamiento; adiestramiento.

trait *n.* rasgo o característica; acquired ____ / ____ adquirido; inherited ____ / ____ heredado.

trance *n. psic.* trance, condición semejante a un estado hipnótico que se caracteriza por la disminución de la actividad motora.

tranquil *a.* tranquilo-a, sereno-a.

tranquility *n.* tranquilidad, descanso.

tranquilizer *n.* tranquilizante, calmante.

transabdominal *a.* transabdominal, a través del abdomen o la pared abdominal.

transaxial *a.* transaxial, a través del axis de una estructura o parte.

transcapillary *a.* transcapilar, que ocurre a través de las paredes de los capilares.

transcript *n.* expediente; copia.

transcutaneous *a.* transcutáneo-a, a través de la piel; ____ electrical nerve stimulation / estimulación eléctrica ____ de un nervio.

transducer *n.* transductor, dispositivo que convierte una forma de energía a otra.

transect *v.* cortar transversalmente.

transection *n.* corte transversal a través del eje largo de un órgano.

transfer *v.* transferir, cambiar.

transfer, transference *n.* transferencia. 1. *psic.* reorientación que hace el paciente de sentimientos negativos o positivos (esp. reprimidos inconscientemente) hacia otra persona. esp. el psicoanalista; 2. transmisión de síntomas o fluidos de una parte a otra del cuerpo.

transferrin *n.* transferrina, globulina beta en

el plasma de la sangre que fija y transporta el hierro.

transfixion *n. cirg.* transfixión, acto de atravesar y cortar al mismo tiempo los tejidos blandos de dentro hacia afuera como en la extirpación de tumores o en amputaciones.

transform *v.* tranformar, cambiar la apariencia, carácter o estructura.

transformation *n.* transformación, cambio de forma o apariencia.

transfusion *n.* transfusión, acto de transferir un fluido a una vena o arteria; blood ___ / ___ de sangre; direct ___ / ___ directa; exchange ___ / exsanguino-transfusión; indirect ___ / ___ indirecta.

transillumination *n.* transiluminación, paso de luz a través de un cuerpo.

transitional *a.* transitorio-a, rel. a transición o cambio.

transitory *a.* transitorio-a, pasajero-a.

translate *v.* traducir.

translator *n.* traductor-a; intérprete.

translocation *n.* translocación, desplazamiento de un cromosoma o parte del mismo hacia otro cromosoma.

translucent *a.* translúcido-a, que deja pasar la luz.

transmigration *n.* transmigración, paso de un lugar o otro tal como las células sanguíneas en diapédesis.

transmissible *a.* transmisible, trasmisible, que puede transmitirse.

transmission *n.* transmisión, acto de transmitir o transferir tal como una enfermedad contagiosa o hereditaria; ___ by contact / ___ por contacto; droplet ___ / ___ por instilación; placental ___ / ___ placentaria.

transmit *v.* transmitir, trasmitir, contagiar; conducir.

transmural *a.* transmural, que ocurre o se administra a través de una pared.

transmutation *n.* transmutación. 1. transformación, cambio evolutivo; 2. cambio de una sustancia en otra.

transocular *a.* transocular, que pasa a través de la órbita ocular.

transonance *n.* transonancia, resonancia transmitida.

transorbital *a.* transorbital, que ocurre o que pasa a través de la cavidad ósea del ojo.

transparency *n.* transparencia; [*slide*] diapositiva.

transparent *a.* transparente.

transpiration *n.* transpiración, perspiración.

transpire *v.* transpirar; [*to perspire*] sudar, transpirar; [*to happen*] suceder, acontecer.

transplacental *a.* transplacental, a través de la placenta.

transplant *n.* trasplante. 1. acto de transferir un órgano o tejido de un donante a un recipiente, o de una parte del cuerpo a otra para sustituir una parte enferma o restituir un órgano a su función normal; 2. parte artificial o natural que se usa como reemplazo; *v.* transplantar.

transplantation *n.* transplantación, trasplantación, acto de hacer un trasplante; autoplastic ___ / ___ autoplástica; heteroplastic ___ / ___ heteroplástica; heterotopic ___ / ___ heterotópica; homotopic ___ / ___ homotópica.

transpleural *a.* transpleural, que ocurre o se administra a través de la pleura.

transport *n.* transporte, movimiento de materiales en el cuerpo esp. a través de la membrana celular.

transportation *n.* transporte.

transposition *n.* transposición. 1. desplazamiento de un órgano o parte a una posición opuesta; 2. cambio genético de un cromosoma a otro que resulta a veces en defectos genéticos.

transposition of great vessels *n.* transposición de los grandes vasos, anomalía congénita en la cual la aorta sale del ventrículo derecho mientras que el tronco pulmonar sale del ventrículo izquierdo.

transsexual *a.* transexual. 1. persona que tiene una urgencia psicológica de pertenecer al sexo opuesto; 2. persona que ha cambiado de sexo sometiéndose a una operación quirúrgica.

transudate *n.* trasudado, fluido que ha pasado a través de de una membrana o ha sido expulsado como resultado de una inflamación.

transurethral *a.* transuretral, que ocurre o se administra a través de la uretra.

transvaginal *a.* transvaginal, a través de la vagina.

transversal *a.* transversal.

transverse *a.* transversal, atravesado-a; ___ plain / plano ___ .

transvestism *n.* transvestismo, adopción de

modales del sexo opuesto, esp. la manera de vestir.

transvestite *n.* transvestido-a, transvestita, persona que practica el transvestismo.

trapezius *n.* trapecio, músculo triangular plano esencial en la rotación de la escápula.

trash *n.* basura, desecho.

trauma *n.* trauma. 1. lesión física causada por un agente externo; 2. *psic.* estado emocional severo.

traumatic *a.* traumático-a, rel. a un trauma.

traumatism *n.* traumatismo.

traumatize *v.* traumatizar, lesionar, lastimar.

traumatology *n.* traumatología, rama de la cirugía que trata del cuidado de lesiones y heridas.

travel *n.* viaje; *v.* viajar, hacer un viaje.

treatment *n.* tratamiento, método o procedimiento que se usa en la cura de enfermedades, lesiones y deformaciones; ____ plan / plan o método de ____; preventive ____ / ____ preventivo; symptomatic ____ / ____ sintomático.

tree *n.* 1. árbol; 2. estructura anatómica semejante a un árbol.

Trematoda *n. Trematoda,* clase de gusanos parásitos de la especie de los *Platyhelminthes* que incluye la duela y los gusanos planos que infectan el organismo humano.

trematode *n.* trematodo, gusano parásito de la clase *Trematoda.*

tremble *n.* temblor, estremecimiento, movimiento involuntario oscilatorio; *v.* temblar; estremecerse.

tremendous *a.* tremendo a, formidable.

tremor *n.* temblor, estremecimiento; alcoholic ____ / ____ alcohólico; coarse ____ / ____ lento y acentuado; continuous ____ / ____ continuo; essential ____ / ____ esencial; fine ____ / ____ de variaciones rápidas; flapping ____ / ____ de aleteo; intention ____ / ____ intencional; intermittent ____ / ____ intermitente; muscular ____ / ____ muscular; physiological ____ / ____ fisiológico; rest ____ / ____ de reposo.

tremulous *a.* trémulo-a, afectado-a por un estremecimiento o que posee las características de un temblor.

trench *n.* trinchera, zanja, foso; ____ back / rigidez y dolor de espalda; ____ fever / fiebre de ____, fiebre remitente transmitida por piojos; ____ foot / pie de ____, infección en los pies por exposición al frío; ____

mouth / infección con ulceración de las mucosas de la boca y la faringe.

trend *n.* tendencia; dirección.

Trendelenburg position *n.* posición de Trendelenburg, posición del paciente en la cual la cabeza descansa en un nivel más bajo que el tronco y las extremidades inferiores.

trepan *n.* trépano, instrumento usado en la trepanación; *v.* trepanar, perforar el cráneo con un trépano.

trepanation *n. cirg.* trepanación, perforación del cráneo con un instrumento especial para reducir el aumento de la presión intracraneal causada por fractura, acumulación de sangre o pus.

trephination *n. cirg.* trefinación, acto de cortar un tejido o un hueso dando un corte circular o de disco, operación gen. efectuada en el cráneo.

treponema *n.* treponema, parásito de la orden *Spirochaetales* que invade a humanos y animales; ____ pallidum / ____ pallidum, parásito causante de la sífilis.

treponemiasis *n.* treponemiasis, infección causada por espiroquetas del género *Treponema.*

triad *n.* triada, grupo de tres elementos que se relacionan entre sí.

triage *Fr.* triage, clasificación y evaluación de víctimas en acontecimientos catastróficos para establecer prioridades según la urgencia del tratamiento, y aumentar así el número de sobrevivientes.

triangle *n.* triángulo.

triangular *a.* triangular.

tribe *n.* tribu, categoría biológica en taxonomía.

triceps *L.* tríceps, músculo de tres porciones o cabezas; ____ reflex / reflejo del ____ .

Trichinella *n. Trichinella,* género de gusanos nematodos, parásitos de animales carnívoros.

trichinosis *n.* triquinosis, enfermedad adquirida por la ingestión de carne cruda o mal cocinada esp. de cerdo que contiene larvas enquistadas de *Trichinella spiralis.*

trichitis *n.* triquitis, infl. de los bulbos pilosos.

trichobezoar *n.* tricobezoar, concreción o bezoar formado de pelo que se aloja en el intestino o el estómago.

Trichomonas *n. Trichomonas,* parásitos protozoarios que se alojan en el tubo digestivo y en el tracto genitourinario de vertebrados; ___ vaginalis / ___ vaginalis, agente causante de la vaginitis.

trichomoniasis *n.* trichomoniasis, infestación por *Trichomonas*.

trichromatic *a.* tricromático-a, compuesto de tres colores.

tricky *a.* engañoso-a; complicado-a.

tricuspid *a.* tricúspide. 1. que posee tres puntas o cúspides; 2. rel. a la válvula tricúspide del corazón; ___ atresia / atresia ___; ___ murmur / soplo ___.

trifocal *a.* trifocal; ___ lenses / lentes ___-es.

trigeminal *a.* trigeminal, rel. al nervio trigémino; ___ cough / tos ___ / ___ neuralgia / neuralgia ___; ___ pulse / pulso ___.

trigeminal nerve *n.* nervio trigémino. *V.* **cranial nerves.**

trigeminus *L.* trigeminus, nervio trigémino.

trigger *n.* impulso o reacción que inicia otros eventos; *v.* desencadenar, iniciar.

trigger zone *n.* área sensitiva que al recibir un estímulo ocasiona una reacción en otra parte del cuerpo.

trigone *n.* trígono, área de forma triangular.

trigonitis *n.* trigonitis, infl. del trígono de la vejiga urinaria.

trimester *n.* trimestre.

trip *n.* 1. viaje; 2. *slang* uso de drogas alucinatorias.

triphasic *a.* trifásico-a, que se produce en tres fases o variaciones, esp. en referencia a las corrientes eléctricas.

triple *a.* triple, que consiste de tres componentes.

triplopia *n.* triplopia, trastorno visual por el cual se producen tres imágenes del mismo objeto.

trismus *Gr.* trismus, espasmo de los músculos de la masticación debido a una condición patológica.

trisomic *a.* trisómico-a, caracterizado por trisomía.

trisomy *n.* trisomía, trastorno genético por el cual una persona posee tres cromosomas homólogos por célula en lugar de dos (diploide), lo cual causa deformaciones fetales serias.

triturate *v.* triturar.

triumph *n.* triunfo, éxito; *v.* triunfar, tener éxito.

trochanter *n.* trocánter, una de las dos pro-

minencias exteriores localizadas bajo el cuello del fémur; greater ___ / ___ mayor; lesser ___ / ___ menor.

trochlea *n.* tróclea, estructura que sirve de polea.

trochlear nerve *n.* nervio troclear. *V.* **cranial nerves.**

trophic *a.* trófico-a, rel. a la nutrición.

tropical *a.* tropical; ___ diseases / enfermedades ___-es; ___ medicine / medicina ___.

tropism *n.* tropismo, tendencia de una célula u organismo a reaccionar de una forma definida (positiva o negativa) en respuesta a estímulos externos.

trouble *n.* aflicción, calamidad, problema; **What is the trouble?** / ¿Qué sucede?, ¿qué pasa? *v.* **to be in** ___ / estar en un apuro; **to be worth the** ___ / valer la pena.

troubled *a.* afligido-a, inquieto-a; preocupado-a.

trough *n.* canal o zanja.

trousers *n. pl.* pantalones.

true *a.* verdadero-a, cierto-a, real; verídico-a.

true pelvis *n.* pelvis verdadera o menor, parte inferior contráctil de la pelvis.

truncal *a.* troncal, truncado-a, rel. al tronco.

truncate *a.* truncado-a, que tiene una parte cercenada; amputado-a; *v.* truncar, cortar, amputar.

truncus *L.* truncus, tronco, torso, el cuerpo humano con exclusión de la cabeza y las extremidades.

truss *n.* braguero, faja para mantener una hernia reducida en su lugar; *v.* ligar, amarrar.

trust *n.* confianza, fe; *v.* confiar, creer en.

truth *n.* verdad; realidad; ___ serum / suero de la ___.

truthful *a.* veraz, verdadero-a; **-ly** *adv.* verdaderamente, realmente.

try *n.* prueba, ensayo; *v.* probar, ensayar, hacer una prueba; intentar; **to** ___ **out** / probar, someter a prueba; **to** ___ **on** / probarse.

Trypanosoma *n. Tripanosoma,* género de parásito protozoario que se aloja en la sangre y es transmitido a los vertebrados por insectos vectores.

trypanosomal *a.* tripanosómico-a, rel. a un tripanosoma o que es afectado por éste.

trypanosomiasis *n.* tripanosomiasis, cualquier infección causada por un parásito flagelado del género *Tripanosoma*.

trypsin *n.* tripsina, enzima formada por el tripsinógeno presente en el jugo pancreático.

trypsinogen *n.* tripsinógeno, sustancia inactiva segregada por el páncreas en el duodeno para formar tripsina.

tryptophan *n.* triptófano, amino ácido cristalino presente en las proteínas, esencial a la vida animal.

tsetse fly *n.* mosca tsetsé, insecto del sur de África, transmisor de la enfermedad del sueño.

tub *n.* tina, bañera.

tubal *a.* tubárico-a; ___ pregnancy / embarazo ectópico en una trompa de Falopio.

tube *n.* tubo, conducto, trompa; drainage ___ / ___ de drenaje; endotracheal ___ / ___ endotraqueal; intestinal decompression ___ / sonda intestinal; nasogastric ___ / ___ nasogástrico; tracheotomy ___ / ___ de traqueotomía; thoracostomy ___ / ___ de toracostomía.

tuber *L.* (*pl.* **tubera**) tuber, tuberosidad; nódulo.

tubercle *n.* tubérculo. 1. nódulo pequeño; 2. pequeña prominencia de un hueso; 3. lesión producida por el bacilo de la tuberculosis.

tubercular *a.* tubercular, caracterizado por lesiones tuberosas.

tuberculin *n.* tuberculina, compuesto preparado del bacilo de la tuberculosis usado en las pruebas de diagnóstico de infecciones de la tuberculosis.

tuberculin test *n.* prueba de la tuberculina.

tuberculocidal *a.* tuberculocida, que destruye el bacilo de la tuberculosis.

tuberculosis *n.* tuberculosis, infección bacteriana aguda o crónica causada por el germen *Mycobacterium tuberculosis* que gen. afecta los pulmones pero que también puede afectar otros órganos; ___ in childhood / ___ infantil; meningeal ___ / ___ meníngea; pulmonary ___ / ___ pulmonar; spinal ___ / ___ espinal; urogenital ___ / ___ urogenital.

tuberculous *a.* tuberculoso-a, rel. a o que padece de tuberculosis o que puede causarla.

tuberculum *L.* tuberculum, tubérculo.

tuberosity *n.* tuberosidad, elevación o protuberancia.

tuberous *a.* tuberoso-a, semejante a una tuberosidad.

tuberous sclerosis *n.* esclerosis tuberosa, enfermedad familiar marcada por ataques convulsivos, deficiencia mental progresiva y formación de múltiples tumores cerebrales cutáneos.

tuboabdominal pregnancy *n.* embarazo tuboabdominal.

tubo-ovarian *a.* tuboovárico-a, rel. a la trompa de Falopio y el ovario; ___ abscess / absceso ___.

tuboplastia *n. cirg.* tuboplastia, reparación plástica de un conducto esp. de una trompa de Falopio.

tubule *n.* túbulo, conducto o canal pequeño; collecting ___ / ___ colector; renal ___ / ___ renal; seminiferous ___ / conducto seminífero.

tuft *n.* penacho, copete.

tug *n.* tirón; estirón; *v.* halar; estirar.

tugging *n.* tirón, acción de estirar con fuerza o tensión.

tularemia *n.* tularemia, fiebre de conejo, infección transmitida a las personas por la picadura de un insecto vector o contraída en la manipulación de carne infectada.

tumefaction *n.* tumefacción, tumescencia, proceso de hinchazón.

tumefy *v.* entumecerse, hincharse.

tumid *a.* túmido-a, hinchado-a.

tummy *n.* pancita, barriguita.

tumor *n.* tumor. 1. bulto o hinchazón; 2. crecimiento espontáneo de tejido nuevo en masa que no tiene propósito fisiológico alguno.

tumoricidal *a.* tumoricida, que destruye células tumorales.

tumorigenesis *n.* tumorigénesis, formación de tumores.

tumor makers, serum *n. pl.* sustancias en el plasma sanguíneo indicativas de la posible presencia de un tumor maligno.

tumorous *a.* tumoroso-a, que tiene la apariencia de un tumor.

tumor virus *n.* virus tumoroso, capaz de producir cáncer.

tuna *n.* [*fish*] atún.

tunic *n.* túnica, membrana protectora; ___ adventitia / ___ adventicia; ___ albuginea / cápsula albugínea; ___ externa / ___ externa; ___ interna / ___ interna; ___ media / ___ media; ___ mucosa / ___ mucosa; ___ muscularis / ___ muscular; ____ serosa / ____ serosa; ____ vaginalis / ____ vaginal.

tunnel *n*. túnel, canal o conducto estrecho; carpal ____ / ____ del carpo; flexor ____ / ____ flexor; tarsal ____ / ____ tarsiano.

tunnel vision *n*. visión en túnel, trastorno frecuente en casos de glaucoma avanzado que produce al paciente una disminución visual considerable tal como si mirara a través de un túnel.

turbid *a*. turbio-a, túrbido-a; nebuloso.

turbinated *a*. aconchado-a. 1. en forma de concha o cúpula; 2. rel. a los cornetes nasales.

turgid *a*. túrgido-a; hinchado-a, distendido-a.

turgor *n*. turgor. 1. distensión; 2. tensión celular normal.

turn *n*. vuelta, giro; turno; *v*. voltear, virar, dar vuelta, torcer; **to** ____ **back** / volver, regresar, retroceder; **to** ____ **down** / doblar; desaprobar, rechazar; [*when referring to one's body*] volverse, darse vuelta, virarse; **to** ____ **into** / volverse, convertirse en, transformarse; **to** ____ **out** / resultar; **to** ____ **pale** / palidecer; **to** ____ **red** / enrojecerse.

turned-down *a*. vuelto-a; doblado-a hacia abajo; desaprobado-a; rechazado-a.

turned-up *a*. vuelto-a, doblado-a hacia arriba.

Turner's syndrome *n*. síndrome de Turner, trastorno endocrino congénito que se manifiesta con deficiencia ovárica, amenorrea, estatura baja y la presencia de cromosomas X solamente.

turning *n*. 1. versión, término obstétrico referente a la manipulación del feto en el útero para facilitar el parto; 2. vuelta; *a*. giratorio-a; **the** ____ **point** / la crisis, el momento decisivo.

turnover *n*. cambio; *a*. cambiado-a de posición; *v*. voltear, cambiar de posición; transferir.

tussis *L*. tussis, tos.

tussive *a*. tusivo-a, rel. a la tos o causado por ésta.

T wave *n*. Onda T, parte del electrocardiograma que representa la repolarización de los ventrículos.

tweezers *n. pl*. pinzas, tenacillas.

twice *adv*. dos veces; ____ **as much,** ____ **as many** / el doble.

twig *n*. terminación o rama diminuta de un nervio o de una arteria.

twilight *n*. crepúsculo; ____ **sleep** / sueño crepuscular; ____ **state** / estado de somnolencia.

twinge *n*. punzada, dolor agudo.

twinkle *n*. guiñada, pestañeo; *v*. guiñar un ojo; pestañear, parpadear; **in a** ____ / en un momento, en un instante.

twins *n. pl*. gemelos, mellizos, jimaguas, uno de dos hijos nacidos de un mismo embarazo; dizigotic ____ / ____ dicigóticos; identical ____ / ____ idénticos; monozygotic ____ / ____ monocigotos; Siamese ____ / ____ siameses; true ____ / ____ verdaderos.

twist *n*. torción, torcedura; sacudida, contorsión; peculiaridad; *v*. [*an ankle*] torcer, virar, doblar.

twitch *n*. tic nervioso espasmódico; sacudida.

tympanectomy *n. cirg*. timpanectomía, excisión de la membrana timpánica.

tympanic *a*. timpánico-a, resonante; rel. al tímpano. ____ **membrane** / membrana ____ ; ____ **resonance** / resonancia ____ .

tympanites *n*. timpanitis, distensión del abdomen causada por acumulación de gas en los intestinos.

tympanitic *a*. timpanítico-a, rel. a la timpanitis o afectado por ésta.

tympanoplastia *n*. timpanoplastia, reconstrucción del oído medio.

tympanotomy *n*. timpanotomía, incisión de la membrana timpánica.

tympanum *n*. tímpano, oído medio.

type *n*. tipo, género, clase, modelo o ejemplar distintivo.

typhlitis *n*. tiflitis, infl. del ciego.

typhoid *a*. tifoideo-a, rel. al tifo o semejante a éste.

typhoid fever *n*. fiebre tifoidea, infección abdominal aguda que es causada por una bacteria de la clase *Salmonella* y que se manifiesta con infl. abdominal, postración, fiebre alta y dolor de cabeza.

typhus *n*. tifus, tifo, infección aguda causada por una *Rickettsia* que se manifiesta con fiebre alta, intensos dolores de cabeza y delirio.

typhus vaccine *n*. vacuna tífica.

typical *a*. típico-a, conforme a un tipo.

typing *n*. tipificación de tejidos, determinación por tipos; blood ____ / determinación del grupo sanguíneo.

U

U *abbr.* **unit** / unidad;   **uranium** / uranio; **urology** / Urología.

udder *n.* ubre, glándula mamaria de la vaca y otros animales mamíferos.

ugliness *n.* fealdad.

ugly *a.* feo-a.

ulcer *n.* úlcera, llaga o lesión en la piel o en la membrana mucosa con desintegración gradual de los tejidos; canker ___ / ___ maligna; chronical leg varicose ___ / ___ varicosa crónica de la pierna; decubitus ___ / ___ por decúbito; duodenal ___ / ___ del duodeno; gastric ___ / ___ gástrica; peptic ___ / ___ péptica; perforating ___ / ___ perforante; varicose ___ / ___ varicosa; vesical ___ / ___ vesical.

ulcerate *v.* ulcerar; ulcerarse.

ulcerated *a.* ulcerado-a, de la naturaleza de una úlcero o afectado por ella.

ulceration *n.* ulceración, supuración; proceso de formación de una úlcera.

ulcerative *a.* ulcerativo-a, rel. a una úlcera o caracterizado-a por una condición ulcerosa; ___ colitis / colitis ___ .

ulcerogenic *a.* ulcerógeno-a, que produce úlceras.

ulcerous *a.* ulceroso-a, rel. a una úlcera o que la padece.

ulerythema *n.* uleritema, dermatitis eritematosa caracterizada por la formación de cicatrices.

ulna *n.* cúbito. *V.* **cubitus.**

ulnar *n.* ulnar, rel. al cúbito o a los nervios y arterias relacionados con éste.

ulocarcinoma, ulocarcinomata *n.* ulocarcinoma, ulocarcinomata, cáncer de las encías.

ultimate *a.* último-a, final; fundamental.

ultracentrifuge *n.* ultracentrífuga, aparato de fuerza centrífuga que separa y sedimenta las moléculas de una sustancia.

ultrafiltration *n.* ultrafiltración, proceso de filtración que deja pasar pequeñas moléculas pero impide el paso de moléculas mayores.

ultramicroscope *n.* ultramicroscopio, microscopio de campo oscuro capaz de hacer visibles objetos que no se distinguen en un microscopio de luz común.

ultrasonic *a.* ultrasónico-a,   supersónico-a; ___ diagnosis / diagnóstico por ultrasonido.

ultrasonogram *n.* ultrasonograma,   imagen producida por medio de ultrasonografía.

ultrasonography *n.* ultrasonografía, técnica de diagnóstico que emplea ultrasonido para producir imágenes de una estructura o de tejidos del cuerpo.

ultrasound *n.* ultrasonido, ondas de frecuencia superior a las del oido humano que se usan en ultrasonografía en procedimientos terapeúticos y de diagnóstico.

ultrasound imaging *n.* imágenes por ultrasonido, captación de imágenes de órganos o tejidos del cuerpo por medio de ultrasonido empleando técnicas de reflejo (ecograma).

ultrastructure *n.* ultraestructura, estructura diminuta que solamente puede distinguirse bajo un microscopio electrónico.

ultraviolet *a.* ultravioleta, que se extiende más allá de la zona violeta del espectro; ___ rays / rayos ___ ; ___ theraphy / terapia de radiación ___ .

ululation *n.* ululación, emisión de gritos o alaridos incoordinados de tipo histérico esp. de pacientes mentales.

umbilical *a.* umbilical, rel. al ombligo; ___ notch / ligamento ___ ; ___ hernia / hernia ___ .

umbilical cord *n.* cordón umbilical, estructura que sirve de conexión entre el feto y la placenta durante la gestación.

umbilicus, navel *n.* ombligo, depresión en el centro del abdomen que marca el punto de inserción del cordón umbilical.

unable *a.* incapaz, inhábil.

unacceptable *a.* inaceptable, no aprobado-a.

unaccustomed *a.* no usual, no acostumbrado-a, desacostumbrado-a.

unadulterated *a.* natural, puro-a, sin mezcla, no adulterado-a.

unaffected *a.* no afectado-a.

unanimous *a.* unánime.

unanswered *a.* por contestar, no contestado-a.

unassisted *a.* sin ayuda, sin auxilio, desamparado-a.

unattached *a.* suelto-a, sin conexión.

unattended *a.* desatendido-a.

unavoidable *a.* inevitable.

unaware *a.* sin conocimiento de causa; que ignora.

unbearable *a.* insoportable, intolerable, insufrible, imposible de soportar.

unbeliever *a.* incrédulo-a.

unbiased *a.* imparcial, sin prejuicios.

unclog *v.* desbloquear, permeabilizar; destupir, destapar.

uncomfortable *a.* incómodo-a, molesto-a, desagradable.

uncommon *a.* poco común, raro-a, extraño-a.

unconditioned reflex *n.* reflejo no condicionado o natural.

unconditioned response *n.* respuesta no condicionada o reacción no restringida.

unconscious *a.* inconsciente. 1. que ha perdido el conocimiento; 2. que no responde a estímulos sensoriales.

unconsciousness *n.* inconsciencia, pérdida del conocimiento.

uncooperative *a.* poco dócil; que no coopera.

uncover *v.* destapar, descubrir, poner al descubierto.

unction *n.* unción, aplicación de un ungüento o aceite.

unctuous *a.* untuoso-a, oleaginoso-a; grasoso-a.

undecided *a.* indeciso-a, indeterminado-a.

undefined *a.* indefinido-a.

under *a.* inferior; *prep., adv.* debajo, menos, menos que; bajo; ___ observation / bajo observación; ___ treatment / bajo tratamiento.

underclothing *n.* ropa interior.

underdeveloped *a.* subdesarrollado-a; en desarrollo.

underdevelopment *n.* subdesarrollo.

underestimate *v.* subestimar; menospreciar.

underfed *a.* desnutrido-a, mal alimentado-a.

undergo *vi.* someterse a; sufrir, padecer, soportar; to ___ surgery / someterse a una operación.

underline *v.* subrayar.

undermine *v.* dañar, debilitar.

undernourished *a.* desnutrido-a; malnutrido-a.

undernutrition *a.* desnutrición.

undershirt *n.* camiseta.

underside *n.* el lado de abajo.

undersigned *n.* el abajo firmante.

understand *vi.* comprender, entender.

understood *a. pp.* de **to understand**, convenido-a, entendido-a, comprendido-a.

undertake *vi.* emprender, iniciar, tomar la iniciativa.

underway *n.* en camino; bajo estudio.

underwear *n.* ropa interior.

underweight *n.* falta de peso, peso deficiente; bajo de peso; de peso insuficiente.

undesirable *a.* indeseable, inaceptable, aborrecido-a.

undetected *a.* no detectado-a, no descubierto-a, inadvertido-a.

undetermined *a.* indeterminado-a.

undeveloped *a.* no desarrollado-a, sin manifestación.

undifferentiation *n.* indiferenciación. *V.* **anaplasia.**

undigested *a.* no digerido-a, no asimilado-a.

undiluted *a.* no diluído-a, sin diluirse, concentrado-a.

undiminished *a.* sin disminución.

undisclosed *a.* no revelado-a, no dado-a a conocer.

undo *vi.* deshacer, desatar; desabrochar.

undress *v.* desvestirse; quitarse la ropa.

undulant *a.* ondulante; ___ fever / fiebre ___. *V.* **brucellosis.**

undulated *a.* ondulado-a, de borde ondulado o irregular.

uneasy *a.* inquieto-a.

unengaged *a.* desencajado-a, fuera de lugar.

unequal *a.* desigual; desproporcionado-a.

unexpected *a.* inesperado-a, imprevisto-a.

unfinished *a.* incompleto-a, sin terminar.

unfit *a.* inepto-a, inhábil, incapaz.

unfitness *n.* ineptitud, incapacidad, incompetencia.

unforeseen *a.* inesperado-a, imprevisto-a.

unfortunate *a.* infeliz, desafortunado-a, desgraciado-a.

unfriendly *a.* poco amistoso-a, poco amigable.

ungrateful *a.* desagradecido-a, ingrato-a.

ungual *a.* ungueal, rel. a una uña.

unguent *n.* ungüento, medicamento preparado para uso externo.

unhappy *a.* infeliz, desgraciado-a.

unharmed, unhurt *a.* ileso-a; *pop.* sano-a y salvo-a.

unhealthy *a.* [*environment*] insalubre, malsano-a; [*person*] enfermizo-a, achacoso-a.

uniarticular *a.* uniarticular, rel. a una sola articulación.

unibasal *a.* unibásico-a, rel. a una sola base.

unicellular *a.* unicelular, de una sola célula.

uniform *n.* [*garment*] uniforme; *a.* uniforme; invariable.

unigravida *a.* unigrávida, mujer embarazada por primera vez.

unilateral *a.* unilateral, rel. a un solo lado.

uninsured *a.* no asegurado-a, sin tener un seguro.

union *n.* unión. 1. acción de unir dos cosas en una; 2. juntura de dos partes cortadas (amputadas) de un hueso o de los bordes de una herida.

uniovular *a.* uniovular, que se desarrolla de un solo óvulo.

uniparous *a.* unípara, mujer que tiene un nacimiento simple.

unipolar *a.* unipolar, de un solo polo, tal como las células nerviosas.

unique *a.* único-a; solo-a; que se distingue de otros.

unit *n.* unidad. 1. estándar de medida; 2. (IU) unidad internacional (UI). *V.* **international unit;** 3. unidad fisiológica, la más mínima división de un órgano capaz de realizar una función; motor ___ / ___ motora.

unite *v.* unir; reunir.

united *a.* unido-a.

unity *n.* unidad; unión.

universe *n.* universo.

universal *a.* universal, general; ___ antidote / antídoto ___.

universal donor *n.* donante universal, persona que pertenece al grupo de sangre tipo O, de factor RH negativo, cuya sangre puede ser dada a personas con sangre tipo ABO con poco riesgo de complicaciones.

universal recipient *n.* recipiente universal, persona que pertenece al grupo de sangre AB.

university *n.* universidad.

unjust *a.* injusto-a.

unkind *a.* despiadado-a, sin bondad.

unlawful *a.* ilegal, ilícito-a.

unlicensed *a.* no acreditado-a, sin licencia o sin permiso.

unlikely *a.* improbable, dudoso-a.

unlucky *a.* desafortunado-a.

Unna's paste boot *n.* bota de pasta de Unna, compresión que se usa en el tratamiento de úlceras varicosas en la pierna, con vendajes en espiral aplicados y cubiertos con la pasta medicinal de Unna.

unnecessary *a.* innecesario-a.

unobstructed *a.* abierto-a, suelto-a; libre; no obstruído.

unofficial *a.* sin autorización; no oficial, se dice de una droga o medicamento no aprobado por la farmacopea o los formularios vigentes autorizados.

unopened *a.* cerrado-a, tapado-a, sin abrir.

unorganized *a.* desorganizado-a; no estructurado; sin orden.

unreal *a.* ilusorio-a, imaginario-a.

unreasonable *a.* irrazonable, intransigente.

unrest *n.* desasosiego, inquietud; intranquilidad.

unsalted *a.* sin sal, que le falta sal.

unsanitary *a.* insalubre, malsano.

unsaturated *a.* no saturado-a.

unstable *a.* inestable.

untiring *a.* incansable.

untreated *a.* no tratado-a.

unwanted *a.* no deseado-a.

up *prep. adv.* arriba, en lo alto.

update *v.* [*to improve*] modernizar; [*documents*] poner al día; arreglar.

upgrade *v.* mejorar.

upgrowth *n.* crecimiento, desarrollo, maduración.

upper *n. pop.* droga estimulante, esp. una anfetamina; *a. comp.* superior, más alto-a.

upper airway obstruction *n.* obstrucción en el conducto aéreo superior.

upper GI *n.* examen radiográfico del estómago y duodeno con ingestión de una sustancia que sirve de medio de contraste.

upper jaw *n.* mandíbula superior.

upper respiratory infection *n.* infección del tracto respiratorio superior.

upper respiratory tract *n.* aparato respiratorio superior compuesto de la nariz, los conductos nasales y la nasofaringe.

upset *a.* indispuesto-a; nervioso-a; disgustado-a; *v.* trastornar; enfadar.

uptake *n.* absorción, fijación o incorporación de alguna sustancia a un organismo vivo; ___ and storage / captura (toma) y almacenamiento.

uranium *n.* uranio, elemento metálico pesado.

urate *n.* urato, sal de ácido úrico.

urea *n.* urea, producto del metabolismo de las proteínas, forma en la cual el nitrógeno se excreta por la orina.

ureal *a.* ureico-a, rel. o concerniente a la urea.

urelcosis *n.* urelcosis, ulceración de las vías urinarias.

uremia *n.* uremia, condición tóxica causada por insuficiencia renal que produce retención en la sangre de sustancias nitrogenadas, fosfatos y sulfatos.

uremic *a.* urémico-a, rel. a la uremia o causado por ella.

ureter *n.* uréter, uno de los conductos que llevan la orina del riñón a la vejiga.

ureteral *a.* ureteral, uretérico-a, rel. o concerniente al uréter.

ureterectasis *n.* ureterectasis, dilatación anormal del uréter.

ureterectomy *n. cirg.* ureterectomía, extirpación parcial o total del uréter.

ureteritis *n* ureteritis, infl. del uréter.

ureterocele *n.* ureterocele, dilatación quística de la porción distal intravesical del uréter debida a una estenosis del orificio ureteral.

ureterocystoneostomy *n. cirg.* ureterocystoneostomía. *V.* **ureteroneocystostomy.**

ureterocystostomy *n. cirg.* ureterocistostomía, transplantación de un uréter a otra parte de la vejiga.

ureterography *n.* ureterografía, radiografía del uréter usando un medio radiopaco.

ureteroheminephrectomy *n. cirg.* ureteronefrectomía, resección de la porción de un riñón y el uréter en ciertos casos de duplicación del tracto urinario superior.

ureterohydronephrosis *n.* ureterohidronefrosis, distensión del uréter y riñón debida a una obstrucción.

ureteroiliostomy *n.* ureteroiliostomía, anastomosis del uréter a un segmento aislado del íleon.

ureterolithiasis *n.* ureterolitiasis, desarrollo de un cálculo ureteral.

ureterolithotomy *n. cirg.* ureterolitotomía, incisión del uréter para extraer un cálculo.

ureteroneocystostomy *n. cirg.* ureteroneocistostomía. *V.* **ureterocystoneostomy.**

ureteronephrectomy *n. cirg.* ureteronefrectomía, excisión del riñón y su uréter.

ureteroplasty *n.* ureteroplastia, cirugía plástica del uréter.

ureteropyeloplasty *n. cirg.* ureteropieloplastia, cirugía plástica del uréter y la pelvis renal.

ureterosigmoidostomy *n. cirg.* ureterosigmoidostomía, implantación del uréter en el colon sigmoideo.

ureterostomy *n. cirg.* ureterostomía, forma-ción de una fístula permanente para drenar un uréter.

ureterotomy *n. cirg.* ureterotomía, incisión de un uréter.

ureteroureterostomy *n. cirg.* ureteroureterostomía, anastomosis de dos uréteres o de dos extremos del mismo uréter.

urethra *n.* uretra, canal o conducto urinario.

urethral *a.* uretral, rel. a la uretra; ____ stricture / estrechez ____.

urethralgia *n.* uretralgia, dolor en la uretra.

urethrectomy *n. cirg.* uretrectomía, excisión parcial o total de la uretra.

urethritis *n.* uretritis, infl. aguda o crónica de la uretra.

urethrography *n.* uretrografía, rayos X de la uretra usando una sustancia radiopaca inyectada.

urethroscope *n.* uretroscopio, instrumento para visualizar el interior de la uretra.

urethrotome *n.* uretrótomo, instrumento quirúrgico empleado en una uretotromía.

urethrotomy *n. cirg.* uretrotomía, incisión efectuada para aliviar una estrechez uretral.

urgent *a.* urgente.

uric acid *n.* ácido úrico, producto del metabolismo de las proteínas presente en la sangre y excretado en la orina.

uricemia *n.* uricemia, exceso de ácido úrico en la sangre.

uricosuria *n.* uricosuria, presencia excesiva de ácido úrico en la orina.

urinal *n.* orinal, vasija en que se recoge la orina; *pop.* taza, pato.

urinalysis *n.* urinálisis, examen de orina.

urinary *a.* urinario-a, rel. o concerniente a la orina. ____ calculi / cálculos ____ -s; ____ infection / infección renal o ____ ; ____ sediments / sedimentos ____ -s.

urinary bladder *n.* vejiga urinaria, órgano muscular en forma de saco que recoge la orina que secretan los riñones.

urinary system *n.* sistema urinario, órganos y conductos que participan en la producción y excreción de la orina.

urinary tract *n.* vías urinarias; ____ infections / infecciones de las ____ .

urinate *v.* orinar, mear.

urination *n.* orina, acto de emisión de la orina; frequent ____ / orinar muy seguido, *Mex.A. pop.* meadera; difficult ____ / orinar con dificultad; painful ____ / orinar con dolor.

urine *n.* orina, orín, *pop.* aguas menores, líquido ambarino secretado por los riñones que se almacena en la vejiga y se elimina en la uretra; clear ___ / ___ clara; dark ___ / ___ turbia; mid-stream ___ / espécimen de ___ a mitad del chorro; murky, hazy ___ / ___ turbia; ___ specimen / espécimen, muestra de ___ ; clean voided ___ / ___ limpia al salir.

uriniferous *a.* urinífero-a, que contiene o conduce orina.

urinogenital *a.* urinogenital. *V.* **urogenital.**

urinoma *n.* urinoma, tumor o quiste que contiene orina.

urobilinogen *n.* urobilinógeno, pigmento derivado de la reducción de bilirrubina por acción de bacterias intestinales.

urodynamics *n.* urodinámica, estudio del proceso activo patofisiológico de la micción.

urodynia *n.* urodinia, micción dolorosa.

urogenital *a.* urogenital, rel. a la vía urinaria o al tracto urinario y genital; ___ diaphram / diafragma ___ .

urogram *n.* urograma, rayos X hechos por urografía.

urography *n.* urografía, rayos X de una parte de las vías urinarias con el uso de una sustancia radiopaca inyectada; excretory or descending ___ / ___ excretora o descendiente; retrograde ___ / ___ retrógrada.

urokinase *n.* urocinasa, enzima presente en la orina que se emplea en la disolución de coágulos.

urolithiasis *n.* urolitiasis, formación de cálculos urinarios y trastornos asociados con su presencia.

urologist *n.* urólogo-a, especialista en urología.

urology *n.* urología, estudio y tratamiento de las enfermedades del aparato genitourinario en el hombre y tracto urinario en la mujer.

uropathy *n.* uropatía, enfermedades de las vías urinarias.

uropyourether *n.* uropiouréter, acumulación de orina y pus en la pelvis renal.

urticaria *n.* urticaria, erupción cutánea gen. alérgica que se manifiesta con ronchas rosáceas, se acompaña de picazón intensa y puede producirse por un factor interno o externo.

usage *n.* uso, costumbre.

use *n.* uso, utilidad, provecho; *v.* usar, emplear.

useful *a.* útil, provechoso-a, práctico-a.

usual *a.* usual, de costumbre; **-ly** *adv.* usualmente, generalmente.

uterine *a.* uterino-a, rel. al útero o matriz; ___ bleeding / sangramiento ___ , sangramiento no relacionado con la menstruación; ___ cancer / cáncer del útero o de la matriz; ___ prolapse / prolapso ___ ; ___ rupture / rotura ___ .

uterosalpingography *n.* uterosalpingografía, examen de rayos X de la matriz y la trompa de Falopio usando una sustancia radiopaca inyectada.

uterovaginal *a.* uterovaginal, rel. al útero y la vagina.

uterovesical *a.* uterovesical, rel. al útero y la vejiga urinaria.

uterus *n.* útero, matriz, órgano muscular femenino del aparato reproductivo que contiene y nutre al embrión y feto durante la gestación; didelphys ___ / ___ didelfo.

uvea *n.* úvea, túnica vascular del ojo formada por el iris, el cuerpo ciliar y la coroide.

uveitis *n.* uveítis, infl. de la úvea.

uvula *n.* úvula, *pop.* campanilla, estructura colgante en el centro posterior del paladar blando.

U wave *n.* onda U, onda positiva que sigue a la onda T en el electrocardiograma.

V

V *abbr.* **valve** / válvula; **vein** / vena; **vide** (see) / vea; **vision** / visión; **volume** / volumen.

vacation *n.* vacación, vacaciones.

vaccinate *v.* vacunar, inocular.

vaccination *n.* vacunación, inoculación de una vacuna.

vaccine *n.* vacuna, preparación de microorganismos atenuados o muertos que se introduce en el cuerpo para establecer una inmunidad en contra de la enfermedad específica causada por dichos microorganismos; BCG ___ / ___ del bacilo Calmette-Guerin, contra la tuberculosis; DTP (diphtheria, tetanus, pertusis) ___ / ___ triple contra la difteria, tétano y pertusis (tos ferina); influenza ___ / ___ contra la influenza; measles virus, inactivated ___ / ___ antisarampión, inactivada; measles virus live attenuated ___ / ___ antisarampión de virus vivo, atenuada; pneumococcal polyvalent ___ / ___ antineumocócica polivalente; poliovirus, live oral trivalent ___ / ___ antipolio trivalente o de Sabin; Salk's antipoliomyelitis ___ / ___ antipoliomielítica de Salk; rabies ___ / ___ antirrábica; smallpox ___ / ___ antivariolosa, antivariólica; typhus ___ / ___ antitífica; typhoid ___ / ___ contra la tifoidea.

vaccinia *n.* vaccina, virus causante de la viruela bovina del cual se obtiene la vacuna contra la viruela.

vacillate *v.* vacilar; fluctuar.

vacillating *a.* vacilante, oscilante, fluctuante.

vacuity *n.* vacuidad, vacío.

vacuole *n.* vacuola, pequeña cavidad o espacio en el protoplasma celular que contiene líquido o aire.

vacuolization *n.* vacuolización, formación de vacuolas.

vacuum *L.* vacuum, vacío, espacio desprovisto de materia o aire; *v.* extraer el polvo con una aspiradora; ___ packed / envasado-a al vacío.

vagal *a.* vagal, rel. al nervio vago o neumogástrico.

vagina *n.* vagina. 1. conducto en la mujer que se extiende del útero a la vulva; 2. estructura semejante a una vaina.

vaginal *a.* vaginal. 1. que posee forma de vaina; 2. rel. a la vagina.

vaginismus *L.* vaginismus, contracción dolorosa espasmódica de la vagina.

vaginitis *n.* vaginitis, infl. de la vagina.

vagolytic *a.* vagolítico, rel. al nervio vago.

vagotomy *n. cirg.* vagotomía, interrupción del nervio vago.

vagrant *a.* errante; suelto-a; libre.

vague *a.* vago-a, indefinido-a; **-ly** *adv.* vagamente.

vagus *n.* vago, nervio neumogástrico.

vain *a.* vano-a, vanidoso-a; **-ly** *adv.* vanamente, en vano.

valgus *L.* valgus, doblado o torcido hacia afuera.

valid *a.* válido-a, valedero-a.

validity *n.* validez.

valient *a.* valiente.

vallecula *n.* valécula, depresión, surco o fisura esp. en referencia a estructuras anatómicas.

valley fever *n.* fiebre del valle. *V.* **coccidioidomycosis.**

valorization *n.* valorización. evaluación.

Valsalva's maneuver *n.* maniobra, experimento de Valsalva, procedimiento para demostrar la permeabilidad de la trompa de Eustaquio o de ajustar la presión del oído medio mediante una espiración forzada con la boca y la nariz tapadas.

valuable *a.* valioso-a, valuable.

value *n.* valor.

valve *n.* (*pl.* **valvae**) válvula, valva, estructura membranosa en un canal u orificio que al cerrarse temporalmente impide el reflujo del contenido que pasa a través de ella; aortic ___ / ___ aórtica; atrioventricular left ___ / ___ atrioventricular izquierda; atrioventricular right ___, tricúspid / ___ atrioventricular derecha, tricúspide; bicuspid or mitral ___ / ___ bicúspide o mitral; ileocecal ___ / ___ ileocecal; pulmonary ___ / ___ pulmonar; pyloric ___ / ___ pilórica.

valvulae conniventes *n. pl.* válvulas conniventes, pliegues circulares membranosos localizados en el intestino delgado que retardan el paso del contenido alimenticio en el intestino.

valvuloplasty *n. cirg.* valvuloplastia, operación plástica de una válvula.

valvulotome *n.* valvulótomo, instrumento quirúrgico que se usa para seccionar una válvula.

vapor *n.* vapor, gas.

vaporization *n.* vaporización. 1. acción o efecto de vaporizar; 2. uso terapéutico de vapores.

vaporize *v.* vaporizar, convertir una sustancia en gas o vapor.

vaporizer *n.* vaporizador, dispositivo para convertir una sustancia en vapor y aplicarla a usos terapéuticos.

variability *n.* variabilidad.

variable *n.* variable, factor que puede variar; *a.* que puede cambiar.

variant *n.* variante, objeto esencialmente igual a otro pero que difiere en la forma; *a.* variable, inconstante, que cambia o varía.

variation *n.* variación, diversidad en las características de objetos que se relacionan entre sí.

varicella *n.* varicela. *V.* **chickenpox.**

varicocele *n.* varicocele, condición varicosa

de las venas del cordón espermático que produce una masa blanda en el escroto.

varicoid *a.* varicoide, que se asemeja a una várice.

varicose *a.* varicoso-a, rel. a las várices o que se les asemeja; _____ veins / venas _____ -s.

varicotomy *n. cirg.* varicotomía, excisión de una vena varicosa.

variety *n.* variedad.

variola *n.* variola, viruela.

variolic, variolous *a.* variólico-a, rel. a la viruela.

varioliform *a.* varioliforme, semejante a la viruela.

varix *n.* (*pl.* **varices**) várice, vena, arteria o vaso linfático aumentado o dilatado.

varus *L.* varus, doblado o torcido hacia adentro.

vary *v.* variar, cambiar; cambiarse; desviarse.

vas *L.* (*pl.* **vasa**) vas, vaso.

vascular *a.* vascular, rel. a vasos sanguíneos; _____ system / sistema _____, todos los vasos del cuerpo esp. los sanguíneos.

vascularization *n.* vascularización, formación de vasos sanguíneos nuevos.

vasculature *n.* vasculatura, disposición de los vasos sanguíneos en un órgano o parte.

vasculitis *n.* vasculitis. *V.* **angiitis.**

vasculopathy *n.* vasculopatía, cualquier enfermedad de los vasos sanguíneos.

vas deferens *L.* vas deferens, conducto excretor de espermatozoides.

vasectomy *n. cirg.* vasectomía, excisión parcial y ligadura de los conductos deferentes para impedir la salida de espermatozoides en el semen, procedimiento gen. usado como contraceptivo.

vaseline *n.* vaselina.

vasoactive *a.* vasoactivo, que afecta los vasos sanguíneos.

vasoconstrictive *a.* vasoconstrictivo-a, que causa constricción en los vasos sanguíneos.

vasodilation *n.* vasodilatación, aumento del calibre de los vasos sanguíneos.

vasodilator *n.* vasodilatador, agente que causa vasodilatación; *a.* vasodilatador-a; que causa vasodilatación.

vasomotor *n.* vasomotor, agente que regula las contracciones y la dilatación de los vasos sanguíneos; *a.* vasomotor-a, que causa dilatación o contracción en los vasos sanguíneos.

vasopressin *n.* vasopresina, hormona liberada por la pituitaria posterior que aumenta la reabsorción de agua en el riñón elevando la presión arterial.

vasopressor *n.* vasopresor, agente que produce constricción en los vasos sanguíneos; *a.* que tiene efecto vasoconstrictivo.

vasospasm *n.* vasoespasmo; coronary _____ / _____ coronario. *V.* **angiospasm.**

vasotonic *a.* vasotónico, rel. al tono de un vaso.

vasovagal *a.* vasovagal, rel. a los vasos y al nervio vago.

vasovagal syncope *n.* síncope vasovagal, desmayo súbito breve debido a un trastorno vasomotor y vagal.

vastus *L.* vastus, dilatado-a, agrandado-a, extendido-a.

Vater's ampulla *n.* ámpula de Vater, punto de entrada en el duodeno de los conductos excretores biliar y pancreático.

veal *n.* carne de ternera; _____ chop / chuleta de _____.

vector *n.* vector, organismo microbiano transmisor de agentes infecciosos.

vegan *n.* vegetariano en el sentido estricto de la palabra.

vegetable *n.* vegetal.

vegetarian *n.* vegetariano-a, persona cuya dieta consiste principalmente en vegetales; *a.* rel. a los vegetales.

vegetarianism *n.* vegetarianismo, método de alimentación que consiste mayormente en una dieta de vegetales y frutas.

vegetation *n.* vegetación, crecimiento anormal de verrugas o excrecencias en una parte del cuerpo tal como se ve en la endocarditis.

vegetative *a.* vegetativo-a. 1. rel. a funciones de crecimiento y nutrición; 2. rel. a funciones corporales involuntarias o inconscientes.

vehicle *n.* vehículo. 1. sustancia sin acción terapéutica que acompaña a un agente activo en una preparación medicinal; 2. agente de transmisión.

veil *n.* velo. 1. membrana o cubierta fina que cubre una parte del cuerpo; 2. parte de la membrana amniótica que cubre la cara del feto; 3. alteración ligera de la voz.

vein *n.* vena, vaso fibromuscular que lleva la sangre de los capilares al corazón.

vena *L.* vena.

vena cava *n.* vena cava, una de las dos venas mayores, la vena cava inferior y la vena cava superior, que devuelven la sangre desoxigenada a la aurícula derecha del corazón.

venal *a.* venal, rel. a las venas.

venepuncture *n.* venipuntura, punción de una vena.

venereal *a.* venéreo-a, que resulta a consecuencia del acto sexual; ____ disease (VD) / enfermedad venérea.

venin, venine *n.* venina, sustancia tóxica del veneno de serpientes.

venin-antivenin *n.* veninantivenina, suero antídoto contra el veneno de serpientes.

venisection *n.* venisección. *V.* **phlebotomy.**

venogram *n.* venograma, radiograma de las venas usando un medio de contraste.

venography *n.* venografía, gráfica e información de un venograma.

venom *n.* veneno, sustancia tóxica.

venomous *a.* venenoso-a, tóxico-a.

veno-occlusive *a.* venoclusivo-a, rel. a una obstrucción venosa.

venotomy *n. cirg.* venotomía. *V.* **phlebotomy.**

venous *a.* venoso-a, rel. a las venas; ____ blood / sangre ____; ____ return / retorno ____; ____ sinus / seno ____; ____ thrombosis / trombosis ____.

vent *Fr.* vent, abertura.

ventilate *v.* ventilar, airear.

ventilation *n.* ventilación. 1. circulación de aire fresco en una habitación; 2. oxigenación de la sangre; 3. *psic.* expresión franca de conflictos emocionales internos.

ventilator *n.* ventilador; respirador artificial.

ventral *a.* ventral, abdominal, rel. al vientre o a la parte anterior del cuerpo humano.

ventricle *n.* ventrículo, cavidad pequeña esp. una estructura del corazón, el cerebro o la laringe; fourth ____ of the brain / cuarto ____ cerebral; left ____ of the heart / ____ izquierdo del corazón; larynx ____ / ____ de la laringe; lateral ____ of the brain / lateral del cerebro; right ____ of the heart / ____ derecho del corazón; third ____ of the brain / tercer ____ del cerebro.

ventricular *a.* ventricular, rel. a un ventrículo.

ventricular septal defect (VSD) *n.* defecto del tabique ventricular.

ventriculitis *n.* ventriculitis, infl. de un ventrículo.

ventriculography *n.* ventriculografía. *V.* **pneumoencephalography.**

ventriculotomy *n. cirg.* ventriculotomía, incisión de un ventrículo.

ventrodorsal *a.* ventrodorsal, rel. a las superficies ventral y dorsal.

venule *n.* vénula, vena diminuta que conecta los vasos capilares con venas mayores.

verb *gr.* verbo.

verbatim *L.* verbatim, al pie de la letra, palabra por palabra.

verdict *n.* veredicto, fallo.

verge *n.* anillo anal; margen; límite; borde; **on the** ____ **of** / a punto de.

verification *n.* verificación.

verify *v.* comprobar, verificar.

vermicide *n.* vermicida, vermífugo, agente destructor de vermes (gusanos).

vermiform *a.* vermiforme, que tiene la apariencia de un gusano.

vermiform appendix *n.* apéndice vermiforme.

vermilion border *n.* borde bermellón, el margen rosado expuesto del labio.

vermis *L.* vermis. 1. gusano parásito; 2. estructura semejante a un gusano tal como el lóbulo medio del cerebelo.

vernix *L.* barniz; ____ caseosa / unto sebáceo, secreción que protege la piel del feto.

verruca *n.* (*pl.* **verrucae**) verruga; ____ filiformis / ____ filiforme; plantaris (plantar wart) ____ / ____ plantaris; vulgaris ____ / ____ vulgaris.

verrucous *a.* verrugoso-a.

versatile *a.* versátil, polivalente; que tiene una variedad de aplicaciones.

version *n.* versión. 1. cambio de dirección de un órgano tal como el útero; 2. cambio de posición del feto en el útero que facilita el parto; bimanual ____ / ____ bimanual; bipolar ____ / ____ bipolar; cephalic ____ / ____ cefálica; combined ____ / ____ combinada; external ____ / ____ externa; spontaneous ____ / ____ espontánea.

vertebra *n.* (*pl.* **vertebrae**) vértebra, cada uno de los treinta y tres huesos que forman la columna vertebral; cervical ____ / ____ cervical; coccygeal ____ / ____ coccígea; lumbar ____ / ____ lumbar; sacral ____ / ____ sacra; thoracic ____ / ____ torácica.

vertebral *a.* vertebral, rel. a las vértebras; ____ artery / arteria ____; ____ canal / conducto ____; ____ ribs / costillas ____-es.

vertebrate *n.* vertebrado, que posee columna vertebral o una estructura semejante.

vertebrobasilar *a.* vertebrobasilar, rel. a las arterias vertebral y basilar.

vertex *n.* (*pl.* **vertices**) vértice. 1. cúspide de una estructura, tal como el punto extremo de la cabeza; 2. punto en que concurren los lados de un ángulo.

vertical *a.* 1. vertical, de posición erecta; 2. rel. al vértice; **-ly** *adv.* verticalmente.

vertiginous *a.* vertiginoso-a, rel. al vértigo.

verumontanitis *f.* verumontanitis, infl. del verumontanum.

verumontanum *L.* verumontanum, elevación en la uretra en el punto de entrada de los conductos seminales.

vesical *a.* vesical, rel. a una vejiga o semejante a ella.

vesication *n.* vesicación. 1. formación de ampollas; 2. una ampolla.

vesicle *n.* vesícula. 1. pequeña ampolla; 2. bolsa pequena de la capa exterior de la piel que contiene líquido seroso.

vesicoureteral *a.* vesicoureteral, rel. a la vejiga urinaria y el uréter.

vesicovaginal *a.* vesicovaginal, rel. a la vejiga urinaria y la vagina.

vesicular *a.* vesicular, rel. a las vesículas.

vessel *n.* vaso, conducto o canal portador de un fluido tal como la sangre y la linfa; blood _____ / _____ sanguíneo; collateral _____ / _____ colateral; great _____-s / grandes _____-s; lymphatic _____ / _____ linfático.

vestibular *a.* vestibular, rel. a un vestíbulo; _____ nerve / nervio _____.

vestibule *n.* vestíbulo, cavidad que da acceso a un conducto.

vestige *n.* vestigio, resto de una estructura que en una etapa previa de la especie o el embrión, tuvo un desarrollo completo.

vestigial *a.* vestigial, rel. a vestigio; rudimentario-a.

vet *n. pop.* veterinario-a.

veterinarian *n.* veterinario-a, persona especializada en veterinaria; *a.* veterinario-a, rel. a la veterinaria.

veterinary *n.* veterinaria, ciencia que trata de la prevención y cura de enfermedades y lesiones de animales, esp. domésticos.

via *L.* via, tracto, conducto.

viability *n.* cualidad de ser viable.

viable *a.* viable, capaz de sobrevivir, término que se usa gen. en referencia al feto o al recién nacido.

viaduct *n.* viaducto.

vial *n.* frasco, ampolleta.

vibration *n.* vibración, oscilación.

vibrative, **vibratory** *a.* vibratorio-a, que produce vibración u oscila; _____ sense / sentido _____.

vicarious *a.* vicario-a, que asume el lugar de otro.

vice *n.* vicio; falta, defecto.

vicinity *n.* proximidad, vecindad; barrio.

vicious *a.* [*ridden by vice*] vicioso-a, depravado-a; **-ly** *adv.* viciosamente, malvadamente.

victim *n.* víctima.

vide *L.* véase.

video *n.* video; _____ tape / videocinta.

view *n.* vista; **in** _____ **of** / en vista de; _____ **point** / punto de vista; *v.* mirar, examinar.

vigil *n.* vigilia. 1. estado de respuesta consciente a un estímulo; 2. insomnio.

vigilance *n.* vigilancia, estado alerta o de atención.

vigor *n.* vigor, fortaleza.

vigorous *a.* vigoroso-a; fuerte; **-ly** *adv.* vigorosamente.

villous *a.* velloso-a, velludo-a.

villus *n.* (*pl.* **villi**) vellosidad, vello, proyección filiforme que crece en una superficie membranosa; aracnoid _____ / _____ aracnoidea; chorionic _____ / _____ coriónicas; intestinal _____ / _____ intestinal.

vinegar *n.* vinagre.

violaceous *a.* violáceo-a.

violate *v.* violar, abusar sexualmente.

violence *n.* violencia.

violent *a.* violento-a.

violet *n.* color violeta; *a.* violeta.

viper *n.* víbora.

viral *a.* viral, rel. a un virus.

viremia *n.* viremia, presencia de un virus en la sangre.

virgin *n.* virgen. 1. sustancia sin contaminación; 2. persona que no ha realizado el acto sexual.

virginal *a.* virginal.

virginity *n.* virginidad.

virile *a.* viril, varonil.

virility *n.* virilidad. 1. potencia sexual; 2. estado de poseer características masculinas.

virilization *n.* virilización, masculinización, proceso por el cual se desarrollan en la mujer características masculinas gen. debido a una trastorno hormonal o al suplemento artificial de hormonas masculinas.

virion *n.* virión, partícula viral madura que

constituye la forma extracelular infecciosa de un virus.

virology *n.* virología, ciencia que estudia los virus.

virtual *a.* virtual, de existencia aparente, no real.

virulence *n.* virulencia. 1. poder de un organismo de causar determinadas enfermedades en el huésped. 2. cualidad o estado de ser virulento.

virulent *a.* virulento-a, nocivo-a, extremadamente tóxico.

virus *n.* virus, microorganismo ultramicroscópico capaz de causar enfermedades infecciosas; atenuated ____ / ____ atenuado; Cocsackie ____ / ____ de Cocsackie; cytomegalic ____ / ____ citomegálico; ECHO ____ / ____ ECHO; enteric ____ / ____ entérico; herpes ____ / ____ herpético; pox ____ / ____ variólico o de Pox; respiratory syncytial ____ / ____ sincitial respiratorio; tumor ____ / ____ oncogénico.

viscera *n. pl.* vísceras, órganos internos del cuerpo, esp. del abdomen.

visceral *a.* visceral, rel. a las vísceras.

visceromegaly *n.* visceromegalia, agrandamiento anormal de una víscera.

viscosity *n.* viscosidad, cualidad de ser viscoso, esp. la propiedad de los líquidos de no fluir libremente debido a la fricción de las moléculas.

viscous *a.* viscoso-a, gelatinoso-a, pegajoso-a.

viscus *L.* (*pl.* **viscera**) víscera.

visible *a.* visible, aparente, evidente; **-ly** *adv.* visiblemente, evidentemente; aparentemente.

vision *n.* visión. 1. sentido de la vista; 2. capacidad de percibir los objetos por la acción de la luz a través de los órganos visuales y los centros cerebrales con que se relacionan; achromatic ____ / ____ acromática; binocular ____ / ____ binocular; central ____ / ____ central; chromatic ____ / ____ cromática; day ____ / ____ diurna; doble ____ / ____ doble, diplopia; field of ____ / ____ campo visual; night ____ / ____ nocturna; peripheral ____ / ____ periférica.

visit *n.* visita; *v.* visitar, ir de visita.

visiting hours *n.* horas de visita.

visual *a.* visual, rel. a la visión; ____ acuity / acuidad ____ ; ____ field / campo ____ .

visualize *v.* visualizar. 1. crear una imagen visual de algo; 2. hacer visible, tal como

copiar la imagen de un órgano en una radiografía.

vital *a.* vital, rel. a la vida o esencial en el mantenimiento de la misma; ____ capacity / capacidad ____ ; ____ signs / signos ____ -es; ____ statistics / estadística demográfica.

vitality *n.* vitalidad. 1. cualidad de vivir; 2. vigor mental o físico.

vitalize *v.* vitalizar, dar vida; reanimar.

vitamin *n.* vitamina, uno de los compuestos orgánicos que se encuentran en pequeñas cantidades en los alimentos y que son esenciales en el desarrollo y funcionamiento del organismo.

vitaminic *a.* vitamínico-a, rel. a las vitaminas.

vitiate *v.* viciar; infectar.

vitiligo *n.* vitiligo, trastorno epidérmico benigno que se manifiesta con manchas blancas en partes expuestas del cuerpo.

vitreous *a.* vítreo-a, vidrioso-a, casi transparente, hialino; ____ chamber / cámara ____ ; ____ body / cuerpo ____ ; ____ humor / humor ____ .

vivifying *a.* vivificador, vivificante.

vivisection *n.* vivisección, corte o sección realizada en animales con fines investigativos.

vocabulary *n.* vocabulario.

vocal *a.* vocal, oral, rel. a la voz o producido por ella.

vocal cords *n. pl.* cuerdas vocales; órgano esencial de la voz; false ____ / ____ superiores o falsas; true ____ / ____ inferiores o verdaderas.

vocalization *n.* vocalización.

vocation *n.* vocación, profesión.

voice *n.* voz.

voiced *a.* dicho, expresado; producido por la voz.

void *a.* nulo-a, vacío-a; inválido-a, sin efecto; *v.* anular, invalidar; evacuar, eliminar.

volatile *a.* volátil, que se evapora fácilmente.

volition *n.* volición, voluntad, poder de determinación.

volume *n.* volumen. 1. espacio ocupado por una sustancia o un cuerpo; 2. cantidad, intensidad; blood ____ / ____ sanguíneo; expiratory air reserve ____ / ____ de reserva expiratoria o aire de reserva; heart ____ / ____ cardíaco; residual ____ / ____ residual; stroke ____ / ____ sistólico; tidal ____ / ____ de ventilación pulmonar.

volumetric *a.* volumétrico, rel. a la medida de volumen.

voluntary *a.* voluntario-a; ____ muscle / músculo ____.

volunteer *a.* voluntario-a.

voluptuous *a.* voluptuoso-a, provocador-a, sensual; **-ly** *adv.* voluptuosamente.

volvulus *a.* vólvulo, obstrucción intestinal causada por torsión o anudamiento del intestino en torno al mesenterio.

vomer *n.* vómer, hueso impar que forma parte del tabique medio de las fosas nasales.

vomit *n.* vómito; *v.* vomitar.

vomiting *n.* manifestación de vómitos.

vomitive *n.* vomitivo.

von Recklinghausen's disease *n.* enfermedad de von Recklinghausen. *V.* **neurofibromatosis.**

voracious *a.* voraz, con un apetito excesivo.

voracity *n.* voracidad.

vortex *n.* (*pl.* **vortices**) vórtice, estructura de forma espiral.

voucher *n.* comprobante.

vowel *n.* vocal.

voyeur *Fr.* voyeur, persona que practica voyeurismo.

voyeurism *n.* voyeurismo, perversión sexual por la cual la contemplación de actos u órganos sexuales induce erotismo.

vulnerability *n.* vulnerabilidad.

vulnerable *a.* vulnerable, propenso a accidentes o enfermedades.

vulva *L.* vulva, conjunto de los órganos femeninos externos del aparato genital.

vulval *a.* vulvar, rel. a la vulva.

vulvectomy *n. cirg.* vulvectomía, excisión de la vulva.

vulvitis *n.* vulvitis, infl. de la vulva.

vulvovaginal *a.* vulvovaginal, rel. a la vulva y la vagina.

W

W *abbr.* **water** / agua; **weight** / peso.

waddle *n.* marcha tambaleante, andar anserino.

wail *v.* lamentarse; gemir.

waist *n.* cintura; talle.

waistband *n.* cinto, cinturón.

waistline *n.* cintura.

wait *v.* esperar, aguardar; **to** ____ **on** / servir, atender a.

waiting *n.* espera; demora; ____ **room** / sala de espera.

waive *v.* diferir, posponer.

wake *vi.* despertar; **to** ____ **up** / despertar a; despertarse.

walk *n.* paseo; caminata; *v.* caminar, andar; **to** ____ **up and down** / caminar de un lado a otro.

walker *n.* andador, andaderas, aparato que se usa para ayudar a caminar.

walking cast *n.* molde de yeso que se adapta para caminar.

wall *n.* pared; tabique; ____ **tooth** / diente molar.

walled-off *a.* encapsulado-a.

wander *v.* vagar; [*to loose one's way*] desviarse, perderse, extraviarse.

wandering *a.* errante, errático-a; desviado-a; ____ **cell** / célula ____; ____ **goiter** / bocio móvil; ____ **pain** / dolor ____; ____ **tooth** / diente desviado.

want *n.* necesidad, falta, carencia; *v.* querer, desear; necesitar; carecer de.

war *n.* guerra.

ward *n.* sala de hospital; ____ **diet** / dieta hospitalaria; isolation ____ / sala de aislamiento; ____ **of the state** / bajo custodia, bajo tutela del estado.

warfarin *n.* warfarina, anticoagulante, nombre genérico de Coumadin, medicamento usado en la prevención de trombosis e infartos.

warm *a.* caluroso-a; caliente; [*lukewarm*] tibio-a; [*character*] afectuoso-a, expresivo-a; *v.* **to be** ____ / tener calor, [*not very hot but feverish*] tener destemplanza, [*weather*] hacer calor; **to** ____ **to** / simpatizar con; **to** ____ **up** / calentar; *adv.* **-ly** afectuosamente, con entusiasmo.

warn *v.* prevenir, advertir, avisar.

warning *n.* advertencia; aviso; [*hard lesson*] escarmiento; ____ **signal** / advertencia; señal premonitoria; ____ **symptoms** / síntomas premonitorios.

warp *n.* torcedura; torcimiento; *v.* torcer; retorcer; perder la forma.

warranty *n.* garantía.

wart *n.* verruga. *V.* **verruca.**

warty *a.* verrugoso-a, rel. a verrugas.

was *pret.* de **to be.**

wash *n.* lavado, baño, lavadura; mouth ____ / enjuague; *v.* lavar; **to** ____ **away** / quitar con una lavadura; [*oneself*] lavarse.

washbasin *n.* lavamanos, palangana, vasija.

washcloth *n.* toallita de manos; paño de lavarse.

washed-out *a.* descolorido-a, desteñido-a.

washstand *n.* lavabo, lavamanos.

wasp *n.* avispa; ____ sting / picadura de ____.

Wasserman test *n.* prueba de Wasserman, análisis serológico de la sífilis.

waste *n.* desperdicio, residuo, gasto inútil; merma, pérdida; ____ **of time** / pérdida de tiempo; *v.* desperdiciar, desgastar, malgastar; **to** ____ **away** / demacrarse, consumirse.

wastebasket *n.* cesto de basura.

wasted *a.* desgastado-a, malgastado-a; [*person*] demacrado-a; consumido-a.

wasting *n.* agotamiento, consunción, pérdida de funciones vitales.

watch *n.* reloj de pulsera o bolsillo; vigilia; *v.* cuidar, observar, esperar; tener cuidado; **to** ____ **one's step** / cuidarse, tener cuidado; ____ **out!** / ¡Cuidado!.

water *n.* agua, líquidos del cuerpo; infusión; ____ **bag** / bolsa de ____; ____ **bed** / cama de, colchón de ____; ____ **blister** / ampolla acuosa; ____ **-cooled** / enfriado-a por ____; ____ **faucet** / grifo, pila, llave; ____ **level** / nivel del ____; ____ **pill** / diurético; ____ **pollution** / contaminación del ____; ____ **purification** / purificación del ____; ____ **tight** / hermético, impermeable; ____ **-soluble** / soluble en ____, que se disuelve en ____; ____ **supply** / abastecimiento de ____; *v.* **to be in deep** ____ / tener dificultades; **to give** ____ / dar ____; **to wash with** ____ / lavar con ____; [*plants*] **to** ____ regar; humedecer; mojar.

watered *a.* aguado-a; diluído-a.

water-electrolyte balance *n.* equilibrio hidroelectrolítico.

water-electrolyte imbalance *n.* desequilibrio hidroelectrolítico.

water-hammer pulse *n.* pulso en martillo de agua.

water intoxication *n.* intoxicación acuosa, retención excesiva de agua.

watery *a.* acuoso-a, aguado-a, húmedo-a; ____ **eyes** / ojos llorosos.

wave *n.* onda, ondulación; ademán de la mano. 1. movimiento o vibración ondulante que tiene una dirección fija y prosigue en una curva de ondulación; 2. representación gráfica de una actividad tal como la obtenida en un encefalograma; **brain** ____ -s / ____ -s cerebrales; **electromagnetic** ____ -s / ____ -s electromagnéticas; **excitation** ____ / ____ de excitación: **high frequency** ____ / ____ de alta frecuencia; ____ **length** / longitud de ____; **short** ____ / ____ corta; **ultrasonic** ____ -s / ____ -s ultrasónicas; *v.* hacer señales o ademanes con la mano.

waved *a.* ondulado-a, ondeado-a.

wavy *a.* ondulado -a.

wax *n.* cera. 1. cera. producida por abejas; 2. secreción cerosa; **ear** ____ / ____ del oído. *V.* **cerumen;** 3. sustancia de origen animal, vegetal o mineral que se emplea en preparaciones de pomadas y ceratos; **depilatory** ____ / ____ depilatoria.

waxy *a.* ceroso-a, céreo-a; [*applied wax*] encerado-a.

way *n.* vía, camino; pasaje; ____ **of life** / manera de vivir; costumbres; ____ **out** / salida; **by the** ____ / a propósito; **in no** ____ / de ningún modo; **out of the** ____ / fuera de curso, desviado-a; lejano-a; **that** ____ / por allí; **the other** ____ **around** / por el contrario; *v.* **to make** ____ / abrir paso.

weak *a.* débil, flojo-a, endeble, enclenque. poco fuerte.

weaken *v.* debilitar; desfallecer; debilitarse; deteriorarse.

weakness *n.* debilidad, debilitamiento, flojera, flaqueza.

wealth *n.* riqueza, abundancia.

wealthy *a.* rico-a, acaudalado-a, adinerado-a.

wean *n.* destetar, quitar el pecho de la madre.

weaning *n.* destete.

weanling *n.* el, la recién destetado-a, desmamado-a.

wear *n.* uso, gasto, deterioro, deteriorización; *vi.* usar, llevar puesto; desgastar; **to** ____ **out** / gastar; gastarse; desgastarse.

wearing *n.* desgaste; pérdida; decaimiento.

weary *a.* cansado-a, fatigado-a.

weather *n.* [*climate*] tiempo; ____ **forecasting** / pronóstico del ____ .

web *n.* red, membrana; **pulmonary arterial** ____ -s / ____ de membranas arteriopulmonares.

webbed *n.* unido-a por una telilla o membrana.

wedge *n.* cuña.

weight *n.* peso.

welcome *n.* bienvenida; *a.* bienvenido-a; agradable; deseado-a; *v.* dar la bienvenida, recibir con agrado; **You are** ___ / De nada; para servirle; no hay de que; **a** ___ **surprise** / una sorpresa agradable.

welfare *n.* bien, bienestar; salud; asistencia; ___ **benefits** / beneficios de asistencia social; ___ **work** / trabajo de asistencia social; ___ **worker** / trabajador-a social.

well *a.* bueno-a; en buena salud; **well-being** / bienestar; *adv.* bien, favorablemente, felizmente; **all is** ___ / todo va bien.

welt *n.* verdugón, roncha.

Western Blot, immunoblot *n.* Western Blot, "inmunoblot", prueba subsecuente para confirmar la infección por el virus VIH en pacientes con evidencia de exposición indicada por un ensayo enzimático inmunosorbente (ELISA).

wet *a.* mojado-a, humedecido-a; *v.* mojar, humedecer.

wet dream *n.* emisión seminal nocturna.

Wharton's duct *n.* conducto de Wharton, conducto excretorio de la glándula submaxilar.

wheal *n.* roncha.

wheat *n.* trigo; ___ **germ** / germen de ___ .

wheel *n.* rueda; *v.* hacer rodar.

wheelchair *n.* silla de ruedas.

wheeze *n.* jadeo, respiración forzada; *v.* jadear.

when *pron.* cuándo; **Since** ___? / ¿Desde ___?; *conj.* cuando; si.

whenever *adv.* cuando quiera; siempre que; ___ **is needed** / siempre que se necesite; ___ **you wish** / siempre que lo desee.

while *adv.* mientras, un rato, algún tiempo; **for a** ___ / temporalmente; **not for a** ___ / por ahora no.

whimper / *n.* quejido, lloriqueo; *v.* sollozar, lloriquear.

whine *n.* quejido, gemido, lamento; *v.* gemir, quejarse, lamentarse.

whiplash injury *n.* lesión de latigazo.

Whipple's disease *n.* enfermedad de Whipple, trastorno causado por la acumulación de depósitos lípidos en los tejidos linfáticos e intestinales.

whirlpool bath *n.* baño de remolino.

whisper *n.* susurro, cuchicheo; *v.* susurrar, cuchichear.

whistle *n.* silbido; *v.* silbar.

white *n.* color blanco; ___ **of the egg** / clara de huevo; *a.* blanco-a; ___ **corpuscle** / leucocito, glóbulo ___ .

white matter *n.* sustancia blanca, tejido nervioso formado en su mayor parte por fibras mielínicas y que constituye el elemento conductor del cerebro y la médula espinal.

whiteness *n.* blancura.

whitish *a.* blanquecino-a; blancuzco-a.

whole *n.* total, conjunto; **as a** ___ / en conjunto; *a.* todo-a; **the** ___ **day** / todo el día.

wholesome *a.* sano-a, saludable.

whoop *n.* estridor, sonido que caracteriza la respiración después de un ataque de tos ferina.

whooping cough *n.* tos ferina. *V.* **pertussis.**

whorl *n.* espiral. 1. disposición de fibras en forma esférica, esp. las fibras cardíacas; 2. tipo de huella digital.

wide *a.* ancho-a; **three feet** ___ / de tres pies de ancho; amplio-a; extenso-a; ___ **open** / muy abierto; **-ly** *adv.* ampliamente, extensamente.

widen *v.* ensanchar, extender.

widespread *a.* extendido-a; muy difundido-a; general.

widow *n.* viuda.

widower *n.* viudo.

width *n.* anchura, ancho.

wife *n.* esposa.

wig *n.* peluca.

will *n.* voluntad, determinación, deseo; testamento. *v.* querer, ordenar, mandar.

Wilms' tumor *n.* tumor de Wilms, neoplasma del riñón que se desarrolla rápidamente y usu. se ve en la infancia.

Wilson's disease *n.* enfermedad de Wilson, enfermedad hereditaria que se manifiesta con serios trastornos hepáticos y cerebrales.

win *vi.* ganar, vencer.

wind *n.* viento, aire; flato, ventosidad.

windburn *n.* quemadura por el viento.

window *n.* ventana.

windpipe *n.* tráquea; *pop.* gaznate.

wine *n.* vino.

wing *n.* ala.

wink *n.* pestañeo; *v.* pestañear.

winter *n.* invierno.

wire *n.* alambre.

wisdom teeth *n.* cordales, muelas del juicio.

wise *n.* cuerdo, prudente.

with *conj.* con.

withdraw *n.* supresión, retracción; introversión; privación; *vi.* retirar, suprimir, descontinuar; privar de; **to** ___ **a product from the market** / descontinuar o suprimir un producto.

withdrawal syndrome *n.* síndrome de privación de una droga adictiva como resultado de la supresión de la misma.

withdrawal treatment *n.* tratamiento de desintoxicación.

within *prep.* dentro de, en el interior de; a distancia de; al alcance de; cerca de; an hour / ____ una hora.

without *prep.* sin, falto de, fuera de; *adv.* fuera, afuera; exterior.

withstand *vi.* resistir, soportar, sufrir.

woman *n.* (*pl.* **women**) mujer.

womb *n.* matriz, útero. *V.* **uterus.**

wonder *n.* maravilla, prodigio, admiración; admirarse, asombrarse.

wonderful *a.* maravilloso-a, asombroso-a, estupendo-a, excelente.

wood *n.* madera.

word *n.* vocablo, palabra, término.

work *n.* trabajo, empleo, ocupación; *v.* trabajar.

work up *n.* 1. preparación del paciente para la aplicación de un tratamiento; 2. obtencion de los datos pertinentes a un caso.

worm *n.* lombriz, gusano.

wormlike *a.* vermicular, vermiforme.

wound *n.* herida, lesión; contused ____ / ____ contusa, lesión subcutánea; gunshot ____ / ____ de bala; penetrating ____ / ____ penetrante; puncture ____ / ____ punzante, con un instrumento afilado.

wrinkle *n.* arruga; arrugarse.

wrinkled *a.* arrugado-a.

wrist *n.* carpo, muñeca. *V.* **carpus;** ____ drop / muñeca caída.

write *vi.* escribir.

writing *n.* escritura, acto de escribir.

wrong *n.* error, falsedad; *a.* equivocado-a; erróneo-a; incorrecto-a; the ____ treatment / un tratamiento ____ ; **the** ____ **side** / el lado afectado, el lado incorrecto; *v.* **to be** ____ / no tener razón; **to go** ____ / [*to fail to understand*] interpretar mal; equivocarse; **-ly** *adv.* mal; incorrectamente, equivocadamente.

X

X *abbr.* **xanthine** / xantina.

xanthic *a.* amarillento-a, rel. a la xantina.

xanthine *n.* xantina, grupo de substancias tales como la cafeína estimulantes del sistema nervioso central y del corazón.

xanthochromia *n.* xantocromía, color amarillento visto en placas de la piel o en el líquido cefalorraquídeo.

xanthochromic *a.* xantocrómico-a, de apariencia amarillenta o relacionado-a con la xantocromía.

xanthoderma *n.* xantodermia, color amarillento de la piel.

xanthoma *n.* xantoma, formación tumoral de placas o nódulos en la piel.

xanthosis *n.* xantosis, descoloración amarillenta de la piel debida a ingestión excesiva de alimentos tales como la zanahoria y la calabaza.

X chromosome *n.* cromosoma X, cromosoma sexual diferencial que determina las características del sexo femenino.

xenograft *n.* xenoinjerto. *V.* **heterograft.**

xenon *n.* xenón, elemento gaseoso, radioisótopo que se encuentra en pequeñas cantidades en el aire atmosférico.

xenon-133 *n.* xenón 133, radioisótopo de xenón usado en la fotoescanción del pulmón.

xenophobia *n.* xenofobia, temor excesivo o aversión a algo o a alguien extraño o extranjero.

xeroderma *n.* xeroderma, piel excesivamente seca.

xerography *n.* xerografía. *V.* **xeroradiography.**

xeromammography *n.* xeromamografía, xerorradiografía de la mama.

xerophthalmia *n.* xeroftalmia, sequedad excesiva de la conjuntiva causada por deficiencia de vitamina A.

xeroradiography *n.* xerorradiografía, registro de imágenes electrostáticas por medio de un proceso en seco usando placas cubiertas con un elemento metálico tal como el selenio.

xerosis *n.* xerosis, sequedad anormal presente en la piel, ojos y membranas mucosas.

xerostomia *n.* xerostomía, excesiva sequedad en la boca debida a una deficiencia de secreción salival.

xiphoid *a.* xifoide, en forma de espada, similar al apéndice xifoide o ensiforme.

xiphoid process *n.* apéndice xifoide, formación cartilaginosa que se une al cuerpo del esternón.

X-linked *n.* caracteres genéticos que se relacionan con el cromosoma X.

X-rays *n.* rayos X (equis), radiografía. 1. ondas electromagnéticas de alta energía de radiación que se usan para penetrar tejidos y órganos del cuerpo y registrar densidades en una placa o pantalla; 2. placa fotográfica o fluorescente que obtiene la imagen de estructuras internas del organismo.

Y

Y *abbr.* **y/o year old** / de un año de edad.

yaw *n.* lesión primaria de la frambesia.

yawn *n.* bostezo; *v.* bostezar.

yaws *n. pl.* V. **frambesia.**

Y chromosome *n.* cromosoma Y, cromosoma sexual diferencial que determina las características sexuales del sexo masculino.

year *n.* año; **at the beginning of the** ___ / a principios de ___ ; **at the end of the** ___ / al final del ___ ; **every** ___ / todos los ___ -s; **last** ___ / el ___ pasado; **New Year** / Año Nuevo; **once a** ___ / una vez al ___ ; **-ly** *adv.* anualmente.

yeast *n.* levadura, hongo diminuto capaz de provocar fermentación que se usa en la nutrición como fuente de vitaminas y proteínas.

yell *n.* grito, alarido; *v.* gritar.

yellow *n.* color amarillo; *a.* amarillo-a.

yellow body *n.* cuerpo amarillo. *V.* **corpus luteum.**

yellow fever *n.* fiebre amarilla, enfermedad endémica de regiones tropicales debida a un virus que es transmitido por la picadura del mosquito hembra *Aedes Aegypti* y se manifiesta con fiebre, ictericia y albuminuria.

yellowish *a.* amarillento-a.

yesterday *n. adv.* ayer.

yet *conj.* todavía; no obstante, sin embargo.

yield *n.* rendimiento; producción; *v.* producir, rendir.

yoga *n.* yoga, sistema de creencias y práctica de meditación y autodominio a través del cual se trata de alcanzar un estado de unión entre el yo y el universo.

yogurt *n.* yogur, leche fermentada por la acción del *Lactobacillus bulgaricus*, a la que se le atribuyen valores nutritivos y terapéuticos.

yolk *n.* 1. yema del huevo; 2. conjunto de sustancias que nutren al embrión.

young *a.* joven; juvenil.

youngster *n.* jovencito-a, muchacho-a.

youth *n.* juventud, mocedad.

Z

Z *abbr.* **z zero** / cero; **zone** / zona.

zero population growth (ZPG) *n.* crecimiento cero de población, condición demográfica que existe en un período de tiempo determinado en el cual la población permanece estable, sin aumentar ni disminuir.

zinc *n.* zinc, elemento metálico cristalino de propiedad astringente.

zinc ointment *n.* pomada de zinc.

Zollinger-Ellison syndrome *n.* síndrome de Zollinger-Ellison, condición manifestada por hipersecreción gástrica, hiperacidez y ulceración péptica del estómago e intestino delgado.

zona *n.* zona. 1. área o capa específica; 2. herpes zóster.

zone *n.* zona, estructura anatómica en forma de banda.

zoograft *n.* zooinjerto, injerto que proviene de tejido animal.

zoster *n.* zóster. *V.* **herpes zoster, shingles.**

zygoma *n.* cigoma, zigoma, prominencia ósea que forma un arco en la unión del hueso malar y el temporal.

zygote *n.* cigoto, óvulo fertilizado, célula fecundada por la unión de dos gametos.

Gramática Inglesa Simplificada

EL ALFABETO / THE ALPHABET

A diferencia del español, en el que cada letra tiene un sonido más o menos definido, en inglés una misma letra puede tener más de una pronunciación de acuerdo con su posición en la sílaba. Esa variación establece la diferencia fundamental en la pronunciación de los dos idiomas y la mayor dificultad que la persona hispano parlante confronta al tratar de aprender la pronunciación de la lengua inglesa. La mayoría de los textos lingüísticos recurren al uso de algún alfabeto fonético que sirve de clave para la pronunciación del inglés y cuyo uso recomendamos al estudiante que quiera perfeccionar la pronunciación. Para los efectos de este diccionario nos hemos limitado a dar una sencilla orientación que ayude al lector a pronunciar aquellas letras y sonidos que más difieren de la correspondiente pronunciación en español y que, por lo tanto, presentan mayor dificultad al hispano parlante. Debemos señalar que esta presentación simplificada de las letras en inglés no abarca todas las posibilidades; las excepciones a las reglas generales son muy numerosas.

El alfabeto inglés tiene veintiséis letras: cinco vocales y veintiuna consonantes. La letra **y**, como en español, puede ser vocal (se pronuncia como la **i** en español) o consonante (se pronuncia como la **y** en ya).

El alfabeto

Letra	Pronunciación aproximada
A	ei
B	bi
C	si
D	di
E	i
F	ef
G	yi (*sonido africado como la* **j** *de Jean en francés*)
H	eich
I	ai
J	yei (*sonido africado*)
K	quei
L	el
M	em
N	en
O	ou
P	pi
Q	quiu
R	ar
S	es
T	ti

U	iu
V	vi
W	doblyu
X	ecs
Y	uai
Z	zi (*sonido parecido a la* s *en mismo o desde*)

La pronunciación del inglés / English Pronunciation

VOCALES

Las vocales en inglés tienen generalmente dos sonidos, uno breve o corto y otro largo. La **e** puede además ser muda al final de la palabra.

Sonido breve o corto: ocurre generalmente cuando la vocal es seguida por una consonante en la misma sílaba.

Letra	*Palabra en inglés*	*Sonido aproximado en español*
a	nap / siesta	sonido intermedio entre la **a** de mano y la **e** de pesa.
	call / llamada	boca (gen. en palabras que terminan en **ll**).
e	bed / cama	frente.
	late / tarde	muda (gen. ocurre al final de la palabra).
i	chill / enfriamiento	sonido intermedio entre la **i** y la **e** en español.
o	compare / comparar	comparar
	hot / caliente	sonido intermedio entre la **a** y la **o** en español.
	move / mover	cura
u	drug / droga	sonido intermedio entre la **o** y la **u** en español.
	full / lleno	**tú**

Sonido largo: ocurre generalmente cuando la vocal es la vocal final de una sílaba, o cuando va seguida de una **e** muda o de una **e** muda y una consonante. Es un sonido vocálico demorado en el cual algunas veces una vocal sencilla tiene un sonido diptongado.

a	basic / básico	ley
e	he / él	sí
i	bite / picadura	hay
o	dosis / dosis	sonido equivalente al sonido del diptongo **ou** en español.
oo	blood / sangre	poro
	book / libro	cura
u	putrid / pútrido	ciudad, la combinación **ew** en inglés también corresponde al sonido **iu:** few / varios.

DIPTONGOS

ou: sonido semejante al diptongo **au** en español o sonido breve semejante a la **o** en español:

mouth / boca	causa
bought / compró	dosis

CONSONANTES

El alfabeto en inglés tiene dos consonantes que casi no se usan en español, la **k** y la **w**; la **ñ**, en cambio, no existe en el alfabeto inglés y las letras **ch**, **ll**, y **rr** no se consideran caracteres propios, sino combinación de dos letras (letra dígrafa). En general, la pronunciación de la mayoría de las consonantes es semejante en ambos idiomas, aunque en inglés la pronunciación de las mismas es más explosiva.

CONSONANTES Y LETRAS DÍGRAFAS QUE MÁS DIFIEREN
DE LA PRONUNCIACIÓN ESPAÑOLA

b: sonido semejante a la **b** inicial en español; es muda en algunas palabras cuando precede a la letra **t:**

	Sonido aproximado en español
bacillus / bacilo	**b**acilo
dou**b**t / duda	(muda)

ch: presenta varios sonidos según su posición en la palabra:

child / niño	**ch**ico
cholera / cólera	cólera
ma**ch**ine / máquina	**sh**shsh! *(semejante al sonido que se emplea para indicar silencio)*

g: cuando le sigue una **e** o una **i** tiene un sonido semejante a la **y** en español *(sonido suave).* Esta regla tiene por excepción las palabras monosílabas:

general / general	**y**eso *(sonido africado)*
giant / gigante	**y**eso *(sonido africado)*
girl / muchacha	**g**ota

en casi todas las otras situaciones tiene el mismo sonido que la **g** fuerte en español:

gastric / gástrico	**g**ástrico
gram / gramo	**g**ramo
guide / guía	**g**uía

gh: en medio de la palabra esta combinación de letras es generalmente muda:

dau**gh**ter / hija

h: sonido aproximado al de la **j** en español pero algo más suave:

hemorrhage / hemorragia   **j**arabe

j: sonido semejante a la **y** en español:

jejunum / yeyuno   **y**eyuno *(con africación)*

ll: sonido igual al de la **l** sencilla:

genera**ll**y / generalmente   genera**l**mente

kn: la **k** es muda:

knee / rodilla   **n**uez

mm: sonido igual a la **m** simple:

i**mm**unology / inmunología   a**m**eba

ph: sonido de **f:**

pharmacy / farmacia   **f**armacia

r: sonido articulado en inglés sin trino y con la lengua situada más hacia atrás de la boca y la parte anterior curvada hacia el paladar sin tocarlo.

su**r**gery / cirugía   ci**r**ugía

rr: sonido igual al de la **r** sencilla:

hemo**rr**hage / hemorragia   ci**r**ugía

s: sonido semejante a la **s** sorda en español en la mayoría de los vocablos:

consult / consultar   consulta
sperm / esperma   esperma

sonido semejante a la **s** sonora de mismo o desde, cuando está entre vocales o antes de la consonante **m:**

disease / enfermedad   mismo
metabolism / metabolismo   desde

al final de la palabra puede tener sonido de **s** o de **z** en inglés:

yes / sí   sí
is / es   (sonido de **z** en inglés)

cuando está seguida del diptongo **io** tiene sonido semejante al de la **y** *(sonido de consonante)*, muy exagerado, o al de la **j** en francés como en **J**ean:

lesion / lesión   lesión

cuando está seguida de la vocal **u** tiene un sonido semejante a la **sh** en inglés:

sure / seguro   **sh**shsh *(como cuando se está silenciando a alguien)*

ss: sonido igual al de la **s** en español:

class / clase   clase

th: tiene dos sonidos. 1. parecido a la **d**; 2. parecido a la **z** castellana:

this / este   de**d**o
therapy / terapia   **z**apato *(con ceceo castellano)*

w: sonido semejante al de la **u** en español como en la palabra h**u**eso:

weight / peso   h**u**eso

z: sonido semejante al que se hace para imitar el zumbido de una abeja

zero / cero   **z**zzz . . .

ACENTUACIÓN DE LAS PALABRAS EN INGLÉS

El acento gráfico no existe en inglés. Las reglas a seguir son pocas pero tienen muchas excepciones:

1. Las palabras de dos sílabas se acentúan generalmente en la penúltima sílaba:

   sw**o**llen / hinchado
   abcess / abceso

2. Palabras a las que se le hayan añadido sufijos o prefijos retienen el acento en la misma sílaba acentuada de la raíz o palabra básica:

   n**o**rmal: abn**o**rmal / anormal
   color**a**tion: discolor**a**tion / descoloración

3. Palabras de tres o más sílabas generalmente tienen una sílaba que se acentúa más enfáticamente, y otra sílaba que lleva un acento menos pronunciado:

   cartil**a**ginous / cartilaginoso

EL NOMBRE O SUSTANTIVO / THE NOUN

Género / Gender

Los nombres o sustantivos en inglés se clasifican en masculinos, femeninos y neutros. El género de cosas inanimadas es generalmente neutro.

Femenino nombre de mujer o animal hembra
la mujer / the woman
Masculino nombre de hombre o animal varón
el hombre / the man
Neutro nombres de cosas, concretas o abstractas
la inyección / the shot   el dolor / the pain

En ciertos nombres se distingue el género por medio de las palabras hembra / female, varón / male, o por niño / boy y niña / girl.

enfermera / female nurse   enfermero / male nurse
bebita / baby girl   bebito / baby boy

Note: En este diccionario se ha incorporado la palabra person / persona a palabras como **chairman,** cambiada a **chairperson,** para evitar el uso exclusivo del masculino en nombres que pueden referirse al sexo masculino o femenino.

Número / Number

El plural de los nombres

> Añada **-s** para formar el plural de la mayor parte de los nombres.

síntoma / symptom   síntomas / symptoms

> Añada **-es** si la palabra termina en **ch, h, sh, ss, x,** u **o.**

punto quirúrgico / stitch   puntos quirúrgicos / stitches
fogaje / hot flash   fogajes / hot flashes
absceso / abscess   abscesos / abscesses
reflejo / reflex   reflejos / reflexes
mosquito / mosquito   mosquitos / mosquitoes

> Añada **-es** si la palabra termina en **y,** cambie la **y** por **i**

deformidad / deformity   deformidades / deformities

> Añada **-es** si la palabra termina en **f** o **fe,** cambie la **f** por **v**

vida / life   vidas / lives
hoja / leaf   hojas / leaves

Plurales irregulares más comunes en inglés

diente / tooth	dientes / teeth	hombre / man	hombres / men
mujer / woman	mujeres / women	niños / children	niño / child
pie / foot	pies / feet	piojo / louse	piojos / lice
ratón / mouse	ratones / mice		

EL CASO POSESIVO DE LOS NOMBRES

El caso posesivo de los nombres en inglés se forma invirtiendo el orden del caso posesivo en español.

> Poseedor + ' (apóstrofe) + s + nombre de lo que posee

la enfermedad de la mujer / the woman's illness

Los nombres que terminan en **-s** y los nombres plurales añaden solamente un apóstrofe al final de la palabra.

> Poseedor + ' (apóstrofe) + nombre de lo que posee

la opinión de los doctores / the doctors' opinion

COMPARATIVO DE IGUALDAD DE LOS NOMBRES

> Singular: **as much** + nombre + **as**

Ella tiene tanta fiebre hoy como ayer. / She has as much fever today as yesterday.

> Plural: **as many** + nombre + **as**

Ella tiene tantos síntomas hoy como ayer. / She has as many symptoms today as yesterday.

EL ARTÍCULO / THE ARTICLE

Los articulos en inglés son invariables en género y número.

El artículo definido / The definite article

> **el, la, los, las** / the

el hospital / the hospital
la medicina / the medicine
los riñones / the kidneys
las recetas / the prescriptions

El artículo definido se omite en inglés cuando:

1. el sustantivo es un nombre común que expresa una idea general.

   una vacuna contra la difteria / a vaccine against diptheria

2. precede a los títulos de Sr., Sra. y Srta., o a cargos dignatarios o profesionales.

   el Dr. Jones / Mr. Jones   el Dr. Jones / Dr. Jones

El artículo indefinido / The indefinite article

un, una / a

una píldora / a pill
un laboratorio / a laboratory
un urinálisis / a urinalysis
un eufemismo / a euphemism

un, una / an

una hora / an hour
un accidente / an accident

1. **a:** Se emplea delante de las palabras que empiezan con consonante o con la vocal **u** o el diptongo **eu** cuando éste se pronuncia como la letra **y.**
2. **an:** Se emplea delante de palabras que empiezan con una vocal o una **h** muda.

USOS DEL ARTÍCULO INDEFINIDO

1. Con nombres que designan empleo o profesión después del verbo **to be.**

   Ella es enfermera. / She is a nurse.

2. En generalizaciones sobre especies o clases precediendo a un nombre en singular; si el nombre está en plural el artículo se omite.

   El mosquito puede transmitir enfermedades. / A mosquito can transmit disease.
   Los antibióticos son indispensables. / Antibiotics are indispensable.

Nota: El plural del artículo indefinido **unos, unas,** se traduce al inglés **some:**

   unas indicaciones preventivas / some preventive indications
   unos procedimientos quirúrgicos / some surgical procedures

EL ADJETIVO Y EL ADVERBIO /THE ADJECTIVE AND THE ADVERB

Los adjetivos en inglés generalmente preceden al nombre y son invariables en género y número.
   Los adjetivos demostrativos son una excepción a esta regla, ya que cambian del singular al plural de acuerdo con el nombre que modifican.

Formación del adverbio / How adverbs are formed

1. Los adverbios de modo que en español terminan generalmente en **-mente,** se forman en inglés añadiendo la terminación **-ly** al adjetivo:

   frecuente / frequent   frecuentemente / frequently

2. Si el adjetivo en inglés termina en **-ble,** la **e** se convierte en **y:**

   posible / possible   posiblemente / possibly

3. Si el adjetivo en inglés termina en **-ic,** el adverbio se forma añadiendo la terminación **-ally:**

   clínico / clinic   clínicamente / clinically

Comparación de los adjetivos y adverbios / Comparative forms of adjectives and adverbs

Tanto los adjetivos como los adverbios admiten grados de comparación.
1. Los monosílabos y algunos bisílabos cortos añaden la terminación **-er** y **-est** a la forma positiva:

a.	frío / cold	más frío / colder	(el) (la) más frío-a / the coldest
adv.	despacio / slow	más despacio / slower	más despacio / slowest

2. Palabras que terminan en **-y** cambian la **-y** en **i** y añaden **-er** y **-est** para formar el comparativo y el superlativo respectivamente:

a.	contento-a /	más contento-a /	(el) (la) más contento-a / the
	happy	happier	happiest
adv.	temprano / early	más temprano / earlier	más temprano / earliest

3. El resto de los adjetivos y adverbios forman el comparativo de superioridad y el superlativo anteponiendo las palabras **more** y **most**.

a.	doloroso-a /	más doloroso-a /	(el) (la) más doloroso-a /
	painful	more painful	the most painful
adv.	frecuentemente /	más frecuentemente /	más frecuentemente /
	frequently	more frequently	most frequently

4. El comparativo y el superlativo de inferioridad se forma anteponiendo las palabras **less** y **least**.

a.	contagioso-a /	menos contagioso-a /	(el) (la) menos contagioso-a/
	contagious	less contagious	the least contagious
adv.	frecuentemente /	menos frecuentemente /	menos frecuentemente / least
	frequently	less frequently	frequently

5. El comparativo de igualdad se forma usando la palabra **as** antes y después del adjetivo y del adverbio.

as + adjetivo + **as**	tan infeccioso como / as infectious as
as + adverbio + **as**	tan temprano como / as early as

ADJETIVOS COMUNES CON COMPARATIVOS Y SUPERLATIVOS IRREGULARES

malo / bad	peor / worse	(el) (la) peor / the worst
bueno / good	mejor / better	(el) (la) mejor / the best
poco / little	menos / less	(el) (la) menos / the least
mucho / much, many	más / more	(el) (la) más / the most

ADVERBIOS COMUNES CON COMPARATIVOS Y SUPERLATIVOS IRREGULARES

lejos / far	más lejos / farther	más lejos / farthest
poco / little	menos / less	menos / least
much / mucho	más / more	más / most
bien / well	mejor / better	mejor / best

PRONOMBRES Y ADJETIVOS / PRONOUNS AND ADJECTIVES

Pronombres personales / Subject Pronouns

1. Los pronombres personales nominativos, es decir los que sirven de sujeto, nunca se omiten en inglés:

(Yo) Tengo dolor / **I** have a pain; **I** am in pain.

El pronombre **I** (yo) siempre se escribe con mayúscula en inglés.

Pronombres personales / Subject Pronouns

Persona	Singular	Plural
1a.	I	we
2a.	you	you
3a.(*m.*)	he	they
3a.(*f.*)	she	they
3a.(*neut.*)	it	they

---

2. Los pronombres que sirven de complemento directo e indirecto siguen al verbo; el complemento indirecto siempre sigue al complemento directo:

La enfermera me dió las instrucciones. / The nurse **gave me the instructions.**
Me las dió. / She gave **them to me.**

Pronombres como complemento

Persona	Singular	Plural
1a.	me	us
2a.	you	you
3a.(*m.*)	him	them
3a.(*f.*)	her	them
3a.(*neut.*)	it	them

---

3. Además de actuar como sujeto o complemento, el pronombre personal en inglés puede también ser reflexivo cuando el complemento es la misma persona que el sujeto:

Él **se** curó a **sí** mismo. / He cured **himself.**

Pronombres reflexivos

Persona	Singular	Plural
1a.	myself	ourselves
2a.	yourself	yourselves
3a.(*m.*)	himself	themselves
3a.(*f.*)	herself	themselves
3a.(*neut.*)	itself	themselves

Pronombres y adjetivos demostrativos /
Demonstrative Pronouns and Adjectives

Los demostrativos son los únicos adjetivos que cambian del singular al plural de acuerdo con el número del nombre que modifican:

Adjetivos demostrativos

este, esta	this
estos, estas	these
ese, esa	that
esos, esas	those
aquel, aquella	that
aquellos, aquellas	those

---

esta enfermedad / **this** disease
estas enfermedades / **these** diseases
esa pastilla / **that** pill
aquellos casos / **those** cases

Pronombres demostrativos

éste, ésta, esto	this one, this
éstos, éstas	these
ése, ésa, eso	that one, that
aquél, aquélla, aquello	that one, that
aquéllos, aquéllas	those

Tome ésta. / Take **this one.**
Tome éstas. / Take **these.**
Ese es mejor. / **That one** is better.
Es aquélla. / It is **that one.**

**Pronombres y adjetivos posesivos /
Possessive Adjectives and Pronouns**

Persona	Adjetivo	Pronombre
Sing. 1a.	my	mine
2a.	your	yours
3a.*(m.)*	his	his
3a.*(f.)*	her	hers
3a. *(neut.)*	its	
Plur. 1a.	our	ours
2a.	your	yours
3a.	their	theirs

---

mi paciente / **my** patient
sus síntomas / **her** symptoms
La medicina es mía. / The medicine is **mine.**
El problema es nuestro. / The problem is **ours.**

Nota: En inglés el adjetivo posesivo se emplea con las partes del cuerpo:

Me lastimé el brazo. / I hurt **my** arm.

Pronombres y adjetivos interrogativos / Interrogative Adjectives and Pronouns

---

Interrogativos / Interrogatives

¿Quién?, ¿quiénes?	Who?
¿De quién?, ¿de quiénes?	Whose?
¿A quién?, ¿a quiénes?	Whom?
¿Qué?, ¿cuál?, ¿cuáles?	Which, what?

¿Quién está enfermo? / **Who** is ill?
¿De quién es la receta? / **Whose** is the prescription?

¿A quién vio ella? / **Whom** did she see?
¿Qué medicina prefiere? / **Which** medicine do you prefer?
¿Qué recomendó el doctor? / **What** did the doctor recommend?
¿Cuál recomendó el doctor? / **Which** did the doctor recommend?
De esos antibióticos, ¿cuáles prefiere? / Among those antibiotics, **which** do you prefer?

Pronombres relativos / Relative Pronouns

que, el cual, la cual, el que, la que, lo que, los que, las que	**that**
que, quien, el cual, la cual, el que, etc.	**which**
quien, que, el cual, la cual, etc.	**who**
que, quien, el cual, la cual, etc.	**whom**
de quien, cuyo, del cual, de la cual, etc.	**whose**

el jarabe que (ella) tomó / the cough syrup **that** she took
la medicina que se recetó / the medicine **which** was prescribed
el paciente que está esperando / the patient **who** is waiting
el paciente que (a quien) la enfermera atiende / the patient **whom** the nurse is helping
el paciente cuya radiografía necesita el doctor / the patient **whose** X-rays the doctor needs

Nota: Las terminaciones **-ever** y **-soever** se añaden a **who, which,** y **what** para formar los pronombres relativos compuestos **whoever** / quienquiera, **whichever** / cualquier-a y **whatever** / quienquiera o cualquier-a.

Pronombres y adjetivos indefinidos más comunes / Most common indefinite adjectives and pronouns

all	todo	many	muchos
another	otro	nobody	nadie
any	cualquier	none	ninguno
anybody	cualquiera	no one	nadie
anyone	cualquiera	nothing	nada
anything	cualquier cosa, algo	one	uno a
both	ambos, ambas	other	otro-a
each (one)	cada uno, cada cual	some	algunos
everybody	todos	somebody	alguien
everyone	todos	someone	alguien
everything	todo	something	algo
	few	poco	
	a few	unos pocos	

EL VERBO / THE VERB

Formas del verbo / Forms of the Verb

Infinitivo	*Pasado*	*Participio*	*Gerundio*
curar / to heal	healed	healed	healing
comer / to eat	ate	ate	eating

Infinitivo / Infinitive   El verbo precedido de la preposición **to:**

examinar / **to examine**

Presente / Present   La misma forma verbal del infinitivo sin la preposición **to** precedida del pronombre correspondiente:

yo examino / **I examine**   nosotros examinamos / **we examine**

Pasado / Past   El infinitivo + la terminación **-d** o **-ed**:

yo examiné / **I examined**   nosotros examinamos / **we examined**

Participio pasado / Past participle   La misma forma verbal que el pasado:

examinado / **examined**

Participio de presente / Present participle   El infinitivo + **-ing**:

examinando / **examining**

Nota: Para formar el pasado o el participio de verbos regulares se añade la terminación **-ed** al infinitivo. Las variaciones a esta regla son las siguientes:

a. Si el infinitivo termina en **e**, se añade **-d** (di**e**, di**ed**).

b. Si el infinitivo termina en la letra **y** precedida de una consonante se cambia la **y** por **i** antes de añadir **-ed** (tr**y**, tr**ied**).

c. Si el infinitivo termina en consonante precedida de una vocal y la sílaba final lleva el énfasis, se dobla la consonante antes de añadir **-ed** (permi**t**, permi**tted**).

Nota: Para formar el gerundio se añade la terminación **-ing** al infinitivo. Las variaciones a esta regla son las siguientes:

a. Si el infinitivo termina en en **-e** precedida de una consonante, la **e** se pierde antes de añadir la terminación **-ing** (aris**e**, aris**ing**).

b. Si el infinitivo termina en **-ie**, la **-ie** se sustituye por la letra **y** antes de añadir **-ing** (l**ie**, l**ying**).

c. En algunos verbos se dobla la consonante antes de añadir **-ing** si la sílaba final del infinitivo lleva el énfasis (spi**t**, spi**tting**), excepto en verbos terminados en **h, w,** e **y** los cuales no doblan la consonante al formar el gerundio.

Tiempos del verbo / Tenses of the Verb

TIEMPOS SIMPLES / SIMPLE TENSES

Toser / **To cough**

Presente / Present   yo toso / I cough
Pasado (pretérito e imperfecto) / Past   yo tosí, tosía / I coughed
Futuro / Future   yo toseré / I will, shall cough

El imperfecto se traduce al inglés con las formas **used to** o **would** para indicar una acción repetida indefinidamente o habitualmente en el pasado.

Yo tomaba la medicina todos los días. / **I used to** take the medicine every day.

El futuro de todas las personas se forma con el verbo auxiliar **will** o **shall** que precede a la forma del verbo en todos los tiempos.

Tomaré la medicina. / **I will take** the medicine.

TIEMPOS COMPUESTOS / COMPOUND TENSES

Los tiempos compuestos se forman con el verbo auxiliar **haber** / to have. (Véase la conjugación del verbo al final de la explicación del verbo.)

Perfecto / Present perfect   yo he tosido / I have coughed
Pluscuamperfecto / Past perfect   yo había, hube tosido / I had coughed
Futuro anterior / Future perfect   yo habré tosido / I will, I shall have coughed

Nota: Además de los seis tiempos indicados, todos los verbos tienen una forma progresiva que indica una acción continuada dentro de la configuración del tiempo a que se refieren. Se forma con el verbo auxiliar **estar** / **to be** seguido del participio presente (gerundio). (Véase la conjugación del verbo **to be** al final de la explicación del verbo.)

Presente	yo estoy tosiendo / I am coughing
Pasado	yo estaba, estuve tosiendo / I was coughing
Futuro	yo estaré tosiendo / I will, shall be coughing
Perfecto	yo he estado tosiendo / I have been coughing
Pluscuamperfecto	yo había, hube estado tosiendo / I had been coughing
Futuro anterior	yo habré estado tosiendo / I will, shall have been coughing

Modos del verbo / Moods of the Verb

INDICATIVO / INDICATIVE

Yo toso / I cough.

La oración interrogativa, negativa y enfática se forma con el verbo auxiliar **to do.** (Véase la conjugación del verbo al final de la explicación del verbo.)

Interrogación: ¿Tose usted por las mañanas? / **Do** you cough in the morning?

Negación: No toso durante el día / I **do** not cough during the day.

Énfasis: Toso mucho por las noches. / I **do** cough a lot at night.

Nota: El verbo **to do** también se emplea para dar énfasis a la respuesta de sí o no a una pregunta:

¿Tose mucho? / Do you cough much? Yes, I **do,** No, I **do** not.

IMPERATIVO / IMPERATIVE

Tosa, por favor. / Cough, please.

Conjugación de un verbo regular

preparar / to prepare

Infinitivo	*Participio*	*Gerundio*
preparar / to prepare	preparado / prepared	preparando / preparing

INDICATIVO

Presente / Present

yo preparo / I prepare	nosotros preparamos / we prepare
Ud. prepara, tú preparas / you prepare	vosotros preparáis, ustedes preparan / you prepare
él, ella prepara / she, he, it prepares	ellos, ellas preparan / they prepare

Pretérito e Imperfecto / Past

preparé, preparaba / I prepared	preparamos, preparábamos / we prepared
preparó, preparaba, preparaste, preparabas / you prepared	prepararon, preparaban, preparasteis, preparábais / you prepared
preparó, preparaba / he, she, it, prepared	prepararon, preparaban / they prepared

Futuro / Future

prepararé / I will, shall prepare	prepararemos / we will, shall prepare
preparará, prepararás / you will, shall prepare	prepararéis, prepararán / you will, shall prepare
preparará / he, she, it will, shall prepare	prepararán / they will, shall prepare

469

Perfecto / Perfect

he preparado / I have prepared
ha preparado, has preparado / you have prepared
ha preparado / he, she, it has prepared

hemos preparado / we have prepared
habéis, han preparado / you have prepared
han preparado / they have prepared

Pluscuamperfecto / Past perfect

había preparado / I had prepared
había, habías preparado / you had prepared

había preparado / he, she, it had prepared

habíamos preparado / we had prepared
habíais, habían preparado / you had prepared
habían preparado / they had prepared

Futuro anterior / Future perfect

habré preparado / I will, shall have prepared
habrá, habrás preparado / you will, shall have prepared
habrá preparado / he, she, it will, shall have prepared

habremos preparado / we will, shall have prepared
habréis, habrán preparado / you will, shall have prepared
habrán preparado / they will, shall have prepared

IMPERATIVO

prepara (tú)   prepare
prepare (usted)   prepare
preparemos (nosotros)   let's prepare
preparad (vosotros)   prepare
preparen (ustedes, ellos)   prepare

En inglés no existe la distinción entre el **tú** familiar y el **usted** formal. La segunda persona del singular es siempre **you**. La segunda persona del plural **vosotros** y **ustedes,** tiene igualmente una sola forma que se traduce también **you.**

La tercera persona singular del presente es la única forma verbal que difiere de las demás al tomar la terminación **-s.** Las excepciones a esta regla son las siguientes:

a. Si el verbo en el infinitivo termina en **-s, -x, -z, -ch,** o **-sh,** se añade **-es:** alcanzar / to reach; he, she, it **reaches.**

b. Si el verbo termina en **-z** precedida por una sola vocal, la **z** se dobla y se añade **-es:** preguntar / to quizz; he, she, it **quizzes.**

c. Si el verbo termina en **y** precedida de consonante la **y** cambia a **i** y se añade **-es:** llevar / to carry; he, she, it **carries.**

Conjugación de los verbos auxiliares / Conjugation of auxiliary verbs

haber / **to have**

Infinitivo	Participio	Gerundio
haber / **to have**	habido / **had**	habiendo / **having**

INDICATIVO

Presente / Present

yo he / I have
Ud. ha, tú has / you have
él, ella ha / he, she, it has

nosotros hemos / we have
vosotros habéis, ustedes han / you have
ellos han / they have

Pretérito e Imperfecto / Past

hube, había / I had
hubo, había, hubiste, habías / you had
hubo, había / he, she, it had

hubimos, habíamos / we had
hubisteis, habíais, hubieron, habían / you had
hubieron, habían / they had

Futuro / *Future*
habré / I will, shall have
habrá, habrás / you will, shall have
habrá / he, she, it will, shall have

habremos / we will, shall have
habréis, habrán / you will, shall have
habrán / they will, shall have

Nota: Para formar los tiempos compuestos se añade el participio de pasado **had** a las formas simples: I have **had**, I had **had**, I will, shall have **had**.

ser, estar / **to be**

Infinitivo	*Participio*	*Gerundio*
ser / **to be**	sido / **been**	siendo / **being**

Presente / *Present*
Yo soy / I am
Ud. es, tú eres / you are
él, ella es / he, she, it is

nosotros somos / we are
vosotros sois, ustedes son / you are
ellos, ellas son / they are

Pretérito e Imperfecto / *Past*
fui, era / I was
fue, era, fuiste, eras / you were
fue, era / he, she, it was

fuimos, éramos / we were
fuisteis, erais, fueron, eran / you were
fueron, eran / they were

Futuro / *Future*
seré / I will, shall be
scrá, serás / you will be
será / he, she, it will, shall be

seremos / we will, shall be
seréis, serán / you will, shall be
serán / they will, shall be

Nota: Para formar los tiempos compuestos se usan las formas simples del verbo auxiliar **to have** y el participio de **to be: been.** I have **been;** I had **been;** I will, shall have **been.**

hacer / **to do**

El verbo **to do** no existe como verbo auxiliar en español; por lo tanto las formas **do, does** y **did** en oraciones interrogativas, negativas, y enfáticas, no tiene traducción al español.

Infinitivo	*Participio*	*Gerundio*
hacer / **to do**	hecho / **done**	haciendo / **doing**

Presente / *Present*
yo hago / I do
Ud. hace, tú haces / you do
él, ella hace / he, she, it does

nosotros hacemos / we do
vosotros hacéis, ustedes hacen / you do
ellos, ellas hacen / they do

Pretérito e Imperfecto / *Past*
hice, hacía / I did
hiciste, hacías / you did
hizo, hacía / he, she, it did

hicimos, hacíamos / we did
hicísteis, hacíais, hicieron, hacían / you did
hicieron, hacían / they did

Futuro / *Future*
haré / I will, shall do
hará, harás / you will, shall do
hará / he, she, it will, shall do

haremos / we will, shall do
haréis, harán / you will, shall do
harán / they will, shall do

Nota: Para formar los tiempos compuestos se usan las formas simples del verbo auxiliar **to have** y el participio de **to do, done:** I have **done,** I had **done,** I will, shall have **done.**

IMPERATIVO / IMPERATIVE
haz (tú) — do
haga (usted) — do
hagamos (nosotros) — let us do
haced (vosotros) — do
hagan (ustedes, ellos) — do

SUBJUNTIVO / SUBJUNCTIVE

El modo subjuntivo se emplea en inglés con mucha menos frecuencia que en español, y para los efectos de este diccionario, no lo hemos incluído.

Verbos irregulares que no forman el participio pasivo o el tiempo pasado siguiendo la regla general / Verbs with an Irregular Preterit and / or Past Participle

Infinitivo / Infinitive	*Pretérito / Preterit*	*Participio pasivo/ Past Participle*
to arise / levantarse, surgir	arose	arisen
to awake / despertarse	awoke, awaked	awoke, awaked
to be / ser, estar	was, were	been
to become / volverse, hacerse	became	become
to begin / empezar	began	begun
to bend / inclinarse, doblarse	bent	bent
to bite / morder	bit	bit, bitten
to bleed / sangrar	bled	bled
to blow / soplar	blew	blown
to break / romper; quebrar	broke	broken
to bring / traer	brought	brought
to build / construir	built	built
to burn / quemar	burnt, burned	burnt, burned
to burst / reventar	burst	burst
to buy / comprar	bought	bought
can *(defectivo, aux.)* / poder	could	—
to catch / agarrar, coger	caught	caught
to choose / escoger, elegir	chose	chosen
to come / venir	came	come
to cost / costar	cost	cost
to cut / cortar	cut	cut
to deal / tratar	dealt	dealt
to dig / cavar, extraer	dug	dug
to draw / dibujar	drew	drawn
to dream / soñar	dreamt, dreamed	dreamt, dreamed
to drink / beber, tomar	drank	drunk
to drive / manejar, conducir	drove	driven
to eat / comer	ate	eaten
to fall / caerse; desprenderse	fell	fallen
to feed / alimentar, dar de comer	fed	fed
to feel / sentir; palpar	felt	felt
to fight / pelear	fought	fought
to find / encontrar, hallar	found	found
to fly / volar	flew	flown
to foresee / prever	foresaw	foreseen
to forget / olvidar	forgot	forgot, forgotten
to forgive / perdonar	forgave	forgiven
to freeze / congelar	froze	frozen
to get / conseguir, obtener	got	got, gotten
to give / dar	gave	given
to grind / moler; pulverizar	ground	ground
to grow / crecer; madurar	grew	grown
to hang / colgar; suspender	hung	hung

Infinitivo / Infinitive	Pretérito / Preterit	Participio pasivo/ Past Participle
to have / tener, haber	had	had
to hear / oír, escuchar	heard	heard
to hide / esconder (se)	hid	hid, hidden
to hit / pegar	hit	hit
to hold / aguantar	held	held
to hurt / lastimar, doler	hurt	hurt
to keep / guardar	kept	kept
to kneel / arrodillarse	knelt	knelt
to knit / tejer	knit, knitted	knit, knitted
to know / saber, conocer	knew	known
to lay / poner, colocar	laid	laid
to lead / dirigir	led	led
to leap / saltar	leapt, leaped	leapt, leaped
to leave / irse, dejar	left	left
to lend / prestar	lent	lent
to let / permitir, dejar	let	let
to lie / echarse, acostarse	lay	lain
to light / encender	lit, lighted	lit, lighted
to lose / perder	lost	lost
to make / hacer	made	made
may / poder	might	—
to meet / conocer	met	met
to melt / derretir	melted	melted, molten
to mistake / equivocarse	mistook	mistaken
must *(defectivo; aux.)* / deber de; tener que	—	—
ought *(defectivo; aux.)* / deber de	—	—
to pay / pagar	paid	paid
to put / poner	put	put
to quit / renunciar, dejar	quit	quit
to read / leer	read	read
to rid / librar, deshacerse	rid, ridded	rid, ridded
to ride / montar, pasear	rode	ridden
to ring / sonar	rang, rung	rung
to rise / alzarse, levantarse	rose	risen
to run / correr	ran	run
to say / decir	said	said
to see / ver	saw	seen
to seek / buscar	sought	sought
to sell / vender	sold	sold
to send / enviar	sent	sent
to set / colocar, poner	set	set
to sew / coser	sewed	sewn
to shake / batir, temblar	shook	shaken
to shine / brillar	shone	shone
to shoot / disparar	shot	shot
to show / mostrar	showed	shown, showed
to shrink / encogerse	shrank, shrunk	shrunk, shrunken
to shut / cerrar	shut	shut
to sit / sentarse	sat	sat
to sleep / dormir (se)	slept	slept

Infinitivo / Infinitive	Pretérito / Preterit	Participio pasivo/ Past Participle
to slide / deslizar (se)	slid	slid
to slit / rajar	slit	slit
to speak / hablar	spoke	spoken
to speed / acelerar	sped, speeded	sped, speeded
to spend / gastar	spent	spent
to spill / botar, derramar	spilled, spilt	spilled, spilt
to spin / dar vueltas	spun	spun
to spit / escupir	spit, spat	spit, spat
to split / partir	split	split
to spread / regar, esparcir	spread	spread
to stand / pararse	stood	stood
to steal / robar	stole	stolen
to stick / punzar, picar	stuck	stuck
to sting / picar, pinchar	stung	stung
to stink / apestar	stank, stunk	stank, stunk
to strike / golpear, herir	struck	stricken
to swear / jurar	swore	sworn
to sweep / barrer	swept	swept
to swell / hincharse	swelled	swollen, swelled
to swim / nadar	swam	swum
to swing / mecer (se)	swung	swung
to take / tomar	took	taken
to teach / enseñar	taught	taught
to tear / rasgar, desgarrar	tore	torn
to tell / decir, contar	told	told
to think / pensar	thought	thought
to throw / tirar	threw	thrown
to understand / comprender, entender	understood	understood
to undo / deshacer	undid	undone
to upset / indisponer (se)	upset	upset
to wake / despertar	woke, waked	waked
to wear / usar, llevar	wore	worn
to weep / llorar	wept	wept
to wet / mojar, humedecer	wet, wetted	wet, wetted
will / (v. aux.)	would	—
to win / ganar	won	won
to withstand / soportar, resistir	withstood	withstood
to write / escribir	wrote	written

Appendix A

Weights and Measures / Pesos y medidas

All equivalents are approximate. / Todas las equivalencias son aproximadas.

Liquid Measure
doses

Líquidos: Capacidad
dosis (sistema métrico)

1	quart / cuarto = 0.946 liter / litro	1000	cc.*
1	pint / pinta = 0.0473 liter / litro	500	cc.
8	fluid ounces / onzas	240	cc.
3.5	fluid ounces / onzas	100	cc.
1	fluid ounce / onza	30	cc.
4	fluid drams / dracmas	4	cc.
15	minims, drops / gotas	1	cc.
1	minim, drop / gota	0.06	cc.
1	teaspoonful / cucharadita de café	4	cc.
1	teaspoonful / cucharadita de postre	8	cc.
1	tablespoonful / cucharada sopera	15	cc.
1	teacupful / media taza	120	cc.
1	cup / taza	240	cc.

*cc. *abbr.* cubic centimeters / centímetros cúbicos

Solids

Sólidos

1	pound / libra	373.24	grams / gramos
1	ounce / onza	30	grams / gramos
4	drams / dracmas	15	grams / gramos
1	dram / dracma	4	grams / gramos
60	grains / granos = 1 dram / dracma	4	grams / gramos
30	grains / granos = 0.5 dram / dracma	2	grams / gramos
15	grains / granos	1	gram / gramo
10	grains / granos	0.6	grams / gramos
1	grain / grano	60	milligrams / miligramos
¾	grain / grano	50	mg.*
½	grain / grano	30	mg.
¼	grain / grano	15	mg.
¹⁄₁₀	grain / grano	6	mg.

*mg. *abbr.* miligrams / miligramos

Other Liquid Measures	Otras medidas líquidas
1 barrel / barril	119.07 liters / litros
1 gallon / galón = 8 pints / pintas (*Ingl.*)	3.785 l*
4 quarts	3.785 l
1 liter / litro	2.113 pints / pintas
1 quart / cuarto	0.946 l
1 pint / pinta	0.473 l

*1 *abbr.* liter / litro.

Avoirdupois Weights	Peso avoirdupois (comercio)
1 ton / tonelada	1016 kilograms / kilos
1 hundredweight = 112 pounds / libras	50.80 kilograms / kilos
2.20 pounds / libras	1 kilogram / kilo
1 pound / libra = 16 ounces / onzas	0.453 kilograms / kilo
1 ounce / onza	28.34 grams / gramos

Length	Longitud
1 mile / milla	1.60 kilometers / kilómetros
1 yard / yarda = 3 feet / pies	0.914 meters / metros
1 foot / pie = 12 inches / pulgadas	0.304 meter / metro
1 inch / pulgada	25.4 milimeters / milímetros
0.04 inch / pulgada	1 milimeter / milímetro
0.39 inch / pulgada	1 centimer / centímetro
39.37 inches / pulgadas	1 meter / metro

Temperature / **Temperatura**

Fahrenheit (F)	Centígrado (C)
32°F freezing point (sea level / nivel del mar)	0°C punto de congelación
212°F boiling	100°C punto de ebullición
Normal Body Temperature	Temperatura normal del cuerpo
Children: 99°F	Niños: 37.2°C
Adults: 98.6°F	Adultos: 37.0°C

Conversion to C		Conversión a F	
subtract 32	−32	multiplique por 9	× 9
multiply by 5	× 5	divida entre 5	÷ 5
divide by 9	÷ 9	añada +32	+32

Cardinal Numerals / Números cardinales

0 cero / zero	30 treinta / thirty
1 un(o), una / one	40 cuarenta / forty
2 dos / two	50 cincuenta / fifty
3 tres / three	60 sesenta / sixty
4 cuatro / four	70 setenta / seventy
5 cinco / five	80 ochenta / eighty
6 seis / six	90 noventa / ninety
7 siete / seven	100 ciento, cien / one hundred
8 ocho / eight	101 ciento uno / one hundred and one
9 nueve / nine	110 ciento diez / one hundred and ten
10 diez / ten	200 doscientos / two hundred
11 once / eleven	300 trescientos / three hundred
12 doce / twelve	400 cuatrocientos / four hundred
13 trece / thirteen	500 quinientos / five hundred
14 catorce / fourteen	600 seiscientos / six hundred
15 quince / fifteen	700 setecientos / seven hundred
16 diez y seis, dieciseis / sixteen	800 ochocientos / eight hundred
17 diez y siete, diecisiete / seventeen	900 novecientos / nine hundred
18 diez y ocho, dieciocho / eighteen	1,000 mil / one thousand
19 diez y nueve, diecinueve / nineteen	1,010 mil diez / one thousand and ten
20 veinte / twenty	1,500 mil quinientos / one thousand five hundred
21 veinte y un(o), veintiun(o) / twenty-one	2,000 dos mil / two thousand
	1,000,000 un millón / one million

Note: **Uno** and **ciento** and its multiples are the only cardinal numbers that change form. **Uno** drops the -o when it precedes a masculine singular noun: one liter of water / **un** litro de agua; but it does not drop the -o in: one out of ten / **uno** de cada diez.

Ciento changes to **cien** before nouns and before **mil** and **millón:** one hundred cases / **cien** casos; one hundred thousand cases / **cien** mil casos.

Multiples of **ciento** agree in gender with the nouns they modify: two hundred cases / **doscientos** casos; two hundred pills / **doscientas** píldoras.

Ordinal Numerals / Números ordinales

The ordinals first to tenth

English	Masculine	Feminine
first	1º primero	primera
second	2º segundo	segunda
third	3º tercero	tercera
fourth	4º cuarto	cuarta
fifth	5º quinto	quinta
sixth	6º sexto	sexta
seventh	7º séptimo	séptima
eighth	8º octavo	octava
ninth	9º noveno	novena
tenth	10º décimo	décima

Primero y **tercero** drop the -o before masculine singular nouns.

the first year / el **primer** año
the third day / el **tercer** día

Note: If a cardinal number and a numeral are used to qualify the same noun, the cardinal always precedes the ordinal.

the first three patients / los **tres primeros** pacientes
Take the first two pills now. / Tome las **dos primeras** pastillas ahora.

In reference to dates, the ordinal **primero** is used for the first day of the month; the cardinal is used for the other dates.

The first of January is the first day of the year / El **primero** de enero es el **primer** día del año.
the fourth of July / el **cuatro** de julio
the third one in line / el **tercero** en línea
the third appointment / el **tercer** turno

Fractions / Fracciones

½	a, one half / un medio, una mitad
⅓	a, one third / un tercio, una tercera parte
¼	a, one fourth / un cuarto, una cuarta parte
⅕	a, one fifth / un quinto, una quinta parte
⅙	a, one sixth / un sexto, una sexta parte
⅛	a, one eighth / un octavo, una octava parte
⅒	a, one tenth / un décimo, una décima parte
⅗	three fifths / tres quintos
⅝	five eighths / cinco octavos
⁷⁄₁₀	seven tenths / siete décimos
0.1	a, one tenth / un décimo
0.01	a, one hundredth / un centésimo
0.001	a, one thousandth / un milésimo

Days of the Week / Días de la semana

Monday / lunes	Friday / viernes
Tuesday / martes	Saturday / sábado
Wednesday / miércoles	Sunday / domingo
Thursday / jueves	

You must return on Monday. / Debe volver el lunes.
On Thursdays the office is closed. / Los jueves la consulta está cerrada.
The test will be next Friday. / La prueba será el próximo viernes.

Days of the week and months of the year are not capitalized in Spanish. / Los días de la semana se escriben con mayúscula en inglés.

Months of the Year / **Meses del año**

January / enero	July / julio
February / febrero	August / agosto
March / marzo	September / septiembre
April / abril	October / octubre
May / mayo	November / noviembre
June / junio	December / diciembre

Make your next appointment for May. / Haga la próxima cita para mayo.
April is a bad month for allergies. / Abril es un mes malo para las alergias.
I saw the patient last September. / Vi al paciente el pasado mes de septiembre.

Expressions of Time / **Expresiones de tiempo**

every hour / cada hora
every (two) hours / cada (dos) horas
once a day / una vez al día
twice a day / dos veces al día
three times a day / tres veces al día
in the afternoon / por la tarde
in the morning / por la mañana
before breakfast / antes del desayuno
with meals / con las comidas
at bedtime / a la hora de acostarse
next week / la semana próxima
in (six) months / dentro de (seis) meses

Appendix B

Topics of Communication
Questions, observations and recommendations to the patient

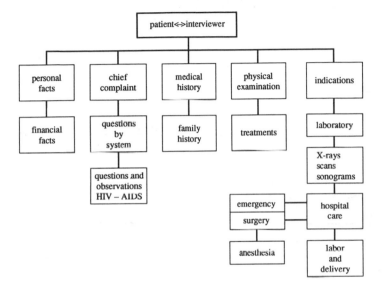

Tópicos de comunicación
Preguntas, observaciones y recomendaciones al (a la) paciente

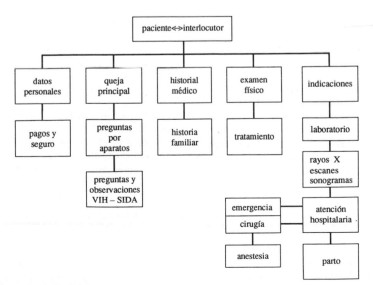

Useful Interrogative Words / Palabras interrogativas útiles	
How many, how much?	¿Cuánto; cuánto-a, cuántos-as?
What?	¿Qué?
When?	¿Cuándo?
Where?	¿Dónde?
Where to?	¿Adónde?
Where from?	¿De dónde?
Who?	¿Quién, quiénes?
Whom?	¿A quién, a quiénes?
Which?	¿Cuál, cuáles?
Whose?	¿De quién, de quiénes?
Why?	¿Por qué?

Personal Facts / Datos personales

Name / Nombre
Age / Edad
Address / Domicilio, dirección
Family members / Familiares

English	*Spanish*
1. Are you the patient?	1. ¿Es usted el (la) paciente?
2. Who is the patient?	2. ¿Quién es el (la) paciente?
3. What is your name?	3. ¿Cómo se llama usted?
4. How old are you?	4. ¿Qué edad tiene?
5. How old is the patient?	5. ¿Cuántos años tiene el (la) paciente?
6. What is your address?	6. ¿Cuál es su dirección?
7. Is this your permanent address?	7. ¿Es ésta su dirección permanente?
8. What is your telephone number?	8. ¿Cuál es su teléfono?
9. Are your parents living?	9. ¿Están vivos sus padres?
10. What is your father's name?	10. ¿Cómo se llama su padre?
11. What is your mother's name?	11. ¿Cómo se llama su madre?
12. Are you married? single? divorced? separated? a widow? a widower?	12. ¿Es usted casado-a; soltero-a; divorcia-do-a; está separado-a de su esposo-a; es viudo-a?
13. What is your spouse's name?	13. ¿Cómo se llama su esposo-a?
14. Do you have children? How many?	14. ¿Tiene hijos? ¿Cuántos?
15. Do they live with you?	15. ¿Viven con usted?
16. Do you live alone?	16. ¿Vive solo-a?
17. What is the name, address, and telephone of a person who can be notified in case of an emergency?	17. ¿Cuál es el nombre, la dirección y el teléfono de una persona a quien podamos avisar en caso de emergencia?

Financial Facts / Aspecto financiero

Medical insurance / Seguro médico
Occupation / Ocupación
Paying the bill / Pago de la cuenta

English	Spanish
1. Do you have medical insurance?	1. ¿Tiene seguro médico?
2. What is the name of your insurance company?	2. ¿Cómo se llama su compañía de seguro?
3. What is the number of your policy?	3. ¿Cuál es el número de su póliza?
4. Do you have more than one insurance policy?	4. ¿Tiene más de una póliza de seguro médico?
5. What is your occupation?	5. ¿En qué trabaja usted?
6. Where do you work?	6. ¿Dónde trabaja?
7. What is the name and address of your employer?	7. ¿Cuál es el nombre y dirección de la compañía o persona para quien trabaja?
8. What is your social security number?	8. ¿Cuál es el número de su seguro social?
9. Do you receive any worker's compensation?	9. ¿Recibe compensación por accidente de trabajo?
10. Are you self-supporting?	10. ¿Se mantiene con sus propios recursos?
11. Who supports you?	11. ¿Quién se hace cargo de sus gastos?
12. Are you eligible for Medicare?	12. ¿Tiene derecho a recibir Seguro Médico (Medicare)?
13. What is your Medicare number?	13. ¿Cuál es el número de su tarjeta de Seguro Médico?
14. Who will pay this bill?	14. ¿Quién es responsable por esta cuenta?
15. How do you want to pay for this bill?	15. ¿En qué forma quiere pagar la cuenta?
16. Will you pay for this bill in a lump sum or would you like to make other arrangements?	16. ¿Pagará esta cuenta en su totalidad o quisiera pagar de alguna otra manera?

Chief Complaint / Queja principal

Present illness / Enfermedad actual
Date and time of onset of illness / Comienzo de la enfermedad
Characteristics of illness / Características de la enfermedad
Frequency of illness / Frecuencia de la enfermedad

English	Spanish
1. What brings you here?	1. ¿Cuál es la causa de su visita?
2. How do you feel right now?	2. ¿Cómo se siente ahora?
3. When did this problem begin?	3. ¿Cuando le comenzó este trastorno?
4. Have you lost any weight recently?	4. ¿Ha bajado de peso recientemente?
5. Is this problem preventing you from working?	5. ¿Este trastorno (este problema; esta condición) le impide trabajar?
6. Is this problem affecting your regular activities?	6. ¿Este trastorno afecta sus actividades diarias?
7. Have you had this problem (symptom; discomfort) before?	7. ¿Ha tenido este malestar (este síntoma; este trastorno) antes?
8. Did it start suddenly or gradually?	8. ¿Le empezó de pronto o gradualmente?
9. Do you have this problem constantly?	9. ¿Tiene este trastorno continuamente?
10. Do you have it every day? How many times a day?	10. ¿Todos los días? ¿Cuántas veces al día?
11. When do you feel worse: in the morning; in the afternoon; at night?	11. ¿Cuándo se siente peor: por la mañana; por la tarde; por la noche?
12. Does it make you feel weak; tired; exhausted?	12. ¿Lo (la) hace sentirse cansado-a; débil; fatigado-a?

13. Do you have fever?
14. Are you in pain?
15. Has any doctor seen you since you became ill?
16. Is your family aware of this problem?
17. Are you taking any medication now?
18. Have you done or taken anything that seems to help you?
19. Have you ever been hospitalized on account of this problem?

13. ¿Tiene fiebre (calentura)?
14. ¿Tiene dolor?
15. ¿Lo (la) ha visto algún médico desde que se enfermó?
16. ¿Está su familia al tanto de este problema?
17. ¿Está tomando ahora alguna medicina?
18. ¿Ha hecho o tomado algo que le mejore?
19. ¿Ha tenido que ingresar alguna vez en el hospital debido a este problema?

Medical History / Historia clínica

I. General Questions / Preguntas generales

II. Review of Systems / Repaso por aparatos

Mouth; ears, nose, and throat; eyes / Boca; nariz, oídos y garganta; ojos
Cardiopulmonary system / Sistema cardiorrespiratorio
Gastrointestinal system / Aparato digestivo
Urinary system / Aparato urinario
Musculoskeletal system / Sistema músculo-esqueletal
Neurological system / Sistema neurológico
Skin / Piel
Genitourinary system / Aparato genitourinario

III. Family History, Past Medical History / Historia familiar, historia clínica previa

I. General Questions / Preguntas generales

English	*Spanish*
1. Have you gained weight recently?	1. ¿Ha aumentado de peso recientemente?
2. Have you lost weight recently?	2. ¿Ha bajado de peso recientemente?
3. Do you have any pain?	3. ¿Tiene algún dolor?
4. Where does it hurt?	4. ¿Dónde le duele?
5. Is the pain sharp; severe; mild; dull?	5. ¿Es el dolor agudo; severo; leve; sordo?
6. Can you describe the pain?	6. ¿Puede describir el dolor?
7. Do you tire easily?	7. ¿Se cansa fácilmente?
8. Do you feel dizzy?	8. ¿Se siente mareado-a?
9. Do you generally sleep well?	9. ¿Duerme bien generalmente?
10. How many hours do you sleep?	10. ¿Cuántas horas duerme?
11. Do you sleep during the day?	11. ¿Duerme durante el día?
12. Do you take any pills to help you to sleep?	12. ¿Toma alguna pastilla para dormir?
13. How long have you had this problem?	13. ¿Por cuánto tiempo ha tenido este trastorno?
14. Are you taking any medication?	14. ¿Está tomando alguna medicina?
15. Are you taking any sedatives?	15. ¿Está tomando algún calmante?
16. Do you have nausea?	16. ¿Tiene náuseas?
17. Have you fainted at any time?	17. ¿Se ha desmayado alguna vez?
18. Have you felt dizzy or have you fainted after eating or exercising?	18. ¿Se ha desmayado o mareado después de comer o hacer ejercicio?
19. Do you suffer from headaches?	19. ¿Padece de dolores de cabeza?

II. Review of Systems / Repaso por aparatos

Mouth; ears, nose, and throat; eyes / Boca; oídos, nariz y garganta; ojos

English	*Spanish*
1. Is there any trouble with your mouth or tongue?	1. ¿Hay algo que le afecte en la boca o la lengua?
2. Have you noticed any bleeding from your gums or mouth?	2. ¿Ha notado si las encías o la boca le sangran?
3. Do you suffer from sore throats? How frequently?	3. ¿Padece de la garganta? ¿Con qué frecuencia?
4. Do you have any dripping or drainage in the back of the throat?	4. ¿Tiene alguna supuración o flema detrás de la garganta?
5. Are you often hoarse?	5. ¿Tiene ronquera frecuentemente?
6. Do you have difficulty swallowing?	6. ¿Tiene dificultad al tragar?
7. Have you noticed any swelling in your neck?	7. ¿Ha notado alguna hinchazón en el cuello?
8. Have you ever had nosebleeds?	8. ¿Ha tenido sangramiento por la nariz?
9. Do you have any difficulty hearing?	9. ¿Tiene alguna dificultad para oír?
10. Do you have ringing in your ears? In the right ear; in the left ear; in both?	10. ¿Tiene zumbido en los oídos? ¿En el derecho? ¿En el izquierdo? ¿En ambos?
11. Have you noticed any secretion from your ears?	11. ¿Ha notado alguna secreción por los oídos?
12. Do you have earaches?	12. ¿Padece de dolor de oídos?
13. Have you noticed any change in your vision?	13. ¿Ha notado algún cambio en la visión?
14. Do you wear glasses or contact lenses?	14. ¿Usa espejuelos o lentes de contacto?
15. Have you noticed any redness or swelling in your eyes?	15. ¿Ha notado los ojos enrojecidos o hinchados?
16. Do you see double?	16. ¿Tiene visión doble?
17. Do you see spots or flashes of light?	17. ¿Ve alguna vez manchas o luces?
18. Have you had pain in your eyes?	18. ¿Ha tenido dolor en los ojos?
19. Do you have any discharge from your eyes?	19. ¿Le supuran los ojos?
20. Have your eyes ever been affected by any sickness or accident?	20. ¿Han sido sus ojos afectados por alguna enfermedad o accidente?

Cardiopulmonary System / Sistema cardiorrespiratorio

English	*Spanish*
1. Do you ever have rapid heart beats?	1. ¿Tiene alguna vez palpitaciones?
2. Have you ever had pain in your chest?	2. ¿Ha tenido alguna vez dolor en el pecho?
3. Do you have any swelling in your legs or ankles?	3. ¿Se le hinchan las piernas o los tobillos?
4. Do you have high blood pressure?	4. ¿Tiene la presión alta?
5. Do you bleed easily?	5. ¿Tiene tendencia a sangrar?
6. Do you smoke? For how long have you smoked?	6. ¿Fuma? ¿Cuánto tiempo hace que fuma?
7. How many cigarettes a day do you smoke?	7. ¿Cuántos cigarros fuma al día?
8. Have you tried to stop?	8. ¿Ha tratado de dejar de fumar?

English	Spanish
9. Have you ever had lung disease?	9. ¿Ha tenido alguna enfermedad de los pulmones?
10. Have you ever had any heart trouble?	10. ¿Ha tenido algún problema del corazón?
11. Do you have frequent colds?	11. ¿Tiene catarros frecuentes?
12. Do you cough up any phlegm?	12. ¿Tose con flema?
13. What does it look like?	13. ¿Cómo es la flema?
14. Have you ever coughed up blood?	14. ¿Ha tenido alguna vez sangre al toser?
15. Have you had any trouble breathing?	15. ¿Tiene algún problema al respirar?
16. Are you short of breath at night; after meals; when you exercise; when you walk; even when resting?	16. ¿Le falta la respiración por la noche; después de las comidas; cuándo camina; aún cuando descansa?
17. Have you noticed any particular sound in your breathing?	17. ¿Ha notado algún sonido diferente al respirar?
18. Is there any position that makes your breathing easier?	18. ¿Alguna posición en especial le facilita la respiración?

Gastrointestinal System / Aparato digestivo

English	*Spanish*
1. Is there any food that disagrees with you?	1. ¿Hay algún alimento que no le asiente?
2. Do you have heartburn?	2. ¿Tiene ardor en el estómago?
3. Do you suffer from stomach aches?	3. ¿Padece de dolores de estómago?
4. Do you suffer from indigestion?	4. ¿Padece de indigestión?
5. Do you drink or eat between meals?	5. ¿Come o toma líquidos entre las comidas?
6. Do you drink coffee? How many cups a day do you drink?	6. ¿Toma café? ¿Cuántas tazas al día?
7. Do you eat fried or fatty foods?	7. ¿Come comidas fritas o grasosas?
8. Do you burp a lot?	8. ¿Eructa mucho?
9. How much milk do you drink?	9. ¿Cuánta leche toma?
10. At what time do you eat breakfast?	10. ¿A qué hora se desayuna?
11. At what time do you eat your last meal of the day?	11. ¿A qué hora hace su última comida del día?
12. Are you constipated?	12. ¿Padece de estreñimiento?
13. Do you have a bowel movement every day?	13. ¿Elimina (obra, está al corriente) todos los días?
14. Are your stools normal? What color are they?	14. ¿Ha notado si el excremento es normal? ¿Qué color tiene?
15. Do you have diarrhea?	15. ¿Tiene diarrea?
16. Have you noticed any blood or mucous in your stools?	16. ¿Ha notado sangre o mucosidad en el excremento?

Urinary System / Aparato urinario

English	*Spanish*
1. Do you have any trouble urinating?	1. ¿Tiene dificultad cuando orina?
2. Do you have to get up to urinate during the night? How many times?	2. ¿Tiene que levantarse por la noche a orinar? ¿Cuántas veces?
3. Do you have back pain?	3. ¿Tiene dolor de espalda?
4. Do you have pain or burning when urinating? Is the color of the urine yellow; murky; milky; pale; reddish?	4. ¿Tiene dolor o ardor cuando orina? ¿Es la orina amarilla; turbia; lechosa; descolorida; rojiza?

5. Do you have blood in the urine?
6. Are you unable to control your urination?
7. Do you urinate very often?
8. Do you pass a little or a lot of urine regularly?
9. Do you have difficulty in starting your urination?
10. Do you have difficulty in having a continuous flow of urine?
11. Have you ever had any kidney problem?
12. Have you ever passed stones?

5. ¿Tiene sangre en la orina?
6. ¿Puede controlar la salida de orina?
7. ¿Orina con mucha frecuencia?
8. ¿Orina mucho o poco regularmente?
9. ¿Tiene dificultad para comenzar a orinar?
10. ¿Tiene dificultad en mantener el chorro?
11. ¿Ha padecido de los riñones?
12. ¿Ha expulsado cálculos alguna vez?

Musculoskeletal System / Sistema músculo-esqueletal

English

Spanish

1. Do you have pain in your joints?
2. Do you have pain in the neck or back?
3. Do your muscles hurt?
4. Do you feel general muscle weakness?
5. Have you noticed any swelling on a bone?
6. Do you have pain in your bones?

1. ¿Le duelen las articulaciones?
2. ¿Tiene dolor en el cuello o la espalda?
3. ¿Le duelen los músculos?
4. ¿Siente debilidad muscular general?
5. ¿Ha notado hinchazón en algún hueso?
6. ¿Le duelen los huesos?

Neurological System / Sistema neurológico

English

Spanish

1. Do you have any feeling of tingling or numbness?
2. Do you forget things easily?
3. Is your memory worse than before?
4. Do you have good balance?
5. Do you have any difficulty walking?
6. Do you have difficulty moving towards the right; towards the left?
7. Have you lost consciousness?
8. Can you feel this?

1. ¿Tiene alguna sensación de hormigueo o entumecimiento?
2. ¿Olvida las cosas con facilidad?
3. ¿Tiene la memoria peor que antes?
4. ¿Tiene buen equilibrio?
5. ¿Tiene dificultad para caminar?
6. ¿Tiene dificultad en moverse hacia la derecha; hacia la izquierda?
7. ¿Ha perdido el conocimiento?
8. ¿Puede sentir esto?

Skin / Piel

English

Spanish

1. Do you have any sores or blisters?
2. Do you have a skin rash?
3. Have you noticed any unusual spots in your skin?
4. Have you had any severe burns?
5. Does anything make you itchy?
6. Are you sensitive to the sun rays?
7. Have you noticed any unusual mole or wart?
8. Have you noticed any discoloration in your skin?

1. ¿Tiene llagas o ampollas?
2. ¿Tiene alguna erupción?
3. ¿Ha notado alguna mancha peculiar en la piel?
4. ¿Ha tenido alguna vez una quemadura grave?
5. ¿Hay algo que le dé picazón?
6. Es sensible a los rayos del sol?
7. ¿Ha notado alguna verruga o algún lunar peculiar?
8. ¿Ha notado algún cambio de color en la piel?

Genitourinary system / Aparato genitourinario

English	*Spanish*

(To a female patient:)

1. How old were you when you had your first period?
2. When was your last period?
3. Are your periods difficult?
4. How long does your period last?
5. Do you ever bleed between periods?

6. Do you have any discharge from the vagina?
7. What does it look like?
8. Do you have any itching or burning in the genital area?
9. Have you ever had a venereal disease?
10. Have you ever had any trouble with your breasts?
11. Have you learned how to examine your breasts?
12. Do you examine your breasts regularly?
13. Do you have any discharge from your breasts?
14. Have you noticed any mass or lump on your breast?
15. Are you pregnant?
16. Have you ever been pregnant?
17. How many times have you been pregnant?
18. How many miscarriages have you had?
19. Have you ever had an induced abortion?

20. How many live births have you had?
21. Did you have any stillbirths?
22. Do you have any problem with intercourse?
23. Do you have any pain during intercourse?

24. Do you use any type of birth control?

(A una mujer:)

1. ¿Qué edad tenía cuando tuvo la primera regla (el primer periodo)?
2. ¿Cuándo tuvo la última regla?
3. ¿Tiene alguna dificultad durante la regla?
4. ¿Cuántos días le dura el período?
5. ¿Sangra alguna vez entre una regla y la otra?

6. ¿Tiene algún flujo o secreción vaginal?
7. ¿Cómo es?
8. ¿Tiene picazón o ardor en alguna parte interior?
9. ¿Ha tenido alguna enfermedad venérea?
10. ¿Ha tenido alguna vez algún trastorno en los senos?
11. ¿Ha aprendido a examinarse los senos?
12. ¿Se autoexamina los senos regularmente?
13. ¿Ha notado alguna secreción de los senos?
14. ¿Ha notado alguna masa o bulto (bola) en los senos?
15. ¿Está embarazada (en estado, encinta)?
16. ¿Ha estado embarazada alguna vez?
17. ¿Cuántas veces ha estado embarazada?
18. ¿Cuántos abortos espontáneos ha tenido?
19. ¿Ha tenido alguna vez un aborto provocado?
20. ¿Cuántos embarazos se le han logrado?
21. ¿Tuvo algún parto no logrado?
22. ¿Tiene alguna dificultad en sus relaciones sexuales?
23. ¿Tiene dolor durante las relaciones sexuales?
24. ¿Usa algún tipo de contraceptivo?

English	*Spanish*

(To a male patient:)

1. Do you have any discharge from the penis?
2. Do you have pain in the testicles?
3. Do you have pain or swelling in the scrotum?
4. Are you unable to have an erection?
5. Do you have a satisfactory sex life?
6. Have you had any venereal disease?
7. Have you fathered any children?

(A un hombre:)

1. ¿Tiene alguna secreción por el pene?
2. ¿Tiene dolor en los testículos?
3. ¿Tiene dolor o hinchazón en el escroto?
4. ¿Se le dificulta tener una erección?
5. ¿Está satisfecho con su vida sexual?
6. ¿Ha tenido alguna enfermedad venérea?
7. ¿Ha tenido hijos?

III. Family History, Past Medical History /
Historia familiar, historia clínica previa

English	*Spanish*
1. Do you have any children?	1. ¿Tiene hijos?
2. How old were you when you had your first child?	2. ¿A qué edad tuvo su primer hijo?
3. Do your children live with you?	3. ¿Viven sus hijos con usted?
4. Are your parents living?	4. ¿Viven sus padres?
5. Are they in good health?	5. ¿Tienen buena salud?
6. Is your father living?	6. ¿Vive su padre?
7. What is his health like?	7. ¿Cómo está de salud?
8. What did he die of?	8. ¿De qué murió?
9. How old was he when he died?	9. ¿Qué edad tenía cuando murió?
10. Is your mother living? What is her health like?	10. ¿Vive su mamá? ¿Cómo está de salud?
11. What did she die of?	11. ¿De qué murió?
12. Did any of your parents, grandparents or close relatives die of, or had any of the following diseases: tuberculosis, heart disease, diabetes, cancer, blood disease, high blood pressure, epilepsy, glaucoma, mental retardation, insanity?	12. ¿Alguien en su familia, padres, abuelos o familiares inmediatos murió de o ha tenido alguna de estas enfermedades: tuberculosis, enfermedad del corazón, diabetes, cáncer, enfermedad de la sangre, presión alta, epilepsia, glaucoma, retraso mental, locura?
13. Have you ever been hospitalized? why? for how long? how many times?	13. ¿Ha tenido que hospitalizarse alguna vez? ¿por qué? ¿por cuánto tiempo? ¿cuántas veces?
14. Have you ever had any of the following illnesses:	14. ¿Ha tenido alguna de las enfermedades siguientes:
amebic dysentery	disenteria amebiana
allergies	alergias
anemia	anemia
appendicitis	apendicitis
arthritis	artritis
asthma	asma
conjunctivitis	conjuntivitis
cancer	cáncer
chicken pox	varicela
chorea	corea
chronic hoarseness	ronquera crónica
chronic laryngitis	laringitis crónica
chronic tonsilitis	amigadalitis crónica
cirrhosis	cirrosis hepática
cystitis	cistitis
diabetes	diabetes
diphtheria	difteria
diverticulitis	diverticulitis
ear infections	infecciones en los oídos
emphysema	enfisema
epilepsy	epilepsia
gallbladder attack	ataque vesicular
gall stones	cálculos en la vesícula

goiter	bocio
gonorrhea	gonorrea
hay fever	fiebre del heno
heart disease	enfermedad del corazón
hepatitis	hepatitis
high blood pressure	presión arterial alta
jaundice	ictericia
measles; German measles	sarampión; rubéola
mononucleosis	mononucleosis
mumps	paperas
scarlet fever	escarlatina
syphilis	sífilis
tuberculosis	tuberculosis
typhoid fever	fiebre tifoidea
valley fever	fiebre del valle
peptic ulcers?	úlceras pépticas?

15. Have any of your immediate relatives been addicted to alcohol, tobacco or drugs?

16. Have you ever been addicted to alcohol, tobacco or drugs?

17. Has anyone in your family died of a heart attack?

18. Is there a repeated history of sickness in your family?

20. Have any of your siblings died?

21. How old was he (she)?

22. Where have you lived for most of your life?

15. ¿Algún familiar inmediato ha sido adicto a bebidas alcohólicas, tabaco o drogas?

16. ¿Ha sido usted alguna vez adicto a bebidas alcohólicas, tabaco o drogas?

17. ¿Algún familiar cercano ha muerto de un ataque al corazón?

18. ¿Hay alguna enfermedad que se viene repitiendo en su familia?

20. ¿Ha muerto alguno de sus hermanos?

21. ¿Cuántos años tenía?

22. ¿Dónde ha vivido usted la mayor parte de su vida?

Laboratory and X-ray Examination / Laboratorio y examen radiológico

English	*Spanish*
1. What type of test are you here for?	1. ¿Qué clase de prueba (análisis) se vino a hacer?
2. Do you have the written request from the doctor?	2. ¿Trae (tiene) las indicaciones del doctor por escrito?
3. Have you had anything to eat or drink this morning?	3. ¿Viene en ayunas?
4. Have you had anything to eat or drink after twelve o'clock midnight?	4. ¿Ha comido o bebido (tomado) algo después de las doce de la noche?
5. Have you ever had an X-ray examination that required either an injection or swallowing any pills or medication before the X-ray was taken?	5. ¿Le han hecho alguna vez una radiografía que haya requerido una inyección o tomar alguna pastilla antes de hacerse la placa?
6. Are you allergic to any medication?	6. ¿Es alérgico-a a alguna medicina?
7. Are you presently taking any medication?	7. ¿Está tomando actualmente alguna medicina?
8. Do you suffer from or have you ever suffered from asthma?	8. ¿Padece o ha padecido alguna vez de asma?
9. Do you suffer from hay fever or from any other allergies?	9. ¿Padece de fiebre del heno o de alguna otra alergia?

10. Do you have any relatives who have allergies?
11. Do you have or have you had: eczema; heart trouble; kidney disorder; liver disorder?
12. Do you have frequent diarrhea or any other digestive problem?
13. Do you feel dizzy?

10. ¿Tiene familiares cercanos que padecen de alguna alergia?
11. ¿Padece o ha padecido alguna vez de eczema; del corazón; de los riñones; del hígado?
12. ¿Tiene diarrea frecuentemente o padece de algún otro trastorno digestivo?
13. ¿Se siente mareado-a?

Ambulance and Emergency Room / Ambulancia y sala de emergencia

English

1. To what hospital do you want to go?
2. To what hospital shall we take him (her)?
3. Do you understand what I am saying?
4. What is your name?
5. What day of the week is it?
6. Who is your doctor?
7. Has your doctor been notified?
8. Are you in pain?
9. Are you having any problem breathing?
10. Have you fainted or lost consciousness at any time?
11. Are you taking any medication?
12. How many pills did you take?
13. Are you allergic to any medication?
14. When did the accident occur? Where did it happen?
15. Did you faint or lose consciousness when it happened?
16. Have you had a tetanus shot?
17. When was the last time?
18. Have you been hospitalized before? for what reason? here? where?

(To a female patient:)
19. Do you know if you are pregnant?
20. Could you be pregnant?

Spanish

1. ¿A qué hospital quiere ir?
2. ¿A qué hospital quiere que lo (la) llevemos?
3. ¿Entiende lo que le digo?
4. ¿Cómo se llama?
5. ¿Qué día de la semana es hoy?
6. ¿Quién es su médico?
7. ¿Le han avisado a su médico?
8. ¿Tiene dolor?
9. ¿Tiene dificultad para respirar?
10. ¿Se desmayó o perdió el conocimiento en algún momento?
11. ¿Está tomando alguna medicina?
12. ¿Cuántas pastillas tomó?
13. ¿Es alérgico-a a alguna medicina?
14. ¿Cuándo ocurrió el accidente? ¿Dónde ocurrió?
15. ¿Se desmayó o perdió el conocimiento cuando ocurrió?
16. ¿Se ha inyectado contra el tétano?
17. ¿Cuándo fue la última vez?
18. ¿Ha sido hospitalizado-a alguna vez? ¿por qué motivo? ¿aquí? ¿dónde?

(A una mujer:)
19. ¿Sabe si está embarazada?
20. ¿Es posible que esté embarazada?

General Statements / Recomendaciones generales

English

1. Make an appointment.
2. The doctor wants to see you in two weeks; right away; in a month; in six months.
3. Follow me, please.
4. Go in this room and undress.

Spanish

1. Haga una cita. (Reserve turno.)
2. El doctor (la doctora) quiere verlo (la): dentro de dos semanas; inmediatamente; dentro de seis meses.
3. Sígame, por favor.
4. Pase a este cuarto y desvístase.

5. Put on this gown.
6. Wait a few minutes.
7. This is not going to hurt you, but it is going to be unpleasant.
8. In this test I am going to take fluid from your spine.
9. This is a cold solution.
10. This machine is to take the mucous from your lungs.
11. I am going to insert this tube to take out the phlegm that is bothering you; to help you void.
12. Leave the cotton; band-aid in place for a few minutes.
13. Breath deeply.
14. Breath deeply and hold your breath.

15. Breath normally.
16. You should eat a light supper the night before the operation (test).
17. You should not eat any greasy foods.
18. You must take these tablets which are especially for this test.
19. The tablets contain a substance that we can trace during the test and that will help make a diagnosis.
20. We are going to take a series of X-rays.
21. After the first X-rays, we will give you a liquid to drink.
22. Drink this liquid, please.
23. After the test, you can have something to eat.
24. We are going to give you a barium enema.
25. We are going to turn the light off.
26. This light is used to examine your intestine.
27. You can use the bathroom here.
28. You cannot drink or eat anything before the test.
29. You can brush your teeth, but do not drink water.
30. Before the test, you cannot eat; drink water or other liquids; smoke; chew gum; take medicine; suck any pills or candy.

31. You cannot take any medicine.
32. You should eat at least two hours before taking a cathartic.
33. I am going to inject this in the vein.

34. This is part of the test.
35. I have to take an X-ray.
36. I have to take one more X-ray.

5. Póngase esta bata.
6. Espere unos minutos.
7. Esto no le va a doler pero le va a causar cierta molestia.
8. En esta prueba necesito sacarle líquido de la columna.
9. Esta solución es fría.
10. Esta máquina es para extraer mucosidades de los pulmones.
11. Voy a ponerle esta sonda para sacarle la flema que le molesta; para ayudarle a orinar.
12. Déjese el algodón; la curita ahí por unos minutos.
13. Respire profundamente.
14. Respire profundamente y aguante la respiración.

15. Respire normalmente.
16. Debe comer una comida ligera la noche antes de la operación (la prueba).
17. No debe comer alimentos grasosos.
18. Debe tomarse estas pastillas que son especialmente para la prueba.
19. Las pastillas contienen una sustancia que se puede rastrear y ayuda a hacer el diagnóstico.
20. Le vamos a hacer una serie de placas.
21. Después de las primeras placas le daremos a tomar un líquido.
22. Tómese este líquido, por favor.
23. Después de la prueba puede comer.
24. Le vamos a poner un enema de bario.
25. Vamos a apagar la luz.
26. Esta luz es para examinarle el intestino.
27. Puede usar el servicio (el baño) aquí.
28. Tiene que estar en ayunas (sin beber ni comer nada) hasta después de la prueba.
29. Puede lavarse los dientes, pero no tome agua.
30. Antes de la prueba usted no puede comer; tomar agua u otros líquidos; fumar; masticar chicle; chupar pastillas o caramelos.

31. No puede tomar ningún medicamento.
32. Debe comer por lo menos dos horas antes de tomar un purgante.
33. Voy a inyectarle esta sustancia en la vena.

34. Esto es parte del examen.
35. Tengo que hacerle una placa.
36. Tengo que hacerle una placa más.

37. Wait to make sure that I do not need to take another one.	37. Espere para comprobar que no tengo que sacar otra placa.
38. You must follow these directions exactly.	38. Siga las instrucciones al pie de la letra.
39. Call tomorrow to know the results of the test.	39. Llame mañana para saber el resultado de la prueba.
40. We will call you to notify you.	40. Lo (la) llamaremos para notificarle.

Commands for Positions and Movements/
Mandatos para posiciones y movimientos

English	*Spanish*
1. Stand here.	1. Párese aquí.
2. Stand here and do not move.	2. Párese aquí y no se mueva.
3. Sit on the table.	3. Siéntese sobre la mesa.

4. Lie down on the table,
    on your back,
    face down,
    on your right side,
    on your left side.
	4. Acuéstese sobre la mesa,
	    boca arriba,
	    boca abajo,
	    sobre el lado derecho,
	    sobre el lado izquierdo.

5. Put your knees against your chest and let your chin touch your chest.	5. Ponga las rodillas junto al pecho dejando que la barbilla le toque el pecho.
6. Put your arms around this machine.	6. Ponga los brazos alrededor de esta máquina.
7. Do not get up, remain lying down.	7. No se levante, quédese acostado-a.
8. Raise your head.	8. Levante la cabeza.
9. Raise your hands.	9. Levante las manos.
10. Raise your right hand.	10. Levante la mano derecha.

11. Raise your left hand
    higher; lower.
	11. Levante la mano izquierda
	    más alto; más bajo.

12. Open your hand.	12. Abra la mano.
13. Close your hand.	13. Cierre la mano.
14. Extend your fingers.	14. Extienda los dedos.
15. Close your fingers one at a time.	15. Cierre los dedos uno por vez.
16. Lift your right leg.	16. Levante la pierna derecha.
17. Lift your left leg.	17. Levante la pierna izquierda.
18. Move your leg.	18. Mueva la pierna.
19. Bend over.	19. Dóblese.
20. Bend over backwards.	20. Dóblese hacia atrás.
21. Raise your buttocks; your hips.	21. Levante las nalgas (las asentaderas); las caderas.
22. Put your hands behind your head.	22. Ponga las manos detrás de la cabeza.
23. Extend your arms, and bringing them towards the front, touch the tips of your index fingers together.	23. Extienda los brazos, traígalos hacia el frente y junte las puntas de los dedos índices.
24. Bend your arm.	24. Doble el brazo.
25. Extend your arm.	25. Extienda el brazo.
26. Squeeze my hand.	26. Apriéteme la mano.
27. Squeeze my hand as hard as you can.	27. Apriéteme la mano lo más que pueda.
28. Make a fist.	28. Cierre el puño.
29. Open your mouth.	29. Abra la boca.
30. Rinse your mouth.	30. Enjuáguese la boca.

General Observations for Medication and Treatment /
Observaciones generales a seguir para medicamentos y tratamientos

English	*Spanish*
1. I will prescribe some medication that should: alleviate the discomfort; relieve the pain; help us determine the problem.	1. Le voy a recetar una medicina que lo (la) va a: mejorar; aliviar el dolor; ayudarnos a determinar cual es el problema.
2. Take the medicine: two, three, four times a day; before, after meals; first thing in the morning; before going to bed; with some solid food; with milk or juice.	2. Tome la medicina: dos, tres, cuatro veces al día; antes, después de las comidas; al levantarse; al acostarse; con algo de comer; con leche o jugo.
3. Always shake the bottle well.	3. Siempre agite bien la botella.
4. Apply: an ice pack; a heating pad to the area.	4. Póngase: una bolsa de hielo; una almohadilla eléctrica en la parte afectada.
5. Take a warm Sitz bath: one, two, three times a day.	5. Dése un baño de asiento caliente: una, dos, tres veces al día.
6. When you lie down, raise your feet above the level of the heart.	6. Cuando se acueste, levante los pies por encima del nivel del corazón.
7. You should: lose weight; exercise more; stop smoking; avoid salt in your diet; eat a more balanced diet; eat more vegetables; eat more fruit and fiber.	7. Ud. debe: bajar de peso; hacer más ejercicio; dejar de fumar; no comer comidas con sal; hacer una dieta más balanceada; comer más vegetales; comer más frutas y fibra.
8. Come back to see me: next week; in ten days; in a month.	8. Vuelva a verme: la semana que. viene; dentro de diez días; dentro de un mes.
9. We still do not know what is causing your illness.	9. No hemos podido determinar todavía la causa de su enfermedad.
10. It is necessary that you get: a blood test; some laboratory tests; a urinalysis; a mammogram; a sonogram; an X-ray; a scan; therapy.	10. Es necesario que se haga: un análisis de sangre; unas pruebas de laboratorio; un análisis de orina; un sonograma; una radiografía; un escán; terapia.
11. Do not eat or drink anything: two hours before the test; after midnight.	11. No coma o tome nada: dos horas antes de hacerse la prueba; después de la medianoche.
12. We will make the necessary arrangements with: the hospital; the laboratory; the therapist.	12. Nosotros haremos los arreglos necesarios con: el hospital; el laboratorio; el (la) terapista.
13. Take the written orders with you.	13. Llévese las órdenes médicas consigo.
14. We still do not have the results of the test (the tests).	14. Aún no tenemos el resultado de la prueba (las pruebas).
15. It is advisable to put you in the hospital for further tests.	15. Es conveniente hospitalizarlo-a para hacer pruebas adicionales.
16. You need an operation.	16. Ud. necesita una operación.
17. We have to operate on your husband (wife, son, daughter).	17. Su esposo-a (hijo-a) tiene que operarse.
18. It is not a serious operation.	18. No es una operación difícil.
19. It is a somewhat serious operation.	19. Es una operación de cierta gravedad.
20. Take your hospitalization and insurance papers with you.	20. Lleve consigo las órdenes de hospitalización y la documentación del seguro médico.

General Recommendations and Observations for the Hospitalized Patient / Observaciones y recomendaciones generales para el paciente hospitalizado

English	*Spanish*
1. Calm down, the ambulance is on its way.	1. Esté tranquilo-a, la ambulancia está en camino.
2. Sit in this wheelchair, please.	2. Siéntese en esta silla de ruedas, por favor.
3. We are taking you to your room.	3. Lo (la) vamos a llevar a su cuarto.
4. We suggest you don't keep any valuables in your room because the hospital is not responsible for lost items.	4. Le aconsejamos que no deje objetos de valor en el cuarto ya que el hospital no se hace responsable.
5. We need a signed consent for your surgery.	5. Necesitamos una autorización firmada para su operación.
6. Push this button for assistance.	6. Puede apretar este botón si necesita algo.
7. Call if you need: to use the bedpan; a sleeping pill; something for the pain; something to drink; an extra pillow or blanket.	7. Llame si necesita: usar el bacín; una pastilla para dormir; algo para el dolor; algo para tomar; una almohada o una frazada (cobija) adicional.
8. You can get out of bed.	8. Puede bajarse de la cama.
9. You must stay in bed.	9. Debe quedarse en la cama.
10. I am the nurse.	10. Soy el enfermero (la enfermera).
11. I need to take your pulse, temperature and blood pressure.	11. Tengo que tomarle el pulso, la temperatura y la presión arterial.
12. I am going to take a sample of blood.	12. Voy a tomarle una muestra de sangre.
13. I need to give you a shot.	13. Tengo que ponerle una inyección.
14. I am going to give you an intravenous feeding.	14. Voy a ponerle un suero en la vena.
15. This will not hurt.	15. No le va a doler.
16. Someone will come to take you to the X-ray room.	16. Alguien va a venir para llevarlo-a a la sala de rayos equis; al laboratorio.

Surgery / Cirugía

English	*Spanish*
1. I am going to prepare you for surgery.	1. Voy a prepararlo-a para la operación.
2. I am going to give you an enema.	2. Le voy a hacer un lavado intestinal.
3. I am going to shave you.	3. Lo (la) voy a rasurar.
4. Your surgery is scheduled for: later; this afternoon; tomorrow morning.	4. Su cirugía va a ser: más tarde; esta tarde; mañana por la mañana.
5. The anesthetist will be here to talk to you and ask you some questions: soon; later; before surgery.	5. El (la) anestesista vendrá a hablar con Ud. y a hacerle unas preguntas: dentro de un momento; más tarde; antes de la operación.
6. Your doctor will be here: soon; later; tomorrow.	6. Su médico vendrá a verlo-a muy pronto; dentro de un rato; más tarde; mañana.
7. You will be discharged: later; tomorrow.	7. Le van a dar de alta: más tarde; mañana.
8. Call your doctor's office and make an appointment: in a week; in ten days.	8. Llame a la consulta de su médico y pida turno para dentro de: una semana; diez días.

Anesthesia / **Anestesia**

English	Spanish
1. I am the anesthetist.	1. Soy el (la) anestesista.
2. I need to ask you some questions.	2. Tengo que hacerle algunas preguntas.
3. Are you allergic to anything? To what?	3. ¿Es alérgico-a a algo? ¿A qué?
4. Are you allergic to any medication? Which?	4. ¿Es alérgico-a a alguna medicina? ¿A cuál?
5. Are you taking any medication? What medication?	5. ¿Está tomando alguna medicina? ¿Cuál?
6. How long have you been taking it?	6. ¿Por cuánto tiempo la ha estado tomando?
7. Are you taking any diuretic?	7. ¿Está tomando algún diurético?
8. Have you had surgery before?	8. ¿Ha tenido alguna operación?
9. What kind of an operation was it?	9. ¿Qué clase de operación fue?
10. Do you remember what kind of anesthesia you had?	10. ¿Se acuerda qué clase de anestesia le dieron?
11. Did you have any trouble with the anesthesia?	11. ¿Tuvo alguna dificultad con la anestesia?
12. What kind of trouble?	12. ¿Qué tipo de dificultad?

Labor and Delivery / **Parto**

English	Spanish
1. When is the expected date of delivery?	1. ¿Cuándo espera dar a luz?
2. Are you having pains?	2. ¿Tiene ya dolores?
3. When did they start?	3. ¿Cuándo le comenzaron?
4. Are your pains spaced at regular intervals?	4. ¿Tiene los dolores a intervalos regulares?
5. How long does the pain last?	5. ¿Cuánto le dura el dolor?
6. How much time is there between pains?	6. ¿Cuánto tiempo pasa entre un dolor y otro?
7. Has your water broken?	7. ¿Se le rompió (quebró) la bolsa de aguas (la fuente).
8. We are going to prepare you for the delivery.	8. Vamos a prepararla para el parto.
9. I am going to do a vaginal examination to determine the progress of labor.	9. Voy a hacerle un examen vaginal para determinar el progreso del parto.
10. Push. Push more. Do not push.	10. Puje. Puje más. No puje más.
11. Do not push until we tell you.	11. No puje hasta que le digamos.
12. Breathe in and out.	12. Respire hacia adentro y hacia afuera.
13. Breathe slowly when you have the contractions.	13. Respire lentamente cuando tenga las contracciones.
14. Breathe normally.	14. Respire normalmente.
15. Breathe slowly and then rapidly.	15. Respire primero lentamente y luego rápidamente.
16. I am going to have to do a cesarean section.	16. Le vamos a tener que hacer una cesárea.
17. Are you going to breast-feed your baby?	17. ¿Va a darle el pecho al bebé?
18. You have a fine baby.	18. Tiene un bebé precioso. [*baby boy*] Tiene una bebita preciosa. [*baby girl*]

Questions on HIV and AIDS / Preguntas sobre el VIH y el SIDA

English	*Spanish*
1. What are the symptoms of AIDS?	1. ¿Cuáles son los síntomas del SIDA?
2. What is the difference between HIV and AIDS?	2. ¿Cuál es la diferencia entre el VIH y el SIDA?
3. How does one get infected by HIV?	3. ¿Cómo puede una persona infectarse con el VIH?
4. Is HIV contagious?	4. ¿Es el VIH contagioso?
5. Can one be infected through saliva; through sexual intercourse; through a blood transfusion?	5. ¿Se puede contraer la infección a través de la saliva; a través del acto sexual; a través de una transfusión de sangre?
6. Can one get the virus from food prepared by an infected person?	6. ¿Se puede contraer la infección a través de comida preparada por una persona infectada?
7. Can one be infected by using the same utensils (glasses, spoons, or other objects) used by an infected person?	7. ¿Se puede contraer la infección a través del uso de los mismos utensilios (vasos, cucharas, u otros objetos) que han sido usados por una persona infectada?
8. Can one be infected by the bite of a mosquito or by any other type of bite?	8. ¿Se puede contraer el virus a través de la picadura de un mosquito o de cualquier otro tipo de picada o mordedura?
9. Is the use of condoms a safe protection? Is there any other type of protection?	9. ¿Es el uso de los condones una protección segura? ¿Hay algún otro tipo de protección?
10. What are the safe sex rules to follow?	10. ¿Cuál sería un comportamiento sexual sin riesgo?
11. What does a positive test result mean?	11. ¿Qué significa un resultado positivo a la prueba?
12. Is the test always right?	12. ¿Es siempre definitivo el resultado de la prueba?
13. Will test results be confidential?	13. ¿Son confidenciales los resultados de la prueba?
14. Is this test the only way to confirm if a person is infected by HIV?	14. ¿Es esta prueba la única manera de saber si una persona está infectada por el virus del VIH?
15. Is there a cure for AIDS?	15. ¿Hay alguna cura para el SIDA?

HIV and AIDS Related General Observations / Observaciones generales relacionadas con el VIH y el SIDA

English	*Spanish*
1. You should be tested for HIV if: (a) you think you may have had any kind of sexual contact with an infected person; (b) you have used intravenous drugs and exchanged needles or syringes with an infected person.	1. Usted debe hacerse la prueba del VIH si: (a) usted ha tenido cualquier tipo de contacto sexual con una persona infectada; (b) ha usado drogas intravenosas o compartido agujas o jeringuillas con personas infectadas.
2. It is very important to follow safe sexual conduct.	2. Es sumamente importante evitar una conducta sexual arriesgada.

3. You are capable of being infected by the virus if you are exposed once.

4. If the result of the test is positive, you should be under the care of an AIDS-knowledgeable health professional.

5. It would be helpful if you joined a support group.

3. Usted puede ser infectado por el virus aunque haya estado expuesto una sola vez.

4. Si el resultado de la prueba es positivo usted debe estar bajo el cuidado de un facultativo-a informado-a sobre el SIDA.

5. Sería ventajoso que usted se asociara a un grupo de sostén.

Appendix C

Signs and Symptoms in Most Common Disorders and Diseases/ Señales y síntomas en desórdenes y enfermedades más comunes

English	*Spanish*
abscess in	absceso
brain	cerebral
breast	de la mama
kidney	del riñón
(throat) tonsilar	amigdalino (garganta)
abnormal color in feces, stools	color anormal en las heces fecales o excremento
black	ennegrecido
pale	pálido
red	rojizo
white	blanquecino
abnormal color in the urine	cambios anormales en el color de la orina
coffee	pardo-negrusco
pale	casi sin color
pink, reddish	rosáceo, rojo
yellow-orange	amarillo-anaranjado
abnormal fatigue	cansancio excesivo
abnormal odor in urine	olor anormal en la orina
aromatic	aromático
foul	fétido
abnormal walking	marcha, andar anormal
accummulation of fluids in	acumulación de líquido en
abdomen	el abdomen
joints	las articulaciones
tissues	los tejidos
absent periods	falta de menstruación
aging, premature	envejecimiento prematuro
anxiety	ansiedad
apathy	apatía
atrophy of muscles	atrofia muscular
asphyxiating episodes	ataques de asfixia
attention span, limited	capacidad de atención limitada
bad breath, halitosis	mal aliento, halitosis
baldness	calvicie
behavior	conducta
belligerent	agresiva, violenta
excited	excitada
belching	eructos, eructación
black-and-blue marks	morados, moretones
blackheads	espinillas

English	Spanish
bleeding from	**sangramiento [sangrar por]**
the ear	el oído
the gums	las encías
the mouth	la boca
the nose	la nariz
the vagina	la vagina
under the skin	debajo de la piel
a wound	una herida
blemishes	**manchas**
blindness	**ceguera**
blind spots	**puntos ciegos**
blisters	**ampollas**
blood clot	**coágulo**
blood in	**presencia de sangre en**
the feces	las heces fecales
the urine	la orina
bloodshot eye	**ojo inyectado**
bluish skin	**piel amoratada**
blurring	**vista nublada**
body odor	**olor fuerte a sudor**
boil	**grano, comedón**
bowlegs	**piernas arqueadas**
breathing	**respiración**
abnormal breathing	respiración anormal
choking sensation	sensación de ahogo
difficulty in exhaling	dificultad al exhalar
difficulty in inhaling	dificultad al aspirar
bronzed skin	**piel bronceada**
bruised body	**contusiones en el cuerpo**
bulbous red nose	**nariz roja y bulbosa**
burning feeling	**ardor; sensación quemante**
cardiac arrest	**paro cardíaco**
cardiac arrythmia	**arritmia cardíaca**
change in bowel habits	**cambio en el hábito de defecar, obrar**
chapped lips	**labios resecos**
chills	**escalofríos**
severe	intensos
cleft lip	**labio leporino**
cleft hands	**manos en garra**
clenched teeth	**dientes apretados**
clotting of blood	**coagulación de la sangre**
clubbed fingers	**dedos en maza**
coated tongue	**lengua pastosa**
coldness in extremities	**frialdad de manos y pies**
collapse	**colapso**
collapsing	**colapso**
knee	de la rodilla
lung	del pulmón
coma	**coma**
common cold	**catarro, resfriado**
constipation	**estreñimiento**
constriction of the penis	**constricción del pene**

English	Spanish
contractions of	**contracciones**
a muscle	de un músculo
the uterus	del útero
convulsions	**convulsiones**
coordination loss	**pérdida de la coordinación**
corns	**callos**
cough	**tos**
dry	seca
excessive	excesiva
coughing up blood	expectoración de sangre
coughing up bloody phlegm	expectoración de flema sanguinolenta
crack in the corner of the mouth	**grieta en la comisura del labio**
cracked lips	**labios agrietados**
cramps	**calambre**
cross-eye	**estrabismo, bizquera**
cyanosis	**cianosis**
cyst	**quiste**
dandruff	**caspa**
deafness	**sordera**
deformity of	**deformidad de**
the bones	los huesos
the fingers	los dedos
the joints	las articulaciones
the muscles	los músculos
dehydration	**deshidratación**
delirium	**delirio**
depression	**depresión**
desintegration of nails	**desintegración de las uñas**
diaper rash	**eritema de los pañales**
diarrhea	**diarrea**
difficulty in	**dificultad al**
breathing	respirar
defecating	defecar, obrar
urinating	orinar
swallowing	tragar
dilated pupil	**dilatación de la pupila**
dimpling	**formación de depresiones u hoyuelos**
discharge from	**supuración por**
the ear	el oído
the eye	el ojo
the nipples	los pezones
the penis	el pene
the vagina	la vagina
discoloration around the eye	**cambio de color de la piel alrededor del ojo**
discomfort	**molestia**
discomfort in passing water	**dificultad, molestia al orinar**
distended abdomen	**abdomen, vientre distendido**
distortion of (visual)	**distorsión visual de**
color	color
size	tamaño
shape	forma
dizziness	**mareo**

English	Spanish
double vision	visión doble
dribbling	goteo
drowsiness	amodorramiento
dry mouth	boca seca
dyspepsia	dispepsia
earache	dolor de oído
echoing sounds	repetición de sonidos
edema	edema
emaciation	emaciación, enflaquecimiento
emotional instability	inestabilidad emocional
enlarged	agrandamiento, engrosamiento
abdomen	del abdomen
eyeball	del globo del ojo
feet	de los pies
heart	del corazón
lymph nodes	de los nódulos linfáticos
erection difficulties	dificultad en la erección
euphoria	euforia
excessive urination	micción excesiva
exhaustion	agotamiento
eyeball	globo ocular
rolled upward	virado hacia arriba
palsied	paralizado
protruding	protuberante
failure to gain weight	no poder aumentar de peso
failure to lose weight	no poder adelgazar
fainting	desmayo
false labor pains	dolores de parto falsos
fatigue	cansancio excesivo, fatiga
feminization	feminización
fever	fiebre, calentura
erratic	errática
high	alta
intermittent	intermitente
persistent	persistente
recurrent	recurrente
fissured tongue	lengua fisurada
flabby skin	piel flácida
flatfoot	pie plano
flushing	rubor
foul breath	aliento fétido
foul taste	sabor (muy) desagradable
fragility of bones	fragilidad de los huesos
freckles	pecas
frigidity	frigidez
frostbite	quemadura de frío, congelación
furred tongue	lengua saburral
hard nodules	nódulos endurecidos
in the face	en la cara
in the head	en la cabeza
hardening of the skin	endurecimiento de la piel
harelip	labio leporino

English	Spanish
headache	dolor de cabeza
hearing loss	pérdida de la audición
heart attack	ataque al corazón
heartbeat	latido del corazón
extra	extra
irregular	irregular
skipped	intermitente
slow	lento
heartburn	ardor en el estómago
heart pain	dolor en el corazón
heart palpitation	palpitación
heavy breasts	senos pesados
height loss	disminución en la estatura
hemorrhage after menopause	hemorragia después de la menopausia
hiccups	hipo
hissing in the ear	zumbido en los oídos
hoarseness	ronquera
hot flashes	fogaje, bochorno
incontinence	incontinencia
of feces	de heces fecales
of urine	de la orina
indigestion	indigestión
inflammation	inflamación
insensibility	insensibilidad
insensitivity to heat or cold	insensibilidad térmica al frío o al calor
insomnia	insomnio
intercourse, painful	coito doloroso
irregular periods	menstruación irregular
jaundice	ictericia
lack of appetite	falta de apetito
large	agrandamiento
head	de la cabeza
limbs	de las extremidades
tongue	de la lengua
lesion	lesión
lethargy	letargo
limping	cojera
listlessness	falta de ánimo, apatía
locked jaw	mandíbula cerrada
locked knee	rodilla bloqueada
loose teeth	dientes flojos
loss of	pérdida
appetite	del apetito
balance	del equilibrio
bladder control	del control de la vejiga
consciousness	del conocimiento
control of muscle tonicity	del control de la tonicidad muscular
coordination	de la coordinación
feeling	del sentido del tacto
libido	de la libido
luster in hair	del brillo del pelo
luster in nails	del brillo de las uñas

English	Spanish
peripheral vision	de la visión periférica
smell	del olfato
voice	de la voz
low birth weight	**peso bajo al nacer**
lumps in	**bultos, masa en**
breast	el seno, la mama
joints	(el área de) las articulaciones
neck	el cuello
pubic area	el pubis
magenta tongue	**lengua magenta**
malocclusion	**maloclusión**
masculinization	**masculinización**
memory loss	**pérdida de la memoria**
menstruation problems	**problemas de la menstruación**
mental ability impairment	**deterioro de la habilidad mental**
moles	**lunares**
mouth breathing	**respiración por la boca**
muscular incoordination	**falta de coordinación muscular**
nasal speech	**habla nasal**
night blindness	**ceguera nocturna**
night urination	**micción nocturna**
numbness	**entumecimiento**
obstruction	**obstrucción**
oozing	**excreción**
pain	**dolor**
dull	sordo
fulminant	fulminante
lancinating	lancinante
intense	intenso, agudo
irradiating	que se irradia, que se corre
mild	leve
persistant	persistente
severe	severo
painful gums	**encías dolorosas**
painful swelling	**hinchazón dolorosa**
paleness	**palidez**
paleness around the mouth	**palidez alrededor de la boca**
pallor	**palidez**
palpitations	**palpitaciones**
palsy	**parálisis**
paralysis	**parálisis**
peeling of the skin	**peladura, descamación de la piel**
pimples	**granos, barros**
pins and needles sensation	**cosquilleo, hormigueo**
polyps	**pólipos**
postnasal drip	**goteo postnasal**
premature aging	**envejecimiento prematuro**
premature beat	**latido prematuro**
premature ejaculation	**eyaculación prematura**
premenstrual tension	**tensión premenstrual**
profuse sweating	**sudor excesivo**
prominence of blood vessels	**prominencia de vasos capilares**

English	Spanish
prostration	postración
protrusion from vagina	protrusión a través de la vagina
puffiness	abotagamiento
pulmonary	pulmonar
abscess	absceso
edema	edema
embolism	embolia
infarction	infarto
tuberculosis	tuberculosis
pyorrea	piorrea
rapid heartbeat	latidos rápidos
rapid loss of vision	pérdida precipitada de la visión
rash	erupción, ronchas
red spots (tiny)	pequeñas manchas rojas
red and swollen joints	articulaciones inflamadas y enrojecidas
relapse	recaída
restlessness	intranquilidad
retraction of the nipple	retracción del pezón
rigidity	rigidez
ringing in the ears	zumbido en los oídos
salivation, excessive	salivación excesiva
salivation and difficulty in swallowing	salivación excesiva y dificultad al tragar
scaled ulcer	llaga con costra
scanty urine	escasez de orina
seizures	ataques, episodios
semiconscious state	estado seminconsciente
shock	shock, choque
shortness of breath	falta de respiración
skin	piel
clammy	pegajosa
cold	fría
moist	húmeda
skin discoloration	cambio de color de la piel
ashen	cenicienta
brownish	cetrina
darkening	oscurecimiento
pale	pálida
pallor (face)	palidez (en la cara)
reddening	enrojecimiento
reddening (flushing)	rubor
yellow-white	blanco-amarillenta
slow clotting of blood	coagulación lenta
slow growth	crecimiento retardado
slow loss of vision	pérdida gradual de la visión
slow speech	habla despaciosa
sneezing	estornudo
snoring	ronquido
softening of	reblandecimiento de
the bones	los huesos
the nails	las uñas
soft ulcerating tumor	tumor ulceroso blando
sore	llaga
sore, hard crusted	llaga de costra dura

English	Spanish
to be sore	estar adolorido-a
sore throat	dolor de garganta
spasm	espasmo
spastic gait	marcha espástica
spasticity	espasticidad
speech difficulties	trastornos del habla
split nails	uñas partidas
sticky mucus	mucosidad pegajosa
stiffening	rigidez
stiff neck	cuello rígido
stuttering	tartamudeo
subnormal temperature	temperatura subnormal
swallowing difficulty	dificultad al tragar
swelling	hinchazón
inside the mouth	dentro de la boca
of the ear canal	del conducto auditivo
of face; of eyes	de la cara; de los ojos
of feet	de los pies
of hands	de las manos
of the lymph nodes	de los ganglios
tachycardia	taquicardia
tingling	cosquilleo
total lack of urination	ausencia de orina
tremor of	temblor en
the fingers	los dedos
the hands	las manos
the lips	los labios
tumor	tumor
twitch	sacudida nerviosa, "tic nervioso"
ulcer	úlcera, llaga
unawareness of surroundings	no saber donde uno se encuentra
unconsciousness	pérdida del conocimiento
unresponsiveness	sin dar una respuesta sensible; sin dar de sí
urgent urination	micción imperiosa
urination, decreased	deficiencia de orina
urination, weak stream	chorro de orina débil
vaginal bleeding	sangramiento vaginal
vaginal discharge	flujo vaginal
varicose veins	venas varicosas
vertigo	vértigo, vahido
vomiting	vómitos, náuseas
waddling gait	marcha, andar tambaleante
warts	verrugas
weakness	debilidad
weight	peso
loss	pérdida de
gain	aumento de
worms	gusanos, lombrices, parásitos
in intestine	en el intestino
in stool	en el excremento
wrist fracture	fractura de la muñeca
yawning	bostezo